FREDERICK JACKSON TURNER

Frederick Jackson Turner in 1910, when he was president of the American Historical Association.

Frederick Jackson Turner

HISTORIAN, SCHOLAR, TEACHER

Ray Allen Billington

NEW YORK   OXFORD UNIVERSITY PRESS
1973

PREFACE

HOW DOES ONE write a biography of such a man as Frederick Jackson Turner? I debated that question a good many times during the half-dozen years that this book has been under way. Turner is known today (to the few who know him at all) as the proponent of two historical concepts that have altered our understanding of the nation's past —the frontier and sectional interpretations. Should a biographer attempt an intellectual portrait, focusing on those two theories and ignoring the irrelevant details of Turner's career? Should he settle for a scintillating little essay of 150 pages describing the genesis, history, and significance of those two hypotheses? If not, how could he justify the pages needed to detail the everyday life and modest accomplishments of a very ordinary college teacher who lived a very commonplace existence? Who today could possibly be interested in the thoughts and aspirations of a man who was scarcely known to all but a handful of his countrymen during his lifetime, who made no dramatic impact on his turn-of-the-century generation, and who has been forgotten by all but American historians today?

Those were the questions I asked myself without finding a satisfactory answer. Satisfactory to myself, that is, for I *wanted* to tell *all* about Frederick Jackson Turner. By this time I had fallen under his spell, as must anyone who reads his letters, and nothing would do but a full-length portrait of the man and his ideas. But how to justify such an extravagance with words? I posed that problem a year or so ago at a session on biography staged by the Southern California Chapter of the

American Studies Association. Professor Leon Howard of the English Department of the University of California at Los Angeles was on his feet with the answer. "Why not," he suggested, "write a biography of a college professor. We have had biographies of statesmen and politicians and athletes and rogues and preachers. Why not, just once, a realistic life of a classroom teacher?"

This, then, is the biography of a college professor. Frederick Jackson Turner was not a typical professor; he did have two original ideas, which is two more than most. Yet his way of life, his ambitions, his hopes and frustrations, were those of the thousands of teachers who labored in the classrooms of his day, and of today. His dream, and the dream of most of his descendants in modern universities, was to broaden man's knowledge by dedicated research and publication. Turner did shed light on America's past with his bold generalizations concerning frontier and section, but these were only fragments of the historical edifice that he wanted to erect. He, and his contemporaries and successors, found instead that their lot was one of repeated interruptions, frustrating demands upon their time, and a disheartening failure to reap the harvest that they expected to nourish the intellects of those about them.

The college professor must be understood not as an ivory-towered recluse, spinning out his fine threads of learning in splendid isolation from the mundane world of affairs, but as a hard-working citizen responding constantly to the demands of the community. Turner was such a man. Hours, days, years of his time went into the trivia of university administration—department meetings, faculty meetings, committee meetings, meetings of every sort that could be devised to torment their victims. More time was dedicated to his students, with an endless routine of classroom preparation, teaching, conferences, thesis and blue-book reading. Like most professors, he succumbed too often to the pressure of town on gown, speaking to women's clubs, service clubs, church clubs, teachers' clubs—all manner of clubs that acted on the theory that the college teacher had nothing better to do than address their membership—without fee. Like most, too, Turner could not resist trying to improve the world, and he occupied himself for months on end battling alumni who sought to professionalize university football or insurgents who fought to wrest control of the American Historical

Association from the Establishment. He, with the rest of his breed, found life a constant battle of the bills as he strove to finance the high standard of living expected of professors with the low salaries that all were paid, at the same time preferring to broaden knowledge with learned articles for non-paying professional journals rather than succumbing to the blandishments of textbook publishers who promised him affluence and a comfortable old age. Frederick Jackson Turner may have been more imaginative than most professors, but his life serves as a case study for the entire profession.

That is the story that I have tried to tell in this book. Too often, perhaps, I have strayed far from the intellectual contributions for which he is justly known to describe his manifold activities as a good citizen and better teacher. My theme, if I have one, is that Turner's desperate desire to write—to popularize the historical concepts and fresh interpretations that crowded his mind—was frustrated by the pressures that have afflicted the academic world from time immemorial, and that afflict it today. When I have discussed his intellectual contributions I have done so in terms of his letters and unpublished essays, acting on the theory that his published works are either well known or readily available.

My effort to depict the many-sided Frederick Jackson Turner accounts for several unorthodox features of this book. Most biographers skip hurriedly over their subject's formative years, to concentrate on his later and more productive life; I have reversed this formula and paid perhaps undue attention to his background in rural Wisconsin, his education at the University of Wisconsin and the Johns Hopkins University, and his baptism into teaching. This has been a deliberate choice, for those formative years not only equipped Turner for his professorial career but were a principal influence in shaping the historical concepts that revolutionized the study of our past. I have also devoted a good deal of space to the routine events of his adult life—the extracurricular concerns that monopolized so much of his time—his passion for fishing and wilderness vacations; his love of "Darling Little Mae" and Dorothy, his lovely daughter; his political beliefs and activities; his devotion to reading and music; his uncanny ability to devise time-wasting pleasures rather than buckle down to the books that he wanted to write. Insignificant aspects in the life of a man whose sole contributions were intellectual, perhaps, but important if we are to understand the whole man, and that has been my purpose.

Turner's magnetic charm, inescapable even to those reading his letters, has made the writing of this book a pleasant task. That pleasure has been heightened by the many friends, associates, and librarians who have given me a helping hand along the way. Their help began more than a decade ago, when the Huntington Library, in January 1960, opened its vast collection of Frederick Jackson Turner papers to scholarly use. I was there, on leave from my teaching post at Northwestern University; so was Professor Wilbur R. Jacobs of the University of California at Santa Barbara, and so was Miss Norma B. Cuthbert, the skilled manuscripts cataloguer on the Library's staff. What thrilling months lay ahead as we read those thousands of pages of letters and unpublished speeches and essays, calling for help now and then with an undecipherable phrase, summoning the others to glory over a particularly important find. My purpose then was to learn something of Turner's views on his frontier thesis for a volume that appeared in 1966 as *America's Frontier Heritage*, but before we finished our labors that fall I was Turner's slave. I had to attempt his biography, even though others were far better equipped for the task.

Other commitments to publishers had to be satisfied first, but when in 1963 the Huntington Library's able director, Dr. John E. Pomfret, offered me a permanent post on the staff as Senior Research Associate I leaped at the opportunity to be closer to sources that would be more and more used in the future. Since that time I have had the joyful experience of almost total immersion in the Frederick Jackson Turner papers; I have also been blessed with release from teaching and academic obligations, and all my time has been free for research and writing. That happy combination has made the Huntington Library an academic heaven, a Valhalla of scholarship beyond compare. So I am particularly grateful to Dr. Pomfret and the Library's trustees for inviting me into paradise, and to Miss Norma B. Cuthbert and her capable successors as custodians of the Turner collections for easing the problems that inevitably arise in using any voluminous assemblage of manuscripts such as those left by a prolific writer. My gratitude extends to Dr. James Thorpe, Dr. Pomfret's successor as Director of the Huntington Library, whose warm friendship and generous aid have brightened my life during his tenure, and to the very capable staff who can now be counted among my most treasured friends.

Their reward should have been release from the barrage of questions that they have answered so cheerfully, now that this book is completed, but I must inflict still more upon them. The first draft of my manuscript, running to some 2000 pages and with from 300 to 400 footnotes to the chapter, has been deposited in the Library for the benefit of those seeking more detailed information than provided by the scant documentation on the pages that follow. I am sure that the Huntington's staff will answer questions concerning this compendium of information about Frederick Jackson Turner as capably as they have my own.

Indispensable as are the Huntington Library's Turner collections, I have traveled a good many miles to supplement them from other depositories. In the many libraries that I have visited—libraries identified in the bibliography of this book—I have been universally welcomed warmly and treated admirably by thoroughly helpful librarians. A few whose aid went well beyond the call of duty deserve special mention. Dr. J. E. Boell, Director of the Archives of the University of Wisconsin, not only guided me through the complexities of the rich collection that he administers, but on my several visits favored me with a desk amidst his treasures where I could sample and copy with a minimum of wasted effort. Miss Josephine L. Harper, Curator of Manuscripts at the State Historical Society of Wisconsin, allowed me equal freedom with the fine collections over which she presides so efficiently. Since my over-long visits to their institutions, both Miss Harper and Dr. Boell have responded cheerfully to my many letters of inquiry—letters usually necessitated by my own deficiencies as note taker. Dr. Clifford K. Shipton, former Custodian, and Mr. Kimball C. Elkins, Senior Assistant, at the Harvard University Archives, gave invaluable aid during a summer spent in research on the papers of the Harvard Commission on Western History, and during subsequent visits called my attention to important materials that might otherwise have eluded me. Dr. L. W. Towner and his capable assistants made the hours that I spent at Chicago's Newberry Library, where much of the preliminary work on this volume was done, as delightful as they were profitable. Shorter periods in the Manuscripts Division of the Library of Congress, the Firestone Library of Princeton University, the Clements Library of the University of Michigan, the Bancroft Library of the University of California at Berkeley, and the Beinecke Library of Yale University were rendered pleasant by the cheerful cooperation of the staffs of those fine institutions.

To all I am grateful; without their help this book could not have been written. Nor would my acknowledgments be complete without particular tribute to one fellow historian who has helped shape my life and thought more than he will ever know. Merle Curti, Frederick Jackson Turner Emeritus Professor of the University of Wisconsin, has been a treasured friend for more decades than either of us cares to remember. During those years he has heightened my enthusiasm for historical studies by his faith in the significance of the past, buoyed my ambition by the energy with which he has pursued his own studies, broadened my vistas by the breadth of his own vision, and provided encouragement and wise counsel by his generous appraisals of much that I have written. More than any man I know Merle Curti personifies the passionate belief in the usefulness of history, the breadth of interdisciplinary imagination, and the freshness of vision that made his teacher, Frederick Jackson Turner, worthy of his mantle among the nation's greatest historians. To him I gratefully dedicate this book.

San Marino, Calif.   R.A.B.
October 1972

CONTENTS

TO MERLE CURTI

whose scholarly attainments and breadth
of historical vision do honor to his teacher,
Frederick Jackson Turner, this book is
gratefully dedicated.

FREDERICK JACKSON TURNER

I

From Boyhood to Manhood

1861–1884

URING his waning years, Frederick Jackson Turner wasted a sizable amount of time poring over genealogical tables and drawing charts of his family tree—not because he had succumbed to the cult of ancestor worship, but because he had found that his forebears had been pioneers, who had shifted westward with the frontier, founding new towns as they did so. This was an exciting discovery to the high priest of the "frontier school," that group of historians which by the 1920s dominated the interpretation of American history. Heredity was less important than environment in Turner's explanation of the nation's past—he spent his life proving that the unique physical and social conditions in pioneer communities helped shape the character and institutions of the people—but he recognized that hereditary factors played their role and must not be neglected. Particularly when the ancestors proved to be as colorful a lot as his own.

They were, Turner found to his satisfaction, Puritan to the core. Humphrey Turner, first of the line to reach America, migrated from England to Massachusetts in 1634, and settled in Scituate. There he lived out his life, as did his son after him, but his grandson John Turner succumbed to the lure of westering and moved on to Guilford, Connecticut. There the Turners tarried for two generations. Then Samuel Turner, born in 1721, took to the road, first to Salisbury, Connecticut, then more northward, still with the New England frontier, to Tinmouth, Vermont. There Samuel prospered, siring six children and adding to the family glory by serving under General Washington at the

Battle of White Plains. The third of his children, Abel Turner, succumbed to the West's magnetism and, with his ten offspring, migrated to Schuyler Falls, in upstate New York. The eighth-born of that numerous brood, also named Abel Turner, was Frederick Jackson Turner's grandfather. The young Abel Turner fought at Plattsburg in the War of 1812. After the war he returned to Schuyler Falls, and in 1818 he married. Abel and his wife had twelve children. One of these, born on September 24, 1832, was named Andrew Jackson Turner, in honor of the President elected that year. Thus did Turner's father come into the world.[1]

Jack Turner, as he chose to be called, was reared in a pioneer community where hard work rather than formal education was the way of life. He learned to fell trees and handle a plow; he later remembered how his arms ached and his fingers bled. Only on rainy days was he happy, for then he could escape to the shop of a printer who let him set type and operate the tiny press. Thus Jack Turner equipped himself for his life's work. He also gave himself opportunity to escape farm drudgery: itinerant printers could always pick up a job in those days and were free to wander where they chose. Jack did wander, first to western Michigan and then to Wisconsin. He arrived at the hamlet of Portage in September 1858 with only ten cents in his pocket. There he spent the winter, setting type on the weekly *Portage Independent.*

Of his several journeys—to Madison and other nearby communities—the most important was to Friendship, in Adams County, a spanking new town built in New England style by a group of speculators under "Squire" Samuel Hanford. There Jack Turner first saw the Squire's daughter, Mary Olivia Hanford, a petite beauty with rich auburn hair who served as the local schoolmarm. "I'm going to marry that redheaded girl," he told a friend, and he did, although it took two years to persuade her. In the spring of 1860 they settled into a modest home in Portage where he divided his time between setting type for the *Portage Record* and serving as clerk of the circuit court. Mary Hanford was to remain at her husband's side until his death in 1905.[2]

Mary's ancestry was as deeply rooted in Puritan New England as her husband's was. The first of her forebears to reach America, the Reverend Thomas Hanford, arrived in 1642. He settled in the frontier community of Norwalk, Connecticut, where he served as pastor for forty years—despite near-dismissal when faulty false teeth led his congregation to believe he had called them "Injun devils" instead of "individuals." The Hanfords were as infected with wanderlust as the Turners; over the next years Thomas Hanford's descendants shifted westward with each generation, through the Delaware Water Gap, first to Delaware County in New York, then on to found the village of Friendship in the northern reaches of the colony. They also, like the Turners, fought the Indians in King Philip's War and the British in the Revolution. And, like the Turners, they sired numerous descendants, including Mary Hanford, who was born at Walton, New York, on April 27, 1838. This was the young lady who with her parents came to Friendship, Wisconsin, where twenty years later she met and married Andrew Jackson Turner. Frederick Jackson Turner, their first child, was born on November 14, 1861.

When, in his later years, Turner speculated on the influences that inclined him toward the study of the frontier, he gave considerable weight to the preachers and pioneers among his ancestors. "Is it strange," he once asked, "that I preached of the frontier?" Perhaps not, but in his franker moments he freely confessed that he knew nothing of his forebears until long after his historial interpretations were commonly accepted. Turner also believed that his New England and New York background made him less provincial, and inclined to a "more dominantly American view."[3] Again, he may have been right, yet during frontier days the most provincial provincials were the products of decades of migration. Proud though he may have been of his heritage, Turner's views owed more to the environment in which he was reared than to remote family connections.

Young Fred was born in November 1861, at a time when the village of Portage was just emerging from its pioneer past and was richer in history and prospects than in achievement. Near the settlement, the crumbling ruins of old Fort Winnebago, built in 1828 to guard the portage between the Fox and Wisconsin rivers that gave the town its name, recalled the not-too-distant day when Marquette and Jolliet passed on their way to the Mississippi and French *voyageurs* sang as they carried packs of Indian trading goods across the two-mile passageway. This meant little to Fred at the time; he testified later that instruction in history was so sparse in the Portage schools that he did not hear of Marquette and Jolliet until many years later. Far more impressive to the lad was the beauty of Columbia County's countryside—rolling hills where forest and prairie mingled and where tiny lakes and sparkling streams beckoned the angler. This was good country and it was filling rapidly; in the fifteen years before 1860 the county's population sky-rocketed from 1969 to 24,421.[4] Central Wisconsin was in its first boom period of pioneer growth.

So was Portage, where 2879 persons lived in 1860, two-thirds of them native-born, and one-third from abroad. All were newcomers; not until 1851 were the last Indian land cessions completed, and not until 1857 was a rail connection established with Milwaukee. Business flocked in then: a four-story flour mill, an iron works, a planing mill on Canal Street, a towering grain elevator near the LaCrosse and Milwaukee Railroad station, two breweries whose output challenged the capacity of the town's citizenry. Portage was a bustling frontier community, bursting with optimism and cockily confident of the future. Every-where were signs of progress: a three-story court house of cream-colored brick, built in 1863; an ordinance banning hogs from the streets, adopted in 1864; six oil lamps set out in 1868 to illuminate the main thoroughfares.[5]

Andrew Jackson Turner, who was prospering with the times, be-lieved in the town's future. So much so, indeed, that in April 1861 he purchased the small newspaper for which he worked, the *Portage Record*, combined it with a struggling rival, and emerged as principal editor of the weekly *Wisconsin State Register*, a lively journal that he continued to own and publish until 1878. In it, seven months later, he chronicled the birth of his first son: "He cannot talk—he has never been known to coo—his eyes do not work perfectly as a pair, but each on its own hook sometimes, so that we have caught him looking both ways at once in evident wonder and distraction. . . . He hasn't advanced far enough yet to discover that night is the time for sleep; (nurse thinks that is one of his worst failings)—and we lack the proof (and rest assured, my dear friends, we have vainly sought for it) that he could tell his father from 'any other man' to save his life."[6] Thus was Freder-ick Jackson Turner introduced to the little community where he was to grow to manhood.

And what a peaceful little hamlet it was. Fall was in the air that No-vember day, with merchants urging sweet cider and choice apples on their customers; L. Funkenstein's emporium advertising winter clothing unequaled for "Fit, Cheapness, and Quality"; the local hardware store boasting "the largest and best assortment of STOVES ever brought to Wisconsin"; the partners Wood, Loomis, and Osborn promising shoppers dry goods "cheaper than can be bought west of New York"; A. A. Kenyon's Livery Stable was eager to show its assortment of harnesses, bridles, and whips, "and perhaps sell a few of them"; and the Portage Brewery urged the thirsty to taste its freshly brewed lager beer. Yet there was little peace beyond the borders of Portage. The first issue of the *Portage Record*, published by Jack Turner on April 17, 1861, described the outbreak of hostilities at Charleston, and by the time Fred Turner was born the Civil War was a grim reality. The *Register* was as uncompromisingly Republican as its owner, trumpeting each northern victory, glorifying John C. Frémont as its favorite hero, and urging "the complete *subjugation* of the rebels; there is no other possible *cure*."

Of all of this turmoil young Fred was happily unaware. He was a healthy baby, gaining weight so astoundingly that in the first ten weeks of his life he grew from eight to thirteen pounds, and even at that age he was able to shake a rattle and "play considerably." His not unprejudiced parents thought him a beautiful baby, with a nicely shaped head, round face, handsome mouth, and "bright blue eyes bright as 'sixpences.' " His lusty appetite for "vituals" persisted; when he was a year old he was still a "great fat baby" who loved life. Young Freddie, as he was called, was probably spoiled by his doting mother and father; a family story describes how, at the age of three, he waited impatiently while a visitor, who could play the accordion and mouth organ at the same time, went through three encores, then pushed his way to the center of the room and sang at the top of his lungs "There'll Be Something in Heaven for Children To Do."[7]

As Fred advanced from babyhood, the larger world of Portage opened before him. The Turners lived in the Fifth Ward, in a modest wooden house on a lot famed for a two-ton boulder that graced the front yard, having been imported from northern Wisconsin at considerable expense. There young Fred spent his boyhood; not until 1882, when he was at college, did they move to a larger brick home on Franklin Street in the Fourth Ward. Despite his father's prominence as editor and publisher of the town's leading newspaper, they were not numbered among the affluent of Portage; Andrew Jackson Turner's name never appeared on the published tax lists of those paying fifty dollars or more, and as late as 1893 their property was appraised at only $1850. Yet they lived comfortably, and even added irregularly to the family circle. Rockwell Lafayette Turner, born in August 1864, soon abandoned his pretentious array of given names for the more prosaic "Will" that he used for the rest of his life. Eight years later, on November 1, 1872, a daughter was born. Ellen Breese Turner, or "Breese" as she was always known, remained through her lifetime one of her older brother's closest companions.

There was much to keep a small boy busy in a town such as Portage, where each season offered fresh attractions. Winter might hold few pleasures for the aging—temperatures regularly skidded to thirty or forty below zero and during one memorable month in 1875 the average reading at sunrise was 7.5 below—but for children the wood-burning stove in parlor and kitchen was a warm spot for games and reading, while milder days provided unparalleled skating and sledding. Spring arrived in late March or early April when the ice "went out" of the Wisconsin River, an event always watched by the citizenry and reported in the local press. With warmer water, the swimming season was at hand; that meant excursions to the "Second White Bridge" over the Fox River or to near-by Silver Lake. "Professor" Clark's Portage Cornet Band began its regular weekly concerts in the village park now. The Fourth of July always meant a parade finishing at the court house lawn, where there was singing by the Portage Liederkranz Society, band music, the reading of the Declaration of Independence, speeches, and in the evening a grand ball at Pettibone Hall with dancing to Schultze's Band. This inaugurated the town's strawberry-and-ice-cream festival season, with every church and most of the charitable societies vying in offering the fattest berries and the richest cream to the customers. The crisp nights of autumn heralded the coming of the Columbia County Fair, with its tents of home-canned goods and splendid floral displays, and its gay carnival atmosphere; then came Halloween, when the boys of the town indulged in their "fantasies," from upsetting privies to suspending a cabbage over a doorway and ringing the bell.

Nor did Portagites have to provide all their own entertainment, for spring, summer, and fall witnessed a constant parade of professional talent. City dwellers who mourned the dullness of the lives of their country cousins would have been astounded at the fare offered in a typical two-week period in 1869: Miller's Athenaeum for five nights, a traveling acting troupe that closed its brief season with a performance of *The Hidden Hand*, Orton's Old Badger Circus for a one-night stand, a demonstration of a patent fire extinguisher by an agent who triumphantly doused a pile of lighted kerosene barrels, a performance by "Blind Tom," a talented piano player.[8] Entertainment might have been unsophisticated in rural America, but Fred Turner and his friends had plenty to keep them busy.

As they grew older, their activities widened. Spelling bees occupied some of their time; in one at the Presbyterian Church between teams of boys and girls young Fred failed on the word "satellite"—a less common word then than today. On a less serious plane, he was one of the younger set who organized a series of "Young Fogy" parties in 1873 —inspired by their elders, who held dances as the "Old Fogies"—to meet fortnightly at Pettibone Hall, where the Virginia reel was performed with the aid of Clark & O'Keefe's band. Parents took pride in watching as their children "waltzed, and swung, and 'hoed 'er down,' in all the exuberance of youthful joy and vigor."[9] They were equally delighted when Fred and his friends decided to enhance the elaborate celebration planned for the Centennial Fourth of July in 1876 by organizing a military company called the "Guppey Guards," so named to honor a civic leader named Joshua J. Guppey. After only a month of preparation they led the grand parade from the Court House to Loomis's Grove for the inevitable speeches. This success assured the Guppey Guards a degree of permanence, particularly after their command passed to the elder Turner, who not only supervised their drills but secured them Springfield rifles and uniforms: gray cloth trimmed with gold lace and dark facings, a black sash with gold edging, and gray caps topped with black and decorated with gilt. This splendid array made the Guppey Guards so attractive to the opposite sex that their annual ball became *the* social event of Portage; young Fred Turner may not have enjoyed the regular drills that won them prizes in state competitions at Madison, but he stayed a member until he left for college.[10]

Growing up in Portage meant not only fun and games, but a surprising number of cultural opportunities. By the time Fred was fourteen he was interesting himself in the oratorical activities that won him modest fame in later years, serving first as a messenger for the Young Men's Lyceum, where debates were held regularly, then when he was only fifteen, delivering one of the "declamations" that honored the Civil

War dead on Memorial Day. At the same time he was reading widely in a variety of books quite unusual for a quasi-frontier town of two or three thousand. The elder Turner owned a respectable library (on one occasion he asked borrowers to return such volumes as *The American Conflict*, *Don Quixote*, *The Federalist*, and Napoleon's *History of Caesar*), which could be supplemented from a permanent circulating library and a traveling library of four hundred works that went on display at John Graham's Drug Store each Saturday. That young Turner used these collections is clear. Starting in 1876, when he was fifteen, he kept a scrapbook in which he pasted items that interested him; these included voluminous extracts from Ralph Waldo Emerson (his favorite author) and from every important literary figure, as well as speeches that would interest a budding orator. A short time later he began contributing a regular "Pencil and Scissors Department" to his father's newspaper, filled with quotations and extracts that he found noteworthy. In the two months the column appeared he quoted extensively from Emerson (most frequently), Goethe, Disraeli, Harriet Beecher Stowe, Robert G. Ingersoll, Victor Hugo, Charles Lamb, Sydney Smith, Daniel Webster, Fielding, Rousseau, Thomas Carlyle, Schuyler Colfax, and a score more.[11] Even as a boy, Fred Turner displayed the unusual talent and catholicity of reading interest of a scholar.

He also excelled in school. He first attended the Franklin Street Primary School, briefly; then he went on to the Intermediate School, under Miss K. C. Wright. Fred was apparently a model student; the one yearly record preserved shows that in 1873 when he was twelve he missed only six of the 49 school days in the spring term—an attendance record bettered by only one other pupil—and earned a top rating of ten in conduct. He next attended Portage's single high school, where he spent the years between 1874 and 1878. This was hardly a lavish institution; built ten years before of the yellow brick for which the city was famous, the building was showing the signs of wear. It had an inconvenient recitation room, poor ventilation, inadequate blackboards, and a furnace that not only smoked and gave little heat but blocked the fire exit route. These physical deficiencies were offset by a rigid curriculum: English grammar, geography, arithmetic, reading, spelling, and map-making the first year; more doses of these subjects plus Latin grammar and United States history in the second; algebra, physical geography, history, botany, German, and Latin through Caesar and Virgil in the third; and, in the senior year, algebra, geometry, astronomy, rhetoric, philosophy, psychology, and German or French.

Fred Turner stood this diet well. During his first term he was one of nineteen on the top honor roll; a year later he tied with his friend Arthur C. Cole at the head of the class with 100 per cent attendance, 100 per cent punctuality, 96 per cent in scholarship, and an over-all average of 99 per cent. These astronomical heights were impossible to maintain consistently; on one marking he fell to a 93 per cent scholastic average and on another to 85 per cent in deportment, but he was almost always first or second in his class. This was no mean achievement; many years later a classmate remembered that "you were the despair of our entire class, because, no matter how diligently we worked, we could never equal the examination marks that you had."[12]

Such a record meant that Fred Turner would receive special distinction when graduation rolled around on the afternoon of Friday, June 28, 1878. The exercises were held in the Court House, specially decorated for the occasion. Flowers decked the speakers' stand, and a banner, bearing the words "Class of 1878" was stretched across the windows. There was standing-room only when Dr. A. C. Kellogg, superintendent of schools, opened the ceremonies, led the audience in singing the class song, and called on the eighteen graduates to deliver the orations that were the final requirement. Fred Turner came fourth, speaking on "The Power of the Press." The local reporter was pleased; "his thought was original, his style clear and forcible, and his manner self-possessed and very earnest." So was his father as he listened to the flow of words: the press was "a necessary adjunct of every free government. . . . the people will make known their power through it, and will resist all tendency toward oppression. . . . as Freedom of the Press increases, so does the freedom of the people. . . . a want of education among the lower classes of the nation is shown by the rise in our midst of Communism, that fell child of ignorance and crime. . . . with the aid of the press, however, that great and long wished for reform—the education of the masses—becomes not only a possibility, but even a probability." These stirring words were more than the three judges could resist. Young Turner proudly carried from the hall not only his diploma, but a set of Macauley's *History of England*, awarded as the first prize.[13]

When, many years later, the historian Frederick Jackson Turner looked back on his boyhood days and tried to isolate the influences that shaped his career, he singled out two that were particularly important: his family and the quasi-frontier atmosphere of Central Wisconsin. When he recalled his family relationships he had surprisingly little to say about his mother. She was apparently a capable housewife, able to enter into the regular discussions about the dining-room table, and wise enough to let her son grow to manhood without any of the oedipal problems common in modern society. Turner's father was of a different stripe. A cockily aggressive runt of a man, so small that he was the constant butt of jokes among his fellow-journalists (one reported seeing him approach two twelve-year-olds, and of hearing one say to the other, "Carry in that hoe or may be that boy that's coming will steal it"),[14] Andrew Jackson Turner was always popular, always sought after, always in the limelight. In public he was gay and outgoing, at his best when bantering with countless friends or haranguing a Republican audience for the Grand Old Party's standard bearer. Yet toward his family, and toward his first-born son, he was shy, almost aloof. Turner remembered him as "the best of fathers to me; undemonstrative, often taciturn, but always kind and full of that deep affection that does not show itself on the surface so much—but which abides."[15] If he learned from his father—and he learned much—it was by example and not by forced feeding.

The example was there, and proved admirable for a future historian. Jack Turner was a newspaper owner and editor by profession, but a politician by instinct, so dedicated to the success of the Republican party that he saw the Credit Mobilier scandal as a Confederate plot and the corruption-ridden Grant administration as "so patriotic, so wise, so beneficent, and so thoroughly American in all its distinguishing features, as to command the admiration of the patriotic men of this country."[16] This proved a handicap to his own office-holding ambitions in strongly Democratic Portage, but Jack Turner's personal popularity won him election after election: as clerk of the circuit court, as a four-term member of the state legislative assembly, as delegate to state and national conventions, as a perennial official of the county Board of Supervisors. His reward came in 1878 when he was named to the Wisconsin Railroad Commission by the Republican governor, a post with such ample financial rewards and speculative opportunities that he sold his interest in the *Wisconsin State Register* to devote full time to his business ventures. Jack Turner could no more abandon publishing and politics than he could vote Democratic; when a rival editor a dozen years later charged that Jack had written nearly every editorial in the *Register* for two decades, he was guilty of exaggeration rather than prevarication, and when the party urged Turner as mayor of Portage in 1881, he was not only elected but performed so effectively that he served for four terms, two of them as the unanimous choice of the voters.[17]

Jack Turner did not set the world afire as either politician or business-man, even though he was a walking encyclopedia of facts and statistics needed in planning any campaign and boasted a gregarious nature that made him a personal friend of every man, woman, child, and dog in Columbia County. In politics he lacked the vision to plan boldly or to place the state and national interest above petty local bickering; in the business world his vision was too broad, his optimism too unquenchable, to succeed. He did prosper in modest ventures, such as a contract to pave a Portage street with cedar blocks at $1.22 a square yard, but when he helped organize the Portage and San Juan Mining Company to develop gold mines in Colorado, or invested heavily in pine lands of northern Wisconsin, or formed the Portage and Superior Railroad Company to build from his home town to Stevens Point and Bayfield on Lake Superior, he did more to help his friends and community than he did himself. He worked hard through a long lifetime, and again and again seemed certain of turning a speculation into a fortune, but he died a relatively poor man, even though he provided comfortably for his family as long as he lived.[18]

In the long run, Andrew Jackson Turner's most significant legacy was his son. Frederick Jackson Turner learned three things from his father that stood him in good stead through his lifetime. One was to appreciate the importance of local history: the elder Turner helped form the local "Old Settlers' Club" to record the impressions of early inhabitants and prepared a number of newspaper articles and pamphlets on the pioneer history of Portage and old Fort Winnebago.[19] More im-portant was the lesson in practical politics that Jack Turner taught his son. Young Fred spent his youthful years in the office of the *Register*, learning to set type and chronicle local news, but learning far more about the community, and about the wire-pulling that went on as politicians vied for office. Lessons continued at the dinner table in the evening, as his father told of the means he had used to harmonize conflicting ethnic groups, or to bring peace to warring religious factions, or to influence the legislature through pressure on this committee or that. Fred was taught much about the formation of the "composite American nationality" of which he would write.[20]

He was taught more as he watched his father pull the strings that elected Republicans to office. Once, when the two were riding among the Baraboo Bluffs, they happened on a country blacksmith shop, covered with pictures advertising Barnum's Circus, where a dozen farmers were gathered for a local caucus. Young Turner watched with admiration as his father leaned against the anvil and spoke persuasively of the candidates he recommended for the next election. "It was so picturesque," he wrote that night, "and so characteristic of our institutions."[21] Here for the future historian to see was the practical working of frontier democracy, and he never forgot the experience. "I understand party politics very much better," he recorded some years later, "from having seen, at close range and from the inside, his own interests in that subject and his skill in shepherding the many nationalities that lived in Columbia County."[22]

If young Fred learned something of local history and politics from his father, he learned far more about the art of fishing—and this was knowledge more essential to his future well-being than the most valuable classroom instruction. Jack Turner was completely irrational in his passion for the out-of-doors and for the three sports that absorbed much of his time: curling in the winter, fishing in the spring and summer, and hunting in the fall. "You know," he warned his son, "it is a cardinal principle with me to never allow anything to interfere with my shooting, fishing, or curling."[23] And nothing did interfere. Every clear winter day found Jack Turner on the rinks of the Portage Curling Club, serving as "skip" with a vigor that overawed his opponents, then leading the competing teams to the famed Haertel's saloon and brewery to drink to success or drown the sorrow of defeat. In the autumn he was as often as not playing hookey from his newspaper office to escape to the headquarters of the Puckaway Club on Puckaway Lake, there to bag his quota of wild ducks and geese; Jack Turner estimated that he spent from ten to twenty days behind a gun each fall, often with his son Fred tagging behind him.

These were satisfactory pursuits, but they paled when the fishing season opened each spring. Jack Turner was a master fisherman, a devoted fisherman, a slightly mad fisherman, who judged his friends by their competence with a rod and who would neglect the most promising business deal for a half-hour on a trout stream. His junior editor reported sadly in the spring of 1867 that Jack had fished but little, having made only four trips to the Tunnel, eight to Briggsville, five to Swan Lake, six to Silver Lake, and thirteen to the "Big Slough," and that he had caught only two thousand trout and a dozen barrels of pickerel. Jack Turner endowed his son with a share of his own piscatorial enthusiasm. When Fred was only five years old, his father sent word that he wanted his "sprouts" brought up properly, "and by all means learned to fish."[24] The boy was "learned to fish," so effectively that his love of lakes and trout streams rivaled that of his father. They made trip after trip together, sometimes to a neighboring stream for an hour's casting, sometimes for weeks on end as they sounded lakes in more distant counties.[25] This apprenticeship left Fred Turner a devoted fisherman, and he remained one through his lifetime.

The stamp of Jack Turner's influence remained on Frederick Jackson Turner throughout his life, but so did the memory of the quasi-frontier environment in which he spent his boyhood. Portage was just emerging from its pioneer past during his impressionable years; in 1870, when he was nine years old, it had no more than 4000 inhabitants, and in 1880 only 4346. All about were reminders of frontier days certain to make their imprint on a small boy. Through the dusty streets each summer lumbered prairie schooners loaded with "emigrants" bound for the free government lands of northern Wisconsin or the Dakotas. Almost every issue of the local newspaper told of Indian outbreaks in the West, flavored with the editor's damnation of the "savages" who began the Modoc War or wiped out Custer's command on the Little Big Horn. Occasionally, events at home reminded him that civilization was in its swaddling clothes: a hunting party was formed to track down a wolf-pack, vigilantes were recruited to help the sheriff capture an over-ambitious horse thief. The wilderness was not quite subdued, and young Turner felt its influence.

Now and then frontier lawlessness touched close to home. Twice in 1869, when he was seven years old, vigilantes turned Portage into a wild-west town—once in September when two hot-headed Irishmen shot it out on the main street (the winner was promptly hanged to a tree by a mob), again a week later, when a notorious troublemaker was arrested after bludgeoning a drinking companion to death (he was dragged from the jail and strung naked from a branch, where his body was found the next morning).[26] These were events that the boy would never forget. Nor did he forget the great lumber rafts that passed the city almost daily during the summer months, bound from the "pineries" of northern Wisconsin to the prairies of Illinois and Iowa, or the journeys that he made with his father to that virgin northern country where the train ran through a narrow aisle cut in the towering forests, or through clearings where homesteaders were building their cabins.[27] The frontier was near and meaningful to Fred Turner.

It was brought even nearer when he mingled with the Indians who clung to their ancestral homes near Portage. Both the Winnebago and the Menomonee had long since been forced to cede their tribal lands, but many refused to move to the Nebraska reservation assigned the tribes, and they continued to hunt along the Baraboo and Wisconsin rivers. There Fred visited their villages on his frequent fishing trips; he saw Indians often in Portage when they came to trade or beg, or to drink themselves into trouble with the authorities. He probably shared the town's satisfaction when troops arrived in 1873 to drive the red men westward, and that December he probably watched as the remnants of the proud tribesmen were marched through the city, herded onto railroad cars, and started toward Nebraska.[28] Certainly he realized that many drifted back, for their villages were common sights even through the 1880s; Fred Turner was often among them, "hearing the squaws in their village on the high bank talk their low treble to the bass of our Indian polesman" as he fished the river, "feeling that I belonged to it all."[29]

He was close to the frontier then, and he was closer as he watched the newcomers to that near-wilderness area merge into the composite nationality that he was later to describe. Roughly one-third the inhabitants of Portage were foreign-born, and the percentage was even higher in the small farm communities that he regularly visited on his fishing trips; in Caledonia, Scots, Welsh, and Germans far outnumbered the few natives, and Lewiston's 234 settlers included 95 Germans, 33 Scandinavians, 35 Irishmen, and 53 American-born. As a boy, Fred Turner was unaware of the census statistics that described this mixing bowl, nor did he realize that, when he was eleven years old, the Portage city council included one native of Ireland, one of Baden, one of Prince Edward Island, one of Prussia, one of Wurthenberg, one of Holland, one of Wales, one of Massachusetts, and one of New York—a mixture to be found only in an emerging community on the fringes of settlement. But he did know that he daily rubbed elbows with men of all hues and backgrounds who were merging into the American society. "It was a town with a real collection of types from all the world," he remembered some years later, "Yankees from Maine and Vermont, New York Yankees, Dutchmen from the Mohawk, braw curlers from the Highlands, Southerners—all kinds. They mixed, too, and respected and fought each other."[30]

These were indelible impressions, and they were still fresh in Turner's mind when he began speculating on the nature of American society. They were part of him, not something he learned from books. They altered his perspective in two significant ways. First, he knew himself to be the product of a social order whose life-patterns and values differed from those of established communities. "I am," he wrote in 1887, "placed in a *new* society that is just beginning to realize that it has made a place for itself by mastering the wilderness and peopling the prairie, and is now ready to take its great course in universal history."[31] Clearly, Turner sensed the differences between the pioneer West and the stabilized East long before he began the studies that led to the frontier hypothesis. Second, his close contact with nature planted in him an almost Emersonian sensitivity to the wilderness; he was doubly aware of the impact of the frontier's closing because he resented civilization's assault on the primitivism that he had enjoyed as a boy. He tended to glorify nature as a generative force, playing a larger role than it actually did in creating new societies. Had Turner been city born and bred he would almost certainly not have evolved his frontier thesis.

Fred had learned much during his Portage years, but now a wider world beckoned. His outstanding high school record meant that he was destined for college, and to central Wisconsin, college meant the University of Wisconsin in near-by Madison. This was a radical step in a day when higher education was for the few, but his father readily agreed, with one strict admonition: "If I supposed you were going to learn to be a loafer, as some boys I know of have done, I should say to you that you *can* be learned at home, at less expense. But that is not what my boy is going for."[32] Nor was it. Young Turner had already shown his mettle by adding a special preparatory "Greek Course" to his heavy senior schedule in high school, mastering Xenophon's *Anabasis*, beginning Homer's *Iliad*, and suffering stiff doses of Greek grammar to meet the university's requirements for its "Ancient Classical Course." He did well, too, with marks ranging from 86 to 95 per cent in what was actually a college-level subject.

In September 1878, Fred Turner entered a strange new world when the train deposited him and five of his classmates at the busy Madison depot the day before classes began. The university was hardly large by modern standards—449 students divided into three colleges—but it was a bit terrifying to one accustomed to Portage's small-town atmosphere. So this newest freshman wandered about in awe. He found a room with board at the usual price of three dollars a week, walked up State Street to the "Hill," and officially enrolled as a "sub-freshman"—a designation alloted to students so poorly trained in small high schools that they entered with less-than-adequate preparation. There were few frills in the courses that busied him that year—Greek and Latin reading and composition, for the most part, with concentration on Cicero, Livy, Homer, and Lysias; solid geometry and trigonometry; general botany; and a touch of oratorical training in the required "rhetoricals." His over-all average, 90.8 per cent, was thoroughly respectable for one with his training; more importantly, he received a baptism in classics that stood him in good stead through his lifetime, endowing him with a sense of the nicety of literary expression, a vigorous prose style, and a storehouse of classical allusions that he used in his own writing.[33]

Fred J. Turner (as he now signed himself) seemed destined for an uneventful four years in college, but the situation abruptly changed during the summer of 1879, when he accompanied his mother and aunt to Omaha, where his father's brother, Charles Turner, lay dangerously ill. Uncle Charlie recovered in due time, but in mid-August Fred was stricken with a mysterious malady. For a time death seemed certain—his father and brother hurried to his bedside, where they stayed until mid-September, when the crisis was passed. Not until October could the boy be returned to Madison, where a Chicago physician diagnosed his ailment as spinal meningitis in its most acute form. His momentary improvement was deceptive, for in November the disease struck with full force again; once more his life was despaired as he grew weaker and weaker. Then, in February 1880, he began to improve. By May Fred was able to ride about the town in a carriage, and by summer he was fully recovered, yet so weakened by the months of pain that a return to college was impossible.[34]

That autumn and winter Turner apparently stayed at home, doing a little tutoring in Greek at the request of the principal of the high school, and gradually regaining his strength. This was an important interlude in his life, for there was little to do but read, which he did—constantly, widely, intelligently. Early in 1881 he jotted down the names of the books he had devoured in the preceding year. The list represented a respectable library: Milton's *Paradise Lost*, eight of Charles Dickens's novels, Taine's *History of English Literature*, Byron's *Don Juan*, Swift's *Gulliver's Travels*, Thackery's *Pendennis*, Hawthorne's *Scarlet Letter*, George Eliot's *Adam Bede*, Irving's *Alhambra* and *Sketch Book*, and scores more. This was solid fare, but far less solid than his more serious self-imposed intellectual diet. The "Commonplace Book" that he kept at the time—an ordinary paper-bound notebook in which he jotted quotations, passing thoughts, and observations on his reading—was filled with translations from the Latin, all carefully signed with "Translated by FJT." Mingled with these were his own random thoughts, largely on literature and the books he was reading, and quotations that pleased him. "Too great zeal in acquiring other's thoughts," he wrote in one moment of near-rebellion, "may . . . lead us to neglect our own and become imitators and not originators."[35] He was to be an originator in the future, but now he was stocking his mind with invaluable learning, sharpening his wits, and perfecting a writing style that was to become his trademark. Turner's forced months of leisure were probably more valuable to him than any number of classes at the university would have been.

He had to finish his education, however, and by the spring of 1881 he was back in Madison for the final term of the college year, taking the usual courses, helping unite two defunct literary societies into the Adelphia Society with such success that he emerged as secretary of the new organization, and delivering Marc Anthony's "Address to the Romans" in the College Rhetoricals so effectively that it was judged "the finest declamation and the best rendered that has yet been heard from the Assembly Hall stage."[36] All this despite bothersome remnants of his illness; twice during the academic year he was forced to return home to nurse himself back to health, and once his father was sufficiently concerned that he warned the professors that his son required special consideration. Yet Fred Turner was on the road to a normal life once more, prepared to resume a full program of studies that fall.

When he enrolled again, on September 6, 1881, the university was little changed; 38 professors were prepared to welcome 401 students, 52 of them in Fred's sophomore class, and the only visible signs of progress were the new paths that led up the Hill to University Hall. The University of Wisconsin, in common with its sister educational institutions, was woefully out of step with the modern world. Theorists in those days held that mental faculties could not be trusted to mature without proper guidance; strict mental and moral discipline was needed to develop the mind. This, rather than the acquisition of knowledge, was the purpose of schooling. Students were not to question or even to reason; learning was by rote, and the classroom a means of testing their ability to recite the set body of material they had memorized. They were never to doubt the rigid prescriptions imposed by their elders. When President John Bascom, one of the nation's ablest and most progressive educators, greeted Fred Turner's sophomore class that fall of 1881, he talked not of the world scene or intellectual values, but of the need to have their food well-cooked but not burned, of the dangers of eating between meals, of the value of healthful exercise, of the virtues of eating slowly, and of the evils of intemperance.[37]

Wisconsin's physical setting was as archaic as its intellectual life. Situated on "The Hill" above beautiful Lake Mendota, it was dominated by University Hall, where most of Turner's classes were held. This venerable building had no central heating until 1883; until that time students sat muffled in overcoats and mittens in classrooms where wood-burning stoves provided more smoke than comfort in temperatures that dipped to twenty or thirty degrees below zero. Hallways had no heat at all; students wrapped themselves in coats and scarfs as they hurried between classes. Such lighting as there was on dark winter days came from flickering gas jets that only seemed to deepen the blackness. Conditions in the university library were even worse. A fee of two dollars combined with the pitifully small collection to discourage student use; in Turner's sophomore year only 39 of some 400 students had "joined" by mid-November, while 180 had enrolled at the free city library.[38]

Yet if Madison offered neither intellectual excitement nor physical comfort, it did provide temptations to which young Turner gleefully succumbed. The local and Milwaukee theaters offered a constant parade of the lowly and near-great, ranging from Buffalo Bill and a full company of Sioux chiefs in *The Prairie Waifs*, through *Uncle Tom's Cabin*, to Edwin Booth in *Hamlet*. During his college years he witnessed Thomas Keene and McCulloch in *Richard III*, Barrett and Booth in *Hamlet*, Fanny Davenport in *As You Like It*, Signor Salvini in *Othello*, Frank Mayo in *The Virginian*, Joseph Jefferson in *Rip Van Winkle*, and a dozen more. Turner could also listen to excellent lecturers, including Bayard Taylor, Henry Ward Beecher, Robert Ingersoll, John Fiske, Edwin Meade, and Matthew Arnold, all within a year.[39]

On a less elevated plane were the student activities that captured the time of the undergraduates. Athletics played a lesser role in those days; an attempt to form a football team in the autumn of Fred's sophomore year ended when someone kicked a hole in the football, but the university did manage to launch a baseball team that suffered ignominious defeats at the hands of the "Racines" and the "Ann Arbors." Things were better the next year, due partly to Turner himself. He was elected to the Athletic Association in September 1882, not because he was passionate about sports, but because this least-prominent of all student activities gave him a chance to serve his college. The Association had much to do; it was an unofficial body entrusted with managing the school's intercollegiate program and, particularly, with exciting enough student interest to field a team to meet Beloit, Racine, and Northwestern, the members of the Western College Baseball League. Turner, acting as vice-president, did his work well, raising enough money to buy uniforms for the team (consisting of nine men and a substitute), arranging adequate time for practice, helping arrange schedules, and even inspiring some interest in a football eleven. College spirit rose during his term on the Association, even to the point where the first college yell—the now-familiar "U Rah Rah Wis-con-sin"—became part of the student vocabulary.[40]

Young Turner was drawn more closely into the vortex of college life when he joined a social fraternity, Phi Kappa Psi, shortly after his arrival in Madison. He was an enthusiastic fraternity man, even to the degree of writing a singularly unoriginal song for the brethren:

> Not Phi Delta nor Chi Psi, drink her down
> Not Beta Theta Pi, drink her down!
> But old Phi Kappa Psi, is the shout we send on high
> Drink her down, drink her down, drink her down, down, down.[41]

Any contribution of this significance deserved recognition, and Turner's came when he was chosen to respond to the toast "Madison" at the annual fraternity "Symposium" at the Park Hotel in November 1882. Despite its name, this was a gala affair with wine, women, and dancing—"the most *recherché*" ever witnessed in university circles, according to the local reporter—and it gave Fred a chance to display some of his most lush oratory: "Although to most of us she is only a foster mother, and on this Thanksgiving night our own household fires are burning in distant places, yet, like the ancient Greeks, we, too, may meet around a common hearth and offer our praises to Madison, the beautiful queen of Wisconsin, throned on the hills, gilded with gleaming lakes and clothed in the robe of rich sunsets."[42]

Fred Turner found his true niche in two other extra-curricular activities that were more to his talents. One, quite naturally, was student journalism. His arrival in Madison coincided with the founding of a weekly campus newspaper, *The Campus*, soon to be renamed *The Badger*, whose second issue, published in October 1881, announced that Fred J. Turner would be one of two exchange editors. From this post he rose to become secretary-treasurer of the Badger Association in his junior year, and president in his senior. This was tantamount to the editorship, and he performed his duties well; *The Badger*'s awareness of the problems that faced students throughout the nation, its crusades to elevate the academic standards of the university, and its professional tone all indicated that Turner was a cut above the usual student journalist of his day.[43]

Even more important than his editorial duties in shaping his future career was Fred Turner's activity as a public speaker. He could not have selected a field better suited to his talents; oratory was the surest road to popularity on the campuses of that day, when the prize speaker was far more acclaimed than the superior athlete. The heart of all social life lay in the "literary societies," whose elected members enjoyed a prestige denied lesser souls, and who in return had to engage in rhetorical exercises, debates, and inter-society oratorical competitions. "They are," wrote one student editor, "the strongholds of a college course, and are, if not quite, almost as important as the college course itself."[44] For some reason Turner was passed by the two prestigious societies at Wisconsin, the Athenean Society and the Hesperian Society, and helped form the Adelphia Society, a poor relation of its more distinguished counterparts. Adelphia had to be content with rented clubrooms in downtown Madison until 1883, when it was assigned a room in Science Hall, and in Fred's senior year it could boast only twenty-three members.[45]

Such fame as Fred Turner won as an orator was not due to his literary society. His supreme moment came at the end of his junior year, when he captured the most coveted of all honors, the "Burrows Prize" (a wretched steel engraving that would grace the walls of the triumphant literary society for a year), in the Junior Exhibition. Five orators vied for this honor yearly, one from each of the literary societies (three for men, two for women), with each nominating its best orator. When Fred Turner was named to represent Adelphia in the spring of 1883, he was assured the most difficult competition of his young speaking career.

Over the next months he filled his Commonplace Book with jottings as his composition took shape. His theme was a happy one—"The Poet of the Future"—for in it he would contrast the sterility of despotism with the cultural opportunities under democracy. "Our poems," he wrote, "live in the grand meter and rhythm of our armies marching to the rescue of the shackled slave and the grandest lyric that ever fell from pen was the Proclamation of Emancipation." This was the message that he brought to the "cultured audience" that packed the University Assembly Hall on the night of May 18, 1883. Turner spoke first, and the knowing realized that the competition was over then and there. "The well rounded figures of his oration," said the local reporter, "the striking metaphors, the graceful gestures, the perfect enunciation, taken in connection with his perfect self-possession placed him far beyond the reach of his competitors." Other speakers followed, but the decision was foreordained. To the audience, Turner's oration was the superior one of the evening in all qualities, and the verdict of the judges was greeted with cheers.[46]

"The Poet of the Future" was a remarkable oration that revealed many of the qualities that were to shape Turner's views during his professional life. Its theme was the twin forces that had remade modern civilization, science and democracy. Science had given man new beauty blessed with utilitarianism; democracy had allowed all mankind to share in benefits reserved for the kings of former ages. Now democracy was waiting for its poet, a poet who would find his inspiration in popular rule and the scientific achievements that rule made possible. "In his lap science will pour her glorious jewels and bid him give to them the setting of his song. In his ear humanity will whisper deep, inspiring words, and bid him give them voice."[47] Turner's oratorical flourishes have little appeal to a modern reader, and his youthful enthusiasm was untempered with realism. But in "The Poet of the Future" he voiced his deep-seated faith in democracy, a faith never to be shaken, and in it he proclaimed his belief in the inevitability of progress. Turner was certain in 1883 that the ordinary people, working through democracy, would eventually achieve a perfect society.

He triumphed in the Junior Exhibition not only because his extra-curricular activities included literary society activities and student editorships, but also because he was spending a great deal of time reading. Whatever the press of other duties, he read constantly, widely, appreciatively. The paper-bound Commonplace Books that he kept through college mirror his changing tastes in authors, and they show, too, how deep his understanding and how thoughtful his speculations were. His tastes embraced the classics—Shakespeare he read daily, with samplings of Carlyle (a perennial favorite), Hawthorne, De Quincey, Goethe, Longfellow, and J. A. Symonds—but he also developed a marked fondness for Herbert Spencer's *Education*, Green's *History of the English People*, and, particularly, the essays of Ralph Waldo Emerson. Emerson was perennially exciting, and through the 1881 and 1882 Commonplace Books are sprinkled quotations from his essays and comments on his ideas. Turner was tuned especially to the Emersonian form of democracy; he heartily agreed with the Sage of Concord that "the artistic idea of our age *is* that of the practical as applied to the people." Here was the germ of the concept that he developed in his "The Poet of the Future," and here was fuel for thought that required more investigation. "Read up on Evolution and apply to this thesis,"[48] he reminded himself.

The formal education prescribed by the rigid requirements of the

Ancient Classical Course that he elected was somewhat less broadening than his own reading. Until the end of his junior year he was classed as a "special student," an inferior designation shared by undergraduates who came from small high schools with inadequate programs in the classics.[49] This did not lighten his burdens; with his classmates he spent the sophomore year reading Horace in Latin, Demosthenes in Greek, Anglo-Saxon texts, and lyric poetry, along with a course in rhetoric, one in oratory, and one in mathematical mechanics. Turner did well, too, ending the year with an average grade of 90.5 per cent, and he would have done even better save for an inability to master mathematical mechanics. According to local legend he was scheduled to fail that course completely, but was given a passing grade when the instructor confused him with another student.[50] In any event, he entered his junior year well equipped in Latin and Greek.

This was just as well, for no sooner did Fred Turner return to Madison as a junior in the fall of 1882 than he discovered a new interest that made the classics seem dull and archaic. He found history, through a remarkable teacher named William Francis Allen. From the time he entered Professor Allen's class, Fred was a lost soul, so absorbed with this exciting new field of learning that all other studies seemed unimportant. He often testified in later life that no other person so greatly influenced his future. "Allen," he wrote in 1920, "has always looked over my shoulder and stirred my historical conscience."[51] This was only a slight exaggeration. That wise and good man shaped his young student into a first-rate historian, equipped him with the tools of the trade, broadened his perspectives, and kindled the enthusiasms that sustained him for the rest of his life.

A transplanted New Englander, a classicist by training and a medievalist by choice, Professor Allen brought to the classroom the rigorous "scientific" techniques he had learned at Harvard and Göttingen, techniques which were then revolutionizing historical studies in the United States. His courses were strictly conventional—in the junior year the students undertook a three-term study of "Dynastic and Territorial History" that surveyed political events from classical times onward, a two-term sequence in ancient institutions, mythology, and art, and the required one-term introduction to American history; in the senior year they worked on a three-term combination of medieval institutions, the English constitution, and the history of civilizations. But whatever the subject, Professor Allen's students entered a world far removed from the usual rote-learning and recital technique then universally employed. In some of his courses Allen lectured, but in most he used the "topical" method, sending undergraduates to the sources to investigate assigned topics, prepare fifteen-minute papers, and present their findings to the class with the aid of a syllabus, charts, and maps.[52] Fred Turner learned history by research in the sources, spiced with the excitement of exploration and the thrill of discovery. Had Professor Allen followed the usual practice of giving textbook quizzes, his prize pupil might have continued the journalistic career that he intended. Instead he found in history an intellectual excitement provided by no other discipline.

The content of Allen's courses was as important to Turner's conversion as the methodology. Professor Allen saw history not as a chronicle of wars and politics, but as a search for the subsurface social and economic forces that shaped political behavior, a concept that was revolutionary in that day. This quest led him into comparative studies, in which he contrasted institutions in ancient, medieval, and modern times for clues to their origin and operation; it also inclined him to a genetic approach that sought to discover *why* and *how* institutional growth occurred. To him, history was an exercise in cause and effect; the historian's duty was not simply to record an event, but to understand the causal forces behind it. "No historical fact has any value," he told his students, "except so far as it helps us to understand human nature and the working of historical forces."[53] These were invaluable lessons for Turner; they not only underlay his whole concept of the nature of history, but inspired him to search for the subterranean currents that explained the American past, thus leading him directly to his frontier and sectional hypotheses.

Professor Allen's research techniques were also progressive for his time. He preached the heretical doctrine that scholars should use every possible tool in their quest for the truth; to him the study of the past required a thorough knowledge of metaphysics, theology, military science, political economy, and jurisprudence.[54] When Turner, in later years, urged historians to use economics, political science, sociology, and anthropology to solve their problems, he was echoing his master. He echoed him again when he used maps to illuminate the nation's expansion and its division into sections. Allen was a pioneer in this technique both in the classroom and research, and he indoctrinated his students in its value. His own studies on the expansion of ancient Rome were based on a series of carefully drawn maps, while the catalogue descriptions of his courses regularly noted that "historical charts and maps are constantly used."[55] Turner later testified that his own passion for mapping all data was inspired by Allen's courses.

The most important lesson learned by young Turner was that the historical process was one of constant growth and relationship. Societies, Allen taught, changed constantly, just as did the biological organisms then being popularized by Charles Darwin and his follow evolutionists. Allen viewed the great breakthroughs in man's progress—the invention of the bow and arrow, the domestication of animals, the smelting of iron ore, the development of the alphabet—as steps in the "evolution of society," each triggering a series of radical changes in the social structure. To him the shift from community to private land ownership was the final step in "the evolution of barbarism into civilization."[56] Allen's course on medieval institutions, which Turner took in his senior year, was largely a study of institutional response to social and economic change. From it Turner emerged with two basic concepts. He saw society as a living, dynamic organism, constantly changing in response to forces governing its evolution. He saw, too, that the pace of change could best be measured by using comparative techniques—the social pressures shaping medieval land tenure, for example, became clearer when contrasted with those governing the land system in a primitive New England or Illinois town.[57] These were essential in Turner's beliefs; his understanding of society as an evolving organism underlay his whole approach to the past, and his application of medieval examples to the American West led him closer to his frontier thesis.

Despite his later, half-joking remarks that he learned so little American history in college that he could approach the subject from a fresh perspective, Turner benefited a great deal from Allen's one-term course on that subject. There he received a surprisingly modern over-all interpretation that even recognized the significance of frontier expansion. Allen viewed the age of colonization as a final phase of the expansion of Europe, and an end-product of the rise of national states, the ferment of the Reformation, and the intellectual explosion of the Renaissance. He pictured the spread of settlement across the continent as a continuation of European expansion, saw the Louisiana Purchase as a watershed in the early history of the Republic, and interpreted even the slavery conflict as a by-product of the westward march. "It must be noted," he told his class, "that it was the *extension* of slavery that thus became the leading issue. The *existence* of slavery in the states was wholly a different question, and one which under our political system could never be more than a moral issue."[58] Allen also recognized that expansion increased the powers of the central government, especially as the demand grew for federal control of slavery in the territories. When his pupil wrote, as he did in 1893, that "loose construction increased as the nation marched westward," he was parroting his master's wisdom.

The books assigned in Allen's courses added to Turner's growing store of knowledge. Most were dreary chronicles; students in the 1880s endured the boredom of the chronological monstrosities that passed as textbooks—one by Alexander Johnson on the *History of American Politics* (1879) was almost universally used—or were sent to pasture in the multivolume works of George Bancroft, John Schouler, Richard Hildreth, and Hermann von Holst. Yet Turner may have found a few volumes more to his liking on Allen's reading lists: the books of Francis Parkman on the French and Indian wars; J. G. Shea's *Discovery and Exploration of the Mississippi River*, which was judged "indispensable to the student of western history"; and Consul W. Butterfield's *Washington-Irving Correspondence*, which was listed as "an important work on the history of the Northwest." These volumes may have stirred Turner's interest in the West, but he learned far more from a less pretentious *History of the United States*, by a young Englishman named John A. Doyle, which was published in 1876.[59]

Doyle's textbook was largely traditional, but he did defy orthodoxy in two ways. He included in the book four colored maps drawn by Francis A. Walker of Yale's Sheffield Scientific School, one showing the territorial expansion of the United States, the other three picturing the westward movement by four-color gradations between the frontier (less than six persons to the square mile) and the fully occupied areas (more than forty-five). Here was a graphic presentation of the expansion process. Doyle also discussed expansion. The story of America would be incomplete, he wrote, without "the history of a movement from the coast towards the west," made by "new settlers, or those born in America who wanted land, gradually moving westward without losing their connection with the original settlements."[60]

No less suggestive were Doyle's speculations on the results of expansion. The westward movement, he wrote, was responsible for "many of the features which distinguish America from the Old World." Because of a frontier, men in America always had the chance to better themselves by moving westward. "Moreover the great demand for labour has given them a free choice of occupation, and thus led to rapid changes. The ease too with which money can be made has led men to concentrate their energies in business, and thus the luxuries and refinement of life has been to a great extent neglected." When free lands were exhausted, all this would change, and the United States become another Europe. These were remarkable statements for that time; in them Doyle isolated many of the characteristics that Turner was to trace to the frontier: the mobility of the people, the greater opportunity for self-advancement, the tendency toward materialism. When Allen recommended Doyle's book as "an excellent English work," he was pointing his student in the right direction.

Allen moved Turner still nearer his future career by directing him into a fascinating research project. This originated in a request from Professor Herbert Baxter Adams of the Johns Hopkins University; could Allen provide information on early land holdings in Wisconsin that would illuminate Adams's study of the origins of New England towns? Allen could; he had six capable students who would be asked to investigate land tenure among the original French settlers. "One of them," he told Adams, "is going to examine the records of Portage where is an old French grant (Grignon)."[61] Turner set to work with enthusiasm, bothering his father and his father's friends with questions, poring over volumes of the *Annals of Congress* and the *American State Papers*, reading reminiscences of old settlers in the State Historical Society library, and combing documents in the Columbia County courthouse.[62] Here was his first chance to apply the techniques he had learned from Allen, and he found the venture exciting.

The result was hardly a historical masterpiece, but it did display the author's skill as an investigator. Turner described the land claim purchased by Augustin Grignon from John Lecuyer, the dispute over ownership that forced Grignon to appeal to a congressional land commission in 1823, the reaction of Lecuyer's heirs, the patent issued by President Andrew Jackson on the commission's recommendation, and the history of the tract from that time on. Little interpretation livened the narrative, nor was interpretation necessary, for the facts spoke for themselves. But the thoroughness of the research, the expertness of the critical evaluations, and the logic of the presentation testified to the fact that Turner has learned his lessons well. Even as a junior in college, he was a capable investigator, viewing history as a record of social growth, and able to picture the evolution of Portage in two generations from an Indian camp site to a settled community.

Turner's study of the Grignon Tract was principally important because it set him to thinking about the differences between land tenure in the United States and that in Europe. Why, he asked himself, was the area about Portage one of small farms, or "peasant proprietorship," instead of great estates? He speculated a great deal on that problem, and he recorded some of his thoughts in his Commonplace Book for 1883. "Investigate land holding peasantry about Madison," he wrote, "(e.g.) just as one would from the remains of ancient land systems (census—Ag[ricultural] Reports—Talks) etc. How many acres average. What kind of houses live in? Food? Manners—sports etc. Need of village system. Significance of Eng." He noted that "if our lands in the west had not been opened to and filled with foreign emigrants it is not unlikely that they would have fallen into the hands of capitalists and have been made into great estates." This, Fred Turner reasoned, would have reversed the democratic trend, "the revolution going on which is to raise *man* from his low estate to his proper dignity." Instead, "such institutions as peasant proprietors" served as a democratizing force, "all the stronger that it works quietly."[63] These were giant steps forward in his thinking: he was relating America's unique institutions to the existence of an area of cheap land, which discouraged aristocratic tendencies.

No less indicative of Turner's future contributions was his discovery of the evolutionary hypothesis and its application to his historical concepts. Society, he saw, was an organism evolving in response to various internal and environmental pressures, just as did the biological organisms described by Charles Darwin and Herbert Spencer. "They have given us a new world," he wrote in his Commonplace Book. Their ideas, if applied to history, would reveal what he called "the persistence of historical forces"; all the past must be restudied "in the light of the development hypothesis."

An intellectual understanding of the past by this key would give so many generalizations that the proper completion of such a work would inaugurate a new era. Science has of late years revolutionized Zoology, Biology, etc. It must now take up recorded History and do the same by it. This I would like to do my little to aid.[64]

These were not unusual beliefs—most of the nation's historians were applying Darwinian techniques in their investigations—but they were hardly to be expected from a college junior in a backwater university. Allen taught him well, and, more than any other teacher, he launched him on the road to his own original interpretations. Turner spoke the truth when he wrote some years later: "I have never, in Johns Hopkins or elsewhere, seen his equal as a scholar."[65]

The stiff doses of history inflicted on Fred Turner during his junior and senior years absorbed most of his time, but there were other courses to be mastered, orations to be prepared, a student paper to be edited, and a modest social life to be enjoyed. The courses could not be neglected—as a junior, he took a sequence in physics, chemistry, and zoology, two courses in English literature, one on the Latin poets, and one in constitutional law; as a senior, the study of political economy, logic and aesthetics, astronomy, and the inspiring lectures by President John Bascom on "Mental and Moral Philosophy." These last he especially enjoyed; President Bascom was a premature Progressive, who glorified democracy and preached that property was usually acquired by happy accident and belonged less to the holder than to society—strong words for that day, and words that vastly influenced young Turner.[66] There were also required courses in public speaking and declamation, where Turner's oratorical skills were further developed. In all he did well; his one undistinguished grade was an 80 in chemistry. All the rest save two were in the 90s, with his marks in Allen's classes usually 97 or 98, and he always was ranked at the top of the class.[67]

There was no question of Fred Turner's graduation with distinction as the spring of 1884 brought his commencement near. With it came the usual round of study, the usual class picnic with its "elegant repast," the usual bickerings that delayed the election of class officers until just before graduation. The senior album described Fred J. Turner as twenty-two years old, five feet eight inches tall, 130 pounds, a lib-

eral in religion and an independent in politics. He was to receive his degree with "Honors of the Second Grade"; only two of the 86 graduating students had earned first honors.[68]

Ceremonies began on Sunday, June 15, when President Bascom
preached the baccalaureate sermon on "The New Theology"; continued through Monday, when seniors read their honors theses to a
sparse audience; and reached the first climax on Tuesday, "Class Day,"
when a room full of sweating parents heard the class prophecy read.
One verse appealed especially to the visitors from Portage:

> *Turner*, "in cloisters immured and to painful study devoting
> Day and night, his patient and innocent life exhausting."
> *Turner*, than whom no senior with loftier intellect gifted,
> Nor with a finer soul, nor in virtue absolute ever.

Then the class valedictorian spoke, the class song was sung, and the parents filed from the hall, with only one more ceremony to be endured.

Commencement day, on Wednesday, was dark and dismal, but Assembly Hall was overflowing when President Bascom, the regents, the
governor, and the faculty filed onto the platform. There was traditional music first, then a prayer, and presentation of flowers to the fem-
inine graduates until "the hall was redolent with their perfumes." Orations, eighteen in all, followed. Turner was the second to last speaker,
but he brought the dozing audience to life with his rich voice, his
forceful gestures, his lush prose. "Architecture through Oppression"
was his theme; the beauty of the past had been created by the toil of
the many for the enjoyment of the few—"millions groaning that one
might laugh, servile tillers of the soil, sweating that others might
dream." Now the age of oppression had passed. "Now the world
begins to see that true progress, true enlightenment, means the progress, the enlightenment of all. . . . When the greatest happiness of the
greatest number shall have become something like reality, when life's
tragedy shall cease to clash with life's romance, and the squalor of the
hovel shall no longer mar the cathedral's beauty, then again may music
'freeze into marble' and forests blossom into stone." This flood tide won
its just reward; the three judges announced that the "Lewis Prize" of
twenty dollars had been awarded to Fred J. Turner of Portage. Fred
Turner walked from the platform, diploma in hand, knowing that he
had won the two most coveted oratorical awards of the university.[69]

Turner left Madison that spring well endowed with learning. He had acquired a thorough grounding in Latin and Greek, and an excellent training in literature; his future writing was to benefit in its crisp style, its colorful metaphors, its freshness of allusion. He had learned something of the natural sciences, and especially of biology; these lessons he was to apply in his total concept of society as an evolving organism, in his belief in the continuity of historical events, and in his unshakable faith in progress. Most important of all, he had been equipped by Professor Allen with a thorough knowledge of historical methodology, an understanding of comparative techniques, and an unquenchable enthusiasm for research into the past. Fred Turner did not know his own future when he boarded the train for Portage that spring day, but it was foreordained. He would be a historian.

II

The Making of a Historian:

WISCONSIN

1884-1888

IN 1884, when Fred Turner graduated from the University of Wisconsin, he was well into his twenty-second year. He had no set plans for the future. History, true, was his passion, but no sensible person would consider a career in a subject that could lead only to boredom or the poorhouse: boredom if he elected high school teaching and was doomed to a lifetime of listening to disinterested students recite memorized passages from a wretched textbook; the poorhouse if he had the audacity to seek a college professorship. There were few opportunities for the historian in those days; not until 1881 did any university establish a professorship in American history, and in 1884 only fifteen professors and five assistant professors of history could be counted throughout the nation. President Eliot of Harvard was not far wrong when he warned two young men that year that to consider history teaching as a livelihood would be "extreme imprudence on their part."[1] Nor was improvement likely. Established professors in respectable disciplines saw history as an auxiliary subject, so unrelated to the main body of classical knowledge that it could be taught by any hack—if taught at all. This was no field for an enterprising young man, if that young man planned to eat regularly.

So Turner reluctantly turned his back on his new love, and instead he weighed two possible careers. One was to capitalize on his fame as a college orator and become an instructor in rhetoric; he was sorely tempted when the regents of the University of Wisconsin offered him an assistant instructorship in rhetoric and elocution that summer, at a salary of $600 a year. But after a few weeks of soul-searching he decided that such a career was not for him. The other was to join with Reuben Gold Thwaites, editor of the *Wisconsin State Journal,* in a glamorous venture. Thwaites, eight years Turner's senior and an experienced newspaperman, had long dreamed of starting his own paper in Colorado or New Mexico, where he could "grow up with the country," and he tried to persuade his young friend to go along as his assistant. Turner listened to tales of the cattle country and the profits to be made from advertising cattle brands, but in the end he decided that the risk was too great.[2] Madison was too attractive to leave, even for the Wild West.

Journalism, however, was an obvious career for a young man whose second home had been a newspaper office. Even before his graduation he had been offered a part-time post as Madison correspondent for the *Milwaukee Sentinel,* and he had accepted with alacrity. That was a busy summer for Fred as he bustled between university and state capitol and city hall to gather news for his dispatches—dispatches not notable for their brevity, as he was paid at space rates. He proved himself an extremely capable reporter, with a nose for news and a willingness to reveal the truth whatever the consequences. In June 1884 he unearthed a plot to unseat John Bascom as president of the university, and in a series of biting articles he showed the flimsiness of the evidence and the prejudiced nature of the charges. Again that fall his snooping revealed a Democratic plan to use the Madison state fair for political purposes, so angering many politicians that they slammed their doors in his face from that time on.[3]

As a reward for his efforts he was dismissed from his post in January 1885, when the state legislature reassembled and a more experienced correspondent was sent from Milwaukee to report its doings. Turner used his father's influence to land a political plum as transcribing clerk of the state senate, then convinced the *Chicago Inter-Ocean* and the *Wisconsin State Register* that he should report Madison's news for their columns. Once more he distinguished himself with his crisp dispatches, his bold denunciation of corruption, and his tenacity in ferreting out information.[4] His reputation was growing, and a career as a newspaperman seemed certain.

Then, overnight, his whole future course was changed. His beloved Professor William Francis Allen was responsible. Long overburdened with an excessive teaching load, and increasingly frail in health, Professor Allen finally won from President Bascom a term's leave of absence that would allow him to renew his acquaintance with Europe's classical antiquities. A substitute had to be found for the spring term, and Allen's prize pupil, who was conveniently at hand, was offered the post. Turner was ready; he had been reading history in every moment of his spare time ("his favorite theme in literature," one of his fellow reporters noted), and was eager to preach what he had been practicing. When the Allens sailed for Italy, in April 1885, Fred Turner was ready to trudge up the Hill once more, this time to face his first class as "instructor in history." "That he will make a success of the branch in which his whole soul is enlisted," wrote one of his friends, "goes without saying."[5]

Turner's weeks in the classroom that spring convinced him that he had found his true vocation, even though he had to labor endlessly to teach classes in dynastic history and medieval institutions in a manner worthy of his mentor. By fall, when Professor Allen returned, Fred Turner was willing to make any sacrifice to continue his studies. There was no opportunity in the history department, where Professor Allen handled all the instruction, but an assistant was needed for Professor David B. Frankenburger in rhetoric and oratory, and even that was preferable to a return to newspaper work. The prospect was hardly alluring. His assignment was to conduct the courses in elocution required of all freshmen and to supervise the "rhetoricals"; this chore meant not only heavy class hours, but listening to the six essays and six declamations required of all freshmen and sophomores each term, and coaching the most talented for roles in the three "rhetorical exercises" where the entire student body assembled to applaud the most successful lower-class orators. "Private rehearsals precede public declamation" read the college catalogue, "and each student has personal criticism passed upon his essay."[6] Turner had to provide hours of individual instruction for more than half of the 416 students enrolled that spring, in addition to teaching a larger-than-normal class load. His "assistantship" had blossomed into a full-time job—and more.

He plunged into this academic maelstrom in September 1885, after finding comfortable quarters in a rooming house at 772 Langdon Street, kept by the kindly Mrs. Bross. The year that followed was one that he would gladly have erased from his memory—no history, little time for pleasure, only the endless monotony of coaching inept pupils in speaking skills ill-suited to their inclinations. Even so, the freshman declamatory contests that ended the school year, in May 1886, showed he had done his distasteful job well. One by one his pupils mounted the stage and spoke: a young lady whose voice broke occasionally as she recited "The Creed of the Bells," a lusty youth who deafened the audience with "The Storming of Mission Ridge," a pretty girl who charmed her hearers with "The Sioux Chief's Daughter," and many more. "The whole programme," reported the local scribe, "spoke well for the efforts of Mr. Fred J. Turner, instructor in elocution."[7] Turner was delighted, of course, but he was also exhausted. When he fled to Portage that summer no history books weighted his suitcases; he was content to escape to the northern lake country, where bass lurked under every lily pad and the trout streams were so overflowing that Fred, his father, and his brother landed as many as 160 a day, some of them well over a pound. This was the life he loved. "Blessed be the woods," he wrote feelingly, "Wish I might never see a city again." Especially when that city was Madison, where classrooms of students had to be taught elocution. "How I dread returning to my work at the University," he confessed as autumn approached. "Yes, I know I ought to be ashamed to say so, but I do."[8]

Fate, in the form of a sudden increase in student enrollment, changed his life for the better. With the freshman class almost doubled, Professor Allen's dynastic history course attracted such a large audience that nearly half were forced to sit on the floor. His complaints, added to those of the students, forced the Board of Regents to divide dynastic history into two sections. Allen, in turn, surrendered the American history courses to Turner, who was relieved of about half his instruction in elocution. This program was preferable to a steady diet of rhetoric and oratory, but Fred Turner soon found that he had not relieved his work load. Fifty-three juniors crowded his upper division history course, and 32 freshmen comfortably filled the room for his lower division offering; in addition, he taught four classes in oratory, each ranging from 31 to 41 pupils. Twelve hours a week in the classroom, 229 students to be taught and examined, eight hours a week in rehearsals for his oratorical students, special coaching for those scheduled in declamation contests—this was the schedule that kept Turner hard at work during the fall term that year.[9]

This baptism into the academic world hardened him for still more rigorous tasks ahead. During the winter and spring terms his teaching load was increased from twelve to fourteen hours—two sections of territorial and dynastic history were substituted for his American history courses—and he held five hours of daily rehearsals for the declamation contests required of all students in oratory. To add to his burdens, Professor Allen fell ill in January, and again in May, forcing Turner to assume his classes and to take on the burden of managing the department for two or three weeks at a time. Yet so eager was Turner to study and teach American history that he responded to a student request that he offer a special advanced course on the Civil War. Twenty students were admitted, though a larger number applied, and sessions were held twice weekly in the rooms of the State Historical Society of Wisconsin, then housed in the state capitol building.[10]

If this were not enough, that academic year 1886-87 added one more burden to his already overflowing schedule. By this time his future was decided: he would be a history teacher, whatever the cost and however poor the rewards. To fit himself for that career advanced work was in order, for a master of arts degree was a necessity and a doctorate in philosophy desirable. The University of Wisconsin could provide the first—it awarded its first master's degree in 1886—and Allen would be a superb director of his master's program. That year Fred J. Turner was listed in the catalogue as a candidate for the degree of Master of Arts, and as spring approached he finally stirred himself into making some progress toward that degree. The sole requirement was an acceptable thesis; with his usual unrealistic optimism he was certain that would be finished by fall, even if part of his vacation had to be sacrificed.[11]

The subject was already decided upon. While poking about in the State Historical Society library, preparing his paper on the Grignon Tract, he had stumbled on bundles of letters from French fur traders in the area, water-stained, tied with leather thongs, and written in what Turner described as execrable French. Here was a glamorous page from the past that had never been turned. Why not write a thesis on the early fur trade of Wisconsin? Such an ambition had been in the back of his mind since 1885, when he had toyed with the idea of a book on the trading activities at Green Bay.[12] Allen gave his blessing, and, in May 1887, Turner began his exploratory investigations. These proved discouraging. He was innocent of any knowledge of French, and even if he had been a master of that tongue the letters were so badly written, and couched in such eccentric grammar, that progress would have been slow. This he discovered when he pressed Therese S. Favill, an attendant at the library who used French expertly, into service. "With my guessing I could get along faster than she could," he reported ruefully.[13] He made some progress over the next weeks, but with the temptations of Lake Mendota in the spring, the pressure of the end-of-year class work, and a natural inclination to avoid unpleasant tasks until the last moment, the work moved very slowly. By summer he found that he had scarcely scratched the surface of the material, and his prospects for a degree were no brighter than they had been a year before.

Two related events that summer of 1887 gave Fred Turner the direction he lacked before. Both had to do with a charming young lady named Caroline Mae Sherwood. The two had met a year before—in late June, 1886—when Mae (as he always called her) visited Madison with her mother to enroll a younger sister in the university. Turner, who knew Mrs. Lucinda Sherwood vaguely, through his parents, gallantly suggested that they put up at Mrs. Bross's boardinghouse, where he was living. That was the happiest suggestion of his life. Madison sweltered in a heat wave, with temperatures in the high eighties and dust ankle-deep everywhere after a two-month drought, but Fred and Mae spent two happy days walking the tree-lined lanes near the city, talking of books and the mysteries of life. Scarcely had she returned to Chicago when she was followed by the first of the hundreds of letters Fred was to write her; "Dear Miss Sherwood," it began, and went on to complain that the days just past had been so enjoyable that the rest of the summer "will be like a plum pudding when all the plums were at the top."[14]

Turner was hopelessly lost at the first sight of Mae. His letters, stiff and formal at first, as befitting that Victorian generation, warmed rapidly, and the "Dear Miss Sherwood" gave way to "Darling Little Mae." There were visits to Chicago, too, at Christmas and Thanksgiving and during the Easter holidays, with walks about the streets of the Kenwood section where she lived, and with them protestations of love. By mid-winter Turner was filling his Commonplace Book with love songs instead of historical jottings:

While thy dear head nestles close to my shoulder
While thy soft bosom is swelling in mine
Ever my thoughts grow bolder and bolder
Closer my face unto thee doth incline.

The next step was inevitable. Fred proposed to Mae on one of their Christmas walks, soberly pointing out that he was a poor risk because his health might fail and his profession was highly unlucrative; Mae was properly Victorian when with a "dark little face" she said a soft "Yes." He went back to Madison the next day and poured out his love in a letter that she always treasured: "I love you as I fancy in the old mediaeval days a Catholic loved the pure face of the Madonna. . . . You seem to me a bit of God's best work. . . . I feel something within me say that I will justify that love if God will let me."[15] They kept their engagement a secret at first, telling only their parents, but by April the news was out and the congratulations were pouring in. Fred Turner was committed to marry Mae as soon as he was able to provide for her.

This gave Turner a new purpose, but such was his love for Mae that he could not resist one last fling before settling into his career. She suffered badly from hay fever and spent part of each summer in the Massachusetts Berkshires; why not forget the labors of the past year and spend an idyllic holiday together? Too, Professor Allen planned to attend the 1887 commencement ceremonies at Harvard that spring, and he urged his young disciple to come along. So the plans were laid: Turner would do his sightseeing at Cambridge and Boston, then join Mae and her mother at Chatham on Cape Cod, where he had found an economical rooming house. After a week or so there they would journey together to Conway, in western Massachusetts, for a few more weeks of pleasure before he returned to work. He would bring along a volume of Tennyson and one of Whittier to read as they walked the New England lanes, and a volume on Tennessee that he had agreed to review. He would also have a French grammar tucked in his suitcase. "I propose to know lots of French before the few weeks of summer life are over," Fred warned, "and you will have to study how to instruct a pupil—dull exceedingly, and very prone to tell his 'Je t'aime' with wordless lips and forget the book in looking at the teacher."[16]

There was little French learned that summer. Fred Turner boarded the train for Chicago as soon as commencement was over, stopped to gape in awe at Niagara Falls, enjoyed the lazy look of the Mohawk Valley, and watched fascinated from the speeding car's windows as the Hudson fell behind and the Berkshires loomed before him. "The hills wrote their rugged autographs against the skyline," he wrote, "the people began to say na-ou, the farms were little patches of stone and daisies turned up slantingly on the hillsides—and I knew I was near New England." Boston was a "veritable Aladdin's palace," and he savored it all —the Common, Faneuil Hall, Old South Church, Bunker Hill, Trinity Cathedral. Harvard's commencement ceremonies were fascinating to one unaccustomed to pageantry; so were the student orations phrased in terse Anglo-Saxon "with none of the bombast that is found in our western college commencements." He loved every moment; "I could gladly pitch my tent on Boston Common for the rest of my days." But Chatham beckoned, and there Turner journeyed on July 1 to join Mae in a succession of heavenly days—dips in the chilly Atlantic, moonlit walks on the beach, gargantuan meals of clams and lobsters, a day with the fishing fleet, where he caught a few cod before succumbing to seasickness. Then the train ride to the northern Connecticut Valley, where a carryall waited to take their little party to the hill town of Conway and Mr. Lyon's boardinghouse, presided over by an eighty-seven-year-old patriarch who inflicted such lengthy prayers on the guests that Turner learned more of the Scriptures than he had in years. The young lovers spent hours strolling down stone-walled lanes, reading Tennyson while they perched on hilltops, stealing an occasional kiss on moonlight walks, visiting historic Deerfield, near by. Never had Fred suffered as when they said their last farewells; even a fishing trip to northern Wisconsin with his father failed to erase the pangs of separation. By August 21 he was back in Madison, sad that "the play time of the happiest summer of my life" was past.[17]

Fred Turner did not realize that he stood on the threshold of a new life. For two years he had dawdled away his time—fishing, talking with friends, playing whist, reading aimlessly—as he followed his daily teaching rounds with little thought of tomorrow. Even now, safely installed in Mrs. Bross's new rooming house at 620 State Street, he found buckling down to his thesis difficult; "I don't accomplish as much as I wish to," he confessed, "for I am sure to come across someone to talk to every hour or so, and besides my work is puzzling."[18] Yet there was no room for laziness in Turner's new life, and the mood soon passed. Suddenly, unaccountably, he found himself moved by a compelling ambition. His eastern trip was responsible; it had shaken him from his comfortable routine and had forced him to take a fresh look at his purpose in life. "I understand myself better since I went to New England," he told Mae. He had been growing provincial, overly ascetic, lazily contented. He had patterned his routine on the monotony of the Midwest countryside. "There were no wide sweeps of water horizontally, no lofty hills, no deep valleys. It was *commonplace*."[19] Now all was changed; that eastern journey had broadened his horizons and stretched his imagination. It had offered him new goals and stirred the ambition that was needed to achieve them. "I have learned the lesson of the struggle that there is in life. . . . I am sure I can make the future my own. If determination will do this for me, it will be done."[20]

Here was a new Turner speaking, one capable of conquering giants. His first task was clear: he must win a permanent teaching post at a reputable university (Wisconsin, if at all possible). This could be achieved only by earning his degree and beginning the publication program that would make him known to the academic world. There was a practical reason for this now, for his good friend and sponsor, President John Bascom, retired that summer of 1887. Bascom's successor, Professor Thomas C. Chamberlin, a locally well-known geologist from Beloit College, was a friend of Fred Turner's father, and received Fred warmly when he called—even listening to a request for a salary increase. Chamberlin listened, but he did nothing. This was discouraging, for Turner's youthful optimism had led him to believe that the new president might make him a professor and head of a new department of American history. Rightly or wrongly, he believed his future to be less secure now than it had been under President Bascom. He felt he had to prove himself to win a permanent spot on the faculty. "Just now," he wrote, "my vision embraces only one object—a *reputation* sufficient as a basis for demands upon the university."[21]

That urgent need taught Turner an important lesson: he could produce books or articles or lectures only under pressure. If something *had* to be done, he did it well and on time. If not, he squandered his working hours on play or makeshift tasks until a deadline loomed. This was to be the pattern of his life, and it was the pattern of that 1887-88 academic year. His daily routine was rigid: rise at 6:45, break-

fast an hour later, classes from 9 to 1, an hour for dinner, classes from
2 to 4, the library for an hour, a walk and tea from 5 to 7, study from
7 until 11, bed at 11:30.[22] Gone from his letters now were accounts
of long walks, of games of billiards, of hours in his canoe on Lake Mendota, of leisurely evenings with friends; they were filled instead with
comments on books read, papers prepared, and progress on his thesis.
What an amazing amount this regime accomplished. During that academic year Turner not only revised his courses to make them more
challenging, but published a number of book reviews and his first
small pamphlet on American history, prepared two major historical
papers for club meetings, wrote an extended article for the *Encyclopaedia Britannica*, and completed his dissertation.

Teaching came first, for he had to prove himself in the classroom to
assure a permanent post on the Wisconsin faculty. Turner was fortunate here, for he was no longer a temporary substitute for Professor
Allen, but a full-fledged instructor with two courses of his own in
American history: "Subcourse IV," an introductory class that met
twice weekly in the fall and winter terms, and "Subcourse V," an advanced offering in which the subject was studied "more largely from
the genetic viewpoint than the preceding, developed by topics." Added
to these were the usual "Rhetorical Exercises" for freshmen, which
took an undue portion of his time. More work was added during the
winter quarter, when Professor Allen succumbed to pneumonia,
brought on by sub-zero temperatures (the classrooms stood at 45°
and students sat wrapped in scarves and overcoats). Once more Turner was asked to take over Allen's courses, in return for some relief from his own rhetorical work. That term he taught his own two
American history courses, with 103 students enrolled, Allen's two
classes in dynastic history, with 74, and four freshman classes in oratory, with 158—a total of 334 students and sixteen hours of instruction,
some of it in medieval history, in which he was ill-prepared. "It was
like floundering in deep water," he confessed.[23] Allen recovered in
time to resume teaching in the spring term, but Turner again added
to his own burdens by offering a course in the Civil War, this time
limited to fifteen pupils who met for two hours weekly. This was a
back-breaking load, but Turner did not mind—so long as he could
study and teach the subject he loved. "I have had delightful work this

month," he wrote Mae in October, "—no elocutionary classes until this week so I have been able to devote my time largely to history."[24]

Such burdens might have justified Turner in parroting a textbook or repeating the lectures he had given the year before, but his materials for each class were specially prepared, usually after extensive reading, and always with fresh interpretations that mirrored his maturing thought. "It demands a year to get fully into the spirit of the thing," he complained, after spending a whole morning and evening preparing a one-hour lecture on the Spanish explorers, "and a lifetime to be an expert on the subject."[25] These efforts were demanded especially for the advanced course, in which the subject was treated from "the genetic viewpoint"; there Turner had his first chance to venture along untrod paths of interpretation. His instructional methods were strictly conventional; he used Alexander Johnston's *History of American Politics* (1879) as his basic textbook (a dull chronicle that devoted a chapter to each presidential administration and piled fact on fact with little concern for causal forces), and required reading in orthodox sources that ranged from George Bancroft and Francis Parkman to current magazine articles. Turner made his own contribution in his lectures and discussion, for there he opened vistas on the past that would not seem out of place in a classroom of today.

He began with some sound words on the nature of history. "Society," the students were told, "is an organism developing upon certain *lands*, with changes at certain *times*. History takes account of these changes and their causes, and needs geography and chronology." To understand the evolution of that organism, the historian must know what it received from the past, how it was affected by surrounding organisms, and the physical conditions in which it developed. Once these were understood, the organism could be studied in four ways: vertically (inheritance), horizontally (interaction of neighboring organisms), physically (the impact of the environment), and sympathetically (understanding the peculiar conditions of the time).[26] Perhaps Turner revealed his immaturity by his pretentious imitation of biological terms, but he was preaching Darwinian doctrine to his students long before the evolutionary theory had altered the viewpoint of many better known historians. He was also showing them that human society was infinitely complex, and could be comprehended only by awareness of the multiple forces operating to cause change.

His fresh interpretations explained the reasons for America's unique course. He saw the nation's history unfolding in a series of chronological stages: *exploration* in the fifteenth and sixteenth centuries, *colonization* by France and England in the seventeenth, *possession* as England ousted France in the eighteenth, *revolution* as independence was won, *federation* as local and national interests were reconciled between 1789 and 1820, *economic growth* as natural resources were utilized in the quarter-century before 1845, *separatism* as the slavery conflict checked the trend toward centralization from 1845 to 1869, and *expansion* between 1869 and 1886 as the West was peopled. Modern scholars might quarrel with the neatness of Turner's categories, but they made far more sense than the division into presidential administrations which was common in his day. So also did the basic theme through which he sought to explain the distinctiveness of America's history. The nation's story, he believed, had to be told in terms of the occupation of the continent, and of the ideas and institutions resulting from that occupation. Chief among these were the concept of democracy and the principle of federation. Turner saw the distinctive "form" of the American past to be "territory growth," the distinctive "idea" to be the relationship between local self-government and the federal authority. The interaction of these forces underlay the federal system of government and, in turn, influenced the conduct of foreign affairs, the slavery controversy, and "western growth." He viewed "land—homesteads—railroads" as instruments of that growth, and worthy of study. These were unusual concepts in a day when every historical work available to Turner viewed the history of the United States from the vantage point of New England and scarcely mentioned the westward expansion of the American people, let alone the impact of the West on the nation.

Sprinkled through Turner's lectures were occasional references that indicated his growing conviction that the frontier had played a part in shaping the past. The Salem witchcraft outbreak resulted from the impact of "the wilderness behind [the] settlements on [the] minds of people from populous England of somber temperament and rigid adherence to [the] Jewish code"; the English, Germans, and Scots-Irish who settled interior Pennsylvania formed a "frontier mixture"; in the lands ceded by the states national sovereignty was elevated above the "historic spirit of State Sov[ereignty]," and served as a strong nationalizing force. These were but a few straws in the wind, significant (if at all) only because of his later theories. Turner's basic views were orthodox, and he gave little attention to social and economic forces, but more than most young scholars of his day he was searching for the causal forces influencing the social organism he was studying.

If he was less bold than he might have been in his teaching, Turner's private speculations on the historical process were more unrestrained. These he jotted as he read. More and more now his home was the library of the State Historical Society, housed in the south wing of the state capitol building, where it overflowed the second floor. Lyman C. Draper, the dedicated wisp of a man who presided over the library's riches from 1854 to 1886, had built its collections from less than fifty volumes to more than 110,000, and he had stocked its shelves with an unrivaled collection of manuscript materials on the early history of Kentucky and Tennessee, newspaper files, government documents, and miscellaneous sources on the older West. His successor, Reuben Gold Thwaites, who took office on January 1, 1887, rivaled his predecessor in energy and in eagerness to aid scholarly investigators. Nowhere could Turner have found more ideal working conditions. Here was a scholar's heaven. "The books," he wrote Mae that year, "stand on their long lines of shelves like great armies; armies made up of the wisest men who ever lived. . . . To sit down on a stool and see the unexplored riches about one, riches that he couldn't begin to dig into in a lifetime, makes him very aware of his *littleness*, too."[27]

Turner's digging was thorough that year, and the more he dug the more he found history irresistible. The more, too, he realized that one aspect of the past fascinated him more than any other. "The more I dip into American history," he told Mae that fall, "the more I can see what a great field there is here for a life study. One must even specialize here. I think I shall spend my study chiefly upon the Northwest and more generally on the Mississippi Valley. The history of this great country remains to be written."[28] A few months later he was still boiling with enthusiasm. "I do not talk anything now but Western history. . . . I have taken a fever of enthusiasm about the possibilities of the study of the great west and of the magnificent scope of United States history in general."[29]

When came this decision? Turner never answered that question satisfactorily, and no one else could even approximate an explanation. His boyhood in Portage's quasi-frontier atmosphere, his awareness of his pioneer ancestors, the jolting realization during his trip to New England that the West was unique, the sectional pride that resented the neglect of his region by New England historians, his belief that the comparative techniques he had learned from Professor Allen could be used to unlock secrets about the American past—all these, perhaps, contributed to Turner's determination to study the West at a time when such an interest was unheard of. He understood the boldness of his decision. "I have," he wrote at the time, "started in a line that is not well travelled and I can see a way of treating it that is out of the usual line."[30]

Did he even then vaguely visualize the theory that was to make him famous? We will never know, but we do know that as he read, new ideas, new interpretations, new plans for research projects, crowded into his mind. We know, too, that a surprising number of these had to do with the role of the West as a formative force. The Commonplace Books he kept that year are filled with notes that mirrored his interests.[31] Some suggested topics worthy of investigation: collate the date of each permanent settlement in Wisconsin with the causes influencing migration; collect the treaties and state papers bearing on the West Florida controversy and show its relation to expansion into Louisiana, Texas, and Oregon; investigate the effect on American nationalism of the Georgia Indian controversy, Daniel Webster's speeches on nullification, the Civil War, and migration into new western states; study the connections between the boundary question, the weakness of the general government, and John Jay's attitude toward the Burr Conspiracy; investigate railroad construction as a consolidating force for the nation and show how railroads introduced groups of foreigners into the United States; explain why the North was so ready to coerce the South in 1860 in terms of Mississippi Valley commerce and the desire to possess the West. These might seem traditional subjects today, promising few riches for the prospector, but in 1887 they were revolutionary.

So were his interests in the formation and structure of western society, and in the role played by immigrant groups in community organization. These stemmed from observations made on his regular fishing trips into backwoods Wisconsin, where he saw recent German arrivals "dispossessing whole townships of Americans and introducing the customs and farming methods of the fatherland."[32] Sights such as these suggested new fields for investigation. How were societies formed in the West? "Need of study of foreign groups," he wrote in his Commonplace Book. "Anthropology, political economy, sociology, politics. Votes by districts. Why are Nor[wegians] Rep[ublican]. Irish Dem[ocrats]?" A short time later he added another observation: "Our composite nationality. Glances through a microscope in the historical laboratory. Biological methods applied to the study of a typical group of immigrants. The Pomeranian settlement at Portage. Evolution." The notations suggest Turner's line of thought. What would be the results, he was asking, as Europeans crowded Yankees from their lands, adjusted to American conditions, and adapted their imported techniques to the differing environment? Would the resulting civilization differ from that of their homelands? If so, what features of the new environment would cause alterations? These were exciting questions. "If I fill my letters with speculations about the evolution of American society from diverse elements of European origin," he warned Mae, "—don't think I am insane or that I love you the less; it will simply be an experiment in enthusiasm."[33] Turner reached no conclusions and was still a vast distance from his frontier hypothesis when he made those observations, but he was groping in that direction.

He was also beginning to build a reputation beyond the borders of Madison. Turner's first ventures into the world of publishing was probably arranged by his mentor; Professor Allen was a tireless book reviewer, and he saw no objection to sharing some of his spoils with his disciple. The reviews gave Turner little chance to expound his own interpretations; he was asked to appraise two volumes on Benjamin Franklin by Edward Everett Hale—*Franklin in France* and *Franklin the Peacemaker*—for *The Dial*, a well-known literary magazine. Thirty pages of notes on the reading done for those reviews attest to the thoroughness of Turner's preparation. This bore sturdy fruit; his judgments were sophisticated, judicious, and properly critical, particularly in pointing out the specific contributions made by each volume.[34] The editor of *The Dial* was delighted, calling it "an excellent article," and Professor Allen was sufficiently impressed to recommend Turner to his friends on the staff of *The Nation*. More reviews followed, most of them short notices that were published unsigned in that worthy journal. One that he particularly enjoyed was a review of James R. Gilmore's *John Sevier*, a book that he found good because it showed that "the valley of the Mississippi is a too much neglected branch of the history of the country," and bad because it stressed boldness of characterization and smoothness of narrative rather than "the accuracy and cautiousness of statement that should mark historical composition."[35] These sound judgments pleased the editor of *The Nation*, who sent on a whole bundle of books for review, as well as Lyman C. Draper, who praised them highly and made cautious suggestions that Turner aid him in editing some of the manuscripts he had gathered, and Reuben G. Thwaites, who thought that his young colleague might join him in writing a history of the state.

Kudos bred kudos, and Turner did not wait long before more came his way. President Chamberlin was the instigator; he had been invited to prepare the article on Wisconsin for the *Encyclopaedia Britannica*, and while he felt competent to do the sections on physiography and geology, he was less certain that he could deal with the history of the state. Would Turner be interested? Turner was interested, even though he was burdened with the excessive teaching load of the winter term and a thesis that demanded attention. He put himself to the task at once, combing census returns and government reports for statistics, digging into the capitol archives, and wringing information from his friends in the legislature. For three weeks he worked steadily until well after midnight; "I feel as though I had been through a threshing machine," he reported to Mae when it was done at last.[36] The result was worthy of the effort. In remarkably few words he sketched the evolution of the state's complex economic and political system from its primitive beginnings, tracing the stages of growth, describing the transition from lead mining to lumbering to agriculture, and showing the effect of the Civil War on the emergence of an industrial-urban civilization.[37] In the article Turner again demonstrated his concept of history as genetic growth, and of society as an evolving organism constantly altered by internal and external forces. One has only to contrast Turner's treatment of Wisconsin with the antiquarian histories of other states in the ninth edition of the *Encyclopaedia Britannica* to realize the extent of his contribution.

More to Turner's liking was his third publication to be completed that busy year, even though the pressure of other duties forced him to delay this until the summer of 1888. Once more Professor Allen was responsible. He had been asked to compile an outline and reading list on the history of the West to be distributed through the National Bureau of Unity Clubs as a guide for women's groups, but was too ill to do a proper job. Turner was delighted to accept an assignment so congenial to his tastes, even though the deadline was only a few weeks away. He soon discovered that he had taken on a major task; only the best books on each subject could be mentioned, but all books had to be read to select those to be included. Yet the work was done on time, and in a manner that won Professor Allen's verdict of "very good."[38]

Outline Studies in the History of the Northwest was hardly a precedent-smashing contribution to western historical studies, but it was the first booklet to bear Turner's name, and it was typically Turnerian in its genetic approach, its stress on geography as a necessary backdrop for historic events, and its emphasis on the stages of growth common to emerging societies. Its fifteen topics (that being the number specified as fitting best into the club year) began with "The Land of the Aborigines" and progressed through "French Exploration," "French Occupation," "French and Indian Wars," "English and Spanish Dominance," "The Northwest in the Revolution," "The Ordinance of 1787," "The Northwest Territory," "The Louisiana Purchase," "Slavery in the Northwest," "The Exploration and Occupation of the Northwest Coast," "The Struggle for Oregon," "The Great American Desert," and "The Alaska Purchase," to "The Northwest of Today." Under each heading the best books were listed and described, a bibliographical exercise that revealed its author to be far better versed in the history of the Old Northwest than of the far western states.[39] Whatever its merits, Turner had produced the first published outline of frontier history. The hundreds that were to follow, from Turner's pen and from the pens of his followers, were to make many improvements but add little to the basic structure.

If Fred J. Turner was gaining his first slight national reputation, his local fame was growing far more spectacularly, and with good cause. He had an irresistible combination of virtues as a public speaker; his melodious voice and training in oratory allowed him to captivate any audience, while his knowledge of western history provided him glamorous subject matter that few Wisconsinites could resist. So it was that he found himself pushed into the limelight on two occasions during that overcrowded academic year, both with exciting results and both adding to his reputation as a student of the West.

The first grew from his activities in the Madison Unitarian Church—strangely enough, for he was a scoffer who had been turned from religion by the "nonsense" preached by his first Sunday School teacher, and he now felt that theology was "about as substantial as an ice to a man who hasn't eaten anything for a month."[40] But Professor Allen was a pillar of Unitarianism, and the minister, the Reverend Dr. J. H. Crooker, was a rationalist whose staunch defense of the University had won him the loyalty of its faculty. When Allen urged his young colleague to join the two young people's clubs sponsored by the church, he readily did so. One, the Channing Club, was devoted to religious discussions and had little appeal to Turner, although he did become a member and participated in at least two lively meetings, one on New England's church history, the other on Benjamin Franklin's religious views.[41] The other, the Contemporary Club, was more to his taste; this was divided into five groups that met fortnightly to hear papers on contemporary history, current literature, social science, modern art, or the latest scientific discoveries. The contemporary history group was made to Turner's inclinations, and he entered into its activities with such enthusiasm that he became the club's president during the 1887-88 year—an office foisted on him, he told Mae, because he dozed off during a long discussion of Rider Haggard's novels and was elected before he could protest.[42]

Turner learned a great deal at the Contemporary Club, and he gave a great deal to it in return. Twice he engaged in discussions that provided background for his later theories—one an analysis of Hermann von Holst's *Constitutional History of the United States,* which he was to recall when, a few years later, he berated that eminent historian for failure to reckon the frontier's significance, another on a lecture delivered in 1887 by Henry George, who spoke on "Land and Labor." Turner paid less attention to that land reformer's views than he should —his thoughts drifted to Mae and how pleasant it would be to be a landowner in a shady part of Mendota's shore—but something of the single tax lodged in his mind, to be unearthed when he pondered the effect of free land on the settlement process.[43]

He was also preparing himself for his major contribution to the Contemporary Club's program. The suggestion came from Professor Allen: why not give a series of lectures on the history of the Old Northwest? Boston's Old South Church was attracting national attention with its scholarly lectures, pleasingly presented; shouldn't some be given at Madison? Then, too, such a series would popularize American history as a field of study, correcting the imbalance that made European history so popular. Turner rose to the bait at once, drafting the surprisingly rich local talent—Consul W. Butterfield, Reuben Gold Thwaites, Allen himself—scheduling dates between January and April 1888, and preparing a syllabus that would guide the audience. These preparations proved so effective that the Unitarian Church was packed to overflowing for the first lecture and even more crowded for the second.[44]

All this acclaim made his own task more difficult. His assignment was the third lecture on "The Ordinance of 1787," a subject not unduly difficult to prepare. Or so he thought as he began writing during the Christmas holiday, well in advance of his March 5, 1888, delivery date; he would have the whole thing done in two days. Two weeks later, as the vacation was drawing to a close, he had "just begun to write a little," and found it "uphill work." Another month and a first draft was ready, but it was a rough first draft with much yet to be done. At that point Turner made a near-fatal mistake: he showed his paper to Allen and Thwaites. "Allen thought I had not prepared the lecture sufficiently; Thwaites thought it was too long. Allen said read your documents in full; Thwaites said cut 'em out and generalize." Caught between this conflicting advice, he followed his own path by trying to "lighten it up" and shorten it a bit. This took time. Two days before that March 5 delivery date he was still at work, fortifying himself with a daily glass of sherry as "a good thing to use for a 'spurt.' "[45]

These heroic sacrifices bore fruit, for he was ready by March 5 to face the audience-jammed church with a completed manuscript before him. Judged by modern historical standards, the result hardly justified the effort. His views were thoroughly orthodox; his oratory embarrassingly ornate. "On the side of Wolfe fought the English language, democracy, and local self-government"; the Revolution was won by "men of the Anglo-Saxon race" who "against the divine right of the King, set the divine right of *man*"; George Rogers Clark was a holy crusader who won the West for the new Republic; the American peace negotiators were "a trio of Americans [who] beat the crafty ministers of France and Spain at their own game"; the unselfishness of "plucky Maryland" forced greedy Virginia to cede its western lands; the Ordinance of 1787 was a "charter of liberty" that struck a death blow at slavery.[46] Turner was treading no new paths when he laid those platitudes before his audience, but they loved it. For an hour and a half they listened enraptured as he read his way through sixty-seven pages of manuscript; then they rocked the hall with their applause. "He is," judged the local critic, "thoroughly conversant with his subject and handled it in a scholarly manner, evincing great enthusiasm and historical research."[47]

Here was glory, and Turner loved it. More was to come over the next days as tributes poured in—from his students, from other lecturers in the series, from Thwaites, who thought he had "made a ten strike." He was in seventh heaven. "I am," he confessed to Mae, "surprised at my love of praise. It is like wine to me."[48] More was to come as the series moved to its triumphant conclusion with a lecture by Professor Allen on "The Position of the Northwest in General History"—a lecture marred by the fact that Allen was ill and asked Turner to read his paper for him. There was no gainsaying that Madison was well pleased with the program; even more gratifying was the fact that it attracted national attention. A number of newspapers noted its success, educators and historians voiced their approval, and the influential *New England Journal of Education* described it as worthy of imitation elsewhere.[49]

There was no time for Turner to bask in his glory; spring was at hand and he still had his master's thesis to complete. He had made precious little progress that academic year, partly because he was juggling a half-dozen assignments in addition to his teaching, partly because the French language required more time for mastery than he could allot. He tried, but there were too many temptations. "If I can possibly find opportunity this term I mean to take up some French studying," he confided to Mae as the school year began. "I need that language especially." A month later he could report some progress: "Last evening I read French—half a dozen pages. It was easy French of course, and I guessed at some things." That spurt did not carry him far. December found him still floundering, and in April, with the thesis deadline only weeks away, he was almost ready to give up. "I must," he told Mae, "learn to read French fluently this summer."[50] No prophet was needed to predict that Turner's dilly-dallying would delay his degree well beyond the 1888 commencement, and perhaps forever.

It might have done so, but for one saving factor. Like many compulsive non-finishers, he could work under the lash; given a deadline and enough pressure, and Turner would respond. This came in the form of an invitation from Professor Allen to read a paper on the Wisconsin fur trade to the prestigious Madison Literary Club, a gathering of the cultural elite of town and gown. Here was a summons that could not be refused; from the day in October when he accepted, Turner knew he *had* to have a paper ready by mid-May of 1888. "I shall," he admitted, "have to do some lively scratching if I don't get picked all to pieces. It will be good exercise for me."[51] All that fall and winter he worked only haphazardly, picking his way slowly through the water-stained pages of trading records, painfully deciphering badly scrawled letters, building a pile of notes so slowly that the end seemed nowhere in sight. Cheerfully optimistic, as usual, Turner was not in the least alarmed—not, that is, until May Day awakened him to the unpleasant fact that his paper had to be delivered in only two weeks and that scarcely a line had been written.

These were the conditions under which he worked best. For the next fortnight Fred Turner lived, breathed, thought, the Wisconsin fur trade. "My room is rustling like a forest with leaves on the price of beaver skins and whiskey, bread and bullets, brass ear knobs and tobacco. . . . The gay chant of the Canadian voyageur rings out . . . in my nightly dreams and I murmur fantastic French in my sleep"— "At present when anyone says 'dear' I think of deer, mention of Martin Luther makes me say 'yes a martin was worth $1.00,' . . . I have hobnobbed with the midnight stars regularly and allowed lessons to care for themselves." Those were the words of a young man who was very hard at work indeed. By the end of those two weeks Turner was in disgrace with his family, his friends, and even with Mae, "and all because I have been trying to get some style and spice and connection into a long row of facts and figures."[52]

His dilemma was as old as Herodotus: should he be dully realistic or imaginatively glamorous as he told his story? Fred Turner knew what he wanted to do. He wrote to Mae:

I am trying to tell how the forest which was to the Englishman a gloomy, repellent, witch haunted realm, lying in its darkness behind his doors, tenanted with lurking foes—not to be entered except with defiant conquering spirit—was to the Frenchman a gay, witching, inviting thing. If it wasn't too flowery I should also like to say that the St. Lawrence flushed an irresistible invitation down its watery course, and whispered to the Frenchman of the Great Lakes from which it came—that the wilderness sang to him in the melody of its waterfalls, thrilled him by the solemn music of its pines, dashed him with the spray of cataracts, awed him by the mystery of its dark glades, and brought him its untutored children to wonder at his goods and call him master—even as Caliban lay at the feet of Trinculo and the potent bottle on Prospero's enchanted island.[53]

He could not do so, of course; one can almost hear him sigh as he went on to say that he had to stick by his facts. Yet the struggle took time. Two days before the paper was due the final draft was only half written; not until minutes before it was to be delivered were the last flourishes added. "I feel," he confessed, "like a Freshman who is coming on with an essay and must write it at twelve o'clock the night before."[54]

Miraculously, Turner was ready when he arrived at the door of Burr W. Jones's Langdon Street home, to find an unusually large audience awaiting him. The next two hours were something less than pleasant to Turner. He spoke well, and the critics named by the Literary Club to comment were extravagant in their praise. So was the local press when it reported the event the next day. He had prepared a "capital" paper that was both "interesting and instructive"; he had "re-peopled the dark forests of early Wisconsin with the now forgotten *couriers des bois;* revived the old Canadian boat songs which were wont in olden times to echo through the gloomy and bluff-girt valleys"; "presented a vivid picture of life at those outposts of civilization."[55] But Turner knew better. "I am not proud over its success," he confessed; in his own mind he had made a reputation "as a digger in fields uninteresting" and had proven that the dry subject could never captivate a popular audience.[56]

Whether he was right or wrong, the Literary Club appearance had forced him to complete his thesis. He read the entire document to Professor Allen a short time later and was duly praised; Allen thought it good enough to be published by the State Historical Society. Allen was right, for despite its overemphasis on detail and its underemphasis on interpretation, "The Character and Influence of the Fur Trade in Wisconsin" was a pioneering work that revealed many of the virtues of Turner the mature historian. His concern was not only with the "what" but with the "why"; his careful study of the state's geographic features allowed him to show that trading routes not only determined the early economic growth of the region, but played their role in international diplomacy. Even more significant was the evolutionary approach he adopted; brushing aside George Bancroft and Francis Parkman, who viewed the fur trade as an insignificant phenomenon, he pictured the trader as a herald of progress and an essential ingredient in the emergence of civilization. "The Indian village," he wrote, "became the trading post, the trading post became the city. The trails became our early roads. The portages marked out locations for canals. . . . In a word, the fur trade closed its mission by becoming the path finder for agricultural and manufacturing civilization."[57] This was state history at its best, unmarred by the antiquarianism so universal in that day, and linking the local events that Turner was studying with the national scene.

It was also the last step in his progress toward the coveted (and in those days, rare) master of arts degree. Fred J. Turner was graduated on a stifling hot day in June of 1888, together with five others who had completed their graduate work, then vanished into the north woods with his father, to enjoy the healing balm of trout fishing. He needed such an interlude, for his future had already been determined—much to his dissatisfaction. He was to continue his graduate work and earn a doctor of philosophy degree, not in his beloved Madison, with Mae in near-by Chicago, but at the awesome Johns Hopkins University, in distant Baltimore. And he was to begin that painful ordeal that autumn.

This thoroughly disagreeable prospect was forced on Turner by President Chamberlin. An able administrator with high ambitions for his little university, Chamberlin recognized the potential skills of his young friend and saw in him a chance to add to the faculty a degree-holder from the nation's outstanding history department. Turner had other ideas. He wanted the doctorate eventually, and he recognized the preeminence of Johns Hopkins, but he also wanted assurance that he could return to Wisconsin as a professor as soon as he had earned his degree.

Or, if this proved unacceptable to the president (as it did), he would stay on as instructor for one more year, but as the head of his own American history department, then accept a leave of absence for study at Hopkins in 1889-90. He was confident that he would succeed. "I have," he wrote Mae, "a line of work mapped out in Western history which is untouched and which I think will prove worth my study and a basis for securing position in some institution if not here [*sic*]."[58]

Turner had rosy dreams, but it was President Chamberlin who had the power of decision, and, in April 1888, he laid down the law. Turner would spend the 1888-89 academic year on his doctorate; he would not be assured a professorship or even a post until he had proven himself; if he did well in competition with the cream of the nation's historians in the East, he *might* be welcomed back as an instructor at a considerably higher salary than he had been earning. Turner had no alternative but to accept this ruling with good grace. He asked only that his leave of absence be kept secret until a substitute could be found who was not sufficiently talented to get a foothold in the department. By June all arrangements were made, and the Board of Regents publicly announced that Turner had been granted leave "to enable him to perfect himself in his specialty at Johns Hopkins University."[59] "It is hoped," wrote the local editor, "that at the end of his course at Johns Hopkins he may return to Madison and again take up his work as instructor of oratory and history, for which he is so well fitted."[60]

Fred Turner must have shuddered as he read those remarks, for he had no intention of suffering through more instruction in oratory, and he was determined to return to nothing less than a professorship. Yet the decision had been made. He would be a university teacher, he hoped at the University of Wisconsin, if not there, then at some other institution. Twice that summer he refused lucrative offers of high school posts—one paying $1400 and the other $1500—even though the temptation was strong to settle into a comfortable existence with Mae at his side.[61] He had to prepare himself for a career in teaching and research, and Johns Hopkins was the ideal training ground. Turner chose wisely, for that year in Baltimore was to be one of the most pleasant, and probably the most significant, of his whole career.

III

The Making of a Historian:

JOHNS HOPKINS

1888-1889

FRED J. TURNER arrived in Baltimore on September 25, 1888, thoroughly dissatisfied with himself and dismally unhappy. He was gloomily aware that he had wasted most of the summer. True, he had completed the syllabus on *Outline Studies of the History of the Northwest*, which was soon to be published, but he had scarcely touched his French studies and had done little of the reading needed to prepare himself for the awesome Johns Hopkins courses. Instead he had squandered weeks on the trout streams of northern Wisconsin and had spent an idyllic fortnight with Mae in the cool forests of northern Michigan, near Marquette. Those were happy experiences, but his conscience burdened him now as he thought of the responsibilities ahead. "I am ashamed of myself at the end of every summer," he confessed, "when I think how very little I have worked. It is a bad habit I have gotten into."[1] He would have to pay for his sins now, and the price would be high.

To add to his woes he was nursing a miserable cold, apprehensive of the new world that he must conquer, and desperately lonesome for Mae. They had parted in New York, she to settle into her hay-fever sanctuary at Conway, he to take "the cars" southward. "You must be with me or I am the most miserable man in the world," he wrote.[2] Sad at heart, he checked into the Carrollton Hotel, reported his presence to the registrar of the university, and spent twelve unhappy hours tramping the streets in search of a room. Never had he seen such run-down, bad-looking, vile-smelling boardinghouses in all his life. All were the same: the haircloth chair on which he was seated while the servant sought out the mistress, the gilt-framed pier glass and sepulchral fireplace, the engravings of Robert E. Lee and "Stonewall" Jackson, the relics of the late departed husband, the mysterious odors that blended garlic, dust, and antiquity. The mistresses were all the same too, drab and yellow in appearance, gushing that they only took in boarders because they were lonely and loved young men, eager to show the cells that they called rooms, and the beds that were perfect racks, built on slabs with a husk mattress covered with quilts that might have covered the limbs of Noah, save that neither flood nor washing had ever touched them. "So I have wandered from street to street all day with almost exactly the same experience."[3]

When he finally came upon the boardinghouse kept by Mary Jane and Hannah Ashton, at 909 McCulloch Street, Turner knew he had found his haven. Mary Jane, who managed affairs, was an "old maid" of some thirty summers, but she was perennially young in her understanding of youth, able to regale them with lively conversation, and sympathetic when they rebelled against long hours of study with pranks and high jinks. His room was comfortable—"the most elegant room for sleeping I have ever found," he reported to his mother—and the meals bountiful—deviled crab, beefsteaks, toasted crackers, rolls, corn cakes, sweet and Irish potatoes, pears and grapes, for breakfast; roast, vegetables, hot breads, and sweets for the noonday dinner; cold ham, tongue, bologna, a box of sardines, and crackers for tea; fish or meat with hot breads for the light supper. Best of all was the companionship. For a half-dozen years Miss Ashton's ample care had attracted history students—Woodrow Wilson, Charles Howard Shinn, Albert Shaw, Charles H. Levermore, and a host more—all of whom made a point of returning to her establishment when visiting Baltimore; Woodrow Wilson was to spend the spring term there, to Turner's lasting benefit. The present company was almost as distinguished: Charles Homer Haskins, the brilliant young medievalist, and Robert K. Aikman of New York University, whose passion for photography sometimes overbalanced his scholarly interests, boarded at Miss Ashton's. Only two old maid spinsters who occupied one of the rooms cast a pall over this lively crew.[4]

His physical needs satisfied, Turner sought out the Johns Hopkins professors who would be his guides. There he experienced a major disappointment. J. Franklin Jameson, who taught most of the American history courses, was to be on leave that year, dooming him once more to heavy doses in two areas outside his major interest: medieval and European history under Herbert Baxter Adams, and political economy under Richard T. Ely. The program that they helped him arrange was memorable both for quantity and variety: the "History of Politics," "Church History," and "International Law" under Adams; "The History of Political Economy," "Elements of Political Economy," and "Special Economic Questions," with Ely; a study of "Social Science" taught by visiting lecturers, and, for some inexplicable reason, a freshman survey of "Advanced Algebra, Analytical Geometry, and Calculus." Capping this strange smorgasbord was the famed history seminar, which met each Friday night from eight to ten, and was taught by the entire department.[5]

Whatever his courses, Turner could learn much, for Johns Hopkins was then an oasis in the intellectual desert of American education. Still in its lusty infancy, it centered within itself the renaissance that was revitalizing the quest for learning in the United States. All was turbulent, all was new, all was exciting, as students and faculty united to push back the borders of knowledge, unhindered by the tradition and lethargy that made such older institutions as Harvard "as solidified as the bones of the Mammoth," in Herbert Baxter Adams's phrase. Hopkins, Turner later remembered, lured students from all the nation and let them form the university; Harvard attracted nationally but forced its undergraduates into the matrix of New England culture.[6] This was not far wrong, for in those days Johns Hopkins approached the ideal of the national university of which George Washington had dreamed. Graduates of ninety-six colleges were enrolled in the graduate school in 1888-89, merging their sectional enthusiasms into a common purpose, and generating a yeasty atmosphere that encouraged adventuring along untrodden intellectual trails.

These were many, for in the 1880s, the whole world of the mind, in both Europe and America, was in ferment, stirred by Charles Darwin's evolutionary hypothesis. As this gained credence, scholars in every discipline reappraised their subjects by applying biological concepts: geologists talked now of the earth as an "organism," economists applied the same term to institutions, and historians applied it to human societies. These were pictured as constantly changing, constantly evolving, for this was the law of the universe. All past knowledge was outmoded; man must restudy every branch of learning for evidence of the growth that was now recognized as the basic fact of life, whether of biological or social organisms. Scholarship was on the threshold of a vast adventure that would reveal the truth for the first time, and in America Johns Hopkins University was the nucleus of that search.

All faculty members and students were aware of this distinction, and all were determined that the university should wear its badge proudly. This meant constant, furious, dedicated work. When Charles McLean Andrews, a contemporary of Turner's, observed that there was "almost a religious fervor among the younger scholars," he was telling only half the truth; that same fanaticism toward learning infected the faculty and drove them to heroic effort. There was competition among the students to excell; there was competition between faculty members; there was competition between students and faculty. Professors—and there was one for every nine pupils—goaded the students to work ever harder, then worked ever harder themselves to keep abreast of the students. "Johns Hopkins," Turner reported after he had been there a few months, "keeps a man at work from morning till after midnight. . . . Here it is a constant race between the professors and the students to see who can do the most work."[7]

The marketplace where they displayed the fruits of their learning was not the classroom (Turner was disturbed to find that lectures—and very dull lectures, at that—were the normal method of instruction, rather than the "topical" approach used so successfully at Wisconsin), but the famed "Seminary" under Professors Adams and Ely. This, the catalogue declared, is not a class but "an association of instructors with the fellows and other graduate students in this department for the prosecution of original studies in American history, institutional, social and economic." Its purpose was not to teach history but to learn history; its students would become master historians by working with master historians, then they would apply the research techniques they learned to problems of their own. Herbert Baxter Adams saw the seminar as a meeting place for scholars who would work cooperatively to unlock the secrets of the past, exchanging views, sharing discoveries, and gaining knowledge by their joint efforts. Here the entire history of the United States—and of the world—would be rewritten.

The seminar's setting was worthy of its objectives. Stretching down the middle of a third-floor room in the university library was a red-topped table strewn with the latest journals and pamphlets, with seats for twenty-four students, each of whom had a drawer for his writing materials. Eight thousand books, arranged in alcoves by subjects, lined the walls; above them were hung portraits of the giants of the historical world—Edward A. Freeman, Lord Bryce, George Bancroft, Hermann von Holst—and interspersed among these were plaster busts of Jared Sparks, Francis Lieber, Alexander Hamilton, and John C. Calhoun. Emblazoned above a bulletin board, in large letters, was the theme of the seminar: Edward A. Freeman's dictum that "History is Past Politics, and Politics Present History." Opening from the main room were offices for instructors; two lecture rooms; a newspaper "bureau," where copies of the latest journals were displayed; and "a geographical and statistical bureau."

Fred Turner found fascinating new interests in every corner of the seminar room, but the "geographical and statistical bureau" excited him most. Here were the raw tools that he was to use through a lifetime devoted to mapping data on political demography and applying statistical techniques to cartography. The room was the creation of the able president of Johns Hopkins, Daniel Coit Gilman, himself a statistically oriented geographer; at his insistence it was equipped with maps, charts, diagrams, atlases, and a series of wall maps that could be used to illustrate the physiographic basis for the history of any nation. Professor Adams heartily agreed with this emphasis; "In the Johns Hopkins University," he wrote, "physical and historical geography are made the basis of instruction in historical and political science."[8] This approach was not completely new to Turner; Professor Allen had relied heavily on the use of maps, and he had infected his prize pupil with his interests. But for the first time Turner could realize the variety of the tools available to the historian interested in the graphic presentation of data. His lifetime use of statistical and cartographic techniques was certainly shaped by his Hopkins experience.

If Turner gained much from Hopkins's "geographical and statistical bureau," he gained far more from the exciting new world of historical studies that awaited him. Professor Allen, gifted though he was, and alert to changing intellectual tides, was too isolated to stay abreast of the latest developments along the eastern seaboard or to be fully aware of progress in allied fields that influenced historical thought. At Madison, Turner had been in a cultural backwash, better supplied than most, but still distant from the populous East, where the winds of change blew most strongly. In Baltimore he was in the center of the academic world, surrounded by the half-dozen historians and political economists who were primarily responsible for these changes. He entered that mainstream, moreover, just at a time when historical scholarship was in the midst of the twofold transformation that ushered in its modern age. On the one hand, it was shedding its "amateur" status and becoming professionalized; on the other, it was shifting from a "romantic" to a "scientific" methodology. Turner was cast into the middle of this revolution, to his lasting benefit.

Professionalism was a natural outgrowth of the multiplication of universities during the late nineteenth century, and of the utilitarian assault on the traditional classical curriculum that followed. With education reaching an ever-widening segment of the population, and with preparation for life rather than for the clergy its objective, historical studies assumed new importance as essential to training for citizenship. For that reason, history courses proliferated; between 1884 and 1894 the number of full-time teachers of history skyrocketed, from twenty to more than a hundred. The reluctant classicist or philosopher who had been sufficient for such instruction in the past would no longer do; departments of history began to appear in the burgeoning graduate programs that were remaking American universities; by the time Johns Hopkins was founded, in 1876, twenty-five institutions awarded the doctoral degree, and more were to come. The trademark of these universities was the historical seminar, introduced into Michigan, Harvard, and Johns Hopkins during the 1870s to train the research-oriented young professors who would staff the growing number of history departments. These scholars, all thoroughly impressed with the quality of their own education, felt vastly superior to the "literary" historians who had long dominated the field—the George Bancrofts, the Francis Parkmans, the William H. Prescotts, the John L. Motleys—and demanded a professional society that would recognize their elevated status. This was formed in 1884, when Herbert Baxter Adams summoned forty-one eminent historical scholars to Saratoga Springs, New York, to draft a constitution for the American Historical Association. By 1890 the association had more than six hundred members, many of them amateurs, but all dedicated to the dual purpose of indoctrinating their countrymen in history and serving as guardians of the nation's cultural heritage.[9] The craft had its guild, and was proudly conscious of its professionalism.

Even more important to Turner was the rise of "scientific" history. This began to emerge in the early 1880s, fostered by a rebellion against the traditional romanticism that had characterized historical studies for generations. America's scientific historians found their inspiration in the theories of two individuals. One was Leopold von Ranke, whose school of German historiography was then in full flower; practitioners of this cult made objectivity their idol and sought to reveal exactly what happened in the past, unmarred by interpretation or evaluation. The other was Charles Darwin, who, along with his fellow biologists was then in the public eye. From the evolutionists, scientific historians adopted a methodology based on experimentation and inductive reasoning, and a concept of society as a continuously evolving organism responding to changing pressures, just as did animal organisms.

Objectivity was the first essential, and to achieve this they had to re-study critically the primary sources that recorded mankind's history, extracting from them exact facts, just as a paleontologist would use fossil remains to reconstruct the precise truth about a phase of animal evolution. These facts should speak for themselves, unmarred by the prejudices or opinions of the investigator. Hypotheses and interpretation were outlawed, lest they distort the objectivity of the interpreter. The sole duty of the historian was to accumulate masses of facts, arrange them in proper order, and allow a synthesis to emerge. Scientific historians saw history as the purest of all disciplines, for it alone was built on inductive reasoning and banned all conjecture.

The evolutionary hypothesis was just as essential to the new methodology. Scholars had to re-examine the past not only to achieve objectivity, but to record the growth of institutions as they responded to internal and external pressures. Historians could reveal the continuous, connected, chain of events through which social organisms evolved from their genesis to the present day. This was a noble ambition, but they soon found it unattainable; nature provided biologists with the succession of fossil remains needed to show the evolution of a species, but man's written records were too few and too recent to allow institutions to be traced to their remote beginnings. The ingenious solution to this dilemma was to adopt the "comparative" technique of the philologists. Linguists taught that similarities in word forms revealed their common origin; why not assume that institutions could be studied in the same way? The scientific historian could compare a modern institution—such as a New England town—with an ancient institution—the medieval German *tun*—and if he found similarities, conclude that the one evolved from the other. This was the twisted logic that fostered the "Teutonic" or "germ" school of history in the 1870s and 1880s. Its members held that the Aryo-Teutonic peoples who had occupied the Black Forest of Germany in the days of Tacitus had developed the democratic institutions later to be shared by Great Britain, Germany, and the United States. The task of the historian was to compare American institutions with those of the ancient Teutons, and when the comparison proved exact, proclaim that he had discovered the "germ" of that institution.[10]

The holy temple of the Teutonists was Johns Hopkins University, and its high priest was Herbert Baxter Adams. Adams's own contribution to the succession of absurdities that they produced was to link select New England towns with the tribal councils of Germanic tribes. There Teutons brandished spears to show their assent, or muttered their dissent. This proved they practiced democracy. So did New England towns. Therefore New England towns were "survivals" of the tribal councils, the flowering of a "germ" that had lain fallow in Anglo-Saxons for a thousand years. So Adams wrote in his *Germanic Origins of New England Towns*. He also added an unbelievable amount of nonsense. The ancient Teutons developed in their *moots* "the seeds of parliamentary or self-government, of Commons and Congresses," the concept of a single head of state, the use of a small council, and the delegation of authority to "a general assembly of the whole people." In these practices "lay the germs of religious reformation and popular revolutions, the ideas which have formed Germany and Holland, England and New England, the *United States*." "It is," wrote Adams, "just as improbable that free local institutions should spring up without a germ along American shores as that English wheat should have grown there without planting."[11] These were the views, weird delusions though they were, that formed the mainstream of American historical thought when Turner entered Johns Hopkins. He was to sit for a year at the feet of the man who had done more to professionalize history, and to popularize the then-accepted Teutonic germ theory, than any other scholar in the nation.

This was the thrilling new world that waited Turner as he settled into the routine of the Hopkins graduate school. His schedule was filled with a constant round of lectures, work at the library, endless reading in the assigned textbooks, and (the brightest spot of all) the seminar. From the first, on October 5, he found those Friday night meetings the most exciting event of the week. Across from him were the older graduate students, sitting in awesome array: Charles L. Smith, who had studied in Germany; Charles McLean Andrews, one of the two university "Fellows," strikingly handsome, with "a dark expression, and finely moulded face"; Charles Homer Haskins, "very young, but a strong man"; others whose names he had not yet learned. Beside him was a fellow-westerner, Frank W. Blackmar of the University of California. Dr. Adams, seated at the head of the table, explained the methods and purpose of the seminar, called on Frank Blackmar to read a paper on "Relation of the State to Higher Education," joined with Dr. Ely in comments that showed how much he knew about higher education, then talked until ten o'clock about his own experiences in adult education at the summer Chautauqua assembly. "A wonderfully energetic man," Turner described him when he wrote to Mae that night, "able to get work out of a crowd."[12]

Evenings such as that, with a dozen men as sharp as himself, were glorious experiences to a young man of Turner's inclinations, and his letters glowed with enthusiasm. "I was," he reported to his mother, "likely to drift into superficial work when I left Madison—now I have caught a little of the spirit of genuine scholarship—and it is rejuvenating." To Mae he was more outspoken: "I am in the full swing of university life and I *like* it! I am becoming to feel like a boy let out of school,—and I really wish to jump and shout aloud in the new freedom and happiness of having pleasant work and *only* pleasant work. I am growing like a plant in the sunshine."[13] When Adams and Ely assured him that he could complete his doctorate in one year—if he learned enough French and German to pass the reading tests—his happiness overflowed. Johns Hopkins was an academic heaven, and all was right with the world.

This exultant mood soon dimmed; as the first excitement died away, he felt a little lost in the impersonal vastness of Baltimore. He was strictly on his own, with no Professor Allen at his elbow to give advice and encouragement, and this heightened his sense of loneliness. Then, too, the excessive number of courses that he had elected proved an impossible burden, and he was daily falling behind in his work. A period of soul-searching and some good counsel from Professor Allen solved his problem; he decided to focus his reading on work for the seminar, the course on the nineteenth century under Adams, and Professor Ely's courses in political economy, in the process dropping church history, and listening to the lectures on Roman history and international law without attempting to do the assignments. This sensible adjustment made life easier, but Turner was still unhappy that his enthusiasm for the West found few sympathizers; only two fellow-students showed a spark of interest, one studying the Spanish missions of California and the other willing to consider a dissertation topic suggested by Turner on the frontier land companies of the post-Revolutionary era.[14] Madison was a happier hunting ground for one of Turner's inclinations.

These dissatisfactions were minor, and they were soon forgotten as he immersed himself in his studies or sought relaxation in Baltimore's abundant culture. Long hours of work, when his brain felt so thoroughly saturated that it would shed any additional information, were balanced with walks about the Maryland countryside, or vigorous daily exercise in the college gymnasium, or musical performances that stirred him to tears of joy; after hearing *Il Trovatore* he felt that he should pawn all his books and become an artist, and he realized after attending a series of six symphony concerts that he had never properly lived before. He spent his Sundays visiting the churches of the city, one by one—Catholic, Protestant, and, most frequently, Quaker—to be overwhelmed by the music and pagentry but untouched by the spiritual appeals. The Quaker services were his favorites, but their drab monotony soon palled; "I don't like colorless things too long," he explained to Mae. "There must be some novelty, some spice about things, or I am in danger of getting ennui."[15] Turner did not know it, but he was admitting one trait that would make it impossible for him to write books that parroted well-known facts of the past.

The Christmas holidays offered fresh diversions, for his flattened pocketbook decreed that he could not go to Chicago to see Mae. Instead, a very lonesome Turner dined that Christmas day at the home of

Dr. Ely, forgot his troubles by immersing himself in Edward Bellamy's *Looking Backward*, and spent a memorable three days at the annual convention of the American Historical Association, in near-by Washington. The papers that he heard intrigued him not at all—they were too detailed and their "facts were not *illuminated*"—but he did enjoy rubbing elbows with the greats of the profession, and he did enjoy giving a paper himself. This was a favor for Professor Allen, who was unable to attend and asked Turner to present the essay that he had previously read to the Contemporary Club on "The Place of the Northwest in General History." Turner did so so effectively that the association's secretary wrote glowingly of the manner in which he had described "that march across the continent which really constitutes America."[16]

He was to perform again during the next weeks, and on no less than three occasions. The first took place without his presence; on January 2 in distant Madison his master's thesis on the Wisconsin fur trade, revised into suitable form, was read to the State Historical Society of Wisconsin by its secretary, Reuben Gold Thwaites. This was an important step in Turner's career, for his thesis could now be published by the society, and he could follow his soon-to-be-usual practice of ordering a hundred copies to be distributed wholesale throughout the profession. Some responded with less enthusiasm than he would have liked —Francis Parkman could unbend only to the extent of finding it "interesting"—but Turner was pleased with the "complimentary letters" that came his way and eager to get on with a publication that "will really justify praise."[17]

His second assignment was more to his liking. The seminar was progressing in its usual confusing way—Turner listened that winter with varying degrees of interest to papers on the statistical techniques of the Interstate Commerce Commission, congressional legislation in Indiana, the relation of the Continental Congress to the colonies, and the history of Greek coinage—but his turn was to come. Two turns, in fact, first with a review of William Barrows, *The Indian Side of the Indian Question*, then, on February 15, with his own paper on "The Influence of the Fur Trade in the North West from the Particular Standpoint of Wisconsin." This was carefully moulded to Johns Hopkins' "scientific" atmosphere; larded with statistics on the quantities of goods sold, and bursting with factual information on the nature of the tribes and traders, it shunned even such interpretation as enlivened his master's thesis. Yet such was the nature of the seminar that his audience found it a lively antidote to constant doses of the "germ" theory. "This," one of the instructors told him, "is the kind of atmosphere in which we can breathe." Those words he never forgot; they encouraged him to generalize and to seek bolder interpretations.[18]

Turner found even greater satisfaction in an extracurricular task given him by Professor Adams. Adams had returned from his graduate study in Germany as an ardent admirer of the German state-administered educational system, which offered a high level of instruction from the primary grades to adult classes. This was beyond the reach of the United States, but when he lectured at the Chautauqua Institute in upstate New York during the summer of 1888, he thought he had discovered an adequate substitute. He would make Johns Hopkins the hub of a nationwide program of adult education, with printed study programs, books specially written for such an audience, lecturers recruited from the graduate students, and examinations set and graded by the university. Eventually this network would be extended through the nation, with all universities participating under Hopkins's direction, and the whole population would be instantly converted into college graduates. "Adams," Turner reported, "found in the Chautauqua school an evolution from the camp-meeting, which in turn came from the hunters' outdoor life, and he insists that the Chautauqua assembly is only another form of the Folk-Moot."[19] With these "germs" it was a laudable institution, deserving support from the graduate students. If Adams had his way, Johns Hopkins would be converted into "a veritable school of peripatetic historians," traveling about the country spreading instant culture.

When Turner offered these wry comments he did not realize that he was to be the principal victim of Adams's enthusiasm. His summons came not long afterward; would he take over as an extension instructor with a modest compensation, sending out lessons to subscribers, reading their papers, and grading their examinations? His first assignment would be to prepare three syllabi on primitive, Chaldean, and Egyptian history. Thus Turner, unable to refuse such a request, added paper-reading and examination-grading to his overcrowded schedule. Nor was this the end, for Adams had still another favor to ask. He had agreed to give a "Teachers' Course of Lectures on American History" to forty or fifty

Washington schoolteachers, but found himself too busy to meet the class regularly. Would Turner give the March lecture on "The Conquest and Organization of the Northwest Territory?" This royal command was less burdensome; Turner had only to polish the lecture on the Northwest Ordinance that he had delivered before the Contemporary Club a year before, but he was terrified when he learned that the audience had swelled to ten times its projected size. "I shiver at the thought of seeing 800 eye glasses all leveled at me," he confessed to Mae. His fears were groundless; his training on elocution stood him in good stead as he led his listeners through the story of the upper Mississippi Valley, from the fall of Quebec in 1759 to the settlement of Marietta in 1788. There was still no hint in his orthodox narrative of the influence of frontiering on men or institutions, but his audience was more than satisfied. "I came, I saw, and I talked the regulation time," he reported, "—and got more than regulation applause."[20]

Recognition such as this—by Adams in selecting his young student to teach extension courses or lecture to such an audience, by Ely in asking Turner to take over his introductory political economy class when he was out of the city—was wonderous balm for the ego. Gone now were the doubts that burdened Turner in September; as the school year progressed he grew more sure of himself, more relaxed, more willing to enjoy the companionship of his fellows. Miss Ashton's boardinghouse offered abundant opportunity. Robert Aikman moved out in February, but Charles Homer Haskins remained, and Woodrow Wilson—on leave from his post at Wesleyan University to give a course on "Administration"—offered an exciting new friendship. "Dr. Wilson is here," Turner reported to Mae in early February, "homely, solemn, young, glum, but with the fire in his face and eye that means that its possessor is not of the common crowd."[21] From that time on, his letters were filled with tales of stimulating conversation over cider and doughnuts, of Wilsonian anecdotes that sent them into gales of laughter, of discussions of a chapter of Wilson's latest book that lasted far into the night, of carefree exchanges of wit and learning. "You would never recognize him as the grave author of a book that has called out the admiration of the ablest statesmen and historians of the world."[22] These were ever-to-be-remembered days—and nights—as the two men matched fine minds and deepened their friendship. They made a perfect pair: Wilson brilliant, inclined to leap to conclusions, an astute political philosopher;

Turner slower of mind but more accurate, exceptionally logical, a social philosopher. The bonds they formed over Miss Ashton's table were to last until Wilson's death, and to give both men intense satisfaction.

Yet all was not scholarly conversation at Miss Ashton's. That winter two of her pretty nieces, Miss Maud and Miss Cora, took up residence there, and on many an evening they inspired high jinks in place of learned discourse. On one memorable occasion, Haskins and Turner, making their regular raid on the kitchen for cider and cake, found the two girls in possession and baptized them with a liberal allowance of flour—to their ill-concealed delight. On another, Mary Jane Ashton treated her boarders to a tempting dish of caramels—heavily laced with red pepper. All were delighted when Miss Cora and Haskins began a gay flirtation, "making large eyes at each other" as he pretended to study. "You would," Turner wrote Mae, "hardly care to hear of my lectures, or . . . of how Haskins and I found Miss Hannah making waffles the other evening, and took possession of the kitchen until it looked like a battlefield, and how Miss Maud threw water over both of us—and all that sort of stuff. It does rest one's brain after a hard study over political economy."[23]

For Turner was studying, and studying harder than ever before. His courses for the second term varied little from those he had elected in September—"History of Politics," "International Law," "Social Science," "Elements of Political Economy," "History of Political Economy," "Special Economic Questions," "American Constitutional Law," elementary mathematics—with an additional twenty-five lectures on "Administration" given by Woodrow Wilson.[24] Even though Turner was auditing some courses and concentrating on those that satisfied his needs, his burden was still great, and it was intensified now by the need to complete all the requirements for the doctoral degree that June. His thesis had to be written; for a time he toyed with a history of government legislation concerning Indians, but common sense prevailed, and, rather than beginning a new topic he settled on revising his study of the Wisconsin fur trade to conform to Johns Hopkins standards. He also had to pass the reading tests in French and German and prepare for searching five-hour written examinations over the fields of his major interest as well as the dread oral examination, which would cover the entire scope of history. Add to these chores reading for his regular courses, grading examinations for extension students in Egyptian or Chaldean history, and keeping abreast of the seminar, and Turner was doomed to some of the busiest months of his life. He survived only by following a rigid schedule: rise at 8:44 each morning, breakfast at 8:45, classes from 9 to 2, dinner and chat with friends at Miss Ashton's from 2 to 3:30, study from 3:30 to 5:30, exercise at the gymnasium from 5:30 to 6:30, supper and talk from 6:30 to 8, and study from 8 to 11:45.[25]

Turner's dreams of a June doctorate, which inspired that Spartan regime, were unrealistic; he might master history and political economy, but French was a major stumbling block, and he had to pass a sight-reading test to qualify for his degree. He simply could not drive himself to study grammar or plod through dull translations when the reading matter of his courses was so enticing. He did make a try that March, but with disastrous results. "The Hopkins instructor," he reported to Mae, "had hard work to keep a sober face when I read some French aloud at his request." Turner did manage to salvage something from this debacle when Professor Ely consented to his taking the examinations in political economy before satisfying the language requirements. This meant he had an added work load, but the reward was worth the effort; with one-third of his examinations completed, he could master French and German while teaching, then return in the spring of 1890 to face the remainder. He would also win the favor of Professor Adams by his industry—an important consideration, for Adams was talking about a textbook in American history and hinted that he might ask Turner to write the section on the Old Northwest. This was necessary to a young man anxious to make western history his domain; "I cannot," he wrote, "let anybody else do my own ground."[26] A bit of slavery was justified to win such a prize. "A Baltimore spring coupled with study necessary to get off my work in Political Economy is not a good thing to grow fat on."[27]

Especially when the preparation of his dissertation was added to his other burdens. This was not a major task; he had only to re-write his master's thesis in terms suitable to the "scientific" tone of Johns Hopkins instruction. The principal shift in emphasis was the association of the trading post as an institution with its "germs" in primitive times. "The trading post," he began, "is an old and influential institution," then he traced its development from the days of the Phoenicians to modern times, showing that early traders pioneered the trails over which Europe was peopled. "The routes of the Migration of the Peoples were to a considerable extent the routes of Roman trade, and it is well worth inquiry whether this commerce did not leave more traces upon Teutonic society than we have hitherto considered."[28] Thus did Turner make his bows to Professor Adams and his "germ" theories—not to cater favors, but because he had to conform to the institutional interpretations so favored at Hopkins, and because he was genuinely interested in the evolution of nongovernmental institutions.

In two other ways Turner's dissertation mirrored the course of his historical thinking while at Johns Hopkins. In his thesis the genetic approach was even more strongly emphasized than in his earlier version; he saw trading posts as "the pioneers of many settlements," furnishing supplies for the miners, lumbermen, and farmers who carried civilization in their knapsacks; he pictured the trappers' trails as "slender lines of Eastern influence, stretched throughout all our vast and intricate water system" over which were to flow agricultural and manufacturing cultures. No less indicative of Turner's altered views was his emphasis on the stages of social growth that occurred along frontiers. Civilization, he believed, progressed in a series of well-defined steps, each building on the one before. Each frontier, he wrote, offered a "prototype" of the frontiers that were to follow, as well as furnishing "an exemplification of all the stages of economic development existing contemporaneously." Traders and hunters were first on the scene, then the cattle-raisers, then the "cultivators of the soil." "The manufacturing era belongs to our own time." The borderlands where "a primitive people comes in contact with a more advanced people," deserved careful study. "As a factor in breaking the 'cake of custom' the meeting of two such societies is of great importance."[29] Turner could never have written these words without his Johns Hopkins training.

If Fred J. Turner had paused to take stock as his Baltimore year ran its course, he would have recognized that he had grown substantially in knowledge, reasoning power, and self-assurance. No longer was he fearful that he might not measure up to the standards of the profession; he had successfully stood the test given by America's greatest historians in America's greatest university. Of this he was fully aware.

"One is at the heart of university life in America here," he wrote that spring, "and very close to German thought, too."[30] Turner realized, too, that he owed his fresh learning and new self-confidence to the four instructors who played a major role in guiding his studies: Herbert Baxter Adams, Albion W. Small, Woodrow Wilson, and Richard T. Ely.

Herbert Baxter Adam's contribution to Turner's emerging beliefs must remain an enigma. That Adams respected Turner highly was made abundantly clear by the posts he offered Turner and by the prospect (which never materialized) of seeking Turner's collaboration in preparing a textbook; that Turner reciprocated this regard was shown by the repeated favorable references he made to Adams in his letters. Never, he testified, had he met a teacher who could inspire his students with such enthusiasm for serious historical work, or demonstrate so successfully the relation between past and present.[31] Yet, in his later years, Turner repeatedly stated that his rebellion against Adams's teaching drove him to develop the frontier thesis. He was particularly irked, he remembered, by his teacher's insistence that further research in American history was unnecessary, as every institution had been traced to its "germ" in medieval Germany; students should turn to European topics instead. If Adams ever told his seminar this (and the records do not reveal such a remark), he had no intention of being taken seriously. In his eyes every town in America housed institutions whose origins could be traced; there were enough subjects crying for investigation to keep students busy for a century. "Institutional history," he wrote in 1884, "was as untouched as were once the forests of America."[32] Nor did Adams turn his back on the West, as Turner later recalled; in 1885 and 1886 he directed the seminar into studies of land legislation, and he repeatedly called attention to the relationship between land and the free-silver question. This was Turner's brand of history.

What Turner remembered as dislike of Adams was probably resentment of the smug self-satisfaction of all eastern historians of that day. New Englanders particularly, and Middle State men to a lesser degree, were indifferent to events beyond the Hudson, and they were inclined to view the seaboard states as the nation's heartland. This bruised Turner's strong sense of local pride. "Not a man that I know here," he wrote Professor Allen, "is either studying, or is hardly aware of the country behind the Alleghenies."[33] When he testified, as he did in later years, that "my essay on the 'Frontier' was a protest against the tendencies of the eastern historians at the time it was written," he was nearer the truth than when he laid his resentment at Adams's doorstep.[34] Adams taught him a great deal, even though his teachings did little to bolster Turner's knowledge of the West.

Turner learned slightly more from Albion W. Small. Later a famed sociologist, Small was at this time an advanced graduate student who had been drafted to give a course on "The Growth of American Nationality" to a small group of Turner's contemporaries. This was admirably suited to Turner's needs; each member of the class was required to search source documents to show how and when sovereign power was transferred from colonies to states, and from states to nation. This gave excellent training in documentary research, but it also required a great deal of thought on the nature of nationalism.[35] The emphasis that Turner later placed on the frontier as a source of a nationalistic spirit in the United States owed something to the strict training he received in Albion Small's course.

Woodrow Wilson taught him far more. Wilson's lectures on "Administration" proved an exciting antidote to some of Adams's Teutonism, partly because they opened new vistas on state-federal relations, partly because they reflected a mild spirit of rebellion against the dominant "germ" theory. Wilson was still a Teutonist; he saw the New England town as "a spontaneous reproduction of the ancient Germanic Mark." But he also told his class that environment altered imported institutions, to the degree that the colonies, "without losing their English character, gained an American form and flavor," because each "borrowed what was best suited to its own situation."[36] Institutions, to Wilson, were not frozen monoliths, but dynamic organisms that responded to external and internal pressures. This was a concept that Turner learned from Professor Allen, but it was strengthened by Wilson's lectures.

Turner benefited even more from his hours of conversation with Wilson, as the two men took long walks about Baltimore or bantered away their evenings at Miss Ashton's boardinghouse. Wilson was an unreconstructed southerner, Turner a loyal westerner; both resented the disrespect shown their sections by easterners. As they sputtered their indignation, they agreed that each had to rewrite the history of the country in a way that would pay proper tribute to his homeland. They also talked a great deal about the nature of nationalism, a subject always of interest to Wilson and very much on Turner's mind now that he was under Albion Small's influence. One important point emerged; both agreed that the role of the West as a nationalizing force had been neglected by historians. If that were the case, had the West—and the process of expansion—influenced the nation's development in other ways? Should not that section's role be investigated in search of truths ignored by eastern-oriented scholars? These were key questions, and their impact on Turner cannot be overestimated. Throughout his lifetime he remained grateful to Wilson for planting many of the ideas that helped shape his frontier thesis.[37]

He was equally grateful to Richard T. Ely, and with somewhat more justification. This eminent economist hardly seemed suited to mould disciples. Overweight, short, with a low squeaky voice and a habit of swinging his glasses on a black cord as he paced about the platform, Ely was far from a sensational lecturer. Yet his ideas were so fresh, so invigorating, that he opened a new world to his students, and particularly to Turner. He was, those students knew, the leader of a group of young economists who were rebelling against the prevailing Ricardian view that man's behavior was governed by immutable natural laws. Man, they held, could better himself by bettering his environment. The duty of the political economist was to point the way by surveying the history of mankind's progress and directing it toward greater reform.[38] These were heretical doctrines for those days—Ely was subjected to periodic witch-hunts as a radical—but they helped reinforce Turner's growing belief that the social order was changeable.

They also led him into a solid diet of political economy, from which he emerged with a number of ideas that he was to weld into his frontier thesis. Ely's technique was to assign books that upheld both the classical and modern viewpoint—for example, John Stuart Mill's *Principles of Political Economy* and Francis A. Walker's *Land and Its Rent* —to supplement these with such varied viewpoints as those in John B. Clark's *Capital and Its Earning* and Henry George's *Progress and Poverty*, and to weave the opposing theories together in his lectures so skillfully that the students scarcely realized they were being converted to the modernist viewpoint. In the more advanced courses Ely's concern was largely with theories of rent; there his students grappled with the obtuse phrasing of Simon H. Patten's *Premises of Political Economy* and listened to their professor compound their confusion as he sought

to reduce a complex subject to understandable terms. From this indoc-
trination Turner emerged with two concepts that vastly influenced his
future thought: the understanding that societies evolved in well-
defined stages, and that land "rents," or values, were determined by a
variety of factors, including the concentration of settlement.

The stages of social evolution had been recognized by political economists since the 1850s, when the German scholar Friedrich List, in his
National System of Political Economy, distinguished between savage,
pastoral, agricultural, agricultural-manufacturing, and manufacturing-
commercial states. Ely, in his books and lectures, adopted and refined
these classifications; he saw civilization emerging through five well-
defined steps: hunting and fishing, pastoral, agricultural, trading and
commerce, and industrial. Each of these he explained in detail.[39] Turner
recognized their significance to American society at once. "Apply in
discussing stages of econ. life," he wrote in the margin of his textbook.
"Instance of Indians and fur traders."[40] Later he was to describe the
march of settlement across the continent in almost identical terms,
with hunters and trappers leading the way, then herdsmen, miners,
pioneer farmers, equipped farmers, and urban dwellers following. We
know today that his classification was oversimplified; men seldom followed the well-ordered schedules that political economists postulated.
But Turner had been introduced to a concept that he could use to
advantage.

Ely also led Turner into the study of the theory of rent. "Rent," as
the term was then used, meant simply the return on land; land that
returned nothing to society, and hence was of no immediate value, was
"free" land. Land was "free" in unsettled or sparsely settled areas; as
population thickened and markets emerged, the land's rent increased
in the form of higher returns and market value. Political economists
quarreled over what determined these increases, or the amount of rent
the land yielded. The classical economists, personified by John Stuart
Mill, argued that land values were set solely by population pressures;
the greater the pressure the higher the return. They bolstered their argument by giving as an example the situation in United States. There
the lands were poorly cultivated and yielded less than their capacity
because land was so plentiful and labor so dear that intensive agriculture was uneconomical. An abundance of land, combined with a scarcity of population and markets, lowered the profit, or rent, that could be

taken, and hence lowered the value of the land. Classicists recognized that there was no completely "free" land in America, but that much was relatively "free" because its value in terms of rent was less than in populated areas.[41]

Arrayed against these theories were those of the "modernists," led by Francis A. Walker, Simon H. Patten, and, particularly, Richard T. Ely. Turner was thoroughly indoctrinated in their views; he carefully read the books of Patten and Walker, and listened with equal care to Ely's lectures. Basic to the modernist interpretation was the belief that land values, or rents, were determined by social as well as physical factors; they held that popular tastes, changing market conditions, inequities in distribution, and the living standards of cultivators affected the quantity of production and consumption, and, hence, determined the rent chargeable to land. Applying these theories to the United States, they recognized that the "marginal lands" on the edge of the cultivated areas provided their owners only a return on capital and labor expended, and hence paid no rent, at least not when compared with lands in thickly settled regions, which did more than "just pay" for their use. The difference between the yield on heavily settled land and the yield on land on the "margin of cultivation" was the amount of rent. When a country was new, thinly settled, and distant from markets, land of high fertility would yield no rent and would be classed as poor, even though that same land, when settled, would be judged "very good" and would return a high rent. In the first stage, when land paid little or no rent, the political economists called it "free land."[42]

From this formidable dose of economic theory Turner distilled a number of concepts essential to his frontier thesis. He learned that returns, or rents, on farm lands were determined by a variety of social and physical factors, including soil fertility, transportation facilities, nearness to markets, and relationship to cheaper lands. He recognized that "free land" in the traditional sense was nonexistent, but that some lands produced such a low rent that they could not advantageously be cultivated. These lands would no longer be free, but would return a steadily increased rent as markets emerged with a growing population. These were essential lessons for Turner in understanding the settlement process in the United States. They are equally important to a modern reader who would understand his frontier theories. When he spoke of "free land" in the West, as he often did, he meant not lands that were actually free, but that paid a lesser return than lands more favorably endowed or situated. He recognized, too, that free lands disappeared as the coming of settlers and markets allowed them to command an ever-increasing rent. These definitions underlay Turner's later thinking, and stood him in good stead as he developed his understanding of American history.

That he had learned them well is shown by a remarkable letter he wrote to Professor Allen that year. "Wisconsin," he told his old mentor, "is like a palimpsest. The mound builders wrote their record and passed away. The state was occupied . . . by the most various peoples of the Indian race. Then came the French. Then a wave of Northern New York and Vermont fur traders—those who lived near the Lake Champlain route or the Great Lakes caught that fur trading spirit. At nearly this time came the miners from the South. Then the emigration from the *New York parallel* again to the farm lands. Now begins the State's policy of attracting immigration," and the coming of Germans in large numbers. Their lower living standards allowed them to displace the Yankees who had settled before them. "I do not," he went on, "regard the movement as entirely to be feared. I think peasant proprietorship is not being weakened by these German settlers. The quick settlement of lands in small farms has, I judge, prevented the absorption of such territory into great estates."[43]

Turner was now aware that society in the newer West was an evolving organism, responding to the repeated intrusion of newcomers from the East or Europe. He recognized that the relative ease with which "free land" could be acquired there served as a democratizing force, checking the growth of "great estates." Most important of all, he had learned that by applying theories learned in the classroom to his native Wisconsin, he could test historical concepts just as a biologist might test a new substance in a test tube. Turner had located the laboratory he was to use through his lifetime. His year at Johns Hopkins, which gave him a new perspective as well as a great deal of learning, made that discovery possible.

Valuable though that year was, Turner was impatient to leave Baltimore that spring of 1889, and to see his darling Mae after what seemed an eternity of separation. Two tasks remained before he could depart.

One—securing a teaching post—had occupied him through much of the spring. Turner knew what he wanted—a professorship in American history at Wisconsin—and he held three aces in his hand when he began his negotiations with President Chamberlin: a solid offer of an instructorship at Ohio State University for one year only, a chance to stay on at Johns Hopkins as Ely's assistant, and a vague hint from Professor Adams that there might be a position open on the Johns Hopkins faculty. He played these cards well, suggesting to his friends in Madison that they might "frighten the authorities" with news of the Ohio State prospect, and allowing his newspaper friends to raise the alarm in the press.[44] "We certainly hope," wrote one editor, "that Wisconsin may not lose the services of so bright a young historical specialist as Mr. Turner, who gives promise of making a decided mark for himself in the early future."[45]

President Chamberlin was no amateur at bargaining, and he refused to be panicked into a decision. He wanted Turner back, but on his own terms: as an assistant professor, who would do some work in elocution. Turner refused to accept; even Ohio State would be preferable to those endless sessions of coaching would-be orators. The negotiations went on until Chamberlin made a compromise proposal: would Turner return as an assistant professor of history with a salary of $1500 a year and the understanding that in a few years he would be elevated to a professorship in charge of the work in American history? Turner accepted, and in due time the formal invitation arrived with the rank and salary assured in return for seven or eight "exercises in history weekly," in addition to some work in civics. That letter was hurried off to Mae in Chicago with a note penned across the top: "Dearest One—" this "settles one of the problems of my life."[46] Fred Turner would return to his Valhalla with his course set. "Now again," he wrote, "I have a goal and a far away one—and I am nearly ready to shoulder my knapsack."[47]

Nearly, but not quite, for one task remained. He had to pass the examination in political economy that would assure completion of his doctorate a year later. Turner studied with assurance as he prepared for that ordeal, but with apprehension, too, for he realized that his whole future depended on the outcome. He was well prepared when he seated himself with the other candidates on June 10 in an empty recitation room, accepted the ten questions from the examiner, and settled down to five hours of strenuous composition. Midway through the morning a boy served them coffee and they talked and gossiped a while, eating sandwiches, and carefully refraining from mentioning political economy, as was the John Hopkins custom. Then it was over, there was a long wait for the result, for Ely was busy as usual. Two weeks later the word arrived: "It can scarcely be necessary for me to let you know that you have passed."[48] Turner had ended his John Hopkins year with a major success. Wisconsin and Johns Hopkins had fashioned a young historian of great promise; now he had to go back to Madison, to prove himself as teacher and scholar.

IV

Teaching—and the Emerging Frontier Thesis

1889-1892

WHEN Fred J. Turner left Baltimore that June of 1889, he was heavily freighted with both learning and ambition. He had to justify his assistant professorship by completing his doctoral degree, winning his spurs as a teacher, and proving himself as a scholar, all within the year. Only then could he persuade President Chamberlin to elevate him to a permanent professorship with a salary that would allow him to marry Mae. Gone now was the lethargy that had slowed his early progress toward his master's degree. "I discover," he wrote, "that my year away has had the effect to stir up the most inordinate amount of ambition in my nature."[1] That was true. The next three years were to be among the most productive—and rewarding—of his life.

In other years Turner would have used the summer to recuperate from his grueling Johns Hopkins ordeal by haunting the lakes of Wisconsin, but Portage seemed dull after the excitement of Baltimore. "You cannot understand how quiet and uninteresting my summer is," he complained.[2] By mid-July he was back in Madison, prepared to buckle down to his tasks, but even that charmed city was less attractive than he remembered it. Mrs. Bross's boardinghouse was so filled with teachers attending summer school that he had to live in a fraternity lodge; most of his old friends were provincial and uninteresting, with only Professor Allen and Reuben Gold Thwaites reflecting the "university atmosphere" to which he was accustomed; and Mae was far away. Never robust, she had tried to build her strength that spring at a health resort in upstate New York that fed its patients codfish and onions; when this medication failed, her mother decided to take her on an extended European tour. They left in May and were not to return until mid-October. Fred Turner was very lonely as he went about his tasks that summer. He spent mornings at the State Historical Society, afternoons studying French and teaching himself typing (with only moderate success), late afternoons on Lake Mendota or exercising in the college gymnasium, evenings at concerts or lectures at the annual Monona Lake Assembly.[3] Always thoughts of Mae haunted him; he spent more time than he should have pressing his married friends for information on the cost of living (a couple could get along on $1000 a year) or calculating the daily income from a salary of $1500 (365 into $1500 = $4.10).[4]

He also thought a great deal about the role of the West in American history, with impressive results. These appeared in a lengthy review of the first two volumes of Theodore Roosevelt's *Winning of the West*, which was published by *The Dial* that August. Turner could not resist displaying some of the nonsense learned from Adams; he wrote approvingly of Roosevelt's descriptions of the "forted villages" of the Kentuckians in which "reappeared the old Germanic 'tun,' their popular meetings, 'folk-moots,' and their representative assemblies, 'witenagemots.'" But he also made some sound observations on the West's influence on the nation's development. There, not in New England, lay the "center of gravity" of the United States. This must be recognized by the younger generation of historians. Once they did so, they would find that beyond the Appalachians "a new composite nationality is being produced, a distinct American people, speaking the English language, but not English." They were forming self-governing communities that were "growing into states of the federal union." In the West, economists would discover forces altering the economy of the nation and of Europe; students of migration would reveal mass movements of people comparable to the *Völkerwanderung* of the Middle Ages.[5] The West had to be understood if American history was to be understood. Here was Turner's challenge to the Wise Men of the East who viewed the United States from the perspective of New England. It was also a watershed in Turner's own development; he remembered later that preparing that review brought home to him "the need of a history of the continuous progress of civilization across the continent."[6] His ambition to study the history of the West was taking a practical direction.

This study had to wait, for the autumn term was at hand, and Turner must return to the academic world. "I feel," he confessed, "much like a man about to plunge into cold water."[7] In fact, he was to experience something like total immersion in a very icy bath. Few students of that day were interested in bettering their minds; they wanted only a college degree that would elevate their social and economic status. To them a "C" grade was just as acceptable as an "A," and much easier to secure; fraternities and clubs ranked far above the classroom in their value scales; and a good time was more desirable than good marks. The handful who showed serious interest were scorned as "grinds" who did not really fit into the lighthearted atmosphere of a university. To make matters worse, there were more students than had been anticipated, for Wisconsin was expanding rapidly; eight hundred crowded the campus that fall, swamping the fifty-six faculty members and over-crowding the boardinghouses—although Turner did manage to arrange a comfortable room at Mrs. Bross's.[8]

These numbers posed problems for Turner and the history department. He had worked out an admirable teaching program. He would offer, in addition to some required sections in Territorial and Dynastic history, a freshman survey in American history, a brand new course in the "Constitutional and Political History of the United States" (which would eventually alternate with another new course in American economic history), and a seminar on the economic development of the Old Northwest.[9] Alas for his well-laid plans! So many students demanded his freshman courses in Dynastic and American history that each course had to be divided into two sections. In the end he taught these four uninspiring classes with sixty uninspired underclassmen in each, the course in constitutional history with seventeen, and the seminar, which attracted only six.[10]

Turner was instantly popular as a teacher. He was nearing his twenty-eighth year at this time, but looked far younger; a persistent Madison legend holds that sophomores mistook him for a freshman that autumn and tossed him into Lake Mendota. He was a strikingly attractive man, of slight build and medium height, with flashing blue eyes, fair hair, a well-trimmed moustache, and a face that glowed with ruddy health. All who knew him commented on his personal magnetism and the deep, vibrant, melodious voice that commanded attention from his classes and charmed his friends. They remembered, too, the quickness of his mind, and the vastness of his knowledge.

Turner's first hint of success as a teacher cemented a resolution in his mind; with a decently paid post and a measure of security, why delay the marriage that he and Mae both wanted? No sooner did she return from Europe that October than he suggested that they marry immediately. She was agreeable; they would live in a large upper room at Mrs. Bross's boardinghouse, with an alcove where Fred could study, and a fireplace to offer cheer. And they would be married in just a month. That arranged, both plunged into the countless tasks required: three hundred invitations to be mailed, a decision to be made about the gloves for the ushers, furniture to be carted from the freight station, wedding presents unpacked, the license to be obtained. Turner hurried through these chores in a haze of happiness. "Everybody looks at me very smiling and cheerful," he reported.[11]

Finally on November 16, 1889, they were married, in a formal ceremony at the Kenwood Evangelical Church. There was a brief wedding supper at the bride's home on Madison Avenue, enlivened by the arrival of a telegram from Turner's class in American history, extending hearty congratulations to their late sovereign and hoping that they could return to their former alliance with him "if no dangerous or hostile alliance be contracted by him during the interregnum."[12] The Turners went on a brief honeymoon in Milwaukee, then attended another reception at the Turner home in Portage, an "uncommonly brilliant" affair, marred by the fact that the groom failed to appear until it was well under way, having been detained in Madison to teach the course of a colleague who was ill. When he did arrive, at nine in the evening, the bridal couple led the way to the dining room, where "a most *recherché* lunch was served in the most dainty manner."[13]

Fred and Mae were married now, but there were problems ahead. Only a few days after their return to Madison he took to his bed with a bad case of measles, and she fled to her mother's home in Chicago, letting her husband know that boardinghouse life was not for her. When he recovered, he went house-hunting, finally finding one at 21 West Gilman Street, at a rental they could afford. This must be properly prepared before Turner could ask Mae to join him; there was a stove to buy, a full-time maid to be hired, the floors stained a color that would please her. Fred Turner was desperately lonely as he went about these tasks, but by the end of January all was ready, and the Turners were able to set up housekeeping in their own home.[14]

Just before they did so an event occurred that changed the pattern of Fred's life. On December 9, Professor Allen, who had taken to his bed with a miserable cold, suddenly died. His passing plunged the university into mourning; classes were canceled, the massive pillars at the entrance to the campus were draped in black, and all social events were put off until after the funeral, three days later. Few wept over Allen's death as much as Turner did, and few were as deeply affected. He had to honor his mentor's memory by seeing to the publication of a book on which Allen had labored for some time, *A Short History of the Roman People,* then in proof form, but with final arrangements still to be made and an introduction prepared. Turner worked feverishly on this task during the next weeks, with satisfactory results. His prefatory remarks were admirably phrased to stress the contributions made by Allen: the blending of political, economic, literary, and religious history into a unified whole; the "policy and process by which the Roman dominion was secured and organized"; and "the social and economic causes of the failure of self-government among the Romans."[15] The study of society as a whole, the importance of expansion, the underlying forces that determined the rise and fall of democratic institutions—there were Allen's themes, and they were the themes that were to occupy his disciple through his lifetime. Turner's tribute mirrored his own historical interests while revealing his debt to his teacher.

Allen's death was tragedy, but it was also opportunity. If Turner could cheerfully cooperate with President Chamberlin by teaching extra courses, and at the same time complete his doctoral work at Johns Hopkins, he might win the professorship that was his goal. The courses were burdensome, even though a graduate student was imported from Harvard to teach some of the elementary work; Turner taught not only his own subjects but sections of the courses on Dynastic and Territorial history, the French Revolution, Nineteenth-Century Europe, a new course on the "History of Society," and the seminar, the latter his own now rather than shared with Professor Allen. This was a killing schedule for those winter and spring terms, compounded by the fact that he was giving his own courses for the first time, and they required extensive preparation. "My courses," he wrote, "are all so nearly new, that I am finding my hands full."[16]

To add labor to labor, he had to win his doctorate that spring or be pushed aside for a more experienced teacher. So he worked furiously on French and German and slaved over the mountains of books that he was expected to know by heart. By the end of May he was ready. Canceling his classes, he set out alone for Baltimore, put up at Miss Ashton's boardinghouse, satisfied his language requirements, and, at four o'clock in the afternoon of the fatal day presented himself to his inquisitors in College Hall. There the entire historical and literary faculty awaited him, seated about a long table, and looking very formidable indeed. Turner was placed at one end; Professor Basil L. Gildersleeve at the other. The written examinations and thesis were satisfactory; would Professor Adams begin the questioning? This went on for three-quarters of an hour, then Ely followed for half an hour and the remaining faculty displayed their intellectual plumage by asking the usual questions to show the depth of their learning. When it was all over Turner left the room, waited those agonizing minutes in the hall, and heard the good news as Professor Adams emerged with his hand extended in congratulations.[17]

Frederick J. Turner (as he now began to sign himself) was a doctor of philosophy, but he was by no means happy with his performance. Later he assured a student who did badly that his examination "could have been no worse than my own experience," taking solace in the thought that his failure "was a spur that sent me further than if I had distinguished myself."[18] Recriminations were for the future, however; he had passed and could return to Madison in triumph. He went home, carrying a box of Maryland crabs to share with Mae, and so excited that he forgot to deposit Miss Ashton's key and left behind his umbrella and glasses. There was still the technical requirement of a published thesis, but this proved easy, for Professor Adams was so pleased with the dissertation completed during Turner's year of residence that he arranged its publication in the prestigious *Johns Hopkins University Studies in Historical and Political Science*. It appeared in December 1891 under the pretentious title, "The Character and Influence of the Indian Trade in Wisconsin, A Study of the Trading Post as an Institution."[19] Turner—the unshakable perfectionist—was not happy with his own words when he saw them in print, but the reviewers were kind, commenting especially on the flowing style that made the book "a popular as well as a scholarly production."[20]

With those coveted letters, "Ph.D.," after his name, he was at last in a position to press President Chamberlin for the professorship that was his goal. This was by no means assured; Chamberlin quite naturally wanted to replace Allen with a teacher of comparable reputation and even asked Turner to recommend a distinguished scholar who would measure up to these standards. Fortunately, Turner's friends rose to the occasion, spurred on by Reuben Gold Thwaites, who broadcast word that Turner might be sacrificed unless the president could be convinced of his future; Woodrow Wilson and Herbert Baxter Adams wrote so glowingly that no administrator could remain unmoved. Of this Turner knew nothing, living through the spring under the pressure of uncertainty, and "growing weary of having to keep one eye off his work to keep his head from the axeman's block."[21] His first glimmer of hope came when the president followed his advice by naming his Hopkins friend, Charles Homer Haskins, to an instructorship in European history. Turner was kept waiting for another year before his goal was achieved, but in the spring of 1891 he was elevated to a professorship, given the chairmanship of the department, and paid a magnificent salary of $2000 a year. At the same time Haskins was granted an assistant professorship. Chamberlin had elected to gamble on the future reputation of these two young men, rather than to recruit an eminent elder statesman. Seldom had a university president chosen so wisely.

With security, an expanding reputation, and an income that would stretch within sight of covering his needs, Turner could face the future with a degree of assurance. Now he could settle to the task of justifying President Chamberlin's faith by devoting himself to teaching and scholarship. His wife was happy to cooperate; Mae was never strong, and she was content to avoid the gay social life of Madison's elite—a wise decision when society's vogue in 1891 was "progressive tiddley winks" and, a year later, "progressive cinch." The Turner's name seldom graced the social columns of the local press; when it did appear, it was usually in a report that Mae was visiting her mother in Chicago. Yet family life was bound to absorb hours that Turner needed for his research—much to his delight. There were luncheons to be given for visiting dignitaries, dinner parties for colleagues, stag gatherings where the living room at 21 West Gilman was filled with friends, talk, and tobacco smoke, and the guests stuffed themselves on grapes, pears, rye bread, mustard, caviar, sardines, marmalade, olives, Edam cheese, and salted almonds, all washed down with beer.[22]

Then the babies came. Dorothy Kinsley Turner was born promptly at noon on September 1, 1890. All went well. "Having babies," the doctor told the proud father, "is Mrs. Turner's vocation." Dorothy grew briskly until she was six months old when near-tragedy struck. A mild cold burgeoned overnight into a severe case of the "grippe" that soon laid not only Dorothy but the maid and the mother low. Turner, aided by his own mother, watched over the baby's bed as she grew steadily worse. Twice during the night of March 24, she seemed on the point of death; each time Turner ran coatless through the night to the doctor's home, overheating himself so badly that he succumbed to the disease the next day. Not until March 28 did the child take a turn for the better, allowing the worn-out father to take to his own bed; not until mid-April was he strong enough to meet his classes. No such disaster marred the arrival of the second child, Jackson Allen Turner, on June 26, 1892. Jack was a husky youngster, and he was the apple of his parents' eye. Happily, his parents could not recognize the prophetic accuracy of his grandmother's proud remark that he was "too angelic to live."[23]

At the same time there were the endless rounds of duties expected of every professor—in the 1890s, as today—at the sacrifice of his own research and leisure. The university called on him to serve on all sorts of committees—to arrange a lecture series, revitalize the student newspaper, aid the literary societies in planning their programs—and to address the students at their weekly convocations, all tasks that consumed an alarming amount of time. The State Historical Society pressed him into service as a "curator" and asked him to serve with a committee on historical monuments. Clubs took their toll: the Madison Lawn Tennis Club, which he joined in 1891; the Channing Club, which he rejoined when he returned to Wisconsin and enlightened with discussions on such unlikely subjects as "Ingersollism," "Religion in Revolutionary Times," and "The Social Life and Religion of Turkey"; the Contemporary Club, which made him its vice-president in 1891 and enlisted him for papers or discussions on "The Chilean Affair,"

"The Political Situation in Europe" ("a profound study," according to
the local reporter); "Australian Federation," "The Relations of Portu-
gal and England," "The Pan-American Congress," and "Turkish Control of the Bosphorus."[24]

Turner's earlier successful lecture series on the Old Northwest was
so pleasantly remembered that he was prevailed on to stage another
for the Contemporary Club on "Crossing the Alleghenies," this time
with a charge of ten cents a head. Once more crowds turned out in
droves, this time to hear of Daniel Boone, George Rogers Clark, the
Kentucky pioneers, and the Battle of King's Mountain; once more
Turner was the star of the show when he spoke on March 4, 1890, on
"The Land and the People." The "panorama of brilliant word pictures" that enraptured his audience contained little new; he told of
the coming of the French to the Mississippi Valley, the invasion of
British traders, the advance of Yankee and Scots-Irish settlers down the
Great Valley. But a new note was apparent. Now his stress was less
on the trader and more on the pioneer farmer. "Indian with his painted
face and eagle feathers, voyageur with his turban handkerchief, his
beaded moccasins and his birch canoe, trader with his peltry-laden
pack horse, all are doomed. For the backwoodsman is in sight; clad in
hunting shirt, axe and rifle in hand, attended by wife and children, he
bears with him the promise of the clearing and the farm, the promise
of local self-government." He was the one who would win the West.[25]
Turner was beginning to focus on those who conquered the wilderness, not those who succumbed to its savagery. Realism was pushing
aside romance, as it had to before he could realize that the frontier
helped mould the American social order.

These extracurricular duties absorbed a fair amount of Turner's
time, but far more went into building a respectable history department
for the university. The time was ripe for expansion. Wisconsin was
growing rapidly, with some two hundred students added to its population each year and the demand for classrooms so great that the regents launched a crash building program during the 1890-91 academic
year. Additional faculty was also needed, and Turner wanted to make
sure his department received its share. President Chamberlin was a
willing ally, for he realized that the university's greatness would be
measured not by its buildings, but by the quality of its instructional
staff. He knew, too, that unless he could attract eminent scholars, the

newly founded University of Chicago, aided by John D. Rockefeller's millions and led by an aggressive president, William Raney Harper, would skim the cream from the prospective graduate enrollment of the Midwest. If the University of Wisconsin was to escape becoming a commonplace undergraduate college, sending its best students to Chicago for their advanced degrees, it must look to its laurels. He and Turner saw eye to eye on the needs of the history department.

They differed on how to meet those needs. Turner wanted two instructors to take over the lower division classes, leaving Haskins and himself to handle the advanced courses. Chamberlin hoped for a mature scholar who would add luster to the university. As they sparred gently, word reached Turner of one man who would more than live up to Chamberlin's expectations, and, at the same time, bring an unbelievable amount of prestige to the department. Richard T. Ely, the nation's foremost economist, was available! The academic grapevine told why. He and Herbert Baxter Adams, both empire-builders, had struggled for years over control of the Johns Hopkins history department. Their battle broke into the open during the 1890-91 school year, when both were offered attractive professorships at the University of Chicago. Each hoped the other would go, for neither wanted to work under President Harper. Ely tried to force Johns Hopkins's hand by resigning, hoping the president would meet his terms and drive Adams to Chicago. Instead, his resignation was accepted, and Adams was elevated to a professorship. Ely had no choice but to eat crow and retract his resignation, but his life was now intolerable at Baltimore. Hearing that Wisconsin sought a prestigious professor, he did not hesitate to tell his former student that he was available.

Turner responded at once, even though such an appointment would deny the department the instructors it needed and doom him to continued lower-level instruction. President Chamberlin was equally interested, but the $3500 salary demanded by Ely was far above Wisconsin's professorial level. Why not, Turner suggested, form a new "School of Economics, Political Science, and History," with Ely as its head? This would justify a dean's salary, and allow Wisconsin to build a graduate program in the social sciences more prestigious than Chicago's. "It will be," he wrote enthusiastically, "the center of postgraduate work for the Northwest."[26] In February 1891, when the Board of Regents gave its stamp of approval, President Chamberlin journeyed eastward, and when he returned, Wisconsin had its new professor. All concerned were delighted, but Ely most of all. With abundant enthusiasm, and little knowledge of midwestern university budgets, he was sure that more instructors and graduate fellows could be added at once to lift some of the teaching burdens from Turner's shoulders. If the legislature would not provide, he would raise the money himself among the region's businessmen, who would be eager to support such a school.

Turner's letters now bubbled with enthusiasm; he wanted to introduce two new courses, one on the "Social and Economic History of the United States," with special emphasis on the progress of western settlement, immigration, internal improvements, land legislation, and labor; the other on "Colonization." "This would be a new course in American colleges, so far as I know, and I think I have some new ideas in regard to the subject."[27] Alas for such grandiose plans! Ely managed to persuade one New Yorker to donate $500, but there the money-raising campaign ended. In the end the changes made were minimal. One assistant professor of economics was added to the staff, Turner became "Professor of American History," and Haskins "Professor of Institutional History."[28] Yet Turner's optimism was unquenched. It was expressed in an article describing the new school which he prepared for the student newspaper. Here a generation of experts would be trained to grapple with the complex political and economic problems arising from the nation's expansion into the world arena. No one discipline would suffice. "The relation of economics to politics and to history, is plain. We cannot hope to understand either the industrial life, or the political life, of a people, while the two are studied apart; each modifies and conditions the other, and both are intimately related to the welfare of the state."[29] Those were sound judgments, and Turner showed the breadth of his vision in making them.

He showed that breadth again when school began in the fall of 1892. Why not, he suggested, enlist the aid of Madison's economic elite by founding a town-gown "Historical and Political Science Association"? Some 150 leading citizens responded to his invitation to meet at the Opera House on the night of November 15, there to adopt the constitution that he had drafted, to listen to an address from Dr. Albert Shaw, editor of the *Review of Reviews*, on "The West as a Field for Economic Study," and to hear Turner himself talk for some time on the importance of the West in history. This was not a trial run for the famed paper that he was to read a year later; instead he argued that the political history of the Mississippi Valley could be understood only against the patterns of trade on the Great Lakes and river systems which determined the course of settlement and urban growth.[30] Turner's every activity during those years was broadening his knowledge and heightening his interest in the West.

So was his teaching. He was not, in this phase of his career, a popular spellbinder; his "History of Society" normally attracted from ten to fifteen students, and his "Constitutional and Political History of the United States" an even smaller number, especially after 1892, when he divided it into two courses, with a solid year on the period to 1815 and another on the years from 1815 to the 1870s. Even his lower division courses were but sparsely attended, with from ten to twenty-five or thirty in each. One term, when he taught only advanced classes, his total enrollment for twelve hours of instruction was sixty-three. His seminar varied from three to nine, all but one or two enlisted from the senior class.[31] This was not the record of a student idol, but the better equipped and more interested recognized that they were listening to a master instructor. The student yearbook for 1891 was still a bit skeptical when it judged that

> Turner, too, was sure to suit
> If "budding state's omnipotence"
> Agrees with your aesthetic sense

but two years later the yearbook's writer made a more mature evaluation: "A man with wonderful energy and power of application, who sees and uses his opportunities, with youth and hope to aid him in the struggle of life, he is certain of success in his undertakings. Though but a few years the senior of the students he teaches, yet he exercises over them a strong and beneficial influence, and commands alike, their confidence and respect."[32]

Certainly those who ventured into his classes were offered a rich intellectual fare. Two of his courses, "Constitutional History" and the "Nineteenth Century," were singled out for special attention. "Constitutional History" he taught as he would a seminar, assigning stiff doses of reading and asking each student to prepare a report that was presented to the class, searchingly criticized, and extensively debated.

Students emerged with a knowledge of the constitutional and political growth of the nation that was not only thorough but up-to-date. To Turner the Constitution was no sacred document, handed down by a benevolent deity, but the product of social and economic forces operating through the colonial era. "The constitutional convention of 1787," he told his class, "was only one stage, not an abrupt unconnected beginning." Nor had its evolution ended with its adoption. "It was still played upon by all the vital forces of American growth and adapted itself to them," particularly to "the needs of the wonderful expansion which is the dominant fact of American history."[33] These were heretical views; little wonder that one student judged his law-school course in constitutional history an anticlimax, after Turner's instruction.

If Turner revealed his unquenchable interest in the evolution of institutions by stressing growth in his "Constitutional and Political History," his course on the "Nineteenth Century" showed his equal concern with the usability of the past. He began with the French Revolution, then only one hundred years in the past, and in lectures and class reports he thoroughly analyzed European diplomatic and commercial interrelationships for the remainder of the century, spending the last weeks on current problems that carried the class down almost to their own day. The second term was devoted to reports. Each student was assigned one nation of Europe and instructed to show how its political, social, and commercial history made understandable its behavior during the preceding decade. This was an intriguing assignment—students talked of forming a "Nineteenth-Century Club," and several eastern colleges imitated Turner's methods—but it also told something of his faith in history as a guide to contemporary conduct.[34] To Turner, historical studies were essential not only for cultural, but also for practical enlightenment; no man was properly educated unless he was sufficiently familiar with the past to apply its lessons to the present. Hence the duty of the teacher was to spark student interest; if this could be done better by studying the nineteenth century than the ninth, so be it. Any history was better than none.

Some history, however, was particularly fascinating, and none more so than the investigation of social and economic forces that underlay political behavior. Turner launched himself into that field in the autumn of 1892, when he added a completely new offering to his list, "The Economic and Social History of the United States." The cata-

logue announcement read: "The subject is studied . . . with reference to the origin and development of the social and economic characteristics of the country." Among the topics to be treated would be
the relationship between physiographic features and political behavior,
changes in thought patterns, the material development of the nation,
and "the process of settlement across the continent." Here, for the
first time in any catalogue, was an announcement that the westward
expansion of the American people would be investigated. A year later
this aspect received even greater stress: "Particular attention will be
paid to the spread of settlement across the continent and to the economic and social causes of sectional and national sentiment."

We have no way of knowing how extensively the westward movement was treated in these early courses, but one or two fragments of
information suggest that it bulked large. One note, which Turner
scribbled as he was outlining his subject matter, shows the nature of
his thinking: "Soc & Ec U.S. Divide up into a series of *studies. Land.*
History of land tenure. Am. problems. Comparative & historical study.
Agriculture. Agrar. politik. Movement of population. Study historically."[35] We know, too, that each student was assigned a broad topic—
immigration, migration, banking, finance, land, internal improvements,
slavery, religion, literature—for special study, then required to present
a report on one aspect of this to the class. At the end of the term all
of the students prepared correlation papers relating the subjects discussed, with Turner serving as listener and interpreter as he knit them
together to show how they supplemented or corrected existing histories.[36] This was exciting; even the uninterested students felt that
they were contributing to knowledge and pioneering a new subject
matter. "History can no longer be studied according to the old
method," wrote a reporter, after listening to some of the reports.
Turner was infecting his followers with his own belief that the enig-
mas of the past could only be unlocked by investigating the subterranean social and economic forces that governed mankind's behavior.

Turner's seminar offered an even more unusual intellectual fare. The
course met weekly in the library of the State Historical Society, still
housed in the state capitol in downtown Madison, and Turner taught it
jointly with Professor Allen until his death, then with Haskins. First
there was a series of lectures on "scientific" history, in which the in-

structors parroted their Johns Hopkins mentors (but with some sensible correctives added), then there were talks on the sources of United States history, then student reports. It was Turner's ambition to study successive periods of the American past, beginning with colonial days, but this proved impossible; the varied interests of his students and his own changing enthusiasms directed investigations into a helter-skelter of topics, often only slightly related. His first seminar, offered in 1890-91, was grandiosely proclaimed as a course on the "Old Northwest," but it was actually on Wisconsin history, and largely on German migration to the state, a subject much on the public conscience as debate went on over the Bennett law, which would require all instruction in the public schools to be in English.[37] A year later Turner made a vain effort to direct attention to the 1830-40 decade, "with particular reference to the reciprocal influences between East and West at that time," but once more student interests and his own universal curiosity about the past generated a variety of papers that defied classification.[38] In 1892-93, the topics were again so diverse that he was hard put to find a central theme when he summarized their contents at the end of the year.

Yet these seminar reports, scattered over time and subject as they were, did mirror Turner's growing passion for the study of the West. Virtually all related in some fashion with expansion, or with the impact of expansion on the nation. Their content varied—"The Migration of German Lutherans to Wisconsin," "The Westward Spread of Population across New York State, 1750-1810," "Iowa's Federal Relations," "The Influence of the Erie Canal on the Economy of New England," "The Relation of the Land System to the Panic of 1837," "The Interpretation of the Ordinance of 1787"—yet an interest in migration, or in the influence of migration, underlay each.[39] Such a list would have been unthinkable in any other seminar in the United States.

The few graduate students attracted to Wisconsin during the early 1890s helped Turner whet his own appetite for studying the frontier. These were not many; there was little about this small backwater college to lure doctoral candidates from the prestigious universities of the East, especially when its regents did not vote to grant that degree until 1893. Emory R. Johnson was Turner's first advanced candidate; he prepared a master's thesis on "River and Harbor Bills" before moving on to a doctorate and, eventually, a professorship at the University of Pennsylvania. On his heels came Kate A. Everest, who earned her master of arts diploma in 1892 and her doctor of philosophy a year later with studies of German immigration into Wisconsin. Turner was delighted with her thesis—it was built on questions and methods uniquely Turnerian. Miss Everest began with a question—why did Wisconsin have a higher proportion of German-born inhabitants than any other state? Then she sought the answer in church and governmental records, printed sources, census returns, and personal interviews. Turner worked along with her, questioning old German settlers and gathering all the information that he could about them.[40] Miss Everest was not destined to make the scholarly reputation of some of the students he trained in later years, but she shared with them an enthusiasm for history that was traceable to her master. The secret of Turner's success in graduate instruction was that he enlisted the student as a co-worker in an exciting quest for truth, glowing with him over each new discovery, talking over the results, and applauding every valid conclusion. Nothing could be more flattering than such intimate attention and such genuine interest. Turner, even in his first assignments as a teacher, showed the qualities that in later years would attract to his seminar the cream of the nation's would-be historians.

Strangely, however, his own thinking about the American past was stimulated less by his pupils during those years than by a troublesome academic chore, forced upon him by the heady idealism of the social reformers who were blueprinting the re-design of society during the 1890s. One of their ideals was instant education for the people; if universities installed adult extension courses, added summer schools to their schedules, and sent their best faculty members into the countryside to spread culture among the common folk, poverty would be wiped out, the success of democratic institutions assured, and morality enshrined. Fred Turner had heard that message preached at Johns Hopkins by Richard T. Ely and Herbert Baxter Adams, and he was ready to help wholeheartedly when Wisconsin turned toward an extension program.

This began in 1859, when "Farmers' Institutes" and "Teachers' Institutes" were inaugurated on the campus, and when the first regular "Teachers' Summer School" began its sessions—a summer school in which Turner taught regularly over the next years. This was only the beginning; the university would not be completely committed until it adopted an "English type" extension program that sent its faculty members in the humanities and social sciences traveling about the state, conducting regular lecture courses and awarding degrees to farmers and townsmen who completed their requirements. Turner was an enthusiastic advocate of such a program, cooperating cheerfully when the president asked him to report on the subjects the history department could offer, and doing what he could to convince Chamberlin to take the plunge.[41] He made a major contribution early in 1891, when he persuaded Herbert Baxter Adams to speak in Madison on "The Higher Education of the People," an address that converted a number of leading citizens to the belief that total education for all the people would make the world a better place to live in.[42]

Something more than the endorsement of an outside educator was necessary to convince university authorities that extension lectures would pay for themselves. Turner saw an opportunity to drive that message home, at least for his own subject, when he was invited to address the Southwestern Wisconsin Teachers' Association, which met in Madison during the late summer of 1890. Here was a chance to show this influential group that history was no archaic exercise in rote memory, preserved in the mothballs of antiquarianism, but a living discipline, spiced with new interpretations and dealing with a subject matter thoroughly relevant to the present. If he could infect the state's teachers with the excitement of research, they would become local ambassadors for the extension lectures that would soon be given throughout the state. This was Turner's hope when he addressed the schoolteachers on a hot August night in 1890 on "The Significance of History," and this was his hope as he improved his remarks for publication in the October and November 1891 issues of the *Wisconsin Journal of Education*.[43] He could not realize as he did so that his masterly essay would one day be seen as a charter of the Progressive school of historiography, and one of the most remarkable articles published in that generation.

Turner's thesis was that the common people were important. Their motives and actions could be understood only if historians focused on economic and social data; all the past must be re-surveyed to show how they lived and worked and played. History could no longer be viewed as past politics; "history is past literature, it is past politics, it is past religion, it is past economics." All were elements in "society's endeavor to understand itself by understanding the past." Modern conditions of industrial growth made this investigation imperative. "Each age writes the history of the past anew with reference to the conditions uppermost in its own times." Thus, history was "ever *becoming*, never completed." American history could be understood only as a continuation of European history, evolving under the impact of New World conditions. It also had to be viewed as part of world history, for the two were too intimately linked to be separated. National history was as outdated as tribal history—"our present life is interlocked with the events of all the world"—and could never be fully understood until global migration patterns and the world-wide impact of American trade and ideals were understood. This could only be accomplished by borrowing from many disciplines, for the source materials that revealed the life of the common people were infinite in number and variety. The task was difficult, but the rewards great. "The priceless service of history" was to show man the richness of his cultural inheritance, to better his life, and to reveal the grandeur of the present.

Had "The Significance of History" been written by a prominent eastern historian and published in a national journal, it might have been hailed at the time, as it has been since, as a blueprint of the "New History" that was to sweep the profession during the next quarter-century. In it Turner advanced most of the concepts that were to be popularized later: "relativism," with its recognition that each age studied the past in the light of its own experiences; "presentism," with its understanding that the principal importance of yesterday was to explain today; "socialism" (as Turner would have phrased it), with its creed that all facets of human behavior should be studied; and "globalism," with its belief that modern trade and communications linked all the world so tightly that no one part could be studied in isolation. These were doctrines destined for general acceptance a generation later. By voicing them in 1890 and 1891 Turner showed himself to be far in advance of his time.

These doctrines had the immediate effect of bringing university extension to Wisconsin—and with it new burdens and challenges. Turner gave his first two extension courses—at Stoughton and Columbus—during the 1890-91 academic year, but not until the fall of 1891, when a full-scale program was inaugurated did he plunge in completely. He offered three lecture series: "The Colonization of North America," "American Development, 1789-1829," and "American Politics, 1789-1840." Hardly lively topics, but Turner was an immense success overnight. Such was the demand that his first lecture in Madison had to be scheduled in the assembly chamber of the state capitol; 500 attended. When he spoke at the Plymouth Church of Milwaukee under the "espionage" (to quote the local scribe) of the Chautauqua Circle, the hall was jammed, and many were turned away. In all, Turner gave courses of six lectures in seven communities that year, with audiences of about 175 persons each. At Poynette, 200 of the town's 600 inhabitants were enrolled. Most simply listened, but the dozens who sought credit proved so numerous that Turner tried to discourage any additions to avoid the paper work that took hours of his time.[44]

This was only one of the hardships of extension lecturing. The pay was little enough—$10 a lecture plus expenses—but for this he was expected to visit seven widely separated communities once each week for six weeks, traveling in cold trains through the sub-zero Wisconsin nights, sleeping in drafty hotel rooms, or with a family in towns too small to boast hotels, talking to large audiences that kept him far beyond his allotted time with questions, dining with prominent townspeople, then catching the train for the long ride home or to the next assignment. This grueling schedule left Turner little time for anything else. "I must," he told a friend that year, "have some time for *intension*."[45] Yet such was his crusading zeal, and such the monetary demands of his growing family, that he followed the circuit until the spring of 1896, although not always at the same furious pace as in 1891-92.

This was fortunate, for his fees were far overbalanced by his rewards. These he gathered as he prepared and revised his lectures on "The Colonization of North America." These lectures spanned several centuries, from the pre-Columbian voyages through the occupation of New England and the conquest of New France, and they required a vast amount of reading in widely scattered books, ranging from Herman Merivale's *Lectures on Colonization and Colonies* (1861) to John A. Doyle's *English Colonies in America* (1887). As he read, Turner more and more directed his attention to the questions of *where* people moved, and *why*. There were clues scattered along the way, and as he digested them he jotted notes that revealed the direction of his thinking. When he learned, from Merivale's *Lectures on Colonization,* that overcrowding drove people to move, Turner listed a series of motives for migration: overcrowding, love of adventure, fear of military service, hope of social and economic betterment, a desire for a more congenial religious climate. When he read, in Doyle's *English Colonies in America,* that physical barriers helped determine the direction of migratory peoples, he picked up his pen and observed that population movements followed the path of least resistance, whether along the lower Danube or the Hudson.[46] Turner was thinking about migration, and storing away tidbits that would be useful in shaping his frontier thesis.

He was also learning another very important lesson. Life in the colonies differed markedly from life in England and Europe. Why? John A. Doyle's *English Colonies in America* suggested that the environment might be partly responsible. In England, primitive societies were formed that evolved over the course of years into full-grown communities, differing from the communities from which they sprang. "We can," Doyle wrote, "trace their life and institutions from the very fountain-head. In their cases we can see those stages of growth going on under our very eyes which elsewhere can be traced only imperfectly and obscurely."[47] Here in America, Turner may have reasoned, was a chance to study universal history in a local laboratory; the evolution of all society could be observed in microcosm in the emergence of a pioneer community. But why did this evolution produce a product so different from its English ancestor? Merivale suggested one answer in his *Lectures on Colonization;* the abundance of cheap land, he pointed out, encouraged farmers to move to fresh fields rather than to manure their worn-out lands. If cheap land encouraged this change in habit, did it encourage others? So Turner must have speculated as he copied out his notes or phrased the sentences that he would someday use in his essays. "Beneath the constitutional forms and ideas," he wrote one night, when marooned in the Atherton Hotel in Oshkosh, "beneath political issues, run the great ocean currents of economic and social life, shaping and reshaping political forms to the changes of this great sea, which changes continuously."[48] This concept, improved in metaphor and syntax, was to become one of the best-known sentences in his essay on the significance of the frontier.

His current thinking found expression in several ways. The syllabi that he prepared for his extension courses mirrored the progress of his ideas. The first, apparently written in 1891, was a highly factual mimeographed production that listed fifteen topics for study, ranging from the geography of North America to "The Colonial Governments," but the second, printed a year later, was more enlightening. "The History of American Colonization," he wrote, "shows how European life entered America and how America modified that life." It could be understood only by recognizing that American colonization was part of the great historic movement known as the Aryan migrations, and that Europe was as profoundly affected as the United States was.[49] Turner, as he read and pondered, was moving toward belief in environmentalism; when he judged that America modified the life and institutions of Europeans he had reached the threshold of his frontier theory.

The lectures that Turner prepared for his extension audiences were designed to cater to their tastes, with a maximum of rhetoric and a minimum of interpretation; the Norsemen were "dwellers of the North," and the "grandeur of the gloomy fjords, . . . the rugged cliffs and lofty mountains stamped their impress on the race"; New Englanders were surrounded by "fogs and snow, and snarling breakers" that "invited no easy life as did the Spanish southland, and no broad plantations stretching along the slow flowing rivers as did the Virginia region."[50] But when Turner paused to think about the colonization process, a very important truth dawned. Colonization, he realized, did not stop with the coast but continued inland as "colonizers" overran the continent. The peopling of America was part of his story.

He voiced these views in a paper on "American Colonization" which he delivered before the Madison Literary Club in February 1891, a paper that anticipated most of the concepts made famous by his 1893 essay on the significance of the frontier. "American history," he told his audience, "is the account of how the environment was occupied by a new organization. It is the history of the application of men and ideas to the physical conditions." Because this was the case, "colonization" must be re-defined to include the migration of any considerable body of people of the same nationality into unoccupied territory. "Taking this liberal use of the term, we may call much of the European settlement of the West, colonization." This deserved investigation.

"We can never understand our country until we know the materials out of which our western states have been constructed." Historians must no longer waste their time on Pocahontas or the name of the first child born in Brown County; they should study "where and by what means the characteristics and the population of western states like Kansas and California and Wisconsin were produced." They should also recognize that colonization from abroad did not end with the Puritans and Cavaliers, but continued through the nineteenth century, as immigrants flooded the seaboard and pushed westward. "They have brought us not merely so much bone and sinew, not merely so much money, not merely so much manual skill; they have brought with them deeply inrooted customs and ideas. They are important factors in the political and economic life of the nation. The story of the peopling of America has not yet been written. We do not understand ourselves."

Such an understanding was imperative, for the "colonizing era" in the nation's history was drawing to a close, and "colonization" was the key to an understanding of that history. "As the occupation of the New World transformed Europe, so the occupation of the Great West has determined the flow of American energies, been the underlying explanation of American political history, and has had profound reactive effects upon the social and economic life of the East." American history would never be understood until the nation's expansion westward had been traced and its impact on the East and Europe appraised. "What first the Mediterranean sea and later the New World were to the Aryan peoples, breaking the bonds of custom, and creating new activities to meet new conditions, that the undeveloped West has been to the American descendants of those Aryans." Yet expansion was too rooted in the nation's character to end. "We have a national self-consciousness, a self-sufficient industrial organization. Will not this organization bud as did the trans-Allegheny organism?" Turner thought that it would, and that American commerce would move outward to dominate markets in Latin America and the Pacific.[51]

When Turner prepared that paper in January 1891, he moved well along the road toward the hypothesis he was to announce two years later. He saw interior settlements as "colonies" of the seaboard, advancing civilization westward just as the English colonizers had in the seventeenth century. He recognized that these new civilizations differed from those that gave them birth, and that these differences were due in part to the influence of different environments. He realized that one period in the nation's history—the period of "colonization"—was ending, and that readjustments had to be made in the social, economic, and political structure. These were basic concepts in Turner's frontier thesis, yet more had to be added before that thesis was completed. He had yet to use the word "frontier," or to understand the process through which expansion went on. He had still to appreciate the alterations in the national character and institutions stemming from three centuries of westering. These next steps would follow easily; he had only to flesh out the skeleton to reach the point where his hypothesis could be pronounced.

His next step came naturally. In the autumn of 1891 the undergraduate newspaper, *The Aegis,* announced a series of articles by faculty members on their research, including one by Turner on "New Aspects of the Early History of Wisconsin."[52] Fortunately, he procrastinated, as usual; by the time his contribution was due he was so deeply immersed in his colonization studies that the essay on Wisconsin no longer excited him. Why not write instead on the reinterpretations that were revising his understanding of American history? This would popularize his department's offerings by demonstrating that the subject provided intellectual attractions without parallel, that its study was an exciting adventure in creative thinking. His was a happy inspiration, for the result was his "Problems in American History," published in *The Aegis* on November 4, 1892, and destined to take its place among the most important contributions made by Turner to the understanding of the past.[53]

Past historians, he charged, had erred in ignoring "the fundamental, dominating fact in United States history," the expansion of population from sea to sea. "In a sense American history up to our own day has been colonial history, the colonization of the Great West. The ever retreating frontier of free land is the key to American development." To investigate the impact of this would be to shed new light on every facet of the nation's past. Politics would take on a new dimension, for "behind institutions, behind constitutional forms, lie the vital forces that call these organs into life and shape them to meet changing conditions. The peculiarity of American institutions is the fact that they are compelled to adapt themselves to the changes of a remarkably developing, expanding people." These changes influenced Europe no less than the United States. "We have to observe how European life entered the continent, and how America modified that life and reacted on Europe." We must appraise the effect on the Old World of free land in the New; we must measure the changes wrought in Europe by American freedom of speech, democracy, and economic progress. These were the "problems in American history" that were crying for a solution.

These problems could be solved only if historians added new tools to their kitbags; those of geologists, mineralogists, biologists, and geographers were essential to understanding the impact of physiographic forces on the settlement process. Only by using such tools could the ebb and flow of expansion be understood, the course of migration plotted, and the extent of regional influences on the social and economic behavior of the people be appreciated. This last was especially important, for the moving frontier left behind a succession of "sections" formed when intruding stocks interacted with the natural environment. These differed one from the other in economic enterprise, governmental practices, and cultural interests. Their continuous pressure on the national government tended, on the one hand, to divide the United States into quarreling factions, each seeking congressional legislation beneficial to its own interests, and, on the other, to unify the nation as people of divergent backgrounds blended into one social order. "State sovereignty is lost in the West, where appears a checkerboard division of states which recruit their population from all parts of the Union."

Sectionalism in all its aspects could be understood only after all manner of subsidiary problems were solved by historians. They must investigate immigration, for the newer arrivals brought habits, ideals, and customs which reacted with the native culture. "We shall not understand the contemporary history of the United States without studying immigration historically." Scholars must study the disposal of the public domain, the building of the transportation network, interstate migration. They must determine the role of free land as a democratizing agent. But, most essential of all, they must view all the past anew from the vantage point of the West. This was the neglected key to American history, and until it unlocked the story of the nation that story would be misunderstood. "What the Mediterranean Sea was to the Greeks," Turner concluded, "breaking the bond of custom, offering new experiences, calling out new institutions and activities, that the ever retreating Great West has been to the United States directly, and to the nations of Europe more remotely."

"Problems in American History" must be ranked with "The Significance of History" as a landmark in Frederick J. Turner's intellectual growth. In that essay he identified the two basic forces—frontier and section—that he believed responsible for much of the distinctiveness of American civilization. Perhaps even more important, he isolated material causes stemming from expansion as basic in the alteration process, rather than mysterious hereditary forces. This was a giant leap forward. So was his insistence that the tools of social and physical scientists be added to the kits of historians, for it was a pioneer insistence on interdisciplinary research. These bold suggestions show Turner as original in thought, rebellious of convention, and inventive in both the concepts and methods of historical investigation. He was not far wrong when he wrote a quarter-century later that, in that one essay, "I said pretty nearly everything I have said since."[54]

His own generation viewed matters differently. Copies of *The Aegis* containing his "Problems" paper were broadcast wholesale among scholars, but with disheartening results; Turner's views were too advanced to be appreciated by most of his contemporaries. Professor Simon N. Patten felt that it provided "a very helpful way of looking at our social problems" (which it did not); Professor Francis N. Thorpe termed it a good outline that would have been improved by the use of some of his own studies on constitution-making; Professor Emory R. Johnson was impressed with the improvement in *The Aegis* since he was a student at Wisconsin under Turner; and Professor Charles M. Andrews was not sure that the profession was ready to write the history of expansion until his own colonial period had been properly investigated. This faint praise, however, was more than offset by a glowing tribute from Herbert Baxter Adams. Adams was not only much interested, and so impressed that he would call its "suggestive views" to the attention of the Hopkins seminar, but he believed its author worthy of a place on the program of the American Historical Association at its next meeting. Would Turner be willing to prepare a paper for the sessions scheduled for Chicago in July 1893?[55] Thus, ironically, the invitation that led to "The Significance of the Frontier in

American History" came from the man whose views Turner later judged so archaic that his frontier thesis was a rebellion against them!

At the time Turner accepted the invitation, he had laid the foundations of his hypothesis, but he had built only a speculative structure. Now he had to add bricks and mortar, in the form of proof, and alter the framework as further study demanded architectural refinements. He had to spend the next months poring over census statistics, maps, and the few books that described western life with any degree of accuracy. He had to probe the works of political scientists, economists, geographers, publicists, and biologists, in search of theoretical justification for his conclusions. Busy times lay ahead.

V

The Genesis of
the Frontier Thesis

1892-1893

MERICANS for generations had been aware that a frontier existed, and that it had altered their lives and institutions.[1] From the days of Benjamin Franklin and Thomas Jefferson they had talked of a "safety valve" in the West that attracted surplus laborers from eastern factories, thus discouraging radical protest. They had linked cheap lands with democracy and had speculated on the uniquely American traits—mobility, inventiveness, individualism, optimism, impatience with authority—traceable to the frontiering experience. One publicist, E. L. Godkin, in an essay on "Aristocratic Opinions of Democracy," published in 1865, anticipated much of what Turner was to say thirty years later. Godkin had held that three centuries of pioneering had bred into Americans a faith in democracy, an individualistic contempt for social authority, "a self-confidence that rises into conceit," "a devotion to material pursuits," "a lack of taste in art and literature," "a prodigious contempt for experience and for theory," and a respect for the practical that made them distrustful of "book-learned" politicians.[2] Yet Godkin, and dozens who preached his message, went unheeded. Why did Turner succeed where they failed?

One answer can be found in the changed social atmosphere of the 1890s. Americans were gradually coming to realize that the frontier was closing, and the era of cheap western lands near its end. How could the nation adjust itself to a closed-space existence? Thinking men believed that for three centuries American prosperity had rested on the exploitation of virgin natural resources, and democratic values

had rested on the equality of opportunity provided by the public domain. Would poverty and despotism be the lot of the United States
now? Some thought it would, and in the crumbling social order about
them they found evidence to bolster their beliefs. A depression gripped
the country between 1873 and 1896, a depression that bore every mark
of permanence. It forced a new mood on the nation. Past depressions
had been endured because renewed expansion would inevitably rejuvenate the economy, but now that hope was glimmering and social critics
sang a new tune. Publicists—such as Henry George or Thorstein Veblen
—preached the inequity of a system that created profits for the few instead of benefits for the many; newspaper headlines told of crippling
strikes, the Haymarket Riot, the shrill demands of the Knights of Labor and the People's party for a more equitable distribution of wealth.
To many Americans these were disturbing portents of a future in a
frontierless land. Class conflict and revolutionary demands threatened
to transform the United States into another Europe.

Actually the frontier did not close abruptly at the end of the nineteenth century, nor did diminishing opportunity there underlie the
social turmoil of those decades. The "Commercial Revolution" was responsible for the social upheaval; the mechanization of commercial in-
terchange brought into the world marketplace agricultural goods from
every corner of the globe to compete with those of traditional pro-
ducers, driving prices downward and disrupting trade patterns. But in
the minds of many Americans the exhaustion of cheap lands and the
depression were inseparably linked. Prophets of doom held that overproduction had driven prices downward, an overproduction fostered
by "a practically unlimited area of fertile land, free as the air we
breathe." They also held that, while prices might recover, prosperity
was a thing of the past, never to be enjoyed again. That prosperity, and
"the comparative freedom from the social and economic problems long
confronting Europe," they laid at the door of "an almost unlimited
area of fertile land to which the unemployed could freely resort." Some
saw the nation's future as one plagued by "social disturbances of grave
significance," a peon-like caste system, and a giant standing army that
would provide work for those who could no longer escape to the frontier.[3]

All of this clamor—and the popular magazines were studded with articles sounding the alarm—focused attention on the frontier and its

passing. So did others, with less lofty designs, who sought to stir national sentiment against continued immigration. The real objective of these zealots was to close the gates against the "New Immigration" from southern and eastern Europe—Italians, Hungarians, and Jews—but they dared not resort to racist tactics and so seized on the closing of the frontier to justify laws against all newcomers. Why share the few remaining lands with the "depraved dregs of European civilization?" "There are no more new worlds," wrote Josiah Strong, a leading spokesman for this view. "The unoccupied arable lands of the earth are limited, and will soon be taken."[4] These were the views not only of bigoted crackpots, but of informed citizens, as well. Francis A. Walker, an educator and statistician, whose works Turner greatly admired, used his presidential address before the American Economics Association to warn that "alien breeds" menaced the nation, since free lands could no longer absorb them. Albert Shaw, a Johns Hopkins friend of Turner's, saw to it that each issue of the *Review of Reviews* that he edited contained at least one article tub-thumping for exclusion.[5] These propagandists symbolized, and encouraged, a groundswell of anti-immigration sentiment that climaxed with the founding of the "Immigration Restriction League" in 1894, just months after Turner read his essay on the frontier.

We can never know the degree to which Turner was influenced by publicists who connected immigration restriction and the depression of the 1890s with the closing of the frontier, but we do know that he clipped articles from Chicago papers by leaders of the exclusion movement, that he included a "free land" period in a section of his economic and social history course that dealt with immigration, and that he directed an undergraduate honors thesis on "The Effect of the Settlement of the Public Domain on Immigration."[6] Certainly any young historian of his sensitivity and interests would have read anything that came his way on the frontier. Whether he did so or not, however, is less important than the fact that this outburst of polemic writings indicated a wave of interest in expansion that had not existed even a decade before. People were ready to ask the questions that Turner was prepared to answer. They would listen when he told them that three centuries of westering had influenced the nation no less than the end of westering was affecting it now. The social atmosphere of the 1890s encouraged Turner's investigations, and assured him a body of readers who would welcome his views.

This was his good fortune. He was fortunate, too, to reach his maturity at exactly the time when the intellectual world was ready to welcome his hypothesis, and when the various disciplines on which he had to lean—history, geography, biology, and statistical cartography—could provide him with the tools he needed in his research. He was equipped, as earlier scholars had not been, to translate his speculations into scientifically based theories backed by impeccable authority.

The revolutionary changes that transformed historical studies during the 1890s benefited him particularly. By this time a group of young professionals were challenging the fantasies of the Teutonists' "germ" theory. Historians who produced learned monographs on the relationship between Saxon tithingmen and New England constables, on the Germanic basis for life in Salem, and on the Kentucky Chautauqua as a survival of the medieval *folkmoot*, could no longer be taken seriously by anyone but themselves. So the attack began, led by Edward Channing and Charles MacLean Andrews, who leveled their lances against the naïve assumption that a modern institution had evolved from a Teutonic "germ" because they resembled each other. As well insist that New England towns descended from Masai villages in Africa as from German *tuns* because both of the earlier models were surrounded by defensive walls. So Channing argued in his *Genesis of the Massachusetts Town*, published in 1891, and Andrews backed his judgment by pointing out that the Connecticut towns he studied were by no means identical to their Germanic ancestors, having been altered by geographic, economic, and ethnic pressures. Their common-sense message deeply impressed the oncoming generation of historians. So did the insistence of other scholars, particularly in England, that politics was not the only clue to understanding human behavior, and that social and economic pressures upon society must also be investigated. When, in his essay on "The Significance of History," Turner quoted approvingly from a book by James E. T. Rogers, *The Economic Interpretation of History*, published in 1889, he was simply moving with the tides.[7]

Turner benefited, too, from the emerging rebellion of midwestern writers against eastern domination. This was long overdue; decades of truckling to New England as the cultural fountainhead of the nation had stifled the growth of native expression in literature and the arts, no less than in history. Hamlin Garland spoke for his section in his *Crumbling Idols,* published in 1894, when he urged his fellow midwesterners to further the coming American democracy by ceasing to worship the "crumbling idols" of the past, to create rather than imitate, and to tap the rich literary resources waiting exploitation in the Mississippi Valley.[8] Turner was to speak for his section when he dedicated himself to showing that the Midwest played an essential role in the emergence of the nation, and that its contribution to national greatness was no less than that of the eastern seaboard. He was responding to an impulse that formed part of the intellectual climate of his region, just as he was responding to the climate of his day. He recognized this. "The ideas underlying my 'Significance of the Frontier,' " he wrote some time later, "would have been expressed in some form or other in any case. They were part of the growing American consciousness of itself."[9]

Historians could rebel against traditionalism, but, to be accepted, their new interpretations had to be bolstered by scientific evidence. Turner's hypothesis, which he developed gradually as he prepared his colonization lectures and his course on economic and social history, was that the frontiering process altered man and man's institutions. This seemed clear to Turner as he read the works of travelers who described the behavior of westerners—a behavior clearly different from that of easterners, who lived in compact communities. But *how* did life on the frontier reshape the pioneers and their institutions?

Turner found his answer in the geographic theory of the day. Since the time of Hippocrates, mankind had believed that the physical environment shaped human behavior, and that variations in climate, topography, and soils determined the nature of the differing civilizations that dotted the globe. This venerable theory—glorified in Turner's day as "environmental determinism"—gained new importance during the controversy over evolution in the 1880s and 1890s. Darwinians, seeking to account for the wide variety of species that had evolved, agreed that these many life forms had been moulded by the equally wide variety of physical environments in which they had existed. This was a common-sense viewpoint, endorsed by Charles Darwin himself. Nor did they stop there. If animal organisms could be so altered by natural forces, so could the supreme animal organism: man. To Turner this meant one thing: the unique social and physical environment of the frontier endowed the pioneers with the distinguishing traits noted by travelers.

That view had the backing of the highest world authority. The crown prince of the environmentalists was the German geographer, Friedrich Ratzel, whose system of "Anthropo-Geographie" was set forth in two fat volumes, published in 1882 and 1891. Man, Ratzel preached, was shaped by the physical world about him, and he succeeded only to the extent that he adapted to his environment. Differences between modern nations were the outcome of earlier migrations into differing regions, each isolated from the others by seas, deserts, or mountains, and each developing differently due to differing physical conditions. These doctrines were universally accepted by American geographers, who parroted them in their books and publications. "That man," declared one in 1889, "has been influenced in his development by his physical, climatic and social surroundings is well nigh indisputable."[10] Textbooks mirrored the universal belief in environmentalism. James A. Dana, revising his well-known *Manual of Geology*, went on record that "favoring conditions in environment" produced "superior races"; a more modern textbook proclaimed that physical forces "determined the pursuits, character, and total life of the people."[11] With geographers standing shoulder to shoulder in this belief, historians had no choice but to follow. They did, almost to a man. "I would not say," wrote Justin Winsor in his *The Mississippi Basin*, "that there are no other compelling influences, but no other control is so steady." When a manual on *How To Study and Teach History*, published in 1893, held that physical conditions created civilizations, shaped their development, and caused their downfall, it simply mirrored the viewpoint of the entire profession.[12] The wonder was not that Turner believed in environment as a moulding force, but that he did not succumb more completely to that belief; he stated repeatedly, and truthfully, through his lifetime that he was not an environmental determinist.

He was on equally sure ground when he accepted the prevailing view that the characteristics and behavioral patterns that the pioneers developed because of their frontier environment were handed down from generation to generation to influence present-day American life. Biologists were not as united behind a belief in the inheritability of acquired characteristics as geographers were in holding to environmental determinism, but Turner had sound scientific backing when he accepted that viewpoint as essential to his hypothesis. His principal authorities were in the ranks of biologists, then much in the public eye as they proclaimed the virtues of Charles Darwin's evolutionary hypothesis. Disciples of Darwin's theory built their case on two "proven" assumptions: that, as species evolved, a process of "natural selection" operated to perpetuate those best adapted to the environment, and that new species broke off from old by a process of "mutation," which was not clearly understood but had been demonstrated by experimental means.

These generally accepted theories were challenged in the 1880s by German scientists, whose experiments suggested that acquired traits were not inheritable; rather, that all characteristics were present in each organism's germ plasm and were passed on from generation to generation without being altered by the environment. These "New Darwinians," enlisted largely from among the younger biologists, went beyond all reason in denying environmental influences, holding that all traits were present in the germ cell at conception, and could never be changed. This overstatement stirred such resentment that opponents of the theory closed ranks; calling themselves the "Neo-Lamarckians," they swung to the view that *all* traits were acquired and passed on to later generations. Environments changed organisms, they insisted, and these changes were passed on to the progeny. This was the view of nine-tenths of the scientists in America and Europe when Turner was formulating his theories. Wrote one: "If there is any principle in inheritance which has appeared self-evident and not requiring any demonstration at all, it is that acquired characteristics *are* inherited."[13] If ever two scientific principles were widely accepted on the basis of unimpeachable scientific support, they were that organisms responded to environmental pressures and that characteristics thus acquired were bequeathed to subsequent generations. This was the state of scientific knowledge when Turner prepared his 1893 essay.

That he was familiar with these developments seems certain. During the months when he was formulating his thesis, he was in almost daily contact with his good friend Charles R. Van Hise, a geologist of repute whose broad interests brought him in touch with the conflicts raging among geographers and biologists over the Darwinian thesis. As a member of the Wisconsin Academy of Sciences, Arts and Letters, Turner heard numerous papers by Van Hise and his fellow geologist, President T. C. Chamberlin, all couched in evolutionary terms, and all extolling environmentalism. There, too, he listened to discussions in which "New Darwinians" and "Neo-Lamarckians" threshed out their differences or struck sparks with their arguments. He was certainly aware of the battle between these opposing schools, for heated articles upholding one viewpoint or the other filled English journals and spilled over into American magazines, many of which he read regularly.[14] His own language suggests his familiarity with this scientific literature, bristling as it did with biological metaphors such as "organism," "plastic," and "adaptation."

We know today that the biologists and geographers led Turner astray, and that the doctrines they preached were false, or not suitable to application to social organisms. By 1910 the scientific world had come to agree that acquired characteristics could not be inherited, and not long thereafter geographers and geologists concluded that the physical environment played a lesser role in altering behavioral patterns than they had formerly believed. These later findings should not cloud the fact that when Turner voiced his thesis he had the best of scientific backing for two of the foundation stones on which it rested.

If he was fortunate enough to voice his views at the exact time they would be most hospitably received, he was doubly fortunate in the progress in statistical cartography that allowed him to illustrate them graphically. Without the efforts of a generation of statisticians and map-makers he could never have visualized the nation's expansion accurately, and without that visual image before him he might never have arrived at his hypothesis. His study of census reports, atlases, and statistical tables allowed him to picture the march of population westward, and to theorize from that picture as his thesis took shape.

German map-makers pioneered the techniques that were to revolutionize their subject in the 1870s and 1880s, but the American who did most to hurry the revolution was Francis A. Walker, eminent educator, statistician, and director of the censuses of 1870 and 1880. Walker sensed the possibilities of the German methods and insisted that they be incorporated in *The Statistical Atlas of the United States Based on the Results of the Ninth Census, 1870*, published in 1874. This bulky volume, which was pivotal in stimulating Turner's interest in the West, contained two features that were particularly useful to him. One was a series of maps showing population density for each decade from 1790 to 1870, shaded to indicate five degrees of concentration between two and six inhabitants to the square mile at the edge of settlement and ninety to the square mile in the populated East. This graphically depicted the westward movement. "The movement of population," judged one reviewer, "seems to take place under our very eyes."[15] Equally important to Turner was an essay on "The Progress of the Nation, 1790-1870," which was based on the maps and which described "the line of continuous settlement" or the "frontier line." There he learned that expansion progressed in set stages, with cattle-raising and other occupations suitable to a sparse population at the outer edge, primitive and technologically advanced farming next in order, and finally an industrialized and urbanized civilization.[16] Here were the "stages of society" that Turner had studied under Richard T. Ely in his political economy courses at Johns Hopkins.

This was enough to excite Turner; he jotted down notes as he read, and he thought well enough of the volume to assign it to his students.[17] His excitement mounted as he read other articles from Walker's pen that traced the westward movement more exactly and noted that it was proceeding at the rate of from seventy to seventy-five feet a day in a direction generally west but slightly north, usually following latitudinal lines.[18] The bulky official report of the 1880 census appealed especially, for its population-density maps were more sophisticated than those of a decade before, and its essay on "The Progress of the Nation" was more emphatic in its description of the westward movement than that in the 1870 census. An article by Henry Gannett, a census bureau geographer, that appeared in the *International Review*, was also useful. "An arbitrary line," Gannett wrote, "must be drawn somewhere beyond which the country must be considered as unsettled, although it may not be absolutely without inhabitants." This, he suggested, might follow the zone occupied by from two to six persons to the square mile.[19] Here was a definition tailored to Turner's needs; he could now visualize a "frontier line" with an exact meaning.

All of these works added something to his knowledge, but none so much as the *Scribner's Statistical Atlas of the United States*, prepared by Gannett and Fletcher W. Hewes, and issued in 1885. This was a key work in the evolution of his thought; he urged it on his students, parroted it in his writings, and almost certainly had it at his elbow when he prepared his 1893 essay. The maps intrigued him especially —maps that vividly pictured in striking color the physical features of the continent, the advance of settlement, the immigration intrusion, the racial composition of the nation. So did the essays: one, on the progress of the nation, spoke of the "westward movement" and the "frontier line"; another, probably by Gannett, described the sequential pattern followed in expansion, with stress on the evolution of pioneer communities from a primitive to a developed economy.[20] Turner's hours of poring over *Scribner's Atlas* taught him a great deal about the nature of the frontier process.

They also alerted him to the value of census bulletins and converted him into a regular reader of their less-than-sparkling prose. This was fortunate, for no one but an avid enthusiast could have been attracted to a four-page pamphlet that reached his desk sometime during the 1892-93 academic year, atrociously printed, and bearing a title designed to repel all but the most dedicated census buffs: *Extra Census Bulletin No. 2. Distribution of Population According to Density: 1890.* Turner turned those pages, and was richly rewarded. He found a colored map showing the population of the United States in 1890 in six degrees of density. And he found also a striking statement: "Up to and including 1890 the country had a frontier of settlement, but at present the unsettled area has been so broken into by isolated bodies of settlement that there can hardly be said to be a frontier line."[21]

We can never know Turner's thoughts as he read those lines. We know what he did; he wrote his name on the first page, labeled the pamphlet "Density," underlined a few passages—but not, strangely enough, the sentence he was to quote later—and filed it away among his notes. Did he realize then that the westward movement was now history, and could be subjected to sociological analysis to reveal its significance? Did he recognize that the American experience capsulized the entire story of society's evolution, and that the lessons he had learned in his Portage upbringing offered clues to the whole nature of civilization? Probably not. Certainly he had the frontier hypothesis well in mind before that census bulletin reached his desk; it had been stated in skeleton form in his February 1891 lecture on colonization, and more completely in his essay on "Problems in American History," which may have been prepared before he saw the announcement of the frontier's closing. More probably, Turner, as a good journalist, saw that announcement as an eye-catching phrase to introduce the essay that was already taking shape in his mind. If so, he was ready now to plunge into the investigations that would add substance to his theories and allow him to present a full-blown hypothesis to the profession.

Turner haunted the State Historical Society library during the next several months. One would like to imagine that he went about his task systematically, reading travel accounts, guide books, western newspapers and magazines, frontier writers, and contemporary observers to find out *how* expansion altered traits and institutions of the pioneers, then studying the works of theorists to understand *why*. It is far more likely that Turner read in a haphazard fashion, mingling contemporary and modern authors, westerners and easterners, travelers and commentators. Certainly he was already familiar with some of the books on which he leaned most heavily, and he had only to dredge their message from his memory. Still, this was no light task. He had to absorb a vast amount of information, assimilate it, sort it, arrange it in an orderly pattern, and interpret it in terms of the national experience. We can appreciate his accomplishment if we recast the evidence that he gathered into the pattern that it assumed in his mind, rather than in the helter-skelter disorder in which he accumulated it.

Observers of pioneer life in early America taught him a great deal. From them he learned that travelers generally noted differences between easterners and westerners, and that western traits exaggerated the national characteristics that Europeans labeled "American." Nationalism was one: frontiersmen, "wholly freed from that local attachment which arises from habit and long residence," demanded services—protection, lands, roads—and there was no power that could provide them "except the general agent of all the states, at Washington."[22] Hence allegiance shifted from the state to the national government. Their mobility accentuated this nationalizing tendency; pioneers were constantly on the move, shifting from territory to territory, and forming no attachment to place.

Most writers agreed that the West also fostered democratic practices; the problems facing pioneers were unique, and required solutions easterners could not understand. So "every new settlement is already a republic *in embryo*." Social democracy was also rooted in the West, for class distinctions seemed meaningless in a land where the turn of a shovel or a fortunate land speculation could transform a pauper into a millionaire. "A pleasing feature of Western life," Turner read in an 1850 issue of *The American Whig Review*, "is the perfect social equality. . . . Strong arms and stout hearts their only wealth; all classes at last salute each other as brothers."[23] Westerners, he learned, were unusually individualistic, marked by an "independence of thought and action"; they were also infected with "a spirit of adventurous enterprise," free to venture into new lands or adopt new ideas, with little respect for tradition. "More new tools, implements, and machines . . . have been invented in this new world," wrote one westerner, "than were ever yet invented in the old."[24] When Turner added inventiveness to his catalogue of western traits he had an imposing list: nationalism, individualism, social and political democracy, mobility, independence, adventurous spirit, and inventiveness. Here was evidence that West did differ from East. Here also was the gallery of frontier traits that he would name in his 1893 essay.

He still had to determine *why* these differences emerged, and the quest for that answer led him into a strange variety of reading matter. Two French theorists whose work Turner read carefully had helpful ideas about western democracy. Emile Boutmy, whose *Studies in Constitutional Law: France-England-United States* appeared in English translation in 1891, argued that in overcrowded Europe strict authority was needed to maintain order, but in America "the vast tracts of land which were without owners" spread the population thinly, rendering force unnecessary. Those newer regions had no aristocratic establishments to be overthrown, and hence turned naturally to democratic practices; democracy would persist so long as men could become owners of the soil by moving a few miles westward. Behind this political democracy was a social democracy that undermined all caste systems and created a unique equality. So argued another French observer, André Churillon, in an article that appeared in the spring 1892 issue of the *Review of Reviews*. This was because opportunity was so abundant on the frontier that class lines could never be drawn; society was fluid, with no "fixity of professions" such as plagued older nations. When all men were potentially equal they were more inclined to treat each other as equals.[25]

Henry George was another theorist on whom Turner leaned. Turner read *Progress and Poverty* first as a graduate student at Wisconsin, studied it more intensely in Professor Ely's courses at Johns Hopkins, and perhaps reviewed it now as he was exploring the nature of the frontier; one note he recorded at this time was a reminder to transcribe a passage from page 349 of his own copy. This passage contained several helpful ideas. In it George reiterated his stout faith in the importance of the environment as a moulding force, and ascribed to "unfenced land" the nation's "general comfort, the active invention, the power of adaptation and assimilation, the free independent spirit, the energy and hopefulness."[26] These were sweeping generalizations, but they bolstered Turner's realization that a connection existed between free land and the frontier characteristics he was isolating.

He gained far more from the volume on *Physics and Politics* by the English political economist, Walter Bagehot. Turner's copy of this work, probably purchased in 1888 or 1889 at the suggestion of Herbert Baxter Adams, is badly worn, tattered from frequent use, and heavily underlined and annotated. It is obviously a book on which he relied heavily. Bagehot believed that the American character was shaped by the centuries-long struggle against the wilderness; those who led the assault became the nation's folk heroes, and their traits, acquired in their conquest, became the traits of all. "The eager restlessness," he wrote, "the high-strung nervous organization, are useful in continual struggle, and also are prompted by it." When Turner finished reading that passage, he reached for his note pad and recorded an idea it suggested to him: "West. Infl[uence] on U.S.—Custom. It stood to East as the sea to Phoenicia, to Egypt, to Greece."[27] Here, in very rough form, was the phrase that he would use in all his basic essays on the frontier.

The characteristics that Bagehot saw emerging in the West he ascribed not only to "colonial" conditions, but also to the mingling of peoples there, creating a fluid social order and lessening the strength of traditionalism. Turner had only to substitute "frontier" for "colonial" to realize that frontiering fostered new traits through intercultural borrowings as well as through environmental pressures. He thought that over and wrote at the bottom of the page: "Influence of West. It was the attractive force to immigration." Bagehot also believed that the newness of the West encouraged alterations in the social structure; in older "arrested civilizations," institutions and habits were too firmly implanted to be changed. The problem, as he saw it, was not to create a new society, but to escape an old one; not of "cementing a cake of custom, but of breaking the cake of custom." That observation inspired another of Turner's notes: "West. Influence on Am[erica]. Breaker of *custom*. The Leavening power in U.S. hist[ory]. Always at the edge of civ[ilization] creating new needs, conditions, opportunities."[28] Here were bits of substance for his theories, dovetailing nicely.

Francis A. Walker added more pieces to his jigsaw puzzle. This eminent political economist and statistician stood high on Turner's list of favorite authors, so he paid attention when he came across a Phi Beta Kappa address on "The Growth of the Nation" delivered by Walker at Brown University in 1889. "The extraordinary progress of the population westward over new lands," Walker believed, was responsible for many of the distinguishing features of the American character. An inventive ability was one; living in a thinly peopled land with few tools and no division of labor, the pioneers had to "make do" by providing for their own needs. "To save time, to diminish labor, to cut corners and break down barriers in reaching an object, to force one tool to serve three or four purposes, and to compel refractory or inappropriate material to answer urgent needs; this was the daily occupation of our ancestors." Pioneer conditions also fostered the extreme nationalism that had become a national characteristic. "No one can doubt that both the increase of our population and its expansion over a continually wider territory, have been the chief causes of the remarkable development among us of that public spirit which we call patriotism." Only when settlers from the "Old Thirteen" met and mingled in the Ohio Valley did this emerge, for only when a people had no history of their own, no local pride, no dependence on a single state's authority, could the nation command their primary affection.[29] Turner borrowed many of his views on frontier nationalism directly from Walker's address.

He borrowed even more from a germinal volume by an Italian political economist, Achille Loria, whose *Analisa della Proprietà Capitalista* was published in Turin in 1889. An economic determinist, Loria believed that human behavior was governed by the relationship between man and the quantity of "free land" available to him. To prove his theories he focused attention on the "colonial" countries, for he shared the common belief that emerging cultures repeated in exact sequential order the steps by which civilizations in older countries had evolved over the centuries. Loria saw industrialism as the final stage in this social evolution, unattainable so long as "free lands" allowed a laborer to change into a proprietor without expenditure of capital. The United States offered a splendid example. He described the dispersal of population westward, the depletion of the soil's fertility by wasteful farming methods common where land was abundant, the importation of indentured servants and slaves in an attempt to offset declining yields, and the final evolutionary stage in which efficiency was heightened by forming great estates, releasing laborers from farms to factories, and inaugurating the industrial era. Loria predicted that the exhaustion of "free land" would lead the United States into a period of social evils such as those plaguing Europe, where economic freedom and democracy were threatened by the plutocrats who controlled farming and manufacturing.[30]

This was grist for Turner's mill, but grist not easily come by. He had no knowledge of Italian, nor was this the sort of book that would normally come to his attention—or to the shelves of the State Historical Society library. In all probability Richard T. Ely brought Loria's book to Turner. Ely was familiar with the *Analisa* when he joined the Wisconsin faculty in the fall of 1892; he was then revising his *An Introduction to Political Economy* to incorporate the system of land economics that Loria set forth. Then, too, Harry H. Powers, a graduate student who was aiding Ely in the revision, had studied in Italy, knew the language well, and was preparing the chapters based on Loria's theories. Turner probably first learned of the Italian economist when he read those chapters in manuscript at Ely's request. He would certainly have recognized the importance of Loria's theories concerning land; in passage after passage Turner read that "free land," rather than protective tariffs, assured high wages for the United States; that "free land" tempered the impact of the class struggle; that the exhaustion of "free land" would alter the nation's economic and political structure.[31] This was valuable information, but clearly incomplete. Nothing would do but that he read the *Analisa* itself.

That he did so, in whole or in part, is certain, for he borrowed not only ideas but phrases and metaphors, from Loria's work. It is very likely that Powers was pressed into service to read the book aloud, translating as he did so, as Turner listened, summarizing on a scratch pad the sections that interested him most. In all probability this took place in

September and October of 1892, for Professor Ely did not arrive in Madison with his pupil until that September, and Turner was familiar with the *Analisa* when he published his "Problems in American History" on November 4 of that year. As he listened, Turner jotted notes applying Loria's theories to his own hypothesis. Loria's description of cheating and speculating during the early colonial period inspired this: "Work up one part on colonial law. Frontier in 1765 regulators etc." Reference to the common law started a new chain of thought: "Too great stress has been laid on the democratic character of the immigrants to America. Free land is the explanation at bottom." Again, when Turner considered Loria's argument on the value of slavery to primitive societies, he added: "The dissolution of a wage society by free land. Anti social tendency. Creation of economic inertia. Satisfaction in small agric[ultural] holdings. Lack of intellectual stimulus arising from contact."[32]

To emphasize these fragments of information garnered from Loria's *Analisa* is to obscure its major contribution to the frontier hypothesis. By the time he encountered that work, Turner understood why men moved West, he was familiar with the routes they followed and their methods of travel, and he had identified certain enduring traits as resulting from the frontier experience. Not until he encountered Loria, however, did he fully comprehend *how* expansion altered the character and institutions of pioneers. Free land was responsible. The abundance of opportunity in the form of readily obtainable natural resources determined the pace of society's evolution, recast British law and custom into an American mould, underlay colonial prosperity, and decided the nature of the labor system. Free land was the synonym for self-advancement on the frontier, and the relatively great opportunity there for economic and social betterment was responsible for the social changes that Turner had observed. This was the arch-stone of his hypothesis, and while others stressed the significance of "free land," none brought the lesson home as forcefully as Loria.

To assign Loria major credit, however, is to deny the indisputable fact that the frontier thesis blended many ideas from many sources. Emil Boutmy, André Churillon, Henry George, Walter Bagehot, Francis A. Walker, and Achille Loria all made their contributions, just as had the dozens of guidebook authors, magazine writers, newspaper editors, and foreign travelers whose works Turner combed for information. None, however, did more than stimulate Turner's imagination and provide him with the facts needed to illuminate his theories. He had arrived at most of his basic conclusions by January 1891, when he prepared his talk on "American Colonization" for the Madison Literary Club, long before he read Loria or many of the other writers who supposedly influenced him most. His reading during 1892-93 was not in quest of a new interpretation, but a search for collaborative evidence to bolster an interpretation he had already arrived at. He studied western travelers and guidebooks, not to learn that westerners differed from easterners, but to discover *how* they differed. He consulted Bagehot and Loria and Walker, not to find a new theory, but to explain how his own theory operated. In essence, the frontier hypothesis was a product of Turner's creative ability. This alone allowed him to provide unity and meaning to speculation about the pioneering past, and to fashion a tentative hypothesis that was worth laying before the profession in the form of a paper on "The Significance of the Frontier in American History."

Turner would have written his essay eventually, for he was too intrigued by his speculations not to share them with the world. But the fact that it was ready for delivery by July 1893 can be blamed on Christopher Columbus. That worthy's landfall was to be celebrated with a World's Columbian Exposition in Chicago, and the Chicagoans would only be satisfied with a world's fair that would outshine any in history. Determined that the fair would not be all amusements and whoopla, they wanted a whole galaxy of cultural attractions, to show that the prairies of mid-America could produce something more than corn and Populists. They must have a series of "Auxilliary Congresses" on literature and the arts, each packed with glittering stars of world renown. One would be a "World's Congress of Historians and Historical Students," arranged by local talent, but enlisting the aid of the American Historical Association, which was invited to hold a special meeting in the city during July. William F. Poole, librarian of the Newberry Library, would prepare a program, aided by a committee from the association led by its perennial secretary, Herbert Baxter Adams.[33]

This proved a near-fatal arrangement, for Adams had a nose-in-air disdain for the outlanders with whom he must work, and he was determined to run his own show, lest the Congress become "a pandemonium or an exhibit of cranks." "Every Chicago man," he complained, "wants the earth and proposes to dump everything into his lakeside show."[34] His solution was to ignore Poole and the Chicagoans completely, arranging for the historians to meet in some quiet spot far from the Exposition's turmoil. Not until President James B. Angell of the University of Michigan, himself a distinguished historian, made a special trip to Chicago was a compromise arranged. Dr. Poole and his local committee would retain their titles, but the program would be drafted by Adams and his fellow association members. "In this way," Adams wrote with obvious satisfaction, "we can capture the historical congress."[35]

All this squabbling took time, and not until late February and early March of 1893 did the first invitations go out, just four months before the sessions were to begin. Adams saw the list of proposed speakers and thought well of it, but he was still skeptical. Few eastern notables would risk their lives by venturing as far west as Chicago, nor would the greats of the profession be appreciated by the motley crew attracted by an overgrown carnival. "I fancy," he sniffed, "people at the World's Fair will not care much about hearing historical papers."[36] One invitation Adams could approve. This was to Turner, who replied on February 23 that he would gladly read a paper on "The Significance of the Frontier in American History."[37]

Other historians were less willing to accept. By March 20 Poole was assured of only four participants, and he had been refused by such notables as Edward Eggleston, Henry Cabot Lodge, Hermann von Holst, and Albion W. Small. This was hardly an impressive beginning; Justin Winsor thought it a "pitiful show," and predicted that the quality of the performers was so low that the committee was unjustified "in asking any reputable writer to take part in the Congress to the extent of reading a paper."[38] Despite these forebodings, the list grew, and it sparkled with a few names acceptable even to that crotchety Bostonian: Moses Coit Tyler, Edward Everett Hale, Ephriam Emerton, Frederic Bancroft, and the Honorable William Wirt Henry. By June twenty-seven scholars had accepted, and Herbert Baxter Adams reluctantly admitted that "we have a large number of good papers and the literary success of the Congress is assured."[39]

Adams could not know as he penned those words that the program was threatened by the loss of the one paper that was to give it lasting significance. On April 23 Turner wrote Poole that he had two fine students—Orin Grant Libby, whose thesis was on the "Geographical Distribution of the Vote on the Ratification of the Constitution of the United States," and Albert Hart Sandford, who had written on "The Judicial Interpretations of the Ordinance of 1787"—who deserved a place. Could their excellent papers be included? Poole was doubtful. This so disappointed Turner that he was willing to make the supreme sacrifice. On May 10 he suggested that were there any question of including Libby's study, "kindly put it in place of my own paper on 'The Significance of the Frontier in American History.' "[40] Fortunately, Turner's academic prestige was sufficiently low that Poole could ignore his request, preferring to sprinkle his program with professors rather than graduate students.

So it was that Turner was among the performers when the historical congress first assembled, on July 10. He and Mae arrived several days before, traveling by train from Madison with their friends, the Reuben Gold Thwaites, the C. L. Hendricksons, and Charles Homer Haskins, and putting up at a University of Chicago dormitory near the fair.[41] Once unpacked, the party joined the throngs gaping at the wonders of the Exposition—all, that is, but Turner. He shut himself in his room to do what he should have done long before: finish the essay that was to be read two days later. "I am," he wrote a friend, "in the final agonies of getting out a belated paper."[42] He interrupted his labors to attend the opening sessions at Chicago's new Art Institute at the foot of Adams Street; there he presumably made his formal bows to the "Committee on Historical Literature," which had assembled in Room 24; lingered only briefly in the Hall of Columbus, where Dr. Poole and a harp soloist held forth; and hurried back to the university dormitory to add the final touches to his paper.

The Historical Congress opened its sessions the next morning, when the members went through the formalities of electing agreed-upon officers, listened to an address by the newly elected president, and settled back to endure the round of papers scheduled for presentation during the next three days. Morning and evening sessions were planned, with from three to five learned papers at each, and only the afternoons free for recovery and glimpses of the Exposition. "It will be seen," wrote the official chronicler of the Congress, "that amateur historians and sensational theorists had no place on the programme."[43] Professionals, their systems inured to such a heavy diet, were numerous enough to provide audiences of from one to two hundred persons for each meeting.

Turner's turn came on the evening of Wednesday, July 12. The day was intolerably hot, but a lake breeze in the late afternoon cooled the air for the thousands milling about the fair grounds, some jamming the lakefront to watch the arrival of the replica of a Viking ship from Norway, more standing in silence as firemen raked through the ashes of a giant storage plant that had burned two nights before. Turner was not among them; he even resisted an invitation extended to the historians to attend a showing of Buffalo Bill's Wild West Show that afternoon. Those last precious hours were needed to put the finishing touches on his paper. So he was ready when the usual audience of scholars and curiosity seekers gathered at the Art Institute that night.

They were a hardy lot, but even their endurance must have been tested by the procession of scholarly papers: Dr. George Kriehn on "English Popular Uprisings in the Middle Ages," Dr. George P. Fisher on "The Social Compact and Mr. Jefferson's Adoption of It," Professor Jesse Macy on "The Relation of History to Politics," Dr. Reuben Gold Thwaites on "Early Lead Mining in Illinois and Wisconsin." Only then did Turner's turn come, with an audience so deadened by this display of learning that he doubtless read only a portion of the lengthy essay he had prepared.[44] For those able to free themselves from the prejudices of that day, even this was enough to show that he was issuing a declaration of independence for American historiography.

Taking his cue from the census bureau's announcement that there "can hardly be said to be a frontier line" remaining, Turner proclaimed his text: "the existence of an area of free land, its continuous recession, and the advance of American settlement westward explain American development." The frontier was one of several vital forces lying behind constitutional forms "that call these organs into life and shape them to meet changing conditions." The nation's institutions owed their originality to the fact that they had been "compelled to adapt themselves to the changes of an expanding people—to the changes involved in crossing a continent, in winning a wilderness, and in developing at each area of this progress, out of the primitive economic and political conditions of the frontier, the complexity of city life." This perennial rebirth of civilization made the frontier—"the meeting point between savagery and civilization"—the area of the "most rapid and effective Americanization." Here new traits, new institutions, were born.[45]

One by one Turner chronicled these traits. In the crucible of the frontier newcomers were Americanized and fused into a mixed race, "English in neither nationality nor characteristics." The result was "the formation of a composite nationality for the American people." The nationalizing tendency was accentuated as the central government broadened its powers to care for its burgeoning settlements. "Loose construction increased as the nation marched westward," transforming the republicanism of Jefferson into the national republicanism of Monroe and the democracy of Andrew Jackson. Then, too, a principal function of the frontier "has been in the promotion of democracy here and in Europe." This frontier democracy, "born of free land," was "strong in selfishness and individualism, intolerant of administrative experience and education, and pressing individual liberty beyond its proper bounds"; it encouraged lawlessness, lax business honor, and harmful currency policies. This in turn alarmed the less democratic East whose efforts to control the West helped explain the political history of the nineteenth century.

Finally, Turner saw the frontier as a spawning ground for many of the social and intellectual traits that distinguish Americans from Europeans. "To the frontier the American intellect owes its striking characteristics:" coarseness and strength combined with acuteness and inquisitiveness; a practical, inventive turn of mind, quick to find expedients; a masterful grasp of material things but lacking in the artistic; a restless, nervous energy; a dominant individualism working for good and evil; and, above all, the buoyancy and exuberance that came with freedom. These were the traits bred into Americans by three centuries of westering.

What would happen to the United States now that the frontier was closing? Turner saw a major shift in the national psychology. Never again would nature yield its gifts so generously. Never again would a stubborn environment help break the bonds of custom and summon mankind to accept its conditions. No longer would frontiering "furnish a new field of opportunity, a gate of escape from the bondage of the past." Now Americans must learn to adjust their economy, their politics, their daily lives to life in a closed-space world. "What the Mediterranean Sea was to the Greeks," Turner concluded, with a final version of his often-used metaphor, "breaking the bond of custom, offering new experiences, calling out new institutions and activities, that, and more, the ever retreating frontier has been to the United States directly, and to the nations of Europe more remotely." Now the frontier was gone, and with its closing had ended the first period of the nation's history.

Turner's essay was to stir controversy for generations to come, but it probably had little impact on the audience that remained as that interminable session came to a close. Those who had not departed or been lulled into indifference by listening to five lengthy addresses were so tuned to the belief that the "germs" of American institutions were generated in the forests of medieval Germany that they simply could not comprehend a doctrine that flew in the face of all tradition and "common sense." One young historian who was present remembered that the audience reacted with the bored indifference normally shown a young instructor from a backwater college reading his first professional paper; he recalled, too, that discussion was totally lacking.[46] Turner must have returned to his dormitory room that night burdened with a heavy sense of failure.

Nor was he heartened by the reaction that followed. Only one Chicago newspaper bothered to mention his address—in a small paragraph on page three. Dr. Poole, who prepared the official report for *The Dial* and *The Independent*, found Reuben Gold Thwaites's dull chronicle of lead mining a valuable contribution and praised another speaker so highly that she gushed her thanks, but he had no place for even a word about the significance of the frontier.[47] Even President Charles Kendall Adams, who was almost certainly in the audience, did not deem the paper worth mentioning when, five days later, he summed up Turner's historical qualifications for the editor of an encyclopedia. Nor did Turner's father: he reported to the home folk that Fred was an admirable guide to the fair—but did not feel that his contribution to history merited even a sentence. Three months later Wisconsin's newspaper revealed the same deplorable judgment. It published a pretentious article on the effects of the Columbian Exposition on historical writing, without mentioning Turner's contribution.[48]

This less-than-enthusiastic reaction portended the fate of the essay when it appeared in printed form, issued first by the State Historical Society of Wisconsin, where it was read a second time in December

1893. Edward Everett Hale acknowledged "your curious and interesting paper," while Theodore Roosevelt congratulated Turner on "striking some first class ideas" and putting "into shape a good deal of thought that has been floating around rather loosely." Frances A. Walker judged "the mere title is a success in itself," but apparently read no further. To Charles M. Andrews it was "extremely interesting," but he envied the "elements of romance" in Turner's materials in contrast with the dry bones of his own colonial period. Even those who stooped to faint praise did so because they saw his ideas as projections of their own: B. A. Hinsdale agreed that easterners needed to learn more about the West; K. C. Lamprecht found in the American experience "a strong similarity in many respects with our colonizing pioneers"; and Achille Loria applauded the publication of a "learned substantiating piece" for his own theories.[49]

Turner, who enjoyed praise rather more than the next man, could find little solace in these offerings, but others gave him genuine satisfaction. John Fiske lauded his "excellent, *admirable* essay," then cast a dash of cold water by adding that for some time he had been "working along toward the same *perspective*." Friedrich Ratzel found it "a very important work," and "an instructive example of the view of the state and its geographic origins." Of all who passed judgment, however, only Talcott Williams, a Philadelphia editorial writer, wrote prophetically that "it seems to me the most informative and illuminating contribution to American history that I have read in several years."[50] Williams was virtually alone in his perception. More typical was the remark of an easterner, that "Turner must be a very provincial type of historian."

This reaction was predictable. New ideas displace old ideas only slowly; man is a conservative creature and changes his mind—and living patterns—reluctantly. Nor had Turner offered the tangible evidence needed to make his thesis convincing. This was not his purpose; he intended only, as he put it, "to call attention to the frontier as a fertile field for investigation," and to "suggest some of the problems which arise in connection with it." Most fatal of all, his youthful enthusiasm had misled him into claiming far too much from what scant evidence he did use. His examples were drawn from one small segment of the frontier—the eastern upper Mississippi Valley that he knew so well—yet he deduced from them a social process that "formed a huge page in the history of society" and luminously revealed "the course of universal history." He was equally at fault when he exaggerated the role of the frontier in American development; to say that the existence and recession of an area of free land *explained* the nation's past was to fly in the face of common sense and known historical knowledge. Turner's generalizations were too sweeping, his assertions too positive, to convince historians who considered themselves exact scientists. Nor did he aid his cause by his imprecise definitions and faulty logic. A writer who spoke of the "frontier" as a line, a region, a place, and a process, or who ascribed to its influence idealism and materialism, nationalism and sectionalism, cooperative enterprise and individualism, would find little following among tough-minded scholars of any generation. Only if a reader looked beyond the exaggerations and loose terminology would he realize the true significance of "The Significance of the Frontier in American History."

In the long run, Turner's faults played only a minor role in the total impress of his hypothesis on the historical profession—save during the period of negative reaction of the 1930s and 1940s, when they provided ammunition for his critics. True, he had solved few problems, but he had asked a number of very pertinent questions. His purpose was not to close, but to open a chapter in American historiography. He offered the profession not a completed historical structure, but a blueprint from which to build one, and he told his fellow craftsmen that, if they built along the lines he suggested, they would understand a great deal more about the *why* and the *how* of their country's past. The true significance of his essay was that it laid down a challenge that was to occupy scholars for generations to come. Few historians have done more—or as much.

VI

The Busy World of the Professor

1893-1903

FREDERICK J. TURNER had written his ticket to fame in his paper on the significance of the frontier, but he had to do a great deal more before the academic world would be ready to award him his due. He had to popularize his theories, and he turned to this task with enthusiasm. He also had to win converts, some from among fellow history teachers, more from the young zealots trained in his seminars. Turner, to find his place in the sun, had to sharpen his teaching skills, win his spurs as a graduate instructor, attract to his classrooms the cream of the Midwest's college crop, and send them forth as missionaries to convert the profession to a belief that the frontier was a basic moulding force in American history. This was no mean assignment.

That Turner succeeded, and succeeded within a remarkably short time, was due to the spectacular development of the University of Wisconsin, no less than to his own talents. Its president, Charles Kendall Adams, who took office in 1892 when President Chamberlin resigned, was as able as his predecessor, and as dedicated to the success of the School of Economics, Political Science and History. During President Adams's ten-year regime the university's student body grew from 1200 to 2000, its faculty from 70 to nearly 200; at the same time he charmed enough money from a responsive legislature to change the campus skyline with a half-dozen imposing new buildings, including a badly needed library. Adams's prime concern was with undergraduate education, and he was tolerant of the social life and athletic contests that increasingly absorbed student attention, but he also stood solidly behind the research activities of his faculty and did his best to staff it with able scholars. The university was a pleasant haven during his years in office.

So was the town of Madison, now earning the designation of city as its population skyrocketed from 13,000 to 19,000 in the decade of the 1890s. All about were signs of progress: the first "horseless carriage" appeared in 1896 (an electric wonder that ran for fifty miles on a single battery charge); an "Edison Parlor" was opened later that year, and there a nickel investment bought a view of a cockfight or a carmencita dance while four phonographs played banjo tunes; the police force got blue uniforms, complete with three-quarter-length coats with brass buttons; a paid fire company with a chemical pumper, was formed; and the city built a sewage disposal plant to save Lake Mendota from pollution. Of all the city's daring innovations, Turner benefited most from the paving of Frances Street, in 1901, for there he had built the house that he occupied for the rest of his teaching days in Madison.

He took this plunge in 1894, buying a lakefront lot at 629 Frances Street for $2000, with the encouragement of a builder who promised him a suitable house for less than $4000. That figure proved as unrealistic as the estimates of most builders; when the Turners moved to their new home that fall their investment was $7906.40, and their mortgage a healthy $6000—a sizable sum for a man with a family and a $2500 salary. The Turners had to go on a regime of skimping and budgeting and overdrawn bank accounts, but they managed to live well: they spent $800 a year for food, fuel, light, and the two servants demanded by academic standards in that genteel age; $500 for taxes and interest; $250 for life insurance payments; $200 for clothing; $100 for doctors and medicine; and a paltry $150 for "sundries," which included trips, pleasure, entertainment, and the books that Turner could not resist buying. Turner hoped to gross an additional $1000 from lecture fees, summer school teaching, and other odd jobs to retire the principal on his mortgage, but that hope was seldom realized.[1]

So the Turner's lived quietly, by inclination as well as by necessity, allowing themselves only such extravagances as membership in the Madison Literary Club, annual visits to Portage, fishing expeditions on Lake Mendota, a camera that earned Fred a considerable local reputation for his "clever work," and, for Mae, membership in the town's Audubon Society and regular bird-watching hikes into the wilds that surrounded the city.[2] This was enough, for their children were a source of never-ending joy. The youngest, Mae Sherwood Turner, born on April 27, 1894, was only a baby, but lively and lovable. Jackson Allen Turner, three years old in 1895, had already proclaimed his intention to be a "foot-ball boy" instead of a professor; his sister, Dorothy, aged five in 1895, leaned in the other direction and could repeat on demand a phrase from one of Dr. Ely's books that "political economy is the housekeeping of the state"—much to her father's delight.[3] Turner was happy with his children and Mae, and needed no other companionship. They were always together, save when Mae visited her family in Chicago or Fred journeyed to the Library of Congress in Washington, as he did in the summer of 1899. They sat by the fireside in the evening, reading, pedaled about Madison's outskirts on their tandem bicycle each morning that the weather allowed, and found happiness in each other.[4]

This was fortunate, for, if Turner was to build the department that he hoped and prove himself as a teacher, there could be little time for play. Building the department was essential; President Adams had encouraged a revision of the curriculum to supplement "required" courses with a series of junior-senior "electives" in each "major" subject. If these were to be properly staffed—and the introductory courses adequately taught—the two-man history department would have to have some help. President Adams was willing, and the money was available. Charles Homer Haskins found his assistant in European history in the capable person of Victor Coffin, a Canadian with German experience and an 1893 degree from Cornell University. He was added to the faculty that year as an assistant professor with responsibility for the freshman and sophomore work in the non-American subjects. Turner preferred to wait for a man who shared his own concepts of history, and such men were rare indeed in that day of Teutonism and the "germ" theory.

They were so rare that in the end he chose one of his own students, Orin G. Libby. Young Libby was ideally suited for his role. An 1892 graduate of the university, his doctoral dissertation, "The Geographic Distribution of the Vote of the Thirteen States on the Federal Constitution, 1787-1788," was so brilliantly conceived and executed that Turner felt it belonged on the program of the 1893 meeting of the American Historical Association. It would, indeed, have been a fit companion for Turner's own essay on the significance of the frontier. Libby, using revolutionary mapping methods, had plotted the vote on ratification by geographic areas, showing how soil patterns and environmental forces shaped opinion on the Constitution just as did economic status. That Turner, rather than Libby, had devised that technique, and would continue to use it in his later seminars, was unimportant.[5] Libby had performed well, and deserved the instructorship that was offered to him in 1895. Turner was shamelessly proud as his protégé continued to pioneer the novel techniques that he suggested, reading a paper before the American Historical Association in 1896 on the need of mapping congressional votes to reveal the sectional foundations for political behavior, and, a year later, introducing a new course at Wisconsin on "American Sectionalism."[6] Libby was following well in his master's footsteps by exploring new methods to show the socioeconomic basis of political decision-making in the United States.

Libby's appointment allowed Turner to broaden his own teaching program—with one significant result. Until 1895 he had had no choice but to offer his traditional subjects: the freshman survey course, his "Economic and Social History" and his "Constitutional and Political History" on alternate years, and two sections of the seminar, one for graduate students, the other for undergraduates, both taught jointly with Haskins. With Libby to shoulder some of the underclass instruction, Turner was free for the first time to specialize in subject matter dear to his own heart. The college catalogue that fall proclaimed a revolution. The "Constitutional and Political History" was abandoned, never to be revived. The "Economic and Social History" was broken into two year-long courses, dividing at 1789. A "Seminary in American History" was introduced, to be taught by Turner without Haskins's aid, and with the announced purpose of studying the political history of the nation by concentrating on successive periods, the first for the 1895-96 academic year to be the era between 1815 and 1820. Turner and Haskins would cooperate in a special course on the teaching of history in the public schools, and would together conduct a "historical conference" for graduate students, who would meet fortnightly to read papers, review books, and discuss current historical literature. The catalogue also announced a completely new course: "History 7. The History of the West," which would meet at noon three times weekly throughout the year. Particular attention would be paid to "the advance of settlement across the continent, and to the results of this movement."[7]

Here was innovation, indeed—this was the first course on the history of the frontier to be offered anywhere—and the local press glowed with pride that Wisconsin's own Turner, "one of the chief exponents of the momentous influence that westward expansion exercised on the course of events in the United States," should be responsible.[8] The introduction of this course did not mean that Turner was succumbing to provincialism or surrendering to sectional pride. His subject matter was to deal not with the "West," but with a succession of "Wests," as the frontier was traced from coast to coast. Too, Turner's investigations increasingly convinced him that the American nationality was a product of the interplay and interaction between the regions of the nation, and that each section had to be understood before their total pattern would become clear. His own decision to explain the "West" to his students coincided with the coming of Professor William P. Trent of the University of the South to offer a one-term course on "Southern Statesmen of the Old Regime."[9] Given the emphasis on regionalism of that day, this was a sensible program.

All of these new and revised courses took a deal of preparation time, but the end was not yet. The Turner budget could be balanced only by adding extra income to his $2100 salary, and this meant work in summer school and extension lecturing. Turner returned to the extension circuit, reluctantly, in the fall of 1893, with his familiar series on "The Colonization of North America" and "United States Politics, 1789-1840," and, in 1895, with a third series, "Western State Making in the Revolution"—the subject of his current research. These seemed sufficiently archaic to discourage any popular audience, but such was his fame that he spent hours during the next years traveling to such unlikely spots as Eau Claire, Wausau, La Crosse, Necedah, and Augusta. Lecturing monopolized far too much of his time during those years, but more had to be spent reading papers, correcting examinations, and drafting the syllabi that were expected in every course. These syllabi appeared regularly—on colonization in 1893, 1894, and 1897; on *American Development, 1789-1829* in 1895—each with up-to-date reading lists, and outlines that revealed Turner's expanding interests. "One cannot understand the history of any people without comprehending their physiographic environment," read one; "The West, a nationalizing force," proclaimed another, and added: "The history of America is the development of democracy in connection with free land."[10] These exercises helped sharpen his knowledge of frontiering, but they took too heavy a toll in his time and energy. The 1896-97 academic year began with the announcement that three of the series' most popular lecturers—including Turner—had withdrawn from the extension staff.

Summer school was not so easily forsaken, even though it meant back-breaking work for modest rewards; he normally taught three courses, which met five or six times weekly for six weeks, for a salary of $300. If Turner had been content to dole out segments of his regular courses, as he did now and then—"American Growth from 1789 to 1829," or "The Beginnings of the West"—he would have more than earned his keep. But that was not his way. These were schoolteachers he was instructing, and he had to equip them to make history live for their students. So he labored over new courses or altered old ones to meet the special needs of his audience. One, on "The Study of History," began with standard lectures on the meaning of history and proper methods of study and teaching, then for four weeks examined intently one segment of European history selected by the class. The purpose was laudable—to illustrate the procedures needed to instruct a class about an era that was not the teacher's specialty—but those eras were not Turner's specialties either, and he had to work with his pupils to offer them a proper model.[11] Equally valuable to the teachers was a course on "The Elements of American History," introduced in 1896, which explored the causal forces shaping the development of the nation, and another, added two years later, on "The History of the West," which capsulized his year-long treatment of the subject into the six weeks of the summer session. These were no light assignments that Turner took on, and because of them he sold his soul to the classroom summer after summer, instead of pursuing research. Nor was that $300 salary, important though it was, solely responsible. Knowledge of history was the torch that would lead mankind from the darkness of ignorance, and Turner's duty was to light that torch for secondary-school teachers no less than for his graduate students.

This same zeal condemned Turner to constant experimentation, as he revised and re-revised his offerings year after year in a perpetual quest for a teaching technique that would make his students realize the importance of historical studies. He gave no set lectures, carefully prepared and written in full, as he had when he first began his career; that method, he told a student, "takes time from more engaging occupations, and . . . is apt to commit you to a settled body of doctrine."[12] Now he began preparation for each class by pulling from his files all the materials that he had gathered on the topic to be surveyed—reading notes, newspaper clippings, chapters torn from books, magazine articles —and reading through the mass of information, sensing new interpretations or fresh organizational possibilities as he did so. These he scrawled on full or half-sheets of paper, together with an outline that he intended to follow—but seldom did. Armed with this material he entered the classroom, spread the outline on the desk with the notes and quotations to be used for illustrations around it, and was ready to begin his lecture. His materials were always fresh, always supplemented with information garnered from recent reading, and always so exciting to Turner that he was able to transmit something of his own enthusiasm to his students.[13] This was a never-ending process, for Turner was a perfectionist, and he constantly reminded himself to make this change or that to improve his instruction. "Change my course in Soc. and Ec. Hist. US into a study of Economic and Social Problems," he wrote one year.[14] In doing this, he sacrificed the writing that would mean his own self-advancement for the benefit of his pupils.

Turner also varied his teaching methods from year to year, as he sought the ideal means of capturing student interest. The "topics" technique, which he had inherited from Professor Allen—each student reporting to the class on a topic he had investigated—he abandoned about the mid-1890s as less suited to testing ability than written term papers based on investigation of the underlying forces that were Turner's principal concern. So his pupils labored over such topics as "Effect of the Revolution on Manufactures," "Literature in the Revolution," "The Threatened Secession of the West," and "Economic Influences on Ratification," all unique for that day, and all designed to test the student's interpretative abilities no less than his industry. So were the examination questions that Turner inflicted on his charges: "Outline the history of the State of Franklin and point out the physiographic factors involved," "What industrial conditions are revealed by the Tariff of 1789?" and "Discuss the relations between the history and physiography of the Blue Grass Country." These were searching inquiries, designed to separate the gifted from the dullards. One student remembered with amusement that after an intense study of the pre-Civil War period the class was asked only one question on an hour examination: "Tell all you know about Kansas."[15]

These examinations—and the total content of Turner's courses—mirrored his objectives as a teacher. He was shaping his students to ask not only the *what*, but the *why* of the past, not only to add a random stone to the mosaic of history, but to understand that stone's relationship to the entire pattern. They had to develop a critical sense first of all; this he instilled by having them read such traditional authors as Hermann von Holst and James Schouler, to discover not only the biases and distortions of the writers, but their failure to describe the "whole life" of the people. Then the students had to grasp the universality of the topic they were studying, no matter how minute. One of Turner's favorite remarks, borrowed from Achille Loria, was that the United States, which was thought to have no history, revealed the hidden, intricate forces that moulded all of mankind's past. "In no other course," one of his students testified, "did I ever get a clearer view of the forces that produce history and of the immense importance of the common impulses of the common man."[16] Turner's concern was never with the period under observation, or even with the total sweep of American history, but with the universal history of mankind.

This was weighty stuff, designed for the serious student and deliberately pitched above the heads of the drones who sought amusement rather than knowledge in the classroom. Turner's purpose was not to entertain but to enlighten, not simply to instruct but to infect his charges with his own fiery enthusiasm for historical studies. Those who succumbed became his disciples, spreading word of his greatness throughout the land, and creating an image of their master as the nation's finest teacher. Some left their impressions behind, Carl Becker in singing prose, Joseph Schafer and Louise P. Kellogg in essays of worshipful adulation, still others in comments less extended but no less adoring.[17] These are the word pictures that have given later generations their impression of Turner as a master teacher beyond parallel.

They are utterly accurate—in the eyes of their creators. They portray a superb lecturer who captivated his students and left them his slaves. His voice was not deep, but it was full, rich, vibrant, musically cadenced. He spoke informally, in conversational tones, always serious but seldom solemn, and never giving the impression of reciting well-prepared remarks. Time and again he paused to illustrate a point on one of the many maps hung about the room, or to search through the stacks of manila folders and sheafs of notes piled on his desk for the apt quotation or the exact statistic needed to illuminate a statement. His lectures were studded with bibliographical information, usually a casual mention that such-and-such a recent book was the best work on the subject. "It gave me the feeling," one student recalled, "that I had to read most of the University library." They abounded in informal stories or bits of verse, and sparkled with references to modern-day problems comparable to those under discussion. His brilliance attracted not the indifferent mass, but the cream of the student body.

Most of all, Turner won his disciples by what he said, not by how he said it. He laid down no unassailable "truths," no dogmatic solutions to historical quandries. He gave his pupils no ordered body of information, weighted with the authority of his own knowledge. Instead, they felt that Turner was not teaching at all; he was himself studying history before their eyes. They shared with him exciting discoveries, and delighted with him when he referred them to their textbook only to point out its errors. Turner taught few facts (indeed, he gave the impression that facts were unimportant), but he taught the students how to select from the infinite variety of facts that composed history the few that had meaning and significance. He showed them that history was no agreed-upon convention, to be learned by rote, but the complex story of interrelating men and events leading to the achievement of noble objectives. He made them realize that the past concealed more questions than answers, that it was something to be delved into, thought about, written about; that it was an exciting world demanding exploration. This was a stirring discovery. "Until then," wrote Carl Becker, "I had never been interested in history; since then, I have never ceased to be so."[18]

Carl Becker and others who testified to Turner's greatness succumbed to his intellectual charm because they were to be historians. His appeal to future lawyers and engineers and bookkeepers was less irresistible. To them the minutes Turner spent in pawing through piles of notes for a usable quotation were not titillating pauses in the quest for learning, but embarrassing interludes. To them the constant bibliographical suggestions were not challenges, but assignments that would discourage the most dedicated student. Turner offered little of the methodical, orderly information desired by unthinking undergraduates; the students left his lectures not with a neatly arranged array of facts that could be memorized at examination time, but with information that had to be digested and questions that had to be answered. He required his students, even his most elementary students, to think, to interpret, to understand the past. This was a difficult assignment, and one from which most of them shied. They were proud that the university boasted a scholar who commanded national attention and published in national journals, but the mass of the students, who had no particular concern for history, showed little inclination to shoulder the heavy burdens required in his courses. Turner, even at the height of his popularity, was no spellbinder who packed his lecture hall and hypnotized his audience with the brilliance of his rhetoric.[19]

That this was Turner's image during the 1890s, at a time when his teaching skills and enthusiasms were at their height, is indicated by both the smallness of his classes and his relative obscurity. Only his required survey course in American history attracted between 50 and 100 students regularly; his "Social and Economic History" began with 41, dwindled the next term to 32, and never again lured more than 30; his "Constitutional and Political History" only once boasted more than 20 (21 enrolled in the fall term of 1895). Even his much-publicized "History of the West" was offered to only 41 students when it was first presented in 1895; this fell to 35 a term later, and it usually attracted less than 30 thereafter.[20] Nor did Turner fare well when judged by another gauge of popularity: mention in the undergraduate publications. His name appeared only infrequently in the yearbook, *The Badger*, and the humor magazine, *The Sphynx*, and then usually as the author of a sufficiently unhumorous remark to suggest that laughter seldom swept his classroom. Thus: from a student asked why Virginia was so named, "After the Virgin Mary"; from one requesting to be excused from an absence, "Because I was sick to my stomach from Professor Turner's class May 20"; from one asked, during a discussion of topics, whether she were the only one who had religion, "Yes, sir, I am afraid I am." The 1896 *Badger* could find nothing more inspirational to say about Turner than:

> It's Dr. Turner who turned o'er the pages
> Which bear written on them the work of ages

He was clearly not a popularizer who bartered intellectual standards for student approval.[21] Turner's later reputation as a master teacher was well-earned, but only among the few who found in history the same stimulus that inspired his own passions.

For those students the rewards were great, for instruction under Turner seemed a talisman to a distinguished career in historical studies. During the 1890s a fair number entered his undergraduate seminar or prepared the "honor's thesis" required for graduation with distinction under his direction. Each student received special attention, yet none was moulded into a replica of the master. Turner's own interest in the frontier was sublimated to allow every student to select a thesis topic that would inspire his best effort, and the variety was infinite: "The National Nominating Power," "The Claims of Georgia to State Sovereignty," "The Pan-American Policy of James G. Blaine," "An Economic Interpretation of the Lead Region of Illinois."[22] Given that free rein, they blossomed, each with an interest in his own historical domain that sent him on to graduate work, and many to leadership in the profession. What other teacher of that day could boast of training such historical giants as Carl Becker, Joseph Schafer, Herbert Eugene Bolton, William J. Hocking, Louise P. Kellogg, Guy Stanton Ford, and William S. Robertson? All of those scholars launched their careers under Turner in the 1890s.

Even more remarkable was the number and quality of graduate students attracted to Madison by his presence. Turner was still a relative unknown during the 1890s, the author of one paper that was only gradually attracting attention within the profession, and a minor faculty member in a backwater college that was overshadowed by the great eastern universities. Yet such was the efficiency of the academic grapevine that by the mid-1890s capable students from throughout the Midwest were journeying to Madison to sit at his feet, and by the end of the century he was luring a few from the East and the Far West. In all, Turner trained or played a major role in training eight doctors of philosophy in history during the decade, and eighteen master's candidates. This was the more remarkable because the doctorate was a little-known degree at Wisconsin, recently introduced and awarded infrequently. Not until 1897 was the history department allowed the fellowships usually needed to attract better students, and then the two allotted it were hardly passports to easy living; for the $400 yearly they paid, the Fellows were expected to spend several hours weekly instructing in the introductory courses. Those who came to Madison under these circumstances were drawn by tales of Turner's excellence, not by the promise of an academic bed of roses.

These tales were persuasive, for his seminar was one of the most remarkable workshops then enlivening the world of historical studies. It met weekly in the library of the State Historical Society, housed in the south wing of the state capitol building, where a long table was set aside for their two-hour sessions, and where the students were surrounded by row on row of books that could be readily consulted. There were not many seminar students—four or five each year before 1895, ten to eighteen thereafter as Turner's fame spread—but they were a well-chosen lot, eager to work at a pace equaling that of their master. He saw to it that each did so, not by force, but by persuasion. The subject matter varied from year to year, changing with Turner's own research interests, but members were allowed to select topics that would interest them within this framework. If a student chose a subject not to his liking he had only himself to blame, and this seldom happened.

So they worked with a will, each digging into the source materials that Turner insisted they use, each reporting his results for general discussion. This was a common practice in other universities; where Turner differed was in his relations with his students. To them he was simply a fellow-researcher, sharing in their excitement when they unearthed an important document, pouncing on each fresh interpretation with an enthusiasm matching their own, suffering their disappointment when their data failed to substantiate their conclusions. Turner did this deliberately, but he was no play actor; he *was* a student, as eager to applaud a find by one of his followers as to cheer one of his own. "Our method," he explained, "is to take the student into the workshop where the chips are flying and where he can see the workman cut his finger and jam his thumb as often as the occasion arises."[23] All were on common ground in that seminar, driven by one common passion—to discover the truth about the past. Turner's function was to provide guidance, to stimulate greater effort by words of praise, to blunt the too-harsh criticism that sometimes greeted a report, and, at the end, to award the able with his blessing or chastise the laggards with mild reproof. Never was there complete rejection. Turner was not interested in punishing the fallen, but in salvaging them for the historical tasks that lay ahead.

These were the techniques that allowed Turner to train more capable graduate students during his first decade in the classroom than many instructors produced in a lifetime. Kate A. Everest was the first of his doctoral candidates, in 1892; then came Orin G. Libby and George H. Alden in 1895, John B. Sanborn and Balthasar H. Meyer in 1897, Paul S. Reinsch in 1898, and Louise P. Kellogg and Charles McCarthy in 1901. All became useful, and some distinguished, citizens, Kate Everest, George Alden, and Orin Libby as teaching historians, John Sanborn and Balthasar Meyer as economists, Paul Reinsch as a teacher and international lawyer, Miss Kellogg and Charles McCarthy as librarians. Turner could justly pride himself on their accomplishments—and did so.

To survey the subjects chosen for investigation by these would-be scholars, or to thumb the theses produced by the eighteen masters trained by Turner during his baptismal years as a teacher, is to recognize both his selflessness and the breadth of his intellectual enthusiasms. He was deeply immersed in his frontier studies at this time, yet not once did the word "frontier" appear in the title of a dissertation he directed, while most were only remotely connected with the West. Instead, they ranged over all American history: "Diplomatic Relations between the United States and Mexico, 1850-1857," "The Attitude of the American Colonies to the English Common Law," "The Origin of the System of Land Grants in Aid of Education," "Congressional Grants of Land in Aid of Railways," "Massachusetts Federalism," "The Colonial Charter," "The Anti-Masonic Party"—the list could be extended, but the point would be the same.[24] Turner's tastes were too catholic to fit into any mould. By giving his students free rein, and by learning with them as they explored the byways of the past, he was broadening his own knowledge of history, and this was one purpose in his life.

All of this took a great deal of time, for he had to keep abreast of the varied topics his students selected, just as he had to spend hours poring over their papers, blue pencil in hand. As Turner waded deeper into the academic stream, however, he discovered that the demands of teaching were as nothing compared to the energy-sapping tasks daily inflicted on professors by their university and community. Outsiders might envy Turner his twelve-hour weekly teaching load, but they knew nothing of the advice he had to give, the lectures he had to deliver, the clubs he had to address, the faculty meetings he had to attend, the committee assignments he had to perform, the departmental duties he had to discharge. All this in addition to the research and writing that he had to do for his own and the university's advancement. Turner, like other instructors from that day to this, found himself increasingly enmeshed in a network of duties that covered the spectrum of the educational process, and went well beyond.

Some of this stemmed from his interest in secondary education. This was genuine; Turner sincerely believed that history instruction on the lower levels had to be improved, and he was willing to labor to that end. So he accepted, even welcomed, a post as one of the university's high school inspectors, who were charged with traveling about the state urging educators to improve their standards. Each school had to be visited yearly, its teaching investigated, its library appraised, and its offerings judged—to determine whether it was worthy of accreditation. This was a time-squandering task; Turner was frequently on the road for a week at a time, traveling from town to town, lodging in inferior hotels or rooming houses, spending hours talking with teachers and principals, and finally getting back to Madison just in time to rush to an eight o'clock class of his own.[25] What he saw on these journeys convinced him that reform was overdue. During the late 1890s he willingly accepted membership on a state committee to standardize instruction in history in the schools, and he used every excuse to preach the need of instilling the normal schools with what he called the "university spirit." Good teachers could never be trained, he believed, until the normal schools were brought into the university's orbit; they should be transformed into respectable academic institutions where would-be schoolteachers would be taught academic subjects, where historians and economists and other academicians would replace professional educators, and where students would be equipped to enter the university for their final training.[26] Turner's recipe for the training of teachers was that of the twentieth century, when normal schools were transformed into state colleges, and finally into universities in their own right.

This concern for secondary education might not have endeared him to the educationalists, but it did enmesh him in the professional teachers' associations and force him to spend too much time at their meetings. He spoke regularly at such gatherings as those of the State Educational Association and the South Side Educational Association of Milwaukee, usually on historical topics that reflected his current interests, but sometimes on broader subjects, such as "Some Relations between the History and Physiography of the United States." He urged on his audiences the virtues of analytical as opposed to narrative history, and the necessity of explaining to their charges the social and economic forces that underlay human behavior.[27] Turner's one-man crusade gave some high school teachers, at least, a chance to hear some very good advice as well as to take some solid doses of history.

It also brought him to the attention of principals, with the inevitable result that he found himself in demand as a commencement speaker at high school ceremonies. This meant more squandered time, for Turner was not one to undertake such tasks lightly, and he prepared each address carefully, sometimes after wide reading in areas not close to his own interests. Two were particularly burdensome: one an address to the Madison High School in the spring of 1895, on "The High School and the City," the other, the dedication of a new high school in Portage, in January 1896. In both he made post-frontier America his theme. The fifty graduates of the Madison school and their parents were told that Americans would develop a social conscience when they could no longer escape society's problems by fleeing to frontiers; then the lakes of Wisconsin would again sparkle unpolluted; no longer would "the central part of our city be overhung with smoke and the air choked with its odors."[28] In that frontierless land, cooperation would supercede individuality, and men would learn to live together in peace. In Portage he again harped on his closed-frontier theme, urging support for higher education to train the scientists and agricultural experts needed for survival in a non-expanding world, diplomats to solve problems created by the international contests for the globe's dwindling resources, social scientists to devise the controls needed in a society where a frontier no longer existed as a "safety valve for social danger, a bank account on which they might continually draw to meet losses."[29] Turner spent a great deal of his energy on those two addresses, and in them he said a good many things that he was to fit into his whole historical framework in the future.

He learned less from another chore demanded by his educational interests. This stemmed from the Wisconsin Free Library Association's decision to equip a number of mobile libraries to travel from town to town throughout the state. In that day of horse-drawn vehicles, heavy books could not be moved. Instead, the commission would prepare fifty-five paperbound volumes dealing with the colonial and revolutionary periods of American history, all small and easily transported. Turner was naturally called into service as a consultant, and he was assigned the tasks of planning the Revolutionary series and of preparing an introduction for the first book, a bibliographical pamphlet of fourteen pages.[30] He did so with no reward, save the satisfaction of knowing that the Wisconsin townsfolk would be subjected to some sound history. To Turner that was enough.

More to his liking, although just as destructive of his research time, were the duties that he owed to (or assumed for) the university. These ran the gamut, from weekly faculty meetings—each lasting two hours or more, and debating every issue from an unexcused student absence to a curriculum revision—through innumerable committee obligations, to preparation of a column on "Progress of the University" for the alumni magazine. Of these none was more disturbing than the need to defend one of his colleagues against the attack of a minor politician. Richard T. Ely was the intended victim; in the summer of 1894 a newly elected state superintendent of public education accused that distinguished professor of favoring strikes, aiding strikers, and advocating "utopian, impractical and pernicious doctrines" in his books and classroom. When the Board of Regents took these charges seriously and named a committee to investigate, Turner rightly feared a witch-hunt that would not only crucify Ely but damage the university. He could meet this danger only by showing the charges to be false. Much of that summer went into writing a lengthy report that not only vindicated Ely, but revealed his accuser as an unprincipled officeholder whose accusations should not be taken seriously. Turner's testimony before the investigative committee helped carry the day; Ely emerged as a brilliant scholar whose views were untainted by socialistic doctrine and who, rather than indoctrinating his students, encouraged them to "look and see things" for themselves. So impressed were the regents that they not only exonerated Ely, but adopted a classic statement on academic rights that has served as a beacon light for freedom of expression since that day.[31]

Turner took satisfaction in Ely's triumph, but he must have been plagued by the realization that some of the unspectacular duties he performed for education were less useful than his own research. Such must have been his frame of mind when he inserted a notice in the student newspaper begging college and high school debaters to stop using him as an information bureau for material needed in their speeches, or when he represented the university at the inauguration of presidents of other institutions, or when he traveled far and wide to speak to alumni groups that cared more about football than learning,[32] or when he opened his home to high school teachers of history and political science seeking to form a state-wide society to encourage research, or to the "Historical and Economic Club" of Wisconsin that lured to Madison history and economics teachers from the normal schools.[33] These were services beyond the call of duty, but Turner was interested in furthering education, and he could no more refuse than could his successors of a later day. Nor could he fail to give endless hours to the committees that made faculty life a burden. He served on a succession of time-consuming bodies that grappled with such diverse problems as the reorganization of the college faculty and the type of degree to be offered by the school of commerce.

These services were irksome to one eager to establish his reputation as a scholar, but no more so than the inevitable invitations to speak before this university society or that. They were many, and all required careful preparation, whether he was addressing a student convocation on "Washington and the West," or a "New Orleans Day" ceremony on Andrew Jackson, or a "Lafayette Memorial Meeting," or the History and Political Science Association on "The Relation between the Physiography and History of the Middle West." Turner gave far too many speeches for his own good, but his time was not completely wasted. As he went through the agony of preparation, his views on the nature of history were sharpened, and his understanding of the frontier deepened.

Turner's interpretation of the past, his lectures showed, was constantly broadening, and his impatience with historians whose focus was narrower than his own was steadily increasing. His most biting invective was reserved for Hermann von Holst of the University of Chicago, and it was unleashed in an extensive review of that distinguished author's *Constitutional and Political History of the United States*, a review delivered before the University of Wisconsin's Historical and Political Science Association in January 1894. Turner spent a vast amount of time on that task, reading all eight volumes carefully, consulting reviews, and laboring long to produce a forty-seven page manuscript that showed how deeply he was committed to a frontier interpretation.[34] Von Holst was wrong, Turner charged, because he totally misunderstood the elements that contributed to American democracy: the evolution of a composite nationality through immigration, freedom from European influences, the spread of settlement westward, the evolution of an industrial society, the emergence of sectionalism, and changing interpretations of the Constitution. Of these omissions, the most fatal was von Holst's failure to understand the "effect of free land in promoting democracy." For *American* democracy differed completely from the European democracy known to that German-born scholar. "It was born from conditions that can never be possible in Europe. It was a democracy that came not from the political theorist's dreams of the primitive German forest. It came stark and strong and full of life from the American forest." Von Holst had written a distorted treatise on slavery; he had not written a constitutional history of the United States.

Turner was perfectly right when he launched those barbs, but he was treading on dangerous ground, for von Holst was one of the nation's most respected historians and a power in the American Historical Association. Turner very much wanted to publish his views, but he was also wise enough to realize the consequences of an assault by a brash young man on the dean of the profession. His doubts were heightened when friends at the University of Chicago told him that von Holst was impatient of anything but praise, and that even a brief newspaper notice of Turner's remarks had created a mild furor on the Chicago campus. So he held firm when the editor of a respectable journal sought publication rights. His views on von Holst remained unpublished during Turner's lifetime.[35]

This was Turner's last foray into personal attack, but he never wavered in his view that the past was far too complex to be explained by a single force (as von Holst had attempted to do in assigning the slavery issue the major role in the evolution of the United States), and that one to be taken into account must be the expansion of the frontier. Historians, he charged in one of his speeches, had almost always erred in refusing to recognize that complexity. "Nothing is so difficult as to discover every motive of a man in any given action and yet nothing is so common even among historians as offhand judgments of events." Those who failed to emphasize this were violating a basic principle of their profession, for if history taught any lesson, it was that "society cannot be explained by a single theory or successfully modified by a single stroke."[36] Historians should realize that expansion was a force to be reckoned with in illuminating the American past. Even modern-day problems were understandable only against that background. The nation's principal need in the twentieth century was to conserve and adapt the early frontier-bred ideals to the changed conditions of contemporary society. The universities must play a major part in solving that problem, and the lead must be taken by western universities, where the social stratification that was already deadening eastern institutions was less advanced.[37] Turner saw America as changing, but he also saw that its direction was—and should be—governed partly by the traits and institutions that had emerged during its pioneering era. This was a theme that he was to stress more and more in the future, as he speculated about the post-frontier world in which he lived.

Less tuned to his own interests were the tasks forced upon him by the community. The State Historical Society demanded a healthy share of his time; he served as curator, arranged a program for the 1899 meeting at Green Bay, and shouldered more than he should of the burden of planning the magnificent new building that was opened on the lower campus in 1900. He was also in demand by the state government when any historic occasion had to be recognized. He was drafted to serve on the committee that planned the celebration of Wisconsin's fiftieth year of statehood in 1898. Turner must have enjoyed naming his father to a speaker's role on the elaborate program held that June, but he paid for that pleasure by being conscripted for the committee that edited the commemorative volume published on the occasion.[38] Turner never complained about these duties, and in some instances he took considerable pleasure in his accomplishments—he judged the State Historical Society's library building as "perfect" and "a delight to the eye and soul," for example—yet now and then he wished that the ivory tower in which he supposedly lived was more impregnable.

This was especially true when the women's and social clubs—those supreme enemies of all academicians—took to his trail. The Contemporary Club, which he had served so well as a graduate student, apparently viewed him as a universal scholar, capable of shedding light on the most obscure subject; he was called upon to speak on such improbable subjects as "Charles Sumner," "The Place of History in Modern Education," and "Drawing in the Public Schools," the last a topic on which he displayed a surprising degree of knowledge. His assignments for the Madison Literary Club were directed toward his own interests, but they still required impressive preparation: "The Louisiana Purchase," "The Origins of Andrew Jackson," "Aspects of Civilization in the Old Northwest," and so on.[39] Whatever the subject, and no matter how alien it was to his own specialties, Turner was able to offer fresh insights and to link his topic with the broader stream of history that he considered important.

This doomed him as a performer before women's clubs, much to his delight. His perfectionism and sound scholarship rebelled against the glamorous popularizations they wanted, as two incidents in which he was involved admirably demonstrate. In 1896, when he addressed the Madison Women's Club on "The Spaniards in North America," Turner made no mention of the romantic *conquistadores,* discoursing instead on the impact of native cultures on Latin America's social structure and the inflationary effect of New World gold on Spain's finances.[40] On another occasion, when he was invited by the Milwaukee Colonial Dames to speak on the "Colonization of the James," he ignored John Smith and other heroes so dear to the hearts of his audience and read a forty-eight page manuscript that explained "the process of actual colonization, the forming of communities, and the social and political life along the lower James." Painstakingly, Turner analyzed the successive waves of settlement in the four river valleys of Virginia in the seventeenth century, and the differing cultures that emerged as man and nature interacted.[41] The excessive amount of research that went into that paper—even to paying $40 for copies of documents that would shed light on the problem—resulted in an essay that could have graced any historical journal, but it must have been received with little enthusiasm by his audience. He received few invitations to address women's groups thereafter.

The kaleidoscope of activities in which Turner was involved during the 1890s did not enshrine him as a hero on the local lecture circuit, but they did bring him his first national recognition—with important results. His fame was beginning to spread—as a scholar whose germinal paper on the frontier was attracting increasing attention, as a teacher whose students sang his praises in a growing number of universities— and with this fame came opportunities to leave Madison for greener pastures. Not unnaturally, the first offer came from Woodrow Wilson, an unabashed convert to the frontier thesis, who was then head of the history department at Princeton. Wilson approached Turner in the fall of 1896: would Turner fill a soon-to-be-created chair in American history, at a salary of $3400? Turner was interested, as anyone earning $2500 was bound to be, but his heart was in Madison and he was too good a bargainer to show any enthusiasm. His cautious response aroused Wilson to his persuasive best, and Turner cast himself in an inquisitorial role as he asked question after question about the library, the living costs, the quality of students (generally considered to be too frivolous at Princeton), the relative advantages of East and West. Wilson parried with skill; the Princeton library was inferior to that of the State Historical Society in Wisconsin, but Turner could have a special fund to buy books; living costs were only slightly higher (houses $500 a year, servants $12 to $16 a month, groceries about the same); he could add another $1500 to his salary by lecturing (Wilson had earned $4000 the year before); the students might be frivolous, but some were serious, and the teaching load would be light.[42]

Turner had to decide between the West, with its "atmosphere of creative activity" and the superb resources of his beloved library, on the one hand, and the admitted prestige of an eastern professorship, on the other. Fortunately, he was spared that decision, for in December 1896, Wilson wrote that the trustees had failed to create the chair in history he had been promised, using lack of funds as an excuse to conceal their real objection to Turner: he was a dangerous religious radical—a Unitarian. Wilson was horrified, and confessed that he would happily leave Princeton if he could. "I am," he wrote, "probably at this writing the most chagrined fellow on the Continent."[43] Turner stayed at Wisconsin, but only after he had used the near-offer as a club over the administration; he asked nothing for himself, but he did request two graduate fellowships to provide readers in his and Haskins's lower-division courses, and $500 a year for books in European history.[44] These minor concessions cost the university little and made a great deal of difference to Turner. His roots were sinking ever deeper in Madison's soil.

This was well, for only a few weeks passed before he was tempted again. The University of Pennsylvania was creating a chair in American Constitutional and Institutional History. Would Turner come East and talk matters over? He did, to such mutual satisfaction that a letter followed him home with a definite offer of a professorship at $3000. But such interest as he had had vanished when Wisconsin agreed to match that salary. Turner had obviously not been tempted seriously, nor was he later that year when asked what terms might lure him to Cleveland's Western Reserve University.[45] He was too happy at Madison to be tempted by any but the offer of the most prestigious post elsewhere.

Such an offer might come soon, but in the meantime Turner had every reason to feel self-satisfied. He was still short of forty years old, yet he was the holder of a professorship in a rapidly growing university at a respectable salary. His articles and reviews were attracting sufficient attention to win him offers from first-rate institutions. The graduate students trained in his seminars were appearing on excellent faculties and spreading his fame as a teacher, resulting in a steadily increasing flow of new and better students into his graduate classes. He lived in a community that was something more than a town but not quite a city, and this he found much to his liking. His home at 629 Frances Street was attracting congenial neighbors who could be counted as intimate friends. His health was sound, and he was able to enjoy canoe trips on Lake Mendota, summer fishing expeditions into northern Wisconsin, and regular exercise on his bicycle or tennis court. He adored Mae and their three growing children. Turner, it seemed, was a man who had everything.

Then tragedy struck. February of 1899 was an unusually cold month even for Madison, with the thermometer dipping to 29 degrees below zero, and sickness rampant. Early in the month the Turner's youngest child, five-year-old Mae Sherwood Turner, contracted diphtheria, a dread killer in those days of scant medical knowledge. The doctors did what they could, but on February 11 little Mae Sherwood died. For two weeks Turner mourned, a broken and disheartened man. Yet more was to come. That October his only son, Jackson Allen Turner, seven years old, complained of intense stomach pains. By the time these were diagnosed as symptoms of appendicitis the appendix had ruptured and inflammation had set in. A doctor came from Chicago to operate, but by this time it was too late. Day after day the lad weakened as doctors did what they could and his father maintained a twenty-four hour vigil at the bedside. The end finally came on the afternoon of Sunday, October 22, 1899.[46] Within a few months the Turners had been reduced from a happy group of five to a bereaved family of three, with only nine-year-old Dorothy Kinsey Turner to comfort her stricken parents.

For weeks Turner remained in seclusion; "I have not done anything, and have not the heart to do anything," he wrote.[47] When he finally returned to his classroom, he was only a walking shadow, his spirit gone. "I would like to go up and shake him by the hand," one of his students recorded. "I guess we all feel the same."[48] Months passed, but friends noted that the sparkle was gone from his eyes, the bounce from his step. Overnight he had been transformed into an older man, haunted by memories that could never be erased. His pride and stamina forced him to continue the routine of life, but Mae succumbed so completely to her grief that she was taken to a sanatarium in Chicago to recover. "Her poor little body could not stand so heavy a load," Turner explained.[49] Not until June 1900 was she able to return home. Turner's last act before she arrived was to erase from the living room wall the marks that recorded the growth of their three children, leaving to the end the most tragic of all: "J A T Jan. 1898. 3 feet 8½ inches."[50]

Marks could be erased, but memories could not. So Turner, living in lonely mourning that spring of 1900 with only Dorothy to comfort him, probably welcomed a situation that required him to make one of his most difficult decisions. This was forced upon him by the master-persuader of the academic world, President William Rainey Harper of the University of Chicago. He had been in touch with Turner in the past, luring him to the campus for a six-weeks summer school assignment in 1898, and a year later for a weekly seminar as a replacement for the ailing Professor Hermann von Holst. These not only allowed Turner to demonstrate his teaching skills, but placed him near at hand when President Harper was ready to make his move. On March 10, 1900, over what was probably an excellent meal at the Quadrangle Club, Harper stated his case: would Turner become head of the Chicago history department at a salary of $4000 and a half-time teaching load for two years, and a full-time salary of $5000 thereafter? Here was an offer to turn the head of any academician, but Turner was not swept away by it. This was a chance to wring favors from the University of Wisconsin, not for himself, but for his students and the history department. He would, he told Harper, make his decision by April 1, but only after consulting his friends in Madison.[51]

Those next weeks witnessed bargaining on both sides that would have done credit to a Near Eastern camel trader. Turner, after consulting his good friends Charles Homer Haskins, Richard T. Ely, and Charles R. Van Hise, told President Charles K. Adams that he would consider staying only if the university guaranteed four things: a full-scale graduate program, the creation of a separate School of History under his directorship, a salary of $3500 commensurate with that post, and a year's leave of absence to allow the Turners to recover from the loss of their children. These terms were approved by the university regents on March 22, after being assured by President Adams that Turner's going would "be regarded as a misfortune, scarcely less than a calamity."[52] With his victim wavering, President Harper swung into action once more. The big guns on the Chicago campus were urged to fire their barrages in the form of letters extolling the virtues of Chicago, and such influential personages as John Dewey, Albion W. Small, and T. C. Chamberlin responded with a will. At the same time Harper multiplied the attractions: a special $30,000 fund to buy American history books for the library, with annual appropriations of $5000 to $10,000 thereafter; a professorship at $3000 for Charles Homer Haskins; a history department expanded to four professors, an associate professor, four assistant professors, and an array of instructors and assistants. "I am hoping," Harper added wistfully, "that you are beginning to see more clearly that the path of duty leads in the direction of Chicago."[53]

Each move on Chicago's part gave Turner a new card to play in his game with President Adams, and he played them well. The welfare of the department, he told the president, required the use of seminar rooms in the State Historical Society library, the publication of a history series in the university bulletin, two additional fellowships, a new assistant professor in American history and an instructor in European history, and that crowning appointment that was the ambition of every professor: a stenographer of his own. If these could be assured, he would agree to stay in Madison. President Adams responded so favorably that five days after Turner laid down his terms, President Harper's assistant wrote coldly: "I beg to congratulate you on your success with the Board of Regents."[54]

Turner's decision was hailed as a major triumph for the University of Wisconsin. His classes greeted his first appearance with "spontaneous and prolonged applause," while the student paper editorialized that "an institution of learning is known much by the members of its faculty," and congratulated the university on holding one of its brightest stars.[55] Turner was delighted with this acclaim, although deep in his heart he realized that he had elected to remain at Wisconsin not because of loyalty, but because his historical ambitions could be better satisfied there than at Chicago. The State Historical Society library offered attractions that could not be duplicated elsewhere; then, too, he feared that administering a large department would take time and energy better spent on research.[56] His commitment now, and for the future, was to historical writing, not to administration.

These feverish negotiations were a godsend, for while they continued there was little time to brood over the loss of his children. With the decision made, and with Mae's return home in June 1900, his problems crowded upon him once more, compounded now with the realization that she needed a change of scene to recover her health. What better way to provide this than a year in Europe? His assured leave of absence for 1900-1901 made this possible. Having made up his mind, Turner threw himself into preparations with the same intensity that had marked his dealings with President Harper. He filled a paper notebook with information on how to transpose miles into kilometers and Fahrenheit temperatures into Centigrade, lists of old masters to buy in reproductions, travel books to be consulted, and notations on the virtues of Pape Roach Seasick Drops. He solicited from the governor a formal document, complete with ribbons and seals, proclaiming Frederick Jackson Turner to be a "gentleman of good character and standing in the community," worthy of attention from American ministers and consuls. He rented the house at 629 Frances Street and made arrangements with two Madison banks to receive the rental money and pay the taxes and insurance.[57]

All was in readiness, but the departure had to be delayed until fall, for the Turners planned to spend $250 a month on the trip and could accumulate that sum only if he taught summer school. This over, they sailed from New York on August 18, accompanied by the array of trunks usual in that day of leisurely travel. They even took Turner's bicycle, which he planned to pedal about Europe. The Atlantic transport *Mesaba* carried cattle as well as passengers, and the odors reminded him more of a farm than the ocean, but he found happiness in the "silvery chasing of the wonderful blue of the waves" and the vastness of the sea. They stayed first in London for a few days, then went on to the Low Countries and took the traditional barge journey up the Rhine before making a short stop-over at Lake Luzerne, where Turner climbed Mount Pilatus. Eventually the family settled into modest lodgings above a wine shop in the village of Wengen, not far from Interlaken, where they could view the splendid whiteness of the Jungfrau at a cost of $3.40 a day for board and room. There they spent the summer, taking long walks into the mountains, visiting Swiss chalets, and listening to the music of the streams and cow bells as Mae recovered her health. But memories faded slowly. "You know what we all felt of heart pain," he wrote his parents, "to be in such a beautiful world without our two children to whom this kind of beauty belonged."[58]

With autumn they moved on, traveling by rail along the Rhone Valley, climbing the Grimsel Pass in a carriage, and finally settling in Bern. There Turner retrieved his bicycle, which had been delayed at customs, and set out by himself to explore the Rhone Valley, where vineyards and orchards and brown-stained houses colored the countryside, and where he could climb to Zermatt to marvel at the Matterhorn. He returned to Bern to find Dorothy and Mae rebelling against the steady rainfall, so they moved on again, to the village of Vevy on the shores of Lake Geneva, for a month of good Swiss food for Mae, tutoring for Dorothy, and extended bicycle trips for Turner into high mountain pastures where each mile was more picturesque than the last. Again they were driven southward when snows mantled the Alps, through the Gothard Tunnel into Italy, with stops at Lugano and Milan. They

settled in Florence, where they stayed until February 1901. Mae and
Dorothy made a valiant effort to master Italian—so they could start an
organ and peanut business in Madison, Turner reported—but he himself
turned to his travels again and pedaled through the rich countryside,
even as far as Pisa, fifty-five miles away.

It was a pleasant life, but by the end of February the Turners were
growing restless and suffering pangs of homesickness. Their funds
were so far exhausted that they had to borrow $200 from the elder
Turner; this financed several weeks in Rome, Sorrento, and Naples
before they finally sailed for home at the end of March. By this time
their financial plight was such that Turner had to leave Mae and Dorothy with Mae's sister in Massachusetts, borrow ten dollars from his
brother-in-law and five from a friend to pay his way to Portage, then
borrow another eighty to transport his wife and daughter to Chicago.
By April 20 he was back in Madison, happy to be amidst familiar surroundings, but saddened at the memories they conjured. His first mission was a pilgrimage to Forest Hills Cemetery with a tribute of Easter
lilies to place on the children's graves. "How much the little place
means to us," he wrote Mae that night. "But Jackson and Tita are not
here."[59]

Turner returned to his native land with a new perspective and altered interests. He had deliberately elected to spend most of his European year in Switzerland and Italy, feeling that they contrasted most
violently with the United States, and hoping that these contrasts would
sharpen his awareness of the distinctive features of American life.
Three differences struck him particularly. One was the compactness
of the European countryside; distances there were so short and the
landscape so varied that the sense of uniformity bred by America's
broad vistas was lacking, with each tiny community sensing its independence from all others. Another was the strong role played by European tradition, which decreed that fixed social customs and crafts
should be perpetuated virtually unchanged from the sixteenth century,
and that the easy democratic practices of his own country would
be lacking. Finally, Turner was impressed with the aesthetic appreciation of Europeans, and Italians particularly, who supported—and
patronized—art galleries and museums and libraries as the Americans
never would. This he also ascribed to the strength of tradition; the peo-

ple of Florence and Rome were inheritors of an artistic heritage that would not develop in the United States for centuries.

Realizing these things, Turner found that his impression of America had altered radically. Some of his reaction was unfavorable; he was shocked by the newness of everything, annoyed by the crassness of the people, and suddenly aware of the overstress on materialism. The nation, he felt, had much to learn from Europe. It had also much to teach. Turner felt his spirit expand when he left the cramped European cities and returned to the vast open spaces of the United States. He was invigorated by the newness of American life, the detachment of the people from tradition, the tendency to look toward the future rather than the past. Here was opportunity, and opportunity not for the few, but for the many.[60] Here, in other words, was a land made different by a frontier that spread the bounties of nature before all the people and invited them to partake of its riches.

Turner turned his back on the most tragic year of his life—a year that saw two of his most treasured possessions snatched from him and his family able to survive only by months of escape in a distant countryside. He returned ready to renew life, but that life would never be the same that he had known. To his friends he was a different man, quieter, more sedate, less inclined to gay remarks or spontaneous bursts of laughter. Some of the sparkle had gone from his eyes, some of the rich timbre from his voice, some of the sprightliness from his walk. This new Turner was more serious, more mature, inclined to view his nation's history from the broader perspective made possible by his year in Europe. He was ready to settle into hard work, for in hard work there was escape from memory, and by hard work he could share his fresh views on the nation's past with the scholarly world to which he was committed.

VII

Broadening Historical Horizons

1893-1910

EACHING, graduate students, departmental building, responding to the endless demands of town and gown—these were only half the burden assumed by any aspiring instructor who entered the academic world in the 1890s. The other was the professional writing that would enlighten the specialists in his field while also enhancing his own reputation in academic life. This came easily to Frederick Jackson Turner. He believed that history was mankind's savior—and he recognized the fact that his understanding of the past was different from, and slightly superior to, that of most of his contemporaries. Research was his passion, and during these early years, at least, he was able to translate his findings into the articles and reviews on which his reputation ultimately rested.

If he had been a practical young man, governed only by self-interest, he would have directed his efforts toward proving the frontier thesis that he had announced so boldly in 1893, but he was not that kind of man. His mind could never be stirred by warmed-over ideas; he was happy only when probing the past for fresh information that would support still newer interpretations. Then, too, Turner's interests were too catholic to be confined within one historical pasture; even this early in his life he saw himself not as a frontier historian or an economic historian, but as an American historian, whose concern was the broad scope of the nation's experience. He was equally excited about *all* the past, not just one compartment. "I don't quite care," he wrote at the time, "to figure in leggins and breech clout all the time."[1] So, instead of buckling down to his frontier studies during these formative years, Turner plunged into research on western state-making, the diplomacy of the early Republic, immigration, and a dozen other topics, all seemingly unrelated, and all only remotely linked with frontiering. To be worthy of his attention they needed only one qualification: they must shed light on the social and economic forces that underlay social evolution.

His breadth of interest and his natural inclination to recognize that a variety of causal forces explained each historical event were bolstered by his encounter with a new theory that the historical profession was to borrow from geology. In 1889, T. C. Chamberlin, friend of Turner and president of the university during his early teaching years, presented his paper on "The Method of Multiple Working Hypotheses," which was later printed in *Science* and, in revised form, in the *Journal of Geology* in 1897.[2] Chamberlin's purpose was to describe a research technique that would allow "the dangers of parental affection for a favorite theory" to be circumvented. He pointed out that if an investigator began his studies with a single hypothesis—that the frontier, let us say, shaped the American character—his mind would happily accept the facts that supported his theory and automatically reject those that did not. This could be avoided only by postulating every single explanation possible for the phenomenon under investigation, then testing each in turn. "The investigator thus becomes the parent of a family of hypotheses; and by his parental relations to all is morally forbidden to fasten his affections upon any one." In fact, he would probably find that an adequate explanation required the coordination of several causal forces operating together to produce a single event.

Here was a methodology made to order for Turner's purposes. He came across Chamberlin's paper soon after it was written, and he cited it frequently thereafter as a testament to which he completely subscribed. Human nature, he insisted, could be understood only by weighing the dozens of forces operating upon it in any given situation. The problem of the scholar was to determine the degree of weight that must be assigned to each, and to do so impartially. Thus one causal force, or several, might be more persuasive than a group of others, but all must be considered: economic, social, cultural, and political. If Turner did not always practice what he preached, and was inclined to allot the frontier a larger role in American history than it deserved, he did so only because he felt that the frontier had been too much ignored in the past. He was aware, as were few of his contemporaries, that not only expansion, but immigration, sectionalism, class conflicts, industrialization, religion, and a host of other forces operated to shape the nation's history.

Turner's thinking at this stage of his intellectual development was nowhere better shown than in the speculations he made on the origins of New England towns as he prepared his course lectures during the middle 1890s. To a modern historian, no subject could be more archaic or insignificant; to Turner's generation, none was more lively or challenging. At stake was the validity of the dominant "germ" theory; Herbert Baxter Adams had built his whole historical structure on his study of *The Germanic Origins of New England Towns*, while his antagonists, such as Edward Channing and Charles McLean Andrews, used these same institutions to launch assaults on the teachings of the Teutonic school. Turner, characteristically, refused to accept the findings of any of the controversialists, reading them first, then plunging into an intensive study of colonial documents so he could draw his own conclusions.

He first analyzed all existing theories: that the New England town was a transplanted Germanic *tun*, that it was modeled on the English parish, that it originated by a process of "constitutional retrogression" when long-forgotten features of medieval German communities were revived amidst comparably primitive conditions, that it duplicated English towns but in an earlier form than they existed in the seventeenth century. None seemed satisfactory to Turner. Surely, he wrote, their origins could be explained by some "simpler and less occult method than by the hypothesis of reversion," then so popular at Johns Hopkins. Were they not, indeed, only the natural product of social evolution under the distinctive environmental conditions of frontier America?

Turner thought that they were. His studies convinced him that one of the characteristics of New England institutions was their adaptability. The settlers, finding themselves in a wilderness environment similar to that of their Teutonic ancestors, adopted many practices that had been suitable in medieval Germany, not because there was a conscious "retrogression," but because they sought practical means of living in a primitive environment. This accounted for many of the similarities that historians had noted: the common ownership of land, a division of tillable fields and pasturage among the villagers, a tendency to deny membership in the community to strangers. These were the products of an abundance of land and a need for defense that existed in both ancient Germany and New England.

To substantiate this belief, Turner examined a number of specific practices of the New Englanders, then found counterparts in the contemporary English scene which they could have borrowed for their own use, or a tendency in human nature that would explain their action. The award of village grants to a group of proprietors, he discovered, was consistent with contemporary practice in the homeland, and was merely applied to the new situation. The practice of restricting community membership was based on the Puritan desire to maintain ecclesiastical purity among true believers The hard line drawn between town proprietors and newcomers who wanted to share their land mirrored the selfishness of human nature, and not a "reversion" to the custom of the *Märker* and *Ausmärker*. The separation of groups from established villages to found their own communities was not a return to the *dörfer* concept of the past, but was caused by the lure of free land and the bitterness of religious conflicts within the older society. Each practice, Turner noted, was "a case of similar causes leading to similar results."[3] New England towns were not patent-office duplicates of either the English parish or the German *tun*, but the product of accepted practices applied in a distinctive environment. This was common sense, but it was also a bold exercise in historical ingenuity for his day.

Turner chose never to publish his speculations on the genesis of New England towns, and he might have gone on garnering knowledge for its own sake had not two unrelated circumstances forced him to take up his pen once more. One was the opening to scholars in 1896 of the splendid "Draper Collection" by the State Historical Society of Wisconsin. This was a treasure trove—four hundred fat volumes of manuscripts accumulated by Lyman C. Draper during a lifetime of collecting, and willed to the society on his death in 1891: letters, documents, reminiscences, interviews, reports, deeds—all the raw materials for the study of the early trans-Appalachian West, and all unused and waiting exploitation! Here were historical riches to occupy Turner for his lifetime. At the same time, he was assured an opportunity to publish what he found under the most auspicious circumstances. In the spring of 1895 a group of the rising new generation of professional historians, distressed that they had no outlet for their scholarly articles save semi-popular magazines, launched the *American Historical Review*, with J. Franklin Jameson of Brown University as editor. An article published in such a journal would be the best way to present Turner's new findings.

The opportunity to do so came knocking at his door. Jameson had never met Turner, but he had heard about him and lost no time in inviting him to submit a contribution for the first issue, preferably in western history. Turner was delighted; here was a chance to use the Draper documents to test his assumptions on the frontier's influence by examining a specific topic in depth. This, he decided, must lie in the late eighteenth century, for by then the coastal colonies were giving birth to new colonies in the interior which were sufficiently free of England's influence that they could respond to environmental forces. There, "the interaction of *American* institutions and political ideas, with free land" could be studied. Hence, he told Jameson, he would explore "State Making in the West, 1772-1789," to determine the extent to which free land altered the colonizing process and shaped the emerging settlements.[4]

This was a larger assignment than Turner knew, and the more deeply he dug into the Draper manuscripts the more he realized that he could neither meet the August 1, 1895, deadline nor tell his story in the sixteen pages alloted him. (His agonized efforts to wheedle more time and space from Jameson were to be repeated with little variation whenever he undertook a writing assignment from that day to his death.) Could he have until August 14? Was there room for an unknown letter of Patrick Henry, and a map? Jameson reluctantly parted with four more pages and promised that August 15 would not be too late, knowing full well that the article would never be finished by that time. Nor was it. The map went off on August 16, half the paper on August 19, another quarter the next day, and the last on August 21—with Turner rushing to the Madison railroad station each night to catch the last mail train. "I undertook a bigger task than I anticipated when I began," he confessed, "and there is some uncanny spell about those Scotch-Irish manuscripts." Optimistically, he had estimated that his manuscript would fill twenty pages. Jameson, more realistic, judged it would reach thirty-five pages in print and crowd out some worthy article—unless it was published in two installments. Turner fought for a time, fearful lest someone steal his ideas and materials before the second part appeared, but he backed down gracefully, muttering that he could not yet understand how his few words could fill thirty-five pages—which they did.[5]

Jameson, still a neophyte in the editorial chair, may have felt relieved when that over-long manuscript went off to the printers, but if he did he sighed too soon. Turner, ever the perfectionist, dawdled so long over each set of proofs that only urgent reminders extracted them from him, again after nightly dashes to the railroad station. Nor did this satisfy him. He had to see the page proof to make sure that he had caught every mistake and to assure himself that the mountain ranges were properly placed on his map; a map without mountains was like Hamlet without the Prince of Denmark. Jameson protested that there was no time. He protested in vain; in the end the proofs were returned, only to prove Turner correct: his mountains were not there. And there were more delays. Only when everything was completed to Turner's satisfaction could the first issue of the *American Historical Review* go to press, its final article (so placed because it came in last) "Western State-Making in the Revolutionary Era" complete with a colored fold-out map—with no mountains.[6]

Turner was still happy with the result, and well he might be; it provided, *The Nation* observed, the "main feast" in an excellent new journal. His story was as fresh in 1895 as it is familiar today—that the new states created by settlers during the Revolutionary era—Vandalia, Wautauga, Nashville, Westsylvania, Franklin, and the rest—demonstrated the significant role played by pioneers in shaping their own governments, the consistency of the trend toward self-determination on frontiers, and the willingness of frontiersmen to accept congressional control as soon as it could be exerted. Turner also proved, to his own satisfaction at least, that westerners, whether from Northeast or Southeast, adopted the same solutions for their common problems, resented the authority of unsympathetic eastern states, and served as a nationalizing force by demanding a place in the central government. These were not insignificant findings, but the article's principal importance was in its demonstration of the fact that solid research in western sources produced both worthwhile results and support for the hypothesis that Turner had presented. Turner had opened a new avenue for historical investigators, and he invited them to share the adventures to which it led.

His next explorations failed to live up to his own promises, for by this time he was so intrigued with the riches in the Draper collections that he was unable to resist burrowing further, whatever the significance of his findings to frontier theory. Fortunately he could do so with some purpose, and without the agonies of composition, for once more J. Franklin Jameson provided him with exactly the task that he most enjoyed. For some time that gadfly of the profession had been urging his colleagues to publish the basic documents of American history, a one-man campaign that bore fruit in 1895, when the National Historical Manuscripts Commission was established. Jameson was chairman, Turner was a member, and modest funds were available for a publications program. They agreed on procedures at their first meeting in New York in June 1896—they would compile a list of manuscripts in public and private depositories, select some of the more significant to be printed in an annual report, and publish only complete documents, rather than summaries. They decided, too, that their first publication would contain documentary materials illustrating the history of Canada, England, New England, the Middle States, the South, and the West. Turner's task, of course, was to compile the section on the West, from the resources of the Draper collection.[7]

Here was an assignment tailored to his interests, and he fell to work with a will, neglecting his friends, his family, and even his classes to spend long hours in the State Historical Society library, joyfully reading document after document and making discovery after discovery that altered the traditional history of the post-Revolutionary era.[8] The whole story, he knew, could not be told within the space assigned him; hence, he settled on the intrigue between Citizen Genêt and George Rogers Clark, as they plotted a campaign against Spain's Mississippi Valley colonies in 1793 and 1794. This was an unknown episode, and the evidence available was astoundingly rich—letters of George Rogers Clark, of Charles De Pauw, of Jonathan Clark, government documents galore, dispatches copied from the Spanish Archives. The French side of the story had to be supplied; Turner spent many hours directing a copyist toward materials in the Archives du Ministère des Affairs Étrangères, then translating and annotating the results. He worked very hard that winter of 1896-97, and before it was over he sent off to Jameson a fat bundle of ably edited manuscripts, ponderously entitled "Selections from the Draper Collection of the State Historical Society of Wisconsin, to Elucidate the Proposed French Expedition under George Rogers Clark Against Louisiana in the Years 1793-94." The manuscripts filled two hundred pages of the *Annual Report of the American Historical Association for 1896.*

Turner's editorial labors added a chapter to the history of the West, but they also wrought a major change in his own scholarly interests. Why bother with proving the frontier hypothesis when the diplomacy of the early Republic offered such a fascinating field for investigation? Here was an unexplored byway paved with unsolved problems, and any unsolved problem was irresistible. Then, too, documents from the French copyist continued to arrive long after the Clark-Genêt correspondence had been sent to the publishers, and these told a story far too important to be discarded. This was the combination of attractions that converted Turner from a frontier to a diplomatic historian, and kept him on that course for the next half-dozen years.[9]

What joy he knew as he read each document from France, hunted down the appropriate supporting information in the Draper collections, added his documentation and introduction, and hurried the result off to the *American Historical Review* or the National Historical Manuscripts Commission! He accomplished little else during 1897 and 1898, but the results were impressive: a long letter from Baron Carondelet on the defense of Louisiana in 1794; the extensive correspondence of the French consul at Charleston, concerning Citizen Genêt's proposed attack on the Floridas in 1793-94; a revealing letter from Thomas Jefferson to George Rogers Clark; a series of documents on the Nootka Sound controversy of 1790, copied from the British Public Record Office, which for the first time satisfactorily explained the shift in the Pacific balance of naval power from Spain to England.[10]

His publications, adding steadily to his reputation, also prepared him for his major task as a diplomatic historian. This came about through a happy accident. As was his habit, Turner sent an offprint of his article on the Nootka Sound documents to the distinguished historian and editor, Worthington C. Ford, and, as usual, he received a guarded acknowledgment, but this time with a difference. Ford had once been

interested in publishing all correspondence relating to the three ministers representing France in the United States during the years from
1791 to 1797—Genêt, Fauchet, and Adet—and had secured copies from
the French archives. Would Turner be interested in seeing any of the
letters? He surely would. He would even be willing to edit the entire
collection—350,000 manuscript pages—if Ford would consent. Ford was
agreeable, and so was the Historical Manuscripts Commission, when
Turner, with his remarkable inability to estimate either space or time,
promised that they would fill only one hundred pages, and would be
ready for publication in the next annual report.[11]

With all obstacles hurdled, and the vast bundle of manuscripts safely
in his hands, Turner was ready to begin his editorial chores by the
end of 1902. These proved formidable. Some documents were missing,
others had to be recopied, more had to be added. Turner wanted the
work done in Madison, where he had a capable copyist, a student
named Homer C. Hockett; the Commission insisted that it be done in
Washington, where their copyist charged only 35¢ for a thousand
words. All of this took a heavy toll in money, patience, and even-
temperedness, as well as unbelievably hard work, until Turner was
forced to flee to Maine for a vacation during the summer of 1903, or risk
a collapse. This meant that deadlines were being missed, and that tensions were mounting. At long last, however, the massive job was done
and the bulky manuscript shipped to Washington. Controversy flared
again when he demanded the services of Homer Hockett to aid him
with the mountains of galley proof, even threatening to hire him with
his own funds if the Commission was too niggardly to pay. Once more
the Commission backed down; Hockett was hired and the proofs were
returned more or less on time to be fitted into the annual report for
1903—which, fortunately, did not appear until late in 1904.[12] There
they filled no less than 1,100 pages, forming an enduring monument to
Turner's industry, no less than to his passion for diplomatic history.

This was Turner's last editorial venture—save for a modest collection
of documents on the Blount Conspiracy of 1795-97, which he gathered
from Paris, London, and New York, and which appeared in the April
1905 issue of the *American Historical Review*—but he would gladly
have gone on had funds been available. His plans were as ambitious as
they were unrealistic: he would edit all correspondence of French ministers to the United States through the Monroe administration, throw-

ing in additional dispatches from the British and French archives, and, for good measure, adding all Russian and Spanish documents that shed light on the Monroe Doctrine.[13] Fortunately for Turner, the Manuscripts Commission failed to catch his enthusiasm; had it done so he might have spent the rest of his days editing documents in diplomatic history.

Even though his editorial plans were dampened, he could continue to write learned articles in the field. These appeared at regular intervals, paralleling his editing assignments. His first, quite naturally, was a thoroughly researched, admirably written, essay on Citizen Genêt's intrigue in the Mississippi Valley, published in the *American Historical Review* in July 1898. He then turned to a subject that occupied him for several years: the diplomatic background of the Louisiana Purchase—a topic of particular appeal in view of the coming centennial celebration. Turner's purpose was laudable—to link the Genêt episode with Napoleon's decision to acquire and sell the territory, thus demonstrating the continuity of events and the significance of the historical antecedents to the purchase—but the complexity of the problem, and the quantities of additional documentary evidence that the French copyist had to provide, involved him in a far longer effort than he had intended. He hoped to reveal his findings to the American Historical Association at its December 1901 meeting, but the paper he prepared for that occasion was so inadequate that he declined to deliver it, trying it out instead on the Madison Literary Club a month later and on the North Central History Teacher's Association in March.[14]

Two more years of research and writing were necessary before Turner was ready to display his brainchild in public. It first appeared as a popular article in the *Review of Reviews* for May 1903, as "The Significance of the Louisiana Purchase." A few months later, and in vastly more sophisticated form, it was presented as a paper on "The Relation of Spain, England, and France in the Mississippi Valley, 1789-1800," before the American Historical Association. It was then published in the *Atlantic Monthly*, where it was printed in the May and June issues in 1904 as "The Diplomatic Contest for the Mississippi Valley." Again, it was recast as a dinner speech when Turner was invited to address a St. Louis celebration of the centennial on "The Historical Significance of the Louisiana Purchase." This time he added oratorical touches that greatly pleased his hearers: "Napoleon gave to the United

States a spacious, a vast way of looking at our destiny, which has yet to work out its full result (Great applause)."[15] Still Turner sought a wider audience, this time among his peers, when his findings were presented in their most sophisticated form in the January 1905 issue of the *American Historical Review* as "The Policy of France toward the Mississippi Valley in the Period of Washington and Adams."

"Now," he wrote a friend, "I am giving up the diplomacy of that period." Then, knowing his own weaknesses, he added, "I hope."[16] He retired to his other interests with a reputation as a master interpreter of American diplomatic history, for his studies added a new dimension as well as fresh interpretations. He demonstrated that European archives held riches essential to the understanding of the nation's foreign relations, that local episodes, such as the Genêt incident, assumed international significance when fitted into the mainstream of events, and that happenings in the back country were often more important to early diplomats than better-known occurrences in national capitals. Here, as in all his investigations, Turner was peering below the surface to find the subcurrents that shaped national action. In bringing this lesson home to craftsmen in the field, he stamped himself as a major contributor to the study of diplomacy.

This is not the reputation that Turner enjoys today, even among specialists in the field; indeed, his diplomatic studies are almost forgotten. Their own excellence doomed them to this fate. Turner's findings were so significant, and his presentations so correct, that they were immediately absorbed into textbooks as part of the acknowledged pattern of history. We view his essays on diplomacy as hackneyed; they are not worth reading because they say nothing new. But they said a great deal that was new to his own generation, which ranked him among the foremost experts in the field. He was so highly regarded that he was invited to deliver two lectures on "The Diplomatic Struggle for the Mississippi Valley" before the Naval War College in Newport, and was twice—in 1906 and 1907—selected as the prestigious Albert Shaw Lecturer in Diplomatic History by the Johns Hopkins University.[17] On a lesser scale, Turner was viewed locally as an expert who could explain such complex issues as the Russo-Japanese War, a reputation built not only on his published works, but on the fact that in 1901 he introduced a course in diplomatic history, the first at Wisconsin and one of the first to be offered at any university in the United States.[18] In his own day, and in both Madison and the wider academic world, Turner was rated a first-rank student of foreign policy.

His contributions in another area, one far distant from frontier history, were less laudable in either motive or result, but they also stamp him as a pioneer in a field not often associated with his name. Turner's venture into immigration history was inspired by a letter that reached him in July 1901, shortly after his return from Europe. Would he prepare a series of articles on the coming of the Italians, Germans, Jews, and French-Canadians to the United States for the *Chicago Record-Herald?* The pay was suitable, and the essays, 2500 to 3000 words each, would not be due for several weeks. Turner, eager to rebuild his bank account after the European venture, accepted, and he immediately plunged into the more-than-necessary research that he expended on all projects, however trivial. For the next weeks he worked long and hard, often until two in the morning, gathering notes, writing drafts, compiling statistics, and even drawing a map correlating German communities in Pennsylvania with the limestone soil areas there—apparently the first of the hundreds of such maps that Turner was to prepare during his lifetime.[19]

He wrought no miracle in the articles that resulted, but they were so vastly superior to most writing on immigration at the time—and for a good many years thereafter—that he must be ranked as a constructive pioneer in this area, no less than in diplomatic history. The clichés and stereotypes of his generation were there—Germans were a "conservative, thrifty and religious folk," Italians were "quick-witted and supple in morals," because they had been taught "self-preservation by deception," Jews were "thrifty to disgracefulness" and their "ability to drive a bargain amounts to genius," the "New Immigration" from eastern and southern Europe brought "a lowering of the standard of comfort," sweatshops, congestion, political corruption, and pauperism—but overbalancing these hostile judgments were words of praise for the recent arrivals that could hardly be duplicated in that day. Turner saw two things about the immigrants that escaped other scholars: that they were the victims of social forces which were responsible for the poverty and crime usually associated with newcomers, and that their material and cultural contributions to American life far outweighed the problems they created during their period of adjustment.[20]

This did not mean that his viewpoint was that of today or that he saw the immigrant as an unalloyed blessing. Wedded as he was to the belief that American virtues were rooted in the rural past, Turner deplored the tendency of newcomers to crowd into cities and live in squalor. But he also realized that immigrants contributed much to America's adjustment to its post-frontier era. They stimulated appreciation of music and the arts. They introduced a Sabbath far more suitable to modern conditions than that of the Puritans. They offered an example in temperance by their adherence to beer and wine. Even the traits of Italians and Jews that were most resented in the United States would soon be abandoned; they were the products of centuries of oppression, and would vanish in the free atmosphere of the New World. Turner did close his eyes to some of the virtues of the newcomers, but he still believed that periodic transfusions from Europe enriched American civilization and should be encouraged rather than prohibited.

His essays not only preached a message alien to that day, but taught his fellow scholars a great deal about the techniques of proper immigration history. Better than any historian of his time, he recognized that the study of immigration must begin in Europe, that there was a significant interaction between geographic and ethnic factors, and that the impact of migration was almost as great on the country of origin as on the country of destination. Turner's description of the coming of the Palatine Germans in the eighteenth century might have been written today, so rich was it in understanding of the political, social, and religious conditions in Germany that underlay the exodus. His explanation of the mass migrations of the 1830s and 1840s laid far more stress on the failure of the potato crop than on the 1848 revolutions, a judgment that is acceptable to modern scholars. He also recognized that artificial inducements—steamship agents, land and immigrant companies, land-grant railroads, and factory owners in search of cheap labor—helped shape migration patterns.

Turner's venture into immigration history wrought no revolution in scholarship; buried as they were in a local newspaper, his articles had no impact on other historians. They are significant only because they reveal the degree to which Turner could generate new ideas on every aspect of the past. He was writing rather good immigration history, and underlining the cultural contributions made by the newcomers, at a time when historians ignored the subject completely, and when the sociologists and publicists who did profess some interest agreed that immigrants carried with them poverty, slums, crime, and immorality, and that this "degenerative breeding stock" was undermining the fiber of the Republic. Turner had an unusual ability to escape the straitjacket of his times, no matter how unique the area into which he ventured.

Those of his fellow craftsmen who refused to follow, and who had the misfortune to write a book that fell into Turner's hands for review, were certain to be reminded of their sins in language more sharp than charitable. Turner was a prolific and highly critical reviewer, for both professional and popular journals, during his early teaching years. Unlike most critics, though he was ruthless, he was also impartial in his judgments; his bludgeon could fall on his closest friend, or a godlike leader of the historical guild, just as it could on an unimportant unknown. All were exactly weighed, and if found wanting in areas that he deemed essential—sound scholarship, careful documentation, recognition of the subsurface economic and social forces shaping human behavior, belief in multiple causation—their errors were paraded and roundly condemned. Turner's book reviews shed light on his historical beliefs, and reveal his convictions, no less than do his other writings of the time.

His particular ire was reserved for those who ignored basic causal forces, and particularly for writers who failed to mention the frontier. "We are now," he wrote in a long review article in the *Atlantic Monthly* in 1896, "coming to recognize the vital forces in American society whose interaction and transformation have called political institutions into life and moulded them to suit changing conditions. Our history is that of the rise and expansion of a huge democracy in an area unoccupied by civilization, and thus affording free play to the factors of physiography, race, and custom."[21] Using these standards, Turner found such eminent scholars as James Ford Rhodes and John W. Burgess sadly wanting. Rhodes, in overemphasizing the slavery controversy, ignored the intimate relationship between the political struggles he described and the subsurface pressures creating those conflicts; Burgess, by concentrating too much on the politics of the middle period, had neglected "the vast social transformations by immigration,

interstate migration, industrial development, revolution of the transportation system, and all the tremendous forces of change involved
in the Westward expansion of settlement." Both were blind to the
multiple forces that created the pre-Civil War social order, forces that
operated particularly during the 1850s. "This," Turner reminded
Rhodes, "was a decade of American expansion and material growth, a
period of the transformation of the social organism by immigration
and industrial change, of the reorganization of sectional relations by
railroad-building, by the revolution of commercial connections, and
by interstate migration." Only the historians who had the power and
the insight to analyze and interpret the economic and social evolution
of American society could understand that complex period.[22] Rhodes
and Burgess, Turner strongly implied, did not.

   Authors who were slipshod in scholarship or antiquarian in method
were just as firmly reprimanded, whatever their status in the profession. Justin Winsor's *Westward Movement* was dismissed as an ill-
digested mass of facts that resembled more a thesaurus than history;
Elliott Coues was soundly castigated for careless editing and faulty
transcription when preparing his collected works of Lewis and Clark;
Alexander Brown was condemned for a multitude of sins—including a
lack of objectivity—in his *English Politics in Early Virginia History*.
This did not mean that Turner was scornful of editors who compiled
documents, or local historians who squandered pages on minute aspects
of the past. Good editing and good local history inspired sincere praise.
Turner found Reuben Gold Thwaites's multi-volume *Early Western
Travels* laudable, partly because it was meticulously edited, partly because it would allow scholars to probe social and economic development on successive frontiers.[23] He had only commendation for studies
that linked minor episodes with the broader stream of history. "The
humblest locality," he wrote in a review of a town history, "has in it
the possibility of revealing in its history, rightly told, wide reaching
historical events." One of Turner's basic principles was that historians
must study the states if they were to understand the nation.[24] Authors
who met those objectives were rightly praised; but antiquarianism was
a sin he never forgave.

   These highly critical standards met their test when Turner was asked
to review the collected works of Francis Parkman. Parkman was a
subjective historian, rarely aware of underlying social forces, and sadly

deficient in scientific research techniques. But he had been an idol of Turner's since graduate-school days. Even so, Turner did not flinch. Parkman, he decided, was faulty in his refusal to recognize social development, the economic relationships between *voyageurs* and merchants, the depressed living conditions in the French parishes, and the class struggle that accounted for so much of French-Canadian history. The charm of his narrative hid the stark grimness of the life he was depicting. Yet all this could be forgiven by a reader swept along by Parkman's style. "He was the greatest painter of historical pictures that this country—perhaps it is not too much to say, that any country—has produced." Parkman might fail to meet the standards of scientific history, but his work would live forever because he was greater as an artist than as a historian.[25] Turner, sensitive to the language as he was, could forgive any author whose words sang as Parkman's did, no matter what his offenses to the canons of objectivity.

Yet he was frank in revealing his hero's weaknesses, just as he had been in condemning Rhodes and Burgess and Coues for their transgressions. This was a practice that made enemies—and friends. James Ford Rhodes apparently forgave Turner his criticisms; the two saw much of each other after Turner moved to Harvard in 1910. Woodrow Wilson proved just as understanding. He had been an admirer of Turner's since their Johns Hopkins days together, and the sentiment was returned with interest; Turner considered Wilson's *Division and Reunion* one of the masterpieces of historical interpretation, and he looked forward to Wilson's next venture—a five-volume history of the United States—as a work that would be "*the* American history of our time."[26] Hence he welcomed the opportunity when the *American Historical Review* asked him to prepare a critical evaluation of the *History of the American People* in 1903. His disappointment mounted as he read. Some features deserved praise; the sentences flowed "so gracefully and buoyantly that the reader easily overlooks the burden which they bear"; no other author had produced "so sustained and vital a view of the whole first cycle of the nation's history." But these virtues were offset by two serious defects. Wilson was "more at home in characterizing political leaders and the trend of events than in dealing with the deeper undercurrents of economic and social change." He was also wrong when he stated that state sovereignty had not changed since the drafting of the Constitution; Turner pointed out that southern views had altered greatly since the 1780s, and that these alterations were traceable to the elasticity written into the Constitution by the framers. He was right, but these were damaging criticisms, for Wilson's concept of state sovereignty was the foundation on which his whole argument rested.[27]

In later years Turner remembered Woodrow Wilson's offense at these judgments, and his own chagrin at having hurt one of his closest friends. He resolved then and there, he recalled, to write no more reviews—a resolution from which he turned on only a few occasions.[28] Yet there is no hint in the contemporary records that Wilson was offended or that he voiced his discontent. He was well aware that his *History of the American People* was a commercial venture, prepared for the popular market, and sadly lacking the refinements expected by his professional colleagues. Wilson visited Madison in April 1903, spent hours with Turner, and departed feeling that their friendship was as intimate as ever—even though Turner, frank as always, almost certainly used the occasion to read his soon-to-be-published review to his visitor.[29] Actually, Turner's decision to review no more books probably followed his meeting with James Schouler at the American Historical Association, after he had castigated that venerable scholar's latest volume as "essentially commonplace." He was, he told a friend, shocked to think of the effect of his harsh judgment on "such a nice old man."[30] Perhaps the memory of this episode flooded back now as he thought of Wilson's reaction to his criticisms. Reviewers, he insisted from that time on, should temper their judgments with praise and always end on a note of commendation rather than faultfinding;[31] better still, they should leave the weighing of their colleagues' scholarship to others.

If frankness threatened to sever Turner's friendship with one future President of the United States, it had the opposite effect with another. His reviews of the third and fourth volumes of Theodore Roosevelt's *Winning of the West* spared no punches; the books were hastily prepared, contained many minor errors, failed to mention the intrigues that divided the western country in the Revolutionary era, and ignored the "land politics" that played such an important role in Congress and at the Constitutional Convention. Roosevelt was also at fault in charging Jefferson with active participation in the Genêt conspiracy; such a rash accusation should not be made unless supported by documents in the Paris archives. Yet there were words of praise as well. Roosevelt had used his authorities "with the skill of a practised historian," and had produced a work of literary merit that added new meaning to a period essential to understanding the truly national history of the United States.

These mixed judgments gave no offense; instead they inspired Roosevelt to ask *The Nation* (where the first review appeared) for the name of its author and to launch an amiable correspondence with him. Their letters reveal something of the political philosophy of both men. Roosevelt cheerfully admitted his neglect of land companies and "land politics"; his purpose was to tell who the frontiersmen were and what they did, leaving to Turner the broader implications of expansion: the interaction of West and East, and the institutional modification that occurred as the westward movement went on. He was also ready to back down in his charges against Thomas Jefferson; he was, he agreed, thoroughly prejudiced in his opinion about the third President, linking him as he did with William Jennings Bryan and the Populist radicals who were threatening to ruin the country.[32] Theodore Roosevelt might retreat, but he retreated gracefully and in good spirit. Turner remained his friend and staunch admirer—and was to be his ardent supporter in the presidential campaigns that followed.

Such was not the case of Edward Channing, another victim of Turner's outspoken reviewing. That bristly New Englander, holder of a Harvard professorship and a rising power in the historical profession, was little inclined to accept criticism from a backlander from remote Wisconsin, yet Turner was no more inclined to respect the demigods of the East than he was his own associates in the West. Less so, in fact, if they failed to recognize the significance of the frontier. This was Channing's sin in his *A Student's History of the United States*, published in 1898. Turner, as usual, found features deserving praise; here was a text that presented history as a discipline of the mind rather than an exercise in rote memory, and it was particularly valuable for the training that it gave on decision-making on political and industrial questions. But these virtues were overbalanced by its complete failure to recognize the significance of the West and South in the nation's history. This was a fatal error; Channing's statements on these important sections were so completely inadequate "as to be misleading, if not entirely incorrect."[33] These were harsh words, and Channing never forgave them. The rift that developed between the two men when colleagues at Harvard—a rift for which Channing was solely responsible —originated in Turner's brutal, but absolutely correct, appraisal of a textbook that was destined to monopolize the market, whatever its merits.

If Turner's outspoken reviews revealed his maturing ideas on the nature and function of history, so did the lectures that he gave during these years, the letters to his friends, and the occasional notes that his reading inspired. To Turner, historical studies were things of beauty, no less than of practicality. "There is," he told an audience in 1908, "a charm in restoring the past, in compelling the procession of leaders of human thought and action again to traverse the stage of human consciousness, in rescuing from oblivion what is worth the memory of the present day. The events of past years, the institutions that have passed away, the life and manner of societies that are gone are a precious heritage, not to be wantonly ignored in the heat and bustle of the day." The scholar who brought that past to life was no idle chronicler. His function was to enlighten those around him, and to help shape the future "as he presents the acquisitions of the past to the consciousness of the men of today."[34]

But history's role was neither to entertain nor to enrich mankind. Turner saw the study of the past as a searchlight into the future, a guide for the public conscience. He was fond of quoting the German historian Johann Gustav Droysen, whose books he read often, that "history is the self-consciousness of humanity." "It is," he told one audience, "humanity's effort to understand itself by understanding its origins, by taking stock of the forces that have made a nation what it is."[35] Hence, while society changed and re-changed with the passing generations, the historian provided the balance wheel that kept men and institutions on an even keel. Men could never break completely with their past; the past was a stubborn force that compelled mankind toward traditionalism, even as they changed with the times.[36]

The importance of history placed momentous responsibilities on the historian. The fragments of the past were so numerous that he could reconstruct falsely if he strayed from objectivity. Turner saw the materials of history as a great heap of tiny pebbles that had to be fashioned into a mosaic. The supreme test of the historical scholar was to find the essential, the really typical and vital, in the mass of evidence that lay before him. If he sought to enforce a creed, a philosophy, a political dogma, or a pet theory, the past had material at hand, "ready for the artful combination and presentation." Nor was the historian a free agent as he went about this task of selection and arrangement. He was a man, a human, affected by his own ideals and experiences, and influenced by the age in which he lived, his class, and his nationality, no matter how he tried to resist.[37] He could minimize these handicaps only by constantly striving for objectivity, however difficult or impossible the quest. This was made especially difficult with the broadening scope of historical studies. Now the narrative was outmoded; scholars must trace each of the interests of society, studying the many activities of the common people that influenced the evolution of the nation. With this new focus, Turner pointed out, all the old materials had to be restudied, archives, monuments and remains re-examined, and new collections made to permit understanding of the nation's growth. Therein lay the joy of investigation. "There are always new harvests to be reaped."[38]

Therein, too, lay the realization that there could be no simple explanation of the past, no single key to the understanding of human behavior, no universal laws of history. In the past, writers had thought they had found the key to the nation's progress in the struggle between Puritan and Cavalier, in the conflict over slavery, in the contest between states and nation, in the rise of democracy. "In truth there is no single key to American history. In history, as in science, we are learning that a complex result is the outcome of the interplay of many forces. Simple explanations fail to meet the case." Turner had no patience with those who sought to formulate laws of human behavior. "The human soul is too complex," he wrote, "human society is too full of vital energy and incessant change, to enable us to pluck out the heart of its mystery —to reduce it to an exact science or to state human development in terms of an equation."[39] Man was a complex animal, fascinating to study, and worthy of the most intense investigation, for nothing was more interesting than human behavior. Individuals were insignificant in this story, and the narrative of events unimportant. Society, ever-changing, restless, mobile, swept by subterranean currents and ruffled by the winds of popular emotion, was the challenge that historians must accept. For in America society had shaped the men. This was Turner's creed.

He stated his beliefs with particular clarity in two papers on "Problems in American History" prepared during these years, one in 1901 for a university function, the other three years later, when he was invited to address a historical congress at the World's Exposition held at St. Louis in 1904, celebrating the centennial of the Louisiana Purchase. Turner was delighted with this latter assignment, partly because he stood to pocket a fee of $150 as soon as his paper was delivered, partly because the similarity between this opportunity and one offered by the Chicago World's Fair of 1893 was too obvious to be ignored.[40] Here was Turner's chance to make another major revelation to the profession. This required careful preparation, even though he would repeat some of the ideas—and even words—he had used in his "Problems in American History" in *The Aegis* in 1892, and restated in a 1901 address to a Wisconsin audience on the same theme.[41] Turner, as usual, arrived in St. Louis with his task still to be completed. He stayed at the Inside Inn (which he renamed the "Thinside Inn" because its walls were so flimsy he could hear every conversation in the room next door), and settled to work while his roommate, Charles Homer Haskins, enjoyed the sights. As usual, too, his essay was ready by 9:30 on the morning of September 25, the day it was to be presented. Promptly at ten Turner entered the hall, to face an audience kept sparse by a driving rainstorm. The quality was high if the numbers were low; he counted the eminent German historian, Karl Lamprecht, among his listeners, and he was well-satisfied that his words would have a decided impact on interdisciplinary studies even beyond national borders.[42]

They did not. Turner was almost as far in advance of his generation in discussing the nature of history as he had been when he had expounded his frontier hypothesis a decade before. His paper, however, offers insights into his beliefs, particularly as they had changed since his original essay on the subject in 1892 and its revision in 1901. Much that he said was familiar. He echoed Achille Loria in proposing that the nation's history capsulized the social and industrial stages that had taken centuries in Europe, and that it offered insights into the evolution of all societies. It should be viewed, Turner thought, not as a narrative or chronicle, but as the record of social transformation to ever higher cultural levels. Loria, however, had ignored the fact that in America there were repeated colonial experiences as new "colonies" were established with every move westward, and that each was modified by the differing physiographic environment in which it grew, and by the character and intensity of the industrial life of its parent society. The study of American history was the study of these transformations, of the expansion and formation of societies, of the interaction of differing peoples, their institutions, their economic activities, their fundamental assumptions. This was the basic problem facing all investigators.[43]

They must also grapple with a whole series of subordinate problems. When Turner wrote his 1901 essay, he pictured these as largely related to expansion. The profession's principal need was a shift of emphasis from New England's internal history to the economic, social, and religious forces that drove that region's multitudes into a Greater New England that formed in the West. Historians should investigate that exodus, which was as important as the coming of the Puritans, and determine its effect on the nation, and on New England. They should pay equal attention to the history of the South, studying the settlement of the upland and the conflicts that developed between that region and the seaboard areas—a subject untouched by scholars. The economy of the southern states was also crying for investigation; the plantation system had to be appraised, the relationship between cotton and slave prices established, and the impact of economic tides on political change studied. Nor should the other sections—the Lake Plains, the Prairie Plains, and the Pacific Coast—be ignored. All should be subjected to the same analysis, from early contacts between Indians and whites through the occupation of the public lands. These, Turner believed in 1901, were the major problems in American history deserving study.

Three years later, his understanding of sections was far more sophisticated. He no longer thought of traditional physiographic provinces, but of interrelated regions forming a "nation of sections," some of them as large as the largest of the European nations, and all rising through successive stages to achieve cultural identity. Sectionalism was a basic fact of American history, no less than expansion, and equally important. Until historians understood how each region was colonized, the contributions made to it by incoming stocks, its industrial evolution, the leaders it had produced, the psychological traits of its people, and its relations with other sections, the history of the United States could not be understood.

This was the fundamental problem as Turner saw it in 1904, but others bulked large. Students must investigate the formation of the

American character for the light it would shed on the evolution of society. They should study the forces operating to create a composite nationality. They should seek to understand the relationships between literature and the other arts, the social and economic conditions that influenced cultural expression, and political action. "We need to give a social and economic interpretation to the history of political parties in this country." This would be possible only if a complex of subordinate problems were solved: the effect of the public domain on legislation, immigration and the European conditions that underlay each wave of migration, the contributions of the Indian and Negro to the nation's civilization, the role of labor in industry and politics. Legal and religious forces still awaited investigation, while the study of the transfer of political power to the common people had only begun. Students should investigate comparative frontiers in Canada, Australia, Russia, and medieval Germany to appraise the uniqueness of the American experience. Whole eras of the past had been neglected: the eighteenth century and "the wonderful development of the nation since the Reconstruction period" were particularly flagrant examples. Similarly, vast areas had been ignored; virtually nothing was known of the history of the region between the Mississippi and the Rocky Mountains. New England had been over-studied, Turner was saying. Now let us broaden our scope and see how the nation took shape.

Because history was no longer past politics, but a study designed to enable a people to understand itself by understanding its origins and development in all the main features of human activity, the past could be understood only by calling into cooperation sciences and methods hitherto little used. Data drawn from literature, art, economics, politics, sociology, psychology, biology, and physiography were grist for the historians' mill, just as were statistics and the techniques of critical evaluation of evidence. "There has been too little cooperation of these sciences and the result is that great fields have been neglected." Too many fertile areas that lay between disciplines had been left uncultivated, too many problems had been studied with inadequate apparatus. Only by the use of all the social and allied sciences could the nation's development be understood.

Here was Turner's concept of history and its problems as he reached the climax of his career. He was still naïve in some of his judgments, still too inclined to accept stereotyped concepts—he had, for example, yet to appreciate the complexity of social evolution, and he pictured progress in the well-defined stages he had learned from Richard T. Ely. But Turner's thought had undergone a remarkable transformation since he had written his "Problems in American History" in 1892. Then the basic, the one essential, problem was to understand the nature of westward expansion. Now he saw expansion as only one element in the equation, important, to be sure, but no more so than sectionalism or cultural influences or economic forces. When Turner admonished his fellow craftsmen to focus on the history of labor, cultural progress, immigration, and social development, he was preaching a doctrine tuned to the twentieth century rather than to the nineteenth. His pleas for an interdisciplinary approach and for the study of comparative history have a more familiar ring in the 1970s than they did in the 1900s. Turner, more than any historian of his day, recognized the complexity of the past, and the need to trace each of the dozens of forces that governed human behavior before that past could be understood.

That he was to spend the rest of his life largely in the study of two of those forces—the frontier and section—did not mean that he was indifferent to the others. During his earlier years he had shown lively interest in immigration, diplomacy, and recent industrialism; for a time he toyed with the idea of dedicating himself to diplomatic history. He was fascinated by every aspect of history, but in the end one captivated him above all others. This was not the frontier; the more deeply he delved into the history of expansion the more convinced he became that its significance was somewhat different than he had first supposed. The primary importance of the westward movement was that it had left behind a series of sections, each differing from the others in racial composition, physiographic conditions, and the psychology of the people. To Turner the formation and interplay of these sections was the real bedrock on which the story of the past rested. Thus, early in his life, he made sectionalism his primary interest. Yet he was too wedded to the frontier concept, and too well known as the father of a theory that was increasingly altering historical studies, to divorce himself entirely from his first love. From this time on, Turner's intellectual life was dedicated to proving the significance of sectionalism, while his public life was dedicated to demonstrating the importance of the frontier.

VIII

Popularizing the Frontier Thesis

1893-1910

WHEN Frederick Jackson Turner first pronounced his frontier hypothesis, in July of 1893, his message fell on deaf ears. To historians in his audience he was an audacious young man from a backwater college whose theories were either incomprehensible or so alien to long-accepted interpretations that they deserved no respect. To the larger public, Turner was a complete unknown, not worthy of mention in the press or even in the more intellectual magazines of the day. In the three years after he announced his theory, neither he nor his frontier thesis was mentioned in the five leading American journals, including the *Review of Reviews*, which abstracted forty others, save in three brief items written by one of his friends.[1] Here was a theory—and its author—that seemed on the way to oblivion.

Then, slowly, the tide turned, as, first, historians, then the reading public, began to realize that Turner's thesis offered reason and hope in an era sadly in need of both. His theories, the nation discovered, not only explained what was happening to the United States in the 1890s and 1900s, but promised that the best of the American past would persist into the twentieth century. This was what the people wanted to hear. A prophet who preached such doctrines, and the disciples who spread his message, was sure to be heard. Turner's theories began to gain support in the late 1890s, and continued to win converts for a quarter-century thereafter, because they fit the public mood so well.

Certainly the American people were ripe for explanations. The world they knew—the comfortable world of the nineteenth century—was

crumbling away. The hard times that had persisted since the Panic of
1873 were deepening into a major depression during the 1890s. On the
western plains, wild-eyed Populists were demanding cheap money and
government meddling in the sacred temples of private enterprise. In the
cities, slums were spreading and class divisions deepening, bolstering the
growing realization that the United States no longer offered equal
opportunity to all. In Washington, reformers were preaching the
heretical doctrine that big business must be controlled for the common
good. Overseas, American war vessels were beating Spain to its knees
and carving out empires amidst the clamor of debate between imperialists and anti-imperialists. These were happenings alien to the nation's
experience. The United States was entering a new era at the turn of
the century, and the people wanted to know why, and what lay ahead.

The frontier thesis offered them no panaceas, but it did provide an
understandable explanation and a great deal of hope. For those who
predicted that empire-building beyond the seas would plunge the
United States into the maelstrom of world politics, the Turnerians
answered that expansion underlay both the strength and liberties of the
nation, and that the newly won empires would nurture democracy and
gird the United States against European meddling. For those who feared
the central government's growing power, they replied that three centuries of pioneering had engrained a belief in individualism so deeply
into the national character that it could never be destroyed. For those
who pictured the deepening gulf between rich and poor as a threat to
democracy, they countered that the frontier faith in equality was too
firmly planted ever to be threatened. Jacob Riis and his fellow reformers might shock the well-to-do with revelations of poverty in a land of
plenty, Charles Graham Sumner and his fellow publicists might offend
the masses by arguing that the social inequalities of the new industrialism were inevitable and must be endured, but Turner provided hope
that frontiering had made all people equal and that the injustices of the
day would soon disappear.

The outstanding feature of the frontier thesis was its optimism. The
frontier was disappearing, but the pioneer experience had bred into
Americans not only value judgments and beliefs that elevated them
above lesser peoples, but a hardihood and an aggressive spirit that would
allow them to protect their way of life and thought against hostile
forces. Turner had pictured a Promethean struggle between man and the

wilderness, with man emerging triumphant. By his victory he had liberated himself from pettiness, embraced the loftiest of ideals, and absorbed power and resolution beyond compare. Whatever the results of the closing of the frontier, Americans had been so endowed by their triumph over the wilderness that they could fashion a new civilization, embodying the best of their pioneer days, but benefiting from the new industrialism. Turner's theories were acceptable—and accepted—because they gave substance to folk myths that satisfied the need of Americans for a rose-tinted view of the future.

They were also appealing because the masses of Americans, living increasingly in crowded cities rather than on farms, were developing a new attitude toward the wilderness at the turn of the century. No longer was the forest the "enemy," as it had been in pioneer days; now it was a haven for peace and relaxation for those seeking escape from the tensions of urban life. This was the change of mood that gave rise to a "wilderness cult" in the United States during the 1890s and 1900s. When Theodore Roosevelt and his fellow conservationists urged the creation of national parks and wilderness areas, they were only recognizing popular demand. So were the leaders of the Boy Scout movement that swept the country in the early twentieth century, and so were "nature writers," such as John Burroughs, John Muir, and Jack London, who glorified the primitive for ever-widening audiences. The back-to-nature movement helped create a ready-made interest in the frontier, endowing the nation's rural past with a halo of romance that it never possessed in reality.[2]

The changing conditions that altered the national viewpoint at the turn of the century created a receptive audience for the frontier hypothesis, but that thesis could not be known until Turner recruited an army of proselytizers to preach his doctrines. This proved easy, for younger historians were eager to embrace an interpretation of American history less absurd than the now-discredited "germ" theory of Herbert Baxter Adams, and broader in scope than the "slavery" thesis argued by Hermann von Holst and James Ford Rhodes. Turner's explanation answered their needs to perfection. It was "scientific" in stressing demonstrable cause and effect. It meshed with the current vogue of Darwinism by emphasizing the development of social organisms, yet it substituted for biological determinism a more reasonable environmentalism. It set forth a hypothesis that demanded testing, thus assuring aspiring scholars subjects for investigation that would occupy them for years to come. It gave scholarly respectability to research into one of the most romantic phases of the national past. And, most important of all, it provided a more rational explanation of the national experience than those current at the time. Little wonder that historians who read Turner's essay were not only converted, but transformed into disciples, eager to spread his doctrines.

Most who did so—whether his students or others who came under his spell—were neophytes in the profession, whose voices were not to be heard until well into the 1900s. For immediate publicists, Turner had to rely on the few established scholars who were swayed by his arguments. Of these none was more important than Woodrow Wilson. Wilson felt a proprietary interest in the frontier thesis; he and Turner had talked of the significance of the West during their hours together at Johns Hopkins, and he had read with enthusiasm the early statement of the theory in the 1892 issue of *The Aegis* that Turner sent him. His chance to parade his new faith came when he was asked to review a traditional history of the United States by Goldwin Smith. Smith was absolutely wrong, wrote Wilson, in viewing American history through New England spectacles. The truly "American" part of America in colonial times was not New England, but the Middle Colonies; during the nineteenth century it shifted beyond the Appalachians, where "not only new settlements, but a new nation sprang up." There the people took on a unique character, and it was this transformation that was the key to understanding the nation's development. "That part of our history, therefore, which is most national is the history of the West."[3]

Turner was delighted, even though Wilson's statement of his thesis, published in *The Forum* in December 1893, appeared before his own paper on the significance of the frontier. He found it "very gratifying," and certain to encourage a more rational understanding of the past.[4] He had reason to be gratified soon again, for Woodrow Wilson was a prolific writer in the popular journals and from that time on used every opportunity to trumpet his young friend's views. His "Calendar of Great Americans," which appeared in *The Forum* a year later, did not include such notables as Alexander Hamilton, John Adams, and John C. Calhoun, because they had never imbibed the "true American spirit" by contact with the wilderness. Later in the decade, when Wilson was invited to address the New Jersey Historical Society on "The Course of

American History," and when he prepared an article for *The Forum* on "The Proper Perspective in American History," he did little more than summarize Turner's views and spice them with rhetorical embellishments that made them more palatable, if less accurate, than they were in their original form. Expansion was "the central and determining fact in our national history," breeding into the pioneers "a new temper, a new spirit of adventure, a new impatience of restraint, a new license of life." In the West, "social distinctions were stripped off, shown to be the mere cloaks and masks they were"; there all men were reduced to equality by the compelling powers of the wilderness.[5] Wilson was so dedicated a convert that he was willing to out-Turner Turner in preaching the frontier interpretation.

His was a lonely crusade at first, for not until after the turn of the century did the younger historians who had been converted to Turner's view begin to make their influence felt—and then largely in professional journals. To capture the public mind, the thesis had to have help from Turner himself, even though he was off on fresh scents and scattering his historical energies into documentary editing, diplomatic history, immigration history, and speculations on the nature of the historical process. This he recognized, and he was never reluctant to take up the cudgels in behalf of his own theories—whenever he could be attracted from his other investigations by a firm invitation with a monetary inducement attached. His writings on the frontier, which originated often as addresses or articles for popular magazines, did little to prove his concepts or add a firm foundation to his beliefs, but they did popularize the hypothesis as the efforts of no other propagandist did.

Reprintings of "The Significance of the Frontier in American History" helped. So long as that germinal essay was buried in the *Annual Report of the American Historical Association* and the *Proceedings of the State Historical Society of Wisconsin* it was available to few readers, but as interest in the theory quickened, so did the interest of other editors in giving Turner's essay wider circulation. Particularly pleasing to Turner was its appearance in 1899 in the *Fifth Yearbook of the Hebart Society*, a publication read by a sizable portion of the nation's schoolteachers. This required special attention; the original essay was refurbished with "Suggestions to Teachers" and a good deal of sound advice on how to approach American history from its "western side." "The spread of settled society into these continental wastelands," the schoolteachers were told, "and the free development of a democracy in relation to unoccupied lands, constitute the peculiar features of our national life."[6] Less to Turner's liking, but more to his amusement, was a request from A. M. Simmons, editor of the *International Socialist Review*, that he be allowed to share the essay with his readers. It was, Simmons assured him, "the first contribution of any significance to the industrial evolutionary treatment of American History." Turner was not sure that he should be used to further views with which he had little sympathy, but he gave his consent, and in 1905 the article appeared, accompanied by a laudatory note proclaiming it "the greatest contribution yet made in the application of the materialistic interpretation of history to American conditions."[7] Two years later it appeared again, this time in a highly respectable book of readings edited by the eminent economist Jesse C. Bullock.[8] This was only the first of a series of reprintings in academic source books that made "The Significance of the Frontier" a familiar phrase among historians, economists, geographers, and sociologists for a generation to come.

Reprintings were well enough, and welcome, but Turner was also concerned with broadening the appeal of his hypothesis among his fellow craftsmen. He found an ally in Henry Morse Stephens of Cornell, a pillar of the profession who had heard so much of Turner's ability that he made a special visit to Madison in 1895 to make sure that the rumors were sound. They were, he found; Turner was going to be heard from, and the sooner the better. Stephens had his chance a year later, when he helped to arrange the program for the meeting of the American Historical Association scheduled for December 1896. Would Turner read a paper reflecting his current research interests? Turner tried to step from the limelight in favor of Theodore Roosevelt or some other authority on the West, but Stephens stood his ground, and by the appointed time Turner had a paper ready on "The West as a Field for Historical Study." Having found it satisfactory in a trial run before the Wisconsin State Historical Society on December 10, he turned it over to Reuben Gold Thwaites for presentation in New York, being unable to afford the journey east himself.[9]

He submitted the paper with genuine apprehension, for he recognized that his subject was alien to the interests of the eastern historical establishment. "I hope," he wrote Morse Stephens, "you can manage to get up a discussion, to prevent the matter from falling with a dull thud."[10]

Turner might have spared himself his fears. A sizable audience listened attentively as his points were made: the role of the West in the election of 1896 proved that the nation's history could not be understood without "extended and earnest historical inquiry into the development of Western society"; this should center on the region between the Mississippi and the Rockies, where a new society was forming; it would be untainted by provincialism, for the West was only a laboratory where the emergence of new societies could be studied in microcosm, revealing truths pertinent to the total evolution of mankind. "The wilderness," Turner wrote, "has been the melting pot and the mold for American institutions; it has been a field for a new species of social life." It deserved study, and was a virgin field for investigators.

Such was the changing atmosphere of the times that this message, far less stirring than that delivered in 1893, was welcomed with enthusiasm. True, the praise of the commentators was directed more toward Turner than toward his ideas: Justin Winsor believed him the one person who had at last grasped the inner meaning of western history; Andrew C. McLaughlin urged the entire profession to accept his challenge and begin research on the story of the West; Woodrow Wilson hailed him as one of the few men in the profession who could combine breadth of comprehension with attention to minute details, who was not afraid of hard work, and who could illuminate his findings by fitting them into the general pattern of history. "Such men," Wilson insisted, "ought to be not only appreciated, but they ought to be loved and supported."[11] Turner was clearly making an impact on his colleagues, and, by doing so, he was widening interest in his frontier theory.

His opportunity to waken the broader public was not long in coming. The first chance was provided by Charles Kendall Adams, who served not only as president of the University of Wisconsin, but also as consultant for *Johnson's Universal Encyclopedia*. When Adams was called upon by the editors to recommend writers in American history, he passed over the shining lights in the field—Justin Winsor, John Bach McMaster, Albert Bushnell Hart—as too busy or too worn with work to lend their talents. Why not try a young man on his faculty named Turner—"a very successful teacher, precise in his methods, and comprehensive in his judgment"? Someone in the editorial office had the good sense to accept this sound advice, and Turner was invited to write an essay on "The Frontier." This was an admirable choice. Turner's article restated his thesis without the rhetorical embellishments and vague metaphors that had marred his original paper; it omitted, too, the extravagant claims for the frontier's influence. He began, as he should have begun his 1893 essay, with a definition of the "frontier"—"a belt of territory sparsely occupied by Indian traders, hunters, miners, ranchmen, backwoodsmen, and adventurers of all sorts"—then traced its movement westward. His estimate of its role in altering the American character was modest; the hardships of frontiering, he concluded, "conduced to an energetic and self-reliant spirit among the pioneers," underlay lawlessness in border communities, and played no small share in developing the practical ability and inventiveness of the American people.[12] This was a fair statement of the frontier theory with which few of Turner's later critics could quarrel.

Encyclopedia articles were well enough, but the emerging response to his ideas convinced Turner that they deserved a wider audience. Why not aim at the very top, and find a place in the columns of the *Atlantic Monthly*, then without peer in its influence on American intellectuals? This meant bringing his theories up to date and applying them to the current scene. Turner spent a good many months at the task, poring over books and articles and census returns to form a picture in his mind of the modern West—its ethnic composition, its industrial potential, its cultural aims. The notes that he jotted mirrored his interests: "West is a region of formation: as an area in US it is like the period of the Middle Ages in Europe," or "Western NY, Penn gave birth to Old Northwest. Old Northwest gave birth to prairie West." Eventually Turner merged the notes into a satisfactory essay that finally reached the desk of a subeditor of the *Atlantic Monthly*. The answer was couched in flattering terms, but firmly rejected the article as not sufficiently timely for the magazine's audience.[13] Turner had suffered his first (and one of his last) setbacks as an author.

He did not have to nurse his bruised ego long. Walter Hines Page, the distinguished editor of the *Atlantic Monthly*, knew of Turner and had read his 1893 essay (Turner had seen to that by sending him a copy). Why not direct this talented historian's writing skills into an article suited to his magazine's readers? Page thought first of an analysis of the contrast between traits of easterners and westerners, and Turner was willing to tackle the assignment, but the nomination of William

Jennings Bryan by the Democratic party in July 1896 changed the situation. Could Turner explain why a major party had embraced Populism, and how the nation should react to its present dilemma? This was a task made to order for Turner's interests, and he went to it with such enthusiasm that by July 29 he could telegraph that the article was on its way to Boston. "Your telegram is a pleasant western breeze indeed," Page assured him.[14] The September 1896 issue of the *Atlantic Monthly* appeared on schedule, with "The Problem of the West" in the place of honor.

The essay was as timely as Page desired, yet it scarcely mentioned Populism and attempted no analysis of current politics. "The problem of the West," Turner began, "is nothing less than the problem of American development." This was his springboard into a thorough discussion of the frontier's influence on traits and institutions: free lands bred into westerners boundless energy, faith in social equality, impatience of restraint, materialistic attitudes, belief in progress. The westerner differed from the easterner; he was "less conservative and less provincial, more adaptable and approachable, less a man of culture, more a man of action." These differences underlay the nation's current problems. The energy bred of expansion could not be stifled with the passing of the frontier. Turner saw demands for a vigorous foreign policy as the inevitable aftermath of the peopling of the continent; these would continue to project the nation's business into overseas markets and the nation's sovereignty over possessions throughout the Pacific. He foresaw equally important changes in domestic policy. By this time Turner realized, as he had not in 1893, that agrarian discontent transcended the demands of a few hotheads for cheap money; it portended a vast social revolution as the country adjusted to a closed-space existence. The outcome would be an extension of government authority in behalf of both the depressed farmers and the workers who could no longer escape to free land. Turner anticipated an era of storm and turbulence as the social revolution ran its course, but eventual benefits to all with the working out of improved social ideals and practices.

If Turner, and Walter Hines Page, had intended to subject public opinion to a form of shock treatment, they succeeded admirably. Only a few days after it appeared, Page wrote to Turner gleefully, "the newspapers here are at once taking up your article for discussion—very favorable."[15] Extracts and summaries dotted the press; the widely read magazine *Public Opinion* reprinted much of the essay, and others reproduced shorter extracts. Editorial writers approved or disapproved as their sectional prejudices dictated. To the *Chicago Tribune*, Turner's essay was a "profound and striking" vindication of the paper's contention that the half-dozen states that it defined as "Chicagoland" would lead the nation into its new era; to the *Boston Herald* and other New England papers, it was a terrifying warning that the center of gravity was shifting westward and that the wild-eyed radicals of the prairies could no longer be ignored.[16] Thanks to the nation's concern over Populism, Turner had won a wider audience for his theories than he could have done with a dozen historical articles.

He had also mightily pleased Walter Hines Page, who now wanted a whole series of articles to shake the national consciousness. For some time Page had been toying with a plan for discussions of the sectional characteristics of the Northeast, South, and Midwest; Turner was surely an ideal analyst for the Midwest. Would he do two or three articles that would explain that region to non-midwesterners? Turner wanted to, but he was filled with doubts. He laid them before Page in a twenty-one page letter. What was the Midwest? What elements should enter into its definition? Geographic? economic? psychological? Probably the best definition would combine physiographic analysis, groupings revealed by congressional votes, crop areas, literary output, and immigration statistics. To pursue this properly would require far more time than Page had suggested. If Page had been a realist, he would have dropped the matter at that point; an author who took twenty-one pages to define his subject—without success—would never be able to appraise the civilization of such a complex area as the Midwest. But Page was persistent. He did not want a complete painting, only a charcoal sketch. Why not simply write about the Old Northwest plus Minnesota? Turner was agreeable. Page was so sure of his man now that he advertised a series of articles by Turner, W. P. Trent, and A. F. Sanborn, to begin in the winter of 1897, articles that would explain the nation to itself as none had in the past.[17]

That was a false hope. Turner wrote one article—"Dominant Forces in Western Life"—which appeared in the April 1897 issue of the *Atlantic Monthly*, but this was hardly an earth-shaking contribution. It was obviously designed as the first of a series; Turner traced migration patterns into the Old Northwest, analyzed the contributions of migrants from the older sections and Europe, and showed their importance in economic development down to the present. These migration patterns he linked with Populism; the older types of farmers who led the way westward were turned back now by arid lands into an industrial society they neither understood nor liked. They could see, as could few others, the sharp contrast between frontier America as a land of equal opportunity, and non-frontier America where class stratification spelled an end to the equalitarian tradition. This, Turner held, was the basis of the revolt that nurtured Populism.

Once more editorial and reader reaction convinced Page that Turner was one of the most valuable assets in his stable of authors, and that he must be encouraged to complete the series that he had promised. Turner was agreeable, promising to have the next article in Boston by June 15, 1897, to appear in the August *Atlantic Monthly*. That date came and went, but no article arrived. A reminder from Page brought no assurance, only a confession that progress was slow, and that writing was a painful process to be avoided if possible. That was the last the *Atlantic Monthly* heard from Turner. Page sent him a "gentle reminder from a hungry editor" a few months later, but there was no response.[18] Turner wanted to publicize his frontier theory, and he was not averse to accepting the modest sums paid to contributors, but he was too much a perfectionist to do a slipshod survey of a complex subject.

A major analysis of the social evolution of one frontier area proved too much of a challenge, but Turner had sensed the national interest in his theories, and he was perfectly willing to seek more acclaim with less ambitious topics. He produced a spate of publications for respectable journals over the next years: "The Middle West" in the December 1901 *International Monthly*, "Contributions of the West to American Democracy" in the January 1903 *Atlantic Monthly*, "The Democratic Education of the Middle West" in the August 1903 *World's Work*. All were gracefully written, all preached the frontier thesis, and all developed aspects of the thesis that particularly interested Turner. They also, it must be confessed, drew heavily on his earlier essays, cataloguing over and over again the traits and institutions that stemmed from the pioneering experience, stressing the significance of free lands as a moulding influence, and striving for current interest by emphasizing that Populism resulted from the exhaustion "of the further free lands to which the ruined pioneer could turn."[19]

The influence of the frontier on American democracy interested Turner particularly, partly because it lent itself to popular treatment at a time when democratic traditions seemed threatened by the rise of big business and big government, partly because he could embroider that theme with a minimum amount of research and a maximum amount of speculation. The very existence of a haven of opportunity in the West, he wrote, prompted economic equality and opportunity, for men would not accept permanent subordination when a promised land of freedom was theirs for the taking. Free lands meant free opportunity, and this distinguished American democracy from the democracies that had preceded it. Its most distinctive feature was the social equality that it fostered; the freedom of the individual to rise in society outlawed European class distinctions and placed all men on a common plane. This conception had vitalized American democracy and brought it into sharp contrast with the democracies of Europe. The passing of free lands would force the United States to readjust its values, but would not doom its faith in human equality. A perennial optimist, Turner predicted that the West would work out a new organization of society that would conserve the democratic ideals of the nation; the western state universities were already pointing the way by substituting for free lands universal education as the key to individual progress. "Let us," he advised, "see to it that the ideals of the pioneer in his log cabin shall enlarge into the spiritual life of a democracy where civil power shall dominate and utilize individual achievement for the common good."[20] This was the democratic gospel according to Turner as his views on the impact of the frontier solidified.

There can be no question that Turner's enthusiasm and an urge to satisfy popular taste led him into exaggerations that he would have avoided if he had confined his writing to scholarly journals. He was even more inclined to cater to the public taste—and bend the truth in doing so—when he took to the lecture platform to explain the frontier thesis. His tendency to employ inexact words and indulge in extravagant metaphors became almost uncontrollable when he was charming an audience or infecting them with his own enthusiasm. He was at his best then, oratorically speaking, and few could resist. "To sit in quiet rapture under the spell of words as harmonious as poetry," exulted one hearer, "falling on the ear in clear and resonant tones, and then to feel, as the moments go by, the heart glow, the mind expand, the fires of aspiration burn because there is added to the beauty of form and expression, thoughts pulsating with life and strength and practical wisdom and moral earnestness—this was the experience of many and the privilege of all who sat in that favored audience."[21] Turner cast a spell; he also fell under that spell himself now and then, and was tempted into extravagances that he would have shunned in a less euphoric situation.

Unfortunately, he was offered ample opportunity to lecture. His fame as a speaker spread rapidly, prompting a series of invitations from universities, teachers' groups, ladies' clubs, and social gatherings; if Turner had been greedy enough to accept all of them, he could have added a healthy sum to his income with commencement and Phi Beta Kappa addresses alone. To catalogue his public appearances during these years would be tedious, but a sampling can indicate the diversity of his audiences: five lectures before the summer school of the University of Pennsylvania in 1894, one at a Lake Forest College ceremony the following April, addresses to the University Club of Chicago, the Northwestern Association of Johns Hopkins Alumni, and the Geographical Society of Chicago in 1897 and 1898, a mounting number of Phi Beta Kappa banquets beginning with one at Minnesota in 1900, talks before such patriotic groups as the Loyal Legion of Milwaukee (which heard a stirring lecture on "The Frontier Soldier") and the Sons of the American Revolution, others to enlighten the Collegiate Alumni Association of Milwaukee or to raise funds for the Portage public library, still more before such diversified teachers' groups as the Janesville public school instructors and the Milwaukee Teachers Historical Club, a number to neighboring colleges and local historical societies, and lectures galore to the students of his own university, where he was in perennial demand as an adornment for celebrations of the birthdays of George Washington and Abraham Lincoln. Lecturing was a profitable business —Turner's fees varied between $50 and $150 for a single performance and up to $500 for a university series—but it also offered an admirable opportunity to propagandize his views. Whatever the announced subject, the frontier could be—and was—glorified as a principal influence in American history, often with the same arguments and sometimes in the same language used in his 1893 essay; when pressed for time Turner was not above borrowing whole paragraphs from that essay, acting on the probably correct assumption that they would be unknown to his audience.[22]

His ability to extract excessive mileage from one theme was admirably illustrated when he was invited to deliver the Phi Beta Kappa address at the University of Kansas on June 7, 1909, for the modest fee of $50—he to pay his own travel expenses. Turner's subject—"Pioneer Ideals and the State University"—proved so acceptable to his audience that he used the same speech on a similar occasion at Iowa a week later, substituting a few sentences on the local scene for earlier remarks on popular sovereignty in Kansas. When called back to the lecture circuit in the spring of 1910, he pulled his manuscript from the files, polished a few phrases, and was ready to deliver it once more, as a Phi Beta Kappa address at the University of Michigan on May 14, as the baccalaureate address at the University of Wisconsin on June 21, and as the commencement address at Indiana University a day later.[23]

Unfortunately for his later reputation, this attempt to satisfy the popular taste did not generate his soundest historical thought. His "Pioneer Ideals and the State University" is a case in point. The theme was a familiar one: the role of the state university in adjusting pioneer traits to a frontierless society. Two traits particularly required alteration. The frontiersman's triumph over the wilderness made him impatient of any governmental restriction on his individual right to control his own economic affairs. With individualism went faith in domocracy, stemming from the abundance of opportunity in the West. "He had a passionate hatred for aristocracy, monopoly and social privilege; he believed in simplicity, economy and in the rule of the people." Now, as the frontier era ended, the West was increasingly dependent on the East; the westerner was surrendering his economic independence to captains of industry, who alone could provide the farm machinery, the transportation, and the agricultural techniques needed for survival. He must find a way of preserving individualism and democracy "without the former safety valve of abundant resources open to him who would take." This must be through governmental legislation. But governmental legislation depended on intelligent legislators and administrators; they must represent all the people rather than the "capitalistic classes" or the "proletariat"; they must be capable of dulling conflicts between classes and convincing the masses that pioneer ideals should be retained in the post-frontier world. These leaders could be educated only in the state universities, for there alone education was dedicated to social needs rather than the training of an elite.[24]

That lecture typified the many public speeches that he gave and the many popular essays he wrote during the years that his frontier thesis was gaining acceptance. In it he said little that was new; he had stressed democracy and individualism as frontier beliefs in 1893 and had pondered the effect of the frontier's closing at least as early as 1896. This lack of originality might be excused on the ground that his audience preferred challenging ideas to fresh interpretations, but Turner was more at fault when he pronounced unsubstantiated theories as indisputable facts. At the very beginning and end of his career he carefully avoided labeling the frontier as a "safety valve" for displaced eastern workers, even though that doctrine had been generally accepted for more than a century. Now, however, he wrote boldly of the West as a "safety valve of abundant resources." This was typical of the overstatement that marked his writing during these years of popularization. Throughout his essays and speeches were evidences of exaggeration, and a willingness to sacrifice historical accuracy for rhetorical effect.

The nature of Turner's scholarly interests made this inevitable, though regrettable. Had he possessed a less mercurial mind, he would have been content to spend his years testing aspects of his frontier thesis and presenting the results in learned papers and monographs. Instead, his inquisitiveness about *all* the past led him into a series of only faintly related quests: western state-making, the diplomacy of the post-Revolutionary period, immigration, and the regional studies that he was soon to publish on the Old West and colonial New England. While thus involved, he was besieged with invitations to write and speak about the frontier. These could not be refused, partly because he was eager to popularize his theories, partly because the monetary rewards were too tempting; a publisher's check for $150 or a fee of $100 for a commencement speech meant a great deal at a time when academic salaries seldom exceeded $3500 a year. Turner found himself in a position where he had to speak or write, but had nothing new to say.

Thus tempted, he could do one of two things. He could abandon his research to supply proof for his frontier thesis—the subject demanded by editors and college administrators—or he could expand and amplify the theories that he had already advanced, basing his expansion on speculation rather than investigation, and building an increasingly shaky structure on an untested foundation. Turner's temperament dictated that he follow the latter course. Rather than forsake his research, he chose to magnify some of the more popular themes mentioned in his 1893 essay—particularly the impact of pioneering on individualism, democracy, and nationalism—using logic and imagination rather than factual evidence to do so. Most of his writing during this period demonstrated how the frontier *should* have shaped the American character and American ideals, not how it *did* shape them, for he advanced not a shred of evidence to substantiate his statements. Unfortunately, Turner's frontiersmen did not always behave as he reasoned they should behave. Modern scholarship has demonstrated that social stratification did exist on frontiers, that racial disharmony in the West rivaled that in the East, that free land was seldom a sufficient magnet to draw displaced workers westward, and that political democracy was lacking in many communities. This Turner recognized or felt instinctively, as the reading notes he kept at the time indicated, but he realized also that his audiences wanted simplicity of statement rather than the carefully qualified admonitions of the professional historian.

That this was a deliberate choice was shown by the contrast between his popular and his professional writing during these years. The latter was of two sorts. On several occasions he was invited to address university audiences—he gave five lectures at the University of Michigan in 1903 on "The Beginnings of the West," two on "Western Society" and "Western Politics" at the University of Chicago in 1909, five on "Western Influences in American History" at the University of Pennsylvania in 1910. These were conventionally phrased, thoroughly unsensational, and distressingly factual, lacking completely the high-flown phrases and imaginative speculations of his public performances. They were also something less than appealing even to university audiences. He found the listeners at the University of Michigan momentarily terrified when he spread his mountain of notes on the table, but reported that they recovered and "stood it nobly." His hearers at Chicago sat patiently as he explained the role of the West in early state-making and politics, but they were hardly enthusiastic. At the University of Pennsylvania the small audience did not dwindle after the first lecture, as he feared it might, but even grew slightly—largely, Turner believed, because of the hostile reaction in the press to his statement that George

Washington was a western land-grabber. Yet the audience was tiny, at best, and made up largely of graduate students from the Midwest and his own friends or former students.[25] Turner was disappointed that he had not appealed to the native Philadelphians, but he had made it clear that he would not cheapen the quality of his scholarship when provided with the right audience.

He made this even clearer when he spoke before two professional organizations, addressing the Ohio Valley Historical Association in 1909 on "The Ohio Valley in the Making of the Nation," and the Mississippi Valley Historical Association a year later on "The Significance of the Mississippi Valley in American History." Both addresses rested on the theme that physiographic conditions altered intruding civilizations; these alterations Turner examined with care, basing his statements on a thorough understanding of the geography of both regions. Both addresses also transcended local history by demonstrating that political and diplomatic events originating in the interior river valleys influenced national politics and diplomacy. And both served as vehicles to reveal the transformations wrought in the American character by the influence of free land. "There has been," Turner told his Ohio audience, "no single element more influential in shaping American democracy and its ideals"; to his fellow craftsmen of the Mississippi Valley Historical Association he added that the true significance of the Mississippi Valley was the development there "by growth among free opportunities, of the conception of a vast democracy made up of mobile ascending individuals."[26] He might have exaggerated the influence of "free land" in the growth of American democracy, but with such restrained statements he was on far safer ground than he was in his public addresses.

Had Turner maintained scholarly standards in popularizing his frontier thesis as he did when speaking to professional colleagues, he would have escaped much of the abuse heaped on him by later critics. He was unquestionably at fault when he succumbed to extravagant rhetoric and unsubstantiated generalizations in magazine articles and public speeches, but so were his later attackers when they accepted these fantasies as his true beliefs. The true Turner could be found only in the *professional* articles and papers that were his major interest. These reveal a scholar well known to fellow historians of his own generation, but scarcely recognizable today—a Turner respected for his meticulous scholarship, the cautiousness of his generalizations, the depths of his research, and the freshness of his interpretations. These were the attributes that won him the respect of his peers, not the popular article in the *Atlantic Monthly* or the audience-gripping commencement address.

They also brought Frederick Jackson Turner to the attention of book publishers, and plunged him into a maelstrom of negotiations that burdened his conscience for years to come. These began when the energetic firm of Henry Holt & Company launched an "American Historical Series," under the direction of Charles Homer Haskins, to produce a series of textbooks stressing social and economic developments. Turner, Haskins told his employers, would be the ideal man for the volume on American history, and they were wise enough to act at once. They had, they assured him, discovered from his publications that he might be the coming man to write the needed college history of the United States. Turner was interested, but his cautious reply suggested that the book would be long a-borning. Writing another narrative history did not appeal to him, and the pathmaker's task was not to be taken lightly. How long a volume was wanted? One that resembled Green's *Short History of England*, or one like Gardiner's *Student History of England*? When must the manuscript be submitted? He had just turned down a similar proposal from the Chautauqua people because they would allow him only eight months. The publishers reassured him: Gardiner rather than Green should serve as the model, no definite deadline was necessary, and the book should contain a liberal supply of facts as well as generalizations. Could he "throw into shape the material for a chapter or two" to let them see what he planned?[27]

This exchange took place in the early spring of 1895. Nine months later a Holt representative who called on Turner was told that the sample chapters were well under way and would be submitted within a few weeks. More months fled by before another polite inquiry brought a less optimistic response. Turner was working on the outline and had a chapter or so under way, but his research was pressing, and he was beginning to wonder if he should not make his reputation as a scholar in a limited field before attempting such a broad treatment. The publisher replied that his position in the profession was already "pretty satisfactorily made," but this flattery had little effect. The more Turner pursued his studies, the more he realized that he was not ready for such a major task. "The subject is growing *as a whole*," he confessed, "and is just now in so formative a condition in my mind that I find it impossible to crystallize any particular portion." Not until he had re-explored all American history in the light of his frontier studies would he feel competent to begin writing. If Holt had another author in mind, they should forget that Turner existed.[28]

These modest disclaimers reveal Turner's perfectionism, but conceal the fact that another publisher was tempting him with a more attractive project. This was the brain-child of Professor W. P. Trent of the University of the South, a friend of Turner, a highly respected author in his day, and a consultant for the Macmillan Company. He suggested to Macmillan that they should enlist Turner, J. Franklin Jameson, Andrew C. McLaughlin, and other young scholars of the rising generation to prepare a series of books on the regions of the United States. Turner was the ideal candidate for the volume on the "Old West"—the area straddled by the Applachian Mountains. Trent had one word of caution that proved prophetic: "His university work and the pleasures of his delightful family life seem to me to interfere somewhat with his concentrating his energies in some one piece of work."[29] George P. Brett, the energetic president of the Macmillan Company, was undeterred. His invitation to Turner went off at once, and brought a predictable response. The subject was a fascinating one, crying for investigation, for the region did have unity and its history would reveal the evolution of the forces in American history to which the term "western" was applied. But a great deal of research was necessary, and Turner could devote his full time to the project only if sufficient inducements were offered. Brett was too canny a publisher to rise to this bait, but he did indicate that a contract would be forthcoming as soon as a portion of the manuscript was submitted. Turner was less than happy with this arrangement, but he promised that Macmillan would have the book within a year or eighteen months.[30]

Assuming this back-breaking task did not deter Turner from listening to the siren call of other publishers. He did decline an invitation, from G. P. Putnam's Sons, to write a two-volume history of the United States for their "Story of the Nations" series, but an editor from Macmillan's juvenile department, Kate Stephens, was more successful. She wanted a book of lively "pen stories" on the Lewis and Clark expedition, running to only 60,000 words, and carrying with it a $250 advance and royalties of 15 per cent after the first 1500 copies. Turner pricked up his ears when he heard those terms, for he knew the subject well and could have a manuscript in Miss Stephens's hands in less than two years.[31]

Rumors that their prospective author was straying from the fold stirred Henry Holt & Company into activity. If, their agent told Turner, he found the entire history of the United States too time-consuming, why not prepare the book in three sections which could eventually be merged into one? This was a suggestion tailored to Turner's temperament. He would be teaching the colonial and revolutionary periods next year, and could simply condense his lectures into the first section. His would be no narrative textbook; it would deal with the development of economic, political, and social institutions, and would show how these emerged from European conditions and were modified by the American environment. "If I am not wrong," he assured the publishers, "it is in this idea of unity and grasp of the essential phases of development, that most of our textbooks are defective." He would have the first section completed in eighteen months, the second a year later, and the third a year after that. What "inducements" did Holt offer to make the work pleasurable? Their terms were generous for that day: the usual royalty of 10 per cent and an advance of $500 delivered in three installments, one at the completion of each section of the book. Turner had a few more questions, but when these were answered, the contract was ready to be signed.[32]

Before Turner could seal the bargain, fate intervened in the person of George Brett of the Macmillan Company. In one of his periodic letters of inquiry on the progress of the book on the "Old West," Brett had the misfortune to mention a rumor that Turner was preparing a textbook; was this true, and if so, could Macmillan be the publisher? Turner, deep in his negotiations with Henry Holt & Company, was interested. Brett might have the volume if terms were satisfactory. What would Macmillan offer? The response was eye-opening: 10 per cent on the first 1000 copies, 12.5 per cent on the next 1500, and 15 per cent thereafter. Turner could also write the book in three installments if he wished, and might condense it into a grammar school textbook that would pay handsome royalties for very little effort.[33]

This was just the ammunition that Turner needed when Edward N. Bristol, Henry Holt's representative, called on him in Madison on October 18, 1897. He would prefer to publish with Macmillan, but would be governed by his prior commitment to Holt if they met Macmillan's terms. Poor Bristol had no choice. The contract, which Turner signed on November 9, provided for the same generous royalties offered by Macmillan, an advance of $1500 paid in three installments on delivery of the three parts of the manuscript, permission to publish a grammar school textbook and other works with other houses, and a commitment by Holt to print a high school textbook that Turner would distill from his larger work. "We want to go on record," the publishers wrote with feeling, "that we have never before risked as high terms on any educational work whatever, and unless there is a revolution in business methods, we do not expect to risk them again." In due course the contract for the high school text was signed, with royalties of 10 per cent on the first 2500 copies and 12.5 per cent thereafter.[34] The Holt editors, despite their complaints, were delighted, as well they might be. The only loser was George Brett. "It seems to us," he wrote bitterly, "that we have been somewhat unfairly treated in the matter of the publication of your College History, in that you have allowed another publisher to revise his offer for the publication of your book . . . without giving us a similar opportunity."[35]

Turner had proven himself a hard bargainer, and he was soon to exercise his skills again, for by the turn of the century he was recognized as the brightest rising star of the profession and fair game for all publishers. Ginn & Company offered him a contract for the grammar school textbook that he had discussed with Holt. A short time later A. C. McClurg Company proposed that Turner edit the works of a western traveler for a series they were planning; he was not interested, but he would like to write a book for them on "Western State-Making." They were agreeable, and another contract was signed, with the manuscript to be delivered within a year.[36] Houghton, Mifflin and Company fell into line next, for one of their editors was Walter Hines Page of the *Atlantic Monthly*, who was an admirer of Turner and determined to add him to that company's stable of authors. Page suggested several subjects—"The Conquest of the Continent," "The Disappearance of the Frontier," "The Extension of the Frontier"—but Turner warmed to none of them, despite Page's repeated assurance that such volumes could be dashed off in a few months from materials already at hand, and that they would assuredly be "the most popular and most influential books ever written in America." A whole generation of eager readers awaited the right book on the frontier, and Turner alone could write it. "The audience you have. They stand ready to give thanks, applause, and gate money." Turner could not resist such honeyed praise. He would prepare a volume, not on one of the suggested topics, but on "The Retreat of the Frontier," and have it ready for delivery within a year.[37]

During these negotiations Turner made the mistake of mentioning his growing interest in George Rogers Clark. Houghton, Mifflin just happened to have an ideal medium for a book on that frontier hero; their Riverside Biographical Series, made up of 25,000-word volumes designed for children, would welcome such a manuscript and pay suitable royalties. Turner not only agreed, he announced still another work well under way: a volume of essays, some published before, but all dealing with aspects of frontier expansion. Would Houghton, Mifflin be interested? They were, only mildly—but they would be happy to publish anything he wrote. So another bargain was sealed. The "Retreat of the Frontier" would be ready within a short time, the book of essays was almost completed, and the George Rogers Clark biography would be in their hands before the year was out.[38]

Turner had, in the five years before the end of the century, established a near world's record for contract signing. He had promised a grammar school textbook for Ginn & Company, high school and college textbooks for Henry Holt & Company, volumes on "The Old West" and the Lewis and Clark expedition for the Macmillan Company, a volume on "Western State-Making" for A. C. McClurg and Company, and a collection of essays on the frontier and books on "The Retreat of the Frontier" and George Rogers Clark for Houghton, Mifflin and Company. Neither the author nor the publishers realized that those contracts were to provide them all with years of embarrassment and discomfort.[39]

The publishers learned their lesson first. They began with reminders that the several manuscripts promised "within the year" were slightly overdue; Ginn & Company inquired politely about progress on the grammar school textbook in December 1901 and suggested that Turner no doubt found himself busier than expected; A. C. McClurg and Company used the same gentlemanly tone in pointing out that they had to have the outline and contents of the book on "Western State-Making" to prepare their 1902 catalogue. Houghton, Mifflin and Company was less gentle, insisting that the George Rogers Clark manuscript must be in their hands by February 1902 if it was to appear that year, and that they hoped to print the other two promised volumes a year later. That February deadline came and went, but no Clark biography arrived at the office of Houghton, Mifflin. Instead, the publisher's letters became increasingly insistent. Turner countered as best he could. "I am so much occupied by my various university duties that I cannot promise the book with certainty as early as you wish it, but I shall do my best to get it into your hands early in the spring," he assured the publishers in January 1902, "—probably in the first part of March or possibly the last of February."[40]

That was as unrealistic as all of Turner's promises. Once more a year passed, and once more the perennially optimistic Houghton, Mifflin editors made their regular inquiries. They very much hoped that the forthcoming volumes could be listed for 1903 publication. Turner was not sure that he could meet the January 1, 1903, deadline that they suggested, but the Clark biography would be in their hands by late February or early March, and the other two manuscripts would follow shortly. By June the editors were growing impatient; they were assured that the whole summer would be devoted to the volumes and that they would be told within a month when each would be completed. Apparently Turner wasted that summer on other tasks, for in October he reported that he was about to start work on both manuscripts, and would submit the Clark biography by the close of the semester. That was his last promise. By the spring of 1904 the Riverside Biographical Series, for which the book was intended, had been abandoned, and with it the last hope that Turner would write a life of George Rogers Clark.[41] Among his papers was a large file drawer packed with notes—hundreds and hundreds of them, drawn largely from manuscript sources—carrying the story of Clark's life only to 1783. Here was a monument to Turner's perfectionism no less than to his impracticality; he had labored endless hours gathering material for a 25,000-word book designed for children.[42]

There was still a spark of life in Houghton, Mifflin's ambitions. The projected volume of essays they were happy to forget, but Turner owed them "The Retreat of the Frontier," as they reminded him periodically. In November 1904, and again in the spring of 1905, they made the usual inquiries, to be told that he had been busy with other writing but would soon turn to the task. That was his last word of encouragement. Three years later Turner was reminded that when last he wrote them, the book was "in the last stages of composition," and asked whether those final pages had been written. There matters rested until 1924, when his retirement from teaching prompted a sly letter from the publishers, who hoped that his new leisure time would allow him to complete the volumes he had promised.[43]

Turner's unhappy relations with Houghton, Mifflin were duplicated with every publisher who cajoled him into a contract. In each instance the story was the same—increasingly demanding letters on the one hand, unrealistic promises on the other, and, finally, silence. Only Holt, lured by the prospect of two lucrative textbooks, continued to make life unpleasant for him—a story that belongs later in this volume. The result was tragedy not only for the publishers, but for Turner. As the months and years slipped by with promises unfulfilled, his mood varied from exuberant optimism to dark pessimism. Sometimes he was confident that he would find the leisure to finish—or even begin—the many books that he desperately wanted to write; then he would fill his letters with happy phrases about manuscripts "nearly finished" or promises that "sometime in the course of the year, I hope to get out a book on the subject."[44] At other times he would sink into despair as he realized that those books would never be written. In those dark periods he brooded long over letters from friends urging him to publish his views, lest others usurp them. Max Farrand warned him in 1905, "You are not getting sufficient credit for your ideas because you delay so long in publication. For goodness sake, hurry up and get out some of those western history books."[45]

This was salt in the wounds, but Turner simply could not respond. He was inclined, during these years, to blame his failure to write on the pressure of university duties; "it is not," he confessed, "an easy task to bring books to fruition when you are running a history department at the same time." His dream was a private income that would free him of all obligations save writing. "As my incomplete books—*unwritten* would be more to the point, loom up before my imaginative vision," wrote Turner to a friend, "I grow more and more covetous of the freedom from University work needed to bring them about." His solution was a best-selling "kindergarten history in words of one syllable, phonetically spelled!" that would shower him with riches.[46]

Actually Turner was as incapable of writing such a primer as he was the textbooks promised to Ginn and Holt. He was a perfectionist by nature and a dawdler by inclination, unable to endure the sustained effort needed to produce a major volume and unwilling to place on record the imperfect account demanded by any broad subject. Not a sentence could be written until every statement it contained had been tested, and repeatedly tested, by reference to the sources. Turner was a glutton for detail and a champion of accuracy, and no man of such temperament could ever complete a textbook. While pleading lack of time to finish his biography of George Rogers Clark, he was writing a whole series of articles reinterpreting the diplomatic history of the Mississippi Valley; while begging for a few hours to work on his textbooks, he was devoting months of patient research to his editorial tasks for the National Historical Manuscripts Commission. Turner's problem was not lack of time, but lack of inclination to undertake a task that he could not complete to perfection.

This doomed any chances that his publishing contracts would be fulfilled, but the death blow to the hopes of the publishers was a new historical interest that obsessed Turner during the opening years of the century. Through his frontier and diplomatic studies he gradually became aware of the fact that the United States was not one nation during its early years, but a complex of regional groupings, or "sections." Sectionalism, no less than expansion, held the key to understanding the nation's past. Once Turner awakened to this realization, he was a lost man. He had found a new subject, one of infinite complexity, that would require a lifetime of investigation for complete understanding. From the day that he awakened to the significance of the section, the frontier was of secondary importance in his hierarchy of enthusiasms. Turner was off to blaze a new trail, one that was to monopolize his attention and affection for the rest of his days.

IX

The Genesis of the
Sectional Concept

1893-1910

FREDERICK JACKSON TURNER rode to fame—and the publishing contracts that plagued his remaining years—on the coattails of the frontier thesis, but even before that controversial theory gained full acceptance he had moved on to a new interest. This was a typical about-face. Others might find satisfaction in tracing migration patterns into the Old Northwest or studying the evolution of democracy in the constitutions of western states, but not Turner. Such investigations, essential though they were to the proof of his hypothesis, posed few intellectual problems. He required new challenges, new interpretations of the American past, new excitements to stir the mind. And he found them all in the study of sectionalism.

His frontier theories led him naturally into this fascinating topic. Westward migration, he knew, spread population across a series of differing physiographic provinces. In each, a distinctive social order emerged; no expert knowledge was needed to realize that New England differed from the South Atlantic states, or the Old Northwest from the lower Mississippi Valley. What caused these differences? Did soils, climate, topography, and precipitation shape the economic, social, and cultural behavior that gave the region its unique character? Or were environmental pressures modified by the ethnic blendings that differed so markedly from section to section? How did the unique combination of natural and human forces that evolved in each section alter political attitudes and cultural expression? Most important of all, how could these sections, each comparable to a European nation, cooperate to achieve national harmony when their differences were so obvious? These were challenging questions indeed. If Turner could determine how sectional compromises shaped the nation's legislative history, how sectional pressures acted as counterweights to excessive nationalism, how internal conflicts were converted from a class to a regional basis, he would have a better understanding of American history. He was on the scent of a subject that made even the frontier seem insignificant.

Nor was it a subject that Turner could possibly ignore. Through his lifetime his concern was not with one facet of American history, but with *all* American history. "I was," he later recalled as he remembered this period of his life, "trying to see it as a whole—on its institutional, social, economic and political side." The frontier was only a part of the past, but the interplay of the sections held clues that would illuminate every aspect, and this was Turner's primary concern. Then, too, he saw history as a spotlight on the present, principally useful for guiding mankind along the road to the future. Sectional forces, he believed, were shaping national policy at the turn of the century (and who could believe otherwise, as rural discontent, urban unrest, and free silver divided the United States into battling regions?); those forces could be understood and modern problems solved only by understanding their role in the past. To Turner the whole national spirit—"Uncle Sam's psychology," he called it—was a product of a federation of sections, and could be diagnosed only by an analysis of how sections were formed and how they interacted.[1] This was an irresistible challenge. "I was," he wrote simply, "forced to undertake a survey of the Regions in American history."[2]

Turner's intellectual curiosity had much to do with exciting his interest in sectionalism, but so did another influence of which he was totally unaware. New ideas, new concepts, new approaches, always rest on a foundation of fact and theory produced by prior investigators, and they emerge because the intellectual atmosphere is favorable to their appearance. Turner lived at a time when scholars throughout the western world were awakening to the significance of regional studies, and when statistical and cartographic techniques had become sufficiently developed to allow them to be pursued scientifically.

Stress on regionalism came naturally to early twentieth-century geographers, who viewed the environment as all-powerful. Sectional studies originated in Europe, where the influence of Friedrich Ratzel, the high priest of environmentalism, was especially strong, particularly after 1897, when he published his influential book, *Political Geography*. This was an eye-opening volume, advancing detailed evidence to show that the growth and character of political units was determined by their position on the earth's surface, their size, the nature of their boundaries, and their distance from oceans.[3] Politics, Ratzel claimed, could be explained only by an analysis of the geographic factors that shaped the attitudes and desires of the people of any natural region. This was an extreme statement, and one to which Turner never subscribed, but it does show the extent to which regional forces were recognized by intelligent men of that day.

Nor was Ratzel alone, for everywhere geographers were focusing on the regions of the world, seeking in them keys to man's economic, social, and political behavior. In France the dominant figure in geographic circles was Vidal de la Blache, whose classic work, *Tableu de la Géographie de la France* (1903), analyzed the regions into which the nation was divided and showed how soils and water supply determined the behavior of each. In England, scholars conducted germinal studies of geographic provinces, or wrote learned articles, such as one on "The Major Natural Regions of the World," by A. J. Herbertson. In the United States, the pioneer investigator of geographic sectionalism was William Morris Davis of Harvard University, who argued so effectively for regional analysis that by the close of the 1890s the American Geographical Society was filling its publications with physiographic data rather than accounts of Arctic exploration.[4] When Turner began his sectional investigations, he was only responding to a climate of opinion that was affecting all scholarship.

Turner was also benefitting from progress in statistical and cartographic techniques that made such investigations possible. Just at this time, soil geography was emerging as a respected discipline; E. W. Hilgard, its pioneer, published his "A Report on the Relation of Soil to Climate" in a bulletin of the Department of Agriculture in 1892. This study was so revealing that two years later the department began a long-term project of mapping the soils of the entire United States. Here were data galore for the sectional historians, for differences in soils and vegetation would explain regional differences in agricultural production.[5] When Turner, in his later studies, equated cultural progress with limestone soil belts, he was building on knowledge supplied him by soil geographers.

He was equally indebted to the statistical cartographers, who taught him how to correlate regional data in graphic form. In this the high water mark was the publication in 1883 of *Scribner's Statistical Atlas of the United States*, ably edited by Fletcher W. Hewes and Henry Gannett. Turner found in this remarkable volume not only the vivid population maps that brought home to him the course of westward expansion, but a number of others that showed county-by county variations in social, economic, and political behavior. One series illustrated the percentage strength of the leading candidate in all presidential elections; another, that of every candidate, by county, in the election of 1880. Turner had only to compare these with soil maps to recognize that a correlation did exist between better soils and political conservatism. Nor did he have to depend on *Scribner's Atlas* alone, for its example was followed in a number of other studies. *Appleton's Annual Cyclopedia* for 1888 printed a map showing the leading presidential candidate's plurality in each county for the period 1872-88; the 1896 edition performed the same service for the McKinley-Bryan contest.[6] When Turner began his sectional studies, the tools needed to translate complex relationships between political, economic, and social behavior into understandable graphic form were at hand.

Census experts came to Turner's aid in still another way. Since the late eighteenth century, when Jedidiah Morse wrote of the "Grand Divisions of the United States" in his pioneering *American Geography*, scholars had recognized that regions, or sections, divided the nation, but those sections had never been exactly defined, nor had their significance been appraised. Not until the publication of *Scribner's Statistical Atlas* were the sections subjected to serious analysis; in a suggestive essay in that volume, "The Natural Grouping of the States," Henry Gannett proposed five divisions: North Atlantic, South Atlantic, North Central, South Central, and West. Each, he found, had distinctive characteristics: thus, the North Atlantic and North Central regions contained 85 per cent of the foreign-born and most of the urban units, the South Atlantic and South Central 90.5 per cent of all Negroes. Gannett's groupings were unsophisticated and his findings unspectacular, but, in a day when the nation conceived of sectionalism in terms of

"North" and "South" alone, he had taken a long step forward. The theoretical foundation was laid on which Turner was to build.

He began the speculations that were to merge into his sectional studies early in his academic career. As an undergraduate he had awakened to the importance of regional forces when Professor William Francis Allen's *History Topics for the Use of High Schools and Colleges* taught him something of the differences between New England and the Old Northwest. As a graduate student at Johns Hopkins, living in a southern environment heightened his awareness of regional differences, while his conversations with Woodrow Wilson deepened his understanding of regional problems. "My studies of sectionalism," he told a friend a few years later, "in the sense of Western, Middle, Southern and New England, rather than of North and South alone, began in that same time."[7] Turner was sufficiently enthralled to prepare a six-page memorandum on "Sectionalization and Nationalization," which he planned to read to Wilson, then use as the basis for one or two articles. All American history, he reasoned, was a struggle between two tendencies—sectionalizing and nationalizing—with the latter gradually prevailing as unifying forces triumphed over those of division. Turner listed those forces: immigration, the navy, free trade agitation, arbitration, growth of commerce, world's fairs, and travel.[8] The projected article was never written, but he was even at this tender academic age thinking of sectionalism as something more than the North-South division that climaxed in the Civil War.

Turner's concern with regional problems in his days as a student produced no tradition-shattering results, but they did spark an interest that he continued to nurture during his early teaching career. He listened intently when one of Allen's students, Humphrey Desmond, addressed the Wisconsin Academy of Sciences, Arts and Letters on "The Sectional Feature in American Politics," then read, annotated, and heavily underlined the published version of the talk, especially the part that advanced the heretical doctrine that the federal Constitution was "a treaty of alliance between two great sections."[9] He copied into his notes occasional phrases that struck his fancy: one, from a volume on *American Constitutional Law*, brought home the fact that "the states had for the most part no boundaries."[10] He eagerly read the essay by

John W. Powell on "Physiographic Regions of the United States" when it appeared in 1896 in a publication of the National Geographic Society. As he did so, Turner recognized its importance, for Powell's analysis was far more sophisticated than any he had read. Powell drew no rigid boundaries, recognizing that regions merged with slow gradations one into the other, but he did distinguish sectional groupings that were more sophisticated than those of earlier geographers, ranging from the "Atlantic Plain," "Piedmont Plateau," and "Appalachian Ranges" on the east to the "Columbia Plateau," and "Basin Ranges," and "Pacific Mountains" on the west.[11] Although excessively detailed, Powell's divisions lent themselves to the type of analysis that Turner was to undertake, and he added them to his vocabulary at once.

But he did this only with variations, for he was far from satisfied. The problem, as he saw it, was to define the "*natural* economic-social-political groups" that formed each section. Such a definition must ignore state lines, but it must also recognize the wide variety of forces that underlay regional psychology. Geographic influences were important, but by no means determinative. Also to be considered were economic activities; congressional votes, which would show how representatives grouped themselves; political behavior, as revealed in state elections; newspaper attitudes; literary output; ethnic composition; and the historical background. Turner was too aware of the nature of sectional divisions in the West of the 1890s to be seduced by a purely geographic explanation. Geographers might merge the area between the Mississippi and the Rockies into the "Plains," but farmers in western Kansas and Nebraska behaved differently from farmers in eastern Kansas and Nebraska. The western farmers raised "more hell than corn," and would continue to do so until a social structure was devised that was suited to an arid climate where irrigation was the way of life and frontier individualism was sublimated to the needs of society.[12] No single mode of analysis would explain western behavior—or the regional conflicts of the past. Sections must be defined in geographic, economic, political, cultural, and psychological terms.

This was a major assignment. Simply to define the regions whose interaction explained the past required years of patient research and analysis. It also demanded recognition of the complexity of forces shaping sectional attitudes, for Turner realized that environmental and ethnic influences blended to create the unique characteristics of each region, and that these characteristics manifested themselves not only in political and economic behavior, but in literature and the arts, education, and every facet of social life. Many years later Turner recalled the problems that he faced in 1895 and 1896, when he began his studies: "I had to have some knowledge of American physiography; I had to know something of demography as well; and I had to recognize that these changes and interrelations affected American social life and characteristics in general: its literature, art, religion, ideals."[13] He had to accomplish all this, moreover, when his energy was directed into the diplomatic studies that were his principal concern, and when sectionalism was more a hobby than a vocation.

Yet it was a hobby that was too fascinating to be shelved, and during the late 1890s Turner launched a systematic program to prepare himself for the investigations he was already considering. This took two forms. One was self-education; he read as widely as he could (though there were few publications on sectionalism), taking notes, analyzing one region after another in his search for the features that distinguished each, learning a great deal about the ice sheets that had transformed North America during the glacial era, and phrasing definitions that approached the exactness he sought. One that impressed him particularly was borrowed from a Phi Beta Kappa address on "Provincialism," given by Josiah Royce: "any one part of a national domain which is, geographically and socially, sufficiently unified to have a true consciousness of its own unity, to feel a pride in its own ideals and customs, and to possess a sense of its distinction from other parts of the country."[14] These were valuable tidbits, but haphazard reading was not enough for Turner. In the fall of 1898 he enrolled in a seminar on physiography given by his colleague Charles R. Van Hise, and he attended regularly through the term as that eminent geologist described the "Atlantic Coastal Plain," the "Piedmont Upland," the "Gulf Plains," and other provinces in intimate detail.[15]

At the same time, Turner was enlisting allies among his students and fellow historians. As early as the spring of 1895 he directed his senior seminar into the study of regionalism, assigning such topics as sectional groupings in colonial times, sectionalism in the Revolutionary period, and evidence of sectionalism in votes on the tariff, internal improvements, and other major issues.[16] Seniors were also encouraged to prepare honors theses on regional topics, or to study voting behavior in presidential elections in terms of sectional influences. One capable undergraduate analyzed members of the Wisconsin state legislature in 1850, 1860, and 1870 according to place of birth, occupation, wealth, and party, then classified the legislators by their voting records on important issues. These pioneer ventures into statistical techniques that were needed to comprehend regional voting patterns—the study of "Demagogics," Turner called it—were ground-breaking studies which cast more light on the principles and methods of political leadership than did any others then under way.[17] Yet they were peripheral to his principal interest in diplomatic history, generated by intellectual curiosity rather than any practical objective.

The only immediate impact of Turner's mounting interest in sectionalism was on the course offerings of his department. In 1896 he encouraged his colleague, Orin G. Libby, to launch a new offering on "American Sectionalism," which dealt with "the geographical distribution of political parties, with special reference to votes in Congress and in the state legislatures." At the same time, Turner's own lectures in his "History of the West" took on more and more of a regional tint. A detailed physiographic map was his most essential tool as he carefully explained each detail. "Notice this map of southeastern Pennsylvania," he told his students. "You see the Susquehanna River and the pink portion, which is the limestone flooring of the Great Valley. . . . Now notice beyond the Great Valley those canoe-shaped regions which constitute the coves or inter-montane valleys beyond. See how the mountains spread in thickly, and how inaccessible to settlement they are."[18] He repeated this stiff dose of geography for each section, as he traced settlement westward. The United States, he told his students over and over again, was nothing more than a "congeries of geographic regions," each as large as a European nation, and American history the story of "the outcome of the interaction of the various sections."[19] Here was a neglected key to understanding the nation's past, and the more Turner read and speculated, the more he became convinced that it alone would unlock secrets that had remained hidden from earlier scholars.

His mounting conviction was shown when he was asked to revise his essay on "The Significance of the Frontier in American History" for publication by the National Hebart Society in 1899. The westward movement was still the all-important fact of American history, but

Turner saw it now as a means of occupying successive physiographic areas, "economically and socially comparable to nations of the old world." "We must," he wrote, "observe how these areas affected the life of the immigrants from the older sections and from Europe." Viewed from this perspective, the study of the frontier became "the fascinating examination of the successive evolution of peculiar economic and social countries, or provinces, each with its own contributions, and individuality."[20] By the turn of the century Turner was convinced that the history of the United States had to be rewritten to reveal the role of sections. He was too absorbed in his diplomatic studies to turn to the task at once, but only an excuse was needed to set him off on the new scent.

This was provided by an ambitious scheme launched by the American Historical Association in 1899. The time was ripe, that body decided, for a multivolume collaborative history of the United States, built on the findings of the "Scientific School" then in vogue. Turner found himself involved as the sole western member of the committee named to plan the series, even though he was determined not to commit himself as an author; he had a work of his own on the stocks—or at least the lumber for one—as well as an abundance of contracts to fulfill, and would never add another.[21] In this laudable determination he reckoned without Albert Bushnell Hart, chairman of the planning committee and eventual editor of the series. Hart wanted Turner on his list, and would move mountains to have him. The stage was set for a battle of wills that could have only one outcome.

One by one Hart played his trump cards. Harper & Brothers had been signed as publishers; that prestigious firm would add glory to the series. A committee of the State Historical Society of Wisconsin was asked to advise on the proper treatment of the West—with Turner a member and principal consultant. The official invitation, mailed on January 2, 1902, was properly baited with flattery: "Yours was one of the first names to occur to my mind as fundamental in any scheme of cooperative scholarship in American history." Would Turner agree to produce a volume—any volume that he wanted to write—for a fee of $1500, half to be paid on delivery of the manuscript? Turner disliked the terms and preferred a royalty arrangement; he also had to consult his other publishers, long-suffering already, but he was interested.[22] This was enough to bring Hart to Madison, to press his case personally with Turner and with Reuben Gold Thwaites, whom he also wanted. He pleaded his cause well; no other historian was so well equipped to reveal the impact of the frontier on American life and to demonstrate the significance of sectional interplay. Turner had only to pick the period best suited to his purpose. This was too tempting to be dismissed. "I am," Turner wrote the next day, "praying not to be led into temptation, and yet there is one field which he proposes to me which may possibly lead to my participation."[23]

Hart had all but landed his victim, and had only to hit upon the right formula to bring him into the net. He found it soon after his return to Cambridge. The larger projects that Turner had undertaken—books that would fit his frontier theory into the broad framework of American history—would take years to complete. Why not interrupt his labors for the brief time needed to dash off a volume applying his concepts to a short span of history? "What I should like from you," Hart wrote, "is not a resumé of the whole result of your studies on western history, but one ship in my squadron, which shall fairly represent your ship yard." A book on the period from 1819 to 1829 would serve as a case study of the importance of expansion and sectionalism; it would also reveal the rise of the western spirit culminating in the election of Andrew Jackson. This combination of temptations was more than Turner could resist. He agreed to add one more contract to the formidable list already signed. He would use the volume to work out his ideas "with respect to the importance of treating American history from the point of view of the existence of great provinces, irrespective of state lines, which have served to determine the development of American conditions."[24]

To describe such a book was one thing; to accomplish the mountains of research and writing necessary was quite another. Turner was sufficiently aware of his own weaknesses to realize that he could stick to his task only by using his classroom as a workshop, where daily assignments would have to be performed. Beginning with the fall of 1903, his "History of the West" took on a new complexion; it was concerned not only with expansion, but also with the "economic, political and social aspects of the occupation of the various physiographic provinces," while his seminar dealt with the administration of James Monroe. A year later, when still deep in research, Turner went so far as to offer a year-long course on the United States from 1816 to 1837, repeating it the year following. Even within this narrow time span, he spent so much time discussing the Missouri Compromise, the election of 1820, the foreign relations of the administrations of Monroe and John Quincy Adams, and the conflict over tariffs and internal improvements before 1829, that he was half way through the second semester before he reached the presidency of Andrew Jackson.[25] Here was concentration with a vengeance, but a concentration that forced Turner to keep his nose to the grindstone.

And the noses of others as well. His students were willing victims, particularly those in his seminars who were forced to sublimate their own interests to study details of the Monroe era, or analyze roll-call votes in Congress for sectional groupings, or list the greats and near-greats of the 1819-29 period with biographical information that Turner might find useful. Select graduate students were pressed into service, several to prepare model tables of contents for a "Proposed History of the United States, 1819-1829," others to produce theses on such topics as "Internal Improvements in the United States during Monroe's Administrations," and "Some Political Aspects of the Press between 1816 and 1830." Solon J. Buck, later to become a prominent historian, was assigned the unenviable task of listing all iron manufacturing plants in Pennsylvania for the decade of the 1820s, as a basis for testing regional opinion on the tariff—a chore only slightly less challenging than those of students made to prepare biographical sketches of all congressmen for the period.[26] During the three years Turner's book was under way, his graduate students received a baptism of fire they never forgot.

Turner's own efforts dwarfed theirs. He spent every spare hour in the State Historical Society library, supervising copyists who transcribed hundreds of items from congressional speeches, newspapers, and *Niles' Register*, or filling sheet after sheet of five-by-eight notepaper with information on internal improvements, the tariff, land policy, foreign affairs, roll-call votes—everything that bore on the sectional alignments of the 1820s. Occasionally Turner tried to bring order to this chaos by using a trial outline: one, which he made in October 1904, listed seventeen chapters and included such topics as "Survey of the Decade in Terms of Literature, Reform, Education, Labor, and American Ideas"; another, done a year later, discarded such peripheral topics to concentrate on the sectional problem in manageable form.[27] Occasionally, too, he was forced to compress portions of his findings into rough drafts, as he did when he delivered five lectures at the University of Michigan that spring on "American Development in the Decade 1820-1830."[28]

If Turner had followed his own inclinations, he would have gone on forever with the research that he loved, but Albert Bushnell Hart had other ideas. His first warning was issued in the fall of 1904; the twenty-odd volumes of the *American Nation* series were being printed in lots of five, and Turner's was in the lot to be published in the autumn of 1905. That meant his maps had to be submitted at once for proper preparation. "At once" to Turner meant six months later, and then only after a wordy exchange over the number to be included; he wanted fifteen, the publishers allowed only nine, and eleven were finally agreed upon. The manuscript proved harder to extract. By July 1905, not a line had reached Cambridge, and Hart was growing desperate. He had to have it by August, he warned; "your volume is becoming the needle's eye for the series." Twice the delivery date had been extended, but that was the end. Turner, tense and overwrought, struck back blindly, accusing Hart of responsibility for the delay, much to that innocent victim's amazement. His assurances smoothed the troubled waters, but he saw that Turner was near the breaking point and had to have some relief. If the chapters already completed could be sent at once, the remainder need not arrive until the end of September. This would mean no vacation, "but I do not see why young fellows like you need vacations."[29]

This was the incentive Turner needed, and all that late summer and fall he worked furiously, rising with the sun, taking a brief dip in Lake Mendota, fishing for pickerel between five and six o'clock, then ascending to the attic study at 629 Frances Street to begin work. There his secretary, a capable student named Merrill H. Crissey, awaited him, and dictation began. Turner paced the floor as he talked, often chewing an unlighted cigar and pausing now and then to consult his notes. When tensions grew too great, or the apt phrase escaped him, or a difficult problem in interpretation proved unsolvable, he would leave the room to pace along the shores of the lake, smoking furiously.[30] So the writing went on, as page followed page and the pile of completed manuscript grew larger. "I am 'pegging away' at my volume for the Hart series," he wrote a friend, "and have a profound respect for a man who has a volume behind him."[31]

By mid-August the introduction and three chapters were on their way to Cambridge, leaving Turner so exhausted that he pleaded with Hart for a little time off to recuperate. This was grudgingly granted; "I hope that you will take the rest, and that the remainder of the book will go the quicker for it." Hart's concern was genuine, for one look at the completed chapters convinced him that he was midwifing a master-piece. Paragraphs were too long, quotations over-abundant, and the whole so bulky that it far exceeded the publisher's space limitations, but these were minor faults when contrasted with the excellence of the product. "No volume which has so far gone through my hands," he assured Turner, "will do more to set in people's minds right notions of how things actually came about."[32] Another chapter, that on the "Far West," which reached him in early September, only confirmed these impressions. Turner's words were worth waiting for.

But not for too long. By early October Hart was cracking the whip once more. All other volumes for the third set of five books were completed; unless Turner's was added in time to go to press by December the publishers stood to lose a healthy sum. These threats produced three more chapters by the end of October and the promise of the remainder by mid-November, a date that Hart reluctantly accepted. Mid-November came, and still no book. "I have been looking out of the window for a week hoping to see the expressman," he wrote on November 21. He did not have to wait much longer. On December 7, 1905, Turner wrote exultantly to his wife: "Finished my rough draft of the last chapter today. Ecco! Selah! Voila! Whoopla! I may drink up the last bottle of Nucleus Club's champagne when I revise the chapter and actually post it." That drink was soon forthcoming, for on December 11 the entire manuscript was in Hart's hands.[33]

If Turner drank that champagne, the celebration was premature, for both his labors and Hart's were far from over. His manuscript was grossly oversized. "I see nothing for it," Hart wrote as he viewed the vast pile of pages on his table, "but to reduce the manuscript to pro-crustean dimensions." Nor was size the only problem. The whole book had to be reviewed to avoid repetition and bring events into consecu-tive order, two chapters lacked point and needed sharpening, dates had to be added throughout to orient the reader, footnotes were too many and too long, the maps were hopelessly overdetailed, transitions had to be supplied and choppy sentences combined. All of this had to be accomplished within two weeks, for January 1, 1906, was the absolute deadline. Thus Hart laid down the law, then tempered his judgment with the words of praise that would inspire Turner to take up his blue pencil: "This piece of work will enhance the large reputation which you enjoy for scholarship and for insight. It is a suggestive, revealing kind of book."[34]

Turner glowed, and accepted the criticism with good grace. He set to work at once, with two stenographers at his side, and, miraculously, completed the revisions on time. Hart was delighted; the manuscript was still too long, but it was publishable if the bibliographical essay could be kept to 3000 words. On January 16 it was shipped to the publishers, and three days later the first payment of $750 reached Madison. If Hart assumed that he was shifting responsibility to Harper & Brothers when he mailed them the manuscript, he was badly mistaken. Galley proofs began to arrive within a few days, and when Turner saw them he was inspired to a new burst of perfectionism. Here was a chance to make all the changes he had longed to make in his manuscript! By February 8 Hart was inquiring anxiously when the first galleys would be returned, pointing out that the whole printing schedule hung in the balance, but not until more than a month later did Turner reluctantly relinquish the last. This taught Hart a lesson. When Turner submitted a bibliographical essay of 6000 words, just double the space allotted him, Hart made the needed deletions himself and did not even send the proofs to the author.[35]

The product was worth the ordeal, and both men were highly pleased. Each recognized the debt owed the other. "One thing I do owe to Hart," Turner confessed to Max Farrand, "and that is the steadfast way he has worked the reel and finally landed the MS. It is a poor sucker instead of a trout, but it fought like the devil against coming to the landing net." Hart, on his part, took pardonable pride in extracting the manuscript from its perfectionist author. "It ought to be carved on my tombstone," he wrote many years later, "that I was the only man in the world that secured what might be classed an adequate volume from Turner."[36] So he had, and revealed himself as a model editor by doing so. No other succeeded, and while Hart did not rely on the technique that rumor ascribed to him—sending so many collect telegrams that Turner was forced to finish the book to avoid bankruptcy—he did display skills in angling that any might envy.

Well might both be proud, for the *Rise of the New West, 1819–1829* was a remarkable volume for its day. Turner's thesis was radically new: beneath the surface calm of the "Era of Good Feeling" were arising disruptive issues and party formations stemming from sectional divisions that were to effect basic changes in the structure of society. To reveal these, he first analyzed the economic and social life of the major sections—New England, the Middle States, the South, the West, and the Far West—in a series of chapters that were unique in their day and have lost little of their charm since. Having set the stage, he described the principal events of the decade, ranging from the Panic of 1819 and the Missouri Compromise through the nullification controversy that signaled the surfacing of the sectional conflict. Yet he wrote no narrative history in the traditional sense. Each episode was analyzed in terms of regional forces, each individual viewed as a symbol of his own section, each congressional act appraised against the sectional divisions that accounted for its success or failure. "I have," Turner wrote, "kept before myself the importance of regarding American development as the outcome of economic and social as well as political forces."[37] This was his purpose, and he succeeded so admirably that the *Rise of the New West* was destined to be read long after most of the volumes in the *American Nation* series were forgotten.

Fortunately, that generation agreed with posterity's judgment. Professional journals were universal in their praise; some few reviewers even understood Turner's purpose, and they pointed out that the history of the nation would have to be rewritten to incorporate the sectional theme. Popular magazines and newspapers echoed this endorsement. "No more profound study of any period of American history has been written," declared *The Independent*, a sentiment that was repeated in *The Nation*, *The Literary Digest*, and every major opinion-making journal.[38] Friends and even distant acquaintances joined in the chorus of approval; the months of agonizing labor must have seemed worth while to Turner as he read James Ford Rhodes's judgment, that the book was "a right grand piece of work," or harkened to his good friend Charles R. Van Hise, who predicted that now other books would follow explaining "the great forces which have moulded the nation, and which will still further mould it in the future."[39]

The publishing world was Turner's now, and the future one of financial security. He had proven himself as an author; now he would complete the college and high school textbooks for Henry Holt & Company, and the grammar school text for Ginn & Company, all within the next year or two. Those volumes would reward him so handsomely that he could abandon teaching for the scholarly researches that were his true passion. So Turner dreamed that spring of 1905 as he labored to complete his *Rise of the New West.*

If those dreams were to come true, he had to have both assistance and leisure, and what was more logical than that this be provided by the publishers who would benefit from his labors? Letters of inquiry to Holt and Ginn brought encouraging responses. Holt felt that he should concentrate on the high school textbook first of all, but had no objections if he worked on the grammar school volume at the same time. They were even willing to discuss a cash advance "to free you from the financial cares that interrupt." Thus encouraged, Turner was ready with his proposition. Would Holt and Ginn together advance him $2000 yearly against royalties for the next two years, with the as- surance that both books would be finished well within that time? This was something more of an investment than either publisher had con- templated. Authorities at Ginn made cautious remarks about a mutual agreement on a lesser figure, but Holt was more specific; they would give him $1000 as an advance by installments on *completion* of each section of the manuscript.[40]

This was hardly the cornucopia envisaged by Turner—he wanted his cash before, not after, the writing was completed—but a crumb was better than no cake at all. He would be ready to start work on the high school textbook in October 1905, and would be willing to devote his full time—even delaying the grammar school text—if the publishers would allow him $500 for assistance. This was a sum worth betting for a Turner book, and Holt agreed. "Luck to us," they wrote, as arrange- ments were made and the check sent in October 1905. They needed luck, for if anything was necessary to show Turner's complete divorce- ment from reality it was this exchange. He opened negotiations with Holt in May 1905, just when Hart was applying pressure for comple- tion of the *Rise of the New West,* and in August, with that pressure still mounting, he assured the publishers that he could begin work on the textbook in October. That was the month when he accepted the Holt check, with the volume for Hart still six months from completion; as he did so, he blithely wrote a friend that he was "looking over the ground for the book," and would devote all his time to it when the other manuscript was completed, "which will be in a few weeks."[41] This unrealistic self-confidence so misled the publishers that by the beginning of 1906 they were briefing their salesmen on the gem that was to come their way, and beginning their advertising campaign.[42]

He was just as unrealistic when he began planning the volume, even with the book for Hart still far from finished. His notes to himself written during these weeks show the type of textbook he hoped to write; "Clothe these factors," he wrote at one time, "and disguise them but keep steadily in mind: Physiography, Economic basis, Political and social and religious ideals and parties"; or "Men—make the *leading characters* in each era and period *live*." This was a large assignment, and so was the time schedule that he prepared early in 1906: the chapters on Spanish colonization would be completed by November, those on the French and early English colonies in December and January, the story of developments between 1660 and 1688 written in February and March, the period from 1688 to 1763 covered between April and June, and the rest of the volume finished that summer.[43] Here was pipe-dreaming, indeed!

Sometime that year Turner did begin work, but the result fell far below his expectations: a four-page introduction, a thirty-four-page chapter on the geography of North America, part of a chapter on the Indian inhabitants, and less than half a chapter on Spanish colonization, all in rough draft with frequent marginal notations suggesting changes. These samples, pitifully few though they were, suggest that the book, if written, would have gained the popularity envisaged by author and publisher. His thesis, set forth in his introduction, was tuned to the times; the spread of civilization westward, he wrote, had been accompanied by the adjustment of peoples to diverse sections. "The evolution, interaction and consolidation of these sections, had made an American nation with a composite people; with institutions mainly derived from Europe and deeply modified to meet American conditions; and with an American spirit and democratic ideals differing from Europe, and fundamentally due to the experience of the people in occupying a new continent."[44] Turner's theme—based on expansion and sectionalism—was to dominate the interpretation of the American past for the next quarter-century. Had his book been completed, it would probably have swept the field and enriched him with the royalties he so desperately wanted.

But that book was never completed. His friends did what they could over the next years, showering him with appeals to bring it on the market for use in their classes, inquiring about the publication date, and pointing out that if he did not produce soon, others less competent would fill the gap.[45] Embarrassing as these inquiries were, they were less humiliating than the recurring reminders from Holt & Company. The company's officials did their best, pointing out the profits that only a book by F. J. Turner could assure, urging him to keep the $500 advance as a gift, promising him the $1500 advance as soon as the whole manuscript was in their hands. "The completed book," they assured him, "would provide a source of revenue for both of us—one likely to last for years."[46] Their pleas were in vain, for not a scrap of manuscript did they see. "Lunched with Bristol of Holt & Co.," Turner wrote his wife in 1908, "—who is a gentleman and didn't worry me." Seven years later he again reported that a Holt representative had called, "to my discomfort."[47]

His pangs of remorse caused him few sleepless nights, however, for by this time he was off on a new quest—one that made textbook writing dull by comparison. This followed naturally on his studies of the Monroe and Adams administrations in his *Rise of the New West*. If the decade of the 1820s yielded so bountifully to analysis in terms of sectional forces, what could be expected of the years between 1830 and the 1850s? That was an era when sectionalism was at its height, yet scholars had been so long blinded by their study of a North-South division that they had completely neglected the more important and more complex alignments that held the key to a true understanding of the period. Here was a virgin field for the investigator. If he could demonstrate that the abrasive issues of the Jacksonian era—the tariff, land policy, finance, internal improvements, expansion—exerted a divisive influence comparable to that of slavery, he would not only advance a logical interpretation of a misunderstood era but prove to his fellow historians that sectionalism was a force to be reckoned with in all ages. Turner was ready to launch a new crusade, and one that promised intellectual pleasures that textbook-writing sadly lacked.

His opportunity came when he was granted leave of absence for the second semester of the 1906-7 academic year. A practical man would have used those months to finish the textbooks. Not Turner. Financial security was nothing when compared with the excitement of research;

he headed for Washington, installed his wife at the Marlborough Hotel, where an excellent cafe provided meals, and established himself in the Library of Congress amidst the books, newspapers, and manuscripts that he loved. There he spent the next months, save for necessary interruptions—a four-day vacation in Virginia with his friend Charles Homer Haskins, a journey to New York to address the annual dinner of the Wisconsin Club, where the audience included "railroad presidents to burn, and all kinds of heavy ordnance," a visit to Johns Hopkins to show his wife and daughter his university and to address the seminar on "American Sectionalism."[48] But work was the order of the day, from nine until six daily, as Turner devoured manuscript collection after manuscript collection, or leafed happily through yellowing newspapers for tidbits on sectional attitudes in the days of Andrew Jackson and Martin Van Buren.

Those were happy weeks for Turner—morning and afternoon spent watching his pile of notes grow steadily, lunch at the "Round Table," where distinguished visitors were invited to meet with the Librarian of Congress, evenings of reading or talk with Mae and Dorothy. Mae's health and the damp Washington weather proved so irreconcilable that she departed for Madison on May 3, leaving Turner even more time for his investigations; he breakfasted heartily at the Marlborough, went without lunch, returned to his rooms for crackers and cheese at supper time, then worked again until ten, when he dined on oysters at Harvey's Restaurant. Even this rigorous schedule left room for homesickness. The treasures of the library, he decided, were too vast to be conquered all at once.[49] Within a few weeks of Mae's departure, he was on his way to Madison, bulging with information and with a bundle of notes that would keep him busy for weeks to come.

Turner's intense study bore important fruit, for it convinced him that no historian, no matter how broad his interests, could understand the complexities of sectional interplay without calling on his fellow social scientists for aid. Geographers were particularly essential for their knowledge of the earth's physical features and climate, but so were sociologists, who could share their understanding of the social order and of the forces underlying social change. Reading in the expanding literature of these two infant disciplines would help, and Turner read every pertinent item that came his way, but progress would be speeded if historians and geographers and sociologists could be brought together to share their knowledge. They might even be persuaded to launch an interdisciplinary investigation into American sectionalism. This was Turner's ideal, and this was the dream that inspired two significant ventures that he undertook during the autumn of 1907.

One was a special session that he arranged for the meeting of the American Historical Association, scheduled for Madison that December. He hoped to attract a handful of eminent geographers to share their findings on the role of physiography in historical causation, but those he wanted proved impossible to recruit, and in the end he was forced to settle for only one. Ellen Churchill Semple, a disciple of Friedrich Ratzel, whose *American History and Its Geographic Conditions* was then in the academic limelight, agreed to present a paper on "Location as a Factor in History." To fill the remaining spot, Turner was forced to turn to his own colleague, Orin G. Libby, who promised to speak on "Physiography as a Factor in Community Life." This was hardly the tradition-shattering session that Turner had hoped for, but he took solace in the belief that the discussion would spark such interest that his fellow craftsmen would join him in appraising the role of sections in the nation's history.[50]

He was to be sadly disappointed. The papers were received with only a modicum of enthusiasm. Miss Semple indulged in overlong generalizations on geographic influences in history drawn largely from her own book, while Libby ascribed the superior culture of the Mandan Sioux to their dwelling place. The discussion that followed was even more disastrous. Professor George Lincoln Burr of Cornell University, its leader, had warned Turner that he would protest against the "misunderstanding or over rating of what calls itself 'the influence of geography on history,'" and he did so vehemently. Human action or causation, he insisted, could not be ascribed to inert objects; when historians gave nature credit for mankind's behavior they were guilty of a fallacy that injured the whole cause of history. Geographic forces might play some causal role, but this was minor; people, not physiography, determined the location of settlements in the United States. Burr's arguments were strongly backed by Henry Morse Stephens, another of Turner's close friends, and even the president of the Geographical Association refused to join the environmentalist cause, confining his remarks to pious words on interdisciplinary cooperation. There was little in that discussion to comfort Turner, let alone provide the tools and comrades needed for his assault on the secrets of sectionalism.[51] He confessed to a friend, "I haven't quite gotten sure of what I think myself on the degree of *control* of geographic factors."[52]

Nor did his second effort—aimed at enlisting the sociologists in his campaign—prove more successful. By a happy coincidence, the American Sociological Society also met in Madison that December of 1907, and Turner readily found a place on its program for a paper entitled, "Is Sectionalism in American Dying Away?" He prepared this carefully, drawing illustrations from the mountain of notes he had gathered in Washington, and incorporating the findings of a fellow historian, Allen Johnson, who had recently sent him an article on "The Nationalizing Influence of the Party."[53] Turner began, quite properly, with definitions; he identified a section as an area that resisted national uniformity, whether by formal protest or unity of opinion or combining votes in Congress; a section was also marked by "manifestations of economic and social separateness involved in the existence in a given region of a set of fundamental assumptions, a mental and emotional attitude which segregates a section from other sections or from the nation as a whole." Having thoroughly confused his listeners, Turner traced the history of sectionalism in America to illustrate the counterbalance between regionalizing and nationalizing forces. Of the latter he isolated two as particularly important—political parties, which served as bonds of union, and small subsections within the larger sections, which tended to make the large sections less stable. These forces had been bolstered in recent years by the unifying influence of industry, communications media, labor organizations, and professional associations, but despite their importance, Turner refused to concede that sectionalism was declining. Instead he saw the nation reaching a state of equilibrium, with a stabilized population pressing on the means of existence; in this condition, sectionalizing forces could operate more effectively than they did during the frontier era, when men were migratory. "National action," he warned, "will be forced to recognize and adjust itself to these conflicting sectional interests."[54]

His audience could not have disagreed with him more. In the spirited discussion that followed, sociologist after sociologist argued that sectional lines would be wiped out eventually by the same nationalizing forces that were even then destroying state lines. "My sociological critics," Turner confessed, "pointed to tendencies toward national consolidation, to the welding together of agencies of communication, credit, and business, and thought they found evidence that sectionalism was doomed and that nationalism, with possible class struggles, would replace the importance of the section."[55] This was a fair appraisal of the reaction. Sociologists, like historians, simply were not convinced that the section was enduring, or that it had played the role in American history that Turner believed it had.

Turner could bow before his critics, or he could try to convince them that they were wrong. He was far too good a scholar to doubt his own findings; the section was important, and the historical profession had to be awakened to its significance. This was to be his personal crusade for the remainder of his days. His duty—to his conscience and his craft—was to produce solid research studies that would convince even the skeptics that American history was actually the story of regional interplay.

His first opportunity came when he was invited to address the State Historical Society of Wisconsin at its autumn meeting in 1908. The paper that he produced for this occasion—"The Old West," he called it—was designed as a case study of one region during the eighteenth century. Turner saw the "Old West"—the Piedmont highlands, the Appalachian Mountain system, the interior valleys, and the New England upland—as a single region, separated from the coastal lowlands by the "fall line" of the rivers, and subjecting newcomers to the full impact of a wilderness environment. His purpose was to show the manner in which these newcomers responded to natural conditions; New Englanders and, particularly, Germans, he proved, changed little, continuing their life patterns and farming techniques in the new setting, while southerners and the Scots-Irish adapted far more rapidly. Yet all were altered to some degree; Palatine Germans might model their barns after those in the old country, but they enlarged their holdings and adjusted to large-scale agriculture; New Englanders might cling to village settlements, but the availability of cheap land bred a speculative spirit among them no less than among southerners. Turner saw self-government and individualism as popularized by frontier opportunity, but he saw also that racial stocks differed in the degree to which they democratized their institutions.

Despite the varying response of ethnic groups to the environment, the "Old West" in Turner's eyes was a distinct section, thoroughly aware of its uniqueness. This was natural; physical conditions there created a different mode of life than that of the coastal lowlands—different agricultural techniques, different governmental patterns, different religious concepts, different social pursuits. Yet Tidewater and Piedmont were united in each colony, with the Tidewater elements dominating the legislative assemblies. Here was a recipe for conflict, as the "Old West" rebelled against Tidewater control in colony after colony. Turner described these clashes in colorful prose, emphasizing especially the Regulators of the Carolinas, who took up arms against an unjust legal and tax system. The "Old West," he was saying, illustrated the whole history of American sectionalism and proved that the subject could not be ignored.[56]

His was an effective argument, for his solid research—in contrast to the unsubstantiated generalizations that marred his lectures on the significance of sections—was convincing to his fellow historians. Their praise was unstinted. Charles M. Andrews considered it one of the most suggestive papers he had ever read, opening a whole new field for interpretation and showing the insufficiency of current understanding of colonial history. "Your monograph on the Old West," wrote Albion W. Small, "makes me feel like thirty cents of which twenty-five are a lead quarter." Carl Becker confessed that his whole viewpoint on early American history was changed by reading the paper, and Max Farrand intended to build an entirely new course on its theme. "The rest of us," he assured Turner, "can potter around and contribute our mites, but you are the man to round up the whole subject." Only crotchety Edward Channing of Harvard failed to join the chorus; he noted that one of his maps of the Carolina settlements had been branded "rather conservative" and wondered testily if Turner had ever tried to draw a similar map.[57]

The essay on the "Old West" climaxed the first period of Turner's investigations into sectionalism, and foreordained his future scholarly career. Historians—and sociologists—had failed to be convinced by his generalizations, but they had warmed to his case study of one section. Hence he must adopt a different approach than the one he had used in presenting his frontier thesis. Instead of arguing for "The Significance of the Section in American History" he must prove his case by analyzing section after section, to demonstrate that the "Old West" was not unique. He must apply what he learned by investigating the inter-action of these sections throughout American history, taking up the story first where his *Rise of the New West* ended. This was the plan that shaped his research interests for the rest of his life; his detailed studies of early New England, the Mississippi Valley, and the Ohio Valley were attempts to duplicate his analysis of the "Old West," while his life-long labors on the sectional problem in the period from 1830 to 1850 were made to confound his critics by rewriting the history of an era in sectional terms. Not until 1925 did he feel that the foundation was firm enough to risk an essay on "The Significance of the Section in American History," and even this was premature. Turner's future as a scholar was firmly committed by 1910.

X

Teacher and Administrator

1901–1910

O SURVEY the contributions made to historical studies by Frederick Jackson Turner during his years at the University of Wisconsin—the pages of well-edited documents, the procession of learned articles on diplomacy, the *Rise of the New West*, the ground-breaking investigations of sectionalism—is to conjure up a vision of a dedicated scholar, withdrawn from the practical world and closeted amidst his documents at the State Historical Society. Such was far from his fate. Like all professors, he was forced to snatch rare moments for research from the mundane duties that busied his days—and, often, his nights. Most of his time and energy went not into the investigations that he loved, but into teaching small armies of undergraduates, ministering to the needs of an ever-increasing following of graduate students, caring for the details of departmental administration, and shouldering the countless duties demanded by his position in the university.

He had little time for social activity, save that demanded by his professorship; the Turners entertained seldom unless a visiting dignitary required recognition, or the arrival or departure of a colleague called for a modest dinner party. They lived quietly in their lakefront home at 629 Frances Street, bicycling together when the weather was suitable, paddling about Lake Mendota in the canoe that was always stored on their front porch, reading before the fire in the "front room," with Turner sitting in his favorite Morris chair, puffing at his pipe or cigar.[1] Now and then Turner sought more active companionship than fragile Mae could provide; he helped organize a curling club (its members were pledged to appear on the Lake Mendota rink two afternoons a week), was a founder of a tennis club, and played an occasional game of golf.[2] Now and then, too, he and Mae spent an evening with their neighbors on Frances Street: the Charles R. Van Hises, the Moses S. Slaughters, the Charles Sumner Slichters. They made a happy company—a historian, a geologist, a Latin scholar, a mathematician—all of an age, all distinguished in their fields, all as passionately fond of camping trips and trout streams as Turner was.

They also lived well, as they strictly upheld the standards demanded of their profession—on a salary woefully inadequate to maintain those standards. Turner was relatively well paid for his day: a salary of $3500 to 1905 and $4000 thereafter, an additional $300 to $500 earned by summer-school teaching, an occasional lecture fee of $50 or $100. But costs were high, and rising. At least one maid was a necessity, both because of Mae's delicate health and because no self-respecting professor could be without servants. Their debts were a constant burden; the $5000 mortgage on their home increased rather than diminished as more borrowing went on. By 1909, Turner's indebtedness reached $10,000 and absorbed $600 yearly in interest charges. In addition, Turner had to pay premiums on life-insurance policies totaling $7000.[3] He could meet his debts only by periodic borrowing, usually a few hundred dollars backed by an insurance policy to replenish an overdrawn bank account. Mae was repeatedly warned to pay cash for nothing that could be charged, and to write no checks until the next installment of salary was deposited. "I paid lots of bills including Oppels $133+," he wrote in 1908. "We shall have the satisfaction of being poor but honest."[4]

Despite their constant flirtation with insolvency, the Turners denied themselves few pleasures that would satisfy their modest desires. Mae's expenditures for clothing inspired occasional mild admonitions, but Turner was inordinately proud of his wife and wanted her to appear at her best. She viewed his reckless purchase of books with the same mixture of disapproval and pride. So their money vanished, but there was always enough to meet some of the bills and occasionally enough to finance a wild extravagance. Such was Turner's purchase in 1908 of a Weber pianola, for the astronomical sum of $950—$150 raised by selling their old Chickering, $100 borrowed from their daughter, the rest to be paid in $25 monthly installments at 6 per cent interest. Turner forgot the belt-tightening needed to meet these payments when he fed a roll into the mechanical monster and annoyed his friends with "The First Heart Throbs" or "Life is a See Saw."[5]

They knew sadness as well as happiness. In the late spring of 1905 Turner's father, Andrew Jackson Turner, contracted pneumonia, rallied, then, on June 10, died suddenly of heart failure. All Portage, and much of the state, mourned his passing, for he was a well-loved man, but Turner mourned him most of all. He had leaned heavily on his father, for friendship and companionship on their fishing expeditions, for sound advice, for the understanding needed in time of doubt or stress. Andrew Jackson Turner's death removed a prop that his son badly needed. Less than a year later, on February 11, 1906, his mother died suddenly of heart failure, at the home of her daughter in Evanston. Only six months were to pass before Mae's mother, Lucinda Allen Sherwood, succumbed on October 22, 1906, after a brief illness.

The Turners received no substantial inheritance from any of their parents. Mae did inherit from her mother some $7000 in Madison real estate and $2340 in insurance, but Turner insisted that she use the income for her own pleasures, and not to lessen pressure on the family budget. His own father's estate amounted to only $15,400, which was divided among the three children. After persuading his younger brother Will not to invest the whole amount in get-rich-quick mining stock, Turner used his share to pay some of his debts, then borrowed his sister's $5000 to retire his mortgage, contracting to repay her in monthly installments of $75.[6]

All this took a heavy toll. Turner appeared in the best of health—he was a robust man in his forties, deeply tanned, bouncy in step—but already the succession of illnesses that were to plague his remaining years were slowing his progress. An appendectomy in 1903, performed in a Chicago hospital with enough nurses in attendance to staff a girl's boarding school (or so he reported to Dorothy), was successful, but months passed before he regained his strength. This, and the passing years, weakened his system so drastically that any sustained period of overwork caused trouble. "I have," he reported to Max Farrand in the fall of 1907, "been hard pressed to do anything but the daily routine of lectures and departmental matters, owing to a condition of half- (or quarter-) health this semester. My thinker has been in a state of mushy inactivity."[7] To make matters worse, his hearing began to fail, even to the point where he considered a hearing aid. Doctor bills were becoming sizable for the Turners, especially since Mae's hay fever showed no improvement and required expensive travel to flee from the Midwest in the late summer and autumn. There was only one remedy, and that was escape into the northern woods, fishing rod in hand. The summers of 1907 and 1908 found the three Turners and the four Van Hises traveling together to the wilds of Canada, renting canoes, hiring guides (one of them "strong as the propeller of an ocean liner") and casting forth from civilization for a blissful interlude. Turner was never happier, as he slept in the open (often in drenching rain), portaged hundred-pound packs from stream to stream, fought his way across wind-whipped lakes or through rock-strewn rapids, or pulled his canoe up a swift-running stream, surrounded by a cloud of mosquitoes.[8] One twenty-pound pickerel landed with a light rod was worth any discomfort. Those summers gave him a transfusion of energy that let him return to his labors in fighting trim.

Summer vacations, no less than bouts of illness or the luxury of a mechanical pianola, cost money, however, and Turner spent his last years in Madison ever-alert to lucrative opportunities. Fortunately, his fame as a historian was soaring, and with it a chance to supplement his regular income with lectures and summer-school teaching in a variety of institutions with salary scales superior to Wisconsin's. Why not capitalize on his prestige to spend summers in mountain areas, where his hours in the classroom would pay for even more hours of camping and trout fishing? This decision led the Turners to a roving life that they thoroughly enjoyed and that paid dividends in health, if not in dollars.

His first opportunity came in the summer of 1902. Would he be willing to give a series of lectures at the Garden of the Gods Assembly and Summer School at Colorado Springs that August? The pay would be minimal—only $100 and transportation—but it would finance a vacation in the Rocky Mountains and remove Mae from the pollen-infested Midwest during the hay fever season. This proved an unhappy bargain. The school's authorities insisted that the Turners journey westward by one rail route rather than another because the discount was greater, pressed a public lecture on Turner in addition to the eighteen he had agreed to give on "The Influence of the West upon the Nation" and "Methods of Teaching History," and then paid him only $50 of the $100 agreed upon.[9] These indignities were forgotten when Turner led Mae and Dorothy into the Rockies, there to marvel at the sight of Pike's Peak and Cripple Creek, to test his skill in swift-running trout streams near Wagon Wheel Gap, and to ride a "cow pony" deep into the wilderness for a week of sleeping beneath the stars.[10]

These pleasures meant that Turner was ready to accept any summer-school assignment that promised equal delights. No comparable offer came his way in 1903—only Cornell sought his services, and even Ithaca seemed unattractive when his friends the Slaughters offered the use of their cabin at Hancock Point, an isolated spot on the Maine coast where forest and sea met. Thence the Turner family departed that June, to spend the next months in loafing and sailing and mountain climbing—but not in writing.[11] The only untoward incident of the summer occurred in Madison, where their house tenants managed to set fire to a waste basket, starting a blaze that made some headway when the fire engines were delayed by an unpaved street.[12] Damage was slight, however. The Turners returned to Madison that fall with renewed energy.

They were soon on their way east again, this time for a longer and more significant stay. Harvard University was their destination. Negotiations that led to this appointment began in the winter of 1902, when President Charles W. Eliot inquired whether Turner would be interested in a one-semester appointment as replacement for an absent faculty member. Turner decided he would be, when assured that the "modern history" mentioned by President Eliot could be American history, and that he could offer the "History of the West." Negotiations almost broke down when a salary of $1500 was mentioned; Turner pointed out that he was earning more than this at Madison and must have at least $2000 to offset travel costs. This was agreed upon, but only with the understanding that Turner help Albert Bushnell Hart teach a seminar on "American History and Institutions." He would also offer a course on "Selected Topics in the Historical Development of American Institutions"—a high-flown title designed to lure a few advanced undergraduates into study of the politics of Monroe's presidency.[13] These details settled, the contract was signed; Turner would teach the two courses agreed upon and aid in Hart's seminar for the second semester of the 1903-4 academic year with a salary of $2000.[14]

The Turners left for Cambridge early in February 1904, happy to be leaving behind them one of the coldest Madison winters in years. They settled comfortably into a rented house at 5 Craigie Street, only a short distance from Harvard Yard. He was welcomed royally, with a round of luncheons and dinners climaxed by a banquet given by James Ford Rhodes at the Examinar Club, "with wine in all kinds of glasses." An extraordinary dinner it was, with Cotuit oysters served with a Chablis, clear green turtle soup with an Amontillado, soft-shelled crabs in horse radish sauce with a Chateau Yquem, cutlets of spring lamb á la Maison Dorèe with a Corte Blauche, frozen Tom and Jerry, roast larded squabs with a Pommard champagne, bombe glacée, fruit, Camembert and Roquefort cheese, ripe olives, and coffee.[15] Madison offered nothing like this.

If this extravagant reception could not turn Turner's head, neither could the modest response to his course offerings. His "Wild West Show," as his friends called it, was smaller than he had expected, while only a handful were attracted by his other classes. Those who did elect his "History of the West" were treated to precious little about the "West"; not until April 13 did he arrive at the end of the eighteenth century in his lectures, and not until May 2 did he close the War of 1812 and begin a discussion of sectional problems that lasted to the end of the month, leaving him only three days to settle the trans-Mississippi West.[16] Undergraduates who expected a glamorous dose of "cowboys and Indians" were disappointed, but they did receive a generous lesson on early expansion and a healthy amount of frontier theory.

Turner embraced Cambridge that spring with somewhat less enthusiasm than Cambridge embraced him. He never felt quite at home there; "I am in the midst of a little too much Harvard to be really homelike," he confessed.[17] He enjoyed the companionship: a May weekend with Albert Bushnell Hart at his New Hampshire summer home, where the two climbed Mount Monadnock; faculty dinners; a doctoral examination in the rooms of Professor Roger B. Merriman, where cold tea was served and the examiners passed a mediocre candidate because they could not bear to think of tears in his pretty wife's eyes. Turner was proud of an invitation to address the Graduate History Club and delighted that "they were polite enough to seem pleased with my account of French *designs*." He was satisfied with the chorus of farewells when time for departure arrived, a chorus joined by the entire history faculty save Edward Channing, who could say nothing more flattering than, "We remember your stay in Cambridge with interest."[18] Yet Turner was not sorry to board the train for Madison that June. "Harvard," he reported to a friend, "has behaved with the discretion and reticence of a New England maiden of two and a half centuries."[19] Boston's chilling social atmosphere was no substitute for the enthusiasm and get-up-and-go spirit that he knew in the Midwest.

Nor did he find the West Coast completely satisfying when he first went there. He had agreed to teach a six-week session at the University of California at Berkeley in the summer of 1904, offering two courses on "The Beginnings of the West" and "The Teaching of American History" plus a seminar on the diplomacy of Monroe's administrations, for a salary of $750. His students may have been disappointed when they found that the West began at Jamestown rather than the Pecos River, and Turner himself was depressed by the condescending attitude of faculty members to the Midwest (Californians recognized only Asia, Boston, and San Francisco, he found, and would send their students to Harvard or Yale but never Wisconsin), but he and Mae and Dorothy thoroughly enjoyed themselves. Best of all was the pack trip into the High Sierra as soon as the last class was over, there to cast for trout in the icy streams near Lake Tahoe and to camp for weeks in the shadow of the snow-clad peaks.[20] That summer Turner began a love affair with the Sierra Nevadas that lasted the rest of his life.

So it was that when Berkeley beckoned again, Turner responded—this time in the summer of 1906—agreeing to offer two courses on "The Advance of the Frontier" and "The Presidencies of Monroe and John Quincy Adams" for a $750 salary and the chance to renew his romance with the high mountain country. This time he and his family journeyed westward by the southern route, stopping to view the wonders of the Grand Canyon ("We saw the world made at sunrise yesterday," he reported), mixing teaching with visits to the experimental farm where Luther Burbank was performing his miracles with hybrid plants, attending the famed "High Jinks" of San Francisco's Bohemian Club in its grove of giant redwoods near the city. Once more the Turners disappeared into the High Sierra as soon as summer school was over, establishing themselves in the Lake Tahoe country, where Turner experienced one of his greatest thrills when he landed a Loch Levin trout fifteen inches long.[21] By September 22 he was back in Madison, after a stopover with relatives in Omaha. "I am now," he reported, "making exploratory casts with the fountain pen but there isn't a good ripple in the ink."[22]

These were happy interludes as well as needed restoratives for Tur-

ner's health, but they were only pauses in the busy academic life that
began with classes each fall. Most of his time from that moment forward was already spoken for by the demands of the classroom and departmental administration, for there was little opportunity for play in
the schedule of a truly dedicated college teacher. Nine-tenths of Turner's waking hours went not into research or trout fishing, but into instruction and efforts to improve the University of Wisconsin and its
educational standards. This was his duty; Turner was emerging as his
university's best-known and most influential professor. He had to use
his position to assure Wisconsin the leadership it deserved, to build a
strong history department, and to train the graduate students who
would preach his doctrines. These were objectives no less important
than popularizing the sectional concept.

His opportunity to secure strong leadership for the university came
in October 1901, when President Charles Kendall Adams resigned because of poor health. Adams's logical successor was Dean Edward A.
Birge of the College of Letters and Science, a respected zoologist, a
brilliant teacher, and a capable administrator who had proven himself
by running the university well during President Adams's illness. Moreover, Birge made no secret of his desire to be elected, and most of the
faculty accepted his nomination as a matter of course. Not so Turner
and a handful of his friends. They liked Birge but were fearful that he
was too unimaginative to build in the traditions of John Bascom, T. C.
Chamberlin, and Charles K. Adams, too immersed in petty details to
provide the bold leadership necessary to create a really great university. Birge could be defeated, Turner realized, only if a rival candidate
entered the field. He was not willing to offer himself, although he was
proposed as a candidate;[23] his own choice was his Frances Street neighbor, Charles R. Van Hise. Turner's role, as he saw it, was to serve as
campaign manager for Van Hise, converting the faculty, button-holing
regents, and swaying popular opinion to his choice. His two assistant
managers were readily enlisted—Moses S. Slaughter, his next-door neighbor, and Charles S. Slichter, whose home was directly across the street
from his and next to that of Van Hise.[24]

The "Frances Street Cabal," as they were called, worked effectively,
marshalling their forces during the months that the regents canvassed
the national scene in a quest for an outsider worthy of the post. Turner
carried the major burden. He worked first with Emil Baensch of Mil-

waukee, president of the Wisconsin Press Association and a major power in Progressive Republican circles, who could influence the state's editors and serve as a pipeline to Governor Robert M. La Follette, then with two of his friends on the regents' selections committee, James C. Kerwin and Arthur J. Puls. Kerwin was particularly cooperative, meeting with Turner in clandestine sessions where he was briefed on arguments needed to convert his fellow committeemen: that choosing a professor from outside the state would be to admit that Wisconsin had none of equal merit; that selecting a president from another university would be unwise, for none of proper excellence would leave his own school; that naming a business leader or a politician would inflict on Wisconsin a man who lacked the university point of view. Nor would Birge do; under his leadership, Turner warned, "we are drifting with the current, taking whatever direction the wind blows, and we are losing ground in competition with other universities. We take second-hand ideas and simply live from hand to mouth."[25] Van Hise alone would provide the imaginative leadership needed.

The majority of the regents were still not convinced, but Van Hise's strength mounted so steadily that by July 1902 the field had narrowed to two men: Van Hise or Henry S. Pritchett, president of the Massachusetts Institute of Technology. A month later Van Hise's selection seemed so certain that a Milwaukee newspaper announced his election. This proved premature; the regents' committee was so hopelessly divided that in April 1903 it reported that no decision could be reached. Instead of naming a new committee, the board took matters into its own hands. A motion to elect Van Hise was made, briefly debated, and voted upon, with ten in favor, three opposed, and one abstaining.[26] Turner had played his role of "King Maker" to its climax.

He must have taken satisfaction that night when he watched from the windows of his home as two thousand students paraded to the Van Hise home, listened to their new president speak briefly on the responsibilities of his post, and heard him saluted by what must be ranked as the most unusual college yell ever to honor a college head:

> Hematite, Biotite, Sis Boom Bah
> C. R. Van Hise Rah Rah Rah

Turner could well be proud, for Van Hise was to earn a place among the greatest university presidents. A top-ranking geologist, he was also a humanist with an awareness of social problems that made him both a center of controversy and a powerful force for good. He saw the university as an arm of the state, to be used to achieve justice for all, extend learning, and conserve natural resources against the inroads of corporate wealth or private monopoly. These were views that hardly endeared him to the large business interests represented within the Stalwart wing of the Republican party, but they won him the support of Progressive Republicans and of most of the faculty.

Turner had indoctrinated the new president with many of his social opinions, and he underlined them again when he spoke at Van Hise's inauguration. The university, Turner declared, existed by the bounty of the state to serve all its people in an atmosphere of learning; it could best do so by training young men and women "to aid in the work of giving intellectual and moral power and high ideals to this vast industrial democracy." Van Hise responded to this challenge magnificently. His inaugural address was a plea for pure research in the humanities and social sciences. A professor could perform no more valuable service for mankind than "his own creative work and the production of new scholars in the laboratory and seminary." "Practical" considerations should be ignored, for no one knew what would be practical in the future; "there is no investigation of matter or force of mind today in progress, but tomorrow may become of inestimable practical value."[27] These were heretical views in a state that saw farmers and engineers as the most useful products of its university, but Turner and his faculty friends were jubilant.

Now the way was clear to build a notable university and a distinguished history department. Turner's advantageous offer from the University of Chicago in 1900 authorized him to establish a School of History independent of the School of Economics, Political Science and History; he was also empowered to select a new assistant professor of American history to supplement the work given by Orin G. Libby and himself, and to hire an instructor in European history to aid Charles H. Haskins and Victor Coffin. George C. Sellery, then completing his doctoral work at the University of Chicago, was chosen for the latter post, but searching out a young man in American history demanded greater effort. Turner spent hours seeking advice from leading authorities before compiling a list of candidates. On it were many of the future shining lights of the profession: Arthur Lyon Cross, Carl Russell Fish, Charles E. Merriam, Carl Becker, and others of only slightly less stature. In the end he chose Fish, then a teaching assistant at Harvard, largely because of enthusiastic recommendations from both Albert Bushnell Hart and J. Franklin Jameson, who had taught the young man as an undergraduate at Brown University. Fish was, Jameson promised, "a really brilliant young man" who saw the West "with the eyes of Hart rather than with the eyes of Channing." This was enough to prompt an offer of an instructorship at $1000 a year, which Fish accepted.[28] The history department, reported the student humor magazine, promised sumptuous repasts with Fish and Sellery for the beginning courses.[29]

Turner had assembled a galaxy of greats and near-greats in his first effort at department-building, but he was to find that the more talented the appointee, the more attractive he was to other institutions. He learned this lesson first from his closest friend, Charles Homer Haskins, when Harvard beckoned with a professorship at $3000 and the promise of $3500 three years hence. Cambridge offered one thing that Madison did not—a good library in medieval history—and Haskins reluctantly decided to accept.[30] "We are all in the dumps," wrote Turner. "It is like breaking up the family."[31] Haskins's replacement proved easy to find, for Haskins himself had a candidate in Dana C. Munro of the University of Pennsylvania. Munro was so doubtful that he balked at coming west for an interview, but he finally succumbed in March 1902. Two weeks later his appointment was announced, with a salary of $3000 and a reputation that the local press was already trumpeting as greater than Haskins's.[32] His arrival allowed a reshuffling of departmental offerings, with medieval history replacing ancient as the required freshman course and modern European history demanded of all sophomores.

It also encouraged Turner to undertake a major revision of the American history staff and offerings. For some time the conviction had been growing that Orin G. Libby must be sacrificed to progress; he was not an easy lecturer, was too specialized to fit well into a superior graduate department, and was lacking in tact and a cooperative spirit; too, his interest in sectionalism duplicated Turner's growing involvement in that field. Worst of all was Libby's increasing tendency to substitute bird-watching for scholarship; he organized a local Audubon Society, lectured widely on migration patterns, gave learned papers on such subjects as "The Nocturnal Flight of Migrating Birds," and spent his Saturdays leading tours for his fellow fanatics rather than working in the State Historical Society library.[33] Such a dilettante had no place in a professionalized department, and Turner did the obvious. His enthusiastic letters of recommendation, stressing Libby's desire to leave because his work was too specialized (a sentiment that Libby hardly shared), brought an offer of an assistant professorship at the University of North Dakota. Thence he departed in the summer of 1902.[34]

Here was Turner's chance not only to make a strong appointment but to create a unique department. He had already indicated its direction when announcing the establishment of the School of History; "Particular attention," this proclaimed, "is given to the study of the evolution of the various sectional groupings—social, economic, and political—in the history of the United States, and to physiographic factors in American development."[35] Now this promise could be fulfilled. Carl Russell Fish had the proper background and interest to offer a course on the "History of New England" to supplement that of Turner on the West. All that was needed was a specialist in southern history, and Turner had just the man in mind. Ulrich B. Phillips, Georgia-born and -bred, a student of William A. Dunning at Columbia, where his doctoral dissertation on "Georgia and State Rights" had captured the coveted Winsor Prize of the American Historical Association, had already attracted Turner's attention as a member of his class during a summer-school teaching stint at the University of Chicago. That brief association led to mutual admiration; Phillips was high on Turner's list of young-men-worth-watching, while Phillips found in Turner's views an inspiration for his whole thesis, as he acknowledged with lavish praise in its preface. Turner was all but committed before he began his quest, but when Dunning heaped unstinted praise on his young protégé, the decision was made. Would Phillips accept an instructorship at $800 a year?[36] Phillips accepted, and joined the faculty in the fall of 1902. He offered only introductory courses at first, but in 1903-4 he introduced his course on "The History of the South."

With his staff assembled, Turner was able to announce the curriculum of his dreams. The introductory work was shifted to his new appointees; Fish and Phillips combined to offer a year course in colonial history, while the beginning survey course (divided now at Jackson's presidency rather than 1812) was in Fish's capable hands. Both offered advanced work in diplomatic history, the economic and social history of the United States, and the usual undergraduate and graduate seminars. The heart of the curriculum, however, was in the regional courses given by the three Americanists: Turner (a westerner) on the West, Fish (a New Englander) on New England, Phillips (a southerner) on the South. Here was a unique array—a cooperative attempt to shed light on the basic forces that Turner believed had shaped the nation's past.[37] If the frontier and the section attracted the attention he believed they would, Wisconsin would be better equipped to train graduate students than any university in the United States.

These rosy dreams were never quite realized. Neither the sectional concept nor the regional studies needed to sustain it rivaled in popularity the frontier thesis, despite all of Turner's propagandizing. Instead, the trend in most universities seemed to be toward topical courses—on diplomacy, economic history, social history, and the like—or chronological courses, covering the colonial era, the Civil War period, or recent events. Eventually Wisconsin was forced to fall into line, abandoning its stress on regionalism to conform to the national pattern.

One reason for this change was the difficulty of holding the stellar performers. Carl Russell Fish was offered a Harvard instructorship as early as 1902; only an assistant professorship kept him loyal to Wisconsin. A year later Bryn Mawr sought his services, but this time Fish decided for prestige rather than more salary and again elected to remain. Phillips was also restive in 1903, for he was conscious that his $800 was less than he deserved, and he was only kept happy with a $100 increase. A double blow fell in 1907 when Fish was nominated to succeed Henry Morse Stephens at Amherst College and the University of North Carolina offered Phillips the headship of its department at $600 more than the $1400 then paid by Wisconsin. Persuasion and slight salary increases frustrated the raiders, but not for long. When Harvard in 1908 sought Fish for a temporary position that held some promise of permanence, he was so sorely tempted that only a full professorship kept him happy. Phillips was less easy to please. He was eager to return to his native South, and when Tulane University sought him as chairman of its department, he succumbed.[38] At the end of the 1907-8 academic year he packed his bags, leaving Turner's triumvirate of regionalists broken— never to be restored.

Turner made an effort to replace Phillips with another historian of the South, but when William E. Dodd of the University of Chicago showed no inclination to leave the Midway and letters of inquiry to major history departments unearthed no candidate worthy of the post, he decided to seek a colonialist and rely on occasional lecturers to enlighten students on southern history. This proved easier. The University of Pennsylvania offered a candidate in Winfred T. Root, who stood head and shoulders above others recommended, a judgment that was sustained when Turner found himself competing with Dartmouth and Princeton for the young man's services. Quick action by the administration brought Root to Madison as a $1200-a-year instructor in the fall of 1908. At the same time, Alfred H. Stone, a southern planter and self-functioning historian of the South and of race problems who had been lecturing at the University of Chicago, was imported to give a course and seminar on southern history for the second semester of the 1908-9 academic year.[39] Turner wanted to have his cake and eat it too.

European history demanded equal attention, and received it. George C. Sellery proved just as attractive to competing universities as the Americanists; Berkeley tried to hire him away in 1906 with an associate professorship at $2400, but the heartfelt pleas of Turner and Munro, a jump in salary to $1800, and the directorship of the summer school at $500 kept him in Madison. Such men could be retained in the future, Turner realized, only by lightening their teaching loads; while the university grew by one-half between 1903 and 1906, enrollment in history courses leaped two-thirds, much of it in the lower division courses, which were taught largely by Europeanists. These figures gave him an irresistible weapon, and his demand for a larger staff produced results. In 1905 he was authorized to add Alfred L. P. Dennis of the University of Chicago as a professor in European history with a salary of $2500 and generous appropriations to buy books in his period. William L. Westermann came in 1908 to teach the ancient history courses; a year later Herbert C. Bell was lured from the University of Pennsylvania, where he was completing his graduate work in French history. Wayland J. Chase also joined the department as a joint appointee with the School of Education; he taught the teaching of history.[40]

By 1910, when Turner left the University of Wisconsin, he had assembled a galaxy of historians who ranked among the finest in the nation. His own studies in frontier and sectional history had already elevated him to the pinnacle of his profession. Carl Russell Fish, although he never blossomed into the authority on New England that Turner hoped he would be, was winning fame for his published works on diplomacy and the Civil War, and for his skill as a lecturer. Winfred T. Root occupied a respectable spot in the hierarchy of colonialists, although his publications record was less than spectacular. In European history, Dana C. Munro's work on the Crusades made Madison a national center for medieval economic studies. George C. Sellery was attracting attention as a brilliant teacher in the field of Renaissance history and as co-author with Monro of a widely used book, *Medieval Civilization*. Victor Coffin, although more inclined to publish manuals and popularized narratives than learned monographs, was well known as a student of the French Revolution. Alfred L. P. Dennis published little while at Wisconsin, but he was recognized as an expert in British foreign relations. William L. Westermann had yet to make his reputation as one of the country's leading classicists, but he was becoming known through his articles on early slavery and the economic history of the Mediterranean basin. Even Wayland J. Chase, although doomed to teach the teaching of history, had scholarly inclinations and was acknowledged to be a capable scholar in the history of ancient and medieval education. The editor of the *Review of Reviews* was not overly wrong when he judged that, at Wisconsin, students "found the very best facilities to be had anywhere for advanced work in American institutional history,"[41] and that their contemporaries in European history were only slightly less favored.

Nor was there any question that Turner had wrought this miracle. True, he had had excellent advice from Munro and the hearty support of the Van Hise administration, but it was Turner who initiated all inquiries, wrote the endless letters needed to seek out the best candidates, suggested the terms needed to capture a new instructor, and made the final decisions. He was a dedicated chairman, firm in the belief that a superior department was as much an accomplishment as a superior book

—and somewhat easier to achieve. His duties were never done, whether spending hours listening to the advice of colleagues and complaints of students, or drafting the innumerable letters that were a chairman's lot, or battling the administration for the funds that would keep his charges contented. Even when he was on leave, the pace continued; during the spring of 1907, when supposedly concentrating on research in Washington, he besieged the temporary chairman, A. L. P. Dennis, with a barrage of daily suggestions and demands. "If we keep this up," wrote Dennis ruefully, "we will have a fat volume of correspondence for the records of the department."[42] Nor could Turner relinquish the helm when Dennis a short time later assumed the official title of chairman. His constant "suggestions"—"I recommend the appointment of So-and-So" (when he had already made the appointment), or "I suggest an appropriation of Such-and-Such" (when he had already made all arrangements with the administration)—left Dennis little to do but rubber-stamp decisions in which he had no part. Turner might be "King Maker" for the university, but he was "King" in his own department, with no nonsense about faculty democracy to curb his powers.

There was nothing selfish in this autocracy. Turner had only two great passions: to understand the past, and to share that understanding with mankind. His own studies were important, but no less important was the training of teachers and scholars who could preach the gospel. His crowning ambition was a department of history that would attract the cream of America's would-be historians, then equip them to carry on the crusade with the same fervor that sustained their instructors. Formal courses taught by the best teachers were needed, but more was required. Turner's desire to provide superior training for his graduate students inspired two additional steps on his part, both time-consuming. One was to direct a steady flow of guest lecturers to Madison; the other, to build a summer session for historical investigation that would lure mature students from the college and university faculties of all the West for refresher courses that would make them more effective propagandists for history.

The lecturers he provided in abundance. Not a year passed but a distinguished scholar was in residence, usually giving a course of six to eight lectures, for an attractive fee that ranged from $200 to $400. To list his guest speakers is to catalogue the eminent historians of that generation—Henry Morse Stephens, William P. Trent, J. R. Jewett, James

Harvey Robinson, Andrew C. McLaughlin, Ettore Pais of the University of Naples, Max Farrand, J. Franklin Jameson, Paul Vinogradoff, Albert Bushnell Hart. Turner chose well, and his visitors provided the graduate students with a rich and varied fare, ranging from "The Social Compact in American History" to "The Rise, Progress, and Significance of Mohammedanism."

He was even more concerned with the excellence of the summer-school offerings. One of Turner's fixed purposes was to create in Madison "a summer center for historical investigation, partly in connection with formal courses, and partly independent of them." This was essential; unless Wisconsin acted, the University of Chicago's excellent offerings would lure the best students, many of whom would stay there to complete their doctoral work. Wisconsin could compete only by improving its own program, giving more advanced work, and advertising the research opportunities offered by the State Historical Society library.[43] Turner practiced what he preached by teaching in the summer session whenever he was not attracted elsewhere; this meant devoting long hours to his courses for a pittance of a salary, when he would have preferred to concentrate on his scholarly investigations. When he could not be in Madison to fill the American history position, he saw to it that someone of comparable worth was recruited in his place: Max Farrand, Andrew C. McLaughlin, George P. Garrison, and Claude H. Van Tyne were all pressed into service. They were chosen partly because Turner saw them, correctly, as rising stars in the historical constellation, partly because their specialities were not regularly taught at Wisconsin, and would broaden the students' knowledge.

This same desire to elevate the tone of history teaching decreed that his interest in secondary education should continue unabated—and that an undue proportion of his time should be squandered on largely indifferent high school teachers. A constant stream of letters from teachers seeking advice flowed across his desk, and all were answered, often at great length. How could American history best be taught in a grammar school? One could use either the "concentric circles" approach, where the whole study was told three times in the first eight grades in varying degrees of depth, or the "cultural period" technique that encouraged the child to build an Indian wigwam or a medieval castle, as his abilities decreed. Turner preferred a combination of the two, and bolstered his judgment with a bibliography that filled page after page.

What was the best method of instruction for fourth-year American history? That question inspired six pages of sound advice, including a careful weighing of the "topical method" against the use of a standard textbook. Where did American history belong in the high school curriculum? In the senior year, because the course was primarily useful in sharpening political judgments and should be taught to mature students. Should the recent past be emphasized? By all means, for there was no better training for citizenship than understanding the elements of the past that were pertinent to the present.[44] So went the advice, in letter after letter. So often was Turner asked for the best books to be used in high school instruction that he prepared a six-page typed list of "Books for a High School Library in American History" that was broadcast wholesale.[45]

Turner's prominence also meant that he was constantly in demand by professional teachers' organizations. He regularly attended meetings of the Wisconsin State Teachers Association and the Wisconsin Teachers Institute, addressing their conventions on "The Teaching of History" or "Essentials in American History." "Advocated more time in history," wrote the secretary of one in summarizing his remarks.[46] Local associations were just as bold in pressing him into service, for talks on "American History in the Public Schools," or "Probable Results of the New Emphasis Placed on History in the High Schools." On a larger scale, he headed a committee of the Wisconsin State Teachers Association in 1903 to plan a high school curriculum that would allot adequate space to history, and for a time he served as an elected member of the six-man Madison School Board.[47] Such was Turner's recognition as an authority on secondary-school history teaching that he was asked in 1902 to lead a discussion of "The Study of History" before the national meeting of the Society for the Scientific Study of Education.[48] Faint honors, perhaps, but they underlined the fact that Turner's commitment to history teaching—on all levels of instruction—was unrivaled.

His purpose, or much of it, was to convert the University of Wisconsin into a mecca that no graduate student in history could resist, and here he succeeded admirably. In his early teaching years he had helped train a truly remarkable group of scholars, including many who were now advancing to the top of the profession, but most had entered his classes as undergraduates more by accident than design and had received their graduate training elsewhere. Now his fame, and the fame of the department, was spreading. Madison was a magnet for an ever-growing number of would-be historians from throughout the West, and even from the eastern seaboard, who came deliberately to study with Turner and his colleagues, sure that advanced degrees from such giants would lead to productive careers in research and the most advantageous academic posts. Each went forth to found his own historical colony, there to recruit still younger students for Wisconsin. Seldom has a teacher, or a department, served so many so well; by the time of World War I, Turner-taught professors or their disciples came close to dominating the profession. "Out of his seminar at Madison," wrote one, "have come almost all of the men who are today reinterpreting American history from the new viewpoint first established by this pioneering scholar."[49]

Why this popularity? What made Turner the premier graduate instructor of his generation? Partly responsible, of course, were the views that he was expounding; the frontier and sectional concepts were new and exciting, a welcome relief from the institutional studies that dominated teaching in a prior generation. Turner offered students not only challenging new trails to follow, but an interpretation of the past that had a persuasive appeal. None thought to question his basic assumptions or challenge the validity of his interpretations—that would come later. Now they joyfully embarked on their explorations, confident that their discoveries would add substance to theories that explained the American past.

Turner's ideas were alluring, but the students who sought his instruction were also attracted by tales of his skill as a teacher—tales that followed the academic grapevine to every corner of the land. He saw the function of the graduate instructor as not to encourage narrow specialization, but to deepen and broaden the student's knowledge and experience. They should be encouraged to read in every field of learning, from the arts to the sciences, and to apply what they learned to historical problems; historians should read history, he counseled only half facetiously, when they were too tired for anything else. Only in this way would their imaginations be stirred, and new vistas open before them. Turner likened the graduate school years to preparation for a voyage of discovery, where the crew learned to navigate and handle the ropes, ready to journey to undiscovered lands. They must be ready to sail boldly before the wind, alert always to hazards that might wreck their vessel, but scorning a course that was slow and safe. They were adventurers, and must find excitement in their venturing. Enthusiasm, given and received, was as much a part of graduate education as learning.[50] Turner fastened the eyes of his students on far horizons, and gave them the courage and skills needed to reach their goals.

These were the views that lured would-be historians from all the land to his seminar. This met weekly in the sumptuous new State Historical Society library on the lower campus, surrounded by the reference books needed to settle any dispute. Candidates were carefully screened to eliminate those who might slow the pace, but they were still embarrassingly numerous; twice Turner admitted twelve, although he usually was able to draw the line at nine or ten.[51] All were set to work on problems geared to Turner's current research interest: the diplomacy of the Mississippi Valley at first, then the Monroe presidency while the *Rise of the New West* was taking shape, and, after 1906, the Jackson and Van Buren administrations. Within these periods each student could select his own topic, so long as it was related to the others. One year, for example, each was assigned three states and asked to show how their internal history mirrored the national scene; again, the focus might be on the first few months of the Van Buren administration. "We spent the year getting him elected," wrote one student.[52]

Turner talked on methodology while the students' papers were being prepared, then the reports began. Each was given the time needed; one, two, or even four two-hour sessions might be allotted a student. Through them all Turner listened intently, pencil poised to jot down a note or a suggestion for improvement; members of his seminar judged the success of their papers by the number of notes that he took. This was a heady experience for the novice historian—the undivided attention of one of the nation's greatest scholars. They were suddenly important, providing Turner with new facts or fresh insights and making their contribution to the world's knowledge. Nor was this a pose on Turner's part. When asked whether he really learned from student reports, he looked surprised and answered, "Why, of course I do."[53] The dozens of pages of notes he took on such occasions (now scattered through his files) testify to the accuracy of that statement.

Turner was a master graduate teacher simply because he was not a teacher at all, but a fellow explorer whose excitement over each new discovery matched that of the discoverer. Never did he inflict his will on his students; he considered their interpretations to be as correct as his own if their methods and sources bore scrutiny. On the rare occasions when he did take exception to an interpretation, he did so gently, probing delicately until the student realized his own error. "By well-directed questions," wrote one after such a session, "he is able to make a person feel cheap for not seeing points that later seem obvious."[54] Turner could ask questions, but never would he answer one. His seminar never found out whether he thought Andrew Jackson's policies good or bad, whether he felt the states had a right to secede, whether he believed the protective tariff was right or wrong. He knew that there was no one truth, and that each student must supply his own answers. Turner treated his students as equals, even while directing their courses. Nothing could have been more flattering—or a greater incentive to be worthy of that equality.

All of this took a great deal of time. Turner himself had to prepare each topic, for he had to read almost as widely as his students did in order to be able to understand and criticize their work. Even when engaged in his own research, the needs of his students were always in mind; he did less writing than expected while at the Library of Congress in 1907, he told a friend, because he could not resist the Jackson and Van Buren manuscripts there when he thought of the seminar on Van Buren's administration he was to give that fall.[55] Each spring he spent hours in screening candidates for admission to the graduate school or for the few scholarships available. No other task took more of Turner's time, and none gave him greater satisfaction; week after week was sacrificed to the ever-growing stack of applications or to a careful reading of the essays and term papers that accompanied them. They pursued him to Washington in 1907, where hours that might have been spent on research were squandered on studying the records of the next year's applicants and writing ten letters on ten successive days—one of them ten pages long—urging his views on the department.[56]

Turner was always ready to fight for his charges. He was perennially dissatisfied that the university allowed the history department only two $400 fellowships, and that the faculty normally granted it funds for only one additional fellowship from the general fellowship funds. This might have been justified, he pointed out vehemently in 1905, if all departments attracted candidates of equal quality, but history's were superior in numbers and merit, and should have a larger share of the pie. Fourteen highly qualified persons had applied for the American history fellowship, all with at least two years of graduate training, many with publications, and most from such respectable institutions as Michigan, Texas, Cornell, and Radcliffe. The system must be changed to allot grants to departments with the best applicants, or the number of fellowships must be radically increased.[57] Turner lost that battle, but his loyalty to his students did not go unnoticed.

That loyalty paid handsome dividends in the superior candidates who earned their doctoral degrees under his direction. Simply to list a few is to underline two things: that Turner had a hand in training a sizable proportion of the historical greats of the next generation, and that he allowed them free rein in selecting their dissertation subjects. Such a list also demonstrates that most of the theses written under his supervision were good enough to publish:

> Joseph Schafer, "The Acquisition of Oregon by the United States."
> Royal B. Way, "Internal Improvements in the United States, 1817-1829."
> Carl Becker, "History of Political Parties in the Province of New York, 1760-1776."
> Charles H. Ambler, "Sectionalism in Virginia, 1787-1860."
> Amelia C. Ford, "Colonial Precedents of the National Land System."
> William V. Pooley, "The Settlement of Illinois, 1830-1850."
> Arthur C. Boggess, "Immigration to Illinois before 1831."
> William J. Trimble, "Mining Advance into the Inland Empire."
> Benjamin H. Hibbard, "The History of Agriculture in Dane County."
> Lewis H. Haney, "Congressional History of Railways."
> John L. Conger, "Nullification in South Carolina."

Such a sampling proves Turner a busy man, and a man of broad interests. An instructor who could supervise master's theses on "The Hawaiian Revolution of 1892" and "The Causes of the Transfer of Literary Supremacy from New York to New England about 1830" was certainly not riding his own hobby horse to death.

The catholicity of Turner's historical interests was nowhere better shown than in his advice to would-be doctoral candidates on suitable dissertation topics. To one he suggested a study of territorial governments revealing the social and economic forces underlying their behavior, an investigation of the reasons for emigration to the United States from one European country, the socio-economic development of any one immigrant group within this nation, some topic within the unexplored history of public lands, the role of a major railroad in encouraging and shaping westward expansion, the exploration of Populist sentiment to decide the importance of local conditions in agrarian unrest, or antislavery agitation in Nebraska, which Turner suspected was as important as that in Kansas. To another he proposed the decline of the New England Federalists after 1812, political aspects of the conflict over Church-State relations in New York or New England, the history of migration from any one New England state before the Civil War, and the history of banking or internal improvements in the Jackson administrations.[58] These were sensible suggestions, and penetrating as well.

They were also time-consuming subjects, for Turner felt that he could criticize a thesis intelligently only by familiarizing himself with the subject almost as thoroughly as its author had. Much of each spring went into that preparation as a prelude to the manuscripts that weighted his desk when the dissertations were submitted. These were read slowly, carefully, critically, each in two or three versions as it approached acceptability; each reading was followed with a long letter of criticism and advice. Then, with the thesis accepted, came the examinations: two long written papers on medieval and modern European history, one on the whole scope of American history, and an oral examination of several hours' duration, concentrating on the special field of the candidate. Those examination rooms were torture-chambers for the examiners no less than the victim, as they sat day after day asking their questions, or day-dreaming of Lake Mendota when other inquisitors took up the burden. Doctoral orals, master's orals, undergraduate honors orals—they went on in merciless procession as commencement day approached.[59]

The sense of relief that Turner must have experienced when that bedlam ended each spring was short-lived, for his obligations to his graduate students did not diminish with their doctorates. Nearly all wanted to publish their dissertations; this meant reading revised manuscripts and interceding with prospective publishers, who sometimes proved reluctant to risk printing the technical monographs that Turner sponsored. Charles H. Ambler's study of sectionalism in Virginia ran the gamut of commercial houses, from Macmillan down, before it was finally accepted, and the fate of most of them was not far different.[60] Articles drawn from theses took more of Turner's time, for each new graduate was unsure of himself and sought the advice of his mentor before risking the judgment of a journal editor. But worst of all were the efforts needed to place each new doctor in a proper academic post —and keep him there in spite of his own faults.

To re-tell the story of Turner's valiant labors in behalf of his candidates would require far more pages than anyone would care to read. He was a master at the art of letter writing, skillfully blending sufficient honesty to create an illusion of impartiality with degrees of praise that correctly mirrored the ability of the candidate. When he told a prospective employer that Charles H. Ambler showed exceptional promise and unusual ability, Ambler got the job. When he confessed to the University of Chicago that Laurence M. Larson bore "the scars of his country training" and might not fit into the urban scene, or when he admitted to the Massachusetts Institute of Technology that Benjamin H. Hibbard was insufficiently experienced in a city environment to be at home in Boston, Larson and Hibbard failed to land the posts, but Chicago and the Institute were convinced of Turner's honesty and could be counted on to take his word when he had a proper candidate for their departments.[61]

Normally such recommendations placed a student in a teaching position that he could hold until he was ready to advance a step on the academic ladder, but every professor has been burdened with some who show an uncanny ability to displease employers, and Turner was no exception. His files bulge with letters written in behalf of students who drifted from school to school (and required a dozen recommendations yearly to win each new post) or who felt themselves superior to the second-rate institution employing them (which they were not) and asked that he write again and again in their behalf. One, however, cost Turner endless hours of letter writing—and was worth it. His heroic efforts in behalf of Carl Becker saved for history one of the discipline's greatest scholars.

Becker earned his undergraduate degree at Wisconsin in 1896, and his master's two years later. Then, on Turner's recommendation, he transferred to Columbia, where he fell under the spell of Herbert L. Osgood and James Harvey Robinson. One year later financial pressures forced him to enter teaching, still without his doctorate. His appearance was against him; he was small and slight, and his country background made him ill at ease at social gatherings. Even worse, he was so retiring that he was dominated by his students. These handicaps doomed him to an almost perpetual job quest until he could prove himself intellectually. He tried first at Pennsylvania State College, then, through Turner's influence, moved to Dartmouth College, where the unruly New Englanders made his life a perpetual misery. In 1902 Becker moved again, to Kansas, after Turner tried in vain to win him a post at the University of Missouri. He did not warm to Kansas, or Kansas to him. His aloofness was interpreted by his fellow Kansans as affected superiority, and his ineptness in the classroom as a sign that he was in the wrong profession. Becker was desperately eager to move on, and Turner was willing to help, even though warning that "the best policy is to *boost* hard and make yourself indispensable by your helpfulness," rather than to nurse discontent.[62]

Becker correctly decided that his indispensability would be improved with a doctoral degree, so he returned to Madison in 1904 and completed his work there three years later. His thesis on political parties in colonial New York, published in 1908, was a landmark in historiography, and it helped convince the University of Kansas that it owned a jewel, even though a rough one. He was made a full professor, with tenure at last, but his ambition to conquer the East remained unfulfilled. Once more Turner (and Becker's own growing reputation) wrought the miracle; his move to Cornell was his last. There he ascended to the very pinnacle of the profession, justifying the faith that had inspired Turner to labor so faithfully in his behalf.

By the time Turner was ready to leave the University of Wisconsin his fame as a graduate teacher was nationwide. Four of his students— W. A. Schaper, Ulrich B. Phillips, Charles McCarthy, and Louise P. Kellogg—had won the coveted Justin Winsor prize of the American Historical Association during the first five years that it was awarded, a record unmatched by any other instructor. The local editor could be forgiven when he lamented that no prize was awarded in 1905 because he had "expected to see Wisconsin add another to her list of victories."[63] Turner's former students were everywhere: three at the University of Kansas, one at the University of Illinois, two at the University of Oregon, two more at the University of Washington, others at California, Kentucky, Indiana, Randolph Macon, Milwaukee-Downer, and the Indiana Normal School. Even more impressive were the accomplishments of those in allied disciplines he had helped train: E. R. Johnson at the University of Pennsylvania, ·B. H. Meyer on the Wisconsin Railroad Commission, Jesse Bullock at Harvard, E. D. Jones at Michigan, P. L. Reinsch a rising star in the field of legal history.[64] "They help explain," Turner wrote, "how the life of a teacher of graduate students checks his own historical output, but furnishes compensations."[65] So it did. He took as much pride in the roster of those attracted to Wisconsin during the 1909-10 academic year—Eugene H. Byrne, A. C. Krey, Edgar E. Robinson, William A. Robinson, Bernadotte E. Schmidt, Allen B. West, Raynor G. Wellington, Melvin J. White, and Edwin E. Witte (all destined to become well-known historians)—as he did in the articles that he published or the one book that he wrote. Wisconsin had earned a place among the top-ranking graduate schools of the nation, and Turner was a prime mover in placing it there.

XI

Undergraduate Teacher and Reformer

1901-1910

𝔇 URING his final years at the University of Wisconsin, Frederick Jackson Turner's greatness as a teacher could be measured by the graduate students trained in his seminars; few college professors of that day—or since—could boast an army of disciples of such quantity and quality. This was well, for his impact on undergraduates, which gradually diminished over his teaching career, continued to decline as his scholarly preoccupations removed him further and further from their world of interest. His reputation reached its nadir late in the decade, when he was burned in effigy on The Hill, the victim of a howling mob protesting a crusade against professionalized football that he headed. Like many college professors, he was the victim of reforming zeal that demanded sacrifices to achieve a better world; like most, he failed and suffered for his efforts.

Turner's research interests, which grew more and more specialized, doomed him to isolation from the great mass of undergraduates. The courses that he offered mirrored his own enthusiasms of the moment, rather than being geared to those of the students. The "History of the West" was offered yearly, together with his seminar, but these were the only stable items after he turned over the introductory survey of American history to Carl Russell Fish. For two years he offered a course in American diplomatic history, then a detailed examination of the period between 1819 and 1837 while he was preparing his *Rise of the New West,* then his old standby on "The Economic and Social History of the United States." Whenever possible he added instruction

259

on the teaching of history. These were hardly designed to lure crowds to the classroom; his "History of the West" attracted between 30 and 65 students yearly, ascending once to 72 and falling to 27; his study of the 1819-27 era began with 52 students but lost much of its following in later years; and his survey of economic and social history did even less well. Once he abandoned the introductory course, Turner taught between 46 and 120 of the 5000-odd undergraduates normally enrolled in the university.[1]

Those who did attend his classes were attracted less by his reputation as a teacher than by either a genuine interest in the subject or a chance to rub elbows with a truly great scholar. He was, unquestionably, a campus showpiece; students whispered among themselves that he had published articles and books, that he had lectured at Harvard, that his writings appeared in the *Atlantic Monthly*, that he walked with the greats of the profession. They were warned that their common practice of calling him "Freddie" in private would not be welcomed in public, and were advised to attend his evening at-homes because "the tradition of the chairs elsewhere he has declined for love of his alma mater makes his nights notable."[2] Yet a popularity poll of the faculty in 1903 did not list his name; to most undergraduates he deserved to be ranked with those who were "so immersed in 'Research' or themselves, that their interest in student life has atrophied."[3]

Turner's reputation was not entirely unjustified, for the more he became immersed in his writing, the more a classroom lecture became an unwelcome interruption. He usually arrived out of breath, his arms laden with great piles of manila folders into which his notes were crammed, and always with the impression that he had been interrupted in more important labors and had grabbed a handful of lecture materials as he fled his office. These were spread on the desk in haphazard disarray as he searched one after the other, seemingly for information needed to start the lecture. As he searched he began to talk, usually with an apology: "As I hope you may remember more surely than I, at our last meeting we were discussing so-and-so." By that time he would have found what he sought—or something else that would do—and could begin. There was little in this procedure to suggest to the indifferent undergraduate that he was listening to a teacher whose concern was his education, and had prepared accordingly.

Even that indifferent student was electrified on the rare occasions when Turner laid his notes aside and lectured extemporaneously, usually during the week or so at the beginning and end of his "History of the West," when he expounded the frontier theory he knew so well. Then his vibrant voice, his radiant personality, the brilliance of his thought and expression, made all his slaves. "What a treat it was to listen to those brilliant lectures of the first three weeks," one recalled. "So well phrased, so comprehensive in their vision, so profound in their thought (at least, it seemed so to us), they practically lifted some of the students out of their seats."[4] If Turner had left his notes at the bottom of the Hill, he would have been a better lecturer.

Such was not his way, for the more he learned, the more he had to share with his classes. His lectures were increasingly crowded with data and details, far beyond the number needed to make a point or justify an interpretation. "Long lists of figures," one student wrote after seeing rows of statistics painfully copied on the blackboard, "all of which show that in spite of large growth of interior, in south, the apportionment of representation had not changed."[5] These were hardly the techniques needed to win friends among indifferent undergraduates; they wanted a clear-cut statement, not an overwhelming mass of un-understandable proof. Turner, ever the perfectionist, could not give it to them.

To picture him, however, as one so absorbed in his studies that he failed to prepare properly for the classroom is to perpetuate a gross error. True, Turner gave his students no set speeches, believing as he did that a too-well-prepared lecture lacked the spontaneity of one delivered extemporaneously on the basis of notes recently reviewed; instead, he maintained an elaborate filing system, so that he could snatch out material for any subject, study it briefly, and speak with the enthusiasm bred of a fresh discovery. Yet no instructor could have worked harder to provide up-to-date and interesting information. He was forever badgering publishers and librarians for illustrative materials to show his classes; one form letter in 1907 requested pamphlets, maps, and pictures from a half-dozen western railroads that would show students their part in settling the West.[6] Turner's collection of "magic lantern" slides was famous; nearly all of the slides were painfully prepared by his own hand to show explorer's routes, trails westward, migration patterns, and whatever else in the expansion process that could be illustrated. Good students found them fascinating, poor students, only boring. The only notes taken by one student after a fifty-minute lecture were: "Slides: mountains and trails."[7]

Turner may not have been a spellbinder, but he had a loyal following, drawn from the ranks of the few undergraduates with a built-in enthusiasm for historical studies. To them he was the world's greatest teacher; from him they learned all that could be learned from any instructor, and in generous measure. He taught most of them few facts, despite the superabundance in his arsenal, but he did instill in them his own faith in history as the panacea for mankind's ills, a realization that the truth about the past was ever-elusive but always worth pursuing, and a conviction that such a pursuit was more rewarding and more pleasureful than any other occupation. Turner was fond of quoting the remark of Dean Basil Gildersleeve of Johns Hopkins, who called himself a radiator rather than an instructor, and insisting that he did little more than radiate enthusiasm for history. "I hope," Turner once remarked, "to propagate inquiry, not to procure disciples."[8] "Whenever I have a ten minutes' talk with Professor Turner," one student wrote, "I feel that I ought to go home, take off my coat, and get down to business."[9]

Loyalty such as this was not inspired by a man who neglected his students, or held himself aloof from their needs. Turner was constantly at the beck and call of undergraduates and graduates alike, stretching his twice-weekly office "hour" into two or three hours to accommodate the lines that queued up before his door, correcting term papers with the same loving care that he lavished on doctoral dissertations, and sharing his valuable time with anyone who needed his help. "No," his young daughter answered, when asked if she wanted to be like her father. "Everybody comes to ask him questions. I want to be like Mother, who doesn't know anything."[10] One of his students remembered with pleasure watching Turner stop to answer a question when on his way to a football game, then become so engrossed that he missed the kickoff.

He was equally concerned with providing students the study-guides needed to lead them through the chaos of his courses. His own outlines, carefully prepared with the launching of each new term, were models of masterful detail, listing the topics to be surveyed in each day's lecture and the illustrative materials to be used. Needless to say, they were seldom followed. As Turner became engrossed in explaining this point or that, all schedules were forgotten, forcing him to compress subjects to which weeks had been allotted into days instead.[11] Each year, too, a new syllabus was drafted, and usually mimeographed, for distribution to the class. This provided a detailed outline, designed to lend unity to lectures that were sometimes disorderly; an oppressively long bibliography; and a listing of current magazine articles and monographs bearing on the subject.[12]

For the more interested listeners, these signposts provided a path through the maze of his lectures that allowed them to concentrate on the flashes of insight that elevated Turner above most of his contemporaries. His interpretations, although commonplace today, were often startlingly fresh, and certainly not to be found in the printed literature. "I am unable to find," he thus told one class in 1902, "any clear evidence that the victory of George Rogers Clark had a vital influence in shaping the negotiations that closed the Revolution." This was an accurate evaluation, yet so far in advance of the times that Turner's own student, James Alton James, upheld the opposite viewpoint when he published his biography of Clark a generation later. Again, Turner anticipated today's historians by urging the study of urban growth as a means of understanding the history of the Old Northwest. "These nuclei of economic and social life," he explained, "show that life in its intensity in a peculiar and interesting way." He told his classes that Marcus Whitman's ride did not save Oregon, that much was to be said for the American cause in the Mexican War, that the Mormons were victims of a clash between streams of northern and southern emigrants no less than of religious persecution, that "Bleeding Kansas" was the battleground between two rival cultures, northern and southern, and between two different sets of social ideals. "The real significance of the slavery struggle in this period," one class was told, "is that it was a contest between expanding sections for the possession of the West." Turner predicted that the last chapter in the history of the West would see the democratic ideals of the pioneers preserved through "socialistic legislation" as the government sought to preserve equal economic opportunity for all the people.[13] Few teachers of his day were capable of such up-to-date interpretations.

Disinterested undergraduates who were unimpressed with these flashes of insight, and who saw Turner only as a research-oriented pedant, were to discover that still another Turner existed, and one even less to their liking. They were to find that a scholar could leave his dusty books to lead a crusade and be converted overnight into a reformer who wielded his sword with such devastating effect that one of the undergraduates' favorite institutions was seriously threatened. The dragon that Turner tried to destroy was college football, and he fought so masterfully that he aroused the ire of the president of the university, offended a sizable proportion of the faculty, and excited the press and the student body so violently that he was pilloried as a villain and hanged in effigy.

Football was sorely in need of reform during the early years of the twentieth century. Unsympathetic spectators saw it as little more than legalized mayhem, a "game" where brute strength was at a premium, where the awesome "flying wedge" was used to batter opponents into submission, and where players were free to cripple a sufficient number of rivals to assure victory. Athletes boasted that they were instructed by coaches to "eliminate" star performers on the enemy's side, and did so by throttling, stamping, or arm-twisting. "The players," one doctor testified, "go on the field expecting to be hurt, and are glad if they come off with nothing worse than a broken bone." Scarcely a major college game was played without at least one participant suffering a concussion or fractured arm. When the 1904 season resulted in 21 dead and more than 200 wounded, the public began to realize that changes were necessary.[14]

Equally alarming was the effect of football on the climate of college campuses throughout the land. Student enthusiasm for the game reached hysterical proportions each autumn; classes were ignored, study forgotten, the library deserted, and all talk was of next Saturday's game or last Saturday's victory. News disappeared from university papers, to be replaced by yells and songs that students were ordered to memorize, demands that they appear at rallies, and praise for the gladiators who won or laments for those who lost. With no rules governing eligibility, even the best colleges hired players openly, used them mercilessly, and sent them on their way after the Thanksgiving game. A player who performed well for a small college one week might be found on the eleven of a major university the next; one team played three others on successive weeks and faced virtually the same lineup each time. Athletes openly sought jobs in good schools, expected to be paid handsomely, and made slight pretense of attending classes. This breakdown of morality was as alarming to critics as the threat to education, the true function of a university.

Conditions on the Madison campus were little better—or worse—than on any other. Football, which began there as a minor sport with less popularity than baseball, had followed the national trend, and by the early years of the century the game was unrivaled as a generator of student enthusiasm. The university was ill-prepared to handle this situation. Its sports program was legally controlled by the "Athletic Association," a private body comprised of student representatives and a handful of faculty and alumni delegates, with the university administration having no direct voice. Such eligibility rules as existed were controlled by an "Athletic Council" selected from the faculty. The game itself was governed by the "Western Inter-Collegiate Athletic Association," or "Big Nine" as it was commonly called, composed of a "Big Four" of western football—Chicago, Michigan, Minnesota, and Wisconsin—and five "minor" schools: Iowa, Purdue, Illinois, Indiana, and Northwestern. Rules of play were established by this body, which was controlled by the athletic directors from each school. With authority divided, with the faculty having no direct voice, and with an undue power vested in student and alumni representatives on the Athletic Council, professionalized football at Wisconsin was given virtual free rein. Nor did the university administration care. President Van Hise was too concerned with weightier matters to interfere, Dean Birge was an unabashed enthusiast, willing to close his eyes to all abuses, and Professor Charles Sumner Slichter, chairman of the Athletic Council, believed that a winning team was essential to a great university.

Fortunately, a national campaign against football brutality was launched in 1904, with *The Nation* carrying the burden of protest at first, and *The New York Times* joining to demand eligibility rules and an end to mass plays. These pleas struck a responsive chord at Wisconsin. The 1903 and 1904 football seasons had been disasters; in 1904 the team lost to every major opponent, the coach resigned before the end of the season, and the graduate manager soon followed him. Virtue was a garb easily donned in such a situation; Wisconsin suffered because its purity doomed it to defeat. Or so the students proclaimed as they raised the hue and cry against professionalism in the Big Nine. "That university that can command the highest priced labor," argued the editor of the undergraduate newspaper, "can admit men of questionable standing with the least pangs of academic conscience and can finally succeed in keeping their deception from their competitors in the cleverest way is always going to win." The chorus of approval from students, faculty, and townspeople made clear that Madison was anxious to clean house—if its victorious neighbors were made to clean house, too.[15] The *Wisconsin Alumni Magazine* was less certain, but even its plea to graduates to recruit football talent was tempered by the warning that they should solicit only players who would be attracted by the "superior educational, social, and athletic advantages of the University."[16]

Turner seemed little concerned as proponents and opponents of Big Time football fought their preliminary skirmishes; during one major mass meeting to whip up sentiment for reform, he was away, addressing a far smaller group assembled to encourage the debating team on the eve of its match with Michigan.[17] Not until the autumn of 1905 did his attitude change, and then largely because a series of articles in *Collier's Weekly*, by a 1905 alumnus, Edward S. Jordan, on graft in college football, brought indisputable proof that Wisconsin's skirts were far from clean. Jordan's revelations were eye-opening: a player had threatened to desert to Michigan on the eve of an important game unless his pay was increased; another, after being expelled, was paid $500 to return; a captain was enrolled in a potpourri of easy courses, including one in football. At the root of these evils, Jordan charged, was a lack of strong leadership by President Van Hise and a faculty so indifferent that the graduate manager was the tool of a grafting athletic ring. Jordan was, predictably, denounced as a traitor to his alma mater, and the Athletic Council, just as predictably, investigated his charges and found them all false.[18]

Both town and gown, however, were left with troubled consciences, and Turner was no exception. The Congregational minister warned from his pulpit that the game must be reformed or abolished; the influential Six O'Clock Club heard a former member of the Athletic Council denounce professionalism; the local press trumpeted the decision of a national magazine not to include Wisconsin (together with Michigan and Minnesota) in its list of amateur teams of 1905, because the school had slipped into the hands of athletic grafters under the "jelly-fish" leadership of President Van Hise. Even the *Daily Cardinal*, usually a staunch supporter, pointed out that Columbia had abolished the game and that others would follow unless major reforms were begun.[19]

This was the situation when Professor Thomas S. Adams, an economist who had replaced Charles S. Slichter as the university's representative on the Western Athletic Association, returned from a meeting in December 1905, sputtering his annoyance. An attempt to change the six months' eligibility rule to a year had failed, he reported, just as had one to alter the rules to lessen brutality; nothing more significant had been accomplished than to set a top limit of fifty cents as the admission price to games. Adams would have none of such chicken-hearted reform. He ended his report to the faculty by proposing a committee of seven to review the whole place of sports in the university and to make appropriate recommendations, a resolution that was adopted after a series of amendments, designed to weight its membership with football enthusiasts, were beaten down. The committee was promptly named by the president, with Frederick Jackson Turner as a member.[20] Even the student newspaper applauded as it urged the members to restore sanity to an "athletic mad" generation.[21]

Turner's selection was indicative of the faculty's mood, for he was known as an unwavering enemy of overemphasis on college athletics. As early as 1898 he had played a leading role when two members of the team were accused of professionalism, and had helped establish their guilt. He had been openly critical of President Van Hise's namby-pamby policy of paying only lip service to reform. He was on public record as believing that football must be underemphasized to restore the intellectual life of universities.[22] So well known was his opposition that athletes shunned his classes; one who wanted to prepare a senior thesis under his direction later recalled that Turner was thoroughly discouraging. "Don't take your thesis under me," he was told, "for I have it in for all football men."[23] That those words were ever uttered may be doubted—Turner leaned over backward to be fair to his enemies—but there could be no question that at least one member of the Committee of Seven would press for drastic reforms.

Turner learned of his new assignment in December 1905, just as Albert Bushnell Hart was wielding the whip to bring him to the wire with his volume on the *Rise of the New West*, but he turned to the task with the enthusiasm of a man who had not a responsibility in the world. A stream of letters went off to friends on the Big Nine campuses: Would they agree that athletics had been overemphasized to the degree that they interfered with the serious functioning of the schools? Would they cooperate in a major reform program? Would they be willing to suspend all intercollegiate contests for two years? The replies were mildly encouraging; Andrew C. McLaughlin, now at the University of Michigan, agreed that the practice of pampering eleven sleek football players was wrong, but he doubted if abolishing sports, even for a few years, would end the evils. Others were more outspoken; Albion W. Small, at the University of Chicago, was particularly insistent that 95 per cent of the faculty felt the tail had wagged the dog too long and that most would favor suspending football.[24] All counseled that positive change could come only through the joint action of the major universities, not by any one alone. This was Turner's clue. Under Turner's prodding, President Van Hise first consulted friends at the University of Chicago; then, with their support, he asked President J. B. Angell of the University of Michigan to call together faculty representatives from the Big Nine to agree on reforms that could be recommended to the faculties of each school. They were to gather at the Beach Hotel in Chicago on January 12, 1906, with a prominent professor and an observer representing each school.[25]

While presidents and deans jockeyed to secure the right delegates, Wisconsin's Committee of Seven held three long meetings, listened to testimony on the state of the university's athletic program, and prepared a report that was submitted to the faculty on January 8, 1906. Their evidence was not too damning: one member of the 1905 team was an out-and-out professional, others were supported by a "corruption fund" illegally raised from alumni, still others were guilty of petty graft when they sold tickets to a major game. These, and other evils, could be met by instructing the university's delegate to the Chicago conference to urge resolutions protesting overemphasis on athletics, and to propose that the Big Nine abolish football for two years "to the end that rational, moral and normal relations between athletics and intellectual activities may develop in each institution." The committee's proposals were adopted by a vote of 48 to 25 after a bitter debate, and Turner was elected Wisconsin's representative to plead the case before the Chicago meeting.[26]

These actions were duly reported in the local press under the headline DOOM OF FOOTBALL NEAR AT VARSITY, TURNER REPRESENTATIVE TO

CHICAGO CONFERENCE. The reaction was predictable. A few alumni urged Turner to end "the worship of the pig skin," but the students rose almost to a man to denounce the villain who would rob them of their favorite sport. His two-year suspension proposal, rumor had it, was only a subterfuge to abolish the game altogether, and this they would have none of. "The student body," warned the *Daily Cardinal*, "demands the continuance of the game and will labor to that end."[27] Turner was painted by undergraduates as an autocrat in control of a faculty Juggernaut bent on crushing student opinion, as so prejudiced that he mistook a football player who said he needed a "pony" to finish his thesis as a cheater when the man only sought a colt to complete his assignment for a degree in agriculture, as an enemy of every form of pleasure. The faculty, an undergraduate publication warned, would soon abolish croquet because of the dangerous implements employed, ping pong because of the inverted posture necessary while hunting the ball under a piano, and marbles because of the chance it might foster gambling.[28] Facetious remarks, perhaps, but they cloaked genuine student resentment, with Turner as its target.

Gradually, the undergraduate demands focused on two points: football should be reformed, not abolished; and they should have a voice in the reforms. Above all, they wanted their representatives to share their views with Turner before he left for the conference in Chicago. This was a reasonable request with which Turner thoroughly agreed. "The professional spirit with its corruption," he told an interviewer, "and the various unhealthy features of intercollegiate athletics must be subjected to clean and effective control by student sentiment and alumni action, quite as much as by faculty representation."[29] The only problem was time, for so little remained before his departure for Chicago that there was no opportunity for the undergraduates to impress their will on the faculty.

Then the unexpected happened. The sudden death of President William R. Harper of Chicago forced postponement of the meeting until January 19, giving the students a whole week to agitate. Within hours eighteen petitions were being circulated, and within days 1500 had signed a request that the faculty hear student views. President Van Hise was sufficiently impressed to call a special meeting of the faculty for the afternoon on January 18, and to preside as student leaders read a series of carefully prepared resolutions. Turner's instructions should be changed, they asked, to urge the Big Nine to reform football rather than to suspend it for two years. The debate that followed was animated, but the decision never in doubt. "Be it . . . resolved," read the official resolution, "that the Faculty declines to modify the instructions to its delegates to the intercollegiate conference."[30] Turner and his fellow reformers had won another victory.

The students might fail to convince the Wisconsin faculty, but neither could Turner convince the Big Nine delegates during two days of heated discussion in a committee room of Chicago's Beach Hotel. When they met on the morning of January 19, he found only two other members willing to abolish football—his fellow delegate from Madison and Professor Albion W. Small of Chicago—and a solid day of persuasion failed to win the remainder completely. "I have," he reported to his wife, "had the most remarkable success in turning an adverse body into a majority of sympathizers—though Wisconsin's proposition will probably lose."[31] He proved a capable prophet. Rather than ending football, the delegates agreed to hold suspension as a threat above the member universities should the recommended reforms be rejected. Those reforms were: a full year of credit-earned residence before participation in any sport, no more than three years of play on any team, no games against high schools or academies, admission prices of no more than fifty cents, training tables to be abolished, a limit of five football games a year, no coaching save by regular members of the instructional staff whose salaries could not exceed those of others of the same faculty rank. At the same time the conference warned the Big Nine rules committee that it must alter play to end brutality. If it refused to act, and if the Big Nine schools failed to accept the recommended reforms, the conference would urge the abolition of football for a two-year period.[32] Turner had carried the day, and carried it with a vengeance.

That his victory would heighten his unpopularity with students and alumni seemed certain. So he was pleasantly surprised when he kept a long-standing engagement to speak to a meeting of the Madison alumni on January 31, on "Intercollegiate Competitive Athletics." Two hundred alumni packed Keeley's Restaurant that night, but their mood was friendly from the start. Applause, not boos, greeted him as he ticked off his points: football ended all education for two months each fall; football was a big business, carried on by professionals, and demoralizing to university ethics; football was a cruel sport that maimed or killed fine young men each year. "Brutality must go," Turner told his attentive listeners; "mercenary professionalism, immorality, deceit, and corruption of student sentiment must go." The Chicago conference had proposed changes that would substitute for organized mayhem a game that students could play, that would be subordinate to intellectual life, that would leave "no slimy trail across the campus, no stain on the fair name of our alma mater."[33] Those stirring words hit their mark. An alumnus who rose to plead that the game be let alone struck not a single spark. Before the alumni scattered that night they voted solidly that football must be reformed or abolished.

The students were woefully disappointed, no less by the turnabout of the alumni than by the acceptance of Turner's reforms by the Chicago conference. "All hail the alumni," proclaimed the *Daily Cardinal* bitterly, "who have succeeded in getting off the 'hurry-up' wagon before it reached the jail!" To them Turner was still the arch villain, bent on destroying a game that they loved. On every campus the story was the same. At Chicago, Albion W. Small reported a bad attack of the blues, while the Michigan delegate was greeted on his return to Ann Arbor as if he had been a combination of Benedict Arnold and Aaron Burr, with a tincture of James Wilkinson added.[34] The reformers had some serious opposition to beat down before their proposals would be adopted.

A more troublesome problem came up as soon as the Big Nine faculties began studying their suggestions. Did the provisions requiring coaches to be members of the instructional staff mean that professionals such as Fielding H. Yost of Michigan and Alonzo Stagg of Chicago must be replaced by amateurs recruited from the faculty? The members, after a hurried exchange of telegrams, agreed that they did not know.[35] Nor were they sure of the interpretation of a number of other clauses that had been hastily framed. Turner did his best to clarify matters when the Wisconsin faculty considered the Chicago Conference report on February 6, 1906, but he had so little success that the only action was a resolution urging a second conference to reframe its recommendations. Once again Turner was named the university's delegate, and once more he set off for Chicago to plead reform.[36] He went with heavy heart, for discouraging news was drifting in from campus after campus: Michigan had rejected the suspension of football by an overwhelming majority, other schools leaned in the same direction, all were confused by the provision that coaches must be members of the faculty and fearful that such a rule would perpetuate the reign of such power-hungry fanatics as Yost and Stagg.[37] The substantial changes recommended by the Chicago conference were ignored as debate bogged down over this one clause.

Turner might have spared himself his doubts, for when the delegates to the second "Conference of College Representatives" gathered on March 9, 1906, all went smoothly. One by one the resolutions adopted earlier were discussed and revised, usually in substantially the same form but with additional clarification. Only the section on coaches underwent major surgery. No coach, it was agreed, could be named except on recommendation of the faculty or president, and all were to be paid modest salaries.[38] With the modification of this basic ruling, the report was ready for faculty action by the Big Nine universities.

Before the report could be considered, a flurry of rumors stirred apprehension on the Wisconsin campus. Local sports writers joined those of the Chicago press in quoting the usual "informed sources" that football was doomed without professional coaches, and that the faculty really intended to abolish the game entirely after the reformed version lost its popularity. Turner was at the center of this storm, fending off interviewers almost daily with the statement that the faculty must speak for itself, but dropping a hint now and then that set the rumor mills grinding. The future of intercollegiate football was by no means assured in Madison, he told one reporter; another learned that the coach would probably be replaced by someone worthy of a faculty post who would de-emphasize the game.[39] To students fearful of the worst these words could be interpreted in only one way. Football was to be abolished!

Their fears were given substance that spring, when the track and crew coaches resigned to accept more secure posts, the baseball coach left to play with a professional team, the graduate football manager submitted his resignation, the captain of the baseball team dropped from school, and the "smashing fullback" of the 1905 eleven announced that he was transferring to the University of Pennsylvania. Those who remained caught the spirit. So few students reported for baseball practice that the season had to be canceled; members of the track team refused to compete in a meet with Michigan until assured that football would not be abolished.[40] Then came word that the Northwestern faculty had voted to suspend football for five years. This was the handwriting on the wall. Mournfully the undergraduates held a mock carnival on the lower campus to watch burly football players meet in fierce games of ping pong and marbles.[41]

An ill-advised move by Dean Birge brought matters to a head. President Van Hise was away, having left behind strict orders that the report of the Chicago Conference not be considered until his return, but Birge was apprehensive of student unrest and wanted a showdown. On March 26 he assembled the faculty members of the Athletic Council to decide between two resolutions: that the Western Conference rules be adopted, or that football be suspended for the 1906 season. They wisely refused to take a stand, deciding instead to wait for the president's return, but the harm was done. All the next day rumors flew about the campus, and that night the students acted. By 9:30 some five hundred had gathered, many carrying rifles or revolvers, to begin a march toward Frances Street shouting "Death to the faculty." Their first stop was Turner's home, which was surrounded. When he appeared on his front porch, the cry went up, "When can we have football?" "When you can have a clean game," he shouted back, "It's been so rotten for the last ten years that it is impossible to purge it." This was the red flag to the bull; for a time his life seemed endangered as Turner vainly tried to point out the evils of the game, and his words were drowned out by hisses and cries of "Put him in the lake." Eventually, the mob drifted on to the home of Dean Birge, who sang a different tune. "You want football," he told them. "I shall take pleasure in conveying your wishes to the faculty when they meet." Cheering, the students pressed on, gathering up wooden fences and board walks as they went, to build a giant bonfire on the campus. Amidst yells and cheers, three faculty members were burned in effigy. The local fire department, summoned to put out the blaze, saved only the last of these from the flames. It bore the name of "Prof. Turner."[42]

This was the troubled campus to which President Van Hise finally returned. He immediately announced that a faculty meeting would be held on April 5, and assured the students that they would be heard before it met. They assembled once more on the night of April 4, a thousand strong, but in a far different mood. Order and contrition prevailed as resolutions were adopted condemning the mob attacks on faculty members, and urging the retention of football after proper reforms improved the game. Their cooperative mood paid dividends. When the special faculty meeting assembled the next afternoon, it listened attentively to a number of petitions—one followed by thirty pages of signatures—pleading the student cause, and heard five student speakers whose sensible pleas made an excellent impression. Then came the voting. The reform suggestions of the Chicago Conference were adopted first, together with a proposal that the Athletic Association provide wholesome sports for the entire student body. The way was cleared now for the key decision: "Resolved that the Athletic Council be instructed to schedule no intercollegiate football games after 1906." The debate that followed was bitter and long, extending well into the evening after a brief adjournment for supper. Like most such issues, it could be settled only by compromise, with the magic formula devised by Professor Dana Munro. Football would continue, but games with the other Big Four schools—Michigan, Chicago, and Minnesota —would not be scheduled for the fall of 1906. For a time division on this issue threatened to continue through the night, but when Turner announced that he was in favor, it was adopted by a vote of 52 to 30.[43] Wisconsin had taken its stand, and it had to wait to see whether the other Big Nine schools fell into line.

Reaction varied with the enthusiasm of the commentator for old-fashioned football. FACULTY KILLS KING FOOTBALL, proclaimed the leading newspaper, but the *Daily Cardinal* happily announced that WISCONSIN MAY PLAY FOOTBALL, and added that "the faculty and students have won their fight for clean and legitimate football." Both were right, for the game would be played, but in a completely new garb. With the other Big Four schools agreeing to cancel all games with each other for at least a year, a "sane schedule" was arranged for the 1906 season, with North Dakota, Lawrence, Iowa, Illinois, and Purdue as opponents. Diehards might talk of "bean-bag football," or gloomily predict that Lawrence would defeat Wisconsin:[44]

> Alas! for our Badger traditions,
> That ever the time should be
> When the Lion of many a gridiron fight
> Shall be swallowed up by a Flea.

But they were to change their tune as that season progressed.

For suddenly, unaccountably, Wisconsin was winning football games, and the students were enjoying the taste of victory. The newly appointed coach had a light and inexperienced squad, but he stressed speed rather than power, with surprising success. With each win enthusiasm mounted, until two hundred rooters made the long journey to Urbana to see Illinois routed. Five victories in a row dried the tears of even the local sportswriters, who admitted that a season which began in gloom and dissatisfaction had ended by demonstrating that "reform football" was a complete success. Even those who speculated that Wisconsin might be the "Champion of the West" that year did not lament that no games were scheduled with Michigan or Minnesota to prove its claim.[45]

Such a spirit sowed the seeds of defeat for Turner's cause, for every victory stirred enthusiasm for more football and more worthy opponents. Why not a six-game schedule for 1907? Why not play at least one of the Big Four? "If we can lick Chicago," wrote a student editor, "reform football is all right." All this would be possible if Turner and his fellow-meddlers would go back to minding their own business, believing that their cause was won. "The many friends of Prof. Turner," one undergraduate declared, "are rejoicing over his recovery from his recent attack of football-phobia, which seems to have become chronic."[46] This was wishful thinking. Turner longed for the day when he could return to his uninterrupted studies, but he was too tuned to the popular mood to leave the ramparts unguarded. "I expect that we shall have to fight to hold things in this satisfactory shape," he told a friend, and fight he did.[47]

His enemies came from within and without. Turner's nemesis on the faculty was Dean Birge, a staunch friend of big-time football, and a clever manipulator of opinion to favor his cause. They clashed that winter when preparing a committee report on the university's athletic code; Birge and the majority who voted with him found it perfectly satisfactory, but Turner and one ally filed a strong dissenting statement. Faculty members on the Athletic Council, he argued, should be increased from three to four, with final authority to rule on interpretations of the code. When these two alternatives—one vesting power in the faculty, the other in the department of physical education—came before the faculty meeting of December 3, 1906, the whole theory of reform was at issue. So bitter the debate, and so even the division, that compromise was necessary. Even Turner saw this, and agreed that he was willing to yield on some points. The solution, shaped by Dean Birge and laid before the faculty on December 10, vested ultimate authority in the entire faculty, rather than in the faculty members of the Athletic Council, whenever differences of opinion developed with the physical education department. Supposedly, Turner had agreed to this settlement, but now he insisted on one amendment; faculty members on the Athletic Council would have power to enforce their interpretation of the rules pending appeal to the whole faculty.[48] He triumphed, but his triumph was short-lived. The Board of Regents, after listening to him plead his cause, reversed the decision, and lodged far more power in the physical education department than Turner thought wise.[49]

Enemies from without the campus were even more threatening. They came from the Big Four universities, where the success of reform football during the 1906 season sparked the same resurgence of enthusiasm that infected the Wisconsin student body. Even Northwestern, which had substituted intramural sports for intercollegiate games, demanded a return to conference play after the local contests revealed some surprisingly good talent. These demands surfaced in December 1906, when representatives of the Big Nine athletic departments, encouraged by the changing climate of opinion, agreed to push for a seven-game schedule providing two were with minor schools, dropped the fifty cent admission limit, and revoked the three-year limit on varsity competition for players enrolled before September 1, 1906. "It begins to look like 'Easy Street' for King Football," wrote one sports editor, with obvious satisfaction.[50]

This prophecy reckoned without Turner and his fellow reformers. Faculty approval was necessary, and at Wisconsin at least there was almost unanimous sentiment against the suggested changes. With Turner leading the attack, they were voted down one by one as students again wailed their resentment.[51] The faculty was happy, but the physical education department pointed out that a real problem remained. The Big Four schools were ready to schedule games among themselves, and some were adopting the seven-game schedule. How could relations be kept harmonious? Another conference was clearly needed, and one was promptly scheduled for Chicago, with each of the Big Nine represented by one delegate from the faculty, and one from the athletic department. Turner and C. P. Hutchins, coach and chairman of the physical education department, journeyed to Chicago together on January 12, 1907, for another day of bickering. Most of the time of this "Peace Meeting," as it was labeled by the press, went into a discussion of picayune regulations governing the treatment of visiting teams; not until late in the day, when Turner had been forced to leave, did they turn to scheduling. He would have been heartbroken at the result: Wisconsin, it was agreed, would play Minnesota in 1907, Chicago and Minnesota in 1908, Chicago and Michigan in 1909, and Michigan and Minnesota in 1910.[52] The faculty still had to give its approval, but Turner recognized the inevitable and fell into line. Instead of opposing, he presented the "Peace Meeting" proposals and personally shepherded them to passage.[53]

Turner raised no white flag with this about-face, but he did sense that support for big-time football was growing and that he could stem the tide only by making some concessions. The 1907 season was a triumphant one, and with each victory student hysteria mounted. It reached a climax on the eve of November 24, when Wisconsin was to play its last game of the season against Minnesota, the first against a Big Four opponent since reform agitation began. By this time the alumni were forming committees to press for a seven-game schedule and the return of a training table, showering letters on the president, and muttering that they would carry their case to the legislature if the faculty did not listen. Their plan was for a giant mass meeting before the big game to protest the "ping pong policy" of the university. "The faculty," read the announcements, "which is apparently composed of men who aim to tie a tin can to college sports, especially football, will be taken to task by former Wisconsin men who are now prominent."[54]

The "giant" mass meeting was not quite as large as expected, but the speeches were fiery enough to please the most avid fan. Speaker after speaker denounced the faculty as "women who wore men's pants," urged naming a full-time coach, and warned the reformers that they should resign if they did not catch the Wisconsin spirit. Resolutions adopted as the meeting drew to a close were less inflammatory, but they requested that a faculty committee of three meet with a similar alumni committee "to consider the best means of improving university athletics."[55] A day later alumni and students—and most of the faculty—watched the eleven battle mighty Minnesota to a 17 to 17 tie and voted the season a success.

The faculty, once more under Turner's leadership, took the alumni's request with proper seriousness. Meeting on December 2, 1907, they listened with approval to a series of resolutions Turner had prepared: the faculty had no intention of abolishing intercollegiate football; it felt the conference rules adequate to govern the game and did not intend to alter them locally; it encouraged the widespread participation of all students in sports programs; it was unswerving in its belief that all athletics "should be justly subordinated to the fundamental purpose of the taxpayers of Wisconsin in creating an institution for the education of youth and for the advancement of knowledge." These, the faculty agreed, would serve as instructions to the three delegates who would meet with the alumni. Turner, naturally, was named chairman of this group, and Professor James F. A. Pyre of the English department and Professor Paul S. Reinsch of political science were named as his fellow members.[56]

The meetings were amiable enough when they began at Turner's home on the night of December 14, 1907. The alumni arrived armed with a set of nonnegotiable demands: a seven-game schedule, a well-paid professional coach, alumni representation on the committees that controlled sports. One by one these points were politely refuted by Turner and his colleagues: they had no control over the coaching staff, which was hired by the president and regents; alumni representation on the Council would create the same problems of divided authority that had been responsible for past difficulties; a seven-game schedule was out of the question. These were the facts of life, and must remain the facts of life if the university was to fulfill its obligations to the state as an educational institution.[57] The alumni, bested at every turn, took refuge in a public statement in which they reiterated their demand for a seven-game schedule and urged that faculty members "known to be bitterly hostile to the declared policy of the faculty in favor of intercollegiate athletic contests" no longer be named to committees governing athletic policies.[58]

The issues were clearly drawn now, with local alumni and a majority of students favoring a seven-game schedule as the first step toward a return to big-time football, and faculty reformers grimly holding the line against them. For a time the faculty viewpoint triumphed. They won a solid victory in January 1908, when delegates from the Big Nine, meeting in Chicago to arrange schedules for that fall's games, voted five to four for a seven-game season, but with the provision that each school must approve by a two-thirds faculty vote. This was a kiss of death, as they well knew. Wisconsin, led by Turner, overwhelmingly favored five games for 1908, even though the alumni petitions had just been presented to the faculty.[59] Chicago, Illinois, Purdue, and Northwestern fell into line, assuring at least one more year for reformed football.

But only one more. That 1908 season was one of the most exciting in years, as opponent after opponent, including Minnesota, fell before the Badger eleven. Again fanaticism soared to irrational levels as the last game approached. This was with Chicago on November 21, with the mythical "Championship of the West" at stake. The campus went mad. Each night for five nights the students shouted themselves hoarse at mass meetings, the last attended by no less than five thousand cheering fans. Turner, listening to the bedlam, must have wondered how so many young men—and old alumni—could be misled into believing that the university's function was to entertain rather than to educate. Ten thousand rabid enthusiasts were on hand that Saturday afternoon to watch Chicago triumph, by a score of 18 to 12. But they were not too disappointed. Big-time football was back in Madison, despite the faculty mossbacks.

It was there to stay, for the success of the 1908 season dealt a death-blow to reform. That winter, one by one, the Big Nine universities voted to restore a seven-game schedule for 1909 and 1910, with only Wisconson doggedly clinging to five games. Turner and his supporters could not keep football reformed forever. No sooner was the 1910 season over than a motion from the Athletic Council authorizing seven games for 1911 was introduced, hurriedly debated, and passed by the faculty with 50 in favor and only 26 opposed. A few months later the regents authorized the president to name the faculty members on the Athletic Council. One by one the reforms won so painfully by Turner were whittled away.

That he won a battle and lost a war was not to his discredit, for other reformers in other days were to prove that no quantity of logic could offset the fanatical desire of youth for victories on the gridiron. Professors might argue that the function of a university was to educate, not match gladiator against gladiator; they might prove that football was a brutal sport that killed or maimed fine young men; they might demonstrate that campus hysteria brought intellectual activity to a near-standstill for two months each fall, at great expense to the taxpayers. Their arguments were irrefutable, but emotions, not logic, governed student conduct on crisp fall afternoons when the honor of the college was at stake. Turner and his fellow reformers had probably saved the necks of a few players by winning rule changes that lessened brutality, and they had certainly dampened campus hysteria for a year or two, to the benefit of a good many who took their education seriously. No other reward could be hoped. Turner had acted as his conscience dictated, but he must have wondered, as he watched the cheering crowds at Camp Randall during a do-or-die battle with Chicago, whether the career of a reformer was worth while.

XII

Leaving Wisconsin

1905-1910

𝕯URING the early years of the twentieth century, Frederick Jackson Turner squandered precious time on football reform and dedicated hours to graduate instruction instead of research. Still, almost despite himself, his reputation was skyrocketing. He contributed precious little to his own ascent; his *Rise of the New West* was a masterpiece, but it was so original that its implications escaped many traditionalist historians; his articles on early foreign policy were too specialized to stir general interest; and his speculations on the nature of sectionalism were too immature to win professional support. Even his article on "The Old West," while appealing to some, was seen by others as an exercise in local history, and of no national significance. Turner was becoming well known not through his own efforts, but because, during those years, historians had awakened to the belief that the frontier thesis was the key to understanding the nation's past, and its author the prophet whose revelation had led them to the ultimate Truth.

For this about-face in national attitude the changing times were largely responsible. As the new century dawned, America was entering its industrial age: mushrooming cities, smoke-belching factories, bitter labor conflicts, the degradation of rural values—all signaled the end of an era that gained in glamour as it receded into the past. Nostalgia for those bygone days underlay the popularity of dime novels with their cowboy fantasies, and of the works of Mark Twain and Bret Harte for readers with more elevated tastes. Historians, grasping for an interpretation more plausible than the now-discredited "Teutonic" explanation of Herbert Baxter Adams, succumbed to this atmosphere in their own way. The frontier was capturing the nation's imagination; perhaps Turner had been right in 1893 when he argued that its significance had not been appreciated.

Particularly because the thesis blended so well with the spirit of Progressivism. Democracy—political and economic—was placed on a pedestal during those years, and Turner told the historians that American democracy was a home grown product of the West. This was a comfortable theory, Jeffersonian rather than Marxist in its implications, offering a safe explanation of the conflict between eastern capitalism and western Populism, between the trusts and the people, between management and labor. Historians could side with the oppressed without tainting themselves with Marxism simply by equating democracy with rural values. Even those who refused to accept environmental determinism—and Turner was in this camp—could use Turner's tools and concepts to stage their own breaks with the past. The young Charles A. Beard was a Turnerian before he sharpened the frontier hypothesis to develop his own "economic determinism." So were Vernon Parrington, who used the thesis to substantiate his progressive interpretation of American writing, Carl Becker, who applied it to the class conflicts of the Revolutionary period, and James Harvey Robinson, who popularized the "New History." Turner might not have convinced all his colleagues that his views were valid, but all were aware that his assault on traditionalism had opened the door to fresh interpretations of the past. And all were grateful.

This acclaim from the younger "Progressive Historians" did not mean that all were swept aboard the Turner bandwagon. Older scholars, and a good many younger ones as well, distrusted the newer interpretations and were inclined to rebel against newfangled ideas that were based more on speculation than evidence. Men of this sort thought it improper to use unsubstantiated hypotheses as the bases for interpretation; they branded as "unscientific" the rewriting of history to conform to a "frontier theory" or a belief in "economic determinism" or a "New History." The stiff-backed resistance of these diehards—and the realization that they were at least partly right—inclined the Progressive historians to exaggerate claims for the validity of their own ideas. The economic factor, or the frontier factor, or the social factor, they argued, shaped *all* aspects of human behavior, not just a few. These over-statements—and Turner's followers were guilty of many of them—did much in later years to discredit the causes for which they stood. Now, however, they only helped popularize the views of the Progressives, and particularly those of Turner.

If the frontier hypothesis won acceptance because the climate was favorable, it also benefited from the proselyting of as dedicated a band of fanatics as ever preached a cause. In the van were Turner's own students, all passionately devoted to their master, all convinced that they had heard the Word and must convert the world. In the long run they did him more harm than good, for their exaggerations eventually helped discredit a theory that was basically sound; "some of my students," Turner wrote ruefully, "have apprehended only certain aspects of my work and have not always seen it in *relation*."[1] That was for the future; now those students formed a Gideon's Army, marching to rid the world of heresy. They were everywhere, for by 1910 several hundred had passed through his seminar and some two score had earned the doctorate under his direction. Albert Bushnell Hart, traveling about the Midwest at this time, found so many in colleges and universities that he accused Turner of monopolizing the field; "wherever I go," he wrote, "they seem to spring out of the ground."[2] All were winning converts and training their own students to spread the Gospel. Scores more manned the high school history departments of much of the Midwest, infecting their charges with the virus of Turnerism even before college age. Nearly all kept in touch with Turner, seeking his advice on a lecture to give or a syllabus to prepare, or enquiring about the latest findings to use in their classrooms. So conscientiously did they assign their master's writings that, when a new instructor arrived at one institution, he found the 1893 issue of the *Annual Report of the American Historical Association* and the copies of the *Atlantic Monthly* containing Turner's essays so tattered from constant wear that they could not be used.[3]

All great teachers have recruited disciples from among their students, but Turner's magnetism extended to a wider circle. He—or his theories—won as converts numerous college and high school instructors who had never entered his classes, and a sprinkling of enthusiasts from beyond the academic ranks: a New York banker who used Turner's ideas as the basis for a book, *The New Frontier;* a political scientist who wrote that the governmental systems of colonial America were chiefly influenced by "an open continent, by the abundance of cheap land, by life in a new country where social rigidity could not by the nature of things be scrupulously maintained."[4] Even John Bach Mc-Master, who, in his multivolume *History of the People of the United States*, had shown little concern with the West, devoted a major portion of his sixth volume, published in 1906, to the frontier. Max Farrand, the most devoted of Turner's admirers, accepted a post at Stanford because he wanted to learn more about the western character at first hand, then moved to Cornell to carry the frontier campaign to the East. So faithfully did Farrand parrot Turner's views that the Northern California Teachers Association thanked him after three lectures on "The West in American History" for "having presented Professor Turner's work in such a clear and interesting manner."[5] This he acknowledged as his due; "the fact is," he wrote Turner, "I have been living on your ideas ever since my summer in Madison."[6] So he had. Farrand was more realistic than modest when he wrote on an offprint of a *Yale Review* article: "Dear Turner, This is really your work, and I am ashamed to send it to you."[7] He, like many another historian of that day, accepted the frontier thesis as the literal truth, to be neither disputed nor questioned.

With the historical profession almost solidly in line, textbook writers awakened to the realization that they had to recast their products to reflect the current trend. This meant a revolution. Through the nineteenth century, high school texts either ignored the West completely or painted westerners as dissolute characters who shamed the glorious New England heritage that had made America great. This view was first attacked by professional historians who were abreast of Turner's theories. John Bach McMaster's *A School History of the United States*, published in 1897, broke the ice by devoting three chapters to the western scene; seven years later, Albert Bushnell Hart, in his *Essentials in American History* urged students to read Turner's essays and saw the West as not only "different from older communities," but the only part of the nation "where democracy was real." With these two eminent historians placing their stamp of approval on the frontier thesis, its general acceptance by textbook writers was inevitable. Roscoe L. Ashley's *American History for Use in Secondary Schools*, published in 1907 and destined to become one of the two most widely used texts for a generation, demonstrated this admirably. The westward movement was the one key needed to understand the past; geographic forces determined the nature of the nation's economy and social structure; the frontier was largely responsible for "the democratic and national spirit of the people."[8]

Turner himself was not sure that this emphasis on his theory was wise. He expressed himself strongly on this point when he was asked to prepare an article for an educational journal on "the value of Western history"—an article that would shift attention from political history in elementary school instruction to "the great human movement of western occupation and development." A place must be found in the curriculum for the study of the frontier, he agreed, but not at the expense of political history—a subject essential to the training of future voters and the conversion of immigrants into informed Americans.[9] His disciples showed less restraint. When the *History Teacher's Magazine* urged its subscribers to read Turner's writings and stress the westward movement as an "important phase in the national development," as it did in 1909, it mirrored the attitude of most of the profession.[10] Even political history should be sacrificed if need be to make room for the study of the frontier, the magazine stated.

Such misguided enthusiasm was to triumph over Turner's moderation, as textbook writer after textbook writer fell into line. For the next twenty years virtually all did so. David S. Muzzey, whose *An American History* first appeared in 1911 and sold millions of copies, based his book on the assumption that "the western-moving frontier was the most constant and potent force in our history." His closest rival, Willis M. West, built his *American History and Government* about the theme that the frontier, and the interaction of the frontier with the older parts of the country, explained the nation's development. These authors typified the dozens of textbook writers whose products flooded the schools through the 1920s. Even older texts were revised to meet the new standards; D. H. Montgomery's *The Student's American History*, which in its original 1897 edition listed only four references to "The West," needed 127 index entries on that topic when it was reissued twenty years later.[11] The influence of Turner's theory on textbook authors can be realized when we understand that only 2.2 per cent of the subject matter in the leading texts published between 1830 and

1870 was devoted to the West, while 93 per cent of those books printed between 1900 and 1925 stressed the frontier as a basic moulding force in the nation's history.[12] When Max Farrand advised Turner, as he did in 1909, that he must "hustle along and get your own text-book out or you will find the field already occupied," he proved an admirable prophet.[13]

Turner never wrote that book, but the dozens of authors who parroted his theories brought him fame unrivaled by any historian of his generation. Thus, early in his career, he was judged by many of his contemporaries as worthy of a place among the immortals. Writing in 1903, when the frontier theory was mushrooming in popularity, Woodrow Wilson branded him "the coming man in American history" and "already in the first class"; at that same time Henry Morse Stephens used the columns of *World's Work* to rank Turner, with Henry Adams, James Ford Rhodes, and Henry C. Lea, as one of the nation's "most important living historians."[14] J. Franklin Jameson, who knew the profession better than any man of that generation, testified before the Massachusetts Historical Society a few years later that Turner outclassed all his contemporaries in combining "accurate scholarship and large views and the power of generalization."[15] Here was high praise from his peers. So was the word from Germany: the great Professor Karl Lamprecht rated the University of Wisconsin among the country's greatest because of Turner's "model historical seminary." Even blustery Edward Channing of Harvard, who could seldom see beyond the Hudson, confided to a graduate student that "Turner and I are the only men in the country who really know the *whole* of American history. Others know it in spots, but we've got it all the way through."[16]

Such acclaim meant a succession of honors, all pleasing to Turner's ego. Prestigious societies invited him to membership: the Massachusetts Historical Society in 1904, the American Antiquarian Society in 1907, the American Academy of Arts and Sciences in 1911, Phi Beta Kappa's newly established chapter at the University of Wisconsin shortly thereafter.[17] He was given his first honorary degree in 1908, when the University of Illinois made him a Doctor of Laws, a distinction that pleased Turner especially because it came from a school whose center for the study of western history was gaining national recognition. Three years later he was awarded the honorary degree of Doctor of Philosophy by the Royal Frederick University of Christiana, Norway.[18]

The popularity of his theory also underlay his rapid rise in the councils of the American Historical Association. As usual with younger men, he began his service to that organization on hard-working committees: the program committee in 1893 and 1897; the Justin Winsor Prize committee in 1898, which gave him the dubious distinction of reading a dozen book-length manuscripts; the nominating committee in 1904, which required a heroic journey to a Chicago meeting on a train delayed fifteen hours by snow and sub-zero cold; the Executive Council in 1895 and 1898, for which he had to travel to New York two or three times a year for wearisome sessions. All this placed a heavy load on his time and pocketbook, for, while bare expenses were paid for meetings of the Council and a few committees, attendance at the association's annual conventions had to be financed from the perennially depleted Turner treasury. Some he simply could not afford; he explained to a friend that he could not attend the Philadelphia meeting in 1903 "without creating hard feelings with my numerous creditors."[19] Others he attended only by practicing rigorous economies; he normally appeared in New York after journeying from Chicago to Toledo by coach, purchasing a Pullman ticket and berth for the overnight stretch to Syracuse, then transferring back to the coach again. Time and again Turner pleaded that committee business be conducted by mail to avoid bankruptcy for members, or urged the Association to be more generous with its travel funds, lest its business be monopolized by the wealthy or those who lived along the eastern seaboard.[20]

The American Historical Association demanded sacrifices, but it also gave Turner a chance to earn a reputation as the most prolific "idea man" of his generation. He was constantly generating plans for projects that would benefit historical studies, some fanciful, but most sound enough to warrant eventual adoption. His ally was J. Franklin Jameson, a born promoter who was at his best manipulating colleagues or congressmen into action, first from his professorship at the University of Chicago, then, after 1905, as director of the historical division of the Carnegie Institution of Washington. They made an ideal pair, Turner proposing plans, Jameson cutting them down to practical size and pulling wires to win their adoption. Without them, historical studies would have lagged seriously.

The causes that they plotted together were many: governmental publication of the early records of the Old Northwest (later to blossom with the publication of the territorial papers of the United States); a national center for historical studies in Washington, where visiting scholars could live cheaply and be modestly subsidized during their sabbatical research leaves at the Library of Congress (still an objective of the American Historical Association in the 1970s); a central university, comparable to the American University of Rome, to bring together the most gifted teachers and advanced students for post-doctoral training (a perennial ambition of historians from the late eighteenth century to the present).[21] "The idea for such a thing," Jameson testified in telling a friend of the proposed historical center, "was suggested to me last year by the fruitful mind of Turner."[22] Even the historical division of the Carnegie Institution was in part Turner's brainchild, although his insistence that it be less a clearing house and more a center for the final training of graduate students got no response from the institution's trustees.[23]

The Turner-Jameson collaboration was more successful when they sought support for publication of the federal government's official records. This had long been one of Jameson's pet schemes; congressional funds and expert guidance from the American Historical Association could produce a series of documents that would provide the profession with source materials for generations to come. After several false starts, the first scent of success came when President Theodore Roosevelt expressed a lively interest. If the Association would name a distinguished committee to plan a publications program, he said, they would be given official status as the Committee on Documentary Historical Publications, with sufficient funds to pay for needed meetings. By March 1908 this blue-ribbon group was ready to operate, with Worthington C. Ford as chairman and a glittering array of members, including Turner.[24] Their assignment was obvious; each member would draft a list of documents in his own field of interest that he thought worthy of government publication.

Most had cut-and-dried tasks, but Turner's was as challenging as it was difficult; he was to select the documents needed to illustrate the social and economic history of the United States. His approach was intelligent: he first sent a letter to some two dozen economists and economic historians seeking their advice, then a more general questionnaire to a wider circle of experts on the nature of materials to be included.[25] The forty-eight tightly packed pages that he distilled from their replies was a pioneering bibliographical survey of major importance. Materials illuminating the social and economic development of the nation, he insisted, were more important than those in military and diplomatic history which had been supported by Congress in the past. Such materials had been neglected because they had to be drawn from all forms of depositories—federal, state, and private—and because they required editing by a number of experts specializing in the many areas involved. To make the task easier, Turner suggested that there be two broad categories: economic materials, including those on land, geography, agriculture, mining and forestry, banking, currency, manufacturing, wages and prices, transportation, and industrial organization; and social materials, divided into such topics as population, social organization, health, criminals and dependents, art and literature. For each of these divisions Turner listed items already published—thus creating a unique and useful bibliography—together with suggestions on the type of sources needed for further study.[26]

This contribution to historical studies was worthy of far greater attention than it received. True, economic materials were paid far greater attention than social; true, too, Turner was unaware of the many facets of social organization that were to fascinate historians of later generations. But as a pioneering bibliographical study, it was a remarkable achievement. A few of his contemporaries recognized its importance. Andrew C. McLaughlin felt that Turner had opened a whole new field of investigation into the relationships between political, social, and economic developments that would make understandable the industrial-urban complex of modern America.[27] Congress was less enthusiastic. The committee's report was accepted by President Roosevelt in November 1908, buried by Congress in Senate Document No. 714, and forgotten. Many years later another committee of the American Historical Association, bent on a similar quest, read it with amazement, branded it a "remarkable document," and regretted that it had had so little effect on the profession.[28] Turner, as was often his fate, was too far in advance of his times to make his impact felt on his own generation.

His contributions were recognized by the intellectual elite among his colleagues, and with that recognition came such honors as they could award. He was, almost from the beginning of his career, welcomed into the tight little inner circle that administered the American Historical Association, and even into the still more exclusive Nucleus Club. The operations of this tiny group were kept secret, lest members take offense at the close interrelationships of the ruling "Establishment," but occasionally word slipped out about the number of bottles of champagne consumed at their annual dinner; on one such occasion Turner left with the wrong overcoat, forcing a colleague to return to Chicago in Turner's own nine-year-old garment.[29] Associations such as these, no less than his own dedicated labors, assured Turner of the highest tribute his contemporaries could pay. This came in 1907 when he was elected to the second vice-presidency of the Association, assuring him the presidency by automatic succession two years later.

This success converted him into a valuable academic property, coveted by university presidents anxious to bolster the prestige of their faculties. To lure Turner from the University of Wisconsin was the ambition of many an administrator during those years; to stay at Wisconsin while benefiting from the bidding for his services was Turner's. With most he had no problems, for his love affair with Madison was too enduring to be disrupted except by the most tempting attractions elsewhere; offers from John Hopkins in 1902 and Amherst five years later were dismissed without a second thought. Two university presidents proved more difficult. Benjamin Ide Wheeler at the University of California and David Starr Jordan at the newly established Stanford University were persistent. Goaded on by two of Turner's best friends—Henry Morse Stephens at Berkeley and Max Farrand at Stanford—they launched a tug-of-war that cost Turner many anxious hours of decision-making and letter-writing before he finally decided against them and for yet another institution.

The negotiations that led to this unexpected result began innocently enough in 1904, when Max Farrand heard a rumor, later proven false, that Turner was considering the directorship of the historical division of the Carnegie Institution of Washington. If he could be lured from Madison by one post, he might by another. So thought President Jordan of Stanford, who was all for wiring him a direct offer, despite the lack of research facilities available at his infant institution. Turner listened with interest when Farrand told him of these aborted efforts, agreed that he must have a good library near at hand, and hinted that more research time than Wisconsin allowed him might make another university attractive. Farrand, sniffing the faint scent of opportunity, went into a huddle with President Jordan, and soon an offer was on its way: Would Turner consider a salary of $5000 yearly, and a guarantee of at least two months free of teaching to pursue his researches in libraries anywhere in the nation? He would not; the salary was not sufficiently above the $4000 paid by Wisconsin to offset moving costs and higher expenses, while the prospect of leaving his family for two months each year was hardly attractive. On the other hand he was deeply in debt and eager to get on with his studies. A whole semester free of teaching each year would certainly be attractive. Max Farrand was so delighted that he replied without consulting his president. A semester-on, semester-off arrangement would be perfectly satisfactory to Stanford. When could Turner come?[30]

Turner went—but to President Van Hise, with Farrand's letter in hand, on a June evening in 1905. He made his position clear: Wisconsin was his true love, but both his wife's health and his own research would be improved by the move. The president, faced with losing his most prestigious historian, acted predictably; if the Board of Regents would not provide the funds needed to give Turner every other semester for research, he would raise the money himself. In the meantime, Turner was to make no promises to Stanford without consulting the Wisconsin authorities. These plans proved short-lived; the regents, although properly sympathetic, showed no inclination to squander their limited funds on research leaves while private donors were impossible to find. Turner was still smarting from the rebuff when President Jordan visited Madison in the spring of 1906, bearing with him a trustee-approved contract with a salary of $5000 and two months of research leave each year. This he laid before Turner in a private conversation, sweetened with his most persuasive eloquence.[31]

Fortunately, a kindly nature intervened before Turner had to decide; no sooner had Jordan returned to California than the devastating earthquake of 1906 leveled San Francisco and laid much of the Stanford campus to waste. "LELAND STANFORD DESTROYED," Turner read in his newspaper on April 19, and he probably was relieved that he was spared an unpleasant decision. If he did so, he reckoned without President Jordan. Even before the dust had settled, Jordan was assuring Turner—in three letters written on three successive days—that the damage was slight, that all would be repaired by the fall of 1907, and that the offer still stood. Jordan's optimism was wasted, for unbeknownst to him, the honors had already gone to his rival. On April 17, the night before the earthquake, Van Hise persuaded the Wisconsin regents to grant Turner a semester's leave each year that he might "advantagously carry to a conclusion [Turner crossed out "carry to a conclusion" and substituted "carry on"] the very important investigations in history upon which he has been engaged for some years."[32] Turner was committed to Wisconsin now, apparently for the rest of his career.

Had Turner been able to forecast his future, Stanford might have seemed more attractive, for already forces were at work within Wisconsin that were to force him to forsake his beloved Madison. A changing political climate was responsible. Since the election of Robert M. La Follette to the governorship in 1900, Progressive Republicanism had dominated the state and university alike, to the growing dissatisfaction of the business and farming interests, who spoke through the Stalwart wing of the party. They had much to be dissatisfied with. President Van Hise, a leading Progressive and a roommate of La Follette's in college, encouraged his faculty to favor humanistic above practical research, and to cooperate with governmental leaders in drafting progressive regulatory measures that encroached on areas traditionally sacred to private enterprise. His noble ideals, which won him the support of his faculties, had little appeal to the majority of Wisconsinites. A farming people with a practical orientation, they increasingly saw Madison's professors as dreamers who wasted tax funds on impractical investigations, fathered such heresies as the income tax and the regulation of public utilities, spent the state's money to train graduate students from other areas, and preached socialism or anarchism in their classrooms. A little head-thumping to bring them to their senses was called for.

So long as Governor La Follette sat at the helm and filled the Board of Regents with his own appointees, these anti-university sentiments were held in check, but in 1905 La Follette was elected to the U.S. Senate, and he relinquished his office to his lieutenant governor, James O. Davidson. A Stalwart of moderate ability and limited education, Davidson made no secret of his belief that the university harbored radicals and idealists who imperiled the state and should be dismissed as soon as possible. Gradually he packed the Board of Regents with men who shared his views: William D. Hoard, who spoke for the dairy industry; Granville D. Jones and Magnus Swenson, who saw Van Hise's support for conservation a threat to their electric power interests; Charles P. Cary, who feared that the university wanted to take over the school system, which he headed as State Superintendent of Public Instruction. The way was paved for a series of confrontations.

The first arose when a temporary deficit allowed the Stalwarts in the legislature to charge financial irresponsibility and name a legislative committee to investigate the university. This committee lost no time in clearing Van Hise when it met in February 1906, but its hearings sent a shudder of apprehension through the faculty. The members, instead of concentrating on finances, welcomed a parade of disgruntled students and townspeople to air their grievances: Professor Ely was away from his classroom half the time, the textbook in statistics was incomprehensible, an instructor's assignments were "too hard," a history professor knew a great deal "but he was too vague for me."[33] This was alarming, but worse was the recurring theme that the faculty spent too little time on teaching and too much on research. Turner especially read the daily reports of the testimony with growing alarm, for his new semester-on, semester-off arrangement was exactly the sort of target the attackers sought. Apparently it did not become a direct issue—Turner's own testimony was confined to a statement on the football situation and a spirited denial that he had used his research time to prepare royalty-paying textbooks—but the wave of the future was clear.[34] That he saw the shape of things to come was shown when Turner sternly told the committee: "I have preferred to investigate and lecture in a university [rather than writing textbooks]; and it seems to me that a university ought to have room, and be able to make provision, for a man with these desires, such that he can continue." Here was a scarcely veiled warning; if the university failed to appreciate humanistic research he would leave, taking with him much of its prestige.

Unfortunately, neither the committee nor the public agreed with him. The committee made its stand clear: "Investigation and research have a proper place in a university, but the training of young men and women is more important to the state than all the other activities in which a university may engage." Its sentiments were echoed—and magnified—by students and townspeople alike. The influential *Wisconsin State Journal*, a mouthpiece for the Stalwarts, harped on the theme over and over again during the next months; what was needed, it insisted, was "a sort of spiritual revival among the faculty" that would focus their energies on teaching instead of useless investigations. The *Daily Cardinal* was just as insistent, likening the faculty to medieval monks who placed themselves on pedestals and scorned ordinary mortals; "Teach," it warned them, "and teach hard." To the *Wisconsin Literary Magazine*, professors were "present day Aunt Ophelias, out of touch with their charges." The *Wisconsin Alumni Magazine* was even more vehement; graduate students were a "foreign element" that should be eliminated, research-minded faculty members were "self-deceiving dreamers who solace themselves with the idea that they are doing for the world a service by their books, while their class work goes unheeded," and administrators were misled simpletons who should see to it that all promotions were based on "good instruction rather than on research work."[35]

These were harsh words, but they could be endured so long as they were not translated into official policy by the Board of Regents. Mounting public sentiment, and the changing political complexion of the board as Governor Davidson's appointees approached a majority, meant that this day was not far distant. This was made clear in June 1908, when Stalwarts on a sub-committee of the regents felt powerful enough to make a direct attack on Turner's half-time teaching and on a similar arrangement enjoyed by Richard T. Ely. The board, it suggested, should "look forward to a discontinuance of said arrangements at as early a date as may be consistent with good faith." Progressives were still numerous enough to prevent the board from adopting such a face-slapping statement, but another that was accepted was almost as insulting: "The ability to pursue original investigation and research work, when not combined with teaching ability, should not constitute sufficient qualification for membership in the faculty of the University." Here was an ominous warning indeed, made more so by a resolution authorizing the Regents' Committee on the State of the University to launch an investigation of professors "who are not giving the proper time and attention to instructional work."[36] To Turner this was a clear indication that he was under suspicion and was to be "investigated."

Little wonder that he was seriously agitated. His state of mind was shown in a twenty-six page letter that he sent to Van Hise, chronicling the success of his students, listing the Winsor prizes they had won, showing their significance in state and nation, quoting their words of praise for his teaching. "When I regret that I have not published more books," Turner assured the president, "I take some heart from these words. . . . Some of these men, at least, are not aware of my 'lack of interest in my students.' If I had been less interested I should have published more books."[37] There was bravado in such a defense, but there was tragedy as well, that a defense should be necessary.

This was only the beginning, for during the 1908-9 academic year the Stalwarts not only won increasing support from the people, but found a leader for their cause. Regent William D. Hoard, former governor of the state, wealthy dairyman, spokesman for the farming interests, and influential publisher of *Hoard's Dairyman*, was ideally suited for this role. A thoroughly practical man, he saw no reason why state funds should be wasted on culture when more farmers were needed; his repeated tune was that money allotted the College of Letters and Science could be better spent on the College of Agriculture. Turner was particularly vulnerable to his charges; he had no shelf of completed books, as Ely did, to prove that he was not frittering away his research leaves instead of sticking to his teaching. Van Hise, anticipating an attack, sought information from Turner on his accomplishments, and was rewarded with the usual bulky documents. Turner was writing a two-volume history of the westward movement, studying the Martin Van Buren administration with his seminar preparatory to a volume on that subject, working up material for a history of the United States since 1865.[38] Yet there was precious little to show in the way of results. Once the assault came, Van Hise would be hard pressed to defend his most prestigious faculty member.

Pressure mounted steadily during the year. Stalwarts in the state legislature, emboldened by mounting public support, proposed a whole array of anti-university measures: crippling amendments to its appropriation bills, a law to admit all high school graduates regardless of qualification, another to merge the university and normal schools under one board, an investigation of fraternities as undemocratic institutions. "I don't like the tone of the thing at all," Turner confided to his wife, and he wrote to Max Farrand: "At present I have a better understanding of the horror of such Federalists as President Dwight for the *spirit* of innovation."[39] He was right, for that spring of 1909 brought the explosion. External critics touched off the fuse: an article by Lincoln Steffens in the *American Magazine*, praising Van Hise and his faculty for making the university a powerful force in the state's cultural progress; another by Edwin E. Slosson in the *Independent*, comparing Van Hise to President Eliot of Harvard as a leader in progressive education; another by Richard Lloyd Jones in *Collier's*, charging the regents with trying to trespass on purely academic ground and dictate what should be taught in the classroom. These hurt the Stalwarts, particularly Richard Lloyd Jones's article, when it was republished in the *Wisconsin Alumni Magazine*. Conservatives on the board were boiling mad as they prepared for their regular meetings in the spring of 1909.

Turner, sensitive as always, realized that an attack was coming and that he would be its principal target. He would, he knew, be blamed for Richard Lloyd Jones's muckraking revelations, for Jones was his former student, and conversations he had had with Turner during a visit to the campus a short time before the article appeared could be interpreted as deliberately planned to supply information about the regents' meddling. In his agitated state of mind Turner transplanted even innocent requests into serious threats: a form letter from the university registrar asking him to describe the allotment of his time between classroom and research became an attack on his light teaching schedule, a regents' resolution to abolish fellowships assigned particular departments an assault on the program he had won for the history department, a questioning of the value of advanced degrees a personal thrust against his role as a graduate instructor. There was only one solution. Wisconsin's future was more important than his own. As a symbol of the humanistic research and graduate instruction that was under attack, he must not give up his research leave in return for a higher salary, as his Progressive friends on the board urged; this would signal the end of pure research everywhere on the faculty. Only by resigning could he save the university from ruin. "I have been so annoyed and irritated," he told Richard T. Ely that spring, "that I would now accept any one of the six calls I have already refused, and do so by wire."[40]

Turner had made his decision, but he was too sane a man to jump without a comfortable net to assure a safe landing. Stanford and the University of California had made clear their continuing interest, and one or the other must be queried as to a permanent post. A decision was easy; Stanford was woefully lacking in the library facilities that were his life's blood, therefore he must choose Berkeley. Having made up his mind, he sent a letter off, in July 1909, to his good friend Henry Morse Stephens, hinting that all was not well at Madison. Stephens responded exactly as he was supposed to respond. "Do I not see between the lines of your letter a little dissatisfaction?" Why not teach the regents a lesson and strengthen the cause of graduate work by going elsewhere? The welcome mat was still out at California, and President Wheeler as anxious to receive him as ever. A full semester off each term might not be possible, but he could be assured a salary of $5000, a teaching load of only a lecture course and a seminar, and the historical riches of the Bancroft Library. Why not follow the star of learning westward? Johns Hopkins led, Stephens pointed out, "Harvard followed and Wisconsin took up the great cause in the history field in the West." Now the center of historical culture was ready to shift once more. Turner could hurry the move by joining the California department. Stephens's plea was seconded by President Wheeler, who dwelt glowingly on the $750,000 library under construction, the generous pension system, and the $750 that could be added to the Turner income each year by summer teaching. He would be in Chicago on September 14, contract in pocket. Could Turner meet him there prepared to sign?[41] Turner agreed, and the time of their meeting was set for three that afternoon.

The six weeks of soul-searching that followed were thoroughly unpleasant ones. From all sides came the inevitable pressures—enthusiastic letters from Berkeley ("I think my cup of happiness would run over, if you were to be my colleague here")—heartbroken pleas from President Van Hise and his Madison friends. Turner's departure would not strengthen the president's hand with the regents, he was told, nor would it aid the cause of graduate studies at Wisconsin. He must stand at Van Hise's right hand as they fought the battle together. Turner was moved by these protestations, but his mind was made up. His only concession was to agree to one more conference with Van Hise after his September 14 meeting with President Wheeler. Above all, he warned, his delay in announcing a decision did not mean that he was seeking further favors from the Wisconsin regents.[42] He was leaving, and no amount of generosity could persuade him to stay.

Turner was leaving, but fate changed his decision on a destination. A letter he wrote to his dear friend Charles Homer Haskins of the Harvard faculty, seeking advice, was responsible. Haskins was vacationing in Meadville, Pennsylvania, when this caught up with him on September 14, the very day that Turner was closeted with President Wheeler in Chicago. Only minutes were required for an urgent telegram—CAN'T YOU DELAY DECISION. IF YOU LEAVE SHOULD LIKE TO SEE WHAT CAN BE DONE ELSEWHERE—and an explanatory letter followed. Haskins and Professor Archibald Cary Coolidge had been plotting for some time to bring Turner to Harvard. An additional professorship in an already well-stocked department posed problems, but Haskins was leaving for Cambridge at once to see if those could be solved. Would Turner give him a few days' grace?

The results were spectacular. Coolidge was elected to lay the case before Harvard's newly chosen president, A. Lawrence Lowell, and he did so eloquently. A once-in-a-lifetime opportunity had risen to improve instruction in American history. Edward Channing and Albert Bushnell Hart were capable, but the number of graduate students had been declining alarmingly as Turner drained the best of the crop toward Wisconsin. Just that year one of their prize students had shifted from European to American history and forsaken Harvard for Madison. Turner might not have written much, but he was a strong man, "perhaps the strongest professor in history in the United States outside of Harvard." No one was more badly needed. President Lowell was impressed, but he was not finally persuaded until Professor Coolidge advanced an irrefutable argument. He would, he said, be willing to guarantee Turner's $5000 salary for the next five years from his own sizable income, asking only that any university funds that became available be used to reduce his payments. The chance to obtain an outstanding professor at no cost was irresistible. Lowell wired that very day; would Turner delay making a decision on California until they could talk matters over?[43]

Fortunately, a meeting between them was already arranged, for Harvard was to inaugurate President Lowell on October 6, 1909, with all the fanfare proper to such an occasion, and Turner was scheduled not only to attend as a delegate from Wisconsin, but to receive an honorary degree. He arrived at Boston's South Station on the morning of October 5, took a streetcar to Cambridge, refreshed himself at the Colonial Club, where he had a room, and made his way to the president's office. Lowell, "very cordial and broadminded," lost no time in making his formal offer, cautioning only that it could not be final until various boards had acted. Turner was still not decided, but his mind was made up during a three-hour luncheon with Henry Morse Stephens of Berkeley, who was also attending the inauguration ceremonies. Stephens was not well enough to continue to administer the California department; Turner would be expected to take charge and to recruit the faculty needed to add luster to the university. Indeed, Stephens might be forced to resign at any time. "I should," Turner explained to his wife, "then be alone with a department to *unmake* and *make*." That unpleasant prospect tipped the scales.[44] He was ready to accept the Harvard offer.

Now Turner could endure the next day's ceremonies with his mind at peace. The formal procession, with its glittering array of uniforms and academic gowns; the inaugural address; the conferring of the honorary degrees, including a Doctorate of Letters to that "pioneer in American history" who had "set forth in memorable pages the vast influence of westward expansion upon the civilization of our country"; the formal luncheon for visiting dignitaries. Only then could Turner break the news to President Van Hise (who urged him to reconsider) and Henry Morse Stephens (who was badly cut, but "took the news like a gentleman"). "So my quarter century of work at Wisconsin closes up," Turner wrote to Mae that night, ". . . They have been rich years—in experience of all things the world offers; and you have been at my side through it all. . . . We shall push on together to see the stars again, knowing that the only real joy is in the effort to fulfill what is best in us."[45]

All was over now but arranging the troublesome details. For a time matters hung in the balance when the official notification made no mention of salary, but that was soon rectified: $5000 annually, the promise of $5500 before too long, the unwelcome news that it would be paid in four quarterly installments. "This makes a long lean period for one coming here from elsewhere," Haskins warned, "but you can on the other hand recognize the arrival of your salary when it comes in such chunks."[46] While the wheels ground slowly in Cambridge, Turner was busy in Madison, placating the losers in the tug-of-war over his services. His letter of resignation, expressing the hope that President Van Hise's "wise and farsighted policy" would be supported by the regents, was graciously answered, but the regents were less courteous; they accepted Turner's resignation without a single word of regret at his leaving. To Turner's relief, President Wheeler of California was as understanding as Van Hise, recognizing that a call to Harvard could not be matched either as honor or opportunity.[47] Turner had left one university and jilted another without making a single enemy.

There was less exultation in Cambridge, and less mourning in Madison, than Turner had hoped. The Harvard Bulletin lived up to his expectations with two full columns on his career and a glowing editorial that lauded his western specialization and branded him one of the few men alive able "to combine the large view with the small one, to combine the general plan and conception with the minute examination of particulars." "You did not get as much space as the Dartmouth game," wrote Haskins as he forwarded these comments, "but you got first place."[48] Madison treated the news less well. The *Daily Cardinal* was so crowded with columns on the coming Minnesota game that it did not even mention the loss of its most distinguished scholar, while the local press found room for only two sparse paragraphs amidst its columns on the BIG GAME. "Prof. Turner," boasted the *Wisconsin State Journal*, "is one of the most scholarly and popular members of the Wisconsin faculty and Harvard has made repeated efforts to induce him to become a member of its faculty." Thus were the great mourned, with a few hurried untruths.

Fortunately, the students and alumni had better sense. No sooner did the significance of Turner's leaving sink home than a cry was raised that was heard even within the sacred cloisters of the regents' meeting-room. The student University Senate and a "Wisconsin Committee of Students" awakened belatedly to his "inspired lectures" and unanimously resolved that his resignation be refused. Newspapers, particularly in Milwaukee, discovered that he was a "rarely inspired teacher" whose loss would be irreparable. Alumni raised their voices in a chorus of protest from Seattle to the eastern seaboard, some demanding that the regents induce Turner to reconsider his resignation, others finding for the first time that he was a scholar of such repute that the university could not possibly part with his services, and all praising his years of devoted teaching. Even the *Wisconsin Alumni Magazine*, although torn between regret that a professor who had achieved so much through the state's bounty should desert, and delight that a Wisconsinite should be in such demand, eventually decided to praise rather than condemn, and hoped that the regents would persuade him to stay.[49]

If there was mourning in the university community, there was even more in the historical fraternity of the Midwest. They voiced their sorrow at the loss of their most eminent representative at a Chicago meeting of the North Central History Teachers Association. The entire program, skillfully arranged by Professor Andrew C. McLaughlin, was one long paean of praise. Turner attended, ate the fifty-cent dinner at the Hutchinson Cafe, and sat in embarrassed delight as a parade of his best friends heaped adulation on adulation, climaxed by a poem "To F. J. T.":[50]

> The frontier weeps, expansion sleeps,
> No scholar's left to learn her.
> For Eastern jeers a Niobes' tears
> Off trots our lovely Turner.

Then came the letters, some spontaneous, others inspired by James Alton James, who urged all former students to write, bound the returns in a red leather cover, and presented the lot at a touching ceremony on the eve of the Turners' departure from Madison.[51] As Turner read those tributes, ranging in praise from high to highest, he must have taken solace in knowing that his efforts had been appreciated by a good many of the region's most eminent scholars, if not by the Board of Regents.

Most of this deluge—of student resolutions, newspaper editorials, letters from friends and former pupils—touched him deeply. All were answered personally—a formidable task, for they numbered more than a hundred—and each with an intimate touch that revealed his affection. "As I read my mail," he confessed to Carl Becker, "I have felt like a ghost caught indecently in pillaging his bodily representative's obituary notices." Yet there was immense satisfaction in what he read, even (as he modestly told James Alton James) if they proved that excellent historical students could "produce very deceptive history." Best of all was the realization that he had left a plentiful crop of scholars in the West to broaden the clearing that he had begun there. "One of the satisfactions I have in changing my residence," he wrote one student, "is that I am not leaving a historical field devoid of explorers."[52] Turner could take pleasure in the indisputable fact that his mark on his native section was too indelible to be erased.

His one fear was that his move might be misinterpreted as desire for greater prestige or financial award than Madison could offer. A few letters bore out that apprehension. Wrote one former student with as little regard for the truth as for grammar: "I reallize [sic] fully that we can not expect a person to make a complete sacrifice of themselves for one's native state, when similar fields of usefulness with more attractive surroundings and better compensation call elsewhere."[53] This cut deeply, for nothing could be further from the truth. Turner would have sold his soul to stay in the Madison that he loved. "I know," he told his wife, "that I have put aside the matter of 'joy of life' for the chance to do the thing that I ought to do." Two of his students, dropping in to bid him farewell, saw him break into tears as he thought of all that he was leaving behind. Turner was not drawn to Harvard by its attractions, as too many thought. He was leaving Wisconsin only because he honestly believed that his move would benefit the university by bringing the regents to their senses. "I feel," he told a colleague, "something like a watch that has been so frequently regulated that at last it can *run*."[54] He ran, but how he hated to do so.

To the few intimates who sensed his true motive, he explained his feelings frankly. At issue was his half-time teaching arrangement. This personified the basic conflict between President Van Hise and his faculty on the one hand and the regents and public on the other. As such, it was a danger rather than a benefit to the university. "I do not," he told a friend, "feel that my research arrangement is desirable for Wisconsin or myself under existing conditions." To bow to the regents and return to full-time teaching would be an admission of defeat for the whole principle of humanistic research. Only if he subordinated his own desires to the good of the university could the regents be awakened to the dangers of their policies; only if he shocked them by leaving would they lessen their attacks on pure research, cease meddling in faculty affairs, end their insistence that the administration be subordinated to the state's school system, and reverse their attempt to elevate practical above cultural instruction. That decision reached, he had only to decide between California and Harvard. California meant "more exploring in new fields and constructing historical clearings and cabins." The time had come "to settle long enough to raise a crop."[55] Harvard offered a better climate for research, and to Harvard he went. In all his reasoning there was not a hint of self-glorification or avariciousness. He wanted to stay in Madison; he could benefit Wisconsin by leaving. His thinking was as simple and honest as that.

Turner's cause could triumph only if his resignation spurred the regents into soul-searching and change, and there seemed little chance of that as he settled to his last year of teaching at Madison. The Stalwarts on the board were as outspoken as ever that fall of 1909; W. D. Hoard was storming about the state demanding more money for the School of Agriculture—the "political Gibraltar of the University," he called it—and C. P. Cary was urging the school superintendents under his charge to rebel against training students for college when most had no interest in higher education. At the other extreme, some of Turner's less moderate friends were itching to use his resignation as a pillory for the regents who had crucified him; Richard Lloyd Jones, who had written the muckraking article in *Collier's* that helped spark the controversy, was ready to prepare a series of exposures that would reveal the board members for what they were: an "ignorant and vicious" crew whose one hope was that democratic education be "throttled and curbed and rebuked and, perhaps, set back fifty years."[56] The battle lines were still tightly drawn, and the quiet reform that Turner wanted seemed far away.

Happily, these extremists no longer ruled, for behind the scenes the moderates on both sides were working quietly toward some solution. The machinery for this was set in motion when the faculty, at the request of the regents, elected a conference committee of nine to meet with a similar committee from the board to discuss the state of the university. When this met on December 10, 1909, the faculty members seized the initiative at once, with a clear statement of their basic grievance. They were, they told the regents, uneasy and dissatisfied following Turner's resignation, and would so remain until the board ceased meddling with individual faculty members. The regents had harried Turner into leaving by first granting, then questioning, his half-time research leaves; by inquiring into his hours of work with an animus that offended him, by distracting him with false accusations until he could no longer carry on his investigations, by creating such a hostile climate that he felt he was no longer wanted. These sentiments were infectious; when a scholar of Turner's status experienced such apprehensions, his doubts were shared by every member of the staff. They had even spread beyond the campus to the point that recruiting a replacement would be difficult.

The regents on the committee listened, then asked the question they were supposed to ask: what have we done to create this atmosphere of doubt and fear? The flood-gates of faculty resentment were opened now, and complaint piled on complaint: the regents had promoted and demoted teachers without consulting the department concerned, they had refused to promote others despite departmental and administrative recommendations, they had imperiled academic freedom by trying to tell the economics department what to teach, they had threatened academic tenure by forcing resignation, they had dealt individually with members of the instructional staff, they had interfered in graduate work by attending doctoral examinations, they had withheld funds from the philosophy department and the economics department and had been unduly generous in supporting "practical" subjects, they had questioned the value of the humanistic research that was the mainstay of any great university. They had, in other words, abused their trust by intruding in the educational processes of the university.

The remedy was as obvious as the malady, and was patiently spelled out by the faculty. Regents should communicate with professors or departments only through the president, they should follow departmental and administrative recommendations on all appointments and promotions, they should bow to the will of the professors on educational matters, they should never interfere in the subject content of any course. Even if an instructor taught socialism or anarchism? asked a regent. No instructor taught socialism or anarchism, he was firmly told, but "you cannot close any field of inquiry without impairing the student's faith in the honesty of teaching." One by one these points were ticked off, until one regent asked plaintively: "What, then, becomes of the powers of the Regents? Are we merely a consulting body?" He was wrong, of course, for the statement finally agreed upon simply recognized a workable division of authority: "The Regents have no intention of interfering with the customary methods of educational administration by the Faculty; they will continue to allow the Faculty the initiative in formulating educational policies; and they desire appointments to be made through the regular channels as developed in the custom of the University."[57] Here was a clear-cut definition of policy, but here also was a crow-eating admission by the regents that they had gone beyond their powers.

Such was the climate caused by Turner's resignation that the statement was adopted without change. The faculty heard the good news at its next meeting; the regents, they were assured, had acted with the best of intentions and with no improper motives; now they agreed to conform to the bylaws of the university. The committee's report to the board, delivered by Frederick C. Thwaits, its chairman and a staunch friend of Turner, was less pussyfooting. The regents had been to blame for Turner's departure and for the campus unrest that threatened the university. They must mend their ways by adhering strictly to the school's bylaws, and by recognizing that educational policy must be determined by faculty and administration. When these recommendations were agreed upon, the battle was over.[58] The faculty had won a clear victory, and Turner was vindicated.

Leaving Wisconsin, Turner soon found, was not easy, and much of the academic year of 1909-10 was squandered on annoying tasks that divided his attention between Cambridge and Madison. Cambridge demanded hours of time. He had to arrange his Harvard courses, first of all. His "History of the West" would be offered, of course, but the seminar posed problems. Albert Bushnell Hart spelled them out: Turner could give his own, or he could participate in a general seminar on American institutions, or he could offer one with Hart. Turner had a better idea; why not a joint seminar by the department's three Americanists, Channing, Hart, and Turner? This suggestion brought an acid rejoinder from Edward Channing: "Possibly you do not know that Hart and I split a few years ago on my initiative for reasons that will be apparent to you after you have been here a year or two."[59] There would be no cooperative instruction in American history at Harvard. Turner would offer his own seminar on the Van Buren administration. The class hours he would leave to the department, but he warned that an eight o'clock class would put him out of business in short order.

Housing for the Turners also had to be found. A preliminary survey that fall indicated that unfurnished houses rented for $900 a year, furnished houses rented for $1000, and Edward Channing's rented for $1500. Such prices were too rich for the Turner bank account, but by spring they realized that they had to make a decision. Their opportunity came when a colleague, Professor Roger B. Merriman, decided to vacate his stately mansion at 175 Brattle Street because of his wife's illness. He offered to rent the house to Turner for only $1000 a year. For a time the Turners hesitated, fearful lest the house be contaminated by disease, but they were soon reassured and sealed the bargain. They would live in unaccustomed style, at least for their first year in Cambridge.

Their financial problems were somewhat eased by developments in Madison. The search for Turner's successor proved easier than antici- pated; Max Farrand (the first choice) was not interested in leaving Yale to which he had just moved, but a rising young star in western history, Frederic Logan Paxson, could be lured from his professorship at the University of Michigan. Paxson proved an ideal choice for all concerned; not only did his recent book, *The Last American Frontier*, assure him a reputation that would attract graduate students, but he was willing to buy the Turner house at the asking price of $13,000— $3000 down and the balance by November 1, 1910.[60] The Turners would have a small backlog of savings to show for their years in Madi- son, even though most of their profits would be swallowed up by re- tirement of the mortgage and moving expenses.

Those troublesome matters settled, Turner settled into a busy spring of teaching and lecturing. That he taught at all was due to his own generosity, for he was due a sabbatical leave, both through his university contract and because he had accumulated credits by summer-school teaching, but he was conscious of the students' needs and offered a semester of his course on Van Buren's administration. At times he must have regretted even this much commitment to the classroom, burdened as he was by lecture engagements long agreed upon: a Phi Beta Kappa address at the University of Michigan in mid-May on "Middle Western Ideals," a paper before the Iowa City meeting of the Mississippi Valley Historical Association later that month on "The Significance of the Mississippi Valley in American History," a commencement address at Indiana University in June. These meant hours of preparation, just at a time when everyone in Madison, apparently, insisted on giving a fare- well party for the Turners. They lived a gay social life that spring, climaxed by a reception at the home of Carl Russell Fish, where students and faculty gave the Turners a silver tea service, and by a departmental dinner with Reuben Gold Thwaites as host, Sellery as speechmaker, and a pair of Zeis binoculars the parting gift. Turner's delight at this hom- age was dampened by one glaring omission: the Board of Regents made not a single gesture to mourn his leaving. That cut deeply.[61]

Summer brought some relief from the social round, but none from the burdens of work. Turner had agreed to teach summer school—the $500 fee was essential to his budget—and he had to use every moment that could be snatched from classroom preparation on a long overdue article for the *Encyclopaedia Britannica*. His labors were magnified by Madison's excessive heat and a prolonged drought that filled the air with dust; they were magnified again when Mae and Dorothy left in early July to find a sanctuary from the hay fever that attacked early that summer, leaving him to endure the final agonies of packing alone. Books—thousands of books—had to be boxed, furniture crated, movers employed, transportation by rail arranged. A complication arose when the company that had sold the Turners their player piano announced that it could not leave the state until the final $458 due was paid, further taxing Turner's time and dwindling bank account. But at last Turner had a van trundle the household goods to the railroad yards—only to discover that the freight car assigned them was too small. A few good cigars and a modestly priced supper bribed the workmen to shift the whole lot by lantern-light, a task that was not completed until ten o'clock on the night of July 30. "I got home," he reported to Mae, "tired enough to sleep."[62]

Nor was the end yet, for Turner had to endure another week of classes before he could follow his furniture to New England. A dismal week it was, with steaming temperatures, a round of dinners with friends, lectures in an oven-like classroom, and, at night, interminable hours on the *Britannica* article. Finally, on August 10, the last task was completed, the last suitcase packed. Turner was ready to leave Madison. As a hired hack carried him along East Washington Street toward the railroad station, he could see workmen beginning to dismantle the horse market that had been a landmark since he could remember—a victim of the automobiles and paved roads that were changing the city's profile. Madison stood on the threshold of a new day when an urban swirl and a gigantic educational institution would replace the tree-shaded streets, the pleasant little college, the leisurely pace of life that Turner knew and loved. He was leaving just in time.

XIII

Harvard Years:
The Academic World

1910-1917

IF FREDERICK JACKSON TURNER had been a prudent and well-ordered man, he would have arrived in Cambridge in mid-August of 1910, ready to join his wife in her hay-fever retreat in the Berkshires and to journey with her to Hancock Point on Maine's cool coast, where she stayed with friends through September. Instead, he had to pay for his sins as a procrastinator. With him came a mountain of notes and a conscience burdened by a scandalously overdue publishing commitment. Instead of relaxing to the murmur of mountain pines, he was doomed to swelter through nights at the Colonial Club and days at the Harvard Library as he ground out page after page for a demanding editor of the *Encyclopaedia Britannica*.

Turner was hardened to the plaints of publishers, but even he admitted that this one had justice on his side. Four years had passed since he had agreed to prepare an article for the *Britannica* on the United States since 1865, with a fee of $500 as the lure. The assignment seemed simple enough at the time—twenty-five pages dealing solely with the political chronicle, to be delivered by October 1, 1907—but Turner had a knack of transforming the simplest task into a model of complexity. Here was a little-known field of marvelous fascination, scarcely touched by historians, and bursting with intriguing problems. So the deadline came and went. Periodic inquiries from the editors grew increasingly peremptory, but not until May 1910 did Turner feel that he had mastered the subject thoroughly enough to put pen to paper. By this time Turner had forgotten the 25-page space limitation, and the New York office had lost the early correspondence where it was specified. Hence they settled on any "reasonable length," which was a green light for a great deal more about the recent United States than the *Britannica* expected.[1]

Turner was at his best when working under the lash, and it was liberally applied. Letters, cables from London, pleas from the New York editors were part of his life as he labored through those hot August days. "Boston is a turkish bath," he reported. "I didn't sleep much last night, but I did get my article along aways, though it is hard travellin' for a man acclimated neither to Boston, nor to work."[2] The results were satisfactory—the first 78 pages sent on August 29, the last of the 194 three weeks later, the bibliography (1250 words longer than requested) by early October, after threats from London that the whole edition was being delayed. Turner had stretched his twenty-five page article into nearly two hundred pages, and a 750-word bibliography into 2000 words—with only the $500 agreed upon as compensation—but he had learned a great deal about a difficult period, and he had produced an article that was viewed by his generation as a major contribution.[3]

He also finished in time to spend three weeks in the Maine woods. Then, in early October, he and Mae and Dorothy moved into their elegant Brattle Street home. They were a bit overwhelmed by its magnificence; Turner was terrified by the dainty antique furniture but delighted at the prospect of keeping fit by walking about in a home that was as big as all outdoors. His friends in Madison took unabashed delight in his plight. "To have a man with your Jacksonian ideas established in a mansion on Tory Row," wrote Reuben Gold Thwaites, "came very near creating heart rupture in this neck of the woods."[4]

Turner had little time to enjoy spacious living, for he had arrived just in time to plunge into the new academic world to which he was committed. And what a fascinating world it was! Harvard, despite its eminence, was a small school by modern standards, with some 2200 students—nearly all of them haughtily indifferent to learning and content with the "Gentleman's Grade" of "C" in their courses. They were rigidly stratified on the basis of wealth and breeding, with the elite concentrated in Mt. Auburn Street's "Gold Coast," the middle group existing in shabby quarters in the "Yard," and the remainder living about Boston and commuting by trolley. Academic requirements were modest; President A. Lawrence Lowell was beginning his attack on the complete freedom of course election that had prevailed under President

Charles W. Eliot, but only gradually were his reforms accepted: "concentration" on a major subject applied first for the class of 1914, a tutorial system at about the same time, common halls for freshmen near the Charles River in 1914, an honors examination for the division of History, Government and Economics in 1917. Turner watched these changes with moderate approval, afraid that they were converting him into a combination of sausage-filling machine and private detective, as he crammed knowledge into reluctant pupils and policed them as they acquired it.[5]

The history department was more to his liking. Two of the Europeanists, his old friend Charles Homer Haskins and his new friend and benefactor Archibald Cary Coolidge, were his particular favorites. Coolidge, especially, proved a tower of strength; he could always be relied upon to convince President Lowell that this project or that of Turner's was worth supporting. His colleagues in American history were of a different stamp. One, Albert Bushnell Hart, was genuinely cordial and did his best to be friendly, but he was so absorbed in university and national politics (he was a fanatical supporter of his Harvard classmate Theodore Roosevelt) and so wrapped up in his writing and editorial chores (930 articles published during his academic years, an average of one every two weeks, and nearly one hundred books, two and one-half a year) that he had no time for companionship. The other was Edward Channing.

Turner spent his years at Harvard trying to understand Channing, and he never succeeded. A chubby dynamo of a man, short and smooth-shaven, Channing was a popular undergraduate teacher, charging his lectures with irony and wit, enlivening them with dramatic techniques, and packing them with demands on the students' time that terrorized all but the most industrious. His horizons, however, never extended west of the Hudson River and seldom beyond the Connecticut. That the frontier had been a force in American history he stubbornly refused to recognize; he only reluctantly admitted that there was a West, and the single chapter on "The Westward March" in the last volumes of his multivolume history of the United States did little more than trace the migration of a few New England families. In that work he deemed Turner's theory worthy of mention only in three footnote references. This was a deliberate slight, but Turner did his best to be charitable. "Porcupinus Angelicus," he called him (behind his back), but he was sincerely eager for a friendship that Channing would never allow. "Channing and I," he told a colleague, "had quite different conceptions of the trend of American history. . . . Nevertheless, I appreciated the scholarship of the man and his New England point of view." Channing was less charitable. "Turner is a dear fellow," he confided to a student, "but he has no idea of the value of time. He has never written any big books."[6]

There was reason for his bristly attitude. Channing, subconsciously or perhaps consciously, recognized in Turner a symbol of the futility of his own life. It was his misfortune that he was never to rise above the "scientific school" of historiography in which he had been reared; unable, or unwilling, to change with the times, he was outmoded before he reached the prime of life. Albert B. Hart offered him no reminders of this, for their views were comparable, but now a vigorous young man had come into the department to challenge his theories, lure graduate students from his seminar, and take over the major task of directing doctoral dissertations. His antagonism was deep, nurtured by his growing isolation from the local and national historical world. This the students sensed. Circulated among them was a cruel satire, purportedly a letter from Channing to the "Star Chamber," demanding that Turner be punished for destroying the sound structure of history that had reached its pinnacle "with the appearance of my fourth volume." "He treats my American history as an amoeba, capable of unlimited division," and had divided it into Old West, New West, Middle West, North West, South West, and Far West. When a copy of this document fell into Turner's hand, he scrawled on it, "Hazing me," but the rift went far deeper.[7]

On the surface, however, all was well, and Turner could begin his Harvard teaching that October with no more than the usual apprehensions. His first lecture in History 17, "The History of the West," went well enough; he found sixty-one students in his classroom, most of them New Englanders with names that spelled eastern conservatism —a Roosevelt, a Frothingham, and a Conant were enrolled—and all were utterly unversed in anything remotely resembling knowledge of the frontier. "They are engaging young rascals," he reported to a Madison friend, "and I foresee that I shall have an interesting experience in attempting to guide them over western trails."[8] Turner led them deep into the wilderness that morning: he gave them a terrifying battery of assignments first—his own essays on "The Significance of the Fron-

tier" and "The Problem of the West," an article in a recent *South Atlantic Quarterly* on the legacy of the pioneers, E. L. Godkin's book,
Problems of American Democracy, and Achille Loria's *The Economic
Foundations of Society*, a look at the maps in the *Census* Atlas for 1900
—then a liberal dose of frontier theory. The frontier was "a zone of
population extending between civilization and the wilderness" where
society was atomized, flying apart into individual particles; frontiersmen were altered by this unfamiliar environment, their behavior dictated by the practical problems of existence. "The course will be the
study of a PROCEDURE rather than a REGION."[9] Here was the gospel according to Turner, a gospel that was as stimulating as it was unfamiliar
to undergraduates nurtured in the belief that the alpha and omega of
American life lay in New England.

If the students found the experience pleasant, so did Turner. The
lads were alert and clever, "if not so steady at the tugs as our western
classes," and many of them were genuinely interested. Those who were
not soon fell by the wayside; the men of large means— the "Mt. Auburn
youth"—departed when they discovered that the way to salvation lay
through the library, but the football team, attracted by the promise of
a diet of cowboys and Indians, "took its medicine like men, and got
good grades."[10] The seminar raised no such problems, even though some
might feel that Turner could have selected a more lively topic than the
election of 1836 as it influenced the Van Buren administration. They
were a capable crew, led by such stellar lights as Samuel Eliot Morison
and Kenneth W. Colgrove, and they did their work so well that Turner
found them not at all inferior to his Wisconsin graduate students.
Only one, R. H. Smith, failed to appear for the second semester, while
the "History of the West" enrollment increased from 61 to 67
students.[11]

With classes under way and the family settled into its temporary
home, Turner could turn to two pressing tasks that plagued him during
his first Harvard year. One was the presidential address that he had to
deliver before the American Historical Association when it met in
Indianapolis that December. He had been increasingly aware of that
responsibility, but had delayed as usual, and when he arrived in Cambridge he was still toying with topics worthy of the occasion. No mere
rehash of his ideas on the frontier and section would do; the traditions

of the association decreed that he must select a subject significant to the entire profession, not just to his own interests. For a time he considered "Changing American Ideals," and "Perspective in American History," but eventually he settled on one more suited to his talents: "Social Forces in American History."[12]

Turner left no record of the train of thought that led him to this topic, but little imagination is needed to reconstruct his trail. As one unusually sensitive to the atmosphere of his day, he recognized that younger historians were on the point of rebellion against the traditional interpretation of the past, and that their revolt was sparked by the spirit of Progressivism that had accompanied Theodore Roosevelt into the White House. To them, no less than to the muckrakers and reformers, social improvement was of paramount importance, so important that history must be converted into an instrument for the transformation of society. Change was occurring, they saw, not by the slow evolution of institutions, but through conflicts of interest and clashes between factions. Had this been the case in prior eras? Was change rather than continuity, conflict rather than consensus, the key to understanding the past? And, if the dynamics of change and conflict could be thoroughly understood, could the lessons learned be applied to the improvement of modern society?[13]

These were challenging questions, and as historians sought answers to them they wrought a revolution in the understanding of the past. Their spotlight was not on the European genesis of American institutions, but on the environmental pressures that adjusted those institutions to the needs of the people; not on the remote past, but on more recent events relevant to today's problems. They saw eighteenth- and nineteenth-century America not as a placid land where institutions evolved slowly, but as a country in a constant state of flux, where conflicts between contending groups underlay progress. The ultimate goal of the nation was not achievement of national unity, as earlier scholars had believed, but social and political democracy. The historian's duty was to reveal the significance of the conflicts that led toward this goal, to show their continuity, and to demonstrate their usefulness to the social reformers of the present.

These views had been Turner's stock-in-trade since 1891, when he prepared his paper on "The Significance of History," but they had taken root slowly through the profession and only now were ready to blossom. At the very session where Turner read his presidential address, James Harvey Robinson spoke on "The Relation of History to the Newer Sciences of Man," touching off a controversy with George Lincoln Burr and other conservatives. In that same year Carl Becker, in an *Atlantic Monthly* article on "Detachment and Writing History," launched an attack on the "objectivists" who believed in the inviolability of "facts," and Lynn Thorndike sharpened the assault by attacking "The Scientific Presentation of History," in *Popular Science Monthly*. These were the shock troops that prepared the way for James Harvey Robinson to issue his collected essays on *The New History* two years later, a volume that gave the movement its name and focus.

The "New Historians" broke sharply with the past. Their emphasis was on events relevant to the present; history they saw as an instrument for reform, not as a subject to be pursued for idle curiosity. They urged less emphasis on political chronicles and more on the social and intellectual record as a means of probing the motives of human behavior and the impact of environmental pressures; their purpose was to understand change as the product of "the underlying forces that surged beyond and behind the visible body politic" (as Turner put it). They thought of themselves as realists, shunning both "barren" empiricism and "grandiose" abstractions. They subordinated the past to the present, and searched for evidence of continuity in the contortions that periodically nudged society into progress. They urged the use of techniques borrowed from other disciplines—sociology, economics, political science, anthropology—as necessary to an understanding of the background of today's problems; the principal purpose of history was not to illuminate former eras, but to synthesize the social sciences and reveal their predictive value in solving the dilemmas of today. History, in other words, was to be broadened, enriched by borrowings from other disciplines, and used to look backward through the eyes of the present.

All this Turner recognized as he gave thought to a subject for his address. What was more logical than that he should issue a manifesto to encourage the surfacing of concepts that he had preached for a generation? Perhaps he was goaded into such a decision when he re-read the 1908 presidential address of George Burton Adams, a conservative who defined history as a "science of investigation" that operated wholly independently of other disciplines to achieve a chronological arrangement of "facts." Such echoes from a bygone day had to be refuted.

Turner began his own address by recognizing that the historical fact was "not planted on the solid ground of fixed conditions." Instead, every investigator was influenced by the times in which he lived; each new generation came on the scene equipped with different insights and prejudices than its predecessors. Turner saw the pathway of history strewn with the wrecks of "known and acknowledged truths" the result of both imperfect analysis and the failure of historians to pay proper attention to the relativity and transiency of their own basis for appraisal. He took no extreme stand for relativism; while skeptical of man's ability ever to learn the exact truth about the past, he still believed that proper methodology and the use of well-formulated hypotheses allowed the truth to be approximated.

Such a methodology required liberal borrowings from other disciplines. Devoting the principal body of his address to a capsule survey of the changes in the American social order since the closing of the frontier, he drew an obvious lesson: that the transformation from a rural to an industrial-urban economy posed problems of such complexity that they could be understood only by scholars well-versed in all the social sciences. Scientists, Turner pointed out, had bridged the gap between disciplines to create electrochemistry, geophysics, astrophysics, and a host of similar cooperative fields; historians must effect alliances with economists, sociologists, political scientists, geologists, geographers, psychologists, and students of the arts if they were to be properly equipped to analyze modern society. This was a belief long preached by Turner, but new to many in his audience; he was the first president of the Association to urge an interdisciplinary approach in his presidential address.

If this was treason to the traditionalists, so were two other points that he emphasized—and that mirrored the views of the "New Historians." History, he insisted, was no mere political chronicle; its principal concern should be the subterranean social forces that determined political events, "shaping and reshaping under the conditions of a nation changing as it adjusts to its environment." Nor were the findings of the historian absolute; the function of the historian was constantly to "rework our history from the new points of view afforded by the present." These heretical views, as offensive to the orthodox as Turner's demand for an interdisciplinary approach, served as an ultimatum to the Old Guard of the profession. Turner had taken his stand for "Progressive History," and opened a new world of interpretation to his younger colleagues.[14] When Waldo G. Leland, secretary of the Association, reported that Turner's address had imposed "new duties" on scholars, he was speaking accurately. So was James Schouler, venerable spokesman for a dying generation, when he complained that history should not be re-written "to suit each new fashion of thought and interest . . . in order to please the coming age."[15] Turner had made no such suggestion, of course, but Schouler's exaggerated alarms typified the panic among the defenders of "Scientism."

James Schouler's carping, and the few echoes that it stirred among his fellow conservatives, was drowned in the chorus of approval that "Social Forces in American History" inspired. Turner was immensely pleased, but his cup of joy overflowed when the applause that greeted his address was interrupted by the arrival of a delegation of his former students, bearing with them a handsome volume with the title *Essays in American History Dedicated to Frederick Jackson Turner*. This had been long a-borning; Charles Homer Haskins made the original suggestion, Guy Stanton Ford assumed the task of extracting essays from a score of former students, and Henry Holt & Company undertook the printing on the theory that, if they could not publish a book by Turner, they would publish one for him. Turner was overjoyed. "I am as pleased as a grandfather with a new grandbaby," he told one of the contributors.[16] He was also embarrassed that his students and the publishers should suffer financially, insisting on sending a check for $8.10 for the six copies sent him—a check that was promptly returned by Henry Holt & Company. As Turner read the essays, he must have had some doubts whether his teaching had succeeded, for few of them were worthy of attention, then or since. Even Guy Stanton Ford, the editor, realized in retrospect that the volume's only virtue was to print Carl Becker's brilliant comments on "Kansas."[17] That Turner's *festschrift* was somewhat more disastrous than most was due to the catholicity of his own interests. The term "frontier" did not appear in the title of a single essay, and only two remotely touched on the subject; instead, they ranged over the whole spectrum of historical interests that Turner inspired in his pupils. Lacking emphasis on the West that the profession associated with his name, and built about no central theme, the volume was quickly—and mercifully—forgotten.

Turner returned to Cambridge from Indianapolis that December, proudly bearing his *festschrift* and with plaudits for his presidential address ringing in his ears, to plunge into a thoroughly disagreeable task that his Harvard appointment required. Even before he arrived in Cambridge, his colleagues, Edward Channing and Albert Bushnell Hart, had offered him an opportunity he could not refuse. The *Guide to the Study of American History* that they had published in 1896 was long out of date; Ginn & Company were eager for a new edition; would Turner join in the revision? He accepted, of course, and the contract was signed in December 1909: 10 per cent royalty to be divided among the three authors, $1000 for secretarial and research aid, a delivery date of January 1, 1911. Turner's assignments were sections on the West and recent history. The triumvirate almost broke up when defining "recent history"; Channing wanted to end in 1898, but Turner insisted on 1910, and he carried the day with Hart's support. So work began, slowly for Turner, whose autumn was occupied with his presidential address; predictably, he was far from done by January 1, but neither were his collaborators. By June 1911, Channing was nearing the end and Hart's portions were in galley proof, but Turner's were still in manuscript, and very rough manuscript at that. Then, too, his sections were running far beyond the word limit that had been imposed. Pressure continued through that summer and into the next school year before Hart's whip-cracking forced Turner to surrender his contributions to the publisher, but the delay was worth while. "I don't know that you have ever rendered a greater service (except your volume in the Am. Nation Series) to the sound understanding of American history," Hart assured him.[18]

These were no idle words, for Turner had made a significant contribution to the "Harvard Guide." His sections on recent history were revolutionary; topics such as "The Trust Problem," "Labor and Injunction," "Conservation," and "American Society in the Twentieth Century" were newcomers to textbooks, and helped shape the teaching of recent American history for a generation. So were the major sections on social and industrial history. His portions on "The West" were less original, largely because he had made the subject familiar to scholars, but they allowed him to garner an unearned increment. A list of the more important books and articles that he had surveyed were brought together in a guide for his students, published in 1911: *List of References in History 17: History of the West*. This modest work of 89 pages was incomplete and was, in Turner's later judgment, an "obvious atrocity,"[19] but it was the progenitor of a whole succession of editions of *List of References* that would be purchased by generations of Harvard students and that would influence the teaching of the subject nationally.

More to Turner's liking was a final assignment inflicted on him by the energetic Albert Bushnell Hart. Would he prepare three articles— "The Frontier in American Development," "Sectionalism in the United States," and "The West as a Factor in American Politics"—for the *Cyclopedia of American Government* that Hart and Andrew C. McLaughlin were editing? The honorarium was generous and the subjects so dear to Turner's heart that he could not refuse, even though he shuddered at the prospect of another deadline. Well he might. The date agreed upon—December 1911—came and went with work scarcely under way; six months later, Hart was warning that the whole volume was ready to go to press and that he must turn elsewhere unless the articles were delivered by June 17, 1912. Turner tried, but he was so deluged by proof on the *Harvard Guide* that not until the end of the month could he write his daughter: "Tonight I start on the race to finish the articles."[20] "Race" was hardly the word; they were not ready for delivery until mid-September and then they were not in publishable form; the 2000 words allotted to the frontier had grown to 2600, the 2000 on sectionalism to 3900, and the 2500 on the West in American politics to 5400. Back they went to him for another month of work before Hart was satisfied.[21] They made but scant contribution, for Turner had said the same things before, but they did compress most of his frontier and sectional theories into a relatively brief space.

The succession of deadlines that kept Turner's nose to the grindstone during his first year in Cambridge meant that his social life was restricted, but with the last galley of proof on the *Harvard Guide* read, and the last encyclopedia article delivered to Hart's office, he could settle into the comfortable routine that was to last until World War I toppled his world into chaos. He and Mae fitted moderately well into Harvard's unfamiliar society and they enjoyed themselves—but again in moderation. The luxurious home of Professor Merriman proved so comfortable that after a year there they moved into a nearby house at 153 Brattle Street that was only slightly less elegant and not at all cheaper; again in 1914 they shifted to a somewhat more modest property at 7 Phillips Place, where the annual rental was only $800. There they lived for the next decade. "We are," Turner reported to a friend in Madison, "well and comfortably housed in our second quarters since the main migration. But it is among other peoples' books and pictures and among other friends and it is not entirely natural yet."[22] Each of these establishments required more care than tiny Mae could give; at least one "Nellie" or "Lizzie" was always in residence and usually two, along with the stenographer Turner needed to drive him to his writing.

These extraordinary expenses doomed him to a constant struggle against bank overdrafts. The $13,000 paid by Paxson for their Madison home was spent before the summer of 1910 was over—$5000 to pay off the mortgage note held by his sister, $4466 to retire miscellaneous debts, a few modest investments—and Turner reached Cambridge with only $300 in the bank and the prospect of borrowing before the first Harvard paycheck came, on December 1. This paltry sum, five shares of American Telephone and Telegraph worth $712 and five of Great Northern Railroad worth $630, a pianola that had cost $950 in 1908 and would sell for less now, a Remington rifle, a Columbia bicycle, a canoe, and a considerable number of books—these were Turner's principal assets after two decades of service to the historical profession. He had also contracted for $17,000 in life insurance that cost him heavily in premiums and was used less as a cushion against the future than as collateral for frequent bank loans.[23] That was all he had. His salary—$5000 a year to 1915 and $5500 thereafter—was adequate for its day, but hardly generous, while other sources of income were almost nonexistent. Royalties on the *Harvard Guide* did not begin until 1920, when he received a check for $13.82, and they never exceeded $35 a year thereafter.[24]

The one bright spot in the Turners' financial future was a speculative stock on which they pinned their hopes for a comfortable old age. President Van Hise was responsible. Hearing rumors of iron deposits in the wilds of Brazil, that eminent geologist made a personal investigation in 1910 that revealed resources as rich as those of Minnesota's

Mesabi Range. Options were taken out, the Brazilian Iron and Steel Company formed, and a few friends allowed to buy stock in a venture that was a gamble, but that promised fabulous returns. Turner contracted for thirty shares, using $500 from the sale of his house as a down payment, and scraping together the remaining $2500 over the next years. His faith in that nest egg was almost pathetic; over and over again he cautioned his family never to sell the "Brazil" stock save as a last resort, assuring them that it would soon pay them $4000 yearly. Alas for such pipe dreams. Every effort to raise the capital needed to develop the properties failed, then the company collapsed completely as Europe plunged into the 1914 war. Turner's hopes of a bountiful retirement and security for Dorothy vanished with his small investment.[25]

The Turners lived always on the brink of debt, but most of their professorial friends were in the same plight, and they saw no reason to complain. They settled into the social life of Cambridge and Boston, as the usual round of dinners, teas, and receptions widened their circle of acquaintances. Friends—the close friends they had known in Madison—were few; Charles Homer Haskins was their sole intimate until his marriage in 1912 added his bride to the little group. Both of the Turners missed the easy give-and-take they had known with the Van Hises and Slaughters on Frances Street, but both were properly respectful of the fashionable events that Bostonians understood so well: stately dinners at the home of James Ford Rhodes, affairs at the Algonquin Club, an evening with Josiah Royce, who was "very bright and interesting," another where Mrs. William James so overawed Turner that he could do no more than admire her conversation "in brilliant spells of silence."[26] "Interesting" experiences, Turner would have labeled them, but hardly the old-shoe friendships that he so enjoyed in the past.

His clubs were also more invigorating than relaxing. Two welcomed him to membership: the Shop-Club, where he matched wits with such lights as Frank W. Taussig, Edwin F. Gay, and Ephraim Emerton in monthly evening meetings where papers were read and discussed; and the Thursday Club, whose members met over an elaborate dinner, plentiful wines, and light conversation before listening to the inevitable essay by one of the members on a topic dear to his research interests. There Turner rubbed elbows with such giants as William James, Harlow Shapley, John Livingston Lowes, and Zachariah Chafee, and there he heard discussions that ranged from "The Old Testament as a German Type" to color blindness in fish (he was delighted to find that they could see the lures that he tied to attract them).[27] There, too, he tried out his own essays; many written during his Harvard years were specifically prepared for this club or that. Historical societies also afforded some relaxation; soon after he arrived, the Cambridge Historical Society enlisted him for a paper on "History and the Local History Society" (spent largely in describing the glories of the State Historical Society in Wisconsin),[28] and over the next years he regularly attended meetings of the American Antiquarian Society in Worcester, where he mingled with such headliners as President Taft and Lord Bryce; the Massachusetts Historical Society, where he advocated enough additions to the list of reference books to bankrupt the organization; and the Colonial Society of Massachusetts, which he served as president in 1914. In a moment of misguided patriotism, Turner even accepted membership in the Bunker Hill Monument Association, only to be called upon as a frequent speaker at their meetings.

These ventures into New England clubland were pleasant enough, but there, too, Turner lacked the intimate comradeship that Madison had provided. So it was that he welcomed the friendship of a lady who seemed utterly unsuited to the role, but who offered him the sympathetic companionship that he needed. Mrs. Alice Forbes Perkins Hooper, wife of "Squire" William Hooper of Boston's elite North Shore, and herself the well-to-do daughter of Charles Elliott Perkins, entered his life shortly after he arrived in Cambridge. She and her husband were having an intimate dinner for President and Mrs. William Howard Taft, and one of her guests had failed her. Could Turner fill in? "I dare say you are old friends." Those arrangements fell through, but Turner and Mrs. Hooper lunched in a less formal setting a week later, and there she unfolded a plan dear to her heart. She wanted to establish a living memorial to her departed father, who had done so much to develop the West by building the Burlington Railroad. A fund to buy books in western history for Harvard's Library had occurred to her. Would Turner approve? Turner did, with enthusiasm, and over the next months they nurtured the plans that culminated in the Harvard Commission on Western History, with Mrs. Hooper its generous angel and Turner its guiding spirit.[29]

The years spent guiding this Commission to its successes in book collecting—and its failure when Harvard officials declined to provide the support it had to have in the inflationary years following World War I —cemented a friendship that was one of Turner's most treasured possessions. They saw each other often, usually over a waffle lunch at Mrs. Hooper's extravagant home, "Elsinaes," in Manchester-by-the-Sea, to talk endlessly of history, of world affairs, of the whole spectrum of art and literature. Mrs. Hooper was a fascinating woman, exceedingly large, crippled to such a degree that she often used crutches, but with a vitality that lured to her home a constant procession of diplomats, college professors, authors, actors, musicians, and unclassifiable characters, all of whom graced her board and refurbished her vast supply of anecdotes and information. "Elsie's house," her mother once declared, "was the only *salon* in Massachusetts." Turner thoroughly enjoyed her remarkable mind, her breezy lack of orthodoxy, her professions of loyalty to the Midwest, where she had spent part of her girlhood. "I really think," he told her once, "I should explode if I couldn't talk out a common point of view with you occasionally. Frankly you are the best thing I have discovered in New England."[30] Mrs. Hooper filled a gap in his life that Madison and his close friends there had provided.

Yet now, as in Wisconsin, Turner found his principal pleasures not in clubs or historical societies or friends, but in the bosom of his own family. He and Mae were inseparable as she watched over his comfort, guarded his health, and ran the household so efficiently that he was free to concentrate on his work. Dorothy, their lone child, was just as adored and just as adoring. Blessed with her mother's petite beauty and her father's wit and charm, she had grown into an irresistible young lady, capable of scattering broken hearts behind her as she moved through circles of Madison and Cambridge. Such a combination meant that she would soon leave them. That day came when she succumbed to the attentions of John S. Main, an old friend of the family, during a visit to Madison in the spring of 1913. Nothing would do but that he visit the Turners that summer to win their approval; they were to be at Kennebago Lake in Maine, and Turner's letter of invitation sounded more like a summons to a fisherman's convention than to the home of the intended's parents. John arrived without the assortment of rods, reels, and flies he had been advised to bring, and with the shameful confession that he fished with worms, but Turner forgave him when he saw the adoration in his daughter's eyes.

That fall the parental consent was formally asked. Turner lectured his would-be son-in-law on the dangers and duties of marriage—"we want you both to be reasonably sure that you have talked out your tastes, your habits, your convictions far enough to be sure that you can both bear and forbear on the matters of divergence; that you love each other well enough to make mutual adjustments; that you do not love an image but the real man and woman"—then wired his consent before his letter could reach Madison. The engagement was announced in November 1913, and in the spring of 1914 they were married. Turner was as happy as his daughter was with the addition to his family. "His only substantial limitation," he told Dorothy, "is that he doesn't know how to fish with a fly. But he seems able to land his trout, and that's something, isn't it?"[31]

That marriage was to bring the Turners sorrow and joy over the next years. Sorrow first in the early spring of 1915, when the first baby was due and Mac hurried to Wisconsin to take charge. Turner, keeping bachelor quarters in Cambridge, was alone when he opened a black-bordered telegram; the child had been born dead. "Your pathetic letter almost broke my heart when I read of our little girl's wonder if she had wanted her baby hard enough," he wrote that night. The tiny body was buried beside the graves of the Turners' own lost children, opening wounds that had never completely healed. Not until a year and a half later were their sorrows swept away with word of the arrival of a handsome grandson on August 8, 1917.[32] Jackson Turner Main, Dorothy named him—a prophetic gesture, for that child was destined to become an eminent American historian.

Turner's joy at the arrival of Jackson Turner Main was touched with pathos, for he was increasingly aware of his own deteriorating health. He made periodic attempts to check the decline; giving up tobacco provided a yearly exercise in willpower that he always lost, while the diets that he inflicted on himself at irregular intervals were either so unrealistic or so temporary that they did little good. Severe colds, influenza, and painful sore throats were Turner's usual winter lot, compounded always by a stubbornly high blood pressure. A worse blow to his ego followed shortly after his fiftieth birthday, when his eyes gave out, requiring that he be permanently dressed in glasses. "By the time you return," he reported to Dorothy, "I shall have false teeth and a long grey beard and a shrill treble voice and a cane and shall need you to help me rise from my easy chair in the corner."[33]

Turner joked about his ailments, but they were no laughing matter. Recurring bouts with illnesses taught him that. In January 1914, a painful carbuncle required lancing under ether and ten days in bed for recovery. A year later a boil in the inner ear erupted into excruciating agony with a fever that shot to 104 degrees, then gave way to erysipelas that began on the face and spread over the body. For a fortnight Turner suffered such torment that his mind wandered as Boston specialists were summoned to save his life. "It was a distinctly rocky road, and I am still more or less shaken up by the journey," he told a friend.[34] Again, in the spring of 1917, he went under the knife for a hernia operation that left him bedridden for three weeks and a walking shadow of himself for a year thereafter.[35] Increasingly slow recovery, no less than the illnesses themselves, showed that Turner was far from the robust person he appeared to his friends.

He believed, with some justification, that his deteriorating health was a by-product of mental strain; whenever he immersed himself too deeply in a problem or grappled overlong with a historical enigma, he ended in bed. His prescription for a cure was based on long experience; a summer in the north woods or the mountains would not only rejuvenate his health but immunize him against illness for the next academic year. Turner saw holidays not as vacations, but as medical necessities; hence he continued the practice, begun at Wisconsin, of accepting summer-school assignments in the West, where he could exchange a few weeks of teaching for an equal time in the Rockies or Sierras.

The universities of Washington and Oregon lured him westward in 1914 with a joint appointment that was hard to resist: fifteen lectures at each on "Phases of the Western Influence in American History," with a total salary of $1200 and time to unwind amidst the rugged beauty of the Cascade Mountains. The cherry on the pudding was an additional payment of all his expenses if he would deliver the commencement address at Washington. Turner did so, very badly he felt, for he had been too busy ending the Harvard year and marrying Dorothy to John S. Main to prepare a proper address on "The West and

American Ideals."[36] The rest of the summer was more satisfactory. Students at Oregon and Washington may not have heard, as their catalogue promised them, "an inspiring lecturer combining in his attitude of mind the qualities of the philosopher, the poet and the statesman,"[37] but they were treated to a first-rate series by a very competent scholar. Turner was happy with the results and with the "good stuff" in his classes.

He was far happier with the weekend expeditions into the Cascades and the ventures he made to nearby trout streams almost every afternoon. His friend and former student, Professor Edmond S. Meany, was his knowledgeable guide, and together they spent so much time in the wilderness that the local press reported that Turner enjoyed fishing more than American history, while a group of like-minded fanatics in Seattle pressed his candidacy for the presidency of the university so seriously that he came dangerously near election before withdrawing. One memorable Fourth of July weekend that Turner called "unextinguishable" ended when he and Meany sat far into the night before a "friendship fire" at the foot of the Olympic Mountains—an event that impressed Meany so deeply that he immortalized it in verse:[38]

> But, O, the throb of ling'ring joy!
> New faith on tiny flames aspire;
> When on the sand from sea-cleansed wood
> We build our sacred friendship fire.

Better still was the escape into the rugged mountains of southern Oregon after the last summer-school class was over, and the weeks spent "beyond the edge of civilization" in the Bitterroot Mountains of Montana, where the Turners lived in sleeping bags, tramped trails blazed by the Nez Percé Indians, caught trout "to suffocation," and absorbed enough of nature's tonic to last through another school year.

They were back again in 1915, this time to Berkeley, where a midsummer meeting of the American Historical Association was scheduled to commemorate San Francisco's Panama Pacific International Exposition. Turner's friend Henry Morse Stephens made the arrangements; six of the nation's most eminent historians were invited to give six lectures each to the California summer school, with an honorarium of $250 each to offset expenses. J. Franklin Jameson, Max Farrand, and

Turner were the choices in American history, with Turner to lecture on the "Study and Sources of the History of the Westward Movement in America." If his usual tendency toward procrastination had not piled duty on duty that spring, and if illness had not again laid him low, Turner might have added a new dimension to his scholarship in those lectures. The last two, he planned, would deal with "The Pacific Coast in the Westward Movement" and "The Significance of the Great Plains, the Rocky Mountains, and the Deserts in American History." They would involve a great deal of work, for he had shamefully neglected the Far Western frontier, but they would lead to papers that Turner saw as equivalents of his essays on the significance of the Ohio Valley, the Mississippi Valley, and the Midwest in American history.[39] If he gave those lectures, as presumably he did, they were so inadequately prepared that he had no urge to publish them; his views on the Far West remain today as obscure as they were during his lifetime.

However successful his course, Turner had a splendid time in California, enjoying the "highjinks" of the famed Bohemian Club in its redwood grove, mingling with old friends at the Association meetings, spending two weeks with a Sierra Club pack train in the High Sierra behind Yosemite Valley, returning strong and healthy and looking very much the woodsman in his bacon-stained khaki trousers, grey flannel shirt, red bandana handkerchief, and much abused sombrero hat. This was happiness. So were the weeks at the end of the summer which he spent with Mae, camping and fishing at Glen Alpine in the High Sierra near Lake Tahoe. A year later the Turners were back again, after the excessive heat of Madison convinced him that he should not spend the summer in research at the State Historical Society as he had planned. Instead, they fled civilization entirely to spend a month in the wilds near Glacier National Park, traveling with three pack horses, led by a delightful guide who wore a Blackfoot hunting shirt. They looked for all the world (as Turner noted) like a caravan out of the Oregon Trail. "I shot the shoots down long rapids on my unhappy back," he reported gleefully to Max Farrand, "fell off wobbly logs, lay down in the Big Badger with a three pound trout at the end of my rod (and kept him from taking the slack he was entitled to) and did all kinds of silly tenderfoot things un-restrained and unmindful of history."[40] The purgatory of Cambridge was endurable for another year after that glimpse of heaven.

To say that Turner saw his return to Harvard each fall as a descent into the inferno would be a slight exaggeration. He was never passionately fond of teaching, but he thoroughly enjoyed contacts with the students and the intellectual challenge that they offered. His duty, as a conscientious instructor, was to teach to the very best of his ability, even though that meant revising and re-revising his lectures in a never-ending effort to make them more appealing and informative. "This lecture work," he told a student, "if adequately done, would engage all of my own energies except such as involved in consultation and advice."[41] Turner practiced what he preached. His lectures were never repeated; all were recast every year with new materials crammed in and older materials revised. His own copy of his *List of References on the History of the West* he filled with suggestions for improvements: "Interpolate a section on Western Constitution Making and Ideals, 1840-1851," and, "Add section on Am. Agricultural competition in Europe and its results." Particular stress was placed on recent events; yearly he re-planned his lectures to include discussion of "Combines," "Progressives," or "Western Ideals" in the period after 1900.[42] Turner believed that past and present merged in the historical process, and he did his best to make this clear, although he was usually so pressed for time that the last two weeks of his course became a jumble of briefly mentioned topics.

If Turner gave a great deal of himself to his students, he expected a great deal in return. His assignments were somewhat stiffer than they had been at Wisconsin: he required 120 pages of reading weekly, a classroom quiz every fortnight, midterm and final examinations, a thesis of at least twenty-five pages each semester. The students' reactions varied with the degree of their enthusiasm for history, just as they had at Madison. A few found his lectures the most inspirational ever delivered. "It is not too much to say," wrote one, "that Turner's class in the History of the West opened to me a new heaven and a new earth"; "he has discovered a new continent for us to conquer," added another.[43] Those not hopelessly infected with a love of the subject were less ecstatic. "Fine course," wrote one at the end of his lecture notes. "Fair lecturer who points out the 'whyfor' of many modern movements."[44] That Turner was no more a modern pied piper at Harvard than he had been at Wisconsin was shown by the declining enrollment in the History of the West: 96 in 1910, 117 a year later, 84 in 1912, 46 in 1913, 38 in 1914, and only 30 in 1915.[45] From that time on, it varied between 35 and 50, and never could be ranked among the popular undergraduate courses.

When, for a brief period between 1914 and 1916, Turner was forced to lecture in the second semester of the American history survey course, "History 32b," he found the audience more receptive. The period, "The History of the United States from 1830," was much to his liking, for his hours of labor on the *Encyclopaedia Britannica* article left him better prepared on recent history than most of his generation was. Building on this solid foundation, supplemented with the additional research that his sense of perfection demanded, he began preparing a set of lectures, each dictated fully, which he hoped to convert into a textbook on "The United States since 1865." As usual, his ambitious program collapsed within a few weeks; he lectured from then on from hastily prepared outlines, and dreams of the book went glimmering. Now, however, the lectures struck a spark. The broad topics that had to be covered did not lend themselves to the statistical illustrations that deadened undergraduates in his frontier course, while Turner's ability to use the past to illuminate the present gave his subject a timeliness that was irresistible, even to dullards. Then, too, he responded to the larger audience by being deliberately appealing; he spiced his descriptions with well-turned phrases, painted personalities with deft strokes, and ventured broad interpretations that endowed the past with new meaning for his listeners.[46]

Here was Turner at his best as an undergraduate lecturer, and the students responded with enthusiasm. Enrollment, a normal 122 the first time Turner lectured, leaped to 186 a year later, when he gave the course for the last time.[47] The students attended regularly, too, and applauded when applause was due. His last lecture brought their approval to a fitting climax. "I've always wanted to carry one course down to date," he began, then deftly described the Federal Reserve and Clayton acts, analyzed recent foreign policy, and appraised Woodrow Wilson's virtues and faults as President. There remained time to glance back over the last quarter-century in quest of a generalization that would give it meaning to the students. "An old order has changed," Turner told them. "Is the United States in the twenty-five years that are to follow to be assimilated into Europe or is a new American democracy to be worked out? And that, I think, is the logical conclusion to this course." Then a word of apology: "I have been somewhat confusing in this course, but I didn't try to be explicit. I tried confusion so that you would have to think out your own conclusions. As Mr. Dooley says, I haven't felt it necessary to do the thinking for your father's sons. And I thank you." Then the class stamped and clapped and cheered as Turner grinned, held out his hand, said "Someone will think I'm a candidate for office," and left the room amidst laughter and applause.[48] Turner had shown in History 32b that he could rival the spellbinders when he forsook details for generalizations and interpretation.

Yet his popularity among Harvard undergraduates never rivaled the acclaim that he received from his graduate students there—and with good reason. To Turner, who passionately believed that a nation could plot its course into the future only if it thoroughly understood its past, every doctoral candidate was a prospective missionary in the cause of national survival. These were men and women worth training, and worth training well. No task was too time-consuming, no duty too unpleasant, if spent in aiding a student who would add his mite to the nation's understanding of itself. When Turner resigned from the Executive Council of the American Historical Association in 1914 so that he could have time to talk to young historians and listen to their papers, he revealed his belief in the importance of historical studies no less than his love of mankind.[49] He revealed that belief again, almost daily, as he neglected his own investigations to read patiently through voluminous dissertations ("I have two big theses on my desk to read and it does look as though I was booked for a long sentence"), or to advise former students on organizing their courses, or to read the manuscripts of their books and articles, or to serve as a brokerage agency as they sought their first jobs or advancement to more prestigious institutions. Nor were these courtesies reserved for his own students. Dixon Ryan Fox, then a beginning instructor, expected only a two-line acknowledgment when he sent an offprint of his first article to Turner, but was delighted to receive a half-dozen pages of mixed praise and criticism in reply.[50]

Turner's appeal to his students stemmed partly from this dedication, partly from the fertility of his mind and warmth of his personality, but more from his humble belief that he and they were equals, working together to discover the truth about the past. A man of lesser breadth might have expected his eminence in the profession to demand respect and obedience from lesser souls, but not Turner. His graduate students were simply fellow investigators, deserving of respect and comradeship. With them he shared board and sometimes bed, feeding the lost souls stranded in Cambridge over the Thanksgiving and Christmas holidays, welcoming them into his home for social occasions, listening to their problems with all the sympathy of a kindly father. Their accomplishments he treasured even more than his own; every printed program of the American Historical Association or Mississippi Valley Historical Association was checked to identify his students, who sometimes numbered a third of those reading papers.[51]

Graduate students responded by flocking into his seminars and vying for the privilege of securing Turner as a thesis director. He gave them virtually a free rein for their intellectual interests: a seminar on the Van Buren administration was abandoned after a year for one on "Selected Topics in the History of the West," and that, in turn, after two years, for "Selected Topics in American History." Turner tried to concentrate on one period each year, sometimes the decade of the 1830s or the fifteen years after 1880, but his usual course was to indicate that topics should be chosen within the 1830-60 span. Within these broad limits, students could select subjects that appealed to their particular interests. In one typical seminar, papers were read on education during the 1850s, the German influence on politics in the years just before the Civil War, the settlement of Wisconsin, Illinois politics of 1850-60, the extension of railroads into northern New England, Mormon institutions, the evolution of New York newspapers, and the emergence of transportation facilities in the South Central states.[52]

This freedom was balanced with sound instruction. Each seminar began with a review of the period to be covered, where Turner spoke informally and the students read widely, as the basis for a two- or three-page table of contents for a history of the United States during those years. Those who intended to map election returns were shown proper techniques and supplied with outline maps ordered from Washington. In the meantime, topics were assigned and research begun. Reports followed after two or three weeks, usually an hour-long presentation of the problems involved, materials available, and progress to that time. Two written papers were required at the end of the term, one covering the topic generally, the other treating a narrow aspect in depth. As these were read, Turner listened, pencil poised to jot down a new idea or bit of information, always ready to offer advice, reprove careless work, or throw out suggestions for fresh approaches or interpretations. "Turner," one student remarked to another as they walked out of such a session, "is as full of ideas as a dog is of fleas."[53] Always his criticism was tempered with an encouraging word of kindness; "you show a subject *opened*, but not conquered," he told one hapless candidate, then added, "you could carry it further by more time and less pressure of other duties, I imagine."[54]

The many who prepared doctoral dissertations under his direction were treated with the same blend of strict discipline and gentle encouragement. Each chose his own topic, for Turner realized that enthusiasm for historical studies multiplied when a student pursued a subject within his own areas of interest. If pressed for suggestions, he normally proposed a subject already familiar to the student; one from Ohio, for example, might be encouraged to write on "Politics of Ohio, 1850-60, with Emphasis on Underlying Social Forces," one from Alabama, on that state's altered political behavior during the 1880s. Turner's function, as he saw it, was to plant the seeds, then shape the plant as it matured. This usually meant drastic pruning; when E. E. Dale wanted to write a history of Oklahoma, Turner gradually narrowed the topic to a study of the range cattle industry there. He insisted on only two qualifications: the subject must be manageable, and it must make a contribution to knowledge. The contribution could be of two sorts, either a "keener criticism and analysis than has been made, or new material handled in an original way."[55] These were sound suggestions, and they saved many a candidate from floundering in an unworkable dissertation subject.

The students responded by producing a series of outstanding theses that helped launch their authors on the road to professional eminence. The subjects ranged over the whole spectrum of American history, just as did Turner's own interests. Some theses were on the West— Solon J. Buck's "The Granger Movement," George M. Stephenson's "The Political History of the Public Lands from 1840 to 1862," Edward E. Dale's "The History of the Range Cattle Industry in Oklahoma," James B. Hedges's "The Development of Transportation in the Pacific Northwest, 1860-1893," Arthur P. Whitaker's "The Old Southwest, 1783-1796." Others explored unknown aspects of the colonial era—Kenneth W. Colgrove's "The Early History of State Instruction to Members of Congress," Daniel H. Bacot's "The Progress of South Carolina during the Confederation and Federalist Periods," Arthur H. Buffinton's "The Policy of the Northern British Colonies toward the French in the Treaty of Utrecht"—or the middle period—Thomas P. Abernethy's "The Formative Period in Alabama, 1815-1828," Arthur B. Darling's "Jacksonian Democracy in Massachusetts," Elwyn C. Gage's "The National Election of 1824." The Civil War era offered subjects for Frederick Merk, "The Economic History of Wisconsin during the Civil War Decade," and H. Donaldson Jordan, "England and the War of Secession." Equally typical of Turner's catholic tastes were the dissertations that he supervised in social history—Colin B. Goodykoontz's "The Home Missionary Movement and the West," Marcus L. Hansen's "Emigration from Continental Europe"—and in diplomatic history—Samuel F. Bemis's "The History and Diplomacy of the Jay Treaty," Thomas P. Martin's "The Influence of Trade in Cotton and Wheat in Anglo-American Relations from 1829 to 1846," and Reginald F. Arragon's "The Panama Congress of 1826."[56] Surely no other instructor of that day allowed his students to range so widely, kept pace with their researches so thoroughly, and directed such a distinguished galaxy of historians as Turner.

Equally remarkable was the disproportionate number of Turner-directed dissertations that blossomed into books. This was no accident. The sound advice given during the selection of a topic (always with publication in mind), the careful supervision during the preparation of the thesis, and the encouragement and help offered as soon as the degree was won all contributed, but particularly the last. Turner had an uncanny ability to diagnose the weakness of a manuscript, and to offer exactly the right advice on improvement. All authors were advised to let the thesis lie fallow for several months; this allowed them to gain perspective and ponder how the subject could be broadened to fit into the pattern of American history. "*Think* about the meaning of it all," he told Thomas P. Abernethy. Then, on re-reading, they would recognize the highlights that deserved greater emphasis, the extraneous materials that should be discarded, the interpretations that had been obscured during the hurry of meeting a degree deadline. They should also keep the needs of the general reader in mind when revising, condensing quotations, eliminating unessential footnotes, sharpening the style, lessening the length.[57] Only in this way could they produce the mature books that would benefit them and the world of scholarship.

If Turner was a master at wet-nursing his doctoral students through the ordeal of the thesis, he was also remarkable in the way he guided them through their final examinations with a minimum of disaster. His instructions were specific: re-read the multi-volume histories by James Ford Rhodes and Edward Channing, be thoroughly abreast of recent monographic literature, know all important articles in the leading journals, be familiar with the bibliographical guides and collections of documentary sources. Those who followed this advice should have had no difficulties, but the few who did flounder by the wayside were always sure of a helping hand. Rarely could Turner convince himself that a candidate should be failed, no matter how superficial his knowledge or how deficient his reasoning powers. One who was unable to name a single important case decided by the Supreme Court was passed; so was one who did not know how to locate materials essential to the study of economic history.[58] Surely, Turner argued with his colleagues, even such men must have some redeeming features and should be saved for the profession.

Turner's kindness indicated no lowering of standards, but only his tendency to associate himself with his students as fellow laborers in historical research. They had worked together, usually for some years by the time the degree was in sight, in class and seminar, and always on a problem that excited the instructor as much as the student. Each was a friend, not a pupil, and deserved to be treated as such. So Turner, remembering always his own miserable performance on his final examinations at Johns Hopkins, was a lion at their sides, hoping for the best, but unwilling to recognize the worst. If even the shakiest candidate could be salvaged, a human being had been aided and another recruit added to the army carrying on the assault against ignorance of history.

His coddling of two students in particular revealed the depths of his compassion. One was Kenneth W. Colgrove, later a prominent political scientist. Colgrove was burdened with a sense of inferiority that was not improved when he did badly on his preliminary doctoral examinations. His thesis satisfied neither him nor Turner when it was submitted in first draft; it was badly written, focused more on background than the topic, and included whole chapters of extraneous materials. Instead of sending it back for complete revision, Turner persuaded the committee that it be accepted and then revised. Then, with the author's self-esteem restored, he suggested the changes needed: drastic reduction of the first chapters with emphasis on essentials, illustrations to relieve the dry narrative, more stress on personalities and human interest, an expansion of the sections at the heart of the study. Colgrove took these criticisms like a man and capably performed the complete rewriting that was necessary.[59] If the thesis had been rejected initially, he would probably have fled the profession. Turner had saved a man, and a good man, for historical studies.

He faced a far more difficult problem with Arthur H. Buffinton. A capable if not overly energetic young man who had earned his master's degree at Harvard in 1909 and was an instructor at Williams College, Buffinton was the first graduate student to see Turner in the fall of 1910. They met in the library stacks on October 4, 1910, to agree upon a thesis topic on the New York frontier in the eighteenth century. For a time all went well, although Buffinton was burdened with a heavy teaching load and showed an obvious inclination to spend more time in the classroom than in the library. By the end of the summer of 1913 he had read all printed documents and secondary works, written 265 pages in rough draft, and had only some newspapers and manuscripts to read. Turner had every hope of seeing the completed dissertation by the spring of 1914, but not a line appeared. Instead, Buffinton sent him letters—telling of a sick colleague whose teaching had to be assumed, or of a new course to be prepared, or of the demands of students on his time. But he would start arranging his notes soon and might get some writing done that summer or fall.

By this time Turner was beginning to recognize the magnitude of the problem on his hands. Buffinton was obviously cast in his own image; he was a perfectionist who found writing difficult and would do anything to avoid putting pen to paper. Theirs was to be a battle of wills, with Turner committed to extracting a thesis, and Buffinton congenitally incapable of submitting one unless driven to do so. Turner could wield the whip better personally than by letter, and he urged his reluctant pupil to spend summers, and even a year's leave of absence, in Cambridge. Buffinton did spend the summer of 1914 at Harvard, but did nothing more than add 66 more pages to his first chapter and make some discoveries ("By discovery I mean that it was new to me, not necessarily to historians").[60] Nor did the next year produce much more, even though he was on leave and under his master's supervision. Chapters were submitted, true, but they were overly long, crammed with unnecessary detail, and so woefully lacking in interpretation that their contributions were lost on the reader. The degree seemed as far away when he returned to Williams that fall of 1915 as it had been five years before.

Nor was there progress as the months—and years—slipped by. Turner urged, demanded, cajoled, appealed, but to no avail. His reluctant charge was as adept with alibis as Turner was with arguments; a new course demanded his attention, a sick colleague had to be replaced, a family situation disrupted his schedule, a bout with illness ended all work. Worst of all, Buffinton discovered that the materials he had already gathered lent themselves to publication, and he began writing articles instead of chapters. They enjoyed only moderate success at first, the *American Historical Review* rejected the first, but it was accepted by *The Historical Outlook*, subjecting him to another Turner lecture on learning to write before he appeared in public. These "Polonius-like dicta," as Turner called them, went unheeded. Buffinton spent the next few years preparing articles, some of them excellent, while the thesis gathered dust in his desk drawer.

As Buffinton's publications multiplied, and as Turner's years at Harvard drew to a close, Turner had an inspiration. If Buffinton would put his printed articles together, write an introduction and some transitional passages, and submit them as his thesis the degree could be granted. Once more Turner reckoned without his pupil's fatal perfectionism; only two of the publications were of high enough quality to please the faculty, Buffinton insisted, and he would be ashamed to let the remainder be seen. That was that, but some good had been done. During the 1922-23 academic year Buffinton did settle into the harness, goaded by regular letters from Cambridge urging him on. As chapters began arriving for Turner's scrutiny, a new problem arose; each of his suggestions for slight revision sent Buffinton to the library for further investigation. "Draw your conclusions now from what you *have*," Turner urged. "If they need verification by further study, do that later."[61] Again, his sound advice went unheeded. Turner learned to keep his suggested changes to a minimum, lest each send his pupil on a time-consuming quest, and to make them in soft pencil on the manuscript so they could be easily erased.

So progress was made as the pile of completed chapters mounted through the summer of 1923 and into the 1923-24 academic year, Turner's last before his retirement. The thesis had to be in his hands by April 1 to assure Buffinton a degree that year, and both were confident; Turner even made arrangements for its reception at the graduate school office and drafted a carefully selected committee of readers to assure its acceptance. April 1 came and went, and no bulky package arrived from Williamstown, but there was still a last chance. Turner would be about Cambridge late that summer and would be glad to help, even though he could not sit on the jury that made the final decision. Miraculously, Buffinton succeeded. Turner had to rewrite much of his summary chapter and do major surgery on a good many other sections, but the result he found acceptable. Before leaving the East that fall of 1924, he saw to it that the proper forms were signed, the committee briefed, and all in readiness for the final act in the drama. "So endeth the *last* lesson," he wrote Buffinton as he told him of these preparations, "and may the Lord have mercy on your soul."[62] That prayer was answered. A few months later Buffinton wrote Turner triumphantly that he had met his committee and they were his. He might have added that under any system of justice that doctorate should have been awarded to Frederick Jackson Turner rather than to Arthur H. Buffinton.

The heroic efforts that won Colgrove and Buffinton their degrees were not typical, of course, but they demonstrate in exaggerated form Turner's dedication to his students and his unshakable determination to see them succeed. He was, by all standards, an outstanding graduate teacher, not solely because his methods were more helpful or his techniques more advanced or his mind more fertile than those of other instructors, but because he saw his students as mirror images of himself and treated them accordingly. If he had maintained a master-slave relationship he would have trained capable investigators; by accepting his students as equals in their joint journeys of exploration into the past he elevated them a step higher, and made them the devoted disciples they proved to be.

XIV

Harvard Years:
Conflict—Academic and International

1915-1920

FREDERICK JACKSON TURNER hoped that after a few years of adjustment to the Harvard scene he would have time to resume his long-neglected study of sectionalism. So he might, had not the orderly world of his dreams been shattered by two conflicts in which he became hopelessly involved. One, the titanic struggle between the Allies and Germany that began in Europe in 1914 and entangled the United States three years later, made such demands on his time and emotions that for two years research was unthinkable. The other, a teapot tempest within the American Historical Association that reached a climax in 1915, was no less fatal to Turner's ambitions.

He had, from the beginning of his professional career, given of himself freely to the association, recognizing this as one of the many time-consuming obligations expected of successful academicians. His years of apprenticeship on burdensome committees meant gradual ascent to the little clique that was in control, with membership on the Executive Council of the association, a post that was his for life after his presidency, and on the Board of Editors of the *American Historical Review*, where he served for two six-year terms. There he joined a tightly knit group of eminent historians who were, in their own eyes, selfless servants of the profession, giving generously of their time and energy to provide leadership and maintain standards. They had, however, drifted into an "Establishment" philosophy and an "Establishment" system of management that operated through a series of interlocking directorships: all officers were named by a nominating committee which was

337

itself appointed by the Executive Council; the second vice-president automatically ascended to the presidency and then to lifetime membership on the Council; the six-man editorial board of the *Review* was self-perpetuating, for it suggested replacements for its retiring members to the Executive Council, which always approved. In effect, some 2800 members of the association were governed by two or three dozen professors from a half-dozen prestigious universities, most of them well advanced in years. A rebellion against such undemocratic procedures was inevitable, particularly in an era of political progressivism when all interlocking directorships, even those operated by staid historians, were fair game for crusaders.

The leaders of the insurgent faction that rose to meet this challenge were an unlikely crew, bound together only by a belief that the "Eastern Establishment" had denied them the acclaim they deserved. At their head was Frederic Bancroft, librarian of the state department, professional gadfly, and a newly elected member of the association's Council; his principal lieutenants were Dunbar Rowland, director of Mississippi's Department of Archives and History, and Professor John H. Latané of the Johns Hopkins history department. Their followers varied in numbers with their changing fortunes, but were recruited largely from the South and West, where resentment against New England's domination of the profession was strongest. To drive the "ring" from power, these rebels believed, they first had to oust J. Franklin Jameson from his editorship of the *Review* and secretaryship of the association. This meant removing ownership of that journal from the Board of Editors, where it had rested since 1895, and vesting it in the association; so long as Jameson operated his own show he was safe from attack. As Jameson's closest associate, Turner could be expected to defend his friend most effectively. Hence, Turner must go.

This decision brought into focus the basic divisions within the association. All agreed that reform was necessary; they differed on the means. Turner was the principal spokesman for the vast majority of members, who were confident that democratization could come from within; they pinned their hopes on a Committee of Nine, headed by Professor Andrew C. McLaughlin of the University of Chicago, which had been created by the Executive Council in November 1914, to propose changes in the governmental structure that would allow greater participation by the membership. The insurgents, on the other hand, were sure that McLaughlin was a tool of the Establishment, and that the Committee of Nine would only whitewash its actions. He and his ilk must be discredited. Bancroft set out to do so; an examination of the association's financial records disclosed that members of the Establishment had been reimbursed for their travel expenses to Council and Board meetings, and that they had even charged an occasional luncheon to the association! These "revelations" he unfolded in a scurrilous pamphlet, published in July 1915. *Why the American Historical Association Needs Thorough Reorganization* was no more sensational than its title; it repeated charges that an inner "ring" controlled the association, maintained that they used funds extravagantly, and argued that the Committee of Nine was rigged by "political hocus-pocus" to vindicate the Establishment. The official nominee for the presidency, George Lincoln Burr of Cornell, must be defeated and a complete slate of reformers elected to the Council.

So long as Bancroft confined his attacks to the Executive Council, he was guilty of nothing but bad taste, for he was a member of the Council and was entitled to examine its records, even though he misused the results. His next assault on the Board of Editors of the *American Historical Review* posed more problems, for he had no official connection with that body and any catering to his demands might be interpreted as tacit admission that the association owned the *Review*—a point that was still in dispute. Yet Bancroft had to attack, for he wanted Jameson's scalp and was convinced that the association would back him when its members found that the editorial board had used expense-account funds for extravagant living. Hence, he had to examine the account books of the Board of Editors. In October 1915 two peremptory letters were sent to Turner, one demanding access to the board's minutes, the other demanding a record of all its financial transactions. Turner was adamant on the minutes; they dealt largely with discussions of articles that had been submitted to the *Review* and making them public would embarrass would-be authors. "I would," he wrote, "as soon open the doors of my house to a fire bug."[1] The financial accounts contained no such confidential information and Turner saw no harm in showing them to Bancroft, although he hesitated lest this be interpreted as truckling to his demands. Jameson had a better idea. Why

Captions for the following four pages

1. Frederick Jackson Turner (right) with his younger brother, Will.

2. Andrew Jackson Turner, father of Frederick Jackson Turner.

3. Turner at the time of his graduation from the University of Wisconsin in 1884.

4. Professor William Francis Allen, Turner's principal mentor at the University of Wisconsin.

5. The University of Wisconsin in 1884, when Turner was a student.

6. Turner (right) and Charles Homer Haskins, a fellow Johns Hopkins student and boarder at Miss Ashton's, who was to become Turner's closest friend and colleague.

7. The Johns Hopkins University seminar room. These students worked for their doctoral degrees with Turner in 1890. Left to right: Charles Homer Haskins, James Albert Woodburn, John H. McPherson, Professor John M. Vincent, Professor Herbert Baxter Adams, Andrew Stephenson (who failed to complete his degree), and Toyokichi Iyenaga.

8. Frederick Jackson Turner in 1893, when he read his paper on "The Significance of the Frontier in American History." Reproduced from the *Badger for 1893*, the University of Wisconsin yearbook, through the kindness of F. Frank Cook, Director of the University Archives.

9. Mae Turner in 1893, with the two oldest children, Jackson Allen Turner and Dorothy Kinsey Turner.

10. Mae Turner about 1905.

11. Frederick Jackson Turner in 1905, as he completed work on his first book, *The Rise of the New West.*

1

2

3 4

5

8 9

10 11

12

13

14

15

16

17

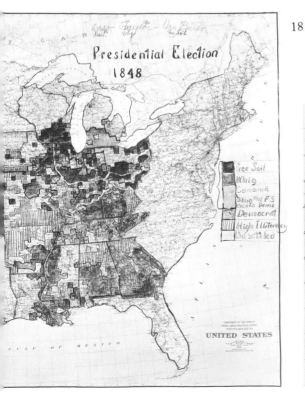

18

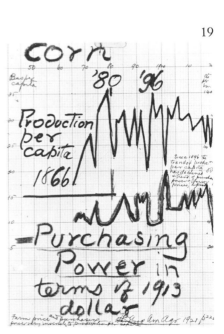

19

Captions for the preceding four pages

12. Turner hanged in effigy by the Wisconsin students for opposing "Big Time" football, as seen by a cartoonist for the *Wisconsin State Journal*, March 31, 1906.

13. The Turners' home at 629 Frances Street, Madison, with Lake Mendota in the foreground.

14. Turner's seminar meeting in the Library of the State Historical Society of Wisconsin in June 1894. Left to right (standing): Emma Hawley (Library staff), W. B. Overson, Orin G. Libby, E. F. Dithmar, Joseph Schafer, C. L. Baldwin, and Florence Baker (Library staff); (seated): Estelle Hayden, Kate Bucknam, Ada Taylor, Annie Pellow, Dena Lindley, Sadie Bold, Flora Barnes, Professor Turner, and Catherine Cleveland. Reproduced from the collections of the State Historical Society of Wisconsin.

15. Mae Turner with their daughter, Dorothy Turner Main, in the early 1920's.

16. The cottage at 2214 Van Hise Avenue, Madison, built by the Turners in 1924 for their retirement years.

17. Turner on a camping trip during the early 1920's.

18. One of the many maps Turner prepared for his studies on sectionalism. This one correlated election returns with illiteracy in 1848.

19. One of the hundreds of charts Turner drew and used in his classes. This one related corn production to population growth.

20. Turner at the door of the Huntington Library, about 1928.

21. The Huntington Library in 1927, when Turner joined the staff. This copy was presented by Turner to his devoted secretary, Merrill H. Crissey.

not send copies to *all* members of the Executive Council and the Committee of Nine?[2] Here was a sensible procedure that was adopted at once.

Copying the records took time, however, and Bancroft was in no mood to take delay lightly. Scarcely a day had passed before a telegram to Turner warned of what was to come:

UNLESS BEFORE 6 P.M. MONDAY NEXT I AM GIVEN PERMISSION TO INSPECT AND COPY CONTRACTS AND NAMES OF FOUNDERS AND GUARANTORS I SHALL PUBLICLY EXPOSE YOU AND THE BOARD'S ATTITUDE.

Those records, Turner explained patiently, were being prepared for distribution and would be in the mail shortly. This kept the peace for only a short time. Then Turner received another telegram:

WHERE ARE COPIES OF CONTRACTS SUPPOSEDLY IN MAIL TWENTY-FOUTH INST?

More telegrams, more accusations, more demands by Bancroft until the missing documents finally reached him. They were, he exulted, just what he wanted. They showed the editors had no financial liability, and hence did not legally own the *Review*.[3] He would expose their perfidy when the Executive Council met on November 26, 1915. This was the prospect that awaited Turner and his colleagues when they journeyed to New York to begin their meetings.

The Board of Editors met first, heard Turner describe his correspondence with Bancroft, and, with blood pressure properly elevated, adopted a series of resolutions denying Bancroft access to the minutes and everything else he demanded. This done, they listened approvingly as Edward P. Cheyney, their secretary, read a report that he proposed be distributed to the association's membership. Cheyney recited the whole sad story of the controversy with Bancroft, denied that the board ever dabbled in association politics, and made it clear that the members never abused the expense-account privileges to which they were entitled. When this was presented to the Executive Council the next day, it was overwhelmingly adopted. The Council, the resolution of adoption read, expressed "its full confidence in the efficiency and unselfish manner in which the board of editors has conducted the affairs of the *Review* since its foundation."[4] Bancroft had suffered a thumping defeat, but such were his illusions that he believed his stand would be vindicated in the association's business meeting, which was to be held a month later. "The rule of Jameson, Turner, McLaughlin and Burr should end this year," he predicted gleefully.[5]

First he had to convince the membership. Using Cheyney's report as a basis, he prepared two pamphlets, which were distributed throughout the association in late November and early December. *The Attempt to Seize the American Historical Review*, and *Misrepresentations and Concealments in Opposition to Reform in the American Historical Association* were typically Bancroft, rambling through page after page of unsubstantiated charges and misleading quarter-proofs. Columns of figures revealed the "exorbitant" sums collected by the "ring" for travel to board meetings; still larger sums, he hinted, had doubtless been used "for purposes both unauthorized and unknown either to the Council or the Association." Turner was Bancroft's particular target now, for he had refused access to the editorial board's minutes. Why had he had concealed those documents unless he had something to hide? Why had he been elected president of the association only after coming to Harvard? Here was proof that the "ring" manipulated its puppets for its own benefit.[6] "Isn't this," wrote Jameson as he finished the last page, "great business for an immortal soul in A.D. 1915, when the whole world is on fire and civilization is going to pieces."[7]

Both sides were prepared when the American Historical Association met at Washington's New Willard Hotel on December 28, 1915. Bancroft and his insurgents were not only housed together at the nearby Albany Hotel, where they could plot their strategy, but they had held a dinner meeting at the Metropolitan Club the night before and assigned each man his role. The Establishment made fewer plans. Some talked of an agreed-upon candidate to defeat Bancroft's bid for reelection to the Executive Council, but Turner ended their plotting by pointing out that this decision was for the membership to make, not the governing clique.[8] The "ring" was willing to let democracy operate at the business meeting, confident that its stand would be upheld.

And it was. Turner was not there when five hundred members crowded into the hotel's ballroom—he had been called to the bedside of his brother, who was critically ill—but he was not needed. The report of the Committee of Nine saw to that, for its recommendations were those long advocated by Turner and other moderate reformers. The members, realizing that democracy could be achieved without adopting the Bancroftians as bedfellows, were in a mood to praise, not bury, the Establishment. They showed their hand when Cheyney opened the meeting by reporting for the Board of Editors. Every mention of Turner or Jameson brought applause, just as did Jameson's own remarks when he rose to underline Cheyney's statement that the board would happily surrender the *Review* whenever the association was ready to assume its financial obligations. The cheers that followed Jameson to his seat brought Claude H. Van Tune to his feet with a ringing resolution; attacks made on the character and motives of certain honored individuals within the past year, he proposed, "meet with our entire disapproval," and "we hereby express our full confidence in the men whose motive and conduct has been thus impugned." The shout of approval was almost unanimous; Bancroft had left the hall and his followers dared not buck the tide.[9]

There was no question of the fate of the Committee of Nine's report now. One by one its recommendations to democratize the association were adopted: there were to be eight, rather than six, elected members of the Executive Council, former presidents were to serve only three years, the powers of the business meeting over the Council were to be enlarged; the nominating committee was to be elected by the business meeting, rather than appointed by the Council; additional nominees were to appear on the ballot when supported by a petition signed by twenty members. The last recommendation was most controversial of all—that proposing ownership of the *Review* by the association—but this too was adopted after a series of crippling amendments were voted down. When, late in the meeting, Frederic Bancroft withdrew his name as a candidate for the Executive Council, he was simply acknowledging that he and his followers had been devastatingly defeated.[10]

Reform from within, cleverly manipulated by Turner, had triumphed over attack from without. Congratulations were in order among the Establishment now, and they flew thick and fast. "I have never doubted the outcome," wrote Turner, "but I confess I had not expected the Three Misquoters to make such an inglorious comic end."[11] Yet scars remained. Turner showed the deepness of his hurt when Charles H. Ambler, one of his former students who had served as a Bancroft lieutenant, attempted to make his peace. His protestations that he had infiltrated the insurgents' ranks solely to urge restraint were brushed aside as hypocritical nonsense. "Let us," Turner told him after an exchange of letters, "not continue the correspondence."[12] Ambler and his fellow conspirators had forever lost the respect of Turner, and of most of the profession.

Despite the pain he had suffered, and despite a year of such total immersion in associational affairs that all research was shelved, Turner was to benefit from the Bancroft rebellion. Now, with victory assured, he could quietly withdraw from the irksome professional duties that had become increasingly burdensome in recent years. This would fulfill a mounting ambition; for some time he had chafed under the endless chores imposed on the editorial board of the *Review*, and he believed that a younger man should take his place. So he welcomed the expiration of his second term, just as he did the recommendation of the Committee of Nine that ex-presidents resign from the Executive Council after three years of service. "For myself," he wrote Jameson, "I have done all that I can, probably, for the Association." He would devote the future to the research he had neglected for so long.[13]

The prospect was doubly alluring, for, as the Bancroft affair neared its climax, negotiations were under way for a full year away from the classroom—a full year to read and think and write. J. Franklin Jameson was responsible, and the Department of Historical Research of the Carnegie Institution which he administered gave the means. Almost from the day Jameson assumed the directorship, in 1905, he had wanted to bring Turner to the Institution, turn him loose on his own researches in the Library of Congress, and have him constantly on tap for discussions on how to revitalize historical studies. Turner was the only man in the United States, Jameson assured the Institution's officers in 1913, who could "wake me and the Department up."[14] Now his chance had come, for Turner was in a mood to leave Harvard for a time, and funds were available. In March 1915 the official invitation arrived, just as the Bancroft rebellion was moving toward its climax. Would Turner be interested in spending six months of the sabbatical year due him in 1916-17 in Washington? The salary would be $600 a month, the duties light, and ample time allowed for research in the Library of Congress.

Turner was delighted. The Carnegie money would let him stretch his scheduled half-year of leave at full pay into a full year at half pay —a whole year to pursue his investigations. When Harvard offered no objections, he accepted eagerly, and in November he received from the president of the Carnegie Institution, Robert S. Woodward, a formal invitation to spend six months in Washington, beginning November 20, 1916. That day Turner noted in his diary "3,600 + 2750 half salary from Harvard = 6350."[15] His Carnegie year promised to be profitable in more ways than one. Jameson was just as elated. "The presence of Professor Frederick J. Turner, of Harvard University, as Research Associate," he wrote in his annual report, "will stimulate all the work of the Department."[16] Turner was able to endure the burdens of Harvard teaching as he buried himself in his many duties during the spring of 1916, dreaming of the fall when his time would be all his own.

Those duties were plentiful, for endless arrangements had to be made. The Cambridge house was to be sublet to a clergyman (though Turner insisted that he would rather fish with a worm than rent to a cleric) who was attracted by the presence of two churches and a theological school nearby, not to mention a front-yard fence built by the Reverend Thomas Hooker in 1632 and an apple tree that was originally in the Garden of Eden. Or so Turner told his daughter. A modest flat or rooming house at no more than $50 a month had to be located in Washington; they settled on a small apartment in the Brighton Hotel, which they rented for nearly $100.[17] Term papers and bluebooks had to be read, oral examinations conducted, theses criticized, and grades reported to the registrar. Then the "Star Chamber Trial"—modified for the occasion—was held. Every professor going on leave, Turner was told, had to be tried by the graduate students and formally expelled from the Yard. In his case a vigilante committee would be substituted for the chamber. He would appear before that august body and accept his fate. He did appear—to be stuffed with soup and shad roe and steak and frozen pudding, then solemnly tried, and banished for a year, although he was allowed to make a statement before his sentence began. Turner enjoyed himself hugely; the students long remembered his booming laugh and beaming face.[18]

The Turners fled Cambridge then, first to Madison, where a personal investigation proved there were no trout in nearby streams, and where the summer's heat drove them westward for a Montana vacation. Such work as was done during those months went into the preparation of five lectures to be delivered at Western Reserve University in late October. Those completed, the Turners settled into their Washington apartment on November 1, 1916, for six months of uninterrupted research. They followed a pleasant routine; each morning Turner and J. Franklin Jameson walked to work together ("thereby," Jameson told a friend, "benefitting the physical health of both, and my mental condition"),[19] then separated as Turner sought out his desk at the Library of Congress and the pile of manuscripts or newspaper file that waited him.

How he reveled in those intellectual treasures as he probed ever deeper into the story of sectionalism in the 1830s and 1840s! But only for a short time, for Turner was emotionally incapable of long periods of sustained work, and temptations were abundant. Scarcely a day passed but he was persuaded to settle down with Jameson and his staff for long discussions of historical problems and the role of the Institution in solving them. Each week he lectured to the department on the economic and social development of the Middle West, a pleasant assignment, but one that required constant preparation.[20] Occasionally he was seduced into delivering other lectures; one he gave before the Harvard Club of Washington in February allowed him to extoll the virtues of the Harvard Commission on Western History. Congress demanded his attention now and then, with a day in the Senate or House gallery, and the conclusion that there was no such thing as a first-class politician; "it is," he reported, "a painful thing to watch."[21] Those were happy months in Washington for Turner, even though they did not produce the great stack of research notes that he had hoped.

He can be excused for not sticking to his last, for the winter of 1916-17 was a poor one for scholarship everywhere. What did the past matter when the whole western world was going up in flames? World War I began in Europe in August 1914, and, although President Woodrow Wilson urged Americans to remain "impartial in thought as well as action," the sinking of the *Lusitania* in May 1915, the *Arabic* crisis a few months later, and the torpedoing of an unarmed French passenger ship, the *Sussex*, in the English Channel in March 1916, drove the United States slowly along the road to war. Passions were heightened by the "rape of Belgium," when German troops overran that small country, and by an effective Allied propaganda that painted the Central Powers as enemies of democracy and civilization. President Wilson's peace efforts, climaxed by his announcement of terms for a "just peace" in January 1917, were answered by Germany's announcement that it was resuming unrestricted submarine warfare against all merchant ships bound for the British Isles. Wilson broke off diplomatic relations at once, at the same time asking Congress for authority to arm American vessels. A filibuster led by Senator Robert M. La Follette defeated that measure, but evidence piled on evidence that the Central Powers would be satisfied with nothing less than total victory, and the President only mirrored majority opinion when he led the nation into war on April 6, 1917.

All of these stirring events Turner watched from his grandstand seat in Washington. As he did so, his views on the global role of the United States were revolutionized. His sympathies, from the very beginning of the war, lay with the Allies; Germany was a monstrous threat to self-rule in Europe, and a German victory would mean a triumph for militarism and autocracy. The Allies had to save civilization and the democratic values that had been bred into Americans by their frontier experience. Turner was so annoyed with Senator La Follette's pro-German stand that he canceled his subscription to *La Follette's Magazine* in the spring of 1916; at the same time he commended Wisconsin's other senator, Paul O. Husting, for the support he rendered England and France.[22] Only an early Allied victory, Turner believed, would check the Balkanization of the United States, as each new crisis drove a new wedge between Irish-Americans and German-Americans and Italian-Americans. This ethnic atomization had to be checked, for America must revitalize postwar Europe by providing a shining example of a successful democracy that unified people from many backgrounds. Not only national survival, but the future peace of all the world, hung in the balance.[23]

Reasoning in this fashion, Turner assumed a strong anti-interventionist stance during the early years of the war. He expressed his views in February 1916, when he spoke at Trinity College on "Why Did Not the United States become Another Europe?" His answer was predictable; Americans had succeeded, as Europeans had not, in perfecting a system of adjustment and compromise that allowed the differing sections to live together peacefully. They had also proven that the oppressed from all the globe could be welcomed and absorbed. This was an example too valuable to be destroyed in any war. The United States had to remain aloof from Europe's holocaust; it had to persist as a bastion of democracy that would serve as a model when reconstruction began. Pressures for intervention were steadily increasing, Turner admitted, but it did not follow that "we should be carried into that maelstrom, and particularly not on European terms. Washington's warnings against entangling alliances still have validity and they gain new force from the awful tragedy which meets our gaze whenever we look across the Atlantic."[24]

There spoke Turner, the Jackson Man, for no backwoods champion of the Hero of New Orleans could have believed more fervently that America's frontier-rooted democracy underlay a governmental system that all the world should—and would—imitate. His were noble dreams, but they were sadly outmoded by the realities of a Europe at war. Not the future, but immediate survival, was the concern of the United States, and as Turner watched events unfold from his Washington vantage point his views changed. By February 1917, two months before war was declared, he believed that "it is time to assert ourselves or bear the stigma of servitude"; a month later he wrote that unless we "strengthen our sinews and harden our tissues and learn our national lesson," Americans would fall before the juggernaut of Kaiserism.[25] To a man with these violent views, the sectionalism of the 1830s was remote and unimportant. "I am finding it difficult to write my historical stint," he confessed. "I want to enlist in spite of my aged imperfections." So strongly did Turner feel that he offered his services for any type of clerical work in the government that would be useful to the army.[26] By the time war was declared, he was ready to make any sacrifices for the holy crusade that was making the world safe for democracy.

Others in Washington shared Turner's views, and through the early days of April the historians among them debated the role they could play in the struggle that had just begun. Jameson, as usual, spearheaded these discussions, and, as usual, Turner bubbled with ideas that his friend could implement. The result was an invitation to a large group of historians to meet in Washington on April 28, 1917, to form an organization that would place the "competence and patriotic good will" of the profession in the service of the government. Two days of discussion gave birth to the National Board for Historical Services, with

James T. Shotwell of Columbia its chairman and Turner among its nine members. Its purposes would be threefold: to channel historical activities throughout the nation into support for the war, to supply the public with trustworthy information on the background and purpose of the conflict, and to father regional or state committees that would organize lecturers and authors to spread information.[27]

From the first, this program raised eyebrows throughout the profession. Would the National Board adhere to canons of objectivity, or would it be simply another propaganda machine for the government? In Turner's mind there was no question that the members were on the side of the angels, and that the use of history to further "present action" was justified. Yet he was haunted by doubts, and protested so vehemently in his campaign to convert the doubters that he revealed his own apprehensions. The Board, he insisted, had a "trust to keep as ministers of historic truth," and this would not be violated. Instead it would only keep alive traditional values and ideals—values and ideals that were often forgotten amid the passions of war. Certainly the truth would not be sullied if the Board emphasized episodes from the past that would illuminate present problems and aid the achievement of a just peace.[28] Turner satisfied his own conscience by such arguments, but converts among his friends were few. Well they might be, for he was arguing that history should be warped to suit the national purpose, even though still wearing the garb of objectivity.

In actual practice, the National Board for Historical Services was neither the propaganda agency feared by its enemies nor the model of impartiality envisaged by its friends. It did perform valuable services by circulating an annotated edition of the President's War Message, placing articles in popular magazines, supplying speakers for numerous occasions, and flooding the news media with historical information needed to make current events meaningful. Yet the profession remained skeptical. Turner's own enthusiasms cooled rapidly; he tried to resign when he returned to Cambridge in May 1917, and even though he was dissuaded from doing so, he played a relatively small role from then on. The atmosphere at Harvard did nothing to rekindle his enthusiasm. Only Edward Channing was outspokenly opposed to the National Board, on the grounds that past precedents did not apply to the present situation—"He explained at some length to me that the submarine had so modified the art of war that the naval and military lessons of the Revolution and Civil War were inapplicable"—but the rest of his colleagues were so cool that efforts to press them into service were soon abandoned.[29] Turner's deep-seated faith in his native land had warped his judgment momentarily, and blinded him to the importance of unvarnished truth, even in periods of national crisis.

That same faith condemned him to some thoroughly unpleasant hours of teaching during the wartime years. Harvard's attitude was very much Turner's own; President Lowell made it clear from the beginning that his sympathies were with the Allies and that the university would do everything possible to speed their victory. By the time Turner returned, in May 1917, the Yard resembled an armed camp, with most of the student body in a Reserve Officers Training Corps and the banks of near-by Fresh Pond so scarred with trenches that pedestrians were unsafe there. Here was an atmosphere to Turner's liking, and he responded predictably. He was too old for military service himself, but he could scrimp to buy Liberty Bonds—and did to the extent of $6000 during the war years—and he could preach that total victory was essential to the survival of mankind. "The world," he wrote in the autumn of 1917, "will not be worth occupying with the kind of Germany that has been revealed at the head of civilization." Anyone who did not make every sacrifice to head off that catastrophe would be judged narrow and selfish in the "Book of Judgment" of history.[30] Turner was determined that he would pass the test.

His own contribution had to be made in the classroom. Regular classes dwindled during the 1917-18 school year; the History of the West shrank to a handful of the halt and the lame, and the seminar disappeared entirely. Rather than mark time, Turner volunteered to serve as instructor in the modified edition of the European history survey that was being peddled to the Student Army Training Corps as "Problems and Issues of the War." This meant that he had to take a major refresher course in a field he had long forgotten; it also meant that he had to read 150 blue books weekly, conduct quiz sections for indifferent students who wanted to be off to the trenches, and grade outline maps for freshmen who located Bohemia in France, Lombardy near Berlin, and Moscow in Italy. He had his finger in the pie, even though he complained that "a pie of 150 papers a week is rather plump."[31]

When peace came in November 1918, it brought a lessening of

frenzy on the Harvard Yard, but it also brought new classroom duties that were only slightly less arduous than those of the war years. These stemmed from a laudable desire of the history faculty to explain America's role in the reconstruction of the world to the returning students. A new course, on the "History of Liberty," was given, starting in the 1919-20 academic year, with a staff of six from the history and government departments. Turner's task was to deliver seven lectures describing and appraising the history of liberty in the United States as revealed in the colonial and Revolutionary eras, the framing of the Constitution, Jacksonian democracy, the period of slavery and reconstruction, the "New Nationalism," and the "safe world" that was beginning with the defeat of Germany.[32] This was a challenging assignment; he would be indoctrinating a considerable proportion of Harvard's students as they prepared themselves for the national stage. No slipshod lectures would do.

Because Turner did take his duty seriously, and continuously revised his offerings, he was forced to do more thinking about the impact of the frontier than he had since the 1890s. When he began, his thoughts were those of 1893, with institutions moulded largely by environmental forces as they took shape in the American wilderness. American liberty, his students were told, was based not alone on Magna Carta or Plymouth Rock or Jamestown. "What is *American* in it is the result of the interaction of the wilderness—vacant land—with the men and institutions." The colonists brought with them a body of habits, traditions, and customs. Some were abandoned, some continued virtually unchanged, and still others thrived as they had not in the less congenial soil of the Old World. These last institutions, developed and transformed by the greater opportunity for the individual existing on the frontier, were those that gave liberty in the United States its unique dimension.

Underlying this greater opportunity were the free arable land and unexploited resources in the zone just west of the settled area, a zone that receded constantly as society was reborn with each fresh advance into the wilderness. This successive rebirth allowed men and their institutions to change as they responded to the environment. "Old institutions were modified, new ones created, new ways of looking upon the world were evolved. The advance was a continuous process of creation, of Americanization, of differentiation from the European type.

The frontier was a gate of escape from custom, class restraints, economic and social burdens." So long as the frontier moved westward, the social order would remain plastic, capable of rapid adaptation. "Crystallization was impossible while the West stood at the border. Society refused to jell."

Of the changes that stemmed from this process, none was more important than the reshaping of the theory and practice of democracy. The West was a land of social equality, where refugees from oppression could begin life afresh. Class lines were less firmly drawn along the frontier, where all could occupy self-sufficient farms, than in the East; attacks on privilege were more common where society was fluid and innovation a daily necessity. Hence the great documents that were mileposts along the road to liberty—the Bill of Rights, the Declaration of Independence, the statutes of civil and religious liberty—could be translated from theory into practice in the newer regions of the West. Had settlement been confined east of the Appalachians, "a modified European type of class rule" would have emerged there; instead, eastern stability was upset and restraints there lessened. The frontier prevented land monopolization, diminished social and class distinctions, and fostered an extended franchise, the disestablishment of churches, free speech, and a free press.

This being the case, what was the prospect for American liberty as the era of free lands drew to a close? Turner had no pat answer to that troublesome question. The people, he noted, were turning increasingly to government for protection from exploitation by business interests, now that escape to free land was impossible. The result was that the state imposed restrictions on the free use of private property as the needs of society took precedence over the interests of the individual. Turner held out no hope for the unrestrained economic liberty of pioneer days. In its place, he predicted, must come an "adjusted liberty" as governmental controls were extended in the interest of society as a whole.

Turner was too wise a man to abide by theories that did not stand careful scrutiny. As he worked and re-worked his History of Liberty lectures, he began to realize that his earlier explanations explained less than he would have liked. The frontier did play a part in the evolution of American liberties, but it was by no means solely responsible. Turner perfected no new hypothesis, but by 1922, when he gave his lectures for the last time, he seemed increasingly aware of the complexity of his subject, and of the danger of oversimplified explanations.

Americans, he taught at that time, generally accepted three forms of liberty to a greater degree than Europeans. First, liberty in the United States was based on the belief that the European balance-of-power system had protected them from aggression and was, in part, the shield behind which their democratic practices had evolved. Second, it rested on a sense of free government, built on a written constitution that employed a system of checks and balances to prevent the concentration of excessive power in any one branch. Third, American liberty exaggerated freedom for the individual, which had been derived partly from English legal concepts of the common law. On this rested the belief that one man was as good as another before the law, that equality of opportunity should be enjoyed by all without social prejudice, and that conditions of bargaining should assure that neither party in a prospective contract be at the mercy of the other. To Turner, at this stage of his thinking, economic opportunity meant not simply an absence of restraint, but a positive complex of conditions resting on law and custom that assured the greatest number of people the greatest opportunity to develop their abilities.[33] He realized, as he had not in 1893, or in 1919, that the frontier had been a significant moulding force, but that its impact was understandable only if other comparable forces were thoroughly understood.

If Turner's frontier theories helped him explain the postwar world to Harvard's undergraduates, his sectional concepts underlay his own thinking on the international problems that plagued the United States between 1918 and 1920. Like most Americans, he viewed with mounting alarm the social ferment that kept Europe in turmoil as reconstruction began; Russia's "Bolsheviki" he saw as heralds of a disorderly future, potentially more dangerous than German "imperialism." Unlike his fellow countrymen, however, he was wise enough to realize that this was social revolution that would eventually culminate in a better world for the masses of people. "A new society must be born in the Old and New World," he predicted.[34] Turner was also alarmed by the curbs on freedom of speech that accompanied the Great Red Scare in the United States, feeling that it was "better to let steam escape than to try to keep it sealed up. . . . The way to make radical revolutionaries is to shut off men who do not think conventionally, from the ordinary avenues of expression." Moreover, what was "wild and dangerous" today might be considered "wise and good" in the future. Yet Turner was shocked by the rapidity of change and the constant threat of violence. The world would be a better place if it could recapture the spirit of the old frontier cabin-raising days—"construction by mutual efforts, toleration and good humor"—even when he knew that those happy days would never return.[35]

His first reaction was a brief escape into isolationism. Better for the United States to retreat into its shell than to risk tainting its democratic institutions by contact with less favored nations. "It would be a pity," Turner wrote early in 1918, "if the United States lost her isolation from Europe so that we could no longer preserve this continent from the struggles for power incident to the application of Old World rivalries to the western hemisphere." A league to enforce peace would plunge the United States into European politics. If Europeans wanted to modify their systems, "let them come to us and follow our practices and system rather than that we should take the burden of the inheritance of the sad old world habits and experiences."[36] Turner, like the pioneers he admired, could dream of an isolated America, just as he could of frontier cooperation, as a panacea for modern problems.

But Turner was a sensible man, and soon discarded such fantasies. The world was shrinking, like it or not; the United States had to learn to live with its neighbors, and this required an effective world organization powerful enough to block future wars. Long before January 1918, when President Wilson proposed an "association of nations" to Congress, Turner was speculating on the basic problem certain to confront such an organization: how to transcend the nationalistic loyalties that were so strongly rooted in European tradition. As early as the spring of 1915 he had found one answer, based, as usual, on the American experience. Any central authority, Turner wrote, must operate directly on individuals, not on nations, and must have control of transportation, business intercourse, tariffs, currency, and banking. This concentration of economic power in the super-government would encourage the formation of political parties across national lines, for the common interests of class groups in England and Germany would be greater than their distinctive interests as Englishmen or Germans. The parties would serve as perpetual bonds of union, as they did in the

United States, where they bound the sections together.[37] These were brave thoughts in a war-torn world where nationalism raged uncontrolled.

These speculations took on new meaning when the President sought to rebuild the world on the foundation of an organization of nations. Turner realized that his views should be shared with the statesmen entrusted with this awesome task, for familiarity with the American experience would help them erect an enduring international body. His public duty was clear. Two remarkable documents resulted. One, filling twenty-three pages in his own hand, and entitled "Syllabus of Considerations on the Proposed League of Nations," was obviously a worksheet for his eyes alone. The other, labeled "International Political Parties in a Durable League of Nations," condensed into seven pages the highlights of his thinking, and was intended for the diplomats then preparing to remake the map of Europe.

In both papers Turner stressed the parallels between the American sections under the federal Constitution and the European nations under a league of states. What, he asked, had held the sections of the United States together? There were many answers—joint ownership of the public domain, fear of outside nations, interstate commerce, the effectiveness of the federal system—but no cohesive force was as strong as political parties. As national organizations, parties forced statesmen to fashion policies beneficial to the entire nation rather than to any one region; they also helped arrange the compromises and concessions that allowed the sections to cooperate together. Hence, party conventions were comparable to international congresses, and agreements that reconciled regional jealousies were similar to treaties. The basis for Europe's political parties had already been laid, with the International Socialists, Industrial Workers of the World, and Bolsheviki on one side, the business combinations and middle-class workers on the other. Some might object to letting the Russian serpent into the Garden of Eden, but it was certain to enter eventually and would be less dangerous if welcomed openly rather than allowed to strike in the dark. Political parties shaped by class interests would emerge only if Wilson's proposed League of Nations operated through a legislative body endowed with real but limited power over fiscal and economic matters. Only this would assure permanence for the League.[38]

These conclusions, Turner firmly believed, might alter the course of history if they could reach the President before the peace conferences began at Versailles. Two emissaries were entrusted with this task. One, Harvard's George Grafton Wilson, carried a copy to Washington in late November 1918, in the hope of handing it to Wilson just before the delegation sailed for France, but apparently he was unsuccessful. Charles Homer Haskins had better luck with the second. As a member of the delegation himself, he was able to slip Turner's memorandum to one of the President's secretaries three days before the party reached Europe.[39] Wilson probably was shown the document, but the tragic events at Versailles gave him no chance to build the effective international organization that he and Turner envisioned. The impotent League of Nations that emerged as a monument to the nationalism and selfishness of the Allied leaders who fashioned the Treaty of Versailles made no provision for a legislative body representative of the people, let alone for the political parties that would assure its permanence.

Yet even this sad shadow of the powerful organization that Turner wanted was too idealistic for the Washington politicians. They were waiting to pounce when President Wilson laid his plans for a League of Nations before them. Turner watched with mounting indignation as they first emasculated, then rejected, the League that he felt would alone assure world peace. The arch-villain in his eyes was Henry Cabot Lodge, a man, "little and spiteful," who played great issues as pawns in a game to satisfy his own wounded vanity and glorify the Republican party. For Turner, alert as always to the forces shaping political decision-making, was utterly convinced by this time that American ideals could best be secured "by cooperative council and concert in the world," not by a head-in-the-sand retreat from responsibility. "Much as we rightfully distrust European diplomats," he wrote late in 1919, "the path of safety may be in forming an international fire service."[40] Yet there was little that he could do save sputter his discontent and vote for Democratic pro-League candidates, even though this meant charges of insanity from his Boston friends. He voted a solid Democratic ticket in 1918 for the first time in his life, and in 1920 was passionately opposed to Warren G. Harding—a "marionette president" who danced at the end of strings pulled by selfish interests.[41] Turner believed that "Henry Cabot Lodge and the good Lord will have an unpleasant half hour if he ever climbs up for the interview."[42]

His complete about-face is nowhere better illustrated than in two Washington's Birthday addresses, delivered seven years apart. In 1916 he could caution that "Washington's warnings against entangling alliances still have validity and they gain new force from the awful tragedy that meets our gaze whenever we look across the Atlantic." But by 1923 Turner was arguing that the first President spoke only for the needs of his day and would not want the judgment of 1796 to control the nation in 1923. Then the United States was weak and isolated; now it was strong, and was faced with the need to survive in a shrinking world. "We have found that when Europe is aflame we cannot find isolation or security. The embers of that volcano fall on our own houses. . . . The world is one, and we cannot escape its misfortunes."[43] Here was a new Turner speaking. The realities of World War I and its aftermath had converted him from a Jackson Man into a Wilson Man.

Yet Turner could never quite fall into step with postwar America. He identified himself so completely with his frontier and frontiersmen that he believed their way of life held the key to happiness; if pioneer ideals could be projected into the present, the nation—and the world —would be better places. When reason governed, as it did most of the time, he spoke as he did in his 1923 Washington's Birthday address; when nostalgia ruled, he looked over his shoulder into a dead past and yearned for it to come alive again. The League of Nations might be a step toward peace, but the real basis for a perfect world was "mutual understanding and good will and 'give' as well as 'take'—the old pioneer custom of the neighborly 'house raising.' "[44] Noble sentiments, those, but totally unrealistic, as Turner well knew. He had to live in the twentieth century, and he was able to enjoy life there more than most of his generation. The League of Nations might be a feeble shadow of the powerful international organization that he sought, social change might be too rapid for his taste, the nation might be less perfect than it had been in pioneer times, mankind might be askew as new wars and rivalries flamed in Europe. But there was work to be done, problems to be solved, a past to be investigated. Turner's interest in politics did not fade with his disillusionment, but his crusading zeal was gone. History would monopolize his energy for the remainder of his days.

The wartime years brought trial and disillusionment to Turner, but they also provided him with a by-product that was one of his proudest possessions—the second (and last) book published during his life-time. This had been long a-borning. For a dozen years his friends—and a good many strangers—had urged him to collect his scattered essays into one volume, where they could be used by students; copies of the original journals in which they appeared were long out of print, while those in libraries were so worn by generations of use that they were almost unreadable. "I have," one professor reported, "spent a small fortune (for a professor) and eighteen months trying to get two copies of each article for my alcove and the end is as far off—as peace."[45] These complaints were based on real need, not flattery; dozens of courses on the History of the West lacked the reading materials necessary for the proper interpretation of their subject matter.

This was recognized by a number of authors and publishers, and they set out to remedy the situation in their own way. If Turner would not republish his essays, they would—and at no profit to him. Scarcely a month passed but a request arrived to reprint this article or that—the McKinley Publishing Company planned a series on "American History in American Schools" and wanted to include "The Significance of the Frontier in American History"; Norman Foerster felt that his forthcoming collection on *American Ideals* would not be complete without "Contributions of the West to American Democracy"; the American Book Company sought permission to use that same essay in a book on "Americanism"; two instructors at Annapolis also wanted it for their volume on *Contemporary Issues and Ideals;* historians galore asked the right to reprint one or the other in collections of documents they were editing. So it went, as Turner's brainchildren appeared in every possible medium, ranging from *Readings in Agricultural History* to *Essays for College English.* One of his former students, Solon J. Buck, had the audacity to announce that he planned to combine a number of Turner's essays and chapters from his *Rise of the New West* into a book of readings for college courses, and that a publisher had assured him that it would have a large market.[46] Turner clearly had to stir himself into action, or he would watch royalties disappear into other pockets.

His opportunity was provided, strangely enough, by the National Board for Historical Services. A bibliography on problems of the peace, prepared by that wartime agency and published in *The Historical Outlook,* listed a number of Turner's articles, praised them as essential to an understanding of the national character, and noted that they "ought to be brought together in a single convenient collection."[47] This sensible suggestion attracted the attention of Edward N. Bristol, the patient Henry Holt & Company editor who had been trying to pry a book from Turner since 1897. Here was his chance. "I wonder," he wrote, "how these essays would comport themselves in one volume? Do they contain duplications?" If not, and if they could be prepared for the press "without any preliminary attention from you to speak of," Holt would be very much interested.[48]

Turner was delighted. He had long contemplated revising his essays into a book on *The Significance of the Frontier*, but, as usual, ambition outweighed accomplishment, and he had done nothing. Now the publishers, fully aware that once he started rewriting he would go on forever, specified that he give them no "preliminary attention" but print them as they originally appeared. This posed problems. On the one hand, he would not be able to eliminate duplicating passages, incorporate modern scholarship, and weld the separate articles into a unified statement of his views on the frontier. On the other, to undertake a complete revision would mean a major delay in publication, and might subject him to charges that he had borrowed too heavily from his own disciples. For once, Turner made the right decision. "I decided," he wrote a friend, "to let them stand much as originally printed with some omission of duplicate passages, and with such indication of time of original publication as would clear up questions of priority."[49] The die was cast. He would have another book, even though an imperfect one.

That decision was reached in record time; Edward Bristol's invitation presumably reached him on the morning of April 24, 1919 (it was mailed from New York the day before), and before the morning was out his reply was on its way. Yes, he agreed that the essays would have some value if published unchanged; to do so would be to mirror the self-consciousness of the American people in successive years and to demonstrate the impact of his ideas on the interpretation of the nation's past. He would be glad to have them published if Mr. Bristol felt they did not duplicate each other too greatly. Copies of the eleven that he planned to include would be sent that afternoon. They must be carefully guarded, for Turner had no others.[50] He was on his way to a new book, he told friends, with publication less than a year away.

His dreams of a handsome volume miraculously produced without his lifting a finger were soon scattered, for even assembling essays for a publisher demanded a fair amount of labor. What about duplication? The Holt editors had no apprehension on that score; a competent historian who had read the collection at their request reported that overlapping passages were few and unimportant. But not to Turner, the perfectionist. Detailed instructions bombarded New York: omit six lines after "Gallatin" in such and such an essay, discard the last two paragraphs on page 23 of another, delete three sentences from still another. Corrections had to be made: substitute Virginia for South Carolina on the last line of page 247. Decisions had to be reached on the order in which the essays would appear. Publisher and author had to stage the usual debate on the number of footnotes to be included. Fugitive essays had to be located; Turner was ready to omit a speech on "Middle Western Pioneer Democracy," which he had given before the Minnesota Historical Society, because he could not find a copy, but one appeared at the last moment. Above all, permissions had to be secured to republish copyrighted items; particularly troublesome was the quest for a vanished former editor of the *International Monthly*, who was only brought to bay just before the volume appeared.[51] There was, Turner decided, no such thing as an instant book. But there were rewards, too, in the form of a contract dated June 10, 1920, promising a fat 15 per cent royalty on all copies sold.[52]

He was to earn his royalties, for in that day of small, efficient publishing houses, there was little rest for the author. Three days after the contract was signed, and just as Turner was to leave for a summer in Maine, the first bundle of galley proofs arrived. He carried them northward in his suitcase, grumbling that he must manipulate a pencil rather than a fishing rod during the next weeks, and settled to his task. A major task it was; Holt was so eager to have a book by Turner on its lists that it made no attempt to standardize footnotes in the manuscript, assuring him that he could care for that slight matter when reading proof. Yet all went so well that just one month and three days after the first galleys were received, the bulky page proofs were delivered at his door. A month later printing began, even though Turner was still discovering corrections that had to be made. *The Frontier in American History* was published on October 6, 1920, less than four months after the manuscript was received and the contract signed.[53]

Doubts beset Turner as he thumbed through his second-born. He liked the dust jacket and found the smooth blue cloth binding attractive, but the quality of the paper was less to his taste, a victim of postwar scarcities and the high cost of living. He was even more apprehensive as he skimmed the contents. "Does it not strike you as frightfully dull and full of repetitions?" he asked a friend. "Honest! I hesitated long over publication because of this doubt."[54] Turner might have been doubtful, but he showed no hesitancy in asking the publishers to send no less than forty-four free copies to former students, friends, and prominent historians. Holt & Company balked at such a wholesale distribution, pointing out that they customarily provided only a few complimentary copies, but they did send him eleven, and he agreed to purchase twenty more at half price.[55] Those went off to a diverse list that ranged from Woodrow Wilson and Lord Bryce, on the one extreme, to his erstwhile student and Bancroftian enemy, Charles H. Ambler, on the other.

The response was worth the effort. True, President Wilson, responded only in a stiff note written by his secretary, an affront that hurt deeply, but Turner had no cause for complaint in the general reaction. From Lord Bryce came four pages of pure flattery, and others were even less restrained—"the most significant contribution of this generation to United States history"; "a new era in American historical interpretation"; "the greatest real contribution that has been made"; "epoch-making essays"; "ideas which changed the trend of historical interpretation in this country"; "conclusions that must influence historians years and decades after you and I are gone"; "I have met no more illuminating discussion of American civilization"[56]—these were the phrases that gladdened Turner as he read his mail during the next weeks. Newspaper commentators were just as flattering: "an historical study of compelling interest"; "the most important single contribution to the subject made in our generation"; "a notable collection of studies."[57] Even the staid Boston press discovered the prophet in its midst. "Professor Turner," announced the *Transcript*, "has pointed the way to a new, and more truly national school of historical research." Little wonder that he chuckled his delight at being found by Boston after living for some years in successful concealment there.[58]

Magazine critics were no less restrained, with emphasis now on the enduring contributions that Turner had made to the study and teaching of American history. "No other teacher of American history," declared the *Review of Reviews*, "has done more to direct the thinking of students and to mark out fields of research than Professor Turner"; *The Nation* agreed that "in giving direction to the methods of investigation in American history and in furnishing new light for its interpretation, the share of Mr. Turner has been the most profound and abiding of this generation." To the *Yale Review*, Turner was responsible for "the most pregnant thinking on American history in the past generation"; to the *Atlantic Monthly*, his book was "a great achievement." Turner clipped all of these heartwarming comments, mounted them on heavy paper, underlined them to call attention to the most favorable passages, adorned them with marginal arrows opposite the very highest praise, and pasted them in a scrapbook, to be re-read when his ego needed rejuvenation. "I am liable," he confessed, "to take myself seriously if my friends and reviewers aren't careful."[59] Yet he loved every word that he read.

Charles A. Beard intruded the one harsh note into this chorus of acclaim. Writing in the *New Republic*, Beard readily agreed that the 1893 essay had "an immense and salutary" influence on historical writing, but he found on re-reading it that Turner's thesis was riddled with overstatements and faulty interpretations. One by one he ticked these off: the existence of an area of free land did not "explain" American development any more than a dozen other factors, including industrialism and the southern plantation system, did; national legislative measures dealing with tariffs and land disposal were "conditioned" no more by the frontier than they were by forces that Turner failed to mention; the "loose construction" of the Constitution was furthered by easterners such as Thomas Jefferson as much as it was by western influences; the thesis paid too little attention to conflicts between capital and labor. Nor was it convincing, for it was built on speculation rather than documentation.[60]

Turner was stung by this attack, as well he might be. "I find myself," he told a friend, "like a great grandfather in reference to the essay on *The Frontier*, quite ready to see its imperfections myself, but disposed to pick up the cudgels when someone else finds flaws in its features."[61] A strong letter answered Beard's points one by one: in the *early* history of the United States free land exerted a greater influence on legislation than slavery or industry did; the West, as the most concerned section, conditioned land legislation far more effectively than the East did; westerners were loose constructionists because this was the expedient position for them to adopt; the frontier served as an effective instrument for Americanization by converting all newcomers into small farmers. He would not compromise with Beard's basic position. "The capital and labor side has an importance which I think emphasizes the importance of the *ending* of the frontier," Turner explained to his daughter, "while he thinks the movement was all along more important than the frontier. The truth is both were related."[62]

Beard was willing to dispute the points made by Turner, but he refused to come to grips with the fundamental issue: to what degree did the frontier and to what extent did economic divisions shape American civilization?[63] This was an insoluble problem, and Beard had no desire to begin an impossible debate with a man he admired as much as he did Turner. He had, he feared, gone too far as it was; for years he regretted that his review had hurt rather than enlightened. "It was," he confessed, "sharper than I should have made it in view of the great service he had rendered to American history."[64] Beard could not know that he had struck the first blow in the assault on Turner's theories, an assault that would crest in the 1930s and 1940s and concern historians for generations to come.

Turner might be annoyed by Beard's criticism, but he was right when he predicted that it would do no harm. Sales were surprisingly good for such a specialized work, reaching 1076 in 1920 and 1345 in 1921, before slipping back to seven or eight hundred yearly.[65] This was not only gratifying, it also allowed Turner to fulfill a long-standing ambition. Since 1905 his conscience had periodically reminded him that he had accepted an advance of $500 from Henry Holt & Company for a textbook in American history that was still unwritten. The publishers were not concerned; as they surveyed sales figures for *The Frontier in American History* in the spring of 1921, they sent back the note he had signed with the word CANCELLED written across the front. Turner would have none of this; the note was promptly returned with CANCELLATION REFUSED added. Nor would he give the Holt editors peace until they allowed him to retire his debt with his first two royalty checks. He received a cash return of only $8.88 on the year of sales that they covered, but he enjoyed far more receiving the much-traveled note with "Paid in full by royalties earned on The Frontier in American History" scrawled across its face.[66] Turner failed his publishers as a profitable textbook writer, but he did set a precedent for honesty that few of his successors were to follow.

His gesture provided a happy climax to the not-too-pleasant experiences he had endured during the years of World War I and its aftermath. Turner had wasted more days than he liked to remember on activities that had contributed to the national welfare but that had not advanced his own researches one whit. Now, with peace restored to the nation, with his affairs in order, and with his Harvard routine established, he could turn eagerly to the investigations into sectionalism that were to occupy his last years as a teacher—and speed his retirement.

XV

Harvard Years:
The World of Scholarship

1917-1924

T O FREDERICK JACKSON TURNER—and to a good many college professors from his day to the present—the duties that occupied
most of his waking hours were roadblocks in the path of his principal objective: to broaden the scope of knowledge by research and publication.
He moved to Harvard in 1910 partly to escape the commitments that
multiplied with the passing years at Wisconsin, but at Harvard he found
himself so involved with his teaching, forming the Harvard Commission
on Western History, and protecting his reputation against the allegations of Frederic Bancroft, that for some years he scarcely put pen to
paper. With the ending of World War I his prospects brightened.
Now, Turner resolved, nothing would stand in the way of his ambitious publication program.

This was already outlined in his mind—he would pile proof on proof
to convince his fellow craftsmen that sectionalism was no less significant
than the frontier in moulding the American past—but his interests were
too catholic, his enthusiasms too mercurial, to let him follow any one
intellectual path exclusively. He was, quite naturally, besieged with
invitations to speak on a spectrum of subjects tangential to his main
interests, and while he had the good sense to refuse many—including
four lectures at the University of London, twelve at the New School
for Social Research (with a $1000 fee), and one before the Montreal
Women's Canadian Club on the current Balkan situation[1]—his resistance
collapsed now and then, with time-consuming results. His fellow historians were particularly hard to deny: Turner was persuaded to address

the annual dinner of the Mississippi Valley Historical Association in 1920 on his early flirtations with western history (and was dismayed when 250 people appeared, instead of the thirty or so for whom he had prepared informal remarks), and the Agricultural History Society, two years later, on "Agricultural History as a Field for Research." The latter assignment pleased him particularly, partly because it gave him an opportunity to catalogue dozens of topics crying for investigation, more because he suddenly realized that he was viewed as the patron saint of that discipline.[2] "It's funny," he confessed to a friend. "I know too little of agriculture to distinguish barley from wheat; but I have started a lot of these men off in historical study of agriculture so they asked me to share myself."[3] These were events pleasing to the ego, but Turner's extracurricular interests led him principally into two bypaths, one focused on the very early period of American history, the other on the very recent.

His excursions into the colonial era began when he was asked to speak before the New England Historic Genealogical Society, in June 1911, on "The Colonial Frontier about 1700." He did so, not very well, he thought, but his tentative explorations into the documents awakened a new interest. Such proof as could be advanced for the frontier thesis he had drawn largely from his midwestern experience; why not dig deeply enough to show that the seventeenth century demonstrated that his theories were valid, just as did the mid-nineteenth? Here was a quest to his liking; Turner spent months searching colonial records for evidence of the frontier's significance, with surprisingly rich results. His findings, delivered before the Colonial Society of Massachusetts, in 1914, as "The First Official Frontier of the Massachusetts Bay," revealed the same reversion to wilderness barbarism, the same succession of frontier types, the same tendency of the newer settlements to serve as a "safety valve" for the old, the same drift toward greater democracy, the same rising spirit of independence, that Turner had observed in his own Wisconsin.[4] His audience was less impressed with the revelations than was Turner—he was not sure that many among those staid Bostonians "understood or enjoyed," and he was conscious that a goodly number listened with stern disapproval as he described their ancestors as wild frontiersmen—but serious-minded historians recognized that he had opened a new vista on the study of the colonial past. Charles McLean Andrews, Samuel Eliot Morison, and Winfred T. Root all testified that they had to recast their thinking to fit the frontier thesis into their interpretations.[5]

Turner was sufficiently gratified to take up the cudgels for the frontier interpretation whenever one of his converts threatened to defect. He did so with a vengeance in 1918, when Charles McLean Andrews was asked by the Massachusetts Historical Society to explain the views of the "Imperial School" that he headed. The colonies, Andrews argued, could be understood only if viewed from the vantage point of London instead of Boston or Williamsburg, and the total pattern of imperial trade and regulation made part of the story. Turner struck back at the next meeting. The "Imperial School" had corrected past distortions, but was guilty of even more when it ignored the "purely American aspects of the subject." The adjustment of the colonists to their new environment could not be ignored. "Was not the more important thing the play of the new influences, the grappling with unaccustomed conditions in surroundings, economic life, the breaking of old customs, the creation of new institutions, the modification of the type?" Boston had a wilderness at its back door no less than an ocean at its front, and each formed part of the equation. Why not view the colonial past from both west and east, from the frontier as well as from the center of empire?[6] Turner may not have swayed his New England audience, but he seriously influenced the study and teaching of colonial history for a generation by these remarks; a "frontier school" not less than an "imperial school" and a "nationalistic school" were to thrive until the 1930s.[7]

He was scarcely less influential when he focused his spotlight on the recent past, as he did frequently during the 1920s. His interest in these later years was natural. During the era of post-World War I disillusionment, the nation turned more and more within itself as it licked its wounds and sought to solve its own problems instead of those of Europe. One of the most serious of those problems was adjustment to a frontierless existence, now that the era of cheap lands was drawing to a close; how to live in a closed-space world, how to feed increasing multitudes with the public domain no longer open, how to apportion the dwindling natural resources equitably—these were questions that plagued solid scientists no less than the sensation-seeking hacks whose lurid tales in magazines and newspapers predicted the imminent starvation of all mankind. Turner, with his proprietary interest in the frontier, listened with special attention to these cries of doom, and he spent far more time than he should reading and speculating on the nation's fate as its people learned to live with fixed borders.

Twice he shared his conclusions with the community, once in 1916, when he addressed social science students of the University of Chicago on "The Last Quarter-Century," again in 1923, when he delivered the Founder's Day address at Clark University on "Since the Foundation." Both required an inordinate amount of preparation—Turner filled folders with notes, clippings, sample pages, and outlines before those two lectures were written to his satisfaction[8]—and for both he had to grapple with some problems that were so difficult that they defied solution. His basic question was readily defined: what would happen now that American society was no longer "undergoing the transformations due to creative interaction with fresh supplies of free land, and natural resources, fresh fields for political and social institutions?" The years since 1890 provided a partial answer; they had witnessed higher living costs, conservation, immigration restriction, and a declining birth rate, as the physical adjustment to a closed-space existence began. But they had witnessed also the rise of monopoly as giant trusts absorbed the remaining natural resources, a tightening of class lines, and an increase in governmental regulation of private enterprise. During those years the nation lost much of its optimistic faith in the future, much of its belief in its mission to remake the world in its own image. These were debits in the balance sheet, but there were credits as well: the mechanical inventions and technological innovations that went with industrialization, the revolutions in transportation that shrank the planet to a quarter its former size, the cultural renaissance that accompanied urbanization, the democratization of politics during the Progressive era. Turner drew no conclusions at the time (he was to speculate far more on the subject in later years), but his message was still clear: the era of expansion had passed and with it one form of life and living; Americans had to adjust to the twentieth century, no matter how deep their nostalgia for the nineteenth.[9]

Turner was safer, and happier, when he stuck to his own last, rather than venturing along the fascinating detour that led him to the present. There his duty, and purpose, were clear—and had been since his *Rise of the New West* was published in 1906. "I am," he wrote as early as 1907, "beginning to see increasingly a great opportunity for a work to fill in between *1815-1850* and I want to do it in the course of a few years."[10] Such a book would not only fill a major gap in American historiography, but provide an opportunity to examine the interplay of sectionalizing and nationalizing forces, to observe the interaction of sections as they bargained and compromised while shaping national legislative programs, to reveal the regional pressures on cultural expression. Gradually the shape of the book formed in his mind—a volume that would describe each of the nation's sections as it existed in 1830 (a more realistic date than 1815), then trace their relationships as revealed in political, economic, and cultural history during the next two decades. Thus was born the image of the book—THE BOOK, his friends were soon calling it—that was to be Turner's *magnum opus.*

This was a major assignment—a volume that analyzed *all* aspects of American culture—and Turner did not approach the task lightly. Much of the needed preparation was already behind him; he had learned a great deal about physical geography while preparing his *Rise of the New West*, and he had done a major amount of thinking about the nature of sectionalism. All that he had learned, however, only proved that he knew too little to draw any conclusions. He had to do more investigation, and a great deal more research, before he could begin to understand the changing sectional pattern in the 1830-50 period, the role of sub-sections within the larger regions, and the correlation between political, cultural, and economic behavior in their relationship with physiographic and ethnic pressures.

Turner spent such time as he could snatch from his many other duties on these investigations, but progress was slow. He had to immerse himself in the literature of a dozen disciplines, from literary history to statistics, with geography the most important; in 1914 he joined the Association of American Geographers, and a short time later he was made a fellow of the American Geographical Society. He had to gather data from an infinity of sources, on everything from county politics to literary productivity; his files grew remarkably during these years as he added folder after folder crammed with notes and charts. As he did so, another stumbling block arose, for the eight- by five-inch sheets on which he recorded his reading notes proved too small to hold the voluminous data he was accumulating, requiring a shift to the larger, typewriter-paper, size. That, in turn, meant that he had to paste his older notes—notes that he had been accumulating since about 1890—on the new sheets, two to a sheet. Even modern newspaper stories that shed light on sectional patterns were grist for his mill; Turner regularly clipped items from the New York, Boston, and Chicago press to be added to his file drawers.[11] This early, he was being overwhelmed by the sheer volume of the research materials he was accumulating.

How to distill meaning from these masses of data? Statistical charts, graphs, and tables of figures were inadequate to reveal the correlations that interested him; maps were the only answer. All his information must be mapped, using the county as the basic unit, for no larger division would reveal the sub-sections formed within sections by environmental and ethnic pressures. Turner was constantly alert to the work of other scholars who might have transcribed some of the information that he sought; letters went off regularly to confirm a rumor that Indiana had available maps showing religious preferences and illiteracy by counties, or that Tennessee had published county maps of the elections of 1824 and 1832, or that an historical atlas being prepared at the Carnegie Institution would contain mappings of the 1850 congressional votes.[12] When he had the good fortune to find a map already prepared (as he seldom did), it filled only a tiny portion of his needs. Most had to be painstakingly constructed from the oceans of information that he culled from newspapers, almanacs, state and local census returns, travel accounts, and a bewildering variety of sources.

They required infinite patience and time, for three types of maps had to be prepared to reveal classifications of data. One group had to show physical conditions—topography, soil structure, economic activities, and ethnic composition; another, cultural factors—denominational preponderance, percentages of illiteracy, numbers of grade school and high school graduates in proportion to the population, newspaper distribution, literary productivity, and the prevalence of libraries; a third, political behavior in each election between 1830 and 1850—which counties were normally Whig or Democratic, and which swung between the major parties. These maps completed, Turner began his correlations, hoping to determine whether the voting patterns resulted from physiographic, ethnic, or economic forces, or whether other social forces were responsible. Did a group of counties in the South that consistently voted Whig vary from that region's traditional Democratic pattern because better soils produced more abundant crops? Or because they were settled from Tidewater Virginia rather than backwoods Tennessee? Or because the percentage of illiterates was low? Or because a majority were Episcopalians rather than Baptist? These were the questions that Turner hoped his maps would answer. Dozens of those maps crowded his files, most crudely drawn, and many designed to shed light on such unlikely subjects as the political sophistication of states with legislative reference libraries as contrasted with those without, and the effect of local-option prohibition on county politics.[13] Hours, days, months of toil went into their preparation, but all seemed worthwhile, for Turner sincerely believed that they would unlock secrets that had eluded historians.

By 1914 Turner was convinced that they had done so, and that he was ready to share his findings with his colleagues. One group, the professional geographers, responded as he hoped they might when he addressed a joint meeting of the Association of American Geographers and the American Geographical Society that spring on "Geographic Influences in American History," showing them some sixty lantern slides of election returns counterposed against maps of soil differences and comparable economic determinants.[14] They were entranced, for here was a whole new field of scholarship that fitted well with the prevailing belief in environmental determinism. "So many problems were opened up by the maps and your explanation of them," one told Turner, "that we could well have spent the remainder of the session in discussing them."[15]

His fellow historians were less impressed when he appeared before them a few months later. The occasion lent itself to drama; the American Historical Association met in Chicago that December, with its evening sessions scheduled for the Art Institute. In that same building, just twenty-one years before, Turner had read a paper on the significance of the frontier that had altered the course of historical studies. Now he would read another on "The Significance of Sectionalism in American History," and again remake the interpretation of the nation's past.

How tragic the difference. Turner argued his cause earnestly; sectionalism, one of the "most characteristic features of all American history," underlay violent eruptions (the Hartford Convention and the Civil War), but it was also a governing force in presidential elections, legislative contests, congressional votes, and the manners, customs, and social traits of the people. All were products of "the reaction between stock and environment," and all demanded further study before the true political history of the United States could be told. Thus, between 1856 and 1908, the lake counties of Illinois, Indiana, and Ohio voted consistently Republican, while the southern portions of those states went Democratic; this did not mean that there was a direct relationship between "hard rocks and Democracy, or glacial lobes and Republicanism," but it did mean that certain types of immigrants were attracted by certain physiographic conditions, and that the combination of geographic and ethnic factors created political attitudes. These were not determined solely by either stock or environment; wealthy property holders within each of the sections or sub-sections tended to unite with comparable property holders in other sections. Political parties mirrored these class divisions just as they did regional groupings; hence, the parties served as bonds holding the union together.[16]

If Turner's paper on "The Significance of Sections" was confused and confusing, so was Turner himself. He had, he realized, attempted too broad a generalization on too scant evidence. Many more elections must be plotted, many more maps drawn, many more examples of ethnic or environmental pressures analyzed before the nature of sectionalism became clear. Were the conflicts that he had described based on regional or class antagonisms? Turner was not sure; his own hesitant suggestion that class lines blurred sectional divisions suggested the doubts that beset him. He was sure, however, that neither his paper before the geographers nor his essay on "The Significance of Sections" deserved publication. The editor of the *Annals of the Association of American Geographers* virtually demanded the former, but Turner could never find the time for revision, and the whole matter was soon forgotten. J. Franklin Jameson, editor of the *American Historical Review*, was even more insistent, embarrassing Turner with letters and telegrams urging the immediate printing of his essay on the significance of sections, even without the revisions the author hoped to make. Instead of leaping at the opportunity to share his theories with the profession, Turner let weeks and months slip by with only an occasional plea for more time to make needed changes. Three years later, Jameson was still pleading and Turner was doing his best to forget the whole matter.[17] He realized, perhaps unconsciously, that mere revision was not enough. He had to do a great deal more work before the complexities of sectionalism could be explained.

In order to do so, he undertook a more searching analysis of the section most familiar to him—the Midwest—over the next few years. His progress was marked by occasional lectures that showed his deepening knowledge—five at Western Reserve University under the McBridge Lectureship in the fall of 1916, when he talked to a dwindling audience on "The Development of the Middle West"; a paper on "The Significance of the Middle West, 1830-1850," delivered before the annual meeting of the American Historical Association a year later; a dedicatory address on "Middle Western Pioneer Democracy," given in 1918, which celebrated the opening of the Minnesota Historical Society's new headquarters.[18] Those lectures also showed, however, that he suffered from a fatal misconception. Turner, despite his protestations to the contrary, still thought in terms of geographic determinism, and he sought explanations for political and social behavior in physiographic pressures, rather than in the many forces responsible. When he could speak, as he did before the American Historical Association, of ethnic streams being "fused in this great geographic melting pot while society was still plastic," or when he told his Minnesota audience that bowie-knife southerners, cow-milking Yankees, beer-drinking Germans, and wild Irishmen were merged into "a new type, which was neither the sum of all its elements, nor a complete fusion in a melting pot" by impact with an unfamiliar environment, Turner was admitting a bias that blocked his understanding of sectionalism. So long as he thought of geographic forces that were strong enough to transcend ethnic differences and that created in each section a standardized community where all lived and voted and thought alike, he was far from his mark.

Turner realized this now and then, and asked himself some very pertinent questions. Tucked among the pages of the paper he gave before the American Historical Association was a single sheet that dramatically revealed his dilemma. "Why," he wrote, "does Indiana not show the same facts in regard to glacial influences as her neighbors on either side?" Why was illiteracy so widespread there? Why did voting patterns there fail to correspond to glacial moraines, as they did in Illinois? Turner had the key to many of his questions when he wrote those words; later investigations showed that Indiana's settlers came primarily from the upland South and did not bow to environmental forces as the environmentalists believed they should. But Turner closed his eyes to this ethnic factor. "Are there," he asked himself, as he sought to answer his own queries, "concealed geographic influences?"[19] He was too wedded to environmentalism as a basic factor, if not as a determinative one, to recognize that the puppets on his stage were responding to pulls from a dozen strings, not just one.

This same prejudice permeated the series of talks that best reveal Turner's views on sectionalism at this stage of his development—the Lowell Institute Lectures delivered in Boston during the early spring of 1918. Turner was delighted when the invitation to participate in this prestigious event arrived, and well he might be; preparing eight lectures on "The United States and Its Sections, 1830–1850" would force him to write most of THE BOOK that would culminate his life's work—the book destined to be published three years after his death as *The United States, 1830-1850: The Nation and Its Sections.* So he spent the next eight months—between June 1917, when the invitation arrived, and February 26, 1918, when he walked on the stage at Huntington Hall— in a desperate effort to produce something worthy of the occasion— and on time. All that summer the fishing rod was forgotten as maps were drawn and re-drawn, pages written and re-written, lectures reproduced. All that autumn every moment that could be snatched from classes and graduate students went into the final polishing that Turner's sense of perfection demanded. Six days before the first lecture was to be delivered, he was still at work. "They are," he reported, "taking every ounce of energy which I can find or borrow." In the end the lectures were completed, and in a form that pleased the select audience that tradition, if not the subject, attracted. "To the cold witness of charts, maps, and statistics," reported the *Boston Transcript*, "he has added the warm color of his own deft and humanly vivid descriptions, moving through the whole with a quiet charm very personal to him."[20] Turner's Lowell Lectures created no sensation in Back Bay society, but they were accepted well.

This was their due, for Turner lavished a great deal of thought as well as time on their preparation, and they revealed exactly the views on sectionalism held at that time. Turner made clear the importance of his findings at the outset; "the frontier and the section lie at the foundations of what is distinctive in American history." No understanding of nineteenth-century politics, or life, or culture was possible without familiarity with sectional interplay. For the sections—and the environmental forces that shaped each—were influential, even if not determinative, in controlling the political, economic, and cultural behavior of the settlers. Ethnic differences, Turner readily admitted, influenced behavioral patterns, but this was largely because geographic conditions attracted differing racial stocks to any region; differences in background might be reflected in voting, but factors of land and climate concentrating different "stocks" at certain places were ultimately responsible.

Hence, American history could be understood only by studying sectional conflicts, and the resolution of those conflicts by adjustment, compromise, bargaining, and, in one case, war. "These relations between sections," Turner told his audience, "are to the United States what international relations are to Europe; the section is in fact a denatured nation." The sections had been held together over the centuries by the Constitution, operating as it did on individuals rather than regions or states, and by the cohesive force of political parties, which ran across sectional borders. Whenever party and sectional lines became practically identical, as they did in the case of New England Federalism and pro-slavery Democracy, the United States faced a situation comparable to that constantly faced by Europe. This meant war rather than peaceful adjustment.

Turner readily admitted that he was asking questions rather than providing answers; sectionalism offered historians a laboratory for the study of the relationship between history and geography and a test tube for the analysis of the relative influence of ethnic and physiographic pressures. Such studies, if made without the taint of "sectional provincialism," would for the first time fully explain the nineteenth century and shed some light on the twentieth. They should be made soon, for at this stage of his thinking, Turner believed that sectional influences were succumbing to nationalizing forces. "The forces of sectional disunion were culled out by the very fact of growth in nationalism, were, in fact, the vain resistance of minority areas to the powerful stream of national tendency." With the passing of the sections, much would go from American life; the richness, the variety, the contradictions of society were, in large measure, the products of regional provincialism. "The sections have saved the nation from deadening uniformity, from unchecked waves of passion, and from the tyranny of a continental majority." The nation would be a poorer land with their passing.[21] This Turner sought to prove to his audience by first capturing the atmosphere of the four sections that existed in 1830—the Northwest,

South, Middle West, and Far West—then describing their clashes and compromises as the political history of the next two decades unfolded.

Even the most enthusiastic among his audience were less excited about Turner's performance than a New York editor was when he read the sketchy accounts that appeared in the press. To Edward N. Bristol of Henry Holt & Company, the Lowell Lectures were a heavensent opportunity: Turner would *have* to write a book. Long before the first was delivered, Bristol had hurried a contract northward—delivery of the manuscript within one year, royalties of 15 per cent of the retail price —and great was the rejoicing when it was returned to New York with that familiar signature.[22] After waiting in vain since 1897, Holt & Company were assured an actual volume from Frederick Jackson Turner, and a very important volume at that.

The publishers cheered too soon, for there was many a slip between a contract and the delivery of a manuscript, as they were to discover again, to their sorrow. Their awakening began in April 1918, shortly after the last lecture was delivered, when they made polite inquiry as to his progress; they wanted to list the volume in their fall catalogue and needed the manuscript soon. It was not quite ready, Turner confessed. Lectures were lectures, and a book was a book; he had to recast them into publishable form. This meant removing some extraneous items designed to be heard rather than read, and adding others calculated to please the eye rather than the ear.[23] If Edward Bristol and his fellow editors had been realists, they would have given up hope then and there. Turner had not written the book they wanted, and he never would; his Lowell Lectures were an artist's preliminary sketch, fresh and radiant, but only an outline; completing the portrait, with all its subtlety and refinement of organization and interpretation, was simply beyond him. Because there were few details in the lectures, they could be completed; because there must be many details in a book, he could go on forever and never finish the writing. At that moment *The United States, 1830-1850* was doomed.

More, the strain of writing and delivering the Lowell Lectures left Turner a sick and tired man. Broken veins in his eyes warned of high blood pressure and weakening arteries; he had to enter on a career of vegetating at once or risk the consequences. "I would," he told Edward Bristol, "give an eye for a worth-while book, or even consent with some serenity to being suddenly snuffed out, but I wouldn't wish to smoke out like a sputtering candle."[24] He was so worn and lethargic that work was impossible. A thorough medical examination showed why; overstrain had reached a point where any effort might prove fatal; even reading and writing could turn an "explosive eye" into a painful carbuncle. The only remedy was to forsake all mental effort for months—perhaps forever. Turner was over the hill and could only hope not to "make too much of a mess of the remainder of the descent."[25]

Only one sanctuary beckoned for that summer of recovery, and that was the snug cottage on Hancock Point, in Maine, which the Turners had visited periodically since 1912. Here was a spot well-suited to his needs, low enough in altitude that his heart would not suffer, as it might in mountain excursions, but primitive enough to satisfy any woodsman. Hancock Point was a tiny backwoods community on Frenchman's Bay, with the usual frame two-story summer hotel, the usual two or three stores, and a dozen or so cottages for escaping Bostonians. Their rented house—"The Moorings," they called it—was a modest cottage, weathered by the salt air, with a hand-painted mantel, a fearsome Baptist clock with painted mottoes, and a broad porch where a sick man could gaze out at the fog-shrouded harbor or read in peace. There were tempting activities, too, that kept a man busy: daily picnics with the neighbors, fishing expeditions on near-by streams, walks along lanes through groves of birch and balsam between banks of wild roses and fireweed and meadow rue, dips in the icy Atlantic waters. There was work to be done of a sort: wood to be chopped, flounder to be caught in the bay, clams to be dug on the tidal flats, lobsters to be purchased for a few pennies from the fishermen. But mostly one could loaf about in old clothes and slouch hat, and call the down easters "Asa" and "Ed," and be called "Fred" in return. Turner loved every minute of life at Hancock Point, so much so that eventually, in 1919, he and Mae sank most of their life savings into purchasing "The Moorings" for $5000, and its furnishings for another $600.[26]

There the Turners went that summer of 1919 for the rest that he badly needed, laden with ice chests and sterillizers and baby carriages and pack sacks stuffed with history notes and trunks and fishing rods and thermos bottles and a baby bed, for Dorothy Main and their grandson were to spend some months with them. Turner's health began to return with his first dip in the frigid ocean (contrary to doctors' orders), but not enough to incline him to work; that summer was spent in unprofitable fishing expeditions, paddling about the bay in a canoe named "Mumps" (because of its bulging sides), and playing with little Jackson Turner Main, who constantly studied his grandfather with "a judicial but penetrating inquiry" that made him "regret the things I have done and left undone."[27] By September Turner was ready to return to the traces, but he still had no more energy than needed to meet his classes and confer with his graduate students.

Nothing was done on THE BOOK in the 1918-19 academic year save a rare scribbled page of suggestions to himself, or a note of statistics to be analyzed later.[28] Nor was the summer of 1919 at Hancock Point any more fruitful, for again Dorothy Main and her son were with the Turners, and again picnics and fishing and loafing and a two-week camping trip to Mount Katahdin monopolized his time. "I didn't find myself able to do any mental work," he reported that fall, "—not having the necessary machine to do it with."[29] The academic year of 1919-20 was little better; that summer Turner once more journeyed to Maine with two packs filled with history manuscript, and once more they were scarcely opened.

The truth of the matter was that Turner had discovered the only recipe for existence that would keep him alive. His sin was neither laziness nor an unconquerable love of the out-of-doors. By this time, his health was so precarious that he ended his teaching each spring totally exhausted and capable of nothing save vegetating. Every fall his first business on returning to civilization was to visit a whole array of doctors—"the ear specialist, who spoke disrespectfully of my hearing; the eye specialist, who discussed the ravages of time; the dentist, who buzzed away at the same theme."[30] Most discouraging of all was the heart specialist, who reported that improvement was too slight to be noticed. Writing on THE BOOK was simply impossible. "Whenever I try to go ahead under full steam," Turner wrote to his publishers, "and that is the way I write most effectively . . . I have landed in the hospital."[31] He might joke of the Hancock Point handyman who always disappeared when most needed, and explained his absence by saying, "B'Gorry, I went fishin'," but vacationing to Turner was a grim necessity—he needed it to stay alive.

Maine's elixir refreshed his body, but as the months passed with no progress on THE BOOK, he grew increasingly despondent, burdened by a sense of failure and oppressed by the realization that his historical findings would never be shared with his profession. So deep was his melancholy that by the spring of 1920 his Harvard friends became concerned lest his emotional problems overbalance his physical. Those problems would continue so long as teaching so sapped Turner's strength that the summer was needed for recovery; his writing could go on only if he escaped from the classroom. A word to President Lowell was sufficient. In April 1920, Turner was told that he would be granted leave for the second half of the 1920-21 academic year without diminution of salary "to enable him to complete for publication one or more books on American history, on which he has been engaged."[32] This time he made no attempt to change the wording of his pardon from "complete for publication" to "carry on," as he had in 1906 under similar circumstances; Turner sincerely believed that with six months of freedom THE BOOK would be ready for the publishers.

How wrong he was. He made his first fatal mistake in February 1921, when his leave began; he would use his freedom not to make the few changes necessary to put his Lowell Lectures in shape for publication, but to convert them into a major book of at least 100,000 words. "This would be difficult," he wrote in a memorandum to himself, "but worth while if possible." Worthwhile, perhaps, but utterly impossible, for the problems that had to be solved for such a thorough study would occupy him forever: sectional rivalries in commerce, the influence of regionalism on literature, the economic impact of the plantation as opposed to the factory, the philosophy of humanitarianism as it varied from region to region. Turner took one look at the questions he had to answer and turned to less burdensome pursuits. He began his leave not by making progress, but by bothering the publishers with useless questions: could they provide an octavo format? would a 120,000-word manuscript be acceptable? how many maps would they allow? would "The United States, 1830-1850" or "The Development of the United States, 1830-1850" be the better title? Better not to settle on the name of the child until it is weaned, they suggested politely.[33] Why not write the book first?

That sensible suggestion did produce an excellent outline—a chapter on the United States in 1830, six more on the six regions that he would analyze, four on the sectional interplay in successive periods between 1830 and 1850—but hardly a word to flesh out the skeleton. Instead,

Turner had to lay the foundation for his interpretations by drawing county-by-county maps to show political behavior, social conditions, and economic activities, then correlate these with maps of natural conditions to show the relationship between physiographic pressures, ethnic forces, and economic pursuits. That took care of the spring. By the time the Turners were ready to leave for Hancock Point in the summer of 1921, he had drawn eight complicated maps that showed such things as the distribution of ethnic groups, political party concentrations, degrees of white illiteracy, the value of farm lands and improvements, and crop specialization. Still to come were ten more that would reveal the presidential vote by counties between 1832 and 1856, as well as other political data.[34] Eight maps—less than half of those needed before analysis could begin—to show for a sabbatical half-year. THE BOOK was still a long way from publication.

Progress ground to a halt during that summer at Hancock Point. "I took a long rest this summer," he reported as he prepared to return to Cambridge, "and feel just now that I know more about trout, canoes, and Fords than I do about maps."[35] Nor was much done during the next two school years, for Turner had found a new plaything and was so fascinated with it that there was little time for serious pursuits. He discovered, during that autumn of 1921, that he had something to tell his friends that they wanted to hear. Not the oft-repeated story of sectionalism in the 1830s—"I am interested in the results myself, but I find when I try it on a class or club that they do not get very excited over it"[36]—but the story of sectionalism in the 1920s. Here was an apt subject: papers were filled with tales of battles between the western "Farm Bloc" and eastern bankers, between advocates of the St. Lawrence Seaway from the Midwest and their opponents from New England, between high-tariff congressmen from the East and low-tariff congressmen from the West. These were matters that Turner understood and could interpret to a wider audience. So he forgot his larger studies as he clipped newspaper items, drew maps showing congressional divisions, prepared correlations to show that the Republican wing of the Farm Bloc was strongest in regions with the greatest number of cars per capita, and drafted talks for his mens' clubs on "Geography of Political Parties," or "Recent American Sectionalism."[37]

These were not completely wasted efforts—save in the eyes of his publishers—for they forced Turner to do a deal of thinking about the nature of sectionalism, and they prepared him to produce one of his most influential, if not one of his most enduring, publications. His speculations led to an about-face in his beliefs. For some time he had been convinced that sectional influences were succumbing to the forces of nationalism, as his Lowell Lectures made clear, but the more he studied modern trends, the less sure he was. By December 1921, he had persuaded himself that sectional conflicts were intensifying, and would continue to divide the nation—that they would, indeed, displace the class struggle as the most divisive force for the forseeable future, for workers would tend to concentrate in certain regions, farmers in others, capitalists in still others, to deepen the antagonisms already created by geographic separatism. Turner envisaged the day when New England, New York, and Pennsylvania would merge into a unit dominated by vested interests and ally itself with the North Central states, when the West would raise the banner of agararian rebellion against the domination of these two regions, and when the South would walk alone as it defended its attitude toward the Negro. As frontier mobility declined, lines between the sections would be ever more tightly drawn, for geographic forces operated more persistently on a stable population than on a migratory one.[38] America's future, he predicted, was one of steadily mounting conflict.

These conclusions were too important to be buried in filing cases. Turner resurrected them in the spring of 1922, first for Phi Beta Kappa addresses at the universities of Michigan and Chicago, then for the commencement address at the University of New Hampshire in June, and finally for an article which he considered his most important contribution since the appearance of *The Frontier in American History*.[39] This last version, Turner felt, was worthy of publication, and in the summer of 1922 a copy of a manuscript called "Sections and Nation" went off to the *Atlantic Monthly*, only to be rejected as unsuited to the publications program of that elite journal. He was hurt by this (his wife immediately canceled their subscription), but he tried again, this time with greater success. The *Yale Review* was delighted to give "Sections and Nation" the place of honor in its October 1922 issue, and there it appeared, on schedule.[40] "I regard it," wrote Wilbur Cross, the editor, "as one of the very best things I have ever published."[41]

There was some truth in these words, for nowhere did Turner better argue the case for twentieth-century sectionalism. He described the regions of the United States first—New England, Middle States, Southeast, Southwest, Middle West, Great Plains, Mountain States, Pacific Coast—each with its geographical peculiarities, each with its unique economic capacities, each with its rival interests, all "partly determined by geographic forces." The gulf between them was not as large as that between European countries, for the regions were not divided by language barriers or memories of historic wars, but they still were shadowy nations that could coexist only by compromise and adjustment, and because they were united by political parties. "Like an elastic band the common national feeling and party ties draw sections together, but at the same time yield in some measure to sectional interests when these are gravely threatened." Congress was comparable to a diplomatic assemblage, arranging ententes and seeking to preserve the balance of power. "We in America are in reality a federation of sections rather than of states. State sovereignty was never influential except as a constitutional shield for the section." Here was Turner's key point, and he used page after page of illustrations from the nation's history to drive it home.

But sectionalism was more than political. A "sectionalism of material interests" could be identified, marked by different types of economic enterprise, as could a "sectionalism of culture" that stamped the people of each region with distinctive traits and interests. Each had its own ideals, New Englanders defending economic conservatism and the protective tariff, midwesterners, the policies favored by the Farm Bloc, southerners, low tariffs and Negro separatism. These ideological divisions, no less than political differences, doomed the nation to a future of conflict, intensifying steadily as the modifying influence of intersectional migration lessened. "The sections are settling down into definite form, and, as they mature, as their physiognomy and character are formed, their differences and even their antagonisms, will become more marked." The nation could survive only if its people ceased to follow an ostrich policy by burying their heads in the sands of the region where they lived. "There must be sympathetic understanding, sacrifices, concessions, and adjustments."[42]

Here was the gospel of sectionalism according to Turner, and an opinion-stirring gospel it was. Nothing that he wrote, and few essays from the pens of historians of his day, excited such comment as did "Sections and Nation." Newspaper editorial writers, ranging from *The*

New York Times to the *Fresno Republican*, joined in a chorus of praise: a "memorable article," "a most absorbing study of political movements," "one of the most striking and valuable articles that has been published in any magazine," a study that would "revolutionize thought on the future development of the United States politically and economically"—these were the phrases that Turner read, clipped, underlined in red, and filed away. He was delighted even with the few dissenting voices. The *Boston Transcript* haughtily insisted that New England was universally loved instead of viewed with suspicion, as Turner implied, while a letter-writer to that same journal thought that his prediction of a future federation of sections "comes pretty close to treason."[43] "By one clipping," he reported delightedly to his daughter, "you will see that I am at least regarded as a proper subject for arrest by the federal and state authorities both. So far I am at large."[44] He was equally pleased by praise from friends and strangers, and especially by enthusiastic comment from such public figures as Walter Lippmann, Senator Irvine L. Lenroot, and the Austrian publicist Josef Redlich.[45]

All of this was very satisfying, but Turner was aware of the fact that essays on modern sectionalism did not bring THE BOOK nearer to completion. It was inching along, particularly during those rare periods when he could find an efficient stenographer. Then he wrote as he liked to write, sitting at a desk buried with notes and charts and maps that he consulted constantly, dictating an overlong and often poorly written text packed with facts and interpretations. This was slow work. "Dictation is hard for me," he confessed to Mae after one day when little progress was made, "and I am rather discouraged to find how much there is to do before the book can be said to be ready. I think I was cut out for a farmer after all."[46] He felt that way even more strongly when he began compressing the gargantuan first chapter to usable size and found the task excruciatingly difficult. At times such as these THE BOOK seemed as far from completion as it had been a decade before, and melancholy gripped Turner. "I don't see how I can do it," he wrote Mae as he prepared to leave for Hancock Point in the spring of 1922. "If I bring up another big lot of notes and take them back again as last year, I might as well confess failure and go out. . . ."[47] Then a burst of progress, when the words flowed and the interpretations fell into logical pattern, would make him happy. Those days, alas, were few.

Still, slowly, almost miraculously, a manuscript took shape. The springs were free now, for Harvard granted him additional half-year leaves from teaching in 1922 and 1923, and the results could be measured in a mounting pile of completed pages. By March 1922, an outline and a rough draft—a very rough draft—of an overlong "Introduction" went to join the previous year's eight maps in the publisher's vault—an "Introduction" that explained Turner's methodology and views on sectionalism.[48] That summer his latest stenographer journeyed to Hancock Point with Turner, to add to the confusion of a household already overcrowded with their daughter and two grandchildren (Jackson was a lively five-year-old now and his sister Betsy was two), the children's nurse, the family cook, and the Turners themselves. Turner insisted on going fishing once a week, much to the disgust of his stenographer—and young Jackson, who wandered in each day to ask politely how many books he and the secretary had written—but dictation was a daily event and the pile of rough-draft pages mounted steadily.[49] Too steadily, for by summer's end Turner awakened to the fact that he had given so little thought to space restrictions that he had enough for several books. "I can see," he admitted to the publishers, "that I have a frightful job of condensation before me," but he would apply the hydraulic press that fall and squeeze it into usable form.[50] He returned to Cambridge in 1922 well-satisfied with the summer's work.

So euphoric was his mood, indeed, that he was bubbling with pipe dreams of a manuscript completed by December—or perhaps November. If the publishers had the whole book by then, could they assure him that proof could be read before his spring leave began? He had plans to do some traveling to celebrate. They could, of course, but the editor who made this solemn assurance must have known that Turner was indulging in fantasy.[51] He discovered this himself when he returned to the classroom and the hours of homework that teaching required; "the crop of theses has been gathering on my table," he wrote a friend, "some 75 of them in all, and I fear the only 'book' will be blue books for the present."[52] The skies brightened with his spring leave of absence (at half pay, this time, but worth it to finish THE BOOK); once more daily sessions with the stenographer were the order of business, and once more the summer at Hancock Point was as profitable as it was busy.

The results were impressive, if not spectacular. Turner was still dwelling in a dream world that April of 1923, when he promised the Holt Company six chapters by the end of May and the remainder by September 1, but during May the first batches of manuscript reached New York. Others followed at regular intervals, until by the end of August three completed chapters were in the publisher's hands. The fourth followed more slowly, but it was virtually finished by October. In all, this burst of energy produced 155 pages of text, after being typed in the Holt office, and very good text it was. Too long, perhaps, but the editors felt that only a few passages needed to be eliminated. They would be happy to have a 200,000-word book, instead of the 100,000 that Turner had planned. "What we want," they assured him, "is the book as you feel it *ought* to be written."[53] This was heady news, and Turner was elated. "The Book will be out sometime within the year," he assured a friend."[54]

That was the high-water mark of progress. Whenever Turner worked too hard, his system rebelled, and so it was now. In May 1923, just as he was settling down with his stenographer at Hancock Point, a siege of influenza and recurring bilious attacks laid him low for a month and drove him back to Cambridge for medical advice. "So far this summer I have been worthless," he confessed at the end of June, and even when his health was restored he was forced to work at a slower pace.[55] Again in December fatigue and a weakened system not only ended all effort but forced the physicians to put him on a comfortless regime. "I am," he told a friend, "still cigaretteless, and pipeless, and cigarless, and even chewless—and cheerless too!"[56] Turner was slowing down, and THE BOOK had to wait.

Worse, he was succumbing once more to the near-fatal disease of perfectionism. Much of his energy during the spring and summer of 1923 went not into writing new chapters, but in revising old ones. The "Introduction" was completely rewritten into sixty-one pages of manuscript—and even this he considered tentative. Chapters I through III were torn apart in a major recasting; through them he sprinkled marginal notes reminding himself to move this paragraph into the sectional surveys and that one into the analysis of the 1830s. Even more fatal was his decision that the maps drawn three years before were in need of updating; would the publishers please return them to be redrawn? The publishers, reluctantly, did so, and he set to work to redo the map on "Distribution of Population" completely and to incorporate fresh material into the others.[57] Once Turner began rebuilding the very foundations of THE BOOK he could go on forever. By November 1923, progress was at a complete standstill.

Even before this breakdown he had come to the conclusion that he had to forsake the classroom to complete his magnum opus. This was not a difficult decision, for Turner was dedicated neither to undergraduate teaching nor to Harvard. Few, save among his closest friends, realized this; those who knew him only casually believed him the most enthusiastic of teachers and the most loyal of Harvardians. The students he found indifferent: "Harvard undergraduates," he once told a friend, "aren't interested in Western history," while the graduate students were no better than those he had taught in Madison.[58] Nor did Turner ever feel really at home in Cambridge. Max Farrand, who was closer to him than any other man save Charles H. Haskins, knew why. "Turner," he once said, "was *recognized* rather than appreciated."[59] Harvard provided him little of the warm companionship, the easy informality, the ego-satisfying adulation that was so abundant in Wisconsin. The East, too, was less to his liking than he would usually admit. "I love my Middle West," he told Carl Becker, and sometimes he wondered why he had ever left there. "I am," Turner confessed, "still a Western man in all but my residence."[60]

True, Turner had twice refused invitations to return to that land of his first love. Both opportunities came in 1913, when he was still under the spell of Harvard's eminence, and neither was of the sort that he could accept. One was provided by the State Historical Society of Wisconsin, when it sought a replacement for Reuben Gold Thwaites; he could return to Madison as superintendent of the society and professor of history at the university with a salary matching that he earned in Cambridge. Turner realized full well that he had neither the talent nor inclination to administer a large library, yet he hesitated so long before refusing that the Madison papers proclaimed his return and the *Boston Transcript* mourned his departure.[61] He listened to the siren call again a few months later, when the University of Chicago offered him its most attractive professorship, with only graduate students to teach and ample time for research. Turner was sufficiently interested to let it be known that he might be persuaded if a suitable salary could be arranged, but negotiations ended when Chicago could offer no more than $5000; Turner's joint Harvard-Radcliffe earnings were $6100.[62] His decision was no indication of his loyalty to Harvard; he might well have returned to the Midwest if the salary had been tempting.

So now, in 1923, his conscience bothered him not at all as he laid plans to escape the classroom forever. One obstacle stood in his way: how could he live on the meager pension that would be his after retirement? As he laid his plans during 1923, his bible was the manual on annuity systems issued by the newly established Carnegie Foundation for the Advancement of Teaching. Every line was read and reread, every margin filled with notes, every blank page crowded with columns of figures, as he tried to balance possible income against probable outgo. The results were not too encouraging. He could count on a pension of $3208.33, royalties of roughly $275 a year from *The Frontier in American History*, $750 from his wife's investments in the Madison Store Company and a few stocks, and $300 from rental of the cottage at Hancock Point, if that became necessary. If worse came to worst, rigid economies could be made. "The Moorings" was worth a good $6000 and could be sold; his life insurance policies, which totalled $22,000 and cost $800 a year in premiums, could be reduced to $9000 on a paid-up basis; in an extreme emergency the $3000 in Brazil stock could be sold at $160 a share and the money reinvested, although this would be done only as a last resort. Turner could also add a bit to the family coffers by lecturing, which was allowed under his retirement plan. All in all, they could count on from $5000 to $5200 a year. That was far less than the $8000 salary paid him by Harvard since 1922, but the Turners could probably afford a small flat in Madison or possibly a tiny house there.[63] Cambridge was out of the question; it was far too expensive.

So the decision was made. "I shall at least not die in the class room," Turner told a friend, "an act for which I have always had a dislike—too spectacular, even if it isn't messy."[64] In April 1923, he submitted his resignation, to take effect on September 1, 1924, a few weeks before his sixty-third birthday.[65] Turner could resign knowing that his shoes were to be well filled. Frederick Merk, a fellow-Wisconsinite who had proven himself a brilliant student when he earned his doctorate at Harvard in 1920, had taught "The History of the West" admirably during the spring terms that his master had been on leave, and he would now take over. His junior rank allowed the department to name another senior professor, and, due partly to Turner's insistence, the post was offered to Arthur Meier Schlesinger of the University of Iowa, a pioneer in the study of social and intellectual history. Schlesinger came to Harvard rather than Columbia, which also sought his services, largely because of Turner's urging.[66]

These matters settled, Turner could begin his last year of teaching confident that a brighter future lay ahead. His conscience decreed that he had to dedicate that year to the classroom rather than THE BOOK, even though materials unearthed in hours of preparation would never be used again. No yellowing notes were used for the first semester of the History of the West, presented at Harvard to fifty-six more-or-less eager students, and at Radcliffe to nine; instead, each lecture was carefully re-prepared, with new information added and old refurbished. "Yesterday," he told a former student, "in preparing a class lecture on the French-English contest for the interior, I had occasion to re-read your Albany, Crane's Southwest in Queen Anne's War, and Volwiler's papers on George Croghan."[67] His seminar was as time-consuming as always, for the eleven enrolled (including such future greats of the profession as John D. Barnhart, James Phinney Baxter III, and R. L. Morrow) roamed widely, forcing Turner to read on such diverse topics as the relation between banking and politics in New England, 1889-96, the southern iron industry, interstate migration into Indiana, and Appalachia politics.[68]

His dedication to his students was again proven during the second half-year. A prudent man would have continued teaching "The History of the West," which was already adequately prepared, but Merk had given that before and was ready to give it again. So it was that THE BOOK was shelved once more, while Turner presented a completely new course on "The History of the United States, 1880-1920." He revealed a great deal about his own enthusiasm for the past when he explained his purpose to the twenty-nine undergraduates who assembled for his first lecture. The modern period, he said, was particularly challenging, bringing into bold relief the problems faced by historians in analyzing any era. Recent events were clouded with the prejudices of class, section, and party; they had to be understood without access to the manuscript records that would allow a view from the inside; they were unbelievably complex and could be comprehended only by destroying the watertight compartments into which knowledge was divided. The students—and Turner—would learn much of economics, even though this was not a course in economics, much of political science, though it was not a course in political science, much of sociology, though it did not deal directly with that subject. "I give the course," Turner confessed, "because I know too little of the period. Want to know more."[69]

So the days and weeks of the 1923-24 academic year slipped away as lectures were prepared, theses graded, doctoral dissertations read and read again. Turner was also to find that retirement involved rituals too traditional to be forsaken, even though his wish was to step across the line unnoticed. He had to talk to the Harvard History Club, and did, in a gay little speech that stressed trivial influences of his boyhood that had stirred his interest in western history. "I enjoyed shocking them," he gloated. "Already I seem to be shedding the academic robe and hood and using my mortar board for a football."[70] He had to sit for a crayon portrait by a gifted portraitist, Alexander James, because his seminar insisted that Harvard should have a perpetual reminder of his services, even though Turner sputtered that the money could be better used to buy books on the frontier.[71] And, above all, he must be the guest of honor at a dinner, where the portrait was presented and proper tribute paid to his years as a teacher.

A gala dinner it was. On May 24 dozens of his friends and former students gathered at the Harvard Club, where the walls of the banquet hall had been decorated with maps and charts showing the migration of Plymouth Rock chickens ("males in blue, females in red, all others in green"), the spread of jackrabbits, the influence of flat feet on the Populist vote, and similar statistical information. They seated themselves at a U shaped table, before place cards on which each was caricatured, with Turner in the middle and two of his dearest friends, Max Farrand and Charles Homer Haskins, on either side. They ate magnificently. Then not one portrait, but two, were presented, that of Turner by Alexander James to the history department, another a cartoon by Julius Klein, a former colleague, to Turner, bearing the title "Westward the Course (History 17) of Empire takes Its Way." Turner's laughter rang out as he studied the details: peaks and prairies from Hoboken to San Francisco staked out with his preemption notices, a caravan of prairie schooners laden with his slides and maps, buffaloes pawing the plains and coyotes saying "woof woof," "open spaces" made by cutting holes in the paper, and his ear, well to the front, labeled the "Frontear in American History."[72]

Then came the speeches. Turner had wanted none, but not even he could overrule tradition. So they rose to speak—Theodore Clark Smith and Verner W. Crane, representing the graduate students of Wisconsin and Harvard; Frederick Merk, to read letters and telegrams from the many who were unable to attend; Max Farrand, in behalf of friends outside the university; Allyn A. Young of the economics department, to present tributes from the non-historians of Harvard. The praise lavished on Turner that night was unrestrained. "Your interpretation of American history," Farrand told him, ". . . has been the determining influence . . . for many years." So it had, but Allyn Young came nearer to portraying the inner Turner than any other speaker—a man passionately interested in the economic, political, and social life of his own generation and of his own country, a man who made large contributions to American history because he asked new and significant questions, a man who used words as an artist would designs to convince his colleagues of theories that revolutionized historical studies.[73] Turner's response to this avalanche of adulation was typical; he deserved less credit than Professor William Francis Allen, who had taught him all he knew, and the students, who had worked with him to unlock the vaults of the past. He had done nothing more than place the keys in their hands. As he seated himself amidst thunders of applause Turner was thoroughly happy. "We had a jolly time," he told a friend, "a real wake with the corpse participating."[74]

Over the next weeks tributes continued to descend on Cambridge, from friends and strangers. The *Harvard Crimson*, which in those days found football more worthy of space than it did professors, awarded him "an enviable niche in the hall of America's great historians." Former students in distant parts kept the telegraph wires humming; six in Minneapolis assured him that he might withdraw from teaching but never from an "abiding place in our esteem and affection"; while Joseph Schafer wired from Madison that his many friends there "are with you in spirits [sic]." Charles Homer Hockett found prose inadequate to express his feelings, and he contributed a page of verse:

> Tense drama of the woods and plain!
> 'Twas but chaotic, meaningless and vain
> Until a Seer arose! To him, All hail, again.

William E. Dodd confided that few men of their generation could retire with the consciousness of so much work so ably done, while Claude H. Van Tyne would "rather have written your comparatively limited number of pages than all the reams of pages of some of the other historical brethren who awe the average student of history." Even the Twin Cities History Club of Minneapolis sent its best wishes.[75] Those were sweet words, and Turner relished them all.

But at long last the tumult and the shouting died, and the Turners could turn to dismantling their house, engaging packers and movers, investigating freight rates, hiring vans, and packing crate after crate with the books that Turner had accumulated in his years at Cambridge. They also had to endure the interminable round of farewell dinners —including a very stiff affair given by the A. Lawrence Lowells—and farewell luncheons and farewell teas. But at last the final goodbyes were said, the furniture loaded, Mae bundled onto a train for Hancock Point, and Turner was alone for a last day of packing. At 2:10 on the afternoon of June 1, 1924, he swung aboard the Boston and Albany's crack "Wolverine," bound for Chicago and Madison, to begin life anew. "It's a good deal like starting life over as a pioneer in a new clearing," he wrote his daughter.[76] His first crop, he confidently believed, would be THE BOOK.

XVI

The Twilight Years

1924-1932

FREDERICK JACKSON TURNER left Boston that June day burdened with many problems, but two of the most pressing had been solved—his immediate financial burdens were to be eased by a lucrative summer-school post in Utah, and his future home was to be a small house in Madison, rather than the apartment he had dreaded. He had reached these decisions amidst the turmoil of departure and was well-satisfied with both, but he was particularly pleased at the prospect of a home of his own near his grandchildren and old friends.

A sensible suggestion from his daughter prompted that move. She had found that the lot next to the elegant home that she and her husband were building on Van Hise Street was for sale for $1400. Land that near the university was always in demand; too, the small house needed by the Turners would be easily rentable to visiting faculty while they were summering at Hancock Point. Here was a prospect too tempting to be denied, and within a week John Main had his instructions: buy at once, with a $200 payment to bind the deal. By April 21 the lot was theirs and house-planning under way. Dorothy Main was instructed to find a good builder who could promise a Nantucket-like cottage, similar to the one illustrated in the latest issue of *House Beautiful*, for no more than $6500. (Frank Riley would do if reminded that the Turners would be more prompt in their payments than they had been when they rented from him the first year of their marriage.) Turner wanted the house to have a basement, for he remembered the cold floors of Portage, but needed no such fancy frills as a sunken

391

bathtub or a tiled bathroom.[1] He would raise the money somehow if construction could begin soon and be completed by November.

Turner was able to assure Dorothy that needed funds could be raised because his last months at Harvard had been brightened by two unexpected windfalls. One could not be collected until the autumn; he was to give five lectures before the Dowse Institute of Cambridge in November, for a healthy fee of $500. The other was more immediately available, for when Turner left Cambridge he was bound for Logan, Utah, and an unbelievably profitable three weeks of teaching. Such an assignment had been farthest from his mind when he laid his retirement plans—his whole purpose was to put the finishing touches on THE BOOK—but he reckoned without the persuasive skills of Elmer G. Peterson, president of the Agricultural College of Utah. Peterson's dream was a "National Summer School" at Logan, staffed by a dozen eminent scholars attracted by the beauty of the Cache Valley and by exceptional financial inducements, and attracting, in turn, at least a thousand students from all over the country. Turner was the one historian who could add the greatest luster to his galaxy of stars, and no price was too high to pay for him.[2]

When negotiations began, in the fall of 1923, Turner had the good sense to refuse a regular six-week appointment at a salary not spectacularly higher than those usually offered, but President Peterson would not surrender. He had mentioned a fee of one-sixth the regular Harvard salary for the full session. How about half that sum for only three weeks of teaching? Turner sharpened his pencils and went to work: one-sixth of $8000 would be $1333, one-half of that, about $666. Add the $300 expense fund that Peterson had mentioned and the figure was $966—or very near $1000. That was too tempting to resist. He would come for that round sum, and would offer two three-week courses, one on "Aspects of the Westward Movement," the other on "The United States, 1830-1850: A Study of Sections."[3] His replacement for the remainder of the six-weeks session, he suggested, might be Frederick Merk, who had taken his place at Harvard. Turner planned to use his three weeks for profit rather than pleasure; he would come west on a special excursion rate that cost only $118.16 for the round trip, live in a dormitory at $35 a month, and eat in a dining room operated by the Home Economics Department at $14 a week. A sizable nestegg would be his reward for that last stint in the classroom.

Turner returned from his three weeks in Logan with a wealth of happy memories, as well as some $700 in savings. He and his colleagues were treated like the lions that they were—"the most eminent faculty ever assembled in the West or indeed, in the nation for summer school courses" according to the college catalogue[4]—and he had a thoroughly good time. His was an instant love-affair with the mountain-rimmed Cache Valley, the orderly community, the neat campus, the kindly people. An earthly paradise, he assured his wife—adding quickly "lacking my particular Eve."[5] Scarcely a day passed but he was entertained or feted, whether by the local Kiwanians, who cheered his talk on "Men with Gifted Feet," or by the Mormon stake, or by the resident faculty, who arranged almost daily tours to scenic spots, or by the town's best fisherman, who served as his guide on the opening day of the season—with no results. Turner was charmed. "I am a Mormon in everything but *revelation*," he reported to Mae after a few days of such treatment. "It is a most lovable, sincere, sound, clean population, and I love them."[6]

Best of all were the classes. Nearly three hundred undergraduates crowded into his two courses to hang eagerly on every word and applaud each lecture. Here was an audience that knew and loved the West as he did and could appreciate him as he wanted to be appreciated. His students refused to let him leave until they had presented him with a handwoven Navajo blanket, along with extravagant praise; the undergraduate newspaper echoed their sentiments when it bade him farewell in an editorial telling how he had "won the hearts and minds of his students here by his patience, sympathy and keenness of suggestion."[7] Turner was overwhelmed; he received more acclaim in three weeks in Logan than he had in fourteen years at Harvard. "Everybody is *too* kindly appreciative of my course," he wrote. "I am utterly spoiled."[8] (President Peterson was wise enough to capitalize on this sense of satisfaction by inviting Turner back for the summer of 1925, this time for one six-week course at a handsome salary of $1500. Mae came with him that year and enjoyed the land and its people as much as he did.)[9]

Much as Turner loved Utah, he was willing to catch the eastbound train, for almost daily bulletins from Dorothy on the progress of the new Madison home had his curiosity at fever pitch. The structure was rising rapidly, she reported, and so were the costs, to the point where they might reach $8000 instead of the $6500 agreed upon. Also, the builder wanted half his payment when the building was half done. Turner arrived in Madison in early July to find the roof nearly on, the outside shingling almost completed, and a sheaf of bills awaiting his attention. High finance occupied his next weeks: an American Telephone and Telegraph Company bond was sold for $1026.79, a share in the Edison Electric Illuminating Company for $964.58, a Northern States Power Company bond for $1000.53, odd shares of stock in three copper companies for $964.58. These modest sums, added to the nearly $700 that he had managed to save from his Utah salary, allowed him to pay the contractor half the final price of $7105.50 on July 19. A like amount had to be raised by October, together with money for moving expenses, furnishings, and a $1000 assessment for street improvements. Turner borrowed $5800 against his life insurance policies at first, then, realizing that his reduced income would never allow him to meet the interest and principal charges on this sum, he reluctantly sold the policies during the summer, keeping only one worth $5000 as a cushion for Mae, should he die suddenly.[10] Turner retired from a lifetime of teaching with a home worth less than $10,000, a cottage in Maine, stock in the Sullivan Machinery Company that paid $220 yearly, royalties of less than $200, and one $5000 insurance policy—these were the total assets of one of the nation's most eminent teachers.

He was ready to recuperate from his financial exercises when he joined Mae at Hancock Point for the last weeks of that 1924 summer, but retiring was a never-ending job and it left little time for the trout streams. Instructions had to be sent to Dorothy on decorations for the house, two van-loads of furniture had to be removed from the Cambridge home before their lease expired on September 1, nearly two tons of books had to be boxed and shipped to Madison—and almost as many to Hancock Point—the five lectures that were to be given in November before the Dowse Institute had to be prepared. As usual, the lecture preparation was left until last, and, as usual, an unexpected cold snap froze the pipes and converted Turner from a scholar into a hewer of wood for the fireplaces and drawer of water for the kitchen sink.[11] He arrived in Boston on November 1 very badly prepared and nursing a severe cold that attacked his vocal cords whenever he used his voice. Turner endured those five evenings but took no pride in his performance; during the first he could scarcely speak above a whisper, in the middle of the second a siege of coughing almost drove him from the platform, and he was able to talk at all during his final appearance because the maid at the Kenmore Hotel prescribed a mixture of egg whites and lemon juice. "It has been a test of my fortitude," he reported, "and of the audience's as well."[12] Turner was utterly exhausted when he left for Madison in mid-November to begin his retirement.

A lively retirement it was. He fell in love with his new home at 2214 Van Hise Avenue on sight. "The Chimney Corner," he named it (after rejecting "The Shack" as discouraging to renters and "The Fisherman's Cottage" as too *House-Beautiful*-like). Small and cozy (Turner's bedroom was so tiny that he considered sleeping with his feet out of the window), and modeled after a Nantucket cottage, it was roomier than its neat shingled exterior suggested, with a great chimney of local limestone, an ample fireplace, and a book-lined study on the southwest side, where it could catch the afternoon sun. "It's like living in a ship's cabin," he reported.[13] But it was vastly superior to any apartment they could have found.

Madison proved a disappointment to the Turners after their high expectations. It had changed in fourteen years, from a friendly college town into an unattractive city peopled by strangers. "New and interesting as a strange land," he found it, and felt himself rubbing his eyes at times—"a later Rip Van Winkle!"[14] So they were content to live their own lives, finding in their family and the little world about them the joys that companions had formerly provided. Turner never tired of watching the antics of the chickadees, nuthatches, brown creepers, woodpeckers, and jays who crowded his windowsill feeding station during the winter, or providing robins with lengths of string for their nests in the spring, or listening to the songs of the meadowlarks on summer evenings. When the sun was warm he enjoyed puttering about the yard, spraying the shingles with a salt solution to imitate the soft grey of the seashore (he never succeeded) or trying to transform sun-baked clay into a green lawn. But the Turners found their greatest joy in their daily meetings with Dorothy and John, who lived next door, and in the grandchildren—Jackson, a studious lad of seven, and Betsy, a carefree four. They were in and out of the Turner cottage all day long, to listen wide-eyed to Puff Puff's stories (so named because he was always puffing on a pipe or cigar) or to gaze enraptured as he fashioned outlandish animals with paper and scissors for "Turner's World Menagerie and Circus," or to watch in awe as those animals were transformed into terrifying creatures with the aid of a magic lantern. Simple pleasures, but they added up to happiness. "Such little things make up our life," Turner told a friend.[15]

That life would have been pleasant, indeed, save for two recurring problems: how to supplement the pittance of an annuity on which they had to live, and how to keep well in Madison's frigid winters. Turner was increasingly concerned with the inadequacy of their income in that day of skyrocketing inflation. Mae did her best to help out, doing without a maid or cook for the first time since their marriage, and finding to her surprise that washing dishes and sweeping the living room rug was not unpleasant; "as thrilling as pioneering," she reported to a friend, then added that it was very elegant pioneering indeed with a centrally heated house, a gas water heater, a water softener, an electric range, a telephone, and electric lights.[16] Even this sacrifice was not enough, and Turner was faced with the uncomfortable realization that he had to add to the family coffers by the only means he knew: teaching, lecturing, and writing.

During the next three years he did far more than he should of all three, but lecturing proved a particular burden. Some of the many invitations that came his way were welcome for the financial returns they promised, some because they encouraged him to explore new subjects, but none was more eagerly received than the first that he accepted on his arrival in Madison. Would he celebrate his return to active membership in the State Historical Society of Wisconsin by delivering the principal address at their annual meeting, in January 1925? Turner would, eagerly. He was well aware that some thirty years before he had revealed the significance of the frontier to an annual meeting of that society. Now he would prepare an equally momentous address on the significance of the section. "I have always tried to have what an astronomical friend of mine calls a 'bright idea' when I have addressed that organization," Turner assured the director. "I should like to do something worth while."[17]

He did his best, but the result was a sad anticlimax. "The significance in American history of the advance of the frontier and of its disappearance is now generally recognized," he began boldly. "This evening I wish to consider with you another fundamental factor in American history—namely, the Section." Then came the usual history of the sectional conflicts of the nineteenth century, the usual predictions that sectional antagonisms would deepen as mobility lessened, the usual plea for governmental policies that would keep friction to a minimum. Turner dwelt more fully now than before on the sub-sections within the sections, whose interests often opposed those of the section itself; he saw them as among the cohesive forces that held the United States together by serving as "a limitation upon the larger section in case it attempts a drastic and subversive policy toward other sections."[18] Yet he had little to add to a story that was already well known to historians and was by no means convincing. The address, printed in the *Wisconsin Magazine of History* and circulated widely throughout the profession, stirred none of the excitement of his frontier thesis. Turner's old Harvard friend, Frank W. Taussig, spoke for most when he complimented Turner on "carrying your old lines of analysis to a further stage."[19] This was an embarrassingly accurate judgment. Turner had little to add to the "old lines" save complicating qualifications that made his argument even less convincing. Yet he was doggedly insistent that his critics were wrong. "I am possessed with the idea," he told a friend, "that twenty years or so from now my Sections paper will travel along with my frontier as interpretations."[20]

The confidence that underlay that statement was further shaken in the spring of 1925, when he was invited to deliver a course of seven lectures at the University of Wisconsin. The chance to serve again as a "special lecturer" in his old department, and the honorarium of $500, were both too tempting to be refused, even though days of preparation were needed. When Turner trudged up the Hill toward Bascom Hall on the afternoon of April 15, carrying his box of slides and numerous notes, his expectations were high: he was sure he would find eager students and faculty swept into conviction by the abundance of proof that he would use to bolster his sectional theories. What he said that day, and on subsequent days, was in his best tradition; again, he traced the history of sectional conflicts, appraised the role of sub-sections, predicted the deepening of regional antagonisms as nationalizing forces weakened the power of the states, and urged governmental policies to maintain national unity.[21] But somehow his listeners failed to catch fire as they did when he talked of the frontier. "His audience dwindled day by day," wrote a former student sadly, "the spark was gone."[22]

Turner might have endured—even enjoyed—the time-consuming

preparation and physically debilitating effort required by lecturing if he had swept his audiences into his own enthusiasm for sectionalism, but, when he could not, each appearance became a greater burden. Yet they had to go on, for fees of the sort he could command were irresistible. So Turner traveled that spring through Illinois, speaking at Knox and Decatur and the University of Illinois on sectionalism, meeting with students, conducting seminars, talking to Harvard and Wisconsin clubs, attending the luncheons and dinners and smokers that were the bane of all intellectual lions. "Bread-and-buttering," he called that swing around the circuit, but cruelly hard work it was, too, when audiences did not respond as they should and diminished day after day. "I shall swear off all talking I think after this," Turner wrote his wife.[23]

That was the last of his moneymaking speaking tours, but by no means the last of the side-excursions that kept him from settling to work on THE BOOK. One that gave him particular satisfaction was a paper he read before the Association of American Geographers, when that body met in Madison in December 1925. Turner prepared his remarks carefully, knowing that his audience would be sympathetic to any discussion of "Geographic Sectionalism in American History"; he would win converts among the geographers if he could not among historians. "I hope," he told a friend at the time, "to awaken the brethren to the intimate relationship between regional geography and American history. Judging from my experience in getting the Frontier idea a hearing, this will take twenty years, and I shall have to lean over the battlements to hear it spoken of as a trite conception."[24] The response was gratifying, for this was one of Turner's most persuasive arguments, and it was greeted warmly. Even his fellow historians showed a spark of interest when the printed version was distributed; Merle Curti felt the same thrill that he had experienced when he read the "Significance of the Frontier," Arthur M. Schlesinger believed that the sectional thesis was now indisputably proven, and Norman Foerster experienced a blinding revelation as the full importance of the sectional hypothesis burst upon him.[25] This was music in Turner's ears, and some compensation for the days of labor that had been stolen from THE BOOK.

Retirement meant a chance to lecture, but it also meant a chance to write—on a variety of topics that promised some financial return or that gave him an excuse not to struggle with the masses of data accumulated for his magnum opus. Two major efforts occupied far too much of his time, one inspired by curiosity, the other by a promise of a $300 fee for what seemed to be a cut-and-dried article that could be written in a few days. The editor of *World's Work* was the tempter; could Turner prepare 5000 words on the changes that had altered the West during the past fifty years? Turner did, but only after using twenty times that number in his early drafts; in his perfectionist mind even such a simple task required reading every scrap of information about the trans-Mississippi country—census returns, state reports, travel accounts, books and magazine articles—and recording what he had learned on hundreds upon hundreds of pages.[26] All of this was compressed into a draft double the size wanted by the editors, then painfully squeezed into the allotted space by casting aside all but the statistics. Turner was not happy with "The West—1876 and 1926" when he finally released it to the mails (he thought it "arid" and too condensed to be readable), but he had performed a remarkable feat of compression; every significant change—in agriculture, industry, politics, social life, and culture— was chronicled in detail.[27] Yet the editors were more than satisfied, as a check for $400 rather than the agreed-upon $300 testified, and Turner had managed to avoid work on THE BOOK for another few months.

He squandered still more time on a paper that could do nothing save satisfy his intellectual curiosity. Ever since 1891, when he had read an article by Henry Cabot Lodge in the *Century Magazine*, arguing that frontier barbarism and materialism stifled the creative spirit in the West, Turner had itched to set the record straight. He could not dispute the basic conclusion, for Lodge's findings were based on an analysis of the 14,243 persons listed in *Appleton's Encyclopedia of American Biography* and were probably correct, but Turner could show that the second generation of frontiersmen contributed as much to the nation's culture as did New Englanders, and at the same time he could demonstrate the relationship between human ability and the geographic environment.[28] He had gathered data casually since at least 1917; now he had the leisure and the excuse to make a thorough investigation. The excuse this time was not even an editor's check, but an invitation to deliver a paper before the Madison Literary Club at its November meeting in 1925. Turner agreed to speak on "The Children of the Pioneers."

He had doomed himself to a major task. Days stretched into weeks,

and weeks into months, as he searched through biographical diction-
aries, newspapers, magazines and books, carefully copying the name
and record of every westerner who had made his contribution to
American life.[29] Eventually his results crammed a whole filing drawer
—all gathered for one presentation before a few friends in a town-and-
gown society. Not a very successful presentation, either. Turner
thought his thirty-three-page manuscript too "listy" and only "tolerated by the friendly gathering."[30] It was crammed with the names of
westerners who had succeeded in business, government, and the arts
but Turner was too good a historian not to distill some meaning from
his columns; his westerners, he believed, gained Lincolnesque stature by
their dedication to the interests of the ordinary people, inventing or
writing or worshipping or painting to glorify and instruct the common
man. Here was a finding worth sharing; "The Children of the Pioneers"
was accepted by the *Yale Review,* if enough names could be squeezed
out to bring it down to 8000 words. It appeared in the July 1926 issue,
enriching Turner by $100 and providing him slight justification for
having indulged his passion for learning while THE BOOK languished.

There was reason for this neglect, for he was finding that retirement
provided no panacea for the illness that laid him low whenever he
became too involved in a major task. Now his health was further imperiled by Madison's frigid winters. Turner's first year in his new home
was divided between attacks of influenza and the lectures that he had
contracted, as progress on his book came to a standstill. When he did
emerge from his bouts with influenza he was so plagued by colds and
so weak that he was afraid to venture outside, lest his staggering give
the neighborhood a bad reputation—or so he reported.[31] Mae was little
better off, particularly during the raw spring of 1925, when recurring
sore throats plagued both the Turners. There could be no relief, the
doctors decreed, until their tonsils were removed. Both were operated
on in Chicago in mid-May, Mae successfully, Turner less so when his
stitches loosened and he was forced to have them replaced, this time
with no anaesthetic. "I don't like to be stitched in the throat without
dope," he told a friend, with masterful understatement.[32]

Better times were around the corner. Turner was greatly cheered
when an unexpected bonanza came his way that spring. Word arrived
that he was one of the first group to be benefitted by Harvard's newly

established Milton Fund—he was to have a grant of $2500 "to complete a History of the United States for the period from 1830 to 1850," with no strings attached save that the money be used to further scholarship.[33] Now a secretary could be hired, a map-maker employed, and necessary office equipment purchased for his cubbyhole in the State Historical Society library. With that nest egg to be drawn upon, and the doctors' assurance of better health with the loss of his tonsils, Turner was ready to begin work on THE BOOK in earnest after his 1925 summer-school stint in Logan. At that time, three chapters and part of the fourth were in Henry Holt & Company's New York vault, together with half-a-dozen manuscript maps; the remainder of Chapter IV and parts of Chapter V were in rough draft. He settled to his task as soon as he proved that all trout had vanished from the streams near Hancock Point. His first move was inauspicious; he asked the publishers to return two of the early chapters for revision! They did so reluctantly, fearing they would never see them again, but by the end of that summer they were revised to Turner's satisfaction and could be returned with the assurance that more had been accomplished on Chapter IV and that Chapter V was virtually done. Turner was confident now that the whole book would be completed by the spring of 1926, and could be announced for fall publication. "You are," he added with a rare touch of realism, "too well aware, however, of my imperfections, to be safe in announcing anything at present."[34]

That warning was as justified as it was unnecessary, for illness and research on "The Children of the Pioneers" monopolized the next winter, with progress on THE BOOK at a dead halt. Summer brought better health, however, and Turner left Madison for Hancock Point in May 1926 confident that the next months would produce an abundance of finished chapters. His dreams were short lived. While in Boston, where he and Mae stopped to see friends, he suffered a painful disturbance of the middle ear, with dizziness and nausea so intense that he was hurried into the Stillman Infirmary for a two-week stay. There he improved until he could walk without staggering, but the deafness remained, to persist for the rest of his days. That summer went not into writing, but into a round of visits to doctors in a vain quest for better hearing, and into the rest he needed to regain his strength. "I haven't," he confessed as they prepared to return home in October, "been able to write a line—or wet a line, except once, with no results."[35]

Winter came early that fall of 1926, as it did often in Madison, with biting cold that kept Turner huddled before an open fire rather than dictating in his office at the Historical Society. As day after day passed with nothing done, he sank into a deepening depression, one that worried Mae and his friends. Clearly, escape to a warmer climate was called for, even though the below-zero state of the Turner bank balance made such a dream unrealistic. Then came a stroke of good fortune. When his sister, Breese De Moe, visited Madison that Christmas, she recognized the problem and the cure; nothing would do but that Mae accept a present of sufficient funds to take the Turners to Florida or Arizona or California. They accepted gratefully, and by mid-January of 1927 they were in New Orleans, basking in the warm sun and stuffing themselves on oysters and fish at Antoine's. The French Quarter was expensive, however, and after a week they were on their way westward, stopping at San Antonio and Tucson, taking life-restoring side-trips under the warm desert skies, and having the time of their lives. Eventually they reached Claremont, California, where they found delightful quarters at 1111 Harvard Street, with a view of the snow-clad mountains from their patio, oranges and lemons on their own trees, and plentiful friends to guide them on tours of the flower-bright countryside.[36] Here was the Eden they had been seeking. Turner sent for the trunkful of notes he had packed and prepared to settle down until summer.

Fate, in the person of Max Farrand, was to prolong that brief visit into a lifetime stay. Farrand, one of Turner's oldest and dearest friends, had just at that time accepted the directorship of the Huntington Library and Art Gallery, the magnificent benefaction near Pasadena bequeathed to the world of scholarship by Henry E. Huntington.[37] Farrand was in the East at the time, but no sooner did he hear of Turner's presence in California than he sent word to George Ellery Hale, a member of the library's board of trustees and an eminent astronomer. Turner was the one person in the world who could be most helpful in transforming Mr. Huntington's rare books and manuscripts into a research library—an ambition dear to both Hale and Farrand. Could the trustees seek him out and convince him to stay on as a senior research associate at $500 a month? Such an appointment would establish a standard that would attract the attention of the entire academic world. Hale acted with an enthusiasm that matched Farrand's own; by March

5 Turner had been brought to Pasadena, persuaded to spend the next month there as consultant, and offered a permanent post as associate for the following winter—a position that he promised to take if all went well. Farrand was delighted. "Congratulate Mr. Huntington and trustees," he wired, "and kiss Turner for me."[38] Turner could not know that he stood on the threshold of some of the happiest—and most tragic —years of his life.

Certainly the month spent at the library that spring was heaven itself. The Turners moved to a small rented bungalow at the "Court of the Oak" in Pasadena on March 15. Each day thereafter he wandered among the books and manuscripts, a sheaf of papers in hand to take notes on the marvels that he saw. Each new box opened sparked his enthusiasm. Materials for his own study were so numerous that he would have to spend a year reading them all. Rare items on the colonial period would allow scholars for the first time to understand the forces underlying political events. The story of the westward movement between the Appalachians and the Rockies would have to be completely rewritten. Such were the riches of the Huntington that it seemed certain to become "a new center of civilization in the United States."[39] As he admired, Turner offered a great deal of sound advice on the library's future. It should build to its strengths when collecting rare items, specializing on the colonial era and the West, but with greater stress on the Midwest and on the recent Far West; the function of history was to explain the present, and modern materials were needed for this. It should collect economic, social, literary, and religious books as well as those in the social sciences; "we need allied workers and allied books, just as the astronomer needs the co-operation of chemist, physicist, geologist, etc. etc., in his work of deciphering the meaning of the heavens." Most of all, the Huntington library required the reference works that were the tools of all scholars; not to buy them on the ground that they were available in other Los Angeles libraries would be equivalent to asking a factory worker to travel ten miles each time he needed a hammer or wrench. The trustees should buy the large sets and the historical journals and the monographs and the government documents (even though they had to build a new wing to house them), and buy them at once. "The nuggets are mined; what is needed is the machinery and the material for treating this gold."[40]

This was sound advice, and much to the library's future benefit. It convinced Farrand and the trustees that Turner was too valuable an asset to be relinquished, just as Turner's months at the Huntington persuaded him that he could be happier in Pasadena than in Madison. His health was better than it had been for years; Mae felt that he had undergone a miraculous resurrection, and he agreed that his weeks at the library had been "a real rebirth of enthusiasm for me."[41] Turner was not so enthusiastic that he forgot to bargain when the trustees offered him a permanent post as senior research associate; he wanted assurance that his principal efforts could be directed toward THE BOOK and that he be allowed to spend his summers in Maine. These terms were thoroughly acceptable and were written into the contract that was signed that summer. Turner was to join the library staff on October 15, 1927, as senior research associate, guaranteeing to spend at least the next six months in Pasadena in return for a salary of $5000 to offset his travel and living costs.[42] The trustees were glad to provide space for his own books and to arrange for the use of a car and driver to transport him between his home and the library if he so desired. On June 28 the local press announced that one of the world's greatest historians would soon add luster to Pasadena's cultural life.

The Turners spent that summer in Maine—a cold, rainy summer that kept Turner before the fire or in bed and confirmed their realization that California was their valhalla—then fled back to Madison in September to rent their home and pack clothes and books and notes for the journey westward. There they found a modest small house at 23 Oak Knoll Gardens for $100 monthly rental, complete with a spreading walnut tree, a sleeping porch, a next-door airedale who trotted in at all hours, and sufficient grackles and mocking birds and milkmen to make alarm clocks unnecessary. Each day Max Farrand called for Turner at nine, drove him to the library, and deposited him at his desk among the riches that he loved. Each noon they munched sandwiches together in Farrand's Gothic office, talking library business as they did so; occasionally Turner broke this routine to join the male staff members in a basement room where they brewed coffee, lunched from paper bags, and talked endlessly of books and history and fishing. "The Huntington Library," he reported happily, "is quite a paradise." He helped make it so. All who worked there fell victim to his gentle charm, his modesty, his patience, his outgoing affection for those about him. Turner contributed a great deal to the library that year—

sound advice, lists of reference works to be purchased, hundreds of his own books that the institution lacked—but his greatest contribution was a practical demonstration of the needs and methods of a research scholar. This was enlightening to the staff, who had been training under Mr. Huntington to care for a collector's library only. Turner gave them advice, gently and with understanding, but he also gave them a lesson in scholarship that was far more meaningful than any amount of counsel. Had he not been in residence, the conversion of the Huntington library into a magnificent research institution would have been far slower and more difficult.[43]

All this Turner greatly enjoyed, just as he enjoyed his new life in California. Friends, new and old, were almost as numerous as in Madison or Cambridge, and sometimes embarrassingly persistent in their attention; every time he started to write, someone dropped in with an invitation to drive to Ojai or Claremont or La Jolla, or a suggestion that they dine at the La Ramada or the La Solano or some other restaurant with a Spanish name and Boston clam chowder at the head of the menu. By the time the Turners started for Hancock Point in May 1928, they had been permanently weaned from the East. That spring they rented their Madison house unfurnished and packed the furniture and books to be sent westward; that summer neither particularly enjoyed the rain and humidity at Hancock Point. Both were happy to reach Pasadena again in early October, there to settle into a larger rented house at 16 Oak Knoll Gardens, where there was room to move about, even though the house next door was so close that, as Turner put it, "we can hear our neighbors change their minds."[44] They were becoming Californians.

Best of all was the sense of financial security that came with the library salary. Turner was forced to surrender his annuity from the Carnegie Corporation, but Harvard continued to pay him $598.32 yearly, the rental of their Madison house added another thousand, royalties brought in a few hundred, and the $5000 yearly from the Huntington relieved them of financial burdens. Turner insisted that his library salary be cut to $3500 after 1929, arguing that he was worth no more at his age and that they could live comfortably on the lesser sum. The soaring prosperity of the late 1920s added to their affluence; in February 1929 an aging relative in the East surprised them with a gift of $2000, while at about the same time they sold their Madison house to their son-in-law for $10,000, with a $5000 down payment and the remainder on a 6 per cent mortgage. These windfalls went into investments, as did most surplus money in that day of a skyrocketing stock market; some to the business ventures of John Main, some into such stocks as Drug Incorporated or the International Match Corporation, some into bank deposits. Their dividends in 1928 reached $1500 and their total income $7915.86—a satisfactory sum for a man who had expected to live on a pittance after his retirement.[45] Mae could even afford a maid now to help her with the work.

Life was good for Turner, but it would have been far better if he had had the willpower to refuse the invitations to write and speak and consult that were the lot of all new lions in a community. Lecture invitations poured in: from the Lincoln Centennial Commission of Illinois, who wanted an address on their hero; from the University of Texas, which would listen to anything he had to say on any subject; from Knox College, which needed a distinguished speaker for its Founder's Day; from DePauw University, where the officials were so impressed with his *The Last Frontier* [sic] that they thought he should deliver the Horizon Lecture Series; from the Pasadena Kiwanis Club which sought a free entertainer for its Washington's Birthday luncheon.[46] These Turner managed to refuse, but he was too neighborly to reject invitations from his new-found friends in Pasadena. His appearances there cost him a great deal of time; during his first two years in California he spoke before students of the University of California at Los Angeles on sectionalism, before the Pasadena Library Club on the value of bibliographies to historians, before the Harvard Club and the Pacific Coast Branch of the American Historical Association on the virtues of the Huntington library, and, in February 1928, in the prestigious Pasadena Lecture Series on Current Topics on "Sectionalism in American Politics."[47] That was the end; from that time on Turner parried all invitations by pleading ill health or the pressures of writing.

The end, that is, until an invitation arrived that could not be refused. The California Institute of Technology had recently added the distinguished political scientist William B. Munro to its faculty. What was more logical than that he cooperate with the two other scholars of equal distinction in the area, Turner and Max Farrand, in a course on history and historical methodology for the culturally deprived engineers? Arrangements were quickly made; for a $500 fee Turner would offer a second-term course on "The Jackson Era, 1828-1838," to be preceded by a term on "The Constitutional Era," with Max Farrand in charge, and followed by another under Munro on "From Cleveland to Wilson." Turner accepted partly because he convinced himself that preparing lectures would force him to get on with THE BOOK, but he was sadly mistaken. Most of that winter term of the 1928-29 academic year went into drafting syllabi, compiling reading lists, selecting source materials for analysis, grading examinations, and enduring ten two-hour sessions with eleven bored undergraduates who were so indifferent that four accepted incompletes and five earned only the grade of "C."[48] Turner could say no more of his last stint in the classroom than that it was "an interesting if fatiguing experience"--and he vowed never to do it again.[49]

Those students he could escape; his doctoral candidates and near-candidates from his Harvard and Wisconsin days he could not. They required constant nursemaiding and were never reluctant to ask for favors. Would Turner support so-and-so for a Guggenheim Fellowship, or for a post in such-and-such college? Would he recommend the best possible man in western history to this university or that? Would he help a worried board of trustees by suggesting an ideal president for the University of Washington—or Indiana, or Iowa? "I feel like a bureau," he confessed after a whole day of such letters.[50] Even those who did not feel themselves worthy of better positions added to his burden by asking him to criticize their articles and lectures and books and to aid them in convincing a publisher of the worth of their products. Turner took such duties seriously, reading each manuscript carefully, taking extensive notes, and writing voluminous criticisms, always leavened with enough praise to encourage the author to greater heights. These were the unsung contributions of the professor—whether retired or not—and were cheerfully rendered without thought of personal gain. Turner differed from his colleagues only in the number and quality of his students, and the greater burdens that they imposed.

But there were dividends to be paid by those students as well, and Turner profited handsomely. He had reached the point of distinction now that tributes were his due, and they came in abundance, largely from those who had been awakened to the excitement of history under his direction. Some dedicated their books to Turner; he was gratified with each recognition and kept careful lists of those who honored him in this way. Others painted flattering pen portraits of their old friend and master; Harold J. Laski, a former Harvard colleague many years Turner's junior, pictured him for the *Century Magazine* as one of the nation's greatest teachers, while Joseph Schafer, in an article on "The Author of the Frontier Thesis" for the *Wisconsin Magazine of History*, sketched him in such glowing colors that Turner was not sure he was the man described. "I look back on that young man," he confessed to Schafer, "with a perhaps pardonable indulgence and a sense of detachment that enables me to read your words without the blushing confusion that would be normal."[51] Of these many tributes, however, Turner was particularly pleased by those from two of his outstanding students, Carl Becker and Merle Curti.

Both wrote with a purpose in mind, Becker to describe his teacher, in a volume on *American Masters of Social Science*, which appeared in 1927, Curti to appraise Turner's methodology in a learned work, *Methods in Social Science, A Case Book*, which was sponsored by the Social Science Research Council and published in 1931. Each made full use of Turner's memory, plying him with questions on the origins of his theories, his philosophy of history, and the techniques that he employed. Turner responded generously with twenty- and thirty-page letters that not only answered his questioners but supplied them with invaluable information on his work, his accomplishments, and his students.[52] Both Becker and Curti used this mine of information wisely, producing model essays that gave Turner his due as a pioneer theorist and trailblazer in the realm of interdisciplinary studies. He was unabashedly delighted. "A premature obituary," he labeled Becker's masterpiece, but confessed that "I have reached the age where that sort of thing from a former student gives me real pleasure."[53] Curti's brilliant appraisal of his historical techniques was just as pleasing. "I would like to have my contributions as a whole seen as you present them," he assured the author, at the same time telling friends that the essay "has set forth my ideas and aims very well."[54] The important thing to Turner was to have his ideas presented so lucidly to an audience of social scientists, but he would have been less than human had he not glowed with pride at such recognition. He must have felt, as he read those two essays, that his life had not been wasted.

Turner must also have been haunted by doubts, for he was sadly aware of the fact that work on THE BOOK was lagging far behind his self-imposed schedules. He had settled in Pasadena in the fall of 1927 glowing with confidence that not only his study of sectionalism in the 1830-50 era would be completed within a few months, but that a whole five-foot-shelf of books would follow: a general volume on sectionalism in American history, another on the struggle between rural and industrial elements, a third on the relations of capital and labor in their class consciousness, and, if possible, "an interpretative general survey of American history coordinating frontier, regional geography, sections, population factors (including immigration), and such religious and art and literary history as needed to explain the other things."[55] THE BOOK had to be finished first, but he thought that would take only a few months. Turner drew up a time schedule that year: April 9 to 30 to revise the introduction and the first two chapters on New England and the Middle States, the four weeks in May for the four remaining chapters describing the major regions, June 1 to July 15 to complete the four chapters surveying the political impact of sectionalism between 1828 and 1844, July 16 to August 15 for the final two chapters carrying the story to 1850.[56] Turner's optimism was irrepressible.

Nor was it diminished by the prospect of a secretary of such terrifying efficiency that Turner would not dare let THE BOOK languish. Merrill H. Crissey had been one of the prods that made the *Rise of the New West* possible when he had worked for Turner as an undergraduate in 1905; the two had drifted apart since Crissey's graduation in 1906, but now he was available again and free to start work on January 1, 1928. He had read of Turner's appointment at the Huntington and would be willing to endure a financial sacrifice to renew their old relationship. Turner pointed out that those sacrifices might be considerable, for he could pay no more than $175 a month from the funds left in his Milton grant and could guarantee employment for no more than six months yearly. Not even these uncertainties could dissuade Crissey. He would arrive on schedule and would be happy to receive any salary that seemed suitable. Turner was assured not only excellent secretarial help, but an adoring slave driver who would be at his side for the rest of his days.

He dusted off his notes and manuscripts in November 1927, confident (as he told a friend) that he would "be able to complete the book within the year."[57] The three chapters and portions of the fourth in the Henry Holt & Company vault had to come back first, together with the half-dozen maps he had sent them some years before, so that he could refresh his memory and make a few changes. The manuscript was returned promptly, with appropriate words of encouragement, but the request for the maps brought an embarrassing admission: both they and the correspondence concerning them had disappeared. This was disaster, even though Turner had photostat copies of all but two. All had to be redrawn before interpretation could go on.[58] By the beginning of 1928 that hurdle was cleared, and work was resumed under the efficient prodding of Merrill Crissey. Their procedures were soon perfected: Turner sat in his pleasant office at the Huntington library, his notes about him, filling page after page with his bold hand; as each was finished, it was copied in triplicate by Crissey on the typewriter, with two of the copies set aside for Turner's corrections. These were many. Scarcely an hour passed but progress halted while Turner searched back through the typed pages to rewrite a paragraph or add a tidbit of information or alter an interpretation. "Though they were presumably copy for the publisher," Crissey wrote sadly as he saw his neatly typed pages torn apart, "the refining process continued, for whenever they were re-read there were further alterations."[59] Often these were time-consuming, requiring a search for confirming evidence, sometimes obtainable only in a distant library. So meticulous was Turner that he once halted progress for days while obtaining data on the 1843 census in Southport, Wisconsin, because his own figures did not jibe with those in an article he had read.

These delays were bad enough, but worse were those that occurred while Turner stopped to dig more deeply into problems that he constantly encountered. Two of those problems were particularly irksome. Turner found that the sections he was analyzing concealed a number of smaller sub-sections that differed politically from the region in which they were located; each of these had to be carefully analyzed and its behavior explained in terms of geographic or ethnic factors— an endless task. He discovered also that most of the secondary books he had counted on to supply incidental information were too inaccurate to be trusted, and that only by digging out every fact himself could he avoid mistakes. This was a fatal realization, for now he had an excuse to bury himself in the riches of the Huntington, his writing forgotten. "The library is as delightful a workshop as ever," he re- ported late in 1928, "but the book moves more slowly than I want it to."[60] Yet it did move; by October 1928 all but the last of the "sec- tional" chapters—that describing the Far West—were "finished." His rash predictions of a book in 1929 seemed within the range of possi- bility.

That burst of activity took its toll, for sustained intellectual effort was fatal to Turner's weakening system. "I have never learned to work moderately when I get interested in a problem," he told a friend that winter, and now he had to pay the piper.[61] The first setback came in February 1929, when he suffered a severe attack of vertigo when leav- ing the library and stopped himself from falling only by grabbing a "No Admittance" sign. Tension, high blood pressure, and a weakening heart was the official verdict; Turner was sentenced to bed for two weeks and warned that he must do no work the rest of that spring. He followed his spartan regime to the letter, but when he failed to improve, the doctors agreed that an infection in his bladder was poison- ing his system. Two operations were needed, one to insert drainage tubes, the other to probe the bladder itself. The first was performed in late April, the second on May 15, both so successfully that by the end of May he could be wheeled into the flowering gardens of the Pasadena Hospital, eat squab for lunch, and resume smoking like an incinerator.[62]

Those gains were deceptive, for no sooner was he out of the hospital than the spells of dizziness began again, accompanied with acute nausea. The doctors allowed him to visit Hancock Point that summer of 1929, partly so that he could consult specialists in Madison and Boston. They could do nothing; a major attack of vertigo in August sent him to his bed for ten days. "I am not worth much," he reported sadly to a friend.[63] Worse was the doctors' prognosis for the future. Turner's attacks stemmed from a malfunctioning heart that was beyond cure. He might be able to lead a normal life for a brief time, but he would never be well, and the end could not be far distant. He returned to Pasadena that September a very sick man; friends noticed his height- ened color, his increasing frailty, the dullness of his eyes, his lack of zest for work.

California's wonders worked their magic, however, and by Novem- ber progress on THE BOOK was resumed, with 485 manuscript pages completed and far more to be done. Procedures had to be changed now, for Turner was too weak to visit the library and dictated to Crissey from a couch in his home. Crissey played a heroic role. Each morning he gathered notes for the day's dictation, transcribed the most essential onto slips of paper, and carried them to the cottage at 23 Oak Knoll Gardens. There Turner examined them and gave his instructions: more information must be found on this subject in such-and-such documents; this book or that must be consulted on the next point to be covered. When Crissey had located all the needed materials and made the necessary notes in his precise hand, he returned to Turner's home, where the notes were filed in proper order with guide-cards of colored cardboard at intervals to indicate dates or topics. With these before him, Turner began his dictation, selecting cards on various subjects to be correlated with others. Progress was slow, for he could work no more than an hour or two before fatigue forced a halt. Crissey then returned to the library to type the day's dictation into a triple-spaced manuscript (with ample room for the inevitable deletions, interpolations, and changes), and to begin research on material for the next day's effort.[64]

So the work inched on, month after month, with no improvement on Turner's part. "The book is moving like molasses," he reported sadly in February 1930.[65] There were interruptions, too, when weakness forced a halt to all writing for weeks at a time, or when friends who had been asked to read chapters sent in their criticism, and revision replaced writing. More than a month went into selecting and polishing a chapter to be published in the first issue of the *Huntington Library Bulletin;* Turner wanted his treatment of the Jackson administration to be used, because he thought it particularly original, but Farrand chose that on New England as the only chapter short enough not to fill a whole issue.[66] Still the pile of "completed" manuscript grew; by the end of March 1930, a "preliminary draft" of all the "sectional" chapters had been typed, rough drafts of those covering the Jackson and Van Buren administrations had been completed, and that on the Tyler administration begun. Only the last three chapters, on Polk, Taylor, and the state of the nation in 1850, were still to be written in their entirety. THE BOOK might yet appear in 1931, if Turner's health held up.

Instead it steadily worsened. Late in March the doctors broke the news to Max Farrand; Turner's heart was growing weaker and might stop at any time. There was no immediate cause for alarm, but his family should be informed, and above all he should not strain himself by visiting Hancock Point that summer. Dorothy responded with her usual good sense; she would tell her father that she was tired of Hancock Point and would like to visit a Pacific coastal resort that summer. This would keep him from traveling without letting him know his true condition. Dorothy might have saved herself the trouble. No doctor's warning was needed to tell Turner that his days were numbered. Painstakingly during those months he was scattering guideposts through his notes for those who might have to complete THE BOOK in his stead; "In case the chapters dealing with the subjects ennumerated on the attached sheet should not be completed . . . ," one began, with instructions following on the treatment he had intended. All were to be placed in the hands of Dr. Farrand, who would find more instructions at the back of a drawer.[67]

The Turners spent that summer of 1930 in a rented house at La Jolla, with Merrill Crissey on hand to continue dictation and Dorothy and her three children—little Lois had been born in December 1928, to complete the Main household—present to add joy and distractions. Turner disliked La Jolla, with its sultry air and well-manicured lawns, but he was convinced that further trips east were too expensive and too tiring to be practical. Then, too, the depression was deepening and the family income shrinking as stocks and bonds abandoned dividends; it declined to $4772 in 1930 and $4312 a year later.[68] Common sense decreed that they should sell their cottage at Hancock Point and buy a modest home in Pasadena rather than pay high rental. That fall they moved into an attractive house at 26 Oak Knoll, with an option to buy at $8500. Buying this proved easier than selling "The Moorings"; Turner made the purchase early in 1931 for $8000—with a $3500 mortgage attached—but a series of prospective customers for the Hancock Point cottage changed their minds as economic conditions worsened. That treasured possession remained in the family to be enjoyed by Dorothy's children and her children's children. Turner managed to sell only his canoe and paddle—for forty dollars.

With the easing of his financial problems came better health; by the end of November 1930, Turner was able to visit the library for a few hours daily, there to dictate from a couch in his office or direct Merrill Crissey's expeditions into the stacks for needed information. By the end of June some 250,000 words had been written, with at least another 150,000 to go, and Turner was inquiring anxiously whether the publishers would accept two volumes. He might have spared his fears. Crissey could not be with him when the Turners established themselves at the Highlands Inn in Carmel for the summer of 1931—a happy one it was, amidst the rocky shores and pine forests and cold fog that reminded them of Maine—leaving Turner nothing to do but resume his eternal revising. Revise he did, so thoroughly that, when Crissey attempted to convert the much-penciled manuscript into legibility that fall, he found 675 pages with passages crossed out or rewritten, whole sections reorganized, and marginal notes in abundance telling him to consult newly published studies or to incorporate fresh information; "add material from Huntington on coal-land prices and coal mining derived from D. Green and Rockwell papers," read one such reminder.[69] Turner even found time to restudy maps and footnotes and propose numerous changes. The "Carmel Revisions," as they came to be known, kept Crissey so busy that fall that there was little time for the main task, yet even then Turner could not accept them as the last word. When the rewritten pages were filed away he marked the folder: "Revised (final?) to page 676." Max Farrand was right when he remarked that THE BOOK would have remained unfinished if Turner had lived forever.

Turner was not to live forever. In October a painful phlebitis of the leg forced him into bed, where he spent most of the next two months, too weak even to dictate. Then, to the surprise of the doctors, his health gradually improved until, in February 1932, he could resume daily visits to the library. These proved to be a mistake, for now he could pursue his researches once more, writing forgotten. One problem intrigued him particularly and must be solved before he dictated the section on the Compromise of 1850: what were John C. Calhoun's motives in swinging to an aggressively proslavery stand? Turner's older interpretation had been upset by manuscripts he had discovered at the Huntington; now he had to re-read the documents and re-formulate his conclusions. By March 14 he had the answer and was able to dictate a memorandum on his findings: "The correspondence with Calhoun in the summer and fall of 1847 shows that he was being pushed to leadership and advice with regard to protecting the South, and that he was not merely initiating a movement of revolt."[70] Noon was at hand by the time Crissey's pothooks recorded this new interpretation, but Turner had one more short letter he wanted to dictate. Marion Sheldon, a former Radcliffe student, had asked him for advice on materials dealing with Silas Wright, a politician whose sketch she was preparing for the *Dictionary of American Biography*. He had replied at length a few days earlier, but now he remembered an additional source she would find useful; *"Niles' Register* (Vol. LXXXII, p. 6, Sept. 4, 1847)" contained a reprint of an editorial from the *Union* on Wright, a biographical sketch from the *Democratic Review*, and other important information. "On the chance that you may not have seen this, I venture to send it on."[71] Those were the last words written by Turner. Typically, they were to a student engaged in a worthy historical task.

He had been in unusually good health and spirits that morning, so there was no premonition of danger when he returned home to lunch with Mae and lie down for a short rest. Yet when she returned from a short walk she found him still in bed, and complaining of a pain about the heart. The physician who was called gave him an injection and assured them both that he would be fine. Turner stirred himself to answer. "I know this is the end," he said. Mae remonstrated, reminding him that small attacks such as this were common, but he repeated: "I know this is the end. Tell Max I am sorry that I haven't finished my book." Then, after a few joking words with the doctor, he slipped into unconsciousness. At 7:30 that night of March 14, 1932, Frederick Jackson Turner died. His heart, too often abused, was unable to overcome the clot that stopped its beating.[72]

Turner was dead, but he had left behind a great deal of unfinished business to be completed by his friends. First, they mourned and paid their tributes. The funeral, held on March 19 in the spacious living room of Max Farrand's home, was a simple Episcopalian service attended by some sixty close friends. Avery Craven, a young historian from the University of Chicago studying at the library that year, prepared the tribute which Farrand read—a moving memorial to a teacher and scholar and friend. Craven, who had studied briefly with Turner at Harvard, harked back to those days: "No man of our day has been more 'borrowed from' and more 'imposed upon' by those who 'get' but give little"—a teacher who inspired his students to his own standards of perfectionism—a scholar who gave of himself freely. "I will never be certain about anything, but never satisfied with anything as long as I am uncertain," said Craven. "That was what Turner did for me."[73] These were words that Turner would have liked.

He would have liked even more the chorus of tribute that rose from friends and strangers. Letters came by the score—so many that eighty-five of the most precious were bound into a book for preservation—nearly all expressing the deep personal loss felt with the passing of a close friend. Editorials appeared in most of the nation's leading journals, venerating the scholar who had opened a new page in American history, and bemoaning the fact that one of such importance should be so little known to the public. Resolutions and memorials were voted by the institutions that he had aided—the State Historical Society of Wisconsin, the American Historical Association, the Huntington, the faculties of the universities where Turner had taught, a dozen more. "The most distinguished Americanist of his generation," they called him, who had "made necessary a reappraisal of the forces of American history" and imbued his students with "the imperative need of integrating the historical with other social sciences."[74] High praise indeed, but revealing of the esteem in which Turner was held by those of his generation who knew him best.

They could not know, those who wrote these words, that Turner was to erect still more monuments to his own memory, for the twist of fate decreed that a man who had been able to publish only two books during seventy-one years on earth would publish two more within little more than three years of his death. The first—a volume of essays similar to *The Frontier in American History* but with sectionalism as its theme—was conceived by Turner in the months before his death; when Merrill Crissey searched his files he found several memoranda listing the eleven articles that might be included and even suggesting a title: "Significance of Sections in American History."[75] Such a command from the grave could not be ignored; on April 6, at a conference of the Huntington library research staff, Max Farrand was instructed to seek a publisher, while Crissey prepared copies of the eleven essays with Turner's corrections. The publisher posed no problems; Henry Holt & Company had waited a generation for a book by Turner and would sign a contract gladly. Preparing the manuscript was less easy, for permissions had to be obtained and a decision made whether to incorporate the often-confusing changes that Turner had noted in his copies of the papers. In the end only factual corrections were made, and in this form *The Significance of Sections in American History* appeared in January 1933.[76]

The volume stirred far less interest than its predecessor of thirteen years before. Such popular journals as thought it worthy of mention were generally favorable, but the tone of the reviewers suggested that they were praising a beloved historian rather than bestowing their benediction on his latest product; of Turner's greatness there can be no question, they seemed to say, but of the book's there was. Fortunately, this opinion was not shared by one of Turner's old Harvard acquaintances, Mark A. DeWolfe Howe, a member of the committee that would select the Pulitzer Prize winner for that year. Turner's book was called to Howe's attention by Allan Nevins when they lunched together just after its appearance; Howe sought it out at once, read it, agreed with Nevins that it was far and away the most significant work in history eligible for the prize. When the award was announced, in May 1933, the book world was astounded; one critic who had never heard of the volume accused Henry Holt & Company of publishing it "almost secretly." Yet Turner's friends were delighted, and Turner's widow enriched by the award of $2000 and the royalty on 700 extra copies sold in the next six weeks.[77]

His friends were to celebrate again, for scarcely was Turner in his grave than the publishers demanded the manuscript of THE BOOK; Turner had assured them only a few weeks before, they said, that it was almost completed. So he had, but he had exaggerated shamefully, as usual. The final three chapters consisted only of outlines, scattered fragments, and a series of memoranda listing subjects to be discussed, while even the "completed" portions were so crowded with penciled changes, marginal suggestions, and scribbled additions that they were almost indecipherable. Months, even years, of patient effort would be necessary to transform this mass into a publishable book, but Avery Craven and Merrill Crissey selflessly assumed that task. Few men have worked harder. They agreed that the volume should be Turner's, not theirs, and that they would make no attempt to include later findings or to complete the unfinished chapters. Yet they had to sort and arrange the fragments that would form the later sections, test every statement for accuracy, check each footnote and add others when they were lacking, choose illustrations, decide which of the marginal suggestions to include, and recast the whole manuscript stylistically.[78] These were herculean labors, done with no thought of reward. Yet they were performed so efficiently that in mid-March of 1934 the 930 pages of text and thirty maps that were to make up *The United States, 1830-1850: The Nation and Its Sections* were in the hands of Henry Holt & Company. The book was officially published on March 28, 1935, just three years and two weeks after its author's death.

To all but the most dedicated Turnerians, it seemed a sad anticlimax to a distinguished career. Its theme was already familiar, while the fine refinements of sectional theory that Turner had intended to develop were either yet to be added or discernible to only a handful of experts. Too, the book showed unmistakable signs of its troubled background; it was often poorly written, marred by a lack of transitions, and lacking in the sense of drama that it might have possessed if brought to the intended conclusion. Throughout were evidences of hasty preparation, needed corrections, out-of-date conclusions, and inadequate analysis. An earlier generation of historians might have accepted these inadequacies for what they were, but those living in 1935 would not. By this time the deepening Great Depression had focused historical interest on new problems; the rural past seemed insignificant in a day when industrial-urban disorganization demanded attention, and the sectional antagonisms of the nineteenth century were inconsequential to men who were dealing with the capitalist-labor conflicts of the twentieth. *The United States, 1830-1850* was a non-functional book at a time when the world was concerned with the malfunctions of capitalism and crying for blueprints for social reform. Such luxuries were out of place in the shattered world of the 1930s.

This did not mean that the reception was universally hostile; Turner was too venerated, and his disciples too numerous, to permit an abrupt about-face in his popularity. Yet such was the spirit of the time that some among the reviewers, at least, were emboldened to say that the great god had nodded. The tone of criticism was set by the *Saturday Review of Literature* when it labeled the volume "disappointing," not simply because of the author's death, but because the sectional thesis did not explain American politics as Turner thought that it did; the reviewer found the chapters on politics hackneyed and the whole book suffering from a midwestern bias. These were harsh words—perhaps harsher than justified—but they only slightly exaggerated the reception that *The United States, 1830-1850* received from all but the most fanatical of Turner's disciples.

These judgments were only a final footnote in the life of a historian who had contributed more to the understanding of the American past than any scholar of his generation. Turner the man was dead, but Turner the speculative historian lived on. His theories on the frontier and section were to influence more students, generate more controversy, and excite more writing after his death than they had when he lived. Turner's legacy was not simply the thin shelf of books and articles produced during his lifetime, but the vitality that he breathed into historical studies, the concepts that brought historians nearer the truth, and the lessons that he taught the men of a younger generation as they attacked the bastions of ignorance with the multidisciplined weapons that he had placed in their hands.

XVII

Frederick Jackson Turner: A Portrait of the Man

WHEN the mortal remains of Frederick Jackson Turner were laid to rest in a Madison cemetery beside the bodies of his two small children, there seemed every reason to believe that he and his theories would soon be forgotten. His sectional concepts had failed to strike a spark and the book that would have given them vitality would never be published. His frontier hypothesis was out of tune with the times, outmoded by a Great Depression that fastened the attention of historians on the urban-industrial world of the present. Many a young scholar labeled Turner a false prophet during those years and rode to fame by proving his theories wrong and his expression of those theories misleading. The frontier thesis, so venerated by Turner's own generation, seemed fated to complete rejection by the next. Turner himself, so respected in his own time, appeared certain to be forgotten.

Yet today Turner lives in the memories of American historians as do none of his contemporaries. More of his books—in paperback editions —are sold now than were published during his lifetime. More articles about him have been written in the past decade than about any former historian, even including Charles A. Beard. Only the papers of Henry David Thoreau attract more scholars to the Henry E. Huntington Library than do the papers of Frederick Jackson Turner. The University of Wisconsin boasts a Frederick Jackson Turner residence hall and a Frederick Jackson Turner professorship. The Organization of American Historians awards its most prestigious prize in his name. When the American Historical Association asked its Executive Council to name the six greatest historians in the nation's history, Turner was the only academic scholar to be ranked first by every member. When the Republic of Mexico invited the United States to select its two most important historians, Turner and Francis Parkman were the nominees; their portraits hang side by side in the hall of the History Commission at the University of Mexico.[1] No fanatical Turner cult exists today as it did in his time, but neither has he been forgotten—as seemed probable in 1932.

Why this about-face? How can one account for the fact that Turner and his concepts are more respected in the 1970s than they were in the 1930s? The persistence of his theories is basically responsible, of course; latter-day students have sought to test his frontier and sectional hypotheses objectively, with neither the blind adulation of his own generation nor the irrational rejection of the next, and have found aspects of them useful in understanding the nation's past. Yet Turner's own image has helped perpetuate his influence, an image preserved by his students and friends to become a permanent part of the folklore of historiography. Turner can be visualized by most Americanists today: a vital man of medium build with penetrating eyes and vibrant voice, radiant with good health, his tanned face and tweedy clothes testifying to his passion for the out-of-doors, fascinating students with his lecturing skills and winning friends with the warmth of his personality—a good man, excessively modest in manner but sparkling with ideas that altered the interpretation of American history. This is the image. How closely does it resemble the Frederick Jackson Turner who lived and thought during the dying years of the nineteenth century and the first decades of the twentieth?

Those who have pictured him for later generations were correct when they stressed the immense charm that won him friends and disciples. Few among his contemporaries combined to such a rare degree the qualities of the scholar with those of a warm, outgoing, fallible, human being. In that era of academic posturing, when the professor was inevitably stuffed-shirtish and disdainful of ordinary mortals, Turner radiated friendship and good fellowship, not just to his peers, but to all about him. His students found him a companion no less than an instructor, always ready to step from the pedestal to become one of them. So did the fishermen and caretakers and ferry-boat operators at his summer home in Hancock Point. Turner was a down-to-earth, old-shoe type of mortal, not through affectation, but because he cast himself in the role of the historical character he most admired: the Jackson Man. His social attitudes were governed by his belief in the goodness and common sense of those about him, whatever their walks in life. Turner was the living embodiment of the frontier egalitarianism that he venerated.

Turner loved the world, and the world loved Turner. Those who met him first were struck by the grey-blue eyes that lighted his face when he smiled, and by the rich timbre of his voice, whether in the low musical pitch of ordinary conversation or the hearty resonance of the lecture platform. Those who came to know him better were impressed by his sympathetic understanding, his eagerness to please, his utter lack of pretense or animosity. Insatiably curious, and thoroughly read on a variety of subjects, Turner was always an interested listener, ready to flatter by the close attention that he paid to any conversation. "His understanding and appreciation of people," one of his friends observed, "must have been one of the secrets of his insight into people in history."[2]

There was no pomposity, no cant, in Frederick Jackson Turner. His happiest moments were spent with guides or lobster fishermen who called him "Fred" rather than "Dr. Turner" and accepted him as their equal. Many letters from distinguished persons were in his files—letters from Theodore Roosevelt, Woodrow Wilson, Lord Bryce, Josef Redlich, and many others—but none was more treasured than a simple note from the caretaker and coach-driver at Hancock Point:

> Dear Friend Turner: Glad to hear from you. Was up at Molasses Pond Saturday after salmon and caught 1 2½ pounder. It did show a great fight. I see one caught weighing 7½.

Details, then, about the cottage, and: "Say Turner when you get here the salmon will still be biting."[3] The "H. W. Johnson" who signed that letter was his sort of a person. Turner was born to live in old clothes, in a remote cabin far from the bustle and tensions of twentieth-century America, amidst the H. W. Johnsons of the world.

To him, all men were equal and all men were good. Few historians of his day enjoyed a wider or more cordial relationship with others in his profession—a profession not without its jealousies and malicious back-biting. All were Turner's friends, none his enemies. Even those who opposed his views directed none of their animosity toward him. Frederic Bancroft attacked Turner for his membership in the "ring" that controlled the American Historical Association, but he had only kind words for Turner the man. In return, Turner saw only good in his enemies; even when he was the victim of Bancroft's most vicious attacks he could muster no more than a tone of annoyance in his letters. Only once was his patience strained. When a very mediocre former student addressed a letter to him as "My Dear Turner"—a form of intimacy reserved in those days for one's closest friends—Turner was sufficiently annoyed to begin his reply "Dear MR. Gochenour," then crossed that out to write "Dear Professor Gochenour." Even this gentle reproof was lost on Mr. Gochenour, who began his answer: "Dear Turner."[4]

His supply of modesty was bountiful—or so the world believed. To those about him, he was the most self-effacing of men, disclaiming glory, abhoring praise, shunning all pomp and ceremony, and shying from the limelight. When elected president of the Colonial Society of Massachusetts, he stirred a palace revolution by refusing to allow the "LL.D." to which he was entitled to be listed after his name, forcing the director of publications to drop the honorary degrees of all past presidents.[5] Yet this façade hid a vast yearning for recognition and a life-size inferiority complex. Scattered through his files are evidences of his need: lists of books dedicated to him, others chronicling the accomplishments of his students, favorable book reviews (and only favorable book reviews) with the most flattering passages underlined in red or identified by a hand-drawn arrow, newspaper columns and editorials that glorified his contributions, also heavily underlined. When historiographical books mentioned his work, each was purchased and the favorable passages identified. In some Turner even added to the index the list of pages where his name appeared that had been missed by a careless indexer. And everywhere he signed his name—a flowing "Frederick J. Turner"—on file covers, pamphlets, blue books, boxes, slips of paper, newspaper clippings, anything with a writable surface. One battered box in which he kept notes he signed no less than a dozen times.

His friends loved him for his modesty, however false it might have been, and they loved him also for the cheerful optimism that was his stock-in-trade. Almost never did he give way to doubt or despair, and then only when progress on THE BOOK had slowed to a standstill. Such moods soon passed, to be replaced with a cheerful belief in the future that was one of his greatest charms—and weaknesses. When Turner wrote his friends, as he did over and over again, that THE BOOK would be out in a year, he was deceiving himself more than he was deceiving them. Like the frontiersmen he so much admired, Turner saw things not as they were, but as they should be. THE BOOK would be finished, the textbook that he longed to write completed, the half-dozen other volumes that he planned speedily written. His reason told him now and then that these were pipe dreams, but reason was brushed aside as too unpleasant a companion. Turner saw the world through rose-tinted glasses, and a happy world it was.

Friends were warmed by Turner's optimism, and they were captivated by his enjoyment of life. He was a contented man who shared his happiness with those about him. His contentment he found in the quiet of his home and the love of his wife, Caroline Mae Sherwood Turner. The Turners were deeply, devotedly, perpetually in love. "Darling Little Mae," as he addressed her in his letters, was his Eve, wherever she was, his Eden. The one unforgettable blot on his happiness was the death of their two small children; the one great joy of his declining years his daughter Dorothy Turner Main and her three offspring. Turner was in the best sense of the word a family man, content with the simple pleasures of home and fireside.

Mae Turner was not an academic helpmate in the traditional sense; she did not type his manuscripts or check his references or read his proofs. She could not even provide Turner with the intellectual companionship that he often required; he found this in his colleagues, his men's clubs, and in his friend Mrs. William Hooper, whose conversations and letters he treasured for their mind-tingling stimulation. But Mae gave him something he needed far more: her devoted attention and a well-run home that left him free for his own studies. This Turner knew, and he was never backward in expressing his appreciation. Mae, in turn, took quiet pride in her husband's happiness and accomplishments. "I know that Fred loved our quiet fireside," she told Max Farrand shortly after his death, "and the logs never smoked. They were dry wood and carefully selected."[6]

On only one point did the Turners differ, and here a mutual truce kept the peace. Mae was ardently religious; Turner felt no need for spiritual comfort. His rebellion against orthodoxy had begun when he rejected the "nonsense" forced on him by a Portage Sunday School teacher; it continued through his college years as he searched for a creed that placed less stress on the supernatural and more on the goodness of man. "If men would simply teach the beauty of right action," he complained at the time, "they would do some good. But they don't—and so myself and a good part of the world, too, drift into paganism."[7] Not paganism, but Unitarianism, eventually attracted Turner and held his interest for the half-dozen years he was in college and graduate school. "My creed," he wrote, "is summed up in the commandment which enjoins love to God, and to man."[8] Even the humanism of the Unitarian Church failed to satisfy his needs; he eventually drifted away, and, through most of his adult life, he worshipped not at all. Mae was distressed, but she was sensible enough to let her husband go his way while she went hers. Their religious differences placed no strain on their love.

Instead, they grew ever closer with the passing years, bound by their affection for their one surviving child as she grew into attractive womanhood, married, and blessed them with three grandchildren. These were the apples of their grandfather's eye. Jackson Turner Main, born in 1917, was a talented lad who inherited a passion for reading and history that rivaled Turner's own. As early as his fifth year Jack rebelled against the naps that interfered with more important pastimes ("I don't go to sleep, you know, I only lie in bed and suffer"); when he was nine he buried himself so deeply in Turner's books while summering at Hancock Point that a dangerous eye inflammation required his hospitalization; by the time he was fourteen he had written a learned paper analyzing the effect of the age of senators on their attitude toward war. Turner was delighted. "I think it fine," he told Jack, "that you should be thinking of the causes that lay behind historical events."[9] He would have been even more delighted if he could have peered into the future to see his grandson a distinguished historian of colonial America and a pioneer in the use of statistical techniques that shed light on "the causes that lay behind historical events."

For his two granddaughters Turner had equal affection, even though they did not share his love of history. Betsy, born in 1920, and Lois, eight years her junior, never knew when the postman would deliver a special letter addressed to them, often with an original poem:

> I love you good, I love you *bad*;
> I love you happy, I love you sad.

Or when their grandfather would welcome them into his study, push his writing aside, and draw a fantastic picture of himself as a fish with a pipe in his mouth. Or charm them with an illustrated verse about the boll weevil:

> He's not the Jabberwock, but he is very evil;
> He never learned to talk; they call him Old Boll Weevil.[10]

Other grandfathers of that day were as devoted as Turner, but few could have been more so. In his expanding family he found happiness, and that happiness made him even more appealing to his friends.

To picture Turner as a devoted grandfather, amusing his grandchildren with pictures and doggerel, is to recognize that he was no inner-regulated scholar who dwelt in the world of the abstract. He was not. Turner lived and wrote with the undisciplined impetuosity of the poet rather than with the restrained exactness of the scientist. Latter-day critics were to bemoan his lack of definitions and quarrel with his imprecise terminology, but neither Turner nor his contemporaries were aware of the fact that he was violating the canons of scholarship. He knew, and they knew, what he meant, even though he varied the meaning of the word "frontier" three times within a single essay. This was the prerogative of the artist, and Turner was as much an artist as he was a historian. His pen-pictures convinced scholars, not through the process of reason, but in exactly the same way that a fine novel or beautiful painting was "convincing." His writings were built on values, not on mechanics, and if no two readers found the same message, no two viewers saw the same thing when they admired a great picture. When Merle Curti accused Turner of being as much an artist as he was teacher or scholar or thinker, Turner was admittedly pleased. "I always wanted to be an artist," he told Curti, "tho' a truthful one."[11] Words were his passion, words that sang, words that set the reader tingling with excitement—these were the words that appealed to Turner, even though they might cloud the exactness of his meaning.

Because he did love words, he played with them, just as would any poet. Phrases that pleased him were borrowed, with proper credit, for his own works; he was particularly fond of Ralph Waldo Emerson's "the nervous, rocky West," and of the lines from Tennyson's "Ulysses" that caught the spirit of pioneering:

> for my purpose holds
> To sail beyond the sunset, and the baths
> Of all the western stars, until I die.

Rudyard Kipling's "Explorer," who fronted death to find the unknown, "lost behind the ranges," was a Turner favorite, as was that author's "The Foreloper":

> He shall desire loneliness, and his desire shall bring
> Hard on his heels a thousand wheels, a people and a king. . . .
> For he must blaze a nation's way, with hatchet and with brand,
> Till on his last-won wilderness an empire's bulwarks stand.

Many a Turner class in the "History of the West" heard the stirring words from Robinson Jeffers's "Californians":

> They rose, and trekked westward the wilderness.
> Now I, the latest in this solitude
> Invoke thee from the verge extreme, and shoal
> Of sand that ends the west. O long pursued
> Where wilt thou lead us now?[12]

Turner believed that the image-charged phrases of a poet could tell something about the frontier that ordinary language could not. He was constantly on the look-out for striking metaphors that would convey the spirit of the westward movement to his readers. The frontier, to Turner, "leaped" over the Alleghenies, "skipped" westward, "passed in successive waves," or "stretched" like a "cord of union" across the backcountry; the California gold rush sent a "sudden tide" of adventurers westward. Once when complimented for calling the mountain folk of the Appalachians "fossil remains of an earlier age," he confessed to rather liking the image himself.[13] Students recalled that phrases such as "we are all poor creatures," or "tickled pink," or "like the breaking up of a hard winter" were used over and over again in his lectures. On Turner's desk when he died was a note correlating features of the American landscape with historical figures:

Washington: the waves of the Atlantic
Jackson: the forest and the Indian
Lincoln: the prairies (waving grass and flowers) . . .
Roosevelt: the Great Plains and the Grand Canyon

None but a man with the soul of a poet could seek such analogies, and seek them so successfully.[14]

Turner did have the soul of a poet and the urge to create beauty with words, whether verse or cadenced prose. His love affair with Mae inspired a dozen poems, all hidden from the world in his Commonplace Books:

> And the lake lies all transfigured
> Silver glories, all its dross
> Every wavelet flashing silver
> Laughing dancing filled with life
> Such the face of my beloved—
> Moonlit waters, dimpling silver
> Dancing eye-eaves when she smiles.[15]

Turner wrote verse, as he wrote his essays, with the passionate convictions of the poet rather than the cold impersonality of the exact scientist.

In his more mature years his enthusiasm for poetry was restrained to reading and memorizing the works of others, but when he did venture into rhyming the result was usually light and gay, as befitting a grown man who must keep his emotions in check. Once, when picnicking with good friends, he jotted down a few lines that revealed a surprising taste for Morris chairs and tasty beverages, rather than the joys of the wilderness:

> Who would break his neck a-rowing
> Raise a thirst and burn his nose
> When the fragrant mint is blowing
> And the whiskey gently flows?
>
> Picnic weather's always nasty;
> Radiators are the thing;
> Better is a flask of Asti
> Than pale water from a spring.[16]

Again in 1907, when walking across a Washington park at dusk, the song of a thrush animated his pen:

> I like little thrushes,
> The song haunts me yet;
> I like little thrushes,
> But mostly *en brochette*.

This success inspired a second attempt:

> I like little crabbies,
> Their gait is so queer;
> But would they be quiet
> If broiled, served with beer?

Thereupon, he wrote his wife, he decided to find out, went to Harvey's Restaurant, and did find out.[17]

Love and laughter inspired most of Turner's attempts at versifying, but once he wrote under a more tragic impulse. The scene that he described was real; during the summer of 1904, when camping in the High Sierra, the Turners stumbled into Desolation Valley, near Lake Tahoe—a vast granite basin swept clean by glaciers and dotted only by a few small lakes or clumps of trees. Mae broke down and wept hysterically; for hours Turner sat beside her to offer comfort before he could lead her away. Both were visibly shaken, for the grim sight brought memories flooding back of their two children who had died so tragically five years before. That winter he tried to capture on paper the emotions that surged through him as he looked:

> Across life's garden, where the flowers grow gay and wanton
> Where high aspiring pines raised up their heads toward God,
> Where tender blossoms dipped their faces in warm mirroring pools,
> Came the grim glacial flood and filled this cup of joy;
> Swept all things clean away—the passions and the pride of life,
> The vital glowing crimsons and the ardent greens of flower-starred
>   meads,
> Swept all things clean and graved the smiles
> To a Medusa face, of calm immobile ash-grey rock.
> And yet, deep opalescent lakes with mystic isles are set within.[18]

None but a man of sorrow, none but a sensitive human being touched with the wand of the poet, could have written those lines. Turner's cheerful, bluff exterior hid a wealth of tragedy and a deep emotionalism that the world seldom saw.

To picture him as a head-in-the-clouds aesthete, however, is to fracture the truth, for Turner was no lofty demigod addicted to Rationalism, Virtue, and Proper Conduct. Name a weakness that distinguished the Imperfect Man from the Perfect, and he had it. His persistent inability to resist temptation was one of his most appealing characteristics. Turner was a feet-of-clay mortal, a hedonist in a Victorian world, a Babylonian in Puritanland, bent on satisfying his appetite for pleasure whatever the consequences. True, he lived a very proper and very respectable life, unmarred by overindulgence save on very rare occasions, and presented a façade of righteousness to his friends. Turner could always be counted on to do the "proper" thing. But never the "right" thing.

He showed this in his appetite for food and drink. Turner was no glutton, but neither could he adhere to a diet, despite constant apprehension about his weight. On one of his several unsuccessful attempts he prepared a menu that provided such bountiful breakfasts and lunches —two slices of bread, oranges, coffee with sugar, and a doughnut in the morning; bread, vegetables, meat, a potato, salad, and pie at noon—that he was left with only 300 of his 1600 allotted calories for dinner and a bedtime snack.[19] Neither was Turner tempted to alcoholic overindulgence—he was defeated for the presidency of the Madison University Club when he ran on a prohibition ticket—but he was always ready for a stimulating cup or three on the proper occasion, despite Mae's disapproval. "The man who drinks champaign [*sic*] pretty regularly," he advised one student, "gets along surprisingly well compared with the man who doesn't."[20]

Turner was a very moderate drinker, but he was a thoroughly immoderate smoker who resisted all attempts at reform with a tenacity that was Mae's despair and his doctor's concern. Cigars, cigarettes, pipes—he used them all with passionate delight. Like Mark Twain, he found that he could stop easily when his wife's pleading became too insistent—he stopped often. And always with the best of intentions. "I should not be greatly astonished," he told Mae on one such occasion, "if I became virtuous and ceased to use the charming but wicked weed altogether. Think of the spring bonnets that would mean for you and Dorothy." That thought suggested a more appealing possibility. If he only smoked expensive cigars he could save even more money by stopping. Therefore he would indulge in very costly ones for a few months before swearing off on the right financial basis. That was the end of that attempt at reform. Turner never did succeed in abandoning tobacco for more than a few days at a time, and he smoked to his dying day with unashamed enjoyment.

His highly stretchable moral fibre decreed that he could never adhere to a budget, manage his finances sensibly, or save money regularly. Who could dislike a man who could begin his married life, as Turner did in the fall of 1889, by buying a paperbound notebook, labeling it "Expense Account, 1890," writing on the first page "In State Bank 78.65. Cash 2.00"—and then leaving the rest of the book blank? That was the story of Turner's life. He was well paid by the standards of the academic world of his day—up to $4000 a year at Wisconsin before 1910 and $8000 at Harvard by the time of his retirement—but he possessed a magician's ability to make money disappear more rapidly than it accumulated. Turner spent his life in an effort to satisfy creditors while balancing a budget, but he never did succeed.

Much of their income went for living expenses, for the Turners believed that life should be enjoyed, not endured. Their homes were comfortable, if not extravagant. Almost always the household ménage included one maid, and often two; sometimes a nurse or cook was added, or a secretary to shame Turner into the writing that he abhorred. At intervals between maids they seldom ate at home, for Mae preferred restaurants to mastering the mysteries of cooking, even when they could scarcely afford such a luxury. Their dinner parties, although infrequent, were usually elaborate. On one occasion seven guests were served soup, a fish course of smelts in tartar sauce, roast chicken with chestnut dressing, beans, browned potatoes, hot rolls, a lettuce and tomato salad, cheese with wafers, a bombe, walnut cake, nuts and candies. On another, Mae's instructions to the serving maids suggested unusual gastronomic delights—and the cultural barbarism inflicted on civilization by Prohibition:

I

Clear soup with egg balls. Crouton sticks. Pass olives.

II

Fillet flounder—sauce tartar. Graham sandwiches. Cucumber
and tomato in French dressing. Pour White Rock.

III

Fillet beef—mushroom sauce. Spinach. Potatoes, currant
jelly. Warm rolls. Pour orange soda.

IV

Lettuce and cellery [*sic*] salad in French dressing
Cheese straws.

V

Ice cream—chocolate cake. Sponge cakes. Coffee after.[21]

That was a lavish dinner to be served by the wife of a professor, even of
a professor at Harvard, and helps explain why Turner spent a good
many hours struggling to keep income and outgo on an even balance.

His problem was confounded by the utter inability of both Turners
to resist the buying urge. His extravagances were fishing apparatus and
books, the latter especially; thousands upon thousands of volumes filled
the Turner homes from basement to attic, many of them multivolume
files of magazines, newspapers, and government documents.[22] His book-
ish tastes were matched by Mae's love of fine clothes—a passion that her
husband thoroughly approved, save at bill-paying time. A gown made to
order for $71.50, a hat for $23.25, another for 25.50, a pair of shoes for
$14.40, a coat for $79.50—costly items for a family with an income of
slightly more than $5000. Each month the bills that poured in from
Boston's department stores threatened to exhaust the bank account completely—and sometimes did: $68.85 due at Stearns, $92.95 at Filene's,
$151.41 at S. S. Pierce's gourmet grocery store.[23] Turner's occasional
attempts to bring the family's expenditures into line were futile, for
every budget that he devised was so unrealistic that it was soon
discarded.

Instead, he was doomed to a constant flirtation with near-bankruptcy.
On many an occasion he paid only half his bills each month, alternating
creditors to keep all more or less satisfied. Even this devious device was
insufficient, and Turner was regularly forced to borrow to pay his
bills—a $200 loan for one month, $1500 for nine more, $700 from the
bank to tide them over until payday—always in the hope of better times

ahead. His letters to Mae when on one of his necessary trips contained regular warnings in oft-used phrases: "Remember the bank account is low," "Ascertain balance if you draw checks," or "Give me a margin of safety if you conveniently can. . . . I am down to about $40."[24] Turner waged his battle with the bills through most of his lifetime, yet he was far too human to change his ways.

He was also human enough to live in a constant state of rebellion against the tension-laden urban life of twentieth-century America. For Turner, life began when he fled civilization; everything about him, from the tweedy clothes that he affected to his tales of the four-pound trout that got away, stamped him as an outdoorsman who could find happiness only in field and stream. So he was, and by necessity, for Turner was both physically and emotionally incapable of living long amidst the bustle of the city. Emotionally, the backwoods offered a haven from a modern industrial society that he neither liked nor understood. "I sometimes am in doubt about 'civilization,'" he once confessed. "Perhaps that is because I like to go trout fishing."[25] Physically, Turner required wilderness life as a tonic to rejuvenate a jaded system worn by the pressures of teaching and writing. Only a few months of either and his whole nature rebelled. Those who knew him best recognized the symptoms—a nervous irritability, a far-away look in his eyes —that meant he *must* find solace in the forest or risk serious disorders. When he wrote, as he once did, that he was "tired of thinking and should like to be a cabbage for a century or two," Turner was not succumbing to indolence.[26] His body and spirit could not endure without periodic refurbishing by the wilderness.

Turner's instincts told him when escape into the forest was necessary; his reason convinced him that the forest should contain a well-stocked trout stream to do the greatest good. He had been, since his earliest youth, a fanatical fisherman who would (as he once said) rather catch three trout on a single leader than study American history—and that, to Turner, was the ultimate comparison. Even as a young man he could write his fiancée that "of all the beautiful things a gleaming, gold and crimson trout throwing himself out of water after a fly is the most beautiful"—then remembered to whom he was writing and added, "almost."[27] As a mature scholar he saved his greatest scorn not for the critics of his theories, but for those misguided souls who thought that the object of fishing was to catch a fish; "it's the getting him with the right thrill—otherwise why not turn Prussian and dynamite him, or kill him with laughing gas, or dam up the brook and shovel him out?"[28] Turner's idea of Heaven, he once confessed, was a good fishing camp in some remote part of Paradise where the work of creation was not too far advanced.[29]

So long as he taught at Wisconsin, escape was easy, for his Old Town canoe was stored on the porch of his Frances Street home, Lake Mendota was at his doorstep, and the familiar streams around Portage were not too distant. But Harvard and Cambridge offered a greater challenge. His canoe went with him (he placed it first, and his Corona typewriter last, on a list of his insured possessions—a fair indication of his scale of values), but the Charles River was a sad substitute for Lake Mendota. Turner did his best. During the summer he slept in a tent on the back porch of his Brattle Street house, "lulled by the lapping of the automobiles and the murmer of the neighbor's maids, and awakened in the early morning by the tinkle of the milkman's bottles."[30] "It seems like a vacation from about 11 P.M. to 7 A.M.," he wrote wistfully.[31] Winters were made endurable by long hours spent discussing the art of dry fly casting with fellow fanatics at the Boston Fishing Club, or reading a new volume on *American Trout Stream Insects*, or, on a mild day, journeying a few miles to make a few casts in a brook that *might* hide a few trout, but never did. Once, when the first hint of spring was in the air, he walked all the way to the Boston aquarium to gaze at a tank of live trout. "I bought a book on dry fly fishing," he reported on a warm March day in 1915, "and the woods and lakes all came back like a healing vision. . . . But I utterly forgot that I was to preside over a meeting of the Colonial Society of Massachusetts."[32] Of all the presents received on his fifty-fifth birthday, the most treasured was a handkerchief from his daughter embroidered with a fishhook monogram. Any reminder of a trout stream was food for Turner's soul.

Summers made life endurable, whether spent in the Rockies or Sierras after a stint of teaching in the West to pay expenses, or at his summer home in the Maine woods. Usually a packsack of notes went with him to Hancock Point, and he always took along a stern ambition to make progress on the lagging book, but his good resolutions faded once he scented a balsam forest or glimpsed a woodland stream. "No, your paper didn't go astray," he confessed to a student whose thesis waited reading. "I did. I wandered off into lobster harbors, and stray islands, and thrush-haunted woods, and rose-lined lanes, and lost myself in the icy waters of the Maine coast, and strayed into the back yard and chopped wood."[33] Turner loved it all—the riotous banks of firewood and meadow rue, the groves of birch and pine, the melodious chant of the hermit thrush at evening. He delighted in defying his doctor's orders by swimming in the frigid waters of the North Atlantic, in digging clams, in chatting endlessly with the down east folk who made him one of themselves. This was Heaven; the classroom was a purgatory to be endured until the next summer. "Opening up Harvard has been something of a job," he wrote one autumn, "and a rather sharp contrast with life by the Hancock Point tides watching time's ceaseless progress to eternity without caring how fast he progged."[34] Turner, like the frontiersmen he studied, could not resist when nature beckoned. His human frailties, no less than his historical theories, endeared him to his generation.

If Turner's love affair with the wilderness stamped him as a spiritual son of the pioneers, so did his views of society and government. Within him were embodied the best—and worst—features of the Jackson Man. He was, to his credit, utterly democratic socially and politically, but he was also inclined toward a myopic nationalism that blinded him to the virtues of other peoples, highly individualistic in an age when the industrial-urban complex outmoded individualism, and prejudiced toward minorities who threatened the traditional "Americanism" that he venerated. All of these traits stemmed from Turner's inherent distrust of the factory and city, both of which threatened the rural values that he deemed essential to the welfare of the Republic. Enemies of those pioneer values were his enemies, whether immigrants threatening established institutions, agrarian radicals endangering the private enterprise system, or reformers preaching the need of a government strong enough to control the marketplace. Turner was as inconsistent in his views as the frontiersmen he emulated; he vacillated between a conviction that the individual should be unrestrained and a belief that government should act forcibly to guard the welfare of the many. Yet he was consistently conservative, living proof of his own thesis that the westerner might favor innovation and democracy, but was basically dedicated to maintaining the status quo.

His love of the United States and of his own Midwest was unshakable. Turner was a fair example of the Jackson Man in his staunch patriotism, his passionate faith in the nation and its freedoms. This did not mean that he was a flag-waving super-patriot; at one time he refused to do a book that would have appeared in a "100% series," and never did he associate himself with the head-in-the-sand isolationists who sought to protect Americans from all contact with other countries. Instead, Turner, as one of his French friends observed, had tried so hard to understand and explain his native land that he had reached a plane of moral nobility somewhat higher than that of his fellow men.[35] With understanding went respect, for the nation and for the midwestern heartland that he believed to epitomize national values. In the Midwest Turner found the free-and-easy social intercourse, the willingness to accept newcomers at face value instead of on the basis of ancestral reputation, that he associated with America's greatness. Easterners were never quite to be trusted; "there is," he wrote, "a love of the whimsical, of the clever thrust, the ironic and cynical, in your unadulterated Boston Yankee" that was almost un-American.[36] Pioneer values, exaggerated though they might be in the West, made that region the symbol of all that was best about the United States.

And of much that was worst, for when Turner borrowed western idealism as the basis of his political philosophy he borrowed prejudice and bigotry as well. Just as the Jackson Man was stirred to nativistic outbursts against the Germans and Irish flooding America's shores in the early nineteenth century, so Turner saw the New Immigrants of the late nineteenth and early twentieth centuries as a menace to traditional values and institutions. They would, he feared, upset the balance between capital and labor that free land had sustained, presaging a destructive class war. In the same way, minority groups of alien race or color must be restrained lest they alter the dominant "American" social order. Turner gave little heed to what he would have called the "Negro Problem," but twice he was asked whether the Fifteenth Amendment's guarantee of the franchise to all was wise, and twice he answered that it was not.[37] His judgment was partly based on his belief that political rights should be granted by state and local governments rather than national, but lurking in the back of his mind was a fear that Negroes and aliens were not quite equal to Yankees.

Turner also shared the prejudices of his day in his attitude toward Jews, bolstered, in his case, by a frontier-like distrust of all aliens whose life-patterns differed from what he considered the norm. His first encounter with their Old World culture came in 1887, when he visited the East and wandered into the Boston ghetto. The very strangeness of the sight was shocking—a street "filled with big Jew men—long bearded and carrying a staff as you see in a picture, and with Jew youths and maidens—some of the latter pretty—as you sometimes see a lily in the green muddy slime."[38] There spoke rural America, with all its prejudices. It spoke again when Turner assured his fiancée that "however you shatter the Jewish jar, the scent of the roses of Israel will cling to it still, and socially I can't say that I ever found one I could be contented with."[39] These were harsh words, but they came from a young man who reflected the bigotry of the times as much as his own prejudice. Certainly he moved a notch or two toward greater tolerance in his later years; in 1922 he disapproved President Lowell's "rather drastic treatment" of the subject when the Harvard faculty debated means of limiting the university's Jewish population, and a few years later he applauded a former student for resigning from the Daughters of the American Revolution to protest that society's anti-Negro bias.[40] Yet his prejudices remained; he might disapprove President Lowell's anti-Semitism, but he also disliked the prospect "of Harvard a New Jerusalem and Boston already a New Cork." "Rejoice in your Maine Yankee neighbors," he wrote his wife at Hancock Point.[41]

Turner's attitude toward minorities was unfortunately consistent, but such could not be said of his political beliefs, which vacillated considerably during the late nineteenth and early twentieth century. Two problems underlay this vacillation. One was his inherited conservatism. Reared in a family that was unimpeachably Republican politically, Turner as a youth found himself torn between the dictates of his heritage and the instincts of a basically liberal young man. The other was the need to fit the pioneer values that he so much admired to the needs of an industrial-urban society. How could the individualism of the frontier—the right of every man to help himself to nature's bounties—be reconciled with the democracy so venerated in the West, now that those bounties were no longer abundant? If the individualistic rights of the few were maintained, the nation's productive resources would be monopolized by industry to the disadvantage of the many; if the welfare of the people was given first priority, individualism must be circumscribed. Which of these frontier values must be sacrificed?

That was Turner's dilemma, and in his effort to solve it he shifted his party allegiance to conform to the ideal that seemed most essential at the time.

His first political experiences were governed more by tradition than reason. He was reared in a household where Republican politics bulked large in the dinner-table conversation, where Republican funds helped pay the grocery bill, and where Satan's disciples—the Democrats—were equated with treason and anarchy. Turner learned his lessons so well that as a senior at the University of Wisconsin he helped form a Young Men's Marching Club to support James G. Blaine in the election of 1884, addressed its members on the virtues of Republicanism, and presumably cast his first ballot against Grover Cleveland. His graduate training changed that; Turner was in full rebellion against parental tradition by 1888, when he voted the Democratic ticket, but his deflection from orthodoxy was brief. During the 1890s alarm over the strident demands of trade unionists and Populists brought his basic conservatism to the fore. In his eyes, the financial chaos threatened by free silver imperiled traditional values no less than the "socialistic" programs of the Pullman strikers or Coxey's Army did. When Turner wrote, as he did in his 1893 essay, that "a primitive society can hardly be expected to show the intelligent appreciation of the complexity of business interests in a developed society" he was offering a text for the times, no less than a judgment on the past. He voted for William McKinley in 1896 —and probably in 1900—as a protest against the monetary "heresies" of the Democrats, and not as an endorsement of conservative Republicanism.[42]

His stay in the anti-Democratic camp was brief, for by the turn of the century a more dangerous enemy threatened frontier values. Turner saw trusts and corporations, symbolized by the giant United States Steel Corporation, which was formed in 1901, as more menacing to democracy and individualism than the Populists were. With this awakening, his opinion of agrarian reformers underwent a remarkable transformation. They became not dangerous agitators, but heralds of an overdue social revolution that would win economic equality for all people; tubthumpers for the Omaha Platform who had seemed dangerously radical in 1892 were now legatees of the Levellers who rose with Cromwell against Stuart tyranny and of the frontier farmers who spoke for liberty in 1776.[43] The business corporation not only posed a greater danger to the individual's freedom of decision than had the agrarians, but threatened to divide the nation into haves and have-nots by wiping out the middle class, where frontier values were best preserved. Turner saw the outcome of unrestrained corporate growth to be a world torn between trust magnates on the one hand and socialist agitators on the other. Neither group was to his taste. "The socialism regime in the hands of its present friends," he wrote a friend, "would be somewhat irksome, and while J. P. Morgan and Carnegie and Rockefeller might make a gilded cage for learning and art, it would be a cage after all."[44] Somewhere between the two extremes lay the course the nation should follow.

Turner found the ideal navigator in Theodore Roosevelt; Roosevelt and his insurgent friends might reap a whirlwind but a worse whirlwind would grow from a Hanna-McKinley planting.[45] Yet even now he could not embrace the President's goals completely, for he realized that trust-busting ran counter to the trends of history and economic efficiency. Turner's political philosophy during the Progressive era was the solution offered by his good friend Charles R. Van Hise, in his influential volume, *Concentration and Control: A Solution to the Trust Problem in the United States*, published in 1911. Regulation, not fragmentation, was Van Hise's plan; he would allow the large corporation to exist, but only under federal controls, thus achieving the economies of large-scale production while protecting the worker and consumer. Embracing such a platform meant a major shift in Turner's thinking. In doing so he was sacrificing the "rugged individualism" of the frontier for the welfare of the consuming and working masses. Popular democracy was given precedence over the right of the individual to use natural resources and laborers as he wished. Turner could vote for Theodore Roosevelt in 1904 and William Jennings Bryan in 1908 with a clear conscience, confident that he was acting in the national good, even though one of his treasured frontier traits had been sacrificed.[46]

This decision placed him squarely in the Democratic camp, for during the next years the Republican party fell increasingly into the hands of the business-oriented conservative wing led by William Howard Taft. Turner did waver during the election of 1912, a contest that fascinated him with its sectional implications. Theodore Roosevelt was nominated first by the Republican Insurgents, and Turner was delighted; as a staunch admirer of the former President and of Robert M. La Follette, his principal supporter, he would cast his ballot for Roosevelt without a second thought. So ardent was Turner's enthusiasm that he shed the cloak of political anonymity that he had always worn on the campus and spoke before the Harvard La Follette Club.[47] When Woodrow Wilson entered the race, however, Turner was less sure. He was pleased with the prospect of a three-way battle—"a prehistoric conflict," he called it, between a mastodon, a bull moose, and a Democratic donkey in a scholar's skin—but now he had to decide between two good friends, both of whom he greatly admired.[48] For a time he debated voting for both Wilson and Roosevelt, with a favorable mention of La Follette, so sympathetic was he to all of their views.[49] Instead, he took up his pen to draw a balance sheet, weighing the merits and demerits of each. His appraisal displayed both his skill as a political analyst and his faith in frontier values.

Taft he eliminated immediately; the election of that paragon of conservative Republicanism would mean control of the economy by the trusts, "tempered by the danger of revolution." As for Wilson, Turner liked him personally but disapproved of his faith in local governments and his willingness to leave trust control to the states. He was fearful, too, that Wilson's political philosophy was outmoded, and he was afraid that the southern Democrats who would ascend to power with him would be so prejudiced by their experiences with slavery and Negroes that they would not respond properly to humanitarian demands for bettering the lot of workers. On the other hand, Theodore Roosevelt's "Square Deal" suggested some sort of "deal" with the captains of industry, while the high tariffs advocated by many of his supporters would imperil the economy.[50] "I shall vote against Taft and Prosperity," Turner told his wife a few weeks before the election, "but aside from voting the Mass[achusetts] state progressive ticket, and the democratic congressional ticket, I'm still undecided."[51] Not until November 2 did he make up his mind, and then because he convinced himself that any Republican victory—even of Republican Insurgents—would mean higher tariffs. Turner voted for Woodrow Wilson and the state Progressive party that year, and was delighted when his candidate entered the White House.

Wilson's progressive domestic program and the lofty idealism that dictated his foreign policy won Turner's heart completely and decided his votes not only during the dying years of Progressivism, but well into the 1920s. He voted a straight Democratic ticket in 1916 for the first time in his life, and in 1920 he favored James M. Cox when party affiliation, affection for the martyred Woodrow Wilson, and a firm belief that Warren G. Harding would ruin the nation dictated his choice. Harding, particularly, stirred Turner's resentment; he would not, he told his daughter, vote for a marionette until he knew who pulled the strings.[52] By 1924 the political apathy that deadened the nation during the "Era of Normalcy" had dampened Turner's enthusiasm for reform. So slight was his faith in any of the candidates in 1924 (including Robert M. La Follette, who ran as a Progressive) that for a time he thought of voting "the straight IWW ticket"—if, that is, he could find anything straight about it—but in the end habit and a somewhat more liberal Democratic platform won his support for John W. Davis.[53] Gone now from letters to friends were spirited discussions of candidates and issues; they were filled instead with delighted comments on the manner in which this congressional vote or that confirmed his views on sectionalism. "The congressional margin is close enough," he gloated after the elections of 1926, "to furnish new material for my (posthumous) magnum opus on Sectionalism in American Politics."[54] Turner, like the nation, had been lulled into indifference by the mediocrities who misgoverned the country during the 1920s.

In this mood his political philosophy underwent a complete about-face. Throughout the Progressive era, whenever he debated which of the frontier values that he treasured—individualism or democracy—must be sacrificed in an industrial world, he had decided that the individual's right to exploitation must be restricted for the benefit of society as a whole—that the ideal of individualism must be subordinated to the ideal of democracy. Now, with prosperity calling the tune, with the masses willing to surrender control to hack politicians who danced on the strings pulled by Big Business, with the democratic ideal buried by popular indifference, such a decision was less easy to maintain. Was democracy the final goal? Or should the industrial barons who seemed able to put two chickens in every pot and two cars in every garage be given a free hand to do as they pleased? Should the frontier goal of individualism take precedence over the pioneer ideal of democracy?

Turner's answer was governed partly by the rise of a new hero who seemed to personify the best of the frontier values that he held so dear. Herbert Hoover had been one of his favorites since the days of the Belgium Relief Program after World War I; Turner deeply admired Hoover's precise mind, his skill as an executive, and his honest expression of principles. That admiration deepened when Hoover responded to a gift of *The Frontier in American History* (a book that he read "with very deep interest") by sending Turner a copy of his own little volume, *American Individualism*.[55] Here was a message that the new Turner could appreciate. "It is," he assured the author, "the platform on which all genuine Americans can stand, a noble statement of the fruits of our past and the promise of our future."[56] Turner was a complete Hoover convert now; with the approach of the election of 1928 he saw his new friend as "a promising sign in the heavens" who would have his vote should the Republicans have the good sense to nominate him.[57]

Turner did cast his ballot for Hoover that year, and when he did so he climaxed the completion of a full cycle in his political thinking. Hoover spoke, and spoke eloquently, for the unrestrained individualism of the frontier past, an individualism free of all governmental interference, an individualism based on faith in the working of natural economic laws under complete freedom in the marketplace. The Turner who embraced these views was not the Turner who applauded the "New Nationalism" of Theodore Roosevelt and the "New Freedom" of Woodrow Wilson, or who built his political edifice on Charles R. Van Hise's platform of governmental control of Big Business. He had realized that his two pioneer ideals—of the economic democracy preached by the Progressives and the rugged individualism favored by Hoover—were irreconcilable in a post-frontier world. So long as the democratic ideal seemed obtainable, as it did during the Progressive era, he could cast his lot with reform, but the negative do-nothingism of the 1920s dimmed his hopes and elevated individualism above democracy in his scale of values. Turner, like the frontiersmen he emulated, made inconsistency a virtue; he was ready, as they had been, to choose the theory that seemed best fitted to the needs of the moment.

One might speculate that if Turner had lived into the 1930s the spirit of reform generated by the New Deal would have rekindled his faith in democracy and reversed his political thinking once more. Perhaps, but probably not, for he could neither have understood nor enjoyed the era that was dawning as he went to his grave. In the largest sense, the world of Frederick Jackson Turner died with him. He knew, and loved, a land where a moving frontier altered men and institutions as it swept westward, where sectional conflicts helped shape congressional legislation and altered the political profile. That nation died when the Great Depression brought into focus the giant social upheaval that had been shaping for a generation. The new America that emerged was adjusted to a closed-space existence, its governmental philosophy was built on the belief that men must be protected from corporate exploitation now that escape to the West was no longer possible, its political processes were reconstructed on the basis of the nationalizing forces that healed sectional divisions. Turner would have felt a stranger in that post-depression world. When he died in 1932, the curtain was already falling on the America that he loved so deeply.

XVIII

The Persistence of a Theory: the Frontier and Sectional Hypotheses

FREDERICK JACKSON TURNER was known during his lifetime, and has been known since, primarily as the progenitor of two ideas, one holding that the frontiering experience helped shape the character of the American people and their institutions, the other that sectional conflicts underlay much of the political decision-making of the nineteenth century. Turner himself strongly resented this image. His concern was with the broad panorama of the nation's history, and his emphasis on frontier and section was only a means of completing the total picture as seen by historians. "It is all one country, acting and reacting," he wrote at one time, "and it is the scholar's duty to see it nationally as well as sectionally."[1] He, more than most men of his day, recognized that the pageant of the past was understandable only through the interrelation of human ideals, economic interests, and cultural ambitions, and that all were so intertwined as to be inseparable. But the fact remains that he did spend most of his lifetime analyzing frontier and sectional phenomena, and that his contemporaries and successors equated him with those interests.

Were those two theories sufficiently meritorious to justify the acclaim they won Turner during his lifetime and the criticism they have engendered since? Certainly no historian rivaled his impact on the profession during the 1910s and 1920s. Americanists almost to a man set out to rewrite the history of the United States within Turnerian guidelines; they discovered that western forces underlay the Revolution, touched off the War of 1812 and the Mexican War, shaped the nature of the

Kansas-Nebraska Act, and brought the slavery issue to a bloody climax in Civil War. The *Mississippi Valley Historical Review*, established in 1907, published so many articles exploring frontier themes that it might better have been named the *Journal of Frontier History*. Southern historians, long absorbed in constitutional history, awakened to the fact that geographic forces were determinant and poured forth books and articles describing economic groupings in the plantation South, exploring conflicts between coast and interior, and analyzing conflict and change in terms of hostility to the planter class. Textbook writers leaped on the van; every text published between 1926 and 1930 made the frontier the focal point of American history, and of the twenty-four most widely used, sixteen cited Turner by name and nineteen accepted the principle of geographic determinism as unassailable.[2] When the *History Teacher's Magazine* published an article on "How to Teach the History of the West in American History" in 1916, the author felt no need to plead his cause and devoted himself entirely to techniques.[3]

Americanists succumbed most completely, but other historians, and men in other disciplines, were not far behind. Medievalists, led by James Westfall Thompson of the University of Chicago, rewrote the story of the Middle Ages in Turnerian language, tracing the expansion of Germany eastward over Slavonic lands in the twelfth and thirteenth centuries, glorifying free land as the causal force underlying migrations, and isolating the same stages of social evolution discernible in the American West. His purpose, Thompson told Turner, was "to interpret the history of the frontier of medieval Germany somewhat as you have interpreted that of the United States"; he succeeded so remarkably that one of his fellow medievalists cried out in protest in 1923 that "while American history is our first business, it is not our sole business."[4] Economists succumbed to the contagion; John R. Commons explained the principal characteristics of the nation's labor movements as products of the frontier, while Selig Perlman built his whole economic theory on the premise that free land produced a working class that was job-conscious rather than class-conscious. Sociologists sprinkled their books with Turner's theories and reproduced his essays in their collections of readings. "I should," wrote Franklin H. Giddings in 1928, "find it hard to think of a scholar who has in my judgment made more significant contributions to the study of those processes of mass activity and organization which go back to frontier environment and experiences."[5] Students of American literature, rebelling against the genteel traditions of their craft, responded with irrational enthusiasm when Norman Foerster in 1926 urged them to recognize the "frontier spirit" as a determinative force in their studies, and they set to work on such books as *The Literature of the Middle Western Frontier*, *The Rediscovery of the Frontier*, and *The Frontier in American Literature*.[6] The whole scholarly world was at Turner's feet by the close of the 1920s.

Nor was the scholarly world alone. Increasingly, the frontier and sectional theories touched the public pulse, the latter especially lending itself to the needs of policy-makers. Publicists and senators praised Turner's views or sought his advice; Walter Lippmann and Charles Merz borrowed his ideas for their widely publicized comments, Newton D. Baker found them essential in the conflict over the St. Lawrence Seaway, Senator Arthur Capper urged them on his constituents, Felix Frankfurter testified to their usefulness even before he ascended to the Supreme Court, and newspapers from *The New York Times* to the *Los Angeles Times* parroted his words in their editorials, approvingly or disapprovingly as their prejudices dictated.[7] When Philip La Follette was inaugurated as Wisconsin's governor in 1931, his inaugural address praised Turner, summarized his views, and concluded that, with the passing of the frontier, "we must find our freedom and make our opportunity through wise and courageous readjustments of the political and economic order of State and Nation to the changed needs and changed conditions of our time."[8] Like it or not (and he liked it a great deal), Turner was a public figure by the time of his death, and his theories the stock-in-trade of politicians and public opinion makers throughout the land.

They made their most impressive impact during the debate over Franklin D. Roosevelt's New Deal. Proponents found them a perfect weapon; so long as free lands existed, laissez faire in government and rugged individualism in business could shape national policy, but with escape to the frontier impossible, the federal government had to provide the security and opportunity that had been found in the West. "Our last frontier has long since been reached," Roosevelt told a Commonwealth Club audience in 1932. "There is no safety valve in the form of a Western Prairie. . . . Our task now is not discovery or exploitation of natural resources. . . . It is the less dramatic business of administering resources and plants already in hand . . . of distributing wealth and products equitably."[9] Opponents of the New Deal found the frontier hypothesis as useful as its proponents did. Governmental meddling in the marketplace, they argued, would undermine the frontier-bred individualism and self-reliance that was the nation's principal strength. Regimentation was no substitute for expansion. The force and sinew of the United States could be preserved only by perpetuating the freedoms of pioneer days.[10] Probably most who debated the merits of New Dealism had never heard of Turner, but his theories were so deeply planted in the public mind that they could be used by all.

Such was their impact, too, on statesmen who argued the course of America's foreign policy. Since the turn of the century, imperialists and anti-imperialists had bent the frontier thesis to their own purposes; the passing of free lands at home, said the former, required the acquisition of new territories and new markets abroad to satisfy the expansionist urge and the needs of the business community; overseas colonies, argued the latter, would undermine the democratic ideals bred of pioneering and rob the Americans of their treasured freedoms. This conflict was updated when President Franklin D. Roosevelt voiced the view that the nation's frontier was the world and urged the American people to join in ending nineteenth-century colonialism everywhere. By the 1930s, Turner's frontier could be used as a basis for a new manifest destiny of the United States beyond the seas.[11]

All of this recognition—by fellow historians, by patrons of other disciplines, by politicians and statesmen—was balm to Turner's soul during his last years. "One of the major satisfactions of Professor Turner's life," wrote his secretary at that time, "must have been the spontaneous evidences of profound appreciation of him . . . that came in a veritable flood during the years of his association with the Huntington Library."[12] Yet the adulation was not without its dangers, for it courted an inevitable reaction. Turner had not, as he freely admitted, advanced an infallible formula for interpreting American history; he had simply proposed an untested hypothesis, to be accepted or rejected after proper research. When a bibliographer suggested listing his 1893 essay as a "Research Paper," he objected, pointing out that "it was really an attempt at interpretation, rather than a piece of formal research."[13] Unfortunately, few of his disciples exercised such caution. To the Turnerian generation the frontier thesis was no hypothesis, but Holy Writ —the Bible and the Declaration of Independence and the Constitution rolled into one—to be literally expounded as Divine Truth.

Nor did Turner help his cause by his own tendency to advance untested generalizations. These appeared largely in the many articles and lectures forced upon him during his prime years by editors and college administrators who demanded that he write and speak about the frontier at a time when his own research was focused on the section. Because Turner had nothing new to say, he was inclined to substitute extravagant rhetoric for investigation, poetic imagery for facts, and elaborate metaphors for soundly based theories. In much of his later writing and speaking he *assumed* that pioneers acted in a certain way, even though he had no proof that they did so. These assumptions, often false, were recorded as established facts, sanctified by his approval.

One example will show how Turner helped dig his own grave. In October 1913, he agreed to give the commencement address at the University of Washington the following June on "The West and American Ideals"—a title that permitted wide-ranging generalizations. Turner hoped to prepare his remarks that winter, but, as usual, he procrastinated, and by spring not a line had been written. The avalanche of end-of-the-year bluebooks and doctoral dissertations, a move from his Brattle Street home to 7 Phillips Place, and preparations for his daughter's marriage doomed all hope of progress before he started west on June 4. There was still a chance during the week scheduled in Madison, but friends and a round of parties decreed that work be forgotten. The Turners reached Seattle on June 15 or 16 with his address still untouched—and commencement only a day or two away. To make matters worse, he had mislaid the package of notes on which it was to be built.[14]

That commencement address, hastily written in a hotel room, was to embarrass Turner when he was alive and give fuel to his critics after his death. Into it he crowded many of the unproven clichés of frontier history. The pioneer "knew not where he was going but he was on his way, cheerful, optimistic, busy and buoyant." He was "an opportunist rather than a dealer in general ideas," but blessed with "a courageous determination to break new paths." American democracy "was born of no theorist's dream; it was not carried in the *Sarah Constant* to Virginia, nor in the *Mayflower* to Plymouth. It came out of the

American forest, and it gained new strength each time it touched a new frontier." In that one inadequately prepared address Turner provided his future critics with enough unsubstantiated generalizations to keep them busy for years.

To his credit, it must be said that he was far from happy with his performance. "I am," he confessed two days later, "still moving by re-flex action after my poor commencement address," adding that he felt like a man who relaxed in the electric chair after the first shock. His one solace was that crying babies in the audience of 2500 drowned out most of his words. "Always," he advised a friend, "take along a supply of babies when you preach."[15] These bantering words hid gen-uine humiliation. At first he refused to allow his paper to be published —"it was written to be spoken," he explained—but when the editor of the *Washington Historical Quarterly* persisted he finally succumbed. Only when he saw his words in print did he realize how seriously he had tortured the truth. His first impulse was to pull out his red pencil to correct factual errors, add marginal qualifications, and scrawl be-side one of the most flamboyant statements "TOO STRONG."[16] Not all of Turner's latter-day essays on the frontier were laden with such distor-tions—his studies of New England, the Old West, and the Midwest were admirably structured on the basis of solid research—but he was far too ready to mouth unsustainable extravagances. He, no less than his overzealous disciples, paved the way for the inevitable reaction against the man and his theories that blossomed during the 1930s.

The Great Depression sparked that assault. In a world beset by a bewildering economic cataclysm, historians began to question the study of a remote agrarian past that bore little relation to the pressing problems of the present. In a world where governmental planning was essential to salvation, a theory that preached the virtues of individual-ism seemed dangerously outdated. In a world that could be saved from totalitarianism only by international cooperation, the nationalism glori-fied by Turner appeared more a menace than a blessing. Did a thesis that was so grossly inadequate to the modern day have any validity for the past? Had the United States ever been the land that it seemed to Turner, or had industry and urbanization and immigration and class conflict played a major role that his teachings obscured? The time was ripe for a complete reorientation of historical studies, with the goal now comprehension of the urban-industrial complex that had gone askew in 1929. This was the mood of American historians by the mid-1930s, but it had been building toward its climax for a decade. As early as 1925 Turner himself predicted that the pessimistic reaction against World War I would generate a sympathetic reaction against pioneer ideals and the rural past, with a new focus on the European experience and the class struggle. "There seems likely to be," he prophesied, "an urban reinterpretation of our history."[17] So there was, and he was its sacrificial lamb.

Fortunately for Turner, death spared him the bulk of the criticism directed against him, but he did live to read the work of two of his attackers. In 1925, John A. Almack, a professor of education at Stanford University, led the way with a discursive article on "The Shibboleth of the Frontier" in *The Historical Outlook*. Turner's theory, Almack argued, combined diluted Marxism and geographic determinism; it was "simply not in accord with the facts" when it preached that the best of the American tradition stemmed from the frontier. Instead, pioneering slowed cultural progress, which was generated instead in factories and cities. Turner's friends hurried to assure him that his critic was an uninformed educationalist who had set up a straw man to knock it down—a man so eager to be a second David that he had constructed a Goliath to fit his stone.[18] Yet Turner was deeply hurt, not at the attack, but because his own essays were subject to such misinterpretation. He held no brief for the frontier hypothesis as sacrosanct and unalterable, and expected it to be criticized. "But the job could have been better done. The idea that I was attributing all that was good in American civilization to the frontier and the backwoodsman in his cabin and that a statistical demonstration that education and ability existed in the east was needed by a Stanford man gives me pain as it shows me how ineffective my mode of statement must be."[19] But he would not reply; those who knew his essays would realize that Almack was tilting at windmills, and those who did not might be curious enough to read them and learn the truth.

He was cut even more deeply by a second criticism, this an article by Benjamin F. Wright, Jr., of Harvard's political science faculty, on "American Democracy and the Frontier," which was printed in the *Yale Review* late in 1930. Aiming his guns at Turner's statement that American democracy originated in the forests of the New World, and ignoring the fact that he had been speaking only of *American* democratic theory and practice, Wright paraded statistics and arguments to demonstrate that democracy had emerged in the Old World and had generally moved from east to west, rather than vice versa. Once more Turner's friends leaped to his support, and once more he assured them that his essays had been misread—"I think Mr. Wright fails to realize that what I was dealing with was, in the first place, the *American* character of democracy as compared with that of Europe or of European philosophers; and that, secondly, whatever may be said regarding the writings and activity of coastal men in promoting it, they had as a background the American western experience and were influenced thereby"—but that he had no intention of replying. If Wright was correct in his strictures, a good many able men had been misled and were capable of taking up the cudgels in Turner's behalf.[20] Besides criticism was healthy, and there was sure to be more of it.

There was more, in mounting crescendo over the next two decades. Critics made their assult on three fronts: they questioned Turner's *statement* of the frontier hypothesis and damned him for inexact usage and failure to define his terms; they challenged a methodology that failed to explain *how* pioneering altered the American character; and they criticized his judgment in overstressing the frontier as a moulding influence, rather than emphasizing eastern-based forces such as capital accumulation, the expansion of domestic and foreign markets, industrialization, urbanization, and class conflicts.[21] The validity of these criticisms calls into question the whole significance of Frederick Jackson Turner in American historiography. Was he as grossly in error as his attackers charged, and, if so, does he deserve the fame accorded him by his contemporaries and later generations? Turner could not answer directly, but he left an abundance of evidence in his letters and unpublished writings to show that his rebuttals would have been generally effective. To reconstruct his replies is to recognize that the frontier thesis, as he understood it, was by no means error-proof, but that it was far less vulnerable than his assailants realized.

True, he did not offer the precise definition of terms that a later generation of scientific historians demanded; Turner defined the "frontier" in his published essays as everything from "the hither edge of free land" to a "graphic line which records the expansive energies of the people behind it." Twice he was forced to grapple with the problem—once in 1894, when he prepared an article on the subject for *Johnson's Universal Encyclopedia,* and again in 1914, when he accepted a similar assignment from the *Cyclopedia of American Government.* Neither was completely satisfactory. That of 1894 was particularly unsuccessful: "those outlying regions which at different stages of the country's development have been but imperfectly settled, and have constituted the meeting-ground between savagery and civilization." His second attempt, made twenty years later, was only a slight improvement: "the temporary boundary of an expanding society at the edge of substantially free lands . . . that zone of settlement nearest the wilderness, wherein society and government are loosely or incompletely organized." Turner had yet to devise a satisfactory definition. "I have never," he admitted in 1926, "published an adequate discussion of this phase of the 'frontier,' with the result that some readers of my first essay seem to think that I imagined all that is significant in American life as having been born on the extreme edge of things."[22]

He did not think that, of course, and increasingly in his later years he groped toward a definition that would convey his true meaning. As he did so, he stressed more and more the concept of a broad, westward-moving zone, rather than a line, a belt in which the stages of civilization were being reenacted from primitive to complex forms. "A zone of population extending between civilization and wilderness," was Turner's description to a Harvard class; a few years later the frontier had become in his mind "a migratory section, rather a stage of society than an area."[23] These definitions made good sense, particularly because they stressed two points on which Turner was emphatic. He had not, he insisted, ever intended to suggest that the "raw outer edge" of the geographical frontier played an important role in American civilization; those who accused him of believing that mental ability or cultural progress moved from the outer edge of society eastward completely misunderstood him. He had, on the contrary, always maintained that "what went on behind the frontier" was of broader significance than what went on on the frontier; national developments in industry, thought, and politics were "deeply influenced by the fact that there was a frontier of settlement which continually opened up new fields for social development."[24] Turner anticipated many modern restatements of his hypothesis when he made those observations.

Whatever his success in shaping his own beliefs on the nature of the frontier, Turner had no trouble communicating with his own generation. To assign three meanings to the word "frontier"—as place, population, and process—was no crime, for the English language bristles with words burdened by a number of meanings. Any reader of his essays knew perfectly well what he meant when a term was placed in context, and saw no contradiction when that term was used in a different context a few paragraphs later. Turner wrote with exemplary clarity for those not seeking a semantic quarrel with him. His real achievement was to make this single word the key to so much of American history, and so meaningful in its separate usages. When he remarked that this aspect of the past could be understood only if "sharp definitions" were sacrificed for "elastic" usages, he was perfectly right.

He enjoyed less success when grappling with the problem of *how* expansion altered American character and institutions. This was basic to his whole theory, and repeatedly asserted: "the settlers transformed the wilderness but in the very process they were themselves transformed," he wrote, or "American character has been formed by this expansion of the social organism."[25] But what wrought this change? Here Turner, in his published writings, was more prone to bald statements than to a search for correct answers. Merely crossing the Appalachians, he suggested on occasion, aroused new ambitions and new social ideals, even though he must have known that conditions west of the range were identical with those on the east. More often he ascribed the alterations to the reversion to primitivism that occurred in pioneer communities: settlers cast off their cultural baggage when they went west, then, as they rebuilt civilization, they adopted practices and concepts adjusted to the new environment. "American social development," he wrote in 1916, "was continually beginning over on the frontier."[26] To accept this simple explanation, however, was to subscribe to the doctrine of environmental determinism, and Turner was too wise to succumb to that doctrine—or at least he did not do so as completely as most of the geographers of his generation did. Frontier culture, he realized early in his career, was the product of three forces: "the European germs, the native races, and the physiography of the new continent."[27] Turner spent much of his life attempting to weigh the exact influence of each.

The "native races"—the Indians—received far too little of his attention; he saw them only as retarding the advance of civilization and "compelling society to organize and consolidate in order to hold the frontier."[28] The relative importance to be assigned "European germs" and the "physiography of the new continent" was at the heart of his problem, and a major problem it was. In his more extravagant moods, as when composing a popular lecture or article, he was inclined to refer grandly to the West as a "huge geographic mould for a new society," and to speak of the manner in which nature "pressed into her mould the plastic pioneer life." These unfortunate exaggerations were not typical, for Turner was constantly aware that people responded in varying ways to an identical environment, or even failed to respond at all. "The different ways in which these different peoples reacted to the same scene interests me," he wrote in 1923. Solving this equation occupied most of his lifetime. He failed, but his speculations brought him surprisingly near a correct answer. He ruled out complete environmentalism at once; "I haven't quite gotten sure of what I think myself on the degree of *control* by geographic factors," he wrote a friend in 1908, but of one thing he was sure: "I think it clear that those who believe in geographic determinism go too far."[29] As proof Turner could, and did, cite case after case in which the invading stock resisted change: Yankees and southern uplanders who clung to their own civilizations even when living side by side in the Mississippi Valley, New England Mormons who transported their ways of life to the arid Great Basin, German farmers in the Great Valley of the Appalachians whose agricultural techniques varied little from those of the Old World, Indian-hating Puritans with an urge for self-government and Indian-loving Frenchmen content with royal absolutism who both occupied comparable geographic regions. "I have the impression," he wrote a former student, "that the provincialism of Oregon rural regions, and in part of Portland, is in some degree a survival of the special type that pioneered that region."[30] The geographic "moulds" that Turner described in his flamboyant moods simply did not operate. There were, he believed, "inherited ideas and customs to consider, and personal leadership too. It is a complex with which we have to deal."[31]

In the end he isolated at least three explanations of the manner in which frontiering changed men and their institutions, all of them based on good sense and ample evidence. First, the mere fact of migration, he believed, affected migrants; it "gave a shock to old conventions, usages, attitudes of mind, fundamental assumptions."[32] Second, migrating stocks tended to seek a physical environment comparable to that left behind, thus allowing the use of skills suited to the area. This accentuated sectional differences and gave the impression of stronger geographic forces than actually existed.[33] Finally, Turner saw that the *social* environment of frontier regions was a major influence in altering traits and institutions, even though the physical environment was not. Men living amidst the relatively greater opportunity provided by "free land" and a fluid social order would develop characteristics and institutions different from those of the cramped East, where a stabilized society and limited economic opportunity firmed class distinctions. "Environment," Turner wrote in 1928, "includes both geographical and social forces, and the physical environment is changed by changing economic forces and interests."[34] Moreover, the resulting changes would influence subsequent generations; children reared in the atmosphere of change and speculation common to frontier communities would view life differently than those raised in settled regions where stability and thrift were the rule. "The ideals of the frontier," he told a Harvard class in 1911, "were handed down to each succeeding generation."[35]

As Turner visualized the frontier process, immigrants reached each new frontier bearing with them traditions, habits, and institutions which transplanted to the new region much of the life and thought of the area they had departed. They also carried with them the seeds of ideals and institutions that had failed to thrive in the East, but that grew rapidly when unfettered by tradition. Even more important, pioneers found in frontier opportunity "occasions for the development of new institutions, the transformation of old institutions, and the greater freedom of the individual man."[36] Turner's emphasis, then, was on change through altered social environments. This would always vary from place to place, for ethnic stocks entering each region would never be identical and physical conditions would differ in degree. Rejecting, as he did, the belief that the physical environment cast all into a common mould, Turner expected that the similarities between frontier areas would be greater than differences, but that in all those areas the cultural traditions carried westward by pioneers would be slightly altered.

Turner came to a surprisingly correct conclusion concerning the frontier process, even though he lacked the statistical tools to determine the relative influence of "stocks" and environment—physical and social —in the resulting equation. His instincts also led him to a reasonably accurate understanding of the nature of the westward movement, and of its significance in American history. He did not, unlike some of his followers, ascribe it undue credit as a moulding force. Only a few months before his death he complained that a critic "incorrectly thinks that I had made the frontier phenomenon the one key to American history." He had not, of course. "It *was* a key, and a neglected one."[37] Turner, by his stress on the West, only tried to achieve a balance that was badly needed. In the same way he avoided the trap of localism into which so many frontier historians have fallen. "The real significance of Western history," he told the American Historical Association in 1896, " is that it is national history." Turner believed, correctly, that "there was no region, class or interest which did not feel the reactions due to this moving frontier. It was not a local phenomenon. It was a national experience."[38] The West's impact on the East was more important than what happened in the West itself. When, late in his career, he read an economist's judgment that "a considerable part of the significance of the frontier lies behind the frontier" Turner added a marginal note: "Perhaps it would be correct to say *most* of its significance."[39] He was no victim of localitis; the broad pattern of American civilization as influenced by westering—and dozens of other factors—was his concern.

Nor was he as guilty of overemphasizing one frontier area, as many of his latter-day critics complained. True, Turner drew most of his examples from the forested upper Mississippi Valley, but he also made serious investigations of the New England frontier, the Old West, the Ohio Valley, and the Mississippi Valley, and was genuinely concerned with the story of expansion into the Far West. He did not, he once assured Herbert Eugene Bolton, fail to recognize the importance of that area, even though he never had occasion to preach about it in an essay. During his late years, particularly, Turner recognized that the Great Plains and Rocky Mountain country had been slighted, and he urged that the oversight be corrected. In 1928, when he was unable to attend a conference on the subject, he sent instead a four-page, single-space list of topics crying for research. "A neglected region (so far as synthesis goes especially)," he called it, "in American cultural, social and economic history."[40] Neglected it might be, but Turner's own reading notes on the Far West, scattered through two file drawers and numbering into the thousands, showed that he was better informed than even his admirers thought possible. So did his occasional speculations. Life in the land of the "league-long furrow," he once observed, required different standards of measurement than life in the Midwest. Then, too, it deserved particular study because the conflict of cultures there—Spanish and English—provided a laboratory to measure the relative influence of hereditary and environmental forces.[41]

Turner made no investigations of the Southwest along the lines he suggested, but he did base revisionist conclusions on two important phases of the migration process on solid research. One concerned the validity of the "safety valve." In his early days Turner accepted this universally held belief—that the West drained excess workers from American factories and thus served as a deterrent to labor radicalism —and incorporated it unthinkingly in his essays. "In Europe," he told a class in 1904, "labor said, raise wages or we will fight. In the United States labor said, raise wages or we will go west."[42] His first serious investigation into the subject apparently began during his research for the *Rise of the New West,* and with it came his first doubts. Could an eastern laborer save enough from his pittance of a salary to migrate? "Compare the cost of taking a Virginia farm in mid-17th century," he noted as a reminder to himself, "an Indiana farm about 1820, an Iowa or Wisconsin farm 1850, a Dakota farm 1890, a Canadian farm 1906." Turner followed his own advice. A folder an inch thick, filled with notes on farm-making costs in the 1850s, allowed him to reach the conclusion he voiced in *The United States, 1830-1850*: that the $1000 necessary to buy and stock a farm in the Midwest was beyond the reach of factory workers and that "direct access to cheap Western lands was not open to the poorer people of the Northeastern states and of Europe."[43] Turner concluded that the frontier was not a direct safety valve a dozen years before economists branded him a false prophet for saying that it was.

He also revised his views on the stages of frontier society that he had learned from Richard T. Ely and had parroted in his early writings. His first doubts arose in 1906, when he was asked to comment on a paper by Edwin F. Gay, read before the American Historical Association, which questioned the whole concept of natural laws in human behavior. Turner refused, pleading inadequate time to assemble the masses of data needed, but his curiosity was piqued and he spent months reading and taking notes. As he read, he recognized that what he had learned on the sequence of frontier types—trapper, cattleman, miner, pioneer farmer, equipped farmer, and town dweller—had to be modified in two ways. First, the stages were not immutable, but were governed by economic needs and opportunities. "Where social pressure or demand from a higher stage exists," he wrote in a note to himself, "there will be an incentive to omit a whole stage (eg in Mountains that bear minerals—or on the great plains when once the RR reaches them)." Second, the steps from stage to stage were taken by intelligent human beings, and hence were determined not by a grand design that shaped the evolution of society, but by the laws of supply and demand. "The 'obvious' stages of 'hunting,' 'pasturage,' and so forth," Turner concluded, "will doubtless go chiming down the ages as the Mother Goose philosophy of history."[44] Those were bold conclusions, challenging as they did a basic belief of historians and political economists of that day.

His curiosity satisfied, Turner turned to more pressing matters, but work on THE BOOK demanded that he again consider the stages of society that unfolded during the 1840s and 1850s. To do so meant further modifications of his theories to include a number of hitherto unrecognized frontier types as investigation revealed the complexity of the settlement process. Land speculators, missionaries, soldiers, gristmill operators, and a dozen more deserved a place with trappers and ranchers and pioneer farmers; land speculators particularly intrigued Turner and inspired bundles of research notes that could have resulted in several ground-breaking articles if he had been so inclined.[45] He also saw that these frontier types advanced westward in no set sequence. "Often," he wrote in 1925, "the economic stages represented by these waves of advancing population were blended or intermixed." This was the case because westward expansion was governed by a variety of factors, including the state of the grain market, transportation facilities, credit, the availability of capital, interest rates, and other man-made influences.[46] Turner was coming to conclusions that were not based on speculation, but on hard research. And they were, like most opinions built on such a foundation, thoroughly accurate.

Unfortunately, he never found time to investigate one aspect of

frontier theory that fascinated him. Did the experience of other frontiering peoples substantiate his findings about the Americans? Were the
peasants who advanced eastward across Siberia, the grain-farmers who
conquered the prairie provinces of Canada, the gauchos who led the
way into the interior of Argentina, the Portuguese who peopled the
sertao of Brazil, and the squatters who drove their sheep through gaps
in the Blue Mountains into the "backs" of Australia altered, as were
Americans, by contact with frontier opportunity? Or did such changes
as took place in their traits and institutions show that ethnic traditions were more important than environmental pressures in governing
human conduct? These questions vastly intrigued Turner, even though
his investigations did not lead in that direction. Others, he hoped, would
carry on the quest, and he particularly urged his own students to do so.
"Russia ought to have its frontier interpretations," he told one; "South
America should be a rich field," he suggested to another. Indeed, the
next and most needed step in frontier studies might well be "the comparison and correlation with the land experiences of other peoples."[47]
Insatiably curious, Turner was an eager student of comparative frontiers, even though he made no contribution of his own.

To summarize his views on the frontier process is to recognize that
they would be accepted by most historians today. He was aware that
environmental forces were not determinant, and that men of differing
races and backgrounds reacted in differing ways to the same geographic
setting. He found in the social environment a far more effective instrument for change than the physical. He viewed the westward movement
as principally significant for its impact on the East, and hence an important national phenomenon. He was emphatic in believing that it was
only one of many influences moulding the nation's civilization. He was
aware that the West was not a direct safety valve luring displaced
factory workers, and that expansion proceeded in no well-defined and
immutable stages. He recognized that the impact of the American
frontier could never be accurately appraised without a study of comparative frontiers. Turner had, in other words, reached conclusions
that were sufficiently accurate to be accepted today.

If Turner stands acquitted, on the basis of his scholarly articles and
privately expressed views, of the lack of understanding of the frontier
process that his critics claimed, did he have a similar understanding

of the impact of westering on traits and institutions? Were his latter-day detractors correct when they argued that democracy did not origi-nate in the forests of the West, but in the cities of the East? Did they err when they charged that not the frontier, but forces stemming from the Revolution produced the intense nationalism of the United States? Were they accurate when they insisted that cooperation was the rule in pioneer areas—with community enterprise underlying everything from cabin-raisings to law enforcement—rather than the individualism that Turner postulated? What in Turner's own theories, voiced in speeches and letters and unpublished essays, can exonerate him of these accusa-tions?

That Turner did exaggerate the role of the frontier as a breeding ground for democratic theory and practice cannot be denied, but neither can his views be understood without a new look at the type of democracy he was discussing. When he wrote, as he did in 1894, and 1896, and 1906, and, finally, in 1914, that American democracy "came from no theorist's dream" but rose "stark and strong and full of life, from the American forest," he was in effect advancing a com-pletely new definition for the benefit of his historical brethren.[48] He was saying, first of all, that *American* democracy (as distinguished from its European ancestor) was unique, and a product of the Jack-sonian-egalitarian-Populist faith in the common man, originating not in the days of Thomas Jefferson, but in the era of Andrew Jackson. As such, his "democracy" shared little with the European-Neo-Federalist concept of the same term, which accepted a rigid class structure, re-fused to treat all men as equals, and retained other relics of an aristo-cratic past. Turner saw the frontier as an enemy of this brand of de-mocracy; there, where "free land" and untapped natural resources opened opportunities for the enterprising, the society (as he put it) was one of "expectant capitalists"—a social order based on the principle of a fair chance for all, rather than arbitrary leveling by external decree or law.[49] American democracy, unlike European, was "the rise of the people to economic and consequently to political power and self-con-sciousness." This was what Turner meant when he wrote that *Ameri-can* democracy emerged from the forest, or that it was due to the ex-istence of "free lands."[50]

Viewed in this light, many of his most extravagant statements take on a more logical meaning. Turner never denied that democracy originated in Europe and that many of its theories and practices migrated from east to west. "It was," he told a Harvard audience, "based not alone on Magna Charta, nor Plymouth Rock, nor Jamestown. What is *American* in it is the result of the interaction of the wilderness—vacant land—with the men and institutions."[51] Rule by all the people as a right, not a concession, was its basic ingredient. This, in turn, underlay two basic changes, uniquely important to the functioning of government in the United States. One was a shift in power from national to local units; frontiersmen believed their problems so different as to require local solutions, and they demanded the right of self-rule, from the days of the Mayflower Compact and Watauga Association down to the end of the nineteenth century. The other was a transfer of authority from an elite group to *all* the people; greater opportunity for self-advancement in the West bred a faith in "King Numbers," whatever the educational or cultural deficiencies of the decision-makers. Turner was fond of quoting a backcountry petition for statehood, arguing that "a fool can sometimes put on his coat better than a wise man can do it for him."[52] Here, in the simple language of the pioneers, was a definition that said a great deal. *American* democracy did differ from the European democracy in which it had originated, and the differences were traceable in part to the frontiering experience.

So did the nationalism that Turner insisted was intensified in the West. This was one of his fundamental beliefs; his essays listed over and over again the factors in pioneer life that heightened loyalty to the central government at the expense of the states: the need for defense and a generous land-disposal system, the lessening of sectional loyalties as men from differing backgrounds met and mingled, the necessity of expanding the constitutional powers of Congress to deal with unanticipated problems originating in the borderlands. When he wrote, as he did early in his career, that "the different sectional colorings were mixed in the palette of the West into a common national hue," he was voicing a sentiment from which he never wavered during his lifetime.[53] Not long before his death, Turner jotted down several reasons for the West's role: the public domain was a common source of revenue, a region to be defended by national armies, an area to be disposed of by the national government, a territory to be governed, a birthplace of new states.[54] Frontiering in his mind was a principal adhesive force creating a strong nation and generating loyalties among its people.

If this were true, how could the frontier generate both nationalism and the localism that was, in his view, a principal by-product of American democracy? Turner never could answer that question satisfactorily, although it plagued him for many years. He tried often enough; the central government "was too remote to lay much restraint upon daily life; and at the same time it was able to furnish them the backing for their designs of building up the region into which the nation was expanding."[55] Such explanations were logical; westward expansion did enhance a nationalistic spirit by diverting attention from Europe to the interior, by deflecting commerce from the sea to the land, by weakening state loyalties, and by enhancing the patriotism of westerners who looked to the central government for protection, aid, and largess. Many a traveler during the nineteenth century commented on the excessive patriotic zeal of the people of the interior as contrasted with the temperate attitude of those who lived on the seaboard. Yet the fact remained that expansion bred sections, and that sections challenged national loyalties. Turner was well aware of this, but he was unable to reconcile the two attitudes. Nor could later scholars; man's unpredictable behavior is seldom based on logic.

Turner faced another dilemma when he stated that individualism was a trait fostered by the frontiering experience. He was perfectly aware of the fact that in all pioneer communities cooperation, rather than freedom for the individual, was necessary for survival; community efforts underlay defense, road and school building, the first governmental structures, and such neighborhood activities as cabin-raisings and logrollings. There was, often, greater restraint on freedom of action in the West than in the East. How could a spirit of individualism emerge from such a setting? Turner defined the term in a peculiarly American way, just as he had democracy. On the frontier, individualism meant only two things: participation in the decision-making process in which regulatory measures were enacted, and freedom from interference in economic affairs by an external government. The pioneer was willing to burden himself with regulatory measures if he knew them to be for the common good, but he did not want a distant congress to limit his money-making capacity in the interest of national welfare. This seemed fair enough in a land where untapped natural resources appeared limitless. "Population was scarce," Turner told one audience, "and there was no multitude of jostling interests, such as accompanied dense settlement and required a complicated system of government."[56] So long as expansion went on, individuals should be free to monopolize the richest bottom land, the finest timber plot, the most valuable mill site, and the most promising ore beds—for just ahead lay other bottom land, other timber plots, other mill sites, other ore beds. They could be sought out by the enterprising without harm to society. This Turner called the "squatter ideal."

That ideal could prevail so long as the westward movement prevailed, but what of the new closed-space world of the twentieth century, where the best of the nation's resources were already in private hands? Had the closing of the frontier burst the bubble of individualistic opportunity? Turner gave a great deal of thought to that question, particularly during the 1920s, when publicists and social scientists awakened to the problems of a frontierless world.[57] How, he asked himself, could the "squatter ideal" be reconciled with the pioneer "ideal of democracy"? If the "squatter ideal" persisted, wealthy individuals and corporations would monopolize the remaining resources at the expense of the general welfare. If the "democratic ideal" endured and the public good was elevated above private interests, the treasured right of the individual to economic freedom would be sacrificed. Which of these ideals must go for the greatest public good? "Time has revealed," Turner told the American Historical Association in his presidential address, "that these two ideals of pioneer democracy had elements of mutual hostility and contained the seeds of dissolution."[58]

He struggled long and hard with this question, filling sheet after sheet with lists of alternatives: on the one side, freedom of action, giving rise to combinations, discrimination, cut-throat competition, and monopoly; on the other, restraint of economic freedom, fostering investigative commissions, legislative controls, and assaults on private property.[59] Which would better perpetuate the pioneer values that gave America its greatness? For a time Turner clung to the hope that business would require no regulation; "in a sense," he told a class in 1902, "a corporation is a socialistic device; Rockefeller, Carnegie, etc. may prove to be pioneers in the direction of social activity."[60] When that hope was shattered, Turner placed his faith in voluntary organization, finding in corporate cooperation, farm associations, and "better business" bureaus the same spirit that motivated the barn-raisings and logrollings in pioneer times, and forseeing the day when they would serve as self-regulating devices for corporations. This dream also proved illusory, as monopolistic trusts continued to place profits above the general welfare. Reluctantly, Turner came to the conclusion that pioneer democracy must take precedent over pioneer individualism, and be preserved by positive government action. Only this could protect the freedom of opportunity formerly provided by free land.[61]

This was a tragic decision for Turner, for it symbolized the passing of the frontier America that he knew so well and loved so much. His values and his ideals were those of the pioneers he studied; the world would never be quite so attractive now that they were outmoded. For Turner had been largely accurate in defining the frontier's influence and isolating the traits and institutional changes traceable to its impact. He had erred in detail, of course, and had been guilty of overstatement in his popular speeches and essays. His tendency to exaggerate, to sacrifice accuracy for a rhetorical flourish, and to generalize on the basis of inadequate evidence cost him heavily in credibility, as his critics of the 1930s and 1940s demonstrated so effectively. But, basically, Turner was right; modern scholars agree that the interpretations embodied in his research papers are for the most part sustainable.

Whatever the detractions of Turner's critics, the fact remains that generations of travelers from abroad have found Americans different from their cousins in Europe or Asia or Africa. Social scientists, using techniques far more sophisticated than those available to Turner, have demonstrated that some, at least, of these differences were exactly those that he ascribed to frontiering. Scholarship since the 1950s has swung more and more to his side, not irrationally, as during his lifetime, but because careful testing has shown him to have been correct. The frontier was an important force—among many—in helping shape the nation's course during the eighteenth and nineteenth centuries. Its passing has created problems that baffled Turner, and that continue to challenge statesmen and politicians as the world seeks to adjust itself to a closed-space existence.

Yet all the scholarship that has been squandered arguing the merits of Turner's frontier thesis—a body of learning that forms a fitting monument to the impact of his theories—only provides a footnote to something that Turner and his generation knew instinctively. Modern Americans living in urban-industrial complexes, to whom the rural past is only a near-forgotten memory, are inclined to forget that somehow the continent was settled, and that this settlement generated social stresses certain to influence those enduring them. No nation could spill a sizable portion of its population into a wilderness for two centuries without being affected by the experience. No people who realized that opportunity for self-advancement beckoned beyond the western horizon could escape changes in mental attitudes and social traits. Such experiences defy historical analysis, but their significance cannot be ignored. One of Turner's students, E. E. Dale, sputtered his indignation at the myopia of his master's critics. Had they seen the territory of Oklahoma grow in seventeen years from a population of a few hundred cowboys and Indian agents to 400,000? Had they seen, as Dale had, 100,000 homesteaders rush into the Cherokee Outlet—to people a region as large as New England within twenty hours? Did they realize that in two decades the population of the Dakotas rose from 14,000 to 719,000, that of Nebraska from 120,000 to a million, that of Kansas from 340,000 to a million and a half?[62] Mass movements of that magnitude made their impact on people and government, even though the extent of that impact defied measurement. Turner knew this, and he was perfectly right in thinking it worth remembering.

He died in 1932, confident that his frontier thesis had bettered man's understanding of the past, and that it would continue as a significant interpretation into the future. This does not mean that he felt it inviolate; Turner was well aware of the inadequacies of his theory. Once, when criticized for overstressing the frontier's influence and for failing to test some of his generalizations, he replied sharply that he was well aware that other forces were just as important, and that he knew the limitations of some of his interpretations better than most of his detractors.[63] But he also knew that his basic premise was correct, and would never be completely invalidated. When he remarked, as he did on one occasion, that his interpretations would become "airy nothings as time goes on," he was being more self-effacing than honest.[64] Only a few months before his death, when reminiscing with his secretary, he stated firmly that the frontier hypothesis, although doubtless calling for reconsideration in detail, was essentially sound.[65] So it was.

The same can be said, although with considerably less assurance, about Turner's second major contribution to historiography: his sectional hypothesis. That he introduced an important concept into American historiography cannot be disputed. Until his day scholars wrote only of the North-South division that had culminated in civil war, closing their eyes to the more numerous regions that clashed and bargained to shape the history of the nineteenth century. For this Turner substituted an understanding of the United States as a "kind of checkerboard of differing environments," from six to ten in number, interacting each with the others much as did European nations. Like European nations, too, they differed not only in political behavior, but in economic structure, psychological attitudes, religious climate, and cultural outpourings. All had to be investigated and understood if one was to appreciate the role they played in the nation's past.[66]

Central to Turner's theory was the concept of conflict, based not on sectional self-seeking, but on the deep-seated belief of each that its culture and economy were superior, and worthy of national adoption. The sections did not fly asunder, however, for two forces held them together. Political parties served as one bond of union, stretching like elastic bands to meet each new crisis, but seldom breaking. "It is not too much to say," Turner wrote in a draft of his last book, "that but for party loyalty, operating as a check on sectional loyalty, this league of sections called the United States might have followed the fortunes of European leagues and alliances."[67] The other unifying force was the existence within each section of sub-sections, or "regions," as Turner called them, which held views antagonistic to the section itself. Often a "region" found more in common with similar "regions" lying outside its section than with its parent section. This complex of cross-lines prevented any major combination of sections from dominating the remainder. The sub-sections, with the political parties, served as a deterrent to separatism. Thus, the history of the United States could never be understood until it was retold in terms of sectional conflict, adjustment, and compromise. "American society," Turner believed, "is the outcome of the interaction of the various sections."[68]

As this belief deepened, the principal passion of Turner's life became the proof of his hypothesis. Here, in his eyes, was a searchlight into the past that had been ignored by his fellow craftsmen. They must be enlightened and converted. His plea was for a common assault on this area of darkness—by historians, geographers, economists, students of literature and the arts, even linguists—for the problems to be solved were too many and too complex for any one investigator.[69] Some few responded to his urging. Many among them had been his students—Charles H. Ambler, Joseph Schafer, Homer C. Hockett, Edgar E. Robinson, and Raynor G. Wellington contributed important findings. Others were younger scholars who were convinced that here was a fruitful field for exploration—Lois K. Mathews, Ulrich B. Phillips, Avery O. Craven, and William E. Dodd accepted Turner's invitation and acknowledged their use of his theories. But in truth the converts were few, and the sum of their findings added up to no very significant reinterpretation of American history. They, like their guide, simply failed to find in the sectional thesis the convincing insights furnished by the frontier hypothesis.

Three obstacles stood in their way, each virtually insurmountable. One was the indisputable fact that the more deeply Turner or his disciples investigated sectional phenomena, the more diffuse and uncertain their findings became. Sections refused to remain well-defined; instead, the more they were studied, the more they overlapped, subdivided, and blurred. Voters failed to respond to environmental or economic pressures as they were expected to, showing a stubborn inclination to cast their ballots for reasons that had no connection with their habitats or means of making a living. This Turner freely admitted. "Generalizations which make physical geography or economic interests alone the compelling explanation of political groupings," he wrote in 1925, "are mistaken. There are also the factors of ideals and psychology, the inherited intellectual habits, derived from the stock from which the voters sprang."[70] In other words, the forces responsible for sectional groupings were not sufficiently consistent to be trustworthy. This being the case, the whole sectional concept was discredited. If geographic or economic influences failed to explain the behavior of some groups, how could they explain others? Why did Mississippians illustrate the hypothesis while North Carolinians did not? Could it be that Turner was wrong, and the sectional thesis was inadequate to the tasks assigned it?

This Turner never admitted publicly, but he was sometimes beset by doubts as his months of research ended in negative or inconclusive results. Wealthy planters with a high literacy rate living in rich-soil regions of the pre-Civil War South *should* have voted Whig; small farmers with low incomes and a low scale of literacy who occupied in-

ferior lands were *supposed* to favor the Democratic Party. Too often
they did not. So many factors entered into political decision-making
that the sectional tests simply did not apply. Turner recorded some of
these in notes that he jotted as he went along. "Impossibility of saying
purely economic determinism," he wrote at one time, "e.g. classification
of votes by agricultural areas when the thing may be areas of stock."
"Voting *habit* and the spiritual element," he noted again. On still another occasion he went on record that "men will vote at times for
patriotic, or religious, or moral motives against their personal interests."[71] Strong leaders, or politicians who deliberately confused issues
to win votes, also distorted the picture, as did political inertia. "The
investigator," Turner confessed to a friend, "must apply the 'multiple
hypothesis' and note the coexistence of more than one influence."[72]
Perfectly true. But to do so meant that the sectional hypothesis failed
to provide an adequate explanation. Emotions, paternal loyalties, ideals,
moral issues, patriotism, and the host of other motives governing human
behavior simply were not measurable in sectional terms. Turner was
honest enough to admit the deficiencies of his thesis, but he would
never agree that they were fatal.

He was unable to prove otherwise, however, because of a second
handicap that doomed his hopes of a sectional reinterpretation of the
nation's history. The maps over which he labored were simply incapable of revealing correlations between geographic and economic conditions, on the one hand, and political behavior, on the other. This
Turner recognized, and during his investigations he listed at least five
reasons for their inadequacy. First, the county units with which he
worked were too large to show the exact relationship between social
factors and vote-distribution; on the other hand, use of a smaller unit,
such as a precinct, posed practical problems that were insurmountable.
Second, the maps created a false impression by making a large county
with a sparse population seem more important than a small county
with a large population. Third, they concealed minorities almost as
large as the majorities that they depicted, and this was a near-fatal
weakness. Using Turner's techniques, a region that was 51 per cent
Whig and 49 per cent Democrat would appear to be all Whig; a
county that barely voted for one party in one election could cast 100
per cent of its votes for that party in the next without altering the
map in the least; a populous city in one corner of a county might

carry the whole county into the Democratic column, when all the rest of that county was Whig. The one way out of the difficulty—to show the size of the plurality by percentage—was virtually impossible to do on a map. The fourth defect listed in Turner's self-criticism was equally serious. In many elections, he noted, candidates deliberately subordinated economic or social issues and appealed to voters through their personalities, thus upsetting all correlations. Finally, strong leaders led voters along paths that defied logic; they often persuaded voters to vote against their own sectional or economic interests, thus removing the counties they led from their natural groupings. Even when the leader correctly mirrored the views of his constituents, his influence was enough to cast doubts on many of Turner's results.[73]

These were grave deficiencies, but they were compounded by the inadequate technique Turner used in his analysis. His elaborate maps failed to reveal the correlations that he sought. No matter how carefully drawn or how small the unit employed, maps were unsuited to the type of statistical investigation he had undertaken, yet he was so wedded to their use that he closed his eyes to more practical methods. Neither he nor his students showed any awareness of the tools available in the early twentieth century; sampling methods, correlation devices, time-series trending, and punch cards for storing and sorting data were all in use at the time, and they were far more suitable to the type of data analysis that interested Turner. Instead, he crowded fact on fact until his maps became undecipherable jumbles of colors and symbols. Even when the maps were kept simple, the visual correlation of two or more to identify patterns of association was almost impossible, unless the degree was so high that it was unmistakable.[74] Turner, using inadequate tools, was unable to demonstrate to fellow historians that the sectional hypothesis was valid enough to justify their attention.

His tragedy was his failure to recognize this. Turner went to his grave convinced that he had altered the profile of American history by the findings his maps revealed, and that the alteration would accelerate as improved cartographic devices were developed. After all, he had demonstrated (at least to his own satisfaction) the direct correlation between illiteracy and poor soil, the close relationship between literacy and glaciated areas, the tendency of counties with dense slave populations to vote Whig, the preponderance of Democratic strength in the barrens of the upland South, and a good many other things that shed light on the past. "I think my studies of 1830-1850," he told a friend just before his death, "will prove that there is a real relation between these areas of party preponderance and areas of physical geography, soils, illiteracy, industries, even literature and religion."[75]

Turner's sectional hypothesis, discredited by the inadequacy of his statistical techniques and by his inability to prove a relationship between geography and political behavior, was cast still deeper into the shadows by the inaccuracy of some of his own predictions. Had he been content to confine his analysis to the pre-Civil War era, where his main interest lay, he would have remained on safe ground, but the present fascinated him no less than the past, and the atmosphere of the 1920s was of a sort to whet that fascination. That was a day of raw regional conflict, with New England and the Midwest snarling over the projected St. Lawrence Seaway, with South and North at arms over the racial issue, with a farm bloc demanding legislation to lift agriculture from its doldrums. To Turner this was sure proof that sectionalism was on the ascent, and that divisions would deepen almost to the point of regional warfare. He watched with excited interest, clipping items from newspapers and magazines, mapping congressional votes, and jamming his files with evidence that would prove his thesis.[76] Every new bit of evidence was proof that sectional divisions held the key to the present no less than to the past.

This was all very well, but when Turner went on to insist that sectional divisions would continue to deepen, he was flying in the face of common sense. True, his reasons were logical. Regional loyalties would intensify as the population stabilized with the closing of the frontier. They would be heightened as mounting population density made each section more aware of the need to guard its own resources and enhanced its political power to do so. Even class and ethnic conflicts, certain to increase with continued industrialization, would add tinder to the flames, for workers and immigrants in one section would be arrayed against farmers and Yankees in another. He summed up his conclusions in 1925: "The significant fact is that sectional self-consciousness and sensitiveness is likely to be increased as time goes on and crystallized sections feel the full influence of their geographical peculiarities, their special interests, and their developed ideals, in a closed and static nation."[77]

Few even among his most ardent supporters could agree with such a prediction. They knew that the very forces Turner isolated as responsible—the closing of the frontier, denser populations, improved transportation and communication facilities, the radio and airplane, industrialization and urbanization—would operate instead as nationalizing pressures that would dampen sectional loyalties. They were right. As regional loyalties gave way to dependence on the national government during the Great Depression of the 1930s and the World War of the 1940s, the sectionalism that had bulked so large a generation before was forgotten. As it passed from the scene, historians turned their attention elsewhere: to the biographical studies popular in the late 1920s, to the economic analysis and investigations of the class structure that captured their interest in the 1930s, to the "consensus" history that dominated the profession during the 1940s and 1950s. In none was there room for Turner's sectionalism. The consensus school, particularly, relegated it to oblivion by glorifying national unity at the expense of all forms of conflict, whether of section, class, group, or ideology. Turner's sectional thesis was as discredited by the end of the 1950s as his frontier hypothesis had been at the close of the 1930s.

Its fate should not be interpreted to mean that the hypothesis lacked some significance or that it will not regain respectability among future historians. Turner exaggerated when he wrote, in 1927, that "the sectional (regional-geographic) factor is as important—for the future, at least—as the frontier doctrine,"[78] but it was a theory that helped explain certain aspects of the past and had to be taken into account in any interpretation of the nineteenth century. Modern historians, equipped now with computers and sophisticated statistical techniques, and substituting tables and equations for maps, have again begun to probe the sectional phenomenon, although with inconclusive results. The day will never come, as Turner hoped it would, when "my Sections paper will travel with my frontier as interpretations,"[79] but neither will the theory be totally forgotten. His was a dual legacy to mankind and the historical profession.

XIX

The Significance of Frederick Jackson Turner in American History

ET US indulge in a very unhistorical speculation. Let us assume that Frederick Jackson Turner's offer to relinquish his place on the 1893 program of the American Historical Association to his student, Orin G. Libby, was accepted by the committee. Let us imagine that he then turned to other investigations, leaving his essay on "The Significance of the Frontier in American History" unfinished. If, as he believed, the intellectual climate was ripe for the announcement of the frontier hypothesis, some other historian would have produced a comparable essay within a few years, and he would have been acclaimed as the father of a thesis that would revolutionize historical studies. Assuming that all of these improbable events had taken place, would Turner's impact on his own generation have lessened? Would he be acclaimed today as one of the half-dozen historians most influential in shaping the study of the nation's past?

Probably not, for the world usually honors the spectacular rather than the enduring, and the frontier thesis captured both professional and popular attention as have few others. Yet a perfectly plausible argument can be made that Turner would have been just as venerated by his colleagues and successors if he had never advanced his famed hypothesis. That hypothesis, and the controversy it aroused, has obscured his many other contributions to historical studies, some of them of broader significance than his theories on both the frontier and section. His proper place in American historiography can never be appreciated until those contributions are known and understood.

To his friends, Turner's appeal lay not only in his unwritten books and scintillating essays, but also in the originality of his ideas as he roamed across the whole field of American history. His mind was a veritable grab bag of fresh viewpoints, constantly replenished by his omnivorous reading and research, and open to all to use as they wished. "I should want," J. Franklin Jameson told his superiors when he assumed direction of the historical division of the Carnegie Institution, "a man overflowing with ideas, . . . who in daily talks would wake me and the Department up, and make suggestions affecting our plans and our thinking. One man in America would fill that bill perfectly, and that is Frederick Jackson Turner."[1] Few of those ideas appeared over his own name; instead, they were seized upon by others and nursed into articles and monographs that probed the borders of knowledge. The dozen books dedicated to him, and the dozens more that acknowledged his help in their prefaces, testified to the fertility of his mind and the breadth of his influence on historical writing in his day.

Two trivial episodes illustrate the freshness of his thought. One occurred when he and Max Farrand visited Independence Hall in Philadelphia. As Turner viewed that historic shrine, a brilliant idea flashed before him; the very shape of the room, he excitedly told Farrand, allowed George Washington to dominate the proceedings as the Constitution was being drafted. Farrand was so impressed that for the next years he taught and lectured that the nation's constitutional structure was determined by the size and shape of the room where its basic document was written. Then came the letdown. "I have just obtained unmistakable evidence," he wrote Turner delightedly, "that the convention *met upstairs*."[2] So much for that theory.

Turner's logic was just as sound—and his conclusions more valid—on a second occasion, when he was called upon to help settle the controversy over the Kensington Rune Stone. His involvement began when the stone's staunchest defender, Hjalmar R. Holand, spoke in Madison in 1910, then entered into a spirited argument with Turner who was in the audience. Fortunately, the local newspaper reporter leaped to the completely false conclusion that Turner was in agreement with Holand, and so stated in his account of the affair. Turner's indignant letter to the editor set the matter straight; "I desire," he wrote emphatically, "to disclaim the utterances attributed to me."[3] This exchange came to the attention of a commission named by the Minnesota

Historical Society to determine the stone's authenticity, and Turner's advice was solicited. His reply, filling four tightly reasoned pages, asked a number of questions so adroitly phrased that the paper is still considered a classic in rune methodology. Did the weathering of the runes and the remainder of the stone reveal age differences? Could the carving have been done while the stone was locked beneath the tree where it was found? Had a stonecutter capable of such neat lettering lived near by? Was there any teacher or minister familiar enough with runes to frame the text who was a friend of the farmer who made the discovery? Were books available on runes? Had a member of the community visited a Minneapolis library where such books could be consulted? So Turner went on, for page after page, urging the use of stonecutters, jewelers, scholars, and skilled lawyers to ferret out the answers. If the investigating commission had followed his advice the Kensington Rune Stone would have been proven a hoax at that time, rather than inviting controversy for another half-century.[4]

These were hardly earthshaking accomplishments, but they demonstrated Turner's ability to summon fresh explanations and apply traditional techniques to unusual problems. He was equally appreciated by his contemporaries for his campaigns to supply researchers with new tools. One effort went toward creating a historical center in Washington where visiting scholars could live comfortably, be supported while carrying on their investigations, and enjoy the stimulating company of a core of permanent senior research associates. J. Franklin Jameson, who was always ready to work for goals inspired by what he called "the fruitful mind of Turner," labored in vain for the enormous sums needed for such a center; not until the 1960s and 1970s did the American Historical Association revive the plan as one of its principal objectives.[5] More successful was Turner's program for an up-to-date atlas of American history, mapping election returns and social data; he made the initial suggestion for such a work to the Carnegie Institution in 1903, converted Jameson to the plan when that energetic promoter became director in 1905, and helped shape the volume when an editor was finally appointed in 1913.[6] Charles O. Paullin's *Atlas of the Historical Geography of the United States*, published finally in 1932, was a monument to Jameson's dogged determination, but it was also a monument to Turner's insistence that such a volume would benefit historical studies.

Far more important was Turner's campaign to provide the profession with a multi-volume biographical dictionary of Americans, comparable to the British *Dictionary of National Biography*. Many had dreamed of such a publication, but the suggestion that led to its completion was made by Turner to the first meeting of the American Council of Learned Societies, in January 1920. They listened with interest, but no one was ready to solicit the enormous sum needed; Turner preached his message annually for two more years before Jameson could be persuaded to head a committee that agreed to try. The first step was to plan a salable product; Jameson, realizing this, extracted enough money from his business friends to call the committee together for a planning session in Washington in April 1923. That was Turner's show. He came with a bulky memorandum which the committee did little more than endorse: the dictionary would include men from all walks of life as well as statesmen; it would be written by scholars and assembled by a staff working under an editor in chief named by the American Council of Learned Societies; it would fill twenty-five volumes of 750 pages each and would cost some $600,000, with more than half that sum going to contributors, who would be paid $20 for each 1000 words. Ultimate authority, Turner suggested, and the committee agreed, would be vested in two groups: a Board of Trustees, made up of prominent business leaders, who would be entrusted with the task of raising money, and a Board of Editors, drawn from the ranks of historians, economists, political scientists, and other social scientists, who would determine editorial policies.[7]

These guidelines established, Jameson, with Turner's assistance and advice, set about finding an angel with the half-million dollars needed. This proved understandably difficult, until the promoters hit on the idea of interesting a prominent newspaper to play the role that the London *Times* had played in financing the *Encyclopaedia Britannica*. *The New York Times* was an obvious target; through the winter of 1923-24 Jameson cultivated the publisher, Adolph S. Ochs, and his right-hand man, John Finley, so persuasively that they agreed to meet with the entire planning committee on April 18, 1924. Plans were laid carefully; authors known to Ochs were persuaded to write the biographies of some of his former friends, every member was instructed to be present and well-informed lest any lack of interest discourage the sponsors, John Finley was even considered as editor but rejected lest this seem too blatant favor-seeking. These tactics triumphed. When Turner and his fellow committeemen left the meeting, they carried a contract in which *The Times* agreed to advance $50,000 a year for ten years to publish a twenty-volume *Dictionary of American Biography*. "I introduced the resolution proposing the undertaking," Turner proudly wrote a friend, "so it gratifies me that a donor has been found."[8] He could not attend the dinner that celebrated the publication of the first volume two years later, but his leading role was not forgotten, as letters from the celebrants testified.[9]

Turner might reveal his commitment to historical studies by sparking such diverse projects as an atlas and a biographical dictionary, but those who would measure the impact of his contributions must turn to the concepts that he popularized to realize the debt due him by the profession. When he began his career, historians believed that a single motivating force dominated each period of the past, whether the urge for democracy in the early years of the Republic or the slavery controversy in later years; attention was focused on the distant past, rather than the near-present; "scientists" believed that they could discover the absolute truth; and all were concerned with politics, to the exclusion of the social forces shaping behavior. When he ended his career, historical studies had come of age, with most of the concepts popular today generally accepted. Neither he nor any other historian was solely responsible for this revolution, but none was more influential than Turner in setting the wheels of change in motion. He, more than any scholar of his generation, helped popularize the basic beliefs that underlie today's interpretation of the past: presentism, relativism, multiple causation, and recognition of the subsurface social and economic pressures determining political behavior.

That Turner should have made his most significant contributions in the realm of the philosophy of history was ironic, for throughout his lifetime he repeatedly professed that he had no philosophy. He told a friend in 1928, "I have never formulated a philosophy of history, or of historical research."[10] Turner protested too much. Actually he was well-versed in the works of the leading authors, past and present, who speculated in that realm; his library contained well-thumbed volumes by R. Rochell, *Die Philosophie der Geschichte* (1878), Johann Gustav Droysen, *Outlines of the Principles of History* (1893), Frederick Harrison, *The Meaning of History* (1896), Charles V. Langlois and Charles Seignobis, *Introduction aux études historiques* (1898), Antonio Labriola, *Essays on the Materialistic Conception of History* (1904), Karl Lamprecht, *Moderne Geschtswissenschaft* (1905), Frederick J. Teggart, *Prolegomena to History* (1916), and a good many more. Turner was more concerned with the nature and purpose of historical studies than he was willing to admit.

His speculations, no less than his own researches, led him to two unshakable beliefs: that multiple causal forces determined each event of the past, and that society could be understood not through studying its institutional or political behavior, but by understanding the subterranean forces governing that behavior. His faith in multiple causation, borrowed early in his career from the writings of his geologist friend T. C. Chamberlin, was fundamental. "In truth," he told an audience in 1908, "there is no single key to American history. In history, as in science, we are learning that a complex result is the outcome of the interplay of many forces. Simple explanations fail to meet the case."[11] If he did not practice what he preached when he overemphasized the significance of the frontier and section, he used overemphasis as a necessary corrective, not because he believed these forces were more influential than others. "The truth is," he confessed in 1922, "that I have found it necessary to hammer pretty hard and steadily on the frontier idea to 'get it in,' as a corrective to the kind of thinking I found some thirty years ago and less."[12] This Turner regretted; in his later years he resented the association of his name with frontiering and sectionalism, and loved to dwell on the contributions he had made to other fields of history. If he had one keystone belief to sustain his historical philosophy, it was a belief in multiple causation.

From this belief stemmed another that was equally alien to the profession when he began his studies. Turner was among the first to recognize that no "fact" cited by historians was immutable, and that all varied through changing interpretation. "Each age," he wrote in his first published essay in 1891, "writes the history of the past anew with reference to the conditions uppermost in its own time." He realized, too, before most of his generation did, that "facts" were altered not only by changing intellectual climates, but by different interpreters; objectivity was a goal beyond the reach of any historian. Each was a man, "played upon by prepossessions, affected by his own experience and his own ideals, dominated—try however he may to resist them—by the influence of his nationality, by the class in which his lot is cast, by the age in which he lives."[13] This was as it should be. Because no two scholars viewed the past through the same eyes, the way was left open for their successors to correct and reconstruct—and be reconstructed. Turner was perfectly right in that judgment; not a theory or factual finding advanced in the past half century but has been revised, and re-revised—including his own.

He was no less committed to the belief that past and present were inseparably linked, the one significant only as a prelude to the other. History was important not as a device for escape into a remote age, but as an essential ingredient in man's understanding of himself and his times. Turner quoted no phrase more often than Droysen's: "History is the self-consciousness of humanity." In his eyes, historical studies underlay the informed citizenship necessary for statesmanlike public decisions, civic responsibility, and cultural progress. They were guideposts along the path to social evolution, counterbalancing revolutionary tendencies, yet pointing the way to constructive change. "The past," he told an audience in 1904, "is so stubborn a thing that much of it flows back in the old channels. History is the minister of conservative reform."[14] Turner saw society, like the cathedrals of medieval Europe, as in continuous construction by successive generations, "still in process of completion."[15] History was the architect, serving as a brake on excessive change, yet encouraging growth and alterations essential to a sound and usable structure.

Because the past's principal importance lay in its illumination of the present, historical studies should concentrate on the portions of mankind's experience that shed greatest light on current problems. Turner held no brief for eliminating the study of remote eras; even the most distant happenings of classical antiquity had some bearing on today. Yet overemphasis on earlier ages was a luxury that the world could no longer afford; conditions in former ages were so different that "lessons derived from anything but the most recent history are apt to be misleading."[16] He regretted that historians played an undue role in reconstructing the world after World War I, when economists and business leaders were better equipped to grapple with the complexities of that troubled era. This was Turner's creed, enshrined in his essays, preached over and over again to his classes. In a day when the usual

American history course ended with the close of Reconstruction, Turner brought his down to yesterday. "It is the contact with the present," he told one of his students, "which gives vitality to undergraduate instruction."[17]

His faith in the usability of the past led him to another realization: that historians had to probe the underlying social and economic forces governing mankind's behavior, not simply the political manifestations of those forces. Turner's concern was the hidden bulk of the iceberg of civilization, not the tiny portion above the surface. He saw social progress as a product of the thoughts and aspirations of the common people, acting in a commonplace way. The historian's duty was to study these ordinary folk, to investigate why they behaved as they did, and to advance approximate explanations; only then would he know how civilization marched, how it altered with the passing of the centuries, how and why governments manifested those alterations. The United States was an ideal laboratory for such an investigation, for he believed, with Achille Loria, that its brief history compressed the evolution of all society. To understand the progress of the common man in America was to understand the emergence of civilization. This, to Turner, was the essence of his chosen subject.

His life was dedicated to the search for such understanding. When he told a publisher in 1897 that the textbook he proposed to write "should give a clear elucidation of the more important lines of development of economic life, political institutions, and social ideals," he was outlining the research program that would occupy the rest of his days—as well as giving a warning that the textbook would never be written.[18] From that time on, he took every opportunity to drive home the message. In classroom lectures, in public addresses, and in essays and books, he preached the doctrine that history was not only past politics, but past economics, past sociology, past literature, past art. History, to Turner, was "the study of all the lines of human activity and social institutions in their development."[19] Understand the life of John and Jane Doe, know their thoughts and aspirations and activities, realize how and why they behaved as they did, and you will unlock the secrets of all past civilizations. That was Turner's credo.

Woe unto those who failed to join his crusade. His cruelest barbs were reserved for authors who skimmed the political surface without examining the subsurface strata, or who oversimplified the past by stressing one causal influence at the expense of others. When Turner condemned one of his contemporaries in 1897 for using only political sources, while neglecting "the vast social transformations by immigration, interstate migration, industrial development, revolution of the transportation system, and all the forces of change involved in Westward expansion," he was arguing for a broader historical perspective, not simply propagandizing for his own frontier thesis. He was doing the same thing when he castigated James Ford Rhodes[20] for overemphasizing slavery at the expense of economic growth, immigration, industrial change, and the evolution of transportation systems; all these, Turner believed, would be accorded a larger place than the slavery issue when future historians appraised mid-nineteenth century development.[21] Nor did he overstress the significance of economic forces at the expense of social ones. "The occupation of the vacant spaces of the vast interior," Turner told a class in 1915, "the economic struggles of conflicting sectional and class interests, the proposals of social reorganization, the humanitarian movements, the profound modification of American stock by new tides of European immigration, the increasing entanglement in world politics brought about by modifications in transportation, communication and commercial connections, in short, the economic and social problems of a Democratic society compelling the possession of its own land, and finding itself involved in the fortunes of Europe and of Asia—these facts may well seem to the future American historian the dominant facts of the second half of the century."[22] So they did.

His stress on underlying social and economic forces did not blind him to the realization that orderly evolutionary patterns could be upset at any time by catastrophic events or the rise of strong leaders. Personality and accident played a part in history, Turner felt, although their influence had been exaggerated by historians and biographers. Yet even here he was quick to point out that something caused the accident, and some social pressures shaped the character of the leader. The more he studied, he wrote in 1928, the more he became convinced that "much of what was regarded as 'sheer accident,' or 'fortuitous circumstances' and 'personality' was really dependent upon preparatory conditions, deep laid tendencies released by the special circumstance on man, rather than the extemporized work of accident or individual." The leader's environment, the society in which he lived, the lesser men whose support he needed, were more important than the traits with which he had been endowed.[23] Turner was too wedded to a belief in social evolution to do more than pay lip service to accident as a causal force in historical determination.

These views doomed Turner to a lifetime of research, with few visible products to show for his efforts. All the relics of mankind must be investigated—not only government documents, but church records, newspapers, magazines, novels, paintings, labor union documents, industrial reports—anything that recorded the hopes or activities of past generations. He saw the materials of history as "a great heap of fragments which must be made into a mosaic." The scholar could not examine every fragment, but he must seek out "the essential, the really typical, the vital, in the mass that lies before him."[24] In theory, this could be accomplished by intelligent sampling; Turner described his own method as one of digging deeply in spots, testing other diggings, and then trying to envisage the historical landscape without being compelled to sink wells every few inches.[25] This was a perfectly feasible technique, but for one fatal defect: he was too much of a perfectionist to stop his posthole digging until every bit of the terrain had been investigated. Turner was a glutton for data; he was even suspicious of ancient and medieval studies because they dealt with such scant materials. Once, after reading two lengthy monographs on the settlement of Missouri and Illinois, he wrote that "when we get similar studies of all the western states" the evolution of societies and institutions there would be better understood.[26] Turner's standards were so high, his sense of perfectionism so demanding, that he never could write history as he knew it must be written.

Despite his own inadequacies, he did prod the profession into a far more sophisticated technique of historical analysis than it had known before his day. He also helped revitalize the study of local history. Properly performed, he believed, investigations on the town, county, and state level would provide historians with the many stones needed to fashion the mosaic of the past. Turner saw the fragments of information dredged out by antiquarians as comparable to the tiny rocks from which geologists deduced important generalizations; as the rocks revealed the evolutionary forces that created the earth, so local records revealed the social forces that shaped society. An item of local history was to Turner a specimen that told its own story, and fitted into the larger picture as well.[27]

Important as such information was, it was only a prelude to the next and most important step the historian must take: the analysis and interpretation that was the essence of history. Turner thoroughly respected narration; he was an ardent admirer of Francis Parkman, whose works he read and regularly assigned to his students. Yet he recognized his own deficiencies as a narrative historian and believed that he, and others less gifted than Parkman, could make their greatest contribution by distilling meaning from the data gathered by researchers. This was the message he preached to his students; "take courage and go ahead," he told one, "seeking the goal of interpretation as well as the facts."[28] Turner followed his own advice. His books and more serious essays, although based on excessive accumulations of data, were also sparked with fresh explanations, most of them commonplace today, but new in their time. "That is the difference between you and me," Max Farrand told him on one occasion. "You have to get your larger and more original point of view. I am content to do what is within my more limited powers."[29]

Gifted as he was in extracting meaning from the past, Turner carefully guarded himself against the cardinal sin of his profession in those days—the danger of over-generalization. This was a tempting bypath; historians thought of themselves as exact scientists and saw no reason why they should not postulate laws of human behavior, just as physical scientists were laying down laws that explained the behavior of the universe. To his credit, Turner refused to succumb to this temptation, for he was wise enough to realize that human conduct was too erratic to sustain predictions. "The human soul is too complex," he told an audience in 1904, "human society too full of vital energy and incessant change, to enable us to pluck out the heart of its mystery—to reduce it to the lines of an exact science or to state human development in terms of an equation."[30] This was good sense. Turner was prone to reckless generalizations when he spoke to popular audiences on the frontier thesis, but when he donned the cloak of the scholar he set a worthy example for his generation.

To sum up his historical beliefs is to realize that he could rub elbows with historians of today without feeling more than slightly outdated.

They would honor him for nursing into reality such useful tools as the *Atlas of the Historical Geography of the United States* and the *Dictionary of American Biography.* They would applaud his belief in multiple causation and his faith in the doctrine of relativism. They would agree with him that the past should be studied to illuminate the present, and that those aspects most useful in understanding modern society deserved greatest emphasis. They would accept his dictum that history was far more than past politics and could be understood only by comprehending the subsurface social and economic currents that shaped political events. They would acknowledge him correct when he cautioned against postulating laws of human behavior. Turner, clearly, outdistanced most of his contemporaries in embracing views considered modern by today's professional fraternity. As a pioneer in popularizing those views, he performed a service respected in his day, but largely forgotten since. Viewed in this light, rather than solely as the father of the sectional and frontier interpretations, Frederick Jackson Turner's significance in American historiography is far greater than his successors have generally realized.

He earned this position because he was one of the few scholars who preached what he practiced. Turner was no narrow specialist, absorbed exclusively in the history of frontier and section. Most of his published essays, it is true, were built on those themes, but he spoke the truth when he pointed out to a friend that "my studies for my college classes and in general have taken a wider scope."[31] Turner's interest was in *all* American history, not any one part. He read constantly, widely, voluminously. Late in his career, when asked to evaluate some fifty books on history that had appeared during the preceding two decades, he reported that he was familiar with all but three, and proved his point by summarizing the merits and defects of each. Again in 1923, when he was called on for a list of the most important recent books on the American past, he was able to name two dozen that he had purchased and read, including such diverse fare as Arthur M. Schlesinger's *New Viewpoints in American History*, James Truslow Adams's *Founding of New England*, John S. Bassett's *Andrew Jackson*, Frederic L. Paxson's *Recent History of the United States*, and James Harvey Robinson's *Mind in the Making*.[32] Turner was interested in *everything* about the past, not in any small segment.

Thumbing the thirty-four commodious file drawers of reading notes that he accumulated before his death makes that clear. Here was no evidence of specialization; every phase of the past, from Christopher Columbus to Herbert Hoover, excited his interest and inspired pages of notes, ending with a sheet or two filled with his conclusions and interpretations. He read on the origins of New England towns, and the Great Awakening, and the laws of trade and navigation, and the military campaigns of the Revolution, and the causes of the War of 1812, and the Mexican War, and Reconstruction, and the Free Silver issue, and Progressivism, and the Venezuela Affair, and the diplomatic background of the Washington Conference of 1922. When Turner spent three class periods proving to the Harvard students in History 17 that Justin H. Smith's conclusions on the origins of the Mexican War were largely wrong, he was simply demonstrating the breadth, not the depth, of his learning.[33] He could have discussed most topics in his nation's history with as much knowledge and good sense as he displayed on that occasion.

Nor was Turner's study of the past dictated by idle curiosity alone. His students, he felt, deserved not textbook pabulum, but the sophisticated treatment that only intense study could provide. And, more important, he found all aspects of the past so fascinating that the urge to investigate each in detail was irresistible. At the height of his career he had irons in so many fires that his colleagues chided him with being a "historical trust magnate" who would leave them nothing to do when he published the results of all his investigations. This Turner cheerfully admitted. "My craft goes tramping about so many ports that I feel unable to chart out a sailing route," he confessed to Max Farrand in 1909. Yet he was unwilling to relinquish any of his staked claims. "Until my studies go farther I can't be sure that it would be wise for me to eliminate any period into which I may need to go in the development of my bent."[34] Nor did that urge for universal knowledge abate. "I sometimes wonder," he told Carl Becker, late in his life, "if after all I have not been simply, rather blindly, trying to explain American history to myself instead of writing history!"[35] That was the story of Turner's life.

Nowhere was his catholicity of interest better shown than in the topics studied by his graduate students. Not one of the dozens he trained produced a dissertation that included the word "frontier" in its title; instead, they investigated economic, social, political, cultural, and diplomatic problems in bewildering variety. Their subjects ranged, chronologically, from the study of primitive Indian tribes to the efforts of post-World War I governments to solve labor problems; geographically from the Atlantic to the Pacific and into Latin America. Once, in a reminiscent mood, Turner jotted down the names of those who specialized in agricultural history (fifteen students), the history of public lands (seven), the history of transportation (six), commerce and internal trade (two), literature and thought (two), religion (three), political history (seventeen), diplomacy (ten), and the history of immigration (seven).[36] "They help explain," he wrote, "how the life of the teacher of graduate students checks his own historical output, but furnishes compensations."[37]

Not only his students', but his own writings and speculations added significantly to knowledge in a number of fields not usually associated with his name. In several he served as a pioneer, plowing new ground and suggesting to his colleagues that here was a field worth cultivating. In all, his germinal ideas stimulated progress, even though his own contribution was slight. Those who reaped the harvest recognized this and acknowledged his leadership; during his lifetime he was glorified by agricultural historians, social historians, urban historians, diplomatic historians, and economic historians as the pioneer who had led them into new areas worthy of exploitation. To understand Turner's significance in American history, one must appraise his impact on these varied fields of learning.

His venture into diplomatic history, early in his career, was a byproduct of his frontier studies; while investigating the peopling of the Southwest during the late eighteenth century he awakened to the superficiality of the books dealing with English–French–American relations. They were inadequate, he realized, because they failed to weigh the forces shaping diplomatic decision-making, particularly those generated along the southern frontier. "I found it necessary," he later remembered, "to go behind the diplomat and the treaties of annexation to the frontier forces and sectional interests."[38] Here was a new approach to diplomatic history—built on the sensible realization that negotiations could not be understood without understanding the forces operating on the negotiators—that was to revolutionize investigation in that field. Just as innovative was Turner's use of documents from

French, Spanish, and British archives; Henry Adams had pioneered in emphasizing foreign sources, but Turner added further proof that they could not be ignored. "It necessitates the rewriting of the diplomatic history of that period," wrote a prominent historian, after reading one of his articles.[39]

That was a fair judgment by a peer. Turner was, to his contemporaries, a diplomatic historian, worthy of all the honors their profession could bestow. In 1903 he was invited to deliver the annual lectures on diplomatic history before the Naval War College at Newport, and did so with success. Twice, in 1906 and 1907, he was asked to give the prestigious Albert Shaw Lectures in Diplomatic History at the Johns Hopkins University, a series that attracted the most eminent students of foreign affairs. Turner refused, despite the lure of a $250 fee for ten lectures, because he felt that he had strayed far from the field and "hardly dare to trust myself to get into the fascinating web again," but the invitations suggest the high esteem in which he was held.[40] So does a proposal made by Samuel F. Bemis, many years later, that Turner prepare the biographical sketches of James Monroe and Daniel Webster for the multi-volume series on the secretaries of state that he was editing. Again Turner declined, but once more the invitation indicates his reputation as a diplomatic historian among those who knew him best.[41]

His contributions to the study of immigration history were only slightly less significant. When he began his investigations at the turn of the century, no subject was less understood; its students were a handful of sociologists who confined themselves to cataloging the evil results of immigration and compiling statistics on the increase in crime, intemperance, and poverty in areas tainted by the newcomers. Turner did not erase that picture, but he did pioneer a more reasonable—and more accurate—understanding of the contributions of immigrants to the national culture. This was a viewpoint that emerged slowly, and largely as a result of his studies. In his early writings, he was inclined to view westward expansion as a product of Anglo-American superiority and to pay little attention to the impact made by later arrivals on the economy and culture. The series of essays on immigration that Turner wrote for the *Chicago Record-Herald* in 1901—"pot-boilers," he called them—mirrored the racial prejudice of that day and gave newcomers a negative mark when weighed against Anglo-Americans. At this stage of his career he was less bigoted than most of his contemporaries, although he still had much to learn.

Yet even at this time he broke with traditionalism, and the gulf steadily widened. His 1901 essays laid down guidelines for future immigration historians: they should investigate the origins of migration in Europe, the impact on European nations of the exodus, the interaction between environmental and ethnic factors in the process of acculturation, the varying abilities of racial types to achieve integration into American society. These were valuable hints, and they helped shape the course of immigration studies. So was Turner's calm analysis of the "extravagant apprehensions" of nativists, who feared the submersion of native stocks beneath the immigrant tide. By the 1910s he was convinced that American democracy and culture were not solely a product of the Anglo-Saxon heritage, but had been enriched by the mingling of peoples from differing backgrounds. "The reaction of these various stocks," Turner wrote in his last book, "with their different habits, morals and religious doctrines, and ideals, upon one another, led to cross-fertilization and the evolution of a profoundly modified society."[42]

As was usual, however, Turner's most significant contribution to immigration history was made not in his own sparse writings on the subject, but through the students he led into the field. His first doctoral candidate, Kate A. Everest, blazed the trail with her study of German migration to Wisconsin, and blazed it so successfully that Turner repeatedly tried to convince others to follow. "The field of immigration offers an excellent opportunity," he told one student as early as 1902, pointing out that it would be necessary to study in Italy or eastern Europe, to understand the forces inducing emigration, and in the United States, to trace the social, economic, and political progress of the newcomers. Twenty years later Turner was still proselytizing: "there is," he assured a student in 1926, "an opportunity to make a national, indeed international, reputation in the history of immigration to the United States."[43] These were tempting inducements, but the expense of foreign travel and the lack of academic interest in immigration history discouraged all but the most dedicated. In the end, Turner trained only three doctoral students in the subject: Kate A. Everest, George M. Stephenson, and Marcus Lee Hansen.

Miss Everest's contributions were minimal, and those of George Stephenson more traditional than inspirational, but in Marcus Hansen

Turner found a disciple worthy of the master. Hansen's doctoral thesis, presented in 1924, mirrored Turner's own views in its skillful handling of "Emigration from Continental Europe, 1815–1860, with Special Reference to the United States." That emigration, the author argued in the best Turnerian fashion, was simply a continuation of the exodus that had begun in the sixteenth century, and could be understood only in terms of the expelling forces operating on the Continent. Too much had been made of differences between the "Old Immigration," from northern and western Europe, and the "New Immigration," from southern and eastern; both were part of a centuries-old migration pattern that had peopled the United States, bolstered its economy, and enriched its culture. Hansen's findings only footnoted conclusions long held by Turner, but they were revolutionary for that day. So Turner recognized as he set to work to win his young disciple a fellowship for a year's study in Europe before converting his dissertation into a book.[44]

If Hansen had had his way, he would have hoarded his findings until they could be used in the several books that he planned to write. Fortunately, Turner had other ideas. He insisted that Hansen prepare an essay at once on "Immigration History as a Field for Research," to waken the profession to the possibilities of immigration studies. Hansen was less sure. Why should he attract others into a field that he found so profitable? That dog-in-the-manger attitude Turner would not tolerate. "The college instructor," he lectured, "finds a part of his pleasure in letting down the bars, in this revelation of what is behind them; and in these indications of how to get at the grass." Moreover, there was room for any number of researchers in immigration history, and such a paper would clarify its author's own thinking, let him survey his materials as a whole, and allow him to develop new hypotheses.[45] Turner was right. The article, published in the *American Historical Review* early in 1927, launched the modern study of immigration history and won its author distinction as a pioneer in a new era of historical research.

It did not, however, win him a job, for Hansen and Turner were to find that few universities shared their enthusiasm for the study of migration. This Turner was determined to change, even though he foresaw the difficulties. "If Chicago, or Illinois, or Minnesota, or Iowa or Wisconsin could only realize the opportunities in such a field," he wrote, "it would be a great thing—but institutions do not as a rule have the constructive imagination."[46] His best chance was to convert one of the midwestern universities, which he felt to be less tradition-bound than those in the East, and long after his retirement he labored to convince his friends there of the merits of immigration history and Marcus Lee Hansen. Even the Huntington was asked to add Hansen to its staff as a research associate; "there is opportunity here," Turner told the director, "for opening a valuable field on the composition of the American people."[47] Eventually a post was located at the University of Illinois, and there Hansen spent the few years until his untimely death, in 1938, as the nation's premier instructor in immigration history. The lusty growth of that discipline during the next decades obscured his pioneering efforts, but the fact remains that the serious study of migration began with this disciple of Turner, under Turner's guidance and inspiration.

Turner also had a slight claim—less valid, perhaps—to the designation of pioneer in the larger field of economic history. Here he was free to admit that his interest in the rural past prejudiced him against the urban-industrial studies that were gaining in popularity in the twentieth century. "One whose activity has been more continuously in an urban environment," Turner wrote in 1922, "would no doubt lay more stress than I have in my published essays on the importance of the economic revolution substantively."[48] This was too modest a self-appraisal. Turner's search for causal forces led him inevitably into investigation of the economic influences that underlay political behavior, at the same time awakening him to awareness of their importance. As early as 1892 he warned his fellow craftsmen that "very often, the cause of great political events, and great social movements, is economic, and has hitherto been undetected."[49] This was Turner's own discovery; he borrowed little from English and German theorists, although he did rely on the works of J. T. T. Rogers, a British pioneer. Instead, he was one of a little group of social scientists at the University of Wisconsin —among them Lester Ward, Richard T. Ely, and John R. Commons— who were the first to recognize that society rested on an economic base and to redirect attention from surface political manifestations to materialistic causes and motives. Of this group, Turner and Commons went further than the others in integrating economics with history.

The results were less than spectacular in Turner's case, for few of his theories were translated into the written essays that would influence his contemporaries. Yet they recognized that something unusual was happening in Madison, and that students trained in Turner's seminars were better versed in economic theory and more aware of the role of economics in shaping public policies than those trained elsewhere. When Charles A. Beard, later to be credited with originating the economic interpretation of American history, wrote, as he did in 1913, that "almost the only work in economic interpretation which has been done in the United States seems to have been inspired at the University of Wisconsin by Professor Turner," he was simply recognizing something known to his generation, but forgotten since.[50] Turner was not the first to realize the significance of economic forces, but he was among the first in America to do so. Beard was perfectly right when he wrote in 1928 that "Mr. Turner deserves everlasting credit for his services as the leader in restoring the consideration of economic facts to historical writing in America."[51]

Nor was Turner, as his latter-day critics often charged, blind to the importance of a Marxian type of class struggle in American history. Turner read widely on the subject and was familiar with the Marxian interpretation; one of the most heavily underlined books in his library was Antonio Labriola's *Essays on the Materialistic Conceptions of History*, published in 1904 to plead the socialist cause. He realized, however, that class conflicts in the United States were a by-product of industrialization, and played a lesser role than sectional divisions in the rural era that was his concern. In 1908 Turner spoke of the "steady stratification of our society by the development of contesting social classes," but he also pointed out that only in very recent times was it possible "to use the words proletariat and capitalistic classes in reference to American conditions."[52] Turner's detractors, with their ex-post-facto approach to industrialism, failed to appreciate this. They also were unaware of the fact that his students were told that the contest between "the capitalist and the democratic pioneer" was a fundamental fact of the nation's past from early colonial days onward. By both recognizing the role of class conflict in history and refusing to exaggerate its importance, Turner came nearer the truth than some of his critics. He was also correct when he reiterated, as he did time and time again in his letters, that he was not an "economic determinist." With an unshakable belief in multiple causation, Turner scorned overemphasis on any one causal force, even one as persuasive as economics. "I tried," he confessed in 1928, "to keep the relations steadily in mind; but it isn't an easy job, and the effort is sometimes conducive to unwritten books."[53] Turner, to his credit, did "keep the relations steadily in mind," and he refused to succumb to the belief that any one force, whether geographic or idealistic or economic, was deterministic.

If his concern with subsurface influences on political behavior made Turner a pioneer among economic historians, it also assured him a place as a trailblazer in the field of social and intellectual history. To him man was the product of social forces, no less than economic, governed always by ideals, cultural aspirations, and relationships with his fellow-men. Turner awakened to that viewpoint with the beginning of his investigations, but not until he prepared the section on social history for the American Historical Association's Committee on Documentary Historical Publication in 1908 did he realize the woeful lack of publication in that field. "One of the most serious gaps in American historical writing," he wrote that year, "is that of accounts of the social thought of the country." This, he was convinced, would be the next important field of investigation cultivated by scholars. "Thank God," he told a friend, "there will be something left for the next generation of historical seekers!"[54]

That "next generation" showed little inclination to leap on the social history bandwagon; not until a quarter-century later did Arthur Meier Schlesinger and Merle Curti (both ardent admirers of Turner) pioneer that new discipline. Turner filled those years with persistent tub-thumping for the subject. More and more social history materials were larded into his lectures; when one of his former students introduced a course in social history at the University of Illinois, he confessed to Turner, "you might initiate some sort of action, if you knew how heavily I was drawing on your writings and suggestions for the back-bone of the course."[55] Every occasion was used to urge investigation into social and intellectual problems. In 1919, when he was asked to suggest programs that might be supported by the Commonwealth Fund, Turner proposed not only "The Formation of Classes and Class Contests" and "The Natural History of Political Parties," but also "American Ideals as Expressed in Literature, Periodicals, Newspapers," "The Study of Common and Higher Education," "The Church Studied as an Expanding Social Institution," and "The Role of the Oriental, Negro, and Indian in American Society." "American history and American literature cannot be understood apart from each other," he wrote in 1923, adding, a year later, that "a valuable study might be made of the pioneer woman and her place in history."[56] One article, published in 1931, contained such an abundance of social history that a friend believed it would convince the profession that "there is little indeed that is new in the gospel of social intellectual history" then being trumpeted by younger scholars.[57]

Turner's concern with social history was a natural by-product of his own probing into the subsurface forces influencing political behavior. His interest in urban history was less clearly related to his own investigations. Yet, throughout his academic lifetime, Turner saw the city as a major force in American life and worthy of far more attention than it was receiving from historians. As early as 1895, when he addressed the graduating seniors of the Madison High School on "The High School and the City," he could picture the center of national power and culture shifting from the country to cities with the passing of the frontier, and urge his young listeners to change their interest from the rural past to the urban future. "As wealth accumulates as Americans cease their feverish rush for exploiting the country," Turner predicted, "and begin looking for means of life as well as means of livelihood, they will more and more combine their activities to make the city a worthier place."[58] These were strange words for a nineteenth-century historian. They forecast an interest in a phase of history that was not even to be defined for a half-century.

Unfortunately, his reading and speculation on urban history was confined to satisfying his own curiosity or enlightening his classes. Turner's focus, naturally, was on the emergence of western cities and their role in the expansion process. On this subject he read widely, filling a thick folder with enough research notes to prepare a respectable book on western urbanization. Perhaps Turner planned such a book at one time; tucked away in his files was an outline on "The Significance of Western Cities, 1820-1830," that listed such topics to be treated as "Nuclei of Regions," "Centers of Dispersion and Collection," "Markets, Local and Internal Commerce," "Infant Industries and Home Market," and "Intellectual, etc. Influence."[59] That book was never written, but Turner's classes heard a great deal about the importance of western cities. "Study the way in which these cities grew," he urged his students in 1902, "what economic force particularly worked upon them; how they became the metropolis of the particular region in which each of them was located, and how they reacted, in turn, upon the area." Such studies would illuminate not only the story of expansion but the entire history of the United States.[60] This was a bold message for the turn of the century.

Nor was Turner's concern only with western cities. In his later years, particularly, he recognized that future historians would find in urban history the same fascination that his own generation had found in frontier history: "there seems likely to be," he wrote in 1925, "an urban reinterpretation of our history."[61] Once, when progress on THE BOOK was discouragingly slow, Turner went so far as to begin an essay on "The Significance of the City in American History." Typically, this progressed no further than a scant outline and notes, but even those fragments suggest the direction of his thinking: "When and how and why did cities become densely populated. . . . How did urban (including alien) ideas, interests and ideals react on frontier and section. . . . Extent to which the cities were built up by movement from interior rural areas to city. . . . Include editors, teachers, preachers, etc. . . . Its counter influence in modifying frontier and sectional traits."[62] That essay, if it ever had been written, might have set the pattern for urban studies, just as his 1893 essay laid down the guidelines for frontier studies.

Turner's interest in urban history—and social history and economic history and diplomatic history and every other kind of history—was unusual, but not surprising. Once he formulated the basic premise of his historical philosophy—that the past could be understood only by analyzing the social and economic forces that shaped political behavior—he was committed to investigating *every* form of human thought and activity. Turner saw man as a puppet, manipulated by a complex of strings, each representing one of the hundreds of forces—social, economic, idealistic, political, religious, cultural—that operated in combination to control his thought and action. His goal was to understand each of those strings and its relation to all the others. That goal was unobtainable, as Turner found when he tried in THE BOOK to interpret even the two decades between 1830 and 1850, but his striving gave him the breadth of knowledge and the universality of historical experience that won him the respect of his peers.

It also decreed him fame as the historical profession's pioneering crusader for interdisciplinary studies. This, too, was the inevitable result of his view of history. Anyone who sought to master the totality of the human experience had to use not one, but a whole trunkful of tools, borrowed from economists, political scientists, sociologists, demographers, anthropologists, geographers, statisticians, psychologists, and all the rest. Turner used them all, many for the first time, so effectively that his friends in the profession sometimes wondered whether he had deserted them entirely. This made no difference to Turner. He was delighted when he overheard a Harvard undergraduate remark that what Turner was doing in the classroom "might be all right, but it wasn't history." He would willingly be branded a sociologist or an economist or a geographer, as he was on occasion, if that label helped him understand the past. "It is the subject that I am interested in," he told a friend, "and I don't particularly care what name I bear." Nor did he. "I am," he wrote in an undelivered lecture, "one of those who believes in breaking line fences, even at the risk of arrest for trespass, or disclosure of being an amateur, or something worse, breaking into the professional's game."[63]

This was the message that Turner preached to his students and colleagues. Underlying his faith in an interdisciplinary methodology were two basic assumptions. One was his recognition that history was the core subject of the social sciences, and hence the most essential of all to understanding human behavior. Others, such as political science and sociology, had splintered from it, but history would always remain the sum total of the parts into which it had divided. The historical scholar, Turner told the Wisconsin Graduate Club in 1897, must draw his data and techniques from these branches, just as from the main stem.[64] Turner's other basic assumption was that, while history was a complex of social sciences, all the social sciences were one, all part of the whole.[65] "The conception of the One-ness of the thing," as he put it to Carl Becker, was forever in his mind. "I have always," he wrote in 1928, "regarded the interdependence of all the social sciences as fundamentally important and, while I realize that there must be also a division of labor, I think that the division has been so sharply made in the past that there has been a loss to students . . . from the water-tight compartments in which the social sciences have previously been divided."[66] Turner saw history as the mother of the social sciences, and he believed that history's destiny was to unite the scattered family for the benefit of all.

He must, then, convince his fellow craftsmen that this was their duty, and his sermons on the value of the interdisciplinary approach were delivered often. His 1904 address at the St. Louis Exposition, on "Problems in American History," laid down the ground rules more specifically than had his 1892 paper under the same title: "data drawn from studies of literature and art, politics, economics, sociology, psychology, biology, and physiography, all must be used. . . . Without the combined effort of allied sciences we shall reach no such results in the study of social development as have been achieved in the physical world by the attack on problems of natural science by the combined forces of physics, chemistry, and mathematics."[67] Again, in his presidential address before the American Historical Association, Turner returned to the theme—the first president of the Association to do so. One of his last professional acts when joining the Huntington library staff in 1927 was to urge the director to buy books in all the social sciences. "We need allied workers, and allied books," Turner pleaded, "just as the astronomer needs the co-operation of chemist, physicist, geologist, in his work in deciphering the meaning of the universe."[68]

Dedicated evangelist that he was, Turner saw to it that his own researches utilized every possible tool, whatever its label. The nature of those investigations meant that he would lower the barriers between history and geography and history and statistics, particularly the former. This he did so successfully with his use of physiographic data and map-drawing techniques that he was hailed by geographers as one of their own. Turner's occasional addresses before geographic societies were notable affairs; when he spoke before a joint meeting of two of the leading associations in 1914, his talk was hailed as the hit of the session and one of the most stimulating ever presented. "Your work," he was assured, "is so sympathetic with respect to geographic factors that it is a pity we do not see more of you and hear a paper every year."[69] He was made a member of the Association of American Geographers—an honor restricted to about one hundred of the most significant contributors to the field—and a Fellow of the American Geographical Society. His passing was mourned by them as sincerely as by historians. "Professor Turner," recorded the *Geographical Review*, "was a rare combination of historical originality with geographical insight. His death is a loss no less severe to American geography than to the study of American history."

He was only slightly less successful in trampling the line fence separating history and statistics. His sectional studies, requiring as they did the analysis of voting patterns, forced Turner to pioneer the empirical investigation of human behavior on the basis of mass data; he was the first historian to attempt a quantitative study of political motivation. He was also the first to employ statistical techniques to establish correlations between economic activity and politics; thus his figures demonstrated the relationship between support for high tariffs and the concentration of wool production in certain areas. The tables and charts used to authenticate his conclusions seem overly simple to today's statisticians, just as the maps that he used to establish correlations between physiographic conditions, economic activity, and political preferences seem overly complex, yet to his own generation they were marvels of ingenuity. Statisticians glorified him, just as geographers did. When the American Statistical Society sought a speaker to celebrate its seventy-fifth anniversary in 1913, Turner was the one selected—"No one," the president assured him, "is better qualified to speak on this subject from the point of view of the historian than you are." When, a decade later, a book was planned on the inter-relationship of the social sciences, Turner was the logical choice for the essay on the connections between history and statistics.[70] He declined both invitations, but the fact remains that contemporaries in both camps saw him as the premier historical expert in the use of statistical techniques.

Geography and statistics might have been most useful to Turner, but political science and sociology were also appropriated for his toolbag, and in both disciplines he won respect and imitators. Political scientists were so impressed with his systems of election analysis that they paid him the tribute of adopting them for their own use; such distinguished students of government as Frederick Ogg, Paul Reinsch, Arthur Holcombe, and Wilfred Binkley acknowledged that the techniques that won them their reputations were borrowed from Turner. Sociologists were always eager to welcome Turner to their meetings and applaud his findings. "Without so describing himself," wrote the dean of that discipline, Franklin H. Giddings, "he is a sound sociologist, and a ground breaking one of first rate importance."[71] Turner was that rare being who ranged so far beyond his own specialty that he could rub elbows with geographers, cartographers, statisticians, political scientists, economists, and sociologists, and feel as much at home among them as he would at a gathering of the American Historical Association.

Therein lay the measure of his greatness. It has been his misfortune to be labeled by later generations as a monocausationist, riding his hobby-horses of frontier and section, and ignoring the broader historical currents that emerged from the industrial-urban world of the twentieth century. No judgment could be more false. Turner, more than any scholar of his generation, recognized the complexity of the historical process and the need of employing every tool available to understand its every facet. He emphasized—even overemphasized—his own special fields of interest, but his fertile mind illuminated every phase of the past, and his research techniques provided colleagues with the methodology that would bring them closer to the truth. The boldness of his imagination gave his fellow craftsmen stately new edifices to build, and the tools with which to build them. Avery Craven, his friend and admirer, summed up the judgment of Turner's contemporaries when he told the mourners who had gathered to memorialize their friend's departure: "He is claimed by the historians, the sociologists and the geographers and yet he was more than any of these. He was a student of the whole field of social sciences and more than any other man I have ever come in touch with, saw the field as one and was able to integrate it."[72] Turner would have loved that epitaph.

NOTES

Chapter I
From Boyhood to Manhood
1861-1884

1. *Turner Family Magazine*, I (Jan. 1916), and *Turner Genealogy, 1628-1919* (n.p., n.d.), 1-7, Frederick Jackson Turner Papers, Henry E. Huntington Library and Art Gallery, TU Box 62 (hereafter cited as HEH TU). See also HEH TU Box K.

2. For Andrew Jackson Turner's reminiscences of his boyhood and early life, see *Portage Daily Register*, July 11, 1891, and letter to his son, Aug. 21, 1878 (HEH TU Box A). For a brief biographical sketch, see *Wisconsin State Register*, Sept. 25, 1880. More complete is Donald J. Berthrong, "Andrew Jackson Turner, Workhorse of the Republican Party," *Wisconsin Magazine of History*, XXXVIII (Winter 1954), 77-86.

3. Turner to Constance L. Skinner, March 15, 1922, HEH TU Box 31; "Notes for Talk to Harvard History Club, April 24, 1924," HEH TU Box 56.

4. Census Office, *Population of the United States in 1860; Compiled from the Original Returns of the Eighth Census* (Washington, D.C., 1864), 527; James S. Ritchie, *Wisconsin and Its Resources* (3rd ed., Chicago, 1858), 132.

5. For a historical sketch of Portage, see *Portage Democrat*, Aug. 31, 1894. See also John W. Hunt, *Wisconsin Gazeteer* (Madison, 1853), 177-78, and *A History of Columbia County* (Chicago, 1880). Items in *Wisconsin State Register* and *Portage Democrat*, too numerous to be cited, provide information on life in the city.

6. *Wisconsin State Register*, Nov. 23, 1861.

7. Mary O. Turner to "Dear Sister Martha," Jan. 22, 1862, HEH TU Box A; F. J. Turner to Caroline Mae Sherwood (hereafter "Mae Sherwood," the name used by Turner), May 9, 1888, HEH TU Box C.

8. This picture of life in Portage reconstructed from files of *Wisconsin State Register*, 1861-80.

9. Ibid. Nov. 22, Dec. 9, 1873. The paper listed forty members of the "Young Fogies," including "Fred Turner."

10. *Portage Democrat,* Oct. 26, 1877.

11. Scrapbook, HEH TU Box 62. Columns in *Wisconsin State Register,* Jan.–Feb. 1878.

12. Loa K. Mausolff to Turner, Nov. 10, 1929, HEH TU Box 42. The *Wisconsin State Register* regularly published high school records.

13. *Wisconsin State Register,* June 22, July 6, 1878.

14. *Wisconsin State Register,* May 23, 1868.

15. Turner to Mae Sherwood, June 15, 1887, HEH TU Box A.

16. *Wisconsin State Register,* June 5, 1875.

17. An appraisal of A. J. Turner's legislative career, taken from the *Milwaukee Journal,* was reprinted in *Wisconsin State Register,* Dec. 26, 1885.

18. Ibid.

19. Ibid. March 11, Aug. 12, 1871; March 16, 23, 1872; Aug. 24, 1899. Berthrong, "Andrew Jackson Turner," 85-86. Turner, "A Talk to a Local Woman's Club," HEH TU Box IV, is on the history of Portage.

20. Turner to Constance L. Skinner, March 15, 1922, HEH TU Box 31.

21. Turner to Mae Sherwood, Sept. 7, 1888, HEH TU Box C.

22. Turner to Joseph Schafer, Oct. 13, 1931. Joseph Schafer Papers, State Historical Society of Wisconsin, MSS IL (hereafter cited as SHSW, Schafer Papers).

23. Turner to F. J. Turner, Feb. 6, 1887, HEH TU Box A.

24. A. J. Turner, letter to *Wisconsin State Register,* June 15, 1867. That journal, Aug. 26, 1865, printed a two-column account by A. J. Turner of "A Trip to the Trout Brooks."

25. Ibid. July 3, 1884; Turner to Mae Sherwood, May 20, 1888, HEH TU Box C.

26. *Wisconsin State Register,* Sept. 18, 25, Oct. 2, 1869.

27. In 1877, and again in 1879, A. J. Turner visited the pineries in connection with land speculations, taking young Fred along. For his printed accounts of these expeditions, see *Wisconsin State Register,* July 28, 1877, July 5, 1879.

28. The *Wisconsin State Register* for 1873 describes in detail the removal of the Indians. See James E. Jones, *A History of Columbia County, Wisconsin* (2 vols., Chicago, 1914), I, 29-31.

29. Turner to Carl Becker, Dec. 16, 1925, HEH TU Box 34A.

30. Ibid. For statistics on ethnic groups in Columbia County, see Census Office, *Statistics of the Population of the United States at the Tenth Census (June 1, 1880). Vol. I* (Washington, D.C., 1883), 446, 534-35.

31. Turner to Mae Sherwood, Sept. 5, 1887, HEH TU Box B.

32. A. J. Turner to Turner, Aug. 21, 1878, HEH TU Box B. In his later years F. J. Turner attached a note to this letter, telling something of his father's boyhood, and adding: "a beautiful example of a tactful parting admonition to a son about to go to college."

33. Frederick Jackson Turner Transcript, University of Wisconsin, University of Wisconsin Archives, Frederick Jackson Turner Miscellaneous File (hereafter cited as U. of Wis. Arch., Turner Misc. File).

34. See *Wisconsin State Register,* Aug. 1879–May 1880.

35. Turner, Commonplace Book, 1881, HEH TU Vol. III (1).

36. *Wisconsin State Register*, April 30, 1881; *University Press*, April 30, 1881.

37. President Bascom's speech is in *The Campus*, Oct. 6, 1881, 6. For the state of college education at the time, see Lawrence R. Veysey, *The Emergence of the American University* (Chicago, 1966), 23-30.

38. *The Badger*, Dec. 7, 1882; Sept. 8, 1883; *University Press*, Jan. 5, 1884.

39. *Wisconsin State Journal*, Sept. 10, Dec. 3, 1881, Jan. 23, 1882. At the back of his Commonplace Book, 1881, Turner listed the concerts, plays, and lectures he enjoyed during the year [HEH TU Vol. III (1)]. *The Badger*, Feb. 23, 1882, 8, notes his trip to Chicago to see a play. For a program of *Othello* which Turner attended in Milwaukee, March 26, 1883, see HEH TU Box 59.

40. *University Press*, Sept. 16, 1882, 5, and *The Badger*, Sept. 30, 1882, 5, describe Turner's election to the Board.

41. Turner, Commonplace Book, 1881, HEH TU Vol. III (1).

42. Turner's speech, *Wisconsin State Journal*, Dec. 1, 1882.

43. *The Campus*, Oct. 6, 13, 1881; *The Badger*, June 23, 1883. For Turner's undergraduate journalistic career, see Fulmer Mood, "Frederick Jackson Turner and the Milwaukee *Sentinel*, 1884," *Wisconsin Magazine of History*, XXXIV (Autumn 1950), 21-28.

44. *University Press*, Nov. 11, 1880.

45. For a history of the university's literary societies, see *Trochos* (April 1884), 72-89; *The Badger*, Jan. 12, May 10, June 15, 1883.

46. For origins of this oration, see Turner, Commonplace Book, 1881, HEH TU Vol. III (1).

47. Turner, oration text, *Wisconsin State Journal*, May 19, 1883; *University Press*, May 26, 1883; *The Badger*, May 24, 1883.

48. Turner listed the books he read in 1881 and 1882 [Commonplace Book, 1881, HEH TU Vol. III (1)].

49. The university recognized three types of "special students": those with inadequate background, those who wished to enter a professional course and needed preparatory training, and those who could not keep up with their regular classes. Turner fitted only the first of these categories (*University Press*, Dec. 27, 1878, *The Aegis*, Sept. 23, 1887).

50. "Frederick Jackson Turner Transcript, University of Wisconsin," U. of Wis. Arch., Turner Misc. File.

51. Turner to Carl Becker, Oct. 26, 1920, HEH TU Box 30.

52. For Allen's teaching methods, see Allen to Herbert B. Adams, Aug. 8, 1886, W. Stull Holt (ed.), *Historical Scholarship in the United States, 1876-1901: as Revealed in the Correspondence of Herbert B. Adams* (Baltimore, 1938), 88; Allen, *University Press*, Feb. 10, 1883; Allen, "Gradation and Topical Method of Historical Study," in G. Stanley Hall (ed.), *Methods of Teaching History* (Boston, 1884), 251-56. Owen G. Stearns, "William Francis Allen: Wisconsin's First Historian," M.A. Thesis (unpubl.), Univ. of Wisconsin, 1955, has been kindly loaned me by the author.

53. Quoted in David B. Frankenburger biographical sketch, William F. Allen, *Essays and Monographs by William Francis Allen: Memorial Volume* (Boston, 1890), 13. For Allen's views on history, see his "The Study of History," *University Press*, Feb. 17, March 2, 16, April 1, 16, May 1, 1874.

54. Allen, "The Study of History," *University Press*, Feb. 17, 1874.

55. *Catalogue of the University of Wisconsin for 1881-1882* (Madison, 1882), 49.

56. Turner, notebooks on Allen's lectures, Frederick Jackson Turner Papers, State Historical Society of Wisconsin (hereafter cited as SHSW, Turner Papers); quotations from Sept. 6, 1882 entry notebook labeled "Ancient Institutions."

57. Notebook, "Medieval Institutions," Oct. 20, 1883, ibid.

58. Allen, "American History Notebook," William Francis Allen Papers, State Historical Society of Wisconsin (hereafter cited as SHSW, Allen Papers).

59. Allen, *History Topics for the Use of High Schools and Colleges* (Boston, 1883); Allen "List of Books for Reference on the History of the United States," *The Badger*, Feb. 15, 1883.

60. John A. Doyle, *History of the United States* (New York, 1876), 7.

61. Herbert B. Adams to W. F. Allen, April 6, 1882; Allen to Adams, April 16, 1882, quoted in Stearns, "William Francis Allen," 241-42.

62. At his son's request, A. J. Turner wrote the son-in-law of Augustin Grignon, April 16, 1883, asking for information [State Historical Society of Wisconsin, Green Bay and Prairie de Chien Papers, Vol. XXVII, 56 (Wis. MSS C)]. For a sound appraisal of Turner's scholarship, see Fulmer Mood and Everett E. Edwards (eds.), "Frederick Jackson Turner's History of the Grignon Tract on the Portage of the Fox and Wisconsin Rivers," *Agricultural History*, XVII (April 1943), 113-14. The essay, reprinted there, originally appeared in the *Wisconsin State Register*, June 23, 1883.

63. Turner, Commonplace Book for 1883, HEH TU Vol. III (2).

64. Ibid.

65. Turner to Carl Becker, Dec. 16, 1925, HEH TU Box 34A.

66. Turner copied many of Bascom's remarks into his Commonplace Book for 1883 [HEH TU Vol. III (2)].

67. For Turner's courses and grades, see "Frederick Jackson Turner Transcript, University of Wisconsin," U. of Wis. Arch., Turner Misc. File, and William F. Allen, "Class Record Books, 1882-1883 and 1883-1884," SHSW, Allen Papers. One of Turner's papers, "Why did Cromwell Fail," is in HEH TU Box 54.

68. "Class Album. University of Wisconsin. Class of 1884," U. of Wis. Arch., IWXF+1884.

69. For Class Day and Commencement ceremonies, see *Wisconsin State Journal*, June 16, 17, 18, 1884, *University Press*, June 21, 1884, and *Wisconsin State Register*, June 21, 1884. His address is in June 21 issue of the last. Ideas and phrases later incorporated in it are in Turner, Commonplace Book for 1883, HEH TU Vol. III (2).

Chapter II
The Making of a Historian: Wisconsin
1884-1888

1. J. Franklin Jameson, "Early Days of the American Historical Association, 1884-1895," *American Historical Review*, XL (Oct., 1934), 2.

2. Frederick J. Turner, *Reuben Gold Thwaites; a Memorial Address* (Madison, 1914), 38. The *Wisconsin State Journal*, June 19, 1884, and *University Press*, June 21, 1884, reported the offer of an assistant instructorship in rhetoric, and his refusal.

3. Quotation, *Wisconsin State Journal*, April 17, 1884. For Turner's activity on the *Milwaukee Sentinel*, see Fulmer Mood, "Frederick Jackson Turner and the Milwaukee *Sentinel*, 1884," *Wisconsin Magazine of History*, XXXIV (Autumn 1950), 21-28.

4. The *Wisconsin State Register*, Feb. 7, 1885, began a column of Madison news signed "F." For Turner's career on the *Inter-Ocean*, see Fulmer Mood, "Frederick Jackson Turner and the Chicago *Inter-Ocean*, 1885," *Wisconsin Magazine of History*, XXXV (Spring 1952), 188-94, 210-18.

5. *Wisconsin State Journal*, April 11, 1885.

6. *Catalogue of the University of Wisconsin for the Academic Year 1885-1886* (Madison, 1885), 9, 64.

7. *Wisconsin State Journal*, May 29, 1886; *University Press*, June 4, 1886.

8. Turner to Mae Sherwood, Aug. 8, 21, 1886, HEH TU Box A.

9. University of Wisconsin, Instructional Report, Fall Term, 1886. Each instructor filed a report each quarter listing courses, hours of instruction, and number of students (U. of Wis. Arch.).

10. *The Aegis*, April 13, May 4, 1887. This was apparently a voluntary extra course, listed in neither the catalogue nor the quarterly "Instructional Reports."

11. *Catalogue of the University of Wisconsin for the Academic Year 1886-1887* (Madison, 1886), 16.

12. Turner to Andrew J. Turner, Sept. 23, 1885, HEH TU Box A.

13. Turner to Mae Sherwood, May 22, 1887, HEH TU Box A.

14. Turner to Mae Sherwood, June 27, 1886, ibid.

15. Turner to Mae Sherwood (n.d.), ibid.

16. Turner to Mae Sherwood, [June 16, 1887], HEH TU Box B.

17. Turner's letters to his mother, father, and sister describing his adventures are in HEH TU Box B; also published in Ray A. Billington (ed.), "Frederick Jackson Turner Visits New England: 1887," *New England Quarterly*, XLI (Sept., 1968), 409-36.

18. Turner to Mae Sherwood, July 25, 1888, HEH TU Box B.

19. Ibid. Aug. 24, 1887.

20. Ibid. Nov. 12, 1887.

21. Ibid. March 10, 1888, HEH TU Box C.

22. Ibid. Oct. 23, 1887, HEH TU Box B.

23. Ibid Jan. 14, 1888, HEH TU Box C. The *Wisconsin State Journal*, Jan. 23, 1888, reported that Turner had assumed the teaching of Allen's classes. For statistics on teaching hours and number of pupils, see Turner, Instructional Report, Winter Term, 1887-1888, U. of Wis. Arch.

24. Turner to Mae Sherwood, Oct. 4, 1887, HEH TU Box B.

25. Ibid. Sept. 11, 1887.

26. Turner, American History Notebooks, 1887-88, HEH, Vol. XIV (1), (2); Vol. XV (1), (2).

27. Turner to Mae Sherwood, Oct. 16, 1887, HEH TU Box B. For a description of the library, see *Wisconsin State Journal*, Feb. 2, 1885. Clifford

Lord and Carl Ubbelohde, *Clio's Servant: A History of the State Historical Society of Wisconsin* (Madison, 1967), is a full history.

28. Turner to Mae Sherwood, Sept. 5, 1887, HEH TU Box B.

29. Ibid. March 25, 1888, HEH TU Box C.

30. Ibid.

31. Turner, Commonplace Book [1886], HEH TU Vol. III (3).

32. Turner to William F. Allen, July 11, 1888, SHSW, Turner Papers, Box II.

33. Turner to Mae Sherwood, [Aug. 21], 1887, HEH TU Box B.

34. Turner, "Review of Edward E. Hale and Edward E. Hale, Jr., *Franklin in France* (Boston, 1887)," *The Dial*, VIII (May 1887), 7-10; "Review of Edward E. Hale and Edward E. Hale, Jr., *Franklin in France*, Part II (Boston, 1888)," ibid. IX (Dec. 1888), 204-6. Copies of reviews, HEH TU Box 54. Turner's careful preparation is revealed in notes summarizing every book or article on the subject then in print (HEH TU File Drawer 4C, Folder: Peace Treaty).

35. Turner, "Review of Gilmore, *John Sevier*," *The Nation*, Oct. 6, 1887, 278.

36. Turner to Mae Sherwood, March 21, 1888, HEH TU Box C.

37. Turner, "Wisconsin," *Encyclopaedia Britannica* (9th ed., New York, 1888), XXIV, 616-19. Reprinted, with editorial notes and introduction, in Fulmer Mood (ed.), "Little Known Fragments of Turner's Writings," *Wisconsin Magazine of History*, XXIII (March 1940), 328-38.

38. Turner described his struggle to finish the work on time in letters to Mae Sherwood, Jan. 22, July 30, Aug. 8, 1888. On its publication, the *Wisconsin State Journal* (Sept. 20, 1888), noted: "He is a very able and industrious young man, and a thorough student. His many friends feel confident that the world will yet hear from him."

39. Turner, *Outline Studies in the History of the Northwest* (Chicago, 1888). A rough draft of what is apparently an early version, labeled "The Development of the Great West," is attached to Turner to William F. Allen, Oct. 31, 1888, HEH TU Box 1.

40. Turner expressed his views on religion in a letter to his mother, Mary O. Turner, July 15, 1887, and in letters to Mae Sherwood, Dec. 12, 1886, Jan. 22, 1888 (HEH TU Boxes A, B, and C).

41. *The Aegis*, April 8, 1887, 10. The Channing Club was described in *Trochos*, III (1888), 161. Turner was also active in the Shakespeare Club (Turner to Mae Sherwood, Dec. 2, 1887, Feb. [9], 1888, HEH TU Boxes B, C).

42. Turner to Mae Sherwood, Sept. 15, 1887, HEH TU Box B.

43. For discussion on von Holst's history, see *Wisconsin State Journal*, Nov. 11, 1886; for Henry George's lecture, ibid. March 23, 30, 1887. Discussion of George's thesis, ibid. April 28, 1887, and Turner to Mae Sherwood, May 11, 1887, HEH TU Box A.

44. *Wisconsin State Journal*, Dec. 31, 1887, Jan. 16, 31, 1888, described the series.

45. Turner to Mae Sherwood, Jan. 7, Feb. 9, 28, March 3, 1888, HEH TU Box C.

46. Draft of Turner's address, HEH TU File Drawer 14A, Folder: Ordinance of 1787.

47. For extended summary of lecture, see *Wisconsin State Journal,* March 10, 1888.

48. Turner to Mae Sherwood, March 10, 1888, HEH TU Box C.

49. *Wisconsin State Journal,* March 27, 1888.

50. Turner to Mae Sherwood, Sept. 4, Oct. 16, 23, Dec. 4, 1887; April 22, 1888, HEH TU Boxes B and C.

51. Ibid. Oct. 16, 1887, HEH TU Box B. See *Wisconsin State Journal,* Nov. 15, 1887, for Turner's talk, "The Fur Trade of Wisconsin."

52. Turner to Mae Sherwood, May 2, 8, 1888, HEH TU Box C.

53. Ibid. May 2, 1888, HEH TU Box C.

54. Ibid. May 12, 1888.

55. For report of meeting and summary of Turner's paper, see *Wisconsin State Journal,* May 15, 1888, *Wisconsin State Register,* May 26, 1888. See also MS, "Journal of the Madison Literary Club, 1877-1903," MSS Division, State Historical Society of Wisconsin.

56. Turner to Mae Sherwood, May 14, 1888, HEH TU Box C.

57. Turner, "The Character and Influence of the Fur Trade in Wisconsin," *State Historical Society of Wisconsin Proceedings,* XXXVI (Madison, 1889), 52-98. Quotation, pp. 97-98. Notes on the geography of the region, probably from reading done at this time, are in HEH TU File Drawer 15, Folder: Physical Geography U.S.

58. Turner to Mae Sherwood, April 13, 1888, HEH TU Box C.

59. *Wisconsin State Journal,* June 20, 1888. Turner described his negotiations with President Chamberlin (Turner to Mae Sherwood, April 13, 19, 22, 1888, HEH TU Box C). By the time he applied to Johns Hopkins the deadline for scholarship applications had passed (ibid. May 23, 1888).

60. *Wisconsin State Journal,* June 8, 1888.

61. Turner to Mae Sherwood, June 15, Aug. 8, 18, 1888, HEH TU Box C.

Chapter III
The Making of a Historian: Johns Hopkins
1888-1889

1. Turner to Mae Sherwood, Sept. 16, 1888, HEH TU Box C.

2. Ibid. Sept. 5, 1888.

3. Ibid. Sept. 26, 1888.

4. Ibid. Sept. 29, Oct. 2, 1888, Jan. 21, 1889, HEH TU Boxes C and D; Turner to Mary O. Turner, Oct. 6, 1888, HEH TU Box D.

5. *Johns Hopkins University Circulars,* VIII, No. 68 (Nov. 1888), 6, listed the students in each class. Turner was the only graduate student in the introductory mathematics class. See also "Transcript of Graduate Record of Frederick Jackson Turner," office of University Registrar, Johns Hopkins. A copy was supplied to the Huntington Library by Irene M. Davis and Ellen G. Klages of that office.

6. Turner, "The West as a Field for the Scholar," apparently a lecture to a Johns Hopkins alumni group (HEH TU File Drawer 15A, Folder: The West as a Field).

7. *The Aegis,* Dec. 14, 1888, 8. For a description of instructional methods at Johns Hopkins, see Hugh Hawkins, *Pioneer: A History of the Johns*

Hopkins University, 1874-1889 (Ithaca, 1960), 220-29; and A. S. Eisenstadt, *Charles McLean Andrews* (New York, 1956), 5-7. Andrews was Turner's contemporary at Johns Hopkins.

8. Herbert B. Adams, *The Study of History in American Colleges and Universities* (Washington, D.C., 1887), 173-92 (quotation, p. 192), describes the seminar.

9. For history teaching at that time see Frederick Rudolph, *The American College and University* (New York, 1962), 334-96. For the origins of the American Historical Association, see David D. Van Tassel, *Recording America's Past. An Interpretation of the Development of Historical Studies in America, 1607-1884* (Chicago, 1960), 171-79.

10. Excellent on American historiography at that time is John Higham *et al.*, *History* (Englewood Cliffs, N.J., 1965), 92-97, 158-60, and two works by Edward N. Saveth, "A Science of American History," *Diogenes*, XXVI (Summer 1959), 107-22, and "Scientific History in America: Eclipse of an Idea," Donald Sheehan and Harold C. Syrett (eds.), *Essays in American Historiography* (New York, 1960), 1-19.

11. Herbert B. Adams, *The Germanic Origins of New England Towns* (Baltimore, 1882), 1. Brief accounts of Adams' career are in Hawkins, *Pioneer: A History of the Johns Hopkins University*, 169-186, and in *Herbert Baxter Adams, Tributes of His Friends* (Baltimore, 1902), 9-49. The best account of the Teutonic school in America is Jurgen Herbst, *The German Historical School in American Scholarship* (Ithaca, 1965).

12. Turner to Mae Sherwood, Oct. 5, 6, 1888, HEH TU Box D. Charles McLean Andrews was a member of this seminar, and he described the meetings in weekly letters to his mother [Charles McLean Andrews Papers, Historical Manuscripts Division, Yale University Library (hereafter cited as Yale, Andrews Papers)]. The seminar's secretary's reports are: Johns Hopkins University, "Seminar Records," Archives of Johns Hopkins University (microfilm copies in Huntington Library).

13. Turner to Mary O. Turner, Oct. 7, 1888; Turner to Mae Sherwood, Oct. 12, 1888, HEH TU Box D.

14. Turner, "Notes for Talks to Graduate Club, University of Wisconsin, December 19, 1908." HEH TU Box 55. For Allen's advice, see William F. Allen to Turner, Oct. 14, 1888; Turner to Allen, Oct. 31, 1888, HEH TU Box 1.

15. Turner to Mae Sherwood, Feb. 3, March 16, 1889, HEH TU Box D.

16. Ibid. Dec. 27, 30, 1888.

17. Ibid. May 14, 1889. The *Wisconsin State Journal*, Jan. 4, 1889, described the reading of the paper. Parkman to Turner, May 2, 1889, HEH TU Box 1.

18. Johns Hopkins University, "Seminar Records, 1888-1889," 420-21. These records are in Wendell H. Stephenson (ed.), "The Influence of Woodrow Wilson on Frederick Jackson Turner," *Agricultural History*, XIX (Oct. 1945), 252 n. 11. The remark praising the paper was made by Woodrow Wilson (Turner to William E. Dodd, Oct. 7, 1917, HEH TU Box 29).

19. Turner to Mary O. Turner, Oct. 6, 1888, ibid. Box D. Turner also described the first seminar in letters to William F. Allen, Oct. 6, 1888, and

Mae Sherwood, Oct. 7, 1888 (HEH TU Boxes 1 and D). John M. Vincent, "Herbert B. Adams," Howard W. Odum (ed.), *American Masters of Social Science* (New York, 1927), 99-127, explains Adams' interest in adult education.

20. Turner to Mae Sherwood, March 29, 1889, HEH TU Box D. A printed program and outline of the lecture is enclosed in this letter. He described his apprehension in letters to Mae Sherwood, Jan. 13, Feb. 8, 13, 1889, HEH TU Box D.

21. Turner to Mae Sherwood, Feb. 13, 1889, ibid.

22. Ibid. Feb. 28, 1889.

23. Turner to Mae Sherwood, Feb. 3, 8, 22, April [?], 1889, ibid. Box D.

24. *Johns Hopkins University Circular*, VIII, No. 71 (March 1889), 54.

25. Turner to Mary O. Turner, Oct. 6, 1888; Turner to Mae Sherwood, [Feb.-March, 1889], HEH TU Box D.

26. Turner to Mae Sherwood, March 30, April [?], 1889, ibid.

27. Ibid. April 14, 1889.

28. The effect of Johns Hopkins on Turner can be realized by comparing the two versions of his thesis, that printed as "The Character and influence of the Fur Trade in Wisconsin," *Wisconsin State Historical Society Proceedings*, XXXVI (Madison, 1889), 52-98, and the doctoral version, "The Character and Influence of the Indian Trade in Wisconsin, A Study of the Trading Post as an Institution," *Johns Hopkins University Studies in Historical and Political Science*, 9th Series (Baltimore, 1891). The quotations are from the latter.

29. Ibid. 89, 104, 168-69, 172.

30. Turner to Mae Sherwood, March 16, April 18, 1889, HEH TU Box D.

31. Turner to Richard T. Ely, Jan. 28, 1902, Richard T. Ely Papers, Manuscripts Section, State Historical Society of Wisconsin, Wis. MSS. MK (hereafter cited as SHSW, Ely Papers).

32. Herbert B. Adams, "Special Methods of Historical Study as Pursued at the Johns Hopkins University and at Smith College," *Johns Hopkins University Studies in Historical and Political Science*, 2nd Ser. (Baltimore, 1884), 15.

33. Turner to William F. Allen, Oct. 31, 1888, HEH TU Box 1.

34. Turner to Helen Solliday, May 27, 1920, HEH TU Box 44.

35. Turner's notes on Small's course, HEH TU File Drawer 15A, Folder: Notes on A. W. Small (18 pp.).

36. Turner's notes on Wilson's course, HEH TU File Drawer 1A, Folder: Mass. Town Lands, "Wilson Lectures at JHU" (6 pp.). Wilson incorporated many of his lectures in *The State: Elements of Historical and Practical Politics* (Boston, 1889).

37. Turner to William E. Dodd, Oct. 7, 1919, HEH TU Box 29.

38. The standard treatment of Ely is Benjamin G. Rader, *The Academic Mind and Reform: The Influence of Richard T. Ely in American Life* (Lexington, Ky., 1966), which deals more with Ely's reform activities than with his economic theories. Ely is also pictured in Oliver E. Baker to Henry G. Taylor, Feb. 19, 1944, SHSW, Ely Papers.

39. Turner copied the list of books assigned by Ely and pasted it in his copy of John Stuart Mill, *Principles of Political Economy* (London, 1886),

Huntington Library, Accession No. 211882. Ely at this time was lecturing from the manuscript of a book: *An Introduction to Political Economy* (New York, 1889); the views that he expressed in his lectures, and probably much of the language, may thus be determined.

40. Note in Simon N. Patten, *The Premises of Political Economy* (Philadelphia, 1885), 69. Turner's copy of the book, with this and other marginal notations, is in the Huntington Library (Call No. HB 171 P 3).

41. Mill, *Principles of Political Economy*, 17, 109, 110, 261.

42. Francis A. Walker, *Land and Its Rent* (Boston, 1883), 21, 25-26, 45-47; Patten, *Premises of Political Economy*, 11-12. Turner underlined a passage in Patten's book stating that intruding lower classes with lesser living standards normally displaced higher classes because they consumed less and hence could sell a larger proportion of their produce. He later used this quotation in a letter to Professor W. F. Allen (Dec. 31, 1888, HEH TU Box 1), discussing the changes in the Wisconsin countryside resulting from the German migrations.

43. Ibid.

44. Turner assumed that he would return to Madison; all through the winter he discussed course offerings with Professor Allen (Turner to William F. Allen, Oct. 31, Dec. 31, 1888, ibid). He told of his campaign among friends in a letter to Mae Sherwood (Feb. 3, 1889, ibid. Box D).

45. *Wisconsin State Register*, Jan. 12, 1889; *Wisconsin State Journal*, Feb. 9, 1889.

46. Thomas C. Chamberlin to Turner, April 10, 1889, enclosed in Turner to Mae Sherwood, April 15, 1889, HEH TU Boxes 1 and D. Chamberlin's final offer to Turner is in Chamberlin to Turner, Feb. 27, 1889, ibid. Box 1.

47. Turner to Mae Sherwood, Feb. 28, 1889, ibid. Box D. Official letter of appointment from Board of Regents, July 8, 1889, ibid. Box 1.

48. Turner left no description of his examination, but the scene can be reconstructed from the account written by Charles M. Andrews to his mother, April 22, 1889 (Yale, Andrews Papers). Turner was informed of his success in Richard T. Ely to Turner, June 27, 1889 (pasted in Turner's copy of Mill, *Principles of Political Economy*, [HEH Accession No. 211882]).

Chapter IV
Teaching—and the Emerging Frontier Thesis
1889-1892

1. Turner to Mae Sherwood, July 4, 1889, HEH TU Box D.

2. Ibid.

3. Ibid. Aug. 2, 1889, HEH TU Box E.

4. Oscar D. Brandenburg to Turner, April 20, 1889, HEH TU Box 1. Professor Brandenburg estimated $240 a year for a house, $130 for a servant, $75 for fuel and light, and $480 for food and drink.

5. Turner, "Theodore Roosevelt, *The Winning of the West* (G. P. Putnam's Sons)," *The Dial*, X (Aug. 1889), 71-73.

6. Turner to Constance L. Skinner, March 15, 1922, HEH TU Box 31.

7. Turner to Mae Sherwood, Sept. 8, 1889, HEH TU Box E.

8. Ibid. Sept. 15, 1889. All universities were increasing rapidly in size at this time. See Lawrence R. Veysey, *The Emergence of the American University* (Chicago, 1966), 264-66.

9. Turner to William F. Allen, Jan. 16, March 14, 1889, HEH TU Box 1.

10. University of Wisconsin, "Instructional Report, Fall Term, 1889-1890." U. of Wis. Arch.

11. Turner to Mae Sherwood, Nov. 19, 1889, HEH TU Box E. They discussed preparations for the wedding in letters of Oct. 21, 25, Nov. 5, 14, 15, 1889, ibid.

12. *Chicago Tribune,* quoted in *Wisconsin State Journal,* Nov. 29, 1889.

13. *Wisconsin State Register,* Nov. 30, 1889.

14. Ibid. Dec. 22, 1889; *Wisconsin State Journal,* Jan. 25, 1890; Turner to Mae Turner, Jan. 25, 30, 1890, HEH TU Box E.

15. William F. Allen, *A Short History of the Roman People* (Boston, 1890), v.

16. Turner to Herbert B. Adams, Jan. 11, 1890, HEH TU Box 1; Univ. of Wis., "Instructional Reports, Fall, Spring Terms, 1889-1890," Univ. of Wis. Arch.

17. Turner left no description of his doctoral examinations, but they probably duplicated those taken by Charles McLean Andrews in May 1889, which Andrews described to his mother in a letter, May 19, 1889 (Yale, Andrews Papers).

18. Turner to Lois K. Mathews, March 21, 1906; Turner to Thomas P. Abernethy, March 12, 1926, HEH TU Boxes 6, 35.

19. Turner delayed publication while he sought permission to add, at his own expense, maps locating Indian tribes and illustrating boundary disputes (Turner to Herbert B. Adams, May 7, Oct. 19, 1891, HEH TU Box 1).

20. *The Aegis,* Jan. 15, 1892, and *Wisconsin State Journal,* Dec. 14, 1891, commented favorably on the book and noted the "charm of an excellent literary style."

21. Turner to Woodrow Wilson, Jan. 23, 1890, HEH TU Box 1.

22. Turner to Mae Turner, Sept. 30, 1891; Oct. 15, 1892, ibid. Box E.

23. Mae Turner prepared two baby books for her children, describing their growth and illnesses (HEH TU Vol. X). See also *Portage Daily Register,* March 17, 19, 26, 28, April 16, 1891.

24. *Wisconsin State Journal,* Jan. 3, 1890, Jan. 16, May 28, June 1, 10, Dec. 8, 1891; Feb. 3, Sept. 26, 1892.

25. Ibid. March 5, 1890.

26. Turner to Richard T. Ely, Jan. 25, 29, 1892, SHSW, Ely Papers, Box 8.

27. Ibid. Feb. 1, 1892.

28. *Wisconsin State Journal,* Feb. 15, April 8, 1892. For a scrapbook containing printed notices of the new school, see SHSW, Ely Papers, Box 8 (16 pp.). The founding of the school is described in Benjamin G. Rader, *The Academic Mind and Reform: The Influence of Richard T. Ely in American Life* (Lexington, Ky., 1966), 106-11.

29. *The Aegis,* April 8, 1892, 447-50 (this was reprinted as a circular and 15,000 copies circulated). *Daily Cardinal,* April 13, 1892.

30. *Daily Cardinal,* Nov. 16, 1892; *Wisconsin State Journal,* Nov. 16, 1892.

31. Univ. of Wis., "Instructional Reports, 1891-1892," U. of Wis. Arch.

32. *The Badger for 1891* (Madison, 1890), 174; *The Badger for 1893* (Madison, 1892), 76-77.

33. Syllabi, HEH TU File Drawer 4D, Folder: Constitutional History Syllabus. Scattered fragments of lectures in HEH TU File Drawer 2C, Folder: Colonial Central Government; File Drawer 3A, Folder: Local Government; File Drawer 12B, Folder: Sovereignty; and File Drawer 15B, Folder: Puritanism, English.

34. *The Aegis,* May 8, 1891, *Wisconsin State Journal,* May 9, June 13, 1891; *Portage Daily Register,* May 11, 1891, described the course and the reaction to it.

35. See HEH TU Box 54.

36. Turner to Merle Curti, Aug. 8, 1928, HEH TU Box 39.

37. *The Aegis,* Oct. 10, 1890.

38. Turner to Herbert B. Adams, Oct. 19, 1891, HEH TU Box 1. *The Aegis,* Oct. 2, 1891, reported the seminar would stress the 1830-40 period. Its operation described, ibid. May 27, 1892.

39. Ibid. May 27, 1892; *Daily Cardinal,* Dec. 13, 1892.

40. Notes, HEH TU File Drawer 6B, Folder: Wisconsin Milwaukee Area. Old Settlers. Turner's early graduate students are described in Fulmer Mood, "The Development of Frederick Jackson Turner as a Historical Thinker," *Colonial Society of Massachusetts Transactions, 1937-1942,* XXXIV (Boston, 1943), 328-31.

41. Turner to Herbert B. Adams, Dec. 8, 1890, HEH TU Box 1.

42. *The Aegis,* Feb. 6, 1891. Address published, *Proceedings of the State Historical Society of Wisconsin,* XXXVIII (Madison, 1891), 93-99.

43. *Wisconsin State Journal,* Aug. 27, 1890; *Wisconsin Journal of Education,* XXI (Oct. 1891), 230-34, (Nov. 1891), 253-56.

44. Turner described his extension experiences in "The Extension Work of the University of Wisconsin," *University Extension,* I (April 1892), 311-24, and George F. Ames (ed.), *Handbook of University Extension* (2nd ed., Philadelphia, 1893). Local newspapers also reported his speaking engagements (see esp. *Wisconsin State Journal,* Jan. 24, Sept. 16, Oct. 22, Nov. 6, 10, 13, 1891).

45. Turner to Herbert B. Adams, Jan. 18, 1892, HEH TU Box 1.

46. Indications of the books Turner read may be gained from a sheet listing books on "Colonization in General," as well as from the syllabi in which he listed readings (HEH TU File Drawer 15D, Folder: Colonization Bibliography). In this same folder are three pages of his reading notes, with the observations quoted above.

47. John A. Doyle, *English Colonies in America. Virginia, Maryland, and the Carolinas* (New York, 1882), 1-2.

48. See HEH TU File Drawer 5D, Folder: Extension Lecture.

49. Frederick J. Turner, *The Colonization of North America* (n.p., n.d. [1891?]); *Syllabus of a University Extension Course of Six Lectures on the Colonization of North America* (Madison, n.d. [1892?]); *The Colonization of North America from the Earliest Times to 1763* (Madison, 1893), HEH TU Vol. VI (1) (2) (3).

50. For Turner's colonization lectures, see HEH TU File Drawer 1E, Folder: Colonization Lecture; File Drawer 15A, Folder: Norsemen as Colonizers; File Drawer 15C, Folder: Spain as Colonizer; File Drawer 15D, Folder: Spain as Colonizer c. 1905-1910; File Drawer 15D, Folder: France as Colonizer; File Drawer 15D, Folder: Colonization Modern England; File Drawer 2D, Folder: Virginia Colonization; File Drawer 15D, Folder: Colonization: Oriental, Roman, Teutonic.

51. This lecture (33 pp.), typed, is in HEH TU File Drawer 15A, Folder: Lecture. American Colonization. Turner notes on the cover that it was delivered February 9, 1891, but prepared in January 1891.

52. *The Aegis*, Oct. 9, 1891.

53. Ibid. Nov. 4, 1892. Turner put a copy of this issue in a manila folder, on which he wrote: "Contains first form of my doctrine of frontier. Prior to my paper in AHA 1893 I had not read Ratzel, or Godkin, or other writer who deals with this problem" (HEH TU Box 54). Also preserved is a copy of the essay on which Turner wrote: "This with the Fur Trade thesis constitute the beginning of my writings on the frontier as a symbol of the western movement & its reactions on the East and the Old World" (HEH Accession Order No. 126772). The essay was reprinted in *The Early Writings of Frederick Jackson Turner* (Madison, 1938), as was his "The Significance of History."

54. Turner to Max Farrand, Oct. 13, 1916, HEH TU Box 26.

55. Simon N. Patten to Turner, Nov. 14, 1892; Francis N. Thorpe to Turner, Dec. 11, 1892; Emory R. Johnson to Turner, Nov. 14, 1892; Charles M. Andrews to Turner, Nov. 29, 1892; Herbert B. Adams to Turner, Nov. 28, 1892, HEH TU Box 1.

Chapter V
The Genesis of the Frontier Thesis
1892-1893

1. The topics covered in this chapter are developed in Ray A. Billington, *The Genesis of the Frontier Thesis: A Study in Historical Creativity* (San Marino, Calif., 1971).

2. Edwin L. Godkin, "Aristocratic Opinions of Democracy," *North American Review*, CCVI (Jan. 1865), 194-232. American writers who speculated on the frontier's influence before Turner are described in Herman C. Nixon, "Precursors of Turner in the Interpretation of the American Frontier," *South Atlantic Quarterly* XXVIII (Jan. 1929), 83-93; English writers are discussed in William M. Tuttle, Jr., "Forerunners of Frederick Jackson Turner: Nineteenth-Century British Conservatives and the Frontier Thesis," *Agricultural History*, XLI (July 1967), 219-27. Ernest Marchand, "Emerson and the Frontier," *American Literature*, III (May 1931), 149-74, cautiously explores Ralph Waldo Emerson's views on the impact of frontiering. Turner was probably unfamiliar with most of his precursors; he first saw Godkin's essay in 1896, read it, chuckled, and said, "Godkin has stolen my thunder."

3. The social background of Turner's essay is admirably described in Lee Benson, "The Historical Background of Turner's Frontier Essay," *Agricultural History*, XXV (April 1951), 59-82.

4. Josiah Strong, *Our Country* (New York, 1885), 160-61. For the relationship between the closing of the frontier and the immigration restriction movement see John Higham, *Strangers in the Land* (New Brunswick, N.J., 1955), 133-41.

5. Benson, "Historical Background of Turner's Frontier Essay," *loc. cit.* 70-76, summarizes these arguments.

6. Newspaper clippings and outlines for the immigration sequence, HEH TU File Drawer 16D, Folder: Immigration Syllabus. The undergraduate thesis on "The Effect of the Settlement of the Public Domain on Immigration" was prepared in 1894 by Court W. Lamoreux.

7. Edward Channing, "Genesis of the Massachusetts Town," *Proceedings of the Massachusetts Historical Society*, 2nd Ser., VII (1891-92), 388-89; Charles M. Andrews, "Some Recent Aspects of Institutional History," *Yale Review*, I (Feb. 1893), 381-410. Andrews' rebellion is described in A. S. Eisenstadt, *Charles McLean Andrews* (New York, 1956), 12-25, 37-60, 79-105. The best general account of this period is John Higham, *History* (Englewood Cliffs, N.J., 1965), 162-70; a special aspect is explored by Robert E. Lerner, "Turner and the Revolt Against E. A. Freeman," *Arizona and the West*, V (Summer 1963), 101-8.

8. This point is well made in Richard Hofstadter, *The Progressive Historians. Turner, Beard, Parrington* (New York, 1968), 49-50.

9. Turner to William E. Dodd, Oct. 7, 1919, HEH TU Box 29.

10. Roland B. Nixon, "Notes on Anthropology," *Bulletin of the American Geographical Society*, XXXI (1899), No. 1, 60. A valuable account of environmentalism among geographers at that time is G. Tatham, "Environmentalism and Possibilism," Griffith Taylor (ed.), *Geography in the Twentieth Century* (London, 1951), 128-62. William Coleman, "Science and Symbol in the Turner Frontier Hypothesis," *American Historical Review*, LXXII (Oct. 1966), 22-49, describes the manner in which Turner was influenced by findings in geography and biology.

11. James D. Dana, *Manual of Geology* (4th ed., New York, 1896), 1034.

12. Justin Winsor, *The Mississippi Basin* (Boston, 1895), dedication; B. A. Hinsdale, *How To Study and Teach History* (New York, 1894), 110-26.

13. Henry F. Osborn, "The Present Problem of Heredity," *Atlantic Monthly*, LXVII (March 1891), 354. *See also* Harland E. Allen, "Hugo de Vries and the Reception of the 'Mutation Theory,'" *Journal of the History of Biology*, II (Spring 1969), 55-65; Edward J. Pfeifer, "The Genesis of American Neo-Lamarckism," *Isis*, LVI (Summer 1965), 156-61, and George W. Stocking, Jr., "Lamarckianism in American Social Science," *Journal of the History of Ideas*, XXIII (April-June 1962), 239-56.

14. Turner joined the Academy as a graduate student in 1887 and was a frequent contributor to its programs thereafter.

15. "Review of: 'Statistical Atlas of the United States. Part II.—Population, Social and Industrial Statistics. Part III.—Vital Statistics,'" *The International Review*, II (Jan. 1875), 131. For the influence of statistical cartography on Turner, see Fulmer Mood, "The Rise of Official Statistical Cartography in Austria, Prussia, and the United States, 1855-1872," *Agricultural History*, XX (Oct. 1946), 209-25, and "The Development of Frederick Jackson Turner as a Historical Thinker," *Transactions of the Colonial Society of Massachusetts, 1937-1942*, XXXIV (Boston, 1943), 283-352.

16. Francis A. Walker, *Statistical Atlas of the United States Based on the Results of the Ninth Census* (n.p., 1874), 1-4.

17. A note jotted by Turner about 1891 reads: "Walker puts body of continuous settlement thus: 1790–83° W. Long. 1810–88°30', 1830–95°; 1850–99°; 1870–99°45'" (HEH TU 3 × 5 Drawer 1, Section: Frontier).

18. Francis A. Walker, "Growth and Distribution of Population," *The First Century of the Republic: A Review of American Progress* (New York, 1876), 211.

19. Henry Gannett, "The Settled Areas and the Density of Our Population," *The International Review*, XII (Jan. 1882), 70.

20. Fletcher W. Hewes and Henry Gannett, *Scribner's Statistical Atlas of the United States Showing by Graphic Methods Their Present Condition and Their Political, Social and Industrial Development* (New York, 1883), copy acquired by State Historical Society of Wisconsin in 1887. Turner, in 1887-88, listed "Scribner's Statistical Atlas" among works assigned his students [HEH TU Vol. XIV (1), American History I].

21. For Turner's copy of this bulletin, published in 1891, see HEH TU Black Box No. 9 (160-68), Item 164.

22. *Observations on the North-American Land-Company, Lately Instituted in Philadelphia* (London, 1796), 113; Henry L. Nelson, "The Growth of Federal Power," *Harper's New Monthly Magazine*, LXXXV (July 1892), 245. Turner's notes indicate that he read these works and all others mentioned below.

23. Francis J. Grund, *The Americans, in their Moral, Social, and Political Relations* (Boston, 1873), 211; "Western Prairies," *American Whig Review*, XI (May 1850), 526.

24. Robert Baird, *View of the Valley of the Mississippi, or the Emigrant's and Traveller's Guide to the West* (Philadelphia, 1834), 101-3.

25. Emile Boutmy, *Studies in Constitutional Law. France-England-United States* (London, 1891), 127-28. Turner copied several passages of this volume into his notes (HEH TU File Drawer 15, Folder: Boutmy). Churillon's essay is on p. 488.

26. Henry George, *Progress and Poverty* (n.p., 1882), 350. This was the note that Turner reminded himself to copy. His copy of the book is heavily underlined in spots (HEH Accession No. 152218).

27. Walter Bagehot, *Physics and Politics: An Application of the Principles of Natural Selection and Heredity to Political Society* (Humboldt Library of Popular Science, New York, 1880), 146. Turner's notes, HEH TU 3 × 5 Drawer No. 1.

28. Bagehot, *Physics and Politics*, 147, 150. Turner's notes, HEH TU 3 × 5 Drawer No. 1.

29. Francis A. Walker, "The Growth of the Nation," *Providence Journal*, June 19, 1889. Turner clipped this address from the paper, pasted it on cardboard, and underlined it heavily (HEH TU File Drawer 15B, Folder: F. A. Walker, PBK 1889).

30. Achille Loria, *Analisa della Proprietà Capitalista* (2 vols., Torino, 1889). An ingenuous argument to show that Turner borrowed most of his thesis from Loria is Lee Benson, "Achille Loria's Influence on American Economic Thought: Including His Contributions to the Frontier Hypothesis," *Agricultural History*, XXIV (Oct. 1950), 182-99.

31. Richard T. Ely, *Outlines of Economics* (New York, 1893), 5, tells of Powers' aid and thanks Turner and Haskins for reading portions of his manuscript.

32. Turner's notes (6 pp.) cover the material on pp. 46-55, Vol. II, of the *Analisa* (HEH TU File Drawer 15A, Folder: Notes on A. Loria).

33. Clarence W. Bowen to William F. Poole, April 14, 1892, William F. Poole Papers, Newberry Library, Chicago, Box: Jan.-April, 1892 (hereafter cited as Newberry, Poole Papers). Bowen was treasurer of the American Historical Association.

34. William F. Poole to C. W. Bowen, Nov. 28, 1892; Herbert B. Adams to Bowen, Dec. 9, 1892. American Historical Association Papers, Division of Manuscripts, Library of Congress, Box 213, Folder: Treasurer's File, 1892 (hereafter cited as LC, AHA Papers).

35. Herbert B. Adams to C. W. Bowen, Dec. 30, 1892, ibid.

36. Herbert B. Adams to C. W. Bowen, March 4, 1893, ibid. Box 213, Folder: Treasurer's File, 1893.

37. Turner to Charles K. Adams, Feb. 23, 1893, SHSW, Turner Papers.

38. Justin Winsor to Herbert B. Adams, March 22, 1893, W. Stull Holt (ed.), *Historical Scholarship in the United States, 1876-1901: as Revealed in the Correspondence of Herbert B. Adams* (Baltimore, 1938), 199.

39. Herbert B. Adams to C. W. Bowen, June 3, 1893, LC, AHA Papers, Box 213, Folder: Treasurer's File, 1893.

40. Turner to W. F. Poole, May 10, 1893, Newberry, Poole Papers, Box: April-June, 1893. This letter, with explanatory remarks, is in W. L. Williamson, "A Sidelight on the Frontier Thesis: A New Turner Letter," *Newberry Library Bulletin*, III (April 1953), 46-49.

41. *Wisconsin State Journal*, May 16, 1893.

42. Turner to Woodrow Wilson, July 16, 1893, HEH TU Box 1. Turner wrote to Wilson four days after delivering his paper, apologizing for not writing sooner because he had been in the final agonies of getting out his paper.

43. "The Auxiliary Congresses," *The Dial*, XV (Aug. 1, 1893), 60. This unsigned article was written by William F. Poole. The congresses are described in *Chicago Tribune*, July 10, 11, and 12, *The New York Times*, July 12, p. 8, and Johnson Rossiter, *A History of the World's Columbian Exposition* (4 vols., Chicago, 1894), IV, 169-73.

44. That he did not read the full paper is suggested by the "Report of the Proceedings of the Ninth Annual Meeting of the American Historical Association," *Annual Report of the American Historical Association for 1893* (Washington, D.C., 1894), 6. This summary omits many points made by Turner in the later published version.

45. Turner, "The Significance of the Frontier in American History," *The Frontier in American History* (New York, 1920), 1-38.

46. This was the impression of Andrew C. McLaughlin, who, many years later, described the scene to Avery Craven, his colleague at the University of Chicago. Craven to author, Jan. 8, 1970.

47. *Chicago Tribune*, July 13, 1893, 3. The letter of thanks to Poole was from Mrs. Ellen H. Walworth of Saratoga, who read a paper, "The Value of National Archives." Mrs. Walworth to Poole, July 26, 1893, Newberry, Poole Papers, Box: April-July, 1893.

48. Charles K. Adams to A. J. Johnson of *Johnson's Universal Cyclopaedia*, July 17, 1893, University of Wisconsin Archives, Presidential Papers 4/8/1, Charles K. Adams, General Correspondence, 1891-1901, Box 5 (hereafter cited as U. of Wis. Arch. Pres. Corr.); Andrew J. Turner to Helen M. Turner, July 23, 1893; HEH TU Box E; *The Aegis*, Nov. 3, 1893.

49. Letters, HEH TU Box 1.

50. John Fiske to Turner, Feb. 6, 1894; Talcott Williams to Turner (n.d.), ibid. Ratzel's comments were in a review quoted in Murray Kane, "Some Considerations on the Frontier Concept of Frederick Jackson Turner," *Mississippi Valley Historical Review*, XXVII (Dec. 1940), 398-99. Ratzel incorporated much of Turner's thesis in one of his own essays. Copy, underlined by Turner to indicate references to himself, HEH TU File Drawer 21C, Folder: Miscellany.

Chapter VI
The Busy World of the Professor
1893–1901

1. Turner wrote these figures on the back pages of a paper notebook, "Expense Account, 1890" (HEH TU Box 61). His home was modest by faculty standards, paying taxes of $71.97 in 1897 and $110.17 in 1899. Other professor's homes were taxed at from $115.80 to $167.30 in the latter year (*Wisconsin State Journal*, May 19, 1897, Feb. 18, 1899).

2. A branch of the society was organized in Madison in December 1897, with E. A. Birge president and Mrs. Turner one of the directors (ibid. Dec. 9, 1897).

3. Turner to Charles H. Haskins, July 16, 1895, Charles Homer Haskins Papers, Firestone Library, Princeton University (hereafter cited as Princeton, Haskins Papers).

4. Mae Turner to Lucinda A. W. Sherwood, Oct. 23, 1897 (HEH TU Box F).

5. Libby's thesis, with an introduction by Turner, was published in 1894. When asked, some years later, whether Turner had suggested the map technique that he used so successfully, Libby escaped into generalizations, replying that "my map on the geographical distribution of the vote on the Constitution was the first effort along that line that I have been familiar with" (Orin G. Libby to Merle Curti, Aug. 24, 1928, HEH TU Box 39).

6. For Libby's later career at Wisconsin, see Fulmer Mood, "The Development of Frederick Jackson Turner as a Historical Thinker," *Transactions of the Colonial Society of Massachusetts, 1937-1942*, XXXIV (Boston, 1943), 331-35.

7. *Catalogue of the University of Wisconsin for 1895-1896* (Madison, 1896), 140.

8. *Wisconsin State Journal*, Nov. 22, 1895.

9. Course announcement, ibid. Feb. 10, 1896. Trent's lectures were later published as *Statesmen of the Old Regime* (New York, 1897).

10. The first quotation is from Frederick J. Turner, *The Colonization of North America. University Extension Department. Instruction by Correspondence* (Madison, [1897]), 1-2; the second from Frederick J. Turner,

American Development, 1789-1829. University Extension Department (Madison, 1895), 12; Turner also prepared a syllabus, *The Colonization of North America from the Earliest Times to 1763. University Extension Department Syllabus No. 23* (Madison, 1894) (HEH TU Vol. VI). The work of the extension speakers was described in *Wisconsin State Journal,* Nov. 30, 1895.

11. For notes Turner used in preparing this course in 1898, see HEH TU File Drawer 1D, Folder: English History. Summer School 1898.

12. Turner to Carl Becker, Nov. 7, 1898, HEH TU Box 2.

13. HEH TU File Drawer 1C.

14. See 3 × 5 file cards, "Program" or "Program Spring," on which Turner listed the lectures to be given each term (HEH TU Box 54). These show that the lectures varied greatly each year.

15. Louise P. Kellogg, "The Passing of a Great Teacher," *Historical Outlook,* XXIII (Oct. 1932), 271. For Turner's thesis topics and examinations during this period, see HEH TU Box 54 and File Drawer 15D, Folder: Notes for Organization of a Class, 1895-1896.

16. Laurence M. Larson to James A. James, May 22, 1910, HEH TU Vol. I, Red Book. This book contains numerous letters written by former students in 1910, when Turner left Wisconsin for Harvard.

17. Carl Becker, "Frederick Jackson Turner," Howard W. Odum (ed.), *American Masters of Social Science* (New York, 1927), 273-318; Joseph Schafer, "The Author of the Frontier Hypothesis," *Wisconsin Magazine of History,* XV (Sept. 1931), 86-103; Kellogg, "The Passing of a Great Teacher," loc. cit., 270-72; Wilbur R. Jacobs (ed.), "Turner As I Remember Him, by Herbert Eugene Bolton," *Mid-America,* XXXVI (Jan. 1964), 54-61. *See also* Wilbur R. Jacobs, "Frederick Jackson Turner—Master Teacher," *Pacific Historical Review,* XXIII (Feb. 1954), 49-58.

18. Quotations from Carl Becker, "Tribute to Frederick Jackson Turner," HEH TU Vol. I, Red Book.

19. This picture of Turner emerges particularly in reminiscences of Guy Stanton Ford, Oral History Research Office of Columbia University, pp. 76-79, 91-92. Ford's less-than-favorable impressions contrast with the remarks he made in his tribute to Turner in 1910 (HEH TU Vol. I, Red Book).

20. University of Wisconsin, Instructional Reports, 1893-1900, U. of Wis. Arch.

21. *The Sphynx,* I (April 13, May 11, 1900), 151, 169; *The Badger for 1894* (Madison, 1893), 252; *The Badger for 1895* (Madison, 1894), 277.

22. The titles of honor's theses were listed in the catalogues of the university.

23. Turner to Carl Becker, Nov. 7, 1898, HEH TU Box 2.

24. Titles of all master's theses were listed in the catalogues of the university.

25. *Daily Cardinal,* March 10, 1897, March 8, 1898. On May 8, 1898, the paper reported that Turner would not meet his classes for a week owing to his absence while inspecting secondary schools.

26. Turner's views on this subject were admirably expressed in Turner to James A. James, Jan. 21, 1894, HEH TU Box 1. Reference to his work on the committee to standardize history teaching is in Mrs. W. A. Noyes to Turner, Aug. 15, 1928, HEH TU Box 39.

27. These lectures were noted in the *Daily Cardinal*, Dec. 11, 1894, Jan. 6, 1897, Jan. 12, 1898; *Wisconsin State Journal*, Oct. 11, Nov. 30, 1901.

28. See MS (28 half-pp.), HEH TU Box 54, and *Wisconsin State Journal*, June 14, 15, 1895.

29. Text of address, *Portage Weekly Democrat*, Jan. 3, 1896, reprinted in Fulmer Mood (ed.), "Frederick Jackson Turner's Address on Education in the United States Without Free Lands," *Agricultural History*, XXIII (Oct. 1949), 254-59. Mood shows that Turner anticipated many of the views on education later popularized by John Dewey.

30. Plan described, *Wisconsin State Journal*, Nov. 23, 1901. Pamphlet, *Free Traveling Library, Series G. Contains a Group of Books Relating to the Revolution. Sent by Wisconsin Free Library Commission* (Madison, n.d.), copy, HEH TU File Drawer 15E, Folder: Wisconsin Library Commission.

31. *Wisconsin State Journal*, July 31, 1894. The controversy is fully described in Benjamin G. Rader, *The Academic Mind and Reform: The Influence of Richard T. Ely in American Life*, 130-58. Turner's efforts in Ely's defense noted in *Wisconsin State Journal*, Aug. 7, 9, 21, 22, 24, Sept. 18, 1894. In his testimony Turner quoted Adam Smith, John Stuart Mill, and other *laissez faire* economists to show they could be accused of statements far more radical than those ascribed to Ely.

32. *Daily Cardinal*, Feb. 20, 1900.

33. Turner represented Wisconsin at the inauguration of the chancellor of the University of Kansas in 1902, and he spoke to alumni groups there (*Daily Cardinal*, Nov. 3, 1902; May 20, 23, 1905).

34. The final volume of this eight-volume history was published in 1902. Turner's notes for his review are in HEH TU 3 × 5 Drawer No. 1. The manuscript of his address of January 23, 1894, is in HEH TU, File Drawer 15A, Folder: Essay on History of US by Von Holst. The meeting was reported in the *Wisconsin State Journal*, Jan. 23, 24, 1894; *Daily Cardinal*, Jan. 23, 24, 1894.

35. When Turner visited Chicago a month later he was told that Von Holst's colleagues were trying to prevent him from seeing the issue of the *Daily Cardinal* in which the essay was summarized. Turner to Mae Turner, Feb. 23, 1894, HEH TU Box F. William P. Trent in 1896 sought to publish the essay in the *Sewanee Review*, which he edited, but Turner refused. It was first published in Wilbur R. Jacobs (ed.), *Frederick Jackson Turner's Legacy: Unpublished Writings in American History* (San Marino, Calif., 1965), 85-104.

36. Turner, talk to Graduate Club early in 1897, "What Is History," *Daily Cardinal*, Feb. 18, 1897.

37. Turner to Alumni Dinner, June 1897, "The University of the Future," summarized in *The Aegis*, Sept. 1897, 10. The notes he used are in HEH TU File Drawer 15B, Folder: The University of the Future.

38. *Wisconsin State Journal*, Feb. 9, June 7, 9, 1897, June 9, 16, 1898.

39. Reports of Turner's lectures, Contemporary Club and Madison Literary Club, *Wisconsin State Journal*, May 17, Sept. 11, Nov. 13, 1894; Oct. 19, 1895; May 9, 11, 1896; Jan. 11, 12, 1897; *Daily Cardinal*, Nov. 13, 1894; Oct. 19, 1895; May 11, 1896; Jan. 12, 1897.

40. *Wisconsin State Journal*, Oct. 15, 1896. Turner's notes for this talk

(16 half-pp.), HEH TU File Drawer 15C, Folder: Talk before Madison Women's Club 1896.

41. Turner not only read widely on early Virginia history, but purchased copies of documents totaling 20,000 words. Address, "The Colonization of the James," HEH TU File Drawer 1D, Folder: Colonization of the James.

42. Correspondence between Wilson and Turner, Nov. 5-27, 1896, Frederick Jackson Turner Papers, Houghton Library, Harvard University (hereafter cited as Houghton, Turner Papers), Library of Congress, Woodrow Wilson Papers, Box 8 (hereafter cited as LC, Wilson Papers). Letters summarized in George C. Osborn, "Woodrow Wilson and Frederick Jackson Turner," *Proceedings of the New Jersey Historical Society*, LXXIV (July 1956), 219-27. The negotiations are described in Wilbur R. Jacobs, "Wilson's First Battle at Princeton: The Chair for Turner," *Harvard Library Bulletin*, VIII (Winter 1954), 74-87.

43. Wilson to Turner, March 31, 1897. Houghton, Turner Papers; Henry W. Bragdon, *Woodrow Wilson: The Academic Years* (Cambridge, 1967), 226, which quotes from Wilson's diary.

44. Charles K. Adams to Turner, May 12, 1897, HEH TU Box 2.

45. John B. McMaster to Turner, April 12, 1897; Simon N. Patten to Turner, May 8, 1897; James Harvey Robinson to Turner, April 12, 1897; Charles C. Harrison to Turner, May 7, 1897; HEH TU Box 2. In December 1897, he was asked by the president of Western Reserve University if he would be interested in moving, and told him that he would not (HEH TU Box 2).

46. *Wisconsin State Journal*, Feb. 11, 20, Oct. 23, 1899; *Daily Cardinal*, Oct. 17, 20, 23, 1899; *Madison Democrat*, Oct. 24, 1899.

47. Turner to Carl Becker, Nov. 17, 1899, HEH TU Box 2.

48. Charles McCarthy to J. Franklin Jameson, March 10, 1900, Elizabeth Donnan and F. L. Stock (eds.), "Letters: Charles McCarthy to J. Franklin Jameson," *Wisconsin Magazine of History*, XXXIII (Sept. 1949), 72.

49. Turner to Woodrow Wilson, March 12, 1900, LC, Wilson Papers, Box 10.

50. Note in Turner's hand, filed with newspaper clippings on children's deaths, HEH TU Vol. X.

51. William R. Harper to Turner, Feb. 14, 1900, HEH TU Box 3. A note attached reads: "March 10, 1900. Pres. Harper in personal interview invited me to accept head professorship in place of von Holst, salary 4000 first 2 years and 5000 thereafter."

52. Charles K. Adams to Board of Regents, March 16, 1900, enclosed in Adams to Turner, March 22, 1900, HEH TU Box 3.

53. Harper to Turner, April 6, 1900, HEH TU Box 3. Haskins had already informed Turner that he was not tempted by a $3000 salary, but that he would move if Turner decided to go. Haskins to Turner, April 4, 7, 8, 1900, HEH TU Box 3.

54. Harvey Pratt Judson to Turner, April 19, 1900, HEH TU Box 3. Turner to Dean E. A. Birge, April 14, 1900, setting forth the terms under which he would stay, U. of Wis. Arch., Pres. corr. Charles K. Adams, Box 6. Rough draft in Turner's hand, HEH TU Box 3.

55. *Daily Cardinal*, April 21, 1900. For a fuller account, Ray A. Billington,

"Frederick Jackson Turner Comes to Harvard," *Proceedings of the Massachusetts Historical Society*, LXXIV (1962), 55-59.

56. Turner to Edward L. Hardy, Feb. 15, 1902, University of Wisconsin Archives, College of Letters and Science, Department of History, Turner Correspondence, 1902-5 (hereafter cited as U. of Wis. Arch., L and S, Hist., Turner Corr.), Box 1, Folder H.

57. Turner to Charles H. Haskins, Aug. 7, 1900. Princeton, Haskins Papers; notebook, HEH TU Box 62.

58. Turner described the family's travels in letters to his mother, father, and sister, Sept. 9, 1900, to March 7, 1901 (HEH TU Box F). Quotation, Turner to "Dear Father," Sept. 17, 1900.

59. Turner to Mae Turner, April 30, 1901, HEH TU Box F.

60. *Daily Cardinal*, April 24, May 3, 1901.

Chapter VII
Broadening Historical Horizons
1893-1910

1. Turner to Charles H. Haskins, July 15, 1896, Princeton, Haskins Papers.

2. T. C. Chamberlin, "The Method of Multiple Working Hypotheses," *Journal of Geology*, V (Nov.-Dec., 1897), 837-48. Paper, Society of Western Naturalists, 1889, reported in *Science*, XV (Feb. 7, 1890), 92-96. *See also* Wilbur R. Jacobs, "Turner's Methodology: Multiple Working Hypothesis or Ruling Theory?" *Journal of American History*, LIV (March 1968), 853-63.

3. For Turner's notes, see HEH TU File Drawer 1A, Folder: New England Towns. He also prepared a brief essay on the subject (HEH TU File Drawer 3D, Folder: New England Towns).

4. Turner to J. Franklin Jameson, June 9, 1895, HEH TU Box 2. Jameson met Turner at the New Haven meeting of the American Historical Association in 1898 (Jameson to Mae Turner, March 17, 1932, HEH TU Vol. V).

5. Extended correpondence between Turner and Jameson, August 16–Sept. 6, 1895, HEH TU Box 2.

6. As the first installment was being printed, Turner was still gathering information for the second (Herbert L. Osgood to Turner, Sept. 19, 1896, HEH TU Box 2; *see also* Notes in HEH TU File Drawers 4B and 4C). At about this time Turner published "The Rise and Fall of New France," *Chautauquan*, XXIV (Oct. 1896), 31-34, (Dec. 1896), 295-300, reprinted in Fulmer Mood (ed.), "An Unfamiliar Essay of Frederick J. Turner," *Minnesota History*, XVIII (Dec. 1937), 381-98.

7. See Waldo G. Leland, "J. Franklin Jameson and the Origin of the National Historical Publications Commission," Ruth A. Fisher and William L. Fox (eds), *J. Franklin Jameson: A Tribute* (Washington, D.C., 1965), 27-36. Minutes of first meeting, J. Franklin Jameson Papers, Library of Congress, Manuscripts Division, Box 7 (hereafter cited as LC, Jameson Papers).

8. Turner to Woodrow Wilson, Dec. 27, 1896, LC, Wilson Papers, Box 8.

9. Many years later Turner told a class that his interest in diplomatic his-

tory had begun when he was reviewing the fourth volume of Theodore Roosevelt's *The Winning of the West* for the *American Historical Review* in 1896. He disbelieved Roosevelt's statement that President Jefferson was personally involved in the intrigues of Citizen Genêt and decided to make his own investigation of the episode (*Kansas City Star*, Jan. 20, 1923; HEH TU File Drawer 15D, Folder: Frontier in American History. Reviews).

10. Notes taken by Turner for his editorial duties, HEH TU File Drawers 5B and 6D. All articles and documents were published in the *American Historical Review* or the *Annual Report of the American Historical Association* between 1897 and 1903.

11. Turner to W. C. Ford, Feb. 19, 1902, U. of Wis. Arch., L. and S., Hist., Turner Corr., Box 1, Folder F. For other letters from Turner to Ford, completing arrangements for publishing the documents, see HEH TU Boxes 3 and 4.

12. Turner to Edward G. Bourne, Feb. 27, Sept. 30, 1903, Jan. 29, Nov. 9, 1904, HEH TU Box 4. Bourne to Turner, March 8, 14, May 1, Sept. 30, Oct. 3, 1903, Jan. 26, Nov. 14, 1904. U. of Wis. Arch., L. and S., Hist., Turner Corr., Box 3, Folder B.

13. Turner to J. Franklin Jameson, Oct. 3, 1905. LC, Jameson Papers, Box 6.

14. *Wisconsin State Journal*, Jan. 14, 1902; *Daily Cardinal*, March 10, 1902. Turner's Notes, HEH TU File Drawer 5C, Folder: Louisiana Purchase.

15. Lecture, stenographic report, HEH TU File Drawer 14C, Folder: After Dinner Speech. Notes used in speaking, HEH TU File Drawer 15D, Folder: Historical Significance of Louisiana Purchase. Draft of article, HEH TU File Drawer 15C, Folder: Early Form of Policy of France.

16. Turner to Max Farrand, April 15, 1905, HEH TU Box 5.

17. Turner to John M. Vincent, March 10, 1907, HEH TU Box 7.

18. Turner discussed the Russo-Japanese War before the Six-O'clock Club of Madison (*Wisconsin State Journal*, Dec. 7, 1904).

19. Turner to Mae Turner, [Sept. 1, 1901, incorrectly dated 1903], describes his long hours of work while preparing these articles (HEH TU Box F). Invitation to prepare the articles, C. H. Dennis, *Chicago Daily News*, to Turner, July 17, 1901, HEH TU Box 1. Extensive file on Irish immigration, HEH TU File Drawer 5A, Unmarked folder. Notes and map on German immigration, HEH TU File Drawer 2C, Folder: Germans to Penn; manuscript of a portion of this article, HEH TU File Drawer 8D, Folder: Germans in West.

20. The articles in *Chicago Record-Herald*, Aug. 28, Sept. 4, 11, 18, 25, Oct. 16, 1901, were clipped by Turner, pasted, and bound (HEH, Rare book Accession No. 126565). Merrill H. Crissey to Fulmer Mood, Jan. 7, 1938, HEH TU Box 52, is a discussion by Turner's secretary of the immigration articles.

21. F. J. Turner, "Recent Studies in American History," *Atlantic Monthly*, LXXVII (June 1896), 837. Turner was invited to review a number of books in ten pages of the magazine, at $8 per page. Horace E. Scudder to Turner, Feb. 7, 14, June 5, 1896, Houghton, Turner Papers.

22. Turner's review of Burgess, *The Middle Period, 1817-1858*, appeared in the *Educational Review*, XIV (Nov. 1897), 390-95, and his review of James Ford Rhodes, *History of the United States from the Compromise of*

1850, Vol. III, in the *Political Science Quarterly*, XI (March 1896), 167-70.

23. Turner reviewed Winsor, *The Westward Movement*, in the *American Historical Review*, III (April 1898), 556-61; Elliott Coues, *History of the Expedition under the Command of Lewis and Clark*, in *The Dial*, XVI (Feb. 1, 1894), 80-82; Alexander Brown, *English Politics in Early Virginia History*, in the *American Historical Review*, VII (Oct. 1901), 159-63; and Reuben G. Thwaites, *Early Western Travels*, in *The Dial*, XXXVII (Nov. 16, 1904), 298-302, XLI (July 1, 1906), 6-10.

24. Review of Mrs. Neville and Miss Martin, *Historical Green Bay, 1634-1840*, *The Aegis*, VIII (April 24, 1894); Turner to J. Franklin Jameson, June 9, 1895, HEH TU Box 2.

25. F. J. Turner, "Francis Parkman and His Works," *The Dial*, XXV (Dec. 16, 1898), 451-53.

26. Turner to Woodrow Wilson, Dec. 24, 1896, LC, Wilson Papers, Box 7.

27. *American Historical Review*, VIII (July 1903), 762-65.

28. Years later Turner told his secretary that "the severance of the warm friendship of many years between Woodrow Wilson and him was caused by adverse comments in his review" (HEH TU Box 35, Folder: Merrill H. Crissey, Drafts of Biographical Data). Turner did review H. M. Chittenden, *History of Early Steamboat Navigation on the Missouri River*, and the latter volumes of Thwaites, *Early Western Travels*, in 1906. He also reviewed J. B. Winslow, *The Story of the Great Court: Being a Sketch of the Supreme Court of Wisconsin*, *American Historical Review*, XVII (July 1912), 859-60.

29. Wilson to Mrs. Wilson, April 27, 1903, copy in HEH TU Box 4.

30. Guy Stanton Ford, "Reminiscences of Guy Stanton Ford," Oral History Research Office, Columbia Univ.

31. So he told his secretary (HEH TU Box 35, Folder: Merrill H. Crissey, Drafts of Biographical Data).

32. Turner's reviews of the last two volumes of Roosevelt, *Winning of the West*, appeared in *The Nation*, LX (March 28, 1895), 240-42, LXIII (Oct. 8, 1896), 277, and in the *American Historical Review*, II (Oct. 1896), 171-76. Roosevelt initiated the correspondence (April 2, 1895). He wrote Turner again April 10, 26, 1895, Nov. 4, and Dec. 15, 1896 (Houghton, Turner Papers).

33. Turner's review of Channing, *A Student's History of the United States*, was published in the *Educational Review*, XVIII (Oct. 1899), 301-4.

34. F. J. Turner, "The Development of American Society," *The [Illinois] Alumni Quarterly*, II (July 1908), 120. He gave a prior version of this talk as the Phi Beta Kappa address at the University of Nebraska, June 10, 1907. MS of lecture, "Social Forces in American History," HEH TU Box 55.

35. Turner owned copies of Droysen, *Grundriss der Historik* (Leipzig, 1882), and *Outline of the Principles of History* (Boston, 1893). Both are underlined and contain his marginalia (HEH Accession Nos. 124357, 124480).

36. F. J. Turner, "The Historical Library in the University," Brown University, John Carter Brown Library, *The Dedication of the Library Building, May the Seventeenth, A. D. MDCCCCIIII. With the Addresses by*

William Vail Kellen, LL.D., and Frederick Jackson Turner, Ph.D. (Providence, 1905), 57.

37. Turner, "Social Forces in American History," HEH TU Box 55.

38. Turner, "Historical Library in the University," *loc. cit.* 50-51.

39. Turner, "Development of American Society," *loc. cit.* 120-21.

40. For correspondence with speakers for the 1904 historical congress in St. Louis, see Albion W. Small Papers, Univ. of Chicago Library, Special Collections Dept., Box I, Folder 9 (hereafter cited as Chicago, Small Papers).

41. This address, bearing a notation that it was delivered in Madison, is in HEH TU File Drawer 14A, Folder: Madison 1901 October 16. A comparison with the 1904 paper shows that the second was re-written from the 1901 version, with more mature insights and interpretations.

42. Turner to Mae Turner, Sept. 17, 21, 23, 25, 1901, HEH TU Box F. Turner discussed the publication of the paper with Albion W. Small, hoping to have it appear in a national journal of prominence. Turner to Small, Oct. 31, 1904; Small to Turner, Nov. 2, 1904. U. of Wis. Arch., L. and S., Hist., Turner Corr., Box 5, Folder S.

43. Turner, "Problems in American History," Howard J. Rogers (ed.), *International Congress of Arts and Science, Universal Exposition, St. Louis, 1904* (Boston, 1906), II, 183-94, reprinted in Turner, *The Significance of Sections in American History* (New York, 1932), 3-21.

Chapter VIII
Popularizing the Frontier Thesis
1893-1910

1. See Lee Benson, "The Historian as Mythmaker: Turner and the Closed Frontier," David M. Ellis (ed.), *The Frontier in American Development. Essays in Honor of Paul Wallace Gates* (Ithaca, 1969), 15-19.

2. See Peter J. Schmitt, *Back to Nature: The Arcadian Myth in Urban America* (New York, 1969); for a more interpretative account see Roderick Nash, *Wilderness and the American Mind* (New Haven, 1967). On the relationships between the closing of the frontier and American foreign policy, see Walter LaFeber, *The New Empire: An Interpretation of American Expansion, 1860-1898* (Ithaca, 1963), 62-72.

3. Woodrow Wilson, "Mr. Goldwin Smith's 'Views' on Our Political History," *The Forum*, XVI (Dec. 1893), 495-97. After reading this review, William E. Dodd asked Wilson whether he had developed the frontier thesis before Turner. He was told that Turner was entirely responsible, and that Wilson's materials were supplied by him (Dodd to Turner, Oct. 3, 1919, HEH TU Box 29). For correspondence, Ray A. Billington, *The Genesis of the Frontier Thesis: A Study in Historical Creativity* (San Marino, Calif., 1971), 181-201. Wendell H. Stephenson (ed.), "The Influence of Woodrow Wilson on Frederick Jackson Turner," *Agricultural History*, XIX (Oct. 1945), 249-53, had earlier reproduced some of the letters.

4. Turner to Wilson, Dec. 30, 1893, LC, Wilson Papers, Box 6.

5. Quotations from Woodrow Wilson, "The Proper Perspective in Amer-

ican History," *The Forum*, XIX (July 1895), 544-59, and "The Course of American History" Wilson, *Mere Literature and Other Essays* (Boston, 1896), 231-32. John Fiske also popularized the thesis. He wrote (March 15, 1895) that he had addressed the Missouri Historical Society on "The Influence of the Frontier upon American Life" [Ethel F. Fiske, *The Letters of John F. Fiske* (New York, 1940), 639].

6. Charles A. McMurray (ed.), *Fifth Yearbook of the National Hebart Society* (Chicago, 1899), 7-41. The different versions of the essay printed at this time are compared by Fulmer Mood in Turner, *The Early Writings of Frederick Jackson Turner* (Madison, 1938), 275-92.

7. A. M. Simons to Turner, Oct. 21, 26, 1905; Turner to Simons, March 30, 1903. Simons first asked permission to reprint the essay in 1903, then again in 1905. U. of Wis. Arch., L. and S., Hist. Turner Corr. Box 5, Folder S. Turner's copy, *International Socialist Review*, VI (Dec. 1905), 321-46, HEH Accession No. 126776.

8. Jesse C. Bullock, *Select Readings in Economics* (Boston, 1907), 23-59.

9. H. Morse Stephens to Turner, Aug. 19, 1895; Turner to Stephens, May 29, 1896. Henry Morse Stephens Papers, University of California at Berkeley (hereafter cited as Calif., Stephens Papers).

10. Turner to Stephens, Dec. 22, 1896, ibid.

11. For Turner's paper and comments that it inspired, see *Annual Report of the American Historical Association for 1896* (Washington, D.C., 1897), I, 281-96.

12. C. K. Adams to W. E. Appleton, July 17, 1893, U. of Wis. Arch., Pres. Corr., C. K. Adams General Corr., Box 5, is Adams's letter of recommendation [Published in *Johnson's Universal Cyclopaedia* (New York, 1894), III, 606-7; reprinted in Fulmer Mood (ed.), "Little Known Fragments of Turner's Writings," *Wisconsin Magazine of History*, XXIII (March 1940), 338-41].

13. Notes, HEH TU File Drawer 15C, Folder: Old Northwest. Notes and Drafts. 1896. The letter of rejection, suggesting other topics on which Turner might write, is Horace E. Scudder to Turner, April 10, 1896, Houghton, Turner Papers.

14. Walter Hines Page to Turner, May 29, July 14, 24, 29, Aug. 6, 1896, ibid. A portion of Turner's manuscript, incorrectly labeled as an early draft of the 1893 essay, is in HEH TU File Drawer 15, Folder: Draft of Turner's 1893 Essay.

15. Page to Turner, Aug. 22, 1896, Houghton, Turner Papers. Turner suggested and was paid a fee of $75.

16. *Chicago Tribune*, Aug. 30, 1896; *Boston Herald*, Aug. 22, 1896. Newspaper clippings, reviews and comment, HEH TU Box 54, Folder: Reviews of Turner's 'The Problem of the West.'

17. Page to Turner, Aug. 22, Sept. 4, Oct. 8, 1896; Turner to Page, Aug. 30, 1896, Houghton, Turner Papers. The *Wisconsin State Journal*, Dec. 3, 1896, printed an advertisement of the series.

18. Page to Turner, Feb. 25, March 26, June 11, July 2, Sept. 9, 1896, Houghton, Turner Papers.

19. Turner, "The Middle West," reprinted in Turner, *The Frontier in American History*, 147-48.

20. Turner, "Contributions of the West to American Democracy," ibid. 268. The *International Monthly* requested another article on "The Comparison of Social Conditions of the East and West" which Turner agreed to do but never submitted. Frederick A. Richardson to Turner, Jan. 3, 10, 1902; Turner to Richardson, Jan. 7, 1902. U. of Wis. Arch., L. and S., Hist., Turner Corr., Box 1, Folder R. Correspondence concerning the *World's Work* article, HEH TU Box 4 and File Drawer 15B, Folder: Jottings on the State University of the Midwest; correspondence with W. C. Cunliff of *World's Work*, U. of Wis. Arch., L. and S., Hist., Turner Corr., Box 3, Folder C.

21. *Evanston Index,* Jan. 31, 1903.

22. This sampling of a few of the speeches given by Turner has been compiled from notices in the *Wisconsin State Journal, Daily Cardinal,* and other newspapers, and from Turner's own notes and correspondence. Typical are: "Notes for Speech 30 Minutes on Frontier Soldier" (HEH TU File Drawer 2E, unmarked Folder); "The Old Forts of Green Bay" (File Drawer 15C, Folder: Address at Green Bay, Wis.); and "George Washington" (File Drawer 15B, Folder: A Talk: Three Pioneers).

23. Correspondence concerning these lectures is in HEH TU Boxes 13 and 14. Turner's honorarium, normally $50, was $150 for the Indiana commencement address. An early draft of the lecture, in which he removed references to Kansas history, is in U. of Wis. Arch., Misc. File: Frederick Jackson Turner.

24. The address was first printed in the *Indiana University Bulletin,* VIII (June 15, 1910), 6-29, and reprinted in Turner, *The Frontier in American History,* 269-89.

25. Turner to Mae Turner, Dec. 1, 2, 3, 1903, HEH TU Box F; April 17, 18, 19, 21, 24, 26, 29, 1910, ibid. Box G. He was paid $500 for the Pennsylvania series.

26. The lectures were published in the professional journals of the sponsoring organizations at the time (reprinted in Turner, *The Frontier in American History,* 157-76, 177-204, quotations, pp. 170, 203).

27. Henry Holt & Co. to Turner, Feb. 14, March 6, 1895, HEH TU Box 63; Turner to Holt, Feb. 26, 1895. Henry Holt & Co. Archives, Dept. of Rare Books and Special Collections, Princeton Univ. Library (hereafter cited as Princeton, Holt Arch.).

28. Holt to Turner, Nov. 16, 1895, Jan. 9, 28, 1895, HEH TU Box 63; Turner to Holt, Jan. 16, Oct. 2, 1896, Princeton, Holt Arch.

29. W. P. Trent to George P. Brett, March 14, 1896, Macmillan Co. Records, New York. Letters, supplied to the Huntington Library by the Macmillan Co. (HEH TU Box 2).

30. George P. Brett, Macmillan Co., to Turner, March 18, April 4, 1896; Turner to Brett, March 28, 1896; William P. Trent to Turner, April 6, 1896, HEH TU Box 2.

31. Kate Stephens to Turner, June 3, 16, Oct. 8, 1897, HEH TU Box 2. In refusing the Putnam invitation, Turner held the door open. He wrote on the last letter, "If details with others not satisfactory will accept offer to make proposals." G. P. Putnam's Sons to Turner, March 27, April 7, Sept. 23, Oct. 10, 1897, HEH TU Box 2.

32. Holt & Co. to Turner, May 27, June 17, July 28, Aug. 19, 1897, HEH

TU Box 63; Turner to Holt, June 11, July 21, Aug. 15, 1897, Princeton, Holt Arch.

33. Macmillan Co. to Turner, Sept. 13, 18, Oct. 14, 1897, HEH TU Box 2.

34. A memorandum (October 18, 1897) filed with his correspondence describes the interview with Bristol. The contract for the college textbook was sent to him on November 3, 1897, that for the high school text (HEH TU Box 63), on September 5, 1900. In the latter contract, he agreed to produce a 200,000 to 250,000-word manuscript within fourteen months.

35. Macmillan Co. to Turner, Nov. 3, 1897, HEH TU Box 2.

36. Reference to the contract with Ginn and Co. is in Ginn and Co. to Turner, Dec. 9, 1901, May 8, 1906, U. of Wis. Arch., L. and S., Hist., Turner Corr., Box 1, Folder G, and Ginn and Co. to Turner, May 8, 1906, HEH TU Box 7. The company archives were destroyed a generation ago, and no copy of the contract has been preserved. Negotiations concerning the "Western State-Making" book are in F. F. Browne to Turner, Nov. 12, Dec. 2, 1901, U. of Wis. Arch., L. and S., Hist., Turner Corr., Box 1, Folder B.

37. Walter H. Page to Turner, Oct. 8, 1897, March 7, 1898, Aug. 18, Oct. 30, 1899, Houghton, Turner Papers.

38. Houghton, Mifflin and Co. to Turner, Feb. 26, May 2, Aug. 5, 1901, U. of Wis. Arch., L. and S. Hist., Turner Corr., Box 1, Folder H.

39. To Turner's credit, he rejected almost as many offers from publishers as he accepted—including the editing of historical works for L. B. Lippincott and Co. and Arthur H. Clark Co.; an updating of Woodrow Wilson's *Division and Reunion* for Longman's, Green and Co.; a history of Wisconsin for Houghton, Mifflin and Co.; a biography of Cyrus Hall McCormick, suggested by his son; a volume on the teaching of American history, suggested by John Dewey for Appleton and Co.; a section on the United States from 1789 to 1850 for the *Cambridge Modern History;* and a volume in the collaborative economic history of the United States, sponsored by the Carnegie Institution of Washington. In rejecting the last, Turner wrote J. Franklin Jameson, "I am already a bankrupt in promises, and have determined not to add to my liabilities this year" (Turner to Jameson, Sept. 28, 1904, ibid., Box 5, Folder J).

40. Turner to Houghton, Mifflin, January 21, 1902, HEH TU Box 3.

41. Houghton, Mifflin to Turner, Sept. 19, Nov. 20, 1902; Turner to Houghton, Mifflin, Nov. 12, Dec. 4, 1902, June 9, Oct. 9, 1903, U. of Wis. Arch., L. and S., Hist., Turner Corr., Boxes 2 and 3, Folder H.

42. Notes, HEH TU File Drawer 13.

43. Houghton, Mifflin to Turner, June 15, Nov. 4, 1904, March 10, 1905, Aug. 21, 1908, May 26, 1924; Turner to Houghton, Mifflin, March 17, 1905. The letters of 1904 and 1905 are in U. of Wis. Arch., L. and S., Hist., Turner Corr., Box 5, Folder H; the letters of 1908 and 1924 are in HEH TU Boxes 11 and 33.

44. Turner to Frank O. Lowden, Jan. 6, 1904. U. of Wis. Arch., L. and S., Hist., Turner Corr., Box 4, Folder L. Turner expressed the same views in an interview (*Wisconsin State Journal*, Oct. 28, 1903).

45. Max Farrand to Turner, Oct. 3, 1905, ibid. Box 5, Folder F.

46. Turner to Max Farrand, Jan. 3, 1905, HEH TU Box 5.

Chapter IX
The Genesis of the Sectional Concept
1893-1910

1. Turner to Constance L. Skinner, March 15, 1922, HEH TU Box 31.

2. Quotation from fragment of lecture prepared about 1922, HEH TU File Drawer 15A, Folder: Piece on Sectionalism.

3. G. Tatham, "Geography in the Nineteenth Century," Griffith Taylor (ed.), *Geography in the Twentieth Century* (London, 1951), 64-65.

4. R. J. Harrison Church, "The French School of Geography," ibid. 75-76; Thomas W. Freeman, *A Hundred Years of Geography* (Chicago, 1962), 82-84. An extreme statement of this point of view, with which Turner was certainly familiar, was James Bryce, "The Relations of History and Geography," *Contemporary Review*, XLIX (March 1886), 426-43. Using English counties as examples, Bryce argued that the economy, and hence political behavior, was the product of geographic conditions. He urged historians to apply this principle to a complete re-study of the past.

5. E. W. Hilgard, "A Report on the Relation of Soil to Climate," U.S. Dept. of Agriculture, *Weather Bureau Bulletion No. 3* (Washington, D.C., 1892), 1-59.

6. Advances in statistical cartography are described in Richard Jensen, "American Election Analysis: A Case History of Methodological Innovation and Diffusion," Seymour M. Lipset (ed.), *Politics and the Social Sciences* (New York, 1969). Turner almost certainly heard Henry Gannett when he delivered two lectures in Madison in 1896, on "Topographical Methods of the Great National Survey" (reported, *Wisconsin State Journal*, April 29, 1896).

7. Turner to William E. Dodd, Oct. 7, 1919, HEH TU Box 29. The influence of Jedidiah Morse and other early geographers on Turner is appraised in Fulmer Mood, "The Origin, Evolution, and Application of the Sectional Concept, 1750-1900," Merrill Jensen (ed.), *Regionalism in America* (Madison, 1951), 5-98.

8. Memorandum, HEH TU File Drawer 15D, Folder: Sectionalism and Nationalism.

9. Turner's offprint, published originally in *Transactions of the Wisconsin Academy of Sciences, Arts and Letters* (Madison, 1888-91), VIII, 7, is in HEH TU File Drawer 14B, Folder: Sectional Feature in American Politics.

10. Quotation from John I. Hare, *American Constitutional Law* (Boston, 1889), I, 13, copied by Turner, along with other quotations and a list of books mentioning sectionalism, on cover of Desmond article (note 9, above).

11. Turner's copy of Powell's essay, 1895 version, underlined and annotated, HEH TU File Drawer L2, Folder: Powell. Before Powell's maps appeared Turner had drawn his own showing sectional divisions, based on contour maps of the U.S. Geological Survey (described in Turner to Woodrow Wilson, Dec. 24, 1894, LC, Wilson Papers, Box 7).

12. Turner discussed this subject in a twenty-one page letter to Walter Hines Page, Aug. 30, 1896, Houghton, Turner Papers (printed in Mood, "Origin, Evolution, and Application of the Sectional Concept," loc. cit. 91-96).

13. Turner to Merle Curti, Aug. 8, 1928, HEH TU Box 39.

14. Josiah Royce, *Provincialism. An Address to the Phi Beta Kappa Society of the State University of Iowa* (Iowa City, 1902), 5. Turner's copy, HEH TU File Drawer L2, Folder: 0501.

15. Turner's notes of Van Hise's lectures, Oct., Nov. 1898, are in HEH File Drawer 12C, Folder: Van Hise Course; 14D, Folder: Lecture Physical Geography; and 15A, Folder: Notes on Van Hise's Lectures. The course was described by the *Daily Cardinal*, Oct. 4, 1898.

16. *Daily Cardinal*, May 15, 1895; *The Aegis*, June 7, 1897.

17. A typescript of the 1901 thesis by William F. Dickinson, "The Personnel of the Wisconsin State Legislature for the Years 1850, 1860, and 1870," is in the State Historical Society of Wisconsin Library. Jesse Macy and Turner discussed some of his student assignments (Macy to Turner, Jan. 28, 1903, Turner to Macy, Feb. 10, 1903, U. of Wis. Arch., L. and S., Hist., Turner Corr., Box 3, Folder M).

18. Undated portion of lecture labeled "History of the West," summer 1902, from lecture notes kept by a student, Homer C. Hockett. Copies of these lectures are scattered through HEH TU.

19. Lecture on "The Upland South: The Colonization of a Province," HEH TU File Drawer 3A, Folder: Formation of the Upland South. Turner in a lecture to the Chicago Geographical Society about this time, postulated the different course of American history if the land had been flat and had had an unvarying climate (HEH TU File Drawer 14A, Folder: Influence of Geography upon the Settlement of the United States).

20. These changes are analyzed in Fulmer Mood, "A Comparison of Differing Versions of 'The Significance of the Frontier,'" Turner, *The Early Writings of Frederick Jackson Turner* (Madison, 1938), 275-92. For a statement of Turner's views on sectionalism at this time, see his review of Ellen C. Semple and Albert P. Brigham, "Geographical Interpretations of History," *The Journal of Geography*, IV (Jan. 1905), 34-37.

21. Turner to J. Franklin Jameson, Jan. 10, 1900, HEH TU Box 3.

22. Albert B. Hart to Turner, Jan. 2, 10, 1902; Turner to Hart, Jan. 7, 1902, U. of Wis. Arch., L. and S., Hist., Turner Corr., Box 1, Folder H.

23. Turner to Jameson, Feb. 4, 1902, ibid. Box 1, Folder J.

24. Turner to Charles R. Van Hise, Dec. 14, 1904, ibid. Box 5; Folder V. Hart to Turner, Feb. 13, March 12, 1902; Turner to Hart, March 8, 12, 1902, ibid., Box 1, Folder H.

25. Courses described in university catalogues for 1904-7. Two half-sheets in Turner's hand, "Program, 1905-1906. 1st Semester. History 14 US 1816-37," HEH TU File Drawer 15B, Folder: Program, U. S. 1816-1837, reveal the schedule of lectures. The last line was prophetic: "Possibly get to 1837."

26. Turner kept most of the materials prepared by his students (HEH TU File Drawer 9B, Folder: Seminary, History 58, 1904; HEH TU Collection of Student Papers, Boxes 1-5).

27. Turner's reading notes, HEH TU Box 55, and File Drawers 5C, 9A, and 9C. The two outlines, Oct. 1, 1904, and Nov. 17, 1905, HEH TU File Drawer 7E, Folder: Table of Contents, 1819-29.

28. These lectures were summarized in the *University of Michigan News-Letter*, Feb. 20, 1905, and the *Daily Cardinal*, March 4, 1905.

29. Hart to Turner, June 3, 9, 24, 1905, HEH TU Box 5. Correspondence on the maps for the period May 11 to July 23, ibid.

30. Reminiscences of Merrill H. Crissey, HEH TU Box 57, Folder: Merrill H. Crissey, Drafts of Biographical Data. Crissey continued to work with Turner until the fall of 1906, when he left to take a position with his uncle in the South.

31. Turner to Hart, Aug. 3, 1905; Hart to Turner, Aug. 16, 1905, U. of Wis. Arch., L. and S., Hist., Turner Corr., Box 5, Folder H.

32. Hart to Turner, Aug. 23, 28, 1905, HEH TU Box 5.

33. Hart to Turner, Oct. 12, 21, 24, 25, 1905, HEH TU Box 5. Turner to Hart, Sept. 29, 1905, U. of Wis. Arch., L. and S., Hist., Turner Corr., Box 5, Folder H. The Nucleus Club was an informal organization of the inner circle that controlled the American Historical Association. The members usually met for a gala dinner after the annual convention (Turner to Mae Turner, Dec. 7, 1905, HEH TU Box G). Turner was asked at this time to allow the *American Historical Review* to print portions of the book before it was published. He and the editor eventually agreed on the chapter on the South, and extracts from the chapters on the West and the Far West. They were printed in January and April, 1906. Correspondence between Turner and J. Franklin Jameson, leading to their publication, is in U. of Wis. Arch., L. and S., Hist., Turner Corr., Box 5, Folder J.

34. Hart to Turner, Dec. 9, 11, 13, 14, 1905, HEH TU Box 5.

35. Hart to Turner, Jan. 10, 16, Feb. 8, 23, 24, March 1, 12, 13, 14, 1906, HEH TU Box 6.

36. Turner to Max Farrand, Dec. 29, 1905; Hart to Farrand, June 2, 1933, HEH TU Boxes 5 and 50A.

37. Turner, *Rise of the New West, 1819-1829* (New York, 1906), xvii.

38. Copies of these reviews and others, HEH TU Box 55.

39. James Ford Rhodes to Turner, July 11, 1908; Charles R. Van Hise to Turner, Oct. 5, 1906, HEH TU Boxes 11 and 7. Sales justified a second printing in 1907, giving Turner a chance to correct some twenty-five minor errors (Turner to Harper & Brothers, Jan. 22, 1907, HEH TU Box 8).

40. Memorandum attached to letter from Holt & Co., May 25, 1905, summarizing letters he had written making these suggestions. Negotiations continued: Holt & Co. to Turner, May 5, 25, June 12, 1905; Turner to Holt & Co., May 25, 1905 (HEH TU Box 63); Ginn and Co., to Turner, May 8, July 27, 1905 (HEH TU Box 7).

41. Turner to Holt & Co., Aug. 10, 1905; Holt & Co. to Turner, Oct. 7, 14, 1905, HEH TU Box 63. Turner insisted on giving the company his personal note, promising to repay the $500 within two years if the book had not appeared (described in handwritten addition to letter received Oct. 14, 1905). His optimistic estimate of his completion date, Turner to Max Farrand, Oct. 13, 1905, U. of Wis. Arch., L. and S., Hist., Turner Corr., Box 5, Folder F.

42. Holt & Co. to Turner, Oct. 26, 1905, HEH TU Box 63. Proof of an announcement of the book was sent to Charles Homer Haskins, editor of the American Historical Series in which it was to appear (proof in Edward N. Bristol to Haskins, May 16, 1907, Princeton, Haskins Papers).

43. Notes and schedules, HEH TU File Drawer 15C, Folder: College History of the US.

44. Drafts of chapters, ibid. The quotation is from the Introduction.

45. William S. Robinson to Turner, Jan. 28, 1907; William R. Shepherd to Turner, Nov. 17, 1911; Homer C. Hockett to Turner, Sept. 27, 1913, HEH TU Boxes 8, 16, 20.

46. Holt & Co. to Turner, Jan. 24, 1911, HEH TU Box 63; Holt & Co. to Turner, Dec. 6, 1915, Princeton, Holt Arch.

47. Turner to Mae Turner, Dec. 30, 1908, March 11, 1915, HEH TU Boxes G and I.

48. Turner to Charles R. Van Hise, March 1, 14, 1907, describe his life in Washington (U. of Wis. Arch., Pres. Corr., C. R. Van Hise Gen. Corr., Box 16, Folder: F. J. Turner). Lectures described in *Daily Cardinal*, April 9, 1907, and arrangements for Johns Hopkins visit discussed in Turner to John M. Vincent, March 19, April 2, 1907, HEH TU Boxes 8 and 9.

49. Turner to Mae Turner, May 4, 13, 1907, HEH TU Box G.

50. Turner to Ellen C. Semple, Sept. 24, Oct. 21, 1907; Turner to C. H. Haskins, Sept. 24, 28, 1907, HEH TU Box 9A.

51. Turner to George L. Burr, Nov. 9, 1907; Burr to Turner, Nov. 13, 1907, George Lincoln Burr Papers, Division of Regional History and Archives, Cornell University (hereafter cited as Cornell, Burr Papers). Turner's report of this discussion, addressed to William A. Dunning, is in HEH TU Box 10 [printed in *Annual Report of the American Historical Association for 1907* (Washington, D.C., 1908), I, 45-47]. For a discussion of the meeting, see H. Roy Merrens, "Historical Geography and Early American History," *William and Mary Quarterly*, XXII (Oct. 1965), 538.

52. Turner to Claude H. Van Tyne, April 25, 1908. Claude H. Van Tyne Papers, Clements Library, University of Michigan (hereafter cited as Clements, Van Tyne Papers). Another session relating geography to history, at the 1908 meeting of the Association, was no more successful. Again, George Lincoln Burr voiced his strong objections to geographical determinism. Turner, who served as discussant, did little more than urge an analysis of "the various divisions of America to see of what economic sections they are composed." He was far from happy with the results (Turner to Mae Turner, Dec. 30, 1908, HEH TU Box G).

53. A copy of this article from the *Yale Review*, Nov. 1906, was sent Turner by Johnson; he followed his usual practice of underlining and adding marginal notations (HEH TU File Drawer L2, Folder: 0090).

54. Typed version, HEH TU File Drawer L3, Folder: 0524; printed in *American Journal of Sociology*, XIII (March 1908), 661-75.

55. Turner in talk to Thursday Club (Cambridge, Dec. 15, 1921, HEH TU File Drawer 14A, Folder: Draft, Revised, Recent American Sectionalism). Discussion summarized, *American Journal of Sociology*, XIII (May 1908).

56. The essay was printed in the *Proceedings of the State Historical Society of Wisconsin for 1908* (Madison, 1908), 184-233. Turner's copy, heavily annotated and with the comment (p. 15), "Add a special paragraph on democracy," HEH Accession No. 126665.

57. Charles M. Andrews to Turner, March 27, 1909; Albion W. Small to Turner, March 22, 1909; Carl Becker to Turner, March 19, 1909; Max Farrand to Turner, March 18, 1909; Edward Channing to Turner, March 19,

1909, HEH TU Box 12. In replying to Farrand, Turner urged colonialists to investigate the eighteenth-century settlement of interior New England—"its relation to land pressure, and to social and economic factors such as the development of proprietary control of town land as a possession instead of a trust" (Turner to Farrand, March 21, 1909, HEH TU Box 12).

Chapter X
Teacher and Administrator
1901-1910

1. Max Farrand to Mae Turner, April 4, 1906, recalled these scenes as Farrand saw them during a two-week visit to the Turner home (HEH TU Box 7).

2. *Daily Cardinal*, March 4, 1910, Jan. 23, 1903. Turner later denied that he ever played tennis as a young man, but his memory was obviously faulty (Turner to Joseph Schafer, Oct. 14, 1931, SHSW, Schafer Papers).

3. Details of Turner's financial arrangements discussed with his brother shortly after his father's death in 1905 (Turner to Will Turner, Oct. 1, 1905, HEH TU Box G).

4. Turner to Mae Turner, June 26, 1908, HEH TU Box G. Entries in his pocket diary (March 11, 1907, Jan. 6, 10, Feb. 10, 1910, numerous other dates) tell of borrowing money to meet immediate needs (HEH TU Box 62).

5. Turner to Mae Turner, April 25, 1909. HEH TU Box G. Entries in his pocket diary (Dec. 15, 1908, Feb. 16, 1910) tell of financial problems related to the purchase (HEH TU Box 62).

6. Accounts of the family finances, Turner to Will Turner, Oct. 1, 1905, Turner to Mae Turner, May 9, 1907, HEH TU Box G. He also listed his assets and liabilities on the flyleaf of his pocket diary for 1908-12 (HEH TU Box 62).

7. Turner to Max Farrand, Nov. 14, 1907. HEH TU Box 9A.

8. The first canoe trip lasted from August 22 to September 4, 1907, the second from mid-July to mid-August 1908. Turner kept a record of the first in day-by-day entries in his pocket diary (HEH TU Box 62). Mae Turner recorded the second in a handwritten diary (HEH TU Vol. XI). He drew $400 from the bank to finance the 1908 journey.

9. The correspondence between Turner and William J. Truesdale, director of the summer school, was extensive, and much of it on Turner's part highly indignant at the treatment he received (U. of Wis. Arch., L. and S., Hist., Turner Corr., Box 1, Folder T). Attached to Turner to Truesdale, March 26, 1902, is a schedule of the sixteen lectures he planned to give.

10. Turner to Max Farrand, Oct. 1, 1902, ibid. Box 2, Folder F; Turner to J. F. Jameson, Aug. 24, 1902, HEH TU Box 3.

11. Turner to Max Farrand, Oct. 17, 1903, ibid. Box 4.

12. *Wisconsin State Journal*, Oct. 24, 1903.

13. Correspondence between President Charles W. Eliot and Turner regarding the position (Dec. 12, 1902–March 10, 1903) is in U. of Wis. Arch., L. and S., Hist., Turner Corr., Boxes 3 and 4, Folder E. Turner's ruffled feelings, arising from the $1500 salary offered, were smoothed by Charles H.

Haskins, who was on the Harvard faculty. He assured Turner that $1500 was the usual compensation for two courses, and that Eliot was astounded to learn that anyone at Wisconsin earned more than this (Haskins to Turner, March 10, 1903, ibid. Box 3, Folder H).

14. Turner to A. Lawrence Lowell, Feb. 19, 1903, ibid. Box 3, Folder F. Official notice of the appointment, April 1, 1903, naming Turner a "Lecturer in History," HEH TU Box 53.

15. Turner to Mae Turner, May 25, 1904. Guests included Edward E. Hale, Josiah Royce, Bliss Perry, Davis R. Dewey, Albert B. Hart, and Frederick P. Vinton. All signed Turner's menu (HEH TU Box 59). Turner described living in Boston in Turner to Reuben G. Thwaites (Feb. 29, 1904, WSHS, Thwaites Papers).

16. Albert G. Waite, "Frederick J. Turner Lecture Notes in History 10b, Harvard University, spring term, 1903-1904" (Harvard University Archives, Call No. HUC 8903.338.10.92). Some of Turner's own notes suggesting the scope of the course are in HEH TU File Drawer 12, Folder: Harvard Lectures.

17. Turner to Mae Turner, May 23, 1904, HEH TU Box F. Mae returned home in mid-May, and Turner spent the rest of his stay in the Colonial Club.

18. Edward Channing to Turner, May 16, 1905, HEH TU Box 5. Turner described the events of that spring in letters to Mae (May 28, 31, 1904, HEH TU Box F). He found Peterboro, New Hampshire, so quiet that when a horse and a bicycle went by he heard a farmer say: "It does beat all what a commotion there is in town tonight."

19. Turner to Edmond S. Meany, April 6, 1904, Roy Lokken (ed.), "Frederick Jackson Turner's Letters to Edmond S. Meany," *Pacific Northwest Quarterly*, XLIV (Jan. 1953), 32-33.

20. Turner to President B. I. Wheeler, Oct. 9, 1903; Turner to H. Morse Stephens, Oct. 22, 1903. U. of Wis. Arch., L. and S., Hist., Turner Corr., Box 4, Folders S and W. Turner to Richard T. Ely, Aug. 30, 1904, SHSW, Ely Papers.

21. Turner to B. I. Wheeler, March 7, 1906, has a note attached, describing the courses Turner planned to give (HEH TU Box 6). Turner described his experiences in letters to Richard R. Van Hise (June 15, Aug. 3, 1906, U. of Wis. Arch., Pres. Corr., C. R. Van Hise, Gen. Corr., Box 16, Folder: F. J. Turner). Turner kept a record of his wilderness experiences in his pocket notebook, May 6 to Sept. 12, 1906 (HEH TU Box 62).

22. Turner to Mae Turner, Sept. 22, 1906, HEH TU Box G.

23. George E. Fellows to Turner, Oct. 26, 1901, U. of Wis. Arch., L. and S., Hist., Turner Corr., Box 1, Folder F. Turner may have remembered a letter received from Birge in August 1901; Birge quoted a student who said that anyone could pass Turner's course by attending his lectures without doing outside reading, and demanded to know if this were true. Such distrust of a faculty member was bound to rankle (U. of Wis. Arch., Pres. Corr., E. A. Birge, General Corr., 1901-3, Series 4/8/1, Box 7).

24. Van Hise's election is described in Merle Curti and Vernon Carstensen, *The University of Wisconsin, 1848-1925* (Madison, 1949), II, 11-13, and Maurice M. Vance, *Charles Richard Van Hise: Scientist Progressive* (Madison, 1960), 70-75.

25. Emil Baensch to Turner, Feb. 7, 1902; John C. Kerwin to Turner, June 6, 10, 19, 1902; Turner to Kerwin, June 11, 1902; Arthur J. Puls to Turner, March 24, 26, 1903, HEH TU Boxes 3 and 4; U. of Wis. Arch., L. and S., Hist., Turner Corr., Box 2, Folder K. In Turner to Puls, March 26, 1903, ibid., is a six-page memorandum, in Turner's hand, on the proper qualifications of a Wisconsin president.

26. *Wisconsin State Journal*, May 28, 1902, April 20, 22, 1903; *Milwaukee Sentinel*, Aug. 13, 14, 1902.

27. Turner's address, *Wisconsin State Journal*, June 7, 1904, Van Hise's address, *Jubilee of the University of Wisconsin* (Madison, 1909), 121-23.

28. J. Franklin Jameson to Turner, May 12, 1900, HEH TU Box 3; Turner to C. K. Adams, May 8, 23, 1900, U. of Wis. Arch., Pres. Corr., C. K. Adams, General Corr., Box 6; Turner to George C. Sellery, May 28, 1901, HEH TU Box 3.

29. *The Sphynx*, III (March 15, 1902), 97.

30. Haskins to President Eliot, Dec. 21, 1901; Haskins to E. A. Birge, Feb. 21, 1902, Princeton, Haskins Papers.

31. Turner to Carl Becker, Jan. 7, 1902, HEH TU Box 3.

32. Turner to Dana C. Munro, March 8, 18, 1902, U. of Wis. Arch., L. and S., Hist., Turner Corr., Box 1, Folder M; *Daily Cardinal*, April 3, 1902.

33. The *Daily Cardinal* printed regular notices of bird walks organized by Libby. He spent the summer of 1899 not in research, but in helping friends dig up the bones of those who helped John Brown at Harper's Ferry, then reburying them at North Elba, beside their leader (ibid. Nov. 13, 1899).

34. Turner to President Webster Merrifield, Feb. 5, 1902, U. of Wis. Arch., L. and S., Hist., Turner Corr., Box 1, Folder M.

35. *Catalogue of the University of Wisconsin for 1900-1901* (Madison, 1901), 175.

36. Turner to William A. Dunning, April 17, 1902; Turner to Ulrich B. Phillips, April 17, May 13, 1902; Phillips to Turner, April 21, May 13, 1902, U. of Wis. Arch., L. and S., Hist., Turner Corr., Box 2, Folder P.

37. One applicant who sought a position and was rejected by Turner was Charles A. Beard (Beard to Turner, April 8, 24, 1903; Turner to Beard, April 22, 1903, ibid. Box 5, Folder B). Turner discussed departmental offerings in letters to Dana C. Munro (April 18, May 6, 1902, ibid. Box 2, Folder M); and in a report on the first two years of the School of History to acting President E. A. Birge (ibid. Box 6, Folder: History Department).

38. Turner sought to forestall these raids by generous salary increases, advancing Fish from $1400 to $1600, Sellery from $1200 to $1500, and Phillips from $1300 to $1400 in 1905, even without outside offers (Turner to E. A. Birge, April 25, 1905, U. of Wis. Arch., L. and S., Dean's Files, Birge Corr., Box 1, Folder T-Z).

39. William E. Dodd to Turner, July 1, 3, 1908, HEH TU Box 11. Herman V. Ames to Turner, May 7, 11, 1908; Turner to Winfred T. Root, May 11, 1908; Root to Turner, May 14, 1908, U. of Wis., Dept. of Hist, Turner Papers.

40. These changes were described in the *Wisconsin Alumni Magazine*, XI (Nov. 1909), 78, and noted in the yearly editions of the university catalogue.

41. Quoted in *Wisconsin State Journal*, June 9, 1904.

42. A. L. P. Dennis to Turner, March 14, 1907, U. of Wis., Dept. of Hist., Turner Papers.

43. Turner set forth his views on the role of the summer session in an undated memorandum (Univ. of Wis. Arch., Summer School File). It is quoted at length in S. H. Goodnight, *The Story of the Origins and Growth of the Summer School and the Summer Session, 1885-1940* (Madison, 1940), 41-45.

44. Turner advanced his views in letters to Ernst Greverus, June 26, Dec. 19, 1901, Mary Peckham, Feb. 14, 1903, and F. O. Holt, Jan. 22, 1909. These, and others like them, are scattered through the files that Turner kept as chairman of the department (U. of Wis. Arch., L. and S., Hist., Turner Corr., Boxes 1-6).

45. Copy, ibid. Box 5, Miscellaneous.

46. Elizabeth Waters to Turner, Jan. 2, 1903; Turner to Elizabeth Waters, Jan. 2, 1903, ibid. Box 3, Folder W. Notices of Turner's lectures to these groups appeared regularly in the *Daily Cardinal* and *Wisconsin State Journal*.

47. Turner resigned in February 1904, when he left Madison to teach a term at Harvard (*Wisconsin State Journal,* Feb. 10, 13, 1904).

48. Nicholas Murray Butler to Turner, Jan. 24, 1902; Turner to Butler, Jan. 30, 1902, U. of Wis. Arch., L. and S., Hist., Turner Corr., Box 1, Folder B.

49. Clarence W. Alvord, "Review of *The Frontier in American History,*" *Mississippi Valley Historical Review,* VII (March 1921), 404.

50. Turner, notes for "Talk to Graduate History Club, December 19, 1908," HEH TU Box 55.

51. "Instructional Reports," U. of Wis. Arch.

52. A. C. Krey, "My Reminiscences of Frederick Jackson Turner," *Arizona and the West,* III (Winter 1961), 379. Turner's seminar topics were listed in the university catalogues, those for the 1909 seminar are in a note in his hand (HEH TU Box 55).

53. "Reminiscences of Guy Stanton Ford," Oral History Research Office, Columbia University, 141.

54. Edwin Witte, "Diary, 1909-1910," Feb. 25, 1910 manuscript, MSS Division, State Historical Society of Wisconsin.

55. Turner to Max Farrand, May 15, 1907, HEH TU Box 9.

56. Turner to Carl R. Fish, March 29, April 3, 1907, HEH TU Box 9.

57. Turner to C. R. Van Hise, May 11, 1905, U. of Wis. Arch., L. and S., Hist., Turner Corr., Box 1, Folder T-Z.

58. Turner to L. E. Aylsworth, Aug. 2, 1902, to W. C. Rice, Nov. 18, 1903, and to J. L. Conger, July 24, 1905, ibid. Box 2, Folder A, Box 4, Folder R, and Box 5, Folder C.

59. Turner described graduate requirements in letters to Carl Becker, Jan. 9, 1904, Judson G. Rosebush, March 2, 1906, and Homer C. Hockett, March 5, 1906, HEH TU Box 6.

60. Charles H. Ambler to Turner, Jan. 13, 1909; Turner to Macmillan Co., Jan. 19, 1909, HEH TU Box 12.

61. Turner to president of the University of West Virginia, June 15, 1907; Turner to J. F. Jameson, July 19, 1902, HEH TU Boxes 9 and 3. Turner to D. R. Dewey, July 23, 1902, U. of Wis. Arch., L. and S., Hist., Turner Corr., Box 2, Folder D.

62. Turner to Carl Becker, April 13, 1907, HEH TU Box 8.

63. *Daily Cardinal*, Jan. 4, 1906.

64. Turner listed some of these accomplishments in a letter to C. R. Van Hise, June 19, 1908 (HEH TU Box 11). The *Daily Cardinal*, Oct. 15, 1908, also catalogued Turner students who were teaching throughout the nation.

65. Turner to Constance L. Skinner, March 15, 1922, HEH TU Box 31.

Chapter XI
Undergraduate Teacher and Reformer
1901-1910

1. Frederick J. Turner, "Instructional Reports," 1901-9, U. of Wis. Arch.

2. *The Sphynx*, III (May 7, 1902), 122; *Wisconsin State Journal*, Sept. 29, 1905.

3. Ibid., May 9, 1903; *The Sphynx*, VI (July 15, 1905), 152.

4. A. C. Krey, "My Reminiscences of Frederick Jackson Turner," *Arizona and the West*, III (Winter 1961), 379. Valuable on Turner as a teacher is Ulrich B. Phillips, "The Traits and Contributions of Frederick Jackson Turner," *Agricultural History*, XIX (Jan. 1945), 21-23.

5. Albert G. Waite, "Frederick J. Turner Lecture Notes in History 10b, Harvard University, spring term, 1903-1904," Harvard Univ. Archives, HUC 8903.338.10.92.

6. Turner to Passenger Traffic Agent, Chicago and North Western Railroad, July 6, 1907, HEH TU Box 9A. Other letters to railroads are in this box, and in Box V, Folder: Transportation, of the Harvard Commission on Western History Papers, Correspondence Ser., Harvard Univ. Archives, Call No. UA III 50 29.12.2.5. (hereafter cited as Harvard Arch., HC on WH Corr.).

7. Waite, "Frederick J. Turner Lecture Notes," Lecture of May 25. Hundreds of slides prepared by Turner are among his papers at the Huntington Library.

8. Quoted in Phillips, "Traits and Contributions of Frederick Jackson Turner," *loc. cit.* 23.

9. Carl Becker, "Frederick Jackson Turner," *Wisconsin Alumni Magazine*, XI (Jan. 1910), 144. This excellent appraisal, written at the time Turner left Wisconsin for Harvard, sheds light on his teaching techniques.

10. Krey, "My Reminiscences of Frederick Jackson Turner," *loc. cit.* 380.

11. One such outline is in HEH TU File Drawer 15D, Folder: Notes for Ec. and Soc. Hist. US, 1815-1850.

12. Mimeographed syllabus, "History of the West, 1909," HEH TU Vol. VI (3) Syllabus of Lectures. History of the West. A shorter syllabus, apparently used about 1904, is also in this folder.

13. Of several sets of lecture notes taken by students in the "History of the West" during these years, the most complete was that of Homer C. Hockett, made during the summer of 1902. Hockett took shorthand well, and he recorded the lectures stenographically. Copies given to Turner are scattered through his notes under the topics covered (HEH TU File Drawer 2E, Folder: Piedmont and Great Valley; Drawer 3A, Folder: Unmarked;

Drawer 3B, Folder: Interior vs. Coast; Drawer 4A, Folder: West in Revolution; Drawer 4A, Folder: Lecture Notes Summer 1902; Drawer 12A, Folder: West. Frontier in N. Eng.; Drawer 15B, Folder: Hockett, Filling in the Southwest; Drawer 15C, Folder: History of West 1902).

14. *The Nation* LXXXI (Nov. 30, 1905), 437-38. This, and other clippings on the football controversy, were pasted by Turner on 5×8 slips of paper, labeled, dated, and filed. U. of Wis. Arch., University Faculty, Athletic Board. Frederick J. Turner File: Football Reform Movement, 1906. Series 5/21/5, Box 1). They provide an excellent history of the subject. The national crusade against professionalized football is described in John H. Moore, "Football's Ugly Decades, 1893-1913," *Smithsonian Journal of History*, II (Fall 1967), 49-68, the local contest in Merle Curti and Vernon Carstensen, *The University of Wisconsin, 1848-1925* (Madison, 1949), II, 536-42.

15. *Daily Cardinal*, Dec. 1, 3, 1904.

16. *Wisconsin Alumni Magazine*, IV (Feb. 1903), 201.

17. *Daily Cardinal*, March 29, 31, 1905; *Wisconsin State Journal*, March 29, 1905. Minutes of the Meeting of the University Faculty, Dec. 12, 1904. Univ. of Wis. Arch. (hereafter cited as U. of Wis. Arch., Minutes, University Faculty).

18. *Daily Cardinal*, Nov. 5, 24, 1905.

19. Ibid. Dec. 7, 1905; *Wisconsin State Journal*, Dec. 5, 11, 23, 1905.

20. U. of Wis. Arch., Minutes, University Faculty, Dec. 4, 1905.

21. *Daily Cardinal*, Dec. 8, 14, 1905.

22. Turner's views on Van Hise, one of his best friends, are in Turner to Mae Turner, May 31, 1904, HEH TU Box F, and on the overemphasis of football, in Turner to Frederick Whitton, Nov. 18, 1904, U. of Wis. Arch., L. and S., Hist., Turner Corr., Box 5, Folder W. Whitton was an official of the Alumni Club of Chicago.

23. Harvey Holmes to Turner, June 23, 1925, HEH TU Box 34. Holmes, a football player, recalled this conversation—but so many years later that its authenticity may be doubted.

24. Turner's letters have not been preserved, but their nature can be inferred from some of the answers he received. See esp. Andrew C. McLaughlin to Turner, Dec. 15, 1905, and Albion W. Small to Turner, [Jan. 1906], HEH TU Boxes 5 and 6.

25. For arrangements for this conference, see Harry Pratt Judson to Van Hise, Dec. 28, 1905; Van Hise to Judson, Dec. 25, 1905; Van Hise to James B. Angell, Dec. 26, 1905, Jan. 3, 1906; Angell to Van Hise, Jan. 1, 5, 1906, HEH TU Boxes 5 and 6.

26. A typed copy of this report is in University of Wisconsin Archives, University Faculty, Sec. of the Faculty. Faculty Minutes, Documents, etc. Ser. 5/2/2, Box 2, Folder: 253-70 (hereafter cited as U. of Wis. Arch., University Faculty, Sec. of Faculty). Action on the report is given in U. of Wis. Arch., Minutes, University Faculty, Jan. 8, 9, 1906.

27. *Daily Cardinal*, Jan. 9, 1906. Student unrest was heightened by newspaper reports, later proven false, that Harvard had abolished football.

28. *The Sphynx*, II (April 7, 1906), 125; *The Badger for 1907* (Madison, 1906), 505.

29. *Daily Cardinal,* Jan. 10, 1906.

30. U. of Wis. Arch., Minutes, University Faculty, Jan. 18, 1906.

31. Turner to Mae Turner, January 20, 1906, HEH TU Box G.

32. Printed minutes of conference (13 pp., untitled), U. of Wis. Arch., University Faculty, Athletic Board, Turner File, Box 1, page 10. Although the members were pledged to secrecy, the *Daily Cardinal* and the *Wisconsin State Journal,* Jan. 22, 1906, published fairly accurate accounts.

33. A typed copy of this Turner speech is in U. of Wis. Arch., University Faculty, Athletic Board, Turner File, Box 1, Folder: Madison Alumni Address. At the bottom, in Turner's hand, are the words: "Passed by an overwhelming majority." The speech was reported in the *Wisconsin State Journal,* Feb. 1, 1906.

34. *Daily Cardinal,* Feb. 1, 2, 1906; Albion W. Small to Turner, Jan. 22, 1906; Andrew C. McLaughlin to Turner, Jan. 26, 1906, HEH TU Box 6.

35. A. H. Pattengill to Turner, Jan. 23, Feb. 3, 1906; Turner to Pattengill, Jan. 26, 1906, HEH TU Box 6.

36. U. of Wis. Arch., Minutes, University Faculty, Feb. 6, 1906.

37. A. H. Pattengill to Turner, Feb. 9, 1906; Andrew C. McLaughlin to Turner, Feb. 10, 19, 1906, HEH TU Box 6. Northwestern, however, voted overwhelmingly against a seven-game schedule. James A. James to Turner, Feb. 19, 1906, ibid.

38. "Report of the Second Conference of Collegiate Representatives," Chicago, March 9, 1906 (5-pp. report, signed by H. J. Barton, secretary). Copy, U. of Wis. Arch., University Faculty, Athletic Board, Turner File, Box 1.

39. *Wisconsin State Journal,* March 13, 15, 1906; *Daily Cardinal,* March 13, 1906. One of the interviewers later recalled that he went to Turner's home expecting to meet a football-devouring ogre, but instead found a sympathetic and rational man who had the best interests of the university at heart (R. D. Hetzel to Joseph Schafer, Aug. 6, 1932, SHSW, Schafer Papers, MSS II). Hetzel was president of Pennsylvania State College.

40. *Daily Cardinal,* March 16, 17, 21, 1906; *Wisconsin State Journal,* March 17, 1906.

41. *Wisconsin State Journal,* March 26, 1906.

42. Ibid. March 28, 1906; *Daily Cardinal,* March 28, 1906.

43. *Daily Cardinal,* April 3, 5, 1906; U. of Wis. Arch., Minutes, University Faculty, April 5, 1906.

44. *The Sphynx,* VIII (Oct. 13, 1906), 21.

45. *Wisconsin State Journal,* Nov. 13, 1906.

46. *The Sphynx,* VIII (March 15, 1907), 133.

47. Turner to James A. James, Dec. 5, 1906, HEH TU Box 7.

48. U. of Wis. Arch., University Faculty, Sec. of Faculty, Faculty Minutes, Documents, etc. Box 2, Folder: 253-70; U. of Wis. Arch., Minutes, University Faculty, Dec. 3, 1906; Turner to E. A. Birge, Dec. 7, 1906. U. of Wis. Arch., College of Letters and Science, Administration. Dean's Files, Box 4, File T (hereafter cited as U. of Wis. Arch., L. and S., Dean's Files).

49. Board of Regents, Minutes. University of Wisconsin Archives, Ser. 1/1/1, Box 6, pp. 517-19 (hereafter cited as U. of Wis. Arch., Regents' Minutes).

50. *Wisconsin State Journal,* Dec. 4, 1906.

51. U. of Wis. Arch., Minutes, University Faculty, Dec. 11, 1906.

52. "Resolutions of the Conference between Representatives of Chicago, Michigan, Minnesota, and Wisconsin" (n.d.), SHSW, Turner Papers, Box II. The new schedules were announced in the *Wisconsin State Journal*, Jan. 28, 1907.

53. Turner had stated in an interview, "I am heartily in favor of the movement, and will speak in favor of it at the faculty meeting." *Daily Cardinal*, Jan. 28, 1907. He did so (U. of Wis. Arch., Minutes, University Faculty, Feb. 4, 1907).

54. *Wisconsin State Journal*, Nov. 19, 1907.

55. Ibid. Nov. 25, 1907; *Daily Cardinal*, Nov. 25, 1907.

56. U. of Wis. Arch., Minutes, University Faculty, Dec. 2, 1907; University Faculty, Sec. of Faculty, Faculty Minutes, Documents, etc., Box 3, Folder: 1-25. A press release, headed "Faculty Favor Athletics," describing the action is in HEH TU Box 55.

57. Manuscript minutes, U. of Wis. Arch., University Faculty, Sec. of Faculty, Faculty Minutes, Documents, etc., Box 2, Folder: 253-70. Attached is a "Supplementary Report" to the faculty in Turner's hand, much underlined and corrected, reiterating his views on de-emphasizing football.

58. *Daily Cardinal*, Jan. 11, 1908; *Wisconsin State Journal*, Jan. 10, 1908. Stephen S. Gregory, chairman of the alumni committee, and Turner exchanged sentiments of mutual gratification after the meeting, although they still differed sharply on naming an alumnus to the Athletic Council (Gregory to Turner, Dec. 16, 1907; Turner to Gregory, Dec. 19, 1907, U. of Wis. Arch., University Faculty, Sec. of Faculty, Faculty Minutes, Documents, etc., Box 2, Folder: 253-70).

59. *Daily Cardinal*, Dec. 2, 1907, Jan. 6, 14, Feb. 25, 1908; U. of Wis. Arch., Minutes, University Faculty, Jan. 13, 1908.

60. Ibid. Jan. 17, June 6, Dec. 5, 1910.

Chapter XII
Leaving Wisconsin
1905-1910

1. Turner to Carl Becker, Dec. 1, 1925, HEH TU Box 34.

2. A. B. Hart to Turner, March 29, 1912, HEH TU Box 17.

3. Edgar E. Robinson to Turner, Aug. 2, 1911, HEH TU Box 16.

4. Guy Emerson, *The New Frontier. A Study of the American Liberal Spirit, Its Frontier Origin, and Its Application to Modern Problems* (New York, 1920); Andrew C. McLaughlin, *Steps in the Development of American Democracy* (New York, 1920), 96-97. Emerson, a Harvard graduate, was a correspondent of Turner's.

5. Max Farrand to Turner, Feb. 23, 1905, HEH TU Box 5.

6. Max Farrand to Turner, Oct. 24, 1903. U. of Wis. Arch., L. and S., Hist., Turner Corr., Box 4, Folder: F.

7. Turner's copy of Farrand, "The West and the Principles of the American Revolution," *Yale Review*, o.s., XVII (May 1908), 44-58, HEH TU File Drawer L2, Folder: 0112.

8. The spread of the Turner thesis in textbooks is described in Henry M. Littlefield, "Textbooks, Determinism and Turner: The Westward Movement in Secondary School History and Geography Textbooks, 1830-1960," Ph.D. thesis (unpubl.), Columbia Univ., 1967. The author has generously allowed me to use his findings. Valuable also is Ruth M. Elson, *Guardians of Tradition: American Schoolbooks in the Nineteenth Century* (Lincoln, Nebr., 1964), based on an examination of about a thousand books used before 1900.

9. Genevieve Melody to Turner, Nov. 5, 1906; Turner to Genevieve Melody, Nov. 21, 1906, HEH TU Box 7.

10. Clarence W. Alvord, "The Study of Western History in Our Schools," *The History Teacher's Magazine*, I (Oct. 1909), 28.

11. Willis M. West, *American History and Government* (Boston, 1913). West apologized for incorporating so many of Turner's ideas, and justified himself only because "yours has been so long delayed" (West to Turner, Nov. 4, 1911, HEH TU Box 16).

12. Irene T. Blythe, "The Textbooks and the New Discoveries, Emphases and Viewpoints in American History," *Historical Outlook*, XXIII (Dec. 1932), 398-99.

13. Farrand to Turner, May 24, 1909, HEH TU Box 12.

14. Woodrow Wilson to editor of *New York Critic*, printed in *Wisconsin Magazine of History*, XXVI (June 1943), 471; Henry Morse Stephens, "Some Living American Historians," *World's Work*, IV (July 1902), 2316-27. Turner wrote Stephens: "I felt rather lonesome in my full-page illustration among the men who have done something. Seriously, however, it is very well worth having friends who believe in you" (Turner to Stephens, March 31, 1902, U. of Wis. Arch., L. and S., Hist., Turner Corr., Box 1, Folder W).

15. J. F. Jameson to Charles Francis Adams, Sept. 12, 1907, Elizabeth Donnan and Leo F. Stock (eds.), *An Historian's World: Selections from the Correspondence of John Franklin Jameson* (Philadelphia, 1956), 108.

16. Lamprecht's opinion quoted in *Wisconsin State Journal*, Feb. 7, 1905, Channing's in Lois K. Mathews to Turner, March 9, 1906, HEH TU Box 6.

17. Turner's diplomas and certificates of election to honorary societies are in HEH TU Box 53.

18. The president, on conferring the degree, noted Turner's battle against the football interests by stressing his "high minded work for the promotion of lofty university ideals" (Edmund J. James to Turner, June 15, 1908, HEH TU Box 11).

19. Turner to Charles H. Haskins, Dec. 16, 1903, U. of Wis. Arch., L. and S., Hist., Turner Corr., Box 3, Folder H.

20. Such a trip is described in Jameson to Turner, Nov. 18, 1902, ibid. Box 3, Folder J.

21. Jameson described Turner's plan to publish the territorial papers in his diary, printed in Donnan and Stock (eds.), *An Historian's World*, 98-99. Their correspondence concerning a historical center includes Jameson to Turner, April 12, 1902; Turner to Jameson, April 29, Nov. 1, 1902, U. of Wis. Arch., L. and S., Hist., Turner Corr., Box 2, Folder J.

22. Jameson to Clarence W. Bowen, Oct. 15, 1901, Donnan and Stock (eds.), *An Historian's World*, 78.

23. Jameson to Turner, April 18, 1905; Turner to Jameson, May 11, 1905, U. of Wis. Arch., L. and S., Hist., Turner Corr., Box 5, Folder J.

24. A brief history of the commission is in Donnan and Stock (eds.), *An Historian's World*, 11-12.

25. A letter typical of the many mailed to historians is Turner to Claude H. Van Tyne, April 21, 1908, Clements, Van Tyne Papers. An example of his second mailing, addressed to "My Dear Professor," is in SHSW, Turner Papers, together with a number of the replies.

26. Turner's draft, with many corrections, HEH TU File Drawer 15C, Folder: Report, Draft by Turner on Social and Economic Documents. Final version (48 pp.), May 9, 1908, ibid. File Drawer 15A, Folder: Report on Documents Economic and Social; published, 60th Cong., 2nd sess., *Senate Document No. 714* (Washington, D.C., 1909), 1-45.

27. A. C. McLaughlin to Turner, Nov. 23, 1908, HEH TU Box 11. McLaughlin urged Turner to address the University of Chicago's social science group, on research in social history.

28. *Annual Report of the American Historical Association for 1917* (Washington, D.C., 1920), 73-74.

29. Turner to Max Farrand, Jan. 3, 1905, HEH TU Box 5.

30. Farrand to Turner, Dec. 4, 1904, June 6, July 2, 1905; Turner to Farrand, Jan. 3, June 23, 1905, HEH TU Box 5.

31. Memorandum (July 1905) attached to Farrand to Turner, June 6, 1905, HEH TU Box 5.

32. Jordan to Turner, April 18, 19, 20, 1906, HEH TU Box 7. Notice from Board of Regents, April 20, 1906, confirming Turner's research leaves, ibid.

33. *Wisconsin State Journal*, Feb. 15, 21, March 7, 1906. Printed *Report of the Joint Legislative Committee on the Affairs of the University* (n.p., n.d.), 1-24, U. of Wis. Arch., Pres. Corr., C. R. Van Hise General Corr., Box 14, Folder: Legislative Investigating Committee.

34. Turner to Senator Wylie, Feb. 22, 1906, HEH TU Box 6. That Turner's leave of absence arrangements were mentioned before the committee is suggested in D. MacGregor to Van Hise, April 16, 1906, ibid. Box 7.

35. *Wisconsin State Journal*, Sept. 24, Oct. 19, 1907; *Daily Cardinal*, March 3, 24, 1906; *Wisconsin Literary Magazine*, V (Dec. 1907), 135-36; *Wisconsin Alumni Magazine*, VIII (Jan. 1907), 145-46.

36. U. of Wis. Arch., Regents' Minutes, Vol. 7, 199, 200. Report of committee, Board of Regents Executive Committee, 1888-1939, Box 11, Folder: Executive Committee Minutes, June 29-July 6, 1908.

37. Turner to Van Hise, June 19, 1908, HEH TU Box 11. Several copies of the letter, one marked "not sent," are in this box. Van Hise replied wryly that he was glad to have Turner's "brief statement," and that it would be useful to him (Van Hise to Turner, June 20, 1908, HEH TU Box 11).

38. Turner to Van Hise, Oct. 12, 1908, ibid.

39. Turner to Mae Turner, May 1, 1909; Turner to Max Farrand, March 21, 1909, HEH TU Boxes G and 12.

40. Richard T. Ely, *Ground Under Our Feet. An Autobiography* (New York, 1938), 196-97. In notes on a draft of his letter to Van Hise of Oct. 12, 1908, Turner wrote that his support for Van Hise's presidency occasioned many of the attacks on him, and that three of his friends on the Board of

Regents had urged him to take a higher salary in lieu of research leaves (HEH TU Box 11).

41. Turner's letters to Stephens have not been preserved, but their tenor can be inferred from Stephens's replies, July 25, Aug. 15, 1909, HEH TU Box 12. The Chicago meeting was suggested in Benjamin I. Wheeler to Turner, Aug. 17, Sept. 3, 1909, ibid.

42. Turner to Van Hise, Sept. 11, 19, 1909; Van Hise to Turner, Sept. 15, 1909, U. of Wis. Arch., Pres. Corr., C. R. Van Hise, General Corr., Box 23, Folder: Executive Committee, Regents.

43. C. H. Haskins to Turner, Sept. 14, 16, 25, 1909, HEH TU Box 12; Archibald C. Coolidge to A. Lawrence Lowell, Sept. 28, 1909; Lowell to Turner, Sept. 30, 1909, A. Lawrence Lowell Correspondence, Harvard University Archives, UA I 5 160, Folder: 881 (hereafter cited as Harvard Arch., Lowell Corr.).

44. Turner to Mae Turner, Oct. 6, 1909, HEH TU Box G.

45. Ibid. Oct. 7, 1909. Copies of printed program for inauguration, and menu and seating list for dinner, HEH TU File Drawer 15E, Folder: Harvard University Inauguration. Diploma given Turner, HEH TU Box 53. Events described, *Harvard Bulletin*, Nov. 17, 1909.

46. C. H. Haskins to Turner, Oct. 21, 1909, HEH TU Box 13.

47. Turner to Van Hise, Nov. 15, 1909, HEH TU Box 13; Van Hise to Turner, Nov. 16, 1909, ibid. Turner was informed that "your resignation as professor of American history was accepted, to take effect at the end of the current college year," with never a word of regret or praise (Board of Regents to Turner, Jan. 21, 1910, HEH TU Box 13).

48. *Harvard Bulletin*, Nov. 17, 1909; Charles H. Haskins to Turner, Nov. 20, 1909. Harvard had just defeated Dartmouth in football, 12 to 3.

49. *Daily Cardinal*, Dec. 16, 1909; Wisconsin Committee of Students to Turner, Dec. 22, 1909, HEH TU Box 13; *Milwaukee Sentinel*, Nov. 28, 1909; *Wisconsin Alumni Magazine*, XI (Dec. 1909), 108-9, 121-25; (Jan. 1910), 142-44, 166-68.

50. A. C. McLaughlin to Turner, Feb. 4, 14, 16, 1910; Edwin E. Sparks to Turner, April 1, 1910, HEH TU Box 14. Copy of printed program, HEH TU Box 59.

51. James A. James to Merrill H. Crissey, July 13, 1934, HEH TU Box 51.

52. Turner to Carl Becker, Jan. 15, 1910; Turner to James Alton James, Jan. 24, 1910, HEH TU Box 15.

53. Charles H. Ambler to Turner, Oct. 26, 1909, HEH TU Box 13.

54. Turner to Charles S. Slichter, Nov. 14, 1909, Charles S. Slichter Papers, U. of Wis. Arch. Turner to Mae Turner, Oct. 7, 1909, HEH TU Box G; A. C. Krey to Max Farrand, June 8, 1932, HEH TU Box 48. Krey recalled visiting Turner and seeing his tears as he thought of leaving Madison. A few students realized the reason for Turner's resignation. One wrote that "the reactionary attitude of the regents" was the only thing that could separate Turner from the library of the State Historical Society (Edwin E. Witte, "Diary, 1909-1910," Nov. 19, 1909, MSS Division, State Historical Society of Wisconsin).

55. Turner to Matthew B. Hammond, Nov. 21, 1909; Turner to Max Farrand, Oct. 28, 1909; Turner to Carl Becker, Dec. 5, 1909, HEH TU Box 13.

For a discussion of Turner's departure for Harvard, see Ray A. Billington, "Frederick Jackson Turner Comes to Harvard," *Proceedings of the Massachusetts Historical Society*, LXXIV (1962), 51-83.

56. Richard Lloyd Jones to Turner, Nov. 15, 24, Dec. 11, 1909, HEH TU Box 13.

57. Two accounts of the meeting were preserved. Paul Reinsch of the faculty kept virtually a stenographic record ("Minutes of the Joint Meeting of the Conference Committee of the Regents and Faculty of the University of Wisconsin," U. of Wis. Arch., Regents, Sec. Papers, Meetings of Board of Regents, 1849-1939. Box 23, Folder: Board of Regents Meeting, Jan. 19, 1910). A briefer account was kept by the regent who served as chairman (Fred C. Thwaits, "Report by the Chairman of the Meeting of the Conference Committees of the Regents and Faculty, held on the afternoon and evening of Friday, December 10, 1909," copy, U. of Wis. Arch., Misc. File, F. J. Turner).

58. U. of Wis. Arch., Regents' Minutes, Vol. 7, 435.

59. Edward Channing to Turner, Dec. 19, 1909, HEH TU Box 13.

60. Frederic L. Paxson to Turner, March 30, 1910, HEH TU Box 14. Paxson paid $100 down, $3000 on June 1, and the balance on November 1, 1910. Turner invested the surplus in American Telephone and Telegraph stock at $142 a share, and in Great Northern Railroad at $126, after paying off his mortgage and other debts (pocket diary, 1908-12, April 12, Nov. 1, 5, and 10, 1910, HEH TU Box 62).

61. Turner to Mae Turner, Aug. 5, 1910, HEH TU Box G.

62. Ibid. Aug. 7, 1910.

Chapter XIII
Harvard Years: The Academic World
1910-1917

1. Charles C. Whinery (*Encyclopaedia Britannica*) to Turner, Aug. 23, 1910, HEH TU Box 14. Correspondence concerning this article is scattered through Boxes 7 to 14, esp. the latter.

2. Turner to Mae Turner, Aug. 26, 1910, HEH TU Box G.

3. Turner's draft of this article, much corrected, is in HEH TU File Drawer 15E, Folder: Encyclopaedia Britannica Article; the manuscript of the bibliography is in HEH TU Vol. VII.

4. Reuben G. Thwaites to Turner, Oct. 10, 1910, HEH TU Box 5.

5. Turner to Frederick Merk, Feb. 17, 1927, Houghton, Turner Papers.

6. Turner to Frederick Merk, March 26, 1931, HEH TU Box 45; E. E. Dale, "Memories of Frederick Jackson Turner," *Mississippi Valley Historical Review*, XXX (Dec. 1943), 347-48.

7. This letter, titled "The Star Chamber, Am. House, Boston," is in HEH TU Box 20. It was written about 1913.

8. Turner to Joseph Jastrow, Oct. 5, 1910, HEH TU Box 15. Data on Turner's classes are drawn from the Harvard University Course Lists (Harvard Univ. Arch., First Half-Year, 1910). These list all students in each course taught at Harvard.

9. Horace J. Smith, Lecture Notes: History of the West. Harvard University, 1910-1911, HEH TU Vol. XXIII.

10. Turner to Homer C. Hockett, Oct. 19, 1910; Turner to August C. Krey, Feb. 6, 1911, HEH TU Boxes 15 and 16.

11. Copies of reports prepared in this seminar by W. C. Hunter and H. R. Townsend, HEH TU File Drawer B3, Folder: Election of 1836.

12. On August 27, 1910, Turner wrote in his pocket diary: " 'Changing Am. Ideals' as subject for Pres. Address. Or 'Perspectives in Am. History.' " HEH TU Box 62.

13. This discussion of Progressive history relies heavily on John Higham, *History* (Englewood Cliffs, N.J., 1965); Edward N. Saveth, "A Science of American History," *Diogenes*, XXVI (Summer 1959), 107-22; Charles Crowe, "The Emergence of Progressive History," *Journal of the History of Ideas*, XXVII (Jan.-March 1966), 109-24; and John H. Randall, Jr., and George Haines IV, "Controlling Assumptions in the Practice of American Historians," *Theory and Practice in Historical Study: A Report of the Committee on Historiography* (New York, 1946), 43-50.

14. Turner, "Social Forces in American History," *American Historical Review*, XVI (Jan. 1911), 217-33.

15. James Schouler to Turner, May 25, 1911, HEH TU Box 16.

16. Turner to Homer C. Hockett, Jan. 3, 1911, HEH TU Box 16.

17. Guy Stanton Ford, "Reminiscences of Guy Stanton Ford," Oral History Research Office, Columbia Univ., p. 269. For Turner's effort to pay for his copies, see Turner to Holt & Co., Jan. 23, 1911; Holt to Turner, Jan. 24, 1911. Princeton, Holt Arch.

18. Albert B. Hart to Turner, May 21, 1912, HEH TU Box 17. Contract with Ginn and Co., Dec. 10, 1909, HEH TU Box 55.

19. Turner to Max Farrand, Oct. 3, 1916, HEH TU Box 26.

20. Turner to Dorothy Turner, June 28, 1912, HEH TU Box H. Hart was a masterful persuader. "Don't spend any more time reading this letter," he wrote on May 21, "for you need it all to finish up your Cyclopedia articles so that I can get them next week" (HEH TU Box 18).

21. Manuscript drafts, corrected by Turner and Hart, HEH TU File Drawer 14C, Folder: Sect. in Am. Hist. MSS, and File Drawer 15E, Folders: West as a Factor in American Politics, and Frontier in American Development. At this time Turner also prepared an article, "The Territorial Development of the United States," for the Harvard Classics University Extension Course [published in William A. Neilson (ed.), *The Harvard Classics University Extension Course, I History* (Cambridge, 1913), 35-40].

22. Turner to George C. Sellery, Dec. 22, 1911, HEH TU Box 16.

23. Pocket diary, June 1, July 8, 1911, and flyleaves of two other diaries for the 1910-11 period, HEH TU Box 62. Details of insurance policies, Phoenix Insurance Co. to Turner, Feb. 17, 1914, HEH TU Box 21.

24. Royalty statements from Ginn and Co. are in HEH TU Box 28.

25. Purchases of Brazil stock listed in pocket diaries, March 25, 1911, March 8, 1913, June 10, 1914, HEH TU Box 62. Turner's optimism that the stock would provide for the family's future is shown in Turner to Mae Turner, July 1, 1912, Jan. 1, 1914, HEH TU Boxes H and I.

26. Turner to Dorothy Turner, Nov. 19, 1912, Nov. 21, 1913; Turner to

Mae Turner, Nov. 16, 1912, HEH TU Box H. Turner recalled Rhodes' generous hospitality in Turner to M. A. DeWolfe Howe, Jan. 9, 1928, HEH TU Box 38.

27. Programs for the 1918, 1923, and 1924 meetings of these clubs, with lists of members, HEH TU Box 59. Turner described meetings to his wife, Jan. 5, 1918, April 16, 1920, HEH TU Box I.

28. Rough notes for this talk, and recommendations to the Massachusetts Historical Society, labeled "Report of the Committee of the Library and the Cabinet," HEH TU Box 56.

29. Turner's relations with Mrs. Hooper and the Harvard Commission on Western History are described in Ray A. Billington (ed.), *Dear Lady. The Letters of Frederick Jackson Turner and Alice Forbes Perkins Hooper* (San Marino, Calif. 1970), 13-74.

30. Turner to Mrs. Hooper, Nov. 5, 1918, HEH TU-H Box 4.

31. Turner to John S. Main, Oct. 24, 1913, HEH TU Box H. Four days later he wrote in his pocket diary: "Wired Dorothy approval of her engagement to John Main," HEH TU Box 62. Turner deplored John's lack of fishing skills in a letter to Dorothy, Nov. 21, 1913, HEH TU Box H.

32. Turner to Mae Turner, March 8, 1915; Turner to Dorothy Turner Main, Dec. 12, 1917, HEH TU Box I.

33. Turner to Dorothy Turner, Nov. 30, 1912, HEH TU Box H. Dieting menu inserted in pocket diary for 1911-12. Blood pressure, recorded yearly since 1918, listed Aug. 30, 1923, HEH TU Box 62.

34. Turner to Mrs. Hooper, June 1, 1915. HEH TU-H Box 3; Mae Turner to Clarence W. Alvord, May 24, 1915, Clarence W. Alvord Papers, Illinois Historical Survey of the University of Illinois, Lincoln Hall, Urbana (hereafter cited as Hist. Survey Univ. of Ill., Alvord Papers).

35. Turner to Dorothy Turner Main, June 13, 1917, HEH TU Box 1, and Mrs. Hooper, June 10, 1917, HEH TU-H Box 3.

36. Turner to Charles H. Haskins, June 18, 1914, Princeton, Haskins Papers.

37. *University of Oregon Bulletin*, XI (March 1914), 14-15, copy, HEH TU Box 56. Turner's outline of lectures that he intended to give, HEH File Drawer 15D, Folder: Lecture Plan. University of Washington.

38. Edmond S. Meany to Max Farrand, Dec. 28, 1932, HEH TU Box 49. Clipping from *Seattle Star*, June 13, 1914, discussing Turner's love of fishing, HEH TU File Drawer 21C, Folder: Miscellany.

39. Turner to Henry M. Stephens, May 14, 1915, Herbert E. Bolton Papers, Bancroft Library, University of California, Berkeley (hereafter cited as Bancroft, Bolton Papers).

40. Turner to Max Farrand, Oct. 13, 1916, HEH TU Box 26; Turner's description of trip above Yosemite Valley, Turner to Mrs. Hooper, Aug. 6, 1915, HEH TU-H Box 3; Turner to Dorothy Turner Main, Aug. 12, 1915, HEH TU Box I.

41. Turner to Thomas P. Martin, Sept. 29, 1916, H.C. on W.H., Corr., Box V, Folder: Extracts from Personal Files.

42. Turner and Merk, *List of References on the History of the West, 2nd Half-Year, 1919-1920*. Turner's heavily annotated copy, with pages inserted on which he has written suggestions, HEH TU Vol. XX (1).

43. Edward E. Dale, "Turner—the Man and Teacher," *University of Kansas City Review,* XVIII (Autumn 1951), 25-26; Lewis D. Stilwell to Turner, April 26, 1924, "Blue Book," HEH TU Vol. II.

44. Horace J. Smith, "Lecture Notes, History of the West, 1910-1911," HEH TU Vol. XXIII.

45. Harvard University Course Lists, 1910-24, record students in each course, and are complete save for the period of World War I. Harvard Univ. Arch.

46. Turner's lectures, varying from finished copies marked "Dictated" to very rough notes, are scattered through a number of folders in HEH TU File Drawer 22A. Reading lists are in File Drawer 22B, Folder: Notes and Other Material 1880-1920.

47. Harvard University Course Lists, Second Half Year, 1914-15, 1915-16, Harvard Univ. Arch.

48. Lecture notes, K. M. Elish, 1915-16, Harvard Univ. Arch., Call No. HUC 8915.338.32.

49. J. F. Jameson to Turner, Jan. 26, 1915, HEH TU Box 23.

50. Dixon Ryan Fox to Max Farrand, Jan. 25, 1933, HEH TU Box 50.

51. Programs scattered through HEH TU Boxes 59 and 60.

52. Turner to Oscar C. Stine, Jan. 17, 1920, HEH TU Box 30. Student papers, some from his Harvard seminar, are in HEH TU Student's Papers (1)-(5). Others are in HEH TU File Drawer B4, Folder: Election of 1836, and F4, Folder: Germans.

53. Frederick Merk to Turner, July 4, 1927, HEH TU Box 37.

54. Turner to Fulmer Mood, Feb. 1922, is a five-page criticism of Mood's seminar paper (HEH TU Box 31).

55. Turner to Arthur P. Whitaker, July 21, 1921, HEH TU Box 31.

56. List compiled from *Doctors of Philosophy and Doctors of Science who have Received their Degree in Course from Harvard University, 1873-1926 with the Titles of their Theses* (Cambridge, 1926), 86-96.

57. Turner to Thomas P. Abernethy, July 16, 1920, Abernethy to Turner, Nov. 29, 1919, HEH TU Box 29; Turner to George M. Stephenson, Feb. 11, 1917, HEH TU Box 27.

58. Turner to Abernethy, Nov. 17, 1921, HEH TU Box 31. For special pleading for students who had written unsatisfactory examinations, see Turner to C. J. Bullock, May 10, 1915, Turner to William S. Ferguson, Dec. 30, 1918, HEH TU Boxes 24 and 28.

59. Kenneth W. Colgrove to Turner, March 29, 1915, Turner to Colgrove, Jan. 5, April 3, June 1, 1915, HEH TU Box 23 and 25.

60. Buffinton to Turner, June 21, 1914, HEH TU Box 21.

61. Turner to Buffinton, Dec. 21, 1922, Feb. 5, Nov. 23, 1923, HEH TU Box 32.

62. Turner to Buffinton, Dec. 12, 1924, HEH TU Box 33. From that time on Turner took puckish pleasure in addressing his student as "Dr. Buffinton."

Chapter XIV
Harvard Years: Conflict—Academic and International
1915-1920

1. Turner to A. C. McLaughlin, Oct. 6, 1915, HEH TU Box 25. Bancroft's letters to Turner, Oct. 5, 1915, ibid. Turner sought Jameson's advice in two letters written on the same day, Oct. 9, 1915 (LC, AHA Papers, Box 283, Folder: T).

2. Jameson to Turner, Oct. 15, 16, 18, 20, 23, 24, 1915, HEH TU Box 25; Turner to Jameson, Oct. 15, 1915. LC, AHA Papers, Box 283, Folder: F.

3. Bancroft to Turner, Oct. 23, 28, Nov. 3, 1915; Turner to Bancroft, Oct. 24, 28, 1915, HEH TU Box 25; Jameson to Turner, Oct. 23, 1915; Turner to Jameson, Oct. 23, 1915. LC, AHA Papers, Box 283, Folder: T.

4. Described in Jameson to H. Morse Stephens, Dec. 1, 1915, ibid. Box 31, Folder: S. The printed minutes are in the *Annual Report of the American Historical Association for 1915* (Washington, D.C., 1917), 75-79.

5. Bancroft to Edgar A. Bancroft, Nov. 29, 1915, Frederick Bancroft Papers, Department of Special Collections, Columbia Univ. Library, Box 1 (hereafter cited as Columbia, Bancroft Papers).

6. Bancroft to William K. Boyd, Dec. 8, 1915, ibid.

7. Jameson to A. C. McLaughlin, Nov. 18, 1915, in Elizabeth Donnan and Leo F. Stock (eds.), *An Historian's World: Selections from the Correspondence of John Franklin Jameson* (Philadelphia, 1956), 186.

8. E. B. Greene to Turner, Dec. 15, 1915; Dana C. Munro to Turner, Dec. 18, 1915; E. P. Cheyney to Turner, Dec. 22, 1915; Turner to G. L. Burr, Dec. 20, 1915, HEH TU Box 25.

9. Printed minutes, *Annual Report of the American Historical Association for 1915*, 49-51. The meeting described by Sidney B. Fay in *The Nation*, CII (Jan. 6, 1916), 22-23, and in Jameson to A. C. McLaughlin, Jan. 4, 1916, in Donnan and Stock (eds.), *An Historian's World*, 189-90.

10. Minutes, second session of business meeting, *Annual Report of the American Historical Association for 1915*, 51-54; report of Committee of Nine, ibid. 69-75. Printed ballot of the nominating committee, committee's report, other papers, HEH TU Box 59.

11. Turner to G. L. Burr, Jan. 8, 1916, Cornell, Burr Papers.

12. Ambler to Turner, Jan. 16, 22, 23, Feb. 5, 1916; Turner to Ambler, Feb. 9, 1916, HEH TU Box 26.

13. Turner to Jameson, Dec. 25, 1915. LC, AHA Papers, Box 283, Folder: T.

14. Jameson to Robert S. Woodward, July 3, 1913, in Donnan and Stock (eds.), *An Historian's World*, 158.

15. Jameson to Turner, March 13, 1915; Turner to Jameson, April 3, 1915, HEH TU Box 23 and LC, Jameson Papers. Robert S. Woodward to Turner, Nov. 15, 24, 1915; Turner to Woodward, Nov. 20, 1915, HEH TU Box 25. Pocket diary entry, Nov. 20, 1915, HEH TU Box 62.

16. Carnegie Institution of Washington, *Year Book No. 15* (Washington, D.C., 1917), 169.

17. Turner to Dorothy Turner Main, April 15, 1916, HEH TU Box I.

18. Place card (rough paper with picture of a coffin pierced by a dagger), together with menu, presented by Professor Emeritus Robert H. George of Brown University to Huntington Library, 1968.

19. Jameson to A. C. McLaughlin, Nov. 20, 1916, in Donnan and Stock (eds.), *An Historian's World*, 202.

20. Carnegie Institution of Washington, *Year Book No. 16* (Washington, D.C., 1918), 151. Syllabus for lecture series, HEH TU File Drawer 15B, Folder: Outline of Talk on North Central States; lecture on "The Middle West, 1830-1850: The Formation of a New Society," TU File Drawer F, Folder: Chap. VII North Central States.

21. Turner to Mrs. William Hooper, March 21, 1917, HEH TU-H Box 3.

22. Turner to Dorothy Turner Main, March 26, 1916; Senator Paul O. Husting to Turner, April 29, 1916, HEH TU Boxes I and 26.

23. Turner to John S. Main, March 31, 1916, HEH TU Box I.

24. Address of Feb. 22, 1916, HEH TU File Drawer 15A, Folder: Trinity College Lecture. Turner expressed many of the same views in a letter to A. C. McLaughlin (March 26, 1916, HEH TU Box 26).

25. Turner to Mrs. Hooper, Feb. 2, 5, 1917, HEH TU-H Box 3.

26. Turner to Mae Turner, July 9, 1917; Turner to Mrs. Hooper, March 21, 1917; Turner to Dorothy Turner Main, April 18, 1917, HEH TU Box I, TU-H Box 3.

27. For history of the National Board for Historical Services, see George T. Blakey, *Historians on the Homefront: American Propagandists for the Great War* (Lexington, Ky., 1970), and James M. Mock and Fredric Larson, *Words that Won the War: The Story of the Committee on Public Information, 1917-1919* (Princeton, 1939), 158-86.

28. Turner to Carl Becker, May 11, 1917; Turner to Max Farrand, May 5, 1917, HEH TU Box 27.

29. Turner to Jameson, May 20, 1917, in Donnan and Stock (eds.), *An Historian's World*, 207-8.

30. Turner to C. H. Van Tyne, Nov. 2, 1917, HC on WH Corr., Box VIII, Folder: TUV. Liberty Bond purchases listed in pocket diary for 1918, HEH TU Box 62.

31. Turner to Mrs. Hooper, Nov. 5, 1918, HEH TU-H Box 4.

32. Many "History of Liberty" lectures, with outlines, reading lists, and revisions, HEH TU File Drawers 10A and 10B. The lecture notes of a student, Frederick Merk, in TU Student's Papers (4), Folder: Merk: History of Liberty Notes.

33. Quotations drawn largely from lecture, "History A. Liberty. Introduction," HEH TU File Drawer 10B, Folder: Liberty, Introduction.

34. Turner to Mrs. Hooper, Oct. 9, 1919; Turner to William E. Dodd, May 26, 1920. HEH TU-H Box 4, TU Box 30.

35. Turner to Mrs. Hooper, Oct. 13, 1917, Oct. 19, 1919; Turner to Dorothy Turner Main, Jan. 26, 1917, HEH TU-H, Box 4, TU Box I.

36. Observations, probably written early in 1918, HEH TU File Drawer 15A, Folder: It Would be a Pity if the United States Lost.

37. Turner to Richard H. Dana, May 3, 1915, Richard Henry Dana Papers, Massachusetts Historical Society, Boston.

38. Turner's rough-draft "Syllabus," HEH TU File Drawer 14A, Folder: Syllabus of Considerations; reading notes, TU File Drawer 14A, Folder: Draft on League of Nations, 1918; versions of final paper, "International Political Parties," ibid. File Drawer 14B, Folder: International Political Parties in a Durable League of Nations," original, LC, Wilson Papers, File II,

Box 157. This copy, interlined and with marginal notes indicating it was carefully read, published in William Diamond (ed.), "Turner's American Sectionalism and World Organization," *American Historical Review*, XLVII (April 1942), 545-51.

39. C. H. Haskins to Turner, Dec. 13, 1918, HEH TU Box 28. Mae Turner to Guy Stanton Ford, April 5, 1942, HEH TU Box 52, and Turner to Mrs. Hooper, May 6, 1920, HEH TU-H Box 5, describe efforts to put the paper in Wilson's hands.

40. Turner to Mrs. Hooper, Oct. 9, Nov. 23, 1919, HEH TU-H Box 4.

41. Turner to Mrs. Hooper, Nov. 5, 1918; Turner to Dorothy Turner Main, Oct. 30, 1920, HEH TU-H, Box 4, TU Box I.

42. Turner to Mrs. Hooper, Jan. 16, 1920, HEH TU-H Box 5.

43. Turner, "Notes for an Address on Washington's Birthday, February 22, 1923," HEH TU File Drawer 15A, Folder: Notes for an Address on Washington's Birthday. He spoke before the Massachusetts Society of the Sons of the American Revolution.

44. Turner to Mrs. Hooper, Feb. 10, 1922, HEH TU-H, Box 5.

45. Archer B. Hulbert to Turner, Jan. 5, 1915, HC on WH Corr., Box 3, Folder: Hulbert, Archer B.

46. Solon J. Buck to Turner, Feb. 26, 1920, HEH TU Box 63.

47. National Board for Historical Service, "Peace and Reconstruction: Preliminary Bibliography," *The Historical Outlook*, X (March 1919), 156.

48. Edward N. Bristol, Holt & Co., to Turner, April 23, 1919, HEH TU Box 63.

49. Turner to Guy Stanton Ford, Nov. 27, 1920, SHSW, Turner Papers, Box II.

50. Turner to E. N. Bristol, April 24, 1919, Princeton, Holt Arch.

51. Letters concerning permission to reprint, HEH TU Box 63. Turner described his efforts in Turner to Lincoln MacVeagh, Feb. 26, March 9, 1920, Princeton: Holt Arch.

52. Two copies of the contract were sent on June 10 and returned same day (Holt & Co. to Turner, June 10, 19, 1920). One copy is in HEH TU Box 63.

53. Turner to Holt & Co., May 19, June 13, 23, 24, 1920, ibid; Holt & Co. to Turner, June 9, 23, 24, July 16, Aug. 14, 30, Oct. 6, 1920, HEH TU Box 63.

54. Turner to Edgar E. Robinson, Dec. 4, 1920, HEH TU Box 30.

55. Lincoln MacVeagh to Turner, Oct. 9, 14, 1920, HEH TU Box 63. Turner's list, TU Box 56.

56. Herbert E. Bolton to Turner, Oct. 23, 1920; Max Farrand to Turner, Nov. 8, 1920; C. H. Van Tyne to Turner, Nov. 14, 1920; U. B. Phillips to Turner, Dec. 16, 1920; Thomas M. Marshall to Turner, Dec. 21, 1920; William E. Dodd to Turner, Feb. 15, 1921; Harold J. Laski to Turner, Jan. 27, 1921, HEH TU Boxes 30 and 31.

57. *Milwaukee Sentinel*, Jan. 30, 1921; *Minneapolis Journal*, March 12, 17, 1921; *Boston Herald*, Nov. 15, 1920. HEH TU File Drawer 15D, Folder: Frontier in American History. Reviews.

58. *Boston Transcript*, Nov. 19, 1920; Turner to Edgar E. Robinson, Dec. 4, 1920.

59. Turner to Mrs. Hooper, Jan. 20, 1921, HEH TU-H, Box 5.

60. Charles A. Beard, "The Frontier in American History," *New Republic*, XXV (Feb. 16, 1921), 349-50.

61. Turner to Mrs. Hooper, Feb. 13, 1921, HEH TU-H, Box 5.

62. Turner to Dorothy Turner Main, Feb. 18, 1921, HEH TU Box I. No copy of Turner's letter seems to have survived, but its contents can be surmised from Beard's reply.

63. Charles A. Beard to Turner, May 14, 1921, HEH TU Box 31.

64. Beard to Merle Curti, Aug. 9, 1928, HEH TU Box 39.

65. Royalty statements, 1921-30, HEH TU Box 56.

66. Canceled note, HEH TU Box 63.

Chapter XV
Harvard Years: The World of Scholarship
1917-1924

1. P. J. Hartog, Univ. of London, to Turner, Dec. 19, 1919, Feb. 2, 1920; Charles A. Beard to Turner, March 13, 1919; James Harvey Robinson to Turner, March 15, May 7, 1919, HEH TU Boxes 29 and 30.

2. HEH TU File Drawer 14A, Folder: Address Agricultural History, 1922; printed in Wilbur R. Jacobs (ed.) "Research in Agricultural History; Frederick Jackson Turner's View in 1922," *Agricultural History*, XLII (Jan. 1968), 15-22.

3. Turner to Mrs. William Hooper, Dec. 19, 1922, HEH TU-H Box 5.

4. A portion of this manuscript comparing conditions in Virginia and Massachusetts, not included in the published version, is in HEH TU File Drawer 3A. The essay, "The First Official Frontier of the Massachusetts Bay," was published in the *Publications of the Colonial Society of Massachusetts*, XVII (Boston, 1915), 250-71.

5. Root to Turner, June 14, 1914; Andrews to Turner, June 15, 1914, HEH TU Box 21. Morison followed one of Turner's suggestions, presenting his findings to the Colonial Society a year later. Henry H. Edes to Turner, Feb. 2, 1915, HEH TU Box 23.

6. Manuscript notes, HEH TU File Drawer 14A, Folder: Turner, What is Colonial History.

7. Turner's influence in fathering the "frontier school" of colonial history is discussed in Wilbur R. Jacobs, "Colonial Origins of the United States: The Turnerian View," *Pacific Historical Review*, XL (Feb. 1971), 21-38.

8. Notes and MS for University of Chicago lecture, HEH TU File Drawer 15A, Folder: Lecture University of Chicago, 1916; for Clark University address, ibid. File Drawer 15E, Folders: Address Clark University, Notes, and Since the Foundation, 1924. The Clark address was printed in *Clark University Library Publications*, VII (Feb. 1924), 9-29.

9. The editor of *The Historical Outlook* sought permission to republish the paper (Albert E. McKinley to Turner, June 30, 1924, HEH TU Box 33). It was printed in *The Historical Outlook*, XV (Nov. 1924), 335-42, under the title, "Since the Foundation of Clark University, 1889-1924."

10. Turner to Max Farrand, May 15, 1907, HEH TU Box 9.

11. For clippings and pasted items on sectionalism see HEH TU File Drawers 16, 17, and 18, esp. File Drawers 14B and 14C.

12. Turner to Logan Esarey, Nov. 24, 1917; Turner to J. Franklin Jameson, Nov. 24, 1917; Turner to George Hempl, Nov. 24, 1917, HC on WH Corr., Box VIII, Folders B, EF, and HIJ.

13. An excellent set of maps prepared at this time is in HEH TU File Drawer 17C, Folder: Sections 1908.

14. No manuscript of this paper has been preserved, but an abstract was published in the *Bulletin of the American Geographical Society*, XLVI (Aug. 1914), 591-95.

15. Isaiah Bowman to Turner, April 7, 1914, HEH TU Box 21.

16. Four manuscript drafts, holograph and partially typed, in HEH TU File Drawer 14A, Folder: Significance of Sections, 1914. A fifth, much re-written, is in HEH File Drawer 14C, Folder: Sections. AHA Chicago Meeting, 1914.

17. Turner to Isaiah Bowman, May 26, 1914, HEH TU Box 21. Turner to J. F. Jameson, Jan. 27, April 15, 30, May 2, 5, 1915; Jameson to Turner, Feb. 2, April 14, 17, 28, May 3, 1915, Feb. 15, 1918. LC, AHA Papers, Box 283, Folder T.

18. Turner to Mae Turner, Oct. 25, 28, 1916 (HEH TU Box I), describe his disappointment at his reception at Western Reserve University. Two drafts of Minnesota Historical Society paper, HEH TU File Drawer 15E, Folder: Significance of the Middle West.

19. Sheet of paper, inserted, ibid.

20. A. Lawrence Lowell to Turner, June 26, 1917, contains the invitation to deliver the lectures (HEH TU Box 27). Turner's remark about the energy required to produce the lectures, Turner to J. F. Jameson, Feb. 20, 1918, HC on WH Corr., Box VIII, Folder HIJ. The *Boston Transcript*, March 23, 1918, contained the favorable remark about them.

21. "The First Lowell Lecture," MS, HEH TU File Drawer E1, Folder: Lowell Lectures, 1918.

22. Holt & Co. to Turner, Sept. 8, 1917; Turner to Holt & Co., Sept. 13, 1917, Princeton, Holt Arch. Contract, HEH TU Box 63.

23. E. N. Bristol to Turner, April 9, 1918, HEH TU Box 63.

24. Turner to Bristol, May 8, 1918, Princeton, Holt Arch.

25. Turner to Mrs. William Hooper, Oct. 9, 1918; Turner to Moses S. Slaughter, Oct. 12, 1918, HEH TU-H, Box 4 and TU Box 28.

26. A description of the Moorings, with a record of the purchase and upkeep, is in a scrapbook in which Turner pasted bills, letters, and receipts (HEH TU Vol. XXI).

27. Turner to Mrs. Hooper, June 19, 1918, HEH TU-H, Box 4.

28. HEH TU File Drawer 11B, Folder: North Atlantic, 1830-1850. Shifting of Population.

29. Turner to Mrs. Hooper, Oct. 9, 1919, HEH TU-H, Box 4.

30. Ibid. Oct. 12, 1920, HEH TU-H, Box 5.

31. Turner to Lincoln MacVeagh, April 5, 1921, Princeton, Holt Arch.

32. Notice of leave of absence, HEH TU Box 56. Turner wrote his wife, "the requirement is *merely* (!) to write a book" (Turner to Mae Turner, April 25, 1920, HEH TU Box I).

33. Turner memorandum, HEH TU File Drawer 10A, Folder: U.S. 1830-1850. New England Politics; letters from Holt & Co. (Lincoln MacVeagh)

to Turner, Feb. 3, March 26, April 4, 8, 1921, HEH TU Box 63.

34. Turner to Holt & Co., May 30, Oct. 10, 1921. Princeton, Holt Arch. Holt & Co. to Turner, May 31, Oct. 4, 1921, July 25, Oct. 31, 1922, HEH TU Box 63.

35. Turner to Merle Curti, Oct. 12, 1921, HEH TU Box 31.

36. Turner to Claude H. Van Tyne, Nov. 1, 1924, Clements, Van Tyne Papers.

37. Turner's notes and drafts, HEH TU File Drawer 12A, Folder: Sectionalism. Harding Administration; 14A, Folder: Draft Recent American Sectionalism; 14B, Folder: Recent American Sectionalism, and 15A, Folder: Talk at Thursday Club.

38. Talk on "Recent American Sectionalism," MS, HEH TU File Drawer 14A, Folder: Draft Recent American Sectionalism.

39. Draft of lecture at Chicago and Michigan, HEH TU File Drawer 14A, Unmarked Folder; drafts of commencement address at Univ. of New Hampshire, HEH TU 14C, Unmarked Folder.

40. Turner to Wilbur L. Cross, July 5, 29, 1922, Yale Review Papers, Beinecke Library, Yale Univ., Folder: F. J. Turner (hereafter cited as Beinecke, Yale Review Papers); Cross to Turner, July 9, 29, 1922, HEH TU Box 31. Sections of MS, much rewritten, HEH TU File Drawer 14A, Folder: Essay on Sectionalism 1920s.

41. Wilbur L. Cross to Turner, Sept. 1, 1922, HEH TU Box 31.

42. Turner, "Sections and Nation," *Yale Review*, XII (Oct. 1922), 1-21.

43. Clippings, HEH TU File Drawer 14B, Folder: Sections and Nation.

44. Turner to Dorothy Turner Main, Oct. 12, 1922, HEH TU Box I.

45. Walter Lippmann to Turner, Feb. 16, 1923; Irvine L. Lenroot to Turner, Dec. 23, 1923; Josef Redlich to Wilbur L. Cross, Nov. 10, 1922, HEH TU Box 31.

46. Turner to Mae Turner, May 20, 1922, HEH TU Box J.

47. Turner to Mae Turner, [May or June 1922], HEH TU Box J. Someone, probably Mrs. Turner, destroyed the last portion of this letter.

48. Copies of "Introduction," HEH TU File Drawer A1, Folder: The United States and Its Sections, and File Drawer A1, Folder: Introduction.

49. For summer's activities, see HEH TU Vol. XXI, The Moorings; Turner to Mrs. Hooper, Aug. 12, 1922, HEH TU-H Box 5.

50. Turner to Lincoln MacVeagh, Aug. 12, 1922, HEH TU Box 63.

51. MacVeagh to Turner, July 25, Aug. 8, 1922; Turner to MacVeagh, July 11, 29, 1922, HEH TU Box 63.

52. Turner to Mrs. Hooper, Dec. 19, 1922, HEH TU-H Box 5.

53. Receipts for insured mail show that Turner sent manuscript on May 3, 5, and 8, August 13, 23, and 30, September 7, 8, 10, 15, and 29, and October 16 and 23, 1923. His illness in June and July accounted for the lack of production at that time (HEH TU Box 63). Holt's reaction to the manuscript is in Lincoln MacVeagh to Turner, May 8, July 12, 18, Aug. 16, 31, Sept. 7, 8, 17, 23, 25, Oct. 18, 26, 1923. Quotation, MacVeagh to Turner, May 4, 1923, HEH TU Box 63.

54. Turner to John M. Gaus, May 9, 1923, HEH TU Box 32.

55. Turner to J. Franklin Jameson, June 26, 1923, LC, Jameson Papers.

56. Turner to Mrs. Hooper, Dec. 8, 1923, HEH TU-H, Box 5.

57. Typical notes, HEH TU File Drawer A1, Folder: US 1830-1850, Folder: Introduction. *See also* Holt & Co. to Turner, Jan. 21, 30, 1924, HEH TU Box 63.

58. Guy Stanton Ford, "Reminiscences of Guy Stanton Ford," Oral History Research Office, Columbia Univ., p. 364.

59. Max Farrand to Mae Turner, [1932], HEH TU Box 49.

60. Turner to Carl Becker, March 10, 1916, HEH TU Box 26; Turner to James W. Thompson, Dec. 29, 1913, University of Chicago Archives, Department of History Papers, Box VIII, Folder 1 (hereafter cited as U. of Chi. Arch., Dept. of Hist. Papers).

61. Turner delivered the memorial address for Reuben Gold Thwaites, who died October 22, 1913. It was printed as *Reuben Gold Thwaites: A Memorial Address* (Madison, 1914). Five days after Thwaites died, Turner was offered the position by President Charles R. Van Hise (C. R. Van Hise to Turner, Oct. 29, Nov. 4, 1913, HEH TU Box 20A). Turner described his reaction in letters to Mae Turner, Nov. 13, 18, 22, 1913, HEH TU Box H.

62. James W. Thompson to Turner, Dec. 18, 1913; Turner to Thompson, Dec. 29, 1913, HEH TU Box 20A; Turner to Andrew C. McLaughlin, Jan. 15, 1914; McLaughlin to Turner, Feb. 10, June 1, Sept. 1, 1914. U. of Chi. Arch., Dept. of Hist. Papers, Box VIII, Folder 1.

63. Turner's copy of Carnegie Foundation for the Advancement of Teaching, *Act of Incorporation, By-laws for the Admission of Institutions and for the Granting of Retirement Allowances* (New York, 1920), 1-25, contains information used in this paragraph (HEH TU Vol. XIX). Additional information is in Turner to Dorothy Turner Main, Jan. 26, 1923 (HEH TU Box J), and Turner's income tax returns for 1924 and 1925 (HEH TU Box 56). His income in 1924 was $8,997.44, on which he paid a tax of $116.88.

64. Turner to Edgar E. Robinson, Nov. 22, 1923, HEH TU Box 32.

65. Harvard Univ. to Turner, May 11, 1923; Turner to A. Lawrence Lowell, April 27, 1923, HEH TU Vol. XIX.

66. Arthur M. Schlesinger, "Reminiscences of Arthur M. Schlesinger," Oral History Research Office, Columbia Univ., pp. 83, 85-86.

67. Turner to Arthur H. Buffinton, Nov. 6, 1923, HEH TU Box 32.

68. Students in Turner's last classes, with the grades assigned them, are listed in Turner and Merk, *List of References on the History of the West* (Cambridge, Mass., 1922), HEH TU Vol. XX (2).

69. "Opening Remarks for First Lecture, History of the US 1880-1920," HEH TU Box 56.

70. Turner to Mrs. Hooper, May 1, 1924, HEH TU-H Box 5. Turner's notes, HEH TU Box 56.

71. Turner to Mrs. Hooper, May 1, 1924 (HEH TU-H Box 5) describes Turner's pleasure at sitting for his portrait. Frederick Merk to "Dear Sir," June 16, 1924, soliciting funds to pay for the drawing, Houghton, Turner Papers.

72. Seating chart for banquet, HEH TU Box 33. He described the evening in letters to Mrs. Hooper, May 1, 1924, and Dorothy Turner Main, April 30, 1924 (HEH TU-H Box 5 and TU Vol. XXII).

73. The speeches were not recorded, but Allyn A. Young later recalled his remarks for Carl Becker (Young to Becker, Oct. 9, 1925, HEH TU Box

34A). The banquet was described in the *Boston Herald*, May 25, 1924, and the *Christian Science Monitor*, May 26, 1924.

74. Turner to Mrs. Hooper, May 1, 1924, HEH TU-H Box 5.

75. *Harvard Crimson*, May 24, 1924. Most of the letters and telegrams were bound into a "Blue Book," comparable to the "Red Book" compiled when Turner left Madison (HEH TU Vol. II Blue Book). Letters from Dodd and Van Tyne, May 24 and June 3, 1924, HEH TU Box 33.

76. Turner to Dorothy Turner Main, May 28, 1924, HEH TU Vol. XXII.

Chapter XVI
The Twilight Years
1924-1932

1. Details of the house planning and financing, Turner to Dorothy Turner Main, April 6, 9, 30, 1924; Dorothy Turner Main to Turner, April 6, 21, 1924; Turner to John Main, April 22, 1924, HEH TU Vol. XXII.

2. Turner's teaching at Logan in 1924 and 1925 is described in Ray A. Billington, "Frederick Jackson Turner and Logan's 'National Summer School,'" *Utah Historical Quarterly*, XXXVII (Summer 1969), 307-36.

3. Elmer G. Peterson to Turner, Oct. 8, Nov. 2, 1923; Turner to Peterson, Nov. 6, 1923, HEH TU Box 32. Turner's calculations were made on the back of one of President Peterson's letters.

4. Agricultural College of Utah, *Bulletin. Summer Catalogue, 1924* (Logan, March 1924), 7.

5. Turner to Mae Turner, June 17, 1924, HEH TU Box J.

6. Ibid. June 29, 1924.

7. *Student Life*, June 23, 1924.

8. Turner to Mae Turner, [July 1924], HEH TU Box J.

9. Elmer G. Peterson to Turner, June 20, Aug. 2, Sept. 20, 1924; Turner to Peterson, Oct. 2, 6, 1924, HEH TU Box 33.

10. Memoranda, "Financing 2214 Van Hise Ave." and "Income Budget, Oct. 1924–Oct. 1925," HEH TU Vol. XXII. Turner discussed finances in Turner to Mae Turner, July 4, 1924, HEH TU Box J.

11. Turner to John Main, Oct. 25, 1924, HEH TU Box J; Turner to Mrs. William Hooper, Oct. 30, 1924. HEH TU-H Box 5.

12. Turner to Mae Turner, Nov. 15, 1924, HEH TU Box J.

13. Turner to Frederick Merk, Dec. 7, 1924, Houghton, Turner Papers.

14. Mae Turner to Mrs. Hooper, March 29, 1925, HEH TU-H Box 6; Turner to Samuel E. Morison, July 30, 1926, HEH TU Box 35A.

15. Turner to Mrs. Hooper, Dec. 23, 1925, HEH TU-H Box 6. Pictures and cut-out animals prepared by Turner to amuse his grandchildren, HEH TU Box 62.

16. Mae Turner to Mrs. Hooper, March 29, 1925, HEH TU Box 6.

17. Turner to Joseph Schafer, March 26, April 5, 1924, HEH TU Box 33.

18. "The Significance of the Section in American History," *Wisconsin Magazine of History*, VIII (March 1925), 255-80.

19. Frank W. Taussig to Turner, April 16, 1925, HEH TU Box 34.

20. Turner to Arthur M. Schlesinger, May 5, 1925, ibid.

21. Several drafts of the lectures given in this series are in HEH TU File Drawers 14C and 15B, Folder: University of Wisconsin Lectures, 1925, and Lecture on Sectionalism.

22. A. C. Krey, "My Reminiscences of Frederick Jackson Turner," *Arizona and the West*, III (Winter 1961), 381.

23. Turner to Mae Turner, March 20, 21, 1925, HEH TU Box J.

24. Rough draft and typed final version, HEH TU File Drawer 14D, Folder: MSS Geographic Sectionalism in American History; published, *Annals of the Association of American Geographers* XVI (June 1926), 85–93. Turner expressed his ambition in Turner to Homer C. Hockett, Jan. 21, 1926, HEH TU Box 35.

25. Merle Curti to Turner, Oct. 6, 1926; Norman Foerester to Turner, Aug. 4, 1926; Arthur M. Schlesinger to Turner, Sept. 8, 1926, HEH TU Box 35A.

26. Hundreds of notes taken by Turner are in HEH TU File Drawer 14D, Folder: World's Work Article.

27. Two drafts, with many corrections, HEH TU File Drawer 15E, Folder: Draft and Final MSS, 1876-1926 Essay.

28. Henry Cabot Lodge, "The Distribution of Ability in the United States," *Century Magazine*, XLII (Sept. 1891), 687-94.

29. Notes taken by Turner fill HEH TU 3×5 File Drawer 8. Two drafts, HEH TU File Drawer 15C, Folder: Turner's Children of the Pioneers, and Folder: Revised Children of the Pioneers.

30. Turner to Prof. Reed, Nov. 11, 1925, Beinecke, Yale Review Papers.

31. Turner to Mrs. Hooper, March 7, 1925, HEH TU-H Box 6.

32. Ibid. April 11, May 16, 1925.

33. President and Fellows of Harvard University to Turner, Feb. 24, 1925, HEH TU File Drawer A1, Folder: Milton Fund. The fund had been established a short time before by William F. Milton with an endowment that provided $50,000 a year for research (*Boston Evening Transcript*, March 5, 1925).

34. Turner, memorandum to Holt & Co., May 28, 1925, HEH TU Box 63.

35. Turner to Mrs. Hooper, Aug. 1, 1926, HEH TU-H Box 6. That summer's events described in "The Moorings," HEH TU Vol. XXI, and Turner to Mrs. Hooper, May 28, July 7, Aug. 1, 29, Sept. 28, 1926, HEH TU-H Box 6.

36. Turner to Dorothy Turner Main, Jan. 23, 27, Feb. 6, 24, March 2, 1927, HEH TU Box K.

37. For the transition of the Huntington Library to a research library, see Ray A. Billington, "The Genesis of the Research Institution," *Huntington Library Quarterly*, XXXII (Aug. 1969), 351-72.

38. Max Farrand to George Ellery Hale, March 7, 1927, HEH TU Box 36. Correspondence between Hale and Farrand, George Ellery Hale Papers, California Institute of Technology, Box 22.

39. Turner to Joseph Schafer, April 24, 1927, SHSW, Schafer Papers. Turner's notes and impressions, HEH TU File Drawer 15A, Folder: Memo by Turner on Research Materials.

40. Turner, "Memoranda" to Farrand, ibid. Many have been published in Wilbur R. Jacobs (ed.), "Frederick Jackson Turner's Notes on the West-

ward Movement, California, and the Far West," *Southern California Quarterly*, XLVI (June 1964), 161-68.

41. Turner to Mrs. Hooper, Easter, April 20, 1927, HEH TU-H Box 7.

42. Turner to Max Farrand, March 8, 19, 1927; Farrand to Turner, March 11, 24, 27, 1927, HEH TU Box 36.

43. Robert O. Schad, "An Impression of FJT at the Huntington Library," HEH TU Box 57, and Mary Esther Jackson, "Reminiscences of Turner at the Huntington Library," Huntington Library Trustees' Files. Lists of books given the library by Turner, HEH TU Boxes 39 and 57.

44. Turner to Dorothy Turner Main, Oct. 3, 28, 1928, HEH TU Box K.

45. Income tax returns, 1927, 1928, and 1930, and list of holdings, March 25, 1929, HEH TU Box 61. He discussed financial affairs in letters to John Main, Jan. 12, March 6, 1929, HEH TU Box K.

46. One folder in HEH TU Box 37 is filled with lecture invitations.

47. For lecture at the University of California at Los Angeles, see HEH TU File Drawer 15A, Folder: Turner's talk at UCLA; for the talk to the Harvard Club, Box 57; for remarks to Pacific Coast Branch, File Drawer 15A, Folder: Talk to Pacific Coast Branch; for lecture, Pasadena Lecture Series, File Drawer 14B, Folder: Sectionalism in American Politics.

48. Mimeographed syllabus, HEH TU Box 57; Turner's lecture notes, HEH TU File Drawer 14B, Folder: Cal Tech Lectures; class lists, HEH TU Box 57.

49. Turner to Mrs. Hooper, Jan. 21, 1929, HEH TU-H Box 7.

50. Turner to Frederick Merk, Jan. 15, 1927, Houghton, Turner Papers. Letters written in behalf of former students fill much of HEH TU Boxes 38 and 39.

51. Turner to Joseph Schafer, [Sept. 1931], HEH TU Box 46.

52. Letters to and from Becker and Curti, HEH TU Boxes 34A, 35, 39, and 40. All reproduced in Ray A. Billington, *The Genesis of the Frontier Thesis: A Study in Historical Creativity* (San Marino, 1971), 221-85.

53. Turner to Dorothy Turner Main, April 25, 1927, HEH TU Box K; Turner to Carl Becker, May 14, 1927, Cornell, Becker Papers.

54. Turner to Merle Curti, Jan. 5, 1931; Turner to Max Farrand, Jan. 5, 1931, HEH TU Box 45.

55. Turner to Max Farrand, March 8, 1927, HEH TU Box 36.

56. HEH TU File Drawer 15B, Folder: Schedule of Writing Deadlines.

57. Turner to President and Fellows of Harvard University, Nov. 22, 1927, HEH TU File Drawer A1, Folder: Milton Fund.

58. Turner to Holt & Co., Nov. 21, 1927, Jan. 9, 1928, Princeton, Holt Arch.; Charles A. Madison, Holt & Co., to Turner, Oct. 24, Nov. 21, 1927, Feb. 3, 1928, HEH TU Box 63.

59. Merrill H. Crissey, "Memorandum on Professor Turner's Writing of His Book," HEH TU Box 49.

60. Turner to Mrs. Hooper, Dec. 27, 1928, HEH TU-H Box 6.

61. Turner to Dorothy Turner Main, March 6, 1926, HEH TU Box K.

62. Ibid. April 25, May 7, 14, 28, 1929, HEH TU Box K.

63. Turner to Merle Curti, Aug. 16, 1929, HEH TU Box 42.

64. Crissey, "Memorandum on Professor Turner's Writing of His Book," HEH TU Box 49.

65. Turner to Joseph Schafer, Feb. 18, 1930, HEH TU Box 43.

66. Turner to Max Farrand, Feb. 4, April 21, 1930; Farrand to Turner, April 18, 1930, HEH TU Box 44.

67. HEH TU File Drawer A1, Folder: Suggestions by Turner for Dedication and Preface, and File Drawer D4, Folder: Turner's Plan for Another to Complete His Book.

68. Income tax forms, 1930, 1931, HEH TU Box 61.

69. Proposed changes for Chapter II, HEH TU File Drawer A1, Folder: Ch. II US 1830-50; for Chapter IV, File Drawer A2, Folder: The Middle States; for Chapter VII, File Drawer A3, Folder: VII North Central States. Memorandum on map revision, HEH TU File Drawer A5, Folder: U.S. 1830-50.

70. Folder "Wilmot Proviso Notes," containing copies of documents that puzzled him, on his desk at the time he died (HEH TU File Drawer D4, Folder: Wilmot Proviso Notes). Last dictated memorandum (Drawer D4 also), labeled: Turner's Last Dictation and Comments by Crissey.

71. Turner to Marion C. Sheldon, March 14, 1932, HEH TU Box 47.

72. Max Farrand to Arthur M. Schlesinger, March 18, 1932, HEH TU Box 47.

73. Max Farrand to John Main, March 19, 1932; *Pasadena Star-News*, March 19, 1932; Avery Craven, "Appreciation of FJT," HEH TU Box 57.

74. Letters of condolence, HEH TU Vol. V; newspaper clippings, HEH TU Box 57; extracts from resolutions, HEH TU Box 60.

75. Memoranda, HEH TU File Drawer L2, Folder: Possible Volume of Essays on Sectionalism, File Drawer 14A, Folder: Possible Volume of Essays.

76. Correspondence, Max Farrand and Holt & Co., concerning publication, HEH TU File Drawer 14C, Folder: Farrand-Holt Correspondence, File Drawer L2, Folder: Correspondence with Henry Holt & Co.

77. Richard H. Thornton to Mrs. Turner, May 18, 1933, HEH TU Box 50A.

78. The labors performed by Crissey and Craven can be realized by comparing the original manuscripts with the published version. See esp. carbons of Chapter IV, HEH TU File Drawer A2, Folder: IV The Middle States.

Chapter XVII
Frederick Jackson Turner: Portrait of the Man

1. W. Paul Resop to Mrs. Turner, July 7, 1940; Paul Knaplund to Howard K. Beale, Merle Curti, and Fulmer Mood, March 8, 1949, HEH TU Box 52.

2. Curtis Nettels to Mrs. Turner, Feb. 8, 1941, ibid.

3. H. W. Johnson to Turner, May 29, 1918, HEH TU Box 28. Mrs. Turner wrote on this letter: "We think this rather nice in that it shows the friendly spirit on both sides."

4. M. L. Gochenour to Turner, June 12, 1912; Turner to Gochenour, July 7, 1912, HEH TU Box 18.

5. Albert Matthews to Turner, Dec. 14, 1915, HEH TU Box 23.

6. Mae Turner to Max Farrand, May 17, 1932, HEH TU Box 48.

7. Turner to Mae Sherwood, Dec. 12, 1886, HEH TU Box A.

8. Turner to Woodrow Wilson, Feb. 5, 1890. LC, Wilson Papers, Box 3.

9. Turner to Jackson Turner Main, Jan. 14, 1932, HEH TU Box K.

10. Turner to Betsy Main, May 16, 1922, Feb. 14, 1923, HEH TU Box J ("Betsy" was the nickname of Elizabeth W. Main).

11. Turner to Merle Curti, June 30, 1927, HEH TU Box 36.

12. Copies pasted by Turner in his copy of *List of References on the History of the West* (Cambridge, Mass., 1922), obviously to be read to the class, HEH TU Vol. III (3).

13. Merrill H. Crissey, "Reminiscences of Frederick J. Turner," HEH TU Box 57, Folder: Biographical and Autobiographical Data. Turner's style is explored by students of literature in Harold P. Simonson, "Frederick Jackson Turner: Frontier History as Art," *Antioch Review*, XXIV (Summer 1964), 201-11, and Merrill E. Lewis, "The Art of Frederick Jackson Turner: the Histories," *Huntington Library Quarterly*, XXXV (May 1972), 241-55.

14. Card, HEH TU Box 47.

15. Commonplace Book for 1886, HEH TU Vol. III (3).

16. Cards, probably written in 1904 during picnic with the Moses S. Slaughters, HEH TU Box 55.

17. Turner to Mae Turner, May 5, 1907, HEH TU Box G.

18. Max Farrand, who was with the Turners, described the scene in a memorandum, May 5, 1932. Memorandum and several versions of the poem, HEH TU Box 55.

19. Menu in pocket diary for 1911-1912, HEH TU Box 62.

20. Turner to Edgar E. Robinson, Oct. 29, 1912, HEH TU Box 18.

21. Household Account Book, 1921-22, HEH TU Vol. XII.

22. Inventory of books at 7 Phillips Place, SHSW, Turner Papers; another of books at Hancock Point, "The Moorings," HEH TU Vol. XXI.

23. Turner, "Miscellaneous Personal Accounts," HEH TU Box H; "Personal and Household Accounts," HEH TU Box G; "Household Account Book," HEH TU Vol. XII.

24. Turner to Mae Turner, August 7, 1913, July 20, 1917, HEH TU Boxes H and I; entries in pocket diary for July 10 and 13, 1911, HEH TU Box 62.

25. Turner to Edward T. Hartman, Jan. 11, 1926, SHSW, Turner Papers.

26. Turner to Mrs. William Hooper, June 19, 1916, HEH TU-H Box 4.

27. Turner to Mae Sherwood, Aug. 8, 1886, HEH TU Box A.

28. Turner to Dorothy Turner Main, April 15, 1916, HEH TU Box I.

29. Turner to Mrs. Hooper, July 13, 1919, HEH TU-H Box 4.

30. Ibid. July 16, 1913, HEH TU-H Box 2.

31. Turner to Dorothy Turner, Sept. 20, 1912, HEH TU Box H.

32. Turner to Mae Turner, March 25, 1915, HEH TU Box I.

33. Turner to Edgar E. Robinson, Oct. 29, 1912, HEH TU Box 18.

34. Turner to Dorothy Turner, Sept. 30, 1912, HEH TU Box H.

35. Bernard Fay, "An Invitation to American Historians," *Harper's Magazine*, CLXVI (Dec. 1932), 30.

36. Turner to Edmond S. Meany, Jan. 11, 1919, HEH TU Box 29.

37. W. E. Green to Turner, Jan. 27, 1902; Turner to Green, Jan. 28, 1902; Turner to R. S. Whitelaw. U. of Wis. Arch., L. and S., Hist., Turner Corr., Box 1, Folder G; Box 3, Folder W.

38. Turner to Ellen Breese Turner, June 30, 1887, HEH TU Box B.
39. Turner to Mae Sherwood, April 19, 1888, HEH TU Box C.
40. Turner to Lois C. M. Rosenberry, April 28, 1930, HEH TU Box 44.
41. Turner to Mae Turner, May 23, 1922, HEH TU Box J.
42. Turner's activities in 1884 were reported in *Wisconsin State Journal,* Aug. 26, 29, Sept. 3, 1884; his vote in 1888, Turner to Mae Sherwood, May 9, 1888, HEH TU Box C. He later recalled that he had voted for McKinley in 1896, but his name is not among those of faculty members supporting the Republican candidate (*Wisconsin State Journal,* Oct. 17, 1896).
43. Turner expressed these views in "Dominant Forces in Western Life," "The Middle West," and "Pioneer Ideals and the State University," published in 1897, 1901, and 1910 [reprinted in Turner, *The Frontier in American History* (New York, 1920), 240, 155, and 281].
44. Turner to Max Farrand, Nov. 24, 1907, HEH TU Box 9A.
45. Turner to Charles S. Slichter, March 16, 1907, U. of Wis. Arch., Misc. File: F. J. Turner.
46. Turner to William E. Dodd, Oct. 9, 1908, HEH TU Box 11.
47. Turner to Mrs. Hooper, June 2, 1912, HEH TU-H Box 1.
48. Ibid. Aug. 8, 1912.
49. Turner to Dorothy Turner, Oct. 11, 1912, HEH TU Box H.
50. Turner to Mae Turner, Oct. 18, 1912, ibid.
51. Ibid. Oct. 22, 1912.
52. Turner to Dorothy Turner Main, Oct. 30, 1920, ibid., HEH TU Box I.
53. Turner to Mrs. Hooper, March 16, Nov. 16, 1924, HEH TU-H Box 5.
54. Ibid. Dec. 14, 1926, HEH TU-H Box 6.
55. Richard S. Emmet (secretary to Herbert Hoover) to Turner, Jan. 15, 27, 1923, HEH TU Box 32.
56. Turner to Herbert Hoover, [Jan. 1923]; a copy of this letter, now in the Herbert Hoover Presidential Library, West Branch, Iowa, has been furnished the Huntington Library by Thomas T. Thalken, director.
57. Turner to Charles S. Slichter, Feb. 14, 1923. U. of Wis. Arch., Misc. File: F. J. Turner; Turner to Mrs. Hooper, May 27, 1928, HEH TU-H Box 6; Turner to Dorothy Turner Main, Nov. 16, 1928, HEH TU Box K.

Chapter XVIII
The Persistence of a Theory: The Frontier
And Sectional Hypotheses

1. Turner to Laurence M. Larson, June 24, 1910, HEH TU Box 15.
2. Irene T. Blythe, "The Textbooks and the New Discoveries. Emphasis and Viewpoints in American History," *The Historical Outlook,* XXIII (Dec. 1932), 398-99; Henry M. Littlefield, "Textbooks, Determinism and Turner: The Westward Movement in Secondary School History and Geography Textbooks, 1830-1960," Ph.D. thesis (unpubl.), Columbia Univ., 1967.
3. Howard W. Caldwell, "How to Teach the History of the West in American History," *The History Teacher's Magazine,* VII (April 1916), 125.

4. Charles H. Haskins, "European History and American Scholarship," *American Historical Review*, XXVIII (Jan. 1923), 215. Thompson's views are expressed in his "Profitable Fields for Investigation in Medieval History," *American Historical Review*, XVIII (April 1913), 490-504, and in his popular textbook, *An Economic and Social History of the Middle Ages, 300-1300* (New York, 1928), 518.

5. Franklin H. Giddings to Merle Curti, Aug. 20, 1928, HEH TU Box 39.

6. Norman Foerster, "American Literature," *Saturday Review of Literature*, II (April 3, 1926), 677-79. For relationship of these books to Turner thesis, see Ray A. Billington, *America's Frontier Heritage* (New York, 1966), 14.

7. Newton D. Baker to Turner, Oct. 8, 1926; Charles Merz to Turner, May 25, 1925; Arthur Capper to Turner, Aug. 4, 1926; Felix Frankfurter to Turner, Dec. 17, 1925, HEH TU Boxes 34, 35, 35A.

8. *Madison Capital Times*, Jan. 15, 1931.

9. *New York Times*, Sept. 24, 1932. For Turner's impact on Roosevelt and the New Deal, see Curtis Nettels, "Frederick Jackson Turner and the New Deal," *Wisconsin Magazine of History*, XVII (March 1934), 257-65, and Steven Kesselman, "The Frontier Thesis and the Great Depression," *Journal of the History of Ideas*, XXIX (April-June 1968), 253-68.

10. James T. Adams, "Rugged Individualism Analyzed," *New York Times Magazine*, March 8, 1934, 1-2, 11.

11. For impact of Turner's thesis on foreign policy, see William A. Williams, "The Frontier Thesis and American Foreign Policy," *Pacific Historical Review*, XXIV (Nov. 1955), 379-95, and Lawrence S. Kaplan, "Frederick Jackson Turner and Imperialism," *Social Science*, XXVII (Jan. 1952), 12-16. Williams, *The Roots of the Modern American Empire* (New York, 1970), uses momentum of expansion created by the frontier to explain much of modern foreign policy.

12. Merrill H. Crissey, "Professor Turner's Last Years," HEH TU Box 57, Folder: Merrill H. Crissey. Drafts of Biographical Data.

13. Turner to Maurice G. Fulton, Oct. 12, 1931, HEH TU Box 46.

14. Turner to Max Farrand, Oct. 26, 1914, HEH TU Box X. Memorandum giving Turner's schedule for summer, HC on WH Corr., Box 5, Folder: Turner, F. J.

15. Turner to Charles H. Haskins, June 18, 1914, Princeton, Haskins Papers.

16. Copy of article, with Turner's notations, HEH TU File Drawer 15B, Folder: Commencement Address University of Washington.

17. Turner to Arthur M. Schlesinger, May 5, 1925, HEH TU Box 34.

18. Arthur M. Schlesinger to Turner, May 2, 1925; Frederick Merk to Turner, May 18, 1925, HEH TU Box 34.

19. Turner to Schlesinger, May 5, 1925; Turner to Merk, May 6, 1925, HEH TU Box 34.

20. Turner to Merk, Jan. 9, 1931, HEH TU Box 45.

21. For the attack on Turner, see Ray A. Billington, *The American Frontier Thesis: Attack and Defense* (Washington, D.C., 1971), and Billington, *America's Frontier Heritage* (1966).

22. Turner to John C. Parish, April 14, 1926, HEH TU Box 35.

23. George W. Bell, "Lecture Notes. History of the West. Harvard University, 1910-1911, and T. C. Smith, "Lecture Notes: The History of the West. Harvard University, 1910-1911," first lecture, HEH TU File Drawer 14C, Folder: Notes on Professor Turner's History of the West.

24. Turner to Luther L. Bernard, Nov. 24, 1928, HEH TU Box 40.

25. "Sectionalism in American History, January 1, 1926," HEH TU File Drawer 14D, Folder: MSS. Geographical Sectionalism in American History; and "Some Sociological Aspects of American History, April 13, 1895," HEH TU File Drawer 15A, Folder: Some Sociological Aspects.

26. Turner, "The Last Quarter Century, 1890-1916," HEH TU File Drawer 15A, Folder: Lecture Univ. of Chicago, 1916.

27. Turner, "Some Sociological Aspects of American History, April 13, 1895," HEH TU File Drawer 15A, Folder: Some Sociological Aspects.

28. Turner, "Summary Hist. 17 1st Half," HEH TU File Drawer 13C, Folder: Turner, Frederick Jackson. Summary of First Term's Work.

29. Turner to Claude H. Van Tyne, April 25, 1908, Clements, Van Tyne Papers; Turner to Arthur H. Buffinton, Oct. 20, 1926, HEH TU Box 35A.

30. Turner to Reginald F. Arragon, July 31, 1924, HEH TU Box 33.

31. Turner to Arthur H. Buffinton, Oct. 20, 1926, HEH TU BOX 35A.

32. Turner, "The Middle West, 1830-1850: The Formation of a New Society," Carnegie Institution Lecture, HEH TU File Drawer F, Folder: U.S. Chap. VII North Central States.

33. Turner to Dorothy A. Dundore, July 22, 1924, HEH TU Box 33.

34. Turner to Merle Curti, Aug. 27, 1928, HEH TU Box 39.

35. George P. Ettingheim, "Notes on Lectures in Turner's 'History of the West Course,' Harvard University, 1911-1912," SHSW, MSS Division.

36. Turner, "Lecture in History of Liberty Series," HEH TU File Drawer 10B, Folder: History of Liberty. Colonial Period.

37. Turner to Isaiah Bowman, Dec. 24, 1931, HEH TU Box 46.

38. Turner, "Lowell Lectures, 1918," First lecture, HEH TU File Drawer E1, Folder: Lowell Lectures, 1918.

39. Notation made while reading Norman Ware, *The Industrial Worker, 1840-1860* (Boston, 1924), HEH TU File Drawer 14C, Unmarked folder.

40. Turner to Colin Goodykoontz, June 21, 1927, Western History Collections, University of Colorado, Boulder. Turner to James F. Willard, Dec. 23, 1929, lists suggested research topics (HEH TU Box 42).

41. Fragment of a lecture on "The Far West, 1830-1850," HEH TU File Drawer K1, Folder: V The Far West; "Memorandum on the Huntington Library," HEH TU File Drawer 15A, Folder: Memo. Turner on Research Materials.

42. Albert G. Waite, "Frederick J. Turner Lecture Notes in History 10b, Harvard University, spring term, 1903-1904," Harvard Univ. Arch., Call No. HUC 8903.338.10.92, Lecture for May 11, 1904.

43. Turner's note, HEH TU File Drawer 7B, Folder: Western Classes; folder with materials on farm-making costs, HEH TU File Drawer F5, Folder: Cost of Moving. Turner's conclusions coincided almost exactly with those of one of his later critics, Clarence H. Danhoff, "Farm-Making Costs and the 'Safety Valve': 1850-1860," *Journal of Political Economy*, XLIX (June 1941), 317-59.

44. Notes, HEH TU File Drawer 7B, Folder: Western Classes.

45. Notes on land speculation, HEH TU File Drawer 3A, Folder: Speculative Land Companies in Virginia, and 7A, Folders: N.Y. Speculation.

46. Lectures on sectionalism for Univ. of Wisconsin, April 1925, notes, HEH TU File Drawer 14C, Folder: University of Wisconsin Lectures.

47. Turner to Arthur H. Buffinton, Oct. 27, 1922; Turner to Frederick Merk, Feb. 17, 1927; Turner to Frank W. Fetter, Oct. 25, 1927, HEH TU Boxes 31 and 37.

48. This phrase, with slightly different wording, was used by Turner in his lecture on Hermann von Holst delivered in 1894, in his "Problems on the West" in the *Atlantic Monthly* in 1896, in his *The Rise of the New West* in 1906, and in his commencement address at the University of Washington in 1914 on "The West and American Ideals." The last is the best-known version.

49. Statement in Turner's first Lowell lecture, 1918, HEH TU File Drawer E1, Folder: Lowell Lectures, 1918. For his interpretation of American democracy, see Irving Kristol, "American Historians and the Democratic Idea," *American Scholar*, XXXIX (Winter 1969-70), 97-99.

50. Turner used the first phrase in his "Essay on von Holst's History," pp. 35-36 (HEH TU File Drawer 15A, Folder: Essay on History of U.S. by von Holst); the second in his Lowell lecture on "The Middle West" (HEH TU File Drawer E1, Folder: Lowell Lectures).

51. Turner, "History of Liberty Lectures," HEH TU File Drawer 10B, Folder: History of Liberty. Introduction.

52. Turner, "Lowell Lectures, 1918. First Lecture," HEH TU File Drawer E1, Folder: Lowell Lectures, 1918; Turner, "Sectionalism in American Politics. Lecture at Pasadena Feb. 20, 1928," HEH TU File Drawer 14D, Folder: Sectionalism in American Politics, 1928.

53. Turner, "Some Sociological Aspects of American History," HEH TU File Drawer 15A, Folder: Some Sociological Aspects of American History.

54. Single sheet of paper, HEH TU File Drawer 5C, Folder: Land Claims and Cessions.

55. Turner, "Lowell Lectures, 1918. First Lecture," HEH TU File Drawer E1, Folder: Lowell Lectures, 1918.

56. Ibid.

57. For Turner's reaction to the closing of the frontier, see Ray A. Billington, "Frederick Jackson Turner and the Closing of the Frontier," Roger Daniels (ed.), *Essays in Western History in Honor of T. A. Larson* (Laramie, Wyo., 1971), 45-56.

58. Turner, "Social Forces in American History," *The Frontier in American History* (New York, 1920), 320.

59. Two half-sheets, HEH TU File Drawer 17B, Folder: US 1890-1909. Bryan-Roosevelt Era.

60. Homer C. Hockett, "Lecture Notes in the History of the West," Lecture of August 6, 1902, HEH TU File Drawer 15C, Folder: Lecture, History of the West, 1902.

61. Lecture notes, HEH TU File Drawer L1, Folder: Sequence to End of Frontier. During the 1920s Turner reversed his position again, to embrace

the "rugged individualism" preached by Herbert Hoover (see above, pp. 441–42).

62. E. E. Dale, "Turner—The Man and Teacher," *University of Kansas City Review*, XVIII (Autumn 1951), 27.

63. Charles O. Paullin to Max Farrand, Oct. 11, 1932, HEH TU Box 49.

64. Turner to Max Farrand, March 23, 1911, HEH TU Box 16.

65. Merrill H. Crissey, "Notes on Frederick Jackson Turner," HEH TU Box 57, Folder: Merrill H. Crissey. Drafts of Biographical Data.

66. Turner's printed articles on sectionalism, with his annotations and corrections, HEH TU File Drawer L1, Folder: Sections. Printed Articles.

67. Handwritten section labeled "Incorporate this in preface or concluding chapter," HEH TU File Drawer A1, Folder: Introduction.

68. Fragment of lecture on "The Upland South: the Colonization of a Province," HEH TU File Drawer 3A, Folder: Formation of Upland South.

69. Talk to Association of American Geographers, 1926. Abstract printed as "Geographic Sectionalism in American History," *Annals of the Association of American Geographers*, XVI (June 1926), 205-6.

70. Turner, "The Significance of the Section in American History," in Turner, *The Significance of Sections in American History* (New York, 1925), 48-49.

71. Turner to Dixon Ryan Fox, March 27, 1919, HEH TU Box 29. Turner's notes on sectionalism, from which these quotations were taken, are in HEH TU File Drawer 18D, Folder: Sectionalism, 1926. With them are numerous clippings on the subject.

72. Turner to Dixon Ryan Fox, March 27, 1919, HEH TU Box 29.

73. Notes listing faults of maps in revealing data, HEH TU File Drawer 10A, Folder: US 1830-1850. New England Politics.

74. An excellent analysis of Turner's problems is in a manuscript article by Richard Jensen, "The Development of Quantitative Historiography in America," which he was kind enough to let me read.

75. Turner to Merle Curti, Sept. 8, 1930, HEH TU Box 44.

76. Merrill H. Crissey, "Notes on Frederick Jackson Turner," HEH TU Box 57, Folder: Merrill H. Crissey. Drafts of Biographical Data.

77. Turner, "Significance of Sections in American History," *loc. cit.* 45.

78. Turner to Norman Foerster, Aug. 6, 1926, HEH TU Box 35A.

79. Turner to A. M. Schlesinger, May 5, 1925, HEH TU Box 34.

Chapter XIX
The Significance of Frederick Jackson Turner
in American History

1. J. F. Jameson to Robert S. Woodward, July 3, 1913, in Elizabeth Donnan and Leo F. Stock (eds.), *A Historian's World: Selections from the Correspondence of John Franklin Jameson* (Philadelphia, 1956), 158.

2. Max Farrand to Turner, Feb. 24, 1908, HEH TU Box 10.

3. *Wisconsin State Journal*, Feb. 3, 7, 8, 10, 1910.

4. Gisle Bothne to Turner, Feb. 4, 1910; Turner to Bothne, Feb. 10, 1910, HEH TU Box 14. Turner's letter has been printed in Theodore C. Blegen

(ed.), "Frederick Jackson Turner and the Kensington Puzzle," *Minnesota History*, XXXIX (Winter 1964), 133-40.

5. J. F. Jameson to Clarence W. Bowen, Oct. 15, 1901, Donnan and Stock (eds.), *An Historian's World*, 78.

6. Turner to J. F. Jameson, Oct. 13, 1905. LC, Jameson Papers. For history of this project, see John K. Wright, Jr., "J. Franklin Jameson and the Atlas of the Historical Geography of the United States," Ruth A. Fisher and William L. Fox (eds.), *J. Franklin Jameson: A Tribute* (Washington, D.C., 1965), 66-79.

7. Turner's "Prior Notes for Meeting of April 6, 1923," and "Minutes of Meeting of Committee on American Biography, April 6-7," are bound with correspondence on the genesis of the *Dictionary of American Biography* in HEH TU Vol. VIII. A history of the enterprise is Dumas Malone, "J. Franklin Jameson and the Dictionary of American Biography," in Fisher and Fox (eds.), *J. Franklin Jameson*, 80-84.

8. Turner to Mrs. William Hooper, Nov. 16, 1924, HEH TU-H Box 5. Committee reports, letters, and copy of agreement, HEH TU Vol. VIII.

9. Jameson to Turner, April 28, 1924, ibid. Waldo G. Leland to Turner, Dec. 15, 1928, tipped into Turner's copy of J. F. Finley, *Dictionary of American Biography* (New York, 1928), HEH, Accession No. 126689.

10. Turner to Merle Curti, Aug. 8, 1928, HEH TU Box 39.

11. Frederick J. Turner, The Development of American Society," *The [Illinois] Alumni Quarterly*, II (July 1908), 120-21.

12. Turner to Arthur M. Schlesinger, April 18, 1922, HEH TU Box 31.

13. Turner, Phi Beta Kappa lecture, Univ. of Nebraska, June 10, 1907, HEH TU Box 55.

14. Frederick J. Turner, "The Historical Library in the University," in John Carter Brown Library, *The Dedication of the Library Building, May the Seventeenth, A. D. MDCCCCIIII. With the Addresses of William Vail Kellen, LL.D., and Frederick Jackson Turner, Ph.D.* (Providence, 1905), 57.

15. Turner, Phi Beta Kappa lecture, Univ. of Nebraska, June 10, 1907, HEH TU Box 55.

16. Turner to Richard H. Dana, May 3, 1915, HEH TU Box 24.

17. Turner to Kenneth W. Colgrove, July 21, 1919, HEH TU Box 29.

18. Turner to Edward N. Bristol, June 11, 1897, Princeton, Holt Arch.

19. Turner, "Historical Library in the University," *loc. cit.* 48-49.

20. Turner, Review of J. W. Burgess, *The Middle Period, 1817-1858, The Educational Review*, XIV (Nov. 1897), 390-91.

21. Turner, "Recent Studies in American History," *Atlantic Monthly*, LXXVII (June 1896), 841.

22. Turner, "Lecture for History 32b," April 12, 1915, HEH TU File Drawer 22B, Folder: Class Lectures. Period 1865-1887.

23. Turner to Merle Curti, Aug. 8, 27, 1928, HEH TU Box 39.

24. Turner, Phi Beta Kappa lecture, Univ. of Nebraska, June 10, 1907, HEH TU Box 55.

25. Turner to Marcus L. Hansen, Jan. 7, 1926, HEH TU Box 35.

26. Turner to E. M. Violette, Jan. 18, 1907, HEH TU Box 8.

27. Turner, "Outline for Address on History and the Local Historical Society," HEH TU Box 56.

28. Turner to T. P. Abernethy, March 12, 1926, HEH TU Box 35.
29. Max Farrand to Turner, Oct. 23, 1909, HEH TU Box 13.
30. Turner, "Historical Library in the University," *loc. cit.* 52-53.
31. Turner to John E. Iglehart, Jan. 14, 1930, HEH TU Box 43.
32. "Answer of Professor Turner," Hist. Survey, Univ. of Ill.: Alvord Papers; Turner to Mr. Holzbog, Nov. 2, 1923, HEH TU Box 32.
33. Note by Fulmer Mood inserted in HEH TU File Drawer D2, Folder: Justice of the Mexican War.
34. Turner to Max Farrand, Oct. 19, 1909, HEH TU Box 13.
35. Turner to Carl Becker, Feb. 13, 1926, HEH TU Box 35.
36. Turner listed his students who had entered various fields (HEH TU Box 56).
37. Turner to Constance L. Skinner, March 15, 1922, HEH TU Box 22.
38. Ibid.
39. Max Farrand to Turner, Feb. 23, 1905, HEH TU Box 5.
40. Turner to Mae Turner, July 14, [1903], HEH TU Box F. Arrangements for the Johns Hopkins lectures are discussed in John M. Vincent to Turner, April 16, 1906, Feb. 25, 1907; Turner to Vincent, May 14, 1906, March 10, 19, 1907, HEH TU Boxes 7 and 8.
41. Samuel F. Bemis to Turner, July 21, 1925; Turner to Bemis, Aug. 13, 1925, HEH TU Box 34A.
42. Frederick J. Turner, *The United States, 1830-1850: the Nation and Its Sections* (New York, 1935), 286. Turner's influence on immigration studies is appraised in Edwin Mims, Jr., *American History and Immigration* (Bronxville, N.Y., 1950).
43. Turner to L. E. Aylesworth, Aug. 4, 1902, SHSW, Turner Papers; Turner to Marcus L. Hansen, June 20, 1926, HEH TU Box 35.
44. Allan H. Spear, "Marcus Lee Hansen and the Historiography of Immigration," *Wisconsin Magazine of History*, XLIV (Summer 1961), 258-68, is brief biography. Carlton C. Qualey, "Marcus Lee Hansen," *Midcontinent American Studies Journal*, VIII (Fall 1967), 18-25, is less flattering.
45. Turner to Marcus L. Hansen, June 20, July 11, 1926, HEH TU Boxes 35 and 35A.
46. Turner to Marcus L. Hansen, Dec. 21, 1926, HEH TU Box 35A.
47. Turner to Marcus L. Hansen, July 22, 1927, HEH TU Box 37.
48. Turner to Arthur M. Schlesinger, April 18, 1922, HEH TU Box 31.
49. *The Aegis*, VI (April 8, 1892), 448.
50. Charles A. Beard, *An Economic Interpretation of the Constitution of the United States* (New York, 1913), 5-6.
51. Charles A. Beard to Merle Curti, Aug. 9, [1928], HEH TU Box 39.
52. Turner, "Development of American Society," *loc. cit.* 133-34.
53. Turner to Merle Curti, Aug. 15, 1928, HEH TU Box 39.
54. Turner to John R. Commons, Nov. 30, 1908; Turner to Carl Becker, March 25, 1909, HEH TU Boxes 11 and 12.
55. Marcus L. Hansen to Turner, Nov. 27, 1929, HEH TU Box 42.
56. Turner to Max Farrand, Feb. 13, 1919; Turner to Dorothy A. Dundore, May 23, 1923; Turner to E. E. Robinson, March 3, 1924, HEH TU Boxes 29, 32, and 33.
57. Merle Curti to Turner, Aug. 18, 1931, HEH TU Box 46.

58. Turner, "The High School and the City," HEH TU Box 54.

59. Notes on western cities, HEH TU File Drawer 6A, Folder: Cities, 1790-1800; "Outline of a possible book," File Drawer 8D, Folder: West Cities, 1820-1830.

60. Homer C. Hockett, "Classroom Lecture Notes, History of the West, August 6, 1902," HEH TU File Drawer 15C, Folder: Lecture History of the West 1902.

61. Quoted in Arthur M. Schlesinger, "The City in American History," *Mississippi Valley Historical Review*, XXVII (June 1940), 43.

62. HEH TU File Drawer 14A, Folder: City, Frontier and Section.

63. Turner to Merle Curti, Aug. 8, 1928; Turner to Luther L. Bernard, Nov. 24, 1928; HEH TU Boxes 39 and 40. Last quotation from pages marked "Omit from lecture on sectionalism" (HEH TU File Drawer 14A, Folder: Talk on Sectionalism, April 1922).

64. *Daily Cardinal*, Feb. 18, 1897.

65. Turner to Carl Becker, Dec. 1, 1925, HEH TU Box 34A.

66. Turner to Luther L. Bernard, Nov. 24, 1928, HEH TU Box 40.

67. Frederick J. Turner, "Problems in American History," reprinted in Turner, *The Significance of Sections in American History* (New York, 1932), 20-21.

68. Turner, "Memorandum to Max Farrand, 1927," HEH TU Box 36; Turner to Max Farrand, March 8, 1927, HEH TU Box 36.

69. Isaiah Bowman to Turner, Feb. 17, March 13, April 7, 1914, HEH TU Box 21.

70. John Koren to Turner, Nov. 18, 1913; William F. Ogburn to Turner, Dec. 15, 1924, HEH TU Boxes 20A and 33.

71. Franklin H. Giddings to Merle Curti, Aug. 20, 1928, HEH TU Box 39.

72. Avery Craven's remarks, delivered by Max Farrand at Turner's funeral service, are in HEH TU File Drawer 57.

BIBLIOGRAPHICAL NOTE

The following bibliographical note makes no attempt to list or appraise the voluminous literature dealing with Frederick Jackson Turner's frontier and sectional hypotheses. This is described in Ray A. Billington, *The American Frontier Thesis: Attack and Defense* (American Historical Association Pamphlet No. 101, Washington, D.C., 1971), and analyzed in Billington, *America's Frontier Heritage* (New York, 1966). Some of the principal articles attacking or defending the frontier thesis have been gathered in George R. Taylor (ed.), *The Turner Thesis Concerning the Role of the Frontier in American History* (Boston, 1949, and later editions); Lawrence Burnette, Jr. (ed.), *Wisconsin Witness to Frederick Jackson Turner: A Collection of Essays on the Historian and the Thesis* (Madison, 1961); Ray A. Billington, *The Frontier Thesis: Valid Interpretation of American History?* (New York, 1966); and Richard Hofstadter and Seymour M. Lipset, *Turner and the Sociology of the Frontier* (New York, 1968).

A largely complete bibliography of Turner's essays, reviews, and other publications, compiled by Everett E. Edwards, is in Frederick J. Turner, *The Early Writings of Frederick Jackson Turner* (Madison, 1938), 233-72. Edwards, however, failed to locate a few items in geographical journals, the most important being a review article, "Geographical Interpretations of American History," *Journal of Geography*, IV (January 1905), 34-37. Turner's essays have been collected and published in Turner, *The Early Writings*, mentioned just above, Turner, *The Frontier in American History* (New York, 1920), and Turner, *The Significance of Sections in American History* (New York, 1932). The most useful articles from these three volumes have been assembled in Ray A. Billington (ed.), *Frontier and Section: Selected Essays of Frederick Jackson Turner* (Englewood Cliffs, N.J., 1961). Other essays, unpublished during Turner's lifetime, have been edited by Wilbur R. Jacobs, *Frederick Jackson Turner's Legacy: Unpublished Writings in American History* (San Marino, Calif., 1965), reprinted in paperback as *America's Great Frontiers and Sections: Frederick Jackson Turner's Unpublished Essays* (Lincoln, Neb., 1969). In addition to his essays, Turner completed two books, *The Rise of the New West, 1819-1829* (New York, 1906; paperback edition, New York, 1962); and *The United States, 1830-1850: the Nation and Its Sections* (New York, 1935).

Since Turner's death in 1932, several of his lesser writings have been edited for publication by Fulmer Mood and Wilbur R. Jacobs. Mood prepared "Little Known Fragments of Turner's Writings," *Wisconsin Magazine of History*, XXIII (March 1940), 328-41; "Frederick Jackson Turner's History of the Grignon Tract on the Portage of the Fox and Wisconsin Rivers," *Agricultural History* XVII (April 1943), 113-20; and "Frederick Jackson Turner's Address on Education in the United States Without Free Lands," *Agricultural History*, XXIII (Oct. 1949), 254-59. Jacobs edited "Frederick Jackson Turner's Notes on the Westward Movement, California, and the Far West," *Southern California Quarterly*, XLVI (June 1964), 161-68; "Research in Agricultural History: Frederick Jackson Turner's View in 1922," *Agricultural History*, XLII (Jan. 1968), 15-22; "*Wider Frontiers*—Questions of War and Conflict in American History: The Strange Solution of Frederick Jackson Turner," *California Historical Society Quarterly*, XLVII (Sept. 1968), 219-36; and "Frederick Jackson Turner's Views on International Politics, War and Peace," *Australian National University Historical Journal*, VI (Nov. 1969), 10-15.

Two volumes of Turner's letters have appeared in recent years: Wilbur R. Jacobs (ed.), *The Historical World of Frederick Jackson Turner. With Selections from His Correspondence* (New Haven, 1968), and Ray A. Billington (ed.), with the collaboration of Walter Muir Whitehill, *"Dear Lady": The Letters of Frederick Jackson Turner and Alice Forbes Perkins Hooper, 1910-1932* (San Marino, Calif., 1970).

A few brief biographical sketches of Turner have been written. Of these the best is Merle Curti, *Frederick Jackson Turner* (Mexico, D.F., 1949). Less comprehensive are Wilbur R. Jacobs, "Frederick Jackson Turner," *The American West*, I (Winter 1964), 32-35, 78-79, reprinted in slightly extended form in Wilbur R. Jacobs, John W. Caughey, and Joe B. Frantz, *Turner, Bolton, and Webb. Three Historians of the American Frontier* (Seattle, 1965); Richard Hofstadter, *The Progressive Historians. Turner, Beard and Parrington* (New York, 1968), which deals largely with Turner's ideas; and Howard R. Lamar, "Frederick Jackson Turner," in Marcus Cunliffe and Robin W. Winks (eds.), *Pastmasters: Some Essays on American Historians* (New York, 1969), 74-109.

Other articles have explored aspects of Turner's life. The most comprehensive of these is Fulmer Mood, "The Development of Frederick Jackson Turner as a Historical Thinker," *Transactions of the Colonial Society of Massachusetts, 1937-1942*, XXXIV (Boston, 1943), 283-352, a germinal study. Less valuable is the same author's "Turner's Formative Period," in Turner, *The Early Writings of Frederick Jackson Turner*, 3-39. Both deal with his education and early teaching career as it influenced his thought. Other periods are described in Ray A. Billington, "Young Fred Turner," *Wisconsin Magazine of History*, XLVI (Autumn 1962), 38-48; Fulmer Mood, "Frederick Jackson Turner and the Milwaukee *Sentinel*, 1884," *Wisconsin Magazine of History*, XXXIV (Autumn 1950), 21-28; Fulmer Mood, "Frederick Jackson Turner and the Chicago *Inter-Ocean*, 1885," *Wisconsin Magazine of History*, XXXV (Spring 1952), 188-94, 210-18; Ray A. Billington, "Frederick Jackson Turner Visits New England: 1887," *New England Quarterly*, XLI (Sept. 1968), 409-36; Wilbur R. Jacobs, "Wilson's First Battle at Princeton: The Chair for Turner," *Harvard Library Bulletin*, VIII (Winter 1954), 74-87; George C. Osborn, "Woodrow Wilson and Frederick Jackson Turner," *Proceedings of the New Jersey Historical Society*, LXXIV (July 1956), 208-29; Ray A. Billington, "Frederick Jackson Turner Comes to Harvard," *Massachusetts Historical Society Proceedings*, LXXIV (1962), 51-83; Ray A. Billington, "Frederick Jackson Turner and Logan's 'National Summer School,' 1924," *Utah Historical Quarterly*, XXXVII (Summer 1969), 307-36; and Max Farrand, "Frederick Jackson Turner at the Huntington Library," *Huntington Library Bulletin*, III (Feb. 1933), 157-64.

A number of Turner's friends and former students recorded their reminiscences, some of which shed a great deal of light on his character and thought. The best of these include: Joseph Schafer, "The Author of the Frontier Hypothesis," *Wisconsin Magazine of History*, XV (Sept. 1931), 86-103; Louise P. Kellogg, "The Passing of a Great Teacher," *Historical Outlook*, XXIII (Oct. 1932), 270-72; Grace L. Nute, "Frederick Jackson Turner," *Minnesota History*, XIII (June 1932), 159-61; Frederick Merk, "Frederick Jackson Turner," *American Historical Review*, XXXVII (July 1932), 823-24; Max Farrand, "Frederick Jackson Turner: A Memoir," *Massachusetts Historical Society Proceedings*, LXV (May 1935), 432-40; Avery Craven, "Frederick Jackson Turner, Historian," *Wisconsin Magazine of History*, XXV (June 1942), 408-24; Avery Craven, "Some Historians I Have Known," *The Maryland Historian*, I (Spring 1970), 1-11; Avery Craven, "A History Still Unwritten," *Western Historical Quarterly*, II (Oct. 1971), 377-83; Edward E. Dale, "Memories of Frederick Jackson Turner," *Mississippi Valley Historical Review*, XXX (Dec. 1943), 339-58; Edward E. Dale, "Turner—The Man and Teacher," *University of Kansas City Review*, XVIII (Autumn 1951), 18-28; Ulrich B. Phillips, "The Traits and Contributions of Frederick Jackson Turner," *Agricultural History*, XIX (Jan. 1945), 21-23; Wilbur R. Jacobs (ed.), " 'Turner As I Remember Him,' by Herbert Eugene Bolton," *Mid-America*, XXXVI (Jan. 1954), 54-61; and A. C. Krey, "My Reminiscences of Frederick Jackson Turner," *Arizona and the West*, III (Winter 1961), 377-81.

Three of Turner's friends recorded their recollections of him for the Oral History Research Office of Columbia University: "The Reminiscences of Frank Maloy Anderson," an important document in the story of the Frederick Bancroft rebellion against the American Historical Association in 1915; "The Reminiscences of Guy Stanton Ford," which contain an excellent account of Turner as a teacher; and "The Reminiscences of Arthur M. Schlesinger."

Any study of Turner's historical and methodological concepts should begin with articles by two of his most gifted students: Carl Becker, "Frederick Jackson Turner," in Howard W. Odum (ed.), *American Masters of Social Science* (New York, 1927), 273-318, a warm portrait of the man and teacher; and Merle Curti, "The Section and the Frontier in American History; The Methodological Concepts of Frederick Jackson Turner," in Stuart A. Rice (ed.), *Methods in Social Science. A Case Book* (Chicago, 1931),

353-67, a brilliant analysis. Rudolf Freund, "Turner's Theory of Social Evolution," *Agricultural History*, XIX (April 1945), 78-87, and George D. Blackwood, "Frederick Jackson Turner and John Rogers Commons—Contemporary Thinkers," *Mississippi Valley Historical Review*, XLI (Dec. 1954), 471-89, deal with Turner's status as a social scientist, and his borrowings and contributions to the social sciences.

Aspects of Turner's background, education, training, and teaching that helped him formulate the frontier hypothesis are investigated in Ray A. Billington, *The Genesis of the Frontier Thesis: A Study in Historical Creativity* (San Marino, Calif., 1971). This volume includes letters written by Turner in his later years in which he speculated on the origins of his thesis; one of these, written to Constance L. Skinner, was earlier published as "Turner's Autobiographical Letter," *Wisconsin Magazine of History*, XIX (Sept. 1935), 91-103. Three important articles on the intellectual climate at the time the thesis was developed are: Gilman M. Ostrander, "Turner and the Germ Theory," *Agricultural History*, XXXII (Oct. 1958), 258-61; which shows that Turner relied more on the germ theory than he would have admitted; Robert E. Lerner, "Turner and the Revolt Against E. A. Freeman," *Arizona and the West*, V (Summer 1963), 101-8, demonstrating that English scholars were rebelling against the overemphasis on political history; and William Coleman, "Science and Symbol in the Turner Frontier Hypothesis," *American Historical Review*, LXXII (Oct. 1966), 22-49, a brilliant analysis of developments in biology and geography as they influenced Turner's thought.

In recent years historians have become aware that Turner's contributions extended far beyond his frontier and sectional theories. Two articles that explore his multitudinous interests in general terms are: Wilbur R. Jacobs, "The Many-Sided Frederick Jackson Turner," *Western Historical Quarterly*, I (Oct. 1970), 363-72, and Ray A. Billington, "Frederick Jackson Turner: Non-Western Historian," *Transactions of the Wisconsin Academy of Sciences, Arts and Letters*, LIX (1971), 7-21. In "Turner's Methodology: Multiple Working Hypothesis or Ruling Theory?" *Journal of American History*, LIV (March 1968), 853-63, Wilbur R. Jacobs argues that Turner was guilty of treating his frontier and sectional concepts as ruling theories, not as hypotheses to be tested, while in "Colonial Origins of the United States: The Turnerian View," *Pacific Historical Review*, XL (Feb. 1971), 21-38, he demonstrates Turner's contributions to the study of the colonial era. Jack Anderson, "Frederick Jackson Turner and Urbanization," *Journal of Popular Culture*, II (Fall 1968), 292-98, examines Turner's published works to show that he was fully aware of the significance of the city in American development. A stimulating analysis of Turner's social thought is Paul M. Maginnis, "The Social Philosophy of Frederick Jackson Turner," an unpublished Ph.D. dissertation submitted at the University of Arizona in 1969.

Wilbur R. Jacobs, "Frederick Jackson Turner—Master Teacher," *Pacific Historical Review*, XXIII (Feb. 1954), 49-58, was prepared before the author had access to the Frederick Jackson Turner papers, and hence needs revision. Turner's inability to write major books is the theme of Ray A. Billington, "Why Some Historians Rarely Write History: A Case Study of Frederick

Jackson Turner," *Mississippi Valley Historical Review*, L (June 1963), 3-27. Indicative of a growing interest in Turner's writings by students of non-historical disciplines are Harold P. Simonson, "Frederick Jackson Turner: Frontier History as Art," *Antioch Review*, XXIV (Summer 1964), 201-11, Merrill E. Lewis, "The Art of Frederick Jackson Turner: the Histories," *Huntington Library Quarterly*, XXXV (May 1972), 241-55; Goodwin F. Berquist, "The Rhetorical Heritage of Frederick Jackson Turner," *Transactions of the Wisconsin Academy of Sciences, Arts and Letters*, LIX (1971), 23-32, and Ronald H. Carpenter, "The Rhetorical Genesis of Style in the 'Frontier Hypothesis' of Frederick Jackson Turner," *Southern Speech Communication Journal*, XXXVII (Spring 1972), 233-48, the first two by professors of English, the last two by professors of speech. Turner's views on one subject are explored in Ray A. Billington, "Frederick Jackson Turner and the Closing of the Frontier," in Roger Daniels (ed.), *Essays in Western History in Honor of T. A. Larson* (Laramie, Wyo., 1971), 45-56.

Revealing as these secondary works are, the basic story of Frederick Jackson Turner's life must be extracted from the manuscript collections in which his letters and documents have been preserved. They have been the principal source used in preparing this book. The "Turner Papers" themselves are deposited in four libraries; in addition, other materials pertinent to his career are in numerous other manuscript collections. In the listing that follows, the "Turner Papers" are first described, then the additional depositories that have been used. In each instance, the italicized phrase in parentheses following each designation is the abbreviation employed in the notes to this volume.

I. Frederick Jackson Turner Papers, Henry E. Huntington Library and Art Gallery, San Marino, Calif. On his death in 1932 Turner willed the Huntington Library all of his letters and documents, as well as his books. Since that time the collection has been greatly increased by gifts of additional correspondence and manuscripts from former students, friends, and especially his daughter, Mrs. John S. Main. Moreover, duplicates have been obtained of the more important Turner letters from other depositories, as well as newspapers, magazines, and other published works essential to the study of Turner's career. These manuscripts, supplemented by Turner's own books with their annotations and marginal comments, make the Huntington Library essential to any serious study of Turner. His papers have been opened to qualified scholars since January 1960, and they have been much used. They fall into several categories:

A Correspondence, Manuscripts and Documents

1. General Correspondence (*HEH TU Box 1 ff.*) Seventy-two flat boxes of letters and related documents, each in a separate folder, chronologically arranged. Boxes 1 through 52 contain letters to and from Turner, Boxes 53 through 57 manuscripts of his speeches and similar items, and Boxes 58 through 62 ephemera, business papers, pages from his pocket diaries, and photographs. Box 63 holds his correspondence with Henry Holt & Co., his principal publisher, much of it photocopied from the Holt & Co. Archives, Firestone Library, Princeton University.

2. Turner-Hooper Correspondence (*HEH TU-H Box 1 ff.*) Alice Forbes Perkins Hooper, daughter of Charles Elliott Perkins and husband of William Hooper of Manchester, Massachusetts, began a correspondence with Turner in 1910 that lasted until his death. This is the only sustained body of letters left by Turner. It is housed in ten boxes, the last two containing typed versions of the manuscripts. The best of these letters have been published in Ray A. Billington (ed.), *"Dear Lady": The Letters of Frederick Jackson Turner and Alice Forbes Perkins Hooper, 1910-1932* (San Marino, Calif., 1970).

3. Family Letters (*HEH TU Box A ff.*) Letters between Turner and members of his family fill eleven boxes, designated A through K. Most important are letters written by Turner to his fiancé between 1887 and 1889, when he was in graduate school.

B   Reading and Research Notes

1. Reading Notes and Lectures (*HEH TU File Drawer 1A ff.*) Turner left the Huntington Library twenty-two file drawers filled with his notes, clippings, manuscripts, lectures, and assorted materials. These are now housed in cardboard boxes, five boxes to each original drawer, designated as File Drawer 1A, 1B, etc. File Drawers 14 and 15 contain many of Turner's speeches and drafts of articles, some unpublished.

2. Notes on Sectionalism (*HEH TU File Drawer A1 ff.*) Twelve file drawers left by Turner were filled with notes on sectionalism which he used in preparing his last book, *The United States, 1830-1850: The Nation and Its Sections* (New York, 1935). They also contain drafts of speeches and other materials essential to understanding his views on the sections. The materials are contained in cardboard boxes, five to each original file drawer, designated as File Drawer A1, A2, etc.

3. Three-by-five file drawers (*HEH TU 3×5 File Drawer 1 ff.*). Nineteen metal 3×5 inch file drawers hold the thousands of brief notes kept by Turner. These include bibliographical cards, research notes, lecture notes, and the like. Drawers 1 and 2 were apparently begun during the 1890s and contain materials important to his early teaching career and the origins of his frontier thesis. Drawers 13 through 19 house the notes used in dictating his last volume.

4. Manuscript volumes (*HEH TU Vol. 1 ff.*) Twenty volumes of albums, scrapbooks, manuscripts, and the like were compiled (and usually bound) by Turner to be shelved separately from his other collections. These include the Commonplace Books he kept as a graduate student, his early syllabi, and the Red Book and Blue Book presented on his leaving Wisconsin in 1910 and Harvard in 1924.

C   Miscellaneous Documents

1. Newspaper and Magazine Clippings (*HEH TU Black Box 1 ff.*). Nineteen black boxes kept by Turner are filled with clippings, pamphlets, magazine articles, and other printed materials, all catalogued and filed by number. In them are some of the census bulletins that influenced his thought on the frontier.

2. Maps (*HEH TU Maps 1 ff.*) Two large boxes hold the many maps drawn by Turner in connection with his studies of sectionalism.

3. Lantern Slides (*HEH TU Lantern Slides 1 ff.*). Lantern slides made under Turner's supervision and used in his lectures fill nine boxes.

II. Frederick Jackson Turner Papers, The Houghton Library, Harvard University, Cambridge, Mass. (*Houghton: Turner Papers*). One box contains letters given to Harvard University by Turner at the time of his retirement. This holds three folders: (1) seven letters from Woodrow Wilson to Turner, 1889-1902, and two from William E. Dodd concerning Wilson's views on the frontier thesis, (2) seven letters from Theodore Roosevelt to Turner, 1894-98, and (3) Letters from Walter Hines Page and other editors of the *Atlantic Monthly*, 1896-99.

III. Frederick Jackson Turner Papers, State Historical Society of Wisconsin, Madison, Wis. (*SHSW: Turner Papers*). Turner presented to the library of the State Historical Society three boxes of papers, most of them related to the state's history. Box 1 contains items associated with Turner's father, Andrew Jackson Turner; Box 2 a few letters and many manuscripts dealing with his teaching at the university, and Box 3 notes taken by Turner while a student, as well as some of the classroom notes used by his professor, William F. Allen.

IV. Frederick Jackson Turner Papers, Archives of the University of Wisconsin, The Memorial Library, University of Wisconsin, Madison, Wis. (*U. of Wis. Arch., L&S, Hist., Turner Corr., Box 1 ff.*). Six boxes of Turner's papers, kept largely when he was chairman of the department of history, are officially catalogued as "College of Letters and Science. Department of History. Turner Correspondence, 1901-1905. Series N 7/16/2. Boxes 1-6." The first five boxes contain letters to and from Turner dealing with departmental and university affairs, but scattered through them are others having to do with his publishing and scholarly activities. Box 6 has one folder of correspondence, but is filled largely with reports and items on the administration of the School of History. In addition to these six boxes, the Archivist maintains a small file of miscellaneous Turner material in his outer office, filed in a desk drawer. This has been referred to as *U. of Wis. Arch., Misc. File: Frederick Jackson Turner*.

While the bulk of the most useful Frederick Jackson Turner materials are included in the four collections described above, other important letters and documents may be found in numerous other collections. The most important of these are:

Charles Kendall Adams Papers, State Historical Society of Wisconsin, Madison, Wisconsin. (*SHSW: Adams Papers*). A sparse collection filling only one box, and covering the years 1872-1902. Many more of President Adams's letters are in the University of Wisconsin Archives, President's File, listed below.

William Francis Allen Papers, State Historical Society of Wisconsin, Madison, Wisconsin (*SHSW: Allen Papers*). One box of papers, covering the period from March 1848 to December 1889, and consisting largely of Allen's diplomas, transcripts, and articles. Included, however, are some of his class record books with notations about Turner and his work.

Clarence W. Alvord Papers, Illinois Historical Survey of the University of Illinois, 418 Lincoln Hall, Urbana, Ill. (*Hist. Survey Univ. of Ill.: Alvord Papers*). This collection contains some thirty letters exchanged between Alvord and Turner between 1908 and 1931. Copies have been supplied the Huntington Library through the kindness of Mrs. Marguerite J. Pease, Director.

American Historical Association Papers, Manuscripts Division, Library of Congress, Washington, D.C. (*LC: AHA Papers*). The Association's papers fill 211 linear feet of shelf space, and contain more than 155,000 items. Materials for the 1892-93 period when Turner was preparing and presenting his frontier thesis are disappointingly few. They are plentiful, however, for the years when Turner was active in the Association, and especially for the 1914-15 era, when Frederic Bancroft staged his rebellion against the establishment. Particularly useful are Boxes 27–31 (Secretary File for 1915), Boxes 243–49 (Executive Council Secretary File), Boxes 255–56 (Minutes of Council Meetings), Boxes 257–85 (Editorial Correspondence, *American Historical Review*), and Box 370, which contains only materials related to the Bancroft affair.

Charles McLean Andrews Papers, Historical Manuscripts Division, Yale University Library, New Haven, Conn. (*Yale: Andrews Papers*). Andrews was a student with Turner at Johns Hopkins University; his letters for the 1888-89 academic year describe the life that Turner knew, although they do not mention Turner.

Frederic Bancroft Papers, Special Collections, Columbia University Library, New York, N.Y. (*Columbia: Bancroft Papers*). Four boxes in this voluminous collection contain letters and documents essential to an understanding of Frederic Bancroft's rebellion against the "ring" that operated the American Historical Association. A microfilm copy of the contents of these boxes has been supplied the Huntington Library through the courtesy of the Columbia University Library.

Carl Becker Papers, Collection of Regional History and University Archives, Albert R. Mann Library, Cornell University, Ithaca, N.Y. (*Cornell: Becker Papers*). Letters to and from Turner and Becker for the years 1896 to 1932 provide one of the richest sources on Turner's historical beliefs. Some of the most important of these, exchanged while Becker was preparing his article on Turner (listed above), have been printed in Ray A. Billington, *The Genesis of the Frontier Thesis: A Study in Historical Creativity* (San Marino, Calif., 1971).

Edward A. Birge Papers, State Historical Society of Wisconsin, Madison, Wis. (*SHSW: Birge Papers*). Birge, a professor of biology, dean, and president of the University of Wisconsin, was not one of Turner's intimate friends, but they shared many common problems during their years together in Madison. The papers fill fifteen boxes, covering the period 1897 to 1948.

Herbert Eugene Bolton Papers, The Bancroft Library of the University of California, Berkeley, Calif. (*Bancroft: Bolton Papers*). Included in this large collection are sixty-six letters exchanged between Bolton and Turner during the years 1909-28. Copies of these have been deposited in the Turner Papers at the Huntington Library through the initiative of Professor Wilbur R. Jacobs.

George Lincoln Burr Papers, Division of Regional History and Archives, Cornell University Library, Ithaca, N.Y. (*Cornell: Burr Papers*). Burr was active with Turner in the American Historical Association, and he was deeply involved in the Frederic Bancroft rebellion. Thirty-eight letters in the collection touch on this episode, including many exchanged with Turner.

Thomas C. Chamberlin Papers, Department of Special Collections, University of Chicago Library, Chicago, Ill. (*Chicago: Chamberlin Papers*). Seven boxes of papers largely dealing with Chamberlin's scientific projects, conservation, and the like. Little on his activities at the University of Wisconsin, when as president he dealt much with Turner.

University of Chicago Archives, Department of Special Collections, University of Chicago Library, Chicago, Ill. (*U. of Chi. Arch.: Dept. of Hist. Papers*). Eight Turner letters have been preserved, two in the President's Papers, written to President William Raney Harper, and six in the Department of History Papers for the period 1912-16.

Richard T. Ely Papers, State Historical Society of Wisconsin, Madison, Wis. (*SHSW: Ely Papers*). This collection of 279 boxes of letters and manuscripts contains more than fifty letters between Ely and Turner, largely for the period 1892 to 1894, when Turner was arranging Ely's transfer to the University of Wisconsin. A "Turner Index" is available on cards, but it is incomplete.

Carl Russell Fish Papers, State Historical Society of Wisconsin, Madison, Wis. (*SHSW: Fish Papers*). This comprises seventeen boxes covering the period from 1891 to 1932. Most of the letters deal with the period after 1910, when Turner left Wisconsin, but some touch on his activities in Madison.

Ginn and Company Papers, Boston, Mass. (*Boston: Ginn and Co.*). Turner's correspondence with this company, dealing largely with the textbook he contracted to prepare for them, was destroyed when the firm moved some twenty years ago. Only one contract, that of 1910 for the volume he prepared with Edward Channing and Albert Bushnell Hart, remains. I am indebted for this information to Mr. Henry M. Halvorson of Ginn and Company.

George Ellery Hale Papers, University Archives, California Institute of Technology, Pasadena, Calif. (*Cal. Tech.: Hale Papers*). Hale, a well-known astronomer and promoter of scientific projects, was influential in bringing Turner to the Huntington Library in 1927. His correspondence, arranged alphabetically under the names of individuals and institutions, contains a great deal of information on the appointment. It is filed under Henry E. Huntington, Max Farrand, Henry M. Robinson, H. M. Goodwin, and Elihu Root.

Harvard Commission on Western History Papers, Harvard University Archives, Widener Library, Harvard University, Cambridge, Mass. (*Widener: HC on WH Corr.*). Twelve boxes of letters deal with the formation of the commission and its operation to 1920; the collection also contains card indexes, lists of acquisitions, and other items. Many of Turner's letters that are included deal with non-commission matters, and were apparently filed by mistake when he was active in the commission.

Harvard University Archives, Class Lists (*Harvard Arch.: Class Lists*). Large scrapbooks in which are pasted printed or mimeographed lists of students enrolled in each class for each term. Some for the World War I period are missing. An important source of information on Turner's teaching at Harvard.

Charles Homer Haskins Papers, The Firestone Library, Princeton University, Princeton, N.J. (*Princeton: Haskins Papers*). This collection contains a number of letters from Turner, largely for the period before 1910. It is, however, disappointing, for Haskins and Turner were intimate friends and wrote often and confidentially. If Haskins had saved more of the many letters he received, the collection would be extremely valuable.

Henry Holt & Co. Archives, Firestone Library, Princeton University, Princeton, N.J. (*Princeton: Holt Archives*). Included are some fifty letters from Turner, largely for the periods about 1897, 1920, and the late 1920s, when he was corresponding regularly concerning his last book. They admirably supplement the letters from Holt & Co. in his own correspondence at the Huntington Library.

Henry E. Huntington Library and Art Gallery, Huntington Biographical File, San Marino, Calif. (*Huntington: Biographical File*). This extensive documentary collection on the history of the Library contains a number of letters from Turner dealing with his appointment and research at the Library. Also included are three volumes of Minute Books of the Board of Trustees for 1919-23, the "Trustees' Files," and the "Hale Letters," having much on Turner's career in Pasadena.

John Franklin Jameson Papers, Manuscripts Division, Library of Congress, Washington, D.C. (*LC: Jameson Papers*). Filling 181 boxes, this is an essential collection in the study of any topic in American historiography for the period between the 1890s and 1921. It includes numerous letters to and from Turner, together with fragmentary information on his 1893 paper, the latter contained in Box 7.

Johns Hopkins University Seminar Records, Johns Hopkins University Archives, The Library, Johns Hopkins University, Baltimore, Md. (*JHU: Seminar Records*). These records, kept by an appointed secretary from within the class, are in two versions, one the handwritten copy taken by the secretary, the other the final typed form. The records of the latter for the 1888-89 year when Turner was in attendance fill pages 387-449 of the minutes book. A microfilm copy is in the Henry E. Huntington Library.

Charles A. Krey Papers, University Archives, University of Minnesota Library, Minneapolis, Minn. (*Minnesota: Krey Papers*). This collection of 278 folders contains several letters from Turner, written to Krey, his former student.

Victor H. Lane Papers, Michigan Historical Collections, Rackham Building, University of Michigan, Ann Arbor, Mich. (*Mich. Hist. Coll.: Lane Papers*). Judge Lane was one of the University of Michigan representatives dealing with the athletic controversy that involved Turner in 1905 and 1906. Several letters from and to Turner shed light on the conflict.

Orin G. Libby Papers, State Historical Society of North Dakota, Bismarck, N.D. (*SHSND: Libby Papers*). Libby, Turner's student and colleague, exchanged many letters with his teacher, but failed to keep a single one. His papers are valuable only for the light that they shed on his own career, of which Turner was particularly proud.

A. Lawrence Lowell Papers, Harvard University Archives, Widener Library, Harvard University, Cambridge, Mass. (*Harvard Arch.: Lowell Papers*). This collection contains a number of letters concerning Turner's appointment to the Harvard faculty and concerning the operations of the Harvard Commission on Western History. I have been allowed access through special action of the Harvard authorities, and particularly through the courtesy of Clifford K. Shipton, university archivist.

Andrew C. McLaughlin Papers, Department of Special Collections, University of Chicago Library, Chicago, Ill. (*Chicago: McLaughlin Papers*). A small collection covering the period 1899-1938, filling only eight boxes. The first three boxes hold letters to and from Professor McLaughlin, some of them from Turner.

The Macmillan Company Archives, New York, N.Y. (*New York: Macmillan Company*). Only three of Turner's letters to George P. Brett concerning a contract for a textbook have survived. Copies of those have been supplied the Huntington Library by Mr. Harry H. Cloudman of the Macmillan Company.

William F. Poole Papers, The Newberry Library, Chicago, Ill. (*Newberry: Poole Papers*). Twenty-six boxes of letter, chronologically arranged, cover the period from 1858 to 1894. Many have to do with Poole's role as chairman of the committee arranging the session in Chicago in 1893 where Turner read his paper on "The Significance of the Frontier."

Dunbar Rowland Papers, Mississippi Department of Archives and History, Jackson, Miss. (*Miss. Arch.: Rowland Papers*). Among the 6000 pieces housed in this collection are some thirty letters to or from Rowland having to do with the 1914–15 rebellion in the American Historical Association.

Joseph Schafer Papers, State Historical Society of Wisconsin, Madison, Wis. (*SHSW: Schafer Papers*). Schafer, as Turner's most loyal student, preserved all letters received from his teacher. These are scattered through the extensive collection of his papers. All to or from Turner have been photostated, and copies added to the Turner Papers at the Huntington Library.

Albion W. Small Papers, Department of Special Collections, University of Chicago, Chicago, Ill. (*Chicago: Small Papers*). Box I of this small collection deals with the Congress of Arts and Sciences at the 1904 St. Louis Exposition where Turner spoke; Small was vice president in charge of arrangements.

Henry Morse Stephens Papers, University of California Archives, University of California Library, Berkeley, Calif. (*Calif.: Stephens Papers*). Several letters from Turner are included, but none dealing with the 1908-9 period when the University of California history department, with Stephens at the helm, was trying to lure Turner to its faculty.

Reuben Gold Thwaites Papers, State Historical Society of Wisconsin, Madison, Wis. (*SHSW: Thwaites Papers*). A number of letters to and from Turner were preserved by Thwaites during his period as superintendent of the State Historical Society of Wisconsin.

Charles R. Van Hise Papers, State Historical Society of Wisconsin, Madison, Wis. (*SHSW: Van Hise Papers*). Most of Van Hise's papers as president of the University are in the university archives, presidential papers (see below), but this collection of nine boxes of correspondence contains some information on Turner.

Claude H. Van Tyne Papers, Clements Library, University of Michigan, Ann Arbor, Mich. (*Clements: Van Tyne Papers*). Of the nine boxes in this collection, four contain correspondence for the period 1901 to 1930, arranged chronologically. Several letters from Turner are included.

Woodrow Wilson Papers, Manuscripts Division, Library of Congress, Washington, D.C. (*LC: Wilson Papers*). A voluminous collection, including a number of letters from Turner during the years 1889-1902. All will eventually appear in the definitive set being edited by Arthur Link, *The Papers of Woodrow Wilson* (Princeton, 1966 ff.).

University of Wisconsin Archives. Included in this invaluable depository are a number of groups of papers essential to the telling of Turner's story. These are:

Board of Regents Executive Committee, 1888-1939 (*U. of Wis. Arch.: Regents Exec. Comm.*). A series of committee reports and documents originating in or submitted to the executive committee of the Board of Regents of the university. Series 1/1/2, Box 1 ff.

Board of Regents Minutes (*U. of Wis. Arch.: Regents Minutes*). Large volumes, handwritten, and with two or three volumes to the year. Paged. Series 1/1/1, Vol. 1 ff.

Class of 1884 Minutes (*U. of Wis. Arch.: 1884 Minutes*). A single paper-bound notebook kept by the secretaries of the class of 1884 during the four years the class was in the university. But few mentions of Turner, who was apparently not active in class affairs. Series: IWXF 1884 X.

College of Letters and Science. Administration. Dean's Files (*U. of Wis. Arch.: L and S, Dean's Files*). Included are numerous letters from Turner concerning departmental and university affairs. The correspondence is largely with Dean Birge. Series 7/1/12-2 and 7/1/2-1.

Instructional Reports, Fall 1886 to Spring 1910. (*U. of Wis. Arch.: Instructional Reports*). Each term instructors reported the courses taught, the hours of instruction, the number of students enrolled, and the like. Those prepared by Turner shed light on his teaching. They are filed in a series of boxes in the university archives.

Minutes of the Meetings of the University Faculty, September 1900–July 1961 (*U. of Wis. Arch.; Minutes of Univ. Faculty*). Volumes 5–7 cover the period when Turner was a member of the faculty. Disappointingly brief, but essential especially for the story of Turner's battle against professional football.

Presidents of the University. General Correspondence (*U. of Wis. Arch.: Pres. Corr.*). Included are 142 boxes of general correspondence to and from the presidents of the university, arranged chronologically with letters filed alphabetically within chronological periods. A number of important Turner letters can be easily located. Numbered as follows: Chamberlin Series 4/7/1; Adams Series 4/8/1; Van Hise Series 4/9/1.

University Faculty. Athletic Board. Frederick Jackson Turner (*U. of*

Wis. Arch.: Athletic Board). A single box filled with clippings and reports concerning the athletic controversy of 1905-7. Obviously prepared by Turner, with annotations in his hand. Series 5/21/5.

University Faculty. Secretary of the Faculty. Faculty Minutes, Documents, etc. (*U. of Wis. Arch.: Faculty Sec.*). Committee reports and other documents submitted to the faculty, arranged chronologically by meetings. Series 5/2/2.

Yale Review Papers, The Beinecke Library, Yale University, New Haven, Conn. (*Beinecke: Yale Review Papers*). A folder labeled "F. J. Turner" contains a dozen or more letters, most of them dealing with the publication of his articles in the *Yale Review.*

Among the manuscript sources used in preparing this book were several sets of student lecture notes taken in Turner's classes, and one student diary. Those that proved most useful were:

K. M. Elish, "Frederick J. Turner Lecture Notes in History 32b, Harvard University, 1915-1916," Harvard University Archives, Call No. HUC 8915.338.32. An excellent set of notes, taken by a student who apparently knew some shorthand, with a number of direct quotations.

George P. Ettenheim, "Notes on Lectures in Turner's 'History of the West' Course," Harvard University, 1911-1912. This full set of notes is owned by the library of Washington State University, Pullman, Wash. A set on microfilm has been supplied the Huntington Library. Full notes, including tables and maps.

Homer C. Hockett, "Lecture Notes, 'History of the West,'" University of Wisconsin, Summer 1902. These notes are scattered through the File Drawers of the Turner Papers at the Huntington Library, filed according to topic. Hockett took shorthand; the notes are full and informative.

Horace J. Smith, "Lecture Notes: History of the West," Harvard University, 1910-11. The author kept full notes, which are bound into a volume with examination questions, the syllabus, and blue books. The notes are in HEH TU Vol. XXIII.

Theodore C. Smith, "Lecture Notes: The History of the West," Harvard University, 1910-11. Careful notes by a good student, in handwritten and typed version, covering the entire year of the course. They are in HEH, TU File Drawer 14C, Folder: Smith, T. C., Student Notes.

Albert G. Waite, "Frederick J. Turner Lecture Notes in History 10b, Harvard University, Spring Term, 1903-1904," Harvard University Archives, Call No. 8903.338.10.92. Some 200 pages of notes on the semester course given by Turner when he visited Harvard University during the 1903-4 academic year. The entire westward movement is covered in one half-year.

Edwin E. Witte, "Diary." Witte was a student at the University of Wisconsin in 1909-10 and kept a full diary, recording his impressions of Turner's seminar and of his resignation from the faculty. The diary is in the possession of the Manuscripts Division, State Historical Society of Wisconsin.

Newspapers

Essential as manuscript sources have proven in preparing this book, many events could not be dated and many others would have escaped notice without a careful reading of the newspapers associated with each phase of Turner's life. The following have proved valuable.

At Portage, Wisconsin, for the period 1861 through 1894:

Wisconsin State Register. This weekly newspaper began publication on March 16, 1861, and a month later Andrew Jackson Turner, Frederick J. Turner's father, became one of the publishers. In February, 1878, he sold his interests to John T. Clark, but the paper continued through the 1890s.

The Portage Democrat. A weekly paper launched on April 13, 1877, to offset the strong Republican bias of the *Register*. Less local news was published and more attention given to political causes. Read through 1894.

Portage Daily Register. The first issue appeared on March 1, 1886, published by the firm then publishing the *Wisconsin State Register*. It contained six columns on four to eight sheets daily. Issues between 1886 and 1894 have been read for this study.

At Madison, Wisconsin, for the period 1881 to 1910:

Wisconsin State Journal. This was Madison's leading paper, rivaled only by a smaller Democratic paper. It was published daily, in from four to twelve pages, and contained a regular column of "University News" as well as coverage of all town events. Numerous speeches and activities of Turner are recorded. Read for the period 1881 through 1910.

At the University of Wisconsin, for the period 1878 to 1910:

The University Press. The first undergraduate newspaper and literary magazine at the University, published by a private group representing the literary societies between 1871 and 1885 as a semi-monthly or weekly journal. Volumes VII through XVIII, covering the period from 1876 to 1886, have been read for this biography.

The Campus. A weekly undergraduate newspaper, started in October 1881 by students who resented the private control of *The University Press*, and published through December of that year. One literary article a week was published in its twelve pages, together with notes, campus news, and editorials.

The Badger. Weekly undergraduate newspaper, successor to *The Campus*, and published by the same group between January 1882 and June 1885. It contained in its eight to twelve pages a "Local" column, news items, editorials, and other features. In September 1885 it merged with *The University Press*.

The Aegis. Published between September 1886 and June 1900, this weekly paper displaced *The University Press* as the official student newspaper of the University of Wisconsin. In 1892, with the establishment of a rival daily paper, it became a bi-weekly publication with greater stress on literary articles, and in October 1895, a monthly literary magazine.

The Daily Cardinal. Published first on April 4, 1892, this daily undergraduate newspaper represented the student body during the remainder of Turner's years at Wisconsin. Issues from the first through 1910 have been read. Although woefully inadequate in reporting local news, it is an essential source for Turner's activities. Copies of this, and of all other university publications, are in the Archives of the University of Wisconsin; microfilm copies have been supplied the Huntington Library.

Magazines at the University of Wisconsin:

The Trochos. A class yearbook containing information on class activities, the faculty, and university affairs. Published between April 1884 and February 1887.

The Badger. A successor to *The Trochos*, published as a yearbook each year by the junior class after February 1888. Read for the period 1888 through 1910.

The Sphynx. The campus humor magazine began publication in September 1899, with the usual jokes, verse, cartoons, and stories. Published every other week, it contained a number of quips involving Turner and one brief item by him. Read for the period 1899 through 1910.

The Wisconsin Literary Magazine. The usual collection of stories, verse, and articles by undergraduates. Published monthly after December 1903. Surprisingly little on Turner or the intellectual atmosphere on the campus. Read through 1911.

Newspaper at Harvard University

The *Boston Evening Transcript.* A daily Boston paper with a great deal of emphasis on Harvard events. Read for specific periods between 1910 and 1924.

INDEX

THE REGISTER
OF EUDES OF ROUEN

NUMBER LXXII OF THE RECORDS OF CIVILIZATION
SOURCES AND STUDIES

THE REGISTER
of
EUDES OF ROUEN

TRANSLATED BY

SYDNEY M. BROWN

Late Professor of History, Duquesne University

EDITED WITH AN INTRODUCTION,

NOTES, AND APPENDIX BY

JEREMIAH F. O'SULLIVAN

Professor of History, Fordham University

COLUMBIA UNIVERSITY PRESS

NEW YORK AND LONDON 1964

To Douglas MacGillvary Brown
September 23, 1920-April 5, 1942

FOREWORD

THIS ENGLISH edition of the *Register* of Eudes, Archbishop of Rouen, was undertaken for the "Records of Civilization" many years ago. The translator, Sydney M. Brown, devoted most of his adult life to the teaching of history. Of a generation whose members served in two world wars, he entered the British air force after his graduation from Bowdoin in 1916; was a Rhodes Scholar at Brasenose College, Oxford, after the First World War; and then began eighteen years of teaching at Lehigh University (1923-41). After service in the United States Naval Reserve in the Second World War, he resumed his academic career at Duquesne University (1947), where he was Professor of History at the time of his death in 1952. The rendering of the *Regestrum visitationum* into English, done over a period of more than twenty years under conditions often adverse to the pursuit of scholarship, was intended as one of his major contributions to his chosen discipline.

At the time of Professor Brown's death, he had completed the preparation but not the revision of his translation and had prepared drafts of some of the notes. His unfinished manuscript was placed by his widow in the hands of Austin P. Evans, Professor of History at Columbia University, who was then editor of the "Records of Civilization." It was through Professor Evans's unflagging interest in the project and his concern for its completion that Professor Jeremiah O'Sullivan of Fordham University was persuaded to revise the English text and provide it with the introduction and notes for which the plan of the edition called.

In his work on the translation, Professor Brown had assistance that he would have wished to acknowledge from Earl Crum, Professor of Classical Languages at Lehigh University from 1923 to 1956; from the Reverend John J. Sullivan, C.S.Sp., formerly Dean of the Graduate School and Chairman of the Department of Classics at Duquesne University; and from the Reverend John P. Gallagher, C.S.Sp., the present Chairman of the Department of Classics at Duquesne. Professor Evans reviewed and made suggestions about the early drafts of the manuscript, providing detailed comments in addition to encouragement and general editorial counsel; after arranging for the

completion of the manuscript—and until his own death in September, 1962—
Professor Evans, though retired, continued to act as the representative of the
Board of Editors in all matters concerning Eudes of Rouen. Although Professor Brown and Professor O'Sullivan never worked together, any acknowledgments offered on Professor Brown's behalf should include mention of the
unselfish service to scholarship Professor O'Sullivan has performed in completing what Professor Brown had begun.

   The edition is appropriately dedicated to Professor Brown's son, who
chose in the Second World War the service his father had chosen in an earlier
conflict and was killed in action in 1942, when in the Royal Air Force.

                                                    HENRY H. WIGGINS
                                                    Assistant Director
                                                    Columbia University Press
Columbia University
in the City of New York
June 15, 1964

EDITOR'S ACKNOWLEDGMENTS

I WISH to acknowledge my debt to that kind and gentle scholar, the late Professor Austin P. Evans; to Dr. Joseph F. O'Callaghan, Fordham University, for aid in comparing Bonnin's published text with the original, MS. 1245; to Dean James E. Tobin, Queens College, for proofreading; to Misses Anne Murphy, Margaret Tighe, and Helena Coen of the Fordham University library staff for procuring books through interlibrary loans; to my wife for typing and retyping the MS.

JEREMIAH F. O'SULLIVAN

Fordham University
Pentecost, 1964

CONTENTS

CONTENTS

INTRODUCTION

IN MANY INSTANCES obscurity is the term most pertinent to the origins of some of the great personages of the Middle Ages. Eudes Rigaud (Odo Rigaldi, to give him his Latin name), archbishop of Rouen, is no exception. Nobody thought of preserving either his birth or his baptismal certificates. The most that can be said with any degree of accuracy is that he was born sometime between 1200 and 1210, in a place called Corquetaine.

Louis Moreri states that Eudes was born at Lyons,[1] while G. G. Coulton avers that Picardy was his place of origin,[2] probably because the authors of *Gallia Christiana* placed Corquetaine in Picardy. The latest, and full-length, biography of the archbishop asserts that he first saw light in the Ile-de-France, at Corquetaine or Corquetelles near Brie-Comte-Robert in the diocese of Meaux, about twenty miles from Paris.[3] The Rigaud family held land at Corquetaine. Who were the archbishop's parents? H. Fisquet says he was the son of Pierre Rigaud, the knight and lord of Corquetaine.[4] Eudes' *Registrum* furnishes more accurate information on his own immediate relatives. He had two brothers and three sisters: Peter inherited the family fief at Corquetaine, and his marriage to Nazarea was performed by Eudes;[5] Adam, like Eudes, was a Franciscan. He was attached to the archiepiscopal *familia* from 1252 until his death in 1269.[6] Eudes' sister Marie became abbess of the famous Paraclete[7] which was founded by Abélard and Heloise. The two other sisters are unknown except by inference. Eudes stayed at the home of his nephew Aumury de Muzy on May 2, 1269. Another nephew, Adam de Verneuil, received from Eudes a prebend as canon

---

[1] *Le Grand dictionnaire historique*, 3 vol. (Amsterdam and La Haye, 1702), III, 264.
[2] *Five Centuries of Religion*, 4 vol. (Cambridge, 1927) II, 202, following *Gallia Christiana*, 13 vol. (Paris, 1850-74), XI, 67.
[3] Pierre Andrieu-Guitrancourt, *L'archêveque Eudes Rigaud et la vie de l'église au XIIIe siècle, d'après le Registrum Visitationum* (Paris, 1938), p. 10.
[4] H. Fisquet, *La France pontificale*, 2 vols. (Paris, 1864-66), I, 123.
[5] See entry in the *Register* for December 1, 1263.
[6] See entry for August 3, 1269.
[7] See entries for June 10, September 28, 1249; January 16, 1253. Marie was the fifth abbess. *Gallia Christiana*, XII, 575.

in Rouen, not because of blood relationship but "by God's direction."[8] Beyond this one appointment, the Rigaud family does not seem to have profited from Eudes' exalted position. The family itself belonged in the social category of *petite-noblesse* and was in a position to afford young Eudes the advantage of education. Of his formative years nothing is known. *Gallia Christiana* makes no mention of his years prior to 1248.

Actually, nothing definite is known about him until he entered the new religious order of Friars Minor of St.-Francis. Here again, the year of his entry into the order is unknown, but it is generally conceded that he was a Franciscan in 1236.[9] Again, where did he enter the order? This is a matter of speculation. The Franciscans had a parish, St-Maclou, in Rouen as early as 1228,[10] and he may have entered there and then gone on to Paris for study. Most probably he met the Franciscans first at Paris and there entered the order which was attracting so many young men and so many brillant minds. If, on the other hand, he entered the order in 1236, without university study, his rise was truly meteoric. The probability is that he had been a student in Paris for some years prior to the year 1236 and that the Franciscans acquired a mind already initiated in the ways of philosophy and theology.

As a Franciscan he studied under the celebrated Alexander of Hales and received the degree of Master in Theology from the university.[11] The Franciscans were forbidden to carry the title of Doctor.[12] Though a newcomer to the order, Eudes, together with Alexander of Hales, John of La Rochelle, and Robert de la Bassée, was appointed in 1242 by the Franciscan General, Haymo, to determine the true interpretation of poverty as that word was used in St.-Francis' Rule. Their findings are known as the Exposition of the Four Masters.[13] The Chapter General which met at Mont-

---

[8] See entries for November 9, 1263; December 5, 1265; December 28, 1266.

[9] P. Féret, *La Faculté de théologie de Paris*, 4 vols. (Paris, 1894-97), II, 303.

[10] M. Julien Loth, *Saint-Maclou de Rouen* (Rouen, 1913), *passim*.

[11] P. Glorieux, *Répertoire des maîtres en théologie de Paris au XIIIe siècle*, 2 vols. (Paris, 1933), II, 31-33.

[12] "Alexandre de Hales", *Dictionnaire de théologie catholique,* 15 vol. (Paris, 1909-50), I, 773.

[13] *Expositio Quatuor Magistrorum super Regulam Fratrum Minorum*, ed. P. L. Oliger (Rome, 1950), pp. 123-68. For the *Regula S-Francisci* (1223), *ibid.*, pp. 173-93. See A. Potthast, *Regesta Pontificum Romanorum*, 2 vols. (Berlin, 1874), I, 614 (7108) for the Bull of Honorius III confirming the Rule of 1223.

There are three Rules of St-Francis dated 1209, 1221, 1223 respectively. Neither

pellier in 1241 ordered each provincial chapter to appoint its most competent friars to draw up a statement on the province's attitude on the relaxation of the Rule on the question of poverty. The *Exposito* of the Four Masters, calling for a literal interpretation of the Rule, was the answer of the Paris Friars.

John de la Rochelle succeeded Alexander of Hales in the Minorite Chair of Theology in 1242. In the same year Eudes was received as a Master in Theology. When John died in 1245 Eudes became the regent of the Franciscan school, an office he filled until 1247.[14] His friend John de la Rochelle had participated in the Council of Lyons in 1244.

The first Franciscan house of Paris dates from 1219, but their large monastery was not begun until 1230. In 1231 Alexander of Hales took the habit, and with him began the Minorite center of studies at Paris. He was a Master in Theology before becoming a Franciscan. His chair was officially recognized and incorporated into the university, and thus began the Franciscan *Studium generale*. Eudes was one of Alexander's first pupils and applied himself to philosophy, theology, and canon law. His philosophical and theological works include *A Commentary of Four Books of Sentences*; *Disputed Questions*; *Studies on the Pentateuch, the Psalter, the Gospel*; and *Sermons*.[15] His *Register of Visitations* affords ample proof of his knowledge of canon law from the Council of Nicaea to the Decretals of Gregory IX, and much of his time as archbishop of Rouen was spent in efforts to enforce that law.

The parish church of St. Mark the Evangelist was founded in Rouen in 1246, and to it came Eudes as superior.[16] Probably he was employed by King Louis IX in the 1247 census of Normandy.[17] When Archbishop Clement of Rouen died on March 5, 1247, Eudes probably attended the

the Rules of 1209 (*Regula Primitiva*) or 1221 (*Regula Prima*) was granted written official papal approbation. They are the *Regulae non-Bullatae*. St-Francis requested official written recognition of his Rule from Honorius III in 1223 (*Regula Secunda or Bullata*). According to this Rule all friars were to live from the work of their hands and from alms in case of necessity. They were never to receive money and never to possess property, appropriated or otherwise.

[14] P. Glorieux, *Répertoire*, II, 25, 31.

[15] *Ibid.*, II, 31-33. For a discussion of Eudes' literary output see P. Andrieu-Guitrancourt, *L'archêveque Eudes Rigaud*, pp. 23-32.

[16] Luke Wadding, *Annales Minorum*, 28 vol. (Quarrachi, 1931-41), III, 183-84.

[17] Charles Petit-Dutailles, "Querimoniae Normandiae" in *Essays in Honor of T. F. Tout* (Oxford, 1924), p. 105.

funeral. Eudes was his successor and was consecrated at Lyons by Innocent IV in March, 1248.[18]

How was he elected? Our only definitive information is his consecration by Pope Innocent IV at Lyons. Innocent, like his predecessor Gregory IX, was well acquainted with the Franciscans. As a matter of fact, he issued during his eleven pontificate years no fewer than eight bulls dealing with the order.[19] John de la Rochelle had attended the Council of Lyons, 1244-45. Many of the men whom Eudes knew at Paris were now confidants of Louis IX, who was a member of the Third Order of St. Francis. Many of them were also in contact with Innocent IV.[20] These were the years of Haymo of Faversham, Adam Marsh, and Robert Grosseteste. There is no evidence that such contacts brought about Eudes' election, but it is probable that Innocent knew about him from trustworthy sources.

Legend entered on the manner of Eudes' choice. The chapter of Rouen met and could not agree, after long deliberations, on a candidate. Finally they agreed that the first cleric who entered the cathedral to pray would be their choice. The first cleric was Eudes Rigaud, who was on his way to preach in the open but who had stepped into the cathedral to visit the Blessed Sacrament.[21] This is probably a mixture of fact and fiction, inasmuch as Eudes had become well known for his preaching in Rouen. He continued to preach after his elevation to the archiepiscopal see; he was well acquainted with the see and with his contemporary ecclesiastics before his appointment. He was probably acquainted with the work of the late Archbishop Clement, who had tried to better the lives of his clergy.

Eudes, a reformer in heart and soul, was cognizant of the works and endeavors of his predecessors. His work as a reformer was well within the framework of papal objectives, especially those formulated during and after the years of Pope Alexander III (1157-81). Alexander III set the pattern for future popes in matters pertaining to centralizing the power of the Church in Rome. His victories in Italy over Frederick Barbarossa contributed to this in no small way. To insure finances for his political activities he multiplied

---

[18] Gams, *Series episcoporum* (Leipzig, 1931), p. 614; *Gallia Christiana*, XI, 67.

[19] Potthast, *Regesta Pontificum Romanorum*, II, 952 (11175); 970 (11422); 1013 (11937); 1014 (11962); 1066 (12653); 1149 (13892); 1152 (13945); 1211 (14691); 1242 (15086).

[20] Robert Menides, "Eudes Rigaud, frère mineur," in *Revue d'histoire franciscaine* (Paris) VIII (April-June, 1931), pt. 2, 18.

[21] Bonnin, *Register*, p. iii.

the exemptions of monasteries from episcopal control, bringing them directly under Rome; in the realm of the secular clergy he reserved prebends to be bestowed at the papal will. On the other hand, he took a strong hand in repressing the venality of higher ecclesiastics. To curb the graver evils in the Church, he convoked the Third Lateran Council (1179), twenty-seven of whose canons deal with matters of discipline, such as luxurious living of prelates, plurality of benefices, bishops who where too young (less than thirty years of age), simony, and the collating of benefices before the incumbent was dead.[22] The main tendencies of the council's legislation were toward centralization and reform. Innocent III (1198-1216) set his heart on bringing about both.

A goodly portion of Innocent's reign was taken up with this task. He appointed directly archbishops, bishops, and abbots, overriding in doing so the decisions of local chapters. But more than anything else, a large portion of Innocent's *Register*[23] is concerned with the moral state of individuals and of the Church at large. The contrast between the asceticism of the Albigenses and the laxity of the clergy as a whole must have been, as it was to Innocent III, patent to all.[24] Among the higher clergy, some were guilty of simony; others did not enforce canon law in all its phases; others were guilty of committing acts of violence, avarice, and greed. Monastic discipline was equally lax. Instances of simony, incontinence, squandering the goods of the house among relatives are many. Even the once great haven of spirituality. Cîteaux, was the subject of discrediting rumors.[25] Reform was a necessity if the Church were to be preserved. As the executor of the plenitude of power, Innocent set his hand to the task.

Innocent realized that a moral reform could not be accomplished without an administrative reform. Thus, appeals to the Roman Curia were encouraged so that in reality it became the court of omnicompetence. Its decisions were in many cases final, as witness the oft-used phrase, *omni appelatione remota* (no appeal allowed), appended to documents. When a

[22] J. D. Mansi, *Sacrorum Conciliorum nova et amplissima Collectio*, 53 vol. (Paris and Leipzig, 1901-27), XXII, 217-23.

[23] *Patrologiae completus cursus,* ed. J. P. Migne, 217 vols. (Paris, 1878-91), CCXIV-CCXVII.

[24] *Ibid.*, CCXVI, 34-35, on reforming abuses among the clergy. See especially the case of Berengarius of Narbonne, bishop, *ibid.*, CCVX, 883-85, noted for avarice and negligence.

[25] *Ibid.*, CCXIV, 1107-08: exhortation letter to the abbots of Cîteaux, la Ferté, Pontigny, Clairvaux, and Morimond.

particular case had to be judged locally he appointed judges-delegate who exercised for that case all the decisive authority of the Roman Curia. In the wide area of moral reform he took into his own hands, in many instances, the examination of candidates for episcopal office, requiring first of all that canon law be observed in the matter of election, that candidates be literate, that they have reached the canonical age of thirty, and that their private lives be above suspicion in the matter of morals. Chapters still elected, but their actions in making the choice, together with the life of the person chosen, were apt to be strictly reviewed in Rome. Once raised to the episcopate, it was the duty of bishops to remain in their dioceses, to visit their clergy in the spiritual sense, and to administer the sacraments. But above all, they were to watch over the lower clergy.

The lower clergy were not, in some instances, an educated and morally disciplined body. Innocent held the bishops responsible for their entrance into the clerical state, especially the priesthood. Vices were to be rooted out and, to aid in this, monthly synods were to be held at which the lower clergy were bound to be present. The canon law on married clergy was to be enforced, and married clerics were to be deprived of their livings. Clerics were to live from the fruits of their prebends and were not to engage in trade; they were not to enjoy plurality of benefices or prebends, and parish priests were to be resident in their assigned parishes.[26] Innocent's concern also extended to the regular or monastic clergy. Abbots and priors were to live with and supervise their communities; neither the abbot nor his community was to dispose of community property without the proper authorization of the chapter of a religious house. A letter addressed to the Benedictine abbots of the province of Rouen recommended the holding of an annual provincial chapter for the "correction of excesses which are committed in your monasteries."[27] The implementation of his decisions, as formulated in the Fourth Lateran Council, are to be found in the national and provincial councils[28] held during his pontificate.[29] Reform from within was one thing, reform from without was quite another. The factors of time, distance, local prejudices, and passive resistance, especially the latter, often reduced the efforts of the supreme external authority to very little account, so much so that while

[26] These reforms were incorporated into the canons of the Fourth Lateran Council. (Mansi, XXII, 981-1058).

[27] PL, CCXVI, 312.

[28] Mansi, XXII, 699-704; 714-22; 763-65; 792-93; 818-44.

[29] Ibid., XXII, 981-1068. On the reforming work of the council see U. Berlière,

the efforts at reform were great and well intentioned, in practice the results were small.

The effort to reform was vigorously carried on by Innocent's successors, Honorius III and especially Gregory IX, whose reforming statutes[30] for the Benedictines, Cluniacs, and Premonstratensians indicate that while Innocent III's efforts pointed the way, there still remained much to be done. The example of the religious life was now to be found not in the old monastic system, but in the ways of the new orders, the Dominicans and the Franciscans. The *Register*, the journal kept by Eudes and his clerks during most of the period from 1248 to 1269, is the fullest and most informative account of actual religious conditions in a given geographical area that the Middle Ages have bequeathed to posterity.

Eudes and his clerks kept a record of his pontifical years which has been given the title by its editor, Bonnin, of *The Register of Visitations of the Archbishop of Rouen*. The major portion is a diary or journal, an *aide-mémoire* or a permanent record of what the archbishop found right or wrong when visiting canonically and what should be done about it. The original manuscript is in the Bibliothèque nationale, Paris, as number 1245 *du fonds latin*.[31] The first folio is lost, and extant entries do not begin until July 17, 1248, though Eudes made his formal entry into Rouen on March 2, 1248. At that time, the archbishop was in the neighborhood of fifty years of age. His own diocese was Rouen, with the suffragan sees of Séez, Avranches, Coutances, Bayeux, Lisieux, and Evreux.

The *Register* is a very human document; as human as the man who dictated its contents to his clerks. Actually, that quality is one of the chief justifications for its translation into English. Throughout the entries, Eudes' sense of justice, impartiality, and forbearance for human frailty are plainly in evidence. Even when one community of religious showed no indication of reforming itself and Eudes departed "sad and frustrated," there was ample justification for harsher words. The *Register* is the mirror of a good man

"Innocent III et la réorganization des monastères bénédictines," in *Revue bénédictine* (Maredsous), XXXII (1920), 22-42; 145-59; A. Luchaire, *Innocent III. Le Concile de Lateran et la réforme de l'Eglise* (Paris, 1898); Philibert Schmitz, *Histoire de l'ordre de Saint Benoît*, 6 vols. (Maredsous, 1948-49), III, 42-80.

[30] *Bullarium Privilegiorum ac Diplomatum Romanorum Pontificum*, ed. C. Coquelin (Rome, 1740), pp. 254-56; 272-74; 278-80.

[31] It was printed as the *Registrum Visitationum Odonis Rigaldi archiepiscopi Rothomagensis*, ed. Theodore Bonnin (Rouen, 1852).

with a knowledge of the ideal and a preoccupation with the observance of the due process of law, but endowed with a sense of balance, especially where human beings are concerned.

In the *Register's* entries can be found a record of the manners, morals, dress, and mores of Normandy in the thirteenth century. Here are glimpses of the daily life of religious, secular and regular; in other words, a glimpse at the life of the church as it was lived in that portion of France. One meets all manner of people: bishops, archdeacons, students, murderers, usurers, holy men and women together with those denounced and charged with waywardness; here is how cases were tried in ecclesiastical courts; here is the community which has books which either does not see to their proper care or lends them without record; here is the man who borrows books and does not bother to return them when duly requested several times to do so; here a picture of the rules of religious life is discernible through Eudes' account of their infractions by the regular and secular clergy.

Many writers have used the *Register* to support their points of view. Leopold Deslisle[32] used it as proof of the low moral state of the Norman clergy. G. G. Coulton quoted from it extensively in his studies of the Middle Ages.[33] Its most understanding student is C. R. Cheney, who analyzed it thoughtfully and prudently in his study of *Episcopal Visitations in the Thirteenth Century.*[34]

Without doubt, caution is necessary when using a document such as the *Register.* There is the inherent danger of reading into it interpretations wholly unjustified. In the first place, it is an eminently private document and was never intended to see the light of publication or to be seen by the eyes of future generations. Secondly, it is a one-sided document in that Eudes caused to be entered not what he found right but what he found wrong. Things were by the very rules of religious life supposed to be right, and there was not much justification for the making of such entries. As such, the Register is somewhat in the category of a police record, and to

[32] Leopold Déslisle, "Le clergé normand au XIIIe siècle, d'après le journal des visites pastorales d'Eudes Rigaud, archevêque de Rouen, 1248-1269," in *Bibliothèque de l'école des chartes* (Paris, 1846), 2d series, III, 479-99.

[33] G. G. Coulton, *Five Centuries of Religion*, 4 vols. (Cambridge, 1927-50), II (1927), 195-238; III (1936), 451-56.

[34] C. R. Cheney, *Episcopal Visitations of Monasteries in the Thirteenth Century* (Manchester, 1931). See in particular his statistical analysis of the *Register* with reference to clerical discipline, alms, and finances, *ibid.*, pp. 168-74.

judge a society from entries dealing with violations of the established order is apt to give an unbalanced picture of that society. Thirdly, every entry which designates a delinquent as ill famed or defamed is not to be taken at face value. Eudes himself did not. Many of the charges were based on rumor or gossip. Eudes recognized this, and no one so charged went without the benefit of an investigation into the facts and without strict adherence to the due process of law. Considering the large number of religious, regular and secular, relatively few were found actually guilty in Eudes' courts of law.

Eudes' preoccupation with canonical justice leads to a very pertinent question. Was Eudes a reformer? Probably in the strictest sense of the word he was not. He did not promulgate or initiate reforms of his own. His efforts were spent in enforcing the canon law of the Church and those statutes promulgated in Normandy by his predecessors. In this less strict sense he was a reformer, in that he enforced reforms initiated by others than himself. He could be very well classified as an analyst of his times. His contacts with Rome were close, yet we do not find him entrusted with diplomatic missions by the papacy. Only in one instance do we find him designated as a judge-delegate by the pope. Usually the decisions of the judges-delegate were final and did not permit an appeal. According to the entry for May 9, 1262, Eudes was the judge-delegate appointed by the pope in the struggle between Jean Leroux, count of Brittany, and the bishops of Quimper and Nantes. All parties were cited to appear before Eudes at Rouen on August 16 of that year. The *Register* makes no further mention of the case.

The *Register* was not kept on a daily basis. There is much evidence that entries were made some time after the actual events. This is quite understandable, especially in the matters of canonical visitations. Eudes generally visited more than one community each day. He and his retinue of four brother Franciscans, a notary, a secretary, a doctor, and a valet, servants, and a few canons of the cathedral of Rouen—his favorite canon seems to have been William of Flavacourt, who succeeded him as archbishop of Rouen (1278-1306)—traveled on horseback. When the prelate's rheumatism became too painful, he rode in a cart. It was not always easy to make formal entries of the day's work. No doubt notes were kept from which the formal entries were later made.

The entries were made by several hands—at least six. Many are entered on the margin or at the bottom of the folio, probably indicating interpolation and afterthoughts. Up to the present, detailed paleographical and critical study of the manuscript is lacking. Numerous questions remain to be answered on Eudes' or his clerks' chronology,[35] place names,[36] and proper names which are at times entered in their French form and again in Latin form.

Order is concerned with the sacraments and matters spiritual. As such, Eudes conferred major and minor orders on clerics, and their powers as clerics flowed from him as bishop. He alone, except for some one specifically delegated by him, consecrated bishops, conferred orders, administered Confirmation, consecrated oils, and installed abbots and abbesses.

Jurisdiction to Eudes implied the power to teach, preach, make ordinances, and administer and judge according to these ordinances. He convoked synods, made diocesan statutes, and allowed dispensations therefrom. He also promulgated and enforced the statutes of provincial and general councils. He appointed priests to parishes and prebends and removed them for cause. He supervised certain hospitals and leprosaries.

As judge, he took cognizance of cases brought to the ecclesiastical forum, be it internal or external.[37] The former dealt with penance, sacramental confessions, matters of conscience, and all private spiritual matters; the latter with public matters of the Church. Eudes or his official dealt with both, while a priest or a penitentiary could be the judge in internal cases.

Aiding him in the administration of his diocese was the cathedral chapter of Rouen, which had its own statutes regulating the niceties of personal and official relations between both parties. Then came the archdeacons, who had their own courts, visited the deaneries, and held synods. Their mandates were carried out by the deans, who were also to supervise the lives of the clergy in their respective deaneries. This was done in the monthly synods.

Eudes also had his curia or court with its officials, such as lawyers, keeper of the seal, recorders, and notaries. Many of his curial officials were permanent, as witness the frequent recurrence of certain names as signatories to documents.

---

[35] For example, the months of December in 1261 and in 1262 were given 32 and 35 days respectively.

[36] The edition of the "Polyptychum Diocesis Rothomagensis" in the *Recueil des historiens des Gaûles et de la France*, 24 vols. (Paris, 1868-1904), XXIII, 228-331, has contributed materially in identifying local Rouen place names, especially parishes.

[37] R. Génestal, La "Privilegium Fori" en France du décret de Gratien à la fin du XIVᵉ siècle, 2 vols. (Paris, 1921-24).

The archdiocese of Rouen comprised the dioceses of Rouen, Lisieux, Evreux, Séez, Bayeux, Coutances and Avranches. Visitations were made in the diocese of Rouen every year. During his pontificate Eudes visited the diocese of Lisieux four times, Evreux three, Séez three, Bayeux three, Coutances three, and Avranches three.[38] The suffragans, jealous of their privileges, real or otherwise, challenged Eudes on his rights of frequent visitation as metropolitan.[39]

As metropolitan, Eudes could preside over the election of bishops in his province, confirm the elections and consecrate the elect, preside over provincial synods, and arbitrate disputes between his suffragans. The suffragans challenged Eudes' jurisdiction on two very essential points: (1) the right to hear cases which had been appealed directly to the archiepiscopal court from the dioceses, by-passing the bishops on the way; (2) Eudes' right of frequent canonical visitation in his suffragans' dioceses.

At the end of the twelfth century episcopal jurisdiction was not integral in many dioceses. Through the centuries, the jurisdiction of the bishops in the West had been undermined chiefly by the archdeacons, who were practically episcopal in jurisdiction but not in order. Their courts were independent of the bishop's court. Moreover, cases were appealed directly from the archdeacons' and rural deans' courts directly to the archbishop's or his official's tribunal without respect to the rights of the local ordinary. This was the case at Rheims, Tours, and Rouen. In the archdiocese of Rouen another personage—the official—had curtailed the juridical and judicial powers of the suffragan bishops. The archbishop seems to have placed his official in every diocese, so that the achiepiscopal court and not the bishop's court became the court of first instance in the diocese, thus practically destroying the episcopal tribunals as cours of first instance. Between the archdeacon and the archbishop, the bishop had practically lost his power of jurisdiction, so much so that the bishops clamored for redress to Innocent IV. This was the reason for Innocent's promulgation of the Constitution, *Romana Ecclesia*,[40] in 1245, which restored jurisdiction in the diocese to the ordinary and also regulated the hierarchy of appeals so that the metropolitan retained

---

[38] O. Darlington, *The Travels of Odo Rigaud, Archbishop of Rouen*, (Philadelphia, 1940), p. 73.

[39] See *Dictionnaire de droit canonique*, ed. R. Naz, 6 vols. (Paris, 1935-), VI (1956), 875-77, for historical treatment on metropolitans; *ibid.*, I (1935), 927-34, for similar information on archbishops.

[40] Mansi, XXIII, 652, 653, 654, 664, 667-69, 670-71, 673. The *Constitutio* origin-

in his own diocese only, and not throughout his province, original juris-diction over appeals. The matter had been raised in the province of Rouen prior to Eudes' time, and an agreement had been reached in 1236 between Archbishop Pierre de Colmieu and Hugh II, bishop of Séez.[41] Accordingly, in principle, there were to be no more appeals from the archdeacons' and deans' courts of the diocese of Séez to the archbishop of Rouen, except through the courts of the bishop of Séez. What of the other dioceses of the province?

Certainly, every bishop in the West was aware of the promulgation of the Constitution, *Romana Ecclesia.* Eudes' *Register* does not afford details beyond the fact that his suffragans appealed to Rome[42] against him and his non-observance of *Romana Ecclesia.* There was nothing strange in such an appeal beyond the presence of the bishop of Séez among the appellants. No reason is given for his presence. His status had been settled long before the papal Constitution of 1245 was published. It may be surmised that his presence demonstrated suffragan solidarity face to face with archiepiscopal authority. Eudes' efforts to arrive at an amicable solution were not successful,[43] and so he took the road to Rome to present his case in person to the pope who had previously consecrated him archbishop. Innocent handed down his decision on July 4, 1254.[44] His lengthy bull forbade the by-passing of bishops in cases of appeal; forbade absolution by the archbishop or his official of those excommunicated by the bishops, their officials, and their archdeacons. The bull was further implemented by an agreement regulating the customs of the province of Rouen reached between Eudes on June 26, 1256, and the bishops of Bayeux, Lisieux, and Coutances.[45] Thus was peace restored on this point of jurisdiction. Intimately interwoven therein was the question of the archiepiscopal right of canonical visitation over his suffragans.

---

ally applied to the difficulties in the archdiocese of Rheims. Later, the pope applied the same remedies to similar situations in Rouen.

[41] See entry for March 2, 1251/52.

[42] See entry for March 2, 1251/52.

[43] At a meeting with his suffragans at Lisieux September 29-30, 1251/52.

[44] See entry for July 4, 1254; also Bonnin, *Register*, pp. 749-54. This decision became an integral part of the *Corpus Juris Canonici* and may be found in *Sext*, Lib. V, Tit. 11, caput VII, *Corpus Juris Canonici*, 2 vols. eds. A. L. Richter and A. Fried-berg, (Leipzig, 1879-81).

[45] See entry for June 26, 1256. For a full discussion of the issues involved and the agreements reached, see P. Andrieu-Guitrancourt, *L'Archvêveque Eudes Rigaud*, pp. 54-93.

In their appeal to Rome on archiepiscopal hearings on appealed cases Eudes' suffragans also complained about his ignoring the decisions of the *Romana Ecclesia* on metropolitan visitations. The papal decision was that the metropolitan should visit his cathedral city and his own diocese before visiting his suffragans' dioceses. This visit should include the large and the small churches, clerics, and laymen. After visiting a suffragan diocese, either in whole or in part, he could not reenter and continue the visit until he had visited the remainder of his province. If there were pressing canonical need to visit a suffragan diocese he was to do so. After having visited his province, he could revisit a suffragan diocese after advising the suffragan of his intensions but would not need the latter's consent. He could begin his visit by covering those places not already visited. Also, he should conduct a canonical visitation of the clergy and people, preach the gospel, and remind all of their duties.[46]

At the provincial council of Rouen in 1252[47] Eudes announced that he was about to proceed to visit his province, "where and when it should be done." His predecessors had visited the suffragans' dioceses every three years, a custom which Eudes appeared about to violate. The suffragans protested against Eudes' "where and when," yet they signed the statutes of the council of Rouen (1251/52). The suffragans then appealed to Rome, and Eudes went in person to present his own case to the pontiff. He won the right to visit where and when he wished. In actuality, it was one thing to win the right to free visitation, another thing to abuse that right. Eudes was too practical a man to abuse authority; thus his visits, as already seen, were not frequent. The provincial council of Rouen, September 12, 1257, confirmed the decree enacted at the council of January, 1251/52, and added that "with the common consent of our brothers the visitation of our province of Rouen must be undertaken by us when it will seem expedient to do so." Having established the right to make canonical visitations at will in his suffragans' dioceses, he proceded to exercise that right, but only within the framework of established custom. The method of canonical visitation in these dioceses did not differ from that used in his own diocese of Rouen. Those visited could be houses of religious or the secular clergy.

The superiors of religious houses were notified of the approximate time

---

[46] This became an integral part of canon law and was entered in *Sext*, Lib. III, Tit. 20, caput I.

[47] See entry for January 22, 1251/52.

of the visitor's arrival, thus allowing no excuse for the absence of the superior. The religious superior was the person responsible for the spiritual and material well-being of the community, and he alone could answer questions pertaining thereto satisfactorily. Thus he was supposed to be present at canonical visitations. On arrival, the visitor was met in procession by the community at large. After this formal reception the visitor met the visitands in chapter and preached a sermon. Then began the visitation proper. In all probability Eudes had a formal set of questions to which he required answers. The whole community was examined openly in chapter.

The questions turned on the observance of the Rule and its observation, the *Opus Dei*, the upkeep of the church and its *ornamenta* (that is, the fabric of the church, its vestments, chalices, altar cloths), and the morality of the community at large. The visitor then called the members of the house singly and in private if he felt the open inquiry was not altogether satisfactory. Thus he had two types of information: the *detecta*, or things revealed openly by the community, and the *comperta*, the things found out by the visitor on examining the individuals. If necessary, he then proceeded to the matter of correction by order, injunction, or compurgation.

The order was given on the spot; it was canonically binding and was to be obeyed by virtue of the rule of obedience. It was usually given in matters relating to the substance of the Rule, for example, violation of the rule on fasting and eating meat. Injunctions were equally binding, but they were presented generally in written form, sealed with the seal of the visitor, and were to be kept for reference in future visitations. Compurgation was used when a visitand was denounced of a grave crime or crimes and had to purge himself therefrom by securing witnesses from his own clerical rank who could swear that he was then telling the truth. When the spiritual side had been looked into, the visitor scrutinized the house's accounts, its debts, the condition of the buildings and of the fabric of the church.

However, there were spiritual islands outside Eudes' jurisdiction of canonical visitation. These were the exempt houses of the Cistercians, the Premonstratensians, the cells and priories of Marmoutier, St-Benoît-sur-Loire and Fécamp.[48]

[48] For houses questioning Eudes' right of visitation see entries for August 22, 1248; June 5, 1250; July 8, 1250; July 12, 13, 1250; July 18, 1250; July 27, 1250; August 30, 1250; June 22, 1252; September 17, 1253; February 5, 1254/55; January 19, 1255/56; October 26, 1256; June 1, 1256; May 22, 1256; May 20, 1256; March 13,

In his visitations Eudes found that certain basic principles of the monastic life were completely disregarded. This was especially and perhaps understandably so in the outside priories. Silence and abstinence from meat in them were practically dead letters in observance. Priests who performed parish work needed to communicate with each other and their parishioners at uncanonical hours and thus violated the Rule on silence. So also did they need sustenance beyond a vegetable diet if their objectives as parish priests were to be attained. But to Eudes they were monks bound to observe silence and to abstain from meat. Another common infraction of the Rule was the presence of lay folk in the cloister and choir. The monastery and priory were part of the social scene in the Middle Ages. They formed an integral part of the local social community, and undoubtedly such intrusions of lay folk into the religious house were of long standing. For all Eudes' efforts in prohibiting such practices he was not very successful in keeping the layfolk out of the cloister. He recognized the difficulty in violating long established practices; he was apt to urge the monks to keep out lay folk but to act with tact and good manners in doing so.

As for the Rule itself, very few of the smaller priories had a copy. The same is true of the reforming statutes of Pope Gregory IX. Despite Eudes' commands and injunctions, very few priories, even by the very end of his journal, had procured a copy of either. The same was true of chalices. The one parish chalice was apt to be the priory chalice, no matter how many monks were in the priory. Even some of the larger monasteries had very few chalices and altars, a probable reminder of the days long past when there were very few priests in the monastery or in the priory.

On the physical side, a few priories were in ruins, "deformed in spirituals and in temporals." The roof was apt to be in sad disrepair, the belfry floor rotten, and the goods wasted. Much of a religious establishment's wealth was apt to be given in part to nephews, cousins, sisters and relatives of all degrees without the consent of the community. With equal abandon superiors loaned out books without receipt. To counteract this practice Eudes demanded that all books be produced in chapter and displayed openly for all to see. The prior of Bourg-Achard loaned a copy of William of Auxerre's *Summa aurea*, and since he did not retrieve it after repeated commands by Eudes, he was disciplined for his disobedience. One would like to know more of the

1257/58; September 14, 1258; April 30, 1258; January 7, 1259/60; October 8, 1259; January 12, 1260/61; September 2, 1260; September 7, 1266; September 19, 1266.

Summa's recipient, Guillaume de Bose. Guillaume also received on loan the glossed Epistles of St. Paul from the same prior. He did not return them.

Of Pope Gregory IX's reforming statutes for the Benedictine Order, two deserve special mention because their application is of recurring interest in Eudes' visitation. One, confession, pertains to the spiritual well-being of the monastic resident; the other, accounting for monastic income, was directed toward the economic solvency of the monastic community.

The Rule of St. Benedict provided for confession of sins by the monk to his abbot. The Cistercian *Usus monachorum* stated the time, place, and manner of confessing. The Cistercian lay brothers confessed seven times yearly. The Constitutions of Lanfranc made provision for frequent confession to the abbot, the prior, and spiritual brethren appointed for this purpose. Gregory IX decreed, as a minimum, monthly confession and Communion for religious. This was the first definite papal legislation on frequency of sacramental confession for all religious. Eudes' task was to enforce this legislation. From his many references to the subject it is evident that frequent sacramental confession was not practiced among religious. The subject crops up in practically every recurring visitation of the houses, and it is clear that the religious did not take kindly to the innovation, even though its source was the Pope. It is not that the religious led bad lives; the new legislation was simply not the accustomed way of doing things. The best weapon for counteracting such innovations was passive resistance.

Pope Gregory's legislation on the economic well-being of religious houses met stiffer resistance than did his statutes on confession. Some of the opposition centered around rents and the uses thereof. These rents were usually legacies for pious uses and were usually connected with *obits*. Provision was made according to the will of the donor that the money be divided among the individual clergy who took part in the ceremony, as in the case of canons, or in procuring additional food, clothing, or other necessities—pittances for the community at large—in case of monks. To avoid fluctuation in values, the chapter of canons or abbot and community of the abbey purchased rent charges, thereby keeping the property and its management within the chapter's or abbey's hands. The rent-charge in this era of agricultural economy was generally always in land. There was also another kind of rent-charge which concerned the investment made directly by the religious community, largely to circumvent usury.

Religious communities had suffered at the hands of lay-abbots, from obligations of hospitality to rich and poor, and from wars, fires, and famine so much so that existence for many was one financial crisis after another. They sold property, loaned it for the lifetime of the lessee, and borrowed from money lenders. Even great and rich abbeys like Bury St. Edmund's in England were in the hands of usurers.

Some found alleviation by appropriating parishes, some sought letters of indulgence for spiritual favors to donors, others dispersed as communities until the particular financial crisis was over. These crises explain why so many houses sought to put themselves under papal protection. Eudes' *Register* records the debts of religious houses in the archdiocese of Rouen in the thirteenth century. Hard money was difficult to obtain even for those who were rich in land; in general, those houses in the hands of prudent administrators managed to survive. Most houses needed wise administrators as much as holy superiors if the temporal side of the establishment were to remain. Among the means of remaining whole in temporals were mortages carrying interest, which were forbidden by canon law and *vif-gages*, or reception of usufructs in return for a sum loaned, which, in practice, somewhat resembled the Roman *beneficium*. The third method, judging by Eudes' *Register*, was the most popular—the purchase of rents, which was really a method of circumventing the mortage, officially condemned by Alexander III in 1179. The decisions of this council were incorporated in *Corp. jur. can., Decretal. Greg. IX*, Lib. v. Tit. 19. The rent was the revenue which the debtor had to furnish the creditors yearly, in money or in kind, as compensation for the creditors' transfer to him of property or capital. Capital was guaranteed by land as collateral. The rent was an annual payment and had many advantages in that it was generally paid in cash; it formed a sure income.

Gregory's statutes demanded that the religious superior and his officers lay bare the monastic accounts at stipulated times and render an account of their stewardship to the community at large. This laid the axe to one of the fundamentals of Benedictinism: the supremacy of the abbot. He could be advised by the *sanior pars* of the community but was not bound to take its proffered advice; he appointed officials within the community. The papal reform statute made the superior and his officials accountable to the community for the goods, income, and disbursements of the house. Eudes indicates, that many houses, large and small, ignored the papal constitution. Eudes was up against passive resistance on a grand scale, a resistance based on the antiquity of the Rule itself and with centuries of tradition behind it. The good Franciscan archbishop tried to enforce the law, but without much success. The monastic attitude that he encountered was but part of the general picture of monasticism in Eudes' time. It is difficult to escape the general impression that monastic obedience to papal commands left much to be desired. In general it is not the monk at large who appears to be at fault, but his superior, probably with the connivance of the former. The monk of today might very well be a superior of tomorrow.

Clerics in the cathedral chapter were supposed to be disciplined by either the bishop or the dean or both; those in the collegiate chapters had privileges guaranteeing them against overmeddling bishops. For the cathedral canons, day-to-day discipline was generally in the hands of the dean until the actual moment of visitation of either the bishop or the archbishop. Eudes found the canons lax in carrying out liturgical services, in the upkeep of the fabric of the church, and in the conduct of their lives as clerics. Some canons were not required to perform in person the liturgical services of their office. These were nonresident canons who deputized substitutes or vicars to perform the offices required. Nonresident canons were quite common in Western Europe, and much as Eudes deplored the practice, he was powerless to do anything effective about its abolition.

The visitation of the secular clergy presented different problem, because they were not a corporate unit, living a community life. Eudes was quite thorough in his visitation of the rural clergy. They met under their deans every month in synod, where discipline was meted out and major cases referred to Eudes. Eudes was present at some of the deans' synods, twenty-four in all, at some more than once. The ground for visitation was prepared ahead of time through notification of the archdeacon and the dean. The synod opened with a prayer and a sermon by Eudes after which he called on reliable and truthful men (*jurati*) present to report on the moral state of the deanery. At any rate, that was the method of procedure followed at the synod of the deaneries of Walmont and Fauville held respectively on April 27 and April 29, 1252. Judging by the findings of each synod, the way was well prepared by the archdeacon, the dean, and the others responsible.

Statistics on the morality of the secular clergy visited by Eudes may be compiled. The validity of such compilations is something else, especially so when on plotting the parishes of the sworn men (*jurati*) on the map, it is found that those charged with uncanonical conduct in the synod are those clergy resident in parishes proximate to those of the sworn men. What of the clergy who lived in distant parishes? For this there is no answer. Such clergy could have been blameless or blameful. Since there is no record either way, the validity of statistics on secular clerical morality as presented in Eudes' visitations is, at best, doubtful.

The terms most frequently employed by Eudes when dealing with his errant clergy were *infamatus, diffamatus,* and *notatus. Infamia*[49] is the partial or total loss of one's good reputation among upright and responsible men. A cleric may be declared *infamatus* (translated "ill famed") after an investigation and trial, but he may also be so designated where an investigation, though not a formal trial, was conducted. A cleric might incur *infamy of the law* when an ecclesiastical court decided that he had lost the good esteem of his neighbors because of his evil deeds. Or he might incur *infamy of the fact,* a matter of public opinion, when upright and honorable men outside an ecclesiastical court held him in bad repute on account of his actions or morality. In either case (of law or of fact) there was an investigation. Such seems to have been Eudes' procedure. A cleric found to be ill famed was to be deprived of his church or benefice.

A cleric was *diffamatus* (translated "defamed") when his good reputation was put in doubt with his ecclesiastical superiors. The *diffamatus* cleric was denounced to his dean, archdeacon, or bishop. An investigation was then ordered by the superior in order to separate fact from rumor. If after the investigation the superior was still in doubt, he generally ordered the cleric to undergo purgation, wherein the cleric was to produce a specified number of character witnesses of his own clerical rank who would swear to his good reputation. *Notatus* (translated "publicly known") implied wide public knowledge of a man's good or bad reputation.

Eudes' terminoloy of accusation presents problems; *infamia* and *diffamatio* seemingly mean one and the same thing. However, even in Innocent III's famous canon, *Qualiter,*[50] it is difficult to say where *infamia* ends and *diffamatio* begins, and the Council of Toulouse[51] defines *diffamatio* in practically the same words used by Innocent III when defining *infamia facti* (infamy of the fact) in his *Qualiter.* It is not surprising, then, to find that Eudes seems to use the terms interchangeably.

[49] Mansi, XXII, 994-95.
[50] Mansi, XXII, 994-95 (canon 8).
[51] *Ibid.,* XXIII, 198 (canon 18).

Ecclesiastical officials in the Middle Ages were an integral part of the public order, and their activities embraced matters secular as well as ecclesiastical. In addition to visiting his archdiocese and administering his own diocese, Eudes was a member of the Norman Exchequer[52] and regularly attended its meetings;[53] he was appointed to the Parlement of Paris and thus became a member of the king's council.

According to Salimbene,[54] Eudes met Louis IX for the first time at Sens in 1249. The chronicle gives a lively account of the affair. Louis was preparing for the Crusade of 1250, from which he was not to return until April, 1254. In the meanwhile Eudes was engaged in the struggle with his own suffragans. After 1254 the meetings of king and archbishop became more frequent. On May 19, 1258, Eudes met in conference with Louis at Poissy and journeyed thence to Paris to sit as a member of the Parlement from May 20 to June 7. From this date he is a confidant of Louis IX. A further indication of this confidence was an invitation from Louis' brother, Alphonse of Poitiers, to visit him.[55] Louis and Eudes are much in each other's company from now on,[56] except when the latter is administering his diocese and province. As friend of Louis and public servant of the crown Eudes participated in the negotiations leading up to the Treaty of Paris (1259) and in raising money to equip Louis' crusade to Tunis (1270).

An uneasy peace existed between England and France after John's loss of Normandy to Philip Augustus. Henry III had tried in 1225, 1230, and 1242 to recapture with armed force what had once been his father's possessions in France. No efforts had been made while Louis was on crusade from 1250 to 1254. Henry's son, Edward I, married Eleanor, daughter of Alphonse X of Castille, and Henry III requested the permission of Louis IX for the royal family to return to London by an overland trip through France rather than traveling the entire way by sea. Louis met Henry at Chartres and

---

[52] Joseph R. Strayer, *The Royal Domain in the Bailliage of Rouen* (Princeton,1936), pp. 17-23. There are also many references to the Norman Exchequer in the same author's *The Administration of Normandy under Saint Louis* (Cambridge, 1932).

[53] October 7, 1258; October 7-10; May 2-4, 1262.

[54] *Chronica* (ed. Holder Egger) in *Monumenta Germaniae* (*Scriptores*) XXXII (Hanover and Leipzig, 1903) 222.

[55] July 27, 1258.

[56] August 22, 1258; February 2, 1258/59; April 23, 1259; September 30, 1260; October 26, 1260; July 22, 1261; June 19, 1262; July 6, 1262; etc. These meetings do not include the sessions of the Parlement.

both traveled together to Paris. Eudes was present.[57] Probably at this meeting the groundwork for the Treating of Paris was laid. Except for one day —September 20—Eudes was in Paris from September 13 to October 1, 1259; Eudes does not give any reason, but undoubtedly the Parlement was in session. Again, from November 10 to November 23 he was in Paris attending the Parlement. Henry III arrived in Paris on November 24 and Eudes read aloud the Treaty of Paris "in the king's orchard" on December 3. Henry then performed the oaths of homage and fealty to Louis. Some difficulty must have arisen in connection with the treaty, because on July 4, 1260, Eudes arrived at Dover, on his way to London, where he remained from July 7 to July 12, as he discreetly expressed it, "on the business of the lord king of the Franks."

The crusade was never far from the mind of Louis IX and found expression in the *Register* of his friend Eudes when at the provincial council of Préaux prayers were ordered throughout Normandy for the successful prosecution of the forthcoming venture.[58] Another council, dealing solely with the crusade, met at Mantes a few months later.[59] Present were not only the suffragans of the archdiocese but representatives of every religious community on whom the conciliar decisions were to be binding. The two exempt orders, the Cistercians and the Premonstratensians, were represented, but they stated that only the decisions of their own abbot-superiors were binding. Thus they could neither promise nor assent to anything. The big problem of the moment was the means of financing the Crusade of Louis IX. The situation was rendered more difficult by demands for money from Rome, not for Louis' venture but for furthering papal policy in Southern Italy and in Constantinople. A council was held at Paris[60] at which the papal legate made clear the needs of the papacy, especially for recovering Constantinople. On the next two days[61] the bishops of France gave their answer, with Eudes as their spokesman. They made clear that the Church in France was already overtaxed and that there was no justification for additional taxes. The needs of Rome were again pressed in a council, held at Paris two years later, at which Eudes was present.[62] One thing is sufficiently clear: there was very

[57] December 7, 1254.
[58] January 25, 1260/61.
[59] April 6, 1260/61.
[60] August 30, 1262.
[61] August 31, September 1, 1262.
[62] August 24, 1264.

little if any relationship between the policy of the papacy and the intentions of Louis IX, whose preparations for the Tunisian crusade were continuing. Eudes was with the king at Gaillon on December 19, 1264, and three days later Giles, archbishop of Tyr, preached the crusade at Rouen.[63] The bishop of Evreux, Ralph de Grosparmi, then joined the archbishop for future consultation until January 2, 1264/65.

On March 24, 1266/67, Louis and his family formally took the Cross, while Eudes with many others did likewise a few months later.[64] He attended two councils with other French bishops to deal with the crusade.[65] Little remained toward the last but to take formal leave and "receive permission" from his flock to leave on the crusade. On November 17, 1269, he preached in the cathedral of Rouen and then set out slowly for Paris, which he reached on December 8. Entries in the *Register* end eight days later, December 16, 1269.

On March 1, 1270, Eudes sailed for Africa with Louis IX and his army. Their first stop was at Cagliari, where Louis annonced that the destination of the crusade was not Palestine but Tunis. On July 15, the army debarked unopposed on African soil. Shortly thereafter the Arabs attacked and inflicted heavy losses on the French. Soon the crusaders' losses from dysentery were greater than those from actual combat with the enemy. Louis fell ill and died on August 25, 1270. Eudes was with his king when he died.

On November 29 the crusading army departed from Tunis for the journey homeward. Louis' bones were brought back to Paris, where amid solemn ceremonies, they were interred at St-Denis on May 27, 1271.

Eudes returned to Rouen on May 31 of that year. He was then in his seventies. He died on July 2, 1276, and was buried in his cathedral church at Rouen. His bones were scattered during the French Revolution, and today no physical trace remains of Eudes and his predecessor-brother-archbishops of Rouen.

[63] December 19, 22, 1264.
[64] June 5, 1267.
[65] December 15-17, 1267; January 29—February 1, 1267/68.

THE REGISTER

1248

IN THE year of our Lord 1248, JULY 17. We arrived at Graville,[1] received our due procuration,[2] and exercised our right of visitation.[3] We found everything in good condition. They have an annual income of about three hundred pounds of Tours;[4] they have no debts. They have enough bread and wine to last them until harvest. The prior from Ste-Barbe[5] together with all the canons of Graville promised to abide by our selection of a prior for them, since the community was then without a prior. After we had received an oath from the canons and had sought their choices individually, we gave

---

[1] Graville-Ste-Honorine, conventual priory of Augustinian canons, dependent on Ste-Barbe-en-Auge (Dom L. H. Cottineau, *Répertoire topo-bibliographique des abbayes et prieurés*, 2 vols. [Macon, 1939], I, 1337.)

[2] Procuration is the right of any ecclesiastical superior on official visitation to receive payment in kind to maintain his retinue of men and animals, or to demand in money a sum equal to the expense incurred should they lodge outside the place visited. Procuration was to be found in the feudal and ecclesiastical orders of society. It found its way into feudal custom and canon law. Actually, it was regarded as a part of the public order, of which ecclesiastical visitation was a part. Thus, papal legates, archbishops, bishops, officials, archdeacons, and deans, when acting in their official capacity of visitors, could and did demand and receive procuration. (*Corpus juris canonici*, ed. E. Friedberg, 2 vols. [Leipzig, 1879-81], *Decretal.*, Lib. III, Tit. 39. This is what Eudes meant when he noted "at the expense of the monastery," "abbot," "prior," "abbess," etc. For non-exempt houses, procuration could not be levied without visitation. (J. D. Mansi, *Sacrorum conciliorum nova et amplissima collectio*, XXII, 1019, Canon 33, Fourth Lateran Council, 1215.)

[3] See introduction, p. xxvii.

[4] The most current monies in thirteenth-century France were the pound Paris and pound Tours. The pound Paris had its origin in royal money; the pound Tours was first struck by the chapter of St-Martin of Tours. The pound Paris was the most stable and thus more valuable. Natalis de Wailly in the Introduction to Vol. XXI of *Recueil des historiens des Gaules et de la France* (Paris, 1885), lxxvii-lxxxi, has a note "Sur la monnaie tournois et la monnaie parisis de S. Louis." He shows that the pound of Tours was worth about 4/5 that of Paris. *Recueil des historiens des Gaules et de la France,* ed. Léopold Delisle and others (Paris, 1868-1904). Etienne St-Martin Saint Léon, *Histoire des corporations des métiers* (Paris, 1897), pp. 172-76, agrees with this figure, as does Philippe Wolff, *Commerce et marchands de Toulouse* (Paris, 1954), p. 307.

[5] Ste-Barbe-en-Auge, an Augustinian priory, founded in the diocese of Lisieux c. 1130. Among its early patrons was Henry II of England. (Cottineau, II, 2604.)

them Richard, the prior of St. Mary Magdalene,[6] as their prior and directed
our letter to the aforesaid prior in the following form:

Brother Eudes, by God's permission the unworthy[7] bishop of the church of
Rouen, to his beloved son Richard, prior of St. Mary Magdalene of Rouen,
eternal greeting in the Lord Jesus Christ. When we came to Graville, in part to
make a visitation and in part to attend to the installation of a prior (for the
community for some time had been deprived of this comfort), we made a
thorough scrutiny of the votes of the brethern, carefully considering everything
that should be considered in the affair, listened to the counsel of good men,
and appointed you as their prior. Wherefore we trust in your devotion to us
and, by virtue of the obedience you owe to us, we order you forthwith to put
your affairs at the priory of St. Mary Magdalene in order as soon and as quickly
as possible, and to hasten to Graville, where you shall perform your pastoral
duties as a good shepherd should. Carry out our command as an obedient son so
that, along with other good shepherds, you may deserve to receive your reward
from God and be commended by us for your merit. We hold by the tenor of
these letters that the brethren of the aforesaid community are bound to show
you the faithful obedience and reverence which is due you as prior. Let it be
distinctly understood that we will inflict adequate punishment upon those who
shall presume to go against our instructions in this matter. Given at Montivilliers six days before the feast of St. Mary Magdalene, in the year of our Lord
1248.

JULY 17. We spent the night at Montivilliers,[8] at the expense of the
abbess. JULY 18. At the same place, at the expense of the abbess. We visited
the monastery and found everything connected with it to be in good condition. In the evening we went on to Lillebonne and slept in the castle.
JULY 19. At Lillebonne. We dedicated the church at Bouville and stayed
the night at Caudebec, at the expense of the parish of Bouville. JULY 20.
We arrived at Jumièges[9] and made a visitation there. We found that Brother

---

[6] A conventual house of Augustinian canons, established in Rouen c. 1154 to care
for the sick. (Cottineau, II, 2545-46.)

[7] See "Minister indignus," Du Cange, *Glossarium*, IV, 415.

[8] A Benedictine abbey founded c. 682, Destroyed by the Normans, it was rebuilt
as a monastery for nuns c. 1030. (Cottineau, II, 1958-59.) This was one of the
richest and most independent-spirited monasteries in Normandy.

[9] Founded as a Benedictine abbey c. 631, it was destroyed by the Normans but
rebuilt about 941 by William Longsword. (Cottineau, I, 1496-99.)

William of Beaunay and Brother William of Bourg-Achard were ill famed[10] of the worst vice;[11] we decreed that they be sent to other monasteries, there to expiate their offenses. Likewise, we found that the subprior was a disturbing element among the brothers; we decreed that he should be removed altogether from the office of subprior.[12] JULY 21. We came to Déville. JULY 22-23. At the same place. JULY 24. We ate at St-Matthieu[13] with the Friars Preachers at our own expense.

Brother Eudes, by God's permission unworthy bishop of the church of Rouen, to all who may see the present letter, eternal greeting in the Lord Jesus Christ. A dispute arose between William Borde, senior, William Borde, junior, and Hays, widow of Ralph Borde, on the one side, and Robert Sain and Alice, his wife, on the other, concerning the charge against the said Robert that he had killed the said Ralph. At length the aforesaid parties came before us, and by their troth corporally given in our hand gave us assurance that they would steadfastly and gratefully abide by any disposition we might make of this matter for the good of the peace. We, therefore, acting with the counsel of good men[14] and diligently examining everyone connected with the quarrel, reached

---

[10] *Infamati.* Their deeds were such that they brought them into public ill repute. *Infamatus* denoted that a trial or inquiry had been held. See Introduction, p. xxxiii.

[11] That is, sodomy. See *The Theodosian Code*, trans. Clyde Pharr (Princeton, 1952), pp. 231-32 (9 : 7, 3; 9 : 7, 6).

[12] Disturbing elements were apt to occur in mediaeval religious communities, and provisions were made to deal with them if they got out of hand. Thus St. Alberic, second abbot of Cîteaux, was imprisoned at Molesme before setting out for Cîteaux: "He labored long to bring about the transfer of the brethren from Molesme to Cîteaux. For this he bore patiently many insults, imprisonments, and blows." "*Exordium Parvum,*" in Ph. Guignard, ed., *Les Monuments primitifs de la règle cistercienne* (Dijon, 1878), p. 67. Cluny made like provisions for turbulent monks. (*Consuetudines Cluniacenses Udalrici Cluniacensis monachi,* in Migne, *PL,* CXLIX, 736.)

[13] A Dominican priory in Rouen. (Cottineau, II, 2546-47.)

[14] The *vir bonus* had his place in the Roman legal system. He was the arbitrator, and when he was called upon to judge a case, though he was not a regularly constituted judge, his decision had the force of law and was binding in law. Cicero's *De finibus bonorum et malorum* and *De officiis* had much to say of the "good man's" function. As such, the "good men" came over into canon law in *Corp. jur. can., Decretal. Greg. IX* Lib. I. Tit. 43. They could be lay or ecclesiastics, depending on the situation. See articles, "Arbitrage," "Arbitrateur," "Arbitre," in *Dictionnaire de droit canonique,* ed. R. Naz, 6 vols. (Paris, 1935), I. 862-901. For the influence of canon on civil procedure, see Yvonne Bongert, *Recherches sur les cours laïques du Xme au XIIIme siècle* (Paris, 1949), especially pp. 159-82. Monastic cartularies constitute an almost untapped source on arbitration as an element of legal procedure.

the following decision, to wit: that the said Robert betake himself overseas within the coming octave of the Assumption of the Blessed Virgin; that he remain there for two years and not return to Normandy within five years of the said octave of the Assumption of the Blessed Virgin, nor, in fact, even after the said five years, unless by special permission of the said William Borde senior, of Eustace of Romilly, and of Stephen Mercer, and unless he shall have brought letters from the Templars or Hospitalers, or other well-known persons, testifying that he had remained overseas for two years. In memory and testimony of this matter we place our seal on the present letter. Given at Déville, the day after the feast of Saint Mary Magdalene, in the year of our Lord 1248.

Brother Eudes, by God's permission unworthy bishop of the church of Rouen, to all who may see this letter, eternal greeting in the Lord Jesus Christ. Be it known that William Borde, senior, Eustace of Romilly, and Stephen Mercer, came before us and pledged their faith with their hands in ours, and having touched the holy Gospels[15] in our presence promised that they would consider Robert Sain to be justly recalled from overseas and that they would do nothing to prevent him from returning freely to his home as soon as he shall have fulfilled the conditions contained more fully in our letter concerning the confirmation of the peace made between the parties. Given at Déville on the morrow after the feast of the Blessed Mary Magdalene, in the year of our Lord 1248.

JULY 25. We arrived at St-Victor-en-Caux[16] and visited there. JULY 26. We arrived at Auffay[17] and visited there. JULY 27. We were at Dieppe, at our expense. JULY 28-29. At Aliermont, at our expense. JULY 30. At Wanchy, at the expense of the priory. No monks there.

JULY 31. At Envermeu.[18] We visited the priory and found that they have an income of four hundred pounds and more. They are burdened with a debt of three hundred pounds. The prior keeps no accounts on the condition of the house; we ordered him to cast his accounts at least four times

---

[15] Taking oath on the Gospels, as a preventive of perjury, is to be found early in the mediaeval period. "[On the contention of two witnesses] they determine that before he takes Communion, he who is being approved shall testify by the four holy gospels..." (John T. McNeill and Helene M. Gamer, *Mediaeval Handbooks of Penance* [New York, 1938], p. 85.)

[16] Originally a priory of St-Ouen-de-Rouen, it became an abbey *c.* 1074. (Cottineau, II, 2915-16.)

[17] A Benedictine priory after 1067; it had been a house of canons regular. (Cottineau, I, 195.)

[18] A Benedictine priory dependent on Bec; it was founded *c.* 1052. (Cottineau, I, 1054.)

a year.[19] Sometimes they eat meat when it is not necessary; we ordered them
to abstain from eating meat.[20]

AUGUST 1. At Le Tréport,[21] at the expense of the monastery. AUGUST 2.
At Eu,[22] at the expense of the monastery of St-Laurent, and we visited there.
AUGUST 3. At the same place, but at our expense. On this day the abbot
took an oath and gave troth that on the fifteenth day before the Nativity of
Blessed Mary he would on our advice resign his monastery, and gave us the
following letter on the matter:

To all who may see this letter, I, Brother Guy, abbot of the monastery at Eu,
give perpetual greeting in the Lord Jesus Christ. The wise man has said: "Let
judgment most severe be passed on those who are presumptuous." So, considering the perilous state of my condition and feeble old age, of my own free
will and, having touched the most holy things, I have sworn and given troth to
my lord the archbishop of Rouen to follow his counsel in resigning or retaining
the abbey which I am directing at present, and to present my decision fifteen
days before the Nativity of the Blessed Mary. I further promise under oath and
troth that I shall never make use of petitions or petitioners to evade the said

---

[19] "In order that the [financial] status of the houses may be known with greater
accuracy, the officials shall, once every three months, in the presence of the abbot or
of the prior if there is not an abbot, and of the seniors [monks] render an account of
their charges [offices], rendering an accurate entry of expenses and receipts." The
Statutes of Gregory IX are published in Bonnin, pp. 644-48. The article here quoted is
on p. 645.

[20] The Rule of St. Benedict (Ch. 36) absolutely forbade the eating of meat except by
the infirm. If full credence is to be placed on St. Bernard, the Rule was not held inviolate at Cluny (*Apologia ad Guillielmum*, in Migne, *PL*, CLXXXII, 911). Bernard's
charge found echo in the reforming statutes of Peter the Venerable (Migne, *PL*,
CLXXXIX, 1029). By the end of the twelfth century, the violation had become so
widespread that prohibition became a part of canon law. It was a question not only
of eating meat but of abstinence in general. Since its earliest days the Rule allowed
only one meal during the period of the Great Fast (September 14 to Easter). This
practice was followed at Cîteaux, but few other monastic establishments observed it.
Two or three meals daily was the general rule. The Rule itself was hedged, in that
meat was not eaten in the refectory but was eaten with the ill in the infirmary, at the
abbot's private table, or in some other "recreation" room. (E. Bishop, "The Methods
and Degrees of Fasting and Abstinence of the Black Monks in England before the
Reformation," *Downside Review*, XLVI [1925], 184-237). A letter of Innocent III of
the abbot of Subiaco "Cum ad monasterium Sublacense" (Migne, *PL*, CCXIV, 1064-
66) on fasting and abstinence found its way into the *Decretales* of Gregory IX, Lib.
III. Tit. 35. cap. 6, and deals not only with food but also with clothing, monastic
poverty, silence, and faithful discharge of offices.

[21] A Benedictine abbey founded *c.* 1053. (Cottineau, II, 3208.)

[22] A conventual house of Austin canons founded *c.* 1119. (Cottineau, I, 1084-85.)

obligation, either by my own act or by means of others. And I further agree, under the binding of the same oath, to make meanwhile no disposition of the goods of the monastery exceeding the value of two silver marks without the advice and consent of those whom the lord archbishop shall assign to me. Given in the year of our Lord 1248, the Tuesday after the feast of Saint Peter in Chains.

We assigned the prior, the subprior, the sacristan, and Roger Lebret to act as counselors to the abbot.

AUGUST 4. We arrived at Foucarmont,[23] where we stayed at the expense of the monastery. AUGUST 5. At Neufchâtel, at the expense of the priory of Nogent.[24] There are no monks there. AUGUST 6. At Neufchâtel, at the expense of the parishioners of St-Pierre-de-Neufchâtel, for on this day we dedicated St-Peter's church.

AUGUST 7. We visited the monastery at Bival[25] and found some of the nuns defamed[26] of the vice of incontinence. This day the abbess resigned the government of the abbey into our hands, and we gave the nuns permission to elect another. They appointed the day after tomorrow for the election. This day we spent the night at Beaubec,[27] at the expense of the monastery.

[23] Originally a cell of Savigny, it joined forces with Cîteaux in 1147. (Cottineau, I, 1202-3.) Note that Eudes received procuration, but dit not visit, officially. With the exception of Cistercian nuns, houses of the Cistercian Order were exempt from the jurisdiction of the local ordinary. The legal principle as the basis of granting exemptions is that nobody may dispense with submission to proper authority, but they can be exempted. The proper authority is the local ordinary (bishop) or religious superior. The pope can not only dispense but exempt from local authority or ecclesiastical superiors. Exemption of religious persons is found as early as the Council of Chalcedon. (Mansi, VII, 359, canon 4.) Benedictine monasteries were not exempt from the jurisdiction of the local ordinary (*Rule of Saint Benedict*, C. 64-. Houses of the Cluniac and Premonstratensian Orders were also exempt. From them, Eudes also collected procuration but did not visit them canonically.

[24] Several religious houses bore the name of Nogent. There was only one priory at Neufchâtel, and that (Ste-Radegonde-du-Mesnil) was a cell of Préaux. (Cottineau, II, 2056.)

[25] St. Mary Magdalena, a Cistercian house of nuns founded *c.* 1130. Note that Eudes made a visitation there. (Cottineau, I, 385.)

[26] The *diffamati* were those who, because of their acts, had been denounced to ecclesiastical superiors, but who may not yet formally have been tried either by their local superiors or by an ecclesiastical court. See Introduction, p. xxxiii.

[27] Originally a daughter house of Savigny, named St. Laurent. It beame a Cistercian house in 1147 when the Savigny congregation joined with Cîteaux. (Cottineau, I, 289-90.)

AUGUST 8. At the same, at the expense of the monastery; on this day, we dedicated the monastery's infirmary chapel of St-Laurent.

AUGUST 9. We were at Beaussault,[28] at the expense of the prior, and we visited the priory. They have an income of . . .[29] [*lacuna in MS*]; they owe twenty-six pounds. We found everything in good condition. This day the prioress of Bival and certain other nuns presented their elect to us through a letter from the community in the following form:

Clemence of Appetot, prioress of Bival, and its entire community, to the reverend father in Christ, Eudes, by the grace of God archbishop of Rouen, greetings and due and dedicated obedience. When a vacancy occurred in our monastery through the resignation of Sister Eleanor, our former abbess, a fact which we believe does not escape your watchfulness, we chose with your permission the Saturday before the Assumption of the Blessed Virgin as the time to elect a suitable person for the monastery. Convening that day in chapter, and invoking the grace of the Holy Spirit, we treated this business. At length, with the common consent and will of the whole chapter, we agreed to give our sisters Matilda of Les Andelys, Joan of Bec, and Matilda of Hoqueville power to provide our monastery with a head and to chose an abbess.[30] They, taking counsel together, have canonically with one heart and one mind provided Marguerite of Aunay for our monastery. Wherefore with care and devotion we beg Your Paternity to confirm the provision made in respect to this worthy person and to bestow the gift of benediction, when it shall seem good to you.[31] Given the Sunday following in the year of our Lord 1248.

[28] St.-Maur-de-Beaussault, a cell of Bec-Hellouin, established before 1141. (Cottineau, I, 312.)

[29] Bonnin states that this lacuna is due to a binder who cut off too much on the margin.

[30] The nuns, in this instance, are seeking confirmation of their act, for no election could be effective without confirmation of, in this instance, Archbishop Eudes. The election in this particular case was "by compromise," or an agreement whereby the electors give to one or more persons the power to proceed in the electors' name to do what the whole body would have done. The election by compromise must be done with the unanimous consent of the three electors, as it was in this case at Bival, "with the common consent and will of the whole chapter." Such an election has the same juridical value as if it had been done by all the electors. In this way the election was canonical. Then follows proclamation of the name of the elect; then, seeking confirmation at the hands of the proper ecclesiastical authority. This confirmation must be given if the election is to be effective and the elect is to take office. In the meantime the proper authority investigates to see if everything was done according to law and propriety, or, as Eudes stated, "we therefore diligently examined both the manner of the election and the elected person and approve and confirm both." (For canon law on such elections see *Corp. jur. can., Decretal. Greg. IX.* Lib. I. Tit. 6. cap. 30.)

We confirmed this election and issued the following letter on this matter:

Brother Eudes, by God's permission the unworthy bishop of the church of Rouen, to his beloved daughters in Christ the prioress and convent of St.-Mary Magdalene of Bival, eternal greeting in the Lord Jesus Christ. When through a vacancy in your monastery, because of the resignation of your former abbess Eleanor, you selected with our permission the Saturday preceding the Assumption of the Blessed Virgin for the purpose of electing another, you convened in chapter, and having invoked the grace of the Holy Spirit, treated the matter of election very seriously, and finally by common council and unanimous will you carried out this matter by allowing Matilda of Les Andelys, Joan of Bec, and Matilda of Hoqueville to act on behalf of all and provide an abbess for your monastery. After treating the matter diligently together, they provided Sister Marguerite for you and your monastery, as you have informed us in the letter received from the prioress and certain other nuns presenting the personage of the elect and humbly supplicating us to deign to confirm the election. We therefore diligently examined both the manner of the election and the elected person, and we approve and confirm both. Wherefore by the tenor of this letter we strongly enjoin all of you to obey and submit to the said Marguerite as is properly due an abbess, and we commit the administration of the temporalities of the abbey to her.[32] And be it known that if any shall be disobedient or rebellious, we shall punish them in such a manner that the punishment of one shall be a terror to the rest. Given at Beaussault, the Sunday before the Assumption of The Blessed Virgin in the year of Our Lord 1248.

AUGUST 10. We were at Saëns,[33] at the expense of the prior; we visited there. We found that they do not observe the fasts of the Rule; we ordered them to observe these more fully. Item, they were in the habit of eating meat quite freely; we bade them abstain from eating meat. Item, they did not observe the rule of silence. Item, there were not three monks there, though there used to be six. Item, they have an income of three hundred pounds and owe as much as forty pounds.

AUGUST 11. We were at St-Lô-de-Rouen,[34] at the priory's expense. We

---

[31] Bonnin is correct when he interpreted the text as *cum visum vobis fuerit oportunum*; the Ms. reads: *cum visum nobis fuerit oportunum*.

[32] She could not exercise jurisdiction over the spiritualities of the abbey until she had been canonically installed by the proper ecclesiastical authority. Marguerite was not yet installed.

[33] Originally a Benedictine abbey, it was destroyed by the Normans, then rebuilt *c*. 1150 as a cell of St. Wandrille. (Cottineau, II, 2873-74.)

[34] A priory of Augustinian canons established *c*. 1114. (Cottineau, II, 2545.)

found everything to be in good condition, except for the fact that they owed four hundred pounds. They have an income of about seventy pounds.

AUGUST 12. At Mont-Ste-Catherine,[35] at the expense of the monastery; we visited there. We found that they sometimes hurry through the Divine Offices, especially the Hours of the Blessed Mary;[36] we enjoined them to say these more slowly. Item, we found that some do not keep silence very well; we enjoined a better observance.[37] We found that some are not willing to accuse their brethren when they break the rule of silence;[38] we enjoined and ordered each to accuse the other without exception. Item, in the outside priories they eat meat freely; we enjoined the abbot to correct this and to see that these priories observe the rules regulating abstinence from meat. Item, we enjoined the abbot to prepare a quarterly statement of the accounts of the monastery. They have had an income of two thousand pounds; they owe nothing, since more is owed to them than they owe. At the same Mont-Ste-Catherine we found that Brother Samson [was ill famed] of having personal property, of being incontinent, and of disturbing the peace. AUGUST 13. We arrived at Déville, at our expense. AUGUST 14-15. At Rouen, at our expense. AUGUST 16. At Déville, at our expense. AUGUST 17.

[35] Originally a Benedictine abbey (Ste-Trinité). (Cottineau, II, 2544-45.)

[36] This is known as the Office of the Blessed Virgin or the Little Office. The first definite mention of this office was by St. Peter Damian, who spoke of its daily recitation by the Camaldolese at Fonte Avellano about 1056. (Migne, PL, CXLIV, 431; ibid., 132; a copy of the office may be found in ibid., CLI, 970-74; "Incipit officium Beatae Mariae Virginis secundum consuetudinem monachorum monasterii Sanctae Crucis Fontis Avellanae.") For further information see Dictionnaire d'archéologie chrétienne et de liturgie, ed. F. Cabrol and H. Leclercq, 15 vols, Paris, 1902-1953, XII, 2012-15.

[37] Rule of St. Benedict, Chs. 42, 48, 52. The Cistercian silence was complete, but an elaborate sign language was used instead. Their rules on silence may be found scattered throughout their Usus monachorum. (Guignard, Monuments, pp. 167-201.)

[38] This accusation should be made in the Chapter of Faults, held immediately after the conventual (High) Mass. The Chapter of Faults was, so to say, the second portion of the chapter, the first being the Chapter of the Rule. For the method of holding both chapters, see Guignard, op. cit., pp. 167-72. In the Chapter of Faults each accused himself and also his fellow-monks of faults. However, "no one is to be accused by more than three, unless, perhaps, by the one in charge of the Chapter ..." (ibid., p. 170). "No one is to accuse another on suspicion alone, but only on what he has seen, heard, or heard referred to." The accuser is not to inflict punishment on the accused. "Whoever is to be beaten, after being ordered by the abbot to undress, must sit in the same place where he is then standing. Taking off his cuculla [choir robe], he places it before him, on his knees. He is to bare his whole body to the waist. With bowed head, he says nothing except 'mea culpa, I will correct myself.' ..." (ibid., p. 171).

At Frênes, at our expense. AUGUST 18. At Pontoise, at our expense. AUGUST 19-20. At St-Denis, at our expense. AUGUST 21. At Gaillonet,[39] at the expense of the priory.

AUGUST 22. At Vesly,[40] at the expense of the priory. We made a visitation there and found a certain monk, Reginald by name, who was unwilling to answer any questions; in fact, he turned his back on us. Item, there was an elder monk there who knew nothing of the state of the house.

AUGUST 23-26. At Frênes, at our expense. AUGUST 27. At Louviers, at our expense. AUGUST 28. At Déville, at our expense. AUGUST 29-30. At Déville. AUGUST 31. At the same place. We visited St-Ouen,[41] at our expense. SEPTEMBER 1. At the same. SEPTEMBER 2-3. At the same. SEPTEMBER 4. At St-Georges-de-Boscherville.[42] We received procuration and visited the place, finding everything in satisfactory condition. SEPTEMBER 5. At Bourg-Achard,[43] at the expense of the priory. We visited there. SEPTEMBER 6. At Ecaquelon, at the expense of the parish. This day we dedicated the parish church of the Blessed Mary. SEPTEMBER 7. At Bec.[44] We visited there and found everything in good condition. They owe only four hundred pounds.

SEPTEMBER 8-9. At Bec, at the expense of the monastery.

SEPTEMBER 10. We came to Corneville,[45] where we received procuration and made a visitation. We discovered, to wit: that they have an income of about two hundred forty pounds and owe one hundred sixty pounds; item, we found two women there who had been received as sisters, and we ordered that no women should be received in the future;[46] item, three of their priories

---

[39] St. Pierre-de-Gaillonet, a Premonstratensian cell of St. Josse-aux-Bois (Cottineau, I, 1240.)

[40] A Benedictine cell of Marmoutier, established about 1063. (Cottineau, II, 3351.)

[41] Established during the reign of Clothair I, destroyed by the Normans and later rebuilt; burned in 1156, 1201, and in August, 1248. (Cottineau, II, 2547-50.)

[42] Originally founded c. 1050 for canons, it became a Benedictine abbey in 1114. (Cottineau, II, 2701-2.)

[43] A priory of Augustinian canons, founded c. 1143. (Cottineau, I, 459.)

[44] A Benedictine abbey founded c. 1034, it gave Lanfranc and Anselm to Norman England. (Cottineau, I, 316-19.)

[45] A house of Augustinian canons founded c. 1143. (Cottineau, I, 879.)

[46] This is an instance of "mixed communities," of which there were many not only in Normandy but throughout western Europe. Sometimes a wall separated the monks from the nuns, as with the Gilbertines in England; sometimes the communities were some distance apart. Both communities had one superior, who was, on occasion, the abbess, as at Fontevrault. This is a subject on which additional research would clarify many points of interest. (F. H. Crossley, *The English Abbey, Its Life and Work in the Middle Ages* [London, 1903]; Dom. U. Berlière, "Les Monastères doubles aux

were being served by only three canons, and we ordered that a companion be given to each of these, or that all three be recalled to the cloister.[47] We found everything else in good condition.

SEPTEMBER 11. We came to Bourg-Achard once again and made another visitation there. We found that lay folk remained in the choir during the divine services; we forbade the continuance of this practice. Item, we decreed that those who were not priests should confess and receive Communion at least once a month. There are certain other matters that must be attended to.

SEPTEMBER 12. At Déville. William l'Orcher, knight, entered an appeal at Déville as expressed in the following terms:

Since William l'Orcher, knight, is in possession of, or so to say holds, the right of patronage of St. Mary's church at Varangeville and did canonically present to you within the time specified by law[48] a person qualified by character and knowledge to hold the said church;

And since you, without reasonable cause, have brought on one futile delay after another, with the intention of allowing the time to run out against the said knight and the cleric presented by him, so that you could confer the said church, which has a fat and teeming income, upon whomsoever you pleased after the proper time had elapsed;

And since you have conferred the said church upon one of your own clerics for the above-mentioned reason, although, as we believe, the time had not yet elapsed;

XII et XIII siècles," *Mémoires publiées par l'Académie royale de Belgique*, 2d ser., XVIII [1924]; M. Bateson, "Origin and Early History of Double Monasteries," *Transactions of the Royal Historical Society*, new ser., XIII [London, 1899], 137-98.)

[47] The Provincial Council of Rouen, held in 1231 under Archbishop Maurice, decreed (canon 37 [Mansi, XXIII, 218] "that all monks who live alone in any place should be recalled to the cloister by their abbots. If the priory is rich enough to sustain two monks, in that case the abbots are to place two monks there." This was in accord with the decree (canon 10) of the Third Lateran Council (1179) (Mansi, XXII, 224). Most of Eudes' conciliar legislation followed closely that of his predecessors, Maurice, Peter de Colmieu, and Clement.

[48] The Third Lateran Council (1179) took up the problem of the right of patronage in an orderly fashion (Mansi, XXII, 336-43; 413-16). The Council of Avignon (1209) decreed (canon 14) that vacant benefices had to be filled within six months (*ibid.*, p. 791). The Fourth Lateran Council, in 1215, decreed (canon 23) that if patrons had not named the candidate for the vacant benefice within three months, the local ordinary could then do so (*ibid.*, p. 1011). Innocent's letter to the bishop of Coventry (1198) states that if the lay patron had not filled the vacancy in four months, the bishop was to appoint (Migne, *PL*, CCXIV, 478-79). For the importance of Alexander III's legislation in the Third Lateran Council, see Paul Thomas, *Le Droit de propriété des laïques sur les églises au moyen âge* (Paris, 1906), 105-47.

Great injury and wrong has been done to the said knight and to the cleric presented by him.

If, indeed, the time has elapsed, no loss should be incurred by the aforesaid, for the said knight was guilty of no delay, but did what was incumbent upon him, and with time to spare.

If tardiness is to be imputed to anyone, it should involve you and your officials rather than him, for at the intercession of the lord of Graville, you yourself, when you were at Bouville to dedicate the church there, and when the office had been vacant for two months or more, admitted to the said knight that time would not run out against him.

I, William, proctor of the said knight feeling that my lord, the said knight has been unjustly injured by the foregoing, supplicate you in every way, my lord of Rouen, to revoke at once the arrangements you have erroneously made with respect to the said church, for the right of collating to the said church has not as yet fallen to you.

Otherwise, my lord, I shall appeal to the Apostolic See, and, in the name of my lord, place both my affairs and the aforesaid church under the protection of the lord Pope, lest you or any other person shall make any disposition of our persons, our goods, or of the aforesaid church until the merits of the appeal shall be fully discussed.

SEPTEMBER 13. We were at Quévreville,[49] at the expense of the steward. No monks there. SEPTEMBER 14. At Pérrièrs, at the expense of the house. No monks there. SEPTEMBER 15. At Beaulieu.[50] They have an income of four hundred fifty pounds; they owe one hundred eighty pounds. Everything is in good condition. SEPTEMBER 16-17. At Déville. SEPTEMBER 18. At Rouen. SEPTEMBER 19. At Rouen. Today we conferred Holy Orders. At our own expense. SEPTEMBER 20. At Rouen. This day we blessed the abbess of Bival.[51] At our own expense. SEPTEMBER 21. At Etoutteville.[52] We visited the priory. We found that they were using feather beds;[53] we forbade

---

[49] A cell of St. Ouen-de-Rouen. (Cottineau, II, 2389.)

[50] A priory of Augustinian canons from St-Lô. (Cottineau, I, 300.)

[51] Margaret of Aunay was elected August 9, 1248. For the ceremonial and prayers at the blessing of an abbess, see M. Andrieu, Le Pontifical romain au moyen âge (Rome, 1940), II, 408-413.

[52] St. Thomas, a cell of the Cluniac priory of Lewes, England. (Cottineau, I, 1082.)

[53] The monk's bed, in conformity with the Rule of St. Benedict (Ch. 55), consisted of a straw mattress, a pillow stuffed with straw, and woolen bed covers. The monks slept in their habits, as do the present-day Cistercians.

any further use of these. Item, they eat meat; we enjoined them to abstain from eating meat. Only two monks were there.

SEPTEMBER 22. We were at Ouville again.[54] We found that the prior wanders about when he ought to stay in the cloister,[55] nor, indeed, does he remain in the cloister one day in five; he does not follow the rule of the monastery; he is a drunkard and of such shameful drunkenness that, because of his inebriety, he sometimes lies out in the fields;[56] he attends festivities, drinking bouts, and banquets given by lay folk; he is incontinent, and his relations with a certain woman in Grainville and with the lady of Routot are subjects of scandal; there is also a certain Agnes in Rouen. Item, Brother Geoffrey is ill famed of the wife of Walter of Ecaquelon, who bore him a son. Item, the sources of income are not well written down; we ordered that they should be better kept. Item, we found that the prior, despite our predecessor's prohibition that he should not undertake the execution of any-one's will, has undertaken that of Dreux.

This day we met John Louvel and told him to appear before us on the feast of St. Remy so that we would have common counsel on his affairs. Item, William, priest of Cailleville, was convicted of drunkenness, and he con-fessed and swore in our presence that if anything more he heard about him on this infamy, and if it be worthy of belief, he will regard his parish as resigned from then on. Item, the priest of St-Vaast-de-Dieppedale was con-victed and confessed that he was guilty of playing ball in public, in which game one of the players was injured, and he swore to us that if he should be convicted of this again he would regard his parish as resigned from that time on. Item, the priest at Ermenouville was convicted of incontinence, and he confessed and swore to us that if any more of this infamy be heard, and if it be worthy of credence, he would regard his church as resigned.

This day we came to Longueil[57] and slept there, at the expense of the house. No monks there.

SEPTEMBER 23. We came to Bacqueville.[58] We found that the monks

[54] A priory of Augustinian canons. (Cottineau, II, 2161.) The prior visit referred to here was probably recorded on the missing folio 1.

[55] The monastery and the cloister were the home of the monk, and he was strictly forbidden to wander therefrom (*Rule of St. Benedict*, Ch. 67).

[56] This manner of conduct was condemned (canon 15) in the Fourth Lateran Council (1215). (Mansi, XXII, 1003).

[57] A dependent priory of Bec. (Cottineau, I, 1648.)

[58] A Benedictine cell of Tiron. (Cottineau, I, 238.)

leave the cloister without permission; that lay folk frequently enter the cloister;[59] that the monks do not observe the fasts of the Rule; that they use feather beds. We decreed that the monks should not leave the cloister without the prior's permission; that lay folk should not enter the cloister. We enjoined that the monks should abstain from the use of feather beds, and that they should observe the fasts of the Rule. Item, we found that Brothers Lawrence and Geoffrey are ill famed of frequenting the town against the will of the prior; they promised that they would so improve their conduct that we should have a good report of them. The priory has an income of two hundred pounds; they owe about forty pounds.

SEPTEMBER 24. At Longueville,[60] at the expense of the prior. They are exempt. This day, at Longueville, the prior of Ouville swore in our presence that he would be entirely amenable to our will, whether in the matter of resigning his priorate or in any other matter.

Item, a dispute arose between Sir John of Dours, lord of Waleincourt, together with his wife Petronilla, and ourselves over the church at Le Gourel, to which they had presented John of Calomchamp, cleric, as priest.[61] At length the cleric renounced and resigned any rights, if he had any, to the said church by reason of the said presentation; and we, the knight, and his wife conferred the church upon him by common agreement. Upon this matter the following letter was prepared:

John of Dours, lord of Waleincourt, and Petronilla, his wife, to all who may see this letter, greeting. Be it known to you that when we presented John of Colomchamp, cleric, to the church of Le Gourel, the said John renounced every right which he might claim by reason of the said presentation, and the Reverend Father Eudes, by God's grace archbishop of Rouen, together with ourselves conferred the said church upon the said John by common agreement, saving to each of us severally whatever right to the patronage of the said church we may

---

[59] I.c., the inner cloister, entrance to which was strictly forbidden to all but the religious of the house, except by special permission of the local superior. Not even religious of other orders, nor ecclesiastical dignitaries except the bishop on visitation, could enter without special permission of the local superior.

[60] A cell of Cluny. (Cottineau, I, 1649.) At this time Eudes must have warned the prior of Duville about observing the Statutes of Pope Gregory IX. See entry for August 8, 1252.

[61] The document does not mention Eudes' legal rights in the matter, yet he must have had some, judging by the agreement reached. Eudes is exercising his right of presentation. Probably Sir John of Dours had presented his candidate without prior consultation with Eudes.

have. In memory and witness whereof we affix our seals to the present letter. Given at Longueville, the Friday after the feast of St. Matthew in the year of our Lord 1248.

Item, this day Walter Charue, seeking absolution from the excommunication by which he was bound for damaging our manor at Aliermont,[62] offered as sureties Michael of Berneval, William Bure, Hugh of Epinay, and John of Dompierre, all of our diocese, and John Black of Orival and John of Frincourt, knights of the diocese of Amiens. They pledged themselves to the extent of fifty silver marks[63] and promised, both on their own behalf and on that of the count of Dreux and his servants, to be amenable to our will in all things. They further agreed that we might hold any of them responsible for the fulfillment of the entire obligation, or any part of it, as we saw fit. The men of the diocese of Amiens placed themselves under our jurisdiction so that we can attend to them as though they belonged to our own diocese.[64] For our part, we absolved the said Walter.

SEPTEMBER 25. We arrived at Dieppe and were at Sauqueville the same day. SEPTEMBER 26. At Aliermont. SEPTEMBER 27. We dedicated the church of the leper house of St. Mary Magdalene of Grenval, and returned to Aliermont, all at our own expense. SEPTEMBER 28-29. At Aliermont. SEPTEMBER 30. We arrived at Déville. OCTOBER 1-2. At Déville. OCTOBER 3. At Rouen, where we slept in the Franciscan monastery. OCTOBER 4. At Rouen. We dined with the Franciscans and went on to spend the night at Déville. OCTOBER 5. At Bonport,[65] at the expense of the monastery. OCTOBER 6. At

[62] This probably refers to the looting of the archiepiscopal palace at Aliermont on the death of Eudes' predecessor, Clement. Such occurrences were quite common on the death of dignitaries—even royalty, as in the case of Henry II of England—whether lay or ecclesiastic. Walter was a vassal of the famous family of Dreux, to whom such conduct seems to have been ordinary. See entry for January 21, 1248-49.

[63] Neither the pound Paris nor the pound Tours was current in Normandy when that duchy was taken from John by Philip Augustus. Philip converted the current Norman coinage of angevins and English esterlins into pounds Tours. Under the coinage reform of Louis IX, 12 pennies Tours equaled a shilling Tours, and 58 shillings Tours equaled a mark Tours. F. Lot and R. Fawtier, *Histoire des institutions françaises au moyen âge*, 2 vols. (Paris, 1958), II, 211-15.

[64] A bishop's jurisdiction is both personal and territorial. Offenses committed in a diocese by those who enter from an outside diocese, even though the act may not be regarded as sinful in their own diocese, may be matters for atonement by those who committed them.

[65] A Cistercian abbey founded *c.* 1190 by monks of Notre-Dame-du-Val (Paris) under the patronage of Richard I of England. (Cottineau, I, 432-33.)

Frênes. OCTOBER 7. At Le Bord-Haut-de-Vigny. OCTOBER 8. At St-Denis, on the eve of the feast of St. Denis. At the expense of the monastery. OCTOBER 9. At St-Denis, on the day of the said feast. At the expense of the monastery. OCTOBER 10. At St-Martin-de-Pontoise,[66] at our own expense. OCTOBER 11. At Genainville,[67] where we found a certain prior and another monk who was staying there. The prior also officiated at Bau, Bouafles, and Guisnes. He did not wish to give us our procuration fee. OCTOBER 12. At Chaumont,[68] at the house of the prior; at our own expense.

OCTOBER 13. At Chaumont, at our own expense. We held a synod for the French Vexin, and received the fees[69] due when the lesser synods are held. On this same day, we visited the priory of St-Martin[-Ouen?]-de-Gisors. We found that the monks, as of custom ate meat, were not accustomed to observe the rules of fasting, wore unauthorized pelisses in violation of the Rule, and slept on feather beds. We ordered them to keep the fasts, to put away their unauthorized pelisses and feather beds, and to refrain from eating meat. Only two monks were in residence. They have an income of forty pounds of Paris; they owed nothing.

OCTOBER 14. We were at Gisors, at our own expense.

OCTOBER 15. We were at Neufmarché, at the expense of the prior, and we made a visitation there. The monks do not keep the fasts of the Rule very well; we ordered them to observe them in the future. They use feather beds; we forbade their further use. Item, they eat meat, which we also prohibited.

OCTOBER 16. At Gournay, at the expense of the chapter of St-Hildevert, where we exercised our right of visitation. [We found that] Firmin, a priest, is noted for drunkenness; we warned him to correct his ways. Item, William, priest of Notre-Dame, is publicly known for incontinence with a certain woman whom, it is said, he has been keeping for the last twenty years; we suspended him until he should clear himself with the seventh hand.[70]. . .

---

[66] A Benedictine abbey originally dedicated to St. Germain. (Cottineau, II, 2334.)

[67] St-Pierre, a cell of Jumièges. (Cottineau, I, 1265.)

[68] St-Pierre-de-Chaumont-en-Vexin. (Cottineau, I, 746.)

[69] These were procuration fees due the visitor on the holding of the lesser or local synod. The archdeaconry of the French Vexin was composed of the deaneries of Chaumont, Magy, and Meulan.

[70] This method of proof was derived from the barbarian legal practices and passed over into canonical practice. It was a form of canonical purgation and included on oath by, in this instance, seven men of equal dignity and profession as the accused. For simoniacs whose crime is not public but who labor under public infamy (*si publica laborant infamia)* there are to be five or six hands. If that number cannot be found,

NOVEMBER 11.[71] At the same place. NOVEMBER 12-19. At the same place. NOVEMBER 20. At Dieppe. NOVEMBER 21-25. At Aliermont. NOVEMBER 26. At Bracquetuit, at our own expense. NOVEMBER 27. At Déville. NOVEMBER 28. At Rouen. [*No entry for November 29.*] NOVEMBER 30. At Déville. DECEMBER 1-3. At la Haye. DECEMBER 4-6. At Frênes.

DECEMBER 7. At Frênes. This day the abbot of St-Ouen-de-Rouen, placed under sentence of excommunication by us for refusing to sing the Litany at the synod,[72] asked to be absolved, according to the Church's form, and we absolved him after he had taken an oath to obey the mandates of the Church. Present were Brother Nicholas, one of his own monks, Master Thibaut, our associate, and Stephen, Henry, Milo, and Evrard, our clerks.

DECEMBER 8. At Frênes. DECEMBER 9. At Mortemer,[73] at the expense of the monastery. DECEMBER 10. At Rouen. DECEMBER 11-12. At Frênes. DECEMBER 13-15. At Sausseuse,[74] at our own expense. DECEMBER 16. At Frênes. DECEMBER 17-19. At Rouen. DECEMBER 20. At Rouen, and we conferred Holy Orders. DECEMBER 21-22. At Déville. DECEMBER 23-27. At Rouen.

DECEMBER 28. At Déville. This day we visited the priory of Mont-aux-Malades.[75] We found everything in good order. The house has an income

---

the accused is to be deprived of his office in perpetuity. (*Decretales* Lib. v. Tit. 3. cap. 13.) Actually, no number was fixed canonically. This would seem to be the sense of the papal decision. (*Ibid.* Lib. v. Tit. 1. cap. 10.)

[71] A lapse of twenty-six days due to the loss of folio 8.

[72] Clergy attended three categories of synods: (1) the Kalends, or monthly chapters called by their deans; (2) the archidiaconal, called by the archdeacon; (3) in the case of Rouen, the archiepiscopal synods which ordinarily met at Pentecost and All Saints. Actually, Eudes called three synods: (1) that of the great archdeaconate of Rouen; [*la Chretienté*] (2) that of the deans of the diocese; (3) that of the parish priests. He decided that the archdeaconate synod (of Archdeacons) would be held on Mondays on account of the confusion wrought by the diocesan or major synod, that the major or diocesan synod (of parish priests) would be held in the cathedral on Tuesdays, and that the deans' synod (of deans) would be held on Wednesdays. There was another council, that of the whole province, which is probably the one referred to here. The provincial council began, with a solemn Mass, followed by a sermon. The deacon then read a passage from the Gospel. This finished, the council's presiding officer intoned the "*Come, Holy Spirit,*" which was in turn followed by the recital of the Litanies of the Saints. Hugh de Comte-Moulins, abbot of St-Ouen-de-Rouen, refused to perform his part in the liturgy and was excommunicated. He sought absolution, which was granted.

[73] Mortemer-en-Lyons. This was originally founded *c.* 1134 by monks from nearby Beaumont-le-Perreux, but became a Cistercian house in 1137. (Cottineau, II, 1990-91.)

[74] A conventual priory of Augustinian canons. (Cottineau, II, 2960-61).

[75] A leprosary established by Augustinian canons. (Cottineau, II, 1891-92.) Its

of twelve hundred pounds; they owe about one hundred twenty pounds. They have movable property worth about four hundred pounds. They owed, when the present prior came, about four hundred pounds.

Item, this day Nicholas of St-Laurent was presented to us for the church of St-Laurent-en-Caux. We examined him and found him to be completely deficient in letters. Since we did not wish to admit him to the said church, for he was already the incumbent of another and larger cure, he appealed to Rome by letter.

DECEMBER 29-31. At Déville. JANUARY 1. At Déville. JANUARY 2. At Déville, and we visited the monastery of Bondeville.[76] JANUARY 3. At St-Matthieu in Rouen.

JANUARY 4. We visited the monastery of St-Amand-de-Rouen,[77] where we found forty-one veiled nuns and six due to take the veil.[78] They make profession only when they receive the archbishop's blessing. We ordered that when they had reached the age for taking the vows, they should wait yet another year before making profession. Sometimes they sing the Hours of the Blessed Mary and the Suffrages[79] with too much haste and jumbling of the words; we enjoined them to sing these in such a way that those beginning a verse should wait to hear the end of the preceding verse, and those ending a verse should hear the commencement of the following

---

name tells its function. Documentary evidence of leprosaries in France is found as early as 1106 and they were probably in existence prior to that date. They were built outside the town or village and were communities with a life of their own. The Third Lateran Council (1179) decreed (canon 28) that they were to have their own chapels, served by either their own or a neighboring parish priest. They also had their own cemeteries. (Mansi, XXII, 230.) Admittance was through the local priest, who turned the formalities over to the bishop, who in turn was advised by a doctor. If the subject were found to be leprous, he or she was then formally separated from the village or town inhabitants in a ceremony which bears resemblance to the Mass of the Dead. Once committed, the ill person was to wear a special garb and was not to return to the villlage or town at any time. It was the task of the local priest to see they did not frequent local taverns. (Jean Imbert, Les Hôpitaux en droit canonique [Paris, 1947], 151-88.)

[76] St-Denis, a Cistercian abbey, founded c. 1150. (Cottineau, I, 419.)

[77] A Benedictine abbey founded c. 1030. (Cottineau, II, 2543-44.) It had been badly damaged by fire in August 1248, and when the flames spread the city of Rouen suffered heavy damage.

[78] For the ceremonial of the blessing of virgins (veiled nuns), see M. Andrieu, Le Pontifical romain au moyen âge, II, 414-18.

[79] The Suffrages were anthems and prayers to the saints said after Lauds and Vespers.

verse.[80] Item, the monastery has one priory, to wit, at Saane[-St-Just], where there are four professed nuns. Item, they have the patronage [81] of ten churches. There are three priests in perpetual residence. They confess five times a year.[82] They do not keep the rule of silence very well; we enjoined them to correct this. They eat meat freely in the infirmary, to wit, three times a week. Sometimes the healthy ones eat with the sick in the infirmary, two or three with one sick sister. They have chemises, use feather beds and sheets, and wear cloaks of rabbits, hares, cats,[83] and foxes; we utterly forbade the use of rabbit skins. The nuns sleep cinctured and in their chemises.[84] Each nun receives a measure of wine, but more is given to one than to another; we ordered that wine should be given to each according to her needs and in equal measure, and if one of them should without permission give a portion of her wine to another outside the house she should compelled by the abbess to go without wine the next day. The monastery has debts amounting to two hundred pounds and an income of one thousand pounds. The abbess does not give detailed accounts to the community at large; we ordered her to cast her accounts each quarter.

This day Nicholas of St-Laurent, priest at Etalleville, came before us and appealed from our jurisdiction to that of the Apostolic See in the following letter:

On the Monday following Christmas Day, you, the lord archbishop of Rouen, without reasonable cause, refused to confer the rectorship of the free and vacant church of St-Laurent upon me, Nicholas of St-Laurent, priest at Etalleville, when I was presented for the said church by William of St-Laurent, knight, who holds the right of advowson. You assumed that I was in some

[80] See the first statute of the reforming decrees of Peter the Venerable (Migne, *PL*, CLXXXIX, 1026), who complained of a like practice.

[81] That is, the monastery is the rector and the churches are served by vicars, who receive a stipend for their services. Usually, the rector received two thirds and the vicar one third of the parish revenue.

[82] Monthly confession was not common until the decrees of Pope Gregory IX. Cistercian lay brothers were to receive Communion seven times yearly, which, of course, required sacramental confession. (Guignard, *Monuments*, p. 281.)

[83] Monastic documents contain many comments on the religious' desire for luxury, especially in matters of clothing. It formed a part of St. Bernard's *Apologia* to William of St. Thierry. (Migne, *PL*, CLXXXII, 912-913). The cat mentioned here is the civet, the skin of which was and still is much sought after for commercial purposes.

[84] Religious slept in their habits, and were to wear their cinctures at all times (*Rule of St. Benedict*, Ch. 22). Eudes was objecting not to the cinctures but to the chemises, which were of linen and worn only by the rich.

way unsuitable, although there was nothing canonically deficient in me. This you should not have done, for your predecessor promoted me to Holy Orders and likewise conferred upon me the care of the Church of Etalleville. Feeling that I have been unjustly injured in this matter, I appeal from your jurisdiction, in writing to the Apostolic See. Furthermore, I appeal lest you should take any action to my detriment, as in conferring the said church upon another, and I request that *apostoli* be given to me.[85]

Although we need not honor an appeal of this kind, we thought that the *apostoli* which he had requested should be given to him.

JANUARY 5. We were at Bellencombre, at our own expense. JANUARY 6. At the same place, and at our own expense. JANUARY 7-11. At Aliermont. JANUARY 12. At Dieppe. [*No entry for January 13*]. JANUARY 14. At the same place.

JANUARY 15. We convoked and visited the priests of the deanery of Longueville[86] at St-Aubin-sous-Aliermont. We found that Richard, priest of Rouxmesnil, kept a certain woman for a long time and had a certain child by her; however, he was disciplined by the archdeacon, and the infamy has ceased. Item, the priest at Appeville is publicly known for drunkenness. Item, we found that the priest at Martigny, who is ill famed of incontinence, neither resides in his parish nor attends the deanery chapters. Item, the priest at Ste-Foy is ill famed of incontinence with a certain woman by whom he has had two sons, and the report is attested by several witnesses; he also sells his grain at harvest time. Item, the priest at St-Germain is ill famed of a certain woman who bore him a son; item, the priest of Le Petit-Torcy is ill famed of the wife of Walter of Laistre; item, the priests at Chapelle-du-Bourgay and at Bois-Robert are ill famed of incontinence. Item, the priest

---

[85] The *apostoli* were letters addressed on the request of the appellant by the judge whose sentence was appealed, to a judge of a higher court. See entry for December 28, 1248. This is an instance of an applicant for ecclesiastical office having an opinion of his own abilities which was at variance with the opinion of his superiors. The *apostoli* had their legal basis in Roman law (*Corp. jur. civ.*, *Digest* Lib. XLIX. Tit. 6. Lex. 1). Gratian reproduced the same text in his *Decretum* (c. II, q. VI, cap. XXI). A formula is reproduced in the 1584 (Lyons) edition of Gratian's *Decretum*, I, 673. Canon law on *apostoli* is to be found in the *Decretales* Lib. II. Tit. 28. cap. 39.

[86] Longueville, together with Eu, Envermeu, Foucarmont, Aumale, Neufchâtel-en-Bray, and Bures, were the component deaneries of the archdeaconate of Eu, diocese of Rouen. The archdeaconates of the diocese were Eu, Grand-Caux, Petit-Caux, Norman Vexin, French Vexin, and the "great archdeaconry" of Rouen (six in all). The deanery of Longueville had forty-two parishes and three chapels.

at Aubermesnil is ill famed of a certain woman; item, the same is true of
the priest at Appeville with respect to the wife of Reialle; item, the priests
at Arques [-la-Bataille] and at Archelles are said to be incontinent; item, the
priests at St-Honoré [-sur-Torcy], Appeville, Arques, La Frenaye, and Les
Authieux are publicly known for drunkenness. We warned and rebuked
them and threatened them that if they were found to be ill famed of these
matters again we would punish them severely. Item, some of the priests
of this deanery did not possess closed gowns,[87] and rode about in short capes;
we forbade absolutely the use of open capes and, under the penalty of twenty
shillings, we ordered them to procure closed gowns before Assumption Day.
Further, we forbade them to go any distance from their homes or to ride
without wearing their gowns, and we enjoined the dean, if they disobeyed,
to collect the above fine without any mercy. Item, there are some who do
not come to the deanery chapters. We enjoined the dean to exact the
penalty without remission.

This day we spent the night at Aliermont.

JANUARY 16. We visited the priests of the deanery of Bures, whom we
had convoked to Meulers. We found that Gilbert, rector of the church at
Freulleville, was ill famed of a certain unmarried woman; item, that the

---

[87] Black cloth or distinct robes do not seem to have been required for the clergy of
the parishes up to the eleventh century. The stole seems to have been the distinguishing mark of clerical attire. By the end of that same century the Council of Melfi
(canon 13) forbade clerics to wear sumptuous and slashed garments (Mansi, XX, 724).
Canon 4 of the Second Lateran Council (1139) forbade slashed and brightly colored
garments to be worn by the clergy. (*Ibid.*, XXI, 527). The canon was repeated at the
Council of Rheims (canon 2) in 1148 (*ibid.*, XXI, 714). The Council of Montpellier
(1195) ordered the rejection of gold and silver ornaments and also decreed that
priests, deacons and subdeacons should wear capes which were closed in front. Capes
worn when journeying to the town or village were to be long and closed. Some capes
were sleeveless, and this was forbidden by canon 3 of the Constitutions of Gallo
(1208) (*ibid.,* XXII, 764). Many local councils legislated on clerical attire: that all
clerics except bishops were to wear colors other than red and green; clerical garb
should reach the feet and not imitate the lay fashion of raising the garments (some
as far as the calf of the leg); tunics and capes should be closed in front. The Fourth
Lateran Council (1215) ordered (canon 16) that clerical garb should be neither too
long nor too short, nor, except for bishops, green or red, and should be closed in
front (*ibid.*, XXII, 1004-6). The same canon forbade sleeveless capes, but only for
those officiating. Evidently the lay style in capes was sleeveless, hence the canonical
insistence on the sleeved mantle or cape. The Council of Rouen (1235) legislated
(canon 36) on the clothes and shoes of the clergy (*ibid.*, XXIII, 378.) The above
formed the basis for the canonical legislation on clerical garb which Eudes endeavored
to enforce.

priest at Ricarville [-du-Val] [was ill famed] of one of his sisters-in-law; but both had been disciplined by the archdeacon. Item, the priest at Pommereval is publicly known and ill famed for frequenting taverns; he does not confess to the penitentiary[88] and is incontinent and a drunkard. Item, William, priest at Mesnières, is ill famed of engaging in trade, and he has farms to which he goes so often that this church services are neglected. Item, the priest at L'Hortier very rarely wears his gown, does not confess to the penitentiary, is grievously ill famed of incontinence with two women by whom he has had many children, and is drunken. Item, the priest at Bures, the dean's associate, is ill famed of a certain married woman. Item, the priest at Aulages is publicly known for drinking and for frequenting taverns. We warned them all as we had warned the priests of the deanery of Longueville; we issued the same orders anent the wearing of gowns and attendance at chapter, and we ordered the dean to exact the fines without mercy. Item, we found that a certain chaplain of Meulers sang a Mass on Christmas Eve for money.

This day we spent the night at Aliermont.

JANUARY 17. We stayed the night at Caule, at our own expense.

JANUARY 18. We visited the priests of the deanery of Aumale, whom we had convoked at Coupigny. We found that Master John, priest of Haudricourt, was ill famed of incontinence with Amelota and with Martina and, although disciplined by the archdeacon, has persisted in his evil conduct. Item, the priest at La Fresnoye is ill famed of incontinence with a certain Emily, a married woman of Aumale; he has been disciplined by the archdeacon. Item, the priest at St-Pierre-d'Aumale, is ill famed of a certain woman, now married, who is said to have borne him a son. Item, the priest of Morvillers is publicly known for his drunkenness and for frequenting taverns; item, he also exacts fees for blessing marriages. Item, the priest at Escles [is ill famed] of a certain unmarried woman. Item, the priest at Villers [is ill famed] of a certain unmarried woman; he was disciplined by the archdeacon. Item, Peter, the priest at St-Valéry, rents arable land for

---

[88] The penitentiary is the vicar-general of the bishop in matters pertaining to the sacrament of penance. His office was made official by the Fourth Lateran Council which decreed (canon 10) that bishops were to appoint aides for preaching, visitation, confession, and penance. The last named is the penitentiary (Mansi, XXII, 998-99). The chief penitentiary then appointed other confessors, with the permission and at the will of the bishop, who were to visit and hear the confessions of the parish clergy.

sowing. Robert of Puys, priest, is publicly known for engaging in trade;[89] he promised to give it up. We warned, rebuked, and threatened them all that if they did not correct their ways and if we should find them ill famed on the above faults, we would punish them more severely. Item, since some of the priests of this deanery rode horseback and appeared in public dressed in unseemly clothing, we instructed those who did not possess closed gowns to procure them before Assumption Day, under the penalty of twenty shillings, to be collected without mercy by the dean. Item, we forbade them to go any distance from their homes without a gown or to ride without one. We enjoined the dean to exact without fail a fine from those who did not attend the chapter meetings, unless they had some good reason for their absence.

This day we spent the night at Caule. We received a letter from the priest at Haudricourt and have inserted it on another page:

John, priest at Haudricourt, to all who may see this letter, greeting in the Lord. Know you that during his visitation of the deanery of Aumale the Reverend Father Eudes, by God's grace archbishop of Rouen, found me to be grievously defamed of incontinence, and after having been disciplined by the archdeacon of Eu I suffered a relapse. I have of my own free will promised the said archbishop that should he find me ill famed of this matter again, I would regard my church as resigned. In testimony whereof I place my seal on the present letter, as well as the sign[90] which I made on it with my own hand. Given at Envermeu, on the feast of the Conversion of Saint Paul, in the year of our Lord 1248.

[89] Trade was forbidden if it was for the purpose of personal enrichment. There is a vast literature, both conciliar and otherwise, on the subject, the substance of which is that trade for trade's sake, if it tends to enrich, is illicit; if engaged in solely for maintenance of person and status, then it is licit. This formed the basis of Gregory IX's formal decretal, "Following the decrees of the Fathers, we forbid, under pain of anathema, monks or clerics engaging in trade for the sake of gain" (*Decretales* Lib. III. Tit. 50. cap. 6). Actually, this prohibition was a reproduction of a letter of Pope Alexander III to the bishop of London (*ibid.*). The Fourth Lateran Council (1215) forbade (canon 16) clerics to undertake secular, especially dishonest, trading (Mansi, XXII, 1003-6).

[90] This may very well mean that the priest could not write his own name. See comparable entries for January 19. Note also that this document is dated the feast of the Conversion of St. Paul, January 25, but is entered in the Register under date of January 18 because it pertains to discipline meted out to a priest on that date, at the synod convoked at Coupigny. The priests' letters dated respectively January 19, 20 and 22 pertain to discipline meted out to priests at St-Léger in the deanery of Foucarmont on January 19, and are entered in the Register under that date.

JANUARY 19. We visited the priests of the deanery of Foucarmont, whom we convoked at St-Léger. We found that the priest at Nesle was defamed of a certain woman who is said to be with child by him; that he is engaged in trade; that he treated his own father, who holds the advowson of his church, in a most disgraceful manner;[91] that he fought a certain knight with drawn sword, making a great clamor, and was supported by a following of friends and relations. Item, the priest at Bazinval is ill famed of a certain woman, and although he has been disciplined by the archdeacon he continues to have relations with her and even takes her to the market; he also frequents taverns. Item, the priest at Vieux-Rouen is ill famed of incontinence, and although he was disciplined by the archdeacon in the matter of one woman he has not ceased to carry on with others; he goes about girt with a sword and wears unseemly clothes. Item, the priest at Bouafles does not wear a gown, is ill famed of a certain woman, and sells his grain at a rather advanced price because of the poor harvest. Item, the priest at Hesmy, reported to be a leper, is ill famed of incontinence. Item, the priest at Ecotigny plays at dice and quoits, and was unwilling to publish the marriage banns of a certain person who had not restored his father's legacy; he frequents taverns, is ill famed of incontinence, and continues his evil ways although he has been disciplined. Item, the priest at Mesnil-David is disobedient and has his children at home and a concubine elsewhere; item, two women fell upon each other in his house; they fought with each other and because one was fond of roses the other cut down the rose bushes. Item, the priest at St-Riquier [-en-Rivière] is [ill famed] of a certain married woman, his parishioner. Item, the priest at La Pierre [-sur-Yères] ran away with a certain woman and, although suspended, continued to celebrate Mass. We ordered the above to appear before us at a later day, when we will deal with them.

Item, Clement, priest at Monchaux, is reported to have children by a certain woman, but rumor also has it that he has reformed since he was disciplined. Item, the priest at St-Remy is publicly known for his inebriety; he does not wear his gown, plays at dice, and frequents taverns, where he often gets into fights. Item, the priest at Guilmerville does not reside in his parish as he should; he does not wear a gown and sometimes loses his clothes in the taverns. Item, Robert, priest of Campneuseville, does not own

---

[91] This was a sin against the fourth commandment, "Honor thy father and thy mother," and usually the offender had to undergo public penance.

a gown; item, John, priest at Hodeng, ill famed of Adina, was disciplined by the archdeacon; item, the priest at St-Martin-au-Bosc is an attorney and a vagebond; item, the priest at Foucarmont is publicly known for incontinence with a certain little old woman, and although he has been disciplined by the archdeacon it is said that he has relapsed; item, the priest at Pierrepont is a drunkard and plays at dice and quoits; item, Master Walter, priest at Grandcourt, is ill famed of his own niece and of drinking too much. We warned all these and threatened them that if we found them to be ill famed of these things again, we would punish them severely. Item, we issued the same orders concerning the wearing of gowns and attendance at chapter as in the other deaneries.

Item, we received the following letter from Gervaise, priest at St-Remy, which is sealed with his own seal:

Gervaise, priest of St-Remy, to all who may see the present letter, greeting in the Lord. Be it known to you that when the reverend father, Brother Eudes, by God's grace archbishop of Rouen, during his visitation of the deanery of Foucarmont convoked to meet at St.Léger, found me ill famed of gambling and of frequenting taverns and disciplined me, I promised and was willing, and still promise, that if he finds me in the future ill famed of these things and I am not able to purge myself, I shall regard my church as resigned. In testimony whereof I have placed my seal on the present letter together with the sign which I have made with my own hand. Given at St-Léger, the Tuesday following the octave of Epiphany, in the year of our Lord 1248.

Item, we received the following letter from Robert, priest of the church of Notre-Dame-de-Mortemer, whom we found to be grievously defamed of unseemly conduct, of pleading in the law courts, of frequenting taverns, and of renewed incontinence with a woman whom he had forsworn.

Robert, priest of the church of Notre-Dame-de-Mortemer, to all who may see the present letter, greeting in the Lord. Be it known to you that I, without any compulsion and of my own free will, have promised the reverend father, Brother Eudes, by God's grace archbishop of Rouen, that whenever he shall so instruct me I will resign my church and will regard it as resigned upon seeing his order. In testimony whereof I have sealed this letter with my seal and with the sign which I have made upon it with my own hand. Given at St-Léger, the Tuesday following the octave of the Epiphany, in the year of our Lord 1248.

Item the priest at Realcamp has once more fallen into sin with his servant, despite the fact that his relations with her have already been a matter of scandal, that he has been disciplined by the archdeacon, that he has forsworn her, and that he has promised to regard his church as automatically resigned if he should associate with her again. It is also a matter of scandal that he sometimes puts aside his garments in the tavern. Item, Robert, priest of Campneuseville, has no gown; he admitted it. We declared the said priest to be *ipso facto* deprived of the aforesaid church.

Item, we found that the priest at Mesnil-David, publicly known for his incontinence and the begetting of many children, who has often been disciplined by the archdeacon, has relapsed; and it is said that he celebrated Mass while under suspension. Wherefore, we ordered him that he must purge himself of these charges before the law or we would institute legal proceedings against him. He replied that he would like to have legal advice on the matter, and we appointed a day for him to give us an answer to the charges.

Item, we have the following letter from the priest at Nesle:

To all who may see this letter I, William, priest at Nesle, give greeting in the Lord. When the Reverend Father Eudes, by God's grace archbishop of Rouen, found me during his visitation of the deanery of Foucarmont to be grievously defamed of incontinence, of inebriety, and of quarreling, I, of my own free will promised him and still do promise that if he should again find me again ill famed for these things I would *ipso facto* regard my church as resigned. In witness and testimony whereof I have placed my seal on this letter, together with the sign which I have made on it with my own hand. Given at Aliermont Saturday, the feast of St. Vincent, in the year of our Lord 1248.

Item, we have the following letter from the priest at Vieux-Rouen:

To all who may see this letter Matthew, parson at Vieux-Rouen, gives greeting in the Lord. Be it known to you that when the reverend father, Brother Eudes, by God's grace archbishop of Rouen, found me during his visitation of the deanery of Foucarmont to be defamed of incontinence and to have been disciplined for this upon other occasions, I voluntarily promised him that if he should again find me delinquent in this matter and I should be unable to purge myself, I would regard my church as resigned from that time on. In testimony whereof, I have requested that this letter be sealed with the seal of the dean of Foucarmont, since my own seal is not at hand. Given at Aliermont the Thursway the feasts of Saints Fabian and Sebastian in the year of our Lord 1248.

This day we spent the night at Caule.

JANUARY 20. We visited the deanery of Neufchâtel, convoking the priests of that deanery to Lucy. We found that the priest at Ormesnil is defamed of the daughter of a certain lady; he has been disciplined by the archdeacon and has sworn to regard his church as resigned. Item, Adam, the priest at Nesle [-Hodeng] was disciplined by the archdeacon for drunkenness and incontinence. Item, the priest at Sommery does not keep residence in his church as he should and goes riding about as a vagabond. Item, the priest at Mesnil-Mauger is reported to buy and sell horses and other commodities. Item, the priest at Ménonval is ill famed of a certain woman. Item, the priest at Fesques attends neither [deanery] chapters nor synods. Item, Master Robert of Houssaye, parson at Conteville, is publicly known for drunkenness, incontinence, squandering, and annoying his parishioners, and for nonresidence. Item, the priest at Maucomble attends the assizes and courts held by laymen. Item, the priest at Lucy exacts thirteen pence from every churched woman, and if a child die before the churching, he does not wish to receive the mother for churching until she shall have paid thirteen pence.[92] Item, the priest at Haucourt buys and holds farms from the abbess of Bival; the priest at Noyers has no gown; the priest at Louvicamp keeps hunting dogs; the priests at Sausseuzemare and at Beaubec have no gowns. We warned them as we had done in the other deaneries, and we imposed a penalty for failure to wear a gown and enjoined the dean to exact this penalty without mercy. This day, we spent the night at Aliermont.

JANUARY 21. At Aliermont. This day we passed the following sentence upon Walter Charue for his part in the affair at Aliermont:

[92] Actually, there were two blessings in this ceremony of purification. The first occurred when the mother was still in bed after the birth of the child. The second occurred in the church. This was the ancient discipline of the church as attested by Gregory the Great, writing to St. Augustine of Canterbury (Migne, PL, LXXVII, 1193-94). A letter of Innocent III in 1214 to the Archbishop of Armagh on the subject found its way into the Decretals (Decretales Lib. III. Tit. 47. cap. 1). Mediaeval ceremonial ritual demanded that the woman come to the door of the church and be met by the priest, who recited Psalm 23, 112, 120, or 122. Then he took her by the hand, led her into the church, saying, "Enter the Temple of the Living God, and pray to the Son of the Virgin Mary who gave you fecundity and the bringing forth of a child," etc. If Mass was to be celebrated, he said the Mass of the Purification of the Blessed Virgin. He then recited more prayers and gave her his blessing, sprinkling her with holy water. (D. Franz, Die kirchlichen Benediktionen im Mittelalter [Freiburg, 1909], II, 232.) No fees were to be charged, but if the woman wished to make an offering the priest was free to accept it.

Since you, Walter Charue, bound by sentence of excommunication as a result of the crime perpetrated at Aliermont by you, along with the commune of Gamaches and several others, have sworn to obey our orders, we impose the following sentence upon you, to wit:

In consequence of the oath on the Sacrament given to us you shall pay damages to the extent of twelve hundred pounds, four shillings, and one penny of Tours, as already determined by inquest, to our servants, and this money shall be paid at Aliermont before Easter. Further, you shall pay thirty pounds of Tours to the woman whose son was killed. Item, to the priest at St-Aubin for damages to his church, thirty pounds of Tours. Item to Nicolas, for divers injuries suffered by him, one hundred shillings. Further since there are many claims for damages which have not as yet been investigated, and as new complaints crowd in upon us every day, we require you to place in our hands one hundred pounds of Tours, from which the said claims shall be settled, or, if anything remains, to be used at our discretion. And we enjoin that these items shall be paid to our servants here, at our manor, and before Easter.

We further enjoin you, by virtue of your oath on the Sacrament, to make twelve solemn or Sunday processions, accompanied by eleven prominent men distinguished by their wealth, birth, or office; that is to say, leaders in their communities. The processions are to be made in the following manner: your eleven associates shall walk with bared heads and feet, clad only in shirt and trunk-hose; you shall walk with bared feet and head, clad in linen drawers and haircloth shirt. Each of you shall carry a wand in his hand and shall receive discipline from priests when the processions are completed. At the time of each procession the people shall be informed of the offense which is being thus atoned. The processions are to be made to the following places: one to the cathedral at Rouen; one to the cathedral at Evreux; one to the cathedral at Lisieux; one to the cathedral at Beauvais; one to the cathedral at Amiens; three to the church at Aliermont, walking with bared feet all the way from the manorial limits to the church; one to the church at St-Aubin; one to St-Vaast; one to the cathedral at Dreux; and one to the cathedral at Gamaches.[93]

By virtue of the said oath, we enjoin you to take all possible precautions that, on the occasion of these processions, no harm shall befall the archbishop of Rouen or his men, either in person or in goods.

We further desire that these processions shall be completed within eight months, unless you are able, on oath, to allege and legally prove some hin-

[93] This was public penance for a public fault, penalty for which was excommunication. Probably Walter and his companions had rifled the archiepiscopal palace and inflicted damage on the manor on the death of Eudes' predecessor. See entry for September 24, 1248.

drance. If it should happen that one of the eleven men should fall sick so that you can in no way fulfill the prescribed sentence, you shall substitute another of a rank equal to that described. But if you can state and prove legally some hindrance we enjoin you by that same oath that within a month after you have been freed from the said hindrance you will begin to fulfill eight processional requirements for eight continuous months.

JANUARY 22. We visited the deanery of Eu at Greny. We found that the priest at Assigny was ill famed of a woman from Meulers and of two sisters. We have a letter from him:

To all who may see this letter I, Baldrick, priest at Assigny, give eternal greeting in the Lord Jesus Christ. Be it known to you that when the Reverend Father Eudes, by God's grace archbishop of Rouen, during his visitation of the deanery of Eu found me to be grievously defamed of incontinence, I promised and still promise him, that should I lapse again, or should he find me again ill famed of these things, I will on the strength of this alone regard my church as resigned. In testimony whereof, I have placed my seal on the present letter, together with the sign which I have made with my own hand. Given at Greny, on the feast of St. Vincent, in the year of our Lord 1248.

Item, we found that the priest at Penly is publicly known for his incontinence with his maidservent and with two others who have borne him two children; item, he is publicly known for his drunkenness; he sells his wine, and gets his parishioners drunk. The same priest at Penly swore to us at our manor of Aliermont, and in the presence of the dean of Eu, Geoffrey, priest at Neuville, the chaplain of the archdeacon of Eu, Master Peter of St-Germain, and Master Stephen of Gien, our clerks, that should we again find him ill famed of these matters, he would *ipso facto* regard his church as resigned. Item, we found the priest at Auberville to be seriously and publicly known for incontinence and to have caused a certain woman to marry one of his servants that he might have freer access to her; item, there is also a rumor concerning an Englishwoman whom he has kept for some time and with whom he had sinned again after he had been disciplined by the archdeacon; item, there is also the daughter of a certain poor woman who lives near the cross.[94] He swore to us that if we should find him again ill famed of the vice of incontinence or of notable remissnes of church duties, for he

---

[94] A reference to the crosses which are to be found, even today, at the crossroads of France.

has not resided in his church as he ought, we would *ipso facto* regard his church as resigned.

Item, the dean is defamed of incontinence, and especially with the wife of the knight of his village; also of extortion, and he is said to have taken forty shillings from the priest at Assigny to overlook the latter's incontinence; item, at Assigny, he churched two prostitutes as though they were virtuous women in order that he might have to do with them;[95] he tries major cases;[96] we will remove him at the right time. Item, the priest at Val-du-Roi, who is at present overseas, is habitually incontinent and, although he has been disciplined three or four times, has again fallen into sin. Item, we have received the following letter from the priest at Cuverville:

To all who may see this letter I, Robert, priest at Cuverville, send eternal greeting in the Lord. I make it known to you that when the Reverend Father Eudes, by God's grace archbishop of Rouen, during his visitation to the deanery of Eu had found me to be seriously defamed of incontinence even after I had received discipline from the venerable archdeacon of Eu, I promised him of my own free will, and still promise, that I would resign my church at Cuverville at the will of the archbishop, and whenever he should ask me to do so. In witness and testimony whereof I have affixed my seal to this letter, together with the sign which I have made thereon with my own hand. Given at Aliermont the Saturday following the feast of St. Vincent, in the year of our Lord 1248.

Item, the priest at Greny is publicly known for incontinence. Item, the priest at St-Sulpice is publicly known for incontinence; he has been disciplined and placed under suspension. Item, the prior of Criel is known to engage in trade; he sells rams. Item, the priest at St-Aignan wears unseemly clothing and is publicly known for incontinence with the wife of Barbarelli of Eu. Item, the priest at Belmesnil [is known] for selling cider, grain, and salt. Item, it is said that the priest at Maraise has a servant-concubine. Item, it is rumored that the priest at Biville sells wine.

This day we spent the night at Aliermont.

JANUARY 23-26. At Aliermont.

---

[95] Prostitutes were excommunicated and could not be churched until absolved. The dean evidently did not have such jurisdiction. Prostitutes wore a special garb and lived in a separate quarter of the town.

[96] Cases specially reserved for absolution to the Holy See or to the local ordinary. (See "Causes majeures," *Dict. de droit canon.*, III, 59-63.)

JANUARY 27. We visited the deanery of Envermeu at Envermeu. We found Reginald, priest at Fréauville, grievously defamed of a certain woman who lives at Pommereval; we have this letter from him:

To all who may see this letter Reginald, priest at Fréauville, sends greeting in the Lord. Know that when the Reverend Father, Brother Eudes, by God's grace archbishop of Rouen, visited the deanery of Envermeu and found me ill famed of incontinence, I promised him in all good faith that should he find me of a certainty ill famed of this matter again and I could not purge myself I would regard my church as resigned. In testimony whereof I have placed my seal on this letter, together with the sign which I have made thereon with my own hand. Given at Envermeu on the feast of the Conversion of Saint Paul, 1248.

Item, René, priest at [St-Pierre-de-] Jonquières, is publicly known for his inebriety. Item, the priest at Les Ifs is mentioned in connection with a certain woman who bore him a child; but he has been disciplined by the archdeacon. Item, William and Ralph, priests at Bailly, are publicly known for their drunkenness; they were corrected by the archdeacon. Item, Robert, priest at Elchiny, [is publicly known] for engaging in trade and for accepting rents. Item, the priest at St-Sulpice is a drunkard. Item, the priest at Sauchy-au-Bosc celebrates Mass though he is under suspension and is ill famed of a woman from Bellengreville and of another from Coqueréamont. Item, vigils are held in his church every Saturday; we ordered the church to be closed at night and forbade anyone to keep vigil there.[97] Item, the priest at Sauchay-le-Bas is a drunkard. Item, the priest at Notre-Dame at Envermeu is gravely and publicly known for incontinence with two women, and there are several others; he still persists in his evil ways and is also noted for drunkenness. Item, the priest at . . . [lacuna in MS] is known to be incontinent, but he has been disciplined. Item, the priest at St-Martin-en-Campagne sells hemp. Item, the priest at Belleville has ships on the sea; he is also ill famed of Bureta, and of frequenting taverns. Item, Vinquenel, chaplain at Bracquemont, is a drunkard. Item, the priest at Martin-Eglise is a drunkard; he has been twice disciplined and has promised the archdeacon that if he should relapse he would regard his church as resigned.

[97] Originally these were "watches," beginning on Saturday night in anticipation of Sunday's services. ("Vigiles," Dict. d'arch. chrét. et de lit., XV², 3108-13.) In the West, they had got out of hand and were marked more by fun and frolic than by devotion. Many councils forbade them, for exemple that of Rouen (1231), which legislated (canon 15) that "vigils were not to be held in churches, except on the feast of the saint of the church." (Mansi, XXIII, 216.)

Item, he is ill famed of incontinence. Item, the chaplain at Douvrend is publicly known for inebriety. Item, the priest at St-Laurent-le-Petit is publicly known for incontinence and for selling the sacraments. Item, the priest at Etrans [is publicly known] for engaging in trade. Item, the priest at Bailleul does not sing Vespers in his church; we enjoined him to sing them every day in his church at Bailleul.

We warned them all and threatened them with severe punishment if we were to find them ill famed of similar offenses in the future. Item, we decreed that each one who did not possess a gown by the middle of August should be fined twenty shillings, and we enjoined the dean to collect this fine without remission. Item, we enjoined and decreed that they should hold the Kalends[98] regularly as is done in the other deaneries, and we enjoined the dean to exact a fine from absentees, and to do this without mercy.

This day we spent the night at Aliermont.

JANUARY 28. We visited the deanery of Bacqueville at Creppeville. We found that the priest at Omonville was ill famed of incontinence, wore unseemly clothes, and quarreled with his parishioners; we have a letter from him which is copied on folio 124.[99] Item, the priest at Auppegard is quarrelsome and scatterbrained, and brawls with his parishioners. Item, the priest at Dènestanville is ill famed of the wife of Gerard of Caux; he has been disciplined. Richard, priest at Calleville, has received discipline for his heavy drinking, but he keeps it up. Item, his associate drinks likewise and is publicly known for incontinence with one of his parishioners. Item, the chaplain of the leper hospital at Auffay does not reside in the church and, although cited, has not appeared.[100] Item, the priest at Benouville does not reside in the rectory. Item, the priest at Baudribosc wears unseemly clothing, conducts himself like a soldier, and is in the habit of taking charge of the lances at tournaments; he does not reside in his church and does not attend the chapters. Item, the priest at Bertreville is incontinent. Item, the priest

---

[98] These were chapters or synods held every month.

[99] The letter to which Eudes refers states that the priest, Hugh of Omonville, offered to resign his church if again found guilty of incontinence. Eudes added, "We sent him to Rome." (Bonnin, p. 661.)

[100] This was apparently an institution of lay foundation. These were served by chaplains appointed with the approbation of the local ecclesiastical authorities. They thus come under the jurisdiction of the local ordinary, who in this case was Eudes, acting in his capacity as bishop of the diocese of Rouen and as archbishop of the archdiocese of Rouen.

at Biville is publicly known for incontinence and drinking; he followed a certain woman through the fields that he might have to do with her. Item, the priest at Imbleville has been disciplined because of a certain woman, and he promised the archdeacon that should he relapse he would regard his church as resigned; item, he is ill famed for engaging in trade. Item, the priest at [Les]-Mesnil is a drunkard and quarrels when he drinks. We warned them and threatened them with heavy punishment should we find them again ill famed of these matters. Item, we made the same regulations concerning gowns and chapters as we had done in other deaneries.

This day we spent the night at Longueville, at our own expense.

JANUARY 29. At St-Just, where we visited the deanery of Brachy. We found the priest at Royville to be ill famed of incontinence with a stone-cutter's wife, who is said to have borne him a child; item, it is said that he has many other children; he is nonresident, plays ball, is nonresident [sic], and rides about clad in an open cape. We have a letter from him which is entered on folio 125.[101] Item, the priest at Gonnetot is ill famed of two women; he went to see the Pope because of this,[102] and it is said that he fell into sin again after his return; item, concerning a certain woman from Waltot. Item, the priest at Venestanville is ill famed of incontinence with one of his parishioners, whose husband, as a result, has gone overseas; he has kept this woman for eight years and she is now pregnant; item, he plays dice and drinks too much; he haunts the taverns, does not keep adequate residence in his parish and rides his horse at will about the country. The penalty which we have imposed upon him is entered on folio 125.[103] Item, the priest at Brachy is [ill famed] of a certain woman, and since she has foresworn his house he goes to eat with her and has his provisions and grain carried there. The chaplain at Brachy frequents taverns. Simon, priest at St-Just, is quarrelsome and argumentative. Item, the priest at Vibeuf frequents taverns and drinks up to the gullet. Item, the priest at Rainfreville drinks too much. The priest at Offranville does not keep satisfactory

[101] The letter promised resignation of his church should he be found guilty of further lapses into incontinence. (Bonnin, p. 649.)

[102] Eudes does not give details on this priest's reason for going to Rome. Probably he had been tried and found guilty in an ecclesiastical court and had been ordered to seek absolution in Rome. This may be an instance of reserved cases. See entry for January 22, above, note 96.

[103] This particular case is not mentioned in the Diffamationes printed in Bonnin, nor is it in the original MS.

residence and went to England without permission. Item, the priest at Ouville has his daughter at home despite the synodal prohibition.[104] Item, the priest at Bourville is a drunkard and is quarrelsome and belligerent. Item, Henry of Avremesnil is ill famed of incontinence. Item, Walter, parson of St-Just, is ill famed of Matilda of Caletot. Item, the priest at Gruchet, being incontinent and disciplined there for, is said to have sinned again. He had a child by a certain woman; the child was sent to be baptized at Luneray. Item, Ralph priest at Essarts, is seriously ill famed of incontinence. Item, the parson of Reuville does not reside in his church. Item, the priest at Gueures il ill famed of a certain woman. Item, Lawrence, priest at Longueil, is keeping Beatrice Valeran, the wife of a man who is outside the country, and has had a child by her.

This day we spent the night at Amfreville, at our own expense.

JANUARY 30. At Amfreville. We visited the deanery of Canville. We found that Adam, parson of Yvecrique, does not reside in his church; he was defamed of the wife of Richard Rufus and of another woman who lives at Vanloyche and who has had a child by him; he frequents taverns though he has wine in his own house; he does not attend the chapters; he is rebellious toward the dean. Item, Master Andrew of Etoutteville is nonresident and quarrels with his parishioners. Master John of Ermenouville [is ill famed] of a certain woman, and because of her he promised to regard his church as resigned should we later find him again ill famed in this matter. Item, the priest at Houdetot does not reside in his church. Two brothers [religious] at Héricourt are drunkards. Item, the priest at Hocqueville frequents taverns. Item, Eustace, priest at Cherville, is a drunkard and, although disciplined, has relapsed; item, he buys more wine than he needs and sells it again. Item, the priest at Hautot is a drunkard. Item, the priest at Fultot does not reside in his church as he ought. Item, the priest at Anglesqueville is ill famed of one of his maidservants. Item, the priest at Flamanvillette is drunken. Item, it is rumored that the priest at Cailleville sometimes buys wine and then resells it. Item, it is rumored that the priest at Iclon keeps his child at home. Item, Gilbert, priest at Canville, was ill famed of incontinence and swore in the presence of the archdeacon that he would regard his church as resigned if he were again ill famed of this.

[104] There is much conciliar legislation forbidding women, including mothers and sisters, to dwell in the homes of clerics. This particular prohibiton refers to canons 40 and 41 of the diocesan Council of Rouen (1235). (Mansi, XXIII, 379.)

Item, the rector of Riville does not present himself for Holy Orders.[105]

JANUARY 31. We came to Valmont[106] and stayed there at the expense of the monastery. We found that knights and laymen enter the cloister and linger about; we enjoined the abbot to do his best to keep them out. Sometimes the monks leave the cloister without permission. They have an income of one thousand pounds; about as much is owed to them as they owe.

FEBRUARY 1. At the same place, and at our own expense. FEBRUARY 2. At Caudebec, at our own expense. FEBRUARY 3-4. At Jumièges, at our own expense. FEBRUARY 5-6. At Ermentrouville, at our own expense. FEBRUARY 7. At Frênes. FEBRUARY 8. At Wy, where we received the measure of oats which the priest at Gadancourt owes us whenever we stay there. FEBRUARY 9. At Cormeilles, in the diocese of Paris, at our own expense. FEBRUARY 10-12. At Paris, at the shrine of Ste-Geneviève. FEBRUARY 13. We were at at Argenteuil, at our own expense. FEBRUARY 14. At Wy, at our own expense. FEBRUARY 15. At Frênes, at out own expense. FEBRUARY 16. At Rouen, at our own expense. FEBRUARY 17. At the same, and this day, being Ash Wednesday, we drove the penitents from the church.[107] FEBRUARY 18-21. At Déville, at our own expense.

FEBRUARY 22. At the same, and this day we visited the deanery of Rouen. We found the priest at St-Sauveur to be ill famed of incontinence with Ermenburge of Bosc and to have been disciplined for this. Item, he promised the archdeacon to regard his church as resigned if he should sin again. Item, it is said that he has kept a woman shut up in his house for two days.

FEBRUARY 23. At the same place.

FEBRUARY 24. At the same place. This day we were at Cailly and visited

---

[105] This refers to major orders (subdeacon, deacon, priest), since he had to be the recipient of minor orders to receive a benefice and its fruits. This particular item is in accordance with canon 57 of the diocesan Council of Rouen (1235), wherein all clerics holding churches were to present themselves for orders at times of ordination. Those ordained were to reside in their churches, except by and with special archiepiscopal permission. Punishment was deprivation of the church. (Mansi, XXIII, 381.)

[106] A Benedictine abbey founded c. 1169. (Cottineau, II, 3289.)

[107] From the first days of the Church bishops imposed penances, heavy and light, to suit the offense. He who had committed grave and *public* sin had to undergo a *public* penance, appearing at the door of the church on Ash Wednesday, dressed in sackcloth and with bare feet, and prostrating himself on the earth. Those who were not to be absolved were driven away; those who were to be absolved were led back into the church. The ceremony is described in Regino, *Libri duo de ecclesiastica disciplina* (Migne, *PL*, CXXXII, 245-46). Eudes was carrying out the ancient canons on penance and penitents.

the deanery. We found that the priest at Grigneuseville has been disciplined by the archdeacon for his incontinence; we have a letter from him. Item, the priest at La Rue-St-Pierre has received discipline from the archdeacon because of a certain little old woman whom he has kept for a long time, also because of his son who lives with him and who is a violator of women, and because of his daughter who is living with him. The priest at Cordelleville is nonresident. We warned them about wearing gowns and attending chapters, under the penalty defined in other synods.

FEBRUARY 25. At the same.

FEBRUARY 26. At the same. This day we attended the chapter of Rouen. We dealt with Master William of Salmonville, canon, who retained by force some of the servants of our official[108] in his house. We received written notice that he would pay the fine. He paid us, and Master William of Saône, archdeacon in the French Vexin, was his surety.

FEBRUARY 27. At St-Matthieu. We conferred the sacrament of Holy Orders at Grandmont. FEBRUARY 28. At St-Matthieu-de-Rouen. *Reminiscere.*[109] MARCH 1. At Louviers.

MARCH 2. At the same. On this day and year appeared before us Sir Walter Dubois, knight; Sir William the Englishman, attorney for the lord of Pinterville; and Rabelle of Villette, for the purpose of obtaining from us a statement as to the rights which they claimed to have in our forest of Louviers. This day having been appointed for this business, in our presence William and Rabelle subjected themselvs to our investigation under the bond of the oath they had taken and by virtue of the obligations they owed to us and as our lieges, whether mediately or immediately, and consented and agreed that we should investigate the matter and, having made investigation,

---

[108] Strangely enough, the *officialis* (or vicar-general) of the bishop is not mentioned in Gregory IX's Decretals. Canons 9 and 10 of the Fourth Lateran Council (1215) formally introduced the *officialis* in the West, though many instances of some abbot appointing another to act as his vicar occur with relative frequency prior to 1215. Canon 9 (Mansi, XXII, 998) decreed that in centers of population where people differed in speech and liturgy, the local bishop could appoint as many vicars-general as would be necessary to care for their spiritual necessities. Probably this is a reference to the Fourth Crusade and the religious consequences of the capture of Constantinople. Canon 10 (*ibid.*, 998-99) exhorted bishops who were themselves unable to fulfill all their episcopal duties to take on preachers, penitentiaries, who would teach and visit the diocese in their name and in their place.

[109] The first word for the Introit for the Mass on the second Sunday of Lent. This is Psalm 24.

render them justice. We called before us our priests, sworn men and worthy of belief, namely, Michael le Bitaut and Master William Landry, canons of Rouen; Roger de Martry; the lord of Folaville; Geoffrey le Bitaut; Alan the forester; Nicholas the sergeant; Geoffrey the forester; Hervert the forester; Roger Boloiche; Peter Berselen; Richard of Hansey; William the Englishman; and Roger the mason. The truth on the foregoing matter having been inquired into and the advice of good men having been had, we determined the foregoing questions and decided in this manner, with Lord William and Rabelle present before us:

In the first place, we said that Sir Walter should have, through the delivery of our steward, whatever is necessary for building on his manor at Louviers: item, enough for building one mill with its appurtenances and one bridge; item, he is entitled to pannage[110] in the forest of Louviers for the use of his own house and of his men, and that without branding; item, we said that he might have from our steward one large and one small beech tree at Christmas time; item, concerning his petition to be permitted to lop off small branches, we said, in ending the matter, that he had no rights to receive any beyond the rights of our customary tenants.

Item, concerning Rabelle, in ending the matter, we stated that after making investigation we found that he had no right to exercise any customary rights in the said forest, nor ought he to have any by law.

Item, concerning the lord of Pinterville, we found that he has the right and custom to use of materials for building and enclosing his manor and for constructing one bridge; at Christmas he receives one large and one small beech tree from our steward; he has pannage for himself and his men; and he must do homage to us. However, we have not yet given our official decision concerning his rights.

These acts were drawn up in our presence, present being Sir Amaury of Meulan, knight; William, archdeacon of the French Vexin, diocese of Rouen; Ralph Pointel, our seneschal; masters Simon of Meinpicy and Peter of St-Germain; Stephen of Gien, dean of Louviers; Eudes, priest at Villers; William of Duyson; Miletus, our clerk; and many others.

MARCH 3. At Frênes. MARCH 4. At St-Germer-de-Flay,[111] at our own expence. MARCH 5. At St-Paul, near Beauvais. MARCH 6-7. At Chaumont, at our own expense.

---

[110] This was the right to put pigs in the forest for feeding.
[111] A Benedictine abbey in the diocese of Beauvais. (Cottineau, II, 2710.)

MARCH 8. At the same, and at our own expense. This day Hugh, sub-prior of St-Martin-de-Pontoise, and Dreux, prior of Tournus, came to us, bringing a letter from their convent, requesting us, since . . . [*lacuna in MS*] [Nicholas], their abbot, had lately died,[112] to give them permission to elect another; we granted their petition.

Item, this day we visited the deanery of Chaumont. We found that Giles, chaplain at Ivry-le-Temple, is ill famed of incontinence with the wife of Garner the carpenter. Item, the dean is ill famed of his maidservant. Item, the priest at Valdampierre does not keep proper residence in his parish as well as he should. Item, Martin, priest at Moulincourt, keeps dogs and goes hunting; he is ill famed of incontinence with Burgetta. Item, the priest at Flavacourt goes hunting. Item, the priest at Lattainville is ill famed of incontinence. Item, the priest at Berville is publicly known for his drinking. Item, the chaplain of Henonville, for drinking. We earnestly warned all these to abstain from such offenses. Item, Adam, priest at Triel, is ill famed of incontinence; we did not warn him for he was absent because of illness. Item, we issued them a general warning against riding or walking abroad without their closed capes, and we enjoined the dean to exact without mercy a fine of twenty shillings from everyone who did not have a closed cape by the time of the winter synod; even if they paid the fine they must buy one. Item, we enjoined the said dean to exact the same penalty, and with-out remission, from all who did not attend the chapters, unless they were absent for a reasonable cause.

MARCH 9. At Etrépagny. MARCH 10-16. At Déville.

MARCH 17. We were at La Salle-aux-Puelles[113] near Rouen, and we found during our visitation that they do not hold their chapter twice a week, as . . . [*lacuna in MS*], the archdeacon, had ordered. Item, lay folk constantly enter the cloisters, the kitchens, and the workrooms; they mingle with the sisters and talk with them without permission. Item, there is overmuch talking in the refectory. The prioress does not audit the accounts with the chapter. The measure of bread has been decreased. We ordered them to hold a chapter twice a week. We prohibited the entry of lay folk into the cloisters

---

[112] Abbot Nicholas II had died on March 5. His successor was Dreux, mentioned above.

[113] This was a leprosary at Petit-Quevilly (Cottineau, II, 2266) for women, founded in 1183 by Henry II of England, and was thereby a secular foundation. The nuns, in this case, were the staff. Thus there is no mention of the revenue of the house, since Eudes is concerned only with the spiritual problems of the nuns.

or workrooms, and we forbade the sisters to talk with any lay folk without receiving permission from the prioress. We forbade talking in the refectory or in the dormitory after Compline unless in a low voice, and briefly.

The ordinance concerning the measure or weight of bread, and concerning bread on Saturday, wine, and general provisions shall remain in force.

We spent the night at Déville, at our own expense.

MARCH 18. We were at the priory of Pré,[114] near Rouen. During our visitation we found that, because of the presence of workmen, the cloister is neither closed nor guarded. For the same reason silence is not observed except in the church and in the dormitory. They often eat with guests. They have cloaks of cat and fox. They do not hold chapter every day, partly because there are so few of them, and partly because of the workmen. They have an income of fifteen hundred pounds of Tours. They owe about five hundred pounds of Tours. They hold patronage of four churches. We issued no ordinances until a community should be formed, which ought to be instituted there before Whitsunday. The prior was not there this day.

This day we were at Déville, at our own expense.

MARCH 19. We visited the chapter at Rouen.[115] We found that they violated their ordinances by talking in the choir. Clerics wander about the church and gossip with women while the service is being celebrated. The statute concerning the processional into the choir is not observed. The Psalms are too briskly run through and sung without pauses. The regulation concerning the Recessional at the Office of the Dead is not observed. When they ask permission to go out they give no reason for their going. Item, the clerks-choral leave the choir without cause and before the end of the commenced Hour, and, in brief, they do not observe several other statutes which are inscribed on the sacristan's tablet. The temporalities are badly managed.

As for persons, we found that Master Michael of Bercy is defamed of incontinence. Item, Dom Benedict, of incontinence. Item, Master William of Salomonville, of incontinence, theft, and homicide. Item, Master John of St-Lô, of incontinence. Item, Master Alan, of frequenting taverns, of drunkenness, and of dicing. Item, Peter of Aulages, of trade. Master John

---

[114] This priory, also called Pré-Rouen, was almost destroyed by fire in 1243; hence the presence of workmen during Eudes' visit. (Cottineau, II, 2546.)

[115] This is the chapter of secular canons attached to the cathedral of Rouen. Practically every such chapter had its own statutes, regulating the *Opus Dei* (the recitation of which was one of their chief duties) and also spelling out in detail their legal relationship to the bishop or archbishop.

Bordez, of trade. It is said that he hands his money over to the merchants in order that he may make a profit. At our own will we sent the aforesaid persons to the archdeacons of Grand and Petit-Caux, and the chapter, through the archdeacons or someone else, should discipline them before the feast of the Assumption; otherwise then and there we would place our hands on them. We ordered them [i.e., the archdeacons] in writing to let us know in what manner discipline had been imposed. Item, we requested the chapter to pay us the procuration fee due for our visitation. The ordinance pertaining to the Divine Office shall continue in effect.

MARCH 19-20. This day we spent the night at Déville, at our own expense. MARCH 20-22. At the same.

MARCH 23. We visited the deanery of Pérrièrs at Champ-d'Oisel. We found that the priest at Champ-d'Oisel and the priest at St-Aubin-la-Rivière had been disciplined by the archdeacon for incontinence. The priest at Pîtres was ill famed of too much drinking; we warned him. Item, we issued the same instructions concerning closed gowns as in the other deaneries. We spent the night at Frênes.

MARCH 24-26. At Frênes. MARCH 27. At Rouen. MARCH 28. At the same. This day was Palm Sunday. MARCH 29-30. At Déville. MARCH 31. At Rouen. APRIL 1. At Rouen. This day we consecrated the holy chrism.[116] APRIL 2-3. At Rouen.

---

[116] Holy oils were used in conferring the sacraments of baptism, confirmation, extreme unction, and holy orders; also in the dedication of churches, coronation ceremonies, blessing baptismal fonts, and reconciliation of heretics. The oils for baptism, extreme unction, confirmation, and holy orders are blessed on Holy Thursday in an elaborate ceremony. (*Dic. d'arch. chrét. et de lit.*, VI², 2777-91.) The Holy Thursday ceremony is described in cols. 2787-90.

APRIL 4. At Rouen. This day was Easter. APRIL 5. We came to Déville. APRIL 6-10. At Déville. APRIL 11. At Bellencombre, at our own expense. APRIL 12-15. At Aliermont. APRIL 16. At Eu, at our own expense. APRIL 17. At Abbeville. APRIL 18. At Montreuil. APRIL 19. At Boulogne. APRIL 20. At Wissant. APRIL 21. We took ship and plied to Dover, and the same day we came to Canterbury and spent the night there. APRIL 22. At Rochester. APRIL 23-24. At London. APRIL 25. At London. This day we swore fealty to the king of England[1] for our land, and the king remitted the arrears due from this land from the date of our consecration. APRIL 26. At London. APRIL 27. At Guilford. APRIL 28. At Blendworth. APRIL 29. At the same, and we received the homages and oaths of our men. APRIL 30. At Windsor. MAY 1-3. At London. MAY 4. At Rochester. MAY 5. At Canterbury. MAY 6. At Dover. MAY 7. We crossed the Channel and spent the night at Wissant. MAY 8. At Boulogne. MAY 9. At Abbeville. MAY 10. At Eu, at our own expense. MAY 11. At Aliermont. MAY 12. At Dieppe. MAY 13-14. At Aliermont.

MAY 15. At the same. Ralph of Aulages, a parishioner of the church of St-Jacques-de-Neufchâtel, who had been excommunicated because of the clerical hearth tax,[2] promised to abide by the mandates of the Church, and he offered as guarantors Gilbert, priest at St-Jacques-de-Neufchâtel, William Vavasseur, and Giles le Bas, parishioners of the said church.

---

[1] Eudes swore fealthy to Henry III of England for the lands which as archbishop he held in Blendworth. An accounting of these lands made by Henry III to Eudes may be found in Bonnin, 777-79. The lands were held in the king's hands until Eudes performed the necessary feudal oath of fealty to the king. Eudes then journeyed to Blendworth, where he received the feudal homage of his own men. Eudes' journey is mentioned by Matthew Paris (*Chronica majora* [London, 1880], V, 72). Blendworth was in Sussex, south of Chichester, but is now inundated by the sea.

[2] *Foagium*, a tax imposed on the hearth of married people, or on those who had been married. The clergy was exempt. ("Foagium," in Du Cange, *Glossarium*, III, 328-29.) Evidently Ralph had refused to pay the tax. However, Professor Strayer states that "it was a payment made to the Duke for his foregoing his right to alter currency." (J. R. Strayer, *The Administration of Normandy under St. Louis* [Cambridge, 1932], p. 46.) See Lot and Fawtier, *Histoire*, II, 174-75, for further information.

On this day and at the same place. Julian Saracen, excommunicated by us on the complaint of the priest at St-Pierre-de-Neufchâtel, sought absolution from us and offered Dreux of Pontoise, the castellan of Mortemer, and Bartholomew Fergant of Longueville as surety that our penalty would be carried out. He swore to abide firmly by our decision, and we absolved him.

Item, Bartholomew Chevalier,[3] excommunicated because he did not wish to compel the said Julian to make satisfaction, sought this day to be absolved by us. He swore in our presence to abide by our decision and gave as pledges in our hand for the fine John of Roie, knight; the castellan of Arques; the castellan of Mortemer; and Bartholomew Fergant. We absolved him.

Item, he sought to be absolved and he offered the same men as pledges for our fine if he should be bound by any sentence either by us or our official. He also swore to abide by the mandates of the Church.

MAY 16-19. At Aliermont. MAY 20. At Bellencombre,[4] at our own expense. MAY 21. At Déville. MAY 22. At Rouen. MAY 23. At Rouen. On the Feast of Pentecost. MAY 24-28. At Déville. MAY 29. At Rouen. This day we conferred Holy Orders. MAY 30. At Rouen.

MAY 31. At the same place. We held a synod of the Greater Archdeanery of Rouen, and we decreed that because of the confusion resulting from the multitude attending the major synod, the synod of the Greater Archdeanery should always be held on Monday. JUNE 1. At Rouen. We held the major synod and spent the night at Frênes.

JUNE 2. At Pontoise, at our own expense. JUNE 3. At Chelles, at our own expense. JUNE 4. At Faremoutiers, at our own expense. JUNE 5. At Treses. JUNE 6-9. At Jardin-Notre-Dame. JUNE 10-12. At the Paraclete, in the diocese of Troyes.[5] JUNE 13. At Nailly, at the expense of the archbishop of Sens. JUNE 14. At Nemours. JUNE 15. Between Essones and Corbeil, in a hospice. JUNE 16-17. At Paris. JUNE 18. At Beaumont-sur-Oise. JUNE 19. At Verberie. JUNE 20. At Noyon. JUNE 21. At Roye.

---

[3] Bartholemew was bailiff of Caux.

[4] St-Martin or Le-Toussaint, a Benedictine priory dependent on St-Victor-en-Caux. (Cottineau, I, 332.)

[5] Eudes' sister Maria had just been elected abbess of this famous monastery, the Paraclete, founded by Abelard in 1131. (*Gallia Christiana*, XII, 575.) Possibly by courtesy of the Bishop of Troyes, he installed his sister while on this visit. (Cottineau, II, 2186.)

JUNE 22. At Amiens. JUNE 23-24. At Aumale, at our own expense. JUNE 27. At Gaillefontaine. JUNE 28. At Buhy.

JUNE 29. At Sérans,[6] where we spent the night. They owe us a procuration fee of seventy shillings of Paris, fodder for our horses, and food for our household. We made a visitation. We found that they use feather beds; we forbade them to use them. They have an income of one hundred forty pounds; they owe about thirty pounds. They owe us a procuration fee of seventy shillings of Paris.[7]

JUNE 30. We visited the deanery of Meulan at Chars. We found that the priest at Courdimanche has occasionally celebrated Mass though he is under suspension[8] and that he has kept a concubine; he rides horseback dressed in a short mantle, and he runs about too much. Item, the priest at Courcelles does not keep residence well nor is he in the habit of wearing his gown. Item, the priest at Hérouville only rarely wears a gown. Item, the priest at Valmondois sells his services; he is noted for having money, is contentious, and is given to drinking. Item, the priest at Vaux is a trader and had, and still has, a certain vineyard which he holds as security from a certain wastrel to whom he has loaned his too precious coins; he does not say his Hours well and sometimes he comes to Mass straight from his bed.[9] Item, the priest at Chars is ill famed of a certain widow; he runs about too much. Item, the priest at Courcelles does not keep residence well, nor does he wear a gown. Item, the priest at Longuesse is ill famed of Eugénie, his parishioner, and has had children by her; he promised us that if he should

---

[6] St-Denis-de-Serans was a Benedictine priory of St-Germer-de-Flay. (Cottineau, II, 3013.)

[7] This and other not unlike entries are difficult to understand, inasmuch as canon law forbade payment of money if food were demanded and received by the visitor, his entourage, and their horses. This was explicitly stated in Innocent IV's *Romana ecclesia* in 1245: "Procurationes autem recipiat, secundum quod est in canonibus constitutum; nullam autem pecuniam ipse vel aliquis de sua familia, occasione alicujus officii aut consuetudinis, seu quolibet alio modo earum nomine, sed in victualibus expensas tantum recipiat moderatas." (Mansi, XXIII, 668.) Note that Eudes' clerk enters the procuration fee twice.

[8] Suspension is a remedial punishment imposed on a cleric by his ecclesiastical superiors. It forbids him to exercise the spiritual functions of order or of jurisdiction. ("Suspense," *Dictionnaire de théologie catholique*, XIV[2], 2864-67; ed. A. Vacant and E. Mangenot [Paris, 1900-50], "Censures ecclésiastiques," II[2], 2113-36; "Peines ecclésiastiques; censures," XII, 624-50.)

[9] Canon 15 of the Council of Rouen (1235) forbade any priest to celebrate Mass without first having said the canonical Hours of Matins and Prime. (Mansi, XXIII, 375.)

be ill famed of these matters again he would regard his church as resigned.

We spent the night at Sérans, at our own expense.

JULY 1. We visited the priory at Parnes.[10]

JULY 2. At Parnes. We visited the priory and received our procuration from it. They have but one chalice and one missal.[11] They do not confess every month as required by the Statutes of Pope Gregory; we enjoined them to confess as the said Statutes require. They have an income of two hundred pounds; they owe about fifteen pounds. They use meat; we prohibited the eating of meat altogether, saving as the Rule permits. They use feather beds; we forbade the use of these, except in cases of necessity.

This day we visited the deanery of Magny, at Magny. We found that the priest at Lainville is a drunkard and incontinent. Item, the prior of Magny is grievously ill famed of a certain woman who is known as "The Mistress" and of the wife of a knight at Etres. The priest at Magny is ill famed of drinking too much, especially with laymen, and of incontinence, and about a year ago he begot a child because of it. Item, the priest at Genainville is ill famed of drunkenness and is useless to his church. The priest at Lierville does not attend the synods. Item, the priest at St-Clair is publicly known for drinking too much at the tavern. We warned them.

This day we visited the priory at Magny.[12] There are three canons there, and they have made profession in their order. They do not observe the fasts of the Rule very well. They receive money for clothing. They have an income of eighty pounds and are in debt up to eighty pounds. The prior is publicly known for incontinence, as we have already been informed by several priests during our visitation of the deanery of Magny. This day we visited the priory at Magny; there were three canons there. They do not observe the fasts of the Rule; they have money to buy clothes. They have an income of eighty pounds of Paris; they owe about eighty pounds.[13]

---

[10] St-Josse, which was a Benedictine priory of St-Evroult. (Cottineau, II, 2225.)

[11] This is a reference to the *missale plenum*, or one book in which were contained all the prayers of the Mass, including those said by the priest, deacon, subdeacon, and choir. It is the union into one book of several books and first appeared about the eleventh century. Prior to this each officiant had a book which contained only his special part. ("Missel," *Dict. d'arch. chrét. et de lit.*, XI², 1479-84.)

[12] A priory of Augustinian canons dependent on Hureil, diocese of Limoges. (Cottineau, II, 1707.) Eudes notes that all three canons have formally professed their vows in the order.

[13] Eudes' clerk repeated this entry for income and debts, as he often does.

From the prior of Magny,[14] whom we found grievously ill famed of incontinence, we have a letter stating that if any further ill fame should arise against him and is supported by the truth, or is of such a nature that he cannot purge himself, he will regard his priorate as resigned by that very fact. And this he swore to us. Item, he also swore to set out for Rome before the octave of the Assumption of the Blessed Virgin and to bring us a letter from any one of the Lord Pope's penitentiaries which made mention of this matter, and furthermore, neither to remain in the said priory nor to return to it until recalled by us.

JULY 3. We visited the priory of Notre-Dame-de-Chaumont.[15] Only two monks are there, and there should be three. They do not confess every month as the Statutes of Pope Gregory require. They have no written copy of their Rule, nor a copy of the Statutes. They do not hold chapter, nor do they receive the minor penances.[16] They do not keep the fasts of the Rule; they eat meat when it is not necessary. They use feather beds, though we had warned them about this before.[17] Instead[18] this time, and in the presence of their own abbot of St-Germer, we enjoined them with firmness to correct their deficiencies. They have an income of one hundred pounds; they owe about thirty pounds.

JULY 4. We visited the priory at Liancourt.[19] Three monks are there. They have an income of one hundred twenty pounds; they owe seventy pounds of Paris. We found some things amiss, to wit, that they eat meat and use feather beds though we had prohibited these things before.[20] This time we forbade them more severely. They owe us a procuration fee of only four pounds of Paris.

JULY 5. We visited the monastery of St-Martin-de-Pontoise,[21] where there

[14] Bonnin properly places this entry in its proper place (about the middle of folio 18) but in MS 1245 it is the last entry in folio 19, i.e., the entry for July 9.

[15] Chaumont-en-Vexin was a Benedictine priory of St-Germer-de-Flay. (Cottineau, I, 746.)

[16] Provision was made in the *Rule of St. Benedict* (Ch. 24) for making satisfaction for minor faults. The subject was not to eat with others at table, nor to intone a psalm or antiphone in the oratory.

[17] The account of Eudes' first visitation of this priory is lost.

[18] Eudes makes the distinction between the unwritten counsel or admonition offered during his last visitation and the written injunction of this visit.

[19] A Benedictine priory dependent on St-Père-de-Chartres. (Cottineau, I, 1600 1601.)

[20] The record of this visitation is also lost.

[21] A Benedictine abbey founded *c.* 1050. (Cottineau, II, 2334-35.)

are twenty-five monks. They have nine priories, and two monks are in each. On Sundays, women and laymen enter the cloister, marching in procession;[22] we forbade them to enter henceforth. They owe pensions up to sixteen pounds of Paris. They have the patronage of thirty churches. In the outside priories they eat meat at any time. We enjoined them to abstain from the eating of meat, save as the Rule permits. They owe about twelve hundred pounds; they have an income of one thousand pounds. We spent the night there and received our procuration.

JULY 6. We visited the Chapter of St-Mellon-de-Pontoise.[23] In the year that has elapsed they have not entirely fulfilled our injunctions.[24] The bells[25] have neither been cast nor hung. The treasurer, just as do the other canons,[26] dose not wish to give any money for the purchase of vestments. Statutory penalties are not exacted for offenses. We strictly enjoined the hebdomadary[27] to exact the required fines without remission and [said] that if he did not do this he should pay the fine from his own accounts. We forbade Henry, chaplain[28] of the king's altar, to give his services in other

[22] The presence of lay folk in so many cloisters is probably a remnant of the times when they had a greater participation in the liturgical life of the Church than in Eudes' day. This procession in question probably began some time in the past and had become customary.

[23] An abbey of Augustinian canons. St. Mellon, bishop of Rouen, who according to P. Gams (*Series episcoporum* [Ratisbon, 1873], p. 613), was bishop of that see, was buried there. (Cottineau, II, 2335.)

[24] This entry implies a previous visitation, but the record is lost.

[25] *Campane*; the Latin word for bell is usually *signum*. The word "clock" is first found in St. Willibald's *Life of St. Boniface* (Migne, *PL*, LXXXIX, 631): "ecclesiaeque cloccum in signum admonitionis sancti corporis." It was the word chiefly in use among chroniclers from the German region. The Campania region was famous throughout the Roman world for its work in bronze and kindred alloys, and this included the making of bells; hence the use of the word *campanae* or *campane*, bells. Bells occupied a strong place in the mediaeval concept of corporateness, and possession of a bell was a *sine qua non* for any kind of community. Not only were bells used in monasteries for calling the monks to the Hours sounding the alarm and calling for help in case of fire, but also they connoted the corporate character of institutions such as the communes.

[26] There were two main divisions of the canonical order; those attached to cathedrals (secular canons) and those who lived a community life under the Rule of St. Augustine (regular canons). The canons of St-Mellon-de-Pontoise fell into the second category.

[27] The official charged with a specific duty or assignment in a religious house for a week's duration.

[28] The word "chaplain" is derived from the name of those priests designated to guard the relics of St. Martin of Tours, principally his cloak (*capa*). In time they became clergy attached to the king, bishop, or lord; in this case, to the king. He was

churches, and we ordered him to sing Mass nowhere else except in his own church, and that assiduously. Item, since Henry, the aforementioned chaplain, had already been absent for five weeks, we ordered Master Richard of Tourny to seize the said altar on our authority if Henry remained away another three weeks. Item, we further ordered him [Richard] to compel the treasurer, by seizure of the revenues which he takes in the church of St-Mellon, to administer in that church the things he should administer in it. Item, Richard of Triel is ill famed of a certain prostitute; however, there was no great scandal, and we warned him to desist. Item, Master Robert is ill famed of the gardener's maidservant, who gave birth to a child and who is still lying in, but there is no great scandal; we warned him to desist. Item, he behaves in a somewhat unseemly fashion, walking barefoot before the door of a certain workroom where prostitutes frequently foregather; we warned him to desist from such things.

This day we spent the night at St-Martain, at the expense of the Chapter of St-Mellon.

This day we visited the prior of St-Pierre-de-Pontoise,[29] where there are five monks. The prior has the cure of souls of the monks. They have no written copy of the Statutes of Pope Gregory. They do not receive minor penances in chapter; indeed, they do not hold chapter. They have an income of two hundred pounds of Paris; they owe in debts up to four hundred pounds of Paris.

This day we visited the archdeanery of Pontoise. Two priests from St-Maclou appeared, as did the priests of St-André, St-Pierre, Ennery, Livilliers, Osny, Génicourt, and Puiseux. We found that the priest at St-Pierre is litigious and quarrels with his parishioners; we warned him to desist. This day, we spent the night at St-Martin-de-Pontoise. The chapter owes us for procuration one hundred shillings of Paris, as well as the use of feather beds, bed covers, and utensils for cooking.

JULY 7. At Juziers, where we visited the priory.[30] Six monks are there, but there should be seven. They do not observe the fasts of the Rule; they eat meat and use feather beds. We enjoined them to observe the fasts of

---

appointed by the patron of the church. In Henry's case, he was outside Eudes' jurisdiction, but he impinged thereon by celebrating Mass in the churches in Eudes' archdiocese.

[29] A Benedictine priory dependent on Bec, founded *c.* 1082. (Cottineau, II, 2335.)

[30] A Benedictine priory of St-Père-de-Chartres. (Cottineau, I, 1503.)

the Rule, to abstain from eating meat, and to give up the use of feather beds. They have an income of four hundred pounds of Tours; they owe nothing, since there is owed to them as much as they owe. We received our procuration there.

JULY 8. We visited the priory of St-Laurent-en-Cornecervine[31] and received our procuration. They are dependent upon the Josaphat monastery at Chartres.[32] Four monks are there; they do not hold chapter. They use feather beds. We enjoined them by all means to refrain from using feather beds, and to receive the minor penances in chapter. Their income amounts to one hundred pounds; they owe forty pounds.

JULY 9. We visited the priory at Villarceaux.[33] There are twenty-three nuns and three lay sisters in residence. They confess and receive Communion six times a year. They have an income of about one hundred pounds, and they owe about fifty pounds. The prioress casts her accounts only once a year. We ordered them to be cast every month by the prioress, by the priest of the house, and by two of the nuns especially elected by the community for this purpose. Item, because of their poor financial condition, we forbade them to receive any nun, even should the abbess [of St-Cyr] send one. There are four nuns who are professed only; namely, Eustacia, Comtesse, Ermengarde, and Petronilla. Many have pelisses of the furs of rabbits, hares, and foxes. They eat meat in the infirmary when there is no real need; silence is not well observed anywhere, nor is the cloister closed off. Joan of l'Aillerie at one time left the cloister and went to live with a certain man and had a child by him, and sometimes she goes out to see the said child; item, she is ill famed of a certain man called Gaillard. Isabelle la Treiche is always complaining about the prioress and finding fault with other sisters. The sister in charge of the cellars is ill famed of a man called Philip of Villarceaux. The prioress is too lenient; she does not administer discipline, nor does she arise [in time for Matins]. Joan of Hauteville wanders beyond the priory alone with Gaillard, and last year she had a child by him.

[31] Also called Le Cornouiller, a Benedictine priory (Cottineau, I, 880). This house has been confused with St-Laurent-en-Lyons, a house of Augustinian canons (*ibid.*, II, 2760).

[32] A Benedictine abbey founded in 1125 by Bishop Geoffrey of Chartres and his brother, Goselin. (Cottineau, I, 1488.)

[33] A Benedictine priory dependent on St-Cyr. (Cottineau, II, 3381.) For St-Cyr, see Cottineau, II, 2646. The relationship between St-Cyr and Villarceaux is made clear in Eudes' letter to the prioress of the latter.

The sister in charge of the cellars is ill famed of Philip of Villarceaux and of a certain priest of her own neighborhood.[34] Item, the subprioress, with Thomas the carter; Idonia, her sister, of Crispin, and this ill fame has arisen within the year. Item, the prior of Gisors often comes to this priory to see the said Idonia. Philippa of Rouen [is ill famed] of the priest at Chèrence, in the diocese of Chartres. Marguerite, the treasurer, is ill famed of Richard of Genainville, cleric. Agnes of Fontenay is ill famed of the priest at Guerreville, in the diocese of Chartres. La Toolière is ill famed of Sir Andrew of Mussy, knight. All of them let their hair grow down to the chin, and put saffron on their veils.[35] Jacqueline left the priory pregnant as a result of her relations with one of the chaplains, who was expelled because of this. Item, Agnes of Mont-Secours is ill famed of the same man. Ermengarde of Gisors and Joan of Hauteville came to blows. The prioress is drunk nearly every night. They manage their own affairs as best they can. The prioress does not get up for Matins, does not eat in the refectory, and does not correct excesses. We considered that an order should be drawn up concerning these things, and we despatched the following letter to the prioress and to the community:

Brother Eudes, by God's permission archbishop of Rouen, etc., to his beloved daughters the prioress and convent of Villarceaux, greeting, etc. Since we found, during our recent visit to your priory, many things that needed to be corrected in the interests of the general welfare, and since we are bound by the command of our office to bring back these things to the status of the Rule, in so far as we can, we will and order above all that the Divine Offices, both in the daytime and at night, be celebrated regularly and at the proper hours as the Rule demands, and that they should be sung with modulation[36] and as order demands; and as soon as the hour strikes all shall hasten at once to the church, unless they are sick or are excused by the prioress or her substitute. Item, we will and decree that the required silence be observed according to the Rule in the choir, the cloister, the dormitory and the refectory, and that there be no talking at all after Compline. Item, we will and decree that all shall sleep together in one dormitory at the same time and that all shall enter and leave it together, and that the keys of the dormitory and of the cloister shall be in trustworthy keeping, nor

[34] Note Eudes' repetition of the charge against the cellaress.

[35] For hair styles of the period see E. Viollet-le-Duc, *Dictionnaire du mobilier français* (Paris, 1872), III, 186-253. The provincial Council of Rouen (1231), canon 39, forbade sumptuous dress for monks, and undoubtedly the same applied to nuns. (Mansi, XXIII, 218.)

[36] Sung with notes, i.e., in plain or Gregorian chant.

shall anyone be permitted to enter the cloister until after Prime, and that suitable and competent inspectresses be appointed for the dormitory and such other places which pertain to the religious life.

Furthermore, we order that no lay or suspect person be received as a guest nor be permitted to sleep within the limits of the cloister. We strictly forbid any sister to leave the cloister without permission and without respectable companionship, nor shall such permission be granted without patent and reasonable cause. Item, we order that no one shall converse with any outsider or with any suspect person without permission and in the presence of some mature sister. We decree that no more saffron shall be placed on the veils, that the hair be not arrayed in vain curls, nor shall silver or metaled belts, or the skins of divers and wild animals be worn, nor shall the hair be allowed to grow down below the ears. Item, we forbid you to continue the farcical performances which have been your practice at the feast of the Innocents and of the Blessed Mary Magdalene, to dress up in wordly costumes, or to dance with each other or with lay folk,[37] neither shall you eat outside the refectory, nor shall you invite any layfolk to eat with you in the refectory. Item, we will and decree that if a quarrel among the sisters should progress from words to blows, each shall be equally blamed and punished in proportion to the violence and malice of the delinquent, by her who shall preside at the chapter on the following day.

Item, until your numbers are reduced to a point consistent with the resources of the priory, we strictly forbid you to receive without permission any expelled sister, any sister who has left the priory without permission, or any novice; nor, in this matter, shall you even obey your abbess [of St-Cyr]. We will and decree that every month, or at least every two months, the prioress shall make a faithful audit of receipts and expenditures, in the presence of three suitable and discreet sisters chosen by you in chapter and of the proctor or curator whom we shall give to you, and that twice a year, or at least once, a general audit of these items shall be made. We warn you collectively and severally that the common life which is to be observed in religion, in clothing, in food, and in other things is to be maintained; nor shall you of your own accord sell or give away any of those things which pertain to the common victualizing or clothing, and if you shall have received anything from friends, you shall apply it to the common use and not to your own. Item, we order and enjoin you to read this present letter in chapter at least once a month, and you may be assured that if we find you negligent in this respect we shall not with a benevolent eye overlook your faults but shall proceed all the more heavily against you with our hand. Given at Sausseuse, on the feast of the Exaltation of the Holy Cross, 1249.

[37] See Karl Young, *The Drama of the Mediaeval Church*, (Oxford, 1933), *passim*. For like prohibitions in the archdiocese of Rouen, see Mansi, XXIII, 377-78.

This day we spent the night at St-Martin-la-Garenne,[38] at the prior's expense, and made a visitation. Five monks are there. The cloister is not kept closed nor is silence observed. They do not receive the minor penances. They do not hold chapter; they omit it because of their small number. They do not have a copy of the Statutes of Pope Gregory; we enjoined them to get one. They have an income of about one hundred fifty pounds; they owe about twenty-five pounds. They have a large supply of food.

JULY 10. We visited the priory of Gasny,[39] where there are four monks. They eat meat and do not observe the fasts of the Rule. They sleep on feather beds. They neither hold chapter nor receive the minor penances. The priory is in the hands of the abbot, who furnishes everything to them.[40] We forbade them to eat meat, save in case of need, or to sleep on feather beds, unless it were necessary. Item, we enjoined them to observe the fasts of the Rule. We spent the night there at the expense of the priory.

JULY 11. We slept at Sausseuse,[41] at the expense of the priory, which we visited. Twelve canons are in residence, and twelve others are in the outside priories. They owe about two hundred sixty pounds; they have an income of four hundred pounds. One canon is dwelling by himself at Valcarbon. We enjoined the prior to give him another canon as a companion, or else recall him to the cloister.

JULY 12. We visited the deanery of Tourny. Master Walter, priest at Mézières, is the penitentiary. We found that the priest at Port-Mort is in the habit of frequenting taverns. The priest at Vernonnet is ill famed of an artisan's wife; item, he thrashed the provost of Vernonnet; he is contentious and quarrels with his parishioners. The priest at Panilleuse is a trader; he buys cows, and he is quarrelsome with his parishioners. The priest at Giverny is ill famed of a certain woman from Rouen, but she is now dead, and he was excommunicated for this for a long time. The priest at Guitry was robbed in a brothel at Les Andelys. The priest at Baudemont does not wear a gown, does not serve with zeal in his church, and is excommunicate. The priest at Bouafles was ill famed of incontinence. We warned them all.

[38] A Benedictine priory dependent on Bec. (Cottineau, II, 2795.)

[39] A Benedictine priory dependent on St-Ouen-de-Rouen. (Cottineau, I, 1258.)

[40] The abbot of St-Ouen-de-Rouen had the disposal of the financial resources of the priory for his own, not the community's use. In return, he was responsible for upkeep of the priory.

[41] A priory of Augustinian canons. (Cottineau, II, 2960-61.)

JULY 13-14. At Frênes.

JULY 15. We visited the deanery of Vesly at Ecouis. We found that Baldwin, chaplain of Herqueville, is ill famed of incontinence. Eudes, priest at Farceaux, is ill famed of a certain Agnes, who is unmarried; he neglects his badly managed church. William, chaplain of Douxmesnil, is ill famed of a certain woman. The priest at Daubeuf, excommunicated for failing to fulfill a crusading vow and to pay the royal tithe,[42] celebrates Mass although excommunicate; he is ill famed of theft and of harboring thieves; he does not keep residence well and neglects his badly managed church. Item, the priest at Noyers is ill famed of a certain woman who is now married; he is a belligerent person. The priest at Bacqueville is ill famed of many women but has none particularly his own. The rector of Herqueville makes no provision for services in his church. The priest at Cuverville sells the holy oils.[43] Peter, priest at Orgeville, confessed to holding and receiving rents. The priest at Chauvincourt is ill famed of incontinence. The priest at La Fontaine does not reside in his church. We warned all those who were present and ordered the dean to cite the priests at Noyers, Daubeuf, and Farceaux. Item, we found that the archdeacon, when visiting three or four churches, receives full procuration fee from each. Simon, priest at Chauvincourt, promised to regard his church as resigned if he should again be ill famed of incontinence and could not purge himself. We enjoined him to go to Rome before the Nativity of the Blessed Virgin and seek absolution from the sentence of Thomas Gallo,[44] both for this irregularity[45] and for the matter of the royal tithe. We enjoined the priest at La Fontaine to build a house in his parish before Christmas so that he might reside and remain there and serve his church as he ought to do. He promised to do this.

This day we spent the night at Frênes.

JULY 16. We visited the deanery of Gisors at Nojeon-le-Sec. Alverius of Ste-Austreberte has with him two nuns in his hermitage; he does not know how to celebrate Mass, and there is danger there. The priest at Puchay was ill famed of a woman called Joan; he was disciplined by the archdeacon.

---

[42] Titles levied by the Crown to support the Crusades of Louis IX.

[43] Oils most frequently used in the parish by the priest are those used at baptism and extreme unction.

[44] Thomas Gallo was an abbot of Verceil, where he died in 1226. He was a learned theologian, cardinal, and papal legate to France.

[45] The nature of the irregularities incurred is not mentioned. For irregularities, see *Dict. de droit canon.*, VI, 42-46.

The priest at Menesqueville is deaf. The priest at Nojeon-le-Sec is ill famed of Phillipa. The priest at Lorleau is ill famed of incontinence. The priest at St-Eloi is ill famed of a woman who lives in the parish of St-Denis-le-Ferment. The priest at Bérnouville used to go hunting with Sir William of Bézu. The dean tries major cases. The priest at St-Martin is ill famed of a woman at Etrépagny who is called Isabelle; he has confessed this. We warned him and all others. We also issued the same decree concerning gowns and attendance at synods that we had done in the other deaneries.

This day we spent the night at Frênes.

JULY 17. At Frênes.

JULY 18. We spent the night at Mont-Deux-Amants,[46] at the expense of the house, and visited it the next day. We found twelve canons there. They have an income of four hundred forty pounds; they owe about one hundred twenty pounds, and about as much is owed to them. One canon dwells alone in the chapel of Autye; we ordered that he be recalled to the cloister or that a companion be sent to him. Everything else we found in good condition.

JULY 19. We spent the night at Gouy, at our own expense. JULY 20-24. At Déville.

JULY 25. We spent the night at St-Victor-en-Caux, where there are nineteen monks.[47] They have two priories, one in England and one this side of the sea. They have an income of about six hundred pounds; they owe about two hundred pounds, but nothing at interest. We found that Robert of St-Amand is a grumbler and an inventor of lies; we warned him.

JULY 26. We spent the night at Auffay,[48] at the expense of the priory, which we visited. There are six monks there. They do not observe the fasts of the Rule very well; they eat meat when there is no need. They owe about one hundred forty pounds; they have an income of about four hundred pounds.

JULY 27-28. At Aliermont. JULY 29. At Dieppe. JULY 30-31. At Aliermont. AUGUST 1. At Longueville, where we dedicated the leper chapel of Longueville to the honor of the Blessed Mary Magdalene. AUGUST 2. At Wanchy, at the expense of the priory. No monks there.

[46] A priory of Augustinian canons. (Cottineau, I, 960-61.)

[47] A Benedictine abbey. (Cottineau, II, 2915-16.) The priory in England was at Clatford, Wiltshire. (W. Dugdale, *Monasticon Anglicanum* [London, 1846], VII, 1054-55.)

[48] A Benedictine priory dependent on St-Evroult. (Cottineau, I, 195.)

AUGUST 3. At Envermeu, at the expense of the priory. We found things in the same condition as at the other visitation, recorded on folio 3.[49] However, they do not eat meat now. There are only eight monks and there used to be twelve. They have no copy of the Statutes of Pope Gregory.

AUGUST 4. We were at Le Tréport, at the expense of the monastery. During our visitation we found twenty monks there. They have four priories. One monk is dwelling alone in the priory of Vireville; we ordered that a companion be sent to him or that he be recalled to the cloister. All but three are priests. They have no set time for making their confession; we ordered them to confess at least once a month, as the Statutes of Pope Gregory require. They have an income of eleven hundred pounds; they owe about four hundred eighty pounds, but nothing at interest. In pensions, they owe thirty shillings to one cleric, and to the son of Sir Robert of Beaumont ten pounds of Paris.

AUGUST 5. We were at Eu and visited there, finding thirty-two canons there. All but seven are priests. There is insufficient provision made for the sick in the infirmary. They have an income of twelve hundred pounds and owe about a thousand pounds. The cloister is not well kept, nor is silence well observed at table. Brother Robert of Dieppe is ill famed of incontinence. The kitchener was unwilling to perform his duties because the abbot took his horse away from him, though he did offer him another.

AUGUST 6. We were at Foucarmont, at the expense of the monastery.

AUGUST 7. At Beaubec, at the expense of the monastery. AUGUST 8. At Bures,[50] where there are two monks. They do not observe the fasts of the Rule, and they eat meat. We warned them to abstain from eating meat and to keep the fasts of the Rule. Their entire income goes to maintain the priory of Pré-Rouen. AUGUST 9. At Bures. AUGUST 10. At Dieppe. AUGUST 11. At Aliermont. AUGUST 12. At Bracquetuit. AUGUST 13. At Déville. AUGUST 14-15. At Rouen. AUGUST 16-17. At Déville.

AUGUST 18. We received our procuration at St-Lô [-de-Rouen], [51] and visited there on the morrow. We found sixteen canons there, and four in the outside priories: two at Thémericourt, and two at Cressy. Nine are priests. They confess three times a year; we enjoined them to confess at least four times a year. The closing of the cloister is not well attended to;

---

[49] See entry for July 31, 1248.

[50] A Benedictine subpriory dependent on Pré-Rouen. (Cottineau, I, 531.)

[51] An Augustinian priory founded c. 1114. (Cottineau, II, 2545.)

lay folk enter at will. We enjoined that the cloister be closed, or that a porter be placed at the door to prevent lay folk from entering freely. They have an income of seventy pounds and owe about fifty pounds; they owe seventeen and a half pounds in annual pensions. They have the patronage of about twelve churches. Robert, a canon, was publicly noted for incontinence with a married woman of Thémericourt; but that was almost two years ago, and he has been disciplined by the prior.

We must appoint someone on behalf of the community to hear the prior's auditing of his accounts.

AUGUST 19. At Mont-Ste-Catherine,[52] at the expense of the monastery. We did not make a visitation because of our ill health. AUGUST 20-21. At Mont-Ste-Catherine, at our own expense.

AUGUST 22. At Noyon-sur-Andelle,[53] which we visited. We found that some of the monks occasionally leave the cloister without permission; we forbade them to do this any further. Item, we found that faults were not well corrected in chapter; we ordered that they be corrected better. Item, we found that some were in the habit of using feather beds; we ordered these to be completely removed. Item, we found that they ate meat frequently and in common; we ordered them to abstain from eating meat. Item, we found that they do not observe the rules of silence very well. Item, we found that they have an income of five hundred pounds and owe about two hundred pounds.

AUGUST 23-24. We were at Frênes. AUGUST 25. At Frênes, where John of St-Martin, knight, presented to us Walter of St-Martin, cleric, for the chapel of St-Martin-le-Gaillard. We issued written orders to the dean of Eu to institute him in the said chapel. AUGUST 26. At Frênes. AUGUST 27. At l'Ile-Dieu,[54] a Premonstratensian foundation, at the expense of the monastery.

AUGUST 28. At Beaulieu,[55] where we found thirteen canons and ten in the outside priories. One canon is dwelling alone at Montmain. We ordered and enjoined that this be corrected. Item, two lay brothers are there. All

---

[52] A Benedictine abbey founded before 1030. (Cottineau, II, 2544-45.)

[53] A Benedictine priory of St-Evroult. (Cottineau, II, 2085.)

[54] A Premonstratensian abbey founded c. 1187 with the aid of King Henry II of England. (Cottineau, I, 1447-48.) Note that Eudes collects procuration but does not visit this house of an exempt order. See entries for July 17 and August 4, 1248.

[55] A priory of Augustinian canons dependent on St-Lô-de-Rouen. (Cottineau, I, 300.) It had a cell in England, Burne or Patrick's Bourne, in Kent. (Dugdale, VII, 1012.)

but one of the canons are priests. They have an income of four hundred fifty pounds; they owe about one hundred sixty pounds, but nothing at interest.

AUGUST 29. At Beaulieu, at our own expense.

AUGUST 30. At Déville. This day, at Pré-Rouen, Sir Nicholas of Hotot, knight, and ourself agreed to submit our quarrel to arbitration. We selected William, archdeacon of the French Vexin, Roger of Breuil, rector of the church at Bretteville, and Sir Robert of Beausemonchel, knight, to wit, that they inquire into the rights of both parties and after finding the truth of the affair, do right to each party to the quarrel. The arbiters promised in our presence to do this in good faith. We, for our part, on our word as archbishop, and Nicholas by oath, promised under penalty of fifty silver marks that without rancor or malevolence to anyone we would regard as valid and acceptable whatever decision the arbiters, or any two of them concurring on a verdict, should reach by arbitration.[56] The abbot of Bec, William of Rouvières; Ansellus of Bray and Nicholas of St-Germain, knights; and William of Cambremer, dean of St-Sépulcre-de-Caen, obliged themselves by their fealty as our sureties, each one obligating himself to a fifth part of the fine or of any defection therefrom, should there be any. Geoffrey Martel, William of Werneval, Peter of Canoville, William of Rouvières, and John of St-Martin, knights, were pledged in like form for Sir Nicholas.

AUGUST 31. At Déville. SEPTEMBER 1-2. At Frênes.

SEPTEMBER 3. We visited the church and chapter of Les Andelys.[57] There used to be eight small prebends;[58] they have been revoked so that there are but two. The two prebendaries are not in residence; we ordered the

---

[56] If there were two arbitrators and there was a divided opinion, there was no decision (*Corp. jur. can., Decretal. Greg. IX.* Lib. I. Tit. 43. cap. 1); but whenever possible, three arbiters were chosen, so that if there were not unanimity then the majority opinion held (*Ibid.*).

[57] Originally founded by Queen Clothilda *c.* 526 as a Benedictine abbey, it became a collegiate church of secular canons. (Cottineau, I, 96.)

[58] The *prebendarii* were those who did not have land of their own but were allowed a portion of the royal lands to support them (*Capitularia regum francorum,* I, Sect. II, 88, in *MGH*). The same use of the term is to be found applying to church lands (B. Guérard, *Cartulaire de l'abbaye de St-Bertin* [Paris, 1841], p. 103). The *prebendarii* were those to whom food was distributed, and this in sufficient quantity for their maintenance. Thus a prebend was a living, or the goods which went to make up that living.

incomes to be seized, since the incumbents are not in residence. The sacristan-matriculary[59] is sometimes quite late in sounding the Hours and is very slow about it; we enjoined him to sound them at the proper times, on pain of being punished by the dean. Two Masses should be celebrated there; but sometimes they are omitted through negligence of the hebdomadary; we decreed that the hebdomadary be fined eighteen pence for every time he omitted celebrating Mass, the fine to be divided among the others. They quarrel and mumble in the choir during the Divine Offices; we strictly forbade this. Item, some of them frequently walk about the church without a surplice,[60] wearing a rochet;[61] others go about in a gown without either surplice or rochet. They make no pauses when singing the Psalms; indeed, they sing them with too great haste; we enjoined the dean to correct this. When singing the psalms, some of them remain sitting in the choir when they should be standing; that is to say, on the feasts of the apostles and at double feasts.[62] We ordered the dean to correct this also. Item, we gave orders that at the time of the greater feasts the sacristan should have the lectern properly covered and should give ear to the lessons. Item, we ordered all those who held churches in the deanery of Les Andelys to attend the synod meetings each month, as they do in other deaneries, and that the dean should punish absentees at the rate of ten shillings for each absence.

This day we spent the night at Frénes, at our own expense.

SEPTEMBER 4. At Vesly, [63] at the expense of the priory. No monks there, though there should be three. SEPTEMBER 5. We sent to the prior of St-

---

[59] The *matricula* was a list of any kind, such as of poor to be fed, or of officials. The sacristan-matriculary was charged with drawing up an official list for sacred services and posting the names of the participants. He was in charge of the sacristy and all matters pertaining to Divine Service.

[60] For the reproduction of the surplice (a garment, usually white, worn over other garments) see Viollet-le-Duc, *Dictionnaire*, IV, 396-98.

[61] This was a white or red knee-length robe with sleeves; see Viollet-le-Duc, *Dictionnaire*, IV, 308-14.

[62] The classification of ecclesiastical feasts on an ascending scale are: simple or lowest rank of feast; semi-double or next higher rank (e.g., Sundays); double of the second class; and double of the first class. The differentiation between feasts is liturgical and is concerned mainly with the recitation of the Divine Office. Those were double feasts where the antiphons for the psalms in the *Opus Dei* were repeated in full before and after the psalm. Double-feast responses were the antiphons before and after the Lessons. For a semi-double or simple feast, only one half of the antiphon was recited before the psalm, but all of its was repeated after the psalm.

[63] A Benedictine priory dependent on Marmoutier. (Cottineau, II, 3351.)

Ouen-de-Gisors[64] to prepare our procuration for us. This he was unwilling to do. This day we spent the night at Chaumont, at our own expense. SEPTEMBER 6. At Pontoise, at our own expense. SEPTEMBER 9-10. At Pontoise, at our own expense. SEPTEMBER 11. At Gaillonet,[65] Premonstratensian Order, at the expense of the priory.

SEPTEMBER 12. At La Roche-Guyon,[66] and we made a thorough visitation.[67] There are four monk-priests. We found all spiritual matters to be in good condition. They informed us that since they had arrived but recently they knew little of the status of the temporalities of the house. At this visitation our associates, Brother William of Guerchy, Brother Walter of Manières, Master Stephen of Lorris, Adam of Sacre, and John of Charité, clerk, were present. Because the monks alleged that they owed us but forty shillings of Paris in procuration, we told them to put this in writing by letter, and we fixed the date for this within the feast of All Saints, at the latest, so that they would not be held for more.

SEPTEMBER 13-16. At Sausseuse, at our own expense. SEPTEMBER 17. At Frênes. SEPTEMBER 18. We conferred Holy Orders at Les Andelys and spent the night at Frênes. SEPTEMBER 19-20. At Sausseuse, at our own expense. SEPTEMBER 21. At Gisors, at our own expense. SEPTEMBER 22. At Argenteuil, at our own expense. SEPTEMBER 23. We attended the burial of Walter, bishop of Paris, of happy memory, in the choir of the cathedral church. This day we spent the night at Gournay-sur-Marne. SEPTEMBER 24. At Coulommiers-en-Brie. SEPTEMBER 25. At Sézanne. SEPTEMBER 26-27. At Jardin-Notre-Dame. SEPTEMBER 28. At the Paraclete. SEPTEMBER 29. At Troyes. SEPTEMBER 30. At Bar-sur-Seine. OCTOBER 1. At Châtillon-sur-Seine. OCTOBER 2. At Chancelles. OCTOBER 3. At Fleury. OCTOBER 4. At Beaune. OCTOBER 5. At Chalon. OCTOBER 6. At Tournus. OCTOBER 7. At Mâcon. OCTOBER 8. At Anse. OCTOBER 9-25. At Lyon. OCTOBER 26. At Villefranche. OCTOBER 27. At Mâcon. OCTOBER 28. At Tournus. OCTOBER 29. At Chalon. OCTOBER 30-31. At Beaune. NOVEMBER 1. At

---

[64] A Benedictine priory dependent on Marmoutier. (Cottineau, I, 1287.)

[65] A Premonstratensian priory dependent on St-Josse-aux-Bois (Cottineau, I, 1240.)

[66] A Benedictine priory dependent on Fécamp. (Cottineau, II, 2485.)

[67] An example of questions asked during a "thorough visitation" may be found in A. H. Thompson, *The English Clergy and Their Organization in the Later Middle Ages* (Oxford, 1947), 293-98. This document lists sixty-six questions which a visitor might ask in whole or in part. They are quite revealing. Undoubtedly Eudes had his own list, and what we have is a précis made by his secretary.

Beaune. NOVEMBER 2. At Fleury. NOVEMBER 3. At Précy. NOVEMBER 4. At Châtillon-sur-Seine. NOVEMBER 5. At Bar-sur-Seine. NOVEMBER 6. At Troyes. NOVEMBER 7-8. At the Paraclete. NOVEMBER 9. At La Croix-en-Brie. NOVEMBER 10. At Tournan. NOVEMBER 11. At Paris. NOVEMBER 12. At Pontoise. NOVEMBER 13. At St-Martin-la-Garenne, at our own expense. NOVEMBER 14. At Sausseuse, at our own expense. NOVEMBER 15. At Mont-Deux-Amants, at our own expense. NOVEMBER 16. At Ste-Catherine, at our own expense. NOVEMBER 17-19. At Déville. NOVEMBER 20. At Auffay, at our own expense. NOVEMBER 21. At Aliermont. NOVEMBER 22-24. At Aliermont. NOVEMBER 25. At Neufchâtel, at the expense of the priory of Nogent.[68] No monks there. NOVEMBER 26. At Déville. NOVEMBER 27-28. At Rouen. NOVEMBER 29-30. At Déville.

DECEMBER 1. At Ouville,[69] where we made a visitation. They have an income of four hundred pounds, and they owe about one hundred eighty pounds. One does not accuse another [in chapter]. We enjoined the prior to prepare a place in some remote part of the house for John Gaul, who had often withdrawn from the order. He was not to be allowed to leave this place. A book should be given to him, that he may sing his Hours. If he should leave, he is to be permanently expelled from the order. Further, we forbade him to talk with anyone, whether canon or secular, without permission from the prior to do so.

DECEMBER 2. We spent the night at Ouville, at the expense of the priory of Etoutteville. The prior was not present, so we did not make a visitation.

DECEMBER 3. At Bacqueville,[70] at the expense of the priory. We found that they use feather beds. We forbade anyone to leave the cloister alone and without permission. They have an income of about two hundred pounds; they owe about forty pounds. The prior does not make up the accounts of the state of the house; we enjoined him to make a quarterly audit of the state of the house.

DECEMBER 4. At Longueil,[71] at the expense of the house. No monks are there. DECEMBER 5. At the same, but at our own expense. DECEMBER 6. At Valmont, which we visited. We found that they do not read the Statutes

---

[68] There is a town, Nogent-en-Bray, a few miles north of Neufchâtel, but I find no mention of a priory. There was a priory at Neufchâtel, Ste-Radegonde-du-Mesnil, but it was a dependent of Préaux-de-Rouen.

[69] A house of Augustinian canons. (Cottineau, II, 2161.)

[70] A Benedictine priory dependent on Tiron. (Cottineau, I, 238.)

[71] A Benedictine priory dependent on Bec. (Cottineau, I, 1648.)

of Pope Gregory; we enjoined them to read them as required. They have the patronage of ten churches. We found things to be in the same condition as at our last visitation, recorded in folio 14.[72] DECEMBER 7. At Valmont. DECEMBER 8. At Montivilliers, at the expense of the monastery. We visited the abbess in chapter. We found everything in good condition. DECEMBER 9. At Graville. They have three priories. One canon is dwelling alone at Bellevue. They owe about forty pounds, but about one hundred pounds are due them. They have sufficient supplies to last until the new harvest. DECEMBER 10. At Beaucamp, at the expense of Sir Geoffrey Paternoster.

DECEMBER 11. At Le Valasse,[73] at the expense of the monastery. Sir William l'Orcher, under sentence of excommunication for obstructing Master Peter of St-Germain in his occupation of the church of Angerville, which we had conferred upon him, because the period in which appointments should have been made had elapsed, came to us, and in the presence of Master William of Saane, archdeacon of the French Vexin; Brother William of Guerche of the Franciscan Order; Master Theobald of Grandville; Arnulf of Jocre; Master Hugh of Courtry, all being our clerks; William of Rouvières and William of Beuzeville, knights; and many other clerics and laymen, sought canonical absolution from us. He promised on oath to make whatever amends we thought fit for the damage sustained by us, as well as for the annoyance caused the said Master Peter, for his excommunication, for carrying away the crops, for the violence, and, in short, for everything pertaining to this affair. He offered as pledges for the fine Nicholas of Hotot and Peter of Gainneville, knights, the chamberlain of Tancarville, and John Malet, all of whom were present and obligated themselves as pledges for seeing that the judgment would be carried out.

DECEMBER 12. At St-Wandrille, at the expense of the monastery.

DECEMBER 13. At St-Wandrille, which we visited. We found that there are twenty-nine monks in residence and there were wont to be forty. They have ten priories. They have only three altars, which is insufficient for the brothers to celebrate Mass; we enjoined them to provide themselves with several altars and in sufficient quantity. There are some who because of this do not celebrate Mass as often as they should. Laymen occasionally enter

---

[72] See entry for January 31, 1248/49.
[73] A Cistercian abbey founded c. 1181. (Cottineau, II, 3268.)

the cloister, especially just now, because of the workmen.[74] They have an income of two hunderd pounds to use for alms. They eat meat in the priories; we enjoined the abbot to correct this and to see that they abstained from eating meat. They have an income overseas of four thousand pounds. The abbot does not cast his accounts each quarter as we had ordered; we enjoined him to make a quarterly audit. They owe only about one thousand pounds. They have a good supply of food, quite sufficient to last until next year. They owe about one hundred sixty-six pounds in annual pensions. We enjoined the abbot to visit the outside priories more often and more diligently. We enjoined the abbot to notify the community, and to do so in writing, how much of their land will be rented out each year. Item, that he make a written record of the debts of the monastery and present it to the community. The record should show what it owes and what is owed to it, to whom it is owed, and who owes to it [the monastery] and how much. Item, we enjoined the abbot to see and search more diligently the coffers and chests of the monks, or to have such a search made.

DECEMBER 14. At Jumièges, at the expense of the monastery. We made a visitation therein, and found that they eat meat in the outside priories; we ordered . . . [lacuna in MS][75] the abbot, to correct these matters more strictly. They have an income of forty-three hundred pounds of Tours; they owe about nine hundred pounds. They owe about twenty-two pounds and thirty marks in pensions. The Divine Office is not said for the sick in the infirmary; we ordered it to be said for them in the future. The monks in the cloister are not well cared for, since they have insufficient bedding; we ordered that bedding be given to each according to his necessity. Item, for a number of reasons we ordered the abbot to remove the kitchener and the cellarer from their offices.

DECEMBER 15. We were at St-Georges[76] and made a visitation there, finding twenty monks. Sometimes they eat meat when there is no need; we forbade the eating of meat, save insofar as the Rule permits. Item, sometimes they eat before the proper hour and without permission; we decreed that he who should eat before the hour should on the very next day observe strict silence,

[74] The abbey had suffered severely from fire and was in the process of being rebuilt.

[75] William IV was abbot of Jumièges from 1240 to 1250. (Gallia Christiana, XI, 196.)

[76] A canons-regular foundation in 1050, it became a Benedictine abbey in 1114. (Cottineau, II, 2701-2.)

and fast on bread and water, and that neither the abbot, the prior, nor any-one else should have authority to modify this penalty without our permis-sion. Item, we decreed that whoever shall not have confessed each month shall incur the above penalty, to begin the first day following the elapsed month. They have an income of fifteen hundred pounds; they owe about two hundred pounds, and four hundred pounds is owed to them. We en-joined the abbot to cast his accounts three times a year, together with some persons elected by the community.

DECEMBER 16-18. At Déville. DECEMBER 19. At St-Matthieu, and we conferred holy orders at Pré. DECEMBER 20. At St-Matthieu. DECEMBER 21. At Déville.

DECEMBER 22. At Déville. This day we were at St-Ouen, and drew up regulations as a result of our findings at our visitation there. The regulations follow:

Brother Eudes, by God's grace unworthy bishop of the church of Rouen, to his beloved sons . . . [lacuna in MS] the abbot[77] and convent of St-Ouen-de-Rouen, eternal greetings in the Lord Jesus Christ. As part of the duty imposed upon us by our office, we made a visitation of your monastery, and we found certain things which we neither can nor should overlook by way of dissimulation, and which must be corrected. Since we found that the sacrosanct and venerable Blessed Sacrament which should be kept with all care and diligence and treated with reverence and honor according to the canons was being improperly cared for, we will and decree that every effort be made to assure its proper care.[78]

Item, we will and decree that you remove the unsuitable and shameful altar ornaments, especially the corporals, in which the real Body of Christ is wrapped, and that each altar be furnished with clean and decent cloths. Since we found that the age-old service of the church was somewhat disturbed, we will and

---

[77] The abbot was Adam.

[78] The reservation of the Eucharist for administration to the sick dates from the early days of the Church, but there is no evidence to prove that the Sacrament was reserved in the church. In Cistercian monasteries it was probably preserved in an aumbry or niche in the wall of the sanctuary. (Marcel Aubert, *Architecture Cistercienne en France* [Paris, 1947], I, 323.) The first official decree for its reservation in the Western Church was promulgated by Innocent III at the Fourth Lateran Council (1215) canon 20. (Mansi, XXII, 1007.) The Sacrament was to be kept under lock and key. Honorius III decreed likewise (*Corp. jur. can., Decretal. Greg. IX.* Lib. III. Tit. XLI. Cap. 10). The Sacrament was wrapped in linen (*pannus eucharisticus*) and placed within a pyx or casket (*capra*), which was molded in the form of a dove and hung from the ceiling. This was the hanging pyx or dove (*colomba*). See A. W. Pugin, *Glossary of Ecclesiastical Ornament* (London, 1846), 120-23.

decree that both the day and night Offices be properly and completely performed in accordance with the ancient custom, unless you shal receive a dispensation.[79]

Item, since there is no exception of persons before God, we will and order you, the abbot, that when monks come to you for admission into the monastery committed to your charge, you will put aside the claims of kindred or of country and admit only such as shall guarantee a vigorous observance of religion and the due performance of the Divine Offices as stated above.

Item, since we have learned that both the priors and the monks dwelling in the outside priories continually violate the statutes of the Rule prohibiting the eating of meat, we enjoin upon you, as abbot, not to delay to discipline this excess, as you wish to avoid the vengeance of God and of ourself.

Item, lest any evil suspicion arise concerning the conduct of monks who have been delegated to perform the Divine Office, we forbid any monk to presume to leave the abbey or wander about the town alone without suitable companionship and without the permission of him whom the Rule allows to grant such permission; if any should presume to do this, he shall go without wine on two successive Fridays, in addition to other penalties which are to be inflicted upon him according to the Rule.

Item, since we found that many, especially the traveling brothers, failed to observe the fasts of the Rule, and that some ate in their rooms, we forbid any exemption from the observance of the Rule to anyone, on any pretext of office or dignity; and he who shall be found culpable shall incur the penalty noted above. We forbid any monk to dwell alone in any of your religious houses or priories, and if there used to be more than two in any of your priories, we will and decree that the original number be maintained, for the service of God should be increased and not diminished. The alms, which we understand has been decreased, should be brought up to the old amount, or increased if that be possible, and should be distributed as the resources of the monastery permit.

Item, we strictly forbid the granting of any more pensions to anyone unless it be by papal authority or permission of a superior, for we have discovered that your monastery is grievously burdened by pensions of this kind.

Item, we will that if you have a written copy of the Statutes of Pope Gregory, of blessed memory, you will have it read both in Latin and in French as required; that if you have not a copy, we enjoin you, the abbot, to have a copy made within a month after the receipt of this letter, to have it read in chapter, and to see that

---

[79] St-Ouen came under the reforming and thus the liturgical influence of Cluny, one of whose features was the continuous recitation of the *Opus Dei*. (*Histoire de l'abbaye royale de St-Ouen-de-Rouen, par un religieux bénédictin de la congrégation de St-Maur* [Rouen, 1662], pp. 145-46; 148-49.)

the rules contained therein be strictly observed, especially in the matter of monthly confessions. And we will and order you to follow the Statute requiring you to make an audit at least three times a year, in the presence of brothers specially selected for this purpose by the community.

Item, since we found that he who ought to give out the new clothing to the others does not give it out at the proper time, and since those who receive new clothing do not surrender the old garments on the receipt of the new, we will that the Statutes regulating this matter be strictly observed, and without favor of persons.

Item, we decree that the things that are necessary be becomingly and well administered in the infirmary according to the needs of the sick and the ability of the house to sustain them. Item, we decree that the same regulations shall be applied to guests.

Item, since no little damage is said to have resulted to the monastery because of the manner in which the chapter's seal is guarded, we order that keys be entrusted to two honest, faithful, and religious persons, elected in common by the community, a third key to be held by the abbot.

Item, since no monk should have any property, or regard anything as his own, we will and decree that no one shall accept any gift from another, or presume to confer a gift upon another, without the special permission of his abbot. And lest anyone attempt to excuse himself for neglecting any of the above charges on the ground of ignorance, we will that this ordinance be read through at least once a month to the brothers in chapter; and be it known that if we find anyone negligent or rebellious in these matters, we will deal with him in such a way that his punishment will be a source of terror to the rest. If, indeed, the abbot or the prior who presides over the chapter is negligent in this respect, we shall punish him more severely.

DECEMBER 23. At Déville. At Rouen. DECEMBER 24. At Rouen. DE-CEMBER 25. Christmas Day. DECEMBER 26. At Auffay, at our own expense. DECEMBER 27-30. At Aliermont. DECEMBER 31. At Le Tréport. JANUARY 1. At Le Tréport, to attend the selection of the abbot there,[80] at the expense of the monastery. JANUARY 2-3. At Aliermont. JANUARY 4. At Longue-ville, at the expense of the house. They are exempt [from visitation]. JAN-UARY 5. At St-Saëns, at the expense of the priory.

JANUARY 6. At St-Saëns, but at our own expense, and we made a visita-tion. They do not always sing the day Offices with modulation; they do not

---

[80] William III succeeded Laurence, who had died in October, 1249. (*Gallia Christiana*, XI, 249.)

confess each month, nor do they receive Communion [monthly]; we enjoined them to correct these things. They have occasionally eaten meat, but they are not eating it now, since they have again been forbidden to do so. The prior does not audit his accounts on the state of the house with the aid of the monks; we decreed that he should compute with the monks, in accordance with the Statutes of Pope Gregory. They do not celebrate Masses as they ought; we ordered them to celebrate more often. There is a young boy there, the nephew of the abbot, and he has been there for two years.[81] The monk in charge of the keys sometimes goes into the town alone on monastery business; we forbade him to go out alone in the future, unless he goes on horseback.

JANUARY 7-8. At Déville.

JANUARY 9. At Bourg-Achard, at the expense of the priory, and we made a visitation therein. We found that there are always ten canons in continual residence. Two canons are dwelling alone in two of their priories; we enjoined that they be recalled to the cloister or be given companions. There are seven [canons] in the outside priories. Some of the monks are negligent in carrying out our former orders[82] concerning monthly confession. They have no subprior; we ordered the prior to appoint one. They have an income of three hundred pounds; they owe about one hundred five pounds; they owe Master William Landre a pension of fifty shillings.

JANUARY 10-11. At Bec.

JANUARY 12. At Bec, which we visited this day. There are ninety-two monks in residence. We found conditions to be the same as at the last visitation recorded on folio 5.[83]

JANUARY 13. At Corneville, at the expense of the monastery. There are but eight canons in residence. Item, we found that some of the canons are dwelling alone in the priories; we enjoined the abbot to give each of them a companion or else recall them to the cloister. They have an income of three hundred pounds; they owe about one hundred forty pounds. They have the patronage of two churches.

JANUARY 14. On the morrow we entered for the purposes of visitation the

---

[81] The provincial Council of Rouen (1231), canon 4 (1231), forbade nuns to take in "little boys or little girls who are fed in the monastery" (Mansi, XXIII, 214). Probably the same prohibition applied to monks.

[82] See entry for September 5, 1248.

[83] See entry for September 7, 1248.

diocese of Lisieux, which occupied our time until February 1.

In the year of our Lord 1249, on the morrow after the octave of the Epiphany, January 14, we entered our province and came to St-Pierre-des-Préaux,[84] where we spent the night at the expense of the monastery, and where we were received with a procession[85] and with the church all decorated. The next day we made a visitation, finding thirty monks in residence. Sometimes they eat meat unnecessarily; we forbade them to eat meat, except under such conditions as the Rule permits. They have an income of eleven hundred pounds; they owe about three hundred pounds. Item, they owe four hundred pounds without interest to a certain Jew, and they do not know whether they will be cleared of this debt or whether they will have to pay it.

JANUARY 15. We spent the night at St-Pierre-des-Préaux at the expense of the monastery of St-Léger-des-Préaux,[86] which we visited this day. We found that they made no profession [of vows] until they received the blessing.[87] They use different food in the infirmary and for the community refectory. We enjoined the abbess to see that the food was prepared in common, both for the community and for the infirmary. Item, they enter the infirmary when there is no real need; we forbade their being sent to the infirmary, except in accord with the Rule. They have an income of about seven hundred pounds; they owe about three hundred pounds. The abbess does not cast her accounts with the community; we enjoined her to compute twice a year with the community concerning the state of the house; we also enjoined that the convent should have a transcript or statement of the accounts. There are forty-five nuns in residence. Some secular girls were there too; we enjoined her to send them all away.[88]

JANUARY 16. We spent the night at Cormeilles,[89] at the expense of the

---

[84] A Benedictine abbey founded in the eighth century. (Cottineau, II, 2356-57.)

[85] That is, in solemn procession. When meeting an ecclesiastical dignitary, the abbot and monastic officials, led by a monk carrying holy water and an aspergillum, led the procession beyond the monastic enclosure. All knelt while the dignitary sprinkled them with holy water. Singing the psalm "Hear, O Israel" if there were one dignitary, or "Let thy loins be girt" if more than one, the procession returned to the monastery with the abbot leading the dignitary by the hand. (Guignard, *Monuments*, 192-93.)

[86] A Benedictine monastery of nuns established *c.* 1050. (Cottineau, II, 2357.)

[87] There was a single ceremony for profession of vows and for the blessing by the local bishop, or by his official, in this particular case.

[88] This was in accordance with canon 4 of the provincial Council of Rouen (1231). (Mansi, XXIII, 214.)

[89] A Benedictine abbey founded *c.* 1050-1060. (Cottineau, I, 875.)

monastery. We found twenty-five monks there. Lay folk sometimes enter the cloister; we enjoined the abbot to provide a better guard for the cloister. They do not confess each month as the Statutes of Pope Gregory require; we enjoined them to observe the Statutes covering this. Traveling monks do not observe the fasts of the Rule; we ordered them to conduct themselves more in accord with the Rule. Item, they occasionally eat meat when there is no need; we forbade them to eat meat except in cases permitted by the Rule. They have an income of about sixteen hundred pounds; they owe about two hundred sixty pounds. The abbot does not audit his accounts as the Statutes of Pope Gregory require; we enjoined him to observe the Statutes pertaining to this more diligently. All of their debts are endorsed with the seal of the chapter. They owe about sixteen pounds in pensions; item, pensions granted by apostolic authority amount to one hundred shillings.

JANUARY 17. At Grestain,[90] at the expense of the monastery, which contains thirty monks. All but four of the monks are priests. They have an income of about two thousand pounds; they owe about four hundred pounds, but about the same amount is owed to them. We enjoined the abbot, the prior, and the other bailiffs to make transcripts of their incomes in a book and then to put them together in one volume. They owe about twenty pounds in pensions. Those dwelling in the priories eat meat and do not observe the fasts of the Rule; we urged the abbot to correct these abuses.

JANUARY 18. At Beaumont-en-Auge,[91] at the expense of the priory. There are fourteen monks in residence. Lay folk sometimes enter the cloister; we enjoined them to appoint a good and suitable person as porter. Item, we ordered the Statutes of Pope Gregory to be read in chapter as those Statutes require. Item, we found that they confess but rarely; we enjoined them to maintain rigidly the Statutes of Pope Gregory governing confession. Item, some of them are negligent in celebrating their Masses. Only the cloistered monks observed the fasts of the Rule, and sometimes even they violate them; we decreed that all should observe the fasts, except those who are dispensed according to the Rule. Item, we forbade absolutely the eating of meat save in cases permitted by the Rule. They do not surrender their old clothes when they receive new ones; we forbade any new garments' being given to anyone until the old ones have been returned. Item, we ordered that as

[90] A Benedictine abbey founded c. 1050. (Cottineau, I, 1342-43.)

[91] A Benedictine priory dependent on St-Ouen-de-Rouen, founded c. 1060. (Cottineau, I, 305.)

many of the capes as are required for riding shall be held in common, nor shall anyone presume to appropriate any of them for himself. They have an income of about seven hundred pounds; they have no debts, since more is owed to them than they owe. Item, we enjoined the prior to cast his accounts more frequently with the community. We corrected Robert of Caudebec, known as the possessor of property, Brother Elias for the same offense, and Hermoland known for his drinking.

JANUARY 19. At St-Hymer,[92] at the expense of the priory.

JANUARY 20. At St-Hymer, and we visited it. There are eleven monks in residence. All but two are priests. They do not have a copy of the Statutes of Pope Gregory; we enjoined them to have the Statutes written out, read as the Statutes require, and to see that the said Statutes are rigorously observed. They do not confess nor receive Communion as the Statutes of Bec require;[93] we enjoined them to follow the Bec Statutes in these matters. Traveling monks do not observe the fasts of the Rule; we ordered that they be better observed. They have an income of about four hundred pounds; they have no debts, since more is owed to them than they owe. The prior does not compute with the community; we ordered him to compute at least twice a year and to prepare a written statement of the accounts of which the community shall receive a copy. This day, we spent the night there, at the expense of the priory. During these two days we spent eleven pounds, fifteen shillings, but we made a voluntary remission of one hundred shillings to the monks for the said expenses; they owe two procuration fees; one for their own priory, and one for the priory of Blangy, where there are no monks because the priory is so poor. The monks have been united with or attached to the priory of St-Hymer.

---

[92] A Benedictine priory dependent on Bec, founded c. 1066. (Cottineau, II, 2733.)

[93] St. Benedict exhorted his monks to confess their faults to their abbots or their spiritual masters. (*Rule of St. Benedict*, Ch. 46.) The *Regularis concordia* (ed. and trans. Thomas Symons [Oxford, 1953], p. xxxix, p. 18) enjoined frequent confession and Communion on its monks. The *Usus* of Cîteaux made provision for frequent confession and Communion (Guignard, *Monuments*, p. 170). The *Constitutions of Lanfranc*, monk of Bec and Archbishop of Canterbury, insist on the necessity for frequent confession and Communion. (Ed. and trans. by David Knowles [Oxford, 1951], pp. 3, 107, 109, 116, 121.) Some of the *Consuetudinarium secundum normam Becci Herluini* has been published in C. Martène, *De antiquis monachorum ritibus* (Lyons, 1960). Certainly Lanfranc's *Constitutions* are based on the customs and usages of Bec. Canon A. Porée's *Histoire de l'abbaye de Bec*, 2 vols. (Evreux, 1901), is still quite useful, especially, I, 475 ff.

JANUARY 21. We came to Lisieux and were received by the chapter with a procession and the church all decorated. We delivered a sermon to the chapter gathered or convoked in the bishop's palace. There we exercised our right of visitation and inquired whether the bishop carried out his episcopal duties. The canons replied that he had not celebrated Mass in the cathedral of Lisieux during the past year; they do not know what he may do elsewhere, and they say that he is unable to exercise such of his episcopal functions[94] as dedicating churches, consecrating the chrism, blessing nuns, and the like.

Item, he does not preach, although he is a most excellent speaker; he is unable to celebrate Mass or visit his churches. Asked in what manner and on whom he confers benefices, they replied that he had conferred them on such as were ill reputed, but that he had later revoked these. The rural deaneries are sold or are farmed for a certain price. Master Nicholas of Cheffreville, archdeacon, does not reside in his church. Asked whether the bishop had an honest household, they replied that they believed so. Asked how the rights and temporalities of the church were preserved, they replied that their forest land had deteriorated in value because of his inefficiency.

Item, [asked] whether he visited the chapter, they replied that he did. Item, asked how the Divine Offices are celebrated, they replied, "Well"; whether money fines were imposed, [they said that] they were properly exacted. Asked how the ornaments[95] were cared for, they replied that there was a sufficiency of ornaments but that they were not kept very clean. Asked if any of the clerics of the church were ill famed, they replied that they were well disciplined by the dean. Item, they replied that the rule of silence was well observed. Item, the clerks-choral and canons leave the choir and wander gossiping through the church while the Divine Offices are being celebrated. The dean told us that he had recently been informed that some of the clerks-choral are publicly known for incontinence, but that he would give this his immediate attention. Item, many of the canons have parochial churches, but they neither reside in them,[96] nor are compelled to. Item,

[94] Bishop William, Pont de l'Arche, was quite advanced in years. See entries for January 31 and February 1 of this year. He became bishop of Lisieux in 1218 and died at the monastery of Bonport in August, 1250. (Gams, *Series Episcoponem*, p. 566).

[95] These were the sacred vessels, "dove," cloths, and vestments used in the celebration of the sacerdotal and episcopal offices.

[96] They have been collated as prebendaries to them, but without cure of souls. They receive a certain income from them.

there is some scandal about the bishop who conferred a prebend on one of his nephews who was ill famed of homicide. Master Simon of Wasvic is a drunkard; so is Master Albert; both of them disturb the choir. Item, Ralph, the bishop's nephew, is ill famed of indecent behavior at the houses of prostitutes and of running about the town at night and visiting brothels. It is said that Vincent is ill famed of incontinence. We warned Master Simon of Wasvic and Master Albert, whom we found publicly known for drunkenness, to live more soberly, and they most sincerely promised to do this; we enjoined the dean to carry out the legate's ruling in these matters with greater strictness. Item, with the approval of the chapter, we set about correcting those things which in our visitation we found to need correction. We acted with the counsel of the dean, the greater archdeacon, and the treasurer, who protested that this procedure should not be regarded as customary, although they admitted that we might administer discipline even without their consent, and for this we expressed our thanks. Item, on their advice we called before us Vincent and Ralph of Pont-de-l'Arche, whom we found grievously and publicly ill famed of incontinence with many women and of running about the town at night carrying weapons. We told them that we would undertake a legal investigation of their incontinence, or, if they preferred, that they might submit themselves of their own free will to our own handling of the matter. They promised that they would abide by our will in the matter, and we enjoined the said Vincent and Ralph to leave the city of Lisieux before Ascension Day and to take up residence in the schools, and not to return to Lisieux without our special permission. They gratefully accepted this punishment and promised to fulfill the conditions imposed. Later, we warned Vincent and Ralph to conduct themselves circumspectly in the meantime, and this they promised to do, pledging one year's income from their prebends as earnest of their good faith. Further, we warned that if in the interim any rumor of incontinence is heard about them, they shall retire from Lisieux within fifteen days of receiving notice from the said dean, archdeacon, and treasurer, and under no circumstances shall they ever return[97] to Lisieux without our special permission and desire. The master of the school[98] [is ill famed] of the miller's wife; John, the

[97] Eudes had carried out his own investigation of their conduct. They were free to choose between a trial and canonical purgation and abiding by Eudes' decision. They chose the latter.

[98] The Fourth Lateran Council (1215), canon 11, decreed the establishment of a school in every cathedral church. (Mansi, XXII, 999.)

bishop's nephew, [is ill famed] of [keeping] birds and dogs; the cantor [is ill famed] of a certain married woman. We found Richard Faiel to be il famed of the wife of Richard the tailor. Called before us, they promised to behave themselves better in the future. Item, we did not believe some other stories which were told us about some of the others. This day our expenses were borne by the bishop.

This day, represented by the archdeacon of the French Vexin, we visited the monastery of nuns at Lisieux.[99] He found that there are thirty-two nuns in residence and that they have an income of five hundred pounds, although they have no written record of it; he ordered the sources of income to be well and carefully entered in a book. Item, since the abbess did not cast her accounts with the assistance of the community, it was enjoined upon her to make an audit at least three times a year, either with the whole community or in the presence of some persons specifically elected by the community. Item, four of the nuns had private incomes which were employed for their own advantage; it was decreed and ordered that these incomes be used for the community. Item, it was learned that they did not observe the fasts of the Rule and were in the habit of eating meat in the infirmary three times a week; they were enjoined to observe the fasts of the Rule more completely and to abstain from eating meat. Item, they receive Communion only four times a year; they were enjoined to receive Communion and to confess once a month. Item, they do not hand in their old garments when they receive new ones; it was ordered that no new clothes be given to anyone unless the old ones have been surrendered.

JANUARY 22. We received procuration from the chapter of Lisieux. JANUARY 23. At Ste-Barbe-en-Auge,[100] at the expense of the priory.

JANUARY 24. At Ste-Barbe-en-Auge, but at our own expense. In the morning we made a visitation, finding forty canons in the community. They have fourteen priories. Sometimes the novices make their profession before the lapse of a year; sometimes they do not make profession even after a year. They have an income of about two thousand pounds; they owe about six hundred pounds. They owe ten pounds to Master John of la Valle; item, the same to Master Simon of St-Pierre. They have the patronage of thirty churches.

---

[99] A Benedictine monastery of nuns. (Cottineau, I, 1626-27.)
[100] A priory of canons regular. (Cottineau, II, 2604.)

JANUARY 25. At Crouttes,[101] where there are but two monks. They do not observe the fasts of the Rule; we enjoined them to observe better the fasts of the Rule. They owe about ten pounds; they have an income of about eighty pounds.

JANUARY 26. At Ticheville,[102] at the expense of the priory. We visited there and found two monks. Sometimes they say Matins without modulation. They do not observe the fasts of the Rule; we enjoined them to observe the fasts of the Rule. They eat meat occasionally; we forbade them to eat meat except when permitted by the Rule. They use feather beds; we prohibited their use. They have an income of about one hundred sixty pounds; more is owed them than they owe.

JANUARY 27. At St-Evroult,[103] at the expense of the monastery.

JANUARY 28. We visited at St-Evroult, where there are thirty-two monks. Lay folk sometimes enter the cloister in going to the church. Almost all are priests. Traveling monks do not observe the fasts of the Rule. Those who are living in the priories eat meat frequently, nor do they observe the fasts of the Rule; we enjoined the abbot to correct this. Item, they use feather beds in the priories. We forbade them to eat meat. They have an income of twenty-seven hundred pounds; they owe seven hundred pounds. They owe about sixteen pounds in pensions. We spent the night there at our own expense.

JANUARY 29. At Bernay,[104] at the expense of the monastery.

JANUARY 30. We visited at Bernay. Fifteen monks are there, whereas before the fire there used to be thirty-five. All but five are priests. Because of the workmen, lay folk enter the cloister. They do not observe the fasts of the Rule, and this is particularly true of the traveling monks; they eat meat occasionally, especially those dwelling in the priories. We ordered and enjoined the observance of the fasts, and we forbade the eating of meat except insofar as the Rule permitted it. They have an income of two thousand pounds; they owe about three hundred pounds. They owe about thirty pounds in pensions; we forbade the abbot and the community to grant pensions to anyone. We spent the night there, at our own expense.

JANUARY 31. We were at Thiberville, as was also the bishop of Lisieux.

[101] A Benedictine priory dependent on Jumièges. (Cottineau, I, 925.)
[102] A Benedictine priory dependent on St-Wandrille. (Cottineau, II, 3157-58.)
[103] A Benedictine monastery of which the historian Ordericus Vitalis was once a member of the community. (Cottineau, II, 2669-71.)
[104] A Benedictine abbey founded c. 1015. (Cottineau, I, 356-57.)

We warned him, in accordance with the apostolic mandate sent to us, and which is incorporated below, to yield the pastoral direction of the church of Lisieux, and to accept such suitable provision as we, acting under apostolic authority, should assign to him from the resources of the said church. The tenor of the apostolic letter was as follows:

Innocent, bishop, servant of the servants of God, to the venerable Brother Eudes, archbishop of Rouen, greeting and apostolic blessing. Notwithstanding the unwillingness of some to bear tales, we must be ever solicitous lest any serious spiritual of temporal damage be incurred by the churches through the incapacity or negligence of their pastors. But indeed, when you were in our presence, you set before us the fact that our venerable brother, the bishop of Lisieux, was so grievously broken by age and weighed down by bodily infirmity that he was no longer of service or able to rule the church of Lisieux or to carry out his pastoral duties. Most humbly you sought advice from us, that provision be made for the welfare of the church and the well-being of the said bishop. Wherefore, desiring at once to preserve the prosperous condition of the said church and to provide the bishop with the boon of quiet and with increased opportunity to improve his health, we instructed your Fraternity, by apostolic writing, and on our behalf, urgently to advise and induce that said bishop to resign his office, and we authorize you upon his resignation to grant him an income from the revenues of the said church sufficent to enable him to live in comfort and decency. Otherwise you shall appoint a cautious and worthy man as his coadjutor, by whose mature counsel and ready aid the said church shall be more wholesomely governed, and you shall curb all opponents with the threat of apostolic censure, without hope of appeal. Given at Lyons, October 21, in the seventh year of our pontificate.

The bishop asked us for a delay until the Monday following the Purification of the Blessed Virgin, when he would give a definite answer whether he would prefer to resign his church on the receipt of an adequate pension or to receive the coadjutor whom we should appoint. We granted the request, and he accepted the conditions.

FEBRUARY 1. While we were at Bec the said bishop sent us the following letter:

To the Reverend Father and lord Eudes, by the grace of God archbishop of Rouen, William, by His grace bishop of Lisieux, sends eternal greeting in the Lord and renders his due and devout reverence and obedience. When, venerable Father, at Thiberville, on the Monday preceding the Purification of the Blessed Virgin, you earnestly advised us, in keeping with the apostolic mandate which you showed to us, to resign our church of Lisieux as the mandate suggested and to accepte the competent income which you would assign, we requested time for deliberation, namely, until the Monday following the said Purification, on which day we would give a definite reply as to whether we would prefer to resign and receive a competency or to accept the coadjutor whom you, acting under the papal mandate, should assign to us. You graciously granted this delay, and we accepted it. Since, indeed, we know that the man diligent in his business is commended by Scripture, and that "a sharp judgment shall be to them that be in high places," considering the irreparable burden of our age, and, above all, fearing lest that which seems to flourish and flower under our hand should actually be tending to decay, and we should be said to seek only what can be done and not what would be of profit, being unwilling to stain our reputation, or rather to allow it to be damaged by reason of our age, and preferring to leave a good example to posterity, we anticipate the day on which we should make our reply, by the tenor of the present letter. We inform you that we prefer to resign our pastoral cure, as is contained in the papal mandate, receiving a competency which you shall assign to us. And, to the end that you shall be no further bothered by this matter, by the tenor of the present letter, we freely resign the pastoral care of the church of Lisieux, which we have governed up to this time, to you, knowing from the papal letter that you are empowered to receive our resignation. We beseech you to make such a liberal provision for us as is consistent with our honor and condition, our infirmity and our age, and which will enable us to live comfortably and decently, in accordance with the papal mandate, and that Your Paternity will present a written statement of your pleasure to the bearer of the present letter. Given at Thiberville, in the year of our Lord, 1249, on the Feast of the Purification of the Blessed Mary.

On March 16 we went to meet the said bishop at Thiberville, and in the presence of F., the dean; A., the cantor; W., the treasurer; Th. of Germany; J. of St-Evroult, archdeacon; W., the sacristan; G., the master of the school; G. of St-Aubin; N. of Pont-de-l'Arche; S. of St-Pierre; William of St-Riquier; W. of Friardel, and N. Sotin, canons of Lisieux, we received the resignation of the said bishop from his own hands, at his instant request, and by apostolic authority pertaining to the cure and not to the dignity, and with the will, counsel, and consent of the aforesaid canons. By the same authority we assigned him, on the usual terms, an annual pension of six hundred pounds of Tours so long as he should live in the provostship of Lisieux, saving twenty pounds of Tours from the goods of the church, to John, the priest at Etrépagny.

FEBRUARY 1 [*sic*]. We were at Bec, at the expense of the monastery.

FEBRUARY 2. At Bec, and it was the Feast of the Purification of the Blessed Virgin. At the expense of the monastery. FEBRUARY 3. At Jumièges, at our own expense. FEBRUARY 4-8. At Déville. FEBRUARY 9. At Rouen. This being Ash Wednesday, we drove the penitents from the church. We ate at Rouen, and spent the night at Déville. FEBRUARY 10-11. At Déville. FEBRUARY 12. At Quévreville, at the expense of the house. No monks are there. FEBRUARY 13. At Noyon-sur-Andelle, where we conferred our benediction upon the abbot of Le Tréport. We spent the night at Mortemer-en-Lyons, at the expense of the monastery.

FEBRUARY 14. At St-Laurent-en-Lyons.[105] Thirteen canons reside in the convent and fifteen in the outside priories. One canon is dwelling alone at Ste-Honorine; we ordered him to be called back to the cloister or that a companion be sent to him. There are ten priests there. The church ornaments are not kept very clean; we ordered the sacristan to keep them clean or be removed from office. One does not accuse another [in chapter]; we decreed that one should accuse another as the Rule requires. Lay folk enter the cloister. The sick in the infirmary are not sufficiently provided for; we ordered that they be ministered to according to their infirmities, insofar as the resources of the house permitted, and that an attendant be provided for them. Item, guests are not well received; we ordered that a canon be appointed to receive them and to deal with them according to his circumstances. They owe about fifty pounds. They have the patronage of three churches. They have an income of about fifty pounds. Brother Simon is publicly known for grave incontinence; so are brothers John of Caux and William of Merey. Brother Peter Beaugener, Adam, and Brother John of Eu are publicly known for insubordination.

FEBRUARY 15. At Bellosane of the Order of Premontré,[106] at the expense of the monastery.

FEBRUARY 16. We visited the chapter of Gournay. We found Firmin, a priest, to be publicly known for drunkenness. Matthew, a canon, is somewhat ill famed of incontinence with a woman from Bosc-Hyons. Item, the dean is publicly known for drunkenness and for infrequent attendance at his church. Some of the canons walk about the town wearing hoods; we forbade them to do this any more. Item, we forbade the clerics to take any more of the burghers' wood at night for burning. Item, we ordered Firmin

---

[105] A priory of Augustinian canons established c. 1150. (Cottineau, II, 2760.)
[106] A Premonstratensian abbey founded in 1195. (Cottineau, I, 336.)

to be removed from office altogether, inasmuch as we had warned him last
year and he had not reformed.[107]

FEBRUARY 16 [*sic*]. At Neufmarché,[108] at the priory of St-Evroult, which
we visited. There are three monks in residence. They do not possess a copy
of the Rule of their order. They do not fully observe the fasts of the Rule.
They eat meat; we forbade them to eat meat, save insofar as the Rule permitted. They have an income of one hundred pounds derived from the
kingdom of France, and another hundred pounds coming from England
They owe about one hundred forty pounds.

FEBRUARY 17. At Pérrièrs, at the expense of the priory. No monks
there. FEBRUARY 18. At Déville. FEBRUARY 19. We conferred Holy Orders
in the cathedral, at Rouen and spent the night at Déville. FEBRUARY 20.
At Déville. FEBRUARY 21. At Mont-Deux-Amants, at our own expense.
FEBRUARY 22. At Sausseuse, at our own expense. FEBRUARY 23. At
Meulan, at our own expense, in the priory of St-Nigase. FEBRUARY 24.
At Paris, in the Temple. FEBRUARY 25. At Corbeil. FEBRUARY 26–MARCH 1.
At Peny. MARCH 2. At St-Maur-des-Fossés. MARCH 3. At Argenteuil.
MARCH 4. At Juziers, at our own expense. MARCH 5-6. At Sausseuse,
at our own expense. MARCH 7-8. At Mont-Deux-Amants, at our own
expense. MARCH 9-12. At Déville. MARCH 13-14. At Bourg-Achard, at
our own expense. MARCH 15. At Le Theil [-Nolent], in the diocese of
Lisieux.

MARCH 16. At the same, and this day, acting under apostolic authority,
we received the resignation of William, bishop of Lisieux, at Thiberville,
and we granted him a life annuity of six hundred pounds of Tours, in the
provostship of Lisieux.[109]

MARCH 17. At Bec. MARCH 18. At Déville. MARCH 19. At Rouen.
MARCH 20. At Rouen. It was Palm Sunday. MARCH 21-22. At Déville.
MARCH 23. At Rouen. MARCH 24. At Rouen. We consecrated the holy
chrism and spent the night at the priory of Noyon-sur-Andelle,[110] at our
own expense. MARCH 25. At St-Martin-de-Pontoise, at our own expense.
MARCH 26. At Pontoise, on Easter Eve, at our own expense.

---

[107] See entry for October 16, 1248.

[108] A Benedictine priory of St-Evroult founded in 1140. (Cottineau, II, 2057.)

[109] See entries for January 31 and February 1, above.

[110] Noyon-sur-Andelle was located in the present-day town of Charleval and is not
distant from Rouen. It is apt to be confused with Nojeon-le-Sec, which is approximately half way between Charleval and Gisors. There is also a Noyon, cathedral city
of the diocese of Noyon, at which Eudes was present on June 20, 1249.

MARCH 27. At Pontoise, on Easter Day, at our own expense. MARCH 28. At Juziers, at our own expense. MARCH 29-APRIL 2. At Sausseuse, at our own expense. APRIL 3. At Mont-Deux-Amants, at our own expense. APRIL 4. At Beaulieu, at our own expense. APRIL 5. At Beaussault, at the expense of the priory, which we visited. They have an income of one hundred pounds and owe about forty pounds. APRIL 6-9. At Aliermont. APRIL 10. We were at Dieppe, and spent the night at Longueville, at our own expense. APRIL 11-15. At Déville. APRIL 16. At Louviers. APRIL 17. At Vernon. APRIL 18. At St-Martin-la-Garenne. APRIL 19. At Juziers. APRIL 20. At Pontoise. APRIL 21. At Paris. APRIL 22. At Corbeil. APRIL 23. At Paris. APRIL 24. At Conflans.

APRIL 25. At Conflans, and this day we wrote the following letter to the lord bishop of Evreux:

Brother Eudes, by divine permission the unworthy minister of the church of Rouen, to the venerable Brother J.,[1] by God's grace bishop of Evreux, eternal greeting in the Lord Jesus Christ. This is to inform Your Fraternity that, the proper time having arrived, we propose to visit your diocese at once, and that on the present Tuesday following the feast of Saint-George we intend to spend the night at Irvy, whence to proceed as God shall inspire us. Given etc.

APRIL 25. At Mantes, at our own expense, whence we proceeded to the visitation of the diocese of Evreux, the report of which begins on folio 59.

APRIL 26. We entered the diocese of Evreux and spent the night at the monastery of Notre-Dame-d'Ivry,[2] at the expense of the house, which we visited the next day. Sixteen monks are there. They have six priories. One of the monks, accompanied only by a cleric, goes every day to the château[3] to celebrate Mass therein. They have an insufficient supply of chalices and missals. At solemn Masses[4] and at the time of the annual feasts, women

---

[1] Jean de la Cour-d'Aubergenville was the forty-first bishop of Evreux (1244-56). (Gams, *Series episcoporum*, p. 550.)

[2] A Benedictine abbey founded in 1076. (Cottineau, I, 1471-72.)

[3] This is the celebrated château of Ivry. The monastery was close by.

[4] The solemn or High Mass was a sung Mass with a full choir; the celebrant was

enter the cloister and the choir; we ordered this corrected and forbade women to enter the choir of cloister in the future. The abbot does not visit the outside priories, and in the outside priories they eat meat whenever they like; we forbade the eating of meat, save as the Rule permits. They have an income of about seven hundred pounds; they owe about three hundred pounds, and they have sufficient provisions. When the present abbot came they owed eight hundred pounds. The almoner is a drunkard. We must speak to the bishop about this monk who goes alone to celebrate Mass at the château at Ivry. Item, [we must also speak to him] about Brother Peter le Cordelier and Simon of Paris, both monks of Ivry.

APRIL 27. At Le Breuil,[5] of the Order of Cistercians, at the expense of the house.

APRIL 28. At Muzy,[6] which we visited. Four monks are there, of whom three are priests. There used to be some silk capes there, but the parishioners and the priests pawned them to get bells made. They do not observe the [papal] Constitution [of Gregory IX] on monthly confession; we enjoined them to observe this more fully. The one who is not a priest does not receive Communion every month; we enjoined both him and the prior to see that he did receive Communion in accordance with the papal statute. The monks walk about the town; this we forbade. Item, we ordered them to send away the maidservant who was there, and that if another be received, she was at least to be older than the present one. They do not observe the fasts of the Rule; they eat meat freely; we enjoined them to observe the fasts and forbade them to eat meat. Some of them wear linen shirts; we forbade the use of linen shirts and feather beds. They have an income of about one hundred sixty pounds, and they owe about one hundred forty pounds. We spent one hundred five shillings, five pence of Paris there [as procuration]. The monks appropriate the oblations,[7] even with the prior's knowledge. The prior never computes with his monks concerning the financial condition of the priory.

APRIL 29. At l'Estrée,[8] of the Order of Cistercians, at the expense of the house.

---

assisted by a deacon, a subdeacon, a thurifer, acolytes, and a master of ceremonies. See Joseph A. Jungman, *Missarum solemnia*, trans. Francis A. Brunner as *The Mass of the Roman Rite* (New York, 1950), I, 195-207.

[5] A Cistercian abbey founded in 1138. (Cottineau, I, 495-96.)

[6] A Benedictine priory founded in 1128. (Cottineau, II, 2024.)

[7] These are the offerings of the faithful.

APRIL 30. At the priory of Heudreville,[9] dependent on the abbey of Tiron, and at the expense of the priory. We visited there, finding four monks in residence, all being priests. They neither confess nor receive Communion each month as the Statutes of Pope Gregory require, nor, as they say, has a copy of the Statutes reached them. They owe about three hundred pounds; they have an income of about one hundred eighty pounds. We enjoined them to confess more often. Item, they use feather beds, a practice which we prohibited.

MAY 1. At Verneuil, at the expense of the manor of Tillières, which belongs to the monastery of Bec. No monks are there.

MAY 2. At the priory of St-Sulpice[10] near Laigle, and at the expense of the priory. Seven monks are there, five of whom are priests. They neither receive Communion nor confess each month as the Statutes of Pope Gregory require; we ordered them to maintain a strict observance of the Statutes covering these matters. Two novices are there; we willed that they be sent back to the abbey. They use feather beds. The prior does not sleep with the others. They eat meat when there is no need; we prohibited the use of feather beds and the eating of meat. They have an income of two hundred fifty pounds; they owe about a hundred pounds. Brother John Chicaut is a sower of discord.

We must speak to the bishop about the two novices at Laigle, and about removing John Chicaut.

MAY 3. We visited the priory of Rai,[11] where there are two monks. They eat meat occasionally; they use feather beds and fail to keep a full observance of the fasts. The prior's companion is so old that he should not be obliged to comply with the foregoing. We forbade the use of feather beds and the eating of meat except when permitted by the Rule. We ordered the fasts of the Rule to be rigorously observed.

This day we spent the night at Lierru,[12] of the order of St.-Augustine, and visited there on the morrow. Ten canons are there, and all but two are priests. They have an income of two hundred pounds and owe about one hundred pounds.

---

[8] A Cistercian abbey founded in 1145. (Cottineau, I, 1077.)

[9] St-Martin. (Cottineau, I, 1413.)

[10] A Benedictine priory, called St-Sulpice-sur-Risle, dependent on St-Laumer-de Blois. (Cottineau, II, 2897.)

[11] A Benedictine priory of St-Taurin-d'Evreux. (Cottineau, II, 2397.)

[12] St-Pierre, situated in the forest of Couches. (Cottineau, I, 1607.)

Since the priory of Rai was poor and had been damaged by fire, and the priory of Lierru was likewise in need, we did not accept full procuration from them. However, we ordered the prior of Rai that, of the amount of our procuration at Lierru, he should pay the prior of Lierru fifty-eight shillings; if he did not do this the prior of Lierru should enforce this payment, on our authority.

MAY 4. At Beaumont-le-Roger, a dependency of Bec.[13] Twelve monks are there. They have no copy of the Statutes of Pope Gregory. They pay the tithe on a declared income of one thousand pounds;[14] they owe about sixty pounds. They owe a pension of sixty shillings to a certain converted Jewess.

MAY 5. At Conches, of the order of St. Benedict.[15] Lay folk enter the cloister and the choir to hear Mass, and sometimes gentlewomen do so too. They do not observe the fasts of the Rule in full, and the healthy ones occasionally eat meat when there is no need. In the outside priories they eat meat whenever they please, nor do they observe the fasts of the Rule. They have an income of twelve hundred pounds, but there is no written record of this. We enjoined the abbot to audit the monastery accounts in the presence of the monks elected by the community. They owe about one hundred pounds. They owe about sixty-two pounds in annual pensions; we forbade them to grant any pensions. Item, our predecessor, P.,[16] by God's grace [cardinal] bishop of Albano, but at that time archbishop of Rouen, had ordered the monks to wear tunics,[17] and we found that some had them, but others did not. We ordered the abbot to provide tunics for all. Item, we forbade lay folk to enter the cloister. Item, we enjoined that the fasts of the Rule be more fully observed, and that the abbot should see to their fuller observance in the outside priories. Item, we forbade the eating of meat as well to those within the monastery as to those dwelling outside, except when the Rule permitted. We ordered a more complete statement of their income to be written out.

---

[13] Founded in 1070, it became dependent on Bec in 1143. (Cottineau, I, 306.)

[14] To the bishop and to the mother house, Bec. ("Dime," *Dict. de droit canon*, IV, 1231-41.) In this instance, it could indicate the royal tithes levied for the Crusades.

[15] A Benedictine abbey founded about 817. (Cottineau, I, 852-53.)

[16] Peter de Colmieu was archbishop of Rouen from 1236 to 1244, at which latter date he was nominated cardinal and bishop of Albano.

[17] The *tunica* was the everyday robe of the monk, with narrow sleeves, as opposed to the choir robe (*cuculla*), with its broad sleeves and hood.

MAY 6. At Evreux, where we were received in the cathedral with a procession. We entered the chapter, and after delivering a sermon we made
a visitation there. Asked whether they wished us to pursue our inquiries
in a general session or by individuals, they replied, after much discussion,
that we might do as we liked. Asked how the Divine Service was performed,
they said that it was well done and that the church had many and sufficient
ornaments. Item, that the offices were performed at the proper hours, unless
the matriculary[18] were remiss, in which event they dined in the presence of
the dean and went without wine on that day.[19] The dean does not perform
his duties and, because of his infirmity, has not done so for a long time.
They courteously and diligently replied to every question asked by us. Item,
the archdeacon, the cantor, the official, Master Auger, and other canons who
were present proposed that the lord bishop should pay the procuration for
our visitation of them, because of certain goods which he had in common
with them; we replied that we should be pleased to have the bishop pay, and
that we did not care who paid, so long as our present chapter visitation was
paid for. We told them to decide this matter for themselves and to take up
the question with the bishop if they wished, as we were unwilling to infringe upon his rights in any way. Item, having inquired from them about
the performance of the Offices and about the church ornaments in general,
we then asked whether, in the church of Evreux, there were any persons ill
famed of incontinence, of drunkenness, of wearing irregular garb, of running
about the town, or of engaging in trade; they replied that there were none
now, since they had just expelled two ill-famed clerks-choral from the choir.
After this we requested them to withdraw, and we then interviewed
them one by one and secretly. Beginning with the cantor, we asked him
whether any of the canons had been publicly known for incontinence, or
for engaging in trade and the like; he said no. We then called Peter, the
archdeacon, who, on being asked the same questions, returned the same answer
as the cantor. Next came Master William of Borcelles, who replied as the
others. Finally we called Master Auger, who answered likewise; but we
reprimanded him for the shape of his tonsure, and the excessively small

[18] The official who drew up the *matricula* or list of officers for the day or week.
He was attached to the sacristan and, in some houses, was the sacristan; thus, he was
responsible for the proper performance of the Divine Offices. As a general rule, he
was the subsacristan.

[19] This is an example of statutory penance local to the chapter of Evreux.

corona[20] which remained. He replied and promised that he would be more than willing to correct this. Asked why he was not a subdeacon, he replied that for some unknown reason he had kept putting it off up to now, and he promised that he would see to it that he became a subdeacon right away.

MAY 7. At La Noë,[21] order of Cistercians, at the expense of the monastery. MAY 8. At Coudres.[22] There are two monks [belonging to the abbey] of Bourgueil-en-Vallée.[23] They use feather beds; they eat meat freely. The priory has an income of four hundred pounds. We prohibited the use of feather beds and the eating of meat, save as the Rule permitted. MAY 9. At Jouy [-sur-Eure],[24] at the expense of the priory. Two monks from Jumièges are there. We found everything to be in good condition. They have an income of about four hundred pounds. MAY 10. At Jouy, at the expense of the priory of le Breuil-Benoît,[25] where there are no monks. MAY 11. At La Croix-St-Leufroy,[26] at our own expense. MAY 12. At the same, at the expense of the monastery, which we visited this day. Twenty monks are there. They have six priories. They eat meat freely in the priories. They have an income of five hundred pounds.

MAY 13. At St-Taurin-d'Evreux,[27] at the expense of the monastery, which we visited. There are twenty-two monks in residence, and three others are elsewhere now, but will return later. They have three priories; all are priests but three. They have an income of fourteen hundred pounds; they owe about two hundred pounds. The abbot does not cast his accounts with any of the brethren elected by the community. They are burdened with many pensions. They have the patronage of eleven churches.

MAY 14. We visited the monastery of nuns at St-Sauveur-d'Evreux.[28] There are sixty-one nuns in residence. The nuns occasionally drink in rooms other than the refectory and the infirmary. Item, they have small dogs, squirrels,

---

[20] The upper part of the head was shaved clean, leaving a crown (*corona*) or ridge of hair between the shaved part and the hair on the lower part of the head, which was close cut.

[21] A daughter house of Jouy, founded *c.* 1144. (Cottineau, II, 2081-82.)

[22] A Benedictine priory founded *c.* 994. (Cottineau, I, 892.)

[23] A Benedictine abbey located between Tours and Saumur. (Cottineau, I, 464-65.)

[24] A Benedictine priory of Jumièges. (Cottineau, I, 1492.)

[25] A daughter house of Clairvaux. (Cottineau, I, 495-96.)

[26] A Benedictine abbey founded *c.* 692. (Cottineau, I, 922.)

[27] A seventh-century Benedictine abbey. (Cottineau, I, 1088-89.)

[28] A Benedictine abbey founded *c.* 1060. (Cottineau, I, 1088.) Note that at the end of the visitation Eudes enters four names but gives no reason therefor.

and birds; we decreed that all such things be taken away. They do not observe the Rule. They have an income of nine hundred pounds; they owe about six hundred pounds. They eat meat when there is no need for it. They have locked coffers; we enjoined the abbess to make frequent and unannounced inspection of these coffers or else have the locks removed. They owe about forty pounds in pensions. Their stock of provisions is low. We enjoined the abbess to cast her accounts at least twice a year in the presence of some sisters elected by the community. Item, we decreed that they were to put away their metaled belts and their unseemly purses. Item, we decreed that the abbess should visit the sisters more frequently and take away the purses and pillows which they make unless they have her permission to possess them.

(Alice of Saussay, Nicholas of Villiers, Beatrice of Lisieux, Mathilda of Bruncourt.)

MAY 15. We were at the palace of the bishop of Evreux, and at his expense. We were honorably received at his special instructions, as we understood. In the evening we sent word to the chapter of Evreux and to all the canons who were in the city and physically able to attend to appear before us in our chambers.[29] When they had appeared we inquired of them in what manner the bishop conducted himself both in his church and in his episcopate, or diocese; how he exercised his pontifical office; his manner of conferring benefices; his general conduct and way of life; and such other things as we thought fitting. They replied that he performed his duties well and conducted himself worthily in everything. We celebrated Mass this day.

MAY 16. We came to Vernon, where we were received in a procession by the chapter of Vernon.[30] We spent the night at the bishop's manor, which is at Viviers, but at the expense of the chapter. We visited the chapter the following day. There are nine canons, of whom only three maintain residence. The bishop has the cure [of souls] of the chapter directly. We

[29] Note that there are two visitations: (1) on May 6, when the chapter itself is visited and inquries are made into its spiritual life; (2) on May 15, when the chapter is visited, but this time inquiries are made into its relations with the bishop, and it was also queried on the bishop as bishop.

[30] This is a reference to one of the two collegiate churches, or churches served by a college of secular priests, in the diocese of Evreux (La Saussaye and Vernon). (Dom J. M. Besse, *Abbayes et prieurés de l'ancienne France*, 8 vols. (Paris 1906-14), VII, 171.)

must speak to the bishop about to whom the patronage of the canons' parishes should belong. Item, also about regulating his way of making visitations there. Item, about the jurisdiction which the dean exercises over the canons, clerics, and vicars of the choir.

MAY 17. At Louviers, at our own expense.

MAY 18. At Daubeuf [-la-Campagne], at the expense of the priory. No monks are there. John of Valmont, curator of the house [priory] of Daubeuf, came to us and made amends for denying to us both entrance to and procuration for Daubeuf. His surety was Geoffrey le Bicauz. We enjoined him to restore to the monks of St-Ouen-de-Rouen the moneys they had sent in lieu of the food which they had not furnished on the preceding day when we had demanded procuration, inasmuch as he is obligated to this whenever we visit there.

MAY 19. At Montaure,[31] at the expense of the priory. We visited there the same day. Four monks are in residence, whereas there are normally three. All are priests. They use feather beds, and some have cloaks trimmed with fox fur. We forbade them to drink in the town, to go about the town, or to use feather beds. They do not observe the fasts of the Rule; we ordered them to maintain a strict observance of the Rule governing the fasts. They eat meat frequently; we ordered them to abstain according to the Rule. They have an income of one hundred sixty pounds. The prior does not audit his accounts with his companions, but only with... [*lacuna in MS*] the abbot,[32] and at that only once a year. We enjoined him to cast his accounts with his companions at least three times a year. The alms they give are small; we enjoined them to give alms more liberally to the poor. Item, that they should not leave the gate of the enclosure, without the permission of... [*lacuna in MS*] the prior. Item, that the prior should supply clothing and shoes to the community as means permit.

MAY 20. At Bonport,[33] at the expense of the monastery, by right of procuration. There came to us André of St-Léonard, a citizen of Rouen. He made amends, and promised that he would abide by our will, on oath taken in our presence, inasmuch as he himself confesses here and now that, armed and with an armed following, he had come at night to our greater mill at Rouen, the one situated by the Rue-du-Bocq bridge, and had carried off

---

[31] A Benedictine priory of St-Ouen-de-Rouen. (Cottineau, II, 1933.)
[32] That is, with Adam, abbot of St-Ouen-de-Rouen.
[33] A Cistercian daughter house of Cîteaux. (Cottineau, I, 432-33.)

grain and flour. By the same oath he promised to perform whatever penalty we laid upon him and to give us sufficient sureties up to one hundred silver marks before next Monday. He offered as his surety John of Val-Richer, nephew of Geoffrey of Val-Richer, who in this instance obligated himself as surety to us for the foregoing and who also pledged himself to the extent of one hundred silver marks.

[*No entry for May 21.*]

MAY 22. Having visited the diocese of Evreux, we came to Rouen and conferred Holy Orders at St-Ouen. We stayed the night at Déville. MAY 23. At Déville. MAY 24. We held the holy synod of the greater archdeanery of Rouen, and we spent the night at Déville. MAY 25. At Rouen. We celebrated Mass and held the greater synod. MAY 26. At Rouen. We ate at the Franciscan monastery, at our own expense. MAY 27. At St-Victor-en-Caux, at our own expense. MAY 28-JUNE 4. At Aliermont.

JUNE 5. At Mortemer-sur-Eaulne, and coming to the local priory of St-Martin,[34] we found three monks there and warned them to receive us both for visitation and for procuration. They denied both obligations; there were present: Brother Harduin, prior of the place; Brother Benedict, prior of Etoutteville; Brother William Tancone, monk of the said place; Master Stephen of Lorris and Master Theobald of Grandville, our companions; Ralph, priest at Le Caule; the dean of Foucarmont; William, priest of Boële, dean of Neufchâtel; and Stephen of Gien and Morel of Chelles, our clerks. We warned them to pay our procuration before the Nativity of Saint John and to make amends for failing to receive us, either for visitation or for procuration, or else, before the said time, to present reasons why they should not at least be held to this.

JUNE 6. At Gournay, at our own expense. JUNE 7. At Chaumont, at our own expense. JUNE 8-9. At Pontoise, at our own expense. JUNE 10. At Argenteuil, at our own expense. JUNE 11. At Pontoise, at our own expense. JUNE 12. At Chaumont, at our own expense. JUNE 13-16. At Sausseuse, at our own expense. JUNE 17. At Mortemer-en-Lyons, at the expense of the monastery. JUNE 18. At Beaubec, at the expense of the monastery.

JUNE 19. At Aumale,[35] at the expense of the monastery, which we visited the next day, finding sixteen monks there. One monk is alone in England; we enjoined the abbot to recall him to the cloister, or else give him a com-

[34] This was a Bec priory which felt it should be exempt. (Cottineau, II, 1991.)
[35] Originally built by Adelise, sister of William the Conqueror, as a house for

panion. There usually are twenty-five monks there. They have only a Latin version of the Statutes of Pope Gregory; we ordered the abbot to have them translated [into French]. They do not confess once a month; we ordered the Statutes of Pope Gregory dealing with this matter to be more fully observed. Lay folk enter the cloister at will, while the monks leave it without permission; we decreed that the cloister should be better kept. Item, we decreed that whoever should leave the cloister without permission should go without wine both that day and the next. Silence is not well kept; we decreed and ordered that it be better observed, and that a daily accusation be brought [in chapter] against those who infringe the rule of silence. The fasts are not well observed, especially by those who travel by horseback; we enjoined them to observe them more fully. They use meat when there is no need; we absolutely forbade them the use of meat. They have an income of fifteen hundred pounds; they owe about thirty pounds in pensions and are burdened with debts to the extent of one thousand sixty pounds. We ordered the kitchener to be sent away from the convent, and that without fail.

JUNE 20. At Aliermont. JUNE 21. At Bellencombre, at our own expense. JUNE 22-24. At Déville. JUNE 25. At Rouen. JUNE 26. At Rouen, and this day, in the presence of the bishops of Bayeux,[36] Avranches,[37] Evreux,[38] and Séez,[39] we consecrated ... [lacuna in MS] as bishop of Lisieux.[40] JUNE 27. At St-Philbert, at the manor of the lord of Avranches. JUNE 28. At Le Theil[-Nolent]. JUNE 29. At Lisieux, and today Lord F., by God's grace bishop of Lisieux, made his first solemn entry.[41]

---

canons, it became a Benedictine abbey about 1130. (Cottineau, I, 204-5.) It had two priories in Yorkshire, Birstall and Witherness. (Dugdale, *Monasticon Anglicanum,* VII, 1019-20, 1056.)

[36] Gui (1241-60). (Gams, *Series episcoporum,* p. 507.)

[37] William V (Guillaume de Ste-Mère-Eglise) (1236-52). Gams, *Series episcoporum,* p. 506.)

[38] Jean de la Cour-d'Aubergenville (1244-56). (Gams, *Series episcoporum,* p. 550.)

[39] Geoffrey de Maïet (1241-58). (Gams, *Series episcoporum,* p. 626.)

[40] Fulk d'Astin (1250-67). (Gams, *Series episcoporum,* p. 566.)

[41] When a bishop was consecrated outside his own diocese, the day of entry into his episcopal church was a day of ceremony. He was met at the outskirts of his episcopal city and, seated on a chair, was borne to the cathedral by the leading citizens of the city. This was the solemn entry spoken of here. The best study on the many aspects of episcopal elections and ceremonial is still Imbart de la Tour, *Les Elections épiscopales dans l'église de France du IX-XII siècle* (Paris, 1891), pp. 319-78.

JUNE 30. We entered the diocese of Séez, and spent the night at St-Pierre-sur-Dives, where was also the lord [bishop] of Séez; but he did not spend the night there. The visitation of the diocese of Séez begins on folio 61.[42]

JUNE 30. We spent the night at St-Pierre-sur-Dives,[43] at the expense of the monastery. The next day we visited it, the lord [bishop] of Séez being present. Thirty monks are there. They have no priories this side of the sea, but they have two in England. Some of them do not confess once a month; we decreed that the Statute of Pope Gregory on this matter be more fully observed. All are priests but three. Traveling monks do not observe the fasts; we ordered that all should observe them. Item, they sometimes eat meat when there is no need; we utterly forbade them to eat meat except when the Rule permitted it. They have an income of about two thousand pounds and thirty marks from England. We ordered that the community elect some of the brothers to audit the abbot's accounts and to be informed about the state of the house. They owe about forty pounds in pensions. Otherwise they owe nothing, for, indeed, money is owed to them. Guests are not particularly well received, because they gave a part of the guest house to a certain layman; we enjoined the abbot to appoint within three days one of the monks to look after the guests more honorably, and to use his own funds if there were a deficit. We forbade him to drink any wine after the third day until he shall have attended to this. The abbot does not sleep in the dormitory, nor does he arise for Matins. He does not cast his accounts with the community. He promised to correct these faults. Item, the abbot promised to show and to reveal to the prior, to the monk in charge of the grain, and to the kitchener, just what [resources] he had, since they had accused him of having many things of which they were in ignorance.

JULY 1. At Pérrièrs,[44] at the expense of the priory. The monks there belong to Marmoutier of Tours and are exempt. JULY 2. At Trun,[45] at the expense of the priory of Coulimer.

---

[42] That is, the entry which follows, June 30. There seems to be no particular reason why Eudes' clerk made special reference here to the folio.

[43] A Benedictine abbey founded in 1046. (Cottineau, II, 2851-52.) It had three priories in England: Modbury (Devonshire), Tutbury (Staffordshire), and Wolston (Warwickshire). Eudes erroneously states that it had only two.

[44] St-Vigor, a Benedictine priory founded before 1076. (Cottineau, II, 2257.)

[45] A Benedictine priory dependent on Troarn. (Cottineau, II, 3228.) Coulimer de-

JULY 3. At Tournai [-sur-Dives],[46] where there are two monks belonging to Croix-St-Leufroy. Although the prior had spoken with us the day before, he was not present when we were there; nay rather, he absented himself. However, we visited the priory as best we could, [questioning] the monk who was the prior's companion. They eat meat when there is no need, and they fail to observe the fasts of the Rule; we enjoined them to abstain from eating flesh, and to observe the fasts of the Rule more strictly. We told the monk who was the prior's companion to inform the prior that he should come to us, wherever we might be, within eight days, to make amends for evading our visitation; and that otherwise we would punish him more severely.

JULY 4. At Planches,[47] at our own expense.

JULY 5. At the same place, but at the expense of the priory, which we visited. There are two monks from St-Père-de-Chartres. They use feather beds. They have no written copy either of their own Rule nor of the Statutes of Pope Gregory in the priory. The prior does not confess once a month, as the Statutes of Pope Gregory require. They do not sing the canonical Hours together. They do not observe the fasts of the Rule. The prior eats meat. They have an income of sixty-four pounds; they owe about twenty pounds. The prior does not compute with his companion concerning the state of the house. We enjoined him to obtain copies of the Rule and of the Statutes. We absolutely forbade the use of feather beds and meat, except as permitted by the Rule. Item, we decreed a stricter observance of the fasts of the Rule, and that they should confess once a month, as the Statutes of Pope Gregory require. We ordered them to celebrate Mass more frequently, ot sing their Hours together, and to sleep together in the same house.

JULY 6. At La Trappe, order of Cistercians, at the expense of the monastery. JULY 7. At Mortagne,[48] at the expense of the dean and chapter, and, at our visitation, we found their income to be insufficient. The statute covering the coming in and going out is not observed.[49]

---

pended on La Couture-du-Mans. (Cottineau, I, 893.)

[46] A Benedictine priory. (Cottineau, II, 3188.)

[47] A Benedictine priory of St-Père-de-Chartres. (Cottineau, II, 2295.)

[48] Ste-Madeleine de Chartrage, a conventual house of canons regular. (Cottineau, I, 713; Besse, *Abbayes et prieurés de l'ancienne France,* VII, 224.)

[49] That is, ingress and exit to and from the chapter's religious establishment without permission of the dean.

JULY 8. At Ste-Gauburge.[50] The monks here come from St-Denis in France.[51] The prior was not there, for, indeed, his own monks had caused him to be summoned to St-Denis. They were unwilling to reply to any of our questions, stating that they were exempt. However, rumors of incontinence and of running about the town are connected with several of the monks of this place.

Thibault,[52] by God's grace archbishop of Rouen, to all the faithful of Christ who may see this letter, greeting in the Lord. Know that a dispute arose between us, on the one hand, and the religious men, P.[53] the abbot and convent of St-Denis-en-France, on the other, concerning visitation and procuration in connection with their priory of Ste-Gauburge, situated in our province, to wit, in the diocese of Séez; we claiming the same visitation and procuration to belong by right to our office as metropolitan, they disagreeing. However, for the good of the peace, a friendly compromise was arrived at in the following way: if it should so please us to visit the aforesaid priory every three years, we shall have the right to do so. We and our successors shall receive, at the time of such visitation, and in the name of procuration, forty shillings, to be paid by the prior or occupier of the said place, from the income of the priory. We agreed that we and our successors shall be content with the said payment and shall have no power to demand or claim any higher procuration. Further, the prior or occupier shall not have the power to deny the house to us or to our successors. To make this agreement duly official it is approved by, and has the consent of, our chapter. In confirmation whereof, we place the authority of our seal and that of the chapter on this letter. Given in the year of grace 1224, in the month of June.

JULY 9. At Dame-Marie,[54] where there are two monks of Jumièges. They do not observe the fasts of the Rule. They have an income of one hundred twenty pounds. We enjoined them to observe the fasts of the Rule more fully. JULY 10-11. At the same, at our own expense.

[50] A Benedictine priory of St-Bonneval, built before 1024, it was given to St-Père de-Chartres by Bishop Yves de Bellême (1034-70); then to St-Denis. (Cottineau, II, 2691.)

[51] Eudes differentiates between Normandy which in 1205 had been added to the French crown's possessions, and France itself. It may also be that he is here referring to the Ile-de-France.

[52] Thibault d'Amiens was archbishop of Rouen from 1222 to 1229. (Gams, *Series episcoporum*, p. 614.)

[53] Peter I was abbot of St-Denis from 1221 to 1247. (*Gallia Christiana*, VII, 385-87.) The documents in the *Gallia Christiana* relating to the dispute do not throw further light on the matter.

[54] A Benedictine priory of Jumièges. (Cottineau, I, 943.)

JULY 12. At St-Martin-de-Bellême,[55] at the expense of the priory. The monks there come from Marmoutier. When they had paid us our procuration fee on behalf of this priory, we told them in the presence of Masters Simon of St-Pierre-sur-Dives, a canon of Lisieux; Robert of Grainville, a canon of Rouen; Thibaut, master of the school at Lisieux; Stephen of Lorris; and our clerks and our companions, Brothers William of Guerches, Peter Belini, of the Order of Franciscans, and Stephen of Gien, our clerk, that on the next day they should be prepared to pay us procuration for St. Leonard's chapel, in the château of Bellême. They entirely denied this obligation. However, we offered them a delay of eight days within which they should present reasons, if any, why they should not be held to this procuration. We asked them if they would accept this postponement. They did not reply to this query directly, but stated that they would take counsel, and then straightway they appealed to Rome, on the grounds that we were demanding this undue and unaccustomed procuration. Returning from their consultation almost at once, they announced that they would neither accept the day which we had proposed, nor would they assign any other reasons. The letter of appeal ran as follows:

Since you, Reverend Father... [*lacuna in MS*] by God's grace archbishop of Rouen, have demanded an undue and unaccustomed procuration from the prior and monks of Bellême, and unlawfully have tried to extort it, the said prior and the monks feel themselves injured, and they place themselves and their affairs under the protection of the Lord Pope, appealing to the Apostolic See in writing, lest you try to take any steps against them and theirs, and herewith they ask you for *apostoli*.

JULY 13. On the next day we questioned them about the state of the house. They replied that they had an abbot and a prior from whom they received correction if there were anything to be corrected there. We told them that they should produce for us before the Feast of the Assumption their privileges, if they had any, showing why we should not exercise visitation there.

We spent the night at St-Grodogrand, at our own expense.

JULY 14. At Alençon,[56] where there are two monks from Lonlay. There

---

[55] A Benedictine priory of Marmoutier. The abbey of Marmoutier enjoyed the privilege of exemption. Its dependent priory was only claiming the privilege enjoyed by its mother house. (Cottineau, I, 331-32.)

[56] A Benedictine priory of Lonlay. (Cottineau, I, 53.)

usually are three monks there; we ordered the number to be completed. They do not observe the fasts of the Rule; we enjoined the prior to observe the fasting rules more fully, and to see that they were observed. They eat meat when there is no need; we prohibited them the use of meat, except as the Rule permitted. They have an income of one hundred forty pounds of Tours; they owe about twenty-five pounds. The prior does not compute with his companion concerning the state of the house; we decreed that all of his companions should be informed of the state of the house.

JULY 15. At St-Martin-de-Séez.[57] Thirty-five monks are in residence. All but three are priests. They do not have a French copy of the Statutes of Pope Gregory. They do not observe the fasts of the Rule in the outside priories; we enjoined the abbot to see that they were observed. They use feather beds in the priories. They eat meat when there is no need; we forbade them the eating of meat, except as the Rule permitted. They have an income of seventeen hundred pounds; they owe about seven hundred pounds.

JULY 16. At St-Gervais,[58] the cathedral church of Séez. Twenty-four canons are in residence. One canon is serving alone in a certain church in the diocese of Le Mans. All but three are priests. Those who are not priests receive Communion only once a year; we ordered them to receive Communion at Easter, Christmas, and Pentecost. The cloister is not well kept; indeed, lay folk enter the cloister. The rule of silence is not observed in the cloister nor in the church. Seculars, both priests and clerics, sit in the choir with the canons. Some of the canons have striped serges; we enjoined the bishop to see that these striped serges were removed. They have an income of about twelve hundred pounds. Some of their churches are served by secular vicars, who do not have the cure of souls; we ordered that these vicars be presented to the bishop and receive the cure of souls from him. Seculars eat in the refectory with the canons. They owe about thirty-three pounds in pensions. More is owed to them than they owe, and they have a sufficiency of provisions. The archdeacons buy their horses to keep as their own.[59] The canons drink in the town. The prior is somewhat negligent and

---

[57] A Benedictine abbey built c. 1050. (Cottineau, II, 2992-93.)

[58] In April, 1226, Geoffrey, archbishop of Rouen, consecrated the cathedral of Séez to SS. Gervasius and Protasius. The Bishop of Séez was Gervase I (1220-28). (Gams, *Series episcoporum*, p. 626.)

[59] The archdeacon made a yearly visitation of his archdeaconry. This he did on horseback. But these canons were part of a community bound by rules of poverty, and

is incapable of exercising his office. Item, we found certain persons there who had been defamed for their acts. The following items are contained in the letter which we sent to the bishop of Séez, in this form:

Brother Eudes, by God's permission unworthy minister of the church of Rouen, to the venerable Brother G[eoffrey], by God's grace bishop of Séez, eternal greeting in the Lord Jesus Christ. Coming to the church at Séez for the purpose of making a visitation, a duty which our office demands of us, we found certain matters requiring correction, at which we neither could nor should connive. Further, since you abide there as a rule, we can accuse you of negligence unless your diligence redeem the blame. We found that the sacrosanct and venerable Blessed Sacrament is so placed on the high altar that those passing through the choir, or praying there, do not have It before their eyes as is meet, so that their devotion may be increased. Item, we found not only that the rule of silence is infringed, but, indeed, that it is hardly observed at all, whether in the church, the cloister, the refectory, or the dormitory. The canons, even in the presence of lay folk, quarrel with one another, and the Divine Office is disturbed. Item, we found that quarrels of this kind are not curbed by anyone. Item, the cloister is very badly kept, and in it the canons gossip and sit with lay folk, nor is there anyone to keep out those who wish to enter. Item, the canons invite seculars, both cleric and lay, and even dubious characters, to eat with them, bringing them into the refectory without bothering to ask permission. Item, no attenton is paid to hospitality, nor is any person appointed to receive the guests, as there should be.

Item, in the dormitory we found unseemly serges and coverlets, that is to say, striped ones. Item, [we found] that many of the canons have been defamed for their acts; indeed, almost all of the archdeacons are publicly known for having property, nor do they compute with the prior concerning the profits from the two archdeaconries. Item, Brother Oliver has been defamed for disobedience or impudence; Gervaise, the cellarer, and the cantor, of incontinence, of too much running about the town and drinking there, very often without any companion and without permission. Item, the same cellarer and cantor frequently absent themselves from Compline and from Matins; item, we found the cellarer to be publicly known for having property and to be negligent in celebrating his Mass, which he omits altogether. Item, we found Hugh Cortillers ill famed of engaging in trade, of possessing property, of incontinence, and of inebriety. Item, we found William of Herbei publicly known for having property and for incontinence; he wears unseemly clothes, to wit, those of many

---

thus no individual could have anything of his own. ("Archidiacre," *Dict. de droit canon.*, I, 948-1001.)

colors, and even wears them when he walks abroad, and without a surplice or frock. Item, we found that when you had sent him to the cloister because of his unseemly bearing, they made him attorney of the assizes,[60] whence he had opportunities for wandering about and falling into his old way of sin. Item, we found that the canons, on going into the town, very frequently stopped for a drink in the houses of the townspeople. Item, we found that in parochial churches they have vicars who have not received the cure of souls, and great danger, therefore, threatens the souls of the parishioners, nor have these vicars been presented to you. In consideration of these things, we order you to correct all of these excesses, and to see that your reformation program is carried out, so that you may not deserve censure for greater negligence. You will inform us in writing of what you have done, so that we may put our hand to it, if necessary. Given at Brieux, the Sunday before the feast of Saints James and Christopher, in the year of our Lord 1250.

JULY 17. We visited the monastery of nuns at Notre-Dame-d'Almenè-ches,[61] where there are thirty-four nuns. All of them own property; they have their own casseroles, copper kettles, and necklaces. Item, they contract debts in town, and eat and sit at table in friendly groups Money is given to each one to provide herself with cooked food and victuals. Many remain away from Compline and Matins, and drink after Compline. Theophana drinks too much. They have no regulation or set time for confessing or receiving Communion. Sister Hola recently had a child by a certain Michael of Val-Guy. Lay folk enter the cloister at will and talk with the nuns. Item, they never eat in the refectory. Denise Dehatim is ill famed of Master Nicholas of Blève. They also quarrel in the cloister and in the choir. Alice, the cantress, had a child by Christian. Item, the prioress had a child some time ago. They have no abbess, for the one they had is lately dead. To procure them an abbess, they agreed on us and the bishop of Séez, and we have the letters of agreement which are entered on folio 126.[62]

This day we spent the night at the monastery of Silly,[63] Premonstratensian Order, at the expense of the monastery.

JULY 18. At St-André-en-Gouffern,[64] of the Cistercian Order, and we

---

[60] These were meetings of the secular courts to which ecclesiastics were often cited, especially from the reign of Philip Augustus on, to defend themselves against royal officials. Strayer, *Administration of Normandy*, pp. 17, 23, 26-30.)

[61] A Benedictine abbey founded c. 769. (Cottineau, I, 62.)

[62] This document is not found in the indicated place.

[63] Notre-Dame-de-Silly-en-Gouffern. (Cottineau, II, 3035-36.)

[64] Affiliated with Clairvaux in 1147. (Cottineau, II, 2588.)

visited the priory of Brieux[65] in transit. Two monks from St-Martin-de-Séez are there. The prior's companion sometimes leaves the priory without permission; we forbade him to do this. He neither receives Communion nor confesses as the Statutes of Pope Gregory require; we decreed that the said Statutes covering these matters be observed. They do not observe the fasts of the Rule, and they eat meat; we ordered them to observe the fasts, and we forbade them to eat meat, except when the Rule permitted. They have an income of about fifty pounds; they owe about twenty pounds, and when by reason of our visitation we requested procuration from the said priory, the abbot and convent of St-Martin-de-Séez absolutely denied the obligation for the priory. At length we agreed upon the bishop of Séez as arbiter in this quarrel, and we have their letter on the matter, as follows:

To all who may see these letters, . . .[66] the abbot and convent of St-Martin-de-Séez, greeting in the Lord. Be it known to all of you by the tenor of the present letter that when the Reverend Father Eudes, by God's grace archbishop of Rouen, in the exercise of his office visited his province while he was in the diocese of Séez, and by reason of visitation sought procuration from the priory of Brieux our monastery, situated in this diocese, a right which he claimed to have, we informed him that for certain reasons we were not obliged to pay this. However, both ourselves and the aforesaid mentioned Reverend Father Eudes compromised upon our venerable Father G[eoffrey] by God's grace bishop of Séez, as arbiter in this disagreement. Under penalty of forfeiting a hundred silver marks, we promised to regard as valid and agreeable whatever disposition he should make of the aforesaid matter. Given in the year of our Lord 1250, on the vigil of the Blessed Mary Magdalene.

This day, which was the feast of St. Margaret, we visited, in passing, the priory of Ste-Marguerite-de-Gouffern,[67] and celebrated Mass there. Twenty-four nuns are in residence. They do not keep [the Rule on] silence. They wander about in the courtyard without permission. Lay folk enter the cloister. They do not wear the same kind of habit, because of their poverty. They have an income of one hundred pounds. We forbade anyone to go into the courtyard without the permission of the prioress, and we ordered the cloister to be better guarded, and that they should observe community life in so far as they were able.

---

[65] A Benedictine priory of Séez. (Cottineau, I, 502.)
[66] The abbot was John II. (*Gallia Christiana*, XI, 722.)
[67] A Benedictine priory of nuns. (Cottineau, II, 2782.)

JULY 19. At St-Jean-de-Falaise,[68] at the expense of the monastery. Premonstratensian canons are there. JULY 20. At the same, and this day we
dedicated the Franciscan church at Falaise and ate there. JULY 21. At
Briouze,[69] where there are two monks from Saumur. JULY 22. At the
monastery of Lonlay [-l'Abbaye],[70] in the diocese of Le Mans, at our own
expense. JULY 23. At . . . [place is erased in the MS].

JULY 24. Here begins the visitation of the diocese of Avranches, in 1250.
At Mortain, where we visited the chapter of St-Guillaume-Fermer. The
chapter comprises sixteen secular canons, but only four are in residence
Jocelin, canon, is publicly known for engaging in trade, and he sends pigs
into the forest to fatten them. Roger, canon, has his daughter, who is fif-
teen or thereabouts, living with him. Firmin, the prior's vicar, is a trader.
We warned all of these. We spent the night at the priory of Rocher [-de-
Mortain],[71] at the expense of the aforesaid chapter.

JULY 25. At the same place, but at the expense of the priory. Monks from
Marmoutier are there. JULY 26. At Savigny,[72] Cistercian Order, at the
expense of the monastery. JULY 27. At St-Hilaire.[73] The monks are from
St-Benoît [-sur-Loire] and are exempt. At the expense of the priory.

JULY 28. At the abbey of Montmorel,[74] Order of St. Augustine. Fifteen
canons are in residence at the abbey, and there are eight in the outside
priories, of which there are four. One canon is dwelling alone in a priory;
we decreed that he be recalled to the cloister or that a companion be given
him. They have an income of about seven hundred pounds of Tours; they
do not owe more than is owed to them and it is collectable. Although the
accounts of the state of the house are frequently cast, no computation is
made in the presence of any canons elected by the community; we ordered
that brothers be elected by the community in whose presence the accounts
should be made up. They owe about fourteen pounds in pensions. They
have the patronage of about ten churches. The lepers are not kept in the

[68] Originally Augustinian (1134), it became Premonstratensian in 1158. (Cottineau,
I, 1102.)
[69] A Benedictine priory of St-Florent-de-Saumur. (Cottineau, I, 507.)
[70] A Benedictine abbey founded about 1020. (Cottineau, I, 1651.)
[71] A Benedictine priory of Marmoutier. (Cottineau, II, 2488.)
[72] Originally dependent on Marmoutier, it became Cistercian in 1147. (Cottineau,
II, 2965-67.)
[73] St-Hilaire-d'Harcourt [du Harcouet], a Benedictine priory. (Cottineau, II, 2728.)
[74] An Augustinian abbey, founded 1160-70. (Cottineau, II, 1967.)

infirmary, as they should be. We ordered that such essentials as his illness required be given to each.

To all who may see this letter, Philip, prior of Les Biards,[75] in the diocese of Avranches, greeting in the Lord. Be it known to you that when the Reverend Father Eudes, by God's grace archbishop of Rouen, visiting his province, demanded procuration from our priory by reason of his visitation, we did not deny it to him so far as our resources allowed; but, pleading the privilege of poverty, we begged him to spare us this fee, and he, moved by our prayers and considerate of our poverty, graciously remitted the fee on this occasion. In witness whereof, we have caused our seal to be affixed to the present letter. Given at Montmorel, the sixth day after the Feast of SS. James and Christopher, in the year of our Lord 1250.

JULY 31. At Sacey,[76] where there are three monks from Marmoutier. We made a visitation. Asked whether they lived in common, they replied, "Yes." Asked whether they clothed themselves from the common resources of the house, they said, "Yes." Asked whether they handed in their old clothes when they received new ones, they replied, "Yes," or that otherwise they got none. Asked whether the prior had the cure of the monks' souls, they answered, "Yes." Asked whether they were all priests, they said, "Yes." Asked whether they all celebrated their Masses, they replied that there was one old man who because of his bodily infirmity does not celebrate. Asked whether they confessed in accordance with the Statutes of Pope Gregory, and likewise as to the statutory recommendations concerning Communion, they replied in the affirmative. Asked in what manner they slept, they replied that they slept on feather beds; we forbade the use of these save in cases of necessity and when the Rule permitted. Asked whether they ate meat, they replied that they did; we forbade the eating of meat, save as the Rule permitted. They have an income of about two hundred pounds; they owe nothing, since much more is owed to them than they owe.

AUGUST 1. At Mont-St-Michel,[77] at the expense of the monastery, and on the following day we visited it, finding forty monks there. Two monks are dwelling alone in outside priories; we enjoined the abbot to give them

---

[75] A Benedictine priory in the diocese of Avranches. (Cottineau, I, 376.)

[76] A Benedictine priory of Marmoutier. (Cottineau, II, 2572.)

[77] This famous abbey began as a hermitage. Richard I, duke of Normandy, settled Benedictines there in 966. (Cottineau, II, 1897-1908.) The abbot at the time of Eudes' visitation was Richard III (1237-64). (*Gallia Christiana*, XI, 522-23.)

companions or to recall them to the cloister. Layfolk and women enter the cloister at will. The monks in the priories do not observe the fasts of the Rule and eat meat whenever they feel inclined to; we ordered the abbot to see that they abstained and to punish abuses of this kind. They have an income of five thousand pounds of Tours; they owe nothing, since much more is owed to them [than they owe].

AUGUST 2. At La Lucerne,[78] Premonstratensian Order, at the expense of the monastery.

AUGUST 3. We came to Avranches and were honorably received with a procession and the pealing of bells. We found four priests there who celebrate High Mass at the high altar, and who perform all priestly functions during the week. Sometimes they say the Office for the Dead *recto tono*.[79] Some of the poor clerks-choral from the choir engage in trade, but the dean does not know their names; we enjoined him to make diligent inquiry and to discipline them.

The chapter attended to our procuration this day.

AUGUST 4. We were with the bishop of Avranches, and visited him.

AUGUST 5. We came to Le Parc, the bishop's manor, at his expense.

AUGUST 6. [Here begins the visitation of the diocese of] Coutances. We entered the diocese of Coutances and spent the night at St-Sever,[80] at our own expense.

AUGUST 7. At the same, at the expense of the monastery. Eighteen monks are in residence. They have three priories, one this side of the sea, and two in England. All but four of the monks are priests. They do not confess every month; sometimes they eat meat freely, and after leaving the refectory. They have an income of about eight hundred pounds; they owe nothing. They pay pensions to the amount of fifty pounds. They have the patronage of twenty-two churches.

AUGUST 8. We spent the night at Villedieu-de-Saultchevreuil[81] and received procuration from the Knights of St. John. Today Master Nicholas of Hotrehan came before us and made the following deposition:

---

[78] A daughter house of St-Josse-aux-Bois. (Cottineau, I, 1668.)

[79] I.e., in plain monotone, without song or notes.

[80] A Benedictine abbey destroyed by the Normans, rebuilt about 1085. (Cottineau, II, 2887-88.)

[81] This commandery was mentioned in an inquiry made by Philip IV in 1292. *Cartulaire général de l'ordre de S-Jean-de-Jérusalem (1100-1310)*, ed. J. Delaville le Roulx, 4 vols. (Paris, 1894-1906), III, 636.

When a vacancy occurred in one of the prebends of the church of Coutances, the venerable father Giles,[82] of blessed memory, by God's grace bishop of Coutances, collated me, Nicholas of Hotrehan, and with his ring canonically invested me with the said prebend and all its appurtenances. By reason of the said prebend, my proctor was specially installed in my name by the bishop's vicar. But the canons of the said church because of greed refused and still unjustly refuse to accede to my request to be admitted to the canonry and to their fellowship. In all justice, I have appealed to the Apostolic See. I have appealed that so long as they spurn me and refuse to accept me or admit me to their body, they be forbidden to proceed to any election or any other common business or management of the chapter in which I might, should, and ought to be present. Further, I have appealed that, by reason of the prosecution of my right to the possession of the said prebend, no executor or any other pass any sentence against me or attempt to do anything prejudicial to my rights; which appeals, legally drawn up by me collectively and severally, I place before you, Reverend Father Eudes, by God's grace archbishop of Rouen, placing myself and my affairs under apostolic protection, and requesting you, in witness whereof, to place your seal on the present letter. Done at Villedieu-de-Saultchevreuil, in the year of our Lord 1250, the Monday preceding the feast of St. Lawrence.

AUGUST 9. At Hambye,[83] at the expense of the monastery, where we found seventeen monks. They have four priories, in one of which a monk is dwelling alone; we enjoined the abbot to recall him to the cloister or to give him a companion. Item, the same with regard to another, who is dwelling alone in another priory near Coutances. They do not have enough chalices, for they have but one. They do not possess a copy of the Statutes of Pope Gregory. They confess but rarely. They do not have private cubicles in the dormitory. They do not observe the fasts of the Rule, and they eat meat at least once a week. They have an income of six hundred pounds, but the sources of income are not well written down. No one is appointed to receive guests. They do not audit the accounts as the Statutes of Pope Gregory require. The monks state that they owe eleven hundred pounds. They have the patronage of six churches. Item, the monks say that the prior should be chosen by the community.[84]

---

[82] Gilles de Caen (1246-48). (Gams, *Series episcoporum*, p. 542.)

[83] A Benedictine abbey of the Congregation of Tiron. (Cottineau, I, 1374-75.)

[84] According to the Benedictine Rule (Ch. 64), all officials were appointed by the abbot.

AUGUST 10. At St-Lô,[85] at the expense of the monastery.

AUGUST 11. At the same, but at our own expense, and we made a visitation. We found twenty-five canons there. All but five are priests. Some with the permission of the abbot do not confess to him; the others do confess to him. In general, they confess only twice a year. Concerning daily affairs, many of them go out to the manor every day, and without permission. They have an income of one thousand pounds, and they owe about one hundred forty pounds. The sources of income are not written out. They owe about eight pounds in pensions. Almost all of them have property. They buy wine even when there is some in the monastery, and each one buys according to his means. The sick are not well cared for; we ordered and enjoined the abbot to see that the sick were treated as their condition warranted and as the monastery could afford. Item, we ordered the shabby infirmary to be altogether removed. Item, we forbade anyone to receive any gift from anyone, be he secular or religious, without the abbot's permission. Item, if they should receive anything with permission, they should hand it over to the abbot at once. Item, women often come to the monastery, enter the rooms, and even drink there; that is to say, some of the more prominent burghers' wives and some of the canons, especially the kitchener, drink with them; we forbade any such admission of women; indeed, we prohibited entry to any woman, and forbade any canon to presume to drink with them. Item, we found that the abbot is rather severe with the relatives of the canons when they come to the monastery to see their relations, and this is one reason at least why they acquire things of their own. Item, when their relatives come, they receive their pittances for subsequent days to give them to their relations; this we forbade. The cloister is not well kept. Lay folk enter the cloister at will.

AUGUST 12-13. At St-Lô, at our own expense. [*No entry for August 14.*] AUGUST 15. At Coutances.

AUGUST 16. At the same, at the expense of the chapter, which we visited. We found twenty-six canons there, and seven rectors:[86] namely, four archdeacons, a cantor, a master of the school, and a treasurer. The master of the school, the cantor, and the treasurer must maintain permanent residence. There are no fines for being absent from the Divine Offices, nor are deficiencies in performing the Divine Offices punished. All of the canons,

---

85 An abbey of Augustinian canons. (Cottineau, II, 2768-69.)
86 "Rectors" in this context means the dignitaries and officials of the chapter.

even those who are not subdeacons, sit in the high stalls,[87] leave the choir whenever they like and without permission, and talk loudly enough to be heard from one side of the choir to the other. They do not visit the treasure room; we ordered them to visit it every year. The church ornaments are not kept clean. Master William of Oissel drinks too much, considering his advanced age. Richard of Tresgoz is a trader.[88] Master Richard of Trigale is a quarreler. Advisard, Thomas Faber, and John Faber are ill famed of incontinence.

AUGUST 17. At St-Pair,[89] at the expense of the priory. We made a visitation and found two monks here from Mont-St-Michel. They eat meat and use feather beds; we forbade the use of both. They have an income of one thousand pounds, of which they send eight hundred pounds to their monastery; they owe nothing.

AUGUST 18. We were at Bricqueville, at the expense of Jean Paisnel, archdeacon of Coutances. AUGUST 19. At Pérrièrs,[90] at the expense of the monastery, or priory. No monks are there.

AUGUST 20. At the monastery of Lessay,[91] which we visited. We found thirty-six monks there. One monk is dwelling alone at St-Martin-des-Iles, and the same condition exists in two other priories; we enjoined the abbot to send companions to them or else recall them to the cloister. They do not observe the fasts of the Rule, and this is particularly true of the traveling monks; we forbade them to eat meat and enjoined them to a fuller observance of the regular fasts. They have an income of fourteen hundred pounds; they owe about four hundred fifty pounds. We enjoined the abbot to cast his accounts on the state of the house in the presence of some of the brothers elected by the community, at least twice a year.

AUGUST 21. At Blanchelande,[92] a Premonstratensian abbey.

AUGUST 22. At St-Sauveur.[93] Here we visited and found that there are twenty-five monks in residence and fourteen dwelling outside. They have

---

[87] The higher stalls were reserved for dignitaries and officials of the chapter.

[88] This is the same Richard who became abbot of Fécamp in 1259 and continued to loan money to prelates and laymen alike. (Léon Fallue, *Histoire de la ville et de l'abbaye de Fécamp* (Rouen, 1841), pp. 208-13.)

[89] A Benedictine priory, dependent on Mont-St-Michel. (Cottineau, II, 2832.)

[90] A Benedictine priory dependent on St-Taurin-d'Evreux. (Cottineau, II, 2249.)

[91] A Benedictine abbey colonized from Bec. (Cottineau, I, 1592.)

[92] This was founded *c.* 1160. (Cottineau, I, 388.)

[93] St-Sauveur-le-Vicomte, a Benedictine abbey founded *c.* 1080. (Cottineau, II, 2880-81.)

six priories. Traveling monks do not observe the fasts of the Rule. The
bread set aside for the poor is so coarse that men cannot eat it; they promised
to correct this. There are two advocates[94] there who spend more than they
should; they are incompetent and noted for incontinence. They have an
income of about one thousand pounds; they owe nothing, and, indeed, a
good deal of the money left to them by their late abbot is still due. The
abbot does not compute the accounts of the house; we ordered him to compute twice a year and the officials to make a written statement of their
accounts each month. They owe about twenty pounds in pensions. In the
outside priories they do not observe the fasts of the Rule and they use
meat; we forbade them to eat meat and enjoined the abbot to see to it that
the fasts of the Rule were observed and that [his monks] abstained from
meat.

AUGUST 23. At Montebourg,[95] at the expense of the monastery. The next
day we visited it, finding thirty-seven monks and four priories. In each
priory there are two monks. Item, one monk is dwelling alone on the Islands;[96] we ordered him recalled or that a companion be given him. All
are priests, with the exception of the novices. They rarely celebrate their
Masses; we enjoined the abbot to correct this. The rule of silence is not
fully observed, especially by those serving in the refectory; we enjoined the
abbot to correct this. They sometimes eat meat contrary to the Rule; we
forbade them to eat meat, save as the Rule permitted. Item, they eat meat
in the priories; we forbade this. Guests are not well received; we ordered
this corrected. They have an income of about three thousand pounds, but
the sources of income are not put in writing; we ordered them to be inscribed
in registers. The officials do not cast their accounts; we ordered a monthly
audit to be made by each official, and a general audit for the whole monastery to be made twice a year, and in the presence of brothers elected
by the community, as the Statutes of Pope Gregory require. They owe
nothing, but they are obligated for about thirty pounds in pensions.

AUGUST 24. At Yvetôt, at the house of the archdeacon, Jean of Essaye,
and at his expense.

---

[94] Many monasteries found it expedient to retain lawyers to deal with secular legal
affairs. This was especially true in France from the reign of Philip Augustus on.

[95] A Benedictine abbey, begun under William the Conqueror and completed under
Henry I. (Cottineau, II, 1939.)

[96] The Islands of St-Marcouf, located off the present town of Quineville on the

AUGUST 25. At Héauville,[97] at the expense of the priory. Two monks from Marmoutier are there. Asked whether they said the Divine Offices together, they replied that they did. They also said that they slept in the same place. They use feather beds. Asked whether they confessed, they said that they did, and to each other. They could not give any information concerning the state of the priory, for the prior was new, having been there only four days.

AUGUST 26. We visited the priory of Vauville.[98] Four monks from [the abbey of] Cerisy are there. They have no copy of the Rule. Item, they use feather beds and eat meat freely; we forbade them to use feather beds or to eat meat, save as the Rule permitted. Item, they do not observe the fasts of the Rule; we ordered them to observe them more completely. They have an income of one hundred forty pounds; they owe about forty pounds. Item we enjoined the prior to compute more often with his monks. We spent the night at Charebec, at the expense of the monastery of Cherbourg.

AUGUST 27. We came to the Augustinian monastery at Cherbourg,[99] and there we spent the night, at the expense of the prior of Vauville. There are twenty-seven canons in residence; one canon is dwelling alone at Barfleur; we ordered him to be recalled or a companion to be given him. All but six are priests. Lay folk freely enter the cloister; we ordered that a porter be appointed to stand at the cloister gate and prevent lay folk from entering. Item, women enter the church and proceed even to the altar; we ordered women to be kept out entirely and that the doors be kept shut to prevent them from coming in. No one is appointed to attend to the reception of guests; we ordered someone to be appointed for this. They have an income of about eight hundred pounds. The abbot does not compute concerning the state of the house; we ordered the bailiff to make a particular rendering of accounts with the abbot every month, and in the presence of some brothers elected by the community, and that twice a year a general audit be made. We found that the wheat in the granary is not measured; we decreed that one of the canons be appointed to receive the grain and measure it. They owe about seven hundred pounds. The abbot is a drunkard. He does not see that the Rule is well observed, does not sleep in the dormitory, does not

---

east side of the Cotentin Peninsula. The parish on the islands was called St-Marcouf de l'Isle. (Cottineau, II, 2781.)

[97] A Benedictine priory of Marmoutier. (Cottineau, I, 1389-90.)

[98] A Benedictine priory of Cerisy. (Cottineau, II, 3306.)

[99] Notre-Dame-du-Vœu, established in 1145. (Cottineau, I, 759-60.)

rise for Matins, and does not eat in the refectory, although he is physically able to do all of these things. Item, he goes riding more than the monastery business requires; he spends money immoderately, has disreputable servants, Beaulabaille, Richard, and Gérard, and is not a wise administrator of the monastery's temporalities. The sick are ill attended. He makes superfluous expenses. Item, the bailiff spends a great deal on behalf of one of his brothers, a cleric, who, it is said, was seized for forgery.

We spent the night here, at the expense of the prior of Vauville.

Statutes for the Monastery at Cherbourg

Brother Eudes, by divine permission unworthy minister of the church of Rouen, to his beloved and venerable son Master John, archdeacon of the church of Coutances, eternal greeting in the Lord Jesus Christ. Visiting our province in the exercise of our office, we came to the monastery of Cherbourg, and found there certain matters requiring correction on which we cannot turn our back and which we neither may nor should overlook. In the first place, we order some alert custodian to be placed over the cloister to prevent, so far as he can do it tactfully, the entry of lay folk. Item, we decree that the doors of the choir be kept closed so that lay folk, and particularly women, shall not enter, for they interfere with the celebration of the Divine Service and disturb the community. Item, as the law requires, we enjoin you to recall the canon who is dwelling alone at Barfleur or else to send him a competent and honorable companion. Item, we urge the appointment of some canon to look out for the guests and to provide for them as is fitting. Item, we decree that... [*lacuna in MS*][100] the abbot shall cast the monastery accounts at least twice a year and in the presence of the community or of some of the brothers elected for this purpose. Item, that the bailiff shall present a statement of income and expenses to the abbot at least once a month, and that specially selected members of the community be present when he casts his accounts. Item, for various reasons we will that the present bailiff be removed from office, nor, under any circumstances, shall he be reappointed without our special permission. Item, we will that some canon be appointed to receive the grain as it is brought in, to measure it, to store it measured in a granary, and to present a more complete statement of the grain consumption each month. Item, we decree that the sick in the infirmary be well and decently attended and treated as their illness demands and the resources of the monastery permit. Item, we enjoined upon [*lacuna in MS*] the abbot to adhere to the custom of the community in church, cloister, refectory, dormitory, and other places, as his duty requires and more regularly than he has been

[100] Robert II (1240?-1281). *Gallia Christiana*, XI, 942.)

doing. Item, we forbade him to have any dogs, except those used only for hunting partridges; indeed, as he promised us, he is to get rid of them within a month. Item, we urged him to get rid of his rather disreputable personal retinue and the unnecessarily large corps of servants which he is said to have employed. Item, we ordered him to choose another room for himself, one that could in no way be reached by lay folk through the cloister, and that the one he is occupying at present be used as an infirmary.

AUGUST 28. At Montebourg, at our own expense. AUGUST 29. At St-Côme,[101] a priory of Cluny, at the expense of the priory. Master Richard English holds the priory. AUGUST 30. At Bohon,[102] where there are eight monks from Marmoutier. All but two are priests. We admonished them, for they are exempt.[103] They have an income of two hundred eighty pounds.

AUGUST 31. At Bohon, but at the expense of the priory of Saintény,[104] since Saintény has insufficient accommodations. We visited the priory of Saintény, where there are two monks from St-Nicole-d'Angers.[105] They have no written copy of the Rule; we enjoined the prior to have one written out in a book. They do not observe the fasts of the Rule; we ordered them to maintain a better observance. Item, they sometimes eat meat; we enjoined them to abstain from eating meat. Peter, the prior's companion, is ill famed of incontinence with a certain married woman; we urged the prior to send him back to the monastery and to get another companion. This day we came to Marchézieux and received procuration from the monastery, or priory.

[101] Originally Benedictine, it became Cluniac in the eleventh century. (Cottineau, II, 2639.)

[102] St-Georges, founded c. 1068. (Cottineau, I, 404.)

[103] Marmoutier waged a running battle with archiepiscopal (Tours) and diocesan authorities to be free of local episcopal restraints, such as visitation, and rights of blessing abbots. In the meantime, this abbey was spreading out and probably had more priories in France and England than any other monastery in France. For their acquisition, see E. Martène, *Histoire de l'abbaye de Marmoutier,* ed. C. Chevalier, 2 vols. (Tours, 1874), chiefly I, 276-545. (Vols XXIV and XXV of *Mémoires de la Société archéologique de Touraine.*) The exemption referred to came by way of Marmoutier's adherence to Cluny when Cluny was in its infancy. The exemptions granted to Cluny became those of Marmoutier, hence the running battle. On April 22, 1220, Honorius III granted a bull to the abbey exempting them and their priories from procuration. (*Ibid.,* II, 195.) Eudes could admonish the monks of Bohon, but his visit could be only unofficial.

[104] This was a Benedictine priory. (Cottineau, II, 2926.)

[105] A Benedictine abbey founded c. 1020 by Fulk Nerra, count of Anjou. (Cottineau, I, 105-6.)

SEPTEMBER 1. We visited Marchézieux[106] and found three monks from Cormery. They have no copy of the Rule; we enjoined them to obtain one. Item, they use feather beds and eat meat; we forbade them the use of feather beds or to eat meat save as the Rule permitted. Item, they do not observe the fasts of the Rule; we ordered them to maintain a better observance. They have an income of two hundred pounds; they owe about sixty pounds. Item, we enjoined the prior to keep his companions informed concerning the finances of the house, that they might know how much they owe and to whom, and how much is owed to them and by whom. We came to St-Fromond this day and spent the night there at the expense of the priory.

SEPTEMBER 2. We visited at St-Fromond,[107] where there are fifteen monks from Cerisy. All are priests. Lay folk sometimes enter the cloister; we ordered them to be kept from the cloister and choir, so far as it could be done tactfully. The monks sometimes go out into the farm without permission; we enjoined the prior not to allow anyone to go out without his permission or that of someone who had that authority. We ordered that if anyone should go out without permission he should be severely punished. Traveling monks do not observe the fasts of the Rule; we urged them to a better observance, and [warned] that if any one were to be delinquent in this matter he would be punished in accordance with the Statutes of Pope Gregory. Item, we found that they use meat once a fortnight; we forbade them to use meat, save as the Rule permitted. Item, we enjoined the prior to appoint a suitable monk to receive the guests and to provide fitting hospitality. Item, we enjoined him to have a complete statement of the priory income written out in a register. They have an income of fifty pounds and owe about forty pounds.

This day we spent the night at Neuilly, in the diocese of Bayeux, and, through the kindness of the bishop, at his expense.

SEPTEMBER 3. Here begins the visitation of the diocese of Bayeux. At Cerisy,[108] where there are about forty monks. All but five are priests. Sometimes they eat meat when there is no need; we forbade them to eat meat save as the Rule permitted. They have an income of two thousand pounds,

---

[106] A Benedictine priory of Cormery. (Cottineau, II, 1738.)

[107] A Benedictine priory of St-Vigor-de-Cerisy. (Cottineau, II, 2682-83.)

[108] St-Vigor, built in sixth century and restored by Duke Robert c. 1050. (Cottineau, I, 656.) The abbot was Osmund (1246-60). (Gallia Christiana, XI, 410.)

but the sources of income are not registered in any books; we ordered them to be written out in registers. They owe about one hundred forty pounds. We ordered the abbot to compute in the presence of brothers elected by the community. They owe about forty pounds in pensions. Item, we found that a certain priory, Marcei [near Mortrée] by name, where there used to be two monks, has been deprived of its servers and handed over to a certain secular called Master Nicholas of Blève.[109]

SEPTEMBER 4. At the Augustinian priory of Le Plessis-Grimoult,[110] at the expense of the priory. Here we found fifteen canons. Some of the canons are dwelling alone in parishes; we ordered that they be recalled to the cloister or that companions be given them. All are priests. They have an income of twelve hundred pounds; they owe nothing in contractual debts. We ordered them to write out their sources of income in registers. They are obligated for about forty pounds in pensions.

This day the prior of La Lande-Patry[111] appeared before us to answer for his priory since it was impossible for us to go there [for a visitation]. Through him we found that the priory has three monks who are priests. They have an income of ninety pounds of Tours. They use feather beds and eat meat; we forbade them to use feather beds or to eat meat except as permitted by the Rule. They have no written copy of the Rule; we enjoined the prior to obtain one or have one written out.

SEPTEMBER 5. We were at the Cistercian abbey of Aunay [Aulnay],[112] at the expense of the abbey.

SEPTEMBER 6. We came to St-Vigor [-le-Grand],[113] near Bayeux, where there are about thirteen monks, of whom six are priests. Chapter is not held daily; we enjoined the prior to correct this. They do not observe the Statutes of Pope Gregory insofar as they pertain to the article of confession; we enjoined them to a fuller observance of this. Silence is not observed in the cloister; lay folk freely talk with the monks in the cloister, nor, indeed, is there a porter at the cloister gate; we enjoined them to appoint a keeper of the cloister gate, to observe the statutory hours of silence, and to refrain

[109] Probably this is the same Nicholas de Blève mentioned in the entry for July 17, above.

[110] St-Etienne, founded c. 1130. (Cottineau· II, 2300.)

[111] A Benedictine priory of St-Vincent-du-Mans. (Cottineau, I, 1548-49.)

[112] It was founded in 1131, came under the influence of Savigny, and thus joined Cîteaux in 1147. (Gallia Christiana, XI, 443; Cottineau, I, 201-9.)

[113] A Benedictine priory. (Cottineau, II, 2916-17.)

from talking with lay folk in the cloister. They walk about the farm freely; we forbade anyone to leave the cloister; they are to go out by the front way and that only with special permission. They eat meat freely and when there is no need; we forbade them to eat meat, except as the Rule permitted. They have an income of six hundred pounds. The prior does not compute with his associates concerning the state of the house; we ordered him to make a general audit, with the assistance of his associates in a body, at least twice a year, and that two copies of this be made, one to remain in the possession of the prior, the other to be given to the community. They return six pounds to their abbey, and they owe pensions.

SEPTEMBER 7. The prior of Le Désert[114] appeared before us, as we had ordered him, to give us certified information concerning his priory, since we could not conveniently go there.[115] Through him we learned that in his priory there are four monks, though there should be six, but that the abbot relieved the priory of two monks because it was grievously burdened. They have no copy of the Rule; we enjoined the prior to seek for one and have it written out. Item, they use feather beds and eat meat; we forbade them to use feather beds or to eat meat except as the Rule permitted. Item, the monks go out beyond the gate without permission; we forbade him to allow this. Item, they do not observe the fasts of the Rule; we urged a fuller observance. They have an income of two hundred fifty pounds; they owe about forty pounds.

This day we were honorably received at the cathedral of Bayeux, and visited the chapter. There are twelve dignitaries there.[116] We asked whether they were bound to keep residence, and they replied that they are said not to be. Four vicars act for the canons in celebrating Mass at the high altar, for, indeed, the canons do not serve at the high altar, save at the time of the great feasts. They have no statutory fines except those relating to non-attendance at the Epistle and Gospel of the Mass. They whisper too much in the choir. Item, we asked who had the cure of souls of the chapter; some said the bishop, others said the dean; we enjoined the chapter to straighten out this matter, and to find out at the first general chapter which of them

---

[114] A Benedictine priory dependent on Troarn. (Cottineau, I, 959.)

[115] It was located to the southwest of Le Plessis-Grimoult, and Eudes was near Bayeux, far to the north.

[116] The bishop, dean, cantor, chancellor, treasurer, two archdeacons, sub- or assistant cantor, master of the schools, custodian, penitentiary, and theologian.

did have the cure of souls. Peter Franchise, the general subdeacon,[117] is publicly known for drinking two much. So far as the canons themselves are concerned: we found that John Rusticus is publicly known for drunkenness; the dean, of evil-seeking, for he lends money to the canons and then sooner or later takes their share of the communal distributions; Jordan, the clerk of John the archdeacon, is publicly known for evil-running about the town at night; Thibaut of Ons, John Rusticus, and William of Clère, all canons, are publicly known for shortening their services. Item, Thibaut and William of Clère hunt with birds and dogs. Jacob Boiscervoise is ill famed of a single charge of usury. Item, John of St-Martin and Ralph Dubois are ill famed of a single instance of incontinence. The temporalities of the chapter are in bad condition, nor does the chapter seem to mind. We enjoined the bishop, the dean, and ... [lacuna in MS] to see that all the above defects were remedied as if we ourselves were present to do so. We received our procuration this day from the chapter.

SEPTEMBER 8. We visited the bishop in chapter and inquired of the canons how the bishop conducted his episcopal duties, his preaching, dedicating churches, ordaining clerics, the collation of benefices and prebends, the induction of clerics to churches and cures, and caring for buildings and revenues pertaining particularly to the bishop. They replied unanimously that he did everything in the very best fashion, and, indeed, we found everything connected with him to be in good condition. This day, it being the feast of the Nativity of the Virgin, we celebrated Mass in the cathedral, wearing pontificals, including the pallium. We received our procuration from the bishop.

SEPTEMBER 9. We were at Douvres, the bishop's manor, through his kindness and at his expense. This day represented by Master William, archdeacon of Eu, we visited the monastery of Longues,[118] which belongs to the Order of Hambye.[119] There are twenty-two monks in residence, which is as many as there ever were. Two of their monks are dwelling alone in

---

[117] The subdeacon who served all the canons but no one in particular when they celebrated Mass.

[118] A Benedictine monastery founded c. 1168. (Cottineau, I, 1648-49.)

[119] Hambye (Cottineau, I, 1374-75) actually belonged to the Congregation of Tiron. Tiron represented one of the many efforts in the eleventh and twelfth centuries to reform monasticism from within. In France the chief efforts centered about Bec, Tiron, Fontevrault, and Savigny; Savigny joined with Cîteaux. The same movement saw the rise of the Camoldoli in Italy, among many other congregations. All were

priories; we ordered that they be recalled to the cloister or that companions be sent to them. They have an income of about four hundred pounds; they owe about forty pounds of Tours and seven measures of grain in pensions. They eat meat when there is no need; we forbade the eating of meat, except as permitted by the Rule.

SEPTEMBER 10. At Ardenne,[120] Premonstratensian Order, at the expense of the abbey.

SEPTEMBER 11. At St-Sépulcre-de-Caen, at the expense of the chapter, which we visited on the morrow. The dean does not keep residence. There is no definite number of canons in the chapter.[121] Everything related to the community we found to be in good condition. The dean is ill famed of a certain woman in Rouen, called Alice au Pie, and contrary to custom receives his share of the communal distribution free and twofold. [122]

SEPTEMBER 12. At the monastery of St-Etienne-de-Caen,[123] at the expense of the monastery. We found fifty-four monks at this monastery, all but eight of whom are priests. The monks in the priories eat meat. They have an income of four thousand pounds of Tours, and of two hundred twenty pounds sterling. We ordered them to enter their sources of income in books. They owe about fifteen hundred pounds, but about five hundred pounds are owed to them. We ordered the abbot and the officials to cast their accounts on the state of the house in the presence of brothers elected by the community. They owe about two hundred pounds in pensions. John Baudre and Thomas of Ostrehan are sowers of discord, authors of wild tales, and disobedient; we warned them sharply, although they already had been warned.

---

basically Benedictine with strong eremitical overtones. For Tiron, see M. L. Merlet, *Cartulaire de l'abbaye de la Sainte-Trinité de Tiron* (2 vols., Chartres, 1883), especially the Introduction. For Savigny, see D. Claude Auvry, *Histoire de la Congrégation de Savigny* (3 vols., Paris and Rouen, 1896). Hambye had six daughter-houses and was called by Alexander III "the head of an order." (Philbert Schmitz, *Histoire de l'ordre de St-Benoît,* 6 volumes [Maredsous, 1948], III, 105.)

[120] Founded *c.* 1121. (Cottineau, I, 137-38.)

[121] In principle, the number of canons was determined by the resources of the church (*Corp. jur. can., Decretales Greg. IX* Lib. I. Tit. 2. cap. 9). Alexander III in 1170 had made the decision when writing to Walter, bishop of Tournai (Migne, *PL,* CC, 677). For further canon law on the certain or statutory number of canons or religious, see *Corp. jur. can. Decretal. Greg. IX* Lib. III. Tit. 5. cap. 22; Lib. III. Tit. 8. cap. 10; also, canon 394 of the modern *Codex juris canonici* (Rome, 1917).

[122] That is, without any deduction of charges.

[123] Founded in 1064 by William the Conqueror. (Cottineau, I, 550-53.)

SEPTEMBER 13. At the monastery of the nuns of Ste-Trinité-de-Caen,[124] at the expense of the monastery. We found sixty-five nuns at the monastery, but there is no certain number of nuns.[125] One does not accuse another [in chapter] save those who are specially deputed to accuse the younger ones. They occasionally keep larks and small birds in cages; we ordered all such small birds to be removed. They do not know what their income is, but they state that more is owed to them than they owe, nor do they know anything about the financial condition of the monastery; nevertheless, the abbess does audit her accounts in her room in the presence of some sisters elected each year for this purpose, and a copy of the computation is on public display in chapter, and this, they say, suffices for them. One hundred sixty pounds sterling of their income comes from England; about twenty-five hundred pounds of Tours is derived from this side of the sea. We told the official of Bayeux to instruct the abbess to make her computations in the presence of sisters elected by the community. Four canons are in residence, and it is said that from the beginning they were priests. It was stipulated that they be priests and that they keep residence in the monastery. The bishop has lately ordered that in the future those on whom these prebends are conferred should swear to take Holy Orders and to maintain residence.

SEPTEMBER 14. At Fontenay [-le-Marmion],[126] at the expense of the abbey. We found twenty-three Black Monks[127] in residence; there should be thirty.[128] All but five are priests. Many of them do not confess each month; we ordered that the statute governing this be observed. Traveling monks do not observe the fasts of the Rule; we ordered that a monk be appointed to attend to the reception of secular guests. They have an income of about nine hundred pounds of Tours. We ordered them to enter the sources of income in registers. Item, we ordered the abbot to make a general audit twice a year, in the presence of brothers elected by the community, and that the other officials should make a monthly one. They owe

[124] Founded by Mathilda, wife of William the Conqueror. (Cottineau, I, 553-54.)
[125] Canon law on the "certain" number applied not only to chapters but to religious houses of all kinds: the number admitted were to be in proportion to the resources of the establishment.
[126] A Benedictine abbey founded *c*. 1050. (Cottineau, I, 1182-83.)
[127] The Benedictines were referred to as the Black Monks and the Cistercians as the White Monks, because of the color of their habits.
[128] This is an instance of a monastery with a "certain" number of monks.

about four hundred pounds, and about twenty pounds in pensions.

On the same day we sent our companion, Master Stephen of Lorris, to to visit the abbey of Notre-Dame-du-Val[129] in our stead. He found thirteen Augustinian canons in residence, of whom all but two are priests. On of the canons is serving alone in a certain church; they were told to give him a companion or to recall him to the cloister. They have an income of about five hundred pounds; they owe about one hundred pounds.

SEPTEMBER 15. At Troarn,[130] at the expense of the monastery. We found forty-four monks in residence. Traveling monks do not observe the fasts; we ordered them to maintain a better observance. They do not observe the fasts in the priories; they use feather beds and eat meat; we forbade them to use feather beds or to eat meat, and enjoined them to observe the fasts of the Rule. They have an income of about three thousand pounds; they owe about three hundred pounds. We ordered them to elect some of the brothers to be present when the abbot and the officials cast their accounts. They owe about thirty pounds in pensions. At St-Hymer, as we were passing through the diocese of Lisieux, at our own expense. The rest follows on folio 30.

On Our Way Back from Our Provincial Visitation

SEPTEMBER 16-18. At Bec. SEPTEMBER 19. At Bourgtheroulde, at our expense. SEPTEMBER 20. At Rouen. SEPTEMBER 21. At Mont-Deux-Amants, at our expense. SEPTEMBER 22. At Sausseuse, at our own expense. SEPTEMBER 23. At Juziers, at our own expense. SEPTEMBER 24. We disinterred or translated the body of Ste-Honorine at Conflans, and we spent the night at Pontoise, at our own expense. SEPTEMBER 25. At Paris. SEPTEMBER 26. At Corbeil, at the house of the Hospitalers. SEPTEMBER 27. At Nemours. SEPTEMBER 28. At Montargis. SEPTEMBER 29. At Bonny. SEPTEMBER 30. At La Charité-sur-Loire. OCTOBER 1-2. At Varzy, as the guest of the bishop of Nevers. OCTOBER 3. At Decize. OCTOBER 4. At Pierrefite-sur-Loire. OCTOBER 5. At Charlieu. OCTOBER 6. At l'Arbresle. OCTOBER 7-NOVEMBER 10. At Lyon.[131] NOVEMBER 11. At L'Arbresle. NOVEMBER 12. At Thizy. NOVEMBER 13-14. At Marcigny. NOVEMBER 15. At Pierrefite. NO-

---

[129] Founded c. 1125. (Cottineau, II, 3254.)

[130] A Benedictine abbey founded c. 1052. (Cottineau, II, 3220.)

[131] Pope Innocent IV issued six bulls on Eudes' behalf during this visit. (Bonnin, pp. 733-36.)

VEMBER 16. At Decize. NOVEMBER 17. At Nevers, with the bishop. NO-
VEMBER 18. At Varzy, with the bishop. NOVEMBER 19. At La Charité.
NOVEMBER 20. At Cosne. NOVEMBER 21. At Bonny. NOVEMBER 22. At
Châtillon. NOVEMBER 23. At Montargis. NOVEMBER 24. At Nemours. NO-
VEMBER 25. At Corbeil. NOVEMBER 26. At St-Denis. NOVEMBER 27. At
Pontoise. NOVEMBER 28. At Juziers. NOVEMBER 29-30. At Sausseuse. DE-
CEMBER 1. At Mont-Deux-Amants, at our own expense. DECEMBER 2-3. At
Rouen. DECEMBER 4-5. At Jumièges. DECEMBER 6. At Déville. DECEMBER 7.
At Mont-Deux-Amants. DECEMBER 8. At Sausseuse. DECEMBER 9. At Juziers.
DECEMBER 10. At Pontoise. DECEMBER 11-13. At Paris. [*No entry for
December 14.*] DECEMBER 15. At Poissy. DECEMBER 16. At St-Martin-la-
Garenne. DECEMBER 17. At the same, and we conferred Holy Orders at
Vétheuil.

DECEMBER 18. At Juziers, at the expense of the priory, which we visited
on the morrow. We found things to be in the same state as that recorded
of the last visitation on folio 19,[132] with this exception, that the prior casts
his accounts on the state of the house only with the abbot; we enjoined him
to associate some of his own more deliberate brothers with him in this matter, so that they might know what they possessed, how much they owed,
and how much was owed to them; and we warned him about the other
matters. There are seven monks in residence.

DECEMBER 19. At St-Laurent-en-Cornecervine, at the expense of the priory.
Everything the same as recorded in the last visitation, on folio 19.[133] DE-
CEMBER 20. At Gaillonet, Premonstratensian Order, at the expense of the
priory. There are four monks here. DECEMBER 21. At Gasny, at the ex-
pense of the priory. Four monks from St-Ouen [-de-Rouen] are in residence.
We found that they sleep in feather beds; we forbade them the use of these.
Item, we enjoined them to read a lesson from their Rule each day after
Prime; item, that they should say their psalms together, and with modulation.

DECEMBER 22. At Noyon [-sur-Andelle], where there are seven monks.
We found things unchanged since our last visitation, which is recorded on
folio 22.[134]

DECEMBER 23. At Rouen, where we sang the *O Virgo virginum*.[135] DE-

---

[132] See entry for July 7, 1249.
[133] See entry for July 8, 1249.
[134] See entry for August 22, 1249.
[135] One of the seven antiphons (one for each day) beginning with "O," sung as
the feast of Christmas approaches. In the sixth century December 18 was designated

CEMBER 24. At Rouen. DECEMBER 25. At Rouen, and it was Christmas Day. DECEMBER 26-28. At Déville.

DECEMBER 29. At Auffay, at the expense of the priory, which we visited, and where we found everything to be as at our last visitation, which is recorded on folio 22;[136] in addition we found that the prior does not confess, nor does he celebrate his Mass as is required by the Statutes of Pope Gregory. We forbade them to eat meat, save as the Rule permitted. More is owed to them than they owe.

DECEMBER 30. At Longueville, Order of Cluny, at the expense of the priory. DECEMBER 31. At Longueil, at the expense of the priory. No monks there.

JANUARY 1. At Dieppe, at our own expense. JANUARY 2-4. At Aliermont. JANUARY 5. At Eu, at the expense of the monastery. JANUARY 6. At the same, but at our own expense.

JANUARY 7. We visited Eu, finding twenty-six canons and one lay brother; there used to be more than thirty. All but seven are priests. They have no stated time for confessing, and some are negligent in making their confessions. Item, we enjoined them to be diligent in redeeming their golden chalice, which they pawned to help out the vicomte. Lay folk enter the cloister, and indeed it is very hard to keep them out. Item, we enjoined the community to elect some of the brothers who would in their stead hear the audits of the convent's bailiffs and abbot.

This day we came to Le Tréport, at our own expense.

JANUARY 8. At Le Tréport, at the expense of the monastery. We visited there, finding twenty-three monks. One monk is dwelling alone in the priory at Eurville; we ordered that he be recalled to the cloister or that a companion be sent to him. There are four novices; all but three of the others are priests.

---

as the feast of the Expectation. Many parts of the Mass and the Divine Office are the same as for the feast of the Annunciation, March 25. The feast of the Expectation was a reminder of Mary's part in the coming feast of the Nativity. During the seven days before Christmas the seven antiphons were said in the Office. They are called "the great O's" because each begins with the invocation O. These date at least from the time of Gregory the Great. From the eighth or the ninth century it became customary to sing them with the Magnificat at Vespers, and this is still the practice, although the number of antiphons is now reduced to one for each of the seven days. At the second Vespers on December 18 the psalm, *O Virgo virginum*, was sung. ("Fête de l'Annonciation," *Dict. d'arch. chrét. et de lit.*, I², 2249-50; Dom Leduc and Dom Baudot, *The Liturgy of the Roman Missal* [New York, n.d.], pp. 62-63.)

[136] See entry for July 26, 1249; actually, the folio is 21.

They do not observe the Statute of Pope Gregory concerning confession very well. One does not accuse another [in chapter]. We want one to accuse another [in chapter]. Traveling monks do not observe the fasts of the Rule; we enjoined a better observance in this respect. They eat meat in the priories; we forbade the eating of meat, and enjoined the abbot to be more diligent in correcting this abuse. They owe about four hundred pounds, but they believe that this year they will reduce this by two hundred pounds.

William of Moncel, a fugitive monk, entered the Le Tréport monastery after being away four years; item, before he entered, the expenses of his novitiate had been paid by the monastery. Once he fled from Le Tréport. Item, he was a tippler, complaining and quarrelsome, and at one time when he was in a certain priory and the prior was unwilling to give him a drink, he went out into the farm and slew two of the prior's swine; he always used to carry a knife. Item, he was publicly known for incontinence.

JANUARY 9. At Envermeu, at the expense of the priory. Eleven monks are in residence, and a twelfth is coming. They owe about two hundred twenty pounds to the abbot, and one hundred pounds elsewhere. Everything else we found to be quite satisfactory.

JANUARY 10. At Aliermont, at the expense of the priory of Wanchy.

JANUARY 11-12. At Aliermont.

JANUARY 13. At Bures [-en-Bray], at the expense of the priory, which we visited. Two monks from Le Pré are in residence. They do not observe the fasts of the Rule; they eat meat, and sometimes because of pressure of business they neither celebrate nor hear Mass. In the presence of the abbot of Bec we admonished them about these things, and about their use of feather beds as well. The priory owes about forty pounds, although the goods of the priory are at the disposal of the priory at Le Pré.

JANUARY 14. At Beaubec, at the expense of the monastery. JANUARY 15. At Neufchâtel, at the expense of the priory of Nogent-en-Bray.

JANUARY 16. We visited the hospital of Nogent where there are three canons, though there should be four. One canon is dwelling alone in a chapel for the dead; we enjoined the prior to recall him or else to give him a companion. We forbade the prior and the canons to dine in the future in the town.

This day we spent the night at St-Saëns,[137] at the expense of the priory,

---

[137] A Benedictine priory of St-Wandrille. (Cottineau, II, 2873-74.)

and this day we visited the nuns' priory. These are about twenty-six sisters in residence, including the lay sisters. They receive presents, which they keep or give away, without asking permission. They have an income of about one hundred forty pounds, and they owe about sixty pounds. They have no wine or cider for drinking, nor have they enough grain to last until Pentecost.

JANUARY 17. We visited the monks, and there were four in residence. Sometimes they do not say their daily Hours with modulation. More is owed to them than they owe. They have an income of three hundred pounds; they do not owe more than thirty pounds. The prior does not compute with his monks; we enjoined him to compute with them frequently.

This day we spent the night at Déville.

JANUARY 18. We visited the leper hospital of Salle-aux-Puelles. They do not keep silence in the refectory. They owe their servants about sixty shillings. They have a sufficiency of provisions. They have an income of about four hundred pounds.

Here follows the ordinance which we drew up here in another year:

Brother Eudes, by divine permission archbishop of Rouen, etc. To all, etc. When in the month of May,[138] 1249, we came to Salle-aux-Puelles near Rouen for the purpose of making a visitation and, convoking the prior, the prioress, the sisters and several other persons dwelling there,[139] made a careful inspection, we found numerous matters as to both spiritual and temporal affairs which de-

---

[138] The prior visitation spoken of here was not made in May, 1249, but on March 17, 1249.

[139] Most of the hospitals and leprosaries were small-staffed, depending upon the resources and endowments of the house. The personnel formed themselves into communities; the men under the prior, the women under a prioress. What rule did they follow? When asked, they claimed the Rule of St. Augustine based on the letters to be found in Migne, PL, XXXIII, 957-65. Jacques de Vitry gives a rather rosy picture of the religious life of such communities: "They live according to the Rule of St. Augustine, without private property and in common under one obedience; and having taken the habit, they promise perpetual continence to God." (Jean Imbert, Les Hôpitaux en droit canonique, [Paris, 1947] p. 267.) However, their way of life seems to have been somewhat haphazard in regard to rules. Thus, the local ordinaries began to insist on statutes for each house. The communities were independent and thus statutes were based on local custom and usages. There is much conciliar legislation on such houses. (Mansi, XXII, 835-36, 913.) It must be remembered that each house was as truly a canonical religious community as was a monastery. Each brother or sister in a hospital or leprosary underwent a year's novitiate, as in a monastery, under

manded correction and reform. For the safety of their souls, we have drawn up the following ordinance which we wish to be scrupulously observed and to be written down as a permanent guide and reminder. First of all, let everyone, clerics as well as sisters, have all things in common and let them live in common; nor shall anyone presume to appropriate anything for his own. Let them have a sufficiency of bread each day. Item, each sister shall have her wine and her pot of beer each day. Item, thrice a week, in the appropriate season, they may have fresh meat, and at the other times, fish once a week. Indeed, on other days let five eggs or three herrings be given to them. During Lent (in the Quadragesimas) let them have fish (if it can be had) on those days when they would ordinarily have meat, and on vigils of solemn feasts they are likewise to abstain from meat. This is to be the general rule. Let the prior see to it that adequate provision is made, as God wills, for those who are sick or have been bled outside the convent. Let him also see that they receive their pittances, but no money, on the stated days. Let him also see to it that the leftover fragments of food are carefully preserved for the poor lepers outside. The food for the clerics and the sisters shall be identical unless it shall seem needful that some change be made, whether for hospitality or other reason, for, indeed, temporal goods have been given to the house for the use of the sick, and not for the benefit of the healthy. The raiment and clothing shall be according to that of your order and uniform, to wit, a russet mantle, and each sister shall receive a tunic and super-tunic every other year. Let them have warm mantles, and new ones every other year. Item, let the prior provide them with sufficient coverlets of fur. Item, let them

---

a master or mistress of novices. At the end of the novitiate, if it were deemed agreeable to the postulant and the chapter, the entrant, now wearing the habit, placed his or her hands between the hands of the local superior and took the three vows of poverty, chastity, and obedience. Before reaching this point, the entrant had to be acceptable to the local ordinary; the entrant had to be free, celebate, without debts, and not a leper. As in the monastery, the religious staff of the hospital or leprosary met in chapter for religious and material purposes. The chapter had a seal whose imprint was necessary for alienations of property. Both males and females attended their separate chapter for religious purposes, but they met as a unit for secular matters. The religious chapter was patterned on its monastic counterpart with its chapter of faults, and imposition of penances; the faults, as in the Benedictine system, being light, grave, and most grave. Their clothing was to be modest in cut and not gay in color. All wore a cross visible on their clothing, thus proclaiming their order. Silence was to be observed in the dormitory; food was to be in common and one was to eat what was given him; nobody was to sleep naked; bathing and washings were frequent. The statutes make much provision for religious exercises, but devotion to their patients seems to have occupied most of their time. (Léon Le Grand, *Status d'Hôtels-Dieu et de leproséries* [Paris, 1901], is a most useful collection. For a general review of the subject see Imbert, *Les Hôpitaux,* pp. 265-277.)

have linen clothing, that is to say, two shirts and two sheets every year at least, and if more are needed for those sisters who may be sick, let the prioress have them made. Let the prioress be considerate and discreet; let her try to understand the condition of the patients and administer to them as the resources of the house permit. Let no sister, upon receiving new clothing, presume under pain of anathema to retain her old garments, especially her linen. In the matter of shoes and their material, let the prior have them made at the discretion of the prioress. Item, let them have two honest and simple maidservants, and a third one if need be, as seems proper to the prior and the prioress. Let the sisters be bled at the proper times, if they so desire, and let them have a competent blood-letter. Let them make confession frequently, and receive Communion at least four times a year; to wit, at Christmas, on Holy Thursday, at Easter, and at Pentecost. Item, the prior and the prioress shall make a monthly audit of expenses and receipts in the presence of the community and shall have the account written out and certified. When the computation has been made, let each retain his (or her) own accounts, so that whenever required by a superior they may be able to give a more certain report on the state of the monastery. Let the prior have the mature and honest society of a small number of clerics and let him get along with as small as staff as possible; and, that no breath of scandal may arise, let everything be done to redound to the glory of God and to the advantage of the sisters, and be an example to all men. Given in the month of August, 1249.

This day we spent the night at St-Lô [-de-Rouen], at the expense of the priory.

JANUARY 19. We visited St-Lô, finding nineteen canons, of whom ten are priests. We enjoined the prior to make an audit with the community as a whole two or three times a year. They owe about five hundred pounds.

This day we spent the night at Jumièges.

JANUARY 20. We visited Jumièges, where there are about forty-eight monks. All but ten or twelve are priests. Some are negligent about celebrating their Masses. Item, many do not confess each month; item, we enjoined the prior, the subprior, and the third prior to tell us who these were. The sick are not well cared for in the infirmary, nor is permission given easily to the sick to be admitted to the infirmary. Item, we ordered that the community should elect some of the brothers to hear every accounting of every official and of the abbot. The cellarer owes about one hundred fifty pounds, when all the credits and debits are considered, and they have a sufficiency of all provisions but wine. The kitchener owes about forty pounds; the chamberlain owes nothing; indeed, two hundred pounds has been owed to that office for a long time, and it has one hundred fifty pounds on hand. As for fasts, we strictly enjoined the new abbot-elect[140] to correct and see that corrections be made, and to attend to those who do not make a monthly confession.

This day we spent the night at Jumièges.

JANUARY 21. We came to St-Georges, at our own expense.

JANUARY 22. At the same, but at the expense of the monastery. Twenty monks are in residence, and all are priests but three. We enjoined the abbot and the prior that those who absent themselves from Compline or leave the cloister without permission be made to fast the next day on bread and water and be held to strict silence. Item, we strictly enjoined them to maintain a fuller observance of the fasts of the Rule. Item, we forbade any monk to accept any gift from anyone, or to presume to keep it, without the permission of the abbot. In the outside priories they eat meat; we imposed the obligation on the abbot to correct this. They owe about one hundred twenty pounds, but about three hundred pounds is owed to them. Item, we enjoined and ordered that someone be elected by the community – either one or two – to hear the accounts of the abbot and of the officials.

JANUARY 23. At Déville, where we at that time confirmed the election of the bishop of Coutances.[141] JANUARY 24. We were at Ste-Catherine, at the expense of the monastery. There was a terrific thunderstorm.

JANUARY 25. We visited at Ste-Catherine, where there are thirty monks. Caleboche and another monk, who are now in prison, sing dissolute songs; we ordered that they be corrected by cutting off their food and subjecting them to flagellation. We decreed that the monastery should bring the number of its monks up to the statutory number. They have four priories. The former prior of Pavilly went to England by himself; we ordered that he be provided with some honest companion either from this side of the Channel or the other. The abbot does not compute in the presence of the community; we ordered that one or more of the brothers, elected by the community, be present when he makes up his accounts. Item, we enjoined them to institute or appoint someone as chamberlain who would provide the others with clothing and shoes and give an accounting to the abbot in the presence of the aforesaid elected brothers. They owe about one hundred

---

[140] William V (1250-65). (*Gallia Christiana*, XI, 196.) As of this date, he was not yet formally installed as abbot. See entry for January 30, below.

[141] John I (1250-74). *Gallia Christiana*, XI, 881.

pounds. They have a sufficiency of provisions. As much, or perhaps more, is owed to them than they owe. They have an income of two thousand pounds. In the priories they use feather beds, eat meat, and fail to observe the fasts of the Rule. We enjoined that these abuses be corrected in accordance with the Rule and the Statutes of Pope Gregory.

On the same day we were at Beaulieu and received our procuration from the prior.

JANUARY 26. We visited Beaulieu, where there are eleven canons in residence. Ten canons are in priories. One canon is dwelling alone at Montmain; we ordered this to be corrected. They owe about two hundred pounds, but the lord of Préaux owes them one hundred forty pounds, though this is a bad debt; other debts, which are collectable, amount to forty pounds. They have an income of four hundred fifty pounds. One sister is dwelling there. We enjoined that no more sisters be received there. They have thirty-four cows, some calves, three hundred sheep, cart horses, and swine.

JANUARY 27. At Pérrièrs, at the expense of the priory. No monks are there. JANUARY 28. At l'Isle-Dieu, Premonstratensian Order, at the expense of the monastery. JANUARY 29. At Mont-Ste-Catherine, at our own expense. JANUARY 30. At the same, and at our own expense. This day we gave our blessing to the abbot of Jumièges at Mont-Ste-Catherine.

JANUARY 31. At Bourg-Achard, at the expense of the priory, which we visited. Nine canons are in residence; we ordered the prior to receive more into the community. The subprior has the cure of souls of the parish of Bourg-Achard, though he has not received that charge from us. Some are somewhat negligent in confessing; we decreed that whosoever should allow a month to go by without confessing should, on the Friday following the last day of the month, fast on bread and water, nor should the prior have any authority to grant a dispensation from this decree. Lay folk enter the cloister and talk therein; we enjoined them to keep lay folk out so far as it was possible, and suggested that some one be appointed to guard admittance to the cloister. They owe about ninety pounds. They have plenty of food, and could sell enough grain to liquidate their debts, or nearly to do so.

On the vigil of the Purification of the Blessed Virgin we were at Corneville, at the expense of the monastery. There are ten canons in residence. In two of their priories canons are dwelling alone. They have an income of about three hundred pounds; their debt is less than one hundred pounds.

We enjoined the abbot to make a special audit with the assistance of some of the brothers elected by the community.

FEBRUARY 1-3. At Bec-Hellouin, at the expense of the monastery. We visited Bec and found everything to be in good condition, except that they eat meat in the priories. We forbade the eating of meat, except as the Rule permitted. FEBRUARY 4. At Wellebotum, at our own expense. FEBRUARY 5. At Mont-Deux-Amants, at the expense of the priory. There are twelve canons there, of whom nine are priests. We found everything to be in good condition. They owe about sixty pounds.

FEBRUARY 6. At Sausseuse, at the expense of the priory. In two of their priories canons are dwelling alone; we enjoined the prior to recall them to the cloister, especially the one at Val-Carbon. Eleven canons are in residence, of whom eight are priests. They owe about three hundred twenty pounds.

FEBRUARY 7. At St-Martin-la-Garenne, where we found things to be just as they were at our last visitation, of which a record is inscribed on folio 20.[142] FEBRUARY 8. At Parnes, and we found things as at our last visitation, of which there is a record on folio 18.[143] We issued the same injunctions, with the addition that we enjoined the prior to procure another chalice, since they had only one. FEBRUARY 9. At Sérans. There are three monks in residence. Sometimes they eat meat; we forbade this, except at such times as the Rule permitted. Item, they use feather beds; we forbade this.

FEBRUARY 10. At Liancourt. They eat meat and frequently use feather beds, nor do they observe the fasts of the Rule. The prior does not sleep in the dormitory with the others, nor does he always eat in the refectory with them. We suspended the prior for the time being, since, although he has been corrected several times, he has not mended his ways.

FEBRUARY 11. At St-Martin-de-Pontoise. There are twenty-six monks in residence, of whom eighteen are priests. One monk is dwelling alone in a priory in the diocese of Beauvais, but he has the bishop's permission. We ordered that one of the gates of the cloister be kept closed to prevent the entry of lay folk, and that a porter be placed at the other to keep them out in as polite a manner as possible. They do not give up their old [clothes] when they receive new ones; we forbade anyone to receive any new clothes until he had first surrendered his old ones. They sometimes eat meat when

[142] See entry for July 9, 1249.
[143] See entry for July 2, 1249.

there is no need; we enjoined them to observe the Statutes of Pope Gregory
on this matter. In the outside priories they eat meat and do not observe
the fasts of the Rule; we enjoined the abbot to correct them. The community has no power of restraint over accounts; we decreed that some of
the brothers be elected by the community to assist at the casting of accounts
and on behalf of the community to have power of restraint over expenditures.
Item, we ordered that all sources of income be written out in several books.
They owe about thirteen hundred pounds, and they have an income of
about twelve hundred pounds. Neither the abbot nor the prior sleeps in
the dormitory; nevertheless the prior has a reason. The prior does not eat
in the refectory, nor does he attend chapter very often. The monks sometimes drink in the cellar; we strictly forbade this and prohibited anyone to
eat or drink outside the refectory, the infirmary, or the abbot's chamber.

FEBRUARY 12. At the same, and we received from the chapter of St-Mellon [-de-Pontoise] for our procuration one hundred shillings of Paris, hay
for the horses, wood, beds, and bedcovers. He who reads the Epistles is
not a subdeacon.[144] The church has not been re-roofed, as we had ordered.[145]
Item, we ordered the chapter to have made as many rochets for vesting as
were necessary. Item, that they begin to repair the roof of the church within
one month. Item, we enjoined Dom Vincent and Dom Robert to tell the
chapter to reform itself, and to correct what should be corrected. We enjoined them to let us know if the chapter did not undertake a reform. The
sacristan's helper is careless about the books, and his clerk is too rude and
ill-mannered and sings the Psalms lopping off the syllables. Herbert, the
vicar of William of Melli, is said to have been apprehended with a certain
married woman; he was treated harshly and put in prison, and paid a fine
to the mayor. Herbert has promised to regard his vicarate as resigned if
he is ill famed of this again, provided, however, the ill fame can be proved.
Robert of Gradu is ill famed of the sister of Master Vincent, and was disciplined by us once before.[146] We gave him the choice of purging himself
as the law requires or of submitting to our investigation. He promised us
to regard his vicarate as resigned if in the future he should eat, drink, or

---

[144] One of the principal liturgical functions of the subdeacon is to assist the
deacon and the celebrant of the Mass. Thus, he reads the Lesson or Epistle of the
day. ("Sous-diacre," *Dict. de théol. cath.*, XIV², 2459-66.)

[145] See entry for July 6, 1249.

[146] *Ibid.*

sleep in the house where Jacqueline, Master Vincent's sister, was, or indeed if he should have anything to do with her. Item, we enjoined him to banish from his house the clerk whom he had, for the latter was publicly known for usury.

FEBRUARY 13. We visited the priory of St-Pierre-de-Pontoise, at Pontoise. There are four monks in residence, but there used to be five. They do not observe the fasts very strictly, and sometimes they eat meat. The prior rides about with the steward. They owe about three hundred pounds. The prior does not compute.

This day we spent the night at St-Denis in France.[147]

FEBRUARY 14. At Paris, at our own expense. FEBRUARY 15. At Pontoise, at our own expense. FEBRUARY 16. At St-Martin-la-Garenne, at our own expense. FEBRUARY 17. At Sausseuse, at our own expense.

FEBRUARY 18. At Evreux, at our own expense. When we had confirmed Master John, the bishop-elect of Coutances, at Déville on January 23 last, we gave a letter to the bishop of Bayeux requesting the latter to summon our suffragans to Rouen to attend the consecration ceremony, as their duty compels them, on the Sunday preceding the Feast of St. Peter's Chair.[148] But when we were at Sausseuse on February 6, Master Matthew of Essaye came to us on behalf of the said bishop-elect and requested us to arrange our affairs for the benefit of the elect and to perform the ceremony at Coutances. However, considering that it would be rather a shame to consecrate him there where the canons did not sing, and because the ritual custom varies in different places, we changed the place of consecration to Evreux. On the Saturday before the Sunday scheduled for the consecration, the lord bishop of Bayeux came to us and stated that we should by no means proceed with the consecration at Evreux, alleging as his reason that it would be prejudicial to the bishopric of Bayeux and a detriment to his jurisdiction.[149] He had not cited our suffragans to Evreux nor could he cite them on such short notice for a ceremony to take place on the morrow. Moreover, the lord bishop of Avranches was absent and he had excused himself as follows:

[147] See above, n. 51.
[148] There are two feasts of St. Peter's Chair: St. Peter's Chair at Rome (January 18), and St. Peter's Chair at Antioch (February 22). Here the latter is referred to.
[149] In the archdiocese of Rouen, the bishop of Bayeux was next in dignity to the archbishop of Rouen.

To the Reverend Father in Christ and my lord Eudes, by God's grace archbishop of Rouen, I, William, by divine permission the humble minister of the
church of Avranches, send greeting and devoted obedience due to my father
and my lord. Since we cannot be present on the Sunday prior to the Feast of
St. Peter's Chair for the consecration of that venerable man, John, bishop-
elect of Coutances, we, in approval of the consecration, beg Your Paternity to
deign to bestow upon him, the elect, the gift of consecration. We consent to
the said consecration. May Your Paternity flourish and be well reverenced in
Christ. Given on Thursday immediately preceding the Feast of the Blessed
Scholastica, the Virgin, in the year of our Lord 1250.

Although the chapter of Rouen earnestly pleaded with us not to infringe
a custom of their church of Rouen, namely, that all conprovincial bishops
should be consecrated at Rouen, we did not harken to them, nor did we
postpone the consecration because of their allegation or supplication. But,
because we did not wish to do anything which would seem to injure the
rights of the church of Bayeux, we postponed the consecration to the following Sunday, and we gave a letter to the bishop of Bayeux the same
Saturday, ordering him to summon our suffragans to attend the said consecration at Rouen.[150]

FEBRUARY 19. At Evreux, and we ate with the bishop-elect of Coutances.
FEBRUARY 20. At Pont-de-l'Arche. FEBRUARY 21-24. At Déville, at our own
expense. FEBRUARY 25. At Rouen, at our own expense. FEBRUARY 26. At
Rouen, where we consecrated the bishop-elect of Coutances. FEBRUARY 27.
At Pont-de-l'Arche, at our own expense. FEBRUARY 28. At Evreux, at our
own expense. MARCH 1. At Muzy, at our own expense. MARCH 2. At Char-
tres, at our own expense. MARCH 3. At the leprosary at Orgères. MARCH 4.
At Orléans. MARCH 5. At St-Benoît-sur-Loire, at the expense of the abbey.
MARCH 6. At Gien. MARCH 7. At Bonny. MARCH 8. At Cosne. MARCH 9.
At La Charité. MARCH 10. At Nevers. MARCH 11. At Decize. MARCH 12.
At Bourbon-Lancy. MARCH 13. At Paray-le-Monial. MARCH 14. At Cluny,
at the expense of the abbey. MARCH 15. At Mâcon. MARCH 16. At Ville-
franche. MARCH 17-APRIL 3. At Lyons. APRIL 4. At l'Arbresle. APRIL 5.
At Thizy. APRIL 6-16. At Marcigny-le-Monial.

---

[150] Eudes was not being dictated to by the Chapter of Rouen. If the bishop-elect
of Coutances was to be consecrated at Rouen, it was because Eudes wished it that
way and not at the behest of the chapter.

APRIL 17. At Pierrefitte. APRIL 18. At Gannay. APRIL 19. At Decize. APRIL 20-21. At Varzy. APRIL 22. At La Charité. APRIL 23. At the priory of Notre-Dame-du-Pré near Donzy. APRIL 24. At St-Sauveur-en-Puisaye,[1] where on the part of the prior of Lewes in England a cleric was presented to us for the church at Etables. APRIL 25. At Cezy, at the expense of the lord bishop of Sens.[2] APRIL 26. At Nailly, at the expense of the lord bishop of Sens. APRIL 27. At Nemours. APRIL 28. At Melun. APRIL 29. At Paris. APRIL 30. At Argenteuil. [*No entries for May 1-4.*] MAY 5. At Pontoise, at our own expense. MAY 6. At Juziers.

MAY 7. At La Roche-Guyon, where we visited the priory. Asked how many monks there were there, they replied four, since the lord of the village had asked for one always to say the Masses for the dead. Asked how the day and night Offices were performed, they replied that they were well done. Asked whether they lived in common, they replied that they did. Asked whether the prior slept and ate with them, they replied that he did. Asked whether they observed the fasts of the Rule, they replied that they did, and at the proper seasons. Asked about confession, they said that all of them celebrated Mass nearly every day, and that before they celebrated they confessed and received penance. We found that they were using feather beds. Asked whether they ate meat, they replied that if any of them ate meat, he was properly punished for it. They have an income of about sixty pounds; they owe nothing.

MAY 8. At Sausseuse.

MAY 9. At the same, and we visited the priory of St-Michel-sur-Vernonnet.[3] Two monks from Montebourg are there. We found that they slept apart, that is to say, in different rooms. They do not say their Hours with modulation, and at times they do not say them together. They do not observe the fasts of the Rule; they eat meat, and people of the world,

---

[1] A Benedictine priory of St-Germain, in the diocese of Auxerre. (Cottineau, II, 2880.)

[2] Giles I (1244-54). (Gams, *Series episcoporum*, p. 629.)

[3] A Benedictine priory of Montebourg. (Cottineau, II, 3340-41.)

clerics, laymen, and women frequently eat with them, and sometimes they eat with lay folk in town. They frequently omit to say Mass on Thursdays. Brother Thomas was a man of property and had gold rings. He used to go out at night, clad in a cuirass, without his monk's habit, and associate with low companions; he has wounded many at night, both lay and cleric, and has himself been wounded and has had the tip of his finger cut off. We ordered the abbot to remove him, or else we would seize the place and expel the monks.

MAY 10. At Sausseuse.

MAY 11. We visited the chapter of Les Andelys and found everything to be in a satisfactory condition. However, the dean requested that a pause be permitted in the middle of the psalmody.[4]

That same day we spent the night at Mont-Deux-Amants, at our own expense.

MAY 12-13. At Rouen. MAY 14-16. At Déville. MAY 17. At St-Victor-en-Caux, at the expense of the abbey.

MAY 18. We visited at St-Victor, and found nineteen monks in residence, almost all of them being priests. They eat meat in the outside priories; we forbade this. We enjoined the abbot to cast his accounts in the presence of a brother elected by the community, who should give a report of the audit to the community. They have an income of six hundred pounds, and they owe about two hundred pounds. We spent the night at Aliermont.

MAY 19-20. At Aliermont.

MAY 21. At Bacqueville, at the expense of the priory. There are four monks there. They do not read the Rule. They have no copy of the Statutes of Pope Gregory. Traveling monks do not observe the fasts; they use feather beds. They have an income of two hundred pounds; they owe about eighty pounds. We forbade them to use feather beds or to eat meat, except as the Rule permitted, and we enjoined them to a fuller observance of the fasts of the Rule.

MAY 22. At Etoutteville. We found the prior dwelling there alone, since his companion died about last Christmastide. The priory has an income of one hundred forty pounds. He eats meat frequently. We enjoined the prior to procure at least one companion before the feast of the Assumption of the Blessed Virgin.

---

[4] I.e., a pause between the ending of each verse of the psalm on one side of the choir and the beginning of the next verse by those on the opposite side.

MAY 23. At Valmont, where there are twenty-three monks. One monk is dwelling alone in England,[5] and another is likewise by himself in a priory.

MAY 24. At Graville, which we visited, finding eleven canons in residence. One canon is dwelling alone at Bellevue. We ordered that a companion be given him, or that he be recalled to the cloister. More is owed to them than they owe. Everything else we found to be in a satisfactory condition. The prior was not in town when we arrived.

MAY 25. At Montivilliers, at the expense of the monastery. MAY 26. At the same, and we visited the abbess in chapter. We found everything there to be in good condition. MAY 27. At Le Valasse, at the expense of the monastery. MAY 28-JUNE 2. At Préaux, at our own expense. JUNE 3-5. At Jumièges, at our own expense.

JUNE 6. At St-Wandrille. There are thirty-three monks there; there used to be forty. One monk is dwelling alone at Marcousy; we ordered him recalled or else provided with a companion. One does not accuse another [in chapter]. Traveling monks do not observe the fasts of the Rule. The abbot does not visit the outside priories often enough; he does not correct faults with impartiality because he tolerates some. The abbot is a wrathful man, and looks it. Item, he gives lands to relatives of his, who administer them badly. Item, he gave or caused to be given to his nephew, who goes riding with him, three additional measures of wheat, although he has his regular wages just as the other servants. Item, we found that the abbot is over-talkative; item, he does not audit his accounts, nor does he know enough about auditing to know exactly what is the state of the house. Item, his relatives, whom he has gathered about him, are disposing of all the monastic properties, as may be seen from the fact that they now have lofty stone houses in place of the miserable ones they once possessed. Item, almost all of the monks have coffers with keys. Item, William of Jumièges struck William of Boisel. Item, a certain carpenter saw John of Saane talking and laughing with a woman in the vestibule near the door of the church; the abbot connived at this, for John is a member of his household. Item, the prior has a scribe in the town, and the office of cantor which he controls is badly carried out because he gives to the scribe the pennies due to the cantor. The sick are ill-attended. The sources of income are not written

[5] In 1170 Henry II gave Stratfield Say (Berkshire) to Valmont. This is probably the priory in question. (Dugdale, *Monasticon Anglicanum,* VII, 1044.)

out. Emelin and John of Châtel do not confess or celebrate Mass as they ought. Reginald of Caudebec is believed to be a leper, but he wears no distinguishing sign,[6] as we had ordered, and he kept in his priory the child he had by a certain woman.

Item about the lighting, which is insufficient; about cleaning the altar things; about lay folk serving in the refectory.

JUNE 6 [*sic*]. At St-Wandrille, and we visited the priory of Bondeville,[7] and among the things needing correction we found that the brothers have keys and their own coffers; that they sleep together in the same place, both day and night, and eat together. Item, the maidservant must be forbidden to eat in the bakehouse which is just in front of the cellar, because of the scandal which might arise. Item, that the nuns shall not sell or dispose of their thread and spindles. Item, some nun to find out how much grain is owed the priory and also to find out the blood connections of the doorkeeper, who is a favorite of the prioress. Item, there is living there a certain daughter of a certain burgess of Vaux who is very simple minded. Item, anent the prioress, we discovered that she did not wish to credit the treasury with the *mine* of barley which the abbot of St-Georges holds and which is in the fee of the nuns. Item, that she is the recipient of personal property, especially of clothing. Item, that some of her favorites are better cared for in the infirmary than others are; indeed, the sick are not sufficiently looked after. Item, when she is in the infirmary she eats at a table by herself, nor does she live in common with the others. Item, she leaves the priory altogether too much, and not on the business of the house. Item, when she goes to Rouen she stays there for three days, or perhaps four. Item, she is quarrelsome and a sower of discord among the sisters, so that she cannot have any peace with the community, or with anyone else. Item, they hold chapter but rarely, and the sisters drink in the granges. We must speak about getting them another confessor in addition to the one they have. Item, that the doorkeeper be changed, for the present one is hardly discreet.

JUNE 7-8. At Déville. JUNE 9. At Rouen. JUNE 10. At the same, and we conferred Holy Orders. JUNE 11-12. At Rouen. We held a synod in

[6] Lepers, Jews, crusaders, and prostitutes were among those who wore a distinctive dress during the Middle Ages. Eudes visited this abbey on December 13, 1249, and made no mention of a leper monk.

[7] This was originally a hospital, and finally a Cistercian priory of nuns dependent on Bival. The "brothers" are probably lay brothers, not choir monks. (Cottineau, I, 419.)

our own hall, because of the vast number of priests and the commotion made by the people.[8] JUNE 13. We held a synod in the church and there appeared before us the mayor and many of the peers and, in the sight of the full assemblage, they sought and obtained absolution. JUNE 14. We were at Rouen and held a synod of the deans, and the peers ate with us.

JUNE 15-16. We were at Déville. JUNE 17. At Auffay, at our own expense. JUNE 18. At the same, where we administered the Sacrament of Confirmation, and thence we proceeded to Longueville, where we paid our own expenses. JUNE 19-20. At Aliermont. JUNE 21. At Aliermont, and here we had ourself bled. JUNE 22. At Aliermont. JUNE 23. At St-Victor [-en-Caux], at our own expense. JUNE 24. On the Nativity of St. John the Baptist, we blessed the abbot of Beaubec, and spent the night at Déville. JUNE 25. At Déville. JUNE 26-28. At Déville. We were grievously afflicted with rheumatism. JUNE 29–JULY 12. At the same.

JULY 13. At Déville, and this day Matthew, called "Le Gros," was absolved from the excommunication inflicted upon him, for that he had imprisoned the servants of the lord archbishop . . . [lacuna in MS].[9] He swore that he would abide by the decision of the archbishop on the case and to make whatever amends the lord should require. As surety, he offered as pledges Geoffrey of Val-Richer, senior, Nicholas Giboy, John of Val-Richer, and Andrew of St-Léonard, who promised that they would see to it that the said Matthew carried out the sentence of the lord archbishop, or that they would do it themselves.

JULY 14-22. At Déville. JULY 23-26. At Ste-Catherine, at our own expense. JULY 28-28. At Mont-Deux-Amants. JULY 29. At Mortemer-en-Lyons. JULY 30. At St-Germer-de-Flay. JULY 31. At Clermont, in the diocese of Beauvais. AUGUST 1. At Compiègne. AUGUST 2. At Noyon. AUGUST 3. At Compiègne. AUGUST 4. At Neuville-en-Hez. AUGUST 5. At St-Germer-de-Flay.

[8] The Pastoureaux overran the town of Rouen on the days Eudes was holding the synod, and he and his clergy took refuge in the archiepiscopal palace. The mayor of Rouen and the communal council (peers) came to apologize for the popular commotion. To show there were no ruffled feelings, Eudes invited them to a banquet. There were one hundred of these peers or jurati, who chose twelve of their number to administer the commune of Rouen. These presented three names to the king, who chose one as mayor. (A. Giry, Les Etablissements de Rouen [Paris, 1883], I, 14-23, 24-46, 204.)

[9] Matthew le Gros was probably connected with the Pastoureaux and the lord archbishop was probably Eudes himself.

AUGUST 6. At Neufmarché. At the expense of the priory. Four monks are in residence. We made a visitation there and found that they are all priests. They use feather beds; we forbade the use of these. They owe about twenty-seven pounds. They do not have a copy of the Statutes of Pope Gregory; we enjoined the prior to have a copy written out.

AUGUST 7. We visited the chapter of St-Hildevert at Gournay. The subdeacon and the deacon are not vested every day; we ordered them to do this. Simon is publicly known of a certain married woman. The dean is ill famed of drunkenness. We enjoined the dean of Bray to summon the chaplain of the leper house at Gournay, who buys up rents and neglects the leprosary, to produce evidence of his rights[10] in the said chapel within forty days, and, further, that he be cited to appear before us to show evidence of the said rights.

This same day we visited the priory of St-Aubin,[11] where there are fourteen nuns. They receive nuns simoniacally; we forbade them to receive any nun without our special permission. We forbade all of them to receive anything from their friends without the special permission of the prioress. They chant the daily Hours without modulation; we enjoined them at least to chant them in low modulation.[12] They owe about one hundred shillings.

AUGUST 8. At St-Laurent-en-Lyons. There are fourteen canons in residence, of whom all but three are priests. One does not accuse another [in chapter]; we enjoined them to accuse each other, and to keep lay folk out of the cloister. They owe about sixty pounds. We enjoined the prior that when ill fame arises about the canons who live in parishes, he make sure there is someone elected by the community to investigate the ill fame. Item, we enjoined the prior to recall to the cloister Brother Robert, who is now living at La Bruyère.

AUGUST 9-10. At Beaubec. AUGUST 11-13. At Déville. AUGUST 14. At Rouen. AUGUST 15. At the same, and we celebrated the Feast of the Assumption. AUGUST 16-17. At Déville.

[10] Each hospital and leprosary had a chaplain. Often the local parish priest acted in this capacity. No matter who served, the rights of the local priest had to be safeguarded against infringement. The chaplain could be appointed by laymen if the hospital or leprosary were directed by laymen, or by the chapter if the institution was in the hands of religious. But in every case, the chaplain served with the consent and knowledge of the local ordinary. (Jean Imbert, *Les Hôpitaux en droit canonique*, pp. 140-47.)

[11] A Cistercian priory of nuns. (Cottineau, II, 2599.)

[12] I.e. sing the introductory verse to the psalm.

AUGUST 18. At the same. This day Robert, called Buquet, and the treasurer of St-Ouen [-de-Rouen] brought us a complete statement of the assets of their house. Their statement is as follows:

This was the condition of the house of St-Ouen-de-Rouen when Hugh, the abbot, died in the year of our Lord 1251. There was owed to the house in good debts 888 pounds and 4 shillings. From the grain there was owed 14 *muids*, 19 *mines*, valued at 110 pounds, 18 shillings, 9 pence, each *muid* being valued at 7 pounds, 10 shillings. Item, from the mixed wheat and rye, 1 *muid*, 2 *boisseaux* worth 4 pounds, 10 shillings. Item, from the oats, 23 *muids*, 4 *setiers*, 3 *bichots*, worth 93 pounds, 8 shillings. Item, from the oats measured as they are at Hez, 9 *muids*, 13 *mines*, worth 38 pounds, 3 shillings. Total 1,136 pounds, 3 shillings, 9 pence. The house owes 1,208 pounds, 5 shillings, 8 pence, leaving a debt of 73 pounds, 23 pence, which the house owes and which is more than the house has.[13] However, it ought to be known that we have 13 good palfreys, not counting our squires' pack horses, the cart and field horses, or the other animals that we have at our house and on our manors. Item, the silver cups of the lord abbot.[14]

AUGUST 19. At Déville. AUGUST 20. At the same, and we administered the Sacrament of Confirmation at St-Vincent-de-Rouen. AUGUST 21. At Bracquetuit, at our own expense. AUGUST 22-26. At Aliermont.

AUGUST 27. At the same, but we went to Sauqueville and visited the chapter. There are six canons in residence, two of whom have common cure of one parish, and if one of these who has the care of souls of the parish is absent, the curacy reverts to the chapter. The prebend is worth fourteen pounds. There is no regular administrator to oversee the morning distribution of grain; indeed, they extort grain from those who owe it whether they have performed their office or not; we ordered the said grain to be handed over to us until we should arrange for a distributor who would give it out as deserved. Sometimes Mass is not celebrated, except the Mass which is celebrated in the parish church, and sometimes the parish has only a high Mass because Dom George, one of those having the cure of souls, is absent

---

[13] According to Eudes' figures, it should be £ 72 1*s*. 11*d*.

[14] "Grain was measured in bushels, quarters, *mines*, *setiers*, and *muids*. The relations between these different measures were not constant, and two measures of the same were not always of the same capacity." (Joseph R. Strayer, *The Royal Domain in the Bailliage of Rouen* [Princeton, 1936], p. 28. In some localities, there were twelve bushels to the *setier*; in others, nine; in others, fifteen and sixteen. Ordinarily two *mines* make a *setier*, and twelve *setiers* make a *muid* (*Ibid.*).

with the consent of the chapter. We decreed that the cantor should receive fifteen pounds from the chaplaincy of the said George, and perform services for it, and that he should have another clerk in addition to the one he has. Item, we found that Ferric, the treasurer, is ill famed of a certain woman called Alice of Garenne. Item, he runs about the town, and goes riding in unseemly clothing, to wit, in a head-covering from which the shoulder cape has been cut off. Master Walter plays dice, frequents taverns, and is publicly known for grave incontinence. The treasurer owes the chapter fifteen pounds, and he promised in our presence that each year he would repay fifty shillings at All Saints', and another fifty at Pentecost, until the whole amount should be discharged.

AUGUST 28. At Bival, where there are thirty-three nuns. They sometimes leave the cloister without permission; we forbade this. Sometimes lay folk enter the cloister, that is to say, the brothers or relatives of the nuns, and also other people; we forbade the admission of any lay folk into the cloister, with the exception of those whom it might be a scandal to keep out. They owe about forty pounds. Silence is not well observed. The sisters have coffers and keys, but with the permission of the abbess. We spent the night at Beaussault.

AUGUST 29. We dedicated the church at St-Aubin near La Ferté-en-Bray, and we spent the night in the priory of La Ferté, at the expense of the parish. AUGUST 30-31. At Beaulieu, at our own expense. SEPTEMBER 1. At Déville.

SEPTEMBER 2. At the same, and this day we visited the priory of Mont-aux-Malades. We found that there are ten canons there. They have two priories, La Ferté-Loupière, in the diocese of Sens, and Houssaye. At La Ferté there should be six canons, but at present there are only four. Chapter is not held every day. The clerics do not receive Communion very often; we ordered the canons who are clerics to confess and receive Communion once a month. They owe about one hundred pounds.

SEPTEMBER 3. At Déville. SEPTEMBER 4. At Mont-Deux-Amants, at our own expense. SEPTEMBER 5. At Sausseuse, at our own expense. SEPTEMBER 6. At Juziers, at our own expense. SEPTEMBER 7. At Pontoise.

SEPTEMBER 8. At Wy, and this day we visited the priory of Villarceaux. There are twenty nuns there. But six of them were not there;[15] one had

[15] I.e., of the community of twenty-six nuns (see Eudes' visitation on July 9, 1249) six were absent at the time of the present visitation.

left and married, and on our mandate and previous orders two had been removed. They owe about thirty pounds and four *muids* of grain. They have five horses, two hundred sheep, and twenty-five swine.

SEPTEMBER 9. At Marcheroux, at the expense of the monastery.

SEPTEMBER 10. We visited the priory of St-Martin-de-Chaumont. We found that [the prior] has no associate; we enjoined him to obtain one before the feast of St. Maclou. Item, he eats meat freely; we absolutely forbade him to eat meat, save as the Rule permitted; item, that he should observe the fasts of the Rule more fully. The priory has an income of about forty pounds and owes about fifty pounds. Item, when by reason of our visitation we sought out procuration from him, he excused himself on the grounds of poverty, though he willingly recognized his obligation in the presence of the archdeacons of Eu and of the French Vexin.

We had ordered Geoffrey, the prior of St-Martin-de-Pontoise, to appear before us on this day to justify himself, in that when the abbot of Pontoise [Dreux] had received permission from ... [*lacuna in MS*], the lord bishop of Meaux,[16] to have no monks in residence for a time at his priory of Moressart, in the diocese of Meaux—the priory being overwhelmed by debts and interest charges—the said prior had sought from the abbot, or had caused to be sought from him, the said priory. Since he was not able to obtain his request, he sent letters to the bishop [of Meaux] stating that this arrangement was disadvantageous to his monastery and that the bishop should recall the monks to the priory; this the bishop ordered done. Item, he sought permission from his abbot to go to Paris, which, it is said, the abbot refused to grant; having obtained, or pretending to have obtained, permission, he went to the bishop of Meaux to see about this matter of the priory, and brought back letters stating that the monks were to be sent to the priory. In our presence he admitted all this, but said that the abbot had given him permission to go to Paris. Having heard his confession, we removed him from his office as prior and sent him to Jumièges with orders to remain there until we should recall him.

This day we spent the night at the priory of Notre-Dame [-l'Aillerie] in the same town, finding three monks there, all of whom are priests. They have an income of one hundred pounds and owe about sixty pounds.

SEPTEMBER 11. At Gisors, at our own expense.

---

[16] Pierre de Cuisy (1223-55). (Gams, *Series episcoporum,* p. 576.)

SEPTEMBER 12. At Vesly, at the expense of the priory. Two monks from Marmoutier are in residence. We asked them whether they celebrated the Divine Offices there, and they replied that they did; whether they celebrated them together, and they replied in the affirmative; whether with due modulation, and they said, "Yes"; whether they celebrated Mass frequently, and they replied that no day ever passed without a Mass. Certain other questions they answered, but some they did not.

SEPTEMBER 13-15. At Sausseuse, at our own expense. SEPTEMBER 16. At Noyon-sur-Andelle. SEPTEMBER 17. At the same, and we conferred Holy Orders. SEPTEMBER 18. At La Ferté-en-Bray, at our own expense. SEPTEMBER 19. At St-Germain-sur-Eaulne, at the expense of the priory of Mortemer [-sur-Eaulne]. SEPTEMBER 20. At Aumale, at our own expense.

SEPTEMBER 21. At the same, but at the expense of the abbey, which we visited. There are thirteen monks in residence, and there used to be twenty-five; two of them are in England.[17] They are all priests but three. Those who are not priests do not receive Communion at the stated times. Item, they confess to one another and without the consent of the elders. We ordered that whoever leaves the cloister without permission should go without wine the following day. Item, lay folk enter the cloister at pleasure and gossip there; we ordered a stricter guard [for the cloister]. Item, they have only a Latin version of the Statutes of Pope Gregory, although we had previously ordered them to get a French copy.[18] The fasts of the Rule are not observed, particularly by those who travel on horseback; item, they eat meat when there is no need: to be explicit, they eat it once every two weeks; we utterly forbade them to do this. Item, sometimes the refectory has no diners at all, since all the brothers are eating in the infirmary; we forbade this custom. Item, lay folk eat in the refectory; we prohibited this. Master Roger, the abbot's clerk, is a dice-player, and a frequenter of brothels; this has been proved to the abbot several times; the same is true of Lagayte; we ordered them both expelled. The community does not make an audit. They have an income of about fifteen hundred pounds. Item, there is too large a secular staff, to wit, six clerks in addition to the said Roger; we ordered all except the essential and respectable ones to be expelled. Item, we stopped the pension of Master Gerard Coispel. Item, the abbot's nephew, who is

[17] They could have been at either Birstall or Witherness. (Dugdale, *Monasticon Anglicanum*, VII, 1019-21, 1056.)

[18] See entry for June 19, 1250.

now twelve years old, is due to receive a pension of one hundred shillings in five years' time or else to be received as a monk. They owe about fourteen hundred pounds of Tours. The abbot does not sleep in the dormitory. Item, in his last accounts the abbot was short one hundred twenty marks, nor has he since accounted for them. Item, Garinet, the abbot's nephew, has more of the abbey property than he deserves; item, he has a certain pack horse which belongs to the monastery. Item, the abbot is inefficient; they suffer many losses because of his inefficiency; he is ignorant. Dreux, one of the monks, is disobedient to the abbot. Neither the abbot nor the prior knows to whom he confesses. Item, he [Dreux] is a fault-finder and a sower of discord. Item, the abbot pledged the income of the church at Heubecourt, valued at forty marks, for three years; item, also his wool, valued at fifty marks, he pledged for two years. The seal of the convent is not well guarded.

[*No entries for September 21-27.*]

SEPTEMBER 28. We dedicated the chapel of the leper house at Aumale. SEPTEMBER 29–OCTOBER 3. At Aliermont. OCTOBER 4. At Ouville.

OCTOBER 5. At Ouville, where there are nine canons in residence and three elsewhere, to wit, two in one of their priories and one at Beaulieu. At one time there were thirteen. They celebrated the dedication of their monastery, although it has not been dedicated. One does not accuse another [in chapter]; we decreed that if anyone should be cognizant of a brother's fault and does not accuse him, he should fast the following day on bread and water. Item, we ordered that the Rule be read in its entirety one day every week, and at table. Sometimes they leave the cloister without permission; sometimes they are punished for this, but not often. They have an income of four hundred pounds; they owe about one hundred pounds, together with a tithe of forty pounds.

Adam,[19] the priest at Yvecrique, offered pledges to us. We gave him permission to attend the schools[20] until the feast of St.-John, provided, however, that he remain in his parish during Lent and give us a bond to the extent of forty pounds, to be used at our discretion if he should behave indecently either at the schools of anywhere else. He pledged his church.

---

[19] See entry for January 30, 1248/49.
[20] This probably means attending for further theological study any of the rising theological faculties of the University of Paris. Rouen had a school, but it was not of much renown.

OCTOBER 6. At Beaulieu. OCTOBER 7. At Nojeon-le-Sec. OCTOBER 8. At Etrépagny. OCTOBER 9. At Chaumont, at our own expense. OCTOBER 10. At the same, and we presided over the holy synod. OCTOBER 11. At Conflans. OCTOBER 12. At Argenteuil. OCTOBER 13-22. At Pré-St-Gervais, near Paris. OCTOBER 23. At Argenteuil, at our own expense. OCTOBER 24. At Pontoise, at our own expense. OCTOBER 25. At Wy, at our own expense. OCTOBER 26-28. At Sausseuse, at our own expense. OCTOBER 29. At Mont-Deux-Amants, at our own expense. OCTOBER 30. At Mont-Ste-Catherine. OCTOBER 31–NOVEMBER 1. At Rouen. NOVEMBER 2-5. At Déville. NOVEMBER 6. At Rouen, and we presided over the synod of the greater archdeanery. NOVEMBER 7. At the same, and we held the greater synod. NOVEMBER 8. We held a synod of deans, and spent the night at Déville. NOVEMBER 9. At Auffay, at our own expense. NOVEMBER 10-26. At Aliermont. NOVEMBER 27. At Dieppe. NOVEMBER 28. At Aliermont. NOVEMBER 29. At Auffay, at our own expense. NOVEMBER 30. At Déville.

DECEMBER 1. We visited the monastery of St-Amand. Forty-four professed nuns are in residence; there are none at Saane.[21] We ordered them to confess and receive Communion once a month. Item, we decreed that, after a year's novitiate they should make their profession, provided that they had attained their fifteenth year. Item, we forbade any nun to give away any of her food, save through the almoner. There is owed to them as much as they owe. We enjoined the abbess, although we had already enjoined her,[22] to draw up a statement of the receipts and expenses of her abbey twice or three times a year, in the presence of sisters elected by the convent for this purpose.

This day we spent the night at Déville, at our own expense.

DECEMBER 2-3. At Rouen.

DECEMBER 4. We visited the priory of Ste-Madeleine[23] at Rouen. We ordered the sisters to hold their chapter every Friday and to confess and receive Communion once a month. They owe about one hundred pounds and have enough grain and foodstuffs to last them until the new harvest. They have an income of one thousand pounds. We spent the night at Déville.

---

[21] At Saane-St-Just was located the priory of Ste-Catherine, dependent on St-Amand. (Cottineau, II, 2569.)

[22] See entry for January 4, 1248/49.

[23] A priory of canonesses regular. (Cottineau, II, 2546.)

DECEMBER 5-10. At Déville.

DECEMBER 11. We visited Pré, where there are eighteen monks. All of them are priests but three. There used to be twenty-five monks there. They owe about six hundred pounds, not counting the abbot's debt,[24] which amounts to eight hundred thirty pounds. Everything else we found to be in good condition.

DECEMBER 12. At the same.

DECEMBER 13. We visited the monastery of St-Ouen-de-Rouen. There are fifty monks in residence. Sometimes they eat meat in their rooms; we forbade this. All but three are priests. They eat meat and break the fasts prescribed by the Rule; we ordered them to observe the Statutes of Pope Gregory in these matters. Item, we forbade them to drink in the town, except in house of other religious.

Note: concerning the priory of St-Giles and of Espaubourg.

DECEMBER 14. At Déville.

DECEMBER 15. We visited the chapter of the cathedral of Rouen, assembled in chapter, and we expounded to the assembly the word of the Lord. We found certain things amiss in the performance of the Divine Offices and in the maintenance of the temporalities, especially in the matter of the English revenues. Item, having inquired into the life and conduct of the bachelors,[25] we found that Videlieu was defamed of frequenting taverns and of incontinence; however, the chapter had already warned him. Item, Rufus, a priest, likewise of incontinence, as is one called White, a monk. Anent the canons, we found Master John of St-Lô defamed of incontinence with a certain woman who is almost blind; we warned him in the presence of the archdeacon, the chief cantor, and the archdeacon of Petit-Caux, whom we summoned and called; but he in reply stated that he had had nothing to do with her since he had been ordained priest, and he added that her husband was dead. We enjoined him, in order to avoid a scandal, to send her out of the town, and he promised to do so. Item, we found Master William of Salmonville defamed of incontinence and of

[24] I.e., a debt to the abbot of Bec. Pré was a priory dependent on Bec.

[25] The bachelor in the ninth century was one who held a piece of land or an office in vassalage. Later, it meant young nobility in training for warfare. The term was transferred to students in training at universities. In this instance, it applies to young men in the process of training to be canons in the chapter. ("Grades théologiques," *Dict. de théol. cath.*, VI[2], 1688-90; "Grades académiques," *Dict. de droit canon.* V, 975-77.)

several other things; and we enjoined him to take up a fixed residence in one place so that he might be able to procure a worthy testimonial of his life and general conduct. He firmly promised us not to depart from Rouen without our special permission and that of the chapter. On this day we were at Déville.

DECEMBER 16-21. At Déville. DECEMBER 22. At Rouen. DECEMBER 23. At the same, and we conferred Holy Orders in our private chapel. DECEMBER 24. At Rouen. DECEMBER 25. At the same, and we celebrated Christmas. DECEMBER 26-27. At Rouen.

DECEMBER 28. At Rouen, and we sent the following letter to all the deans of our diocese:

Brother Eudes, etc., to his beloved sons, all of the deans constituted in the city and diocese of Rouen, eternal greeting in the Lord Jesus Christ. By reason of the exigencies of church business and of many matters needing attention we have decreed the convocation of a provincial council to which our venerable brothers the suffragans of the archdiocese of Rouen, the abbots, archdeacons, deans of churches, conventual priors and chapters, and the other collegiate bodies both secular and religious of the province of Rouen are held to appear. Wherefore we order each and all of you to cite the abbots, deans, archdeacons, conventual priors, chapters and convents and other collegiate bodies, secular and religious, in his deanery to appear at Rouen on the present feast of St. Vincent, either in person or represented by suitable proctors, and to appear on time so that on this same day we may hold a sacred council. You will reply in writing informing us of your action. Given, etc.

We sent the following letter to the bishop of Bayeux:

Brother Eudes, etc., to the venerable Brother [Guy], by God's grace bishop of Bayeux, eternal greeting in the Lord Jesus Christ, and true charity in the Lord. To deal with urgent business of the church and with other necessary matters we have by decree convoked a provincial council at which our venerable brothers the suffragans of the church of Rouen, the abbots, archdeacons, deans of churches, conventual priors and cathedral chapters and other collegiate bodies, both secular and religious, of the province and diocese of Rouen are obliged to attend. Wherefore, in accordance with custom and pertinent to your dignity we order Your Fraternity to cite our venerable brothers the suffragans of the church of Rouen, the abbots, priors, deans, archdeacons, the cathedral chapters, convents, and other collegiate bodies, both religious and secular, to appear promptly at Rouen, either in person or by sufficient representation, on the feast of St. Vincent, so that we may hold a sacred council on this day. You too will be present at the said place, on the said day and hour, and you will inform us in writing of your action. Given, etc.

DECEMBER 29-30. At Rouen.

DECEMBER 31. At the same, and we sent out the following letter to the lord bishop of Bayeux:

Brother Eudes, by God's permission unworthy bishop of the diocese of Rouen, to the venerable Brother [Guy], by God's grace bishop of Bayeux, in the bonds of true charity sends eternal greeting in the Lord Jesus Christ. Recently we sent you a letter openly declaring our intention to convoke a provincial council, and we requested you to cite our venerable brothers the suffragans of the church of Rouen, and to ask the chapters of the cathedral churches, as is the custom and consonant with our dignity, namely, that the suffragans appear in person, the chapters through suitable proctors, at Rouen on the feast of St. Vincent to celebrate with us a provincial council, and that they appear on time so that we might hold the council on this stated day. Further, that you should be present in person at the stated place, and on the said day and hour. We also intend, with the assistance of our council and of our other venerable brothers, to discuss with the archdeacons of the cathedral churches and also with... [lacuna in MS] the abbots and conventual priors of the province of Rouen, with the exception of those bodies adhering to the discipline of Cîteaux,[26] certain matters which are known to be of particular interest to the aforesaid individuals and which cannot be conveniently treated without their presence. We request you to announce in your diocese, and to have our venerable brothers announce to the aforesaid persons in the other dioceses that they should be present at the said day and place, either in person or represented by suitable proctors, if they wish to do so and believe that their interests are involved, so that we may proceed to deal with the said business with the aid of your counsel and that of our other suffragans, considering the honor of God and the advantage of souls. You will notify us by letters patent what you shall have done in this matter. Given at Déville, the Sunday after Christmas, in the year of our Lord 1251.

JANUARY 1. At Rouen, and on this same day the following letters were sent out from our curia:

Brother Eudes, by divine permission the unworthy bishop of the diocese of Rouen, to all constituted deans in the city and diocese of Rouen, eternal greeting in the Lord Jesus Christ. To deal with urgent business and other necessary

---

[26] The Cistercians were an exempt order, i.e., they were directly under the Pope and thus not within the spiritual jurisdiction of the local ecclesiastical authorities.

matters affecting the Church, we have ordered a sacred provincial council to be convoked at Rouen on the day of the current Feast of St. Vincent. On the said day and at the same place we intend, with the counsel of our venerable brothers the suffragans of the church of Rouen, to consult with the abbots and conventual priors of the province of Rouen, with the exception of the Cistercians, about certain matters which are known to affect the said individuals, and without whose presence negotiations cannot conveniently proceed. We request each one of you to inform all the abbots and conventual priors in his deanery, with the exceptions of the Cistercians, to be present at the said day and place, either in person or represented by suitable proctors, if they so desire and believe that their interests are involved, so that we may be able to proceed and, with their advice and the counsel of our brothers the suffragans of the church of Rouen, may so handle the aforesaid business that it will redound to the honor of God and to the comfort of souls. You will inform us by letters patent what disposition you make of this matter. Given at Déville, the second day in the octave of the Nativity, in the year of our Lord 1251.

JANUARY 2-3. At Rouen. JANUARY 4. At Jumièges, at our own expense.

JANUARY 5. At Bec-Hellouin. This day Master John, cleric was presented to us by John of Muchegros, esquire,[27] for the church of Muchegros, but was rejected. Since we did not wish to receive the said John, he appealed both on his own behalf and on that of the said esquire. But since John, esquire, was a minor and also excommunicated and had not yet done homage to the queen for his land, and since the church itself stood in our patronage, we were not willing to admit John the cleric to that church.

JANUARY 6-10. At the same. JANUARY 11. At Pont-Authou, and we dedicated the local church. JANUARY 12. We dedicated the church of Berville, and spent the night at Boissey [-le-Châtel], at the expense of the parishioners of Berville. JANUARY 13. At Jumièges, at our own expense. JANUARY 14. We dedicated the high altar at Jumièges, and we spent the night there, at our own expense. JANUARY 15-20. At Déville. JANUARY 21. At Rouen.

JANUARY 22. At Rouen, and this day we celebrated the sacred provincial council, there being present the venerable brothers the suffragans of the church of Rouen, together with the proctors of the cathedral churches of

---

[27] The Latin is *scutiferus,* which means a gentleman generally less than fourteen years old, and thus a minor, who had reached the stage of shield-bearer in his military training. Eudes gives no reason for Esquire John's excommunication.

this province, with the exception of the chapter of Evreux, which, although on our authority invited to attend the council by our venerable brother Guy, by God's grace bishop of Bayeux, as were the other chapters of our province, nevertheless did not send any proctor as the council demanded.

On this same day, seated in council and in the presence of the afore-mentioned venerable brothers whose advice we sought, we determined the question of a resumed provincial visitation as follows: We stated unequiv-ocally that we may proceed to visit our province when and where it may seem best to us. Item, in the same council, in the presence of the afore-said brothers and the representatives of the said chapters, and with their advice, inquisitors, proved and honest men, were elected who, as is con-tained below, should in their own diocese make inquiries as to what is being done in the matter of reforming morals and of correcting abuses, and at the next provincial council should make a report as to matters needing reform or discipline, in accordance with the decree of the general council.[28] For the diocese of Rouen, James of Rouen and William of Eu, archdeacons, were elected as inquisitors; for Bayeux, Master Adam, dean of Noron, and Ralph, dean of Bavent; for Evreux, Master Stephen, archdeacon, and Giles of Biville, canon of Evreux; for Lisieux, Master Richard of Woelen, priest at Canapville, and Master Robert, priest at Courbepine; for Avranches, Master William of Tour and Master John, archdeacons; for Séez, Master Nicholas, parson of the church at Moulins, and Amidieu, dean of Argentan; for Coutances, Robert le Sor, dean of les Puits, and Robert Piedfust, dean of Carentan. The seating order of the bishops at the sacred council was as follows: we sat in the middle; on our right came in order the lord bishop of Evreux, and the bishop of Lisieux; on our left sat the lord bishop of Séez, and after him, the bishop of Coutances. The council's business having been finished, we retired, singing the *Te Deum*.

JANUARY 23. At Rouen. JANUARY 24. At Déville. JANUARY 25. At Auffay. JANUARY 26-28. At Aliermont. JANUARY 29. At Aumale. JAN-UARY 30. At Amiens. JANUARY 31. At Bapaume. FEBRUARY 1. At Cam-brai, at the abbey of St-Aubert. FEBRUARY 2. At the same, but at the house of the bishop, and at his expense. FEBRUARY 3. At Vaucelles, a Cistercian house. FEBRUARY 4. At St-Quentin. FEBRUARY 5. At Nesle. FEBRUARY 6. At Montdidier. FEBRUARY 7. At Conti. FEBRUARY 8. At Aumale. FEBRU-

---

[28] That is, canon 8 of the Fourth Lateran Council. (Mansi, XXII (994-95.)

ARY 9-11. At Aliermont. FEBRUARY 12. At Auffay. FEBRUARY 13. At Déville. FEBRUARY 14. At Rouen, and this day we drove the penitents from the church. FEBRUARY 15. At Mont-Deux-Amants, at our own expense. FEBRUARY 16. At Sausseuse, at our own expense. FEBRUARY 17. At Juziers, at our own expense. FEBRUARY 18. At Argenteuil. FEBRUARY 19-20. At Paris; at St-Maclou. FEBRUARY 21. At Argenteuil. FEBRUARY 22. At Pontoise, at our own expense. FEBRUARY 23. At Gisors. FEBRUARY 24. At the same, and we conferred Holy Orders. FEBRUARY 25. At Noyon-sur-Andelle, at our own expense. FEBRUARY 26. At St- Matthieu d'Ermentrouville.

FEBRUARY 27. At the same. This day at Ermentrouville we handed over Thibaut of Château, a cleric pledged to a crusade, whom we had kept in detention at our manor at Rouen as a suspected homicide, to Geoffrey of Val-Richer, senior, Reginald of Château, Bertin of Château, Andrew of St-Leonard, and Clement of Senots, all citizens of Rouen, under the following conditions which we put in writing: to wit, that the said citizens, collectively and severally, promise to return the said Thibaut to us at our manor at Rouen on the day following the octave of Easter, or upon our order, and in the same condition as he is at present.[29] This is supported by a corporate oath taken by each one of them with his hand in ours, and under pain of forfeiting one thousand pounds of Tours, to be paid by each one in shillings. He will appear on this day to hear the decision which we shall have reached after we have made inquiry into the homicide which the said Thibaut is said to have committed, unless, within the Sunday on which the *Isti sunt dies*[30] is sung, the said citizens deserve to obtain the complete liberation of the said Thibaut from us.

FEBRUARY 28. At the same.

MARCH 1. At Beaulieu, which we visited on the following day. We found that there are twelve canons there. One canon is dwelling alone at Montmain; we gave strict orders to the prior to send him a companion before Easter. All but two are priests. They owe about two hundred pounds; about two hundred pounds is owed to them, but they still owe two years of the royal tithe. With the exception of oats, they have sufficient provisions to last until the harvest.

---

[29] This could mean many things, including the prohibition of promotion in clerical orders.

[30] Passion Sunday.

MARCH 2. At Quévreville, at the expense of the priory. No monks are there.

At the same.[31]

We, Pierre,[32] by divine mercy the elected [archbishop] of Rouen, and Hugh,[33] by His grace bishop of Séez, make known to all who may see the present letter that a dispute arose between us concerning ourselves and our bishoprics because we, the elected [archbishop] stated that the archbishop of Rouen, at the time of making his visitation in the diocese of Séez, was competent to take cognizance of the cases and complaints of the subjects of the bishop of Séez on the simple complaint of a plaintiff. Item, that the archbishops of Rouen, and any of their officials, have the power to allow appeals from the archdeacon or from the rural deans of the diocese of Séez, through by-passing the bishop, and that the archbishops of Rouen and their officials, by sentence of excommunication and suspension or by any other method, may compel the subjects of the bishop to receive their delegations; and that they may administer punishments and execute sentences, issue citations and test evidence. We, the bishop of Séez, deny all of these claims.

However, by common consent and mutual agreement we compromised in this matter, and selected Hugh [of Pisa], archdeacon of Rouen, and Master William, the official of Séez, both venerable men, to act as arbiters; and each of us, on our own behalf and that of our dioceses, promised in full, and under penalty of two hundred marks, to abide by and to uphold forever whatever these men should decree in the aforesaid matter or should be pleased to ordain in this peace, arbitration, or judgment.

We will the penalty to apply to us and to our successors, to be enforced against us or our successors, and to be carried out with no exceptions whatsoever, if any of us or of our successors shall fail to observe the arbitration or judgment, or if we should act against the decision. We obligate ourselves and our successors, under the same penalty, to have this promise ratified by our chapters and to promulgate the decison of the aforesaid arbiters.

We desire also that the decision shall remain firm and stable, even though it should be violated in any way and the fine paid. In testimony whereof we add to the present letter the authority of our seals. Done in the month of March, on the feast of St. Benedict, in the year of our Lord 1236.

---

[31] See Introduction, pp. xxv-xxvii, for discussion of the conflict between Eudes and his suffragans.

[32] This was Pierre de Colmieu, archbishop of Rouen from 1237 to 1244, when he was made cardinal of Albano. (Gams, *Series episcopurum*, p. xxii, p. 614.)

[33] Hugh II (1228-40). (Gams, *Series episcoporum*, p. 626.)

In the name of the Father, and of the Son, and of the Holy Ghost, Amen. The following agreement was reached with respect to the venerable fathers, Pierre, by God's grace archbishop-elect of Rouen, and Hugh, bishop of Séez, by us, Hugh, archdeacon of Rouen, and Master William of Rouris, the official of Séez:

We, Pierre, by the Divine Mercy the elected [archbishop] of Rouen, and Hugh, by His grace bishop of Séez, make known to all by the present letter that a dispute arose between us, etc., as above, and on down to the end, i.e., "on the feast of St. Benedict". We, after diligent deliberation and consideration discussing the circumstances of the aforesaid business, and desiring the peace and quiet of the said venerable fathers, their dioceses, and their subjects, arbitrate and declare that under the aforesaid penalty, neither the archbishop of Rouen nor any official of his shall receive appeals made, or to be made, from archdeacons or rural deans of the diocese of Séez, through by-passing the bishop of Séez.

Item, under the same penalty we decide and declare that the archbishop of Rouen, or his official, has the power to compel the subjects of the bishop of Séez to receive subdelegates, to draw up writs and citations, to carry out sentences, and to hear testimony; and to excommunicate, suspend, or in any other way coerce any who are hostile or disobedient, except that they shall not be held, at the order of the said archbishops or their officials, to cite anyone beyond the diocese of Séez, unless he should persuade them that there was reasonable cause; nor shall the bishop of Séez attempt in any way to prevent them from carrying out their duties as stated.

Item, under the same penalty we declare and decide that when the archbishop of Rouen shall again visit the diocese of Séez, he may take cognizance of cases which are brought before him by simple complaint affecting subjects of the bishop of Séez, so long as he remains in the diocese of Séez.

And lest the parties be aggrieved, we decide and declare under the same penalty that the said archbishop is not to inject himself into those cases once he is outside the diocese of Séez, but that when he or his officials leave the diocese he will hand over in their entirety the cases already begun before him, and likewise the enforcing of the judgment of those cases which have been decided, to the bishop of Séez, unless provable suspicion be lodged against the latter; in that case, the said archbishop shall consign the said trials and enforcement of judgments to some one of the subjects of the bishop of Séez, and the bishop himself will be liable to receive the same actions as the said archbishop, just as was stated above, deemed consigned to himself into those cases already begun or terminated before him beyond the diocese of Séez, if the parties should consent thereto.

In making these statements we do not intend to derogate or detract from the agreement made by the venerable father, lord of San Sabina,[34] between the aforesaid archbishop and bishop, or new agreement or addition [codicil] made afterwards about it between themselves. The said elected archbishop and bishop, however, have entirely approved the decision and aforesaid statement and have expressly ratified it. In view of this, we have deemed that the present document should be strengthened with our seal. Done in the year of our Lord 1236, in the month of March and on the feast of St. Benedict.

To all who shall see this document the official of Rouen gives greeting in the Lord. Be it known that we, in the year of our Lord 1251, on the Friday after the Sunday on which *Reminiscere*[35] is sung, have seen and carefully inspected certain letters sealed under the seal of the venerable men, Gilbert, the prior, and the whole chapter of the church of Séez as it appears at first glance and which read as follows:

To all who shall see these documents Gilbert, prior, and the whole chapter of the church of Séez, [give] greetings in the Lord.

Let everyone know that we regard as ratified and as permanent the agreement made in the Roman Curia through John of happy memory, bishop of San Sabina, between the venerable father Hugh, our bishop, and our church as party of the first part; and the proctors of Maurice[36] of happy memory, the archbishop of Rouen, on his behalf and on behalf of the church of Rouen, as parties of the second part; and likewise that the agreements and additions entered into on this agreement afterwards, through our aforesaid bishop and reverend father, Pierre, archbishop of Rouen, the then elected successor of Maurice, and the agreement made by the venerable men, Hugh of Pisa, archdeacon of Rouen, and William, the official of Séez, between the said reverend fathers, Pièrre, elected archbishop of Rouen and Hugh, our bishop, concerning the fact that the same elected bishop stated that the archbishop of Rouen, at the time of visitation, could, in the diocese of Séez, take cognizance of cases and complaints of the subjects of the bishop of Séez brought on simple complaint to the bishop, and that the archbishops of Rouen and their officials could entertain indiscriminately appeals taken from the hearing of the archdeacon or the rural deans of the diocese of Séez, by-passing the bishop, and that the archbishops of Rouen and their officials could compel the subjects of the bishop to receive

---

[34] John VII (1227-33), cardinal priest of San Sabina. (Gams, *Series episcoporum*, p. xiii.)

[35] The second Sunday of Lent.

[36] Maurice, archbishop of Rouen (1231-35), the predecessor of Pierre de Colmieu. (Gams, *Series episcoporum*, p. 614.)

judges, enforce judgments and issue citations, and follow up the execution of imposed sentences and hear testimony. We hold these as ratified and firm and become answerable under the penalty set forth in the decision for observing all the aforesaid without violation; and should it happen that the aforesaid agreements, written in may leaves, be transcribed in one document, we will willingly attach our seal to it when we shall be required to do so by the venerable father, the archbishop of Rouen. And in order that these agreements remain ratified and permanent, we have deemed that these writings should be signed with our seal. Done at Séez, in the year of our Lord 1238, on the Saturday after the Ascension of our Lord. What we have seen we attest under the seal of the curia of Rouen. Dated on the said day and year.

To all who shall see these writings Guido, by the grace of God bishop of Bayeux; William, of Avranches; John, of Evreux; Godfrey, of Seéz; Fulk, of Lisieux and John, of Coutances, bishops, [give] greetings in the Lord.[37] Be it known that we have appointed Simon, cleric, the bearer of these present letters, our proctor for setting forth before the reverend father Eudes, by the grace of God archbishop of Rouen, the grievances done to us, our churches, and our subjects by the same, and by his officials and agents, against the spirit of the Constitution of Rheims and also against justice, and to appeal from him and his officials on behalf of us, our churches, and our subjects, from each and every grievance which he shall propose, and lest he presume to aggrieve further in the aforesaid or other ways ourselves, our churches, and our subjects, or to do anything in our disfavor or that of our churches or our subjects, he, Simon, is to seek and obtain *apostoli* from the archbishop and his aforementioned officials. Given in the year of our Lord 1251, on the day following the feast of St. Vincent.

To the most Holy Father and Lord, Innocent, by the grace of God supreme pontiff of the Holy Roman church, Brother Eudes, by the permission of God unworthy bishop of the church of Rouen, devotedly kisses your blessed feet. Be it known to Your Reverend Holiness that Simon, cleric, being duly constituted in our presence proctor of our venerable brothers the suffragans of the church of Rouen, four of the same being present, to wit, of Bayeux, Séez, Lisieux and Coutances, in the year of our Lord 1251, on the Monday after the Sunday on which *Reminiscere* is sung, has set forth in these words that the said

---

[37] Guido of Bayeux (1241-60). (Gams, *Series episcoporum*, p. 507; William V of Avranches (1236-52) (*ibid.*, p. 506); John of Evreux (1244-56) (*ibid.*, p. 550); Godfrey of Séez (1241-58) (*ibid.*, p. 626); Fulk of Lisieux (1250-67) (*ibid.*, p. 566); John of Coutances (*ibid.*, p. 542).

suffragans, their churches, and their subjects were aggrieved by us, our officials, and our agents. These are the grievances which the archbishop, his officials, and his agents inflict on the suffragans and their subjects; they receive appeals lodged by the suffragans' archdeacons and other subjects, the suffragans themselves being by-passed. They cite and commit to the archbishop cases which are in the hands of the suffragans without giving a provable or law-worthy reason therefor. Item, when an appeal is made from an interlocutory or definitive sentence, although the other party deny the appeal or deny that the appeal was entered within the ten-year period, or propose something similar, nevertheless they prevent sentence from even being carried out in the case. Item, although objection be made before the sentence was rendered that an appeal as made from an unjust or less law-worthy case, and although the appeal, as if having emanated from a provable case, be not received, and though they may not have begun to investigate, on the bases of the case laid before them, whether it was true or not, in both instances they prevent the case from proceeding further; indeed in every instance of appealed cases, on the very first citation, they impede further legal procedure in the case. Item, against the third party who attempts anything in a case in which an appeal was made, they lay claim to and exercise jurisdiction. Item, they rescind or declare that on legal grounds sentences of excommunication, suspension, and interdict imposed by him from whom the appeal is made are null even though they have no jurisdiction over the appeal. Item, whether or not an appeal is made, with the consent of the clergy, of even of clerics and laity, they, without the consent of their ordinaries, investigate judicially the cases of both. Item, they compel the subjects of the suffragans to execute their decrees and precepts and to give testimony in cases which have fallen to them by way of appeal. Item, they force the officials and other subjects of the suffragans, in matters of simple complaint, to appear in their presence. Item, they reduce sentences imposed by the suffragans' officials, archdeacons and subjects of the suffragans who have jurisdiction, and by-pass those who have imposed excommunication. Item, they reprimand and censure the officials of the suffragans and their other subjects, because they are unwilling to answer in the presence of the complainants. Item, they hear, through simple complaint, those who make accusation about the suffragans, be the latter exercising contended or willing jurisdiction. Item, they seek money damages for themselves in appeal cases. These things having been proposed, the same proctor [Simon] appealed to the Apostolic See in these words: "Because you, Lord Archbishop, and your officials and your agents have aggrieved and are aggrieving your suffragans, their churches, and their subjects in the aforesaid matters, contrary to right and contrary to the tenor of the Constitution of Rheims, and lest you any further aggrieve these same churches and their subjects, for these very subjects and churches I, Simon, proctor of the said suffragans, appeal here and now in writing to the Apostolic See and seek *apostoli* from each and every of the aforesaid grievances." After these things, the same proctor, there and then, made another appeal in these words: "Item, since by old and approved custom, the archbishop of Rouen for the time being is obliged to await the lapse of three years after his visitation before he may repeat the visitation of his province, and since you, contrary to the aforesaid custom, have definitely announced that you will repeat the visitation whenever it pleases you, and lest you again begin to make the aforesaid visitation before the stated time of three years, I, the aforesaid Simon, proctor for these dioceses and their subjects, appeal in writing to the Apostolic See and here and now seek *apostoli*." But we did not deem that these appeals should be deferred to for several reasons, some of which we have caused to be noted below. We did not defer to the first appeal, for when on the very day before the lodged appeal the four above-mentioned brothers, in our presence, as it was said, had explained to us the aforementioned articles, we sought of the same four individually that they explain to us whether each of them had been aggrieved by us, our officials, or our agents in all the aforesaid articles, or in some, or in that which he would say, offering to give to each of them the proper remedy for these wrongs about which he would say he was aggrieved; we offered diligently this same offer to them and their proctors after the appeal. None of them wished to point out a certain article or articles [and say] in which one or in which ones he would declare that he was aggrieved, nor was there any one of them who would say he was aggrieved in all articles. The proctor, indeed, on behalf of the aforesaid suffragans, on being asked by us about the aforesaid, in the aforesaid form, was unwilling to give a definite answer. Item, [we did not defer] because many of the aforesaid articles contained falsehood within them. Several articles, by old and approved custom, pertained to us and our church. Indeed, some things contained in the same articles, inasmuch as they were consonant with law and with reason, could by no means be considered as grievances. [We did not defer] to the second appeal inasmuch as it was interposed contrary to law and because it is not the custom that the proctor make allegations on what constitutes custom; and because in this case we do not believe that that custom has a place, we did not deem that the appeal should be deferred to. Given in the year of our Lord 1251, the Friday after the feast of the Blessed Matthew the Apostle.

MARCH 3. At Noyon-sur-Andelle, at the expense of the priory. Seven monks were there. We found everything in good condition, except that the sacristan, although he is believed to be a good man, does not confess as the Statutes of Pope Gregory require; we enjoined him to confess in accordance with the said statutes. They have an income of about five hundred pounds, and they owe about two hundred sixty pounds.

MARCH 4. At Déville, and the lord bishop of Beauvais[38] was with us. MARCH 5-6. At Louviers. MARCH 7. At Sausseuse, at the expense of the priory. Thirteen canons are in residence. Two canons dwell alone in two of the priories. Eight priests are there. They owe about as much as [is reported] in the other visitation, contained on folio 34.[39]

MARCH 8. At Gasny, and we visited there. Some of them use feather beds, but, as they say, because they need to; we enjoined them to read a section of the Rule after Prime. Item, we found that they do not fully observe the fasts of the Rule; we enjoined them to be more observant. Item, sometimes they eat meat; we forbade them to eat meat, except as permitted by the Rule. Item, there are three monks there, whereas in another year there were four, but they told us that there was no definite number, for the abbot sends monks there as he sees fit, sometimes more, sometimes fewer. All of the income is for the use of the monastery of St-Ouen [-de-Rouen], except what is needed for the maintenance of the monks dwelling in the priory.

MARCH 9. At St-Martin-la-Garenne. We found four monks there, all of whom are priests. There used to be five. Two of them, that is to say, William the sacristan, and Richard the bell ringer, are topers and are light-headed. They [the monks] do not confess each month as the Statutes of Pope Gregory require; they eat meat at times when there is no need. Item, although they are often present in the choir, some of them do not sing when the Hours are being sung. Item, they go off to the Seine without getting permission from the prior. They owe about eighty pounds. With the exception of oats, they have sufficient provisions.

MARCH 10. At Juziers. MARCH 11. At the same, at the expense of Gaillonet.

MARCH 12. At the same [Juziers]. The Rule pertaining to the keeping of the cloister is not observed. They use feather beds; the abbot says that this is an old custom. Six monks and a prior are in residence. We advised them to use mattresses of straw. They do not observe the fasts of the Rule, nor do they abstain from meat; we ordered the one to be observed and ab-

---

[38] William of Grez (1249-1267). (Gams, *Series episcoporum.*, p. 511.)
[39] See entry for February 6, 1250/51.

stinence in the other. We received procuration.

MARCH 13. We received procuration at St-Laurent-la-Garenne. We ordered them to read the Statutes of Pope Gregory. They use feather beds. We advised them to do without them, and to abstain from eating meat as well except when permitted by the Rule. They owe about thirty pounds. They have enough wheat and wine, but only a little oats.

MARCH 14. At Parnes, where we made a visitation. The prior has not yet bought the chalice, although we had already ordered him to buy one.[40] They pay twenty pounds in tithes. Five monks are in residence. No chapter is held, nor are minor punishments administered. They do not observe the Statutes of Pope Gregory regarding confession; we enjoined them to adhere strictly to these statutes. They eat meat; we enjoined them to abstain, except as the Rule permitted them. They owe about thirty pounds; however, they already have their full supply of grain. Item, we enjoined the prior to buy a chalice and a missal.

This day we came to Sérans and visited there. They have no copy of the Statutes of Pope Gregory; we ordered them to buy one, or to have a copy written out. Item, we enjoined them to confess to their prior at least once a month, according to the statutes of the Rule. They do not observe the fasts of the Rule; we enjoined them to observe them as the Rule require. They eat meat; we ordered them to obey the Rule concerning abstinence.

MARCH 15. At St-Martin-de-Pontoise, and we made a visitation. There are twenty-seven monks in residence. All but ten are priests. They owe about eleven hundred pounds. They had not entered their income in several books, as we had already ordered them to do;[41] we enjoined them to write them out. Item, we forbade them to receive Geoffrey, the former prior, or Stephen, his companion, whether as monks or otherwise, without our consent. The abbot does not visit the outside priories often enough. The abbot's relatives are a burden to the monastery and to the priories, especially that of Tourny. The prior does not eat in the refectory, and indulges in somewhat dainty food; we enjoined him to correct these things.

MARCH 17. We visited the chapter of St-Mellon. They have only a few rochets and amices; the chapter ought to procure a sufficient supply. We found everything else to be in a sufficiently good condition. We stayed the night at St-Martin, and for procuration they paid us one hundred shillings

[40] See entry for February 8, 1250/51.
[41] See entry for February 11, 1250/51.

of Paris and provided us with straw, beds, fodder for the horses, and wood.

MARCH 18. At St-Martin, at our own expense.

MARCH 19. At Liancourt, which we visited. They eat meat whenever they are bled, and, to be sociable, whenever the monks from their abbey[42] come to visit them. We reproved them and forbade them to break the Rule for the sake of being sociable. They owe fifty pounds, but about twenty-seven pounds are owed to them. Some of the monks are at their abbey.

MARCH 19. At Mortemer-en-Lyons, at the expense of the monastery.

MARCH 20. At Pérrièrs, at the expense of the priory. There are no monks there at present.

MARCH 21. At Ste-Catherine, at the expense of the monastery, and we visited it this day. Thirty-two monks are there. One does not accuse another [in chapter]; we ordered each one to accuse the others. One of the monks is dwelling [alone] in the priory of Villaines; we decreed that a companion should be given to him within a month after Easter. We also ordered a chamberlain[43] to be appointed to distribute clothing and shoes. Item, we ordered that the goods intended for the poor be distributed without diminution.

MARCH 22-27. At Rouen. MARCH 28. At Rouen, and we consecrated the holy chrism. MARCH 29. At Rouen.

---

[42] St-Père-de-Chartres.

[43] The chamberlain had charge of clothing and personal necessities of the monks; clothing included bedding.

1252

MARCH 30. At Rouen. Now begins the year of our Lord 1252. It was Easter. MARCH 31. At Rouen. APRIL 1-5. At Déville. APRIL 6. At the same, and, at Bondeville, we received the resignation of the prioress [of that priory]. APRIL 7. At St-Lô [-de-Rouen], at the expense of the priory.

APRIL 8. We visited there, finding eighteen canons in residence. Eleven of them are priests. We ordered them to place the most holy Body of our Lord Jesus Christ properly and in a becoming manner on the altar. One does not accuse another [in chapter]; we ordered them to accuse each other mutually. Item, [we ordered] them to keep lay folk out of the cloister, so far as this could be done tactfully. They owe about four hundred pounds, and about three hundred pounds is owed to them, payable before the feast of the Assumption of the Virgin. They have an income of seven hundred pounds. We spent the night at Ste-Catherine.

APRIL 9-10. At Gouy, at our own expense. APRIL 11-12. At Déville. APRIL 13. At St-Georges [-de-Boscherville], at the expense of the monastery.

APRIL 14. We visited there, and we found that there are twenty monks in residence, and eight outside. One monk is dwelling alone at St-Martin; we ordered that a companion be given to him, or that he be recalled to the cloister. Item, we ordered and commanded the abbot to be very strict in giving the monks permission to go beyond the cloister, and we forbade the prior to give such permission to anyone, in the absence of the abbot, provided, however, that the abbot is due to return within a very short time. Item, we ordered, as ordained for every Saturday, that one was to wash the feet of another.[1] We strictly forbade any monk to carry anything at all away from the refectory, or to give away any of the food placed before him, but [ordered] that all remnants should be devoted to alms. They owe about sixty pounds, and about two hundred pounds is owed to them. Whenever the abbot is away, the sick are improperly cared for. This day we spent the night at Déville.

[1] The *Rule of St. Benedict* (ch. 35) ordained that the members of the community wash their feet every Saturday. For a fuller treatment of the washing of the feet see "Lavement des pieds," *Dict. de théol. cath.*, IX[1], 16-31.

APRIL 15-17. At Déville.

APRIL 18. At Jumièges, at the expense of the monastery. On the following day we visited there. We found forty-seven monks in residence, and the temporalities in good condition.

APRIL 19. At St-Wandrille, at the expense of the monastery. APRIL 20-21. At the same, and at our own expense.

APRIL 22. At the same, at our own expense. This day we made visitation there and found thirty-four monks in residence. The abbot visits the priories but rarely. The candle which was wont to burn before the Blessed Sacrament is no longer alight; we ordered it to be lit and kept burning in the future, as was the practice hitherto. When the outside priors come to the monastery, they neither sleep in the dormitory, eat in the refectory, nor stay in the cloister; we ordered that when they do come to the monastery, they arise for Matins, and in every way conduct themselves as do the members of the community, whether in the refectory, the dormitory, the cloister, or the church. Item, we ordered that one accuse another [in chapter], and that, if anyone knew of another's delinquency and did not report it, he should be punished. They owe about four hundred pounds, and about eight hundred pounds is owed to them. They have enough wine, grain, meat, and oil to last until the harvest, and a sufficiency of woolen and linen clothing.

APRIL 23. At Lillebonne, at the expense of the priest of St-Denis, and this day we dedicated the said church [of St-Denis]. APRIL 24. At Le Valasse, at the expense of the monastery. APRIL 25. At Trouville, at the expense of the parish. This day we dedicated the church of Notre-Dame at Trouville.

APRIL 26. At Valmont, which we visited this day. We found twenty-two monks there. All but four are priests. One does not accuse another [in chapter]; we ordered mutual accusations. They go out from the cloister to the farm without permission. Item, we enjoined the abbot to see to it that the monks observed the fasts according to the Rule, whether they were within the monastery or outside, and we ordered them to abstain from meat altogether.

APRIL 27. At the same, at our own expense. This day we visited the priests of the deanery of Valmont. The sworn men[2] were Master Michael of

---

[2] The *jurati,* or sworn men, were drawn from within the ecclesiastical territorial jurisdiction; in this case the deanery of Walmont. Their function was to assist in the judgment of cases, and an oath was taken to do right. Regino's *De ecclesiastica*

Angerville; Henry, priest at Daubeuf-Serville; Master Nicholas of Frober-
ville; William, priest at Bertreville; Baldwin of St-Pierre-en-Port; and Peter,
priest at Butot. John, priest at Valmont, publicly ill reputed of incontinence,
gave a letter to the archdeacon of Grand-Caux, to the effect that he would
regard his church as resigned if he were again so defamed; item, William,
priest at Auberville-sur-Veulettes; item, Ranulf, priest at Maniqueurville;
item, Walter, priest at Thiouville, Richard, priest at Toussaint, is ill famed
of a certain married woman whom he took with him to Maromme; he has
permission to attend the schools at Rouen and is a vicar at Maromme. The
archdeacon, whenever he visits four churches, receives procuration from one,
and then exacts a money payment from the rest in the name of procuration;
item, he asked for a subsidy from the priests when he went away to the
schools. We warned Peter, priest at Hanouard, to stay in his church, and
not go riding about in a short coat and a detached head dress, and with a
sword; he promised to do this. The priest at Bordeaux, is publicly known
for engaging in trade. The priest at Hanouard carries weapons, and wears
a short coat and detached head dress. The priest at Criquebeuf, when he
was dean, sealed up the grange of Master John of Mauconduit. The said
master broke the seal of the dean. The rector of Criquebeuf does not keep
good residence.

APRIL 28. At Beusemonchel, at our own expense.

APRIL 29. At the same, at our own expense, and, at Yébleron, we visited
the deanery of Fauville. The sworn men were Master William, priest at
Vattetot; Master Robert, priest at Valliquerville; Reginald, priest at Auzouville; Ralph, priest at Auberville; Ralph, priest at Normanville; and Master
John of Hautot-le-Vatois. Henry, priest at Ecretteville, is ill famed of the
wife of Robert Dubois, and, recently, on Palm Sunday, the said Robert found
him one night in one of his hedged enclosures [near a house], and they
came to blows; item, he is publicly known for drinking. William, the chaplain of Sir Jordan of Valliquerville, is defamed of a woman who bore him
a child. Master Nicholas, priest at Normanville, is defamed of incontinence,
and he has many children. Roger le Paiges, cleric, has a certain maidservant
in his parish at Ecretteville, and he has kept her for eight years. The prior
at St-Maclou [-la-Brière] is ill famed of a certain married woman; he has

---

disciplina (in Migne, *PL*, CXXXII, 281) gives the function of the *jurati* and their
place in the synodal proceedings. In Regino's time, the ninth century, the *jurati*
numbered seven.

been disciplined by the archdeacon. Hugh, the chaplain of Lanquetot, is a drunkard. The archdeacon sought a subsidy from his priests when he went away to the schools. John, priest at Hattenville, is ill famed of a certain unmarried woman, the daughter of one of his female parishioners, by whom he has had two children; he has been disciplined by the archdeacon, but it is rumored that he has since relapsed. The priest at Yébleron does not serve his church very well, for he sometimes omits the canonical Hours, and he frequents taverns; we forbade him to enter any tavern within a league of Yébleron under the penalty of ten shillings for each time that he should enter a tavern within the league, this fine to be collected by the dean, whom we enjoined to exact it without any remission. The priest at Bolleville is a drunkard. John of Ray, priest at Hautot, is a trader. The chaplain of the leperhouse at St-Amator is ill famed of a certain woman who is now married; however, the scandal has stopped. The dean reported that John, the priest at Hattenville, obligated to the archdeacon, because of his incontinence, offered a surety of ten pounds in case he should fall again into sin, and that it is rumored that he has so fallen. Manasse, priest at Gruchet, [is held] to resign his church for incontinence. Stephen, priest at Raffetot, to resign his church. Enguerrand, priest at Cléville, is pledged to the loss of his benefice for incontinence. Ralph, priest at Veauville, who knows that he is pledged to lose his benefice. Richard, priest at Yébleron, is pledged to the archdeacon, to what extent he does not know, for his incontinence and his frequenting of taverns; he does not keep residence, rather, he runs all over the country. Richard, called Port, priest at Les Baons, is likewise obligated for incontinence. William, priest at Ricarville, [is obligated] to a fine of ten pounds for incontinence. William, the chaplain of Sir Jordan of Valliquerville, is obligated, but he does not know to what amount. Walter, priest at Guillerville, [is obligated] to a penalty of ten pounds for his incontinence with the wife of Henry Taber, his parishioner. Ralph, priest at Grandcamp [is obligated] to the loss of his benefice because he used to have an unmarried maidservant, called Bisevaque. We must inquire about the wassail drinkers.

To all who may see this, Henry, priest at Ecretteville, sends greeting in the Lord. You will know that when the venerable Father Eudes, by God's grace archbishop of Rouen, visited the archdeanery of Grand Caux, he found me grievously defamed of the wife of Robert Dubois, my parishioner. Of my own free will I have promised that if I should again be defamed of the vice of incontinence, and could not purge myself canonically, I would automatically regard my church as resigned from that time on. In witness whereof I have sealed the present letter with my own seal and that of the dean of Foville. Given at Beusemonchel, on the Monday following the Sunday on which the *Cantate*[3] is sung, in the year of our Lord 1252.

APRIL 30. At Montivilliers, at the expense of the monastery. We visited the abbess and found everything connected with her office to be in good condition.

MAY 1. At Graville, at the expense of the priory. We visited there, and found eleven canons in residence. One canon was with Master William of Fontaine; we enjoined the prior to recall him to the cloister. At Bellevue there is not a sufficient stock of provisions, even for one canon. Because of the relics,[4] lay folk remain in the choir while the Divine Offices are being celebrated; we ordered the relics to be displayed on another altar, and that by all means the lay folk should be kept out of the choir. Item, we forbade the canons to talk with lay folk in the cloister. Item, we ordered one to accuse another [in chapter]. They owe about forty pounds.

MAY 2. At Graville we visited the deanery of St-Romain [-de-Colbosc]. The sworn men were Master William of Cerlangue; the priest at St-Giles; the priest at l'Eure; the priest at Buglise; the priest at Ternemare and the parson of Etainhus. The priest at L'Oiselière is defamed of a certain parishioner of Les Trois-Pierres, that is to say, the wife of Daniel; we warned him. Item, the priest at Gommerville, ill famed of the daughter of the dean of Gommerville, gave us a letter obligating himself to a penalty of twenty pounds. Aubin, priest at [St-Sauveur-d']-Emalleville, is defamed of the wife of Walter Deschamps, his parishioner, and of several others; we warned him. Alexander, priest at Sainneville, [defamed] of one of his parishioners named Ermenburge, obligated himself to the archdeacon to resign his benefice. Item, Master Paris, priest at St-Vigor [-d'Ymauville], has been disciplined by the archdeacon; he is ill famed of incontinence and is a drunkard, a trader, and a usurer; we warned him about this. William, priest at Etainhus, has merlins and falcons and is defamed of a certain widow, who is his pa-

---

[3] The Introit for the Mass of the fourth Sunday after Easter.

[4] The relics here referred to are those of St. Honorine. For the life of St. Honorine, see *Acta sanctorum,* vol. III, February 27 (pp. 682-84). Ste-Honorine-de-Graville is now in the diocese of Paris under the name of Conflans-Ste-Honorine. The relics of St. Honorine are still in the church, which was built in the eleventh century.

rishioner; he had obligated himself to the archdeacon to a fine of ten pounds. We warned him. Item, the priest at Manéglise has for a long time been ill famed of a certain married woman, his parishioner; he obligated himself to the archdeacon to lose his benefice. Item, Durand, priest at Manneville [-la-Goupil], [is ill famed] of a certain spinster, his parishioner, because of which he obligated himself to the archdeacon to a penalty of twenty pounds, after taking the Cross; he later relapsed with a certain woman near Paris. Ralph, priest at St-Aubin-Routot, is ill famed of a certain married woman; we assigned him the day following the synod and before conferring ordinations for the purpose of purging himself. The priest at Virville is a drunkard; we enjoined the priest at [Parc-d'] Anxtot to collect five shillings from him for every time that he should get drunk, and another five whenever he should enter a tavern within a league [of Virville]; item, we enjoined him [the priest of Anxtot] to summon the chaplain of the leper house to appear before us at Valmont. The chaplain of the leper house at Virville is ill famed of incontinence. The chaplain of Ecrainville is ill famed of incontinence. The chaplain of Epretot is ill famed of a certain woman, with whom he was found, as it is rumored.

This day we spent the night at Montivilliers.

MAY 3. At Valmont, at our own expense. MAY 4. At Flainville, at the expense of Master John of Flainville. MAY 5. At the same, but at the expense of the parish of Sotteville, the church of which we dedicated. MAY 6. At Longueil, at the expense of the priory. No monks are there. MAY 6. At Aliermont.

MAY 7. At Bures, at the expense of the priory. At Bures, Master Walter of Longueil, called "the Child," a cleric, came to us and of his own free will abandoned any claim which he might have to the church of Boardiville. He withdrew from ligitation and resigned. He also promised on oath never to revive his claim to the said church, nor in any way impede from occupying it peacefully whomever we should by our authority install in it; that he would be amenable to our mandate, would obey whatever discipline we should impose because of his embezzlement of the income of the said church, and would make amends for this and for the evil things he has said about us. Present at this meeting were: Master Jacques, archdeacon of Rouen; Master Simon, archdeacon of the French Vexin; Master Stephen Lorris, canon of Rouen; Dom Nicholas Site, priest; Stephen, priest at Blenelle; the dean of Bures; and William, former dean of the same place.

MAY 8. At Neufchâtel, at the expense of the priory of Nogent. No monks are there.

MAY 9. We visited the hospital at Neufchâtel. Four canons are in residence. The prior's relatives visit him too often, especially the priest of Menouval, who abuses the hospital property and receives goods, even the ploughs of the house; and the priest of Obermesnil, his nephew, Peter of Rièvrecourt, cleric, and William of Beaurepair, who work there and require a very unnecessary amount of food and drink. The prior has never visited the sick during his entire lifetime. The prior often stays alone in a certain manor called "Le Chaser"; he was often bathed there, and there was a certain woman who stayed there and caused suspicion. Item, he quietly leaves the dormitory at night and goes no one knows whither; item, it is reported that he goes at night into the wall-enclosed walk of Walter Froitier.

This day, we spent the night at Beaubec, at the expense of the monastery.

MAY 10-12. At Aliermont.

MAY 13. At Envermeu, at the expense of the monastery. We visited it and found that there are ten monks in residence, and there should be twelve. Some of them do not confess, as they should, in accordance with the Statutes of Pope Gregory; we enjoined them to confess more often, and to observe the Statutes of Pope Gregory more fully. Lay folk sometimes sit and talk with the monks in the cloister; we forbade this. They owe two hundred twenty pounds to the abbot of Bec, and sixty pounds to others. The prior makes no audit. They have an income of about four hundred pounds.

[No entry for May 14.]

MAY 15. At Foucarmont, at the expense of the monastery. MAY 16. At Tréport, at the expense of the monastery.

MAY 17. We visited at Le Tréport, where there are twenty-two monks. All but seven are priests. One does not accuse another [in chapter]; we enjoined them to correct this. Traveling monks do not observe the fasts prescribed by the Rule; we enjoined them to correct this. They have four priories, of which three are in the diocese of Rouen and one in that of Amiens. Those who are dwelling in the priories eat meat and do not observe the fasts of the Rule; we ordered that the abbot, who was at that time in England,[5] be notified of this, and that he correct these abuses according to the Rule. They have an income of eleven hundred pounds; they owe three hundred pounds,

---

[5] Probably visiting the monastery's priory at Hastings. (Dugdale, *Monasticon Anglicanum*, VI, 168.)

but about two hundred pounds is owed to them. This day we spent the night there, at our own expense.

MAY 18. At Eu, at our visitation, we found thirty-two monks in residence. All but nine are priests. They have not yet recovered the gold chalice;[6] we enjoined them to warn the vicomte to return it and [warned] that he would be excommunicated unless he did. The cloister is not protected from lay folk; we ordered them to keep them out so far as it could be done tactfully. They owe eight hundred sixty-eight pounds. About four hundred pounds are owed to them. They have an income of nine hundred pounds. We praised them for selling ten acres of their woodland, and for taking advantage of the right granted to them in a special charter of freely selling and acquiring property. They do not cast their accounts according to the statute requirements [of Pope Gregory]; we enjoined them to observe the Statutes in this matter, to elect some members of the community to assist at the audit, and to make a written copy, so that one record might be in the hands of the community, the other in those of the abbot. This day our expenses were paid by the abbey.

MAY 19. At the same. MAY 20. At Dieppe. MAY 21. At Longueville, at the expense of the priory.

MAY 22. At St-Saëns, at the expense of the monks' priory. This day we visited the nuns' priory. There are as many nuns as lay sisters in residence, namely, twelve of each, one brother, and a priest; we ordered the priest to be removed, because of his ill fame. Sometimes they eat in a certain room; we forbade them to do this in the future. We forbade anything to be brought away from the refectory, unless it be brought to the prioress to distribute as she sees fit.

MAY 23. We visited the monks of St-Saëns. There used be five monks there. We told them to increase their alms, and to bestow it at least twice a week to all who should come to the gate. About six hundred sixty pounds more is owed to them than they owe. We enjoined the prior to associate with himself some, or all, of his companions in the work of casting his accounts. No one except the abbot[7] knows the state of the prior's accounts or of his conscience.

We spent the night at Déville.

MAY 24. At Déville. MAY 25. At Rouen, and this day we conferred Holy

---

[6] See entry for January 7, 1250/51.

[7] The abbot of St-Wandrille, of which St-Saëns was a dependent priory.

Orders. MAY 26-28. At Rouen. MAY 29–JUNE 2. At Déville. JUNE 3. At Ste-Catherine, at our own expense.

JUNE 4. At Mont-Deux-Amants, at the expense of the priory. We found that . . . [*lacuna in MS*]. We ordered the canon who is staying at Graville with the priest to be recalled. Thirteen canons are there. Item, we ordered that better provision be made for the sick as far as the resources of the house will allow.

JUNE 5. At Sausseuse, at our own expense. JUNE 6. At Juziers, at our own expense. JUNE 7. At St-Cloud, in the diocese of Paris, at our own expense. JUNE 7. At Corbeil. JUNE 9. At Melun. JUNE 10. At St-Jean-du-Jard, in the monastery, at our own expense. JUNE 11. At Villeneuve-St-Georges. JUNE 12. At Paris, at the home of John Grivel. JUNE 13. At the same, and we ate with the Franciscans. JUNE 14. At Pontoise, at our own expense. JUNE 15. At Chaumont, in the French Vexin. JUNE 16. At Saucy, in the Norman Vexin. JUNE 17-21. At Déville.

JUNE 22. At the same. Hither came Peter, a monk of Gisors, whom we, carrying out the apostolic mandate, had warned to appear before us before the feast of the Nativity of St. John the Baptist, along with his prior, to make amends for their contempt and lack of obedience when we arrived at the priory of Gisors on July 17, for we found the doors locked and entry denied to us.[8] Meantime, he had made no amends, either for himself, or for the prior. Once again we warned him that he and the aforesaid prior should appear before us to make amends for the foregoing.

JUNE 23-26. At St-Matthieu. JUNE 27–JULY 1. At Déville.

JULY 2. At Déville. When . . . [*lacuna in MS*][9] the abbot of Fécamp, acting under apostolic authority, had conferred the church of Auberville-sur-Veulettes upon R., cleric, and the said cleric had failed to take the oath of obedience to us, or do the other things required by the custom of the church of Rouen, we caused the income of the said church to be seized for our use by the dean of Valmont. On JULY 2, the said cleric having appeared before us and having taken the oath of obedience to us and performed the other things required by the custom of the church of Rouen, we directed the said dean to permit him to enjoy the goods of the said church in peace, and to supply him with anything of which he stood in need.

[8] Eudes began his visitation of the deanery of Gisors on July 16, 1249. On July 17 he was at Frênes.

[9] William III (1227-60). (*Gallia Christiana*, XI, 209-10.)

JULY 3-4. At Déville. JULY 5. At Ste-Catherine. JULY 6. At Louviers. JULY 7. At Sausseuse. JULY 8-9. At Meulan. JULY 10-12. At Pontoise, at the court of the queen.

JULY 13. At the same, and we presented the following letter to the queen:

To all who shall see this letter, Brother Eudes, by divine permission the unworthy bishop of the church of Rouen, eternal greeting in the Lord Jesus Christ. When we requested the royal bailiff of Caux to conduct, or to have conducted, at our expense from the king's prison to our prison at Rouen the prisoners taken by him, we did so because they are such as should be handed over to us by reason of the ecclesiastical jurisdiction which we have over them. When we stated that the said bailiff was obliged to do this, he denied his obligation and refused to comply with our request. Afterwards, at the request of the Lord Pope, made to our excellent lady Blanche, by God's grace illustrious queen of France, through that religious man Brother John of Limoges, the papal penitentiary and nuncio, the said lady queen conceded that the surrender of the said prisoners should be carried out, at our expense, by the said bailiff or his servants until the coming feast of All Saints, and after that date for a period of two full years, or for two months after the return of the king to Paris, if it should happen that he should return before the said time, so that by this concession of the lady queen, and by the arrangements made for the detention up to the stated period, no prejudice may, in any sense, accrue to the lord king. We gave our consent to this, reserving our right if anyone should contest the said detention. In memory of this, we have caused this letter to be confirmed with the authority of our seal. Given at Pontoise, in the month of July, in the year of our Lord 1252.

This day we spent the night at Marines, at our own expense.

JULY 14. At the same, at our own expense. JULY 15. At Chambly. JULY 16. At Creil. JULY 17. At Compiègne. JULY 18. At Noyon, in transit. JULY 19. At Montdidier. JULY 20. At Poix. JULY 21-22. At Aumale, at our own expense. JULY 23–AUGUST 3. At Aliermont. AUGUST 4. At Wanchy, to receive our procuration. AUGUST 5-6. At Aliermont.

AUGUST 7. At Longueville, at our own expense. At this place Ralph of Atre, cleric, swore in our presence to abide by the verdict that was imposed upon him for having maimed or mutilated Henry Omet. As his guarantor, Reginald of Fleur, of Martigny, offered himself to the extent of sixty pounds. He [Ralph] holds a manse in the parish of Notre-Dame at Aliermont, worth five shillings.

AUGUST 8. At Ouville, at the expense of the prior of Etoutteville, to collect our procuration. This day at Longueville, before we went away, we warned the prior and the community once again to assemble in chapter or in some other suitable place, to hear the papal mandate sent to us concerning the observance of the Statutes of Pope Gregory. Since they refused to do this, we pronounced the following excommunication against them:

Since we, acting legally and under apostolic authority, issued a personal warning at Longueville to ... [*lacuna in MS*], the prior and community of the said place, members of the Benedictine Order, that they should convene in their chapter, or in some other suitable place, to hear the apostolic mandate directed to us, and they contumaciously refused to comply, despite the fact that we had granted them several delays in this matter, we in consideration of their stubborness have suspended, in writing, the aforesaid prior for himself, and the cellarer of the said place for the community, and we proclaim them suspended. Done at Longueville, the fifth day before the feast of St. Lawrence, in the year of our Lord 1252.

Item, this same day, we visited the prior of Etoutteville, at Ouville. He says that he has an income of one hundred fifty pounds. In addition to this year's tithes, he owes about forty pounds. Item, they do not observe the fasts of the Rule, and they eat meat freely; we warned him to observe the Statutes of Pope Gregory, to procure and keep a copy of the Statutes. Item, we understood that he had been defamed of a certain woman called Honoria; we warned him to correct his life and to avoid her. We ordered them to procure a copy of the Statutes of Pope Gregory, to read them and observe them.

AUGUST 9-11. At Déville.

AUGUST 12. At the same. This same day, after examining his offenses, we suspended, in writing, Walter, the priest at Theuville, particularly since we found him to be guilty of wounding Gerard of Theuville, a layman.

AUGUST 13. At the same. AUGUST 14. At Rouen, on the vigil of the Assumption. AUGUST 15. At the same, on the feast of the Assumption, and the bishop of Séez was present.

AUGUST 16. At St-Matthieu. This day we handed the following writing to Master Nicholas of Blève and to Gerard of Corgeon:

This will be the authority of the mediators, over those articles concerning which there is disagreement in dealing with them. If, with the common consent of the parties, they cannot come to any agreement, they may turn to one party or the other, or temporize, as may seem good and equitable to them.

AUGUST 17. At the same. AUGUST 18. At Déville.

AUGUST 19. At the same. This day Herbert, priest of Bernomesnil, resigned the church of the said village into our hands, there being present: Brother Adam Rigaud; Simon, the archdeacon of the French Vexin; and Master William of Jordan.

AUGUST 20. At the same. AUGUST 21. At Auffay, at our own expense. AUGUST 22-23. At Aliermont.

AUGUST 24. At the same. This day, using these words, we excommunicated G[eoffrey], priest at Grigneuseville:

We excommunicate, in writing, Geoffrey, priest and rector of the church of Grigneuseville, because on the day following the Assumption of the Virgin, which had been assigned to him for purging himself of the charge of homicide for which he had been defamed, and on the Saturday following, he sought from us a postponement of the said purgation, and, not having obtained it, he contumaciously withdrew from the village although we had forbidden him to leave it without our permission. Nor did he purge himself. Done at Aliermont, on the vigil of St. Bartholomew in the year of our Lord 1252, and in the presence of Robert and Geco of Baaly, clerics; Brother Theobald of Taverny; Master Peter of Aumale; Master Stephen of Lorris; and William, archdeacon of Eu.

This same day, after [his] excommunication, a certain cleric entered an appeal on his [Geoffrey's] behalf, making known his proctorship in the following words:

To all who may see this, Geoffrey, rector of the church of Grigneuseville, greeting in the Lord. Know you that I appoint my beloved Simon, cleric, the bearer of this letter, as my proctor in my appeal from any injury which may be done to me by the Reverend Father Eudes, by God's grace archbishop of Rouen, or by his official. I shall willingly regard as valid whatever decisions the said proctor, in my name, shall consider should be made about any matter or legal procedure brought by them, be it by reason of their office or be it a legal process instituted in their presence at the instance of anyone whomsoever. Given in the year of our Lord 1252, on the Thursday following the Assumption of the Blessed Mary.

He instituted his appeal, alleging false grievances.

AUGUST 25-27. At the same.

AUGUST 28. At Bacqueville, to receive our procuration. This day we visited

Sauqueville.[10] Six canons are in residence, of whom two, acting in common, have care of souls, and if either of them be absent the cure reverts to the chapter. They do not celebrate two Masses every day. Item, they have few *Lives of the Saints*[11] or [other] books. Dom Walter still plays dice. The treasurer does not keep residence, nor does he officiate as treasurer. The chapter had decreed that whosoever should help with the harvest from the feast of St. Michael to the Nativity of St. John[12] should receive full commons[13]. The treasurer and Dom Walter receive it, but have not earned it. Dom Ferric and Dom Walter frequent taverns. We gave orders that no one should receive any share of the distributions who did not deserve it, and we appointed Dom Gilbert as distributor. Item, we ordered books to be bought with the pennies which the treasurer gives.

This same day we visited the priory of Bacqueville, and we found that four monks are there and that all are priests. They do not confess to their prior; we ordered them to confess. Item, they have no copy of the Statutes of Pope Gregory; we ordered them to look for one, to get it, read it, and observe it. They do not read the Rule. They do not observe the fasts very well, and sometimes they eat meat; they use soft feather beds; we ordered them to do without them. They have an income of about two hundred pounds; they owe one hundred pounds. We forbade them to eat meat except as the Rule permitted. Item, we forbade them to use feather beds.

AUGUST 29. At Auffay,[14] at the expense of the priory, and we visited [there]. There are six monks. They have an income of about four hundred pounds. They read their Rule but rarely. They have a copy of the Statutes of Pope Gregory, but they do not observe them very well; we ordered them to read and observe them, and to have both a Latin and a French version.

[10] This house is not mentioned in either Besse, *Abbayes et prieurés de l'ancienne France*, or Cottineau.

[11] Each monastery and order was apt to have its own lives of the saints. The oldest collection was the *Depositio martyrum* (fourth century). The long article, "Culte des saints," in *Dict. de théol. cath.*, XIV[1], especially cols. 941-46, contains much useful information, as does the article "Saint" in *Dict. d'arch. chrèt. et de lit.*, XV[1], especially cols. 439-49.

[12] May 8-June 24.

[13] Each chapter had food which was community property and which was called "commons." Each full member was entitled to his share of commons. However, each was obligated to perform certain functions in return. If the functions were not performed, he was not to receive commons.

[14] The entry gives the Latin name as Altifagium. It was also called Aufayum (see entry for December 29, 1250).

Some of them do not confess every month; we ordered this to be corrected. They do not abstain from eating meat, because of the sick who are there; we ordered them to abstain, except as the Rule permitted them to eat it. They owe more than two hundred sixty pounds.

This day we invested Everard, our cleric, in the name of Master Terry of Cortenay, with the prebend which belonged to Dom Robert Lorgier. Brothers Adam and Harduin were present. After December 29 we can return [to Auffay] for, except for the present, it will have been two years since we were last here.

AUGUST 30. At St-Victor [-en-Caux], at the expense of the abbey, and we visited [it]. There are eighteen monks in residence, and two in England.[15] Almost all of them are priests. We ordered the Statutes of Pope Gregory to be read and observed. Lay folk enter the cloister; we ordered them to be kept out. With the exception of the abbot, who labors under an infirmity, and those whom he invites, they observe the Statutes covering the eating of meat. They have an income of about six hundred pounds; they owe about two hundred pounds. We ordered a monthly audit to be made in the presence of [brothers] elected by the community. The abbot does not sleep in the dormitory, because of the infirmity from which he suffers. We ordered them to obtain the Statutes of Pope Gregory, to read and observe them.

This same day John of Paletot, knight, pledged us to make whatever amends we should require for having kicked Master Peter of Torcy, rector of the church of Torcy, in the churchyard of the said church, as he admitted in our presence to have done. He offered as guarantors Sir William of Bloseville, Sir Robert of Muchedent, and Sir John de Muchedent, knights, and John of Neville, damoiseau,[16] who promised that the said knight would also make such amends to the said Master as we might decree.

AUGUST 31. At Beaubec, at the expense of the monastery. SEPTEMBER 1. At St-Laurent-en-Lyons, at the expense of the monastery.

SEPTEMBER 2. At the same, and we visited there. Thirteen canons are in residence; there used to be fourteen, but one has been sent to a certain priory, where another was dwelling alone. One does not accuse another [in chapter]; we ordered this to be corrected. They owe about one hundred sixty pounds. We gave orders that Brother Peter, who resides at St-Crispin, should cast

---

[15] Clatford Priory in Wiltshire was a dependency of St-Victor. (Dugdale, *Monasticon Anglicanum*, VII, 1054-55.

[16] A gentleman attached to a lord but not yet knighted.

his accounts twice a year. The prior says that the aforementioned Brother Peter will repay one hundred pounds which the house has loaned him. The capes and pelisses are not distributed quite on time.[17]

SEPTEMBER 3. At Beaussault, at the expense of the prior. Two monks are there. They eat meat very frequently; we ordered them to procure a copy of the Statutes of Pope Gregory, to read them and observe them, as well concerning the eating of meat as of other things. We ordered them to procure and read a copy of the Rule. They have enough wheat, although it is of the old crop. They owe nothing except twenty pounds to their abbot and then pounds to the prior.

We visited Bival. Some of the nuns have their own food and prepare it themselves; we ordered all such things to be carried to the [common] pantry. They have coffers and keys, but they hand the keys over to the abbess whenever she desires them. We forbade them to introduce any lay folk into the cloister. Item, we forbade any of them to eat with lay folk. The rule of silence is not well observed; we ordered this to be corrected. They leave the cloister without permission; we ordered them to be prevented from doing this. They owe forty pounds, and sixty *minae* of wheat. They are bringing up ten young boys;[18] we ordered these to be removed. There are thirty-two nuns. Sister Egide of Saussay and Sister Isabelle of Tarines are disobedient. We forbade them to receive anything from their friends without permission, or to omit the service of Compline because of the presence of guests, whoever they might be. We stayed the night at Bellosane, by right of procuration.

SEPTEMBER 4. We visited the convent of St-Aubin. There are thirteen nuns. We forbade them to eat meat, especially in the presence of lay folk. Item, we forbade anyone to receive permission to eat with her relatives or others, unless the prioress or subprioress is present. They owe twenty pounds. The harvest is good. They lack a treasurer.

This same day we visited the chapter of Gournay. Five of the nine canons are in residence. They intone the Psalms too rapidly; we enjoined them to sing the Psalms with due observance of the pauses. This same day the prior of Neufmarché gave us procuration there.

SEPTEMBER 5. We spent the night at Mortemer and visited at Neufmarché. They have no copy of the Rule; we ordered them to obtain one and read

---

[17] This refers to the yearly distribution of clothing to the monks.

[18] The presence of boys in religious houses of nuns was forbidden by canon 4 of the Provincial Council of Rouen (1231). (Mansi, XXIII, 214.)

it. We forbade them to eat meat, except as the Rule permitted, since the healthy ones occasionally eat meat. They owe about forty pounds; they have an income of about two hundred pounds.

SEPTEMBER 7. At Les Andelys, at our own expense. SEPTEMBER 8. At the same, and we celebrated the Nativity of the Virgin. SEPTEMBER 9-17. At Sausseuse.

SEPTEMBER 18. At Les Andelys, at our own expense, where, on that day, we visited the chapter. We found everything in good condition. We ordered them to obtain some lanterns.[19] We ordered the deacon and the subdeacon to serve in their respective orders every day, if it should be necessary, and they are not legally prevented from so doing. We ordered Tierce to be sung before Mass and Sext immediately after Mass, unless it be a fast day. We also ordered that the bell be rung for Nones at an hour such that, if there is necessity or time demands it, Vespers may then be sung after Nones.

SEPTEMBER 19-20. At Ste-Catherine, at our own expense. SEPTEMBER 21. At the same, and we conferred Holy Orders. SEPTEMBER 22. At Roven. SEPTEMBER 23. At Déville. This day the archbishop's quartan fever began.[20] SEPTEMBER 24-26. At the same. SEPTEMBER 27. At Bourg-Achard, at our own expense. SEPTEMBER 28. At Cormeilles, in the diocese of Lisieux, at our own expense. SEPTEMBER 29-30. At Lisieux, to deal in the making of peace with our suffragans about those matters in which they say ... [*lacuna in MS*].[21] OCTOBER 1. At Le Theil[-Nolent]. OCTOBER 2-3. At Bec-Hellouin. OCTOBER 4-14. At Déville. OCTOBER 15. At Mont-Ste-Catherine, en route to St-Thibault. OCTOBER 16. At Noyon-sur-Andelle. OCTOBER 18. At Etrépagny. OCTOBER 19. At Chaumont. OCTOBER 20. At Pontoise. OCTOBER 21. At the priory of L'Estrée, near St-Denis. OCTOBER 22-24. At St-Maur-les-Fossés. OCTOBER 25. At Courquetaine. OCTOBER 26. At Rampellon. OCTOBER 27. At Bray-sur-Seine. OCTOBER 28. At Villeneuve-l'Archevêque. OCTOBER 29. At Rougemont. OCTOBER 30. At Brinon-l'Archevêque. OCTOBER 31–NOVEMBER 1. At St-Thibault-aux-Bois. NOVEMBER 2. At Rouvrais. NOVEMBER 3. At Vézelay. NOVEMBER 4. At Clamency. NOVEMBER 5. At St-Amand. NOVEMBER 6. At Gien. NOVEMBER 7. At St-Benoît. NOVEMBER 8. At Orléans. NOVEMBER 9. At Blois. NOVEMBER 10-11. At Tours. NOVEMBER 12. At Vernon, with

[19] This may very well have been for the lighting of the church during the early morning Divine Office.
[20] A reference to the severe rheumatism from which Eudes suffered.
[21] This probably refers to the appeals listed under March 2, 1251/52.

the lord archbishop of Tours. NOVEMBER 13. At Neuville, a possession of the abbey of Marmoutier. NOVEMBER 14. At Vendôme. NOVEMBER 15. At Bonneval. NOVEMBER 16. At Chartres, at the abbey of St-Jean-en-Vallée.[22] NOVEMBER 17. At Bu. NOVEMBER 18. At Ivry, at our own expense. NOVEMBER 19-28. At Sausseuse. NOVEMBER 29. At Pontoise, and this day was buried Blanche, queen of France, at Maubisson, in the nuns' church, and we were present at her burial.[23] NOVEMBER 30. At Gassicourt, near Mantes, in the diocese of Chartres, with the abbot of Cluny. DECEMBER 1. At Sausseuse.

DECEMBER 2. At Les Andelys. On the following morning, . . . [lacuna in MS], priest at Barentin, came to us at our house, on the steps leading to the upper hall. He was then living at Gournay, and although we had ordained him two years ago, he has not yet celebrated his first Mass, nor does he reside in his church as he had sworn to do. We warned him to fit himself for celebrating and to celebrate, and in the future to take up his residence in person in the church of Barentin, as he ought to do.

DECEMBER 3. At Ste-Catherine, at our own expense. DECEMBER 4. At Déville. This day we gave orders that the said priest of Barentin should be warned by the dean concerning the aforementioned matters.

DECEMBER 5. At the same. This day, in writing, we suspended Walter, rector of the church at Flavacourt, in the archdeaconry of the French Vexin, from his office and from his right to receive the usufruct of this benefice, until such time as we should make other disposition of him and of the matter itself. He was defamed of incontinence with a certain woman named Mathilda, and although he had confessed this ill fame to us before, and had voluntarily admitted the truth of the charge, we suspended him. His confession was made and suspension decreed in the presence of William the treasurer and Master Stephen of Lorris, canon, both of Rouen; John, the canon of the prebend of Quinze Marcs; Henry, priest at Maneville; and Stephen, priest at Blenelle.

DECEMBER 6-7. At the same. DECEMBER 8. At Bellencombre, at our own expense. DECEMBER 9-20. At Aliermont.

---

[22] An Augustinian foundation of about 1099. (Cottieau, I, 714-15.)

[23] Other contemporaries date Queen Blanche's death as of December 1, 1252 (Matthew Paris, *Chronica majora*, V, 354), but Eudes states that her burial took place on November 29, 1252. Maubisson was a Cistercian abbey of nuns founded by Queen Blanche in 1241, near Pontoise, in the diocese of Rouen. (Cottineau, II, 1790-91.)

DECEMBER 21. At the same. This day Ralph of Boscregnoult, knight, pledged us that he would make whatever amends we should determine, for he had, as it is said, come to hunt in our preserve, and had violently seized and caused to be taken from our men certain hoes, mattocks, and nets. And because our men took these things away from those who had hunted in the said preserve, this knight had caused our men to be beaten. Richard of Dun and Geoffrey of Millemesnil, knights, stood as guarantors for the pledge.

DECEMBER 22-23. At the same.

DECEMBER 24. At the same. This day Miles, rector of the church of Saussay, directed the following appeal against the venerable Master Peter of Porte, archdeacon of Rouen, in the Norman Vexin:

I, Miles, rector of the church, appeal to you in writing, Reverend Father, lord archbishop of Rouen, against the venerable Master Peter of Porte, archdeacon of the church of Rouen, in the Norman Vexin, by reason of the following: That is to say, because the said archdeacon, installed outside the diocese of Rouen, has imposed the sentence of suspension upon me for certain matters over which he claims jurisdiction by reason of the said archdeaconry, whereas the said archdeacon neither can nor should exercise jurisdiction, even though he may have it, beyond the diocese or even beyond his archdeaconry. Item, I appeal in writing against him, inasmuch as the said archdeacon, although I have never been convicted nor pleaded guilty, nor have I been condemned by any competent judge, has suspended me unjustly for a sum of money or share, which the said archdeacon claims to belong to him as the annate from the church of Saussay, during the time that the church was vacant and which he said is still unpaid to him. Item, Reverend Father, I appeal in writing and in person, and for the above-mentioned reasons, and urge in justification of the facts that the said archdeacon be restricted, he being installed beyond the diocese of Rouen, and that there is danger in delaying [my restitution]. I ask an immediate *apostoli.* Done this said day and year.

The same day Miles asked us to give him the benefit of relaxing the sentence of suspension imposed by the venerable Master Peter of Porte, the said archdeacon. He asked us to lift the weight of the same unjust sentence, to declare and cause to be declared the suspension null, especially since there is danger in delay and the archdeacon in question is outside the limits of the diocese of Rouen. Presenting his arguments, Miles swore, as he should, that he would abide by our decision in his appeal against the archdeacon.

Brother Eudes, etc., to the dean of Gisors, greeting, etc. Miles, the rector of the church at Saussay of our diocese, appealed to us in writing on the eve of the Nativity against the venerable Master Peter of Porte, archdeacon of the church of Rouen, in the Norman Vexin, for the reasons noted above. The said Miles humbly besought us to grant him the benefit of a remission of the aforesaid suspension, as stated above. And we, realizing the danger of a delay if the said rector should remain any longer bound by the said sentence of suspension, particularly during these solemn days when it is essential that the said rector visit the flock committed to him and reveal the divine [mysteries] to them, decided that the sentence, insofar as it actually related to him, should be relaxed, after we had first received from him a sworn oath to abide by the decision that will be given. We command you to pronounce the suspension of the sentence. Dated at Aliermont, on the vigil of the Nativity, in the year of our Lord 1252.

Simon, archdeacon of Eu; Master Stephen of Lorris, canon of Rouen; Peter of Aumale; Dennis, rector of the church of Cormeilles; Brother Hardouin; and Everard, called "the count's son," were present at the appeal and the request.

DECEMBER 25–JANUARY 12. At Aliermont. JANUARY 13. At the same, and our fever grew doubly severe. JANUARY 14-15. At the same. JANUARY 16. At Auffay, at our own expense.

JANUARY 17. At Déville, and this day we issued the following written sentence:

In the year of our Lord 1252, the Friday following the ocatave of the Epiphany. We caused Henry, rector of the church of Bracquemont, to be legally collated to the said church, and although he was not present, we ordered the publication of the edict of citation or calling to the said church, requiring him to return to the said church and take up his personal residence therin, as he ought to do and as the care of the said church requires. The said Henry did not care to obey. More than six months ago, after he had deserted the said church, we, as we may legitimately do in such cases, ordered him to be summoned peremptorily by the dean of the said place, and in the said church, to appear before us at Rouen or vicinity on the Friday following the octave of the Epiphany to hear our judgment in this matter; but he did not appear either in person or by proctors. Whereupon, judging him to be contumacious, we have declared the said Henry deprived of his church by definitive sentence. Done the said day and year, in the presence of the following witnesses: Master Stephen of Lorris; Manasses, parson of the church of Genesville; Master Peter of Aumale; Everard "the count's son"; Master Henry, the physician; and Stephen, the priest at Blenelle.

JANUARY 18. At Déville.

JANUARY 19. At the same, and this day John of La Crique, esquire, presented John of Mont-Richard, cleric, to us for the church at La Crique. There were present: Hilary, prior of Salle-aux-Puelles; Hugh, the almoner; the parson of Bardeville; Walter, cleric; and Master Peter of Aumale.

JANUARY 20-23. At the same.

JANUARY 24. At the same. Walter, priest at Herecourt, has for many years been ill famed of incontinence, and is still so, albeit he has been warned many times about this. However, after the said warnings he promised us that he would resign his aforesaid church at our command, if it should happen that he should be again defamed of this crime and the ill fame should be substantiated, and he could not purge himself of the said vice. Today he appeared before us and confessed that after all the warnings and the promises he had made he had scandalously suffered a relapse, and he resigned his church into the hands of the venerable Master Simon, archdeacon of Eu, who was given our authority to receive it in our behalf. Present were: Reginald, the archdeacon of the place; Master Stephen of Lorris, canon of Rouen; and Gooscy, the cleric of the aforementioned Reginald.

JANUARY 25. At Déville. This day Geoffrey,[24] priest at Grigneuseville, has with noisy insinuation been grievously defamed of the murder of Roger of Cottévrard, although when an investigation was legally conducted we were not fully convinced that the aforementioned crime had been committed by this priest. However, as a result of the inquiry and the confession made in law by the priest himself, and the insinuations of the people noisy with scandal, the said priest stands gravely defamed of the said homicide. We peremptorily appointed a certain day upon which he was, in accordance with the rules of his order, to purge himself with the twelfth hand.[25] But since the said priest failed in the said purgation, we ordered him to be cited peremptorily before us on the Friday following the feast of St. Vincent, either at Rouen or wherever we should happen to be, to hear our judgment in the matter. The said priest did appear before us on the stated day at Déville. But because he contumaciously withdrew, we judged him contumacious and considered him as convicted of the said offense, and by definitive sentence we this day deprived him of the said church and declared his final

[24] See entry for August 24, above.
[25] His order was that of priest, and thus he was obliged to procure twelve priests as his canonical compurgators.

separation therefrom. The following witnesses were present: Master Simon, archdeacon of Eu, in the church of Rouen; Stephen of Lorris, canon of Rouen; Peter of Aumale; Philip, then chaplain at Déville; Hugh, our almoner; John, canon of Quinze-Marcs; and Denis, rector at Cormeilles.

JANUARY 26. At the same. These are the names of those who were present at the agreement made between us on the one side, and Walter of Atre, esquire, on the other, concerning the right of patronage of St. Peter's church at Touqueville; we [agreed] on the venerable men William, treasurer of Rouen, and Reginald, archdeacon of Petit-Caux. The arbiters of the aforesaid [Walter] were Masters Simon, archdeacon of Eu; Hugh of Auvergne, Gilles of Picardy, and Stephen of Lorris, canons of Rouen; and Peter of Aumale.

JANUARY 27–FEBRUARY 2. At Déville. FEBRUARY 3. At Ste-Catherine, at our own expense. FEBRUARY 4. At Louviers. FEBRUARY 5-6. At Sausseuse, at our own expense. FEBRUARY 7. At St-Martin-la-Garenne, at our own expense. FEBRUARY 8. At Meulan. FEBRUARY 9. At St-Germain-en-Laye. FEBRUARY 10-12. At Paris. FEBRUARY 13-26. At Nogent-sur-Marne, near Paris. FEBRUARY 27. At Argenteuil. FEBRUARY 28. At Pontoise, at our own expense. MARCH 1-2. At Meulan. MARCH 3. At St-Martin-la-Garenne, at our own expense. MARCH 4-5. At Sausseuse, at our own expense. MARCH 6. At Les Andelys. MARCH 7-8. At Mont-Deux- Amants, at our own expense. MARCH 9-14. At Rouville, near Pont-de-l'Arche. MARCH 15. At the same, and this day the lord bishop of Euvreux acted for us at the sacrament of Holy Orders at Les Andelys. MARCH 16. At the same: that is to say, at Rouville. MARCH 17-22. At the same.

MARCH 23. At the same. This day Walter, priest at Flavacourt in the archdeaconate of the French Vexin, a man often and gravely defamed of incontinence, in the presence of several witnesses—to wit, Master Henry of Babille, our physician, and Stephen of Gien, priest and our chaplain—voluntarily resigned his aforesaid church into the hands of Master Simon, archdeacon of Eu, who had our instructions and authority to accept his resignation.

MARCH 24-30. At Rouville.

MARCH 31. At the same. This day we excommunicated in writing Stephen, priest at Menucourt, in the deanery of Meulan, for this reason: that as his faults merited, he had been for a year or thereabout under a sentence of excommunication laid on him by ourselves. In contempt of that sentence, Stephen had celebrated Mass several times. We also ordered the aforesaid church to be seized by the dean of Meulan. Item, this same day, in the presence of Stephen, archdeacon of the French Vexin; Stephen of Gien, priest; and Everard, all clerks of ours; Robert, clerk of the said archdeacon; and Henry Muchegros, our sergeant; Simon, the archdeacon of Eu, acting in our behalf, warned him to conduct himself in such a way that he might be able to celebrate Mass and administer things divine.

APRIL 1-13. At Rouville, APRIL 14. At Quévreville, at the expense of the priory. No monks there. APRIL 15-18. At Ermentrouville. APRIL 19. At Déville.

1253

APRIL 20. At Déville. It was Easter Sunday. APRIL 21–MAY 2. At the same. MAY 3. At Auffay, at our own expense. MAY 4-5. At Aliermont.

MAY 6. At the same. On this day Master Robert of Avranches, cleric and proctor of [our] beloved children, the venerable men Geoffrey, treasurer; John, archdeacon; Alan, master of the school; Nicholas of Godfried; Master Peter May; Philip of Fontenay; and Richard Tibout, all canons of Avranches, came before us, and in the presence of [our] beloved son Simon, archdeacon of Eu in the diocese of Rouen, and of brothers Adam Rigaud and Harduin, Friars Minor, showed us a letter, sealed, as it appeared at first glance with the seal of the said venerable men, the canons of Avranches. The tenor of the letter was as follows:

To the Reverend Father and Lord Eudes, by God's grace archbishop of Rouen, his devoted Geoffrey, treasurer; John, archdeacon; Alan, master of the school; Nicholas of Godfried; Master Peter May; Philip of Fontenay; and Richard Tibout, all canons of Avranches, give greeting and reverence due to a father and owed to a lord. Your Paternity is advised that we have appointed Master Robert of Avranches, cleric, as our proctor, in order to convey to you notification of the election made by us in the church of Avranches of the venerable man, Master Richard,[1] the Englishman, as bishop and shepherd, and to convey to you the appeal interposed by us on this affair, and also to renew the aforesaid appeal to you, or to introduce the appeal, if that seems a fitting thing to do. We will regard as valid and hold acceptable whatsoever the said Master Robert, acting for us and our adherents, shall arrange in this business. In testimony whereof we place our seal on the present letter. Done in the year of our Lord 1252, the Tuesday after *Quasimodo*.[2]

The said proctor, on the day and at the place aforesaid, in our presence and in that of the above-mentioned, appealed to the Apostolic See, as follows:

Since that cautious and discreet man, who is to be commended for his habits

---

[1] Richard IV, Lainée (1253-57). (Gams, *Series episcoporum*, p. 506.) No reason is given for this appeal, but probably only a portion of the chapter of Avranches participated in the election; hence the appeal to Eudes. (*Gallia Christiana*, XI, 485-86.)

[2] The Tuesday after the first Sunday after Easter.

and his knowledge and who is circumspect in temporal matters, Master Richard, called the Englishman, canon of Avranches, has been canonically elected as bishop and shepherd of the church af Avranches by the discret mcn G., treasurer; J., archdeacon; A., master of the school; Nicholas of Godfried; Master Peter May; Master P. of Fére; Richard Tibout; and Philip of Fontenay, canons of Rouen, an appeal is made in due legal form on their behalf to the Apostolic See, lest anything be attempted against the election of the said Richard canonically made by them, during this appeal or to their prejudice. I, Robert of Avranches, cleric, constituted proctor in this matter of the said electors, in your presence, Reverend Father, introduce the said appeal, lest anything be attempted aginst the said election or to the prejudice of the said electors, and once again, in writing, I appeal to the Apostolic See.

MAY 7-27. At Aliermont. MAY 28. At Grigneuseville. MAY 29. At Déville.

MAY 30. At the same. This day, that is to say, the Tuesday before Pentecost, we examined Geoffrey, cleric, presented to St. Richard's church at Harcourt, on the passage: *omnia autem aperta et nuda sunt eius oculis*.[3] Asked what part of speech *aperta* was, he replied, "A noun"; asked if it might be any other part of speech, he said, "Yes, that is to say, a participle." Asked from what verb it was derived, he said, "From this verb: *aperio, aperis, aperii, aperire, aperior, aperieris,* etc." Asked for the formation of *compati*, he said, "*Compatire,* from *cum* and *pateo, pates, patui, patere, patendi, patendo, patendum, passum, passu, patiens, passurus, pateor, pateris, passus, patendus.*" Asked what *pateo, pates,* meant, he answered, "To open" or "to suffer."[4] Asked what part of speech *absque* was, he said, "A conjunction"; asked what kind, he said, "Causal." Examined in chant,[5] he did not know how to sing without solfeggio or note, and he was even discordant in solfeggio or note. We therefore, both because of this insufficiency, and because, after an investigation which we had caused to be made about him, he was found to be ill reputed of incontinence and of quarrelsomeness, did

---

[3] Heb. 4:13. "All things are naked and open to the eyes of Him with whom we have to do."

[4] The candidate was weak in conjugating irregular verbs. The present perfect of *aperire* is *aperui,* not *aperii.* The infinitive of *compati* is *compatescere* (a derivative of *patere*) not *compatire.* The candidate intended *passum* and *passu* to be the supine in *um* and in *u* of *patere,* but *patere* has no supine. The present participle of *patere* is *patens,* not *patiens.* *Patere* has no future or past participles.

[5] For chant in the Middle Ages see "Chant romain et grégorien," *Dict. d'arch. chrét. et de lit.,* III[1], 256-321; also, "Chantres," *ibid.,* III[1], 344-365.

not think he should be admitted to the said church. Those present were: Brother Osmond; Brother Walter of Minières; Brother Roger, his relative, all Friars Minor; Ralph, priest at Déville; Master Maur, our physician; Master Peter of Aumale; Stephen, priest at Blenelle; and Everard, son of the count, our clerks.

MAY 31–JUNE 7. At the same. JUNE 8. At the same. This was Pentecost. JUNE 9-15. At the same. JUNE 16-17. At St-Matthieu.

JUNE 18. At the same. On this day Roger of Sorebin, rector of the church at Limésy, submitted himself to the will of the lord archbishop in the matter of making amends, for that he had not presented himself for Holy Orders, as by oath he was held to do.[6] By an official letter, sealed with his seal, Roger agreed that he should be *ipso facto* deprived of the said church if he did not present himself for successive orders. His obligation is contained on folio 127.[7]

JUNE 19-21. At the same.

JUNE 22. At a gathering of the people and clergy of Rouen at the Mare-du-Parc, near Rouen, we preached a sermon and issued the following written condemnation of heresy against John Marel, a heretic whom we had long detained in our prison:

In the name of the Father, and of the Son, and of the Holy Ghost, Amen. John, called Marel, obstinate in thinking and asserting things contrary to the Catholic faith, frequently and legally heard, unwilling to retract the errors confessed by you, after canonical warning, and legally excommunicated by the Church, we, on the counsel of prudent men, declare you a heretic and condemn you for the crime of heresy.[8]

We spent the night at Déville.

JUNE 23-27. At the same. JUNE 28-29. At Louviers. JUNE 30. At Frênes.

JULY 1. At the same. On this day John of Mussegros,[9] esquire, took a solemn oath to abide by our decision, after an inquiry is made, as to both the possession and the proprietary rights of the advowson to the church of

---

[6] The synodal statutes of Rouen (1235) required clerics who had churches to proceed to holy orders. (Mansi, XXIII, 381.)

[7] Eudes deprived him of his church. See Bonnin, pp. 653-54.

[8] This is the final stage of the legal inquisitional process into the orthodoxy of the individual's beliefs. Eudes was the final judge. The punishment usually was death by fire or long years of imprisonment.

[9] See entry for January 5, 1251/52, where the name is Muchegros. Mussegros is the present-day spelling.

Mussegros. Item, he agreed to restore, or so far as possible would see to the restoration to the rector of the fruits and revenues received by any other than the rector instituted in the said church by our authority. Item, in the matter of his clandestine marriage with Jeanne of Bois-Bernard: item, he took oath that he would not withdraw from our decision, nor try to avoid it, on the grounds that he is under age. We therefore decreed, in his presence and with his consent, that he would allow ecclesiastical functions to be celebrated in the future in the church by the aforesaid rector. Concerning the other matters aforementioned, at John's suggestion the following obliged themselves to us as pledges, each one to the extent of one hundred pounds to be paid in full: Richard of Blarru and Adam of Frênes, knights; Robin of Frênes and William of Clery, esquires. Present at these negotiations were: Master Simon, the grain steward of St-Martin-de-Tours; William, dean of Les Andelys; Master Robert, canon of the same; Albert, priest at Frênes, the rector of the chapel of Mesnil-Bernenguel; Miles, vicar of the church at Les Andelys; Master Peter of Aumale; Master Henry Babille and John Gibose, physicians; and Stephen of Gien, priest and Everard, our clerks.

JULY 2-8. At the same.

JULY 9, that is to say, the Wednesday following the octave of SS. Peter and Paul. Some time ago the priest of Le Mesnil-Verclives had been gravely denounced for incontinence before us. In his presence we made an investigation of the charges, first submitting to him a list of the matters we wished to investigate. On this Wednesday we published the results of our inquiry, the priest being again present before us at Frênes. The inquest revealed that he gave scandal and is gravely defamed of incontinence; we pointed out to him that he had to undergo canonical purgation and assigned to him the day after the feast of St. Peter in Chains for this purpose. However, the said priest stated that he wished to speak against the aforesaid investigation.

JULY 10-12. At the same. JULY 13. At Gouy. JULY 14. At Déville.

JULY 15. At the same, where was made the appeal contained in the attached schedule, together with the deposition of those who appealed, which are likewise entered in another schedule affixed to the same folio:[10]

Lord Archbishop, you have aggrived and are aggrieving the suffragans of the province of Rouen by absolving provisionally[11] and without any knowledge

---

[10] See Introduction, pp. xxv-xxvii, for a discussion of this conflict between Eudes and his suffragans.

of the case their subjects who assert that they have appealed to you from them
[the suffragans] or their officials contrary to justice, by usurping to yourself
power of this kind and thereby weakening their jurisdiction and prejudicing
ecclesiastical liberty, whereas none of your predecessors used this power; and you
have again usurped this power after an appeal made on their behalf from you
to the Apostolic See because you revoke without jurisdiction the sentences imposed by them and their officials by appealing such cases to yourself or to your
court, or you reduce such sentences contrary to the spirit of the Constitution of
Rheims, and you have even begun to act thus after a journey undertaken by
their proctor for the purpose of forwarding the said appeal. On account of
these grievances, and lest you should attempt further such, I, William, their
proctor, appeal to the Apostolic See on their behalf and seek *apostoli.*

Lord Archbishop, you have aggrieved and are aggrieving the chapter or
church of Avranches by absolving provisionally without any knowledge of the
case the subjects of the chapter or of the church who assert that they have
appealed to you from them [the chapter?] or their officials contrary to justice, by
usurping to yourself power of this sort and thereby weakening the jurisdiction
of the said chapter and church and prejudicing ecclesiastical liberty, since
none of your predecessors used this power; and you have again usurped this
power after an appeal made on their behalf to the Apostolic See, because you
revoke without jurisdiction the sentences imposed by them and their officials
by appealing such cases to yourself or to your court, or you reduced such sentences contrary to the spirit to the Constitution of Rheims, and you have even
begun to act thus after a journey undertaken by their proctor for the purpose of
forwarding the said appeal. On account of these grievances, and lest you attempt
further such, I. William, proctor of the said chapter and church, appeal to the
Apostolic See on their behalf and seek *apostoli* here and now.

To all who shall see these letters Guido of Bayeux, John of Evreux, Godfrey
of Séez, Fulk of Lisieux and John of Coutance, bishops, [send] health in the Lord.
Be it known to all of you that we have appointed our beloved Master William
of Fontaines, bearer of the present letters, as our proctor in our appeal from the
Reverend Father Eudes, by the grace of God archbishop of Rouen, his officials,
or his agents, for the reason that these same absolve provisionally the subjects
of the aforesaid bishops, who assert that they have appealed from the aforesaid
bishops or their officials, contrary to justice and [tending to bring about] the

---

11 *Absolvendo ad cautelam,* i.e., provisionally. ("Absolution," *Dict. de droit can.,*
I, 122.)

weakening of their jurisdiction and prejudicing the ecclesiastical liberties of Normandy. [We have appointed William also] to act concerning other grievances affecting us individually and collectively, whatever this same William will deem should be done, by entering an appeal touching the aforesaid grievances, and we wish this to be known to all concerned. Given in the year of our Lord 1253, in the month of June.

To all who shall see these letters the dean and chapter of Avranches [send] health in the Lord. Be it known to all of you that we have appointed our beloved Master William of Fontaines, bearer of the present letters, as our proctor in our appeal from the Reverend Father Eudes, by the grace of God archbishop of Rouen, his officials, or his agents, for the reason that these same absolve provisionally the subjects of our church who assert contrary to justice that they have appealed to the aforesaid archbishop or his officials from us or the officials of the court of Avranches, thereby weakening the jurisdiction of the said church of Avranches and prejudicing the ecclesiastical liberties of Normandy. [We have appointed William also] to act on other grievances touching us and our church, as he sees fit. We will hold as ratified and acceptable whatever he shall deem should be done about the foregoing by appealing. Given at Avranches in the year of our Lord 1253, in the month of July.

JULY 16-19. At Déville. JULY 20. At the same, and there we consecrated the new abbess of Fontaine-Guérard,[12] where there had never yet been an abbess. JULY 21-22. At the same. JULY 23. At Gouy.

JULY 24. At Frênes. We had appointed the day following the feast of St. Peter in Chains[13] as the time when the priest of Le Mesnil-Verclives should appear before us at Rouen to purge himself of the vice of incontinence, of which, after a personal investigation, we had found him culpable; but we have postponed this to the Monday following the Assumption of the Blessed Virgin.[14]

JULY 25. At Chaumont. JULY 26. At Chambly-le-Haubergier. JULY 27. At Creil, in the diocese of Beauvais. JULY 28. At Compiègne. JULY 29. At Noyon. JULY 30. At Montdidier. JULY 31. At Poix. AUGUST 1. At

---

[12] A Cistercian house of nuns founded in 1198 and raised to abbatial status in 1253. (Cottineau, I, 1173.) The first abbess was Ida (1253-56). (*Gallia Christiana*, XI, 320.)

[13] August 1. This refers to the entry of July 9, above.

[14] August 15. Note how careful Eudes is to observe due process before imposing the final sentence.

Foucarmont. AUGUST 2-3. At Aliermont. AUGUST 4. At Dieppe. AUGUST 5. At Ouville, at our own expense. AUGUST 6. At St-Wandrille, at our own expense. AUGUST 7. At Corneville, at our own expense. AUGUST 8. At Pont-Audemer. AUGUST 9. At Bec-Hellouin, at the expense of the monastery.

AUGUST 10. At the same, and at their expense. Today Elias, priest at Bosc-Regnoult, and Roger, priest at St-Paul in the deanery of Bourgtheroulde, voluntarily resigned their churches into the hands of Simon, the archdeacon of Eu, who on our authority and on a special mandate received from us had accepted these resignations. Present at this action were: the deans of Bourgtheroulde and Pont-Audemer; Masters Peter of Ons, the official and a canon of Rouen, and Peter of Aumale, our companions; and Masters William and Richard, clerks of the abbot of Bec.

AUGUST 11-13. At Déville. AUGUST 14. At Rouen. AUGUST 15. Assumption Day. AUGUST 16-17. At Déville.

AUGUST 18. At the same, and here appeared before us the priest at Le-Mesnil-Verclives, publicly ill reputed of incontinence, especially with a certain woman named . . . [*lacuna in MS*]. He promised us on oath that should he be again ill famed of her, or anyone else, and could not purge himself, he would regard his church as resigned from that time on, and he agreed that we could pronounce him to be so deprived. However, we enjoined him, in view of his offenses, to make a pilgrimage to St-Giles[15] and to St-Amator before Christmas.

AUGUST 19. At Noyon-sur-Andelle, at our own expense. AUGUST 20-23. At Frênes. AUGUST 24. At Sausseuse, at our own expense.

AUGUST 25. At La Roche-Guyon. We received a procuration fee of forty shillings of Paris from the monks, and this sum is due to us when we come here once a year. We found things to be as they were at our last visitation, a record of which is entered on folio 36.[16]

AUGUST 26. At St-Côme-de-Meulan, at our own expense. AUGUST 27. At St-Germain-en-Laye. AUGUST 28-29. At Paris, and we stayed the night at St-Maclou. AUGUST 30. At St-Denis. AUGUST 31. At St-Martin-de-Pontoise, at our own expense.

[15] St-Giles [-du-Gard], abbot and confessor whose feast day is September 1. For his life and miracles, see *Acta sanctorum*, September, I, 284-304, and *Butler's Lives of the Saints*, ed. Herbert Thurston and Donald Attwater (4 vols., New York, 1956), III, 457-58. His was a favorite pilgrim and penitential shrine. The shrine of St-Amator was near Cahors.

[16] See entry for May 7, 1251.

SEPTEMBER 1. At the same, but at the expense of the monastery, which we visited and where we found twenty-three monks in residence. One monk is dwelling alone at Valmondois; we enjoined the abbot to send him a companion before Michaelmas, or else to recall him to the cloister. The prior does not sleep in the dormitory; we ordered him to sleep there with the rest of the community. We forbade the prior and all the others to eat or drink in any rooms except the refectory, the infirmary, or the abbot's room. In the priories they do not observe the fasts of the Rule, nor do those monks who travel on horseback; we enjoined the abbot to see that everybody was more strict in the observance of these things, unless there was valid reason for the contrary. They owe about twelve hundred pounds, and another three hundred payable with interest due at the Pontoise fair;[17] they have an income of about fifteen hundred pounds of Paris.

This day Stephen, priest at Menucourt in the deanery of Meulan, who had been suspended and excommunicated by us, sought absolution and swore to abide by any decision we made, and to obey our will and command. He offered as pledges Simon Bogot and Robert, called Binet, of Meulan.

SEPTEMBER 2. We visited the chapter of St-Mellon. There is a deficiency of amices and rochets; we ordered them to have some made. As a result of the carelessness of the assistant sacristan in charge of vestments and copes, the silk copes and ornaments are not well cared for and are dirty; we gave orders that they be cleaned and more diligently looked after. There is a deficiency of bells, both large and small ones, and of benches and of wood for making them, and there is strife in the matter of who should make them; we must notify the chapter that we are having the aforesaid made.

This day we spent the night at St-Martin and, for procuration, we received from the chapter one hundred shillings of Paris, straw, couches, and wood. There was some contention about hay.

Note: we must see about appointing proctors, about wood for the benches, about the large and small bells, rochettos, amices, the chapter house, and coffers.

SEPTEMBER 3. At the same, at our own expense, and we visited the priory of St-Pierre-de-Pontoise. We found their temporalities to be in good condition. They owe the abbot two hundred forty pounds, and an hunderd pounds elsewhere.

---

[17] Repayments of loans were commonly made while fairs were being held. Loans were also entered into on such occasions.

SEPTEMBER 4. At Juziers, at the expense of the priory. Seven monks are there. They have an income of about four hundred pounds. Sometimes they eat meat; we forbade them to eat it save as the Rule permitted. Item, they use feather beds.

We informed the priest at Santeuil [of our decision] on Simon and John of Us, esquires, who forcibly took from the house of the priest of Us, and rode off with horses belonging to the dean of Meulan, who was staying at Us on business for the archdeacon of the French Vexin, and who have promised to abide by our disposition of the said matter. [We have sentenced] each of them to proceed in procession to the church at Us on one Sunday and to the church of Notre-Dame-de-Pontoise on another, with bare feet, clad only in a shirt and trunk-hose, without belt or headdress, and carrying rods in their hands. We order that the said priests of these churches announce when this is done.

SEPTEMBER 5. At Gaillonet, of the Order of Premontré, where we received our procuration. SEPTEMBER 6. At St-Laurent-en-Cornecervine. We found conditions to be the same as at our last visitation,[18] except that they no longer eat meat unless there is need. SEPTEMBER 7-8. At Sausseuse, at our own expense.

SEPTEMBER 9. At Gasny, where there are three monks. They do not say their Hours very frequently, in part because of the infirmity of those sent there to convalesce, and in part because of the pressure of business. We found other things to be the same as is reported on folio 45.[19]

SEPTEMBER 10. At St-Martin-la-Garenne. Four monks are there, and there used to be five. They owe one hundred twenty pounds of Paris. Item, they occasionally eat meat when there is no need; we forbade this. Whenever the prior goes to Normandy[20] he remains a goodly while, and he rides about freely. Item, he sometimes goes to the house of Lady Alice, the wife of Lord Thibaut, and she occasionally comes to the priory, either to rest her horses or for some other reason. Sometimes the prior drinks at her house, and sometimes she drinks in the priory, and once she and another woman ate in the priory. Item, the prior receives many knights in the guest house; we forbade the prior to consort with such people in the future, especially with

---

[18] See entries for July 8, 1249.

[19] The folio number is 44, and the date is March 8, 1251/52.

[20] St-Martin-la-Garenne was a dependent priory of Bec, and this would account for the prior's ramblings in Normandy. St-Martin-la-Garenne was in the French Vexin.

the knights and the aforementioned lady. We instructed them to abstain from meat, save as the Rule permits. Item, they do not observe the fasts of the Rule in their completeness; we enjoined them to a fuller observance.

[*No entry for September 11.*]

SEPTEMBER 12. We visited the priory of Villarceaux. In residence are twenty nuns, two lay sisters, and two priests. The letter containing our ordinances is not read every month.[21] Whenever they are bled, they do not chant the Office with modulation. They sing vulgar songs at the feast of the Innocents. The prioress does not compute as we had ordered; she does not eat very often in the refectory; she rarely arises for Matins; she is remiss in holding chapter, and she fails to hear Mass daily.

This day we were at Parnes, and we made a visitation. Four monks from St-Evroult are there, but there used to be five. They eat meat and use feather beds. They owe about twenty pounds; they have an income of two hundred pounds. We found that everything else about them was in good condition.

SEPTEMBER 13. We were at Sérans-le-Bouteiller and, for procuration, we received six hundred shillings of Paris, domestic utensils, forage for the horses, straw for our men and beasts, and wood. We made a visitation. Four monks from St-Germer are there. They eat meat and use feather beds. They owe about twenty-five pounds. They have no copy of the Statutes of Pope Gregory; we ordered them to procure one, to read it, and to observe it.

SEPTEMBER 14. We were at Marcheroux, at the expense of the monastery. They are Premonstratensians.

SEPTEMBER 15. We were at Chaumont, at the expense of the priory. There are three monks in residence, as there should be. They use feather beds; we ordered them to use mattresses of hair. They do not observe the fasts very well; we ordered an improvement. They do not read any martyrology,[22] nor do they have a copy of the Statutes of Pope Gregory; we ordered them to obtain one, to keep it, and to read it. They have a copy of the Rule; we ordered them to read it. Sometimes they drink at the priest's house; we ordered them to correct this. They eat meat three times a week; we forbade them to do this and ordered them to abstain from it altogether. They owe about sixty pounds; they have an income of one hundred pounds.

---

[21] Eudes had visited the priory on July 9, 1249. They had not corrected their method of celebrating the feast of the Holy Innocents.

[22] The martyrology is a collection of the lives of the saints for every day in the year. The appropriate lives for the day are read in either the chapter or the refectory.

SEPTEMBER 16. We were at the same, and we visited the priory of St-Martin. The present prior came before the feast of the Purification and found enough grain to last a whole year; but the priory owes twenty pounds, and it ought not to owe so much. They do not all sleep in the same place; we ordered this corrected. They have an income of about forty pounds. They do not observe the fasts of the Rule; we ordered them to correct this. We enjoined them to follow the Statutes of Pope Gregory about abstaining from meat and gave orders that offenders should be punished with the penance required therein. They have no [copies of the] Rule nor [of the] Statutes; we ordered [that copies be procured] before Christmas and that they be read.

This same day we visited the prior of Liancourt, at his expense and that of his companions. They have no copy of the Statutes of Pope Gregory; we ordered them to find one and procure it before Christmas, and to observe it. They owe about sixty pounds; they have an income of from one hundred twenty to one hundred forty pounds.

This is the inventory of the Maison-Dieu at Chaumont, made on the octave of the Nativity of the Blessed Mary, 1253, by Master Peter of Aumale, at the command of the lord archbishop: Concerning spiritual matters, we found that the priest does not have the cure of the brothers of the said house;[23] he celebrates the Divine Service with sufficient regularity; he eats there and lives in common with them and does as much for them as the poor resources of the place permit. Of immovable property they have about eighty *jugera*[24] of land. They have an income of about fifty shillings of Paris, but they owe almost as much. They have nine cows, one hundred forty sheep, two hundred forty rams, six horses, and twenty pigs, including the large and small ones. Item, they receive two *muids* of wheat annually from a certain mill at Chaumont. Item, they own the wool from all the sheep and rams mentioned above, and which is valued at thirty-five pounds of Paris. They owe about twelve pounds of Paris. We enjoined William, the priest of the place, to prepare, with the assistance of the brethren, a statement of the expenses and receipts of the house; but, on this account,

[23] He was not responsible for their spiritual wellbeing in the administration of the sacraments and thus was not answerable to the local ordinary. Evidently the priest of the parish in which the hospital was located had the cure of souls of the hospital personnel and patients.

[24] The *jugerum* was approximately two acres.

he is not to forego casting his accounts with the priest and the mayor of Chaumont, as the archdeacon has ordered.[25]

SEPTEMBER 17. We were at Vesly, at the expense of the prior, and we warned the monks to observe the Statutes of Pope Gregory. We enjoined the dean of Gisors to instruct them to send the prior of Gisors to us, or to our official if we should happen to be absent from Rouen or vicinity, before the coming feast of Saint Remy, to answer whether he would be willing to admit us for the purpose of investigating his priory with reference to the observance there of the Statutes of Pope Gregory, as the Lord Pope has commanded.

SEPTEMBER 18. We were at Noyon-sur-Andelle, at the expense of the prior. They have an income of about forty pounds. They do not know how much they owe, but, with the exception of oats, they have enough grain in the barns to last out the year. Sometimes they eat meat when there is no need; we ordered them to correct this, or else undergo the penances exacted by the Statute [of Pope Gregory].

SEPTEMBER 19. At Ste-Catherine[-du-Mont], at the expense of the monastery.

SEPTEMBER 20. We visited the same. One monk is dwelling alone at Caudecote; we ordered that a companion be given him. One does not accuse another [in chapter]; we ordered this corrected and that those who were negligent be punished. The Statutes of Pope Gregory are not read three times a year; we ordered them to correct this. Item, we ordered that alms be distributed without any diminution in amount. They have an income of two thousand pounds; they do not owe any amount which it would hurt them to pay. The abbot says that Samson, the monk who resides at Chapelle-en-Bray, is defamed of having property, that he is suspected of incontinence, and that he has been holding the church at Hodeng in fee.[26] Item, Lawrence the priest who is staying at Pavilly, is gravely ill famed of incontinence; item, he bought a secular garment. Item, Bartholemew, the prior of St-Aubin, is ill famed of a certain married woman, and also of having property. The same is true of the prior and subprior of Laurent, of Brother Geoffrey

---

[25] Chaumont's hospital administration was in the hands of the mayor and of the superior of the resident religious. This was a very common type of hospital administration. Chaumont had an elected mayor since 1182 by virtue of a charter granted by Philip Augustus. (Bonnin, p. 168, n. 1.)

[26] He is holding it at farm or in fee, i.e., he is to serve it but has another do so for a price.

of Longueville, and of Samson. The infirmary has no courtyard. There is an epileptic there; this must be attended to. The bailiff of Laurent likewise. The prior of Chapelle reports that Samson is a man of property, that he has been holding the church at Hodeng, [in fee], and that he is in the habit of receiving oblations with the bishop's permission; item, he is litigious, dissolute, and rebellious. Item, the prior of Pavilly says the same of Lawrence.

This day at St-Matthieu, Master Matthew, then rector at Thièdeville, resigned [his church] into our hands, placing in our hands the hat[27] of Master Peter of Aumale. There were present: Reginald, archdeacon of Petit-Caux; Masters Jean of Flainville, Hugh of Rosay, Robert of Sens; and the said Peter of Aumale, all canons of Rouen.

SEPTEMBER 21. We were at St-Matthieu in Ermentrouvile, and we conferred Holy Orders at Pré. On this same Saturday, that is to say, the one after the feast of the Exaltation of the Holy Cross, we dined at St-Matthieu.

SEPTEMBER 22. At the same, and we celebrated the feast of St. Matthew.

SEPTEMBER 23. At St-Lô-de-Rouen, at the expense of the prior. There is no subprior; we ordered them to choose one. There are seventeen canons. Rarely does one accuse another [in chapter]; we insisted that this be corrected. We gave orders that lay folk be kept out of the cloister. They owe about three hundred pounds; they have an income of about seven hundred pounds. The prior does not compute with the community; we ordered him to cast his accounts with the assistance of some of the brothers elected by the chapter. The sick are not well cared for and are too speedily removed from the infirmary; we ordered this corrected. Dom William is at present defamed of a certain woman, and of previous relations with another.

SEPTEMBER 24. At Pérrièrs-sur-Andelle, at the expense of the priory. No monks are there. This day William, called Enguelart, former priest at Les Noyers, promised and took oath in our presence that if he should again be found ill famed of incontinence he would, without the clamor of a trial, submit to whatever disposition we should make of him personally or of his benefice.

SEPTEMBER 25. We were at Beaulieu, at the expense of the priory, and we made a visitation. We found fifteen canons there. A certain canon who is serving the church at Bois l'Evêque does not carry out all the due ecclesiastical offices there. All but three are priests. The prior goes away

---

[27] The hat was held to be the symbol of his church, and in giving up the hat he resigned his church. It is comparable to seisin of tenure by the rod, by the sod of earth, etc.

too much and, quite often, to no useful purpose. He does not always eat in the refectory; indeed, he scarcely eats there at all, although he has no reason for staying away. The prior has two of his nephews in the service of the house, and they perform their services in a more rebellious way than do the others. One of the nephews, Thomas by name, is ill famed of incontinence; he dines in his room too often and too well. Item, their acquaintances do much damage to the place. The sick are not properly attended. They owe about two hundred pounds. No one knows anything about the financial state of the house. Some of them think that they owe about four or five hundred pounds. They have a sufficiency of wheat and oats; they have no wine. The vines have been burned. The prior's accounts are not sufficiently complete. They have an income of four hundred fifty pounds. The sources of income are not written down. The prior waxes wrathful after eating; he does not often hold chapter. They do not observe silence very well. The prior received four hundred pounds from the sale of the woods and the tithes of Préaux. The subprior is unworthy, partly because he has been defamed of incontinence, partly because he does not observe silence very well, and in consequence he does not dare to discipline the others. Item, the subprior sometimes stays away from Compline. Item, Ralph, who resides at St-Jacques-de-Neuville, is ill famed of incontinence. The prior, once angry, remains so. Those who make trips on horseback stay away from Compline and often eat and drink too much. They have an income of six pounds derivable from the prior's country,[28] but which is never entered in the accounts.

Note: the letter of the prior and of the chapter dealing with the accounts is contained in the next folio.

This same day we enjoined . . . [lacuna in MS], the prior of Beaulieu, to appoint a new subprior and a new bailiff, to cast his accounts more diligently, and to stay in the cloister. The chapter of Beaulieu sent us the following letter:

The prior and the bailiff of Notre-Dame-de-Beaulieu, in the presence of the entire community of the said church, prepared a statement of the accounts on the Friday following the feast of St. Michael, in the year of our Lord 1253. The members of the community present were: Dom Richard, then subprior; William, called de Garde; G. of Cany; N. called Hongrie; Julian; Clement;

---

[28] The word *patria* is used here to mean the district in which he was born.

Henri of Cambremer; William of Fleury; Richard Boss; Richard of Bois Oisse; John of Faverole; Ralph of Fontaines; G. of Remfreville; and R. of Yerville. Account was taken of all receipts and expenditures, of all moneys owed and owing, and it was found that they owe about four hundred sixty pounds and are owed about two hundred fifty pounds. In witness whereof . . . [*lacuna in MS*].

This same day William of Haricourt, damoiseau,[29] in the presence of Sir Bartholomew of Capeval and Sir John of Rivage, knights, presented as a second incumbent to the church at Haricourt Robert of Rivage, priest. There were present: Master William of Carville; William Bryne, priest; Master John of Fry; William, priest at St-André; Jude, priest at Pubeu; Master Henry, the physician; Brother Walter of Minières; Brother Lawrence of Chambly; Master Peter of Aumale; Geoffrey, who had been presented as first incumbent to that church; and the two knights. The said Robert was willing and expressly agreed that we should create a pension of twelve pounds a year out of the income of the said church for Walter, the former rector of the place. The pension is to continue as long as he shall live, or until some competent benefice is assured to him. Robert gave us a letter covering this.

SEPTEMBER 26. At St-Saëns, at the expense of the prior. Three monks are there; there used to be five. Two of them are at the abbey; they will return before long. The prior does not celebrate Mass very often; we ordered him to correct this. We ordered the prior personally to appoint the monks in charge of the keys and the mill. About forty pounds more is owed to them than they owe. We ordered that the monks be informed as to the finances of the house, in the matter both of debts and of the indentity of their creditors. The prior does not cast his accounts in the presence of anyone; we ordered this corrected. They have an income of three hundred pounds.

SEPTEMBER 27. We were at Neufchâtel, at the expense of Bernard of Hongrie, because of the manor he holds there. This same day, we visited the nuns at St-Saëns. In residence are eighteen nuns, three lay sisters and one lay brother. They have four carucates[30] of land and an income of one

[29] See above, August 30, 1252, n. 16.
[30] A carucate of land was the amount of land that could be cultivated by a plough in a year. It varied from district to district according to the length of the perch, or rod; a basic unit of measurement in length and was anywhere from 80 to 120 acres.

hundred pounds. They owe about eighty pounds. They cannot support a refectory, but they all eat together in the infirmary, and even the healthy ones eat meat. They have coffers, and they keep whatever is given to them. The prioress does not attend choir very well. They do not observe silence when they eat in the infirmary. The prioress does not dare to discipline the others inasmuch as she is as much an offender herself. The Rule is not observed. No chapter is held. The Divine Offices are not well performed.

SEPTEMBER 28. At Bures, at the expense of the prior. We visited there and found two monks. They use feather beds when there is no need. They do not celebrate Mass every day. They do not observe the fasts of the Rule. Sometimes they eat meat. They have no copy of the Rule or of the Statutes [of Pope Gregory]; we ordered these defects corrected.

This same day we visited the hospital at Neufchâtel, where there are four canons. They owe about seventy pounds; they have about forty pounds on hand, reckoning both money and wool. They have a sufficiency of provisions, that is to say, of wheat, oats, and meat. Two sisters are there. They have an annual income of above two hundred pounds in rents and tithes. There used to be six [canons there], and at one time there were eight.

SEPTEMBER 29–OCTOBER 1. At Aliermont, at our own expense

OCTOBER 2. At Longueil, at the expense of the priory. This day the dean of Longueville resigned into our hands the church of Etrans. There were present Masters John of Flainville and Peter of Aumale.

OCTOBER 3. At Bacqueville, at the expense of the priory. Four monks are there, including the prior; all of them are priests. They have only one chalice. They do not confess often enough, and but rarely to the prior. They use feather beds; they do not hold chapter; they do not read the Rule; they have no copy of the Statutes of Pope Gregory, nor have they ever had one, as they say. We ordered correction in these matters. Sometimes they break the fasts, even the healthy ones; we ordered this corrected. All the monks break the fasts occasionally when there are guests; we forbade this to be done. Item, sometimes they offend by eating meat; we ordered that this be corrected. No computation is made except in the presence of the abbot or those making an official visitation. They have an income of two hundred pounds, and as much, or perhaps more, is owed to them than they owe. With the exception of wine, they have sufficient provisions.

OCTOBER 4. At Ouville, at the expense of the prior. Twelve canons reside there. Women sometimes enter the cloister; we ordered them to take heed that no more enter. They do not accuse each other [in chapter]; we gave orders that anyone who knows [of any offense] and will not present an accusation shall suffer the same penalty as the actual offender. They owe one hundred twenty pounds. They have a sufficiency of wheat and oats, but very little wine, to wit, only four *muids*. They have an income of four hundred pounds. The sick are not well attended. Seculars dine too often in the refectory; we ordered this corrected.

OCTOBER 5. We were at Etoutteville, at the expense of the prior, and we visited there. Two monks are there; we ordered that they should acquire a third before Christmas. They do not observe the fasts of the Rule, nor do they abstain from meat; they have no copy of the Statutes of Pope Gregory. We commanded them to correct all of these abuses, to procure a copy of the Statutes and to read it, and to observe the fasts; and that if anyone should offend, he should be required to fulfill the statutory penance. They owe twenty-three pounds. They have the parochial tithe,[31] forty acres of ground, and forty-three shillings in money rents.

OCTOBER 6. At St-Wandrille, at our own expense.

OCTOBER 7. At the same, but at the expense of the monastery. There are six novices who are in their year of probation. About forty monks are in residence. One monk is alone at Roony. One does not accuse another [in chapter] except for insulting gestures, quarreling, and affronts. We ordered this corrected. They do not observe silence very well; we ordered them to correct this. Some of them do not observe the fasts of the Rule very well. We ordered them to watch carefully lest either the staff[32] or the laborers frequent the taverns or play dice. They owe four hundred forty-three pounds, sixteen shillings, one penny; two hundred sixty-seven pounds, fifteen shillings is owed to them. They have not yet begun to consume this year's wheat, and they have enough wheat and oats to last out the year. The sick and the guests are insufficiently looked after; we enjoined that this be cor-

[31] The parishioners paid tithes to the monks who have cure of the souls in that parish.

[32] *Familiares.* In general, the familiars of a religious establishment were the secular persons attached to its service, either in the interior of the house as servant boys or in its rural dependencies as day laborers. They could be the abbot's personal servants also. Dom U. Berlière, *La Familia dans les monastères bénédictins du moyen âge* (Brussels, 1931), is a short but very clear treatment of the subject. Since they were directly attached to the religious house, their conduct was expected to be above reproach.

rected. We ordered the prior to hear confessions. It is reported that the monk in charge of the baking and distribution of bread favors his relatives with monastery property, and to the detriment of the house; the same is reported of the prior. The prior receives money for Mass and spends it as he pleases. The prior of Tiegeville is keeping one of his nephews who is ill famed of incontinence; we forbade Robert, the abbot's nephew, to receive any prebend, bread, or wine in the monastery. Item, the kitchener is ill famed of the wife of the abbot's nephew and of a certain woman in Caudebec.

OCTOBER 8. We came to Bourg-Achard, where our expenses were paid by the priory.

OCTOBER 9. We visited the same. They do not confess every month; we enjoined them to correct this. We forbade them to talk with anyone in the cloister or to permit any secular to sit in the cloister. They owe two hundred pounds. They have a sufficiency of wheat, oats, and pigs; they have no wine. The prior is a wrathful and quarrelsome man, and is readily moved to begin lawsuits. They till the soil and labor on Sundays and feast days. The sick are badly attended. The sick do not confess to any of the brothers. They have a certain sumptuous but quite useless manor. The monastery roof needs repairing. One of the prior's brothers is there, but he does nothing and is dishonest; his name is Robert. They have an income of three hundred pounds. The prior has a common pasture worth sixty pounds. About fifty pounds is owed to them. The amount used for alms is very small. Robert Macue was defamed of incontinence with a certain spinster. The prior is ill famed of La Cornue and Alice of Bouquetot. Brother Walter, the cellarer, is suspected of possessing property. Item, the prior was ill famed of Audrey, the mercer's wife, who is now dead.

This same day we came to Pont-Audemer to treat of peace between us and our suffragans.[33]

OCTOBER 10. At Pont-Audemer. OCTOBER 11. At Bec-Hellouin. OCTOBER 12-15. At Louviers.

OCTOBER 16. At the same. This day Thomas, priest and rector of the church of St-Jean-Baptiste-de-Tragarville, resigned this church into the hands of the treasurer of Rouen, who had been appointed on our authority and in

[33] See documents under the entry for March 2, 1251/52, for the dispute between Eudes and his suffragans.

our place to receive this resignation. Present were: Masters Robert of Sens and John of Flainville, canons of Rouen, and Brother Harduin.

OCTOBER 17-26. At Louviers. OCTOBER 27. At Martot. OCTOBER 28– NOVEMBER 5. At Déville.

NOVEMBER 6. At the same. This day the rector of Senots was deprived of his church as is herewith reported:

For that the rector of the church at Senots had been in due legal form and solemnly warned by the authority and special mandate of the Reverend Father Eudes, by God's grace archbishop of Rouen, to maintain personal residence in the said church, which he had sworn to do at the time of his institution therein, and as the cure of the church requires; and for that he has scorned to observe either the said oath or warning, nor has he attempted to reside in the said church although more than six months have passed since the issuance of the said warning; and further, for that the said rector, on the authority of the aforementioned Reverend Father, was peremptorily cited to appear before him on the Thursday following All Saints, either at Rouen or in the vicinity, and was ordered to be prepared to stand trial in the aforesaid matters, but failed to appear before the said father, who, on that day, was at Déville:

Therefore we, Simon, the archdeacon of Eu, acting on the special authority entrusted to us by the aforementioned Father, do declare the said rector absent by contempt and to be regarded as contumacious, and by definitive sentence we deprive him of the said church and declare him to be so deprived.

Present were: Master Hugh, canon of Rouen; Master John of Paris, canon of Les Andelys; Master Henry, surnamed Blesus, the physician; Dom John and Dom Morel, canons of Quinze-Marcs; Everard, William of Plessy and Dom Hugh, the almoner, our clerks; and John of Musenay, rector of Bernouville.

NOVEMBER 7-19. At Déville.

NOVEMBER 20. At the same. This day William of Vardes, presented for the church at Amécourt, was examined in the passage from the legends of the Purification, *illa namque salus,* and construed the passage as follows: "*illa,* that one; *salus,* salvation; *generata,* engendered; *de Virgine Maria,* of the Virgin Mary; *hoc est,* that is; *die,* the day; *quadragesimo,* of the period of forty days; *Maria,* O thou Mary; *genetrice,* mother; *hodie,* today; *ab ipsa,* from her; *deportata,* carried; *ad templum,* to the temple; *ipsius,* of him; *ut ipse,* that he; *redemptor noster,* our father; *sit,* may be; *presentatus,* presented; *sic,* in such a manner; *cum substancia nostre carnis,* in the substance of our flesh; *etiam,* but; *adimplet,* he fills; *ipsam,* her." Asked what this meant in French, he said that he did not understand the sense very well.

Asked what part of speech *adimplet* was, he said, "A verb," and he conjugated it well. Asked what is the word *urnis* which had been left out, he said that it meant "the breasts." Item, asked what part of speech was *genetricis*, he said, "a noun," and declined it as follows: nominative, *hic genetrix*; genitive, *huius genetricis*; dative, *huic -trici*; accusative, *hanc -tricem*; vocative, *-trix*; ablative, *ab hoc -trice*. He said that it had no plural. Present at this examination were: Master Simon, archdeacon of Eu; Stephen, his clerk; Master Peter of Aumale; and Hugh of Courtrai, canons of Rouen; Dom Hugh, the almoner; and Everard, the clerk of the lord archbishop.

This same day Master Thomas, surnamed Ratel, rector of the church of St-Léger-au-Bosc, in the deanery of Foucarmont, voluntarily resigned his church into our hands. Present were: Brothers Adam Rigaud, Roger Rufus, and Harduin, of the Friars Minor; Master Simon, archdeacon of Eu; Master John of Paris, a canon of Les Andelys; Dom Hugh, our almoner; and our clerks, Everard and Morel.

NOVEMBER 21-29. At Déville. NOVEMBER 30. At the same. The feast of St. Andrew. DECEMBER 1-2. At the same.

DECEMBER 3. At the same. This day in our hall at Déville and in the presence of the abbot of Beaubec, the treasurer of Rouen, and many others, John of Meisnil-près-Portmort and William of Fleury rendered homage to us for the fiefs which they hold of us. And since the said William had not yet paid the relief due from his fief,[34] we ordered him to pay it as he ought to do, and within fifteen days.

DECEMBER 4-7. At the same.

DECEMBER 8. At the same. This day Adam de la Houssaye resigned whatever rights he possessed or might claim to possess in the church at La Crique, and returned to us his charter of investiture. Present were: Simon, archdeacon of Eu, and Masters Hugh and Peter of Aumale, canons of Rouen.

DECEMBER 9. At the same. This day the suffragans of the church of Rouen sent to us the following notice:

May it be agreeable that the matters which form the object of appeal, as well as the form of the appeal itself, together with the arguments which either party may care to advance (even though there is no proof that you have

---

[34] Relief was paid when a new tenant took over a fief on the death of the previous tenant. It was the equivalent of modern death taxes and was supposed to be paid before the newcomer was invested with the holding or fief. Eudes had knights who held fiefs from him as their feudal overlord.

examined them), be presented in such a way that no mention is made of the discussions which have been held about reaching an agreement among ourselves, and be forwarded to the Pope in writing, that he may decide or determine the matter as may appear best to him. [May it be agreeable] that if either party should desire a copy of the reasons advanced by the other party, he may have the same, and may reply to it in writing, if he should so desire. [Finally, may it be agreeable] that if ... [lacuna in MS] [Eudes], the archbishop, should desire not to make a copy of the reasons for the other party, they shall not be obliged to make a copy of their reasons for him.

We sent them the following note:

It is agreed that both parties should send [their arguments] to the Curia, and that the Lord Pope, simply, and without the bother of a formal trial, shall, upon hearing and considering the various arguments, dispose of the controversy in every detail as shall seem to him most suitable for restoring the peace.

DECEMBER 10. At St-Victor-en-Caux, at the expense of the abbey.

DECEMBER 11. At the same, and we made a visitation. Fifteen monks are in residence, three are at St-Thomas, and two are in England. All are priests but three, and of these two are deacons, the other a subdeacon. They report that the Statute concerning the eating of meat is well observed, except by the abbot because of his infirmity. The abbot does not cast his accounts with the assistance of any brothers elected by the community; we ordered this corrected. They owe about two hundred pounds. They lack wine. The sacristan is negligent about celebrating Mass. The abbot has ten or twelve silver dishes, three great silver goblets, and silver spoons.

This day we came to Auffay; our expenses were paid by the priory, and we spent the night there.

DECEMBER 12. We visited there. Six monks are in residence. They are negligent about confessing; we enjoined the prior to see that they confess at least once a month, and to deprive of wine anyone who should be negligent in this matter until such time as he should come to confession. They owe about one hundred fifty pounds. They do not read the Statutes of Pope Gregory; we enjoined them to correct this. We enjoined that whenever the prior should make a detailed audit of the income, some of the monks should be present.

That same day we spent the night at our manor at Aliermont.

DECEMBER 13-15. At Aliermont. DECEMBER 16. At the same. This day the letter concerning the manor at Croixdalle was prepared, which you may find on folio 156.[35]

DECEMBER 17. At Longueville, at the expense of the priory. Here the lord archbishop read, corrected and authorized the oath to be taken by the retailers of Dieppe. This you will find in folio 156.[36]

DECEMBER 18. At Déville. DECEMBER 19. At Ermentrouville. DECEMBER 20. At the same. This day we conferred Holy Orders at Gramont. DECEMBER 21. At the same, and we preached in the church at Rouen.

DECEMBER 22. At the same. This day Roger, priest at Aubermesnil, in the archdeanery of Petit-Caux, resigned his church into our hands, and we received his resignation. DECEMBER 23. At Rouen, and this day we began the O Virgo.[37] DECEMBER 24. At Rouen. DECEMBER 25. At the same. We celebrated Christmas. DECEMBER 26. At Louviers. DECEMBER 27. At Evreux, to negotiate for peace with our suffragans.

DECEMBER 28. At Pont-de-l'Arche, where we received the following letter:

Albert,[38] notary of the Lord Pope, and legate of the Holy See, to his beloved son in Christ, Nicholas of Hermenville, cleric of the diocese of Rouen, [sends] greeting in the Lord. Your forthright petition exhorts us to grant you a special favor. Wherefore we, heeding your prayers, and by the authority that we wield, grant that you may freely receive and hold an ecclesiastical benefice, even though it may involve a cure of souls, if such be offered you canonically, notwithstanding your lack of years, for you have almost completed your twentieth year.[39] Let no man violate this instrument of our concession or presume to contest it. If, however, any man should presume to make the attempt, let him know that he will incur the wrath of the Almighty and that of SS. Peter and Paul, His apostles. Given at Meaux, on December 10, in the eleventh year of the pontificate of the Lord Pope Innocent IV.

---

[35] This document is given in full in an appendix to Bonnin and deals with the properties of the archbishopric. Bonnin, pp. 769-73.

[36] Bonnin, pp. 766-68, 783-85.

[37] On the "great O's," see above, note 135 to entry for December 23, 1250.

[38] Albert, cardinal and apostolic delegate.

[39] Canon law demanded an age of twenty-five years for one having jurisdiction or cure of souls (Corp. jur. can., Greg. IX Lib. I. Tit. 6. cap. 7-14). For one who was being given a benefice without cure of souls, an age of seven years and the order of tonsure were required (Corp. jur. can., Sext Lib. I. Tit. 2. cap. 9). An age of fourteen and tonsure were required to become part of a cathedral chapter, while twenty-one was the age required for the holding of office in such chapters.

We received the following as well:

Nicholas of Hautot, knight, to the Reverend Father and Lord Eudes, by God's grace archbishop of Rouen, [sends] greeting with all reverence and honor. I present my beloved and faithful cleric, Nicholas Maquereau, to you for the church at Hautot, now vacant, the advowson to which I know belongs to me. and I humbly beseech that you will deign and be willing to admit him to the said church. May Your Paternity grow strong in the Lord. Given the Friday before Christmas, in the year of our Lord 1253.

DECEMBER 29. At Rouen, and in the chapter concerning the business of Guy of Bourton.[40] This day Nicholas, priest vicar of Carville, promised that he would offer no further obstacles to Thibaut of Falaise in procuring and in remaining in peaceful possession of this church. He gave surety for himself and his followers and promised that he would commit no injury or cause any to be committed.

DECEMBER 30. At Auffay.[41] DECEMBER 31. At Aliermont. JANUARY 1. At the same. JANUARY 2. At Foucarmont. JANUARY 3. At Poix. JANUARY 4. At Montdidier. JANUARY 5. At Noyon. JANUARY 6. At the same. This was Epiphany. JANUARY 7. At Compiègne. JANUARY 8. At Senlis. JANUARY 9. At Chambly. JANUARY 10. At Pontoise. JANUARY 11-12. At Paris. JANUARY 13. At St-Maur-des-Fossés. JANUARY 14. At Courquetaine. JANUARY 15. At Rampilon. JANUARY 16-17. At the Paraclète. JANUARY 18. At Troyes. JANUARY 19. At Bar-sur-Seine. JANUARY 20. At Châtillon. JANUARY 21. At La Perière. JANUARY 22. At St-Seine. JANUARY 23. At Dijon. JANUARY 24. At Auxonne. JANUARY 25. At Dole-sur-le-Doubs. JANUARY 26. At Salins. JANUARY 27. At the same. We could not proceed because of the heavy snow. JANUARY 28. At the same. JANUARY 29. We sent Arnoult[42] away because he was sick, and we spent the night at Levier. JANUARY 30. At Pontarlier. JANUARY 31. At Cossonay. FEBRUARY 1. At Lausanne.

[40] See entry for May 29, 1254, where the name is Guy de Bourbon.

[41] Here Eudes began a journey (from December 30 to March 11) to Rome to seek a solution from the Pope in person to the troublesome problem of jurisdiction over his suffragans. For a man suffering from rheumatism such a journey in the winter must have been especially difficult. For a prelate so zealous in the discharge of his duties in his archdiocese, the time consumed in travel to Rome must have seemed costly. However, he did have the satisfaction of having his position vis-a-vis the visitation of the dioceses of his suffragans upheld by the Pope (see Introduction, p. xxvii.

[42] Possibly a servant; no other mention is made of him.

FEBRUARY 2. At the same. Here we celebrated the feast of the Purification of the Virgin Mary. We preached a sermon and celebrated Mass, wearing the pallium at the request of the bishop.[43]

FEBRUARY 3. At Villeneuve. FEBRUARY 4. At Granges. FEBRUARY 5. At Sion. FEBRUARY 6. At Leuk. FEBRUARY 7. At Brigg. FEBRUARY 8. We climbed the mountains and came to Divoire. FEBRUARY 9. At Domodossola. FEBRUARY 10. At Palenzano. FEBRUARY 11. At Gallarato. FEBRUARY 12-13. At Milan. FEBRUARY 14. At Bergamo, and this day we crossed the [River] Adige at Trezzo, but not without danger. FEBRUARY 15. At Brescia. FEBRUARY 16-17. At Mantua. FEBRUARY 18. At Massa. FEBRUARY 19. At Ferrara on the Po. FEBRUARY 20. At San Giorgio. FEBRUARY 21-24. At Bologna. FEBRUARY 25. At Imola. FEBRUARY 26. At Cesena. FEBRUARY 27. At Rimini. FEBRUARY 28. At Fano. MARCH 1 At Cagli. MARCH 2. At Eugubio.[44] MARCH 3-6. At Assisi. MARCH 7. At Perugia. MARCH 8. At Todi. MARCH 9. At Narni. MARCH 10. At Citta Castellana. MARCH 11. At Rome, in the section of the city called St. Peter's. MARCH 12. We went to the Lateran and kissed the foot of the Lord Pope. MARCH 13—APRIL 11. At Rome.

[43] John de Cossonay, bishop of Lausanne (1242-73). (Gams, *Series episcoporum*, p. 284.)

[44] Probably Gubbio.

APRIL 12. At Rome. This day was Easter Sunday, and here begins the year 1254. APRIL 13-19. At Rome. APRIL 20. At Sutri. APRIL 21-27. At Viterbo. APRIL 28. At Orti. APRIL 29. At San Gemini. APRIL 30. At Bevagna. MAY 1-28. At Assisi.

MAY 29. At the same. This day Dom Guy of Bourbon, dean of Rouen, with his hand upon the Holy Gospels, promised us that obedience, reverence, and fidelity which his predecessors owed to the archbishop of Rouen, and he swore to take a more complete oath when we should come to Rouen. At this oath were present: Masters Robert and Peter, canons of Rouen; Brothers Harduin and Walter of the Friars Minor; Master William, canon of Anis; and Philip of Sixchamps, rector of Lie.

MAY 30. At the same. This day Peter of Aumale, canon of Rouen, on our special mandate, received nine sworn witnesses through whose evidence he was convinced that Herbert of Hoville, priest in Rome, had been canonically ordained as acolyte and subdeacon by the cardinal bishop of Praeneste,[1] and, on the Saturday before Easter, as deacon and priest by the bishop of Pinna.

MAY 31. At the same, and this day was Pentecost. JUNE 1. At the same. This day the Pope left Assisi. JUNE 2. At Bevagna. JUNE 3. At San Gemini. JUNE 4. At Città Castellana. JUNE 5-8. At Rome. JUNE 9-10. At Praeneste. JUNE 11-19. At Anagni.

JUNE 20. At the same. This day Master Peter of Aumale, canon of Rouen, on our special mandate, received sworn witnesses through whose evidence he was convinced that Roger Basin of Valmont, priest in Rome, had been canonically ordained as priest, the Saturday after Pentecost, by the bishop of Pinna and Adria.[2]

JUNE 21–JULY 3. At Anagni.

JULY 4. At Anagni. Today the papal decision in the matter of the

[1] Simon de Brie who later became Pope Martin IV (1281-85).
[2] The Provincial Council of Rouen (1231) forbade (canon 10) ordinations except by the ordinand's ordinary. (Mansi, XXIII, 215.)

dispute between us and our suffragans, which was the occasion of our visit to the Curia, was handed to us. It is to be found near the end of the Register.[3]

JULY 5-7. At Anagni. JULY 8. We left the Curia and proceeded to Burgo Novello. JULY 9-10. At Rome. JULY 11. At St. Peter's castle. JULY 12. At Sutri. JULY 13. At Viterbo. JULY 14. At Montefiascone. JULY 15. At Aquapendente. JULY 16. At Radicofani. JULY 17. At San Quirico. JULY 18-19. At Siena. JULY 20. At Marti. JULY 21. At Pisa. JULY 22. At Lucca. JULY 23. At the March of Sarzana. This day we crossed by the Bertrand gate. JULY 24. At Bracco. JULY 25. At Sestri. JULY 26. At Recco. JULY 27. At Genoa. JULY 28. At Recenso. JULY 29. At Saono. JULY 30. At Cortemiglia. JULY 31. At Carentina. AUGUST 1. At Asti. AUGUST 2. At Turin. AUGUST 3. At San Ambrogio. AUGUST 4-7. At Suse. AUGUST 8. We crossed at Mont-Cenis, and came to Termignon. AUGUST 9. At St-Michel. AUGUST 10. At Aiguebelle. AUGUST 11. At Chambéry. AUGUST 12. At La Tour-du-Pin. AUGUST 13. At St-Antoine-de-Vienne. AUGUST 14. At Vienne. AUGUST 15. At the same, and we celebrated the feast of the Assumption of the Blessed Mary. AUGUST 16. At Lyons. AUGUST 17. At Bragelle. AUGUST 18. At Thizy. AUGUST 19. At Marcigny. AUGUST 20. At Pierre-fitte. AUGUST 21. At Decize. AUGUST 22. At Nevers. AUGUST 23. At Cône. AUGUST 24. At Gien. AUGUST 25. At Lorris. AUGUST 26. At Cepoi. AUGUST 27. At Nemours. AUGUST 28. At Melun. AUGUST 30. At Paris. AUGUST 31. At Senlis. SEPTEMBER 1. At Compiègne. SEPTEMBER 2. At Noyon. SEPTEMBER 3. At Villeneuve-du-Roi. SEPTEMBER 4. Beauvais. SEPTEMBER 5. At Gisors. SEPTEMBER 6. At Noyon-sur-Andelle. SEPTEMBER 7. At Ste-Catherine. SEPTEMBER 8. We were received with a procession at Rouen, and this day in the cathedral church we celebrated mass in pontificals.[4]

SEPTEMBER 9. At Déville. This day, of his own free will, Robert Hélène resigned the church at St-Aubin-d'Hoquetot into our hands. Present were:

[3] Bonnin, pp. 749-54. This long papal bull forbade that bishops be by-passed in cases of appeal and forbade absolution of those excommunicated by their own bishop, officials, or archdeacons. The bull was further implemented by an agreement regulating the customs of the Province of Rouen. See entry for June 26, 1256, which confirmed Eudes' right to visit his province as he saw fit; in practice, he did so only at three-year intervals.

[4] Eudes departed from Rouen on January 29, 1253/54 and did not return until September 8, 1254. Thus he was away for 252 days, about 120 of which were spent near the Pope.

the archdeacon; Masters Robert and Peter; Dom Ralph of Quévry, canon of Rouen; and many others.

SEPTEMBER 10-16. At Déville. SEPTEMBER 17. At St-Saëns, at our own expense.

SEPTEMBER 18. We visited the nuns of St-Saëns. In residence are fifteen nuns, two lay sisters, and one lay brother. One nun is dwelling alone at St-Aubert. We enjoined that another nun be sent to her. When they leave the priory the nuns sometimes stay away for two weeks or even longer, and by themselves. Since the one was stolen from the chapter, they have no French copy of the Rule. They sometimes eat meat when there is no need, but this is because of their poverty. They have keys, but they say that they keep what is under key with the permission of the prioress. They owe about one hundred pounds. They have four carucates[5] of land and one hundred pounds in rents. A nun assists the priest at Mass.[6] We enjoined them to correct all of these things. Their priest is incontinent; we enjoined them to get another. Dom Luke, the priest, is their confessor. The prioress eats in the infirmary more often than she does in the refectory. We enjoined them to correct all of these matters.

We spent the night at Neufchâtel, at our own expense.

SEPTEMBER 19. At the same, and we conferred Holy Orders. SEPTEMBER 20. At Aliermont.

SEPTEMBER 21. At the same. This day we invested Morel, our clerk, with the prebend which had belonged to Master Peter, called L'Archevêque, in the name of Master John, surnamed Bordet, canon of Quinze-Marcs. Present were: Brothers Harduin, Adam, and Walter, of the Friars Minor; and Morel himself, our clerk.

SEPTEMBER 22. At the same.

SEPTEMBER 23. At Auffay, at our own expense. This day at Aliermont Master Walter, called le Gros, canon of Sauqueville, resigned into our hands the share which he had in the church at Criquetot. Present were: Master Robert, canon of Rouen; Brothers Harduin, Adam, and Robert; and Everard, rector at Cravençon.

SEPTEMBER 24-26. At Déville. SEPTEMBER 27-28. At Louviers. SEPTEMBER 29-30. At Frênes. OCTOBER 1-2. At the same.

---

[5] See entry for September 27, 1253, note 30.

[6] No woman was to presume to ascend to the altar or to minister to a priest (*Corp. jur. can., Decretal. Greg. IX* Lib. III. tit. 2. cap. 1).

OCTOBER 3. We visited the chapter at Les Andelys[7] Four vicars are there, one of whom sings Mass daily at La Culture, while another sings Mass at Ste-Madeleine. The other two sing Mass at the church in Les Andelys, one of them celebrating the morning Mass, the other the High Mass. They do not celebrate High Mass, as is ordered, with deacon and subdeacon, for their parishioners. The canons requested us to be permitted to sing Nones immediately after Mass, and we consented, since more would be present at Nones [at that hour] than if Nones were sung at another hour. The vicars do not wish to receive their capes at the order of the dean, nor to sing the Responsaries;[8] we ordered this corrected. They are too fast in chanting the alternate verses of the Psalms; we enjoined that this be corrected. Some of them do not confess to their dean; we enjoined them to confess to him in the future, at least once a year, or at all events to confess with his permission. Master Robert is a drunkard. Dom Peter, the sacristan, is also a toper, and quarrelsome withal. Dom Miles is too hasty of temper. The common pennies,[9] and those which are owed to the church, are badly looked after; we enjoined them to collect these. Item, Master Richard does not reside in his church, although he is bound to, unless he should be at the schools or on pilgrimage; but he is neither at the schools nor on pilgrimage; indeed, some counsel should be taken that this statute of the chapter be observed.

This day we spent the night at Sausseuse.

OCTOBER 4. At Sausseuse.

OCTOBER 5-6. At Frênes. On the latter day Gilbert, priest at Boisemont, took oath and promised that without the clamor of a trial he would regard his church as resigned should he again fall back into the sin of incontinence of which he had been denounced, and should he not be able to purge him-

[7] This was a chapter of canons not bound to residence. Their duties were performed by vicars, each of whom received a portion of the revenues of the benefice of the canon for whom he was substituting.

[8] They did not wish to wear the cope, or cape, for liturgical services. There are three methods used to describe the usages of liturgical chant: (1) direct, or the chant as a whole; (2) antiphonary, or alternating choirs; (3) responsonary, or the choir responding to one voice. In the last, one voice intoned, the choir answered, and so on alternately. This could also apply to the portions of the Mass, e.g., the Gradual, the Gospel, the Preface, where answers are necessary. ("Chape," "Responsorial," *Dict. d'arch. chrét. et de lit.*, III[1], 365-81; XIV[2], 2389-93.) Possibly the canons did not wish to pay the customary fees demanded by the dean. ("Chape, droit de," *Dict. de droit canon.*, III, 519-21.)

[9] The donations made by the faitful and deposited in the money box of the church for the common use of the canons. A separate box was for the church use.

self. He promised that he would never reassert a claim to the said church. William, priest at Ecouis, took the same oath. We have letters of resignation from both of them. William, rector of the church at Fontenay, made the same promise, and he is suspended until the feast of All Saints. Item, Master John, rector of the church at Sauchy, put up a forfeit of ten pounds to be used at our discretion, if he should again be denounced for incontinence and be unable to purge himself legally.

OCTOBER 7. At the same. This day Peter, priest of St. Peter's at Pont-St-Pierre, swore and promised that he would regard his church as resigned and would not reassert any claim to it should he again be ill famed of incontinence; we have his letter covering this.

OCTOBER 8. At Gasny, at the expense of the priory, which we visited. This time only two monks were there and neither of them was well; the prior was not there. Sometimes they eat meat when not permitted by the Rule; we forbade them to eat meat save as the Rule permits. They do not have suitable clothing or books; we enjoined the monk who was present to tell the prior to see that this state of things was corrected. At this place we commenced to collect our procuration fees for this year. Our total procuration expense was four pounds, twelve shillings, four pence, all of Paris.

OCTOBER 9. At Juziers, at the expense of the priory. Total expense for procuration: one hundred eighteen shillings, eight pence, of Paris.

OCTOBER 10. At the same, but at our own expense.

OCTOBER 11. We visited the same. At this time there were only five monks in residence, and of these three were priests. One had gone away with the former prior, who has now been made an abbot. They are short one priest; we enjoined the cellarer and the sacristan to tell ... [lacuna in MS], the abbot, to give them a priest, and to take his nephew back to the abbey[10] so that there he might learn his religious duties.

This day we spent the night at the abbey of St-Martin-de-Pontoise, at our own expense.

OCTOBER 12. We celebrated the holy synod in the church of St-Martin-de-Pontoise, and this day we also spent the night at the aforesaid abbey, and at our own expense.

OCTOBER 13. At the same, at our own expense.

OCTOBER 14. At Juziers, and this day the canons of Gaillonet paid us

[10] St-Père-de-Chartres. on which Juziers depended.

one hundred ten shillings of Paris as our procuration fee, although, had we desired it, they should be held for all that we expended that day, for they owe full procuration. However, since they are poor, and since we had a large following with us on this occasion, we remitted them the balance.

OCTOBER 15. At St-Martin-la-Garenne. This day Stephen, priest at Commeny, who had abjured his concubine, by whom he had had children, and who had in good faith promised . . . [*lacuna in MS*], the archdeacon of the place, that should he fall into sin with her again, he would regard his church as resigned, and who later did relapse, as he confessed before us, was warned by us to resign his church. Present were: the said archdeacon and the treasurer; Master Peter of Aumale, canon of Rouen; Brother Walter of the Friars Minor; and Morel, our clerk. Stephen asked that a time be set for the consideration of this matter, and we granted that he might come for this purpose to the synod at Rouen; meanwhile we suspended him. This day, we received our procuration there. Our expense total was six pounds, twelve pence of Paris.

OCTOBER 16. At the same, but at our own expense.

OCTOBER 17. At the same, and we visited there. Five monks are in residence; all of them are priests. They do not observe the fasts of the Rule; they eat meat when there is no need; we enjoined them to observe the statutes of the Rule covering these matters. Three times a week they dispense alms to all who may come to the gate. They owe about one hundred twenty pounds. The prior is supporting one of his relatives at the schools at Paris out of the priory revenues. We enjoined them to read the Rule, to wit, one chapter every day after Prime; to read the martyrology also. This day we received our procuration at Sausseuse. Our expense total: one hundred eighteen shillings of Paris.

OCTOBER 18. We visited at Sausseuse, where there are twelve canons. One canon is dwelling alone at Valcarbon, another is at St-Sulpice, and a third at Haricourt; we enjoined the prior to recall them to the cloister, otherwise we would take this matter in hand ourself. The prior does not visit the priories once a year.[11] Investigating the conduct of the canons dwelling there, we enjoined him to correct this, to wit, that he should visit them at least once a year. Each day they give alms to everyone who may come. There are three sisters and one brother there. They owe three hundred pounds and more.

---

[11] This was not in accordance with the reforming statutes of Pope Gregory IX. (Bonnin, p. 648.)

We sentenced Brother Richard of Vernon, who had been rebellious and disobedient to the prior and to his companions in the priories, to eat in the refectory at the bench[12] until such time as he should be released by us or by the prior, to whom we later gave authority to do this. Brothers Adam, Eudes, Richard, and Eugene are quarrelsome, and Eugene is too greedy. Brother Adam is ill famed of incontinence. Brother Thomas of Auvergne has property and is ill famed of incontinence. The prior is negligent in visiting and in disciplining the canons of the priories, and in punishing the quarrelers; and since he had been remiss in handling the rebellion of Brother Richard of Vernon, we enjoined him to undergo suitable penance.

This day we spent the night at Frênes.

OCTOBER 19. At Frênes. OCTOBER 20. At Pont-de-l'Arche, to negotiate peace with the lord of Ivry. OCTOBER 21. At Ermentrouville. OCTOBER 22. We slept at Rouen. OCTOBER 23. At Rouen, and we celebrated the feast of St-Romain. OCTOBER 24. At Ermentrouville. OCTOBER 25. We preached a sermon to the burgesses of Rouen and spent the night at Ermentrouville. OCTOBER 26. We held the synod of the greater archdeanery in the cathedral at Rouen, preached a sermon, and spent the night at Ermentrouville. OCTOBER 27. We held the major synod, preached a sermon, and spent the night there.[13]

OCTOBER 28. We held the synod of deans, to whom we delivered our mandate concerning the canons regular: that is to say, that whenever canons regular who have a cure of souls in churches shall be removed by their superiors from the said churches, no other person charged with the cure of souls shall be dispatched there who does not bring with him a letter from us. Further, the deans shall seize all churches into our hand, after a month's time, unless someone bearing our letter shall have been installed there.[14] Item, we enjoined them, that after each time Holy Orders are conferred, they shall seize the churches of all persons and spare not those who

---

[12] For those who had been denounced in the chapter of faults and were deemed quilty by the superior. They ate at a separate table apart from the community.

[13] *Ibidem* in the next could refer either to Rouen or Ermentrouville.

[14] Canon 18 of the Provincial Council of Rouen (1231) decreed that no one, not a priest, having the cure of souls may receive his church in vicarage; nor can a priest who has the cure of souls do so except he be a perpetual vicar, and even in that case he can enter into his vicarage only with the special consent of the bishop. (Mansi, XXIII, 216.) Eudes did not want the canons regular farming out their quondam parishes.

have not presented themselves for Holy Orders, even though the said persons assert that they have permission from us or from the Pope, unless they shall see our letter granting such permission. We issued the same injunctions anent those who do not reside in their parishes. Item, we enjoined them that whenever they should seize any property into our hand, they shall not return it without our mandate, and that they shall keep for us whatever income may accrue during the interim. We particularly enjoined each one of them to inform us by letter, and before Christmas, what and how many properties he had seized into our hand, and the reasons therefore. Item, we enjoined them to seize the churches of those who, without reason, handed their churches over to a vicar for a month or two, and then went wandering about the country, to return to their churches later and stay a week and hand them over again. These we do not judge to be keeping residence. Item, that they should exact a fine of five shillings from those priests who wear short coats. Item, in the absence of the deans themselves, they shall not permit their clerks to carry out their investigations, for they [the clerks] are not bound by oath to us as the deans are. Item, that they shall not have as assistants in making investigations or instituting appointments to office of this kind any priests indifferently, but only such as are discreet. Item, as ordered in our statute, they shall enter in some large book of the church all possessions and rents, and other facts.

This day we appointed the Saturday before the feast of St. Andrew as the day when the priest at Nesle, in the deanery of Neufchâtel, shall purge himself by the oaths of ten men of his order of the vice of incontinence, and that with his sister.

We spent the night at Ermentrouville.

OCTOBER 29-31. At Déville. NOVEMBER 1. At the same, and we celebrated the feast of All Saints. NOVEMBER 2. At St-Wandrille, at our own expense. NOVEMBER 3. At the same, and at our own expense. This day, we confirmed the election of Geoffrey of Nointot as abbot of this place.[15] NOVEMBER 4. At Jumièges, at our own expense.

NOVEMBER 5. At the same, at the expense of the monastery, which we visited this day. Fifty monks are there, and all are priests but eleven. There are some who do not confess once a month; we enjoined these to drink no wine, except at breakfast, until they had conferred with us or one of our

---

[15] Geoffrey II (1255-88). (*Gallia Christiana*, XI, 181.)

penitentiaries about this. Every day they give alms to all comers. The sick are well taken care of. We enjoined that in the future some one of them, on behalf of the community, should have a transcript of the record of the accounts. They owe nothing. The amount of our procuration was seven pounds, six shillings, seven pence.

NOVEMBER 6. At St-Georges,[16] at the expense of the monastery. The amount of our procuration was one hundred ten shillings, five pence.

NOVEMBER 7. We visited at the same. Eighteen monks are in residence; one is in England,[17] and two are at St-Nicole-de-Londe. Silence is not well observed in the cloister or in the church. The cloister is not well kept from outsiders. Those who have been bled eat three times a day, leave the cloister, and enter the orchards and farm, and this without permission. They do not confess as they are compelled to by the Rule; we enjoined that, under pain of suspension, all who had not yet confessed to the abbot should do so before Christmas. There are some who do not confess once a month; we enjoined these to speak to us or to our penitentiaries about this before we should leave the abbey. They do not observe the fasts of the Rule; we enjoined that all the food left over from meals should be given to the poor, and not to the servants of the monks, as they had been in the habit of doing. Robert le France is a sower of discord, or a talebearer; Brother Nicholas Carpenter is suspected of having property. The said Robert rarely sings Mass, rarely confesses.

NOVEMBER 8-10. At Déville.

NOVEMBER 11. At the same. This day we cited by word of mouth Ascelin, priest at Aubermesnil, to stand trial on the Saturday before the feast of St. Andrew on the matter of the offenses which are entered in the other Register.[18] Present at this citation were: ... [lacuna in MS], the archdeacon; Peter of Aumale, canon of Rouen; Brother Harduin; and Morel, our clerk. Item, tomorrow will be devoted to hearing testimony about his crime.

NOVEMBER 12. At the same.

NOVEMBER 13. At Noyon-sur-Andelle, at the expense of the monastery. Total [for procuration]: one hundred seven shillings, nine pence.

[16] St-Georges-l'Abbaye [-de-Boscherville], a Benedictine abbey. (Cottineau, II, 2701-2.)

[17] Possibly at Edith Weston (Rutlandshire), which was a priory of St.-Georges. (Dugdale, *Monasticon Anglicanum*, VII, 1052.)

[18] This register has never been located and is presumed lost. See below, May 18, 1255, n. 6.

NOVEMBER 14. We visited at Noyon-sur-Andelle. Seven monks are there. They do not observe the Statutes of Pope Gregory covering the fasts and the eating of meat very well; we enjoined them to correct these things. They owe one hundred eighty pounds; however, as yet they have not received their English moneys, which amount to one hundred pounds.[19] Ralph of Falaise is negligent in singing Mass; we enjoined the prior to ask [Ralph], as soon as he shall arrive, why he sings Mass so little and to warn him to correct this. We also enjoined the prior not to drink any wine until he has done this after Ralph's arrival.

This day we stayed the night at Mortemer.

NOVEMBER 15. At Vesly, at the expense of the priory. Total [for procuration]: four pounds, ten shillings, six pence.

NOVEMBER 16. We visited there, but there is neither a prior nor a monk in residence. We ordered the dean of Vesly to seize the abbot's grange if he did not install monks and a prior there before Epiphany.

This day we spent the night at Parnes, at the expense of the priory. Total: [For procuration] one hundred nine shillings.

NOVEMBER 17. We visited at Parnes, where there are four monks. All are priests. They use meat and have feather beds; we forbade them to eat meat, except as the Rule permits them to do so. The monks and the priests have only one chalice; we enjoined the prior to buy one worth at least one hundred shillings of Paris, and we told the prior that we would lend him this amount until Pentecost. They owe thirty-five pounds.

This day, we spent the night at Sérans-le-Bouteiller. For procuration we received seventy shillings of Paris, cooking utensils, fodder for the horses, straw for our men and beasts, and wood.

NOVEMBER 18. We visited there. Only three monks are there, and there should be four; we enjoined them to tell their abbot, from us, to give them another monk. They use meat; we forbade them the use of meat, except as the Rule permits them. They have no copy of the Statutes of Pope Gregory; we enjoined them to get a copy written out.

This day we spent the night at Chaumont, at the expense of the priory of Notre-Dame. Total for procuration: six pounds, four shillings, three pence.

[19] Hendred, in the diocese of Norwich, was an affiliate of Noyon-sur-Andelle and was assessed in 1254 at a valuation of £10/10/0. (W. E. Lunt, *Valuations of Norwich* [Oxford, 1926], p. 611.)

NOVEMBER 19. We visited the priory of St-Martin-de-Chaumont, where there are two monks. They have a copy neither of the Rule nor of the Statutes of Pope Gregory; we enjoined them to see that they procure these. They eat meat when there is no need; we forbade them absolutely to eat meat except as the Rule permits them to do so. They owe twenty pounds of Tours. They have an income of about forty pounds. The prior, in truth, owes us procuration, but because of the poverty of the priory, we have remitted this for five years; however, lest we might lose our right to this, we enjoined the prior to pay to our clerk forty shillings of Paris towards our expenses.

NOVEMBER 20. We visited the priory of Notre-Dame-de-Chaumont. They eat meat; we forbade them to eat meat, except as the Rule permits. The fasts of the Rule are not very well observed; we enjoined them to a fuller observance.

This day Master Peter of Aumale, at our special mandate, visited the Maison-Dieu at Chaumont.

NOVEMBER 20. We spent the night at Liancourt. For our procuration they owe us only four pounds of Paris. This day we visited there and found three monks in residence, as is normal. They eat meat; we forbade them to eat meat save at the Rule permtis it. We found Thomas, a member of the staff and a relative of the prior, gravely defamed of incontinence, to wit, with two women of this village, one of them a married woman, the other a single woman. Item, this year he brought a woman from Frênes into the priory, while the prior and his companion were away at Chartres, although a novice was staying there, and right in front of the novice he brought her into the dormitory to have to do with her. He had relations with her in the very dormitory where the novice was sleeping. Item, he made her sleep the whole night in the priory despite the novice. Item, he bestows the goods of the house upon his concubines in the village. Because of these things we ordered the prior to remove him without question from his guest house before Christmas.

NOVEMBER 21. At St-Martin-de-Pontoise, at our own expense.

NOVEMBER 22. We visited there, at the expense of the monastery. Twenty-five monks are in residence, but the abbot should send three of them to priories. There is one deacon, one subdeacon, and two novices; all of the others are priests. They do not read the Statutes of Pope Gregory; we enjoined them to correct this. We forbade all rooms for eating purposes;

that is to say, [we ordered] that the monks should not eat anywhere but in the refectory, the infirmary, or in the abbot's room with the abbot himself. They owe eleven hundred pounds, of which six hundred pounds are at interest. They have an income of fifteen hundred pounds or thereabouts. Total for procuration: six pounds, seventeen shillings, four pence.

NOVEMBER 23. We visited the priory of St-Pierre-de-Pontoise. Five monks are there. They do not read their Rule; we enjoined them to read it. They do not possess a copy of the Statutes of Pope Gregory; we enjoined them to get one and to read it. They owe three hundred pounds to the abbot, and another hundred pounds elsewhere. They have an income of three hundred pounds. The priest at St-Pierre quarrels with his parishioners; item, he sings his Vespers while the monks are chanting [theirs], so that one disturbs the other; item, he ought to be singing Mass at the hour when he is singing or beginning to sing Matins; item, if any of his parishioners says anything to him, he takes off his vestments and stops celebrating Mass.

This day we visited the chapter of St-Mellon. Nine canons and the treasurer are in residence. Each one has his own vicar, since all of them are priests. They ought to have a deacon and a subdeacon. They are deficient in altar cloths, and there is also an insufficient number of albs and amices. We forbade the further use of silken capes. They are short of chasubles, bells, benches, and the wood for making the frame for the bells. One of the canons told us that they had agreed in chapter to set aside up to sixty pounds from their prebends to satisfy these wants and that they should have them by Christmas. Item, they have ordered the treasurer to see to these things himself. Luke, the chaplain, is known for incontinence, and sometimes he walks about the village in a supertunic. The said Luke, being on oath, admitted that he has been ill famed of two women, one of whom is now dead, and that of her, as he believes, he had a child, whom he has had brought up; also of the other woman who is still living, and that recently. We warned Luke to keep away from her; otherwise, should we hear that he had been ill famed of this matter again, we would proceed against him, as the law requires. Present at this admonition were: Master Peter of Aumale, canon of Rouen; Brothers Harduin and Walter; Master Richard of Sap; and Morel, our clerks. Dom Vincent, a vicar, requested us to restore to him the fruits [income] of two prebends which we had caused to be seized and promised that he would answer to us for the value of the fruits.

This day we spent this night at St-Martin [-de-Pontoise], and received for procuration one hundred shillings of Paris, which is the amount they owe us. They also are obliged to provide quarters furnished with beds, wood, cups, drink, and cooking utensils.

Note: The lack of a proctor, the roofing of the monastery, Bible.

NOVEMBER 24. At Wy. The priest owes us a *muid* of oats each year when we come here.

NOVEMBER 25. We visited at Villarceaux. There are twenty nuns and two lay sisters. When they have been bled they say the Divine Offices without modulation.[20] They confess five times a year at least, that is to say, according to their custom, at five annual feasts. Their book of homilies[21] and their silk copes have been pawned with the prior of Sausseuse. They owe eighty pounds. The prioress rarely arises for Matins, nor does she often eat in the refectory. She receives and spends without the knowledge of the nuns. She does not often come to chapter; we warned her to correct these faults. Item, we gave orders that one of the nuns should be elected by the community to attend the prioress when she receives [money]; that she was to keep one key [of the treasury] and the prioress another; that she was to know exactly what went into [the treasury] and that the prioress was to spend nothing without her knowledge.

This day we spent the night at St-Laurent-en-Cornecervine at the expense of the place. Total [for procuration]: four pounds, six shillings.

NOVEMBER 26. We visited there and found four monks. Sometimes they use feather beds. We found everything else to be in good condition, except that they owe forty pounds and have no funds for planting vineyards. Archbishop Hugh[22] had decreed that if, by God's grace, it should ever happen that homes were built and men dwelt in the forest of the villa of Court Cervine, such dwellers should be the parishioners of the prior of St-Laurent

[20] See above, July 9, 1249, n. 36.

[21] A homily is an explanation of a biblical text, particularly of the Gospels and Lessons (Epistles) read on Sunday by the priest to the people and explained by him. In the Middle Ages, collections of homilies were made largely on the model of Paul the Deacon's *Homilliarus, hoc est praestantissimorum ecclesiae patrum sermones sive conciones ad populum.* (Migne, *PL,* XCV, 1159-1566.) It was a book of sermons for Sundays and feast days of the saints, and used as such by the preaching clergy and as spiritual reading by others. Such collections, and there were many, were to be found in every religious community during the Middle Ages.

[22] Hugh, archbishop of Rouen (1130-64). (Gams, *Series episcoporum,* p. 614.)

and their tithes should be his, saving the archiepiscopal rights. Archbishop Robert[23] confirmed this.

This day we spent the night at La Roche-Guyon, and for procuration we received forty shillings of Paris as well as the other things to which we are entitled there.

NOVEMBER 27. At Frênes. NOVEMBER 28. At Ermentrouville.

NOVEMBER 29. At the same. This day at our palace at Rouen, Richard, rector of the church at Nesle, who had been personally and peremptorily cited to appear before us at Rouen on the Saturday before the feast of St. Andrew to purge himself, with the aid of ten oath helpers of his order, of the vice of incontinence with Mary, his own sister, and with the wife of his nephew, seeing or recognizing that he would not be able to purge himself in this matter took oath that he would submit to whatever punishment we should inflict for the said crime whether as regards his estate, his body, or his church. Present at this action and oath: the archdeacon Reginald, Brother Harduin, Master Richard of Sap, and the priest at Berville.

NOVEMBER 30. At Mont-Ste-Catherine, at the expense of the monastery, which we visited this day. There are twenty-six monks in residence. The abbot does not visit the priory of Vilaines, because the monks are poor; we ordered this corrected. Certain ones are ill famed of incontinence and of other offenses, as is reported at the other visitation.[24] The abbot says that they have promised to reform; we enjoined him to make this his particular duty. Lay folk enter the cloister. We gave orders that the cloister be better kept. The Statutes of Pope Gregory are not read; we ordered them to be read at least three times a year. They eat meat in the priories; we enjoined the abbot absolutely to forbid them to eat meat, save as the Rule permits them to do so. They do not receive any guests unless they be monks. Item, we enjoined them that some one be elected by the community to assist the prior when he makes his special and general audits. Item, it has been nearly a year since the abbot has made an audit; we ordered him to cast his accounts before Christmas or go without wine on Christmas Day. The abbot is such a wrathful and bitter man that when he presides in chapter no one dares accuse another because of his severity. The sick are wretchedly attended, nor is there any one to look out for them; indeed there is not even an infirmary. Item, he [the abbot] forbids any sick brother to have anything but

---

[23] Robert, archbishop of Rouen (1208-22). (Gams, *Series episcoporum*, p. 614.)
[24] See entry for September 20, 1253.

bread and water. Guests are not well provided for. The cellarer is careless about serving wine to guests; item, [the guests] get wine in unequal a-mounts. The monks are not sufficiently well clothed or shod. Item, the abbot compels his monks to be bled in Advent[25] and then to attend Matins and all other Hours. Item, nothing is given to the bled monks, except in the measure that it is given to those who are not bled. We received procuration. Total: seven pounds, five shillings, six pence.

Memo: John of Servaville, subprior; Robert of Bos-Herbert.

DECEMBER 1. At Pont-de-l'Arche anent our business with the lord of Ivry.[26] DECEMBER 2. At Quévreville, and we received procuration there. Total: eight pounds, seven shillings, three pence. DECEMBER 3. At Mont-Deux-Amants. DECEMBER 4. At Le Bord-Haut-de-Vigny. DECEMBER 5. At St-Denis in France. DECEMBER 6. At Paris. DECEMBER 7. We went to meet the king of England, who was en route to Paris.[27] DECEMBER 8-11. At Paris. DECEMBER 12. At St-Denis in France. DECEMBER 13. At Pontoise. DECEMBER 14. At Limay. DECEMBER 15. At Gaillon. DECEMBER 16. At Louviers. DECEMBER 17-18. At Ermentrouville. DECEMBER 19. We conferred Holy Orders at Grandmont. DECEMBER 20. At Frênes. DECEMBER 21. At Chaumont. DECEMBER 22. At Chambly. DECEMBER 23. At St-Leu-d'Essérent. DECEMBER 24. At Creil with the lord king. We celebrated Christmas. DECEMBER 25. At Creil. DECEMBER 26. At Chaumont. DECEMBER 27. At Frênes. DECEMBER 28. At Pont-de-l'Arche. DECEMBER 29. At Mont-Deux-Amants, at the expense of the priory.

DECEMBER 30. We visited there. Twelve canons are in residence, of whom

[25] This abbot was acting contrary to general monastic practice in bleeding. The general rule was that monks were not bled during Advent, the three days before Christmas, Lent, Easter, Pentecost, or special feast days.

[26] See entry for October 20, 1254. There is no explanation of the nature of the business to be contracted.

[27] Henry III, king of England, became the brother-in-law of Louis IX by his marriage to Eleanor of Provence. At this particular time, Henry's son Edward was at Bordeaux for his marriage to Eleanor of Castille. Here he was joined by his father. Edward requested permission from Louis to travel overland and thus avoid a long sea journey for his bride. Louis invited him to Paris. Thus Henry III, his son, Edward, and his bride stopped off at Paris on the invitation of the king of France. Archbishop Eudes attended the gathering as a vassal of both kings. At this stage, he does not seem to have been in the special entourage of Louis. Probably at this meeting of the crowned heads of both countries there was laid the basis for the Treaty of Paris (1259). On December 24-25, Eudes was with Louis IX, and his close association with the king can probably be dated from this time.

eight are priests. They owe about one hundred pounds; one hundred pounds of collectable debt is owed to them, and there is also a bad debt of fifty pounds. The sick are ill-attended. Brother William Barbot becomes wrathful after drinking wine. Item, Matthew is a grumbler. This day, we spent the night at Pont-de-l'Arche.

DECEMBER 31. At Bec-Hellouin. JANUARY 1. At the same.

JANUARY 2. We visited there and found about eighty monks in residence. They do not read the Statutes of Pope Gregory; we enjoined them to read them. In the priories they do not well observe the fasts of the Rule, and they eat meat. All other things are in good condition.

JANUARY 3. At Pont-Audemer.

JANUARY 4. Here begins the visitation of the diocese of Lisieux. We visited at Grestain, where there are twenty-eight monks. We enjoined them to accuse one another [in chapter], for they were not in the habit of doing this very well. Two monks who serve the church sleep in it. At least three times a week they dispense alms to all comers. They have an income of two thousand pounds. They owe but forty pounds, and more than that is owed to them. The abbot, who is very old and nearly blind, does not celebrate Mass; however, he receives the Blessed Sacrament every Sunday. We received procuration there this same day. Total: one hundred thirteen shillings, five pence.

JANUARY 5. We visited the abbey of St-Léger-des-Préaux. Forty-five nuns are there, which is the number required by their statute. They take but three vows; to wit, renunciation of property, chastity, and obedience. We forbade them to celebrate the feast of the Innocents because of the customs contrary to the Rule. The nuns go out alone to the homes of relatives. We forbade them to do this in the future. They do not all eat the same food in the refectory; we ordered them to serve the same food to all, so far as that was possible. The abbess does not compute with the community; we enjoined her to draw up a statement of expenses and receipts several times a year, and this with the assistance of some of the sisters elected by the community. The abbess does not eat in the refectory save at the time of the great feasts. This same day we received procuration at this abbey. Total: six pounds, fifteen shillings, seven pence.

JANUARY 6, that is to say, on the feast of the Epiphany, we visited the abbey of St-Pierre-des-Préaux. Thirty monks are there. All are priests but five. Those who are not priests receive the Blessed Sacrament every Sunday.

One of the monks is sleeping alone in the cellar; we enjoined that either another should be sent to sleep there with him, or that he not be permitted to sleep there in the future, since it is unbecoming for a monk to sleep alone. They do not observe the fasts in the priories, and they eat meat there; we enjoined the abbot to see that this was corrected. The only alms supply consists of the leavings from the table and eighteen small loaves of bread a day. They owe about four hundred pounds. We received procuration there this same day. Total: six pounds, seven shillings, one penny.

JANUARY 7. We visited the abbey of Cormeilles, where there are twenty-four monks. They have only one priory in the kingdom, to wit, the "Egyptian."[28] All are priests, with the exception of two novices. They rarely sing private Masses; we enjoined the abbot to have this corrected, even by holding back their wine if necessary. The Statutes of Pope Gregory are not read; we enjoined them to read them at least three times a year. One does not accuse another [in chapter]; we enjoined the abbot to correct this. Alms are given daily to all comers. They owe about six hundred pounds and more. A former abbot is staying at Paris with two monks, and he has an income of two hundred fifty pounds; nor does he submit any account of his income. We must speak about this to the lord bishop. The same abbot is ill famed of incontinence. This same day we received our procuration there. Total for procuration: seven pounds, less nine pence.

Note: we must speak with the lord bishop about the former abbot of Cormeilles.

JANUARY 8. We received procuration at Beaumont-en-Auge. Total for procuration: six pounds, four shillings, ten pence.

JANUARY 9. We visited the priory of Beaumont, where there are thirteen monks. There are some who do not celebrate their Masses even once every two weeks. Item, they are negligent about confession; we enjoined the prior to correct these things, and to be diligent about it. The Statutes of Pope Gregory are not read; we ordered them to be read as the Statutes require. The cloister is not well kept from outsiders. Item, the monks leave the cloister and walk about the farm alone and without permission; we ordered the prior to correct this. They are all too remiss in observing the fasts, and at times they eat meat; we ordered Pope Gregory's Statutes covering these matters to be observed. We ordered the prior to prepare an itemized statement of his accounts three or four times a year.

[28] Ste-Marie-Egyptienne, near Pont-Audemer. (Cottineau, II, 2787.)

This day, we received procuration from St-Hymer. Total: six pounds, eighteen shillings, one penny.

JANUARY 10. We visited at St-Hymer. In residence are twelve monks and a layman who wears a monk's garb; we enjoined them to bring their number up to the statutory figure, that is to say, to thirteen. They do not read the Statutes of Pope Gregory; we enjoined them to read them three times a year. All but two are priests; they eat meat very freely, to wit, half of them during one week, the other half during the next; we enjoined them to observe their Rule and Pope Gregory's Statutes in this matter. About as much is owed to them as they owe; they have an income of about four hundred pounds.

This same day we received procuration from the priory of Blangy, from which priory, because of the poverty of the place, the monks have been recalled to the priory of St-Hymer. Total for this procuration: six pounds, five pence.

JANUARY 11. We came to Lisieux and visited the abbey of the nuns. There are twenty-eight nuns who have their proper habits, as they ought to have. They confess too rarely; they promised us that in the future they would both confess and receive Communion at least once a month. Three times a week they go into the infirmary to eat meat there. Three of them have some income of their own; we enjoined these not to keep this, except on the order of their abbess. They have an income of five hundred pounds. We enjoined the abbess to cast her accounts with the assistance of some of the sisters elected by the community. They owe about thirty pounds. Item, we enjoined the abbess that sometime she should collect from each nun the keys of her coffer, and to inspect these coffers to see whether they had any personal property. Two or three of the nuns are not on speaking terms with the others. This same day we received procuration from the bishop, but we could not find out how much we spent, because our servants could not find anyone who was willing to compute our expenses.

JANUARY 12. We preached a sermon in the hall of the lord bishop to a gathering of members of the chapter, of clerks-choral, and certain others. After the sermon, and when the clerks-choral and others had gone away, we made an investigation concerning the general state of the church; the performance of Divine Offices at the church itself; the books; and the ornaments, of which they had a sufficient number. We found that they chant the Psalms too hurriedly, and that sometimes there are done in the church the small penances which are exacted from those canons who receive commons[29] but not from the others; we enjoined that the ordinance of the legate[30] concerning this matter be observed by them. Subsequently we called in each rector or canon separately and made inquiry concerning the conduct and habits of the canons and clerics of the said church, and we discovered that Nicolas Corpin had been denounced for incontinence, as was William le Turc; and so was Stephen, the official of the dean, of a certain Wilhelmina and of yet another. Item, the same of Stephen, the dean's clerk, of a mother and her daughter. Item, the same is true of the canons, that is to say, of John Coypel and certain others. On the basis of this inquiry we enjoined that the canons make a diligent investigation on their own part, and that if they found these things to be true, to correct them. For, since we did not have full proof of these things, we were unwilling to go ahead and discipline the aforesaid abuses. This day after dining, we revealed to the bishop and to certain of the canons some secret things which demanded correction. This day the chapter gave us procuration, and there dined with us, the precentor, Archdeacon Nicholas, Archdeacon William, and the official of Lisieux. Total for procuration: eleven pounds, seventeen shillings, five pence.

JANUARY 13. We received procuration at Ste-Barbe. Total: seven pounds, less fifteen pence.

JANUARY 14. We visited there. They have one canon dwelling alone in a certain priory, but there is a reason for this, so we permit it for the present. Thirty-four canons are in residence. All are priests, with the exception of the novices. Sometimes the novices make their profession before the end of the year;[31] we enjoined the prior to observe the written Rule in this matter. All the novices, according to custom, receive Holy Communion every Sunday, having made their confessions previously. They are diligent in putting aside one-tenth of all the grain that is used in the house, and they distribute it as alms. They are obligated for an old debt of six hundred pounds and also for a new one of three hundred pounds; but the prior does not believe that any more of the old debt will be demanded again.

[29] See above, August 28, 1252, n. 13.

[30] Probably this refers to statutes drawn up by Pierre de Colmieu, archbishop of Rouen (1237-44). For a short biography see "Colmieu (Pierre de)," *Dictionnaire d'histoire et de géographie ecclesiastique,* ed. A. Boudrillart and others (Paris, 1912), XIII, 274-75, and the bibliography appended thereto.

[31] I.e., before the end of their year of probation.

This day we received procuration at Crouttes. Total: six pounds.

JANUARY 15. We visited there. Two monks from Jumièges are in residence. They have an income of one hundred forty pounds. Sometimes they eat meat; we forbade them to eat meat, save as the Rule permits. They owe about sixty pounds; likewise, about sixty pounds is owed to them. However, they have this year's grain and all of last year's.

This day we visited at Tichreville, where there are two monks from St-Wandrille. On some days Mass is not celebrated by either of the monks; we enjoined them to make arrangements so that Mass is celebrated daily by at least one of them. They have only such ornaments, books, and chalices as belong to the parish. They have no copy of the Rule; we ordered them to have one written out, and that quickly. They do not observe the fasts of the Rule well, and they eat meat when there is no need; we enjoined them to a better observance of the fasts, and to abstain from meat as the Statutes of Pope Gregory require. They have an income of eighty pounds;[32] they owe about thirty pounds. We enjoined them to procure books, vestments, and a chalice, so that they can celebrate Mass whenever they desire without using the ornaments of the parish. Total for procuration: seven pounds, eight shillings.

JANUARY 16. We visited the abbey of St-Evroult. Thirty-three monks are in residence. They have nine priories. Eighteen of them are priests. They do not read the Statutes of Pope Gregory; we enjoined them to read these three times a year. One does not accuse another [in chapter]; we ordered this corrected. Traveling monks and those who are in the priories do not observe the fasts of the Rule; we enjoined that this be corrected. Sometimes they eat meat, especially in the priories; we enjoined them to observe Pope Gregory's Statutes in this mater. They owe ... [lacuna in MS]. This day we received procuration there. Total for procuration: nine pounds, fifteen pence.

JANUARY 17. We received procuration at Bernay. Total for procuration: six pounds, six pence.

JANUARY 18. We visited there, where there are seventeen monks. They have two priories this side of the sea, and one in England.[33] We enjoined

---

[32] According to the visitation of January 26, 1249/50, the priory had an income of £160. The manuscript spelling of this date is Ticheville.

[33] Bernay had two priories in England: Eye in Suffolk and Everdown in Northamptonshire. (Dugdale, *Monasticon Anglicanum*, II, 775, 1051.)

the abbot to visit the priories in this kingdom at least once a year. All but one of them are priests. One does not accuse another [in chapter]; we ordered this corrected. Sometimes the bailiff eats and drinks in the seneschal's room; we ordered this corrected. They eat meat when there is no need; we enjoined them to observe Pope Gregory's Statutes in this matter. On Mondays and Saturdays alms are given to all comers, on Tuesdays to all lepers, and on Thursdays to all poor scholars. They owe two thousand pounds.[34] We enjoined the abbot to associate with himself some of the brothers elected by the community in taking in receipts, whether from loans or any other source, incurring any expenses, or in making a statement of expenses. They have an insufficient supply of wine.

This ends the visitation of the diocese of Lisieux.

Returning from our visitation of the diocese of Lisieux, we received procuration at Corneville. Total for procuration: six pounds, less one penny.

JANUARY 19. We visited at Corneville.[35] They have three canons dwelling alone in three parishes of our diocese. Ten canons are continuously in residence in the abbey itself. All are priests but three. Those who are not priests receive Holy Communion only three times a year. One does not accuse another [in chapter]. They leave the cloister without permission; we enjoined that this be corrected. They have no infirmary. Alms are given to all comers three times a week. They owe about one hundred pounds; one hundred sixty pounds is owed to them in accounts receivable. The chapter house, the monastery, and the stables need reroofing; we enjoined the to correct this. Brother Henry did not wish to take a priory when the abbot ordered him to do so. He was disobedient. William Mignot, who was the bailiff, resigned his office without permission, on the ground that his time was too valuable, and was unwilling to assume it again even at the abbot's command. Item, after he gave up his office as bailiff, he bought a cape which he did not wish to hand over to the abbot. Item, Thomas has his own cape which he likewise is unwilling to give to any of his fellow canons. Convoking the entire community in chapter a bit later, we compelled the said Henry to accept penance for the aforementioned disobedience, ordering him to receive discipline every week day from the abbot or the hebdomadary,

---

[34] This was probably due to the repairs necessitated by the great fire reported on January 30, 1249/50.

[35] An Augustinian house colonized from St-Vincent-du-Bois c. 1143. (Cottineau, I, 879.)

and to fast on bread and water the first three Fridays of Lent. Item, we enjoined the abbot to seize the capes of the said William and Thomas and, by virtue of obedience, he was not to return them again, but only such capes as might be given to anyone, and, further, to take away from them the keys of their boxes and coffers.

This day we received procuration today from Bourg-Achard. Total: six pounds, seven shillings, seven pence.

JANUARY 20. We visited at Bourg-Achard. Eleven canons are there, and one from Ste-Madeleine at Rouen. They have one of the canons dwelling alone in a priory or parish; we enjoined the prior either to give him a companion or else to recall him to the cloister. Those who are not priests receive Holy Communion only three times a year; we enjoined these to do so at least once a month. Both the priests and the others confess too rarely; we enjoined both the priests and the others to confess at least once a month. In general, alms are given to all comers; that which is left over from the refectory and by the guests is given to the lepers. They owe about one hundred pounds, and about as much is owed to them. They have sufficient provisions to last until the new harvest. We learned afterwards that the canons who have cure of churches return from their churches to the priory whenever they desire, spend money at their own discretion, and do not go over their expenses with the prior; we enjoined the prior to see to it that this was corrected.

This day we spent the night at Déville.

JANUARY 21. At Déville.

JANUARY 22. We visited at St-Amand. Forty-four nuns are there, and they agreed that four more will be there. The older ones accuse the others [in chapter], but that is all; we enjoined them all to accuse each other [in chapter] without exception. They take three vows, that is to say, of obedience, poverty, and chastity; we enjoined the abbess that when they were being professed[36] no additional vows were to be taken. Item, we enjoined the abbess to collect all the keys of the coffers several times a year, to inspect these coffers to see if any personal property was being kept therein, to do this when the nuns were not present, and, if anything needed correction, to correct it. The abbess has not drawn up an account for the last three years. They have an income of twelve hundred pounds; they owe four

---

[36] For the ceremony of profession see Andrieu, *Le Pontifical romain au moyen âge*, III, 411-25.

hundred pounds, because of the aquaduct which they have just built and which they needed. They neither confess nor receive Holy Communion every month as we previously ordered them to do;[37] we enjoined them to do so the first Sunday of the month, after previously confessing their sins to their confessor. We enjoined the abbess to write out a statement of receipts and expenses and to cast her accounts two or three times a year in the presence of some of the nuns elected by the community. We enjoined the nuns that if it happened that they made alms purses, they were not to be given away save with the permission of the abbess, nor indeed should they keep them for themselves.

This day we spent the night at Déville, at our own expense.

JANUARY 23. We visited the priory of St. Mary Magdalene at Rouen. Ten canons and one sick man are there. The Statutes requiring the holding of chapter on Fridays, and of confessing and receiving Holy Communion once a month, are quite well observed so far as the sisters[38] are concerned. We enjoined the prior to associate some elected member of the community with him whenever he casts the accounts with the canon who purchases for the community. Brother Nicholas of Godarville has been sent to Bourg-Achard because of his incontinence. Roger of Berville would willingly stir up trouble if he could find any confederates.

This day we spent the night at Déville, at our own expense.

JANUARY 24, that is to say, Sexagesima Sunday. We preached in the cathedral at Rouen and ate at our palace there, and later we returned this day to Déville to spend the night.

JANUARY 25-27. At Déville.

JANUARY 28. We visited the abbey of St-Ouen-de-Rouen. There are fifty monks attached to the abbey, including those who are present at St-Michel. Thirty-five are in priories. One monk is dwelling alone at St-Giles; we enjoined the abbot either to recall him to the cloister or to send him a companion. All are priests but eleven. There are some who do not confess once a month; we enjoined the confessors to give us the names of those, before they dined. Item, some are inexcusably negligent in celebrating Masses; we enjoined these to speak with us about this matter before we left the abbey. They do not observe the fasts of the Rule in the priories, and

[37] See entry for December 1, 1251.

[38] Since Ste-Madeleine was a hospital, sisters were in residence as part of the community.

they eat meat, as they occasionally do at the abbey; we enjoined the abbot to see that they observed the Statutes of Pope Gregory in this matter. Item, we enjoined them that no one was to absent himself from Compline, or to drink after Compline. Item, we enjoined them not to eat in rooms, or with guests, though they might provide the guests with their requirements. They keep their pelisses because they have to, for they do not receive a new one every year, but only one every two years. However, the monk in charge of the clothing told us that they never return them, and therefore we enjoined them that whenever they wish to be rid of these, they should hand them over to the monk in charge of the clothing shop or to the almoner. They owe two thousand three hundred thirty-three pounds, six shillings, two pence, over and above what is owed to them. The abbot is negligent about attending chapter; rarely eats in the refectory, and seldom arises for Matins. The kitchener and the other officials cast their accounts only three times a year; that is too seldom. The sick are not well cared for, nor do they have an infirmary. The same abbot has conferred, by his own seal, three more pensions on three advocates.[40] The chapter seal is very freely employed in conferring benefices and pensions. We enjoined those negligent in confessing and in receiving Communion to undergo the penance which we deemed should be imposed. They have keys for their boxes and for their coffers. One hundred shillings were found in the coffer of Brother Roger de St-Aniane. Item, he is a sower of discord. We enjoined the confessors to warn those who were negligent in confessing to make their confession within three days, or to take their wine from them until such time as they did confess; similarly they should, each month, take wine away from all who had not confessed. Later we issued the same order to the abbot and to the entire community. Item, we gave orders that anyone who had not celebrated Mass at least once during the week should abstain from wine until he should have done so. Item, we commanded that whoever should absent himself from Compline without manifest cause should be punished for a grave fault. Item, we ordered that whoever had no further use for his pelisse should surrender it to the monk in charge of the clothing shop or to the almoner.

---

[40] Most monasteries found it expedient to employ lawyers, due to the pressure of civil administrators. This was especially so in France after Philip Augustus. For the role and function of the lawyer, see "Avocat," *Dict. du droit canon.*, I, 1524-28. Paul Fournier, *Les Officialités au moyen âge* (Paris, 1880), has valuable material on the subject.

Item, we strictly forbade any monk to presume to eat or drink anywhere but in the refectory, the infirmary, or in the abbot's room, under any circumstances whatsoever, and not even with the guests unless these were the guests of the abbot, when, with the abbot's permission, one or two at the most might keep him company. However, we willed that the guests be suitably cared for by some honest servant. Item, we strictly ordered the kitchener to prepare his accounts in the presence of the abbot and some of the brothers elected by the community, once an week if possible, or at least once every two weeks; that three copies be made of this account, one to be kept by the abbot, one by the kitchener, and the third by the elected members of the community. Item, we strictly ordered that a general audit of the abbey finances be made at least three times a year in the presence of the abbot and some of the brothers especially elected for this purpose by the community, and that copies be made, as was stated in the case of the kitchener. Item, we strictly ordered that the seal of the chapter be applied to no document until after great deliberation, especially when the business concerns the conferring of benefices, pensions for a life time, or manors granted for a lifetime. Item, we ordered the abbot, at least three times a year, and when all were assembled in chapter and had no warning of what was toward, to collect the keys of every box and coffer, and while all remained in chapter, to go and make a personal inspection or have one made to discover if there were any personal property being kept under key, and that if he should find any, he whose property was found under key should be punished for a grave fault and everything taken away from him. Item, we ordered that the Office of the Hours be said daily to the sick, and that, likewise, Mass be celebrated daily in the infirmary chapel; that the Epistle and the Gospel be read to those who are not able to come to Mass, if they wish to hear them. Item, we strictly forbade officials to give anything in the future to the monks, and the monks to request anything from the officials, as both have been in the habit of doing, and we forbade them to receive anything from now on. We issued a general order, applicable to the traveling monks and to those who are staying in the priories, that the Statutes of Pope Gregory be observed. Item, we gave orders that every official should present a statement of his accounts at least three times a year, and that if he has any balance he should turn it over to the abbot, or keep it, with his permission.

This day we spent the night at Déville, at our own expense.

JANUARY 29. We visited at Mont-aux-Malades, where there are ten canons in residence. Item, they have ten canons in priories. All those who are in residence are priests, with one exception; we enjoined the prior that he who is not a priest should be made to confess and receive Communion once a month. There are four communities; one is composed of canons, one of healthy brothers, one of male lepers, and the fourth of female lepers. Seventeen male lepers are there, and fifteen female. The leprosary owes nothing beyond what is owed to it. With the exception of wine, they have sufficient provisions to last them until the new harvest, and they have enough wine to last until August. They have an income of about one thousand pounds.

This day we spent the night at Déville, at our own expense.

JANUARY 30. We visited the priory of St-Lô-de-Rouen. Seventeen canons are dwelling there. One does not accuse another [in chapter]; we enjoined them that, as a matter of obedience, whosoever was culpable in this respect should speak to us about it before we left the house. The cloister is not well kept; we strictly enjoined them that it should be watched more diligently, and that a guard should be placed at the cloister gate. They owe about four hundred pounds; they have an income of seven hundred pounds. The meals served in the rooms are of too sumptuous a nature. The prior rarely computes [his accounts]. We gave strict orders that none of the priests stationed in the parishes should retain possession of any property, whether rents or pennies,[41] without the permission of the prior, nor should they purchase for themselves any special wine or meat. For this reason we forbade all of them to presume to have any property, even were it only a penny. We strictly forbade all eating in the rooms, and this applies to the relatives of the canons and townsmen. We absolutely forbade women to eat in the rooms [of the priory]. Item, that some shall not eat after the others in the refectory. Item, we forbade any of them to eat or drink in any place other than the refectory, the infirmary, or the prior's chamber. Item, [we enjoined] that each month the prior should make up his accounts in a full parliament,[42] in the presence of all the canons or at least in the presence of some of the brothers elected by the community. Item, that no one, after eating, shall drink unless there be a real need for this, and then he shall go and drink in the refectory accompanied by the monk who is managing the refectory. Item, that no one,

---

[41] The pennies donated by the parishioners and put in the poor box.
[42] *Prior computet in Pallamento.*

save only the priest of the parish, shall presume to talk with women or even with strange men in the monastery; and he, as soon as he shall have celebrated Mass, shall return to the cloister, unless [delayed] by confessions or such parochial matters. Item, that no one shall presume to talk with women or with anyone else at the door of the monastery or courtyard without permission. We especially enjoined that whosoever should be found guilty of doing this should go without wine for a day. Item, in the presence of the entire community we ordered the prior to see that all these matters were diligently attended to, for if we should find that any of the canons had been guilty of the aforementioned things, and had not been disciplined by the prior, we would punish the offender for his offenses and the prior for negligence. This day we received procuration there. Total: six pounds, ten shillings.

JANUARY 31. We attended the first entrance of the Friars Minor into their new manor. After preaching to the people we celebrated High Mass in the said house. We spent the night at our manor at Rouen.

FEBRUARY 1. This day Master Richard of Sap, acting on our special mandate, and in the presence of the abbot of Aumale; Brother Gerard, his monk; Master Thibaut of Falaise; and Morel, canon of Quinze-Marcs, instructed Roger, rector of Limésy, to submit to our decision in the matter of making amends for the fact that he had failed to be ordained, for although he had sworn that he would present himself for ordination, he had not done so. He was ordered to pay forty pounds to us before Palm Sunday as a fine, or else legal proceedings would be commenced against him.

FEBRUARY 2. At Rouen. We celebrated the feast of the Purification of the Virgin. FEBRUARY 3-4. At Frênes.

FEBRUARY 5. In the presence of all our associates, we issued a verbal warning to the prior of Gisors to receive us at his priory both for visitation and procuration. He, offering no reason, asked for a delay until next Tuesday before replying to this.

This day we were at Chaumont.

FEBRUARY 6. At Pontoise. FEBRUARY 7. At St-Denis. FEBRUARY 8-11. At Paris. FEBRUARY 12. At St-Denis. FEBRUARY 13. At Pontoise. FEBRUARY 14. At Magny. FEBRUARY 15. At Frênes. FEBRUARY 16. At l'Ile-Dieu. Total for procuration: one hundred shillings, less eleven pence. FEBRUARY 17. At Pérrièrs. Total for procuration: six pounds, six pence.

FEBRUARY 18. At Beaulieu, which we visited. Thirteen canons are in residence; eleven are outside, both in England and in Normandy. Twice a week alms are given to all comers. They owe about two hundred pounds. They lack both wine and meat, and also money for setting out vineyards. But an old debt of one hundred pounds is owed to them as well as another one hundred pounds which will come due before August, so that they will be able to purchase their supplies and have their vineyard set out. We received procuration there this day. Total: six pounds, five pence.

FEBRUARY 19. At Rouen. This day, at our hall at Rouen, Master Simon of Vatteport submitted the following appeal:

Lord Archbishop, a long time ago I, Master Simon of Vatteport, cleric, was presented to you for the church of St-Martin-de-Daubeuf in the Vexin, then free and vacant, by William of Daubeuf, the true patron of this church, and by Damoiselle Margaret, his mother and guardian or curatrix of the said patron. Somewhat later I, Master Simon, received your letter of inquiry. The investigation willed and ordered by you was duly carried out and the result submitted by me to you. However, you, unjustly, did not desire to receive me for the said church: Wherefore, considering that I have been injured not a little, I appeal to the Apostolic See in writing, and place both myself and the said church under the protection of the Lord Pope.

FEBRUARY 20. We conferred Holy Orders at St-Clément [in Rouen]. This day Master Richard of Sap peremptorily assigned the Friday before Palm Sunday to the priest at Domcourt on which to reply to witnesses and the statement of witnesses. The same to the priest at Moincourt to answer the statements of witnesses.

FEBRUARY 21. At Noyon-sur-Andelle, at our own expense. FEBRUARY 22. We received procuration at St-Laurent-en-Lyons. Total: seven pounds, two shillings, ten pence.

FEBRUARY 23. We visited at St-Laurent. Fourteen canons are there. Fifteen are in priories; one canon is dwelling alone; we enjoined the prior whom we had previously enjoined on this matter[43] to sing seven penitential psalms and the Litany for his disobedience, and to receive private scourgings during the coming Lent. One of the canons is negligent in making confession, and he is a priest; we enjoined the subprior to send him to us before we left the house. They owe one hundred ten pounds. The canon in charge of the bread does not perform his duties very well. Furthermore, he is ill famed

---

[43] See entry for September 2, 1252.

of incontinence; we enjoined the prior to remove him definitely from office, and that before Martinmas. We enjoined the prior to give to the community, more satisfactorily in the future than he has been wont to do, the pittances for the double feasts[44] and for the three double responses.

This day we received procuration at Neufmarché. Total: one hundred two shillings, four pence.

FEBRUARY 24. We visited at Neufmarché, where there are four monks. We enjoined them to have at least one Mass celebrated daily at the high altar by some one of them. They have no copy of the Statutes of Pope Gregory; we enjoined them to obtain one and to confess in the manner described therein, to observe the fasts as enacted therein, and to observe the Statutes concerning the eating of meat; and if they failed in this to undergo such penances as the said Statutes require. They owe about forty pounds; they have an income of about two hundred pounds. We enjoined the prior to celebrate Mass at least once a week, or, if he cannot do this, to receive Communion at least once a week. Item, we enjoined him to cast his accounts of receipts and expenditures in the presence of his companions several times a year.

This day we visited the chapter of Gournay. We found there the dean and Master Simon; the others are not residents. We ordered Dom Robert, the hebdomadary, to assume the office of precentor. We found everything else to be in sufficiently good condition at present. This day we spent the night in the same town, at our own expense.

FEBRUARY 25. We visited the convent of nuns of St-Aubin, where there are fifteen nuns. We forbade them to receive any more nuns without our special permission, and we did this because of their poverty. We enjoined them all to wear the same kind of scapular[45] in the future. Item, we enjoined the prioress that when the novices reached their fourteenth year she should cause them to take three vows, namely, of obedience, of chastity, of poverty: that is to say, that they will live without possessing anything of their own. If they are not willing to vow these things, they shall return to the world, and a like procedure shall be followed with respect to those already received.

---

[44] The great feasts such as Christmas, Easter, Ascension Thursday, Epiphany, Purification, Annunciation, Pentecost, St. John the Baptist, All Saints, etc.

[45] The scapular is mentioned in the *Rule of St. Benedict* (Ch. 55) in connection with the tunic and the *cuculla*. It was a sort of coverall to keep the tunic clean while working in the fields. As the word indicates, it fell to the knees from the shoulders.

Note: they should be provided with a chaplain who shall receive his cure of souls from us. They owe more than thirty pounds of Paris. Agnes of Pont and Petronilla are not speaking to one another. Alice of Rouen is incontinent; she lately had a child by a certain priest of Beauvais. We issued a strict prohibition, and especially to the prioress, that none of the nuns' relatives should in the future sleep in the convent, and that if it be at all possible they should neither eat nor drink there; but if it should happen [that anyone did], then none of the nuns should eat or drink with them. Item, concerning the cleric who is staying there. We gave orders that Richilde, the cellaress, be removed from office. Item, we ordered Agnes of Pont, who is quarrelsome and a sower of discord, to put aside her hatred for Petronilla; and if she should not wish to do this and to amend her ways in certain other respects, we will and order that she be definitely removed from the community.

This day we spent this night at Bellosane, at the expense of the house. Total [for procuration]: four pounds eleven shillings, eight pence.

FEBRUARY 26. We received procuration at Beaubec.

FEBRUARY 27. We visited at Bival, where there are thirty-three nuns. We forbade them to receive any more without our special mandate, and we ordered them to send back to their homes a girl whom they had promised William of Possy to accept, and another. Because of their poverty we do not wish them to receive these girls on any condition. We forbade any of them to eat with seculars from now on. We enjoined the abbess to undergo minor penance for having permitted some of the nuns to eat with seculars since our last visitation,[46] and we promised her that we would punish her for a grave fault[47] if she should be found guilty of this matter again. They receive Communion seven times a year, and they confess at least as many times, and sometimes more often. Item, we enjoined the abbess that the nuns should not take the vows until they were fourteen years old. There were groups of two there who had not been speaking to each other; we made them make up even to the extent of kissing each other on the mouth, and we forbade them ever to mention the cause of their disagreement under pain

---

[46] See entry for September 3, 1252.

[47] Punishment for grave fault implied banishment from the common table and from common prayer (*Rule of St. Benedict*, Ch. 25). On the method of making satisfaction for grave fault see *ibid.*, Ch. 44.

of excommunication[48] for her who should make mention of it, and we enjoined the abbess to notify us. They owe fifty pounds, not counting the wages of the servants. Just after Pentecost Sister Isabelle had a child by a certain priest.

This day we spent the night at Beaussault, at the expense of the house. Total: [for procuration] four pounds, ten shillings of Paris.

FEBRUARY 28. We visited at Beaussault, where there are two monks. They have no copy of the Rule; we ordered them to see that they got one. Item, we enjoined them to observe the fasts of the Rule more fully. They eat meat freely; we enjoined them to observe the Rule in this regard, and, because of their offenses, we enjoined them to undergo the penance contained in the Statutes of Pope Gregory, and [we warned] that if they should not do this, and we found them to be delinquent again, we would punish them for a grave fault. They owe about forty pounds.

This day we spent the night at Neufchâtel. We received procuration there because of our manor at Nogent. Total: ten pounds, four shillings, five pence.

MARCH 1. We visited the hospital at Neufchâtel, where there are four canons. We enjoined them to chant their Hours, both during the day and at night,[49] with modulation, unless they should be prevented by sickness. They owe forty pounds. They have sufficient supplies, that is to say of wheat, oats, wine, beer, and cider. They have four hundred sheep, forty head of cattle, fifty pigs, and twenty-five horses, both large and small.

This day we visited Reginald, a monk of Préaux, the companion of the prior of Ste-Radegonde. They do not have a daily Mass in his priory; we enjoined them to correct this. They do not observe the Rule either as to fasting or as to the eating of meat; we enjoined them to accept the penance contained in the Statutes of Pope Gregory, should they be delinquent in this, and [we warned] that if he was not willing to do this, we would proceed against him more severely. A certain young woman is staying in his priory to prepare their meals; we ordered her to be definitely removed; and, since the prior was at St-Saëns, we enjoined the said Reginald to tell him all about these things for us.

[48] This would be grave fault according to the *Rule of St. Benedict* (Ch. 44) for which the penalty was, at times, excommunication or being cut off from the community until suitable satisfaction had been made.

[49] That is, beginning with Matins about 2 A.M. and continuing through the day to Compline, the last office for the day.

The same day we received procuration at Bures. Total for procuration: six pounds, twelve shillings, nine pence.

MARCH 2. We visited the two monks staying there [at Bures]. They have no copy of the Rule; we enjoined them to tell the prior of Pré for us to get them one. They use meat when there is no need; we enjoined them to undergo the penance written down in the Statutes of Pope Gregory covering this, whenever they should be delinquent in this matter; otherwise, we should punish them. They do not observe the fasts; we ordered this corrected. Item, women sometimes eat with them; we ordered them to keep the women away.

This day . . . [*lacuna in MS*], the dean of Rouen, seized at Tristeville fifteen pounds in rents which his men of St-Vast owed us, and he forbade them to pay this sum to us and took it himself from these men.

We spent this night at Aliermont.

MARCH 3. At Aliermont. This day Simon, rector of Vimerville, of his own free will resigned the church of Vimerville into our hands. Present were: the treasurer; Masters John of Flainville and Peter of Aumale, canons of Rouen; Brother Harduin of the Friars Minor; Master Richard of Sap; Master Abraham, rector at Grandcourt; John of Boves; and Morel, our clerk.

This same day Master Robert, rector at Rupefort, since he had heedlessly disregarded his oath and had not presented himself for Holy Orders nor taken up personal residence in his church, as he was by oath held to do, swore to abide by our decision in this matter. We at once enjoined him, by reason of the said oath, to pay to us or at our command the sum of fifty pounds of Tours for his offense, and that before the coming Michaelmas unless we should grant him a delay. He readily offered as sureties for the payment of the said fifty pounds at the said date Master Gilbert, rector at Seneville in Grand-Caux, and Dom Henry, rector at Magneville. Present were: the treasurer Masters John of Flainville, Peter of Aumale, and Giles of Picardy, canons of Rouen; Master John, canon of les Andelys; Master Abraham, rector of Grandcourt; Master Richard of Sap; Brother Harduin of the Friars Minor; Everard and Morel, our clerks; and John of Boves, our bailiff.

MARCH 4. At Aliermont. MARCH 5. At the same, but at the expense of Wanchy. The sum which Michael paid: eight pounds. MARCH 6. At the same, but at our own expense. MARCH 7. We received procuration at St-Victor-en-Caux. Total: seven pounds, seven shillings, five pence.

MARCH 8. We visited there, finding sixteen monks. One of them, because of his ill health, is not able to celebrate Mass very often; we ordered him to receive Communion frequently. Three times a week alms are given to all who ask for them. Traveling monks do not observe the fasts of the Rule, but they say the Statute concerning the eating of meat is well observed; we ordered the fasts of the Rule to be observed, both by the traveling monks and by the others. The abbot cast his accounts at Michaelmas, and this was the state of affairs: they owe but fourteen pounds, and there is owed to them a debt of one hundred pounds hanging over from last year, as well as the entire income for the present year. The abbot is ill famed of incontinence with a certain woman who, it is said, is at La Bargue, and he had a child by her. He rarely arises for Matins, confesses infrequently, and does not often eat in the refectory.

This day we spent the night at Longueville, at the expense of the house.

MARCH 9. We visited at Sauqueville. We ordered that the distributions should be made in common to all residents, and not to any others. The treasurer frequents taverns and does not keep residence; we gave orders that they should seize his prebend if it should come into the hands of the chapter, and also his share of the candles, until such time as he should receive other orders from us. We committed the care of their souls to Luke, the priest at Colmesnil, until we revoke that commission. When the treasurer does come to the church, he does not wear a cape. We ordered Ralph of Cliville to seek out a suitable chaplain to serve in his stead. Dom Walter frequents taverns. It is rumored that the treasurer, after renouncing a certain woman, has relapsed with her since his renunciation. We enjoined and warned the said Walter to keep away from taverns in the future. Item, we warned Gilbert, denounced for incontinence, to abstain therefrom. We gave orders that two parochial Masses shall be celebrated for the parishioners on the morning of each day, as well as another Mass [conventual] at the high altar. Item, we enjoined them to wait until one verse [of a psalm] has been finished before beginning the next one. Item, we enjoined the precentor to have a tablet [of offices and officers] placed in the church from now on.

This day we spent the night at Longueil, at the expense of the house. Total for procuration: seven pounds, eleven shillings, four pence.

MARCH 10. We visited there. Four monks are in residence, but there is no prior. There is some trouble about the institution of a prior, for the lord of the village wishes to see installed a prior of his own choosing, while the abbot of Tiron desires to install his own choice. Ralph, who is administering the temporalities of the place at the orders of the lord of the village, has been excommunicated by his abbot and by the official of Rouen. We warned them to abstain from eating meat, as the Rule requires, or that otherwise we would punish them as transgressors of the Rule. Item, inasmuch as the said Ralph has been a frequent offender, we ordered him to fast on bread and water for four Fridays before Pentecost. We strictly forbade women to eat at the house in the future. Likewise we ordered them to observe the Rule concerning the observance of the fasts. They owe about thirty pounds. Total for procuration: one hundred thirteen shillings, three pence.

MARCH 11. At Ouville. We received procuration. Total for procuration: six pounds.

MARCH 12. We visited there. The sick who cannot celebrate Mass do not confess or receive Communion often enough; we ordered this corrected. Item, we ordered one to accuse another [in chapter]. Item, women sometimes enter the cloister; we forbade them to enter the cloister in the future. Item, sometimes the canons go out of the cloister and towards the garden without permission; we enjoined them to correct this and to punish those who should prove delinquent. They owe about eighty pounds.

This day, at Etoutteville, we visited two monks of the Order of Lewes,[50] who are staying there. We found that they are about twenty pounds in debt, not counting the one twelfth which they owe to their abbey.[51] There ought to be three monks there, but because of an old debt, there are now only two. We made inquiry as to the becoming way of life of the servant body, asking whether women ate at the place and such other questions as we are in the habit of asking. Present were: Masters Peter of Aumale and William of Dènestanville; the priest at Doudeville who is dean of the place; Brother Harduin; and Morel, our clerk. The prior, however, protested the privileges of his order,[52] that this visitation should in no way be prejudicial to him. After his protestation he replied to all questions asked of him, and

---

[50] Of the Order of Cluny.

[51] This probably refers to St-Louis' assessement on ecclesiastical institutions to defray the expenses of his Crusade. The larger institutions, in turn, assessed the dependencies.

[52] They were Cluniacs and thus claimed exemption from visitation.

we found that everything was in a satisfactorily good condition. Total for procuration: one hundred four shillings, six pence.

MARCH 13. At Ermentrouville. MARCH 14. At Bourg-Achard. MARCH 15-16. At Bernay. MARCH 17. At Bec. MARCH 18. At Ermentrouville, near Rouen.

MARCH 19. At the same. We peremptorily assigned the Monday after the feast of St. Mark the Evangelist to Dom Amaury, priest of Courdimanche, as the day on which he should appear before us at Rouen or vicinity, if we should be there, or before our official if it should happen that we were away, for the purpose of undergoing purgation, with the twelfth hand of his order, in respect of certain crimes for which we, upon legal investigation, found him to be defamed. Present at this assigning were: Masters Stephen, the archdeacon of the French Vexin; the official of Rouen; John of Flainville and Peter of Aumale, canons of Rouen; the dean of La Chrétienté at Rouen; Hugh, our almoner; and Richard of Sap, Everard, and Morel, our clerks.

MARCH 20. At the same. In the year of our Lord 1254, the Saturday preceding Palm Sunday, postponed from the preceding Friday, which Friday was assigned to ... [*lacuna in MS*],[53] the abbot of St-Victor-en-Caux, to deal with the inquiry into his incontinence, which the duties of our office compel us to undertake against him, and especially as the day on which the said abbot shall reply whether he wishes to submit to our discretion in this matter or prefers to have the business settled by judicial process. Presented before us according to due legal process, the said abbot replied that he preferred a trial according to law and requested, before anything else, that the key to the chapter seal be restored to him. He alleged that, by our order, it had unjustly been taken from him while the case was still pending. This done, we appointed for the trial the Monday after the Sunday on which the *Jubilate*[54] is sung, that is, if it is not a ferial day; or the next non-ferial day, if the said Monday should be a ferial day; on that day we shall proceed on the business of the investigation and we shall consider the restoration of the key as the law will dictate. The trial will be held before us, or if we should happen to be away, before our official, whom we especially appoint to act in our stead. It was expressly agreed that we might consult witnesses before the said day, summoning the said abbot to appear at such

[53] William, abbot of St. Victor-en-Caux, who subsequently abdicated on December 17, 1255.
[54] The third Sunday after Easter.

examination, and whenever we deem it expedient. In the interim we shall have the said key placed in the possession of the said official. Present at this hearing and on the day and year aforesaid were: Masters John of Flain ville, John of Putot, the said official, and Peter of Aumale; Morel, our clerk; and Richard of Sap, canon of St-Candide-de-Rouen.

MARCH 21. That is to say, on Palm Sunday, at the same. We preached a sermon at St-Gildard and celebrated High Mass at the cathedral of Rouen.

MARCH 22. At the same. On this day, and in our presence, Sir Herbert of Villers appointed Reginald of Villers, esquire, to act as his attorney at the assize of Les Andelys, in his action against certain persons and until further notice. Present were: the abbot, the prior, and the precentor of St-Ouen-de-Rouen; Roger of Les Andelys and divers other monks of the same place; Master Peter of Aumale, canon of Rouen; and Master Richard of Sap and Morel, our clerks.

MARCH 23-25. At the same. MARCH 26. At the same, and at Rouen, where we blessed the Holy Chrism. MARCH 27. At the same.

MARCH 28. At the same. Now begins the year 1255. This day we celebrated Easter.

MARCH 29-31. At Frênes. APRIL 1. At Frênes. APRIL 2. At Le Bord-Haut-de-Vigny. APRIL 3. At Pont Charenton. APRIL 4. At Corbeil. APRIL 5. At Melun. APRIL 6. At the same. We celebrated the nuptials of the king's daughter with the king of Navarre.[1] APRIL 7. At Corbeil. APRIL 8-9. At Paris. APRIL 10. At Pontoise. APRIL 11-12. At Sausseuse. APRIL 13. At Louviers. APRIL 14-17. At Frênes. APRIL 18. At Déville.

APRIL 19. At the same. This day we pronounced the following sentence:

In the year of our Lord 1255, on the Monday following the Sunday on which the *Jubilate* is sung. In the name of the Father, and of the Son, and of the Holy Ghost, Amen. In the business which, by the demands of our office, we have undertaken against Henry, priest of the church at Avremesnil, who was obligated to resign the said church whenever he should be requested by us to do so, as is very evident from his letter concerning this, we, after consultation with good men and after considering all aspects of the case, with scrupulous observance of all legal requirements have declared the said Henry deprived of the said church by definitive sentence. We have many times and in proper legal form asked the said Henry to resign the said church but he, in violation of justice, has refused to do so, without presenting any reason why he is under no obligation to be so held. Present at this were: Master Peter of Ons, canon and official of Rouen; Master Richard of Sap, our clerk; Sir Robert of Normanville, knight; Clement of Senoz, citizen of Rouen; Brothers P. Hurcet, Robert of Ouville, Harduin, and Walter, our chaplains and members of the Friars Minor; Master Abraham of Dieppe; Dom Ralph, priest at Déville; William of Plessy, Everard, and Morel, our clerks; Master John of Paris, canon of les Andelys; Peter Faber and William of Betencourt, citizens of Rouen.

APRIL 20. At the same. This day, we promulgated the following sentence:

[1] Thibaut V, king of Navarre and count of Champagne, married Isabelle, second daughter of Louis IX. Later, Thibaut accompanied Louis on the crusade and was with him when he died. Thibaut died in 1270 and his queen in 1271.

In the year of our Lord 1255, on the Tuesday following the Sunday on which the *Jubilate* is sung. In the name of the Father, and of the Son, and of the Holy Ghost, Amen. This concerns the action which we, by the demands of our office, are undertaking against Stephen, priest of the church at Commeny, in the matter of depriving him of the said church. The said Stephen duly confessed that a long time ago he had, in our presence and in all good faith, promised that venerable and discreet man Master Stephen, the archdeacon of the French Vexin, that should he sin again with a certain concubine of his by whom he had had children and whom he had abjured, he would regard his aforesaid church as resigned. As he confessed that he had sinned with her after making the said promise, we warned him frequently and according to due legal form to keep the said promise. Despite such warning he refused to do what justice required, and was preremptorily ordered to stand trial in this matter before us at Rouen, or vicinity, on the Monday following the Sunday on which the *Jubilate* is sung. But he contumaciously absented himself. After consultation with good men and after considering all aspects of the case, and with a scrupulous observance of all legal requirements, we declare him to be deprived of the said church by definitive sentence. Given at Déville the Tuesday after the aforesaid, in the year of our Lord 1255, and in the presence of the following witnesses: Brothers Adam Rigaud, Harduin, and Ralph of Nef, of the Friars Minor; Masters Richard of Sap, John of Paris, and Reginald of Vicomte; Stephen, rector at Neuville-en-Bois; Hugh, our almoner; and Everard and Morel, our clerks.

APRIL 21. At Frênes. APRIL 22. At Pontoise.

APRIL 23. At the same. The following agreement was reached between the lord king and ourself: that a certain suitable person shall be delegated by the archbishop of Rouen to take up personal residence at Pontoise to hear all cases affecting the burgesses of Pontoise that pertain to the ecclesiastical forum and that are brought on the simple complaint of the parties intending the action, and to decide such cases unless they deal with forgery, sacrilege, heresy, usury, or simony, which must be heard before the archbishop of Rouen or his official and not before the aforesaid delegate. They can not bring other cases before the archbishop or his aforesaid official on simple complaint beyond the *banlieue* of Pontoise. However, proper and free appeal from the aforesaid person is permitted in all cases pertaining to his jurisdiction, in matters of both damages and sentences, from him to the aforesaid archbishop and his official. Further, the aforesaid person shall be obliged to observe the reasonable and ancient customs in the interest of the burgesses.[2]

APRIL 24. At the same. This day the priest at Domcourt instituted an appeal.[3] APRIL 25. At Magny. APRIL 26-28. At Frênes. APRIL 29. At the same. This day Nicholas appealed. APRIL 30. At the same. MAY 1-3. At Frênes.

MAY 4. At the same. We condemned the priest at Gressenville to pay us a fine of twenty shillings of Tours for being without a clerk since the feast of St. Martin Hiemalis,[4] as he himself confessed in proper legal form in our presence. Anent this fine, we personally enjoined the dean of Gamaches, who was then with us, and who had warned the said priest about this before, to receive a satisfactory surety from him, so that whenever we should demand it the fine could be paid. Nevertheless, we enjoined the said priest to provide himself with a suitable clerk before the holding of the next synod.

MAY 5-10 At Frênes. MAY 11. At Sausseuse. This day we visited Brother John, the prior of St-Michel-de-Vernonnet, whom we found to have been dwelling there alone for a long time. Thereupon we enjoined him to see his abbot before the feast of St. Peter in Chains about giving him a companion or recalling him to the abbey. And we gave him a letter, which we directed to the abbot,[5] to the effect that, unless he did this, we would take such proceedings against him as the law dictated. Item, we found that he eats meat when there is no need, that he does not observe the fasts of the Rule, and that he has a copy neither of the Rule nor of the Statutes of Pope Gregory. In the presence of the treasurer of Bayeux, of Brother Walter of Minières, and of Morel, our clerk, we warned him to refrain from eating meat, as the Statutes of Pope Gregory require, and that if he should prove delinquent in this, to undergo the penance prescribed in those Statutes. We

---

[2] There is a question whether the archdeaconry of Pontoise had been given to the diocese of Rouen by the French crown prior to Eudes' pontificate. Dom Michel du Plessis (*Description historique de la haute Normandie* [Paris, 1740], II, 175 ff.) denies it, and this after a thorough examination of the documents. What is clear is that Eudes did not exercise jurisdiction therein until his agreement with Louis IX in 1255. The best work on the question of the archdeaconry of Pontoise is by R. Genestal, "La Patrimonialité de l'archidiaconat en Normandie," in *Mélanges Paul Fournier* (Paris, 1929). Evidently the archdeaconry, up to this point, was in the hands of the king, a layman, and thus was held contrary to canon law.

[3] See entries for March 19, 1254/55, and May 27, 1255.

[4] There were two feasts of St. Martin: November 11 (*hiemalis*, winter) and July 4 (*callidus*, summer).

[5] The abbot of St-Wandrille.

warned him to observe the fasts as the Statutes demand and to procure a copy of both the Rule and the Statutes. Item, we warned him that women should not eat with him at the house in the future; item, that he should not eat in the village if it be not with religious persons or such as could not occasion any evil speaking; nor should he eat with such as these very often.

MAY 12. At St-Martin-la-Garenne, at our own expense. MAY 13. At Meulan. MAY 14. At St-Cloud. MAY 15. At Paris. MAY 16. We were at Paris with the lord king, at the feast of Pentecost. MAY 17. At the same. MAY 18. The lord king gave to us and to our successors the archdeanery of Pontoise, with all its appurtenances, in which is contained the churches listed at the end of the *Registrum ecclesiarum*.[6] See the letter on this below.

MAY 19-25. At Paris. MAY 26. At Pontoise.

MAY 27. At Gassicourt. This day Amaury, formerly the priest at Domcourt instituted the following appeal from our sentence:

Reverend Father, archbishop of Rouen, you have seriously infringed my rights in that without canonical warning you have sentenced me, Amaury, priest at Domcourt, to undergo the trial of purgation with twelve priests. Wherefore, I appeal in writing from you to the Apostolic See, and I seek *apostoli* which shall be given to me at once. If you shall deny me this, I appeal once again and in writing, and place myself and my church under the protection of the Lord Pope. Given in the year of our Lord 1255, on the Thursday after Trinity.

MAY 28. At Pacy. MAY 29. At Evreux. MAY 30. At Beaumont-le-Roger. MAY 31. At Bernay, to treat of peace with our suffragans. JUNE 1. At Bec. JUNE 2-8. At Déville.

JUNE 9. At the same. We ordered the abbot of Valmont[7] that he should not obey or permit any of his monks to obey the abbot of Hambye if he should come to the abbey of Valmont, and, as he had been in the habit of doing for a long time, if he should attempt anything against the abbot or any of the community, to the no little prejudice of his abbey and of our jurisdiction, he was not to be obeyed. When we issued these orders there were present: Masters John of Flainville and Peter of Aumale, canons of Rouen;

---

[6] The *Receuil des historiens des Gaules et de la France*, XXIII, 228-329, includes a *Polyptichum Rotomagensis ecclesiae*. The editors are of the opinion that this valuation or register was compiled by Archbishop Pierre Colmieu (1236-44). Possibly this is the *Registrum ecclesiarum* to which Eudes is refferring. The letter on Louis IX to which Eudes refers is not to be found in the Register.

[7] As head of the order, Hambye claimed jurisdiction over Valmont.

Master William of Dènestanville, canon of Bayeux; Brothers Adam, Harduin, and Walter of Minières, of the Friars Minor; and Morel, our clerk. Furthermore, we sent a letter to the prior and community of Valmont, informing them that if the aforesaid abbot of Hambye should demand of them anything more than he was entitled to by ancient custom, they were not to obey him; that even if the abbot of Valmont should command them to obey the said abbot, they were in no way to obey their own abbot.

JUNE 10. At the same.

JUNE 11. At the same. This day William, called Crespin, paid homage to us at our hall at Déville. Present and seated with us at table were Simon, archdeacon of Rouen; Reginald, archdeacon of Eu; Masters John of Flainville, Peter of Ons (our official), and Peter of Aumale, canon of Rouen; Sir Ralph of Dangute, knight; the dean of La Chrétienté of Rouen; the prior of La Salle-aux-Puelles; Brothers Adam Rigaud, Peter Hurtet, and Walter of Minières, of the Friars Minor; William, and Everard, and Morel, our clerks; Geoffrey, our steward, William, our baker, Peter of Frênes; our sergeants, and many others. We ordered him, as he was bound to do, to draw up an account of the lands he held from us, and this before the holding of the assize.

JUNE 12. We visited at Bondeville. In residence are thirty nuns, five lay sisters, two just received, three brothers, and three clerics. They receive Communion seven times a year. We enjoined them to receive Communion at least every two weeks from now on, which they promised us to do. One sister is dwelling alone in one of their granges, and one of the brothers is dwelling there alone also; on account of suspicion, we enjoined them that the sister be recalled to the house or that a companion be given to her. We forbade the sisters or any of the servants to eat in the bakehouse from now on. They owe about fifteen pounds. With the exception of potables, they have sufficient supplies to last them until the new harvest. We found that the prioress was quarrelsome and of an evil tongue, that she had no idea how to maintain discipline, and that she was even scorned by the sisters. We warned the prioress about this and advised her to improve her conduct in the future. We ordered the prioress and the subprioress to send away their grandnieces and a certain other girl.

This same day we examined Geoffrey of Tourville, cleric, presented to us by Thomas of Pavilly, damoiseau,[8] for St. Mary's church at Pavilly, who

8 See above, August 30, 1252, n. 16.

beginning at the passage *Factum est autem cum filii Dei venissent quadam die,*[9] when he came to *circuivi terram et perambulavi* and was asked to decline *circuivi,* did so as follows: *circuo, circuis, circuivi, circuere, circuendi, circuendo, circuendum, circuitum, circuitu, circuens, circuiturus, circuor, circueris.* Asked what conjugation it was, he replied, "the third." Asked what part of speech *coram* was, he said, "A preposition." Asked, further, what part of speech *stetit* was, he answered, "a verb." Asked to decline it, he replied: *sto, stas, steti, stare, standi, stando, stantum, statu, stor, staris, status sum, stari.* Asked what part of speech *factum* was, he said, "A participle." Asked of what tense, he said, "The preterite." Asked of what signification, he said, "Neuter." Asked from what it was derived, he replied, "From *facio, facis.*" Asked to decline this verb, he responded: *"Facio, facis, feci, facere, faciendi, faciendo, faciendum, factum, factu, faciens, facturus, fio, fis, factus sum, fieri, fictus, fiendus."* Item, being examined in the passage *Jurat Valerianus,*[10] he read it very badly and construed it in this manner: *"Valerianus,* Valerian; *jurat,* swears; *sponsus,* thou spouse; *podere,* to put forth; *nulla,* nothing; *detegere,* to discover. *Illa ait,* etc."

This same day Richard, priest at Nesle in the deanery of Neufchâtel, resigned his church, as he had of his own free will sworn and promised to do. Present were: Master Simon, archdeacon of Rouen; Master Reginald, archdeacon of Eu; and Master Stephen, archdeacon of the French Vexin; and Masters Giles the Picard, John of Flainville, Robert of Grainville, Peter of Aumale, and Peter of Ons, our official, all canons of Rouen. This same day we stayed this night at Déville.

JUNE 13. At Guoy. Here begins the visitation of the diocese of Evreux.

JUNE 14. We entered the diocese of Evreux and spent the night at Montaure.[11] Total of our expenses: seven pounds, seven shillings, three pence.

JUNE 15. We visited there. Only two monks are there, but there should be three at least. They have but one chalice, which serves the priest of the parish as well as the monks. They have no copy of the Rule; we enjoined them to get one. Sometimes women eat with them; we enjoined them not to allow women to eat with them at their house in the future. They eat meat freely; we enjoined them to abstain as the Rule requires, and further that

[9] Job 2:1.

[10] I have been unable to identify this passage.

[11] A Benedictine priory of St-Ouen-de-Rouen, founded *c.* 1063. (Cottineau, II, 1933.)

if they should be delinquent in this, to fast on the following Friday, as is laid down in the Statutes. They have an income of one hundred sixty pounds; they owe only thirty pounds. Item, we enjoined the prior to cast his accounts with the occasional assistance of his companion.

This day we spent the night at Daubeuf. No monks are there. Total of expenses: . . . [lacuna in MS].

June 16. We visited the priory of Beaumont-le-Roger. Nine monks are there; all but two are priests; there should be twelve, but because of the destruction of the place by fire there have been only nine since the fire. All of them eat meat three times a week; we ordered them to abstain from it completely, except in such cases as permitted by the Rule. We ordered that they should fast on bread and water on the following Friday if they should be delinquent in this matter, as is set down in the Statutes of Pope Gregory. They owe about two hundred pounds; they have an income of one thousand pounds. They talk with lay folk in the cloister; we forbade the prior to allow this practice to continue. Expense total: seven pounds, nine shillings, five pence.

JUNE 17. We visited the priory of Lierru, of the Order of St. Augustine. Seven canons are staying there; all of them are priests. They give alms to all comers three times a week. They have an income of about two hundred pounds, they owe about sixty pounds. Expense total: six pounds, five shillings, three pence.

JUNE 18. We visited the abbey at Lyre,[12] where there are sixty monks, of whom twenty-two are priests. The Statutes of Pope Gregory are not read; we enjoined them to read them at least three times a year. Traveling monks do not observe the fasts; we enjoined them to observe the Rule in this regard. They eat meat in the priories; we ordered this corrected. They have an income of two thousand pounds; they owe about twelve hundred pounds. We enjoined them that a general audit be reported to the chapter, in the presence of all; item, that particular audits be made at least once a month in the presence of the abbot and some of the members elected by the community. We enjoined the grain master to make up a statement of his receipts. Item, that the abbot had at one time contracted a loan without the consent of the chapter;[13] item, that he raged against the brothers who had

---

[12] A Benedictine abbey founded *c*. 1046. (Cottineau, I, 1694.)

[13] No prelate or superior could rightfully contract loans without the consent of the chapter (*Corp. jur. can., Decretal. Greg. IX* Lib. III. Tit. 10. cap. 1).

been corrected in chapter; item, that he was negligent in looking after the needs of the sick. We warned him about these things and ordered him to correct them, else we would proceed against him as the law permits.

JUNE 19. We came to St-Sulpice-près-Laigle, and received procuration. Expense total: six pounds, eight shillings, six pence.

JUNE 20. We visited the priory of Rai,[14] where there are two monks. They do not sleep in the same room because the prior's room is too small. The prior promised to correct this as soon as possible. Three times a week they give alms to all comers. We enjoined the prior's companion, who is not a priest, to confess and receive Communion once a month. They do not observe the fasts of the Rule; they eat meat when there is no need; we enjoined them to correct these things, as the Rule and the Statutes require. They owe about sixty-five pounds; they have an income of eighty pounds, or perhaps more. Since the accommodations were inadequate, the prior made arrangements for us at St-Sulpice. Total for procuration: six pounds, two shillings; but inasmuch as the prior was poor, we had sixty shillings given back to him.

We visited the prior and the monks of St-Sulpice the same day. Seven monks are there, of whom two have not yet made profession in the Order, although one of them was advanced to priesthood. We enjoined the monk who is not a priest to confess and receive Communion at least once a month in accordance with the Rule. They do not read the Statutes of Pope Gregory; we ordered them to read these twice a year. They use linen shirts; we forbade the professed monks to use these. They do not observe the fasts of the Rule, and all of them eat meat when there is no need; we warned the prior and the monks to observe the Rule in abstaining from meat, and to undergo the penance provide in the Statutes should they be delinquent in this. Item, that they observe the fasts of the Rule.

JUNE 21. We spent the night at Breteuil, where the steward of Tillières gave us procuration, his manor belonging to the abbot of Bec. Total for procuration: eight pounds, seventeen shillings, two pence.

JUNE 22. We visited the abbey of Conches. Twenty-eight monks are there; all but two are [professed] monks. We ordered them to read the Statutes of Pope Gregory at least three times a year. Four times a week alms are given to all comers, twice a week to clerical scholars, and once a week

---

[14] A Benedictine priory dependent on St-Taurin-d'Evreux. (Cottineau, II, 2397.)

to lepers. The fasts are not observed in the priories, and they eat meat there; we enjoined the abbot to see that the fasts are more completely observed in the priories, and to forbid them to eat meat except in such cases as the Rule permits. Item, we enjoined the abbot to make a general audit of the house affairs twice a year in the presence of some of the members elected by the community, and that audits of the various offices likewise be made in the presence of elected brothers at least once a month. They owe about three hundred pounds, and they have an income of twelve hundred pounds. Expense total: seven pounds, ten shillings, eight pence.

JUNE 23. At La Noë, a Cistercian foundation.

JUNE 24. We received procuration at the abbey of St-Taurin, but we did not visit it this day because of ill-health. Expense total: seven pounds, seven shillings, nine pence.

JUNE 25-29. At the same, and at our expense.

JUNE 30. We visited there. The abbot was in Le Cotentin at this time. Twenty-eight monks are there. The Statutes of Pope Gregory are not read; we enjoined them to read these twice a year. They have no chamberlain; we enjoined the prior to tell the abbot for us to appoint a chamberlain for them. They owe about two hundred pounds, but they have sufficient supplies to last until the new harvest. This day we spent the night there, at our own expense.

JULY 1. We visited the abbey of St-Sauveur. They sometimes leave the cloister without permission; we enjoined them to correct this. Sixty-one nuns are there. We enjoined them all to eat the same food in the refectory. Item, that the nuns in the infirmary who are not lying in bed shall eat the same food together at one table; those who are confined to their beds may eat apart and in [their] beds. We enjoined the abbess to inspect the coffers of the nuns more frequently, taking the keys to the coffers when they least expect it, and to search for any property, and to punish her under whose key any property shall be found. Item, we ordered them to turn in their old clothes when they receive new ones. Once more we enjoined them to put away their metaled belts.[15] We enjoined them to send away all children who were not veiled. We advised them to confess and to receive Communion once a month. We forbade them to receive the relatives of the nuns in the guest houses of the abbey, either for sleeping or for eating; item, we forbade the nuns

---

[15] See entry for May 14, 1250.

to eat with them. Item, we ordered a general audit of the abbey affairs to be made twice or three times a year and with the assistance of some sisters elected by the community, and the report to be announced in chapter; item, that particular audits be made in the same way and every month, and that two copies of these be made, one to be retained by some sister elected by the community, the other to be given to the abbess. They have an income of one thousand pounds; they owe two hundred fifty pounds. Today we received procuration from the abbess of St-Taurin. Expense total: seven pounds, five shillings.

JULY 2. We visited the chapter of Evreux after we had preached a sermon in chapter before the canons and clerks-choral. After the latter had withdrawn we visited the chapter. We asked them as a body if the Divine Office was celebrated both day and night, at the proper hours and with due modulation, and they replied, "Yes." Item, we asked them if they had a sufficiency of ornaments and books; they said that they had. Item, we inquired whether any of the clerks-choral were ill famed of incontinence; they replied that none was at present, and they added that whenever any one was defamed of this vice, or any other, he was very well disciplined by the hebdomadary and the chapter, so that none of them dared to do anything publicly or indulge in any conduct which might give rise to suspicion. We then asked them to withdraw, and we consulted with them individually and secretly, beginning with the precentor. We asked him whether any of the canons suffered from the vice of incontinence, or of drunkeness, or of engaging in trade, or of anything else from which infamy might arise; he said that there was none at present, save only Geoffrey of Courcelles, who had once been touched by the vice of incontinence but had been disciplined. He believed that the infamy had now ceased. Then we summoned all the others privately and secretly, and they all returned the same answers. This day the aforesaid chapter gave us accommodations in the bishop's palace. Total for procuration: ten pounds, twelve shillings.

JULY 3. Having called Archdeacon William, the treasurer, and several others into our room we made inquiries about the bishop, and we found everything to be quite satisfactory. We received procuration from the bishop[16] this day, although he was absent. Total for procuration: nine pounds, nine shillings, ten pence.

---

[16] John de la Cour d'Aubergenville (1244-56). (Gams, *Series episcoporum*, p. 550.)

JULY 4. We visited the abbey of Croix-St-Leufroy. Twenty monks are there, and all but four are priests. We enjoined the abbot to visit all his priories at least once a year, or to see that they were visited. They do not observe the fasts in the priories, and they eat meat in them; we enjoined them to correct this. Item, we enjoined the abbot to have individual audits made every month in the presence of the elected members of the community. They owe about three hundred pounds; they have an income of five hundred pounds. Total for procuration: nine pounds, ten shillings, five pence.

JULY 5. We visited the prior of Jouy. Two monks are there. They do not observe the fasts very well; we enjoined them to observe the Rule in this matter. Sometimes they eat meat when there is no need; we enjoined them to observe the Statutes of Pope Gregory about this. Total for procuration: six pounds, five shillings, five pence.

JULY 6. We visited at Coudres. Two monks from Bourgueil are there. The priory has an income of four hundred pounds, two hundred fifty pounds of which they, as of custom, pay their abbey. We enjoined them to a stricter observance of the fasts of the Rule. We forbade them the use of meat, save as the Rule permits. Total: eight pounds, two shillings, three pence.

JULY 7. We visited the priory at Heudreville. Five monks of the Order of Tiron are there. All are priests. They have no copy of the Rule; we ordered them to obtain one. They use feather beds. We forbade them to eat meat, except as the Rule permits. Three times a week they give alms to all comers. They owe about one hundred pounds; they have an income of about one hundred eighty pounds. Total for procuration: six pounds, eleven shillings, four pence.

JULY 8. We visited the priory at Muzy where there are four monks from Coulombs. Because of the smallness of the rooms they do not sleep together. They use feather beds. They have no copy of the Rule; we enjoined them to procure one. One of them wears a linen shirt; we forbade him to do this. They eat meat freely; we utterly forbade them to eat meat save insofar as the Rule permits. They owe about three hundred pounds; they have an income of about one hundred sixty pounds. They have no provisions. Total for procuration: six pounds, two shillings, four pence of Paris.[17] Note: We must speak with the bishop concerning Muzy with reference to its burdensome debt and about reducing the number of monks there.

[17] See July 17, 1248, n. 4, and September 24, 1248, n. 63.

JULY 9. At L'Estrée, a Cistercian foundation, at the expense of the monastery. JULY 10. At Breuil, a Cistercian foundation, at the expense of the monastery.

JULY 11. We visited the abbey of Ivry, where there are thirteen monks. All are priests. They eat meat when there is no need; we forbade them to use meat save as the Rule permits. The sources of income are not written down, nor does the abbot cast any accounts; we enjoined them to correct this. They owe about three hundred pounds. No one is placed in charge of the infirmary; we enjoined the abbot to put someone in charge, and, at his own expense, to provide him with everything needful. Total for procuration: seven pounds, ten shillings of Tours.

JULY 12. We visited the chapter of Vernon. We did not find any canons there, but only vicars. There are nine canons connected with this church, but they do not reside in it.[18] Item, there are nine vicars in residence, of whom five are in priests' orders, two are deacons, and two are subdeacons. Two masses are sung daily by the vicars, a High Mass, and a Mass of the Blessed Virgin; the parish priest also celebrates a parochial Mass each day. This day we received our procuration from the chapter, and at the bishop's palace. Total for procuration: nine pounds, two shillings, three pence of Paris.

JULY 13. The steward of Bailleul gave us procuration at Sausseuse, because the priory there has no monks, nor does the place offer sufficient accommodation for us. Total for procuration: seven pounds, three shillings, five pence of Paris.

JULY 14. At Le-Bord-Haut-de-Vigny, at our own expense. JULY 15. At Senlis, where the lord king was lying ill. JULY 16-19. At the same. JULY 20-22. At Pontoise.

JULY 23. While we were passing through the village of Bray, the parishioners came before us and accused their rector. They said that he was in the habit of roaming about the town at night ready armed; that he was quarrelsome and abusive towards his parishioners, speaking scornful words about them, and that he was ill famed of incontinence. We cited the said priest before us at Sausseuse, and in the presence of the prior of the place, Brother Adam Rigaud, Brother Harduin, and Master Richard of Sap, we warned him about these matters and advised him to abstain from such con-

---

[18] Though he could do nothing to correct it, Eudes did not care for the practice of non-resident canons.

duct in the future, else we would take such proceedings against him as the law requires. This day we had transported from Courdimanche to Wy and handed over to the priest there two albs, two amices, three chasubles, one chalice, one silver cross, one breviary[19] in two parts, one missal, one gradual, and a portable altar.

JULY 24. At Frênes. JULY 25. At Louviers. JULY 26. At Evreux, to come to an amicable settlement with our bishops. JULY 27. At the same, about the lawsuit between us and the lord of Ivry. JULY 28. At Louviers. JULY 29. At Frênes.

JULY 30. At the same. This day Robert, rector of St. Peter's Church at Neaufles, near Gisors, resigned his church into our hands. Present were: Master Peter of Aumale, canon of Rouen, and Albert, cleric; Archdeacon Reginald; Brother Alexander of La Croix; Everard and Morel, our clerks; and Enguerrand, cleric, of Frênes.

JULY 31. By horseback to Port-Mort. We warned Amaury, whom our official had deprived of his church at Courdimanche, not to enter the church again as rector, nor to make use of any of the goods or fruits of the church; otherwise we would take such proceedings against him as the law requires. Present were: Simon, the archdeacon; Master Peter of Aumale, canon of Rouen; Brothers Adam, Harduin, and Walter, of the Friars Minor; Dom James, rector of St. Mary the Little; Stephen, clerck of the said archdeacon; Hugh, the almoner; Everard and Morel, our clerks; and several others.

We spent the night at Vernon.

AUGUST 1. At Vernon. AUGUST 2. At Frênes. AUGUST 3. At Ste-Catherine. AUGUST 4. At Déville. AUGUST 5. At Auffay. AUGUST 6-9. At Frênes.

AUGUST 10. At the same. This day Henry,[20] former priest at Avremesnill, swore while touching the Holy Gospels that he would restore to us, or at our order, the property which he had taken from the said church, after he had been deprived thereof, or goods of equal value. He promised that he would offer no further objections either to us or to our agent in the matter of his removal, or to anyone whom we should canonically install in the said church. We should enjoy a free and quiet possession of the fruits of the

[19] The word *breviarium* has many meanings. In all probability, the meaning here is in reference to the Books of Hours, or books containing the Divine Office. In general, the missal or mass book was not one book in Eudes' time, but a series of books: lectionary, gospel book, gradual and Canon of the Mass.

[20] See entry for April 19, 1255.

said church. He offered as pledges Richard of Dun and William Buhere, knights. This he swore in the presence of the aforementioned pledges; Masters John of Flainville and Peter of Aumale, canons of Rouen; Richard of Sap, William of Ville-en-Colle, and Abraham of Grandcourt, rectors; Brothers Adam and Harduin of the Friars Minor; and Morel, our clerk.

AUGUST 11. While we were on the road near Torcy, Richard of Dun and William Godrain [Buhere ?], knights, pledged themselves, with hands placed in ours, to a forfeit of eighty pounds, equally divided between them, and payable on the strength of the said oath, if the above-mentioned Henry should again interfere with the fruits of the church at Avremesnil, or should disturb it in person or by means of any agent, or should in the future revive any claim to the aforesaid fruits.

This day we visited at Auffay, where there are six monks. They do not read the Statutes of Pope Gregory; we enjoined them to correct this. They do not observe the statutes pertaining to confession and the use of meat; we enjoined them to a full observance of these Statutes. They owe two hundred pounds.

AUGUST 12-13. At Déville. AUGUST 14. At Rouen. AUGUST 15. At the same. We celebrated the feast of the Assumption. AUGUST 16-17. At Déville. AUGUST 18. At Frênes. AUGUST 19. At Genainville. AUGUST 20. At Pontoise. AUGUST 21. At Corbeil. AUGUST 22-23. At Melun. AUGUST 24. At Paris. AUGUST 25. At Pontoise. This day at St-Martin, Dom Amaury, erstwhile priest at Courdimanche, withdrew in its entirety the appeal which he had made regarding our sentence and regarding our official because our official had deprived him of the said church.[21] Item, he promised not to interfere personally or through any other person in the fruits, the buildings, or any things pertaining to the said church. He obligated himself to us with movables and immovables to the value of twenty pounds as a forfeit should he be delinquent in any respect concerning these matters. Present were: Master Peter of Aumale, canon of Rouen; the treasurer of St-Mellon-de-Pontoise; Master Richard of Sap; Brother Walter of Minières; Sir Rigaud, knight;[22] Peter of Mesnil; John, a priest; the master of St-Lazare-de-Pontoise; Benedict, rector of St-Ouen, near Pontoise; Guy, his chaplain; Dom Hugh, the almoner; and Morel, our clerk.

---

[21] See entries for March 19, 1254/55, and May 27, 1255.
[22] Probably Eudes' brother, the father of Adam, the Friar Minor, who was in the *familia* of Eudes and whose signature is on many of Eudes' documents.

AUGUST 26. At Genainville.

AUGUST 27. At Frênes. This day, about noon, we invested Morel, our clerk, with the Rouen prebend which belonged to Master William Picard and was held by Jordan, the brother of Dom John Gaetani,[23] cardinal deacon of St. Nicholas in the Tullian Prison. Present were: Brothers Adam, Harduin, and Walter, of the Friars Minor.

AUGUST 28-31. At Déville. SEPTEMBER 1. At St-Wandrille, at our own expense.

SEPTEMBER 2. We visited there, where there are thirty-six monks. One monk is dwelling alone at Betteville. We enjoined the abbot to visit the priories every year. One does not accuse another [in chapter]; we enjoined them to correct this. Traveling monks do not observe the fasts, nor do those who are in the priories, and these also eat meat. The house would be in good condition as far as its finances are concerned if it could collect the money which is due it from England.[24] As much is owed to them as they owe. We ordered the officers to draw up a statement of the accounts of their offices. We received procuration there this day. Total for procuration: eight pounds, four shillings, three pence.

SEPTEMBER 3. At Le Valasse, of the Cistercian Order. SEPTEMBER 4. At Graville, at our own expense. SEPTEMBER 5. We dedicated the church at Rouelles, and this day we spent the night at Graville at the expense of the parishioners of Rouelles. Total: eight pounds, two shillings, six pence.

SEPTEMBER 6. We visited at Graville. We ordered one to accuse another [in chapter]. Ten canons are residing in this priory, and one is alone at Bellevue; we ordered him recalled to the cloister or a companion given him. They owe about fifty pounds; they have an income of three hundred pounds. We received procuration there this day. Total: seven pounds, seven shillings, five pence.

SEPTEMBER 7. We visited the abbess of Montivilliers. We found everything regarding her in good condition. They have an income of twenty-five

---

[23] John Gaetani was named to the titular church in Rome of St. Nicholas in the Tullian Prison in 1244. Later, he became Pope Nicholas III (1277-80). ("Nicolas III," *Dict. de théol. cath.*, XI[1] 532-35.)

[24] England was feeling the political unrest which culminated in the Provisions of Oxford. For background see M. Powicke, *The Thirteenth Century*, vol. IV of *The Oxford History of England* (Oxford, 1953); also, F. M. Powicke, *King Henry III and the Lord Edward* (2 vols. Oxford 1947) Vol. I, which has an excellent account of the reasons for baronial discontent with Henry's domestic and foreign policies.

hundred pounds; they owe one hundred ninety-three pounds, seven shillings, but four hundred forty nine pounds, fourteen shillings, six pence is owed them. We received procuration there this day. Total: seven pounds, fourteen shillings, six pence.

SEPTEMBER 8. At the same, but at our own expense.

SEPTEMBER 9. At the same. Reginald Bernenguel appeared before us and admitted that he had prevented his men from performing their due services to the priest at Auzouville, and he pledged himself to accept whatever penalty we should impose. He offered William of Hatantot as his surety, up to forty pounds.

SEPTEMBER 10. At Valmont.

SEPTEMBER 11. We visited and found twenty-three monks in residence. One does not accuse another [in chapter]; we enjoined them to correct this. Twelve priests are there, and that is enough to care for the regular services. We enjoined them to observe the fasts rigorously. They eat meat; we forbade them to eat meat except as the Rule permits. Alms are given three times a week to all comers and to lepers on other days. They do not observe the fasts in the priories, and they eat meat; we enjoined them to correct this. The abbot does not compute.

SEPTEMBER 12-13. At the same. SEPTEMBER 14. At the same. We assigned to Walter, priest at Theuville, the Thursday after the feast of St. Matthew the Apostle as the day when he should stand trial by investigation or purgation for the vice of incontinence. SEPTEMBER 15. At St-Wandrille. SEPTEMBER 16. At Déville. SEPTEMBER 17. At St-Matthieu. This day Master Robert, rector at Roquefort, justified himself for not taking [Holy] Orders, on the grounds of his ill-health. SEPTEMBER 18. We conferred Holy Orders in the cathedral of Rouen, and spent the night at St-Matthieu.

This day ... [*lacuna in MS*], the rector at Rive, swore that if he did not take priests' Orders before Christmas Day, he would consider his church as resigned, and without the publicity attendant on a trial. Present were: Masters Simon, archdeacon of Rouen; John, canon of Soissons; Richard of Sap, dean of Gamaches; Brother Harduin of the Friars Minor; Brother John of Perugia, Hospitaler; Dom James, rector of St. Mary the Little; and Stephen, rector at Neuville.

SEPTEMBER 19. At St-Matthieu. SEPTEMBER 20. At Frênes. SEPTEMBER 21. At Gisors. SEPTEMBER 22. At Beauvais. SEPTEMBER 23. At La Neuville. SEPTEMBER 24. At Noyon. SEPTEMBER 25. At La Neuville.

SEPTEMBER 26. At Beauvais. SEPTEMBER 27. At Gisors. SEPTEMBER 28-
29. At Frênes. SEPTEMBER 30. At Louviers. OCTOBER 1. At Bourg-Achard.
OCTOBER 2-3. At Pont-Audemer.

OCTOBER 4. Although Matthew, the nephew of Master Peter, was found
to be otherwise satisfactory, we did not wish to admit him to the church of
Flaines, because of the protest of the monks of Aumale, who made him swear
that he was contemptuous of the things which his predecessor had kept in the
aforesaid church.

This day we spent the night at Préaux.

OCTOBER 5-9. At the same. OCTOBER 10. At Bourg-Achard. OCTOBER 11.
At Louviers. OCTOBER 12. At the same. This day we visited the bishop of
Evreux, who was lying ill at Brosville. OCTOBER 13-20. At Frênes.

OCTOBER 21. At the same. This day Gilbert of Boisement was cited to
appear before us or our official at Rouen on the Wednesday before the
vigil of St. Martin *Hiemalis* in order to hear the law on the investigation
which had been made concerning him, and also about some letters which
he gave to us, sealed with his seal.

OCTOBER 22. At Sausseuse, at our expense.

OCTOBER 23. At Gasny, where we visited this day. Three monks are there.
They have no decent vestments [for services in the church], nor books. They
do not observe the fasts of the Rule. All of them eat meat, and they use
feather beds; we enjoined them to correct all of these things and to undergo
the penalties described in the Statutes of Pope Gregory should they be
delinquent therein. Total for procuration: sixty-nine shillings.

OCTOBER 24. We visited at St-Martin-la-Garenne. Five monks are there,
but the prior was not present when we made our visitation. We enjoined
them to accept the penance prescribed in the Statutes if they should be at
fault in eating meat. They owe one hundred twenty pounds. Everything
else we found to be as already described in the Register.[25] Total for procuration: four pounds, eight shillings, ten pence.

OCTOBER 25. At Gisors, where we received procuration. Total for procuration: six pounds, six shillings, ten pence.

OCTOBER 26. We visited there and found six monks in residence. They
use feather beds. They make a practice of eating meat three times a week,
that is to say, on Sunday, Tuesday, and Thursday. They have no copy of

[25] See entry for October 15, 1254.

the Statutes of Pope Gregory; we enjoined them to procure the aforesaid Statutes and to undergo the penalty prescribed therein as often as they offended against the Statute concerning the eating of meat. They owe about one hundred fifty pounds, but there is owed to them about eighty pounds They have an income of four hundred pounds.

This day we celebrated the holy synod of the Vexin, at Meulan.

OCTOBER 27. We received procuration at Gaillonet. Total for procuration: four pounds, nineteen shillings, one penny. OCTOBER 28. At Genainville OCTOBER 29. As Sausseuse, at our expense.

OCTOBER 30. We visited there and found eleven canons in residence. The rule of silence is not well observed; we enjoined them to correct this. They owe three hundred pounds and more. With the exception of oats, they have a sufficient store of provisions. They have an income of four hundred pounds. Everything else we found to be in good condition. We received procuration there this day. Total: four pounds, four shillings, one penny.

OCTOBER 31. At Les Andelys. NOVEMBER 1. At the same. We celebrated the feast of All Saints. NOVEMBER 2-6. At Frênes. NOVEMBER 7. At St-Matthieu. NOVEMBER 8. We held the sacred synod at Rouen. NOVEMBER 9. We continued the synod and spent the night at Ermentrouville. NOVEMBER 10-11. At Déville. NOVEMBER 12. At Auffay. NOVEMBER 13. At Aliermont. NOVEMBER 14. At Dieppe.

NOVEMBER 15. At Envermeu, where we visited. Ten monks are there; there used to be twelve, but, as the prior told us, the abbot is going to send two directly. They do not read the Statutes of Pope Gregory; we enjoined them to read these twice a year. They eat meat when there is no need; we enjoined them to correct this, and to undergo the penalty prescribed in the Statutes if they should be delinquent in this. They have an income of about three hundred pounds. We received procuration there this day. Total for procuration: seven pounds, fourteen pence.

This same day Roger of Corqueterville, esquire, and William of Buhere, knight, made recompense to us for that the said Roger and the son of the said William had gone hunting in our preserves, and each served as the surety for the other.

NOVEMBER 16. We received procuration at Le Tréport. Total: seven pounds, eight shillings.

NOVEMBER 17. We visited there and found twenty monks in residence. They do not read the Statutes of Pope Gregory; we enjoined them to read these twice a year. One does not accuse another [in chapter]; we enjoined the abbot to appoint a supervisor who should keep a lookout for the offenses of the others and accuse them. The fasts are not observed by the traveling monks nor by those who are in the priories. Item, they eat meat in the priories; we enjoined them to correct this. The officials of the house make no statement of their accounts; we enjoined them to draw up a statement of receipts and expenditures once a month, in the presence of the abbot and some of the brothers elected by the community; item, that a general audit concerning the state of the house be made at least twice a year in the presence of the abbot and the elected brothers. The abbot ought to consider carefully, and before Christmas, the matter of his unjust exaction of tithes on newly cultivated ground[26] belonging to certain of his parishioners, and to submit a definite report on this to us. Since the prior does not keep to the cloister very well, but rides abroad altogether too much and on the baldest of excuses, and since he frequently dines in his rooms and very often remains away from Compline, we warned him to refrain from these violations of the Rule, or that otherwise we would institute proceedings against him as the law requires. Present were: . . . [lacuna in MS] Master John of Soissons, Brothers Adam and Harduin, and Morel, our clerck. Item, we also warned the cellarer, who had given some of the abbey goods to his relatives.

This day we spent the night at Eu, at our own expense.

NOVEMBER 18. We visited at Eu. Twenty-eight canons are in residence; there used to be thirty-two. One of the lay brothers there confesses and receives Communion too rarely; we enjoined them to correct this. Alms are given to clerics on Monday, Wednesday, and Friday; to other poor people on Tuesday, Thursday, and Saturday; on Sunday those who are ashamed to beg receive alms at a hospice in the town. They owe three hundred eighty pounds, but at least as much, if not more, is owed to them. The canon in charge of clothes is negligent in giving out clothing; we warned him about this. We received procuration there this day. Total: six pounds, seventeen shillings, two pence.

NOVEMBER 19. At Foucarmont, at the expense of the abbey. NOVEMBER 20. At Aumale, at our own expense.

NOVEMBER 21. We visited there. Sixteen monks are in residence; eleven are priests. Two of their monks are in England. Silence is badly kept.

[26] *Novales* (new lands), land hitherto uncultivated and thus not subject to tithes.

Almost all of them make a practice of going out in the manse without getting permission. One does not accuse another [in chapter]. The cloister is not well kept. Those who go beyond the gate of the house without permission are not regarded as runaways. Almost all of them have coffers. Those who are not priests confess and receive Communion too infrequently, to wit, only twice a year. One confesses to another and without permission. The Statutes of Pope Gregory are not read; we enjoined them to read the Statutes twice a year. The fasts of the Rule are not observed, and sometimes they even eat after Compline. They eat meat twice a week or oftener. Sometimes, indeed, frequently, the refectory has no monks at all. Two of the monks are not on speaking terms with each other, and some of the others play dice. They owe twelve pounds, most of it at interest. The abbot makes no audits in the presence of brothers elected by the community, either of particular offices or of the house as a whole. We received procuration there this day. Total: one hundred twelve shillings, five pence.

NOVEMBER 22. At Mortemer-sur-Eaulne. Two Cluniac monks are there. We received procuration there this day. Total: eight pounds, nine shillings, one penny.

NOVEMBER 23. We visited the abbey of Bival, where we found discord and quarrels, whereupon we caused the authors of these disorders to be brought forth in a cart.[27] We enjoined the abbess to see to it that the orders of Archdeacon R., described in our other visitation,[28] be strictly carried out. Item, we earnestly enjoined upon her that no one should presume to go beyond the gate of the cloister without permission, and that no one should write a letter or have one written unless it be submitted to the abbess, and that whosoever should offend in any of these two matters should be punished as for a grave fault. [We enjoined her] that if she did not do this we would institute proceedings against her as is required by law. We received procuration this day at St-Saëns. Total for procuration: nine pounds, five shillings, six pence.

[27] In all probability, the disturbers of the peace had been incarcerated. "In these days such a cart served the same purpose as does a pillory now . . . whoever was convicted of any crime was placed upon the cart and dragged through all the streets and he lost henceforth all his legal rights . . ." Riding in such a cart implied loss of dignity. (Chrétien de Troyes, *Arthurian Romances*, trans. W. W. Comfort [London, 1928], p. 274.)

[28] See entry for February 27, 1254/55. The archdeacon was empowered to enforce Eudes' legislation. However, Archdeacon R. is not explicitly mentioned in either the visitation of September 3, 1252, or that of February 27, 1254/55.

NOVEMBER 24. We visited at St-Saëns. Four monks are in residence; there used to be five; they must get a companion as soon as possible. More is owed to them than they owe. Everything else we found to be in good condition.

This day we spent the night at Déville.

NOVEMBER 25. At Déville. NOVEMBER 26-28. At Rouen. NOVEMBER 29–DECEMBER 1. At Déville. DECEMBER 2. At Bellencombre.

DECEMBER 3. We visited there, finding four canons in residence. There are five male lepers, one female leper, two sisters [nuns], four brothers, and one [porter] at the gate. We enjoined the prior to hold a chapter once a week with all the brothers present. They have an income of about two hundred pounds. They have a little wheat, which will not last until the feast of St. John, but they have enough oats and barley to last out the year. They owe about forty pounds.

This day we spent the night at Aliermont.

DECEMBER 4-8. At Aliermont.

DECEMBER 9. This day, in St. Mary's church at Aliermont, Sir Ralph of Bailleul made recompense to us for having hunted in our forest at Aliermont. Sir Roger of Freulleville and John Lovel were his pledges. Sir Geoffrey of Miromesnil made recompense also, with Sir Geoffrey of Chapelle and Sir Michael of Berneval as his sureties. Present were: the aforesaid pledges; Sir John of Rivage and Sir Hugh Tesson, knights; Masters William of Dunestanville, John of Soissons, Richard of Sap; and several others. The recompense you may find imposed upon Sir Nicholas of St-Beuve in folio 157.[29]

DECEMBER 10. At Bellencombre. DECEMBER 11. At Pavilly. DECEMBER 12. At Jumièges, at our own expense.

DECEMBER 13. We visited there and found fifty-four monks in residence. Some of them do not celebrate Mass every week, or even once every two weeks; we issued an injunction that these should drink no wine, except at breakfast, until they shall have talked with us or one of our penitentiaries about this. Some do not confess every month; we enjoined them to correct this. Those who are in the priories eat meat; we enjoined them to correct this. We received procuration there this day. No amount was reckoned, because they did not wish to make any computation.

[29] The amount of the fine is not mentioned. (Bonnin, p. 789.)

DECEMBER 14. At St-Georges, at the expense of the abbey. Total: seven pounds, three pence.

DECEMBER 15. We visited there and found eighteen monks in residence. One does not accuse another [in chapter]; we enjoined them to correct this. They have an income of eleven hundred pounds; more is owed to them than they owe. Everything else, with Gods grace, we found to be in good condition.

This day we spent the night at Déville.

DECEMBER 16. We visited the abbey of Ste-Catherine. Twenty-eight monks are in residence. One does not accuse another [in chapter]; we enjoined them to correct this. We enjoined them to draw up a statement of the general financial condition of the house twice a year and in the presence of some of the brothers elected by the community. The abbot had made no computation of the moneys from England, nor of the costs of the buildings; we enjoined him to correct this. Brother Samson is ill famed of possessing property; we enjoined the abbot to punish him well and severely. Total for procuration: eight pounds, five shillings, three pence.

DECEMBER 17. William, the abbot of St-Victor [-en-Caux], at our hall at Rouen, resigned the administration of his abbey into our hands. Present were: the treasurer; Master Stephen, archdeacon of the French Vexin; Master Peter of Ons, official and canon of Rouen; Masters John of Soissons, Richard of Sap, Philip of Fontenay, and Ralph of Agarne and many others.

We spent the night at St-Matthieu.

DECEMBER 18. We conferred Holy Orders at Grandmont and spent the night at St-Matthieu.

DECEMBER 19-22. At St-Matthieu. DECEMBER 23-24. At Rouen. DECEMBER 25. At Rouen this day we celebrated Christmas. DECEMBER 26. At Déville. DECEMBER 27. At the same. On this day we invested Master Richard of Etaples with the prebend of Quinze-Marcs. Present were; Brother Harduin and Morel. DECEMBER 28-29. At Déville. DECEMBER 30. At Séez, on the feast of St. Vincent. In the palace of the bishop of Séez, Master Richard of Etaples, using his hat as a symbol, resigned the prebend of Quinze-Marcs. Present were: Brothers Harduin and Walter, of the Friars Minor and Morel, our clerk. DECEMBER 31—JANUARY 4. At Déville. JANUARY 5-6. At Bourg-Achard, at our own expense. JANUARY 7. At Bec. JANUARY 8. At Orbec, at our own expense. Here begins the visitation of the diocese of Séez. JANUARY 9. We entered the diocese of Séez and spent the night at St-Pierre-sur-Dives,[30] where we received procuration. Total for procuration: six pounds, six shillings, six pence.

JANUARY 10. We visited there. Thirty-eight monks are in residence. All are priests but six. Because of the workmen, the cloister is not well guarded. The Statutes of Pope Gregory are not read; we enjoined that the Statutes be read as the Statutes themselves require. We forbade them to eat meat except as the Rule permits. We enjoined the abbot to have individual accounts of the offices drawn up every month with the assistance of brothers elected by the community, and two copies to be made of this: one copy to remain in the possession of the community, the other to be given to the abbot. Further, that a general audit be made twice a year and in the manner aforesaid.

This day we spent the night at Pérrièrs, at the expense of the priory.[31] Total: one hundred three shillings, ten pence.

JANUARY 11. Although they are exempt, we, in the absence of their prior, warned the two monks from Marmoutier who are staying there so to conduct themselves during their residence that no evil report of them should reach our ears, since, by reason of offenses committed within our archiepiscopal province, we would undertake proceedings against them as is required by law.

This day we spent the night at Trun,[32] at the expense of the priory at Coulances, where there are no monks. It is dependent upon Jumièges.[33] Total for procuration: nine pounds, six shillings, seven pence.

JANUARY 12. At Tournai [-sur-Dives].[34] Two monks from Croix-St-Leufroy are there. The priory is without vestments, chalice, and books; we advised the prior to procure some vestments other than the vestments belonging to the parish. The monks dine in the village with some of the married squires, and the squirres with their wives dine in the priory. Because this seemed perilous to us, we enjoined them to abstain from such conduct.

---

[30] A Benedictine abbey founded c. 1040. (Cottineau, II, 2851-52.) It had at least two priories in England: Modbury (Devonshire) and Tutbury (Staffordshire). (Dugdale, *Monasticon Anglicanum*, VII, 1042; III, 388.)

[31] St-Vigor, a Benedictine priory dependent on Marmoutier, founded c. 1076. (Cottineau, II, 2257.)

[32] A Benedictine priory dependent on Troarn. (Cottineau, II, 3228.)

[33] One of the better histories of Jumièges is by Julien Loth, *Histoire de l'abbaye royale de Saint-Pierre-de-Jumièges*, 3 vols. (Rouen, 1885). For references to the priory of Coulances, see *ibid.*, 1, 255, 272; II, 113, 137, 199, 205, 253, 291.

[34] A Benedictine priory dependent on Croix-St-Leufroy. (Cottineau, II, 3188.)

They have an income of eighty pounds; they owe ten pounds. They do not observe the fasts of the Rule; we enjoined them to observe these as the Rule requires. They eat meat; we forbade them to eat meat, except as the Rule allows. Because of his ill-health the prior does not celebrate Mass; we enjoined him that if he were unable to celebrate Mass, he should receive Communion at least once a month. We received procuration there this day. Total for procuration: seven pounds, eighteen shillings, four pence.

JANUARY 13. We received procuration at Planches.[35] Total for procuration: one hundred fifteen shillings, ten pence.

JANUARY 14. We visited there. Two monks from St-Père-de-Chartres are there, but the prior's companion had gone to Chartres just then. They celebrate Mass too rarely, nor do they confess often enough; we enjoined them to confess as is set forth in the Statutes of Pope Gregory. They have no copy of the Rule, nor do they observe the fasts of the Rule; we enjoined them to observe this more strictly. They eat meat freely; we forbade them to eat meat, except as the Rule permits. Women often dine with them in the priory; we advised the prior to restrict this practice insofar as he could.

This day we spent the night at La Trappe, a Cistercian house.

JANUARY 15. We visited at Mortagne.[36] As yet there is no definite number of canons. Twenty chaplains are obligated to reside there, each with his own clerk-choral. There are statutory penalties against those who are negligent in coming to the Hours, and against those who talk in choir loudly enough to be heard three stalls away. The parish priest has the care of the canons' souls. They follow the Uses of Chartres. The chaplain who is obligated to celebrate the morning Mass each day is, because of this obligation, excused from attending the Hours. But actually he does neither the one nor the other, that is to say, he neither celebrates his Mass nor comes to the Hours. In consequence of this we enjoined the bishop to see that this was corrected. Don Nicholas Pilate, priest, is ill famed of incontinence and of playing dice. Master Philip of Fontaine is ill famed of incontinence with the wife of the skinner. Item, Guylot of Mont-Isembert is ill famed of incontinence. The lord bishop promised us that he would correct these things satisfactorily. We received procuration there this day at the expense of the chapter. Total nine pounds, two shillings, ten pence.

[35] A Benedictine priory established c. 1065. (Cottineau, II, 2295.)
[36] See entry for July 7, 1250. See also the article "chapitres de chanoines," *Dict. de droit canon.*, III 530-95, on the subject of canons.

JANUARY 16. We spent the night at Ste-Gauburge and received the forty shillings which they owe us for procuration.

JANUARY 17. We called before us Brother Walter the Englishman, Brother William of Perche, Brother Peter of Malo, Brother Martin of Paris, and Brother Guerin. The prior had gone to the Curia [at Rome]. The monks come from St-Denis in France. All the buildings, including the monastery, are in need of reroofing; they told us that this was the fault of the prior. We asked them whether they slept together in the same room; they replied that they did. Item, they stated that they had no copy of the Statutes of Pope Gregory. They answered that all of them were priests. They replied that the prior had the care of their souls. Because of the ill-repute connected therewith, we forbade them to wear barracan[37] in the future. Item, the monks run about the town and without permission; we enjoined them to correct this. Item, they have some rabbit dogs; we prohibited these. They give alms three times a week to all comers. From Christmas to Sexagesima they eat meat freely; but they say that at other times they never eat it without the permission of the prior, unless they are feeble or ill. They do not keep well the fasts of the Rule; we enjoined them to correct this. They owe only forty pounds, as they say, and since the buildings threaten to fall down, we ordered them to repair them. There used to be six in residence, but one has gone to the abbey [St-Denis], and he ought to be back shortly. They answered all of our questions both as to temporalities and spiritualities. Present were: . . . [lacuna in MS], the precentor; Master Richard of Sap, canon of Rouen; Masters John of Soissons and John of Les Andelys, canons; Brothers Harduin and Walter of the Friars Minor; and Morel, our clerk. Although Brother Martin said that we ought not to visit them because they were exempt, yet when they had read the letter formerly drawn up by Archbishop Thibaut and P[eter], the abbot, together with the community of St-Denis, they conceded that we were empowered to exercise a visitation. You may find this letter above, on folio 59.[38]

This day we spent the night at Dame-Marie.[39] Total for procuration: seven pounds, eighteen shillings, two pence.

JANUARY 18. We visited there. Two monks from Jumièges are there. Sometimes the prior eats with the knights in the village, and sometimes the

[37] Goatskin clothing which was forbidden because of its luxury.
[38] See entry for July 8, 1250.
[39] A Benedictine priory dependent on Jumièges. (Cottineau, I, 943.)

women together with their lords dine at the priory. We told the prior to abstain from this practice so far as he could do so with tact. Alms are given to all comers three times a week. They have an income of one hundred pounds and more. Sometimes the prior remits sixty pounds to the abbey, sometimes he sends more, occasionally less.

This day we received procuration at St-Martin-de-Bellême. Total: seven pounds, two shillings, three pence.

JANUARY 19. Since by common and customery right it is within our power when visiting the diocese of Séez to visit all religious places, and to receive procuration from them, we turned aside and visited the priory of St-Martin-de-Bellême, and we warned, and by this writing still warn, the prior and the monks of the said place to receive us for the visitation under the authority of common law[40] and to answer us about the state of their house. Item, we warned, and by this present writing still warn, the prior and the monks that they should receive us for the visitation and procuration of the priory of St-Leonard-de-Bellême, especially since the bishop of Séez is reported to receive two procurations in these two places, and the prior, Geoffrey by name, says that he holds the administration of both priories.[41] Because, after the aforesaid legal warnings, we did not wish to punish them, we, with their consent, appointed the Monday following the Sunday on which the *Reminiscere*[42] is sung as the day upon which they, after due deliberation on this matter, should appear before us at Rouen or wherever we should happen to be, and show cause why they should not be held accountable for the foregoing. Present at these arrangements were: Brothers Geoffrey, the prior aforesaid; William, sacristan of St-Leonard; William, cellarer of St-Martin; Clement; and many others. Done on the Wednesday before the feast of St. Vincent, in the year of our Lord 1255.

This day we spent the night at Loony, at the house of Sir William of Nonry, knight.

JANUARY 20. We received procuration at Alençon.[43] Total for procuration: six pounds, nine shillings, five pence.

JANUARY 21. We visited there. Three monks from Lonlay, in the diocese

---

[40] General, or common, ecclesiastical law is applicable to the whole Church and is habitually observed by all. ("Droit canonique," *Dict. de droit canon.* IV, 1447-48.)

[41] St-Martin-de-Bellême was a dependent priory of Marmoutier and claimed exemption on the basis of exemption granted to the mother monastery. (Cottineau, I, 331-32.)

[42] The second Sunday in Lent.

[43] St-Léonard, a Benedictine priory dependent on Lonlay. (Cottineau, I, 53.)

of Le Mans, are there; two of them are priests, the other is a child,[44] and
still wears shirts. They do not observe the fasts of the Rule; we enjoined
a better observance. They eat meat in common; we forbade them to eat
meat except as the Rule permits. They have a copy neither of the Rule nor
of the Statutes of Pope Gregory; we enjoined them to obtain copies of both
and to obey them more fully. Women occasionally eat in the priory; we
forbade them to eat there in the future. They owe thirty pounds, and have
not enough provisions to last until harvest.

This day we spent the night at Séez, at the bishop's palace, and at his
expense.

JANUARY 22. We visited the chapter at Séez, the bishop being present.
Twenty-four canons are there. Those who are not priests confess and receive Communion only once a year; we told the bishop to take counsel and
attend to this matter. They have coffers; we enjoined the prior to make
more frequent inspection of these coffers lest there be any property therein,
and to correct such matters if he should discover anything needing correction.
General alms are dispensed only once a week. They have some churches
where there is nobody charged with the cure of souls, despite the fact that
we had warned the lord bishop about this on our other visitation;[45] because of this we retain the rights of appointing priests to these churches.
They owe about seven hundred pounds; they have an income of twelve
hundred pounds. There is no continuous reading in the refectory, the lectern is poor, nor can the reader be heard plainly; we enjoined the bishop
to correct this. At the request of the bishop and the chapter we postponed
the appointments to the above-mentioned churches until the time of the
synod, and they promised to install proper priests in charge before that time,
or that otherwise we might make such disposition of them as we wished.
These are the churches in question: Fleure, Francheville, Frioux, Colom-
bière, Aunay, Le Mesnil-Guyon, Alode, Ste-Scolasse, Courevêque, Telliers,
Mesnil-Bernard, Bonne-Foi, St-Gervaise-de-Séez, St-Julien-de-Merule, Barville, St-Germain-d'Origny-le-Butin, St-Jean-du-Forêt, St-Quentin-le-Petit,
St-Quentin-de-Blavont, Le Pin, Verceville, Condé, Vaast, Costes, Arènes,
Avèrnes, Néaufles, Trois-Aulage, Voire.

JANUARY 23. We visited the abbey of St-Martin-de-Séez.[46] Thirty-four

---

[44] A child was one not yet seven years old and in this instance probably an oblate.
[45] See entry for July 16, 1250.
[46] Founded c. 1050 from St-Evroult. (Cottineau, II, 2992-93.)

monks are there. All but seven are priests. We enjoined them to read the Statutes of Pope Gregory three times a year. They have seven priories in France.[47] One monk is dwelling alone in a certain priory; we enjoined that he be recalled to the cloister and the priory given to a certain priest, because the place is so poor that it cannot support two monks. We issued a general injunction that all monks who are dwelling alone anywhere be recalled to the cloister or that companions be sent to them. The priories do not observe the fasts of the Rule; they eat meat; we enjoined them to correct this. Total for procuration: ten pounds, nine shillings, five pence.

JANUARY 24. We received procuration at Almenèches.[48] Total for prouration: six pounds, eleven shillings, two pence.

JANUARY 25. We visited there. Forty-seven nuns are in residence. They leave the cloister and wander out in front of the granary without permission; we enjoined the abbess to have this corrected. In the dormitory they have rooms with locks. They have their own maidservants who do not serve the whole community. They do not eat from the common dishes, but they have their own plates. Each one receives her own loaf of bread, and keeps what is left over; we enjoined the abbess to give them their loaves without favoritism, and to collect what is left over. They do not live on the same income; in short, they do not live in common at all. The nuns eat with their friends whenever the latter visit the monastery. On the days when they eat meat, the refectory is deserted. They have an income of five hundred pounds, and an additional twenty-five marks from England; they owe sixty pounds, but they do not have sufficient provisions. The lord bishop of Séez drew up a very good ordinance for them, which because of their poverty they do not observe and which we caused to be read in our presence. We enjoined them to observe it, at least in all cases from which their poverty might not excuse them, as, for example, in the matter of dogs.

This day we spent the night at Silly, a Premonstratensian foundation.

JANUARY 26. We spent the night at St-André-en-Gouffern, a Cistercian house.

JANUARY 27. We visited at Briouze.[49] Three monks from Saumur are there. They have no copy of the Rule; we enjoined them to procure one. They do not observe the fasts of the Rule; we enjoined these to be more

---

[47] That is, outside Normandy.
[48] A Benedictine priory, supposedly founded by St-Evroult. (Cottineau, I, 62-63.)
[49] A cell of St-Florent-de-Saumur. (Cottineau· I, 507.)

fully observed. They eat meat on Sunday, Tuesday, and Thursday; we forbade them to eat meat, except as the Rule permits. They have an income of one hundred pounds; they owe forty pounds. We received procuration there this day. Total: six pounds, two shillings.

JANUARY 28. At St-Jean-de-Falaise, where there are Premonstratensian canons. On behalf of the priory of Brieux, . . . [*lacuna in MS*], the abbot, and the convent of St-Martin-de-Séez gave us the following letter:[50]

To all who will see this letter, John, the abbot, and the convent of St-Martin-de-Séez, give greeting in the Lord. We inform all of you that when the Reverend Father Eudes, by God's grace archbishop of Rouen, was visiting the diocese of Séez, he requested procuration from our priory of Brieux in the name of visitation, and we were prepared to give him the said procuration if he desired it. But he, in view of the poverty of the place and in answer to our petition, remitted to us and to the prior of the place the said procuration for this time. In testimony thereof, we, . . . [*lacuna in MS*], the abbot, and the convent of St-Martin-de-Séez, and the prior of the said place, have caused our seals to be placed on the present letter at the request of the said Father. Given at Séez the Monday following the feast of St-Vincent, in the year of our Lord 1255.

We read this letter at Almenèches in the presence of . . . [*lacuna in MS*], the precentor of Rouen; Masters John of Soissons and John of Les Andelys, canons; Dom Stephen, priest of Blenelle; Brothers Harduin and Walter; and Masters Nicholas Bocel, Robert of Les Andelys, and Morel, our clerks. At Séez, on the Wednesday before the Purification and in the presence of Master Guy of Merule, precentor; Master John of Soissons, canon; Osmond, clerk of this bishop; Dom Matthew, his chaplain; and the archdeacon of Séez, we warned the lord bishop of Séez that, in all places where there used to be monks but are none now, he should strive to bring the number up to the former total, and wherever the number has been reduced, he should see that the old number is restored.

JANUARY 29. At St-Pierre-sur-Dives, at our own expense. JANUARY 30. At Lisieux, at our own expense. JANUARY 31. At Préaux, at our own expense. FEBRUARY 1. We received procuration at Corneville. Total for procuration: seven pounds; two shillings, six pence.

FEBRUARY 2. That is to say, on the feast of the Purification of the Virgin.

[50] See entry for July 18, 1250.

We visited there. Eight canons are in residence. In one parish a canon is dwelling alone. One does not accuse another [in chapter]; we enjoined them to correct this. Those who are not priests receive Communion only three times a year. We enjoined the abbot to make a statement of receipts and expenditures in the presence of the entire community, or at least before some of the brothers elected by the community, and to have copies made, of which one shall remain with someone elected by the community, and another to be given to the bailiff. They owe sixty pounds, and are without sufficient provisions to last out the year. This day we spent the night there, at our own expense.

FEBRUARY 3. At Bec. FEBRUARY 4. At Bourg-Achard, at our own expense. FEBRUARY 5-9. At Déville.

FEBRUARY 10.

In the year of our Lord 1255, on the Thursday following the octave of the Purification of the Blessed Virgin Mary, I, Thomas, priest and former rector of the church at Belenne in the diocese of Beauvais, presented to the Reverend Father Eudes, by God's grace the archbishop of Rouen, by the prior of Longue-ville-Girard, the rightful patron of the church of St-Médard, for the free and vacant church at St-Médard-près-Beauvais, appeal in writing to the Apostolic See. I appeal from the interlocutary decision of the said Father who by inter-locutary decree unjustly decided that I should not be admitted to the said church of St-Médard, although I had been canonically presented. This deci-sion was made on the grounds that I could not see well enough, or that my eyes were not good enough to allow me to carry out the duties incumbent upon the priest charged with the cure of souls of a parish, although I, Thomas, can see well enough to read and to attend to all the ecclesiastical duties which have to be done by a priest charged with a cure of souls, and I offered to demonstrate this and to prove it, and I still offer to give sufficient proof. Because of this I, Thomas, feeling that I have been unjustly oppressed, appeal in writing from the aforesaid grievance to the Apostolic See, and request that sealed *apostoli* be given to me. If he should refuse this, I make a further appeal in writing to the Apostolic See on this account.

He had been examined the day before on Naaman's letter[51] and had been found deficient in vision, either for administering a cure of souls or for performing ecclesiastical duties. Present were: Simon, the archdeacon; Master

---

[51] IV Kings 5. Naaman, general of the army of the king of Syria, brought a letter to the king of Israel in these words: When thou shalt receive this letter, know that I have sent to thee Naaman, my servant, that thou mayest heal him of his leprosy.

Richard of Sap, canon of Rouen; Master Peter Hasart, dean of La Chrétien-té, ... [*lacuna in MS*], the dean of Pont-Audemer; Brothers William of Pérrièrs, John of Cottévrard, Harduin of Yvrique, and Walter of Minières, of the Friars Minor; and Peter of Mesnil.

FEBRUARY 11-12. At Déville. FEBRUARY 13. That is to say, on Sep-tuagesima. We preached a sermon in the cathedral at Rouen and spent the night at Ermentrouville. FEBRUARY 14. At the same. FEBRUARY 15. At the same. This day Richard of Sierville, priest, read to us the following, by way of appeal:

Lord Archbishop, I, William of Sierville, cleric and part patron of the church of St-Philbert-de-Sierville, have been especially appointed by my brother Robert as proctor for this appeal to the Apostolic See on my own behalf and on that of my brother Robert of Sierville, knight, who is also part patron of the said church. Because you, without suitable cause, refused to admit Richard of Sierville, priest, a suitable person, presented by us to you for the free and vacant church of Sierville, I request that *apostoli* be given for myself and the said knight.

I, too, my lord, Richard of Sierville, priest, appeal from you to the Apostolic See because you refused and did not wish to receive me into the said church after my legitimate presentation by the aforesaid William and Robert, and I request that *apostoli* be given to me. And, my lord, the aforesaid appeals are made in writing.

To the reverend father in Christ, Lord Eudes, by God's grace archbishop of Rouen, Robert of Sierville, knight, and William of Sierville, cleric, patrons of the church of St-Philbert-de-Sierville, in the deanery of Pavilly, greeting and the reverence and devotion due to a lord and father. We inform Your Pater-nity that we, by common agreement, present to you Richard of Sierville, cleric, and bearer of the present letter, a laudable and upright man, for the free and vacant church at Sierville, the advowson of which is known to belong to us, and we humbly beg Your Paternity that, diligently moved by divine piety, you will receive the aforesaid cleric into the aforesaid church. Given in the year of our Lord 1255, on the Sunday following the Nativity of the Blessed Virgin Mary.

To the reverend father and lord in Christ, Eudes, by God's grace archbishop of Rouen, Robert of Sierville, knight, and William of Sierville, cleric, patrons of the church of St-Philbert-de-Sierville, in the deanery of Pavilly, greeting and reverence and devotion due to a lord and father. We inform Your Paternity that we, by common consent, presented to you Richard of Sierville, a cleric at the time we gave him a letter of presentation, now a priest, the bearer of this letter, and a worthy and upright man, for the free and vacant church at Sierville, the advowson of which is known to belong to us. You will see all this contained in the letter given to this cleric by us, and attached to the present writing. We most humbly implore Your Paternity that, diligently moved by divine piety, you will receive into the said church at Sierville, the said Richard, now a priest, whom we, by common consent, present to you for the aforesaid church at Sierville, now free and vacant, and of which the patronage is known rightfully to belong to us. Given in the year of our Lord 1255, on the Monday preceeding Christmas.

In the said year, on the Wednesday before Christmas, the said priest was presented to us for the aforesaid church, at Ermentrouville.

On the said day and year, the said cleric who claimed to be part patron of the church at Sierville, showed us the following letter, sealed, as it appears at first glance, with the seal of his brother Robert, knight:

To all who may see this, Robert of Sierville, knight, greeting in the Lord. You will known that I have appointed William of Sierville, cleric, my brother, and the bearer of this letter, as my proctor in presenting Richard of Sierville, priest, a worthy and upright man, to the church of St-Philbert-de-Sierville, a half advowson of which is known to belong to me, and also, if it should be necessary, in making an appeal in my behalf to the Lord Pope, or the Roman Curia. I will treat as valid and acceptable whatsoever, in any of the above matters, the said William, cleric, shall perform for me or cause to be done. And I signify this to all, sealing the present letter with my seal. Given in the year of our Lord 1255, the Monday before Christmas.

FEBRUARY 16. At the same.

FEBRUARY 17. At the same.

Brother Eudes, by God's will unworthy bishop of the church of Rouen, and Fulk, by God's grace bishop of Lisieux, to all who may see this letter send eternal greeting in the Lord Jesus Christ. You will know that a dispute arose between us, inasmuch as we, the bishop of Lisieux, in our name and in that of our diocese of Lisieux, claimed right, episcopal jurisdiction, and parochial rights over William, surnamed Choplilart, and his men of Longuemare, as belonging to us and our diocese. Whereas we, the archbishop of Rouen, acting in our own name, saw that this was contrary to the interests of the diocese of Rouen and so stated that the aforesaid belonged to us and our diocese. However, for the sake of peace, we agreed to submit our contention to the arbitration of those venerable and discreet men, Master Simon, archdeacon of Rouen, and Master William of Saon, archdeacon of Eu, in the diocese of Lisieux, promising, in good faith, to maintain inviolate whatever disposition the said two arbiters should agreeably make or arbitrate or order done concerning this contention, by way of making peace or rendering a decision; further agreeing that a penalty of one hundred pounds of Tours, to be rendered in shillings, shall be paid by the party refusing to accept the said arbitration, formal statement, or ordinance of the said peace, or failing to carry out the said arbitration or formal statement or establishment thereof.

If the said two arbiters are unable to come to any agreement in this matter, we desire that a third arbiter, namely, he who is at present the precenter of Rouen, be added to the two arbitrators in this business. The decision of the majority, their judgment or arbitration over the aforesaid dispute, we promise to honor under the aforesaid penalty and in the manner aforesaid. We further desire that this matter shall be cleared up before the coming Nativity of the Blessed Virgin Mary, unless a delay is granted, at our consent. In witness whereof, etc. Given in the year of our Lord 1255, in the month of February.

FEBRUARY 18. At Ste-Catherine, at our expense. FEBRUARY 19. At Frênes. FEBRUARY 20. At the same. We received the following letter.

To all who will see the present letter, the abbot and the convent of St-Ouen-de-Rouen give greeting in the Lord. You are to know that we appoint the bearer of this letter, our beloved Master Bernard of Gisors, cleric, as our proctor in making an appeal to the Reverend Father Eudes, by God's grace archbishop of Rouen, that the monks of St-Victor-en-Caux not be permitted to elect or demand any person to be created as their abbot who does not come from the monastery of St-Ouen-de-Rouen. We shall regard as valid and acceptable whatever the said proctor shall find it expedient to do or have done in our behalf and that of our monastery, both in this matter itself and in whatever other contingencies may arise because of this appeal. By the tenor of the present letter we signify this to all concerned. Given in the year of our Lord 1255, the Saturday before the feast of St. Peter's Chair.

This same day the proctor submitted the following appeal:

I, Bernard of Gisors, proctor of the abbot and the convent of St-Ouen-de-Rouen, and in their name, submit to you, Reverend Father, archbishop of Rouen, that the said religious are and have been in possession of such a privilege, that the monks of St-Vistor-en-Caux, of your diocese, elect and have elected, or demand and have demanded, as a person to be made their abbot whenever an abbot was to be chosen, someone from the bosom of the monastery of St-Ouen-de-Rouen. Wherefore in your presence, I appeal in writing to the

Apostolic See, against the said monks of St-Victor, in the name of the afore-said abbot and convent of St-Ouen, and that you shall neither confirm as abbot of St-Victor, nor bestow the gift of benediction upon, anyone at the election or demand of the said monks of St-Victor who is not elected or demanded from the bosom of St-Ouen-de-Rouen, and I request *apostoli.*

Present were: Simon, the archdeacon; William, the treasurer; P[eter], the archdeacon of Grand-Caux; Ralph of Chevry, canon of Rouen; Robert and Morel, our clerks; and many others.

FEBRUARY 21. At Frênes. FEBRUARY 22. At Genainville. FEBRUARY 23. At Pontoise. FEBRUARY 24–MARCH 2. At Paris. MARCH 3. At St-Denis. MARCH 4. At Pontoise, at our own expense.

MARCH 5. At Pontoise. This day the following profession was made to us:

I, Ascius, the elected and confirmed shepherd of the monastery of St-Victor-en-Caux, promise reverence and obedience to you, Father Eudes, archbishop of Rouen, to your successors, and to the church of Rouen. And this I confirm with my own hand.

MARCH 6. We visited the chapter of St-Mellon-de-Pontoise. We decreed or enacted that whosoever shall not have entered the choir before the [sing-ing of] the first Gloria of the first Psalm shall be regarded as absent. We decreed or enjoined that the established penalties for minor offenses be enacted and firmly exacted. They have only two graduals and two anti-phonaries; they have no psalters beyond the ones which we found deficient at the other visitation.[52] Luke, the vicar, celebrates Mass outside the church at St-Mellon in violation of his oath. He is still ill famed of incontinence, as he was at the other visitation. Item, he walks about the town in a short gown and knee-length tunic; item, he is in the habit of leaving his duties without permission. Item, Dom Vincent likewise leaves his duties; we en-joined them to observe fully their required tasks. We forbade all of them to walk about the town or any other place dressed in short gowns, except for reasonable cause. Item, we forbade the said Luke to celebrate Mass any more in the chapel of the château, and we threatened him with due punish-ment should he presume to disobey. Moreover, he gave us a letter stating that he would regard his vicarate as resigned if he should again offend. For procuration the chapter owes us one hundred shillings of Paris, as well as

---

[52] See entry for November 23, 1254.

accommodation, including wood, beds, cups, dishes, and cooking utensils.

This day we visited the priory of St-Pierre [-de-Pontoise]. Five monks are there. They owe three hundred pounds to the abbot and another sixty pounds elsewhere. We enjoined them to read a chapter of the Rule every day after singing the psalm *Preciosa* at Prime.

Seven [pounds], fifteen shillings, four pence.

Note: about the priory of Valmondois, entered into without permission.

MARCH 7. We visited the abbey of St-Martin-de-Pontoise. It has been split.[53] Only nine were in the convent; two were in the infirmary, of whom one is a leper, the other is ill. We forbade the abbot to receive anyone as a monk, or to accept anyone as a guest, without our permission, unless he is of the household of the king, or such a one to whom hospitality could not be denied without violating the spirit of hospitality. The monks have coffers and keys; we enjoined the abbot to make unannounced inspection of these coffers, collecting the keys, several times a year, in order to remove any property. At the time the community was divided, it owed fourteen hundred pounds, and even now it owes thirteen hundred, but it has both wine and wheat available for sale, to the value of five hundred pounds, of which they may devote two hundred to laying out vineyards, and three hundred to paying off their debts. In the presence of Master Simon of Rouen, Master Peter of Ons, archdeacon of Grand-Caux, and the provost of Pontoise, we forbade the abbot, under pain of excommunication, to receive any one as a guest whom he might refuse without grievous hurt to the abbey. Item, under the same penalty, to grant any new pension without our mandate; item, to bestow, for the next three or four years, any of the buildings of the monastery upon any burgess or other person, without our mandate. Item, because we had heard certain other things about the incontinence of the provost of St-Martin-de-Pontoise, we warned him, in the presence of the said archdeacon, and of Morel, our clerk, to refrain from frequenting the house of Agnes of Maudestor, or visiting a certain woman of Beaumont, who was staying at Val-Girard-en-Pontoise, and a woman who lives at Chapelle, and one other; and that if we heard he was again ill famed of incontinence, we would proceed against him as the law require. Total for procuration: seven pounds, fifteen shillings, four pence, but we had thirty-five shillings and four pence remitted to them.

[53] One group sent out to dependent priories.

MARCH 8. At the same. MARCH 9. At Chaumont [l'Aillerie], at our expense. MARCH 10. At the same, but at the expense of the priory. Total for procuration: six pounds, eighteen shillings.

MARCH 11. We visited there. Three monks from St-Germer-de-Flay are there. They do not observe the fasts of the Rule. They eat meat freely, much as seculars do. They told us that eating meat is not an essential of the Rule, and that the Lord Pope had granted them a dispensation from those things which are not an essential of the Rule; therefore we have permitted it for the present. It is a practice of theirs that he who wishes to receive little round loaves may have them. They owe about eighty pounds.

This day we spent the night at Gisors.

MARCH 12. At the same. Today in our presence Garner of Chaumont, and Adeline, his wife, swore to show each other marital affection from now on. MARCH 13. At the same. MARCH 14-15. At Frênes. MARCH 16. At Frênes, with the Lord King. MARCH 17. At Mortemer. MARCH 18-19. At Gouy. MARCH 20-23. At St-Matthieu. MARCH 24-25. At Bec. MARCH 26-29. At Pont-Audemer. MARCH 29. At Bourg-Achard. MARCH 30. We visited there. There are ten canons; two have died recently. All but three are priests. We enjoined them to confess at least once a month. One hundred pounds is owed to them, and this is more than they owe; they have sufficient provisions to last until the new harvest. The prior does not look out for the clothing of the canons very well; he is either too severe or too slow in giving it out; we enjoined him to correct this. Item, we enjoined the prior to give each canon a pelisse every other year. We received procuration there this day. Total: eight pounds, eleven shillings, four pence.

MARCH 31. At Ermentrouville. APRIL 1. We conferred Holy Orders at Pré, and spent the night at Ermentrouville. APRIL 2. At Ste-Catherine, at our expense. APRIL 3. We received procuration at Quévreville. Total: eight pounds, eleven shillings, one penny. APRIL 4. At Frênes.

APRIL 5. At L'Ille-Dieu, a Premonstratensian house. When we arrived there to make a visitation, they showed us the transcripts of two letters. The first had a seal and ran as follows:

To all who may see this letter, G., by God's grace called the abbot of Laon, vicegerent of the abbey of Prémontré, and the chapter general of this order, give greeting in the Lord. Know that we have an indulgence, granted to the entire order by the Lord ... [lacuna in MS], Pope, under the following terms: All monasteries both of Prémontré itself and its monasteries shall be uniformly visited in head and members every year by visitors appointed at the chapter general and by none other who are not Premonstratensians. A diligent investigation shall be made, openly and in secret, by sworn witnesses, as seems fit.

Item, we saw the other transcript which was unsealed, and ran as follows:

Innocent, bishop, servant to the servants of God, to his beloved children, the abbot of Prémontré, his co-abbots, and all the convents of the Premonstratensian Order, greeting and apostolic blessing. For the honor of the Divine Name, Whose praises you foster with your watchful diligence, the Apostolic See graciously grants you the means whereby your way in religion may follow after ever-increasing grace and be the wherewithal for tranquillity of soul. The following is the status of the monastery of Prémontré, which is at the head of your entire order. After it was brought into being, as you assert, there was decreed by the three first abbots who were the annual visitors [of Prémontré] that all other monasteries of that order were always to be visited or corrected by the abbots, priors, and visitors of Prémontré or by others designated by them and by no other except on the mandate of the Holy See. In a privilege conceded to the said order by the Holy See, it is expressly stated that if there is anything to be corrected either in the persons or monasteries of the order it must be referred for a hearing to the general chapter at Prémontré,[54] so that there, in accordance with justice and due consideration, it can be corrected. We therefore, answering your prayers because of your holiness, concede to you, by virtue of apostolic authority, that Prémontré and other monasteries, just as in the past, so in the future, may only be visited or corrected by its abbots, visitors, and others designated by the order, and by no other, without mandate of the Holy See making full and express mention of this Bull. Therefore to no one among men is it lawful to infringe on this our charter of privilege or rashly presume to violate it. If anyone presume to attempt it, let him know that he will incur the wrath of Almighty God and His blessed Apostles Peter and Paul. Given at Lyons on September 1, in the eighth year of our pontificate.

Total for procuration: six pounds, five shillings, two pence.

APRIL 6. We received procuration at Pérrièrs. Total: seven pounds, nine shillings, eight pence.

APRIL 7. We visited at Beaulieu. Thirteen canons are in residence; nine are priests. One does not accuse another [in chapter]; we enjoined them to

---

[54] Privilege granted to the order by Innocent II on May 3, 1134. (Migne, *PL,* CLXXIX, 204-06.) The same privilege granted that no archbishop, bishop, or prelate could place the houses of the order under interdict, or excommunicate them, "since your excesses can and should be corrected by the common chapter held at Prémontré." (*Ibid.*)

correct this. They owe two hundred forty pounds, but a good and collectible debt of about one hundred pounds is owed to them. No almoner is there. Item, the poor people have no house where they may go when it rains. We forbade anyone to give any alms to their servants or others. Item, we enjoined the prior to institute an almoner. We received procuration there this day. Total: seven pounds, nine shillings, five pence.

APRIL 8-10. At Rouen.

APRIL 11. We visited at St-Lô-de-Rouen. Eight canons are there at present; all of the others were withdrawn at the order of the bishop of Coutances. One accuses another [in chapter]. All but one are priests. They owe six hundred forty-eight pounds. We received procuration there today. Total: eight pounds, seven shillings, one penny.

APRIL 12-15. At Rouen.

APRIL 16. At Rouen. APRIL 17-18. At Déville. APRIL 19. At Déville. In the year of our Lord 1256 William Crispin sent us the following document:[1]

These things William Crispin holds of the archbishop of Rouen. La Buscalle entire, and in demesne; Cherbie entire; all that my lord Aden of Cardonnei holds at Ronqueroles, at Hannesis, at Guisegnies and at Travailles; all that my lord Maheu of Hannesis-le-Wiel holds at Hannesis of the fief of La Buscalle; all that Peter Malfillastre holds at Hannesis of the fief of La Buscalle; all that Sir Peter of Villers holds at Guisegnies and at Pavée of the fief of La Buscalle; all that Maheu of Daubeuf holds at La Buscalle of the fief of La Buscalle; all that my lord Eudes of La Gripière holds of my lord Adam of Cardonnei of the fief of La Buscalle.

APRIL 20. At Déville. APRIL 21. At Jumièges. APRIL 22. At Pont-Audemer. APRIL 23. At Beaumont-en-Auge. APRIL 24. At Troarn. APRIL 25. At Caen. APRIL 26. At Falaise.

APRIL 27. At Falaise. This day we promulgated the following sentence:

In the year of our Lord 1256 on the Thursday after the feast of St. Mark the Evangelist, after the election at Montivilliers of Julianne, prioress of the same monastery, and who was presented to us by Master John of Harfleur, priest and especially appointed proctor of the community of the said monastery for this business, we diligently examined the aforesaid election and inspected the letters sent to us regarding the election itself, and we considered those things which might and ought to weigh with us, in the presence of Julianne and the aforementioned proctor, and, acting on the advice of good men, we decided not to accept the aforesaid election, since there is a possibility that it was uncanonically carried out. However, considering the suitableness of the said Julianne, the profit and peace of the said monastery, and the fact that the power of collating to the monastery has fallen on us anyway, we are collating and placing her over the said monastery.

[1] William Crispin had become a vassal of Eudes on June 11, 1255. At that time, Eudes asked William to draw up a statement of the lands to be held. The holdings are listed. Evidently, William was living at La Buscalle, inasmuch as that was demense land.

APRIL 28. At Falaise. APRIL 29. At Condé. APRIL 30. At Tinchebray. We blessed the abbess of Montivilliers.[2]

MAY 1. Here begins the visitation of the diocese of Avranches. We entered the diocese of Avranches and visited the priory of Aries.[3] Fifteen nuns of the Order of St. Benedict are there. All of them do not confess to their own priest; we enjoined them to correct this. We found there a certain prioress who was of little knowledge and who was unable to inform us about the amount of her resources. They have an income of one hundred twenty pounds. Because of their poverty, they are not held for procuration.

This day we spent the night at the priory of Notre-Dame-du-Rocher-de-Mortain,[4] and, visiting there, we found nine monks from Marmoutier, who are exempt. However, they gave us information concerning the state of the house, as to both spiritual and temporal matters, nor could we discover anything notable which needed correction. They have an income of one hundred forty pounds and possess two manors in England. We received procuration there this day. The sum which we spent for procuration: eight pounds, five shillings, eleven pence.

We visited the chapter of St-Firmin. There are fifteen secular canons and a prior; six canons are in residence. Firmin, the prior's vicar, leases the prebends from the canons. Morel, clerk-choral, is a brawler. Reginald of Stampe, canon, is ill famed of incontinence and has with him a child, whom he is bringing up. Bartholomew, the precentor's vicar, sometimes gets drunk, and he does not arise for Matins. Roger, canon, sometimes frequents taverns. John, the dean's vicar, is a drunkard. In the matter of the potations of Bartholomew, the precentor's vicar, and of John, the dean's vicar; and of the drinking by Roger, canon, in taverns; and of the incontinence of Reginald of Stampe, we warned the said Bartholomew, John, Reginald, and Roger to abstain from such practices. Item, we warned the chapter to punish these men for these offenses. Item, we warned the chapter to discipline Morel, the clerk-choral, who is a brawler and abusive, and Firmin, the vicar, for his leasing of prebends, and to correct them as the law requires, or otherwise we would place a heavier hand upon them all. This day

---

[2] For the ceremonial and prayers used in the blessing of an abbess, see Andrieu, *Le Pontifical romain au moyen âge*, III, 409-10.

[3] No record of this priory is found in either Cottineau or Besse, *Abbayes et prieurés de l'ancienne France*.

[4] A Benedictine priory, dependent on Marmoutier. (Cottineau, II, 1989.)

we received procuration from the chapter but at the house of the prior, Roger. This prior, at our request, offered his house for this time most graciously, for he was in no way held to do this. Total for procuration: eight pounds, ten shillings, seven pence.

MAY 3. We received procuration at Savigny, a Cistercian house.

MAY 4. We visited the priory of St-Hilaire. Three monks from St-Benoît-sur-Loire are there. They do not observe the fasts of the Rule, and they eat meat freely; we enjoined them to correct these things. They give alms to all comers twice a week. They have an income of one hundred pounds; they owe sixty pounds. We received procuration there this day. Total for procuration: six pounds, seventeen shillings, one penny.

MAY 5. We visited the priory at Les Biards.[5] We found one monk there alone; his companion had returned to the abbey, during the past Lenten time, in order that he might be ordained to the priesthood. But, as the prior said, he, or another, ought to return very shortly. He does not observe the fasts of the Rule, and he eats meat freely; we enjoined him to observe the Rule in these matters more fully. We received procuration there this day. Total for procuration: four pounds, thirteen shillings, nine pence.

MAY 6. We visited the priory of St-James-de-Beuvron. Seven monks from St-Benoît-sur-Loire are there. They confess too rarely; we enjoined them to make more frequent confession. Item, they do not observe the fasts of the Rule, and they eat meat; we warned them to maintain a fuller observance of these two rules. In reply, they stated that these two articles did not form an essential part of the rule, but it was purely a matter of conscience, and that the Pope had granted them a dispensation in these things which are not of the substance of the Rule. They have an income of two hundred twenty pounds. We received procuration there this day. Total for procuration: six pounds, three shillings.

MAY 7. We visited the abbey of Montmorel, of the Order of St. Augustine. Sixteen canons are in residence, six are in three of the priories, and one is dwelling alone in England. They give alms to all comers three times a week. They owe one hundred sixty pounds, but indeed quite as much is owed to them; however, that debt is not as collectible as the one they owe. Total for procuration: six pounds, thirteen shillings, seven pence.

MAY 8. We visited the priory of Sacey. Three monks from Marmoutier are there. They do not observe well the fasts of the Rule, and they eat

5 A Benedictine priory of La Couture-du-Mans. (Cottineau, I, 376.)

meat when there is no need; we enjoined them to a fuller observance of the Rule in this matter. Item, since we found that in the church the Blessed Sacrament was placed in a window in such a way that they must turn their backs upon it whenever they say their Hours, we ordered them to place it honorably upon the altar, in some tabernacle or pyx. They have an income of two hundred pounds; more is owed to them in a collectible debt than they owe. Total for procuration: six pounds, seventeen shillings, one penny.

MAY 9. We received procuration at Mont-St-Michel. Total: nine pounds, seventeen shillings, four pence.

MAY 10. We visited there. Forty monks are in residence; all but ten are priests. John, who is in charge of the infirmary, neither celebrates Mass nor receives Communion; we enjoined them to correct this. The abbot is too severe; no one is admitted to the infirmary without his special permission; we enjoined him to be more considerate of the sick and weak, even if they have not asked permission from the abbot. We enjoined the abbot that all computations, both particular and general, always be made in the presence of members elected by the community. They owe three thousand pounds. In the presence of the vicar of Avranches, and of the abbot, a complaint was lodged against the abbot in chapter that he was a destroyer of the goods of the monastery, to wit, that he had dowered in marriage several of his nieces; that he had maintained one of his nephews in the schools for a long time, and at enormous expense defrayed by means of goods of the abbey, and he bought for him a most beautiful copy of the entire *Corpus*[6] without the wish or consent of the community that he had incurred canonical excommunication for laying violent hands upon several priests;[7] and many other enormities were alleged against him. Since the vicar stated that until now he had never heard anything about these matters, we enjoined him to make a diligent inquiry on the spot into their truth; to correct them as they should be corrected in law, or that, if he did not, we would take up the matter with a heavier hand. Item, we enjoined the abbot to dismiss from his service John Pofunée, esquire, who was found to be hurtful to the abbey in many ways. We had issued like orders at our other visitation, but they had not yet been carried out.[8]

[6] The *Corpus Legum*, which included the *Decretum* of Gratian and the *Decretales* of Gregory IX.

[7] It is forbidden, even for an abbot, to strike a priest in anger. *Corp. jur. can., Decretal. Greg. IX* Lib. v. Tit. 39, deals with all the variations of the subject.

[8] See entry for August 1, 1250.

This day we spent the night at Avranches at the palace of the bishop, and received our procuration from him. Total: six pounds, four shilllings, nine pence.

MAY 11. We visited the chapter. By God's grace, we found everything to be in good condition except that a certain Nicholas, who had recently received a benefice in that church worth ten pounds, was publicly known for engaging in trade The dean and chapter promised us that they would correct this satisfactorily and quickly. We received procuration this day from the chapter. Total: nine pounds, six shillings, eight pence.

MAY 12. At La Lucerne [-d'Outremer], a Premonstatensian house. Total for procuration: one hundred nine shillings, two pence. This day Peter of Gamaches, knight, swore in our presence that because of the beating of a certain messenger bringing a letter to our curia, he would abide by our decision up to the amount of one hundred pounds. He promised on oath to give us pledges for this, either to our official or to the dean of Gisors. Item, he also swore on oath to produce his brother Matthew before us. Item, that if it were possible he would bring his stepson, provided that he be given a safe-conduct going and coming. Present were: A., the dean; Nicholas of Godfried, canon of Avranches; Peter, archdeacon of Grand-Caux, canon of Rouen; Brothers Harduin and Walter; and R., clerk of the lord bishop of Avranches. The said Peter stood to the law in our presence on the aforementioned charge and was found not guilty. But since, as they have confessed to us, his brother, Matthew, and Renaud, his stepson, were guilty of the stated offense, we condemned them to pay us fifty shillings, for which he constituted himself the surety and principal debtor for the money, which was to be paid to us on behalf of the squires. Item, the squires swore that they would make three penitential processions, in bare feet and clad in shirt and trunk hose, on three Sundays, under penalty of paying us twenty pounds; for this penalty the said knight agreed to be a guarantor and principal debtor.

MAY 13. Here begins the visitation of the diocese of Coutances. We visited the priory of St-Pair. Two monks from Mont-St-Michael are there. Women sometimes eat with the monks at the priory; we ordered them to abstain from this practice so far as they tactfully could do so. Twice a week bread is given as alms to all comers. They do not observe the fasts of the Rule. They eat meat freely; we ordered this corrected. The priory is worth about one thousand pounds to the abbey, not counting the food for the priory monks.

We received procuration there this day. Total for procuration: one hundred seventeen shillings, eight pence.

MAY 14. We received procuration at Villedieu-de-Saultchevreuil, at the house of the Hospitalers. Total for procuration: seven pounds, thirteen shillings, nine pence.

MAY 15. We visited the abbey of St-Sever. Eighteen monks are there. All but six are priests. The morning Mass is occasionally omitted; item, they chant their Hours with too great precipitancy; we enjoined them to correct this. One does not accuse another [in chapter]; item, we enjoined them to correct this. Alms are given to all comers three times a week. They owe one hundred forty pounds and have an income of eight hundred pounds. The sick are badly provided for; we enjoined them to correct this. Item, we enjoined the abbot to make his computations in the presence of certain brothers elected by the community. We received procuration there this day. Total for procuration: seven pounds, twenty-three pence.

MAY 16. We visited the abbey of Hambye. Eighteen monks are there. They confess too rarely; we enjoined them and those who are not priests to confess at least once a month. In the priories they eat meat and fail to keep the fasts of the Rule; we enjoined them to correct this. They owe one hundred pounds. We received procuration there this day. Total: seven pounds less three pence.

MAY 17. At Coutances, where we received procuration from the lord bishop.[9]

MAY 18. We visited the chapter of Coutances. We found that the canons freely leave the choir without need and without permission. Item, that they talk loudly from stall to stall. We found Andrew of Boum, John of La Croix, and Ralph of St-Sauveur, clerks-choral, to be engaged in trade. Item, Peter, called "Domine," a canon, is publicly known for drunkenness. And since there was a dispute between bishop and chapter as to which of them should discipline these offenses, we enjoined both to undertake to settle this dispute or that otherwise we would take a hand in it. The following agreement was reached by them in our presence:

Be it known to you that a controversy arose between the venerable father J[ohn], by God's grace bishop of Coutances, on the one side, and the venerable men, the chapter of Coutances, on the other, because the chapter claimed that

---

[9] John, bishop of Coutances, 1251-74 (Gams. *Series episcoporum*, p. 542).

the Father had injured them, inasmuch as he had, on his own authority, unjustly occupied a certain house and garden contiguous to the house allocated to the treasurer of Coutances. Moreover, there is another house, located in front of the doors of the church, which the chapter states that it bought with its own money; and yet another house in which John, archdeacon of Avranches and canon of Coutances, lived, and which the bishop did not wish to be transferred to the control of the chapter since he [the bishop] held it in fee except for milling rights. In addition, he held back last Christmas a corrody worth ten pounds annually which is to be paid at Christman time. For the bishop it was stated that he had the cure of souls of all the canons of the chapter of Coutances as well as of the clerks-choral, which right the chapter denied and thus injured him. To settle these matters, the said Father and chapter agreed as follows: that the treasurer of Avranches should act as arbiter for the bishop, and Roger, archdeacon of Coutances, should do the same for the chapter, both being discreet men; if these two are unable to resolve these matters either in whole or in part, they shall call in a third arbiter, namely, the dean of Bayeux, and the decision of two or three of these judges shall prevail. It is further agreed among the parties that the party who is not favored by all the arbiters, or the decision of two of the three of them, shall be held to pay two hundred marks to the other party; and that the decision shall be reached by the arbiters within a year from the date of the drawing up of this instrument by the parties, unless the time limit is prolonged by mutual consent. The said arbiters must swear that they will faithfully bring this matter to a termination.

MAY 19. At Pérrièrs at the expense of the priory. No monks are there. The place belongs to the abbey of St-Taurin-d'Evreux. Total for procuration: six pounds, eleven shillings, eight pence.

MAY 20. We received procuration at Blanchelande, a Premonstratensian house. Total for procuration: one hundred eleven shillings, six pence. This day, by word of mouth, we warned the prior of St-Germain-sur-Ay,[10] to receive us for the purpose of making a visitation at his priory next Monday, or that otherwise we would institute proceedings against him as the law requires. Present were: ... [lacuna in MS], the abbot of Blanchelande; Peter, archdeacon of Caux; Richard of Sap, canon of Rouen; Brothers Harduin and Walter and Morel, our clerk.

MAY 21. We visited the abbey of Lessay. Thirty-four monks are there. With respect to spiritual concerns, we found that, through God's grace,

---

[10] A Benedictine priory dependent on Mont-St-Michel. (Cottineau, II, 2709-10.) See entry for June 1, below.

everything was in good condition except that occasionally the officials broke the fasts when there were guests; we enjoined them to correct this. They have an income of fifteen hundred pounds; they owe about three hundred pounds. We ordered the officials to cast their accounts at least once a year. We received procuration there this day. Total for procuration: seven pounds, seven shillings.

MAY 22. We visited the abbey of St-Sauveur, where there are thirty monks. All are priests but five who are dwelling in priories. We enjoined the abbot to punish those who broke the fasts or ate meat. Traveling monks do not observe the fasts of the Rule; we enjoined them to correct this. More is owed to them than they owe. Total for procuration: six pounds, three shillings, eight pence.

Since we had ordered Thomas, prior of Ste-Hélène,[11] and Martin, prior of St-Germain-en-Hague,[12] to receive us for visitation and for such procuration as the facilities of their houses allowed, the said priors appeared before us at Héauville on the Wednesday before Ascension and stated that they were not obliged to receive us for visitation or to provide procuration for us, inasmuch as never before had they been visited by an archbishop of Rouen nor had they given such a one procuration. Item, they had never been visited by a bishop of Coutances, nor had they granted him procuration. After this they took an oath on their word as priests to speak the truth, and they stated the case as before, adding that Gillain,[13] former bishop of Coutances, had at one time ordered the prior of Ste-Hélène to receive him for visitation and procuration, which the prior had utterly refused to do. Item, John, who is now the bishop of Coutances, once commanded the prior of Ste-Hélène to accommodate him at his house for the purpose of sleeping and eating at the expense of the bishop, which the prior utterly refused to do, telling the bishop, when he asked the reason for his conduct, that he had refused him hospitality, though at the bishop's expense, in order that the bishop might not be able to say in the future that the priory had at one time received a bishop for visitation and procuration. Having made these statements, they placed themselves at our discretion and under our instructions in this matter. Present were: Martin, prior of Héauville; Dom Robert

---

[11] Located at Omonville. (Cottineau, II, 2725.)

[12] This is properly St-Germain-des-Vaux. (Cottineau, II, 2707.) It was dependent on St-Paul-de-Cormery, diocese of Tours.

[13] Bishop of Coutances from 1246 to 1248. (Gams, *Series episcoporum*, p. 542.)

le Sor, canon of Coutances; Master Bartholomew of Coville, P[eter], archdeacon of Caux, R[ichard] of Sap, canon of Rouen, Dom Ralph of Boum,
rector of Heauville, Brothers H[arduin] and W[alter], and Morel, our
clerk, and many others. This being done, we told them [the priors] that
we would make inquiry into the truth of these matters, and would suspend
any action in the matter until we had investigated the truth of the situation
more completely.

MAY 23. We received procuration at Héauville. Total for procuration:
six pounds, seven shillings, nine pence. Two monks from Marmoutier are
there. Because they were exempt, they did not wish to answer any questions
about themselves or concerning the state of the house; however, we warned
them to live without scandal, because if they committed any delict, we had
the authority to proceed against them.

MAY 24. We visited the priory of Vauville. Four monks from Cerisy
are in residence. They have no copy of the Rule; we enjoined them to
take pains to procure one. They do not observe the fasts of the Rule; we
enjoined them to a fuller observance. They eat meat freely; we enjoined
them to keep entirely away from meat, except as the Rule permitted them
to eat it. The prior does not draw up his statement concerning the revenues
of the house with the assistance of any of his companions, nor are they aware
of the things he does; we enjoined him to prepare a statement of receipts
and expenses and to have a written record of this prepared. Total for
procuration: one hundred shillings less six pence.

MAY 25. We visited the abbey of Cherbourg. The cloister is not well
kept, and lay folk talk with the canons and pass through the cloister to do
so. The canons possess coffers, but neither the abbot nor the prior inspect
these; we enjoined the abbot or the prior to investigate them. Whenever
they eat meat they all leave the refectory. Some of them have unauthorized
serges, and pelisses of rabbit fur; we ordered these removed. The abbot is
occasionally immoderate in his drinking. He does not sleep in the dormitory
frequently enough; when he does not sleep in the dormitory, he does not
arise for Matins. He never casts his accounts with the community. The
bailiff casts his accounts only once a year; the other officials compute only
with the bailiff. The sick are ill provided for. We enjoined them to correct
all there things. They have an income of seven hundred pounds. Twenty-
six monks are in residence. They owe about five hundred pounds. They
confess infrequently; we enjoined them to correct this. Several women, and

young ones at that, reside within the walls. Total for procuration: nine pounds, five pence.

This day the prior and cellarer of this place sought official absolution from us from the excommunication placed upon them by Master Philip of Fontenay, on apostolic authority. They offered Dom Robert, called Le Sor, canon of Coutances, as a pledge that they would abide by the decision, and, having accepted their oath to that effect, we absolved them.

MAY 26. We received procuration at Montebourg. Total for procuration: nine pounds, five pence.

MAY 27. We visited there. Thirty-two monks are in residence. Since the prior of St-Michel-près-Vernon[14] in our diocese has been behaving very badly, we enjoined the abbot to remove him from his priory; otherwise we, because of his offenses, would remove him therefrom in disgrace. Alms are given to all comers three times a week. Although the sacristan and the monk in charge of the infirmary have sufficient resources, they never prepare any statement respecting the finances of their offices; we enjoined them to prepare such a statement at least once a year and in the presence of the abbot and some of the brothers elected by the community. Those who are in the priories eat meat and do not observe the fasts of the Rule. The abbot does not visit his priories every year; we enjoined him to visit them, or have them visited once a year, and to have all abuses corrected. The abbot does not compute; we enjoined him to cast his accounts at least once a year in the presence of brothers elected by the community. Item, that the officials should cast their accounts of expenses and receipts once a month in like manner, and in the presence of brothers elected by the community.

This day we received procuration at Carentan, at the expense of the priory of St-Côme,[15] which is at present pledged to a certain Lombard.[16] Total: seven pounds, eighteen shillings.

MAY 28. We received procuration at [St-Georges-de-] Bohon.[17] Eight monks from Marmoutier are there. They are exempt; however, we admonished them to live without scandal. Total: seven pounds, eight shillings, eight pence.

---

[14] St-Michel-près-Vernon was a priory of Montebourg.
[15] St-Côme-du-Mont, a Cluniac priory. (Cottineau, II, 2639.)
[16] An Italian banker, who loaned money usually at interest.
[17] A Benedictine priory of Marmoutier. (Cottineau, I, 404.)

MAY 29. We received procuration at Saintény. Total for procuration: seven pounds, four shillings, one penny.

MAY 30. We visited there. We found two monks from St-Nicole-d'Angers. They do not observe the fasts of the Rule, and they eat meat freely; we warned them to observe their Rule more completely in this matter. They have an income of one hundred forty pounds; they owe twenty pounds, over and above twelve pounds which they are obliged to pay at once.

This day we visited the priory of Marchézieux. Three monks from Cormery are there. The prior does not sleep with the others; we enjoined him to correct this. They have no copy of the Rule; we enjoined them to procure one. They do not observe the fasts of the Rule and they eat meat freely; we enjoined them to observe the Rule more fully in these matters. They have an income of two hundred pounds; they owe about one hundred pounds. Total for procuration: seven pounds, seven shillings.

MAY 31. We visited the priory of St-Fromond. Thirteen monks from Cerisy are there. All are priests. The abbot should send two more monks there shortly. In the hour set apart for conversation, the monks leave the cloister and go out to the farm, and without permission; we forbade this. Alms are given to all comers daily. When there are guests several of them [the monks] break the fasts of the Rule. Once a week they all leave the refectory and eat meat together in the infirmary; we enjoined them to correct this. They have an income of five hundred pounds; they owe one hundred forty pounds. Robert, who is a cleric and relative of the prior, and who serves in the refectory, is ill famed of incontinence. The prior casts no accounts. The convent seal is kept by the prior alone. We enjoined the prior to prepare a statement of the house finances twice a year and in the presence of brothers elected by the community; that he should dismiss the said Robert; item, that the convent seal should be kept under two keys, of which the prior should have one, the other to be kept by some brother elected by the community. We received procuration there this day. Total for procuration: seven pounds, eight shillings, three pence.

JUNE 1. We visited the abbey of St-Lô, an Augustinian house. Twenty-four canons are there. Alms are given to all comers three times a week. They have an income of seven hundred pounds; they owe about two hundred pounds. By God's grace, we found everything to be in good condition. Total for procuration: six pounds, eighteen shillings, four pence.

La Bloutière[18] is a priory situated near Villedieu-de-Saultechevreuil and belongs to the Augustinians. Because of its poverty we did not visit it, nor did we receive procuration from it.

St-Nicole-du-Bois-Roger is a priory situated near Coutances which belongs to Cormery. Because of its poverty we did not, at this time, visit it nor receive procuration there.

Savigny is a priory situated near Coutances which belongs to the abbey of Ste-Barbe. Because of its poverty we did not, at this time, visit it nor receive procuration there.

At Fontenay, on the feast of Pentecost, in the year of our Lord 1256, Brother Gilbert, called Caple, the prior of St-Germain-sur-Ay, at the mandate of the abbot of Mont-St-Michel-in-Peril-of-the-Sea, and in his presence, sought from us official absolution from the suspension under which we had placed him for his refusal to admit us to his priory for visitation and procuration. We absolved him after the prior had sworn to obey our will in this matter of the visitation and the procuration which we had sought from his priory.[19] In the matter of the procuration which he owed to us, we enjoined him to pay forty shillings of Tours to the abbot of St-Sauveur, who gave us procuration on the day when we came to the priory. However, we made it clear that we did not wish the receipt of this forty shillings to be of any prejudice to us in the future, for we are entitled to exact full procuration from this priory whenever we visit it, should we so desire. Present were: . . . [lacuna in MS], the said abbot; P[eter], archdeacon of Caux; Master Richard of Sap, canon of Rouen; William of Bretteville, knight; Brother William of Philbec, subprior of Mont-St-Michel; Robert, called Miles, cleric; Brothers Harduin and Walter of Minières, of the Friars Minor; Master John, canon of Les Andelys; Hugh, rector of the church of Foucescalier; and Morel, rector at Us, and Robert, called Campsore, our clerks.

JUNE 2. We spent the night at Briquessard. JUNE 3. At Fontenay. JUNE 4. At the same. We celebrated the feast of Pentecost, and absolved the prior of St-Germain-sur-Ay, as stated on the preceding page.[20] JUNE 5. At Troarn JUNE 6. At Pont-l'Evêque. JUNE 7. At Pont-Audemer. JUNE 8. At Jumièges. JUNE 9. At Déville. JUNE 10. At Déville. This day we conferred

---

[18] This priory was decidated to St. Thomas à Becket. (Cottineau, I. 399.)

[19] See entry for May 20, above.

[20] This is another indication that the Register was not compiled on a day-to-day basis. The absolution took place on June 4, which was the date on which the feast of Pentecost fell in the year 1256, yet the terms of the absolution are entered under the date of June 1.

Holy Orders. JUNE 11. At Déville. JUNE 12. We held the sacred synod of the Greater Archdeaconry and spent the night at Ermentrouville. JUNE 13. We held the Greater Synod and spent the night at Ermentrouville. JUNE 14. We held the synod of the deans in our palace at Rouen. This day Maurice, rector of the church at Boisemont, resigned into our hands the chapel at Guillaume-Mesnil.

JUNE 15. At Déville. John, rector of the church of St-Etienne-de-Wylebo [Wellbotum?] resigned his church into our hands. Item, William, rector of the church of St-Maurice-de-Marcouville, in the deanery of Bourgtheroulde, resigned his church into our hands. Present were: the archdeacon Simon; ... [*lacuna in MS*], the treasurer; Arnulf, archdeacon of Petit-Caux; Master John of St-Lô; Master Lawrence of Ricarville, canon of Rouen; Master Philip of Fontenay; and Morel, our clerk.

JUNE 16-18. At Déville. JUNE 19. At Pont-de-l'Arche. JUNE 20. At Louviers. JUNE 21-23. At Frênes. JUNE 24. At Bonport. JUNE 25. At Bourg-Achard. JUNE 26. At Pont-Audemer. This day peace was concluded between us and our suffragans. JUNE 27. At Bec. JUNE 28. At Louviers. JUNE 29. At Sausseuse.

JUNE 30. At St-Laurent-en-Cornecervine, where we visited. Four monks from Val-Jehosafat-de-Chartres are there. Three are priests. They owe seventy pounds. We found everything to be in a sufficiently good state. Total for procuration: one hundred shillings, four pence of Paris.

JULY 1. At Le Pecq. JULY 2-6. At Paris. JULY 7. At St-Denis. JULY 8. At Conflans-Ste-Honorine. JULY 9-11. At Pontoise.

JULY 12. We visited the hospital at Pontoise. Ten brothers are there, including the priest. There are five sisters. Sometimes the brothers eat in the town. We found nothing there in good order. This is the income which the said house is reported to possess: twenty-four acres of land in four places in the dioceses of Paris, Beauvais, and Rouen; sixteen acres of vineyard, less one which is said to have been taken from them; sixteen pounds in rents; three acres of meadow; one mill worth twelve *muids* of grain; the tithe from Anery worth six *muids,* two-thirds of which are in wheat and one-third in oats; at Us, six *sétiers* and five *mines* of wheat, and five *mines* of oats.[21]

JULY 13. At Wy. The priest at Gadancourt owes us an annual rent of a *muid* oats whenever we come to Wy. JULY 14. At Genainville. JULY 15.

[21] For explanation of the units of measurement, see above, August 18, 1251, n. 14.

At Marines, at our expense. JULY 16. We dedicated the church at Marines. JULY 17. At Liancourt. For procuration we received four pounds of Paris, accommodation, and utensils as agreed upon in our agreement.

JULY 18. We visited there. Three monks are there. Brother William of Orléans does not confess to his prior. A certain novice leaves the house without permission. They eat meat freely; we forbade them to eat meat except as the Rule permits. They do not observe the fasts of the Rule; we warned them to observe the Rule in this matter. They have an income of one hundred twenty pounds; they owe one hundred pounds. We enjoined the prior to order the abbot to remove from the priory, before the feast of the Assumption of the Virgin Mary, both Brother William, who is ill famed of incontinence and of several other vices, and the novice who is incapable of assisting others in their duties; otherwise we ourself would remove the said Brother William from the priory and in disgrace.

This day we visited the priory of St-Martin.[22] Two monks from St-Magloire-de-Paris are there. They owe about eight pounds, but about four pounds are owed to them; they have an income of about forty pounds. The prior is ill famed of a certain Isabelle, from Chaumont, who gave birth to a girl by him. We received forty shillings of Paris as procuration.

JULY 19. At Ressons, a Premonstratensian house.[23] Total for procuration: six pounds, four shillings, one penny.

JULY 20. At Neufmarché. Five monks from St-Evroult are there. They do not sing Nones in the monastery, although they sing the other Hours there; we enjoined them to correct this. They use feather beds; they have no copy of the Rule; they eat meat freely; we enjoined them to see that all these things were corrected in accordance with the Rule. Brother John of Auffay and Brother Alexander are not very obedient. Item, Brother John is quarrelsome, and an immoderate drinker; we warned him to abstain from both of these offenses, or that otherwise we would institute proceedings against him as the law requires. Total for procuration: six pounds, sixteen shillings, four pence.

JULY 21. We received procuration at St-Laurent-en-Lyons. Total for procuration: seven pounds, fifteen pence.

JULY 22. We visited there. Fourteen canons are in residence. One does

[22] St-Martin-d'Es, a Benedictine priory dependent on St-Magloire-de-Paris. (Cottineau, II, 2789.)
[23] Established c. 1150. (Cottineau, II, 2450.)

not accuse another [in chapter]; we enjoined them to correct this. One of the lay brothers has rancor toward another; we enjoined the prior to have the cause of rancor removed and minor penances inflicted upon both parties at the next meeting of the chapter. They owe one hundred sixty pounds. The sick are ill provided for; capes and pelisses are not distributed on time; we ordered this corrected. This day we received procuration at Bellosane. Total for procuration: one hundred thirteen shillings.

JULY 23. We visited the priory at St-Aubin, where there are fifteen nuns. They do not always say their Hours with modulation. There is a parish there, but it has no priest in charge. We forbade the relatives of the nuns to sleep at the priory or to eat or drink with the nuns therein. Item, we forbade them to receive anyone as a nun without our special permission; if they do receive such a one, she is not to be regarded as a nun. They owe somewhat over forty pounds. We, at the time, took the veil away from Alice of Rouen and from Eustasia of Etrépagny because of their fornications. We sent Agnes of Pont to the leper house at Rouen, because she had connived at Eustasia's fornication, and indeed had even arranged it, as the rumor goes; further, she gave the said Eustasia, as report has it, some herbs to drink in order to kill the child already conceived within the said Eustasia. We removed the prioress from her office. Until a new prioress shall be instituted, we have suspended punishment of Anastasia, the subprioress, who is ill famed of incontinence.

This day we visited the chapter at Gournay. Three canons are in residence; there are five learning to be canons and one wandering monk. We found evertyhing to be in good condition.

This day we visited the hospital of the Hôtel-Dieu at Gournay, where there are four brothers, one chaplain, and three sisters. The brothers and sisters are received there with the consent of the brethren of the house, the chapter, and the burgesses of Gournay. The brothers sometimes drink in the taverns and eat in the town without permission; we warned the dean of Gournay to discipline the brothers who offend in these matters. The house is worth about one hundred pounds. We forbade the chaplain to hear the confessions of the brothers or sisters, or the sick who are in the house, without our special permission or that of the priest of St. Mary's, in whose parish the said hospital is located.

JULY 24. We received procuration at Vesly. Total: six pounds, fourteen shillings, eight pence.

JULY 25. We visited there. Three monks from Marmoutier are in residence. They have but recently arrived.

JULY 26. At Parnes. We issued a warning to Sir Eustace of Noyers, knight, who was defamed of adultery. Present were: Peter, archdeacon of Caux; Richard of Sap, canon of Rouen; Brothers Harduin and Walter; and Morel and Robert, our clerks. Total: six pounds, seven shillings, seven pence.

JULY 27. We visited there, and the prior of La Chapelle was present. Five monks are in residence. At La Chapelle we promised the prior that we would lend him six pounds of Paris until the feast of the Purification of of the Virgin so that he might purchase a chalice which his priory lacked. We enjoined each one of the monks to confess at least once a month and warned the prior that if we found him negligent in this again we would punish him for it. They eat meat freely; we forbade them to eat meat save as the Rule permits. The priory of La Chapelle owes about fifty pounds and has an income of forty-five pounds.

This day we received procuration at Sérans-le-Bouteiller. For procuration we received seventy shillings of Paris, domestic utensils, fodder for the horses, straw for man and beast, and wood.

JULY 28. We visited there. Three monks from St-Germer are there. They do not observe the fasts of the Rule. They eat meat freely; we enjoined them to observe the Rule in this matter. They owe forty pounds; they have an income of one hundred twenty pounds.

JULY 29–AUGUST 3. At Frênes.

AUGUST 4. At the same. This day we enjoined Master Vincent, called Grossim, and forbade him any further exercise of certain privileges conceded to him by the count of Eu, of which he claimed to be the executor, until such time as he should receive permission from us. We warned him that if he disobeyed our mandate we would institute proceedings against him as must be done according to law.

On this same day Peter Carnifex, of the parish of Muchegros, pledged himself, under penalty of twenty pounds and in accordance with the uses and customs of Normandy, and on the Holy Gospels swore, that he would never again do any harm to Gerard, or cause any harm to be done to him by anyone else; and that if anyone did desire to injure Gerard, and he should learn of it, he would give Gerard information about this. Peter Bunel, in our presence and at the request of the said Peter Carnifex, constituted himself surety for this pledge.

AUGUST 5. At Frênes. Matthew, brother Peter of Gamaches,[24] knight, and Peter's stepson were brought before us, sworn, and, by virtue of the oath which they took, were asked whether they had beaten a certain messenger, bringing a letter to our curia at Rouen, and if so, in what manner they had thrashed him. They replied that they had beaten him by striking him on the head, shoulders, and arms with two rods, and by throwing him to the ground. Asked whether they knew he was a messenger of the archbishop of Rouen, they said that they neither knew it nor believed it, but that they had harassed him because a woman had told them that he was a messenger bringing a citation against Sir Peter. Asked whether they had acted at the command or desire of the said knight, they said, "No"; indeed, they believed that they had displeased him, since he had run after them, and not being able to catch up with them, he cried out when they were beating the messenger: "You are doing me an injury." After this they swore to abide by whatever sentence we should lay upon them for their offense, and they offered Sir Peter as their guarantor to the extent of ten pounds for each of them. Thereupon we designated the Monday in the vigil of the Assumption of the Virgin Mary, as the date upon which they might hear our sentence at Rouen. Present were: Peter, the archdeacon; Master Richard of Sap, the dean of Gamaches; Miles, priest at Saussay.

AUGUST 6-10. At Frênes.

AUGUST 11. We visited the priory of Noyon-sur-Andelle, finding seven monks there. All but one are priests. We forbade them to eat meat save as the Rule permits. They owe one hundred twenty pounds. Total for procuration: six pounds, twelve shillings, nine pence.

AUGUST 12. At Ste-Catherine, at our expense. AUGUST 13. At Déville.

AUGUST 14. At Rouen. Here we found the following letter:

Alexander, bishop,[25] servant of the servants of God, to his beloved son, Master John of Putot, rector of St. George's church near Fontes, in the diocese of Rouen, greeting and Apostolic blessing. At the intercession of our beloved son, ... [lacuna in MS], the abbot of Fécamp, we are pleased to grant to you, as a special favor, that you may provide a suitable vicar to serve the church of St-Georges-près-Fontes, in the diocese of Rouen, which has the cure of souls, so that you may take up residence in the schools for five years, or for such a period as the abbot may request. Further, you may enjoy the full revenue of the

24 See entry for May 12, above.
25 Alexander IV, 1255-61.

said church as though you were in personal residence; nor shall you be compelled to assume any higher orders in the interim, nor take up any personal residence in your parish, despite the oath which you have said that you took concerning the taking of successive orders and of taking up your personal residence in this church. Moreover, if the Apostolic See should ever grant to the local diocesan the right to compel personal residence by the parish rectors of his diocese, despite indulgences of this kind, we, by apostolic authority, make an exception in your case. Therefore, no one shall be permitted to infringe this our charter of concession, nor shall anyone presume to do so. If anyone should so presume to attempt this, let him know that he will incur the warth the Omnipotent God and that of the Blessed Apostles Peter and Paul. Given at Anagni, September 12, in the first year of our pontificate.

AUGUST 15. At Rouen. We celebrated the feast of the Assumption. AU-GUST 16. At Pont-de-l'Arche. AUGUST 17. At Vernon. AUGUST 18-19. At Louviers. AUGUST 20-21. At Pont-de-l'Arche. AUGUST 22. At Frênes. AUGUST 23. At Louviers. When the king's castellan of Vaudreuil seized William, called Pipuet, esquire, and William of Contemoulins, esquire, in the preserves at Vaudreuil, they escaped from the hands of the castellan's servants and came to Louviers. The castellan followed them to this our town and captured them there, although he could not legally do so, and carried them off to prison at Vaudreuil. When this came to our attention, we realized that his acts were prejudicial to us and our diocese, for the full jurisdiction over the said town pertains to us. We approached the king, and having presented the case to him, we obtained the following letter by request:

Louis, by God's grace king of the Franks,[26] to ... [lacuna in MS], the bailiff of Rouen, greeting. We have been informed that our castellan of Vaudreuil captured, within the jurisdiction of our beloved and faithful [Eudes], the archbishop of Rouen, to wit, in his town which is called Louviers, two men who had been taken by his sergeants in the preserves of the sergeants of the said castellan. We command you to restore the said two men to the said town [Louviers] if it be possible and as should be done, lest by this occurrence it should result that the jurisdiction of the archbishop be restricted in the future. When you have done this, report the fact by letter to the aforementioned archbishop. Given at the abbey of Notre-Dame-Royale, near Pontoise, in the year of our Lord 1256.

On Wednesday, on the vigil of St. Bartholomew, in the said year of the

---

[26] It is interesting to find the old formula being still used in official documents.

Incarnation of the Lord, William of Les Voisins, then bailiff of Rouen, came to Louviers and in our presence at our palace there, and acting under the royal mandate already described, restored to us the said two esquires who had been captured in the said town. Present were: We, Eudes, archbishop of Rouen; Peter, archdeacon of Caux; Richard of Sap, canon of Rouen; Brother Harduin of the Friars Minor; Bartholomew, called Fergant, vicomte of Pont-de-l'Arche; Sir Geoffrey of Roncherolles, knight; John, his brother; Ralph, the bailiff's clerk; Robert of Les Andelys; and Hugh (our almoner) and Morel, our clerks; Roger of Martry, Ralph Bitaud, and William Anglais, provosts of Louviers, and several others. We then confined the said esquires in our prison. Having first accepted their pledges that they would stand trial before us or before our bailiff, if anyone desired to prosecute them on the charge for which they had been apprehended, we released them. Their pledges were Sir Geoffrey of Roncherolles and John, his brother; these men also offered themselves as sureties for satisfaction of any fine we might levy on them.

AUGUST 24. At Frênes. AUGUST 25-27. At Ste-Catherine. AUGUST 28. At Frênes. AUGUST 29. At Genainville. AUGUST 30. At Pontoise. AUGUST 31. At St-Denis. SEPTEMBER 1-9. At Paris. SEPTEMBER 10. At Asnières. SEPTEMBER 11. At Verberie. SEPTEMBER 12. At Noyon. SEPTEMBER 13. At Montdidier. SEPTEMBER 14. At Conty. SEPTEMBER 15. At Aumale. SEPTEMBER 16-18. At Aliermont. SEPTEMBER 19. At Dieppe. SEPTEMBER 20. We received procuration at Longueville. SEPTEMBER 21-30. At Déville. OCTOBER 1. At Bourg-Achard. OCTOBER 2. At Pont-Audemer. OCTOBER 3. At Lisieux. OCTOBER 4. Here begins the visitation of the diocese of Bayeux. OCTOBER 5. At Val-Richer.[27] We received procuration at Fontenay. Total for procuration: six pounds, eight shillings, two pence.

OCTOBER 6. We visited there, finding twenty-five monks in residence. They have two priories in Normandy and one overseas in England. We enjoined them to read the Statutes of the Pope as the said Statutes require. They do not confess every month; we enjoined them to correct this. We enjoined the abbot to make frequent inspection of such coffers as were provided with keys, so that he might remove any property. We forbade them the use of meat, except as the Rule permits. They owe something over one thousand pounds; they have an income of one thousand pounds.

---

[27] Established as a daughter house of Clairvaux in 1146. (Cottineau, II, 3264.)

This day we reached and received procuration at Barbery [Barbeaux],[28] a Cistercian house.

OCTOBER 7. We visited the abbey of Notre-Dame-du-Val, an Augustinian house. Fourteen canons are there; all but one are priests. We enjoined the novice to confess and receive Communion at least once a month. They have an income of three hundred pounds and more; they owe one hundred fifty pounds. They are spending many pounds on the repair of their buildings and monastery. Total for procuration: six pounds, eight pence.

OCTOBER 8. We received procuration at le Plessis-Grimoult. Total for procuration: seven pounds, seven shillings, eight pence. OCTOBER 9. We spent the night there at our own expense.

OCTOBER 10. At the same, and at our expense. We visited. Nineteen canons are there; all are priests. They owe about three hundred pounds; they have an income of about twelve hundred pounds. Canons are dwelling alone in some of the parishes; we enjoined that they be recalled to the cloister or that companions be given to them.

OCTOBER 11. We spent the night at Belle-Etoile, a Premonstratensian house. Total: one hundred four shillings, eight pence.

This day we visited ... [lacuna in MS], the prior of La Lande-Patry. Three monks from St-Vincent-du-Mans are there. They eat meat freely; we forbade this, save as the Rule permits. The house has no copy of the Rule; we enjoined the prior to get one, or to have one written out and so procure one. They have an income of ninety pounds; they owe about forty pounds. Then the prior gave us the following letter:

To all who will see the present letter, I, Thomas, prior of La Lande-Patry, in the diocese of Bayeux, greeting in the Lord. You are to know that when the Reverend Father Eudes, by God's grace archbishop of Rouen, visited the diocese of Bayeux, he sought procuration from our priory, in the name of that visitation which he exercises over me and my companion, as his duty is. I, fully recognizing my obligation to pay the said procuration, yet because we are burdened with some debts, besought the archbishop to be gracious enough to remit this obligation on this occasion; which request he, in his mercy, granted. In witness whereof I present the present letter sealed with my seal. Given at Belle-Etoile, the Wednesday following the feast of St. Denis, in the year of our Lord 1256.

Present were: Guy of Merule, precentor; Peter of Ons, archdeacon of

[28] Originally of the Congregation of Savigny. (Cottineau, I, 261.)

Grand-Caux, in the diocese of Rouen; Brother Harduin of the Friars Minor; and William of Plessy, rector at Gaynneville, and Morel, rector of Us, our clerks.

OCTOBER 12. We visited the priory at Le Désert. Six Benedictine monks from the abbey of Troarn are there. They do not confess often enough; we enjoined them to correct this. They have no copy of the Rule; we enjoined them to correct this. They have no copy of the Rule; we enjoined the prior to get one or to have one written out. They do not observe the fasts of the Rule; we urged them to correct this. They eat meat freely; we absolutely forbade them to eat meat save as the Rule permits. They have an income of three hundred pounds; they owe about thirty pounds. We received procuration there this day. Total for procuration: seven pounds, twelve pence.

OCTOBER 13. We spent the night at Aunay, a Cistercian house.

OCTOBER 14. At the same. The prior of Cahagnes,[29] an Augustinian house, appeared before us and swore to abide by our decision for that he had refused to receive us for visitation and procuration. In defense, he stated that the bishop of Bayeux had never received procuration there. We told him that we would investigate the truth of this matter, and that if we found, upon inquiry, that the bishop had ever received procuration there, we would exact a fine for his unwillingness to receive us for procuration.

We received procuration this day at Cerisy. Procuration: six pounds, ten shillings, ten pence.

OCTOBER 15. We visited this abbey. Thirty-two monks are there. One monk is dwelling alone in a certain priory, located on an island; we enjoined them to send him a companion or to recall him to the cloister. Alms are given daily to all comers. The fasts of the Rule are not observed in the priories, and they eat meat in them; we forbade the use of meat, save as the Rule permits. They have an income of two thousand pounds; they owe one thousand twenty pounds for their mitre,[30] and sixty pounds in other debts.

---

[29] An Augustinian priory dependent on Notre-Dame-du-Val. (Cottineau, I, 556.)

[30] It was not uncommon for abbots to request and receive the privilege from the pope of wearing a mitre. Its cost may be accounted for by its precious stones. However, the authors of *Gallia Christiana,* Cottineau, and Dom Besse do not make mention of the abbots of Cerisy being mitred, nor is there any mention in A. Potthast's *Regesta pontificum Romanorum* (2 vols. Berlin 1874-75, Vol. II), of popes granting such a privilege.

OCTOBER 16. At Longues, which is a dependent of Hambye. Total for procuration: seven pounds, two shillings, three pence.

OCTOBER 17. We visited there, where there are eighteen monks. They have two priories. Ten of them are priests. Sometimes they eat meat, particularly in the priories, nor do the priories keep the fasts of the Rule; we enjoined them to observe the Rule more fully in these matters. Alms are given daily to all comers. They have an income of three hundred fifty pounds; they owe about forty pounds.

This day the lord bishop of Bayeux gave us procuration with all honor, in consequence of the visitation which we exercised with respect to him.

OCTOBER 18. We visited the chapter of Bayeux. We asked who had the cure of their souls; some said that it was the bishop, others the dean. We found certain defects, namely that they rush through the Hours, that the ornaments are dirty, and that the bishop has usurped certain rents which the chapter has from the assart[31] in the forest at Neuilly. Everything else, by God's grace, we found in good condition. We received procuration this day from the chapter at the bishop's palace.

OCTOBER 19. We received procuration at St-Vigor. Total: seven pounds, ten shillings, eleven pence.

OCTOBER 20. We visited there. Twelve monks from the abbey of St-Benigne-de-Dijon[32] are there. They leave the cloister and go out into the farm as they like and without leave; we enjoined them to correct this. They have two priories in which monks are dwelling alone; we enjoined them to give these monks companions, or recall them to the cloister. They eat meat when there is no need; we enjoined them to observe the Rule covering this. Traveling monks do not observe the fasts of the Rule; we enjoined them to correct this. They have an income of six hundred pounds, and they owe two hundred pounds.

This day we spent the night at the bishop's manor at Douvres, through his kindness.

OCTOBER 21. We received procuration at Ardenne, a Premonstratensian house. Procuration: six pounds, eleven pence.

OCTOBER 22. We visited the chapter of St-Sépulcre-de-Caen. One dignitary is there, that is to say, the dean. There is as yet no certain number of canons. Luke, called Capet, runs about the town disgracefully and gets in-

---

[31] Wood on wasteland cleared for the purpose of cultivation.
[32] A Benedictine abbey. (Cottineau, I, 966-68.)

toxicated very easily; but then he is weak in the head. Total for procuration: nine pounds, fourteen shillings, six pence.

OCTOBER 23. We visited the monastery of nuns at La-Trinité-de-Caen. The abbess was in England at the time.[33] We found seventy-two nuns there. One does not accuse another [in chapter]. The rule of silence is not well observed; we enjoined them to correct this. They take three vows at the time of their being blessed; to wit, the vows of obedience, chastity, and poverty, but no other vow. The young nuns keep larks, and at the feast of the Innocents they sing their Office with farcical improvisations; we forbade this. They have paid three hundred fifty marks to the Roman Curia. About as much is owing to them as they owe. Total for procuration: seven pounds, six shillings, four pence.

OCTOBER 24. We visited the abbey of St-Etienne-de-Caen, where there are sixty-three monks. All but three are priests. In one of the priories there are rabbit dogs; we forbade the monks who are staying there to become hunters. There are some who do not confess every month; we enjoined them to correct this. It used to be their practice that all those ministering [to the celebrants] at all Masses, save those [Masses] for the dead, received Communion, but this practice, through negligence, has gradually been abandoned; we enjoined the abbot and prior to have this custom more fully observed by all. The cloister is badly kept; we enjoined them to correct this. Traveling monks do not observe the fasts of the Rule; we enjoined them to correct this. In the priories they do not observe the fasts of the Rule and they eat meat freely; we enjoined them to correct this. They owe fifteen hundred pounds, but about as much is owed to them; they have an income of four thousand pounds. Total for procuration: seven pounds, ten shillings, ten pence.

OCTOBER 25. We visited the Maison-Dieu at Caen. Seven canons are there. The prior was not there. The brethren receive Communion and confess twice a year, to wit, at Advent and at Lent. They have an income of one thousand pounds and another five hundred for daily alms; they owe two hundred pounds, and they have their annate money on hand.

This day we spent the night at Troarn, at our own expense.

OCTOBER 26. We visited there, finding forty monks. All but six are priests. Those who are not priests receive Communion every Sunday. Travel-

---

[33] Julianne de St-Sernin (1247-64). (*Gallia Christiana,* XI, 433.) She may have been visiting Horstede in Norfolk, where the house had a priory. (Dugdale, *Monasticon Anglicanum,* VII, 1057.)

ing monks do not observe the fasts of the Rule. In the priories they do not observe the fasts of the Rule, and they eat meat freely; we enjoined them to correct this. They owe about four hundred pounds; they have an income of about three thousand pounds. Total for procuration: eight pounds, twelve shillings, eight pence.

When we were visiting in the diocese of Bayeux, we warned Brother Henry, prior of Cahagnes,[34] of the diocese of Bayeux, to receive us for visitation and procuration, but he refused to do this, stating that he was not under obligation to do so, and alleged in justification that, in his time, the bishop of Bayeux had never visited him, nor had he ever received procuration there from him nor, as far as he knew, from any of his predecessors. However, the prior swore to abide by our decision in this matter, and we, after diligent investigation, discovered that the bishop of Bayeux had visited there many times and had received procuration. This being the case, we peremptorily cited the said prior to appear before us at Troarn on the Thursday before All Saints to hear our judgment, and the said prior having come before us at the said time and place, we gave orders that the prior and his successors should be obliged to receive us there for visitation and procuration. We ordered the prior to pay us a fine for having given us offense by unjustly refusing to receive us on the aforementioned business. Present were: Peter, archdeacon of Grand-Caux; Richard of Sap, canon of Rouen; the prior of Ste-Barbe; Hugh, rector at Foucescalier; Reginald, rector at Giverny; Morel of Us; Robert Scansore; ... [lacuna in MS], the abbot of Troarn; and many others. Thereupon, and at the said time and place, the said prior recognized that he was obligated to the foregoing and to the payment of full procuration if we should desire to exact it. He agreed to pay whatever fine we should desire for the offense shown to us. However, we forbore to exact this penalty until such time as we should think best. Present were the aforesaid archdeacon, Richard; William, the prior of Troarn; Brother Harduin of the Friars Minor; and Morel and Robert, our abovementioned clerks. The said prior, before the aforementioned witnesses, swore that he would pay the said fine to us, whenever we should ask him to do so.

OCTOBER 27. At Pont-l'Evêque, at our expense. OCTOBER 28. At Pont-Audemer. OCTOBER 29. At Bourg-Achard. OCTOBER 30. At Déville. OCTOBER 31. At Rouen. NOVEMBER 1. At Rouen. We celebrated the feast of

---

[34] See entry for October 14, above.

All Saints. NOVEMBER 2-5. At Déville. NOVEMBER 6. We held the sacred synod at Rouen, and spent the night at St-Matthieu. NOVEMBER 7-8. At Rouen. NOVEMBER 9. At Frênes. NOVEMBER 10. At St-Germer-de-Flay. NOVEMBER 11. At Bulles. NOVEMBER 12. At Gournay-sur-Aronde. NOVEMBER 13-23. At Noyon, on the business of the inquest held on the body of St. Eloi.[35] NOVEMBER 24. At Verberie. NOVEMBER 25. At Louvres, in the diocese of Paris. NOVEMBER 26-28. At Pontoise. NOVEMBER 29. We received procuration at Gasny. Total for procuration: one hundred nine shillings, three pence.

NOVEMBER 30. We visited there. Four monks are in residence, one of whom is ill. They stated that they had remedied the lack of books, and the lack of the minor ornaments, but not the major ones; we enjoined them to procure the things still lacking.[36] Some of them do not observe the fasts of the Rule; they eat meat; we enjoined them to correct this, and to fulfill the penalties described in the papal Statutes, if they should be remiss in these things. Alms are given to all comers twice a week. We received procuration this day at Mont-Deux-Amants. Total for procuration: six pounds, eight shillings, seven pence.

DECEMBER 1. We visited there, finding twelve canons. We enjoined them to read the Rule through at least once a week. They owe about one hundred fifty pounds, since some one has recently loaned them one hundred pounds, of which amount they have retained some as cash and invested some in cattle which they have at present. The sick are ill provided for; we enjoined them to correct this. We particularly enjoined the subprior to be diligent in visiting the sick and to make such provision for them as the illness of the patient seemed to render expedient. They do not get their clothing as soon as they need it, for it is given to them after too long a delay; we enjoined them to correct this.

At Ste-Catherine, at our own expense.

DECEMBER 2. At Rouen. DECEMBER 3. That is to say, the First Sunday in Advent, and we preached to the people in the cathedral. [No entry for December 4]

---

[35] St. Eloi, Bishop of Noyon (590-660). Eudes assisted in the investigation preliminary to his formal canonization. (Butler's Lives of the Saints, ed. Thurston and Attwater, IV, 455-58; "St. Eloi" in Dict. de théol. cath., IV², 2340-50; Dict. d'arch. chrét. et de lit., IV², 2674-87.) His feast is celebrated on December 1.

[36] See entry for October 23, 1255.

DECEMBER 5. Nicholas, the abbot of St-Ouen-de-Rouen, had been summoned peremptorily to appear before us on the day following the first Sunday in Advent, to give reasons for his contempt and disobedience in failing to appear at the synod held at All Saints just passed, and to make amends, as justice requires, for such disobedience. On the said day, the abbot, as the law requires, appeared before us, and apologized for his disobedience. Placing his hand on his breast, he swore to obey our commands in the matter of the amend. Present were: Peter, the archdeacon of Caux; Masters Robert of Sens, Richard of Sap, canon of Rouen, John of Soissons, canon and then Official of Rouen; Brothers Lawrence and Richard, monks of St-Ouen; Martin, the abbot's clerk; Morel, our clerk Philip; a servant of the curia of Rouen; Brother Denis, prior of the monastery at Frênes in the diocese of Amiens; and many others.

This day we visited the monastery of St-Ouen, where there are fifty monks. Some of them confess too rarely, despite the orders which we issued at our other visitation.[37] Item, they do not obey our mandate concerning the celebration of Masses, to wit, that whoever should fail to celebrate Mass at least once a week should abstain from wine until he shall have sung one. Those who have been bled wait as a body until curfew before going to bed. In the priories they eat meat and observe the fasts of the Rule badly. The general audit of the house is made too infrequently, that is to say, but once a year, and then it is vaguely done, whereas we had ordered them to cast their accounts three times a year. Item, the same is true of the kitchener and the other officers, although we had ordered them to cast their accounts at least three times a year. Item, although we had forbidden any monk to receive or request anything from the officials, this order is not obeyed, but they say that they do this because when, for any reason, they have permission to leave the house, the abbot does not give them anything for their expenses, and so, they say, that they are obliged to ask and receive [expense money]. At the time of the last feast of the Apostles Peter and Paul they owed seven thousand two hundred forty pounds, seven shillings, eleven pence; however, there is owing to them, in both good and bad debts, sixteen hundred seventy-five pounds thirteen shillings, so that their liabilities exceed their assets by five thousand five hundred sixty-four pounds, fourteen shillings, eleven pence. The prior does not keep to the cloister very well. The treasurer is not very competent. The abbot knows too little about the temporalities; he

[37] See entry for January 28, 1254/55.

changes the officials too readily. In defiance of our command, one monk is dwelling alone at St-Giles.[38]

DECEMBER 5-6. At Déville.

DECEMBER 7. We visited the abbey of St-Georges-de-Boscherville. Twenty-one monks are there; all but six are priests. One does not accuse another [in chapter]; we enjoined them to correct this. We enjoined them to hand in their old clothes whenever they were issued new ones. Alms are given to all comers daily. They owe two hundred pounds; three hundred pounds is owed to them. Total for procuration: seven pounds, eight shillings, eight pence.

DECEMBER 8. We received procuration at Jumièges. Total for procuration: seven pounds, fifteen shillings.

DECEMBER 9. We visited there. Fifty-one monks are in residence; all but thirteen are priests. Some are negligent in celebrating Mass; we enjoined them to correct this. There are some who do not confess every month. They have certain houses in which there used to be monks, but in which there are no monks now; we took this matter under advisement. Alms are given daily to all comers, but, as they say, the amount is less than it used to be. We enjoined them to prepare two copies of every audit, of which one should remain in the possession of the community, the other in that of the abbot. More is owed to them than they owe. We warned the abbot and the prior to see that the kitchener and the precentor confess often enough, and that the subcellarer celebrates Mass more frequently, for we had found them negligent in these matters, and unless the latter manifestly corrected themselves on the above faults, the former were to report them to us before Easter. Item, we warned the said abbot and the prior to pay better attention to the bestowal of alms, for we found negligence in the administration of this work. Item, we warned the abbot and prior to replace the monks in the priories.

This day we spent the night at St-Wandrille, at our own expense.

DECEMBER 10. We visited there, finding forty monks. One does not accuse another [in chapter]; we enjoined them to correct this. Traveling monks and those dwelling in the priories do not observe the fasts of the Rule. They eat meat; we enjoined them to correct this. Alms are given daily to all comers. They owe about five hundred pounds, and about five hundred

[38] See entry for December 13, 1251.

pounds is owed to them. The sick are ill provided for and the infirmary is in poor condition; we enjoined them to correct this. We received procuration there this day. Total for procuration: ten pounds, seventeen shillings.

DECEMBER 11. At Le Valasse, a Cistercian house. DECEMBER 12. We received procuration at Graville. Total for procuration: six pounds, eleven shillings, two pence.

DECEMBER 13. We visited there. Twelve canons are in residence. One canon is dwelling alone at Bellevue. We strictly forbade women to eat in the house of the canons in the parishes. Three times a week alms are given to all comers. They have an income of three hundred pounds; they owe fifty pounds to a certain priest.

DECEMBER 14. This day we spent the night at Montivilliers, at our expense.

DECEMBER 14. [sic]. We visited the abbess[39] who had but lately been established there; we warned her to sleep in the dormitory and eat in the refectory, as is fitting; to see that frequent confessions were made, and to draw up her accounts very often. They owe two hundred pounds, but quite as much is owed to them. Total for procuration: nine pounds, five shillings, ten pence.

DECEMBER 15. At Valmont, at our expense.

DECEMBER 16. We visited there, where there are twenty-six monks, thirteen of whom are priests. Some leave the cloister without permission; we enjoined such offenders to be punished. We enjoined the abbot to collect the keys of the coffers from time to time, and to inspect them with the object of removing any property. Layfolk eat in the refectory; we forbade this for the future. One monk is dwelling alone at Val-St-Jacques; we enjoined them to correct this. We received procuration there this day. Total for procuration: seven pounds, ten shillings, one penny.

DECEMBER 17. We received procuration at Etoutteville. Total: seven pounds less a penny. The prior is a squanderer of the priory goods; he is quarrelsome, and is almost always excommunicate; he celebrates Mass all too seldom.

DECEMBER 18. We dedicated the church at Rocquefort and received procuration there this day. Total for procuration: nine pounds, thirteen shillings, eleven pence.

---

[39] Julianne. See entry for April 27, above.

DECEMBER 19. We visited at Ouville, where there are twelve canons. One does not accuse another [in chapter]. The sick are not well provided for; we enjoined them to correct this. Alms are given daily to all comers. The total income is not written down; we enjoined them to correct this. They owe one hundred ten pounds; they have an income of four hundred pounds. Total for procuration: eight pounds, seventeen shillings.

DECEMBER 20-21. At Déville. DECEMBER 22. At Rouen. DECEMBER 23. We conferred Holy Orders at Rouen. DECEMBER 24. At Rouen. DECEMBER 25. At Rouen. We celebrated the feast of the Nativity. DECEMBER 26. At Frênes. DECEMBER 27. At Le-Bord-Haut-de-Vigny. DECEMBER 28. At St-Denis. DECEMBER 29-31. At Paris. JANUARY 1. At St-Denis. JANUARY 2. At Pontoise. JANUARY 3. At Chaumont. JANUARY 4. At Gournay. JAN-UARY 5. At Beaubec. JANUARY 6. At the same. We celebrated the feast of the Epiphany. JANUARY 7-10. At Aliermont. JANUARY 11. At the same. The steward at Wanchy gave us procuration. Total for procuration: nine pounds, seventeen shillings, eleven pence. JANUARY 12. We received procuration: nine pounds, seven shillings.

JANUARY 12. We received procuration at Bures. Total for procuration: nine pounds, seven shillings.

JANUARY 13. We visited the two monks who are staying there. They do not observe the fasts of the Rule; we forbade them [to violate the fasts] just as the Rule forbids them to. They use meat when there is no need; we forbade them to eat meat at all, except as the Rule permits. They have no copy of the Rule; we enjoined them to procure one. The prior of Pré receives about six hundred pounds from them. We warned the prior and his companion about the aforementioned abuses. Present were: the treasurer and Master Robert of Sens, canon of Rouen.

This day we visited the prior and the three canons at the hospital. They confess too rarely; we enjoined them to correct this. Everything else is in good condition. Five sisters are there. They owe about forty pounds.

This same day we received procuration at Neufchâtel from the lessee at Nogent. No monks are there. Total for procuration: nine pounds, two shillings, five pence.

JANUARY 14. We received procuration at Beaussault. Total for procuration: six pounds, eighteen shillings, one penny.

JANUARY 15. We visited the two monks staying there. Mass is sometimes omitted in this priory, because of the pressure of work. Three times a week alms are given indiscriminately to all comers. The rules of fasting are not well observed, and they make a general practice of eating meat. They do not possess their own copy of the Rule; we enjoined them to procure one. We enjoined them to obey the Rule in the matter of the fasts and the eating of meat. They owe one hundred pounds; they have an income of about one hundred pounds.

This same day we visited the abbey of Bival. Thirty-four nuns are there, but included in this number is the prioress of St-Aubin.[40] They receive the Body of Jesus Christ regularly seven times a year, but they confess more frequently. They owe one hundred forty pounds, but sixty pounds is owed to them. They have tranferred, without our consent, the manor of Pierrement, which is worth one hundred forty pounds, to Master William of Viviers for fifty pounds. We enjoined them to observe rigorously the orders laid down by R., the archdeacon, a report of which is contained in the record of our other visitation.[41] We strictly forbade any of them to presume to go beyond the cloister gate without permission, or to write any more letters or to have any letters written for them, without showing them to the abbess. We dismissed the priest, because of scandal connected with the nuns and the people, although we did not find anything bad about him that could be proved. Florence has recently given birth to a child there, and the entire house has been ill famed because of this.

This same day we received procuration at Mortemer-sur-Eaulne, where there are two Cluniac monks. Total for procuration: eight pounds, fourteen shillings.

JANUARY 16. We received procuration at Aumale. Total: eight pounds, seven shillings, seven pence.

JANUARY 17. We visited there. Seventeen monks are in residence; all but five are priests. One does not accuse another [in chapter]; they confess too rarely; we enjoined them to correct these things. We particularly forbade anyone to possess linen clothing or to go into any room after Compline to eat or drink. In this matter we forbade the abbot to presume to absolve anyone who should be delinquent in this regard, and we retained the sole privilege or authority to grant such absolution. Item, we told the abbot that we did not wish him to have the authority to grant permissions to stay away from Compline. Alms are given three times a week to all comers. We en-

---

[40] St-Aubin was also a Cistercian house. (Cottineau, II, 2599.)
[41] See entry for February 27, 1254/55.

joined the abbot to have a statement of the income written out. Item, we enjoined the officials to prepare a statement of the receipts and expenditures at least once a month, and this in the presence of brothers elected by the community. Item, that the abbot, at least twice a year, should make an audit of the monastery finances, and in the presence of brothers elected by the community; that two copies of this should always be made, one to remain with the abbot, the other to be given to the members elected by the community. With respect to all of the foregoing, we drew up a written ordinance which, sealed with our seal, we gave to the abbot, and which is to serve as a basis for our visitation next year. They owe eight hundred eighty pounds. The abbot has granted four acres of free land on burgage tenure[42] to one of his relatives. Since this transaction was prejudicial to the interests of the monastery, and the abbot had no written approval of this from the community, we enjoined him to revoke this grant. Item, we instructed the abbot to grant no more long-term leases of land without the consent of the community. Item, since the visits of the nurse, Alice Telière, to the abbey had become a matter of scandal, particularly because, as rumor has it, she used to sleep with the abbey laborers, we enjoined the abbot not to allow her to enter the abbey again on any condition. Item, since the porter was defamed of theft, we enjoined the abbot to make an investigation into the truth of this report and to remove him entirely from the hospice, if the report were found to be correct.

This same day we spent the night at Foucarmont, a Cistercian house.

JANUARY 18. We spent the night at Eu, at our own expense.

JANUARY 19. We visited at Eu, where there are twenty-eight canons. The Rule is not read every week; we enjoined them to correct this. All but nine are priests. They owe one hundred seventy pounds. They are short of wine. Everything else is in sufficiently good condition. The abbot and the community, to the prejudice of the archbishop and the archdeacon, have appropriated certain churches in their patronage to their own use, and without permission from the diocesan. In connection with this, they said that they possessed these privileges and letters from archbishops; whereupon we appointed the Friday after Ash Wednesday as a date on which they should produce all the documents they had supporting this claim. Total for procuration: seven pounds, nine shillings.

JANUARY 20. We visited the abbey at Le Tréport. One does not accuse an-

42 The customs governing the holding of land or houses in boroughs.

other [in chapter]. They retain their old pelisses when they are given new ones; we enjoined the abbot not to give them any new ones unless they surrendered the old ones. In the priories they do not observe the fasts of the Rule; they eat meat; we enjoined them to correct this. Even in the abbey itself they eat meat at the abbot's discretion; we enjoined the abbot that he should see that the Rule covering this be observed more strictly. They owe about three hundred pounds. Because the abbot had not compelled the observance of the ordinance which we had drawn up at our last visitation[43] concerning the audits of the officials, we made him receive penance in our presence, and we enjoined upon him the performance of the penance which we saw fit to impose and promised him that we would punish him for grave fault should we again find him negligent in this matter. Furthermore, we forbade the abbot to permit the priors to give any more money to any of the monks. We received procuration there this day. Total for procuration: eight pounds, eight shillings, four pence.

JANUARY 21. At Criel, at our own expense.

JANUARY 22. We visited the priory at Envermeu, where there are twelve monks. They eat meat when there is no need; we enjoined them to observe the Rule concerning this more fully. They owe one hundred forty pounds in addition to two hundred pounds which they owe to their abbot. We warned the prior and his companions about making frequent confession, since we had found them delinquent in this.

This day we received procuration at our manor at Aliermont, but at the expense of the priory. Total: eight pounds.

JANUARY 23. We received procuration at Longueil. Total for procuration: ten pounds, eight shillings, nine pence.

JANUARY 24. We visited at Bacqueville. Four monks of Tiron are in residence. They use feather beds; we enjoined them to correct this. There is one person there who is not a priest; we enjoined him to make monthly confession and to receive the Body and Blood of Jesus Christ every month. Three times a week alms are given to all comers. They do not observe the fasts of the Rule; they eat meat freely; we enjoined them to observe the Rule more fully in these matters. Brother John Pligaut, prior, Brother Luke of Nogent, Brother Herbert of Chartres, Brother Stephen of Chateaudun, these we warned about the aforesaid things. The sources of income are not written

---

[43] See entry for November 17, 1255.

out; we enjoined the prior to have them written out. They owe one hundred fifty pounds; they have an income of two hundred pounds. We received procuration there this day. Total for procuration: nine pounds, eleven shillings, nine pence.

JANUARY 25. We spent the night at Auffay. Total for procuration: eight pounds, eight shillings, nine pence.

JANUARY 26. We visited there, finding five monks from St-Evroult. We admonished them to confess at least once a month and to observe the Rule in the matter of keeping the fasts and concerning the eating of meat. They said that their conscience was clear in these matters. They have an income of four hundred pounds; they owe two hundred pounds.

JANUARY 27–FEBRUARY 2. At St-Victor-en-Caux. FEBRUARY 3. At Rive. FEBRUARY 4. At Frênes. FEBRUARY 5. At Genainville. FEBRUARY 6. At Pontoise. FEBRUARY 7-18. At Paris. FEBRUARY 19. At Pontoise. FEBRUARY 20. At Genainville. FEBRUARY 21. At Frênes. FEBRUARY 22-24. At Déville. FEBRUARY 25. That is to say, on the First Sunday in Lent, at Rouen. We preached in the cathedral. FEBRUARY 26-28. At Déville.

MARCH 1. We visited at St. Mary Madgdalene [of Rouen]. Twelve canons are in residence there. There is no subprior. All but three are priests. As is customary with them, all those who are not priests, both brothers and sisters alike, confess and receive Communion thirteen times a year. We enjoined the prior to collect the keys from all several times a year and without notification, so that he might inspect their coffers to see if there were any property. Twenty-four sisters are there. They owe about fifty pounds. Brother Peter Goiers is disobedient, nor does he wish to correct his offense of incontinence, of which he was ill famed at Foville. We enjoined the prior that more frequent individual audits should be made.

This day we spent the night at Déville, at our own expense.

MARCH 2. We visited at Pré. Eighteen monks are in residence; all but four are priests. Alms are given to all comers three times a week. Sometimes they eat meat when there is no need, but, as they say, they eat only a little; we enjoined them to observe the Rule more fully in this matter. Item, we enjoined the prior to see that the fasts of the Rule were more fully observed in the priories. They have an income of about one thousand pounds; they owe the abbot seven hundred pounds, and one hundred pounds elsewhere.

This day we spent the night at Déville, at our own expense.

MARCH 3. We conferred Holy Orders at Déville. MARCH 4. We received procuration at Ste-Catherine. Total for procuration: eleven pounds, seven shillings, eight pence.

MARCH 5. We visited there, finding thirty monks, of whom eighteen are priests. We enjoined the abbot to draw up a general financial statement at least twice a year. They have an income of one thousand pounds; they owe five hundred pounds, but some debts are owed to them.

This day we spent the night at Frênes.

MARCH 6. We received procuration at Sausseuse. Total for procuration: six pounds, fifteen shillings.

We visited there. Twelve canons are in residence; all but three are priests. Silence is not well observed. The subprior is too lenient in giving the canons permission to leave the cloister; we strictly enjoined him to correct this. Some of the canons, to wit, Brother Matthew and Brother Philip, dine at the house of a certain layman at Le Til; we enjoined the prior to see that this matter was corrected at the first chapter at which these two were present. There are two brothers and two sisters at the house. They owe about two hundred pounds; they have an income of four hundred pounds. This day we spent the night there, at our expense.

MARCH 8. We spent the night at La Roche-Guyon, and for procuration we received forty shillings of Paris, as well as certain other things which they owe us.

MARCH 9. We visited the priory at St-Martin-la-Garenne. Five monks from Bec are there. Alms are given three times a week to all comers. They eat meat when there is no need; we enjoined the offenders to perform the penance laid down in the Statutes [of Pope Gregory]. They have an income of one hundred forty pounds; they owe sixty pounds. We received procuration there this day. Total for procuration: seven pounds, sixteen shillings, two pence.

MARCH 10-11. At Gisors. MARCH 12-13. At Gournay.

MARCH 14-15. At Mortemer. MARCH 16. At Gouy.

MARCH 17-18. At Rouen. MARCH 19-21. At Pont-de-l'Arche.

MARCH 22. At [Champ-d'] Oisel.

MARCH 23-26. At Déville.

MARCH 27. At Déville, and the lord king was with us this day and slept at our manor.[44] MARCH 28-30. At Déville. MARCH 31. At Rouen. APRIL 1. At Rouen. Palm Sunday. APRIL 2-6. At Déville. APRIL 7. Here begins the fifty-seventh year.

[44] Louis and his entourage had been traveling in Normandy. Eudes actually met him at Pont-de-l'Arche on the 19th and conducted him as a guest to the archiepiscopal manor at Déville.

APRIL 8. We celebrated Easter at Rouen. APRIL 9. At St-Victor-en-Caux, the king remaining at Auffay. Today we dined with the king at Arques. APRIL 10-12. At Aliermont, the king staying at Arques. APRIL 13. At Longueville, where the king was also. APRIL 14-15. At Neufchâtel, the king abiding there as well. APRIL 16. At Mortemer-sur-Eaulne, with the king. APRIL 17. At Gournay, the king being there too. APRIL 18. At Gisors, and both the king and queen were there. APRIL 19. At St-Martin-de-Pontoise, at our own expense. APRIL 20-22. At Paris. APRIL 23. At St-Germain-en-Laye. APRIL 24. At St-Martin-de-Pontoise, at our own expense. APRIL 25. At Gisors. APRIL 26. At Frênes. APRIL 27. At Pont-de-l'Arche, where the queen was staying. APRIL 28. At Rouen, and the queen was also there. APRIL 29. At Frênes, with the queen. APRIL 30—MAY 5. At the same. MAY 6-7. At Déville.

MAY 8. We received procuration at St-Saëns. We visited the priory of nuns at St-Saëns this day. Sixteen nuns are there. One nun is dwelling alone at Ste-Austreberte; one sister and a brother are staying at a priory, and they have a chaplain. Sometimes, because of their sickness, they say Matins and their Hours without modulation.[1] We admonished them [the nuns] not to receive anything or retain anything without the permission of the prioress. They confess at least seven times a year. They owe two hundred twelve pounds. The king has given them Equiqueville which with all its appurtenances is worth one hundred thirty pounds from another source, and four carucates of land which are worth forty pounds; so that all in all they have an income of two hundred seventy pounds. Total for procuration: eight pounds, eighteen shillings, four pence.

To the monastery of nuns at St-Saëns belong altogether two hundred forty-five acres of [arable] land, plus eight acres of meadow; of the arable some one hundred fifteen acres are sowed with grain, wheat, barley, and also legumes. They have a cash income of one hundred forty pounds, sixty-two

---

[1] See above, July 9, 1249, n. 36.

shillings, eight pence. Their income in wheat is eight *muids*; in oats, sixty-six;[2] in capons, two hundred twenty; in sheep, eleven hundred; item, they also have a cash income returnable with the capons and sheep of twenty-seven shillings and six pence. Item, they have a mill at Equiqueville and a wood of which they do not know the size; the priest at Equiqueville has a tithe in the said mill. Item, they possess rights of *pannage*,[3] milling, and straw rents, but they do not know the worth of these. Item, they have a mill at St-Saëns which is worth very little. Item, they have fifty-seven sheep there, twelve plough horses, and a plough team of four oxen; item, they have eighteen animals, both cows and oxen. Item, they have only two *muids* of wheat to last them until August. They have nothing to drink. Twenty-six pounds, five shillings, two pence is owed to them. Their total debt is two hundred thirty-four pounds, three shillings, three pence.

MAY 9. We visited the monks of St-Saëns. Four monks are there; there used to be five. They do not observe well the fasts of the Rule; they eat meat when there is no need; we enjoined them to be more observant of the Rule in these matters. More is owed to them than they owe. Everything else is in good condition. This day we spent the night at Aliermont.

MAY 10-12. At Aliermont.

MAY 13. At the same. This day Sir Fulk of Sauchay made recompense for having gone hunting in our forest, and, in the king's presence, he offered as his surety Sir Jordan of Valliquerville.

MAY 14. At the same. This day Master William Pinel entered the following appeal from us and against us to the Apostolic See:

I, William Pinel, cleric, proctor of Robert of St-Riquier, Simon of Rouen, Robert of St-Amand, William of Coudray, Gilbert of Rouen, Robert of Capremont, Roger of Caux, Hugh of Frênes, John of Contemoulin, and Reginald of Breuil, monks of St-Victor-en-Caux, and of those associating with them, do assert that you, my lord, Reverend Father, made a provision of fifty pounds of Tours, together with the priory of St-Thomas, for William of Dune, former abbot of the said abbey of St-Victor-en-Caux, to the enormous hurt and injury of the said monastery; and that, despite an appeal entered against this by the said monks, you compelled or wished to compel, by virtue of your office or by the seal of your office, the present abbot to pay the said provision, though the obligation has not been acknowledged or admitted, and the proper legal

---

[2] On units of measurement, see above, August 18, 1251, n. 14.

[3] The right to put pigs into the forest, where they fed on roots, nuts, etc.

procedure has not been observend. Wherefore I, the proctor of the said monks, feeling that they have been unduly aggrieved by you, appeal in writing to the Apostolic See on behalf of them and those associating with them, and I request *apostoli*. Should you deny this to me, I enter a further appeal in writing.

We considered this appeal to be frivolous, but inasmuch as it contained, as we thought, more inaccuracies than anything else, we permitted the said proctor to have his petition sealed; but later on he refused to take it away with him. Present at this were: Brother Philip of Caen, of the Order of Preachers, Master P[eter], archdeacon of Grand Caux, Brother Walter of Minières, Brother Peter Hurtet, and Dom Willard, prior of Salle-aux-Puelles.

MAY 15. At Neufchâtel. MAY 16. At Gournay. MAY 17. At Gournay. We celebrated the feast of the Ascension there this day.

MAY 18. We visited the priory of Chaumont. Three monks from St-Germer are there. Sometimes the prior goes for two weeks without cele-brating Mass; we enjoined him to correct this. They do not observe the fasts of the Rule; they eat meat freely; we enjoined a fuller observance of the Rule in these matters. They owe forty pounds, and they have neither wheat nor oats; they have an income of one hundred forty pounds. Total for procuration: seven pounds, six shillings, three pence of Paris.

MAY 19. We received procuration at Gaillonet. Total for procuration: seven pounds, twelve shillings, two pence. MAY 20. At St-Germain-en-Laye. MAY 21-22. At Paris. MAY 23. At Paris, and on this day, Thomas of Le Fossé, priest, entered the following appeal:

Reverend Father, archbishop of Rouen, I, Thomas of Le Fossé, priest, pre-sented to St. Mary's Church at Boville by that noble lady, Dame Rohaysia of Angerville, to whom belongs the right of presenting to the said church, appeal to the Apostolic See for the protection of my rights acquired by your presenta-tion of me and by the renunciation of any other [right of] presentation made or to be made by any other person. I appeal that you shall not admit any other person to the said church, or confer it upon any one else to my prejudice; and I place my person, my legal position, and my goods under the protection of the Apostolic See. I request, nay, demand, *apostoli*, and should you deny me this, I enter an instant appeal.

Present at this were: Simon, archdeacon of Rouen; Masters John Cholet, and John of Beauvais; Brother Eudes, monk of St-Lucien-de-Beauvais; Aymon, canon of St-Aignan-d'Orléans; Dom Jacques, archdeacon Simon's priest; Morel, our clerk; and Ralph Migarel, priest.

MAY 24. At Paris. MAY 25. We received procuration at St-Martin-de-Pontoise. Total for procuration: nine pounds, eleven shillings, five pence.

MAY 26. We visited there. Nineteen monks are in residence. In the priories they do not observe the fasts of the Rule and they eat meat freely; we enjoined the abbot to see that the Rule was better observed on this matter. We enjoined the abbot to have a statement of the house income written out in some book, which book should remain in the possession of the community. They owe one thousand pounds, but they have also been obliged to borrow two hundred pounds to defray the expenses of the vineyards and for harvesting; however, at the present time some twenty-five *muids* of wheat is owed to them. They have a certain chamber called "Bernard's Room," in which they drink almost as much as they do in the refectory; we strictly and particularly warned the abbot about this, and enjoined him that under pain of grave punishment he must not permit anyone to eat or drink there, or anywhere else but in the infirmary, the refectory, or the abbot's room. We enjoined him that if this were not done, we would take proceedings against him as the law requires.

MAY 27. We celebrated Pentecost there.

MAY 28. We visited the priory of Juziers. Six monks are there; all are priests but one, who confesses and receives Communion once a month. They use feather beds; they do not observe the fasts of the Rule, and the use meat freely; we enjoined a fuller observance of the Rule. Alms are given daily to all comers. They owe two hundred pounds, but sixty pounds is owed to them; they have an income of four hundred pounds. They owe about thirty pounds in pensions, not counting a pension which they owe to the abbey. We received procuration there this day. Total for procuration: ten pounds, four shillings, one penny of Paris.

MAY 29. At Sausseuse.

MAY 30. We visited the Maison-Dieu at Les Andelys. Robert of Sideville, the prior, is there alone without a companion. There is one sister there who is quite old, and a young maid servant. The house has an original income of sixty-five pounds, and through a gift of the lord king a recent one of fifty pounds of land in the provostship of Les Andelys. They have sufficient wheat to last until the new harvest. They owe about six pounds; at the present moment they have received some forty pounds of Tours from the royal sources of income. They have spent the other income already. We strictly forbade the prior to receive any one as a brother or sister without our special permission. This day we spent the night at Frênes.

MAY 31. We received procuration at Quévreville. Total for procuration: ten pounds, eleven shillings of Tours. JUNE 1. At Déville. JUNE 2. At the same. We conferred Holy Orders. JUNE 3. At St-Matthieu. JUNE 4. At the same. We conferred Holy Orders. JUNE 5. At the same. JUNE 6. We issued a mandate to the deans to the effect that they should immediately convoke all abbots, priors, priests, and such as owe attendance at a holy synod, to attend the holy synod on the Tuesday following All Saints; item, that whenever a synod is held, the deans of the church of Rouen should cite all priests and should report to us the names of those who are absent when the synod of deans is held.

On which day the following appeals were entered at St-Matthieu:

Since you, O Reverend Father, archbishop of Rouen, have unjustly and without reasonable cause refused to admit me, Brother Richard of Sommery, monk, to the free and vacant parochial altar of St-Ouen, after I had been presented by those religious men, the abbot and convent of St-Ouen aforesaid, who, by an indulgence granted to them by the Apostolic See, are the true patrons of the said altar, I, feeling that I have been unduly aggrieved, and acting on the mandate of the said abbot and convent, appeal in writing to the Apostolic See and request *apostoli*. And I place myself and the said altar under the protection of the Apostolic See.

Since those religious men, the abbot and the convent of St-Ouen-de-Rouen, the patrons of the church of St-Pierre called Honoré-de-Rouen, presented me, Richard of Ecales, cleric, to you, Reverend Father, archbishop of Rouen, to the free and vacant church aforesaid, and you unjustly and without reasonable cause refused to admit me to the said church at their presentation, I, feeling that I have been unduly aggrieved, appeal in writing to the Apostolic See and request *apostoli*. And I place myself and my church aforesaid under the protection of the Apostolic See.

To all who may see the present letter, we, N[icholas] by God's grace abbot of St-Ouen-de-Rouen, and the convent thereof, give greeting in the Lord. Know you that we appoint our beloved Nicholas of Frênes, cleric, the bearer of this present letter, as our proctor in all causes or matters affecting us and our monastery, as well in judicial business as in other things; in entering appeals or in challenging verdicts; in prosecuting appeals, whenever he shall feel or be convinced that we and our monastery are injured by any persons or in any way, or that we and our monastery are being prejudiced. We will regard as valid and acceptable whatever he, as proctor, shall do for us and our monastery in the foregoing matters. We present this information, by means of the present letter, to all whom it may concern. Given in the year of our Lord 1257, on the Wednesday after Trinity [Sunday].

Since the Apostolic See has granted an indult to those religious men, the abbot and convent of St-Ouen-de-Rouen, that when the rector of the parochial altar established in the monastery shall resign or die, the abbot and convent shall have this altar served by one of the brothers, and shall not be obliged to present some secular cleric for the said altar, for the advowson is known to belong to them;

And since, Reverend Father, archbishop of Rouen, on the death of Roland, the former rector of this altar, they presented Brother Richard of Sommery, one of their monks, for the free and vacant altar, and under the aforesaid indulgence, you, unjustly and without reasonable cause, refused to admit the said monk to this altar at their presentation;

I, Nicholas of Frênes, cleric, proctor for the said monks, feeling that my aforementioned lords and the said monk have been unduly wronged by you, enter an appeal in their name and in writing to the Apostolic See, and I request *apostoli*. Further, I place my lords and their monastery under the protection of the Apostolic See.

Since those religious men, the abbot and convent of St-Ouen-de-Rouen, presented to you, Reverend Father, archbishop of Rouen, Richard of Ecales, cleric, to the free and vacant church of St-Pierre, called Honoré-de-Rouen, the right of patronage over which is known to belong to them;

And since, Reverend Father, you, unjustly and without reasonable cause, refused to admit this cleric to the said church at their presentation, to the prejudice and injury of the said monks:

I, Nicholas of Frênes, cleric, and proctor of these monks, considering that my lords have been unduly aggrieved in this matter, appeal in their name, and in writing, to the Apostolic See, and I request *apostoli*. Further, I place my lords and the aforesaid church under the protection of the Apostolic See.

Alexander, bishop, servant of the servants of God, to his beloved children, ...[*lacuna in MS*], the abbot and convent of the monastery of St-Ouen-de-Rouen, of the Order of St. Benedict, greeting and apostolic blessing. Desiring that the liberties, immunities, jurisdictions, honors, and all other rights which adorn the said monastery shall in all ways be preserved, we, by the authority of the present letter, concede that you may freely enjoy all the graces and indulgences which, collectively or separately, have been granted to you or to your monastery by the Apostolic See, and without any contradiction whatsoever, and notwithstanding any letters which may have emanated from this See curtailing such graces or indulgences, or which may be issued by the said See in the future and do not make full and express mention of this letter.

Further, we pronounce as null and void whatever sentences of excommunication, suspension, or interdict shall be directed against you, or any of you, contrary to such graces and indulgences; and we declare them revoked if perchance they have already been issued.

No one shall be permitted in any way to infringe or rashly oppose this our charter of concession, constitution, and revocation. Should anyone presume to attempt this, let him know that he will incur the wrath of the Omnipotent God and that of the holy apostles, Peter and Paul. Given at the Lateran, February 11, in the third year of our pontificate.[4]

JUNE 7-8. At Louviers. JUNE 9. At Limay. JUNE 10. At St-Germain-en Laye. JUNE 11-14. At Paris. JUNE 15. At Pontoise. JUNE 16. We visited the chapter of St-Mellon-de-Pontoise. Those holding prebends are not held to residence.[5] In residence are ten vicars, one deacon, one subdeacon, and two chaplains. The deacon and the subdeacon sometimes do minor penances.[6] All of the deficiencies which we discovered here at our other visitation[7] still exist, except that of the bell tower, which has been entirely repaired, and the monastery roof, which has been partially repaired.

We visited the priory of St-Pierre this same day. Five monks are there. All are priests. We enjoined them to read a chapter of the Rule every day after singing *Preciosa* at Prime;[8] the prior agreed to this. They eat meat when there is no need; we enjoined them to observe the Rule in this matter, and to accept the penance contained in the Statutes of Pope Gregory if they should be delinquent. They owe forty pounds, not counting their debt to the abbot. This day we received from the chapter for procuration: one hundred shillings of Paris and accommodations including straw, wood, beds, cups, dishes, and other domestic utensils.

JUNE 17. At Auvers [-sur-Oise], at our expense. We conferred the

---

[4] February 11, 1257. (Potthast, *Regesta*, II, 1369 [16727].)

[5] They could enjoy most of the fruits of the prebend and appoint a vicar or his substitute to fulfill their duties in chapter or at the Divine Office.

[6] Each chapter had its statutes, violation of which incurred satisfaction or penances.

[7] See entry for March 6, 1255/56.

[8] A versicle, "preciosa in conspectu Domini mors sanctorum ejus" (Precious in the sight of the Lord is the death of His saints), is said just after the psalms at Prime and just before reading the Martyrology.

sacrament of Confirmation there. JUNE 18. At Le Fäy [-aux-Anes], at our expense, JUNE 19. At the same, but this day we conferred the Sacrament of Confirmation at Ivry [-le-Temple].

JUNE 20. We were received at the priory of St-Ouen at Gisors. We obtained from the prior for procuration one hundred twelve shillings of Paris, which is all that he owes, and should he give us more it would be of grace and not of obligation.[9]

JUNE 21. We received procuration at Pérrièrs. Total for procuration: eight pounds, eighteen shillings, eight pence. JUNE 22. We received procuration at L'Ile-Dieu. Total for procuration: six pounds, nineteen shillings, six pence. JUNE 23-24. At Frênes. JUNE 25. At Gournay. JUNE 26. We dedicated St. Mary's church at Gournay. Total for procuration: eight pounds, five shillings, three pence. JUNE 27. At Beauvais. JUNE 28. At Clermont. JUNE 29. At Compiègne. JUNE 30—JULY 1. At Noyon. JULY 2. At Noyon, in the matter of the body of St. Eloi, which lies there.[10] JULY 3. At Montdidier. JULY 4. At Poix. JULY 5. At Mortemer-sur-Eaulne. JULY 6-9. At Aliermont. JULY 10. At Aliermont. We dedicated the church at Tristeville. JULY 11. At the same.

JULY 12. At the same. We dedicated the church of the leper hospital at Arques. This day Cardon of Pierrecourt swore to submit to our sentence for having maliciously pounded at night on the door of the priest at Hibouville. Present were: the archdeacon of Eu; Master Richard of Sap, canon of Rouen; Brother Adam; Sir William Buhere and Sir Michael of Berneval, knights; Morel, our clerk; and many others.

JULY 13. We dedicated St. Nicholas' chapel in the woods at Sauchay. This day we spent the night at Dieppe, at the expense of the prior of the same place. JULY 14. At St-Victor-en-Caux, at our expense.

JULY 15. We visited there. Twenty monks are in residence, and two are at St-Thomas; all but three are priests. There is small provision made for alms, and no general donations are made. We enjoined the abbot to prepare a financial report of the general state of the house twice a year in the presence of brothers elected by the community, and to have individual audits made every month in the presence of the elected brothers. They owe about eighty pounds. We ordered the abbot to impose penance of grave fault upon

[9] See entry of February 5, 1254/55.
[10] See above, November 13-23, 1256, n. 35; below, August 23, 1258, and February 16, 1260/61.

the prior and certain others who came to blows while the abbot was away
and to continue the penalty until he should receive further instructions from
us. But since Brother Simon, the prior, Brother John of Contemoulin,
Brother Gilbert of Rouen, and Brother Robert of Capremont performed the
penance unwillingly, we revoked it, reserving the right to inflict such other
penalty as should seem expedient to us. These are the names of those who
appealed against us in the matter of making provision for William, the
former abbot:[11] Brothers Simon of Rouen, Robert of Riquier, John of Contemoulin, Hugh of Frênes, Gilbert of Rouen, Robert of St-Amand, Clarem-
baut, Robert of Capremont, William of Coderay, and Roger of Caux. We
received procuration there this day. Total for procuration: ... [*lacuna in
MS*].

JULY 16. At Déville, at our own expense.

JULY 17. We visited the priory of St-Lô-de-Rouen. We found eleven
canons there; five have been sent to other abbeys and priories to relieve the
burden of debt which afflicts the house. All but one are priests. One does
not accuse another [in chapter]; we enjoined them to correct this. We enjoined them to cease using private rooms. They owe four hundred pounds,
but they have nearly enough provisions to last until the new harvest. We
found something amiss concerning the keys of the cellar, for a certain cleric
was in the habit of carrying them about, and sometimes when it was time
for luncheon or dinner, he was absent. Item, there was no one to look out
for the sick in any competent way; we enjoined the prior to have this corrected. We received procuration there this day. Total for procuration: ...
[*lacuna in MS*].

JULY 18. At Bourg-Achard, at our expense. JULY 19. At Bec-Hellouin.

JULY 20. We visited there, where we found about eighty monks. We
found everything to be in good condition, except that those in the nonconventual[12] priories do not keep the fasts of the Rule and eat meat freely;
we enjoined the abbot to discipline them for this.

JULY 21. We received procuration at Corneville. Total for procuration:
six pounds, sixteen shillings, ten pence of Tours, of which amount we remitted to them one hundred shillings. We visited there this day. Nine

---

[11] See entry for May 14, 1257.

[12] Priories in which, because of the small number of monks, the regular liturgical
observances of the Divine Office were not carried out. Many times such establishments
were cells inhabited by two monks.

canons, including the abbot, are there. One canon is at Colletot, another is at another priory, and each is alone. Item, they celebrate three Masses each day and with due modulation.[13] One does not accuse another [in chapter]. Seven priests are there. Those who are not priests receive Communion three times a year; the novices confess when they please; we enjoined their master to be solicitous in providing for them to go to confession. The canons occasionally leave the cloister to watch the workers engaged at the house; we enjoined them to correct this. The canons possess coffers; we enjoined the abbot to inspect them frequently. The church income was written down on rolls; item, they owe about thirty-five pounds of Tours, over and above what is owed to them. They have almost enough wheat and oats for the use of the community and the servants to last until the new harvest. They have two casks full of cider. Two lay sisters are there. Item, the people of the parish often come and enter the monastery to hear Masses and the service, or to strike the two bells which they [the parishioners] possess in the monastery tower; we ordered them to construct a partition between the bells, so that the canons might sound their own bells more freely and be able to concentrate upon the divine cult with more quiet. Item, guests occasionally eat there, and one or two of the canons eat with them; we enjoined the abbot to prohibit the canons from eating with the guests in the future.

JULY 22. That is to say, on the feast of St. Mary Magdalene. We spent this night there, at our own expense. This same day William Bernard swore in our presence to treat Emeline, called Noble, his wife, and whom he has several times put away from him, with marital affection. He gave, in addition, a pledge to continue in this course under a penalty of one hundred shillings. His sureties were Walter of Chemin and Richard of Buez, both of whom live at Corneville. Both gave their pledge under a penalty of twenty pounds of Tours.

JULY 23. We received procuration at Bourg-Achard. Total for procuration: nine pounds, seven shillings, seven pence. We visited there this day and found ten canons; all but one are priests. There is no subprior; we ordered the prior to appoint one. One does not accuse another [in chapter]; we enjoined frequent and mutual accusation and that corrections be made. Almost all of the canons fail to observe the rule of silence; we enjoined them under pain of excommunication and by their oath of obedience to observe the rule of silence carefully, telling them that should we find one or

[13] See above, July 9, 1249, n. 36.

more guilty of breaking this rule, we would punish him or them as guilty of a grave fault. They have an income of about three hundred pounds; they owe one hundred pounds of Paris, and two hundred pounds of Tours is owed to them. They have sufficient wine to last until Michaelmas, but they do not have enough wheat and oats to last until the new harvest. We forbade the prior to go riding alone in the future, to eat outside the priory in the town, or to permit any woman to eat at the priory. We enjoined him to confess more frequently than was his practice, to wit, at least as often as he should happen to celebrate Mass.

JULY 24. At Pont-de-l'Arche. JULY 25. At Frênes.

JULY 26. We received procuration at Vesly. Total: eight pounds, eight pence of Paris. This same day we absolved the prior of Vesly, formerly prior of Gisors, from the sentence which, under apostolic authority, we had imposed upon him a little while ago[14] for failing to observe the Statutes of Pope Gregory. Item from the sentence we imposed upon him in the matter of the procuration from the priory of Gisors, in which matter he was never willing to stand trial. Item, from the sentence imposed upon him by the archdeacon of the place [Gisors], because of a certain tax for the procuration of the said archdeacon which the said priory owed, and which tax he did not wish to recognize. We absolved him provisionally from these; that is to say, he swore in our presence that he would abide by the decision reached about the foregoing. Present were: Master William, the treasurer; and Robert, the archdeacon of the Norman Vexin, in the church of Rouen.

This same day Master John, priest at Suzay, confessed to us that he had once again fallen into sin with a certain woman of whom he had already been defamed, for which he had been admonished and because of which he was obligated to pay ten pounds. But we, desiring him to undergo purgation, admonished him to give us a letter promising to regard his church as resigned. When he had agreed to this request, we appointed the Monday before Assumption as the day on which he should appear at Rouen, or vicinity, to answer questions about this and other offenses and obey the sentence.

JULY 27. We received procuration at Parnes. Total: one hundred fifteen shillings, eight pence. We visited there this day, finding four monks. Because they were then repairing St. Mary's chapel, they do not sing Matins with modulation.[15] They eat meat freely because it has been their custom,

[14] See entries for September 17, 1253; February 5, 1254/55.
[15] See above July 9, 1249, n. 36.

but it is not according to the Rule. They owe about twenty pounds. We enjoined them to abstain from eating meat. Everything else we found in good condition.

JULY 28. We visited at Villarceaux, where there are twenty nuns. They do not have sufficient books; they lack two antiphonaries. The gate looking towards the fields is open too often; we ordered it closed. They owe eighty pounds; they have six horses, sixteen cows, thirty-four swine; but they have no provisions. The community has four maidservants for general work, and one for the infirmary. They have a niece of the prior of Vesly there, at present in secular garb; in chapter they knelt and besought us for permission to receive her, because the prioress and community had promised to give her the veil. Item, the prioress swore to show us all obedience and reverence in whatever we, in conscience, should think it best to enact for them. Item, we enjoined her to remove, or to have removed, all of the servants who were in the house, both male and female, with the exception of this niece.

This same day we spent the night at St-Laurent-en-Cornecervine, at their expense. Total for procuration: one hundred six shillings, one penny. We visited there this day. Four monks are there, including the prior. We found everything in satisfactory condition.

JULY 29. At Wy. We conferred the Sacrament of Confirmation and spent the night there. The priest at Gadancourt owes us an annual rent of a *muid*[16] of oats, whenever we turn aside to Wy.

JULY 30. We visited at Sérans-le-Bouteiller, where there are three monks from St-Germer-en-Flay. They use feather beds; they do not observe the fasts of the Rule; they use meat whenever they please. They owe about fifty pounds of Paris; they have a sufficiency of provisions. We received procuration there this day, and for this we had seventy shillings of Paris, fodder for the horses, straw for men and beasts, domestic utensils, and wood. They did not wish to pay for hay bought outside the town, saying that this was not included in the letter sealed with the seal of Thibaut, former archbishop of Rouen, a transcript of which letter they showed to us. For they said that they were not obligated for anything not contained in the said letter. A transcript of this letter is copied out below, on the last folio.[17]

JULY 31. At Liancourt. For procuration we received four pounds of Paris, accommodation and utensils, as is set forth in the agreement. We visited

---

[16] See above, August 18, 1251, n. 14.
[17] Bonnin, p. 776.

there this day. Three monks are there. They use feather beds and do not observe the fasts of the Rule; we enjoined them to correct this as the Rule requires. They eat meat freely; we forbade them to eat meat save as the Rule permits. They owe one hundred pounds of Paris; they have sufficient provisions. Everything else we found to be in good condition.

AUGUST 1. At Notre-Dame-de-l'Aillerie-de-Chaumont, at our expense.

AUGUST 2. At the same. We visited St-Martin-d'Es, where there are two monks, both of whom are priests. The prior does not celebrate Mass every week. They have an income of forty-five pounds; they owe thirty-three pounds. They use feather beds; we ordered this corrected. They do not sleep in the same place; we ordered them to correct this. We spent the night at l'Aillerie, at our own expense.

AUGUST 3. We received procuration at Ressons. Total: one hundred fourteen shillings, two pence.

AUGUST 4. We received procuration at Marcheroux, and this day we sent John of Graye, cleric, whom we have appointed our proctor, to the Roman Curia. Total: six pounds, six shillings, two pence.

AUGUST 5. We received procuration at Neufmarché. Total for procuration: eight pounds, sixteen shillings, eight pence.

This day Girard, priest at Martigny, appeared before us and confessed that he had kept a certain woman, called Mathilde, who was also one of his parishioners, for three years, and also that he had several times known another young girl. We assigned to him the day after Assumption for proceeding against him as the law requires on his admissions which were made with due regard for legal process, in our presence. He then promised, by letter, to regard his church as resigned if it should happen that he sinned again.

We visited there [at Neufmarché] this same day. Four monks from St-Evroult are there; all are priests but one. The parish priest eats at their table, and the parish Mass is always celebrated in the monks' choir; the parishioners complained about this; we enjoined the prior, in the presence of the local archdeacon, to build a special altar before the Cross, on which the parish priest should celebrate Mass every day, and that the monks should find a clerk to assist the priest. They eat meat in common; we forbade them to eat meat save as the Rule permits. About as much is owed to them as they owe. Everything else we found to be in good condition.

AUGUST 6. At Gournay, at our own expense, and we visited the chapter.

In residence are four canons and five students. We found everything to be in good condition.

We conferred the Sacrament of Confirmation this day at the monastery of St-Hildevert. We found only two canons there, to wit, Matthew and Master John of Paris.

This day we visited the leper hospital at Gournay. The chaplain there is maintained at the expense of the house. The arrangement is unsatisfactory: the dean of Gournay and certain burgesses are the proctors of the house and of the master; a certain leprous cleric is lessee. They owe about sixteen pounds.

We also visited the Maison-Dieu this same day. In residence are six brothers, six sisters, and one chaplain; the brothers and sisters are accepted there with the consent of the brothers of the chapter of Gournay and of the burgesses. They all eat in common, the brothers, the sisters, and the priest. The sick are ill provided for. One of the sisters there was destroying and even pilfering the goods of the house. They do not observe any Rule. They do not discipline each other. They do not sleep in one and the same place. Some of them sleep with their wives there and whenever they please.[18] They confess whenever and to whomsoever they please. They have no parish, nor do they desire to have one.

AUGUST 7. We visited the priory of nuns of St-Aubin. Fifteen nuns are there, but we found only twelve. Eustasia of Etrépagny was a wanderer; Alice of Rouen was in grave fault. We forbade the prioress and the community to receive anyone as a nun, or to veil anyone, without our special knowledge and command; and that if they did so, we would not regard the one received as a nun. We expressly forbade the relatives of the nuns to sleep in the house, or to eat or drink at the house with the nuns. There is a parish there, and the priest lives at their house and celebrates Mass for them. They owe about one thousand pounds. The above-mentioned Eustasia was pregnant when she departed; she left and it was said that she gave birth to a child which she had by John, the chaplain at Fry. We ordered them to procure some clerk to assist the priest, and to do this before the feast of St. Remy.

---

[18] These religious-minded brothers and sisters serving in the hospitals and leprosaries contracted temporary vows and were free to marry when the period of the vow's duration was terminated. Many remained at the hospitals or leprosaries even after they married.

AUGUST 8. We received procuration at St-Laurent-en-Lyons. Total: eight pounds, three shillings, five pence.

AUGUST 9. We visited there. Fifteen canons are there; all but two are priests. When the canons return to the cloister from the priories they do not celebrate Mass as frequently as they should. The novices confess only once a year; we ordered them all to confess once a month. One does not accuse another [in chapter]; we enjoined them to correct this. We ordered the prior to hear the confessions of the lay brothers. They owe about two hundred eighty pounds. Brother Peter Beaugendre was suspected of possessing property; we expressly enjoined him to free his conscience in this matter, to celebrate Mass more often than was his practice, and to confess to the prior.

We received procuration this day at Bellosane. Total: one hundred eleven shillings.

AUGUST 10. We received procuration at Beaulieu. Total for procuration: seven pounds, nine shillings, seven pence.

AUGUST 11. We visited there. Fifteen canons are in residence; eleven are priests. There are three sisters as lay sisters, two maidservants, and two lay brothers. They owe one hundred fifty-three pounds and fourteen shillings; thirty-two pounds of a good and collectible debt is owed to them. They have an income of four hundred fifty pounds. Other things we found to be in a sufficiently good condition. The prior had kept one canon for a long space of time at Montmoy, although the cure of souls had not been granted to him; he accepted a penalty for this, and we enjoined a penance upon him. This day we lunched at Carville, at the house of the treasurer,[19] though at our expense. We spent the night at Déville.

AUGUST 12. At Déville, and we preached a sermon in the churchyard of St-Gervaise.[20] AUGUST 13. At the same. AUGUST 14. At Rouen. AUGUST 15. At Rouen, where we celebrated the feast of the Assumption of the Virgin. The lord archbishop of Sens was staying with us. AUGUST 16. At Déville. The lord archbishop of Sens was with us. AUGUST 17-21. At Frênes. AUGUST 22. At Frênes. This day we visited the chapter at Les Andelys. Four vicars are there; one celebrates Mass daily at La Culture, another at La Madeleine, and two in the church. They do not have the required Mass.[21] Dom Peter is not

---

[19] That is, the treasurer of the cathedral of Rouen.

[20] This was undoubtedly a sermon preached in the open. Many churches in Europe are in the center of the cemetery or churchyard.

[21] That is, conventual Mass, at which the community was present daily. Usually

constant in sleeping in the sacristy as he is held to do. Some of the chaplains of the church hear the confessions of parishioners without the dean's permission and this they should not do. Dom Peter does not show the necessary diligence in the training of the boys in the song schools. Master Robert is a drunkard. Dom Miles is regarded as suspect concerning Emmaline of Haqueville; Dom Peter Robilgart was thrashed by two women, and these had a battle between themselves because of him. We gave instructions that certain vicars should not invite men to eat with them and bring their wives, nor should any other woman eat with them.

AUGUST 23. We visited the priory at Noyon [-sur-Andelle], where there are seven monks. They have coffers and keys; we enjoined the prior to collect the keys occasionally and to look into the coffers to see if any property was there, and to correct whatever he found to need correction. They use meat freely; we forbade them to eat meat save as the Rule permits. A general distribution of alms takes place on Sunday; on other days to all travelers, or certain dishes of food to the people living in the vicinity. They owe ninety pounds. Total for procuration: eight pounds, seventeen shillings, three pence.

AUGUST 24. At Déville.

AUGUST 25. We visited the chapter at Rouen. Present were: Simon of Rouen, Reginald of Petit-Caux, Robert of the Norman Vexin, Stephen of the French Vexin, archdeacons; the treasurer; the precentor; the chancellor; and the subcantor. We preached the word of God before the entire chapter and the clerks-choral. Then we entered the chapter and visited, examining them first of all as a body. We admonished them to warn the dean to keep residence in the church, and to get themselves promoted to such [Holy] Orders as the administration of heir dignities required. We warned them to allow and pass as binding, whatever ordinances the treasurer and archdeacon Reginald should issue. This over, we called in the chancellor and the subcantor separately and in that order, then the others two at a time, and we made inquiries into the conduct of persons. We found nothing that was not good. Item, we admonished them to compel certain ones to take deacons' Orders.

AUGUST 26. We visited St-Amand. Forty-five nuns are there as well as four girls who have been promised that they would be received before any

---

it was a High or Solemn Mass. Even though the priests celebrated privately, they were obliged to hear the community Mass.

others. They have seven maidservants. Silence is badly observed, especially in the monastery and in the dormitory. The abbess does not eat in the refectory; whenever she eats in her own chamber she always has certain ones as her companions, and does not call the others for such recreation. When the nuns are in the infirmary, they have no one to read the Divine Office to them. We enjoined the abbess not to be ready or lenient in granting permission to the nuns to undertake traveling, but to be stern and to give them permission to go only for a definite time. We forbade them to appoint any almoness or to give alms without consent. Item, we forbade them to receive anything from their relatives without permission.

AUGUST 27. At St-Saëns.

AUGUST 28. At Longueville. Total for procuration at Longueville: seven pounds, eighteen shillings.

AUGUST 29. At Sauqueville. The treasurer, Ferric, does not keep residence, although he is obligated to do so. Item, he is publicly known for incontinence with Aubrey of Canay. Walter, called "Gros," does not keep residence. We ordered the bailiff to seize their revenues. The canons perform no other services than as parish priests. It is not known whether Gilbert, the deaf canon, has been corrected about his incontinence. We spent the night at Aliermont.

AUGUST 30—SEPTEMBER 3. At Aliermont. SEPTEMBER 4. At the same. Today Robert Pichet, of St. Mary's parish, Geoffrey, a parishioner of the same church and Reginald Pate swore in our presence that they would obey our orders and will, and would likewise accept whatever penalty we should desire to impose as a result of the things they said and did against the priest at St. Mary's.

SEPTEMBER 5. At Aliermont. SEPTEMBER 6. At Anglesqueville. SEPTEMBER 7-8. At Jumièges. SEPTEMBER 9-11. At Pont-Audemer. SEPTEMBER 12. We presided over the sacred provincial council at Pont-Audemer. Present were [the following]: on our right sat Gui, bishop of Bayeux, and next to him Fulk, bishop of Lisieux (there being no bishop just then in the church of Evreux; had there been one, he would have been seated between Bayeux and Lisieux); on our left sat Richard, bishop of Avranches, Geoffrey, bishop of Séez, and John, bishop of Coutances, in that order. We opened the council by preaching a sermon. Then a letter from the bishop of Bayeux calling and authorizing the council was read. Thirdly, the lists of proctors of the catedral chapters were read. Fourthly, the statute drawn up in the general council[22] concerning the convocation of annual councils by archbishops and their suffragans, which is to be found under the title "On Accusations,"[23] and other statutes of the same general council which seemed pertinent, were read. The proctors were: for the Rouen chapter, William, the treasurer of Rouen; for Bayeux, Master Peter of Locelles, the official of Bayeux, and a canon of Bayeux; for Avranches, A., the dean of Avranches; for Evreux, the official, and Master John of Meulan, canon of Evreux; for Séez, Master Nicholas of Blève, canon of Bayeux; for Lisieux, Master William, dean, and Nicholas, archdeacon of Gacay in the church of Lisieux; and for Coutances, Master Harvey Paste. Fifthly, the inquisitors appointed at the last provincial council were asked to report; all were negligent except the inquisitor of Rouen. Thereupon we appointed others: to wit, G.[William], the treasurer, and Robert, the archdeacon in the Norman Vexin, for the diocese of Rouen; Stephen, dean of Marais, and Master Adam, dean of Noyers, for Bayeux; Alfred, dean of Genet, and Henry, dean of Mesnil-Gilbert, for Avranches; William of St-Just, dean of Vernon, and Nicholas, dean of Lyre, for Evreux; Master Nicholas, rector of the church of Moulins, and Amidieu, dean of Argentan, for Séez; Gilbert, dean of Bernay, and Nicholas, dean of Cormeilles, for Lisieux; and Nicholas, dean of Cenilly, and Robert, called Piedubois, dean of Carentan, for the chapter of Coutances. Sixthly, we enacted the statutes which were read to the sacred council and which ran as follows:

It is the pleasure of the sacred council that the [statutes] below be observed in strictness, in such manner that the Reverend Fathers, Eudes, by God's grace archbishop of Rouen, his suffragans, and their subjects are in no way obliged to observe them as newly enacted statutes, that is, as regards those which have already found expression in [canon] law, in the Statutes of Pope Gregory IX or in episcopal synods.

We will the observance of the statute promulgated at the Council of Lyons dealing with procurations owed by reason of visitation, and receivable by the archbishop and bishops; we also will that the statute be observed which prohibits the inflicting of burdens under the pretext of performing their duties.[24]

We will that the statute of the general council against those who form leagues,[25] together with the statutes against the liberties of the Church which

[22] The Fourth Lateran Council.

[23] *Corp. jur. can., Decretal. Greg. IX* Lib. v. Tit. 1. cap. 25.

[24] *Romana Ecclesia*, promulgated by the Council of Lyons of 1245 (Mansi, XXIII, 668).

[25] In September, 1235, the principal barons of the realm met with St. Louis at

have been published with frequency and solemnity, be read in synods and in parochial churches, and that those who transgress such statutes be canonically punished by the bishops.

We decree the pronouncement of a general excommunication against secular powers who seize clerics with greater violence than the resistance of the arrested one justifies, or who hold them contrary to the request of an ecclesiastical judge, and then after the charge is proved that [the secular powers] be individually declared excommunicated.[26]

We strictly forbid that a secular judge be brought in by ecclesiastics in cases pertaining to the Church, especially to cases relating to personal actions.[27]

St-Denis in Paris. From their assembly emanated a catalogue of baronial grievances to Gregory IX against the bishop of Beauvais and the archbishops of Tours and Rheims, who were accused of undermining royal and baronial authority by making cases involving laymen and clerics justiciable in ecclesiastical courts. Gregory answered (Potthast, *Regesta*, I, 858) that such royal and baronial attitudes saddened him, "that you and the barons of your realm, seeking to reduce the Church to servitude, have drawn up a statute contrary to the liberties of the Church, so that the men under your jurisdiction are not bound to answer in ecclesiastical courts." Gregory then asked Louis IX and his baronage to revoke the decision of this baronial confederation. The movement spread throughout France, and many provincial councils excommunicated the makers of such statutes, e.g., the provincial council of Béziers, 1246. (Mansi, XXIII, 696.) Canon 18 decreed that, after legal admonition, the writers of *Statuta* which were contrary to the liberties of the Church were to be held excommunicate. Probably Eudes is referring to such councils when he speaks of the decree of a general council. The Council of Lyons (1245) did not act specifically against the *statutarii* or confederation. In November, 1246, the *statutarii* elected four representatives to carry on its business. Those who were intimidated by excommunication were to be deprived of their standing in the baronial confederation. The barons now drew up a manifesto in Latin and in French, setting forth their grievances against the Church. Both versions may be read in Matthew Paris, *Chronica Majora*, IV, 591-93. Pope Innocent IV answered in January, 1247, by excommunicating the members of the confederation. (Potthast, II, 1047.) The bull may be found in B. Guérard, *Cartulaire de l'eglise Notre-Dame de Paris* (Paris, 1850), II, 389-90. It is clear that a situation had arisen in France not unlike that leading up to the Constitutions of Clarendon in England (1164). The bill of particulars indicated that jurisdiction over cases was the main issue. A further bull of Innocent IV (June 20, 1252) indicates that the movement was in full vigor, with the barons forbidding the payments of rents to ecclesiastical owners and forbidding the donation or transfer of property to the Church. (Potthast, II, 1207.) On July 7, 1257, Alexander IV ordered that the excommunication pronounced by Innocent IV should be repeated in provincial councils and diocesan synods. (Potthast, II, 1384.) This accounts for Eudes' decrees at the provinvial councils over which he presided. As Eudes' document indicates, the struggle for the courts went on in Normandy, too.

[26] Provincial council of Rouen (1231), canon 28 in Mansi, XXIII, 217.

[27] *Ibid.*, XXIII, 216-17 (canons 23, 26). Personal actions in this instance are actions of the clergy as clergy.

We decree that abbots, priors, and other ecclesiastical persons who receive major tithes from parochial churches be compelled to restore the fabric, ornaments, and books in proportion to the tithes they receive therefrom.

We will the synodal statute, that is, that ecclesiastics to whom come the mandates of different judges, judges-delegate, conservators, or executors should look with care at the names of the judges of the diocese, and at the names of the places to which the judges cite them, and make sure that the authenticity of the names and places is strictly observed.[28]

We forbid any Christians, male or female, to work for Jews in their homes, or presume to dwell with them, and we order that Jews be compelled to wear visible signs by which they may be distinguished from Catholics.[29]

We strictly forbid the holding of vigils and dances in cemeteries and holy places and order transgressors to be canonically punished.[30]

Clerics who are in churches, and especially the unmarried ones, are to be admonished to wear a suitable tonsure; clerics who have taken the Cross are to be compelled to wear the Cross in a conspicuous place.[31]

We will the observance of the statute of the general council regarding gilded saddles, reins, spurs, and pectoral crosses gilded or otherwise superfluously decorated, whose use is forbidden to clerics, and also [the observance of the statute] regarding the closed garments which priests should wear.[32]

We forbid beneficed clergy or those already in Holy Orders to become attached or addicted to hunting or hawking.

We decree that the certain number of religious shall be reestalbished in those abbeys and priories whose resources have not been diminished, unless some delay be granted by the express permission of a superior, and for reasonable causes.[33]

We will and command that the statutory law forbidding a monk to dwell anywhere alone be observed.[34]

Monks dwelling in nonconventual priories shall be warned under threat of suspension and excommunication, as may seem expedient, that they are expected to strive to keep the Statutes of Pope Gregory covering the eating of meat, making confession, and observing the fasts.[35]

---

[28] *Ibid.*, XXIII, 215 (canon 9).
[29] *Ibid.*, XXIII, 219 (canon 49); *ibid.,* XXII, 1055 (canon 68).
[30] *Ibid.*, XXIII, 216 (canon 14).
[31] Fourth Lateran Council. Mansi, XXII, 1003-6 (canon 16).
[32] *Idem.*
[33] *Corp. jur. can., Decretal. Greg. IX* Lib. III. Tit. 5. cap. 25; Lib. III. Tit. 8. cap. 10; Lib. III. Tit. 7. cap. 2; also canon 394 of the modern *Codex juris canonici.*
[34] Mansi, XXIII, 218 cannon 37).
[35] *Ibid.*, XXIII, 218 (canon 38).

We order that regular clergy shall not live with secular clergy, except by special permission of their diocesan.

The statute forbidding religious to contract loans beyond a certain amount, without the permission of their abbot, shall be strictly adhered to.[36]

We decree that rural deans who exercise jurisdiction shall neither excommunicate nor suspend except in writing.

We decree that priests shall not cease to publish excommunications, be the parties ever so reconciled, until a legal absolution of the excommunicated ones shall be established.

We will that absolution from excommunication be made with due solemnity.

We forbid priests from presuming to pronounce general excommunications, except for robberies and vandalism, and after a sufficient warning to the offender.[37]

Seventhly, with the common consent of our brothers, we decreed that the visitation of the province of Rouen may be recommenced by us whenever such shall seem expedient. The provincial council being thus celebrated, and without any discord, we retired singing *Te Deum laudamus* and came before the altar of St-Aniane, where, at the completion of the Psalm, we offered the suitable prayers.

It is to be noted that before we sat in council we celebrated Mass in pontificals, our suffragans standing by, but not vested as for the celebration of Mass; two canons of Rouen, one deacon, the other a subdeacon, were so vested. Mass being celebrated, we and our suffragans being properly clothed, we took our seats, and the deacon, in proper vestments, read the Gospel, beginning: "Jesus appointed," et cetera. We then with loud voice began the *Come Holy Spirit*. This completed, the precentor of Rouen and the precentor of Lisieux, both in surplices, sang the Litany. Then, having repeated the *Lord's Prayer* in a low voice, we uttered the prayer *Adsumus*.[38] After this we preached our sermon, and then were carried out the other things in the order mentioned above.

These are the grievances inflicted by the secular court upon the bishops of Normandy, and on which counsel was taken by the archbishop of Rouen and his suffragans:[39]

---

[36] *Ibid.*, XXIII, 213-14 (canons 1-3).

[37] *Ibid.*, XXIII, 215 (canon 5).

[38] The prayer said at the beginning of a synod may be found in Andrieu, *Le Pontifical romain au moyen âge*, II, 78, III, 596. The Gospel read was Luke 10 : 1.

[39] The basic agreement on secular and eccleciastical jurisdiction in Normandy was reached in 1190 between King Richard I of England and Walter of Coutances, arch-

First, that they cite bishops or cause them to be cited by one sergeant, albeit they are in the habit of being cited by four knights. Let this be referred to the king.[40]

Item, they seize clerics although they are not discovered in the very act of committing the offence. Let justice be done.[41]

Item, that they do not wish to bring to justice or seize excommunicated clerics, at the mandate of the bishops or their officials. Let this be referred to the king.[42]

Item, the lands of crusaders and of clerics which are in the keeping of the Church, they detain in the hand of the king, as well as the uncollected fruits, and they are unwilling to hand them over at the mandate of the bishops. Let justice be done by those who are in right of possession on this matter.[43]

Item, they delay investigation, beyond the first assize, of the goods of those whom they call "usurers"; and this is in violation of ancient custom. Let the kind be approached.[44]

Item, they hold inquests of *Harou*, and on such an occasion they demand a fine from the clerics and force them to pay with their lands; and they do the same with crusaders.[45] Let justice be done.

Item, if a cleric, against the wish of the bailiff, summons any layman to an ecclesiastical court, the bailiff seizes the land of the cleric and arrests his relatives, but will not swear that he had made these seizures for the said reason. Let

---

bishop of Rouen. Clerics were not to be arrested by secular authorities except for homicide, theft, and arson; otherwise, they were to be handed over without delay to the eccleciastical courts. Wills, alms, etc., were to be dealt with solely in ecclesiastical tribunals. (Matthew of Paris, *Chronica majora*, II, 368.) This agreement remained in force when Philip Augustus took Normandy from John in 1204. (*Coutumiers de Normandie,* ed. E. J. Tardif [Rouen, 1881], cap. 57, 23.) Normandy, as Eudes and his suffragans testify, was following the pattern being observed in the rest of France in the thirteenth century. The baronage was setting up its own rules independent of engagements entered into between ecclesiastical authorities and the Crown, but probably with the tacit agreement of the latter.

[40] This was in violation of cap. 28 of the *Coutumiers de Normandie*.

[41] Mansi, XXIII, 217. (Canon 28.)

[42] *Corp. jur. can., Decretal. Greg. IX* Lib. v. Tit. 40. cap. 27. Innocent III decreed that excommunicated clerics degraded for certain crimes in an ecclesiastical court were to be handed over to secular courts. See also *ibid.* Lib. v. Tit. 27. cap. 2.

[43] Mansi, XXIII, 217. (Canon 27.)

[44] This was a violation of cap. 49 of the *Coutumiers de Normandie*.

[45] The custom of *Haro* or *Harou* presupposed a grave and flagrant crime and was the "hue and cry" set up by the intended victim of the crime. All lords to whom Philip Augustus gave rights of high justice could hear such cases. The accused was brought without delay before the justice, and Norman custom allowed that clerics accused by *Haro* were to be tried before a secular court and without benefit of clergy.

justice be done if the land belongs to the Church. Item, they retake and reseize the clerics, crusaders, and incomes of the church, once taken by them, and afterward released, and will not return them. Let justice be done.

Item, they are unwilling that the agents of the bishops be present at the summons issued by the king, albeit they attended formerly. Let the king be approached.

Item, they are unwilling to observe the ordinance of King Philip regarding questions of rights of patronage.[46] Let the king be informed.

Item, they refer these disputes from one assize to another, following within eight days, in another baillage, and in another diocese.[47] If this involves an ecclesiastic and a layman, this practice shall not be tolerated.

Item, if the rector of a church claims that he has been despoiled of last year's tithe due from a layman, and the layman replies that his is a lay fief, the bailiff does not permit this case to be aired in an ecclesiastical court.[48] Let justice be done.

Item, they disseize ecclesiastics and their men of their franchises, their rights, and their accustomed usages; and since they say that this matter concerns the lord king, they will not hear them, nor show them justice, but send them to the lay court.[49] Let justice be done.

Item, they investigate perjuries and adulteries, and punish them in violation of the liberty of the Church. We do not believe that this is being done, but it ought not to be tolerated if it is done.

Item, they will not make investigation as to whether a church has held property in free alms for thirty years.[50] Let the king be approached.

Concerning herbs, fruits, and the trees in churchyards. Let a definite statute be drawn up.

Concerning the grievances of the Templars. Let counsel be taken about what can be done.

Concerning the tithes of lambs which laymen are unwilling to keep until they are old enough to live without their mothers. This is unjust.

SEPTEMBER 13. At Jumièges, at our expense. SEPTEMBER 14. At the same. We dedicated the altar of the abbey infirmary. At our own expense. SEPTEMBER 15. At Jumièges. SEPTEMBER 16. At St-Wandrille. SEP-

[46] *Coutumiers de Normandie* cap. 23, 57.

[47] *Ibid.* cap. 55.

[48] Anything dealing with ecclesiastical tithes was supposed to be tried in an ecclesiastical court. *Corp. jur. can., Decretal. Greg IX* Lib. III. Tit. 30, deals with the subject of tithes.

[49] *Coutumiers de Normandie* cap. 21.

[50] *Coutumiers de Normandie* cap. 72

TEMBER 17. At Bourg-Achard. SEPTEMBER 18. At Louviers. SEPTEMBER 19-21. At Frênes. SEPTEMBER 22. We conferred Holy Orders at Les Andelys, and we slept at Frênes. SEPTEMBER 23-24. At Frênes. SEPTEMBER 25. At Sausseuse. SEPTEMBER 26. At Genesville. SEPTEMBER 27. At St-Germain-en-Laye. SEPTEMBER 28. At Paris. SEPTEMBER 29. At Paris. We celebrated the Mass of the Angels[51] at the royal chapel. SEPTEMBER 30. We celebrated the Mass of Relics[52] in the same chapel. OCTOBER 1. At Paris. OCTOBER 2. At St-Denis. OCTOBER 3. At Pontoise. OCTOBER 4. This day we celebrated the Mass of St. Francis at the house of the Franciscans and dined with them in the refectory. OCTOBER 5. At Meulan. OCTOBER 6-7. At St-Martin-la-Garenne. OCTOBER 8-9. At Sausseuse. OCTOBER 10. At Vesly.

OCTOBER 11. We held a synod at Gisors, and spent the night at Vesly. OCTOBER 12. At Gisors. OCTOBER 13-18. At Frênes. OCTOBER 19. At Sausseuse. OCTOBER 20. At Vernon. OCTOBER 21. We dedicated the royal chapel at the château of Vernon. OCTOBER 22. At St-Illiers. [*No entry for October 23.*] OCTOBER 24. At Mantes. OCTOBER 25-26. At Pontoise. OCTOBER 27. At Paris. OCTOBER 28. At St-Denis-en-France. OCTOBER 29. At Le Bord-Haut-de-Vigny. OCTOBER 30. At Frênes. OCTOBER 31. At Rouen. NOVEMBER 1. At Rouen. We celebrated the feast of All Saints. NOVEMBER 2-5. At Déville. NOVEMBER 7. At our hall at Rouen. The priest at Gondecourt resigned his church into our hands. Present were the archdeacon of Rouen and several others.

This day we enjoined the deans to set a suitable time within which priests who do not have capes shall procure them; and that unless they do acquire them, the deans shall seize their fruits[53] and buy capes for them. Item, we enjoined the deans to exact fines from those who do not attend the chapters, and we gave half of these fines to them, until we think such an order should be revoked.

We warned canonically Master William Revel to show us obedience and reverence as he ought to do.

On the same day we pronounced the following sentence in these words and in writing:

---

[51] The feast day and Mass of St. Michael the Archangel.

[52] This Mass is celebrated in commemoration of the saints whose bodies or relics are preserved in the church.

[53] I.e., the revenues of their churches.

In the name of the Father, and of the Son, and of the Holy Ghost, Amen. In the year of our Lord 1257, on the Wednesday following the feast of All Saints. Since John, the chaplain of the chapel at Vaudrimare, is reported to have abandoned this chapel in a fraudulent manner, whereby the said chapel has been defrauded of Divine Service, we caused him to be cited canonically and warned to return to the said chapel and to serve in it as right demands. After waiting until more than six months had elapsed, and [finding] that he did not care to perform the aforementioned duties, we caused the said John to be legally and peremptorily cited to appear before us at Rouen on the said Wednesday to stand trial in this matter. As he was absent on the said day, we, going into the whole business as usage demands, and considering what might and should influence us, on the advice of good men, and with the counsel of the wise, have pronounced the said John contumacious, and sentence him definitively to be deprived of the said chapel.

NOVEMBER 8. At Frênes. NOVEMBER 9. At Le-Bord-Haut-de-Vigny. NOVEMBER 10-21. At Paris. On this date we began to exact this year's procurations. NOVEMBER 23-28. At Paris. NOVEMBER 29. At-Le-Bord-Haut-de-Vigny. NOVEMBER 30. At Frênes. DECEMBER 1. At Rouen. DECEMBER 2. At Rouen. The first Sunday in Advent; we preached in the cathedral at Rouen. DECEMBER 3. We entered the chapter of St-Ouen and treated of those matters which pertain to the payments due from the abbey. We spent the night at Déville. DECEMBER 4. We received procuration at St-Georges. Total for procuration: nine pounds, four shillings, seven pence.

DECEMBER 5. We visited there, finding twenty-two monks; all but five are priests. We enjoined them to give up their old clothes upon the receipt of new ones. Alms are given daily to all comers. More is owed to them than they owe; they owe about sixty pounds.

This day, we received procuration at Jumièges. Total for procuration: nine pounds, seventeen shillings, three pence.

DECEMBER 6. We visited there. Forty-seven monks are in residence. Some are negligent in making their monthly confession; we enjoined the prior to speak to us about this before we left the house. We enjoined them to write out their sources of income. We warned the abbot in full chapter for the second time to place monks in those priories where there have been monks within thirty years; this was the second warning.[54] Alms are given daily to all comers.

---

[54] See entry for December 9, 1256.

This day we spent this night at St-Wandrille, at our expense.

DECEMBER 7. We visited there, where are forty monks. One does not accuse another [in chapter]; we enjoined them to correct this. All but nine are priests. In the priories they do not observe the fasts of the Rule, and they eat meat; we enjoined them to correct this. Alms are given daily to all comers. More is owed to them than they owe: about one thousand pounds. The infirmary is in a wretched state, and the sick are ill provided for; we enjoined them to correct this, that is to say, to construct a new place to serve as an infirmary. Item, we commanded, since the monk in charge of the infirmary has but a small income, that when his money has been expended and he has checked his accounts with the abbot, the latter should give him money for expenses from his own account, and pay whatever has been borrowed for the use of the sick, and that the infirmarian should account for how much and for what purpose the money has been spent and borrowed. This day we received procuration there. Total for procuration: eleven pounds, seven pence.

DECEMBER 8. At Le Valasse, a Cistercian house. DECEMBER 9. At Tancarville, through kindness.

DECEMBER 10. We visited at Graville, where there are eleven canons. They have recently sent one canon to Beaulieu to be the companion of the prior there. We strictly forbade women to eat in the future at the houses of the canons in the parishes. Alms are given three times a week to all comers, and on Fridays to lepers. They owe one hundred fifty pounds to a certain priest; they have an income of three hundred pounds. Roger is suspected of incontinence; we enjoined the prior to investigate the truth of this, and to discipline him should he need correction. Total for procuration: eight pounds, seven shillings, two pence.

DECEMBER 11. We visited the abbey at Montivilliers. One does not accuse another [in chapter]; we enjoined them to correct this. They confess and receive Communion every month. They asked us for permission to have keys, but we absolutely refused. They owe two hundred sixty pounds for vintage; but about three hundred sixty pounds is owed to them from last year. We forbade the nuns to act as godmothers in the future. Total for procuration: ten pounds, sixteen shillings, seven pence.

DECEMBER 12. We spent the night at our expense at Valmont.

DECEMBER 13. We visited there, where there are twenty-seven monks. One does not accuse another [in chapter]; we strictly enjoined them to correct this in the following manner, to wit, that he who does not accuse his companion of an offense shall incur the same penalty as the perpetrator would merit. Some leave the cloister withour permission; we strictly enjoined them to correct this. They have keys; we strictly enjoined that they be taken away. Alms are given three times a week to all comers. They eat meat too often; we enjoined the abbot to see that the Rule was observed in this matter, and we also enjoined him to see it was enforced by those who are dwelling in the priories. They owe three hundred pounds, but nine hundred pounds is owed to them in arrears; two hundred pounds of this is a bad debt; the balance is collectible. We forbade the abbot and community to obey the abbot of Hambye in any matter prejudicial to us and to the church of Rouen, or to receive him should he come there to make visitation or administer discipline. We forbade them these things by virtue of obedience and under pain of suspension, and we enjoined them to appeal to us under a form which we gave to them, should he try to exercise his power of visitation or discipline. This day we received procuration there. Total for procuration: eight pounds, eleven shillings, ten pence.

DECEMBER 14. We received procuration at Ouville and visited there. Ten canons are in residence; all but two are priests. One does not accuse another [in chapter]; we enjoined them to correct this. Alms are given once a day to all comers. One of the lay brothers is lying ill at the house. They owe about one hundred twenty pounds. They have sufficient wheat and oats to last until the next harvest. About sixty pounds is owed to them. Total for procuration: eight pounds, six shillings, eight pence.

DECEMBER 15. At Aliermont.

DECEMBER 16. At the same. This day, at our hall, a certain fowler named Hardy, in the service of the countess of Dreux, made amends for the fourteen partridges which, as he confessed to us, he had taken with dog and falcon in our preserve.

Item, this day and in our presence William of Moutiers, son of the late William of Moutiers, knight, and Miles, called Balainne, both squires of the said countess, Robert Tassel, William, called Esperon, and Gilbert, called Gualove of St-Aubin, at the king's mandate, made amends for their offense in hunting illegally and against the prohibition of our sergeants in our forest at Aliermont. It should be known that Walter Charue stood surety for the fine of the aforesaid Hardy. The said Robert, William, and Gilbert of St-Aubin stood as guarantors for the two esquires, and each of the three vouched for the others. Present at these proceedings were the venerable men W[il-liam], the treasurer of Rouen; Master John of Neuilly-en-Thelle, canon of St-Mary's church at Beauvais; Michael, the chaplain of the said threasurer; Brother Walter of Minières; Everard, our clerk; Walter Charue; Sir Ansel, then chatelain of Arques; G. [Walter] of Villers, then bailiff of Caux; Reginald of Tremblay, our sergeant; Peter of Mesnil; and many others, to wit, Sir Alerin of Fontaines, Sir John of St-Martin, Sir Ralph of Bailleul, and Sir Robert of Fressenneville, knights.

DECEMBER 17-18. At Aliermont. DECEMBER 19. At Auffay, at our ex-pense. DECEMBER 20. At Déville. DECEMBER 21. We attended the opening of the Dominican monastery; we celebrated Mass, preached a sermon, and spent the night at Déville. DECEMBER 22. We conferred Holy Orders at Rouen in the Franciscan monastery, and dined with the Franciscans.

This day, after Vespers, in our palace at Rouen to be exact, in the am-bulatory Stephen, priest at Fontenay, not wishing to await judgment for being gravely defamed of incontinence and having twice failed to purge himself, submitted himself completely to our will and command concerning his status, and promised to resign his church without the publicity of a trial whenever we should so desire and deem expedient. Present were: Reginald of Petit-Caux and Robert of the Norman Vexin, both archdeacons in the church of Rouen; Master Richard of Sap, canon of Rouen; John Cholet; Morel, our clerk; the official of Rouen; and many others. In the presence of these wit-nesses he swore all the aforesaid with his hand on his breast.

DECEMBER 23. At the same, and we performed our O.[55] DECEMBER 24. At the same. DECEMBER 25. At the same. We celebrated the feast of the Nativity of the Lord. DECEMBER 26. At Couronne. DECEMBER 27. At Bourg-Achard. DECEMBER 28. At Pont-Audemer.

DECEMBER 29. Here begins the visitation of the diocese of Lisieux. We visited the abbey of Grestain, where there are thirty-two monks. Some of them occasionally remain away from Compline; we enjoined them to correct this. Alms are given twice a week, to wit, on Mondays and Thursdays, to all comers. We enjoined the abbot to enjoin upon the monks dwelling in the priories to abstain from eating meat and to observe the fasts of the Rule. We enjoined him to discipline those who were delinquent. They have an income of sixteen hundred pounds; they have sufficient provisions to last

[55] See above, December 23, 1250, n. 135.

until the new harvest; they owe four hundred pounds, but about six hundred pounds is owed to them. On the same day we received procuration there. Total for procuration: nine pounds, five shillings.

DECEMBER 30. We visited the abbey of St-Pierre-les-Préaux. The prior was not there at the time. Thirty monks are in residence. We enjoined the abbot to visit the priories overseas at least once a year.[56] One does not accuse another [in chapter]; we enjoined them to correct this. One monk is sleeping alone in the cellar. In the priories they do not observe the fasts of the Rule, and they eat meat; we enjoined the abbot to see that the Rule is observed in these things. They owe about three hundred pounds, but they have already collected all of this year's fruits. We enjoined all the officials to make up the accounts required by their offices. We received procuration there on the same day. Total for procuration: nine pounds, eighteen shillings, two pence.

Note: On December 31, while we were still at Préaux, we appointed the vigil of Septuagesima, as the day when a certain squire of Neville should appear at Rouen or in the vicinity, to hear our decision concerning the fine to be made for having thrashed a servant bringing a letter to the court at Rouen.

DECEMBER 31. We visited the abbey of St-Léger [-des-Préaux]. Forty-five nuns are there; that number is certain. We enjoined them to take only the three vows, to wit, concerning property, obedience, and continence. They do not all eat the same food. There are six maidservants. They have coffers and keys. They have two small dogs and three squirrels. The nuns go outside the main abbey when they can and return whenever they like. They owe about one hundred fifty pounds, and they have sufficient provisions. They do not hand in their old clothes when they receive new ones. The abbess does not sleep with them in the dormitory; she rarely eats in the refectory, and attends chapter infrequently. We forbade the use of individual dishes in the kitchen; we urged them to get rid of as many of the horde of maidservants as they could conveniently and to remove the dogs and squirrels. We enjoined the abbess to inspect the coffers frequently during the year and to discipline any property owners, should there be such. We received procuration there on the same day. Total for procuration: seven pounds, nineteen shillings.

---

[56] There are at least two priories of this abbey in England: Monkstofte and Stour.

JANUARY 1. We visited the abbey of Cormeilles. Twenty-five monks are there; all are priests, with the exception of the novices. Alms are given daily to all comers. Traveling monks do not observe the fasts of the Rule; we enjoined them to correct this. As much is owed to them as they owe, and they have sufficient provisions. By apostolic authority they owe in pensions thirteen pounds to archdeacon Nicholas, ten pounds to archdeacon Girard, and one hundred shillings to a certain other person. The former abbot went to Rome.

JANUARY 2. We received procuration at Beaumont-en-Auge. Total for procuration: nine pounds, sixteen shillings.

JANUARY 3. We visited there, where there are thirteen monks. The Statutes of Pope Gregory are not read; we enjoined them to read the Statutes. They confess too rarely, and some do not celebrate Mass often enough; we enjoined the prior to have these things corrected. The cloister is badly kept, and the monks freely go out into the farm and without permission. They do not observe the fasts of the Rule, and they eat meat too often; we enjoined the prior to correct this. They have an income of seven hundred pounds. They have sufficient provisions to last until the new harvest. They owe two hundred pounds, but they are due to receive four hundred pounds before the feast of St. John.[57]

On the same day, we received procuration from the priory of Blangy, but at St-Hymer. Total for procuration: eight pounds, ten shillings, eleven pence.

JANUARY 4. We visited the priory of St-Hymer. Eleven monks are there, but there used to be eight; all are priests. They eat meat when there is no need; we ordered them to observe the Rule in this matter. They have an income of four hundred pounds; they owe about one hundred pounds, and they must buy about one hundred pounds worth of wheat. The prior is supporting one of his nephews at Paris out of the goods of the priory, but they say he does this with the permission of his abbot. We received procuration there on the same day. Total for procuration: thirteen pounds, three shillings, eight pence.

JANUARY 5. We visited the abbey of Lisieux, where there are thirty-two nuns. One nun was alone at the house of some relative of hers who was lying ill; we enjoined the abbess not to permit them to leave the abbey alone again. They confess and receive Communion every month. They have cof-

[57] This must be the feast of St. John the Baptist (June 24), not of St. John the Evangelist (December 27).

fers; we enjoined the abbess to inspect these several times a year to remove any property. Three of them have their own incomes; we enjoined the abbess that they were not to do anything with these incomes without her permission. We forbade them to have keys to the cubicles in the infirmary. They have an income of five hundred pounds, and they owe twenty-four pounds. They have enough wheat to last until the new harvest.

We received procuration this day from the bishop and at his palace; but his staff did not wish to prepare any statement of expenses.

JANUARY 6. After a procession in the church of Lisieux and being present in person, we preached a sermon to the canons of the church and to the people. When this was done we celebrated High Mass in pontificals. Then, the bishop and the canons being assembled in the vestry, which they use as a substitute place for holding chapter, for they have no other chapter house, we visited them. We found a lack of deacons, but they promised us that, after considering this matter among themselves in chapter, they would cause certain ones to be advanced to the diaconate. We found other things, to wit, that Ralph, called Coypel, a canon of Lisieux, was defamed in that he, either in person or with accomplices, had offered violence to a certain woman, intending to force her into his house at Lisieux that he might satisfy his lust with her. She resisted their efforts, and when she began to cry out, Ralph or his accomplices throttled her so violently that the woman is said to have died shortly afterwards. Item, Vincent of Pont-de-l'Arche, a canon of Lisieux, is gravely defamed anew of a woman whom he put aside for a little while, but later, after her husband's death, this woman conceived a child by him. In writing, we warned the bishop and the dean of Lisieux that he or they to whom the disciplining of these matters belonged should investigate the truth of this charge; should he find it to be as reported, he or they should inflict such punishment as the law demands. We added that should we find them negligent or remiss in this matter, we would put our hand to it. Total for procuration: fifteen pounds, seven shillings, six pence.

JANUARY 7. We received procuration at Bernay. Total for procuration: nine pounds, eleven shillings, ten pence.

JANUARY 8. We visited there. Twenty-seven monks are in residence. They have one priory with seventeen monks in England; two priories in Caux, and one in the diocese of Evreux. All are priests except the novices and two others. On Mondays and Fridays alms are given to all comers, on Tuesdays to all lepers, on Thursdays to poor scholars. Those dwelling in the priories do not keep the fasts of the Rule, and they eat meat; we enjoined the abbot to have this corrected. They have an income of two thousand pounds; they owe about five hundred pounds.[58] They have sufficient provisions to last until the new harvest, with the exception of wine, but of this they have about enough to last until Pentecost.[59]

JANUARY 8. [sic]. At Bec-Hellouin. JANUARY 9. At Louviers. JANUARY 10. We visited at Gasny. Three monks are there and have but lately arrived, the prior most recently of all. They lack books [for services]; we enjoined the prior to have this condition corrected. We admonished the prior to live according to the Rule of St. Benedict, and to make his monks do so as well. Item, we admonished them to observe the fasts of the Rule, and to abstain from meat except in those cases permitted by the Rule. Alms are distributed twice a week to all comers. Total for procuration: eight pounds, fifteen shillings, three pence.

JANUARY 11-13. At St-Germain-en-Laye. JANUARY 14-15. At Paris. JANUARY 16. At Montlhéry. JANUARY 17-20. At Paris. JANUARY 21-22. At Pontoise. JANUARY 23. At Mantes. JANUARY 24-27. At Vernon. JANUARY 28-31. At Frênes. FEBRUARY 1-2. At Sausscuse. FEBRUARY 3-4. At Louviers. FEBRUARY 5. At Ste-Catherine. FEBRUARY 6. That is, on Ash Wednesday, at Rouen. We preached a sermon there. FEBRUARY 7. At Bonport. FEBRUARY 8. We received procuration at Mont-Deux-Amants. Total for procuration: seven pounds, eight shillings, eight pence. FEBRUARY 9. We visited there. Fifteen canons are in residence. They have four priories. One does not accuse another [in chapter]; we enjoined them to correct this. The canons are not well equipped with clothes and shoes; we enjoined correction of this. Alms are given daily to all comers. They owe two hundred pounds; one hundred fifty pounds in a collectible debt is owed to them and another one hundred pounds of a bad debt; we enjoined the prior to make out a separate statement for all debts.

This day, we spent the night at Rouen.

FEBRUARY 10. That is, the first Sunday in Lent. We preached in the cathedral.

FEBRUARY 11. We visited at Bondeville. In residence are thirty nuns, five lay sisters, and three lay brothers. They have pawned two chalices to meet

---

[58] According to the entry for January 18, 1254/55, the debt was £2,000.

[59] At this point (January 8) Eudes evidently cut short his visitation of the diocese of Lisieux and did not resume it until April 3, 1258, right after Easter.

their obligations; they still have two: one is a small and poor thing, the other is good enough. They have coffers and keys; we enjoined that the keys be taken away. They receive Communion every month. There are five young girls there who have not been received. The nuns go to Rouen very frequently. They owe about one hundred forty pounds, but they have bought land which is worth three hundred pounds. They farmed out a certain tithe for three years for seventy-five pounds, but which has a normal annual value of forty pounds. We accepted the resignation of Marie, former prioress, and immediately after hearing the votes of all the nuns who wished to have a voice, we gave them Comtesse as their prioress, inasmuch as many of them agreed upon her. Their receipts and expenditures are written out on the last page of the preceding folio. These are the properties and rents of the house at Bondeville:

Ninety-three pounds of Tours.

Thirty *muids* of communal grain.[60]

They believe that they have about seven *muids* of their own wheat in their grange at la Heuze.

In the abbey grange about one *muid* of barley; in the other granges none.

At the abbey are two carts, with six horses; one riding horse; six cows, and fourteen bullcalves. In the granges they have two hundred sixty-four sheep; item, twenty-seven cows in the grange at la Heuze; item, thirty small pigs; item, three ploughs altogether, but each using three oxen; item, four small colts.

These are the debts of the house, from the statement drawn up in the presence of the community.

Two hundred twenty pounds in cash, and two *muids* of barley; servants' [wages] for harvest time; item, they have only enough oats to last until seeding time. They use at least sixty-eight *mines* of wheat a month; item, in the cellar they have six casks of wine and two of cider; item, they do not think that the buildings can be repaired for [less than] eighty pounds of Tours; item, after Easter it will be necessary to purchase for the house all victuals but bread, peas, and legumes.

This day we spent the night at Déville.

FEBRUARY 12. We received procuration at Auffay. Total for procuration: eight pounds, fourteen shillings, nine pence.

FEBRUARY 13. We visited there. Six monks from St-Evroult are there.

[60] See above, August 18, 1251, n. 14.

We admonished them about observing the fasts of the Rule and about eating meat, as is contained in the Rule. They owe one hundred forty pounds. One of them is not a priest. They replied that in the matter of observing the fasts and of eating meat they had a good conscience.

This day we spent the night at Beaubec.

FEBRUARY 14. We received procuration at Beaussault. Total for procuration: six pounds, fourteen shillings, one penny of Paris.

FEBRUARY 15. We visited there, where there are two monks from Bec-Hellouin. They do not possess their own copy of the Rule; we enjoined them to seek one. Mass is sometimes omitted in the priory; we enjoined that this be corrected. Alms are given three times a week to all comers. They do not observe the fasts of the Rule very well; we enjoined them to observe the Rule in this matter. They eat meat, but they have a good conscience in this. They owe sixty pounds to the abbot, and about ten pounds elsewhere.

Note: about having essentials; about a confessor; about an audit; about gifts; and about receiving [novices] without the assent of the community.

This day we visited the abbey of Bival, where there are thirty-three nuns. According to their Rule, they receive Holy Communion seven times a year; but they confess more frequently. Two maidservants and one [lay] sister are there, as well as two other [laysisters] whom the abbess has sent to procure necessities for the sick. The abbess gives each nun twelve shillings a year for clothes, and each one keeps for herself what is left. The sources of income are written out in a certain roll. They owe sixty pounds; they do not believe that they have enough grain to last until the new harvest.

This day we spent the night at Neufchâtel, at the expense of the priory at Nogent. Total for procuration: nine pounds, fourteen shillings, four pence.

FEBRUARY 16. We conferred Holy Orders there. On this day Master John of Neuilly-en-Thelle and the treasurer of Rouen, at our command, visited the hospital at Neufchâtel. They found everything to be in a sufficiently good condition, except that, as they say, the sick are not well looked after. They have sold about two hundred pounds' worth of their woodland, of which amount they have already received sixty pounds. We enjoined the prior to buy a chest provided with two keys, of which he should have one and the dean of Neufchâtel the other. In this box should be placed all the moneys received from the said woodland, and they should be kept intact and not spent without our consent.

This day we received procuration at Mortemer-sur-Eaulne. Two English monks from Lewes are there. Total for procuration: nine pounds, fourteen shillings.

FEBRUARY 17. We received procuration at Aumale. Total for procuration: seven pounds, twelve pence of Paris.

FEBRUARY 18. We visited there, where there are nineteen monks. One does not accuse another [in chapter]. All but six are priests. The cloister is badly kept; we enjoined them to correct this. They have no charity for each other; we admonished them, as well as we could, to correct this. We enjoined them to turn in their old clothes upon receiving new ones. We enjoined them to make transcriptions of their charters in some book set apart for that purpose. They owe six hundred pounds, one hundred pounds of which is owed to a certain burgess; it would be better for them if they owed this money at interest. The English prior came from England without permission and borrowed thirty-seven marks to defray his expenses. They do not get their clothes until after much altercation; we enjoined them to correct this. They have enough wheat to last until the new harvest. They say that they can pay off about three hundred pounds of Tours this year. We strictly prohibited them from receiving any more monks in the future without the consent of all. If this should cause any discord among them, nothing at all should be done save through us.

This day we spent the night at Foucarmont.

FEBRUARY 19. We received procuration at Eu. Total for procuration: nine pounds, twelve shillings, four pence.

FEBRUARY 20. We visited there. Twenty-eight canons are in residence; all but seven are priests. Eleven canons are dwelling outside. We enjoined them to read the Rule once a week. Lay folk frequent the cloister and the church altogether too much; we enjoined them to be restrained so far as this could be done tactfully. Three times a week a general distribution of alms is made to all comers, and three times a week to clerics. They have enough wheat to last until the new harvest; they may sell about four hundred pounds worth of it; they have enough wine to last them until after the harvest. They owe four hundred pounds, but about four hundred pounds in arrears is owed to them. Through God's grace, everything is in a sufficiently good condition. As yet they have not paid us well for the churches appropriated to them on our authority.

This day we received procuration today at Le Tréport. Total for procuration: nine pounds, nineteen shillings, ten pence.

FEBRUARY 21. We visited there. Twenty-one monks are in residence; all but four are priests. One does not accuse another [in chapter]; we enjoined them to correct this under this penalty, that he who shall see a companion offend and not accuse him shall fast or abstain from wine that day. They have eleven monks in priories. A general distribution of alms is made twice a week. They owe two hundred pounds. Total for procuration: ten pounds, seven shillings, four pence.

This day we received procuration at Envermeu.

FEBRUARY 22. We visited there, where there are twelve monks. We enjoined them to observe the Rule in the matter of eating meat. A general distribution of alms is made thrice a week. They owe one hundred fifty pounds, in addition to two hundred pounds which they owe to their abbot; they have an income of three hundred pounds in these parts, and of fifty marks in England. In the last six years they have received nothing from England, except eighteen marks this year and five marks in some previous year.

This day we received procuration at Bures. Total for procuration: ten pounds, seven shillings, ten pence.

FEBRUARY 23. We visited. Two monks from Pré are there. Mass is occasionally omitted; we enjoined them to correct this. They do not observe the fasts of the Rule; they eat meat; we enjoined them to observe the Rule in this regard, or to accept the penalty contained in the Statutes, or to seek permission from their abbot in this matter, for he can at least grant them a dispensation from the statutory penalty.

This day we received procuration at Aliermont from the steward of the priory at Wanchy, and we slept at Aliermont. Total for procuration: ten pounds.

FEBRUARY 24-26. At Aliermont, at our expense. FEBRUARY 27. We received procuration at Longueil. Total for procuration: ten pounds, seven shillings, six pence. FEBRUARY 28. We received procuration at Flainville, on the account of the priory at Etoutteville, from Master John of that place, who then held the said priory in farm. MARCH 1. We received procuration at Bacqueville. Total for procuration: nine pounds, thirteen shillings, seven pence.

MARCH 2. We visited there, where there are three monks. They use feather beds. Occasionally women from the town eat with them; we ordered this corrected to wit, that they shall not invite them to dine in the future. They eat meat freely. The sources of income are not written down; we enjoined the prior to have them written down. They owe about eighty pounds. Hubert of St-Aubin and Thomas of Rouen, monks, were staying with Robert of Gonnetot, then prior, at the time of the visitation.

We spent the night at Déville.

MARCH 3. At Rouen, where we preached a sermon in the cathedral.

MARCH 4. We received procuration at Ste-Catherine. Total for procuration: nine pounds, six shillings, two pence.

This day, in our hall at Rouen, Nicholas of St-Laurent, priest, came before us and specifically and expressly renounced all rights which he claimed or said that he had in the church of St-Laurent-en-Caux, and made amends to us for charging that we had rashly and unjustly disputed about this church. He submitted himself to our will in the matter of the expenses which we had incurred by reason of our dispute with him in the case of the said church. On the Holy Gospels he took oath that neither in person nor through the agency of any other would he offer any obstacle in the complete and peaceful enjoyment and possession of the said church to Master Henry of Yvesmesnil, instituted by us as priest in the said church. Present were: the venerable men Master William of Saane, treasurer of Rouen; Master John of Flainville, canon of Rouen; Master John of Neuilly-en-Thelle, canon of Notre-Dame-de-Beauvais; the prior of the Maison-Dieu at Rouen and the prior of Salle-aux-Puelles; Master John of Soissons, canon and official of Rouen; Everard and John, our clerks; and Master Henry, the aforementioned priest.

MARCH 5. We visited at Ste-Catherine. Twenty-five monks are there; all but eight are priests. We ordered the abbot to prohibit the prior or monk dwelling at Caudecote from hearing the confessions of the parishioners of Dieppe and from performing for them the sacraments of the Church.[61] One does not accuse another [in chapter]; we enjoined them to correct this. We gave orders that all should receive Communion at least once a month. They owe about four hundred pounds; some debts are owed to them. According to what the abbot told us, the prior at Pavilly behaves very badly.

This day we spent the night at Noyon [-sur-Andelle], at our expense.

---

[61] The Fourth Lateran Council (1215) decreed (canon 21) that all the faitful were bound to confess, at least once yearly, to their own parish priest. (Mansi, XXII, 1007-10.) Each bishop approved the priests for his diocese and they, except in case of necessity, could not confess or absolve others than their own parishioners. (Louis Thomassin, *Ancienne et nouvelle discipline de l'église,* ed. M. André [Paris, 1864], I, 388.)

MARCH 6-8. At Frênes. MARCH 9. At Sausseuse, at our own expense.
MARCH 10. We received procuration there. Total for procuration: eight
pounds, two pence of Paris.

MARCH 11. We visited there. Thirteen canons are in residence; all but
four are priests. A general distribution of alms is made daily to all. They
have two lay brothers and two lay sisters there. They have but little oats.
They owe one hundred forty pounds. Everything else is in good condition.

This day we received procuration at St-Martin-la-Garenne. Total for procuration: seven pounds, ten shillings, eleven pence.

MARCH 12. We visited there. Five monks from Bec are in residence. A
general distribution of alms is made three times a week. They sometimes eat
meat when there is no need; we enjoined them to abstain from eating meat,
except as the Rule permits. They owe about forty pounds; but before harvest
time they will sell enough of their produce, over and above what they will
eat themselves, to equal that amount. The prior has two nephews who are
scholars at Paris and to whom he is giving support out of the priory goods,
but the prior says that he has the abbot's permission.

This day we spent the night at La Roche-Guyon, and for procuration we
received forty shillings of Paris from the monks of Fécamp who are dwelling
there.

MARCH 13. We admonished the aforementioned monks that they should,
before the Pentecostal synod, show us cause, if they have any, why we should
not visit them and receive full procuration from them; otherwise we should
proceed against them as we deem expedient. Present were: G. [William],
the treasurer; R[ichard] of Sap, canon of Rouen; Master John of Neuilly-
en-Thelle; Brothers Harduin and Walter of the Friars Minor; and Morel,
our clerk.

We spent the night at Frênes.

MARCH 14. At Frênes. MARCH 15. At Mortemer. MARCH 16. At Rouen.
MARCH 17. That is to say, on Palm Sunday, at Rouen. MARCH 18. At
Déville. MARCH 19. At the same, but we dined at the house of the Preaching
Friars. MARCH 20. We dined at the house of the Friars Minor and slept at
Rouen. MARCH 21-23. At Rouen.[62]

[62] There are no entries for March 24 through April 2. Easter Day was on
March 24.

APRIL 3. In the year of our Lord 1258. We received procuration at Ste-Barbe.[1]

APRIL 4. We visited there. Thirty-two canons are in residence; all but seven are priests. They have an income of two thousand pounds; they owe about seven hundred pounds. They have no provisions of any kind, that is to say, neither wine, nor cider (*siceram*), that is, *sidre*, nor meat. The prior does not sleep in the dormitory. This day we spent the night there, at our own expense.

APRIL 5. We received procuration at Crouttes.

APRIL 6. We visited there. Two monks from Jumièges, to wit, Duresque and a certain other, are there. Except when both happen to be journeying on horseback at the same time, Mass is celebrated daily in the chapel. They have in income pertaining to their sustenance about one hundred pounds; more is owed to them than they owe.

This day we had breakfast at Canapville, at the bishop's house and through his kindness.

This same day we visited the priory of Ticheville, finding there two monks from St-Wandrille. They have two women with them; one is young, the other about thirty years of age; we warned them to send these women away and to get another or others who would not arouse suspicion. They have an income of about eighty pounds. They eat meat freely and when there is no need; we warned them to abstain from eating meat, in accordance with the content of the Rule. They do not observe the fasts of the Rule; we enjoined them to correct this. They owe about sixty pounds. We received procuration there this day.

APRIL 7. We visited the abbey of St-Evroult. Thirty-one monks are there. They have nine priories this side of the sea. One does not accuse another [in chapter], except in the matter of silence. Traveling monks do not ob-

---

[1] Sometime between Easter and this appearance at Ste-Barbe, Eudes had attended a meeting of the Exchequer at Caen, See L. Delisle, *Cartulaire normand de Philippe Auguste, Louis VIII, Saint Louis et Philippe le Hardi* (Caen, 1852), "Mémoires de la Société des antiquaires de Normandie," 2d ser., VI (1852), No. 539, n. 3.

serve the fasts of the Rule; they eat meat for two days when they have been bled; it does not bother their consciences. They eat meat in the priories; we enjoined them to observe the Rule covering this. Alms are given daily to all comers. They have an income within the kingdom of France of two thousand pounds; almost as much is owed to them as they owe.

[*No entries for April 8-23.*]

APRIL 24. Visitation of the diocese of Evreux.

We entered the diocese of Evreux and received procuration at Beaumont-le-Roger. Total: nine pounds, eighteen shillings, six pence. We visited there, finding five monks; there should be twelve, but because of the new buildings which they are constructing the number has been lessened. They eat meat at least twice a week; we enjoined them to abstain save as the Rule permits. The property and income of the house are not entered in writing; we ordered the prior to have all sources of income written out. They have an income of about one thousand pounds; they owe three hundred pounds. They have sufficient provisions to last until the new harvest.

APRIL 25. We received procuration at Daubeuf from a certain lessee of that place. We made no computation there, for we were not able to find out the price of things. APRIL 26. We received procuration at Montaure.

APRIL 27. We visited there, where there are three monks. They had[2] but one chalice [which must serve] for the monks as well as for the priest of the parish. They have an income of one hundred sixty pounds, on which they pay the tithe; they owed about fifty pounds, and about thirty pounds were owed to them. Brother Roger of Les Andelys was then prior of the place. We found everything else to be in good condition. Total for procuration: nine pounds, eleven shillings, five pence. This day we received procuration at La Croix-St-Leufroy. Total: nine pounds.

APRIL 28. We visited there after preaching a sermon. Twenty-four monks were in residence; all but three were priests. We enjoined the abbot to visit all of his priories or to see that they were visited. We ordered the abbot to compel those monks who traveled by horseback to observe the fasts according to the Rule, and to forbid the monks from dining with the lay folk who came to their house. They owed about one hundred pounds.

This day we received procuration at the priory at Jouy. Total: nine pounds, seven shillings.

---

[2] The change of tense indicates probably that the actual writing of the entries of the Register did not take place until some time after the actual visitation.

APRIL 29. At the same. We received procuration from the lessee of Bail-leul, since there were no monks at the priory of the said Bailleul, nor did the house provide sufficient accommodation for us. Total: eight pounds, eight pence.

We visited the said priory at Jouy, where there were two monks. They have an income of four hundred fifty pounds, of which they remit as much as they can to the abbey. They sometimes eat meat when there is no need; we enjoined them to abstain as the Rule required.

APRIL 30. With God's grace, we preached the word of God in the chapter of Evreux to the resident canons and clerks-choral. When this was finished they all left the chapter room, leaving us and our companions behind. A little later, desiring to make visitation as our office requires us to do, we called in those venerable men, the dean, the treasurer, and Stephen, the arch-deacon of the said place, one by one, and diligently inquired from each of them whether the Divine Office was performed at the proper hours and with required modulation[3] both by day and by night; whether they had ornaments, books, and vestments suitable for the Divine Service; whether the lighting of the church was well and competently attended to by those responsible for this duty; whether the priest-canons willingly celebrated their Masses in the church. All three replied unanimously that all of these matters were very satisfactory. Item, we asked them whether any canon, cleric, or even chap-lain in that church were publicly known for the vice of incontinence, for any business undertakings, or for anything else; they replied that, through God's grace, there was none at present, and that when anyone connected with the church, whether canon or clerk-choral, was defamed of the vice of incontinence, of inebriety, or any act that brought notoriety, the heb-domadary and the chapter punished him most severely. They believed that all ill fame had ceased. Item, some of the seniors grumbled and claimed that we were not empowered to visit the province until after we had visited the prominent places of our own diocese. However, we showed them our charter of privilege, and had it read aloud in full chapter, whereby we may do this without any interruption, or, even if we are interrupted by a sum-mons from the king, the queen, or the Pope, we may resume and enter upon our [suspended] visitation.[4] With God's grace, we found everything else to

---

[3] See above, July 9, 1249, n. 36.

[4] This document is printed in full in Bonnin, (p. 743), and reference is made to it by Pope Innocent IV in a letter to Eudes, Bonnin, p. 754.

be in good condition, and we received procuration from them this day at the palace of the bishop. Total: twelve pounds, nineteen shillings, three pence.

MAY 1. We visited the abbey at St-Sauveur, where there were sixty-three nuns. There was an insufficient supply of books [for the Divine Service]; we ordered them to procure them. Silence was not well observed; we ordered this corrected. We advised them to confess every month. We enjoined them not to keep any dogs, birds, or squirrels, and to get rid of those they had. Individual nuns have individual coffers; we ordered the abbess to have these opened and to see what was contained in them. We enjoined them to put away their metaled belts. Item, they did not turn in their old clothes when they received new ones; we gave orders that no nun should presume to give away any old clothes without the permission of the abbess. Item, we ordered that relatives of the nuns should not be received to spend the night there or to dine. Item, that individual audits should be made every month. Item, we ordered them to be sure to send away all the little girls who had not taken the veil. They owed about three hundred pounds; they have an income of one thousand pounds. We enjoined the abbess to keep the nuns from acquiring possessions of any kind. We received procuration from them at St-Taurin. Total: ten pounds, four shillings, two pence.

MAY 2. Ascension Day. We preached the Word of God in chapter, and then we visited the abbey of St-Taurin. The abbot was not in the house at this time. Twenty monks were there; six had died; we advised them to have some new monks professed. All but eight were priests. They had sufficient provisions to last until the new harvest; they believed that they owed nothing. Everything else we found to be in good condition. They have an income of about fifteen hundred pounds. We received procuration from them today. Total: ten pounds, thirteen shillings, but we caused thirty-three shillings to be remitted to them.

On this day we took part in a procession with the canons, and, by God's grace, we celebrated Mass in the cathedral at Evreux.

MAY 3. We visited the abbey at Conches. Twenty-eight monks were there. We enjoined the abbot to visit all of his priories more frequently than had been his practice. Alms are distributed four times a week: twice to scholars-cleric, and as many times to lepers. The fasts were badly observed in the priories; we enjoined the abbot to enact as best he could fuller decrees about this in a general chapter, to see that they were observed, and to inflict a penalty upon those who were delinquent in this respect and in the eating of meat. They had sufficient provisions to last until the new harvest; they owed nothing. This day we received procuration there. Total: ten pounds, sixteen shillings, ten pence.

MAY 4. We visited the priory at Lierru. Nine canons of the Order of St. Augustine were there; five were priests, and there was one novice. Several of them possessed coffers which the prior had not yet inspected; we ordered him to find out what was contained in them at once, and to clear them of any property. Item, we ordered all of them to receive Communion on the first Sunday of every month, and to make very frequent confession. They have an income of about two hundred pounds; they owed about thirty pounds. The prior was supporting his own brother, a dishonest person and of bad reputation, in the house; we ordered him sent away. The provision for the sick was bad; we ordered this corrected. This day we received procuration there. Total: eight pounds, twelve shillings, two pence.

MAY 5. We visited the abbey at Lyre. Forty-two monks and four lay brothers were there; twenty of them were priests. They use meat in the priories; we enjoined the abbot to inflict punishment upon those who ate meat when there was no need and who conducted themselves in violation of the Rule. About as much was owed to them as they owed. With the exception of wine, they had enough provisions to last them until the new harvest. They have an income of two thousand pounds. The abbot used to leave the house and wander about more frequently than the business affairs of the house warranted. We received procuration there this day. Total: ten pounds, eleven shillings, two pence.

MAY 6. We received procuration at St-Sulpice-près-l'Aigle, and we visited there this day. Eight monks were there; all but one were priests. We ordered the monk who was not a priest to confess at least once a month. They were using feather beds. The prior was not sleeping in the dormitory with the monks. They do not observe the fasts required by the Rule; more and more frequently they ate meat when there was no need; we absolutely forbade them to eat meat except as the Rule permits, and [warned them that], if they were delinquent they should be punished. They have an income of two hundred fifty pounds; more was owed to them than they owed. With the exception of wine they had enough provisions to last until the new harvest. Total: nine pounds.

MAY 7. We received procuration there from the prior at Rai, inasmuch as the accommodations at Rai were insufficient for us. Total: eight pounds, six shillings. Because of the poverty of the house we had sixty shillings remitted to the prior.

MAY 8. We visited the aforesaid priory at Rai, where there were two monks; that is to say, one and the prior. They ate meat, and we left this matter to their conscience. They have an income of eighty pounds; they owed about thirty pounds.

We received procuration this day at the royal castle near Breteuil from the steward of the priory at Tillières. Total: twelve pounds; we caused sixty shillings to be remitted to him.

MAY 9. In the morning we ate at the manor of Sir William of Minières, knight, and we spent the night at the priory at Coudres, and received procuration there. Total: seven pounds and seventeen pence.

MAY 10. We visited this priory. Two monks were there; to wit, one with the prior. Alms are given daily to all comers. They did not observe the fasts of the Rule; they ate meat freely; we enjoined them to abstain as the Rule demands, and to observe the fasts more completely. They have an income of four hundred pounds; they owed nothing except to their abbot of Bourgueil, to whom they are obliged to remit annually as much as they can.

We received procuration this day at Heudreville. Total: eight pounds, sixteen shillings, eight pence.

MAY 11. We visited there. Three monks of the Order of Tiron were there; all were priests, and had recently arrived there. They use feather beds. Item, they had two maidservants in their house, a thing which much displeased us, and indeed we told them that this was not safe for them, because of the evil which might perchance arise therefrom. They did not observe the Rule; they ate meat whenever they liked, and when there was no need; we ordered them to correct this in accordance with the Rule and the statutes of the Order of Tiron.[5] They have an income of three hundred pounds. Alms are given three times a week to all comers. They had sufficient provisions to last until the new harvest; they owed about one hundred pounds.

---

[5] Not unlike Bec, Savigny, or even Cluny, Tiron was a congregation of Benedictines with its own customs and usages. For the material wealth of the congregation, see M. L. Merlet, *Cartulaire de l'abbaye de la Sainte-Trinité de Tiron*. For a list of the congregation's abbeys and dependencies, see *ibid.*, I, cxvi-cxxviii.

This day we visited the priory at Muzy.[6] Four monks from Coulombs were there. They had no written copy of the Rule, nor of the Statutes of Pope Gregory; we enjoined them to seek these out at once, to live according to the Rule, and to conduct themselves as the Rule required. Because of the smallness of the house, they were not sleeping together. They used feather beds. Alms are given to all comers three times a week. They had one maid-servant; we ordered her sent away. They did not observe the fasts; we gave orders that they be scrupulously observed. They ate meat freely; we expressly forbade them to eat meat except as the Rule permits. They owed two hundred forty-two pounds; they had no provisions. The prior, together with his whole household, was then under excommunication, as a result of a judgment and because of the royal twelfth.[7] The affairs of the priory were vilely and shamefully handled, and the place showed disgraceful evidence of collapse and ruin. Their own abbot of Coulombs was present at this visitation, and we consulted with him and asked him, considering the state of the place, to try and reform it in every way possible. Item, there was a certain insane monk there, Dom Simon by name, who was thoroughly deranged, and a living scandal to all monks; we admonished the companions of the prior to strive to have him confined to the cloister or sent to the infirmary. We received procuration from them this day. Total: seven pounds of Paris.

This same day we moved on to the priory of St-Georges-sur-Eure.[8] We found two monks there, to wit, the prior and one monk, who was not a priest. They had no copy of the Rule, nor did they live as the Rule requires; they did not get up for Matins; indeed, they said their Hours in their room and without modulation.[9] The prior rarely or never celebrated Mass. In fact, we found that they conducted themselves, and had conducted themselves, most evilly. The house was dirty and dilapidated. They had a certain maidservant; we ordered her removed without fail. They owed about one hundred pounds; they have an income of about fifty pounds. We enjoined the prior to pause in his evil ways and to reform himself by discipline according to the Rule.

MAY 12. The day of Pentecost. We joined the monks in a procession at

[6] A Benedictine priory dependent on Coulombs. (Cottinea, II, 2024.)

[7] Levies by the king on ecclesiastical property for the Crusade. Payment was enforced by the ecclesistical powers.

[8] Cottineau, II, 2704.

[9] See above, July 9, 1249, n. 36.

Ivry, and a little later, while the people and the monks were standing in the body of the church, we preached the Word of God. With His assistance we celebrated High Mass. After Mass we visited the monks in chapter. Eighteen monks were there; all but four were priests. Women were in the habit of entering the choir and the cloister very often and at will; we enjoined the abbot to correct this, and to keep them away from the means of access and approach. The priors living outside ate meat; we ordered the abbot absolutely to forbid them to eat meat, except as the Rule permits. Item, we ordered that the audits be cast in the presence of the seniors elected by the community, and at least once a week or once a month. They owed about three hundred pounds. They had sufficient provisions to last until the new harvest. They had an income of about eight hundred pounds. We received procuration there this day. Total: nine pounds, four shillings, four pence.

MAY 13. We preached the Word of God at St. Mary's church at Vernon to the people and the vicars present, and through His grace we celebrated High Mass. Then we made a visitation. We found only vicars there. There are nine canons in this church, but they are not resident; of them, five are in priests' orders; two are deacons, two are subdeacons, and one has been very recently appointed. Two Masses are celebrated daily by the vicars; that is to say, a High Mass, and a Mass of the Blessed Virgin; the priest of the parish celebrated a parochial Mass every day. The clerics were publicly known for drinking; we warned them to moderate their wine, and to abstain from wine and from all illicit things. John Borguenel, a canon of the house, was personally present at this visitation. They gave us procuration this day at the bishop's house. Total: ten pounds, eight shillings, nine pence.

MAY 14. At Frênes. We were bled today. MAY 15-17. At Frênes. MAY 18. With God's grace we conferred Holy Orders at Les Andelys, and we spent the night at Sausseuse, at our own expense. MAY 19. At Poissy, at the royal palace. MAY 20-21. At Paris, because of the Parlement. MAY 22. At Paris. Because we could not be present at the sacred synod at Rouen in person, we caused it to be held and celebrated by the treasurer of Rouen, acting for us.

MAY 23-27. At Paris, because of the Parlement.

MAY 28. This day Henry, rector of the church at Cahagnes, acting as proctor for Reginald, rector of the church at Travailles, came before us, with a letter from the official of Rouen concerning the resignation of the said church into our hands, and in the name of the said Reginald, he resigned the said church.

MAY 29. At Paris. MAY 30. At the same. This day Master Nicholas, called Gibbouin, was presented to us by the religious, the abbot, and the community of St-Ouen-de-Rouen, for the church of Neuville-Champ-d'Oisel. MAY 31– JUNE 5. At Paris. JUNE 6. At the same. This day William Crispin presented Roger de Val to us for the church at Bailly. This same day G., priest at Ambleville, resigned his church into our hands. JUNE 7. At Paris. JUNE 8. At Pontoise. JUNE 9. At Chambly. JUNE 10. At Verberie. JUNE 11-12. At Noyon. JUNE 13. At La Neuville-du-Roy. JUNE 14. At St-Quentin-près-Beauvais. JUNE 15. At Caulincourt, at one of the manors of the bishop of Beauvais, at his expense, he being there at the time.

JUNE 16. At Gaillefontaine, where we celebrated a parish Mass, and, God aiding, we preached a sermon this day.

This day Master Walter of Hupeignies, rector of St. Mary's church at Mortemer, came before us and voluntarily resigned his church into our hands.

This day, after our siesta, we proceeded in person to the monastery of nuns of Clairruissel,[10] and there, with God's assistance, we preached a sermon.

JUNE 17. At Aliermont.

JUNE 18. At the same. Today John, the son of Sir Fulk of Sauchay, knight whom our men had caught, came before us and made amends for having gone hunting in our forest at Aliermont without our permission or that of our resident lessee, and for having forcefully seized and carried off a hare. For all of these aforesaid things the aforesaid Fulk, knight, his father, Sir Nicholas of St-Saëns, knight, and Sir Nicholas Mahomet, knight, stood as sureties to us.

JUNE 19-24. At Aliermont.

JUNE 25. At Aliermont. This day we enjoined the priest at Auffay to pay us forty shillings of Tours before the feast of the St. Mary Magdalene, and to submit to a discipline at the synod held in his deanery, clad in shirt and trunk hose, and in the presence of the priests attending the synod of that deanery, for having struck one of his parishioners with his fist in his church aforesaid, and for having quarreled with the prior of the said place.

JUNE 26. At Dieppe.

JUNE 27. We visited the priory of St-Saëns. Three monks were there with the prior. The prior does not celebrate Mass as often as he ought and could; we counseled him to celebrate Mass more frequently. They ate meat there

[10] Attached to Fontevrault c. 1140. (Cottineau, I, 798-99.)

when there was no need; they did not observe the fasts of the Rule very well; we ordered this corrected. More was owed to them than they owed. We found everything else to be in good condition. This day we received procuration and spent the night there. Total: nine pounds, seventeen shillings, two pence.

JUNE 28. We visited the nuns at St-Saëns. Fourteen were in the community at this time, two being at Ste-Austreberte. Silence was badly observed, we ordered this corrected. A lay sister was there. They had wheat enough for the needs of the community until the new harvest. They owed about sixty-eight pounds. Item, there were two little girls there whom the prioress and some of the nuns asked us to allow them to receive and veil; but we did not listen to their prayers in this matter, and ordered them to send these girls away within the next eight days; we enjoined them not to presume to receive anyone without our special permission. This day we spent the night at Déville.

JUNE 29. At Déville. We celebrated the parochial Mass here in pontificals, and, with God's assistance, we preached a sermon, it being the feast of Saints Peter and Paul. JUNE 30–JULY 1. At Déville.

JULY 2. In the chapel of our manor at Rouen we listened to and considered the statements made before us on behalf of the prior and chapter of Séez, in the matter of their election of Master Thomas of Aulnay as bishop of Séez.[11] After a diligent inquiry into the manner of conducting the election, into the character of the elected one, and into the observation of the canonical process, after taking counsel with good men, we, by our metropolitan authority, confirmed this election as canonically carried out and the elected person as suitable.

This day we spent the night at Quévreville, and received procuration there from the lessee of the place. Total: eight pounds, eighteen shillings, eight pence.

JULY 3. At Noyon [-sur-Andelle], at our expense.

JULY 4. The summer feast of St. Martin. We celebrated the parochial Mass at Perrièrs, and administered Confirmation there, with God's help. We received procuration there this day from the lessee of the house belonging to St-Ouen-de-Rouen. Total: nine pounds, nine shillings, two pence.

JULY 5. At L'Ile-Dieu, at the expense of the abbey. Total for procuration:

[11] Ordained to the priesthood by Eudes December 21, 1258, and consecrated bishop the next day.

eight pounds, eighteen shillings. JULY 6. At Bonport, at the expense of the abbey. JULY 7. At the priory of Montaure, in the diocese of Evreux, we performed the marriage ceremony for William of Premery, our panteer,[12] and Joan.

We spent the night at Pont-de-l'Arche.

JULY 8-10. At Frênes.

JULY 11. At the same. This day Miles, priest and vicar of St. Mary's church at Les Andelys, came before us and confessed that within the past fortnight he had carnally known a certain woman of whom he had been frequently and shamefully ill famed. As he said, he had known her several times. He promised, with his hand on the Holy Gospels, that he would perform and observe whatever we should be led to command or do in this matter.

JULY 12. At Frênes. JULY 13. At Sausseuse, at our expense. JULY 14. At the same, at the expense of the parishioners of Ecos. This day, with God's aid, we dedicated St. Denis' church at Ecos.

JULY 15. At the priory of St-Ouen-de-Gisors, where the prior had but lately arrived. From him we received as our procuration seven pounds of Tours, which amount we receive every year when we come there.[13] Once a year the prior who should happen to be at the said place is obligated to pay us our procuration, but no additional payment unless it should be through liberality and graciousness.

JULY 16. Turning aside to the house of nuns of Gomerfontaine,[14] we preached a sermon in chapter, with God's aid.

This day we visited the priory at Chaumont[-en-l'Aillerie]. Three monks from St-Germer-de-Flay were there. Alms are given once[15] to all comers. They eat meat in common with unconcern and more often than is necessary; we ordered them to abstain according to the Rule. They do not observe the fasts of the Rule; we ordered this corrected. They owed about one hundred pounds. The prior's companions were very disobedient to him in some matters. We received procuration there this day. They have an income of one hundred forty pounds. Total: eight pounds, nine shillings, six pence.

JULY 17. We received procuration at Gaillonet from the Premonstraten-

---

[12] The supervisor of the bread.
[13] See entry for June 20, 1257.
[14] A Cistercian abbey om nuns, founded c. 1207. (Cottineau, I, 1299.)
[15] The text does not indicate whether alms were distributed once a week or daily.

sian monks of this place. Total: seven pounds, twelve shillings, nine pence.

JULY 18. We received procuration at Juziers, and visited there. Five monks were there; all but one were priests. All use feather beds. Some of them had boxes and chests with keys; we ordered the prior to have these opened, to inspect them frequently and to clear them of any property. Alms are given daily to all comers. Item, sometimes the prior, or some of the monks, ate with the guests, in the morning, at midday, or at whatever hour they might arrive; we gave orders that the monks should eat at stated and determined hours and provide for the guests as seemed expedient. They did not observe the fasts of the Rule very well. They owed about two hundred sixty pounds and one *muid* of wheat; they have an income of four hundred pounds. They ate meat freely, but they said that they had privileges and indulgences to do this. Item, we ordered the prior to contribute to the repair of the bell tower and to the adornment of the monastery. Item, women were in the habit of entering the monastery and cloister at will; we ordered the prior to try to keep the gates and the entrances closed, so that the said women should not have such facility of access to them. Total: eight pounds, one penny.

JULY 19. We visited the abbey of St-Martin-de-Pontoise. Twenty-two monks were in residence; three of them were novices. Some were dwelling alone in priories, a fact which much displeased us. Those who are not priests confess and receive Communion once a month. The prior was not present at this time, and it was said that he rarely arose for Matins, and that similarly, when he came back from outside, he rarely ate in the refectory. He was acting for the prior of Chambly, and simultaneously was exercising the office of prior [of St-Martin-de-Pontoise]. They owed eight hundred pounds. and they were compelled to negotiate a loan of one hundred pounds to defray the expenses of getting in the wheat this coming harvest, and perhaps some more for the gathering of the grapes. They did not have wheat enough to last until the new harvest. Since some of them were ill famed of incontinence, and the house was in bad condition, we sent Brother Adam Rigaud and Master Richard of Sap there to investigate the condition of the house. A little later, and while we were still there, when their investigation of the place had been completed, we having considered what we felt to be expedient for reforming the state of this monastery, were led, on the counsel of good men, to draw up the ordinance which is entered on the next page.[16]

16 See entry for August 7, below.

Total for procuration: seven pounds, eleven shillings, two pence.

JULY 20. At St-Germain-en-Laye, where we found the king and queen. JULY 21. At the same. JULY 22. The feast of St. Mary Magdalene. We celebrated High Mass in pontificals at the royal chapel in Paris, God permitting. The king was there present, as were many prelates of France who had come to attend the Parlement, and, with God's aid, we preached a sermon. JULY 23-25. At Paris. JULY 26. At Neuville-St-Georges. JULY 27. At Corbeil, where we talked with the count of Poitou and his wife.[17] JULY 28. At Melun. JULY 29. At Nemours.[18] JULY 30. At the same, and we celebrated High Mass at the nuns' monastery. When this was finished, we preached a sermon, with God's assistance. JULY 31. At Cheroi. AUGUST 1. At Nailly, at the manor of the venerable father, . . . [lacuna in MS],[19] the archbishop of Sens. We stayed with him and at his expense.

AUGUST 2. On the vigil of the Invention of St. Stephen. We accompanied the venerable Father, William, archbishop of Sens, along with a very great multitude of horsemen, that is to say, of clerics and burgesses of Sens, as far as the monastery of St-Pierre-de-Sens, whose monks, that is to say, the abbot and community, solemnly received the said Father with a procession. The said father spent the night there, but we, with God's grace, celebrated Vespers at the cathedral and spent the night at St-Remy, at our own expense.

AUGUST 3. We were at the cathedral church at Sens, together with the venerable Fathers, the bishops of Auxerre, Meaux, Nevers, Troyes, and Beaune. This day the canons of Sens received the above-mentioned Father, the archbishop, at his first entry with a procession.[20] We lunched and dined with him, and we spent the night at St-Remy, at our own expense.

AUGUST 4. At Montereau-Fault-Yonne, at the château of the king of Navarre.[21] The venerable Father, the bishop of Auxerre, was with us. AUGUST

[17] Alphonse, second brother of Louis IX. Louis gave him Poitou on the occasion of Alphonse's marriage to Jeanne, daughter of the count of Toulouse.

[18] An Augustinian priory founded c. 1170, near Fontainebleu. (Cottineau, II, 2046.)

[19] William de Brosse (1258-67). (Gams, Series episcoporum, p. 629.)

[20] The first entry of an archbishop or bishop into the cathedral of his see was a solemn occasion. He was met outside the city walls, seated in a chair, and borne in procession on the shoulders of the prominent town dignitaries to the cathedral's doors.

[21] Thibaut V, king of Navarre and count of Champagne, who was a cousin of Louis IX. This was the year in which Eudes was made a member of the Parlement of Paris, but on what date there is no precise information. It may well have taken place in May, when Louis and his queen met Eudes at Poissy, (see above, May 19). From this time on, Eudes was a member of the Parlement, and his official and private

5. At Courquetaine, at the house of our brother, Sir Peter Rigaud, knight, the said bishop being with us. AUGUST 6. This day at Paris, and we dined with the said Father, the bishop.

AUGUST 7. At St. Martin's abbey at Pontoise. This day we enjoined the abbot of the place, by virtue of his oath of obedience, to order . . . [*lacuna in MS*], the former steward of the grain, to remit in its entirety whatever property he might have, and that within eight days; after which he should send him to some house belonging to the order, that he might stay there and live according to the Rule until he should deserve to be recalled by us to his monastery. Item, that he should dismiss Peter, his servant, and Eustace, the custodian of the house at Celles, from their offices and from his service. Item, that without delay he should seek out and call to him some prudent man, a cleric or a secular priest, whose aid and counsel he should use in handling the temporal affairs of his abbey. Item, we willed and ordered that our vicar at Pontoise should be present at his audits, and that he should draw up a statement of all receipts and expenditures, both large and small, in the presence of the entire community, and at least once a month; that copies should be made of these, of which the abbot should have one, and the vicar one, the other to remain in the possession of the community. Item, we enjoined the abbot to interest himself personally in the sales and measurings of wheat, wine, and their other products and not to appoint another grain steward without special permission.

These are the debts owed by the abbey of St-Martin-de-Pontoise on the Saturday preceding the feast of St. Mary-Magdalene, in the year of our Lord 1258:

At the fair next coming: one hundred twelve pounds of Paris.

Item, to Master Ralph of Montesland: fifty pounds of Paris.

Item, to Bernard of L'Ile: ten pounds of Paris.

Item, to Adam of Livillier: one hundred five pounds of Paris.

Item, to Ralph of Stampe: fourteen pounds of Paris and two *muids* of winter wheat.

Item, to Robert Fovetel: fifty-three pounds of Paris.

---

meetings with the king became more frequent. There is no record in *Les Olim* of the decisions taken at the meeting of 1258, but Eudes was present. He took part in the debates and delivered a sermon to the other members. A short time after the sessions of the Parlement, Eudes was a guest of Alphonse of Poitou. He was with the king in September to inspect the relics of St. Eloi. Their meetings and conversations became more and more frequent as Eudes' private advice was sought.

Item, to Ralph Coguet, thirty-one pounds.

Item, to Henry of Attrebate: two hundred twenty pounds and six shillings of Paris.

Item, to William of Liancourt: eighty pounds.

Item, tot William Paline: twenty pounds.

Item, to the abbot of St. Catherine's: twenty pounds of Paris.

Item, to John, called Pire: twenty pounds of Paris.

Item, to [other] creditors: thirty pounds of Paris.

Item, to the servants: thirty pounds of Paris.

Item, to Bertha: eleven pounds of Paris.

Item, to John, called Ast: forty-five pounds of Paris.

Item, to Robert le Chambelene: forty-eight pounds of Paris.

Item, to Ralph Théophile: one hundred pounds of Paris.

Total: one thousand twelve pounds,[22] and two *muids* of wheat.

Sir William of Gisors: fifty-eight pounds of Paris.

Item, the farmers of Bantelu: fourteen pounds.

Item, the farmer of Vallangoujard: ten pounds.

Item, the farmer of Laria: eight pounds.

Item, Henry Heraut: eight pounds.

Item, the farmer of Hérouville: six pounds and six shillings.

Item, other farmers: seven pounds.

Item, Marchmont and Bovethus: nineteen pounds.

Item, Henry of Pierrelaye, Junior: three pounds.

Item, there is owed to them seven *muids* of winter wheat.

Total: one hundred twenty pounds, and twelve *muids*; and they have in cash seventy-three pounds and six shillings.[23]

We attached and assigned to the abbot as his assistant Dom Honduin, priest at Frémecourt, to aid him in administering his temporalities and to act as his proctor; and we received his oath that he would be faithful in carrying out these things.

AUGUST 8. At Genainville, the said bishop being with us. AUGUST 9. At Frênes, the said bishop being with us. AUGUST 10. At Ste-Catherine, the said bishop being with us. AUGUST 11. We, with God's aid, preached a sermon in the atrium of St-Gervaise, and we spent the night at Déville. The said

[22] The correct total would seem to be £1,077-6s.

[23] The correct total would seem to be £133-6s., and seven *muids* of wheat.

bishop was with us. AUGUST 12-13. At Déville. The said bishop was with us.
AUGUST 14. At Rouen. The Reverend Fathers, the bishops of Beauvais and
Auxerre, were with us, and the bishop of Beauvais celebrated Vespers at the
cathedral this day. AUGUST 15. In the company of the said bishops we celebrated the feast of the Assumption of the Blessed Virgin Mary at Rouen.
The said bishops spent the night at our palace, while we slept at the house
of the precentor.[24] AUGUST 16. At Déville, with the said bishops. AUGUST 17.
At Frênes, with them. AUGUST 18. At Chaumont, with them. AUGUST 19. At
Bresles, at the manor of the bishop of Beauvais, at his expense. He was
present, and the bishop of Auxerre as well. AUGUST 20. We and the bishop
of Beauvais ate with the bishop of Auxerre at Gournay-sur-Aronde, and spent
the night there. AUGUST 21. At Noyon. AUGUST 22. At the same, the king
of France being there, together with many prelates of France. AUGUST 23. At
the same. We opened the reliquary in the church of the cathedral in which
the body of St. Eloi is said to rest. In it we found some bones wrapped in
leather, together with some writings. The said bishops of Auxerre and Beauvais were present. AUGUST 24. At Compiègne; there we spoke with the king.
AUGUST 25. At Pont-Ste-Maxence. With God's aid, we celebrated Mass in
the parish church, and we preached the Word of God; there were very many
parishioners present. AUGUST 26. At Beaumont-sur-Oise. AUGUST 27. At Pontoise.

AUGUST 28. God granting, we propounded His Word at St-Mellon-de-
Pontoise, and we made a visitation. The prebendaries are not held to keep
residence. One canon, namely Dom Luke, was present and was in residence
at the time. In residence are ten vicars, one deacon, one subdeacon, and two
chaplains. No syndic or his proctor was there; we gave orders that one
should be appointed. They did not possess sufficient altar cloths or ornaments; we ordered this corrected. The reliquaries, in which the bodies of
certain saints and that of St. Mellon are said to rest, have rotted away and
are so consumed by age that they will hardly allow being touched with the
hand; we gave orders that this should be corrected, and that the books be
bound. We enjoined the said Dom Luke that, in the future, chapter should
under no circumstances be held anywhere but in St-Mellon, or in the town
of Pontoise; we enjoined him to see that the ornaments, the altar linen, and

---

[24] This was Gui de Merle, who later became bishop of Lisieux (1267-83). (Gams,
Series episcoporum, p. 566.)

the old altar cloths were folded, preserved, repaired, and maintained in a cleaner and better condition than had been the practice. Item, the vicar of Master Peter of Mincy was the only one to be obstinate and rebellious in not observing certain regulations of the chapter. We decreed that as often as it was evident that he was delinquent, he should pay a penny a day. We also decreed that the chapter Statutes be written out. Item, Dom Peter, the vicar of Master William, is publicly known many times over for incontinence, for unseemly behavior, especially for garrulousness, and for going about at night; we gave orders that all vicars should walk decorously through the town, should maintain better silence in church than was their practice, and should obey the precentor in performing the Divine Office, and that the precentor should supervise and regulate the Divine Office. Luke, a vicar, was shamefully ill famed of a multitude of enormities. Although we warned him many times before about these things, he has not reformed. Ralph, the vicar of John of Montluce, was in the habit of going about the town in a buckled supertunic; we enjoined him to wear a closed gown as befits a priest. Item, we warned Henry, the vicar of Master Peter of Mincy, not to obstruct the Divine Office as he formerly had done, and to conduct himself in a harmonious manner with his associates; we warned Robert of Gradu about these same things. Item, the said Peter, vicar of the said Master William, confessed that he had kept Petronilla for a long time, but that he had not known her carnally since she had married. A little later he swore on the Holy Gospels, with his hand on his breast, and promised us that should we again find him guilty of incontinence so that he could not canonically purge himself, he would regard his benefice as resigned. Present were: brother Adam Rigaud; Master Richard of Sap, canon of Rouen; Master Ralph of St-Gildard; and John of Morgneval, our clerk.

This same day we visited St. Peter's priory. Five monks were there; all were priests. They had invited some people to drink with them but each paid for his own; we ordered them that they must not presume to do this again. The prior had a certain nephew to whom he made bountiful grants from the goods of the priory, and this without receiving permission from his abbot; we ordered the nephew sent away and ordered likewise that the prior make no further gifts to him, for he was reported to be incontinent. The prior was not present there.

This day for procuration we received from Dom Luke, canon of the place [St-Mellon-de-Pontoise], on behalf of the chapter, one hundred shillings of Paris, the amount which they owe to us each year, together with accommodation, straw for beds, wood, cups, dishes, and other domestic utensils. We spent the night at St. Martin's, near Pontoise.

AUGUST 29. At Le Bord-Haut-de-Vigny. We received procuration at Vesly from the local prior.

AUGUST 31. We visited the priory at Noyon [-sur-Andelle]. Six monks were there, and the prior had sent one to England. There should be seven. All were priests. They ate and had eaten meat when there was no need; we forbade them to eat meat, save as the Rule permits. They have an income of five hundred pounds; as much was owed to them as they owed; but they were continuously obliged to put aside about one hundred pounds for improving the vines for the coming year.

This day Alice, the prioress of St. Paul's near Rouen, was presented to us by the prioress of Montivilliers, for she had just been elected by the community of Montivilliers. We received procuration this day from the prior of Noyon [sur-Andelle].

SEPTEMBER 1. We confirmed the election made, in accordance with law, at Montivilliers by the prioress and community, of Alice, prioress of St-Paul's near Rouen, while we were at Noyon [-sur-Andelle].

This day we spent the night at Ste-Catherine, at our own expense.

SEPTEMBER 2. Eudes, Warner, and Henry, priest-vicars of the church of Notre-Dame-la-Ronde, and Robert, rector of the said church, came before us and swore on the Holy Gospels that they would observe the ordinance drawn up for the reformation of the said church with the assent and approval of the king, and that they would not contravene it in the future. Present at this oath taking were the venerable men: Simon, the archdeacon; William, the treasurer of Rouen; Peter d'Ons, the archdeacon of Greater Caux in the same church; and Geoffrey Revèlle, dean of the church of Notre-Dame-le-Ronde.

This day we spent the night at Déville.

SEPTEMBER 3. We received procuration at St-Victor-en-Caux.

SEPTEMBER 4. We visited there, where there were twenty monks; two of them were in England. All but six of them were priests. A certain cleric from Bourg-Baudoin, Nicholas by name, who, as the monks stated, had been staying there for twenty weeks, was ill famed many times over of the vice of incontinence and had notoriously and scandalously cohabited with both married and unmarried women of the town. The abbot had not made a general audit with the community for more than a year; he had ill provided for the sick; he rarely or never arose for Matins, unless it be for the Matins with the Twelve Lessons;[25] he did not come to the refectory, nor had he ever slept in the dormitory. Alms were badly dispensed, and the amount had been diminished. We enjoined the abbot to correct all of these things, to remove the said Nicholas, cleric, and to correct the other useless servants, novices, and the ill famed. Item, we ordered the abbot to draw up a general statement concerning the finances of the house, with the assistance of the community or of some of the brothers elected by the community, and this within the next eight days; that he should transmit to us under seal of the convent the account thus made by them. Item, we ordered him to have certain business transactions and duties, such as those of the kitchener and of the man in charge of the grain, attended to by some of his own monks and not by secular clerics; and that the daily expenses should be put in writing; that an account of these should be made and returned in the presence of the abbot and some of the brothers elected by the community. The said abbot sent to us at Aliermont, within the prescribed eight days, the audit made with his community and under the seal of the said community. This is contained on the following page under the sign +.[26]

We received procuration this day at Longueville.

SEPTEMBER 5-7. At Aliermont. SEPTEMBER 8. The Nativity of the Blessed Virgin Mary. We celebrated Mass and preached a sermon at St. Mary's church at Aliermont. This day, with God's assistance, we blessed the abbess of Montivilliers in the above-mentioned church.[27]

SEPTEMBER 9-12. At Aliermont.

+ In the year of our Lord 1258, on the Tuesday following the Nativity of the Blessed Virgin Mary, the abbot of St-Victor-en-Caux in the presence of his community drew up an estimate of the assets of the said house, in terms of the wheat and money of the year just past:

Value of grain was: one hundred fifteen *muids*, that is to say, thirty *muids* of mixed grain, twenty-five *muids* of barley, and sixty *muids* of oats.

Consumption of grain was: for milling, thirty-eight *muids*; for brewing, twenty-eight *muids*; for the prebendaries, thirty *muids*; in pensions, two *muids*; in seed, eight *muids*; by sale, nine *muids* of oats.

[25] The Office recited on solemn feasts, e.g., Christmas, Easter, Pentecost, Ascension.
[26] Below, entry for September 9-12.
[27] Alice, who was elected on September 1, 1258.

The value of the money was: four hundred fifty pounds, and one hundred pounds from England: total, five hundred fifty pounds.

The total of monetary expense for the kitchen, for wine, for buildings, for the shoeing of horses, for the clothing and shoes of the monks, for servants' wages, for Abbot William's pension,[28] for the forty pounds for the royal tithe, for purchase of land: six hundred four pounds and fifteen shillings. Therefore the expenses have exceeded the assets by fifty-four pounds, fifteen shillings.

Such is the state of the house; one hundred twenty pounds in grain and money is owed to the house, and the house owes one hundred forty-four pounds.

SEPTEMBER 13. At Beaubec.

SEPTEMBER 14. We came to the priory at Sigy,[29] proposing, with God's grace, to exercise our office of visitation there, and we warned the prior of the place to admit us for procuration, since we were prepared to perform that which our office made incumbent upon us. This the said prior did not wish to do, but rather desired to appeal, and that in writing. We found the doors of the priory fast closed, and in no wise did he permit us to enter.

We received procuration at Beaulieu. Total for procuration: eight pounds, twelve shillings, two pence.

We visited there this day. Fourteen canons were there, and all but two were priests. No prior was there, the last one having died within the past month; we gave them permission to elect [another]. Three lay sisters were there and two maid servants. They were not certain about the state of the house but they believed that they owed somewhat over fifty pounds, although to whom they did not know. We ordered them to elect someone as prior as quickly as possible, to be solicitous about conferring together to determine how much they owed, to whom, and for what, and to certify all this to us, under seal of the chapter, before the day of election [of the new prior].

SEPTEMBER 15. We received procuration at St-Laurent-en-Lyons.

SEPTEMBER 16. We visited there. Fourteen canons were in residence; all but two were priests. We ordered those who are not priests to receive Communion every month, and that the statutes of the Rule be read frequently in chapter. Item, we ordered one to accuse another [in chapter]. They have six lay brothers and four lay sisters. They owed one hundred pounds. All of the canons asserted that Brother Peter Beaugendre had been present at the time and place that a certain cleric had been despoiled by robbers, that

---

[28] Abbot William had resigned December 17, 1255.
[29] A priory of St-Ouen-de-Rouen. (Cottineau, II, 3034.)

he had given counsel and aid in this crime, and that he had threatened the prior he would kill him and burn down the house.

This day we spent the night at Gournay, at our own expense.

SEPTEMBER 17. We visited the chapter at Gournay. Nine canons are there. In actual residence we found only Matthew and Master John of Paris, with the dean. We found everything to be in good condition. However, the chapter was burdened with many debts. We ordered them to hang something, or to have something constructed, beside the High Altar to receive the pyx wherein the Body of the Lord rests.

This same day we summoned the brethren of the Hôtel-Dieu of Gournay to the monastery of St-Hildevert, and there appeared before us the chaplain of the said house, together with three brothers, and they informed us that in their house were six brothers and six sisters. As [a source of] income, they have the custody of the mill at Welebue and eighteen *muids* of wheat; at Cuigy, twenty *mines* of wheat and oats. They do not observe a rule.[30] They owed fifteen pounds; in income they have, counting all things together, about sixty pounds. They have one meadow and one wood. The brothers and sisters confess to whomsoever they desire; they belong to no parish. Item, we ordered the deans of Cuigy and Gournay to act for us in requiring the brothers and sisters of this house, by statute, to bind themselves by a vow of chastity, to live without possessing property, and to eat in common.[31] Item, that the chaplain of the place should have the cure of souls, and because of this, they should make some satisfactory arrangement with the priest of St. Mary's, in whose parish they dwelt.[32]

This day we visited the priory of nuns at St-Aubin. Fifteen nuns were there. There is a parish there and a parish priest, and he celebrates Mass at the priory. We forbade the prioress to receive anyone, nor to give the veil to anyone, without our special mandate. We informed her that if they should do so, we would not regard the one so received as a nun. We expressly forbade relatives to eat or drink in the house, and the nuns [to eat or drink] with them.

This day we caused the leper house of St-Aubin to be visited by Dom

[30] Most of the hospital staffs professed to follow the Rule of St. Augustine, but few actually did observe it.

[31] The main points of the Rule of St. Augustine.

[32] Everything was done to safeguard the rights of the parish priest from trespass by outsiders where cure of souls was concerned.

Willard, prior of Salle-aux-Puelles. He found there three brothers, three sisters, and a chaplain. There was a certain leprous cleric there, Nicholas by name, who had governed the house for a long while; he frequently ate in the village with the said chaplain and took away the goods of the house. We gave orders to the said Nicholas to give up his business affairs, and, to the chaplain, to cease eating with the lepers. They had six horses, two hundred ewes, six cows; they owed twenty pounds. They had, as they believed, sufficient provisions to last until the new harvest. Item, to see how he would do in these things, we assigned to them for the purpose of transacting business and having land cultivated in season, one Geoffrey, who used to stand before the door of their house.

This day we received procuration at Neufmarché.

This same day we visited there. Three monks were there; there should be four. All were priests. They had no written copy of the Statutes of Pope Gregory. They observed the fasts of the Rule badly; we ordered this corrected. They used meat freely; we forbade them to eat meat save as the Rule permits, and we left it to their consciences whether they should approach their abbot in connection with those things in which they had erred, that he might grant them a dispensation, or whether they should accept the penalty contained in the Statutes. On his own authority, the abbot of St-Evroult had appropriated to his abbey the income of a certain manor near the abbey which the count of Roumare had conferred upon the priory at Neufmarché. He wished the income of the said priory to be applied to his own use.

SEPTEMBER 18. We visited St-Martin-d'Es. Two priest-monks were there. Because of the prior's illness, they do not sleep in one place. The prior was suspended because of the royal tithe. They owed twenty pounds; they have an income of about forty-five pounds.

This day, in the name of procuration, we received four pounds of Paris from the prior at Liancourt, the amount which, as is contained in the agreement, we should receive from him every year, in addition to housing and the use of utensils. This day we spent the night there.

SEPTEMBER 19. We visited the said priory at Liancourt. Two monks and a prior were there. They use feather beds. They observe the fasts of the Rule badly. Also, they eat meat when there is no need, but in this matter they said that they had their abbot's permission. They have an income of one hundred pounds; they owed one hundred pounds. They thought they had sufficient provisions.

This day we spent this night at Sérans [-le-Bouteiller], and for procuration we received seventy shillings of Paris, forage for the horses, straw for man and beast, domestic utensils, and wood. This is the procuration which is due us annually.

SEPTEMBER 20. We visited there. Three monks from St-Germer-de-Flay were in residence; all were priests. They sleep on feather beds and eat meat when there is no need; we ordered them to correct these things after taking counsel with their abbot. The sources of the house's income were not written down; we ordered them to have them written out. They owed about fifty pounds; they had enough provisions, as they believed.

Brother Eudes, by divine permission the unworthy bishop of the diocese of Rouen, to his beloved children in Christ, the subprior and convent of Beaulieu, eternal greeting in the Lord Jesus Christ. Since we are led to provide Brother Richard, called Du Bois, one of your own canons, for you and your house and are committing to him the cure of your souls, we order you to receive him as prior and as such to obey him henceforth. Otherwise we shall impose the sentence upon you which the law demands, and with God's authority we shall have that sentence strictly carried out to a proper fulfillment. Given and done at Sérans-le-Bouteiller, the Thursday after the octave of the Nativity of the Blessed Virgin Mary, in the year of our Lord, 1258.

This day we visited the priory of St-Laurent-en-Cornecervine. Three monks were there with the prior. The fasts of the Rule were not well observed. They ate meat, and they said that they had an indulgence to do this. They owed thirty pounds, and about ten pounds was owed to them. They had sufficient provisions. We found everything else to be in sufficiently good condition.

This day we spent the night at Juziers and received procuration from the prior of St-Laurent-en-Cornecervine.

SEPTEMBER 21. With God's aid we conferred Holy Orders at Juziers, and we spent the night at Frênes, near Meulan. SEPTEMBER 22-29. At Paris. SEPTEMBER 30. With God's help we celebrated High Mass and first and second Vespers in the royal chapel, on the Feast of Relics. The king was present, as well as some of the prelates of France. OCTOBER 1. At Paris.

OCTOBER 2. At Paris. This day, and by our order, we had made an examination of the investigation done by the dean of Valmont touching the life, morals, way of life, and other attributes of Robert of Ros, a priest presented to us for All Saints' church. The investigation revealed that the said priest had received his [Holy] Orders from an outside bishop without obtaining permission from the bishop of his own diocese, and for this reason we were unwilling to admit him to the said church.

OCTOBER 3-5. At Paris. OCTOBER 6. At St-Cloud, and the king was there. OCTOBER 7. In the company of Master Eudes of Lorris, we journeyed to the meeting of the Exchequer at Caen and spent the night at Mantes. OCTOBER 8. At Evreux. OCTOBER 9. At Beaumont-le-Roger. OCTOBER 10. At Lisieux. OCTOBER 11. At Troarn. OCTOBER 12. At Caen. OCTOBER 13-17. At Caen, attending the Assize of the Exchequer. OCTOBER 18. At Lisieux. OCTOBER 19. At Bec-Hellouin. OCTOBER 20. At Déville. OCTOBER 21. At Rouen, and we spent the night at the royal castle because of business connected with the Exchequer. OCTOBER 22. At the same, but we slept at our own manor. OCTOBER 23. We celebrated the feast of St. Romain and spent the night at the royal castle. OCTOBER 24-26. At the same. OCTOBER 27. With God's aid, we preached a sermon at Notre-Dame-de-Rouen, and we spent the night at Ermentrouville. OCTOBER 28. At the same. OCTOBER 29. We held the sacred synod of Rouen.

OCTOBER 30. On this day we did not accept the excuse of the abbot of Jumièges for being absent at the celebration of the said sacred synod. On the following day and in our chamber, which adjoins the chapter house of the church, we enjoined the deans who appeared before us to exact the statutory fines in full from the priests who, without legitimate excuse, did not attend the meetings of the chapters and the deans' synods, [informing them that] otherwise we would exact and receive the full penalties from the deans themselves. Item, we ordered them to compel the priests, especially those with the cure of souls, to wear closed gowns. Item, this day we sentenced Arnulf, rector at Fréauville, to undergo purgation with the seventh hand[33] for the vice of incontinence of which he was ill famed many times over, and for this we assigned to him the day on which the next Christmas ordinations are conferred.

This day we spent the night at Frênes.

OCTOBER 31. At Frênes. NOVEMBER 1. We celebrated the feast of All Saints and Mass in the parish church, and there, with God's help, we preached a sermon.

NOVEMBER 1. [sic]. We received procuration at Parnes and visited there this day. A new prior was there, and three monks with him. Some of them

[33] See above, October 16, 1248, n. 70.

used feather beds. Alms are given three times a week to all comers. Sometimes they used meat when there was no need; we warned the prior that they should abstain from meat as the Rule requires. They owed about one hundred pounds of Paris. They had but little wine; they believed that they had enough wheat and oats to last until the new harvest.

NOVEMBER 2. At St-Martin-de-Pontoise, at our own expense. NOVEMBER 3. At Paris. NOVEMBER 4. At the same. This day and of his own free will Guy, former rector of the church at Hadencourt, resigned his church into our hands. NOVEMBER 5-7. At Paris. NOVEMBER 8. At the same. This day being the anniversary of the death of King Louis,[34] we celebrated Mass at St-Denis, and the king, his son, was present. NOVEMBER 9-19. At Paris. NOVEMBER 20. At St-Martin-de-Pontoise, at our expense.

NOVEMBER 21. At the same. This day, having called before us the rectors and chaplains of the archdeaconry of Pontoise, we held a synod with them. In their presence, we commissioned Master Ralph, our vicar, and Reginald, priest of St-André-de-Pontoise, to act for us in making visitations, and to correct such things as seemed to need correction within the aforesaid archdeaconry. Item, we forbade the chaplains of collegiate churches within the said archedaconry to celebrate their Masses before the churches' rectors, having read the Gospels, had finished preaching to the people; the said rectors had made no little complaint to us about this. Item, we earnestly enjoined upon and commanded the aforesaid rectors of such churches to begin their Masses in good time, so that, having celebrated them according to the proper manner, the said chaplains should be able to celebrate their Masses at suitable hours. Item, we enjoined the chaplains to be present along with the aforesaid rectors at the service and the processions, especially on Sundays and festal days. Item, [we enjoined] that they should give assistance to the rectors in times of need, in baptisms, and in the visitation of the sick, as well as in celebrating the Office of the Mass and in confering other Sacraments.

NOVEMBER 22. We spent the night at Wy and received from the priest at Gadancourt a *muid* of oats, which the said priest is held to give us each year when we come to his place.

NOVEMBER 23. We visited the priory at Villarceaux. The prioress was not there. The number of the professed nuns was twenty-two, of whom five were absent. [There were] three lay sisters. They said that there should be twenty,

---

[34] Louis VIII died on November 8, 1226, at Montpensier in Auvergne.

but the prioress had received two against the will of some of the community, and had, against our prohibition,[35] increased the number by two. They believed that they had enough wheat and oats to last until the harvest time. They had eight cows, four calves, six horses, and three colts. They did not know how much they owed, and they were not too sure about the state of the house. After a while we, considering the fact that the prioress, in opposition to our mandate, had received the said women, that is to say, one from Mantes, as a lay sister, and the niece of the abbot of Jumièges as a nun, with the dean of Magny acting as our agent, issued the following warning to the prioress to send the aforesaid women away:

Brother Eudes, by God's permission the unworthy bishop of the church of Rouen, to his beloved son in Christ, the dean of Magny, eternal greeting in the Lord Jesus Christ. When we recently exercised our function of visitation at the priory of Villarceaux, as our office compels us to do, we discovered that the prioress of this priory had received a certain woman from Mantes as a [lay] sister, and the niece of the abbot of Jumièges as a choir nun of the said place. This was contrary to a prohibitive order which we had given to the prioress and her convent at our last visitation, to wit, that they should not presume to receive any one as a choir nun or [lay] sister of their monastery beyond the number of persons whom they had, without our special license. Our desire in this was to provide for the utility of this monastery, since its resources hardly suffice for a small number of persons; but since this action has been taken both to the prejudice of the priory and in our despite, and as we do not wish to connive at this evasion of our prohibition aforesaid, we order you, by the tenor of the present letter, to go in person to the aforesaid prioress and convent and warn this prioress, on our authority, to send the said women without delay to the abbey of St-Cyr, on which they are dependent; if the prioress received them at the order or with the consent of that abbess, the expenses of the journey shall be borne by that abbess. But if you shall find that the said woman of Mantes was received without the knowledge of the said abbess, and the said niece with her [the abbess'] knowledge, then you shall admonish the said prioress to reduce that woman to the estate which she occupied before, and send the niece to the aforementioned abbess as above set forth. Furthermore, do you admonish the said prioress and convent without delay to expel from the house the young boys whom they have been bringing up, despite our prohibition made to them a long time ago. You may use our authority to compel the prioress to carry out the aforesaid, threatening whatever censure

[35] See entry for July 28, 1257.

seems fitting to compel obedience. Do not delay or postpone to inform us faithfully whatever you do or whatsoever you shall discover. Given, etc.

This day we spent the night at Gasny, at our expense.

NOVEMBER 24. We preached a sermon in the church at Guiseniers, and, God permitting, we heard Mass there, and this day we spent the night at Frênes. NOVEMBER 25-28. At Frênes. NOVEMBER 29. At Pont-de-l'Arche, at the royal castle. NOVEMBER 30. Here, with God's assistance, we blessed the marriage between Roger of Préaux and the daughter of the late Nicholas Arrod of Paris. This day we spent the night at Rouen. DECEMBER 1. The first Sunday in Advent. We preached in the cathedral at Rouen and spent the night at our manor. DECEMBER 2. At Déville. DECEMBER 3. We received procuration at Jumièges.

DECEMBER 4. After propounding the Word of God, we visited there. Forty-nine monks were there. We enjoined the prior to be solicitous in seeing that one accused another [in chapter]. Thirty of them were priests. Item, several of them were negligent in making monthly confession as we had ordered them to do;[36] we enjoined the prior to speak with us about this before he ate. Item, the officials and the bailiffs did not turn in their old clothes to the almoner when they received new ones, and the abbot said that this was because he had given them permission, and he believed that they customarily gave their old clothes to the poor. We ordered the abbot not to allow diminution in the amount of bread for alms, or in the measures of wine served to the individual monks in the refectory. Item, the abbot told us in chapter that he had restored two monks to Genainville, as we had several times admonished him to do. Item, he likewise promised us to restore two monks to Guiseniers before the next harvest. There was a certain monk there, Hamo by name, who irreverently and inanely uttered words of contumely in chapter, a thing which mightily displeased us. Item, the abbot and prior said that they could not restore any monks to Cottévrard because of the poverty of that house. Item, the sick were badly provided for; we ordered them to correct this as soon as possible. Alms are given daily to all comers. This day we spent the night there, at our expense.

DECEMBER 5. We received procuration at St-Wandrille.

---

[36] See entry for December 6, 1257. Mention of the two monks at Genainville (below) probably refers to the same entry. The two monks had not been placed at Guiseniers by December 31, 1259, nor by January 6, 1260/61, nor by December 30, 1261.

DECEMBER 6. We visited there, after preaching a sermon in the chapter. We found thirty-five monks there. The abbot, who had gone to England, had taken three monks with him, and there were two leprous monks at Mont-aux-Malades. All but four were priests. Item, certain of the monks were in the habit of dining with the guests and until such a late hour that they could not attend Compline; we ordered the prior to guard against this more diligently, so that [such monks] should not miss the conventual Hours. Item, we enjoined him to make an audit every six weeks, either in the presence of the community or in the presence of some of the brothers elected by the community. They owed about seven hundred pounds; moreover, they had a certain manor at Ste-Austreberte, which certain heirs of the late John Marshal were holding, but from which they had received nothing for several years. Item, they were entitled, by custom, to the hides, blood, and the four feet of certain animals, and they are not entitled to more. Item, the abbot married off his nephew and his niece after he had become abbot, and some believe that he endowed them with some of the goods of the abbey. We must talk with the abbot about all these things, warn him, and see that more frequent audits are made.

This day we celebrated high conventual Mass and spent the night there at our own expense.

DECEMBER 7. At Déville.

DECEMBER 8. We visited at Mont-aux-Maladies. Ten canons and their prior were in residence. There were nineteen male lepers, fifteen female lepers, and sixteen sisters in good health. There are four communities: one of the canons; one of the brothers in health; a third of the male lepers; a fourth of the female lepers. They owed about three hundred pounds. They had sufficient provisions to last until the new harvest. Everything else, with God's grace, we found to be in good condition.

This day we spent the night at Déville, at our own expense.

DECEMBER 9. After propounding the Word of God, we visited the house at Salle-aux-Puelles. There we found ten leprous sisters and one in good health. The prior is the proctor and administrator of all the goods of the house. They always sing Matins at midnight, for which the sisters rise when they wish but cannot be compelled to do so. Item, on Wednesday, Fridays, and Saturdays, to wit, on each of these three days, or on other days when they do not eat meat, each one has five eggs and three herrings. On other days they have portions of meat. We ordered the prior to give them their pittances without any retraction or diminution, as was wont to be done. They had cows, swine, sheep, and horses and mares in the forest; from the vicomté[37] they receive five hundred pounds annually; they have a grange at Quévilly of which they estimate the annual value to be thirty pounds, and they have land beyond the gate; they also have meadows which are quite sufficient for pasturing their domestic animals for the use of the house. They owed nothing; however, the prior told us secretly that he had, as well in good debts as in cash in hand, about eighty pounds of Tours and more. Where upon we ordered him to see that the infirmary was better provided for.

This day we spent the night at Déville, at our expense.

This same day, when Florent, priest, and rector of the church at Limay, came before us, he voluntarily confessed that he had committed adultery with one of his own parishioners. We ordered him to set out for Rome to visit the portals of Saints Peter and Paul before the octave of the coming Epiphany, and to bring us a letter from the papal penitentiary that the journey had been thus accomplished. In the meanwhile [we ordered that] he should see that his church was provided for.

DECEMBER 10. We visited the priory of Notre-Dame-de-Pré. Fourteen monks were there; all were priests but two. We gave orders that the Statutes of Pope Gregory be read more often. Before the house was burned[38] there were twenty-four monks there. Item, they did not observe the fasts well; we ordered this corrected. Alms are given three times a week to all comers. They owed about seven hundred pounds to their abbot; however, the abbot has received on their behalf some sixty marks sterling in England. They owed about four hundred pounds in other debts. They believed that they had enough provisions to last until the new harvest. Everything else we found to be in sufficiently good condition.

On that day we spent the night at Déville, at our expense.

DECEMBER 11. We visited the house of St-Mary-Magdalene-de-Rouen. There we found in residence ten canons and twenty-four sisters. Six lay brothers were there, but all of them do not stay in the house. One canon was dwelling alone at St-Nicole-de-Beauvais. The prior had not inspected the coffers of the canons and of the sisters, as we had ordered him to do before;[39]

---

[37] The vicomté of Rouen.
[38] It had been burned in 1243.
[39] See entry for March 1, 1256/57.

we again ordered him to make frequent inspection to see that they did not have any property. They owed about eighty pounds. Item, the brothers and sisters make a practice of confessing and receiving Communion thirteen times a year. Item, we gave orders that individual accounts of daily expenses should be diligently made up in the presence of the more reliable brothers and sisters of the house. We expressly forbade the prior to receive clerics or laymen in the house as guests under any conditions, nor to allow laymen to eat with him or with the brothers there. Item, we forbade him to receive or establish any more sisters, canons, or lay brothers without our special permission.

This day we spent the night at Déville, at our expense.

DECEMBER 12. We visited St-Amand. Forty-four veiled nuns and six about to take the veil were there. We issued orders that all, and particularly the young ones, should confess and receive Communion at least once a month. Item, that one should pardon the fault or offense of another before presuming to receive Communion. Item, that she who watches over the entrance to the cloister, or the gate, should be diligent in preventing any nun from talking alone to a layman, but should be present herself. Item, we ordered the abbess to inspect the nuns' coffers frequently, and not to allow them to have any property. They have five maidservants. Item, we forbade the nuns to give away any alms-bags, frill-collars, cushions, or other such things, without the permission of the abbess. Item, we enjoined the abbess to draw up more frequent statements of the daily expenses in the presence of the seniors of the community. They owed about four hundred pounds because of costly construction work.

This day we spent the night at Déville, at our own expense.

On the same day Sir Hugh of Fonts, knight and lord of St-Richard, took issue with the presentation made by the abbot of St-Victor-en-Caux to the church of St-Richard, stating that he was the patron of the said church.

DECEMBER 13. After preaching a sermon, we visited the abbey of St-Ouen-de Rouen. Fifty monks were in residence, and thirty were outside. Traders and apothecaries were in the habit of coming there, entering the cloister and offering things for sale to the monks; we forbade them to permit this practice in the future. All but six of the monks were priests. Item, as we had expressly done before,[40] we forbade the monks to eat with lay folk within the enclosure of the monastery. Item, in the priories they eat meat and badly observe the fasts of the Rule. Item, the funds for alms were too small;

[40] See entry for January 28, 1254/55.

rarely were alms bestowed, and then were given only to a few; indeed, the almoner was hard put to it to find paper [wicks] (*papiros*) for the chapter and oil for the four lamps. We advised the abbot to question the almoner about these things, to give him the free and common incomes, and to try to increase the amount of available alms. They owed five thousand, eight hundred twenty-seven pounds, twelve shillings, six pence; there was owed to them three thousand ninety-three pounds, eleven shillings, eleven pence, so that after collection is made the excess of their debts over what is owed to them is two thousand seven hundred twenty-eight pounds and seven pence.[41] Furthermore, since we heard that the prior, in the abbot's absence, rode about too frequently from place to place, to wit, to Roncherolles and St-Michel, we ordered him to be more diligent in staying in the abbey, and especially when the abbot was away. Item, we forbade him to eat with the guests as was his practice. Item, we enjoined the kitchener to be most diligent in seeing that the food and dishes for the sick and infirm in the infirmary be prepared at the proper hours, for this had occasionally been done very irregularly and carelessly. We warned them all to admit us for procuration and visitation at the priory at Sigy;[42] some of them did not give any definite reply to this.

This day we spent the night at Déville, at our expense.

DECEMBER 14. We received procuration at St-Georges. This day we were bled. DECEMBER 14-18. At the same, at our expense.

DECEMBER 19. We first preached a sermon and visited there. Thirty-five monks were in residence. Nicholas of Rouen was at Le Tréport. All but five were priests. We enjoined them to accuse each other [in chapter] and to dispense more alms. More was owed to them than they owed. We spent the night at Déville, at our expense.

DECEMBER 20. We visited the priory of St-Lô-de-Rouen. Sixteen canons were in residence, and four were in their outside priories; all but one were priests. We ordered the prior to give frequent warning to his canons to celebrate their private Masses more often than was their wont. We enjoined the prior and subprior to punish those whom they knew had not accused their associates, since we found them deficient in this. Item, we ordered the prior to inspect the coffers and boxes of the canons and not to permit them to have any property. They owed three hundred fifty pounds. They had enough

---

[41] The correct figure would seem to be £2,734-7d.
[42] See entry for September 14, 1258.

wheat to last until the next harvest, but not enough oats; they had enough wine. They have an income of seven hundred pounds. They never made any general distribution of alms, because of the debts with which they have been burdened for a long time. The sick were badly provided for, although we had ordered them to attend to this before.[43] This day we received procuration and spent the night there.

DECEMBER 21. We conferred Holy Orders at the Franciscan monastery at Rouen and spent the night at Ermentrouville. Among the ordinands, the bishop-elect of Séez was ordained to the priesthood.[44]

DECEMBER 22. In the presence of the bishops of Lisieux, Coutances, and Avranches, and the said bishop-elect, and of the clergy and people, we preached a sermon in the cathedral of Rouen. This finished, we, as God's agent, consecrated the said bishop-elect, and then we dined with him and the above-mentioned bishops at our palace. We spent this night at Ermentrouville.

DECEMBER 25. We celebrated the feast of the Nativity, and the said four bishops were present with us at the feast. DECEMBER 26. At Déville. DECEMBER. 27. At Auffay, at our expense. DECEMBER 28–JANUARY 5. At Aliermont.

JANUARY 6. We reached the priory at Envermeu, where we visited the priests of the deanery of Envermeu, and we found that the priest at Wanchy was ill famed of a certain widow of Rouen and had had a child [by her]. Item, the priest at Douvrend was ill famed of incontinence, and had had a child. Item, the priest at Martin-Eglise was held suspect of a certain maidservant who was staying at his house. Item, the priest of St. Mary's at Sauchay was ill famed of many women. Item, the priest at St-Sulpice was ill famed of incontinence, of frequenting taverns, and of not wearing a closed gown. Item, the priest at Bellengreville was contentious and was wont to quarrel with his parishioners. Item, the priests at Derchigny, St-Martin, Boissay, and Arques were traders and merchants. Item, the priest at St-Laurent-le-Petit was ill-famed of incontinence. Item, the priest at Parfondeval and Master Michael of Jonquières celebrated Mass twice a day. Item, we decreed that all should obtain closed gowns before Lent, and that unless they had done so by that time they should not presume to celebrate Mass without our permission and that of the dean. Item, we ordered the chapters and deans'

---

[43] See entry for July 17, 1257.

[44] This was Thomas of Aulnay, whose election had been confirmed by Eudes on July 2, above.

synods to be held every month as had been the custom. We cited some of the priests to appear before us on another day. Item, the priest at Bailly was incompetent; we gave orders that he should have a coadjutor.

JANUARY 7. On the following day we enjoined the priest of Martin-Eglise to put out of his house the maidservant who was waiting upon him and of whom he was held in suspicion. Item, [we ordered] the priest of Notre-Dame at Sauchay to send away his children whom he had at home, and not to receive in the future or have with him a certain woman from Dieppe, or a certain candlemaker; further, that he should have himself absolved from the excommunication placed upon him because of the tithe, and to do this before mid-Lent. Item, we enjoined the priest at St-Sulpice to keep away from taverns, to stop drinking up to his gullet, and to get himself a closed gown before the coming Lent. Item, we enjoined Crabell, the priest at Derchigny, to stop trading and to give up his business transactions. Item, the priest at St-Laurent-le-Petit, that he should procure a closed gown and keep away from a certain married woman whom he had known before he became a priest. Item, we ordered the priest at Bellengrèville to stop quarreling with his parishioners.

JANUARY 8. Arnulf, rector of a certain portion of St. Peter's church at Fréauville, appearing before us as the law requires at our hall at Aliermont, of his own free will resigned his said portion into our hands. Present were the venerable men R., archdeacon of Petit-Caux; Master John of Neuilly-en-Thelle, canon of Rouen; Brothers Adam Rigaud and Harduin; and the dean of Envermeu, and John of Morgneval, our clerks. Today Nicholas of Capeval, junior, made amends to us for having hunted partridges in our preserves with a dog.

We spent the night at Aliermont.

JANUARY 9. In the church of Notre-Dame-d'Aliermont we visited the priests of the deanery of Bures. We found that John [Greek], priest at Equiqueville, had been gravely ill famed of a certain young girl, by whom he has had a child; item, that he used to sell wine to his parishioners and was publicly known for playing dice. We enjoined him to forbid this girl to hold any further relations with him, to give up selling wine as had been his practice, and to keep away from dicing. Item, we found the priest at Aulages to be ill famed many times over of Mabel, a married woman. Item, the priest at Melleville was a spendthrift. Item, the priest at Ricarville was under suspicion concerning his sister-in-law. Item, the priest at St-Martin was under suspicion because of the nuns of St-Saëns who frequented his house too often. Item, we gave orders that the chapters and the dean's synods be held more frequently.

This day spent the night at Aliermont.

JANUARY 10-13. At Aliermont.

JANUARY 14. We visited the priests of the deanery of Longueville. We found that the priest at La Chaussée sometimes received prostitutes, and he was ill famed because of this. Item, the priest at Rouxmesnil was publicly known for divination and he was keeping his own daughter at his house. Item, the priest at Appeville was a drunkard and a sot. Item, the priest at St-Aubin wore unseemly garb and seldom, if ever, wore a closed gown. Item, the priest at Bois-Hulin was quarrelsome and celebrated Mass very rarely, and he said that he could not because of the pains in his head and the weakness of his eyes. Item, the priest at Castenay was a dice player and was keeping his daughter at home. We corrected all these things, and ordered the above to amend their lives. Item, we ordered the priests, collectively and individually, to refrain from shameful, scurrilous, and unseemly words, especially before lay folk, and we ordered those who did not have closed gowns to buy them before mid-Lent.

JANUARY 15. At Eu, at our own expense.

JANUARY 16. We visited the priests of the deanery of Eu at Eu. We found that Baldwin, priest at St-Remy-les-Champs, was gravely ill famed at incontinence, and he gave us a letter stating that he would resign his portion whenever we should so desire. Item, Master Matthew, his associate, was a vagabond and a player of dice. Item, the priest at Aubermesnil was ill famed of incontinence. Item, Geoffrey, priest at Val-du-Roi, is incontinent; we ordered the dean to investigate this matter, especially about a certain woman from Gamaches. Item, the chaplain of Sir John of St-Martin was ill famed of many women and of trading. Item, the priest at Binville is quarrelsome. Item, the priest at Sept-Meules was ill famed of Euphemia; he is held to pay us ten pounds of Tours should he happen to relapse. This day we spent the night there [at Eu], at our own expense.

JANUARY 17-18. At Aliermont. JANUARY 19. At Mortemer-sur-Eaulne, at our own expense.

JANUARY 20. We visited the priests of the deanery of Neufchâtel in St. Mary's church below Mortemer castle. We found that the priest at Beaubec was publicly known for incontinence, but he had been disciplined by the archdeacon. Item, the priest at Sausseuzemare was ill famed of a certain married woman. We forbade them all to visit taverns, and we ordered all of them to procure closed gowns.

JANUARY 21. We visited the priests of the deanery of Foucarmont in the same church. We found that the priest at Mesnil-David was ill famed of a certain woman from La Boissière, and because, when brought into our presence he would not admit the truth of this, we ordered the dean to make an investigation to determine whether the said woman from La Bossière was in the habit of being with the said priest, whether any other woman had been with him in a suspicious manner during the past year and more, and whether there was any scandal about these things or any one of them. We assigned for this examination the Vigil of St. Agathe, and we gave him a written notice containing all the preceding articles. Item, the priest at Guilmerville was ill famed of much unbecoming living, and we ordered the dean to inquire whether the said priest was a drunkard, whether he frequented taverns, whether he conducted himself evilly and in an unbecoming way throughout the nearby villages, and whether there was any scandal about these things. For this inquiry we assigned the Wednesday after Purification. Item, Dom Durand, priest at Mortemer, was ill famed of incontinence, of trade, and of collecting market tolls. Item, he sold wine at his house. Item, he took in guests for pay, and he held vicarages. We forbade him to do any of these things, and we ordered him to get rid of the vicarage belonging to Master Eudes of St-Denis. Item, the priest at Le Caule was ill famed of a certain woman; we ordered him to keep away from her. Item, the priest at Bosc-Geffroy dined with the priest at St-Riquier, against the order of the archdeacon, and this after a penalty had been imposed. Item, the priest at Preuseville. Item, the priest at Monchy did not reside in his church, was frequently under suspension, and, as it was said, was a player of dice. Item, the priest at Vieux-Rouen was keeping his children at home. Item, the priest at Aubéguimont pays little attention to the chapters and dean's synods, and he has been warned about this; however, he gave us in private some reasons for his absence from these. Item, the priest at Le Caule does not attend chapter well, nor did he reside in his church as he should have done. Item, he shared in the sale of woodlands; we enjoined him not to interest himself in the sale of woodlands or of any other things and to reside in his church as he should. This day we spent the night there [Foucarmont], at our own expense.

JANUARY 22. At the same, and we preached in the hall of the castle.

JANUARY 23. We visited the priests of the deanery of Aumale and found that William, priest at Fouilloy, was incontinent. In our presence he confessed that he had known one of his married parishioners carnally. Because of this he promised us to regard his church as resigned before the coming Pentecostal synod, whenever we should require this of him. We warned those priests who did not have closed gowns to procure them before mid-Lent.

JANUARY 24-26. At Aliermont. JANUARY 27. At Bellencombre, at our expense. JANUARY 28. At Beaulieu, at our expense. JANUARY 29-30. At Frênes. JANUARY 31–FEBRUARY 1. At Vernon. FEBRUARY 2. At the same. We celebrated the feast of the Purification of the Virgin in the royal chapel, in the presence of the king, and, God permitting, we preached a sermon. Item, we bestowed the gift of benediction upon Brother Hugh, the abbot of Bellosane. FEBRUARY 3-5. At the same, and the king was there as well. FEBRUARY 6-7. At Frênes. FEBRUARY 8. At Ste-Catherine. FEBRUARY 9. Septuagesima Sunday; we preached a sermon in the cathedral at Rouen and spent the night there.

FEBRUARY 10. We cited the clerics of Albano[45] to appear before us. We found they had been conducting themselves becomingly and well and were still so conducting themselves. However, since their rents were coming in badly, assigned as they were to ruinous buildings, we appointed Stephen, the archdeacon of the French Vexin, to act as their mentor, counsel, and manager for a year.

We spent the night at Gouy.

FEBRUARY 11-13. At Frênes. FEBRUARY 14. At Genainville, at our expense. FEBRUARY 15. At Poissy. FEBRUARY 16-21. At Paris.

FEBRUARY 22. At Paris. Today we examined William, priest, presented to us for the church at Rotois. Present were: Simon, archdeacon of Rouen; Master Peter of Aumale, canon of Rouen; Brother Adam Rigaud; and John of Morgneval, our clerk. He was examined in a passage from the Book of Genesis,[46] to wit: *Ade vero non inveniebatur adiutor similis eius, inmisit*

---

[45] A college of ten chaplains founded in 1244 by Pierre de Colmieu, archbishop of Rouen, after his promotion to the cardinalate and his translation to the bishopric of Albano.

[46] Genesis 2:20-21. "But for Adam there was not found a helper like himself. Then the Lord God cast a deep sleep upon Adam and when he was asleep, He took one of his ribs and filled up flesh for it."

ergo Dominus Deus soporem in Adam, cumque abdormisset, tulit unam de costis eius, et replevit carnem pro ea. Asked how to construe and expound this in the French tongue, he said: *"Ade,* Adam, *vero,* in sooth, *non inveniebatur,* did not find, *adiutor,* a helper, *similis,* like, *eius,* himself." Asked how to conjugate *inmisit,* he did it thus: *"Inmitto, -tis, -si, -terre, -tendi, -do, -dum, inmittum, -tu, inmisus, inmittendus, -tor, -teris, inmisus, -tendus."* Item, he said: *"Dominus,* Our Father; *inmisit,* sent; *soporem,* sleep *(encevisseur) in Adam,* ... *[lacuna in MS].* Item, asked how to conjugate *[declinaret] replevit,* he replied as follows: *reppleo, -ples, -vi, -re, repleendi, -do, -dum, repletum, -tu, replens, repleturus, repleor, -ris, -tus, repleendus."* Item, we made him reduce *repleendi* to syllables, and he said: *"Re-ple-en-di."* He was examined in chant on *Voca operarios,*[47] but he did not know how to sing.

FEBRUARY 23-26. At Paris. FEBRUARY 27. At St-Cloud. FEBRUARY 28. At Poissy. MARCH 1. At Mantes. MARCH 2. At Vernon. MARCH 3-7. At Frênes.

MARCH 8. At Frênes. This day John, chaplain of Monchy, in our presence, voluntarily resigned his chapel into our hands. Present were: Brothers John of Rouen, Adam Rigaud, and Harduin of the Friars Minor; Everard, canon of Nogent-le-Rotrou, and Master Gervais, called Rasoir, our clerks.

MARCH 9-12. At Frênes.

MARCH 13. At Frênes. This day Nicholas of Condé, proctor of Fécamp, in our presence instituted the following appeal from us:

Inasmuch as you, Reverend Father, archbishop of Rouen, unjustly and without reasonable cause have refused and still refuse to receive to the free and vacant church of All Saints at Fécamp, Robert of Courcelles, priest, canonically presented to you within the statutory time by that religious and honest man, W., by God's grace abbot of Fécamp, to whom the advowson of the said church is known to pertain, to the no small prejudice and hurt of he said abbot and the monastery of Fécamp:

I, Master Nicholas of Condé, cleric and proctor of the said abbot, feeling that he and the said monastery have been unduly aggrieved in this matter, appeal in writing to the Apostolic See, in the name of the abbot and the monastery of Fécamp, and request *apostoli* immediately; and I place the aforesaid church of All Saints and the right which we have in it under the protection of the Lord Pope.

---

[47] Matthew 20:8. "Call the laborers and pay them their hire," etc.

In the year of our Lord 1258, on the Wednesday before the Sunday on which *Oculi mei*[48] is sung, Master Nicholas of Condé, cleric and proctor of the abbot of the monastery of Fécamp, appealed in the name of this abbot and the monastery of Fécamp from us, and the complaints are contained in the schedule hereunto annexed, and in the form contained therein.[49] We are not obliged to defer to this appeal, inasmuch as the aforementioned Robert of Courcelles has been twice examined by our advisers and found deficient in letters.

MARCH 14-19. At Frênes.

MARCH 20. At Frênes. This day Master Hugh, who was acting as rector of the church at Barville, admitted that the resignation which he had made to us at Juziers of the aforesaid church was valid. This appears in the letter which he drew up and which is sealed with his own seal. Present were: Brother Adam Rigaud; Master John of Neuilly-en-Thelle, canon of Rouen; and Everard, canon of Nogent-le-Rotrou, Master Gervais, and Henry of Les Andelys, our clerks.

MARCH 21-28. At Frênes. MARCH 29. Today Fulk, by God's grace bishop of Lisieux, acted for us at the ordinations conferred at Noyon-sur-Andelle. MARCH 30–APRIL 12. At Frênes. We spent so long a time at Frênes because of the infirmity in our leg.

[48] The Third Sunday in Lent.
[49] The appeal is entered neither in the MS of the Register nor in Bonnin's appendices.

THIS is the fifty-ninth year.

APRIL 13. At the same [Frênes], and this was Easter Day. APRIL 14-19. At Frênes.

APRIL 20. We received a letter from our lord the king, asking us to hasten to him at Fontainebleau without delay as soon as we should see his letter, for he was seriously ill. Ignoring the severity of our own infirmity, we made haste and spent that night at Genainville, where we received another special messenger bringing us a letter from the king urging us not to proceed further, for that, with God's grace, he felt better and was convalescing. So we remained where we were.

APRIL 21. At Genainville, at our expense.

APRIL 22. This third day we received a letter from the king stating that he was ill again, and that he was very much afraid that he was about to die. Having read this, we immediately took our way to him, though not without great travail, hastening along with the aid of horses and a wagon. This day we spent the night at Paris.

APRIL 23. At Fontainebleau, where we found the king in bed, but with God's grace, in sufficiently good health. APRIL 24-27. At Fontainebleau. APRIL 28. At Melun. APRIL 29. At Villeneuve-St-Georges. APRIL 30. At St-Cloud, where we were so seriously attacked by fever and rheumatism that we were compelled to stop and go to bed, for we could not proceed any further. MAY 1-13. At St-Cloud, because of our illness.

MAY 14. At the same. This day John of Rotois, esquire, was brought before Adam Rigaud and Master Richard of Sap, canon of Rouen, and, in the presence of the dean of Foucarmont, he [John] claimed to be the patron of the church at Rotois and requested that the said dean be admitted to the said church, saying that he had himself presented the dean for this church on the Friday preceding last Quinquagesima.[1] The said Brother A. and Master R. did not believe that the said presentation had been made to the said dean on the stated Friday, but that, in fact, the right of bestowing the

---

[1] February 22, 1258/59.

said church had devolved, through lapse of time, upon the archbishop, and so they were unwilling to admit the said dean to the said church. However, they conceded to the said esquire that time should not count against him from that day [May 14] until the Tuesday [June 3] next after Pentecost, but rather that he would have the same right in the aforesaid church as he had on the Wednesday [May 14] before the Rogations[2] began, and the said deans [*sic*] [Adam and Richard] assigned to the said esquire the said Tuesday [June 3] [for him to appear] before the archbishop wherever he [the archbishop] should be, to perform what, by reason [of the foregoing], should be done as the law requires.

MAY 15-31. At St-Cloud. JUNE 1. This was Pentecost. JUNE 2-6. At St-Cloud. JUNE 7. This day our venerable brother Thomas, by God's grace bishop of Séez, conferred Holy Orders for us at Pré, near Rouen. JUNE 8-15. At St-Cloud. JUNE 16-20. At Paris. JUNE 21. At St-Cloud. JUNE 22. At Poissy. JUNE 23. At Mantes. JUNE 24. At Vernon. JUNE 25-27. At Frênes. JUNE 28. At Gouy. JUNE 29. At Rouen, and, with God's help, we celebrated High Mass in the cathedral, and all the resident canons and clerks-choral dined with us this day. JUNE 30—JULY 7. At Déville.

JULY 8. We visited the priory at St-Saëns. Three monks were there with the prior; all were priests. They ate meat when there was no need, and without the permission of their abbot. More was owed to them than they owed. The prior did not celebrate Mass very often, although we had warned him several times about this.[3] Other things were in sufficiently good condition. We received procuration there this day. Total for procuration: eight pounds, seven pence.

JULY 9. We visited the nuns at St-Saëns and preached there. Fifteen nuns were in residence; two were at Ste-Austreberte. They frequently omitted singing their Hours with modulation. Some of them remained away too long when they received permission from the prioress to go out; we gave orders that an earlier time for returning be imposed upon such as these. They owed about one hundred pounds. Joan Martel was rebellious and disobedient and quarreled with the prioress; she rode out on horseback to see her relatives, clad in a sleeved gown made of dark material; she had her own mes-

---

[2] The Rogations (Gallican Litanies, or Minor Litanies) date from the episcopate of St. Mamert of Vienne (474). They consisted of three days of fast, during which processions were made and the litanies sung, on the three days before Ascension Thursday. ("Rogations," *Dict. d'arch. chrét. et de lit.,* XIV[2], 2459; X[2], 1740-41.)

[3] See entry for September 26, 1253.

senger whom she often sent to her relatives. Nichola gave birth to a child in the priory on Ash Wednesday, and it is said that the father is Master Simon, the parson at St-Saëns. The child was baptized at their monastery and then sent away to one of the mother's sisters; the mother lay there and was churched at the monastery; at the time of the delivery she had two midwives from the village. Item, she bore another child once before and of the same Simon. A portion of food was given to each, but they did not hand in the fragments for alms; indeed, they sold or gave what remained to whomsoever they wished. The prioress was under suspicion because of Richard of Maucomble; she was also reported to handle the goods and affairs of the house very badly, and to conceal some of the fruits and rents. This same Richard slept at the house with the brother and relatives of the prioress, and had often eaten there. The community promised and agreed to receive and veil four nieces of some of the nuns, provided that we would agree; each of the nuns had letters from the community covering this concession. We, in full chapter, broke and tore to pieces these letters, being highly annoyed at a concession of this kind. Once again we expressly forbade them to receive or veil anyone without our special permission. Indeed, having heard that the prioress had been inefficient in business deals and in handling affairs, and was still incompetent, we desired to get an audit from her, and to assist at this audit we deputed the priors of Salle-aux-Puelles and of Bellencombre.

This day we spent the night at Bures and received procuration there.

JULY 10. We visited at Bures, where there are two monks from Pré. Alms are given three times a week to all comers. They do not observe the fasts of the Rule, because, as they said, of their various occupations. They ate meat when there was no need; we enjoined them to abstain as the Rule requires, or to seek a dispensation from their abbot who, it is said, is able to grant them dispensation in this matter; however, they should refer this to their own consciences. They owed about twenty pounds. Total for procuration: eight pounds, nine shillings.

On the same day we administered Confirmation in the parochial church at Bures.

We received procuration this day at Wanchy. Total for procuration: . . . [lacuna in MS].

JULY 11. We administered Confirmation in the parochial church at Wanchy and spent the night at Aliermont. Total for procuration: seven pounds, nine shillings, three pence. JULY 12. At Aliermont. JULY 13. At the same. This day we cited Walter, the priest at Binville, to appear before us at Rouen on the Tuesday before Assumption of the Blessed Virgin Mary, to answer charges. JULY 14. We received procuration at Mortemer-sur-Eaulne from the lessee of Master Eudes of St-Denis, who holds the said tenement for life. Total for procuration: eleven pounds, nineteen shillings, ten pence.

JULY 15. We visited there, where there were two monks from Lewes. They were not dwelling in charity, but in rancor. Brother Eudes of Mortemer was not eating with Brother William the Englishman, nor was he singing his day or night Hours with him; but he used to eat in the château or in the village taverns. We enjoined him to conduct himself in a more charitable, courteous, and friendly manner towards the said William and to eat and to sing his Hours with him in the future. Furthermore, since we saw that the buildings were somewhat decayed, and that the chancel of the monastery had not been repaired as we had ordered done at our other visitation,[4] we ordered Dom Durand, priest at the said village, and at that time vicar of the said house, to undertake the repair of the entire manor himself, as to both the roofing and the rebuilding, and to do this from the goods and assets of the rents, and to pay nothing more to Master Eudes of St-Denis [the lessee] until the houses had been suitably repaired.

We received procuration this day at Aumale. Total for procuration: seven pounds, ten shillings, nine pence.

JULY 16. We first preached a sermon there and made a visitation. Seventeen monks were there; three were in England. We gave orders that the Statutes of Pope Gregory be observed. Item, that they should not lend the books of the monastery to anyone without a receipt or a definite letter promising a return, and that the [register] in which the books of the monastery are listed be read out at least once a year. Item, we ordered the abbot to make a frequent inspection of the coffers of his monks lest they should be in possession of any property, and to open these within a month. Alms are given thrice a week to all comers. They owed four hundred forty pounds; they had seventy pounds of Paris in cash, and two hundred fifty *mines* of wheat available for sale, over and above the amount needed for food until the feast of St-Remy; they had enough wine to last until the new harvest,

---

[4] Though Eudes had many times received procuration from this priory, there is no earlier record of a formal visitation of the house. See entry for June 5, 1250. It was a Cluniac priory and thus claimed exemption from canonical visitation.

and clothes and shoes until the said feast. We ordered that no new clothing be issued unless the old clothes were returned. Dom Eustace was gravely ill famed of a certain woman, because of whom he had received discipline before; he promised us be would stay away from her in the future. We ordered the abbot to carry out the penalty which had been instituted against him because of this fault. Item, we ordered the abbot to speak more kindly with his monks, and to be more courteous in disciplining them, as he might well do in true charity. Indeed, we at the time removed William the Englishman from the abbey because he was contentious and had had words with the abbot, and had complained to the king; we ordered him transferred to Jumièges, and to remain there until he should be recalled by us. This day we spent the night there, at our own expense.

JULY 17. We visited the nuns at Bival. There were thirty-three of them. There were also three maidservants and one lay sister. We forbade the abbess to permit any nun to go out alone, or to give them permission to visit their relatives, except for a very limited period. According to the Rule of their order they receive Communion seven times a year, but they confess more frequently. The sources of income were written out in a certain roll. They owed fifty-six pounds in addition to the amount which they owed to their servants. The abbess gives to each nun twelve shillings a year for clothing alone, and each one keeps for herself what is left over. They had little wheat. We ordered the accounts to be cast in the presence of the community, or of some of the sisters elected by the community.

We visited Beaussault this day, where two monks from Bec-Hellouin were in residence. They had a written copy of the Rule. Alms are given thrice a week to all comers. They owed about two hundred pounds to their abbot, and twenty pounds in other debts. They eat meat, but they say they do this with their abbot's permission, and they have a good conscience in this regard. About one hundred twenty pounds, in both good and bad debts, was owed to them. They had more horses than they should have had, a fact which displeased us. We received procuration there this same day. Total for procuration: seven pounds, five shilling, six pence.

JULY 18. At St-Germer-de-Flay, at our own expense.

JULY 19. We visited the priory [of Notre-Dame-de-l'Aillerie] at Chaumont-en-Vexin. Three monks from St-Germer-de-Flay were there with the prior. Alms are given three times a week to all comers. They did not observe well the fasts of the Rule, and they ate meat freely and without scruple when there was no need, but their conscience was good in this matter; we told their abbot, who was present at this visitation, that he should take counsel on these two articles, and then act as seems suitable to God and the safety of their souls. They owed about one hundred pounds; they have an income of one hundred forty pounds. We received procuration there this day. Total for procuration: eight pounds, thirteen shillings, one penny.

JULY 20. We preached a sermon in the parish church at Gisors and conferred Confirmation there.

This day we spent the night at the priory of St-Ouen-de-Gisors, and for procuration we received seven pounds of Tours from the prior; this is the amount in which the said prior is held to us annually in the name of procuration, but only when we turn aside once a year to come to this place.

JULY 21-27. At Frênes. JULY 28-29. At Louviers. JULY 30. We received procuration from the vicar of the house at Quévreville.

JULY 31. We visited the priory of Mont-Deux-Amants. They have four outside priories. Fourteen canons were in residence; all but two were priests. Silence was badly observed, and some were ill equipped with shoes and clothing; we ordered the old clothes to be turned in upon the receipt of new ones. The sick were badly provided for; we ordered this corrected. An altercation broke out in our presence because some of them claimed that in times of convalescence some were better provided with food than others. Very few things were done in charity among them. More was owed to them than they owed. We forbade the prior to be so easily moved to contentiousness as he had been, and not to go to Rouen as often as he was in the habit of doing. We ordered him to see that the sick were better provided for, and that the sources of income were written out again in a clearer manner, and that a transcript of this, or the book in which they were written out, be shown to all the canons and kept in a public place. Item, we ordered him to make better provision for the clothing of the canons than had been done. We received procuration there this day. Total for procuration: nine pounds, five shillings.

AUGUST 1. We received procuration from the vicar of the house at Pérrièrs. Total for procuration: eight pounds, five shillings, six pence. AUGUST 2. We dined with the king at Château-Gaillard, and we spent the night at Frênes. AUGUST 3. At Lyons-la-Forêt, where the king was staying. AUGUST 4. At Gournay, with the king. AUGUST 5-6. At Gisors, with the king. AUGUST 7-8. At Frênes. AUGUST 9. At Déville. AUGUST 10. With God's aid, we preached a sermon at the Franciscan cloister, and we spent the night at Déville. AUGUST 11-13. At Déville. AUGUST 14. At Rouen, and with God's aid we propounded His Word before the Rouen chapter.

This day on our mandate, our official of Rouen and the archdeacon appointed the day after this coming Michaelmas as the time when Richard, priest at Calleville in the deanery of Bacqueville, should hear our decision in the matter of the incontinence for which he was publicly known and ill famed; he had confessed this in our presence.

AUGUST 15. We celebrated the feast of the Assumption of the Blessed Mary at Rouen.

AUGUST 16. At Rouen. This day we sentenced Hugh, priest at Claire, to purge himself with the seventh hand[5] of priests of a charge of incontinence; we appointed the day of the octave of the Nativity of the Blessed Virgin Mary as the time for doing this, either before us at Rouen or before our official at Rouen. Present was Master Simon, archdeacon of Rouen.

This same day Master Geoffrey, rector of the church at Canonville, was brought before us and made his amends for having abandoned his aforesaid church for a long time, for he had gone to Boulogne without obtaining permission from us. He promised to accept our decision in this matter.

AUGUST 17. We blessed the nuns of St-Amand-de-Rouen, and spent the night at Ste-Catherine, at our expense. AUGUST 18. At Frênes. AUGUST 19. We dined with Sir Simon of Montfort[6] at Neaufles castle, and we spent the night at Chaumont. AUGUST 20. At Bresles, at a manor belonging to the bishop of Beauvais, and at his expense. AUGUST 21. At Gournay-sur-Aronde. AUGUST 22. At Noyon. AUGUST 23. At Compiègne. AUGUST 24. At Neuville-en-Hez. AUGUST 25. At Chaumont. AUGUST 26-28. At Frênes. AUGUST 29. We received procuration at Vesly, where there are two monks from Marmoutier. Total for procuration: six pounds, eight shillings, nine pence. AUGUST 30. At Vernon, where the king was staying. AUGUST 31. With God's aid, we blessed the nuns of Le Trésor-de-Notre-Dame at their own monastery and in the presence of the king. We dined at Bray-sur-Baudemont, and we spent the night at Vernon. SEPTEMBER 1. At the same. This day Peter, the clerk of the bailiff of Gisors, offered us Sir Eudes of Villers, knight, as his surety that he would hand over to us, whenever we should so desire, the goods of Robert Billette. SEPTEMBER 2-3. At Vau-

---

[5] See above, October 16, 1248, n. 70.
[6] Simon de Montfort, earl of Leicester and count of Eu.

dreuil, with the king. SEPTEMBER 4-5. At Pont-de-l'Arche, with the king.

SEPTEMBER 6. At Ermentrouville. This day we pronounced the following sentence:

In the name of the Father, and of the Son, and of the Holy Ghost, Amen. Because Henry, rector of the chapel of Bellencourt, who had been cited by our mandate which carried a specified time limit and which had been publicly read in the chapel by the temporary dean of Chaumont, and who had been waited for six months or more beyond the citation date, made no effort to return to the chapel or even to reside there, as is now made clear by letter patent of the said dean who is now with us;

And because, though peremptorily cited to appear before us this present Sunday to hear the law in this matter, he has not appeared either in person or by representative;

We, by definitive sentence, deprive the said Henry, contumaciously absent, of the said chapel and grant the patron of the said chapel permission to present some other suitable person.

SEPTEMBER 7. At Rouen, and with God's grace we preached a sermon before the king in the cathedral. SEPTEMBER 8. At Rouen, and we celebrated the feast of the Nativity of the Blessed Virgin Mary, and the king dined with us in the Great Hall. SEPTEMBER 9. At Pont-de-l'Arche. SEPTEMBER 10. At Frênes. SEPTEMBER 11. At Gisors. SEPTEMBER 12. At Pontoise. SEPTEMBER 13-18. At Paris. SEPTEMBER 19. At Meulan. SEPTEMBER 20. With God's aid we conferred Holy Orders at Juziers priory, and we spent the night at the priory of St-Nicaise at Meulan, at our own expense. SEPTEMBER 21–OCTOBER 1. At Paris. OCTOBER 2. At St-Martin-de-Pontoise, at our own expense.

OCTOBER 3. We visited there. Twenty monks were in residence; three others had gone to Rome and had appealed from the abbot and against him. They have twelve priories, in each of which there should be monks. At this time there were no monks at Boiriz;[7] we ordered the abbot to place two monks there without delay. There was no prior; we ordered the abbot to appoint someone as prior. They had no provost, nor anyone in charge of the granary. Those who are not priests receive Communion once a month. We enjoined the abbot to impose such salutary penance as he deemed advisable upon those, especially in the outside priories, who ate meat when

---

[7] Cottineau does not mention a monastic foundation thus named.

there was no need, and who did not observe the fasts of the Rule. They had a good deal of wine and wheat but did not know how to compute its worth. They owed thirteen hundred pounds after paying off interest and comparing the amount which they owe with the amount which is owed to them. Harduin, priest, was there, both by our mandate and with the consent of the abbot and community, to assist the abbot in handling and managing the business of the abbey. We received procuration there this day. Total for procuration: seven pounds, five shillings, seven pence.

OCTOBER 4. We preached in the Franciscan cloister at Pontoise, and, with God's aid, we celebrated High Mass. We dined with them in community, it being the feast of St. Francis.

OCTOBER 5. After expounding the Word of God, we visited the chapter of St-Mellon. Two canons were in residence, Dom Luke and Master Robert; [there were] nine vicars and two chaplains. There are ten prebends there. The [liturgy] books were badly bound. There was such a dearth of altar cloths that the altar often remained bare because of this defect. Item, Robert of Manières was contentious and quarreled with his associates; we warned him to restrain himself from quarreling and from using insulting words in the future. The vicars were in the habit of going about the town dressed in short coats; we expressly forbade them to wear them in the future, [threatening] otherwise that they would be taken away from them and employed for the support of the fabric of St. Mellon's church. We gave Dom Luke, canon of St-Mellon, the authority and power to coerce these [vicars] in this regard, by ecclesiastical censure if it should be necessary. The chaplain of Dom Richard, the sacristan, did not provide the church sufficiently with the things which he should provide for it, that is, candles for those singing in the choir. He was negligent, that is, in lighting the candles, in ringing the bells, and in preparing and bringing in the book of Lessons at the appropriate hours; we warned the said Dom Richard that he should attend to all of these things through his chaplain, and that he should work more diligently and better than was his practice. Item, Ralph, priest and vicar of John of Montluçon, voluntarily confessed that for a long time he had kept a woman called "La Maréchal", and that he had known her carnally within the past six weeks, and had been gravely ill famed of this. He admitted this ill fame and, with his hand on his breast, swore on the Holy Gospels that he would regard his benefice as resigned if we should find him again defamed of this "La Maréchal" or any other woman, and he could not purge himself canonically. Item, Peter, priest and vicar of Master William, was gravely defamed of a certain woman named Petronilla, and this ill fame was fully established by all the vicars of this church of whom we required an oath in this matter and carefully examined each one separately. We sentenced him to purge himself with the seventh hand of priests,[8] which he was not willing to do, believing that he could not find suitable compurgators; however, he humbly besought us to deal mercifully with him. We, taking compassion upon him, imposed the following penance in writing, to wit, that he should take his way to Mont-St-Michel-in-Peril-of-the-Sea and to St-Giles before the coming feast of St Andrew and bring back to us letters which would be worthy of belief and which showed that he had completed this pilgrimage as the law requires. Indeed, with hand on breast, he swore upon the Holy Gospels, as he had promised and sworn at our other visitation,[9] touching the Holy Gospels and his hand on his breast, that without the publicity of a trial he would regard his benefice as resigned from that time on, if it should happen that he be found ill famed again of the said Petronilla or of any other woman, and the charge was provable; he also promised not to revive any claim to his benefice. Present at this visitation were: Master John of Neuilly-en-Thelle, canon of Rouen; Brother Harduin of the Franciscans; Master Gervais Rasoir and John of Morgneval, our clerks; and the two aforesaid resident canons.

This day we visited St. Peter's priory. Six monks were there; all were priests. The prior had but lately arrived. They used meat when there was no need. The sources of income were not written down; we ordered this done. They owed three hundred pounds. They complained greatly because women entered their choir and chancel and disturbed their prayers; they asked that we take this under advisment.

This day we spent the night at St-Martin, where for procuration we received from Dom Luke, canon of St-Mellon, in the name of the chapter of St-Mellon, one hundred shillings of Paris, which amount, together with wood, platters, cups, straw, beds, and cooking utensils, the said chapter owes us annually for procuration.

This day the rents of Roger, chaplain of Notre-Dame-de-Pontoise, were handed over to us. First, four pounds in rents on the house of Eudes of Les

---

[8] See above, October 16, 1248, n. 70.

[9] See entry for February 12, 1250/51. Peter and Herbert seem to be one and the same.

Andelys, in the town of Foleny. William Bridard of St-Martin, four shillings. Item, eight shillings on an arpent at Osny and which is in essart. Item, two *muids* of wheat from the mill at Bicherel and one *muid* from the grange of Ymereche in the town of Chauvincourt. Item, fifteen shillings in rent from Walter the mason. Item, seven shillings on the rent of the house of Roger the mason; sixty shillings rent on the house of Ralp le Quartier. Four shillings on the house of Ronge Loche situated in the town of La Cavetèrie. Seven shillings from Thibaut, son of Grube, for two parcels of land in the gardens of Barre; two shillings of rent from the garden of Lady Adine la Leveline.

OCTOBER 6. We visited the priory of Cornecervine. Three monks from Notre-Dame-de-Josaphat-de-Chartres were there. They used feather beds, ate meat, and did not observe the fasts of the Rule. They had an income of about one hundred pounds, of which they remited ten pounds to their abbey. They owed about thirty pounds. We received procuration there today. Total for procuration: seven pounds, five shillings, eight pence.

This day, we, acting in mercy, published the sentence of purgation with the seventh hand[10] of priests against the priest at Calleville, in the deanery of Bacqueville, who was gravely ill famed of incontinence, although he had failed in a former purgation. For his purgation we appointed the day following the Rouen synod.

OCTOBER 7. We visited the priory of St-Martin-la-Garenne, where there were six monks from Bec. They ate meat repeatedly when there was no need, nor did they observe the fasts of the Rule very well. The prior was under suspension for failure to pay the royal tithe and had endured the said suspension for a rather long time, and because of this he had not celebrated Mass for almost three months; we imposed upon him a suitable penance, and ordered him to pay off the said tithe as soon as possible and to obtain absolution. About as much was owed to them as they owed. The sources of income were not recorded; we ordered them written down. We received procuration there today. Total for procuration: seven pounds, six shillings.

OCTOBER 8. With God's grace, we celebrated the sacred synod of the French Vexin at Vetheuil.

This day we spent the night at La Roche-Guyon, and for procuration received from the Fécamp monks, who are staying there, forty shillings of Paris, in which amount the said monks are annually held to us for proc-

[10] See above, October 16, 1248, n. 70.

uration, in addition to shelter. The same day we warned the said monks to show to us, before this coming Christmas, whatever privileges or instruments they possessed, demonstrating why we should not visit them,[11] and why they should not at least be held for full procuration. The prior was sick.

OCTOBER 9. We visited the priory at Gasny, where there were three monks. The prior was lying ill at St-Nicaise. We found the house to be badly and negligently administered. The lands had not yet been tilled,[12] although the time for sowing seed had almost passed.[13] We were unable to find out anything about the state of the house. The roof needed repair; the sewer adjoining the chamber was almost in ruins; we ordered them to take up the matter with the abbot [of St-Ouen-de-Rouen]. Item, the abbot goes there too often and so impoverishes the priories. We received procuration there this day.

OCTOBER 10-11. At Frênes. OCTOBER 12-16. At the royal castle at Rouen, on business of the Exchequer. OCTOBER 17. At Pinterville, near Louviers. OCTOBER 18. At Evreux. OCTOBER 19. At the same. With the favor and assistance of God, we consecrated Ralph[14] as bishop of Evreux, our beloved brothers in Christ, the bishops of Lisieux and Séez, cooperating. Present at this ceremony, which took place in the monastery of St-Taurin, were the king and the venerable Fathers, the archbishop of Rheims and the bishop of Orléans.

OCTOBER 20-22. At Frênes.

OCTOBER 23. At Frênes. This day William, priest at Châtillon, having been brought before us, promised and swore, with hand on breast and touching the Holy Gospels, that he would abide by our will for having, been, it is said, a perjurer, in that he absented himself from his church for a long period. We assigned the day of the coming Rouen synod as the date for our decision.

---

[11] Fécamp was an exempt abbey, and its daughter house, Roche Guyon, claimed the same privilege.

[12] Tilling the soil in preparation for sowing winter crops of wheat, rye, etc. Usually all crops were in the soil by Martinmas (November 11).

[13] Reading *tempus sationis* in the MS for *tempus sanationis* of the published text.

[14] When John de la Cour d'Aubergueville, bishop of Evreux, died in June, 1256, one group of the canons of the cathedral chapter elected Ralph de Grosparmi. At the same time, another group elected Ralph d'Aubusson. The result was a quarrel between both candidates which kept the see of Evreux without a bishop until October 19, 1259. Ralph's election was finally confirmed, and he held the bishopric from 1259 to 1263. (Gams, *Series episcoporum*, p. 550.)

OCTOBER 24. At Ste-Catherine, at our expense.

OCTOBER 25. We visited the abbey of Ste-Catherine, where there were twenty-six monks and four novices. We ordered the abbot to have these latter make profession at the earliest time possible. There was no guardian at the entrance to the cloister. Monks were dwelling alone in the priories of Caudecote and Villaines; we enjoined the abbot not to allow any monk to remain alone in any of his priories, but to make such disposition of them as should seem proper in accordance with the will of the Lord. They owed seven hundred pounds. All of the monks complained greatly that the staff of the monastery, of the abbot and of the bailiff, came every day through the cloister to the refectory seeking food and drink, and that the monk in charge of the refectory was bound to serve them with portions of meat; because of this there was good reason for grumbling and murmuring. The abbot told us that he could not easily correct this situation. We received procuration there this day. Total for procuration: ... [lacua in MS].

OCTOBER 26. With God's aid, we preached a sermon in the cathedral in honor of St. Romain, whose festal day occured last Thursday. We spent the night at our manor at Rouen.

OCTOBER 27. We visited the priory at Auffay, where there were five monks from St-Evroult; all were priests. They ate meat when there was no need; we forbade them to eat meat save as the Rule permits. They did not observe the fasts of the Rule very well. They owed about one hundred fifty pounds. They had, as they believed, sufficient provisions to last until the new harvest. We received procuration there this day. Total for procuration: six pounds, fourteen shillings, seven pence.

OCTOBER 30. At the same. Today William Buhère of Hibouville, knight, made amends to us for that his son, Walter, had gone hunting with a dog in our warren at Aliermont. His sureties were Reginald of Aliermont, cleric, and Bartholomew Taupin of Envermeu.

OCTOBER 31. At Dieppe. NOVEMBER 1. At the same. By God's grace, we celebrated the feast of All Saints'. We sang High Mass in the parish church and preached there. NOVEMBER 2. We received procuration at Longueville. Total: ... [lacuna in MS]. NOVEMBER 3. At Déville. NOVEMBER 4. With God's aid, we celebrated the sacred synod at Rouen.

This day Master Hugh, priest, former rector of the church at Ternemare, resigned his church into our hands.

NOVEMBER 5. We held the synod of deans in our chamber. We ordered them diligently to carry out the mandates of our official, for several of them had been negligent in this. Item, we ordered them to have the synodal statutes read aloud in chapters and deans' synods twice a year, that is to say, once between synods.

On this Wednesday, in a full synod of deans, and in the presence of the venerable and discreet men: G., the treasurer; P[eter] archdeacon of Petit-Caux; J., our official; and Master John of Neuilly-en-Thelle, canon of Rouen, we deprived William, priest at Châtillon, of all the fruits pertaining to his church for three years, because he had not wished to reside in the said church for the whole space of the said three years, but had boldly deserted it, running about here and there, trying his best to annoy us. We enjoined him to receive four disciplines at the first four chapters and deans' synods, in the presence of each and all of the priests of his deanery there attending; item, we enjoined him never to leave his church again for more than two days without special permission from us or from our official. Item, with hand on breast and touching the Holy Gospels, he swore before us that he would never offend in this way again.[15]

This day we spent the night at Déville.

NOVEMBER 6. We visited the nuns at Bondeville.[16] In residence were thirty-two nuns, of whom two were novices; three lay brothers; and seven lay sisters, two of whom were simple-minded [fatue]. Lay folk, that is to say, friends and relatives of the nuns, entered the cloister at will, and conversed in the gardens and guest reception rooms of the priory; we ordered the prioress to see that lay folk were kept out of the cloister, the dormitory, and the refectory, and not to permit lay folk to eat in the house with the nuns, nor to speak with them save in some public place, as, for example, the parlor. Item, they observed silence badly; we ordered this corrected. Lucy was rebellious against the prioress and addressed insults to her in the refectory; she was quarrelsome and wrathful. We enjoined her to keep silence on three Fridays. We forbade the prioress to be lenient in giving the nuns permission to go out and gave orders that none should go out without a companion. They had coffers with keys; we ordered the prioress to inspect these and to have the keys taken away. We gave orders that the sources of income be entered in some book, and also that the places from

---

[15] See entry for October 23, above.

[16] Bondeville was a Cistercian priory for nuns. (Cottineau, I, 419.) In the context, *sorores* and *fratres* are undoubtedly lay sisters and lay brothers.

which the income is derived be likewise recorded. They owed two hundred pounds. Item, we ordered the private accounts to be drawn up in the presence of some persons elected by the community. Item, since the prioress had yielded to the clamor of the nuns and had given them her convent seal without our knowledge and order, we sentenced her to receive one discipline[17] in chapter in the presence of the community. Item, we enjoined Brother Roger to obey the prioress humbly in all things, for he had been disobedient and rebellious toward her.

This day we gave John, called "The Greek," rector at Equiqueville, permission to go to Rome, and we freed him from the obligation to maintain a personal residence in his church until after the feast of St. Remy. With hand on breast, he swore and promised us that he would not request the Roman Curia for an extension of this privilege of non-residence. Present were: Master John of Neuilly-en-Thelle, canon of Rouen; Brothers Harduin and Nicholas of Montebourg; Peter Louvel; and John of Morgneval, our clerk.

NOVEMBER 7. At Frênes.

NOVEMBER 8. We visited the priory at Parnes, where there were three monks with the prior. We ordered one of the young monks to confess once a week and to receive Communion once a month. They ate meat freely, but they say that their conscience is good in this matter. They owed about four pounds. We received procuration there this day. Total for procuration: six pounds, ten shillings.

NOVEMBER 9. At Poissy. NOVEMBER 10-23. At Paris, because of the Parlement. NOVEMBER 24. At St-Denis, with the king of France, whom we accompanied to meet the king of England.[18] NOVEMBER 25. The king of England was received with a solemn procession at the church of St-Denis by its monks. The king of France, we, and many others were present. We spent the night there. NOVEMBER 26. The king of England was honorably received with a solemn procession at the cathedral of Paris by the citizens. He had come to conclude a peace between himself and the king of France.

NOVEMBER 27–DECEMBER 2. At Paris. DECEMBER 3. In the apple or-

---

[17] The discipline was a whip or scourge of leather or of cords, used either by the individual in self-mortification, as was the case of the prioress in this instance, or inflicted in public as a punishment meted out by a superior. Since the prioress had no superior in the convent, the penance would be self-inflicted, and in public, as ordered by Eudes.

[18] Henry III (1216-72).

chard[19] of the king of France, in the presence of the kings of France and England, and of many barons and prelates of both realms, we read aloud and made public the agreement made between the two kings. And here the king of England did homage to the king of France.[20]

DECEMBER 4-5. At Paris. DECEMBER 6. We dined with the king of England at St-Germain-des-Prés. DECEMBER 7-9. At Paris. DECEMBER 10. At St-Germain-en-Laye. DECEMBER 11. We received procuration at Juziers. Total for procuration: seven pounds, sixteen shillings, two pence.

DECEMBER 12. We visited the priory at Juziers. The prior was not present. Seven monks were there; all were priests, with the exception of one novice, who had been admitted to the novitiate. We ordered this novice to confess and receive Communion once a month. They ate meat freely and used feather beds. Item, they held court in the cloister, and they had a prison adjoining the cloister, where malefactors and thieves were confined. We ordered them to hold court somewhere else, far from the church, and to build their prison beyond the consecrated ground and beyond the churchyard. Item, the cellarer told us that he had heard from the prior that they did not owe ten pounds more than was owed to them.

We received procuration this day at the priory at Gaillonet, a Premonstratensian house. Total: six pounds, seven shillings, six pence.

DECEMBER 13. With God's help, we bestowed our benediction upon Simon, abbot of Marcheroux, at Wy, and preached a sermon there to the entire parish. We spent the night there and received a *muid* of oats from the priest at Gadancourt, which this priest owes us once a year when we turn aside to Wy.

This day a certain priest, presented by us for the church at Château-Baudemont, and whom we found to be ill-equipped for the cure of souls, appealed to us in writing.

DECEMBER 14. We received procuration at Sausseuse. Total for procuration: seven pounds, five shillings, two pence.

DECEMBER 15. We entered the chapter of Sausseuse, and, having preach-

---

[19] *Pomerium* may well mean here an open space within and without the walls of the town.

[20] Eudes is silent about the part he played in bringing the two sovereigns together, but it is probable that he was the go-between. In July of the following year Louis IX sent him to England to iron out some difficulties which had arisen about the treaty of 1259. For the Treaty of Paris see Mikhail Gabrilovic, *Etude sur le traité de Paris de 1259* (Paris, 1899), pp. 5-48.

ed a sermon, we gave our attention to the election of Brother Peter of Liancourt, who had been elected as prior by five of the brothers proceeding by way of compromise instead of by all of them. Taking under advisement this election and the manner in which it was held, and having examined the prior-elect, we confirmed his election as valid, and enjoined the community to regard Peter as their prior and also to give him their obedience. We then investigated the state of the house but were unable to obtain complete information. However, we discovered that they owed forty pounds of Paris to Master Robert of Grainville, a canon of Rouen, that they had no money for pruning their vineyards, and that they lacked many horses. Not so long ago there had been eight good horses there. Then we ordered the prior to visit the outside priories and to see that their buildings were repaired, for it had been intimated to us that they were in a ruinous state.

This day we slept at Frênes.

DECEMBER 16. We received procuration at Noyon-sur-Andelle. Total: ... [lacuna in MS].

DECEMBER 17. We visited there, where there were six monks from St-Evroult. The prior was ill. They ate meat freely; we forbade them to eat meat except as the Rule permits. They had suffered heavy losses in England. Because of the prior's illness, we were unable to get full information about the state of the house.

At this place John of Bray, priest, whom we had not wished to admit to the church at Baudemont, although he was presented by the king, withdrew the appeal he had entered against us at Wy. We were not obliged to defer to this appeal for, upon examination, we had found him to be too deficient in letters to have a cure of souls.

DECEMBER 18. We received procuration at L'Ile-Dieu. DECEMBER 19. At Déville. DECEMBER 20. God assisting us, we conferred Holy Orders at the Dominican monastery at Rouen; we dined with them, and slept at our manor at Rouen. DECEMBER 21. God assisting us, we preached in the cathedral and spent the night at our manor. DECEMBER 22. We dined with the Franciscans at Rouen. DECEMBER 23. At Rouen, and we made our O.[21] DECEMBER 24. We promulgated the following sentence from our hall at Rouen on the vigil of the Nativity:

In God's name, Amen. Because Geoffrey, rector of the church at Panilleuse,

[21] See above, December 23, 1250, n. 135.

has been cited according to law by our mandate, and the edict of citation has been read publicly in the said church, to the effect that he should return to this church which he had before deserted and take up personal residence therein as the cure of a church requires, and having abandoned it for more than six months has not seen fit to obey our order:

Although peremptorily cited to appear before us at Rouen, or wherever we should be, on the Tuesday before Christmas, to stand trial in this matter, as is evident from the report of our dean of Baudemont, the judge appointed to attend to this, the said Geoffrey did not appear, either in person or by proxy on this day, nor indeed up to the third hour of the following day, for we waited for him until then:

Wherefore, not wishing that the said church should any longer be deprived of its rector, we, by definitive sentence, declare the said Geoffrey deprived of the said church, and we grant to its patron the liberty of presenting a suitable person.

Present were: Masters Richard of Salmonville and John of Neuilly-en-Thelle, canon of Rouen; Brother Adam Rigaud of the Friars Minor; John of Morgneval, our clerk; Master Michael of Equiqueville; Pochard, cleric; Clement of Senots; and many others.

DECEMBER 25. We celebrated Christmas at Rouen. DECEMBER 26-27. At Déville. DECEMBER 28. This day Andrew, a member of the Order of the Penitence of Jesus Christ,[22] in our presence renounced every right which he had or might have in the church at Criquebeuf, which he had held for many years. DECEMBER 29. We received procuration at St-Georges. Total for procuration: nine pounds, ten shillings.

DECEMBER 30. After preaching, we visited there. Fourteen monks were in residence; two were at St-Nicholas, and four in England; all but four were priests. Alms are given daily to all comers. One hundred pounds of Tours in excess of their debts was owed to them, not counting the fact that the collectors of the tithe asked eighty pounds of Tours from the abbot, as dating from the period of the last abbot. We ordered the abbot to look after those who have been bled, better than was the custom. Item, we found one cleric, Lawrence by name, defamed of incontinence. He had kept a certain woman

---

[22] Reading *de ordine poenitentiae Jesu Christi* in the MS for *de ordine Provincie Jesu Christi* of Bonnin. These were the Friars of the Penitence of Jesus Christ, also called Friars of the Sack. The order was founded shortly before 1251 and disbanded by order of the Council of Lyons, 1274. See Richard W. Emery, "The Friars of the Sack," *Speculum*, XVIII (1943), 323-34.

for fourteen years; we ordered the abbot to conduct a thorough investigation and to do what seemed best, so that scandal and the occasion of scandal might be removed. Item, we gave orders for the cellarer to keep the keys of the doors at night.

This day we spent the night at Jumièges, at our own expense.

DECEMBER 31. We visited there. Fifty-two monks were in residence; six of them were novices. No monks were at Cottévrard, nor at the manor at Guisenières. The fasts of the Rule were ill observed in the priories; similarly, the monks dwelling in the priories ate meat; we enjoined the abbot not to allow them to eat meat except as the Rule permits, and to punish those who were delinquent in this. They did not owe much; about two hundred pounds was owed to them. Alms are given daily to all comers; we ordered the abbot not to allow the amounts given for alms to be diminished. We received procuration there this day. Total for procuration: twelve pounds, sixteen shillings, seven pence.

JANUARY 1. At St-Wandrille, at our own expense.

JANUARY 2. We visited there, finding forty-two monks; all were priests but four, and eight others who were novices. We gave orders that the monks should dine with the guests at night less often than they do, so that they do not miss Compline. Item, that the abbot should increase the amount set apart for alms. Item, we ordered the individual audits to be made up once a month, and this in the presence of some to the brothers elected by the community. They owed five hundred pounds. Item, they were accustomed to receive the hides, blood, and feet of certain animals; the abbot was engaged in litigation about this with the abbot of Royaumont.[23] Item, he was in litigation with the heirs of John of Fonts, lately slain, over a certain manor at Ste-Austreberte, which the aforesaid heirs were holding to the prejudice of the church at St-Wandrille. We received procuration there this day. They did not wish to reckon the expenses.

JANUARY 3. We received procuration at Le Valasse, a Cistercian house.

JANUARY 4. We received procuration at Graville. Total for procuration: eight pounds, sixteen shillings.

JANUARY 5. After preaching a sermon, we visited there. Nine canons

---

[23] A Cistercian abbey built c. 1228, a daughter house of Cîteaux; it was founded by Louis IX in the diocese of Beauvais, near Versailles. (Cottineau, II, 2558; A. Dimier, Saint Louis et Cîteaux [Paris, 1954], pp. 52-81.) See entry for December 6, 1258/59, regarding St-Wandrille's litigation over the manor of Ste-Austreberte.

were in residence. The prior had sent one to Bellevue to be the associate of the prior there. We forbade women to eat with the canons who had cure of souls. Alms are given thrice a week, and to lepers on Friday. About sixty pounds of collectible debts was owed to them in excess of what they owed. They intend, with God's aid, to invest two more canons before the coming feast of the Purification, and so there will be twelve.

This day spent the night at Montivilliers, at our own expense.

JANUARY 6. That is to say, on Epiphany, God helping us, we preached a sermon at the monastery at Montivilliers before the nuns and the people of the town, and we celebrated High Mass in pontificals. This day we received procuration there. They did not wish to compute.

JANUARY 7. We entered the chapter of the nuns and with God's aid preached His Word to them in chapter. Then, desiring, with God's help, to perform our duty of making a complete visitation, both in head and in members, as our office requires of us, it was urged on the part of the abbess and community that the archbishop of Rouen had never been in the habit of visiting them as a community, but only through the abbess. After a great deal of altercation, we asked them collectively and singly whether they would receive us for the purpose of making a full visitation; through their spokesman, Master Robert, their cleric, they replied, "No," adding that they would never consent that we exercise the office of visitation there, except in the matters concerning the abbess alone, and they rested their case upon charters, custom, and privilege. However, we warned them to make us amends for this disobedience, rebellion, and contempt before the coming Ash Wednesday.

This day we spent the night at Valmont, at our own expense.

JANUARY 8. After preaching a sermon to the chapter there, we visited them. There were twenty-six monks; one was simple-minded; we gave orders that he be well watched and guarded, lest he escape. All but six were priests. There was one novice who did not wish to receive Communion once a week as we had ordered at our other visitation;[24] we repeated our command that all novices confess and receive Communion once a week.[25] One

---

[24] This novice has not been mentioned in prior visitations to Valmont, January 31, 1248; December 6, 1249; May 23, 1251; April 26, 1252; September 11, 1255; December 16, 1256; and December 13, 1257.

[25] Probably this refers to his injunction issued on December 6, 1249, to read the Statutes of Pope Gregory. None of his visitations refers specifically to confession and Communion in the visitations of Valmont.

does not accuse another [in chapter], as we had ordered; we again issued explicit orders that one should accuse another [in chapter], and that the penalty which the perpetrator of the offense received should also be imposed upon him who did not accuse his companion.[26] Item, some of them had coffers in the dormitory, with keys; we ordered the keys taken away. Item, some of them had themselves bled without the abbot's permission; we advised them to determine amongst themselves at what periods of the year and how often it should be permitted to anyone to undergo bleeding; that those who are bled be better treated than had been customary, and that they be not obliged to rise for Matins unless they so desired. Alms are dispensed three times a week. Item, we ordered all income of the monastery, as a whole and in detail, written out in three registers. There was owed to them about three hundred pounds of Tours in good and bad debts. We received procuration: nine pounds, six shillings, three pence.

JANUARY 9. We received procuration at Ouville. Total for procuration: eight pounds, fifteen shillings.

This day, in the upper hall of the priory at Ouville, where we slept this night, we invested with our ring John of Morgneval, our clerk, in the name of Master Simon of Pincesais, with a prebend of Rouen, which the said J[ohn] had erstwhile resigned into our hands. Present were: Master John of Neuilly-en-Thelle, canon of Rouen; Brothers Harduin, Nicholas of Montebourg, and Walter of Manières; and John of Morgneval, the clerk aforesaid.

JANUARY 10. After first preaching in chapter, we visited them. Eleven canons were present; all but three were priests. We enjoined the subprior to see that one accused another [in chapter]. Item, we ordered the prior to make frequent inspection of the canons' boxes and coffers, and to remove the keys; item, that he have silence observed. They had two lay brothers. Alms are given daily to all comers. They owed about sixty pounds; they had, as they believed, sufficient provisions to last until the new year.

This day we came in person to the priory at Etoutteville, and found only one monk from Lewes there, together with two laymen who were keeping the said house for Gilbert of Wyanville, cleric, who leased it from the prior of Lewes. There should be at least three monks there, and we gave orders that these should be restored. We found the manor in bad condition; we ordered it repaired. Later we had the goods of the said priory seized by the

---

[26] See entries for September 10, 1255, and December 12 and 13, 1257.

vicomte of Malepreux until such time as the state of the house was reformed.[27]

This day we spent the night at the priory at Ouville and received procuration from the stewards of the said house at Etoutteville. Total for procuration: ten pounds, eight shillings.

JANUARY 11. We preached in the parish church at Bacqueville and received procuration this day at the local priory. Total for procuration: eight pounds, six shillings, four pence.

JANUARY 12. We visited there, finding four monks from Tiron, all very old and feeble. They ate meat freely. We ordered them to confess before celebrating their Masses. The lord of the village was held to pay them one hundred shillings of Tours each year, but they had received none of this for three years; we ordered the prior to demand this of the lord. They owed about sixty pounds.

We received procuration this day at Longueuil, from the lessee of the house belonging to Bec. Total for procuration: nine pounds, four pence.

JANUARY 13. We received procuration at Envermeu. Total for procuration: nine pounds, three shillings, ten pence.

JANUARY 14. We preached in chapter and then visited the priory at Envermeu. Twelve monks were there; all but two were priests. We ordered the prior to take away the keys and inspect the coffers of the monks. They owed one hundred sixty pounds; sixty pounds was owed to them. We found everything else to be in sufficiently good condition.

This day we received procuration at Le Tréport. Total for procuration: nine pounds, nine shillings, six pence.

JANUARY 15. We visited there, finding twenty-three monks. One of them was the chaplain of the count of Eu; he went riding with the count. They had four priories, and there were monks in each of them. One did not accuse another [in chapter], although we had expressly enjoined upon them before to rectify this abuse and to see that this was done.[28] We gave orders that old clothes, especially the pelisses, be turned in upon the receipt of new ones. Item, the monks requested that tunics be given to them in place of the pelisses. Alms are given to all comers four times a week, that is to say, thrice to laymen and once to clerics. We ordered the abbot to

[27] This is an example of Archbishop Eudes invoking the secular power in an eccleciastical matter.

[28] See entry for February 21, 1257/58.

see that the Rule, so far as it pertained to the eating of meat and the observance of fasts, be maintained in the priories, and to inflict such penance upon the transgressors as should seem expedient. They owed three hundred pounds; the count owed them sixty pounds and more, nor were they able to recover this. They have enough provisions for the year.

Note: concerning their having tunics ... [*lacuna in MS*].

We spent this night at Eu, at our own expense, and there we heard reports of the death of Louis, the eldest son of the king.[29]

JANUARY 16. We began our journey to the king and spent the night at Aumale, at our own expense, where we received the following letter:

Louis, by God's grace king of the Franks, to his beloved and faithful Eudes, archbishop of Rouen, greeting and affection. It has pleased God, Whose Name be blessed above all, that our beloved first-born son, Louis, should depart from this life. Not only bodily affection and the bonds of nature had attached him to our heart by a certain tie of spiritual affection, but also the very nature of his worthy talents and innocence of life had rendered him most dear and lovable to us.

Although we have the firmest hope in God for his eternal salvation, not only because of his conduct which was commended by all, but also because of the laudable and faithful end which he had, we earnestly ask and request you in particular to pray to the All-Highest for his soul, and to arrange that, in all the religious and conventual houses of your Province a spiritual offering of Masses and prayers shall be offered for him, for the sake of Divine Mercy and for the love of us. Given at Paris, the Monday after Epiphany.

JANUARY 17. At St-Lucien-de-Beauvais where, our old rheumatism attacking us once again, we were unable to proceed further, but were compelled to take to our bed. JANUARY 18-23. At the same. JANUARY 24. At Gisors, at our own expense. JANUARY 25. At Frênes. JANUARY 26. At Pont-de-l'Arche, and there we found the king. JANUARY 27. We and our venerable brother, the bishop of Evreux, were at Bec-Hellouin. JANUARY 28. At Pont-Audemer. On this day we had caused our venerable brothers the suffragans of the church of Rouen to be cited there to celebrate the sacred council.

JANUARY 29. In the morning we went to the church of St-Aignan, and before we took our seat in council, we celebrated Mass in pontificals. Present were our venerable brothers our suffragans, who were not vested for

[29] Louis was born in 1244. He was affianced to his cousin Berengaria of Castille. The marriage was to have taken place in the summer of 1260.

celebrating Mass, but with the deacon and subdeacon so vested, Master John of Porte, archdeacon of the Norman Vexin, acted as deacon. Because we did not have a canon of Rouen present, we caused Master Thomas of Falaise, canon of Lisieux, to be vested as subdeacon. After Mass had been celebrated, we and our suffragans, all dressed in pontificals, took our seats on the dais, and there the deacon, suitably vested, read the Gospel, to wit. "After these things, the Lord appointed also other seventy-two" [30] This completed, we commenced in a loud voice the *Veni Creator Spiritus*. When this had been sung, two clerics in surplices sang the Litany before the altar.

Then, having repeated the Lords Prayer in a low voice, we said the prayer *Assumus*. Following this, we with God's aid preached a sermon. Then the letter to the bishops of Bayeux convoking the council was read, and a rescript was read as well. Thirdly, the list of proctors of the cathedral chapters was read. Fourthly, that statute of the constitution drawn up by the general council concerning the annual celebration of councils by archbishops and their suffragans, which is contained in the titulus *De Accusationibus*, and which begins, *Sicut olim*, was read; other statutes of the same general council which seemed advisable were also read, as were the decrees on intemperance, drunkenness,[31] etc.

The proctors were: For the chapter of Rouen, William, the treasurer, and John of Porte, archdeacon of the Norman Vexin; for the chapter of Beauvais, Master John of Carmont, archdeacon, and Nicholas of Blay, sacristan of the same church; for the diocese of Evreux, R[ichard] of Val, treasurer of the said church; for the chapter of Lisieux, Master Lawrence Roman, sacristan, and Richard of Houlant, canon of Lisieux; for the chapter of Coutances, Master Hervey Paste; for the chapter of Avranches, A., the dean of Avranches; for the chapter of Séez, Master Nicholas, dean of All Saints at Mortain; the proctor for the bishop of Beauvais was Master Girard of Corion, archdeacon of Beauvais.

Then the inquisitors who had been appointed by the last provincial council, were asked if they had anything to present. Some of these were absent, and the ones who were present replied that they did not wish to give a report while their colleagues were absent. We then appointed others, to wit: for the diocese of Rouen, the deans of Neufchâtel and Pont-Audemer; for the diocese of Beauvais, the deans of Mery and Vaux; for the diocese

---

[30] Luke 10:1.
[31] Canon 15 of the Fourth Lateran Council (1215). (Mansi, XXII, 1003.)

of Avranches, the rectors of Parreigny and Dragey; for the diocese of Evreux, the deans of Laigle and Ivry; for the diocese of Lisieux, the deans of Pont-Audemer and Bernay; for the diocese of Séez, the deans of Macé and Annebec; for the diocese of Coutances, Dom Robert le Sor and William, rector of the church at Saire.

It should be known that at this council our venerable brothers sat by us in this order: on our right hand, Ralph, the bishop of Evreux, and Fulk, the bishop of Lisieux (Gui, the bishop of Beauvais, who was absent, would have sat immediately beside us and before these two bishops, had he been present); on our left hand, Richard of Avranches, Thomas of Séez, and John of Coutances.

Sixth, the following statutes were recited and read:[32]

It is the pleasure of the sacred council that the following statutes be strictly observed, so that the Reverend Fathers Eudes, by God's grace archbishop of Rouen, and his suffragans, and their subjects shall in no wise be bound to observe them as though they were new statutes, that is, as regards those which have already found expression [in canon law], in the Statutes of Pope Gregory IX, or in episcopal synods.

We will that the statute of the council of Lyon concerning procurations receivable by archbishops and bishops due for visitations, and concerning the elimination of the evils of procuration, caused by the pretension of their official entourage, be observed.

We will that the statute of the general council against those who form leagues, and the statutes issued with prejudice to the liberties of the Church, be frequently and solemnly promulgated in synods and parish churches, and that the transgressors of this statute be canonically punished.

We decree that secular powers who seize clerics with more violance than the resistance of the defendant justifies, or who detain such beyond, or in opposition to, the request of the ecclesiastical judge, be declared excommunicated canonically in general, or individually after definite evidence is procured.

We strictly forbid the employment of secular judges by ecclesiastical persons in any cause affecting a church, especially in personal actions.

We decree that abbots, priors, and other ecclesiastical persons who receive the major tithes in parish churches shall be obliged to restore the fabric, books, and ornaments, in the same proportion as they receive the tithes.

We will that the synodal statute, to wit, the ecclesiasical persons to whom

---

[32] The decrees are practically a copy of those of the synod of September 12, 1257. See above, pp. 322-328.

come the mandates of various judges, delegates, conservators, or executors shall diligently inspect the names of the judges of the diocese, and the places to which they cite, and take care that their authenticity be strictly observed.

We forbid any Christian, male or female, to work for any Jews in any hospice, or presume to dwell with them; and we order all Jews to wear some obvious signs, that they may be distinguished from Catholics.

We strictly prohibit the holding of vigils or dances in churchyards and sacred places, and we order transgressors to be canonically punished.

Clerics, especially the unmarried ones, shall be solemnly warned in churches to wear a suitable tonsure; [clerics] who have taken the Cross[33] shall be obliged to wear a cross openly.

We will that the statute of the general council prohibiting to clerics the use of gilded saddles, cingles, bridles, spurs, and other superfluities, and the clauses covering the garments to be worn by clerics, be observed.

We forbid beneficed clerics, or those in holy orders, to become enamored of, or addicted to, hunting and fowling.

We decree that the certain number of religious be maintained in all abbeys and priories whose resources have not been diminished; unless, perchance, by the express permission of the Superior, and for reasonable cause, the present number be maintained temporarily.

We will and command that the legal requirement that no monk shall dwell anywhere by himself be observed.

Monks dwelling in nonconventual priories shall be warned under threat of suspension and excommunication, and shall be induced by whatever means shall seem expedient, to strive to observe the Statutes of Pope Gregory covering the eating of meat, confessions, and fasting.

We decree that regulars shall not dwell with secular folk save with the special permission from the Diocesan.

The statute forbidding monks to contract loans above a certain amount, without the permission of their abbot, shall be strictly observed.

We forbid all rural deans who have jurisdiction to issue any sentences of excommunication or suspension, except in writing.

We order that a priest should not cease from the publication of a sentence of excommunication, even though the parties are reconciled, until he is legally sure of the absolution of those excommunicated.

We will that absolution be made with due solemnity.

We forbid priests to pronounce general sentences of excommunication, save in the cases of theft and rapine, and after sufficient warning.

---

[33] That is, the clerics who have pledged themselves to go on Crusade. Those who had done so wore a cross prominently on their robes.

Item, we then decreed that chaplains to whom churches are temporarily entrusted shall be diligently examined as to their fitness in letters, conduct, and ordination.

Having completed these matters, and the council having been harmoniously celebrated, we withdrew, singing *Te Deum laudamus,* and as the *Te Deum* was finished we reached the altar of St-Aignan, and there we offered suitable prayers.

JANUARY 30. At Jumièges, at our own expense. JANUARY 31. At Déville. FEBRUARY 1. With God's grace, we preached at the cathedral in Rouen and celebrated High Mass, and we spent the night at our manor. FEBRUARY 2. At the same, and there we celebrated the feast of the Purification of the Blessed Virgin.

FEBRUARY 3. Richard, priest-rector of the church at Calleville, in the archdeanery of Petit-Caux, was brought before us, and he proved that he had been prevented from purging himself canonically of the vice of incontinence of which he had been ill famed. We had assigned to him the day following the synod just held, to purge himself with the seventh hand of priests.[34] Item, we assigned him the Monday following the *Laetare Iherusalem*[35] to purge himself in a similiar way, with the seventh hand of priests, of this vice, at Rouen, or wherever we should be near by, or before our official, if it should happen that we were away.

This day we dined at Franqueville, at the manor of Peter Blondel, a burgess of Rouen, and we spent the night at Frênes.

FEBRUARY 4-6. At Frênes. FEBRUARY 7. We began our journey to Chartres, and spent the night at Vernon. FEBRUARY 8. At Pacy. FEBRUARY 9. At Ivry. FEBRUARY 10. At Bu. FEBRUARY 11. At the abbey of Notre-Dame-de-Josaphat, at our expense.

FEBRUARY 12. We visited the shrine of Notre-Dame-de-Chartres, and spent the night at St-Pierre-en-Vaux.

This day sixty-six of the canons of Chartres assembled to elect a bishop, and proceeded by the method of scrutiny;[36] Master Peter of Mincy, dean of Chartres, was elected by thirty-nine votes. The others appealed.

FEBRUARY 13. Having heard and understood this discord which arose out of the election, we went to the cathedral, desiring to bring the canons

---

[34] See above, October 16, 1248, n. 70.
[35] Fourth Sunday of Lent.
[36] The usual method of election to ecclesiastical office by secret ballot.

into concord once again, and, God favoring us, we offered ourself as a mediator, actuated for the good of the peace and by zeal for charity. On this same business we remained there this day and during the following days, sleeping at the bishop's manor. Finally, in our presence, they unanimously consented to the said election.

[*No entry for February 14.*]

FEBRUARY 15. At Néauphle-le-Vieux. FEBRUARY 16-27. At Paris, because of the Parlement. FEBRUARY 28. At St-Denis. MARCH 1. At Pontoise.

MARCH 2. We spent the night at Sérans-le-Bouteiller, where we received seventy shillings of Paris from the local prior, in which amount the prior is annually held to pay us when we come to visit this place. In addition, we received domestic utensils and dishes, fodder for the horses, straw, wood, and coal such as might be found in the village, as is contained in the letter of agreement copied out on the last page of the Register.[37] An altercation arose between our clerk who acts as *maître d'hotel* and the prior who was there at the time, about seeking in the town for feather beds, wood, cooking utensils, hay, and stabling for the horses. We thoughtfully consulted with our associates about all of them and concluded that the prior was obliged to provide us with all of these things with the exception of the feather beds, since there was no mention of anything but straw mattresses in the agreement.

MARCH 3. We visited there, finding three monks from St-Germer-de-Flay; all were priests. They did not observe the fasts of the Rule. They ate meat freely. They owed about fifty pounds. Everything else we found to be satisfactory.

This day we visited St-Martin-d'Es, where were two monks from St-Magloire-de-Paris, old and feeble, poor and thin. They were unable to live in accord with the statutes of their order. They owed about twenty pounds and had a meagre supply of provisions.

On the same day we visited the priory at Liancourt and found the place desolate; there was no prior there, he having recently withdrawn. He had sent only two monks there, and these, as they said, did not have enough to sustain themselves; the house owed about one hundred pounds, and they did not have any provisions. We sent a letter to the abbot of St-Père-de-Chartres urging him to labor with all solicitude for the bettering of the

[37] Bonnin, p. 776.

condition of this place, and to make such regulations as would lead to spiritual and temporal improvement. The two monks had no idea why the prior had left.

This day we spent the night there, and for procuration we received four pounds of Paris, in which amount they are held each year for procuration when we visit there. In addition, we are entitled to shelter and the use of utensils.

MARCH 4. We visited the priory of Neufmarché, where there were four monks from St-Evroult. They ate meat freely, although they had received no permission to do this either from us or from their abbot, but the prior said that his conscience was good in this matter. The parish priest belonged to their table. Alms are given on Sundays to all comers, and on other days to distressed persons. The prior had recovered and had lost again the twenty-five pounds annual income from Gonneville, which the count of Roumare had conferred upon the said priory, for the abbot of St-Evroult had for many years appropriated this revenue for his own use. This day we received procuration there. Total for procuration: nine pounds.

MARCH 5. We preached the Word of God, and visited the chapter at Gournay. We found only two canons residing there with the dean, to wit, Master John of Paris and Master Thomas. There was strife between the canons and the dean, because, as the canons said, the dean had no stall of his own in the choir, had no authority, nor ought to have, to discipline either them or the clerks-choral of the church; they did not regard him as the dean of the church, but thought him to be only the dean of La Chrétienté,[38] or a rural dean. The dean replied to the contrary. At the canons' request we appointed the abbot of Bellosane as their confessor.

This day we inquired about the condition of the leper hospital at Gournay, and we found a certain leprous cleric who wished to be included in the allotment of portions; they had no wheat for eating, no oats for sowing, and they owed fifteen pounds.

We visited the Hôtel-Dieu the same day, and, upon investigation, we found that when the brothers of the house, but who live outside it, came to Gournay, they did not wish to sleep at the hospital, but spent the night in the houses of the burgesses; we ordered the dean to compel them to spend the night at the hospital whenever they come to Gournay.

[38] See above, December 7, 1248, n. 72. La Chrétienté was the chief archdeaconry of the diocese of Rouen.

This very day we visited the nuns' priory at St-Aubin, after we had pronounced God's Word. Sixteen nuns were there. The prioress was away. At our last visitation we forbade them to receive or give the veil to anyone without our special mandate.[39] However, despite our command, they had received as a nun and bestowed the veil upon a certain girl, to wit, the daughter of Sir Robert, called Malvoisin, knight. When we asked them why they had presumed to do this, they replied that urgent necessity and poverty had so compelled them, and that in consideration of their consent, the father of this girl had given and endowed them with an annual income of one hundred shillings, and they had a letter to prove this. They added that they had done this without the consent or wish of the prioress. We, realizing and considering that they had not done this without the vice of greed and of depraved simony, subsequently ordered the dean of Bray, by letter patent, to admonish, as the law requires, the said nuns to remove this girl from their house before Ascension Day and, having taken away the veil from her, to return her to her father's house. Upon the prioress we enjoined and caused to have enjoined a penance which seemed expedient because she had allowed such a crime, and likewise upon the nuns for their boldness in undertaking such a matter. A certain parish priest was there at their expense, who celebrated Mass for them and who also served the local parish, where there were fifteen parishioners. They had no provisions, and were in debt.

This day we spent the night at Bellosane, at the expense of the abbey.

MARCH 6. At Beaubec, at the expense of the abbey. MARCH 7. At Foucarmont, at the expense of the abbey. Today Fulk of Sauchay, knight, made amends to us because he and his son, John, had gone hunting in our preserves at Aliermont, and had taken a hare. MARCH 8. We received procuration at Eu. Total for procuration: nine pounds, six shillings, four pence.

MARCH 9. Having propounded the Word of God, we visited there, finding . . . [lacuna in MS] canons. We gave orders that lay folk be kept away from the cloister and the choir; item, that they should try to arrange some other route so that lay folk would not proceed to the Blessed Sacrament through the choir. They did not have suitable vestments or church ornaments, nor did they possess books suitable for reading in the refectory; we advised them to procure a scribe. Thrice a week a general distribution of alms

[39] See entry for September 17, 1258.

is made to all comers, and thrice to clerics. About one hundred fifty pounds more was owed to them than they owed. They had sufficient wheat and oats to last until the new harvest, but they had not enough of wine. The canons were ill equipped with clothing; we ordered this corrected. If the revenue or offerings at the reliquary for this purpose were insufficient, it should be made up from the common fund; item, we ordered the keeper of the reliquary to provide the clothing needed by the canons more readily than had been his wont, and to do this without murmuring. Item, we ordered him to render an account at least once a year of all incomes, oblations, rents, or other moneys which came into his hands because of his office, in the presence of some brothers elected by the community, and to prepare an itemized list of expenses, for oil, for the lamps, or other things. Item, we gave orders that the chalices and all books should be openly displayed to the community once a year, and that a list of these, collectively and singly, be entered in some schedule or large book, as the majority of the community should decide; that the vestments be renewed, and kept clean. Item, that the charters of grants to the church be preserved, as we had ordered before,[40] in a coffer under four keys.

This day we spent the night at Aliermont, at our expense.

MARCH 10. We received procuration at Neufchâtel from Reginald of Aliermont, who was at that time lessee of the priory of Nogent. Total for procuration: twelve pounds, eight shillings, nine pence.

MARCH 11. We visited the hospital at Neufchâtel, where there were four priest-canons. We ordered Brother Hugh, called Dominus, to confess more frequently than had been his custom. We ordered the prior to make frequent inspection of the canons' coffers. They believed that they had enough provisions to last until the new harvest, and that more was owed to them than they owed. A little while ago they sold about four hundred pounds' worth from a certain wood; of this sum they spent, on the advice of the local dean, some two hundred pounds in buying lands and rents; the balance they had on hand, in cash and credits.

We received procuration this day at St-Victor-en-Caux. Total for procuration: eleven pounds, twenty-two pence.

MARCH 12. After preaching God's Word, we visited this abbey, where there were twenty monks. The abbot had sent one monk to dwell alone

[40] See entry for January 19, 1256/57.

at a certain place in the county of Eu; we ordered the abbot to send him another monk as companion, or to recall him to the cloister and have the place served by a secular priest. The alms quota had been diminished, nor was there any definite day for distribution; we ordered them to decree some regular day upon which a general distribution should be made. Item, we gave orders that Nicholas of Bourg-Baudouin, cleric, whom we had caused to be sent away from there once before[41] because of his ill fame, should no longer be permitted to live there, either at harvest time or at any other period. They owed about one hundred twenty pounds, but about twenty-four pounds more than this was owed to them. A certain secular cleric had carried the keys of the granary, and the monks complained about this; however, we decreed that one of the monks should have another key, so that neither could sell or measure the grain without the other.

On the authority of the late Pope, we imposed the following penance upon Girard of Montiavoul, Roger of Montiavoul, and Peter of Essarts, who killed a certain lay brother of Marcheroux: that, shoeless and with naked feet, clad only in trunk-hose, with halters tied to their necks, and bearing rods in their hands, they should walk in procession on Palm Sunday to the church of the place where they had committed the homicide; that, before the doors of this church they should be whipped by priests singing the Penitential Psalm, and should publicly admit their offense and declare the reason why such penance had been imposed upon them; that they should do the same at Gisors on the octave of next Easter; the same at Chaumont two weeks after Easter; at Frênes, on the Sunday following. Item, that they fast every Friday for ten years, and visit the shrine of St. James[42] before the feast of St. John the Baptist.

On this same day we spent the night at Déville.

MARCH 13. At Rouen. MARCH 14. With God's aid, we preached in the atrium of the cathedral, celebrated High Mass in this church, and slept at our manor.

MARCH 15. That is to say, the Monday after *Laetare Iherusalem*,[43] which day we assigned to Richard,[44] priest at Calleville, to appear before us, and purge himself with the seventh hand of priests[45] of the vice of incontinence

[41] See entry for September 4, 1258.
[42] St. James of Compostella in Spain.
[43] Fourth Sunday in Lent.
[44] See entry for February 3, above.
[45] See above, December 16, 1248, n. 70.

of which he was many times defamed. The said Richard came before us in person, saying that he was unable to find compurgators, and thus failed in his purgation. It must be known that, a little while before, he had been many times accused and also defamed of a certain woman, and had sworn and promised the local archdeacon that he would regard his church as resigned whenever we should so desire, if he should again be found ill famed and guilty in this matter, and could not purge himself canonically. But later, however, he relapsed, and, being defamed, we had required him to undergo a canonical purgation, in which he utterly failed, as he himself confessed before us, and so had twice failed to purge himself. He confessed that he had known this woman carnally. We assigned him the Saturday before Palm Sunday as the day on which he should come to Rouen, or wheresoever we might be in the vicinity, or to our official, should we be absent, to hear our verdict.

This day we spent the night at Déville.

MARCH 16. We received procuration at Beaulieu. Total for procuration: eight pounds, eleven shillings, five pence.

MARCH 17. After preaching a sermon, we visited the local priory. Ten canons were in residence, and there were eleven elsewhere. One, who belonged to their table, was dwelling alone at the manor of the lord of Préaux, and the other ten in priories. We ordered the prior to inspect the canons' coffers two or three times a year. There were four lay sisters there, and two lay brothers. Alms are given thrice a week to all comers. We enjoined the prior to have all sources of income, in gross and in detail, entered upon rolls and in registers. They owed five hundred pounds. They did not have sufficient provisions to last until the new harvest, and they believed that it would be necessary for them to spend one hundred pounds for wheat and oats before the harvest time. They had nine casks full of wine. Item, later, hearing that Brother Julian had said shameful and reviling things to his prior, and was disobedient and rebellious, we ordered him to receive three disciplines in chapter in the presence of the community, and to eat three times from the floor of the refectory; we reserved further penalty until such time as we see fit to impose it.

This day we spent the night at St-Laurent-en-Lyons and received procuration there. Total for procuration: ten pounds, two shillings, six pence.

MARCH 18. We visited the priory of St-Laurent-en-Lyons. Thirteen canons were in residence. They had six outside priories. All but one were priests.

They had six lay brothers. Two of the canons, led astray by a certain levity of spirit, had gone away and were vagabonding. We ordered the lay brothers to confess and receive Communion at least four times a year. Alms are given to all comers three times a week. They had two maid-servants. They owed fifty pounds. They had sufficient supplies to last until the new harvest. Item, one did not accuse another [in chapter]; we ordered this corrected, so that he who did not accuse another should receive the same penalty as the offender. Furthermore, Brother Richard of Eprèville performed a clandestine marriage between a certain man and his own daughter, whom he had begotten after he had become a monk and after receiving priestly orders; because of this, we enjoined the prior to recall this Richard to the cloister, and on our behalf to suspend him from celebrating Mass and and from performing any office to be held in his order. Item, that he be placed in grave fault for forty days and be not permitted to leave the cloister during the said penance, nor even when it had been completed. Item, one of the canons was suffering from epilepsy; we advised the prior not to allow him to celebrate Mass.

This day we spent the night at Mortemer-en-Lyons, at the expense of the abbey.

MARCH 19. At Frênes. MARCH 20. With God's aid, we conferred Holy Orders at Les Andelys, and slept at Frênes. MARCH 21. At Frênes. MARCH 22. At Frênes. Today Thomas, called Cousin, former rector of the church at Berville, voluntarily resigned this church into our hands. MARCH 23-24. At Frênes. MARCH 25. That is to say, the Annunciation of the Blessed Mary. We celebrated High Mass in the church at Les Andelys, preached there, and spent the night at Frênes. MARCH 26. We spent the night at Boos. MARCH 27. At Rouen. MARCH 28. Palm Sunday. We walked in the Procession, and preached in the atrium at St-Gildas. MARCH 29. We ate with the Dominicans. On this same day Richard, rector of the church at Calleville, voluntarily resigned this church into our hands.[46]

We spent this night at Déville.

MARCH 30. We visited the monastery of St-Ouen-de-Rouen. Sixty monks were there, of whom twenty were novices. Those who were dwelling in the priories ate meat at will; we enjoined the abbot to visit them and correct those who were delinquent. Item, we ordered the abbot to summon,

---

[46] See entry for March 15, above.

and to have summoned, some of the elder brothers of the community to hear the daily and individual audits drawn up by the kitchener, the monk in charge of the granary, the infirmarian, and the other officers of the house; that the full report be read out in the presence of the community from time to time, and that a copy of the audit be entered in writing. Item, we discovered that the abbot was given over to wine, was a drunkard, and grew loquacious after dining; that he made hasty promises, and was frivolous; we privately admonished him about all of these things and rebuked him. Item, we forbade that the parish churches to which the abbot and community had the right to collate should, in future, be conferred under the seal of the community alone, as had been the practice. Item, the infirmary was badly managed; we ordered this corrected. Item, we gave orders that guests and their retinues be better provided for with food than had been the case. Item, since we heard some more about the incontinence of the sacristan, we privately warned him to be careful. They owed about two thousand two hundred forty-five pounds, nine shillings, ten pence.

We dined this day at the Franciscan monastery and slept at Déville.

MARCH 31. We visited the priory of St-Lô [-de-Rouen]. Twenty canons were dwelling there; six of them were novices. We enjoined the prior and the subprior to punish those who did not accuse their companions [in chapter], with the penalty which should fall on the offender. Item, we ordered the prior to make frequent inspection of the canons' coffers. A general distribution of alms was never made; we ordered them to enact that alms be given so far as it were possible to do so. Item, we ordered that whenever the individual audits are drawn up in the presence of some of the brothers elected by the community, an official account should be prepared once a year, and the full report read out to the community. They owed one hundred eighty pounds; however, they had enough on hand, in debts, rents, or salable goods, to pay this off during the year. We received procuration there this day, but slept at our manor at Rouen. Total for procuration: ten pounds, two shillings.

APRIL 1-3. At Rouen

APRIL 4. With God's grace we celebrated Easter at Rouen. APRIL 5. At Martot, at the manor of the abbot of Bec. APRIL 6. At Pinterville. APRIL 7. At Brosville, at the expense of the bishop of Evreux. APRIL 8. At Condé [-sur-Iton] at the expense of this same bishop. APRIL 9. At Dreux. APRIL 10. At Chartres. APRIL 11. At Chartres. We were present at the reception of Peter de Mincy, by God's grace the [new] bishop.[1] APRIL 12. At Janville. APRIL 13. At Jargeau. APRIL 14. At Gien-sur-Loire. APRIL 15. At Villa Catuli [Villecien?], a manor belonging to the bishop of Nevers.

[No entries for April 16-17.]

APRIL 18. At St.-Pierre-le-Moûtier. APRIL 19. At Moulins-sur-Allier. APRIL 20. At St-Pourçain. APRIL 21. At Aigueperse. APRIL 22. We were bled at Mont-Ferrand, and spent the night at Clermont [-Ferrand] at the bishop's manor, though at our own expense. APRIL 23-24. At Clermont [-Ferrand]. APRIL 25. At Issoire. APRIL 26. At Vieille-Brioude-de-St-Julien. APRIL 27. At Notre-Dame-le-Puy, and we kissed the relics there. APRIL 28. At Luc. APRIL 29. At Genolhac. APRIL 30. At Alais. MAY 1. At Nîmes. MAY 2. We visited the shrine of St. Giles, and, with God's grace, we celebrated Mass on the altar beside which rests the body of the saint. We dined this day with the venerable Father, the archbishop of Narbonne, and spent the night at the abbey.

MAY 3. With God's aid, we celebrated Mass at Notre-Dame-de-Vauvert, and spent the night at Nîmes. MAY 4. At Bagnols. MAY 5. At Montelimart. MAY 6. At Valence. MAY 7. At Roussilon. MAY 8. At Lyons. MAY 9. At Lyons. We dined with the Franciscans. MAY 10. At L'Arbresle. MAY 11. At Charlieu. MAY 12. At La-Mote-St-Jean. MAY 13. At Mont-Ecosse. MAY 14. At Moulins-en-Gilbert. We celebrated the feast of the Ascension, celebrated Mass, and preached in the parish church. MAY 15. We visited the shrine of St-Leonard at Corbigny, and spent the night there. MAY 16. At Asquins-sous-Vézelay. MAY 17. At Reigny, at the manor of the bishop of

---

[1] Through the conciliatory mediation of Eudes, and in his presence, Peter de Mincy had been elected on February 12, 1259/60.

Auxerre. MAY 18. At Neuville-Royale, where we met the king. MAY 19. At the same, with the king. MAY 20. At Sens, with the king. MAY 21. At Montereau, with the king. MAY 22. At Melun, with the king. MAY 23. At Corbeil. MAY 24. Pentecost. We preached in the royal chapel at Corbeil, and, with God's grace, celebrated High Mass before the king, and dined with him. MAY 25. We dined with the king at Villeneuve-St-Georges and spent the night at Paris. MAY 26. At Meulan. MAY 27. At Sausseuse. MAY 28. At Frênes. MAY 29. With God's assistance we conferred Holy Orders at Les Andelys, and spent the night at Frênes. MAY 30. At Frênes. MAY 31. At Rouen, where we were received at the cathedral with a procession upon our return from our pilgrimage to St-Giles. The chapter and the burgesses dined with us. JUNE 1. With God's grace we celebrated the sacred summer synod. JUNE 2. We held a synod of deans and slept at Rouen. JUNE 3. At Frênes. JUNE 4. At Magny. JUNE 5. At Pontoise. JUNE 6-16. At Paris, because of the Parlement. JUNE 17. At St-Germain-en-Laye. JUNE 18. At Pontoise. JUNE 19. At Genainville. JUNE 20-22. At Frênes. JUNE 23. At Ermentrouville. JUNE 24. At the same. To wit, on the Nativity of St. John the Baptist. JUNE 25. At Auffay. JUNE 26. At Aliermont, where we were bled. JUNE 27-28. At Aliermont. JUNE 29. At Gamaches, on the feast of SS. Peter and Paul. We preached in the parish church and celebrated Mass. JUNE 30. At Rue-sur-Mer. JULY 1. At Montreuil. JULY 2. We had breakfast at Boulogne, and slept at Wissant. JULY 3. At Wissant. JULY 4. With God's help we crossed the sea, and we slept at Dover. JULY 5. At Canterbury, where, with God's grace, we celebrated Mass in St. Thomas' church. JULY 6. At Rochester. JULY 7-12. At London, on business of the King of the French.[2]

JULY 13. At London. Today we exchanged the fruits of Master Richard of Salmonville's prebend for those of the prebend which belonged to Dom Benedict, and we conferred upon Amaury of Montfort the prebend which Richard renounced.

JULY 14-19. At London. JULY 20. At Rochester. JULY 21. At Canterbury. JULY 22. At Dover, on the feast of St. Mary Magdalene. JULY 23. At Wissant. Before we left this place, we received the homage of the abbess

---

[2] Though contemporary documents do not give much information on the visit, Eudes came to England in connection with the difficulties which had arisen about the executions of the Treaty of Paris (1259). See Powicke, *The Thirteenth Century*, pp. 121-28, 161.

of Préaux, in the diocese of Lisieux, for that which she holds of us at Bouafles. JULY 24. At Boulogne. JULY 25. At Montreuil. JULY 26. At Abbeville. JULY 27. At Eu, at our own expense. JULY 28. We dined with the count of Eu at his manor, Le Parc, and spent the night at Dieppe. JULY 29. At Dieppe. JULY 30-31. At Aliermont. AUGUST 1. At St-Saëns, at our own expense. AUGUST 2. At Frênes. AUGUST 3. At Vernon. AUGUST 4. At Pontoise. AUGUST 5. At Boulogne, near St-Cloud, at the manor of the abbot of St-Victor. AUGUST 6-7. At the same. AUGUST 8. We had breakfast there, and spent the night at St-Germain-en-Laye. AUGUST 9. At the same. This day was born the Lady Agnes,[3] daughter of the queen. She was baptized by the bishop of Paris, and, God be praised, we were present at this baptism. AUGUST 10. At Meulan. AUGUST 11. At Vernon. AUGUST 12. At Frênes. AUGUST 13. At Gouy, at our own expense. AUGUST 14. At Rouen. We preached to the canons and clerks-choral in chapter, and we installed Amaury of Montfort as canon. AUGUST 15. By God's grace, we celebrated the feast of the Assumption of the Blessed Mary. AUGUST 16-17. At Déville. AUGUST 18-19. At Martot. AUGUST 20. At Frênes.

AUGUST 21. At St-Laurent-en-Lyons. We came there this day because the canons were at strife over the election of a prior, but by God's grace we restored concord among them, and with the common consent of all we provided them with a prior, to wit, their subprior.

AUGUST 22. At Frênes. AUGUST 23. At Martot. AUGUST 24. At Bec, at the expense of the house. AUGUST 25. At Arbec. Here we entered the diocese of Séez. AUGUST 26. We received procuration at St-Pierre-sur-Dives. Total for procuration: nine pounds, four shillings, ten pence.

AUGUST 27. We visited there, where were thirty-six monks. The cloister could not be kept because of workmen. They had not confessed very often; we ordered the abbot to persuade them to confess at least once a month, as is contained in the Statutes of Pope Gregory. They have an income of three thousand pounds; more was owed to them than they owed. A complaint was made in chapter that, at the urging and suggestion of some of the community, they had granted letters of the community together with letters of the abbot to some of their servants, providing annual pensions for them because of their valued service. We advised them to be careful in the future not to grant letters to anyone so readily. Item, we privately advised the ab-

---

[3] Agnes married Robert II, duke of Burgundy, in 1279 and died in 1327.

bot to inform some of the more trustworthy members of the community concerning the state of the house at more frequent intervals. We found other things to be satisfactory. Their bishop had visited them during the Lent just passed.

This day we spent the night at Pérriès and received procuration there. Total for procuration: seven pounds, five shillings, eight pence.

AUGUST 28. Although they were exempt, we warned the prior and the two monks of Marmoutier who were dwelling there to be very careful to abstain from doing things forbidden by the Rule and to conduct themselves in such a manner that we need not be compelled to undertake such action against them as the law requires because of any offense committed within our province [Rouen].

We received procuration at Trun from the proctor of the house at Coulances, which is subject to Jumièges. There are no monks in residence. Total for procuration: seven pounds, four shillings, eight pence.

AUGUST 29. We received procuration at Tournai on the feast of the Decollation of St. John the Baptist. With God's grace we celebrated Mass in the parish church and preached there. Total for procuration: seven pounds, fourteen shillings, ten pence.

AUGUST 30. We visited the priory at Tournai, where there were two monks from Croix-St-Leufroy. Because of his infirmity the prior did not celebrate Mass, and he was negligent about receiving Communion; we ordered him to receive Communion at least once a month. They did not observe the fasts of the Rule very well; we ordered them to observe these as the Statutes of the Rule require. They ate meat freely; we forbade them to eat meat save as the Rule permits. The monks sometimes ate at the houses of the knights of the village, and the knights with their wives ate with the monks; we ordered them to avoid doing this as much as they could. They have an income of eighty pounds; they owed thirty pounds.

We received procuration this day at Planches, where there were two monks from St-Père-de-Chartres. Because of his advanced age the prior rarely celebrated Mass. They had no copy of the Rule, they confessed too infrequently; they ate meat and did not observe the fasts of the Rule; we enjoined them to correct all these things in accordance with the Rule, and to observe them henceforth. Lay folk, both men and women, frequently ate with them. The prior's companion was not a priest. They have an income of one hundred forty pounds; they owed forty pounds. The prior, because of his advanced age, and his companion, Brother Warren, because of his unseemly conduct, should have been removed. Total for procuration: seven pounds, eight shillings, eight pence.

AUGUST 31. We spent the night at La Trappe, a Cistercian house, at their expense.

SEPTEMBER 1. We visited at Mortagne. As yet there was no certain number of canons there; however, we found that there were about one hundred, and that there were officers there, to wit, a dean, a chancellor, a provost, and a precentor, who are compelled to maintain residence; twenty-one of them were chaplains, all of them are bound to personal residence, and they receive "commons", or daily distributions. There were statutory penalties against the negligent. The disciplining of the clerks-choral is in the hands of the dean. At both day and night Offices they follow the Uses used at Chartres for entering the choir, and performing other liturgical Uses. The parish priest has the cure of the canons' souls. Each chaplain is obliged to have his own clerk. One of the chaplains, who is held to celebrate morning Mass every day, felt that he was greatly burdened, and on this account he did not attend the Hours very often, nor did he frequent the choir; we told him to ask for the assistence of his associates in bearing this burden. Some of them were ill famed of incontinence, but the bishop had disciplined their excesses, and the ill fame had died out for some little time now. Colin of Buat, a very young canon, because of his lasciviousness, was somewhat ill famed of incontinence; he was also accused of getting into quarrels and of going out at night. Scandal had arisen because of his conduct. Furthermore, it should be noted that, at the instance of a certain man, we had Luke, chaplain at All Saints, summoned before us to answer to this man for a horse which he had injured, although it was in good condition when he took it from the man; an agreement was reached between them when they appeared, according to law, before Master John of Neuilly-en-Thelle, our associate, who was acting for us. They agreed to submit their case to the archdeacon of Corbonne and two others. In this manner we exercised jurisdiction there.

This day we spent the night at nearby St-Giles, at the expense of the chapter. Total for procuration: nine pounds, six shillings.

SEPTEMBER 2. We spent the night at Ste-Gauburge, and for procuration we received from the prior of the place forty shillings which he owes us in the name of procuration. He cannot refuse us shelter, and we cannot demand

anything more from them, nor are they held for anything more to us unless
it be by special favor. However, seeing that by the tenor of the agreement
which is entered on folio 61[4] we are entitled to visit this place every three
years, we warned Henry of Cergy, then prior of the said place, to receive
us for visitation; this he absolutely refused to do, stating that they had
privileges of exemption. We harmoniously agreed to discuss this matter at
St. Denis with their abbot on the day following the feast of St. Denis, at
which time the written agreement should also be read.

SEPTEMBER 3. We visited the priory of Dame-Marie, which is a cell of
Jumièges. Two monks were there. Alms ought to be dispensed three times
a week. They are obliged to remit all of their surplus provisions to their
abbot, and this year they had given him sixty pounds. We found everything else, as to both spiritual and temporal things, to be in good condition.
We received procuration there on that day. Total for procuration: seven
pounds, three shillings.

SEPTEMBER 4. We received procuration at St-Martin-de-Bellême, where
there were two monks from Marmoutier. Total for procuration: seven
pounds, five shillings, nine pence.

SEPTEMBER 5. We visited the priory at Alençon, where were three monks
from Lonlay, in the diocese of Le Mans; two of them were priests, the
other an acolyte, who wore a linen shirt. They did not have written copies
either of the Rule or of the Statutes of Pope Gregory; we ordered them to
seek and procure these and to observe what is contained therein as completely as they could. They ate meat freely, and they did not observe the
fasts of the Rule; we ordered this corrected. We forbade the prior to
permit his companions to run about the town, or to permit women to dine
in the priory or even to converse there. They owed twenty-five pounds.
We received procuration there this day. Total for procuration: seven pounds,
three shillings.

SEPTEMBER 6. We spent the night at the bishop's palace, at his expense.
We did not reckon our expenses.

SEPTEMBER 7. We visited the community at Séez, in the presence of the
bishop. Thirty-three canons were there. Those who were not priests received
Communion only once a year and confessed but three times yearly. We
enjoined the bishop and the prior to take this under advisement and to pass
statutes requiring more frequent confession and Communion. Lay folk con-

---

[4] See entry for July 8, 1250.

versed with the canons in the cloister about their business deals and trans-actions: we gave orders that lay folk be kept out of the cloister and that silence be observed there. The lectern in the refectory was in need of repair. The canons had coffers; we ordered the prior to inspect these frequently in order to remove any property. The archdeacons had not yet drawn up their accounts with the prior. A general distribution of alms should be made once a week. More was owed to them than they owed, and they had a year's rent on hand. The prior was afflicted with a quartan ague, which had been bothering him for two years, so that he was rarely able to celebrate Mass. Dom Hugh became drunk very easily and had a weak head for wine. We enjoined the bishop to be very diligent in seeing that all property was taken away from them. Robert of Logy was a man of property and sold his old pelisses and tunics which he did not turn in when he received new ones. The canons complained that the prior ate, and was still in the habit of eating, outside of the regular hours, to wit, before Mass and after Com-pline; we discovered that he did this because of his infirmity and by reason of necessity, but we ordered him to refrain from doing this so far as he was able. There was dissension among them at being obliged to sell their old clothes in order to buy more suitable garments. Some of them had but one pelisse and one tunic every two years; we advised the prior to provide them all with white super-tunics, if they wished them. We received procuration there that day, but we did not compute.

SEPTEMBER 8. We visited St. Martin's abbey at Séez, after first preaching in chapter, God aiding us. Thirty monks were there. They have seven priories in France.[5] One monk was dwelling alone in one of them; we gave orders that he be recalled to the cloister or that a companion be sent to him, as the resources of the priory should dictate. All but three of the monks were priests. A general distribution of alms is made once a week. They ate meat in all of the priories. They owed one thousand pounds, but they had one hundred marks in ready money on hand. We found every-thing else to be in good condition.

This day, that is to say, the Nativity of the Blessed Mary, we celebrated High Mass in pontificals, with God's grace, and received procuration there. Total for procuration: fifteen pounds, ten shillings, eight pence.

SEPTEMBER 9. We visited the abbey of nuns at Almenèches, after we

---

[5] I.e., outside Normandy.

had, with God's grace, expounded His Word. Forty-two nuns were there. We gave orders that in chapter the Rule should frequently be read in Latin and explained in French. They were in the habit of confessing to whatsoever traveling brother they pleased; we told the bishop, who was present with us at this visitation, to appoint some definite confessors from the Franciscan or other Order as he should deem expedient. The refectory often remained deserted, that is to say, they did not eat there as a body, but ate meat here and there in the rooms, in sociable groups of twos and threes. Several of them had their own rooms; they also had five maid-servants. We ordered the abbess to be careful in granting the nuns permission to go out, to wit, that she should impose a definite time for their return. Each one received one loaf of bread a day, and whenever anything was left over, they kept it. We gave orders that alms be given; we advised them to eat and live in common, and to give up their individual rooms. Because of their poverty they did not observe the Rule. They owed five hundred pounds. Since we could not spare the time to break our journey and undertake a reformation of their state, which they needed, we told the bishop to consult and treat with the abbess and, after studying the ordinance which G.[6] of good memory, former bishop of Séez, had drawn up for them as a way of life, to issue such orders as he should deem both useful and becoming for the monastery and favorable to the salvation of the nuns, insisting so far as possible upon an observance of the Rule. This day the bishop of Séez and we dined there, at the nuns' expense. Although they are obligated to us for full procuration, because of their poverty we overlooked this, being content on this occasion with the aforementioned dinner.

On the same day we spent the night at the abbey of Silli[-en-Gouffern], a Premonstratensian house, at their expense.

SEPTEMBER 10. We visited at Briouze, where were three monks from [St-Florent-lès-] Saumur. They did not observe the Rule, nor did they have a written copy of it. They did not sleep together in one place, because the house was too small. They ate meat freely and fasted rarely, if at all. Oliver, the prior's associate, frequently went hunting, going after partridges with net and falcon, and he had a certain contraption in which the falcons were caged; these things much displeased us, partly because he did them publicly and partly because of the scandal. The prior had two Breton squires and his own sister with him, and, so far as we could see, they were not of any service

---

[6] Geoffrey de Maiet (1240-58).

either to him or to the house. The prior's two associates were improperly clothed; we ordered the prior to correct this. They owed about thirty pounds We received procuration there this day. Total for procuration: six pounds, five shillings.

SEPTEMBER 11. We spent the night at St-André-en-Gouffern, a Cistercian house. We ate in the refectory with the community. SEPTEMBER 12. We celebrated the parish Mass, preached, and with God's grace, conferred the Sacrament of Confirmation at Necy.

This day we came in person to the priory of Brieux and visited it. Two monks from St-Martin-de-Séez were there. The prior's companion was tonsured only as a clerk and could not be promoted because of his deficiency in letters. They ate meat, did not observe the fasts, and had no written copy of the Rule. They had an income of not over sixty pounds, and since the house could not accommodate us, we spent this night at the royal castle at Falaise. Although the prior was obligated to us for full procuration, we released him this time, because of the poverty of the priory, for one hundred shillings of Tours.

SEPTEMBER 13. We spent the night at St-Jean-de-Falaise, which is a Premonstratensian abbey, at the expense of the abbey. There were with us there this day, our venerable brothers, F[ulk] the bishop of Lisieux, R[ichard], the bishop of Avranches, J[ohn], the bishop of Coutances, and Thomas, bishop of Séez. They consulted with us about the matter of those who had taken the Cross,[7] about married clergy, and several other things.

SEPTEMBER 14. We spent the night at Canapville, at the manor of the bishop of Lisieux, and at his expense. SEPTEMBER 15. At Bec, at the expense of the monastery. SEPTEMBER 16-17. At Martot. SEPTEMBER 18. With God's grace we conferred Holy Orders in the royal chapel of the castle at Pont-de-l'Arche, and spent the night at Martot. SEPTEMBER 19. We spent the night at Frênes, and we had as our guest our venerable brother Ralph, by God's grace bishop of Evreux. SEPTEMBER 20. At Vernon.

SEPTEMBER 21. We spent the night at Meulan, to wit, on the feast of St. Matthew the Apostle and Evangelist. On this day while we were riding

---

[7] *Super negotio crucesignatorum* may well indicate a discussion of those who had taken the crusaders' vow and had purchased their release with money, much to the scandal of many. Or it refer to the forthcoming papal levy for the crusades. A cursory examination of Vol. I of the *Calendar of Papal Registers* (ed. W. H. Bliss. London, 1894) reveals a large number of men in England who had vowed to go on this crusade, redeeming their vow for ready cash.

between Mantes and Juziers, we came upon some ploughs being employed in working and turning the ground; we had the horses of the ploughs led away to Meulan, because they [the owners] had thus irreverently presumed to labor on the feast of so great a Saint. It should be known that John, called Poilecoc, of Mantes, and John, called Li Cointes, of Issou, in the deanery of Magny, who owned the said horses, came to us and, pledging their faith, promised to obey our will in this matter. Matthew of Marche, provost of Meulan, offered himself as surety for John, [called], le Cointe [*sic*], and Laurence, called Galon, of Meulan did likewise for John [called] Poilecoc; both pledged their faith and promised that they would make proper amends to us if the said John and John would nor or could not satisfy us.

SEPTEMBER 22-28. At Paris. SEPTEMBER 29. We ate at the convent of the Franciscans. SEPTEMBER 30. With God's grace we celebrated High Mass at the royal chapel, in honor of the feast of the Relics, and dined with the king. OCTOBER 1. At St-Denis-l'Estrée. OCTOBER 2. At Asnières, with the lord king.

OCTOBER 3. In the company of the king, our venerable brother the bishop of Evreux, and with many nobles and others being present, we carried in procession the bones of a virgin—to wit, one of the eleven thousand virgins,[8] named Barge—from Asnières to the abbey at Royaumont, where we were met with great veneration and with a procession by the abbot of Clairvaux and the abbot and community of Royaumont. The bishop of Beauvais was also present. These [those at Royaumont] received the bones of the virgin, which were encased in a reliquary, with great honor. The abbot of Clairvaix preached a sermon. With God's grace we celebrated High Mass in the said monastery.

This day with God's grace, we spent the night at Chambly with the Masters of the Exchequer, and at the king's expense.

OCTOBER 4. At Gisors, at the expense of the king. OCTOBER 5. At Frênes, at our own expense. OCTOBER 6. At Déville. OCTOBER 7-9. We sat as one of the Masters of the Exchequer, at Rouen, and spent the nights at Déville. OCTOBER 10. We spent this night at our manor at Rouen. OCTOBER 11. At Bec-Hellouin with the other Masters of the Exchequer, at

---

[8] The martyrdom of the eleven thousand virgins of Cologne is commemorated on October 21. Nothing certain is known of them. The Roman Martyrology simply says, "At Cologne, the birthday of SS. Ursula and her companions, martyrs."

the king's expense. OCTOBER 12. At Lisieux with them. OCTOBER 13. At Caen. OCTOBER 14-17. We sat in the Exchequer at Caen, with the other Masters. OCTOBER 18. At Lisieux, with the Masters of the Exchequer. OCTOBER 19. We received procuration at Corneville.

OCTOBER 20. We visited there. Ten canons, including the abbot, were in residence; and ten were outside, and some of these had been given the cure of souls, others had not; we ordered the abbot that canons staying in parishes should have the cure of souls and that he should see to this before the next synod. Two canons were dwelling alone in two outside priories. One did not accuse another [in chapter]. We gave orders that those who were not priests should receive Communion at least once a month. Item, we ordered the abbot to inspect the canons' coffers frequently in order that he might take away any property. The abbot was a new one, and did not know very much about the state of the house as yet; however, he told us that they owed one hundred forty pounds. They had, as he thought, enough provisions to last a year. The buildings needed roofing repairs, and even the roofs of the monastery were leaking in an unbecoming way.

OCTOBER 21. At Couronne. OCTOBER 22. At Rouen, this being the vigil of St. Romain. OCTOBER 23. With God's grace we celebrated the feast of St. Romain. OCTOBER 24. With God's help we preached in the cathedral of Rouen, and slept at Frênes. OCTOBER 25. At Chaumont. OCTOBER 26. Although we had purposed to celebrate the sacred synod there, with God's assistance, we were obliged to alter our plans, for the king informed us in writing that as soon as we received his letter we should hasten to him at Creil, where he was lying ill. Not daring to neglect this request, we left the greater part of our retinue behind at Chaumont, as well as our brother in Christ, Brother Nicholas Montebourg, who, by God's grace, preached for us in the synod. We hastened on to the king at Creil this same day, where we spent the night with a few of our staff, and without our equipment, for our companions and brothers, along with the rest of our staff, had spent the night at Chambly.

OCTOBER 27. We spent the night, all our staff being with us, at Paris. OCTOBER 28-30. At Paris. OCTOBER 31. At Senlis. NOVEMBER 1. On this feast of All Saints, we celebrated High Mass, with God's help, at the Franciscan monastery, and the king was ill there. NOVEMBER 2. At Compiègne. NOVEMBER 3. Noyon. NOVEMBER 4. At Neuville-Royale. NOVEMBER 5. With the bishop of Beauvais at his manor at Beauvais, and at his expense.

NOVEMBER 6. We spent the night at Gisors at the priory of St-Ouen, and from the prior we received seven pounds of Tours, in which sum the prior is held to us annually, whensoever we should turn aside to this place once a year.

NOVEMBER 7. At Frênes. NOVEMBER 8. At Rouen. NOVEMBER 9. With God's grace we celebrated the sacred synod at Rouen. NOVEMBER 10. We held the synod of deans in the chamber of our associates. This day the chaplain of the leper hospital of Beaumont voluntarily resigned his office.

On the same day we spent the night at Ste-Catherine, at our expense.

NOVEMBER 11. We received procuration from the lessee of the house at Quévreville, at Quévreville. Total for procuration: ten pounds, five shillings.

NOVEMBER 12. We preached in the chapter at Mont-Deux-Amants, and visited there. They have four houses outside, in which there are canons. Fourteen canons were in the priory; all were priests. They left the cloister more often and more readily than they should do. One did not accuse another [in chapter]; we issued orders that he who did not report a delinquent should incur the same penalty as the delinquent. Alms are given daily to all comers. They complained that the prior did not collect the income of the house very well; we ordered the prior to be more solicitous than he had been about procuring and collecting the rents, and that he should provide the canons with better clothing. They owed two hundred pounds, and they did not have enough oats to last until the new harvest. Total for procuration: nine pounds.

NOVEMBER 13. We received procuration at Vesly, where are two monks from Marmoutier. Total for procuration: seven pounds, fifteen shillings. NOVEMBER 14. We received procuration at Parnes. This day with God's grace we preached and conferred the Sacrament of Confirmation there. Total for procuration: seven pounds, ten shillings.

NOVEMBER 15. We visited the priory at Parnes, where there were four monks from St-Evroult. We ordered the junior monk to confess and receive Communion once a month. They ate meat when there was no need and used feather beds. They did not observe the fasts of the Rule very well. Alms are given thrice.[9] They owed fifty pounds. They had a supply of provisions sufficient for one year.

---

[9] Again, Eudes does not specify whether alms were given three times weekly or daily.

NOVEMBER 16. At St-Martin-de-Pontoise, at our own expense. NOVEMBER 17. At Paris, because of the Parlement. NOVEMBER 18. At Paris. Today we conferred the church at Magneville upon Master Gervaise, our clerk. NOVEMBER 19-20. At Paris, because of the Parlement.

NOVEMBER 21. At Paris. Today Ralph, rector of St. Blaise's church at Le Parc, resigned his church into the hands of Brother Walter of Manières, our chaplain, who received authority from us to accept this. Present were: Masters John of Manières and Morel, rector at Us; and John of Morgneval, our clerk.

NOVEMBER 22-23. At Paris. NOVEMBER 24. At Meulan. NOVEMBER 25. At Vernon. NOVEMBER 26. At Frênes. NOVEMBER 27. At Rouen. NOVEMBER 28. To wit, on Advent. With God's grace we preached in the cathedral at Rouen and celebrated High Mass.

NOVEMBER 29. At Déville. It should be noted that Walter, priest at Bray-sous-Baudemont, brought before the synod of the Fench Vexin because he had been many times defamed of incontinence and of many other excesses or crimes, confessed all and each of the following in the presence of Archdeacon Stephen, Master John of Neuilly-en-Thelle, and Brother Adam Rigaud, who stood as our representatives there. He confessed that he had been defamed of one of his parishioners whom he had already abjured and he admitted that this ill fame was supported by truth. Item, he confessed that he was defamed of having constructed a certain wax figure for purposes of witchcraft, but on oath he said that he knew nothing about this except on hearsay from a certain woman who had conceived and borne him a child and who had two other children. Item, he admitted being the father of these children. Item, he admitted that he was defamed of the shame of usury and of shady transactions. Item, he admitted coition with a certain woman named Cretelot. Item, he admitted intercourse with another woman within the past fortnight. Item, he admitted having torn the supertunic of a certain woman who, he said, was a prostitute and with whom he had cohabited several times. Item, he admitted that he went to the assizes at Gisors upon citation by the bailiff. Item, he admitted that he led the dancing at the marriage of a certain prostitute whose marriage he had himself performed, and whom he, together with some of the neighboring priests, had known at night, each of whom was acting with evil intent. The said Walter, priest, was peremptorily and personally cited to appear before us on a definite date, to wit, the day after Advent, at Rouen or wherever we should be in that vicinity, to reply to these charges. He did appear before us at Déville. He did not wish to resign his church when we wished him to do so, wherefore we declared him deprived of the church as follows:

In the name of the Father, and of the Son, and of the Holy Ghost, Amen. We, Brother Eudes, by God's permission the unworthy bishop of the diocese of Rouen, deprive you, Walter, rector of the church of Bray-sous-Baudemont, of that same church, in that you are publicly known for the crime of incontinence as is abundantly clear from your confession made according to due process of law. Though admonished many times, you have remained incorrigible. We deprive you of the faculties of celebrating Mass in our diocese.

Present at this depriviation were: Masters William of Denestanville, canon of Bayeux, and John of Neuilly-en-Thelle, canon of Rouen; Brothers Peter Hurtet and Harduin of the Franciscans; Willard, prior of Salle-aux-Puelles; and John of Morgneval, clerk.

NOVEMBER 30. William, priest at La Fontaine, whom we had considered contumacious because he did not wish to appear before us on the preceding day although he had been cited, put in his appearance. We assigned him the day on which the next ordinations were to be conferred, to hear our will on the matter.

We received procuration this day at St-Saëns. Total for procuration: seven pounds, seventeen shillings.

DECEMBER 1. We visited the priory at St-Saëns, where there were three monks with the prior; all were priests. They said that they ate meat in accordance with the Statute of the Rule. More is owed to them than they owe and they have a sufficiency of provisions. Other things were in a satisfactorily good condition.

This day we also visited the nuns at St-Saëns. There were fourteen nuns, and two were at Ste-Austreberte; but since the house at Ste-Austreberte had but a very slim revenue and could not support two nuns so that they could live there comfortably and becomingly, we ordered the prioress to recall them, and forbade her to send any others there, because of the dangers involved. We forbade them to receive or give the veil to anyone without our special permission. We decreed and ordered that they abandon their custom of giving a portion of bread to each, but that the cellaress should provide a sufficient amount of bread for them all and should give it to them in common. We expressly forbade anyone to go out alone. We ordered them to send away all the secular little girls, except the sister of William of Pommeraie, whom we were quite willing they should receive if it seemed expedient to them and not burdensome to the house. They owed about three hundred fifty pounds; they had an income of four hundred fifty pounds. Then the prioress returned her seal to us, and withdrew from all functions because of her infirmity. We released her from office and gave the nuns permission to elect another. Shortly afterwards they elected Joan of Morcent, whom they presented to us, and whom we, after investigating the merits of the election and of the elected one, confirmed.

We received procuration at Bures. Total for procuration: eight pounds, six shillings.[10]

DECEMBER 2. We visited the priory at Bures, where there were two monks from Pré. They ate meat when there was no need, and did not observe the fasts of the Rule very well, but they said this was because of the large staff which they had there, and because of their various occupations. We ordered them to speak with their abbot about this. Alms are given thrice a week to all comers.

This day we spent the night at Aliermont.

DECEMBER 3. At Aliermont. DECEMBER 4. At the same. This day we received procuration from the lessee of the estate at Wanchy. Total for procuration: seven pounds, nineteen shillings, five pence. DECEMBER 5. At the same. DECEMBER 6. To wit, on the feast of St. Nicholas. With God's grace we celebrated High Mass in pontificals at St. Nicholas' church, and preached there. DECEMBER 7. At the same. DECEMBER 8. To wit, the Conception of the Blessed Virgin Mary. We celebrated Mass in pontificals, and preached in St. Mary's parish church at Aliermont. DECEMBER 9. At the same. DECEMBER 10. We received procuration from the lessee of the priory of Mortemer-sur-Eaulne. Total for procuration: ten pounds, nineteen shillings, six pence. DECEMBER 11. We visited the said priory, where there were two monks from Lewes. Master Eudes of St-Denis holds the priory for life. DECEMBER 12. At Aumale, at our own expense. DECEMBER 13. After we had, with God's grace, first preached a sermon in chapter, we visited the abbey of Aumale. There were seventeen monks in residence and three

---

[1] Eudes' chronology is off here in that he has thirty-two days for December. If the separate entry, "At Rouen," for IX Kalends January (December 25) is dropped, the chronology comes out right. The scribe began the month of December with V nones rather than IV nones, the latter being correct.

in England. They had no prior. All but four were priests. They were not scrupulous about turning in their old clothes when they were given new ones. We ordered the abbot to inspect the monks' coffers frequently to be sure that they had no property. A general distribution of alms was made once a week; it should be made three times. We ordered that their sources of income be written out in a register and read out frequently to the community in chapter. They owed five hundred fifty pounds, mostly to the Lombards. By a letter binding on the convent they are obligated in three hundred pounds for . . . [*lacuna in MS*], the count of Aumale, in England.[11] As a result of all this we believed that the abbot became, according to the Decretal,[12] suspended according to law from the administration of temporalities and spiritualities. Since the abbey had been burdened by him, we enjoined him to free his abbey from this obligation. We received procuration there this day. Total for procuration: seven pounds, nineteen shillings.

DECEMBER 14-15. At Aliermont. DECEMBER 16. We received procuration at Longueville. DECEMBER 17. We visited the priory at Auffay, where there were five monks from St-Evroult with the prior; all were priests. They ate meat twice a week. They owed about one hundred pounds, and they had sufficient supplies to last until the new [harvest]. Other things we found to be in good condition. We received procuration there this day. Total for procuration: nine pounds, fifteen shillings.

DECEMBER 18. At Déville. DECEMBER 19. With God's aid we conferred Holy Orders at the monastery of the Franciscans, dined there with them, and spent the night at our manor at Rouen. DECEMBER 20. With God's grace we preached in the cathedral and spent the night at our manor. DECEMBER 21. We dined at Rouen with the Dominicans and spent the night at Déville. DECEMBER 22-23. At Déville. DECEMBER 24. We made our O[13] and spent the night at our manor at Rouen. DECEMBER 25. With God's aid we celebrated the feast of the Nativity at Rouen. DECEMBER 26. At Déville. DECEMBER 27-28. At Frênes. DECEMBER 29–JANUARY 1. At Martot. JANUARY 2. We received procuration at the abbey of Ste-Catherine.

---

[11] Baldwin de Bethume sided with John against Philip Augustus and was deprived of the title of count of Aumale. Residing in England, Baldwin used the title, as did his descendants. Joan of Dammartin, daughter of Ralph of Dammartin and wife of Ferdinand, king of Castille, enjoyed in France the revenues of Aumale.

[12] *Corp. jur. can., Decretal. Greg. IX.* Lib. III. Tit. 24. cap. 1-4.

[13] See above, December 23, 1250, n. 135.

Total for procuration: ten pounds, sixteen shillings, four pence.

JANUARY 3. With God's grace we first expounded His Word in chapter and visited. Twenty-five monks were there. The abbot was very ill and could not attend chapter. There was no porter at the entrance to the cloister. We ordered the bailiff to enter the sources of income in some schedule or register. Because of the abbot's absence we could not obtain any definite information about the state of the house. This day we spent the night at St-Georges, at our expense.

JANUARY 4. We visited there, where there were twenty-three monks. We ordered the abbot to see that confessions were made frequently. It was not customary for one to accuse another [in chapter]; we enjoined the abbot to correct this. Those who were bled were not well cared for. Only the tenth part of the bread cooked at the house was given in alms. More is owed to them than they owe, and they have plenty of provisions. We received procuration there this day. Total for procuration: eight pounds, eleven shillings.

JANUARY 5. We spent the night at Jumièges, at our expense.

JANUARY 6. That is to say, Epiphany. With God's grace we celebrated the high conventual Mass. Afterwards, we preached a sermon in chapter and then visited the monks. There were fifty-two; there were eight novices there. They did not observe the fasts of the Rule very well in the priories. About as much was owed to them as they owed, and they had many supplies. Other things were in good condition, except that the abbot refused to return the monks to Guisenières. We received procuration there this day. They did not compute expenses.

JANUARY 7. We visited at St-Wandrille, where there were forty monks. One did not accuse another [in chapter]. All but eleven were priests. Alms are given daily to all comers. They owed about three hundred pounds. They had enough provisions to last out the year. Every thing else we found to be in good condition. We received procuration there this day; they were unwilling to compute.

JANUARY 8. We spent the night at Le Valasse, a Cistercian house, at the expense of the monks. JANUARY 9. With God's grace we preached and conferred the Sacrament of Confirmation at the parish church at Tancarville, and spent the night at the chamberlain's house, and at his expense. JANUARY 10. We received procuration at Graville. Total for procuration: eight pounds, nine shillings, five pence.

JANUARY 11. After preaching in chapter, we visited there. Thirteen canons were in residence; all were priests except the novices who were then there. One did not accuse another [in chapter]; we gave orders that he who did not accuse a delinquent should incur the same penalty as befell the delinquent. Alms are given three times a week to all comers. They owed forty-six pounds. Brother Ralph of Ansetot secretly removed some napkins without the prior's permission; he hid them for many days and denied that he had done so. However, he admitted his offense to us in chapter and then asked us to impose penance upon him. We ordered the prior to punish him as a possessor of property, according to the Rule of his Order, and to do this before the next Purification. Item, since Thomas of Bec and Thomas of St-Sauveur had not yet performed penance and had not been disciplined for the charge of ill-fame for which they had been judged many years ago, we ordered the prior to impose such a penalty upon them, that they and others would dread to be delinquent in the future.

This day we spent the night at Montivilliers, at the expense of the monastery.

JANUARY 12. We entered the chapter of the nuns of Montivilliers and, with God's aid, we preached. We had come to them again as we had done at our other visitation,[14] namely, to visit them in head and members; but they were unwilling to admit us for this purpose, saying that they were exempt and that we could not visit anything there, except the abbess. However, after much altercation, to remove all cause of contention they voluntarily agreed to submit to our will, as is more fully contained in the following letter which they gave to us, sealed with the seal of the abbess, for that is the one they use:

To all who may see these presents, the abbey of nuns of the monastery of Montivilliers, greeting in the Lord. Know you that contention arose between the Reverend Father Eudes, by God's grace archbishop of Rouen, on the one hand, and us, on the other, turning on the right of [general] visitation which the said father claimed by common law to have with respect to us. This we absolutely denied to the said Father, stating that we were wholly exempt from his jurisdiction. However, we submitted to his will to the extent that we will be held to strict observance of such ordinances as the said father, considering those things which should be considered, should, in God's interest, establish, saving the right of our liberty and of our abbey in all other matters in which it

[14] See entry for January 7, 1259/60.

should be saved. In testimony whereof Alicia, our abbess, has affixed her seal to the present, for hers is the seal we use. Given on the Monday after the Resurrection, in the year of our Lord 1260.

We, however, read aloud the following written statement to them in attendance upon us in full chapter after inspecting certain privileges, particularly a certain definitive sentence of Pope Innocent III,[15] in which he declared that the abbey of Montivilliers was subject to the archbishop of Rouen, in the same way as other monasteries were subject to their diocesan bishops, saving certain articles which he [Innocent] defined in another decree and which pertain to certain churches and the collations thereof, the obedience of their clerics, the assizes of clerics or laymen, and things of that sort:[16]

In the name of the Father, and of the Son, and of the Holy Ghost, Amen. When a dispute arose between us, on the one hand, and the abbey of Montivilliers, on the other, over the right of visitation, which we declared we possessed with respect to the said abbey and which the said abbey wholly denied, the said abbey submitted to our will as is more fully contained in their letter. And we, after hearing and considering whatever might and should influence us, especially the definitive sentence of Pope Innocent III, promulgated about this matter, declared that the full right of visitation over the said nuns belonged to us in the name of our diocese of Rouen.

We ordered them all, by virtue of their oath of obedience, to reply truthfully to whatsoever questions we should ask of them. We inquired how many nuns were there; they said that there were fifty-nine, and that the statutory number was sixty. Four of them were at St. Paul's near Rouen; we ordered the abbess to be diligent in visiting them. We ordered them to make arrangements for a better ringing for the Hours, so that they would not say their Hours, Masses, and Compline with too great haste or precipitancy, and that there should be light during the entire performance of the Office. They should receive Communion once a month. They had coffers equipped with keys; we ordered the abbess to remove the keys, and

---

[15] Such a document does not seem to be mentioned in Potthast, *Regesta*, I, 1-468, which contains a register of documents emanating from the Roman Curia during the pontificate of Innocent III.

[16] Potthast, *Regesta*, I, 434 (4979). Among other grants to the abbess by Innocent, she was given the right to inspect and visit churches subject to Montivilliers, and the right to compel the clerics therein to take Holy Orders.

to make frequent inspection of the coffers. All were clothed in common; we ordered them to turn in their old garments upon the receipt of new ones. The alms supply had been diminished because the nuns gave to the maidservants and other designated persons the remnants of their portions, that is to say, of their bread, wine, and cooked food, all of which should be given away as alms. We ordered the abbess not to permit the continuance of this practice, and to be heedful and diligent in this matter. Item, at the feasts of St. John, St. Stephen, and the Holy Innocents they conducted themselves with too much hilarity and sang scurrilous songs such as burlesques, canticles, and cantatas; we ordered them to behave more decorously and with more devotion in the future. They had maidservants in common. They did not observe the fasts of the Rule. Item, those who ate twice a day ate so late that they could not enter the dormitory at an hour proper to those who fasted; we ordered this corrected; item, [we ordered] that all the healthy ones should eat together. We forbade them to eat in the refectory in little groups or cliques, but to take their seats at table haphazardly, and to eat the same food. Alms were given three times a week, and the abbess was obliged by tradition to feed thirteen poor people every day. Item, we ordered the abbess to attend chapter more often and to adhere to community life in better fashion than had been her wont; that she should give ginger to the nuns, as she used to do. Item, we ordered the cantress to procure an ordinal of Hours at the expense of the abbess. Item, we ordered the abbess to provide the nuns with pelisses, cloth for their needs, and other things, with more regularity than she had been doing. Item, that she behave more courteously and affably towards the friends of the nuns, especially in the matter of admitting them. They owed Thomas, called The Cleric, some two hundred sixty pounds, and one hundred forty pounds in another debt. They had supplies in plenty. About four hundred pounds was owed to them. We received procuration there this day. Total for procuration: nine pounds, seven shillings, two pence.

JANUARY 13. We spent the night at Valmont, at our expense.

JANUARY 14. We visited there. Twenty-four monks were in residence; one was simple-minded; four were in outside priories; all but six were priests. One did not accuse another [in chapter], although we had ordered this done on several occasions.[17] Alms are given three times a week to all comers. Some of their servants frequent taverns and spend their time in immoderate

---

[17] See entry for January 8, 1259/60.

drinking; we ordered the abbot either to send them away or to administer suitable discipline. We gave orders that the sources of income be written out in some folios; item, that individual accounts be drawn up once a month, and that a record of these be made. About three hundred pounds in debts both good and bad was owed to them; they owed about eighty pounds. We received procuration there this day. Total for procuration: eleven pounds, twelve pence.

On this same day Sir John of Resenclion, knight, appeared before us and made amends for having beaten a certain cleric who was bringing a letter to our curia. Ralph of Canonville and John of Maleville, knights, stood surety, under his agreement, for a fine of one hundred pounds.

On this same day Roger Martel, rector of the church at Angerville, came before us and swore to all the articles of the oath customarily taken by rectors of churches. Present were: Master John of Neuilly-en-Thelle, the dean of Valmont; Master John Mauconduit; and John of Morgneval.

On this same day Thomas Houffray [Humphrey], cleric at Vylemerville, appeared us and under penalty of twenty pounds of Tours abjured Valentina, the wife of William Trenchant, of the same place.

JANUARY 15. We received procuration at Ouville. Total for procuration: eight pounds, thirteen shillings, nine pence.

This day Roger of Sérans, priest at Limésy, whom we had suspended for contumacy because he had not wished to appear before us on the day when he had been peremptorily and personally cited to appear, and did not send anyone to answer for him, came before us. He swore to abide by our will and mandate, and it should be noted that when he had been accused and also defamed of the vice of incontinence, especially with the wife of Peter of Vicquemare, cleric, he was put under oath by Master John of Neuilly-en-Thelle, who was acting for us, and, on oath, he said that he believed that he had been defamed but that the ill fame ceased within the month. We peremptorily and personally appointed next Thursday for him appear before us at Rouen, or wherever we should be in the neighborhood, to answer any questions which we put to him concerning this ill fame and the truth of the matter, or any other charges.[18]

This day Master Adam, rector at Yvecrique,[19] who had been cited before us on several occasions but had not wished to appear, did present himself

[18] See entry for January 19, below.
[19] See entry for January 30, 1248/49.

before Master John of Neuilly-en-Thelle, who was acting in our place, and promised to obey our command concerning his remissness. Under oath he admitted that he had been excommunicated on three occasions, that he had not celebrated Mass now for almost a year, and that he had served in his church only at Christmas. Item, that within the past week he had eaten and drunk in a tavern with Robert Gondree, John Huese, and one other. Item, that since Advent he had baptized children; that in Advent he had heard the confessions of women in labor, but that he had not administered the Eucharist since Michaelmas, except to the said women, and this because of necessity, as he said. We peremptorily and personally cited him to appear before us at Rouen, or wherever we should be nearby, on next Thursday, to hear our judgment and will, so that, whether he should or should not appear, we would proceed against him as the law requires.

We visited Ouville, where there were ten canons; all but one were priests. They had two lay brothers. We ordered them to place their reliquary outside the choir or chancel in such a manner that lay folk would not pass freely in front of the canons and could not speak with any canon as they passed. Item, we ordered one to accuse another [in chapter], and that the house income be written out in records. They owed sixty pounds; they paid a tithe on four hundred pounds annual income.

JANUARY 16. We received procuration from the lessee at Etoutteville. Total for procuration: eleven pounds, sixteen shillings, three pence. JANUARY 17-18. At Dêville.

JANUARY 19. To wit, the feast of SS. Fabian and Sebastian. Roger of Sérans, priest at Limésy, appeared before us at Dêville.[20] He had already confessed to us in our presence and at our order that he had been, after due process, defamed of incontinence, but that the ill-fame had ceased for a month now. We, however, ordered him to purge himself of this ill-fame with the tenth hand of priests,[21] and we assigned him the day after the coming Ash Wednesday to perform this.

This day we spent the night at Dêville.

JANUARY 20. We came to the cathedral at Rouen to visit there, and with God's grace we preached in chapter to the canons and the clerks-choral. When we had finished, we proceeded to make our visitation in the presence

[20] See entry for January 15, above.
[21] See October 16, 1248, n. 70. It was up to the decision of the ecclesiastical superior to designate the number of compurgators required by the defendant.

of the archdeacons of Rouen and of the Norman Vexin, the treasurer, the precentor, the succentor, and the other canons, sending away the clerks-choral and chaplains. However, we postponed our visitation until the morrow, and spent the night at Déville.

JANUARY 21. We returned to the aforesaid chapter and warned them in common to compel their chaplains to celebrate their Masses more regularly and frequently than had been their practice and to frequent the chapter. Item, we ordered them to exact the statutory penalties for minor offenses, as is contained in the tables of the sacristan; item, we ordered the succentor to see that the Sequences[22] were improved. Then we called them individually before us and asked of each whatever we wished; and, God helping, we did what we saw ought to be done.

This day we spent the night at Couronne.

JANUARY 22. At Bourg-Achard, at our own expense.

JANUARY 23. We visited the priory there. Fifteen canons were in residence, and nine in priories. Seven of those in residence were novices; they were, according to the prior, disobedient and intractable, behaved insolently, and were incorrigible. Six were priests. We enjoined the prior to impose such a penalty upon infractions of silence or other customary observances of the Rule that through fear of the penalty or by a withdrawal of wine or food, they should dread to be delinquent. As much or more was owed to them than they owed. They had sufficient provisions to last out the year. We ordered the prior to provide the canons with better clothing than he had done and to provide the sick with better food and necessities. Item, we warned the aforesaid novices to be diligent in reforming their conduct, and to learn the Offices, service, and observances of their Order with humility, or that otherwise the prior, relying upon our authority, would expel them. Item, we were pleased to permit Dom Geoffrey, who had been vagabonding for a long time, to be received again, saving subjection to regular discipline. We received procuration there this day. Total for procuration; nine pounds, six shillings, seven pence.

JANUARY 24. At Pont-Audemer.

JANUARY 25. At the same. This day we caused our venerable brothers the suffragans of the church of Rouen to convene here in order to discuss the

---

[22] Sequences were poems or songs which followed the Alleluia and were sung during the Mass and became a part of the liturgy. For a full explanation, see "Sequence," *Dict. d'arch. chrét. et de lit.*, XV[1], 1294-1303.

holding of the council which is to take place tomorrow.

JANUARY 26. We came to the church of Notre-Dame-de-Préaux at Pont-Audemer, accompanied by our venerable brothers in Christ, and with God's help we celebrated the Mass of the Holy Ghost in pontificals, assisted by a deacon and subdeacon suitably vested, to wit, Master Richard of Salmonville as deacon. Since we did not have a canon of Rouen with us, we had Master Thibaut of Falaise, canon and official of Lisieux, vested as a subdeacon. At this celebration of the Mass our suffragans stood by, clothed in albs and choral capes. Mass having been celebrated, we and our suffragans mounted the dais which had been erected by the monastery gates, and from there was read the Gospel, to wit: "After these things, the Lord appointed also other seventy-two,"[23] which was read by the deacon who had been vested for Mass. When this had been read, we began the *Veni Creator Spiritus* with loud voice. When this had been sung, the precentor of Rouen and some other canon intoned the Litany. The Lord's Prayer, spoken in subdued tones, followed, and we then offered the prayer *Assumus*. Then with God's aid, we preached. The sermon being finished, the letter of convocation and the rescript were read, as afterward were the letters of the proctors of the cathedral chapters; then [was read] the Statute promulgated in the general council concerning the holding of annual councils by archbishops and their suffragans and which is contained in the decree title "On Accusations" and beginning [with the words] *Sicut olim*; also the decree "On Intoxication and Drunkenness".[24]

The proctors for the cathedral chapters were: for Rouen, G. of Saane, treasurer, and Robert, the precentor; for Bayeux, A., the succentor of Bayeux, and Osbert of Canonville: for Evreux, Girard, dean of Evreux; for Lisieux, Masters Giles of Val-Tort and Th. of Falaise; for Avranches, Master William, the archdeacon of Avranches; for Coutances, Master H., the master of the schools; for Séez, William, the archdeacon of Exmes.

Next we asked the inquisitors who had been appointed at the last council if they had anything to report, but only a few of them were present and we did not get anything from them. Then, by common consent, we ordered the archdeacon of each diocese to inquire into his archdeaconry and to give us a report at future councils of whatever should be referred to us either by

[23] Luke 10:1.
[24] See above, January 29, 1259/60, n. 31.

them or by another. After this, all of the following statutes were read:[25]

It is the pleasure of the sacred council that all which is contained below should be scrupulously observed, so that the Reverend Father Eudes, by God's grace archbishop of Rouen, his suffragans, and their subjects shall nowise be obligated to the observance of these as if they were new statutes, namely, as regards those which are found in [canon] law or expressed in the Statutes of Pope Gregory IX, or in the episcopal synods.

We will that the decree of the Council of Lyons, dealing with the procura-tions which should be received by archbishops and bishops by reason of visita-tion, and with the intolerable abuses sometimes imposed by the officials in their entourages, be observed.

We will that the statute of the general council, directed against those who form leagues and the statutes drawn up with prejudice to the liberties of the Church, be promulgated frequently and solemnly in the synods and the paro-chial churches, and that transgressors be canonically punished.

We decree that such secular authorities who seize clerics with greater violence than the resistance of the defendant justifies, of detain them for a long time or in despite of the ecclesiastical judge, shall, after the fact has been clearly proved, be declared excommunicated canonically in general or individually.

We strictly forbid any ecclesiastical person to admit a lay judge in any cases pertaining to the Church, and particularly in any personal actions.

We decree that abbots and priors, and other ecclesiastical persons who receive greater tithes in parochial churches, shall be obliged to restore the fabric, books, and keep ornaments in repair, in such proportion as they share in the tithes.

We will that the synodal statute, to wit, the one stating that ecclesiastical persons to whom come the mandates of various judges, delegates, conservators, or executors, shall diligently inquire into the names of the judges of the diocese, and the places to which they cite, and assure themselves of the authen-ticity thereof, be strictly observed.

We forbid any Christian man or woman to work for Jews in houses, or presume to dwell with them, and we decree that Jews shall be obliged to wear some distinctive signs, whereby they may be distinguished from Catholics.

We strictly forbid any vigils or dances to be held in churchyards and sacred places, and require that transgressors be canonically punished.

Let the clerics, particularly the non-married ones, be solemnly warned in the churches to wear a befitting tonsure; and let all men who have taken the Cross be obliged to wear a cross in some conspicious place.

We desire that the statutes of the general council concerning the possession

[25] For the most part, the decress are a repetition of the council of September 12, 1257. See above pp. 322-28.

of gilded saddles, harness, spurs, girths, and other superfluities which are forbidden to clerics, and [those] concerning the wearing of closed gowns over their garments, be observe.d

We forbid the beneficed clergy, and those in holy orders, to yearn for, or habitually indulge in, the pleasures of hunting and hawking.

We decree that the certain number of religious persons shall be maintained in all abbeys and priories whose resources have not been diminished, unless perchance, by the express permission of the superior, and for a reasonable cause, a temporary delay be granted.

We will and command that the published law be observed forbidding any monk to dwell alone anywhere.

Let all monks dwelling in nonconventual priories be warned with threat of suspension, excommunication, or by such means as seems expedient, that they should strive to conduct themselves according to the Statutes of Pope Gregory, observing his regulations concerning the eating of flesh, making confession, and keeping the fasts.

We decree that the regular clergy shall not dwell with secular folk, except with the special approval of their diocesan.

The statute drawn up limiting the amount of money to be borrowed by monks without the permission of their abbot is to be strictly observed.

We decree that rural deans who exercise jurisdiction shall not excommunicate or suspend except in writing.

We decree that priests shall not cease from the publication of sentences of excommunication, even though the parties may have come to an agreement among themselves, until they are, according to law, sure of the absolution of those excommunicated.

We will that absolution to be carried out with due solemnity.

We forbid priests to pronounce general sentences of excommunication save for thefts or destructions, and after suitable warning.

We decree that chaplains to whom churches have been temporarily entrusted shall be diligently examined as to their knowledge of letters, their moral conduct, and their ordination.

Item, we decree that canons regular, to whom the cure of souls is to be committed, shall be very diligently examined as to their command of letters and as to their life, morals, conduct, and marriage.

Item, we decree that a special Mass be celebrated for every deceased archbishop and every deceased bishop of the province of Rouen, in every cathedral, conventual, collegiate, and parish church of this province.

Item, since it is a work of charity to weep with the weeping, and to open the bowels of compassion for those who are afflicted, we, moved by fraternal affection for our brethren who are dwelling in lands oversea, in Constantinople, and in the Morea, and are oppressed by grievous burdens, decree that throughout the entire province there shall be sung before the Lord, once a day, at the Mass of the day, and just before the *Pax Domini*, the Psalm *Deus venerunt gentes*,[26] with the Lord's Prayer, versicles and usual prayers, for the Holy Land.

These things being completed, and the council, by God's grace, celebrated in all concord, we departed, singing *Te Deum laudamus*, which as we finished brought us before the altar of the Blessed Mary, where we offered suitable prayers.

JANUARY 27. This day we spent the night there.

We spent the night at St-Philbert, at the manor of the bishop of Avranches, and at his expense.

JANUARY 28. With God's grace we visited the abbey of Bec, preached a sermon in the chapter, and visited there. About eighty monks were there. According to custom, one did not accuse another [in chapter]. We enjoined the master of the novices to try to correct the novices' way of life and to instill in them the spirit of the discipline of the Rule. Item, we ordered the abbot to have the income of the monastery written down in some register or record. With God's grace we found all other things to be in sufficiently good condition, save that the monks in the priories eat meat freely.

JANUARY 29. At Martot. JANUARY 30. At Frênes. JANUARY 31. At Les Andelys. FEBRUARY 1. We celebrated the feast of the Purification of the Blessed Virgin Mary, preached, with God's grace, a sermon in the church at Les Andelys, and spent the night at our new residence.[27]

This day Walter of Courcelles, knight, paid us a fine for having contracted a marriage without publishing the banns in church.[28] The fines for this sort of thing should be imposed and exacted by us. Sir Robert of Croisy, knight, and Sir John of St-Clair, knight, presented themselves as his sureties.

FEBRUARY 2. We visited the canons and clerics of Les Andelys. Two

---

[26] Psalm 78, "O God, the heathens are come into my inheritance," was to be sung just before the *Agnus Dei*.

[27] Eudes had just completed a new residence on the archiepiscopal manor at Andeli. (Bonnin, p. 380, n. 1.)

[28] The banns of marriage, then as now, were the notification by ecclesiastical authority of a forthcoming marriage. Canonical legislation of the eight and ninth centuries ruled that before the blessing could be given for a marriage, an investigation of the parties had to be made by a competent ecclesiastical authority, who was generally the parish priest. (Mansi, XIII, 847-848, canon 8).

canons were dwelling with the dean, to wit, Masters Robert and Ralph. There are six prebends there, but one of them is still a whole one,[29] and will be divided after the death of Master Robert. Of the six canons one ought to be [a priest] [*lacuna in MS*], two ought to be deacons, and three, subdeacons. There are four vicar-priests there, of whom one celebrates Mass every day at La Couture and another at Magdalene; the remaining two stay in the church, hear confessions, and assist the dean in administering the other Sacraments of the Church. Two other vicars are there, a deacon and a subdeacon, and these are required to vest themselves every day for High Mass. The dean has the cure of the souls of the clerics of the chapter and of the parishioners, and even of some of the nearby villages. We ordered Dom Peter Robillard, the sacristan, to employ decent and suitable clerics to teach in the song-schools, to sleep in the monastery, and to be more permanent than some others whom he had had before. Item, we forbade the priors of St-Léonard and of the hospital to permit the parishioners of the town to come to them to hear Mass, especially on Sundays and holy days, but to send them to their own parish church. Item, with the consent of the dean and of the canons, we ordered them to hold a general chapter twice a year, to wit, on the day following the Nativity of the Blessed Mary, and on the morrow after Low Sunday,[30] imposing a fine of twenty shillings of Paris to be paid by every canon who absented himself. Other things, with God's grace, we found to be in good condition.

We received procuration this day at Sausseuse. Total for procuration: seven pounds, six shillings, eight pence.

FEBRUARY 3. We visited the priory there, where we found twelve canons, of whom six were priests. There were two lay brothers and two lay sisters there. Because of the excessive number of poor people who attend, they distribute alms only twice a week. We gave orders that the income of the house be entered in a register or record. They owed five hunderd pounds of Paris, almost all of it to Master Robert of Grainville.

FEBRUARY 4. We visited the priory at Gasny. Two monks were there with Brother Roger of Les Andelys, then prior of the place. They observed the fasts of the Rule badly and ate meat. We forbade the prior to invite women to dine at the priory, or to eat with them in town. They owed two hundred

---

[29] Held by a canon who has no vicar, chaplain, etc., and to whom all the revenues accrue.

[30] First Sunday after Easter; also called *Quasimodo*.

pounds and more. The prior believed that they had sufficient provisions to last out the year. Total for procuration: seven pounds, fifteen shillings, ten pence.

FEBRUARY 5. We came to the priory at La Roche-Guyon, and found that the monks from Fécamp who were there were living quite out of accord with the Rule, nor did they have a sufficiency [of provisions] for their maintenance. The prior was not there.

This day we visited the priory at St-Martin-la-Garenne. Three monks were there; there should be six, but because of the very bad weather the prior had sent three of them back to the abbey; and because of the scarcity of goods they sometimes ate meat when there was no need and did not observe the fasts of the Rule very well. They owed their abbot some two hundred forty pounds. With God's grace we found other things to be in good condition. We received procuration there this day. Total for procuration: nine pounds, ten pence.

FEBRUARY 6. We celebrated a parish Mass at Limay, and with God's aid we preached there and administered Confirmation. We spent the night at Juziers, at our expense.

FEBRUARY 7. We visited the priory at Juziers. Six monks were in residence, of whom one had been received there last Advent; however, he should be sent to the abbey during the coming Lent. They freely ate meat by the abbot's order, and they had pelisses trimmed with rabbit fur. They did not observe the fasts of the Rule. All but one were priests. They owed about one hundred pounds; about forty pounds was owed to them. We received procuration there this day. Total for procuration: seven pounds, fourteen shillings, four pence.

FEBRUARY 8. We came to the priory of St-Laurent-en-Cornecervine and visited there. Three monks from Ste-Marie-de-Josaphat, in the diocese of Chartres, were there. They ate meat and used feather beds, but, as they said, with the knowledge of their abbot. They did not observe the fasts of the Rule. The buildings were in a ruinous state, but the prior told us that he would have them repaired at once. They had much wine which they were unable to sell as they needed to do.

This day we received procuration from them at Juziers. Total for procuration: seven pounds, eleven shillings.

FEBRUARY 9. We received procuration at Gaillonet from three canons of the Premonstratensian Order who were dwelling there.

FEBRUARY 10. We spent the night at Wy, where we received a *muid* of oats from the priest at Gadancourt, for the rector at Gadancourt owes us this when we make our annual diversion to Wy.

FEBRUARY 11. We visited St. Martin's abbey near Pontoise, where there were twenty-two monks in residence. We forbade the monks to have their own cups, but ordered that the cellarer should give to each of them whatever he desires they should have in common. Ten of them were priests. Dom Walter was at Jumièges. They owed fourteen hundred pounds, nine hundred pounds of it at interest. Item, we gave orders that Brother John, called Haubert, be recalled from the priory at Tours to the cloister, that he might be subjected to severer discipline.

This same day we summoned before us the priests of the archdeaconry of Pontoise, and we ordered them to convene once a month before our vicar, hold their synods, and observe the synodal statutes. We received procuration there this day. Total for procuration: ten pounds, twelve shillings, six pence.

FEBRUARY 12. We visited the chapter at St-Mellon. The canons in residence were Master Robert and Dom Luke, nine vicars, and two chaplains. There are ten prebends. Two of the vicars are there, of whom one should be a subdeacon, the other a deacon. They had neither a copy of the Lives of the Saints, nor a Bible; we ordered Dom Luke to try to procure a sufficient number of Lives of the Saints. In this matter an inquiry was ordered by the king to find out whether the treasurer or the chapter should provide the books. Item, we ordered Luke to buy cloth with what chapter moneys he had on hand, and to have albs, altar cloths, amices, and such things made. Item, we ordered that they be purchased with the treasurers' rents of twenty pounds. He had put this sum aside for purchasing wax candles, and the chapter had received the money. Item, they did not have an ordinal; some of them sang their Hours according to the use of Paris,[31] others according to that of Rouen; we told them that we would give them an ordinal containing the use of Rouen, which we desired them to follow always. Item, Luke, a vicar, was incontinent and defamed of incontinence; we ordered our vicar to make an inquiry into this. Item, because of their murmurings, we forbade the distribution of the Mass pennies [to the canons]. Item, we ordered Dom Richard to permit the chaplains to celebrate their Masses in the morning

---

[31] The liturgical practices; unfortunately, Eudes does not say what they were. However, see "Paris," *Dict. d'arch. chrét. et de lit.*, XIII[2], 1892-97, for further information on this subject.

before the bell was rung for Prime. Item, that the chaplains should celebrate their Masses in a low voice, so as not to disturb those who were chanting the Psalms in the choir.

We spent this night at St. Martin's and received from Dom Luke, canon of St. Martin's, one hundred shillings of Paris, in the name of the chapter, as well as dishes, wood, cups, straw, beds, and cooking utensils for which the chapter is held each year for procuration.

We dined this day in the house of the Franciscans.

FEBRUARY 12. We visited St. Peter's priory, where there were six monks from Bec-Hellouin. They sometimes ate meat when there was no need. All were priests. They owed two hundred sixty pounds, of which one hundred seventy-two was owed to their abbot.

FEBRUARY 13. We celebrated the parish Mass, preached, and with God's aid administered Confirmation at St-Maclou.

We spent the night at St. Martin's, at our own expense.

FEBRUARY 14-15. At Paris, to attend the Parlement.

FEBRUARY 16. At Paris. This day, we issued the following announcement:

In the name of the Father, and of the Son, and of the Holy Ghost, Amen. Since we, Brother Eudes, by Divine permission the unworthy bishop of the diocese of Rouen, had been appointed arbiter by the parties concerned in the dispute which arose between the dean and the chapter of Noyon, on the one hand, and the abbot and convent of St-Eloi-de-Noyon on the other, concerning the proper resting place of the body and relics of St. Eloi the Confessor,[32] we, by apostolic authority, decree that those who are in possession of the body and relics of the said saint should keep and venerate them; further, that the canons, dean, or chapter should make no attempt to move or translate the chest or contents within ten days, either personally or through agents, until all expenses contracted be settled satisfactorily to all concerned.

FEBRUARY 17-24. At Paris.

FEBRUARY 25. At Paris. This day the priest at Bois-Asselin set out for Rome with a letter containing an appeal which we have interposed against Peter of Ferentino in the matter of a prebend at Les Andelys.

Today John, the former rector at Osny, voluntarily resigned his church into our hands.

FEBRUARY 26-28. At Paris. MARCH 1. At Paris. This day Stephen, former rector of Vesly, resigned this church, [of Vesly] into our hands of his own

[32] See entries for November 13-23, 1256; February 1-2, 1257/58.

free will. MARCH 2. At St-Martin-de-Pontoise, at our own expense. MARCH 3. We received procuration at the priory of L'Aillerie at Chaumont. Total for procuration ... [*lacuna in MS*].

MARCH 4. We visited the priory, where there were three monks from St-Germer-de-Flay. Alms were given every Sunday to all comers. They did not observe the fasts of the Rule. They ate meat freely. They owed seventy pounds.

This day we visited the priory of St-Martin-d'Es, where there were two monks from St-Magloire-de-Paris. They owed fourteen pounds. They had a scant supply of provisions; they were very poor.

This day we spent the night at Liancourt, where we received from the prior four pounds of Paris, the amount in which, in addition to shelter and domestic utensils, he is held to us for procuration.

MARCH 5. We visited the priory at Liancourt, where there were three monks from St-Père-de-Chartres; all were priests. They observed the fasts of the Rule badly; they ate meat three times a week, with their abbot's permission, as they said. They owed two hundred pounds; they had a sufficiency of provisions.

This day we visited the priory of Sérans, where there were three monks from St-Germer-de-Flay. They ate meat; they observed neither the fasts nor silence. We ordered the prior frequently to inspect the coffers of his companions. They bestow alms three times a week. They owed about sixty pounds; they had enough provisions to last out the year. This day we received from the prior of this house seventy shillings of Paris, in which amount the said house is annually obligated to us for procuration, in addition to supplying us with dishes, common utensils, fodder for the horses, and such straw, wood, and coals as may be found in the town.

MARCH 6. At Bray-sous-Baudemont we absolved William of Buhy, esquiry, from the excommunication by which he had long been bound at the instance of Baldwin of Buhy; we made peace between them.

We lunched this day at Le Trésor and spent the night at Vernon. We fixed the amount of the fine of the said William at sixty pounds of Paris.

MARCH 6. At Pinterville. MARCH 7. At the same, and there we received homage from our men for the manor which we had purchased from Peter of Meulan. MARCH 8. At Ste-Catherine, at our own expense. MARCH 9. To wit, on Ash Wednesday; with God's grace we preached in the cathedral, celebrated Mass, and spent the night at our manor there. MARCH 10. At

Déville. Today we made a concession to Master Martin, who had been presented for the church at Manteville, that time would not run out against him for that church before the vigil of St. Matthew.

MARCH 11-12. At Déville. MARCH 13. With God's grace we preached and celebrated a High Mass in the cathedral at Rouen on this, the first Sunday in Lent, and we spent the night at our manor there.

MARCH 14. We issued the following pronouncement:

Whereas Philip, called Butler, rector of the church of Mézièrs, has absented himself for the last eight or nine months from the said church, thus rashly going against the oath he swore to us;

And we have caused him to be cited publicly in the said church to return to his church and to reside there;

And he, perservering in his evil way, has neither cared to come nor to take up his residence;

And although we have cited him many times before, and although we for the last time cited him to appear before us at Rouen on the Thursday following Ash Wednesday to stand trial in these matters, he neither came nor sent any representative; yet we in graciousness awaited his appearance until the morning of the following Monday:

Therefore, we confirm his contumacy in God's presence, and herewith sentence the said Philip to be deprived of the aforesaid church for his long, continued contumacy, for refusal to appear in person or by proxy when cited and waited for, for the violation of his oath, and, for so long a time, failure to reside in his church.

Present were: Master John of Porte, archdeacon of the Norman Vexin; Master John of Neuilly-en-Thelle; Master Richard of Salmonville, the greater archdeacon; the official of Rouen, and many others.

We received procuration this day at Noyon[-sur-Andelle]. Total for procuration: nine pounds, seventeen shillings, eight pence.

MARCH 15. We visited the priory of Noyon-sur-Andelle, where there were seven monks from St-Evroult; all were priests. They ate meat when there was no need, often three times a week. They owed two hundred twenty pounds; there was owed to them, as well in England as in these parts, eighty pounds. They had sufficient provisions to last out the year. With God's grace we found other things to be in good condition.

This day we received procuration from the lessee of the house at Pérrièrs, to wit, the Ides of March. Total for procuration: nine pounds, sixteen shillings, seven pence.

MARCH 16. We spent the night at L'Ile-Dieu, at the expense of the abbey.

This day we examined Nicholas, called Quesnel, a cleric presented to us for St. Mary's church at Vinemerville, in the passage, *In principio creavit Deus celum et terram*,[33] and he construed as follows: "*Deus*, God, *creavit*, created, *celum*, the heaven, *et terram*, and the earth." We had him decline the noun *Deus*, which he did quite satisfactorily, except when he came to the accusative plural, he said, "*Deos or Dos.*" Item, we asked him what part of speech was *inanis*; he said, "a noun," and yet he said that there were two parts, and he declined it thus: In the nominative, *hec inanis*, in the genitive, *huius -nis*, in the dative, *huic -ni*, according to the third declension, except that in the vocative plural he said, "*O inane*"; however, he said that *inanis* meant "an evil thing." He replied quite well as to the accent of the middle syllable. Item, we asked him what part of speech was *ferebatur*; he said that it was a verb, and that it meant "he carried." He conjugated *fero, fers* as far as the supine, which he omitted, saying that there was none. The participles he gave as *ferens, ferturus*; the verb he said was of neuter gender, in the conjunctive mood, and past perfect in tense. Item, he conjugated *dixit* quite well. He conjugated the verb *fiat* as follows: *fio, fis, fui, esse, fiendi, -do, -dum, factum, -tu, fiens, facturus*.[34] We asked him whether it had a passive, and he said that it did not, for that it was of neuter gender. We asked him for the sense of these words: *Et vidit lucem quod erat bona*,[35] and he answered, "It was a good thing to do." Item, he conjugated *divisit* as follows: *divido, divisis, divisi, dividere*, quite well until he reached the passive, when he said *divideor*,[36] *divideris*, with a drawn-out middle syllable. We asked him of which conjugation it was; he first said that it was the third and then that it was the fourth, and he said that he knew the fourth, for it puts its genitive in *i* and its dative in *o*. Item, he declined *hic vesper* according to the third

---

[33] Genesis, I, 1.

[34] A strange confusion of the verbs *facere* (to do, to make) and *esse* (to be).

[35] Genesis 1:4.

[36] *Divideor* would be second conjugation, passive voice; whereas *dividere* is third conjugation.

declension, giving *o vespere* as the vocative. He did not wish to chant, and said that he knew nothing about chant.

And then and there he said:

Seeing that you, Reverend Father, by God's grace archbishop of Rouen, are unwilling to admit me, Nicholas, called Quesnel, cleric, to the church of Notre-Dame-de-Vinemerville as rector, or even to confer the said church upon me, judging me to be insufficiently lettered, although I, the said Nicholas, have been presented to the said church by its true patron, and the said church stands free and vacant; and because you have desired your investigation to be made into the aforesaid matters, particularly with respect to my morals, decency, and life, [although] the truth of the right of patronage was fully demonstrated to you: I, the aforesaid Nicholas, now feel myself aggrieved in this matter, and, by the authority and at the request of John, called Quesnel, patron of the said church, appeal in writing to the Apostolic See, and request that you give me *apostoli* duly sealed; which if you refuse to give and seal for me, I again appeal in writing to the said Apostolic See, and, by the authority of the said patron, place myself and the aforesaid church under the protection of the Pope.

We did not think it proper to defer to that appeal, inasmuch as in our examination we had discovered him to be completely deficient in letters, that is, he knew neither how to read competently nor to construe, nor was he willing to chant. Present at this examination and appeal were: the abbot of l'Ile-Dieu; Master John of Neuilly-en-Thelle, canon of Rouen; and Brothers Harduin and Walter of Minières, of the Friars Minor.

MARCH 17. After propounding the Word of God, with His Grace, we visited the priory of Beaulieu. Ten canons were in residence, two of them being novices; we ordered these novices to confess and receive Communion once a month. Item, we ordered the prior, although we had given him a similar order at our other visitation,[37] to inspect the coffers of the canons more frequently. There were four lay sisters and three lay brothers. They owed five hundred pounds. We received procuration there this day. Total for procuration: nine pounds, five shillings, nine pence.

MARCH 18 . At Déville.

MARCH 19. With God's grace we conferred Holy Orders at the Dominican convent at Rouen.

This day Master John, former rector of the church of Notre-Dame-de-

---

[37] See entry for March 17, 1259/60.

l'Aillerie at Chaumont, voluntarily resigned his church into our hands. Item, Henry of Bailleul, erstwhile rector at Vauville, likewise resigned his church.

Our long-lived rheumatism attacked us again this day, and we spent the night at Déville.

MARCH 20-24. At Déville. MARCH 25. At Déville, to wit, on Annunciation Sunday. MARCH 26-28. At Martot. MARCH 29-30. At Frênes. MARCH 31. We spent the night at Mortemer-en-Lyons, at the expense of the abbey. APRIL 1. At Montmain, at our own expense.

APRIL 2. At our palace in Rouen. This day Arnulf, priest, rector of the church at Roncherolles-en-Bray, came before us and submitting himself completely to our will and in every other way to our disposition or command, took oath, with hand on breast and on his word as a priest, that he would regard his church as resigned whensoever it should please us, or that he would gratefully receive whatever pension therein we should deem fit to grant him. Present were: Master Adam, archdeacon of Rouen; Master John of Porte, archdeacon of the Norman Vexin; Master John of Neuilly-en-Thelle, canon of Rouen; and the dean of Ry.

To all to whom this may come, Thomas, priest, rector of the church at Lyons, gives greeting in the Lord. Know you that for many years there has worked against me, and still does, the ill fame of the vice of incontinence, in particular with a certain woman named Malot, and that I have often been accused of this to the Reverend Father Eudes, by God's grace archbishop of Rouen. Realizing that the said father can proceed against me in these said matters with all harshness, I have promised the said Father, and with hand on breast have taken oath on the Holy Gospels, that I will, without the publicity of a trial or attempt at reclamation, regard my aforesaid church as resigned from the moment the said Father desires, and whensoever I shall be required so to do by him.

Present were: Master John of Porte, my archdeacon; Masters J[ohn] of Neuilly-en-Thelle, Richard of Salmonville, canons of Rouen, and J. and P., clerks of the said Father. In testimony whereof I have given this letter, sealed with my own seal and with my own hand, to the said Father. Given at Rouen the Saturday before *Laetare Hierusalem*, in the year of our Lord 1261 [*sic*].

APRIL 3. That is to say, on the Sunday on which *Laetare Hierusalem* is sung, we with God's grace preached in the morning at the cathedral, and spent the night at Pont-de-l'Arche.

On this same day, acting on sound advice concerning the resignation by Master John, the rector of the church of Sensay into the hands of the archdeacon, to wit, Master John of Porte, we have approved the said resignation.

APRIL 4. We spent the night at Vernon. APRIL 5. At Mantes.

APRIL 6. We were there in the morning for the purpose of celebrating a sacred council which, with God's aid, was celebrated.

This same morning we came to the church of St-Aubin at Limay, beyond the bridge at Mantes, accompanied by our venerable brothers in Christ, our suffragans, and there with God's aid we celebrated the Mass of the day, not, indeed, in pontificals, or with vested deacon and subdeacon, but simply, as is the daily use. Our venerable brothers attended Mass but were not vested. When Mass had been sung, we, together with our venerable brothers, proceeded to hold the sacred council in the same church. We opened the council, God aiding us, by revealing how the most wicked Tartars had destroyed, and were, from day to day, striving to destroy the Holy Land, and how the Pope and the king of France willed and ordered that the Holy Land be supported by manpower and by works of mercy. Next we had cited the proctors of every diocese in turn, as well those representing religious bodies, both regulars and seculars, and we enjoined them to give us the letters of proxy which they had in their possession. When the letters of proxy had been given in, we decreed, with the consent of the sacred council, that all who were absent, or who appeared without sufficient authority, or who had sent representatives insufficiently instructed, should be punished canonically, and that in such matters as the whole body of statutes of the council or of the Parlement assembled before the king, they should be proceeded against in the matters treated in the council just as though they had been present in person at the sacred council. This being enacted, we caused to be read in council: first, the Pope's letter mentioning the destruction of the Holy Land; second, we caused to be read another of the Pope's letters which treated of the preaching of a crusade, and of this second letter we had a copy written out for all of our aforementioned suffragans. Then, with the advice of our aforesaid brothers, we decreed and ordered that all those who did not wish to go to Paris to attend the Parlement before the king of France, assigned to the day when *Isti sunt dies*[38] is sung, to hear what should be ordained and enacted at the said Parlement, should elect suitable and good persons and

---

[38] Passion Sunday. See *The Hereford Breviary* (London, Henry Bradshaw Society, 1904), Vol. XXVI (edited from the Rouen edition of 1505). Passion Sunday fell on April 10 in 1260/61, so that the council was held in Paris between April 10 and April 15.

legalize their status with letters patent. They should attend the said Parlement at Paris in person to represent them and to hear, forward, and refer to them whatsoever is ordained and decreed in that Parlement. After counsel had been taken, all and several of our own diocese unanimously chose us, and every diocese chose the bishop of that diocese, and everyone promised that whatever should be recorded and related by us and by our aforesaid venerable brothers, our suffragans, to each and all of them concerning the statutes or other actions of the said Parlement, they would firmly observe, and would do whatsoever we and our aforesaid suffragans should deem ought to be done concerning what is decreed therein. There was one exception: the Cistercian and Premonstratensian monks replied that their superior abbots would attend the Parlement at Paris, and that without the consent of these superiors they could not promise or assent to anything. Nevertheless, we enjoined them to send, with the assent of their superior abbots, some of their own monks from each diocese to the Parlement at Paris, that they might hear what might be ordained and decreed.

This day we orally assigned to our venerable brother in Christ . . . [*lacuna in MS*],[39] the bishop of Coutances, the Monday following *Quasimodo* as the day when he should appear before us at Rouen, or before our official, should we happen to be absent, to see about the benefit of absolution for the Friars Hermits of St. Augustine.

When all this had been done, we spent the night at Meulan, going by water, along with our venerable brother . . . [*lacuna in MS*], the bishop of Evreux.

APRIL 7-15. At Paris. APRIL 16. At Meulan.

APRIL 17. That is, on Palm Sunday. We came in the morning to Juziers, and there we adored the Cross in procession; afterwards, we preached in the local church, and then we celebrated Mass there. This done, we returned to Meulan and spent the night there.

APRIL 18. At Pacy. APRIL 19. At Pinterville. APRIL 20. At Rouen.

APRIL 21. At the same. This same morning we went to the churches of Ste-Catherine, St-Ouen, St-Amand, and St-Lo[-de-Rouen], and granted absolutions, as is the custom. Later on, having placed the penitents in the cathedral, we preached to them, and granted solemn absolution. Later, with God's aid, we blessed the sacred chrism and did such other things as was fitting.

[39] John.

APRIL 22. At Rouen. This day with God's aid we held a service in the cathedral of Rouen.

This day Ralph, rector of the church at Ganseville, voluntarily resigned his church into the hands of Brother Adam Rigaud, who had been appointed by the lord archbishop to receive this resignation. Present were: Peter of Osny, archdeacon of Grand-Caux; Master Richard of Salmonville, Master John of Neuilly-en-Thelle, and Master G. of Flavacourt, canons of Rouen; and William le Turc, clerk.

APRIL 23. At Rouen.

APRIL 24. That is to say, the day of the Lord's Resurrection. With God's grace we celebrated High Mass at the Franciscan monastery, and the bishop of St-Malo, who, with the bishop of Avranches, was visiting us, celebrated High Mass for us at the cathedral.

APRIL 25. At Déville, and the said bishops were with us there. APRIL 26. At Martot. APRIL 27. At Beaumont-le-Roger, to attend to the business which concerned us and the bishop of Lisieux. APRIL 28–MAY 3. At Martot. MAY 4-7. At Frênes. MAY 8. At Pont-de-l'Arche. MAY 9-13. At Rouen, where we sat at the Exchequer with the other masters. MAY 14. At Bec-Hellouin. MAY 15. At Lisieux. MAY 16-20. At Caen, to attend the meeting of the Exchequer. MAY 21. At Troarn. MAY 22. At Lisieux. MAY 23. At Beaumont-le-Roger. MAY 24. At Pinterville, where we entertained at our expense the bishop of Evreux and the other masters of the Exchequer. MAY 25. At Martot.

MAY 26. We came to the priory of St-Lô[-de-Rouen], and having with God's grace preached His Word in chapter, we visited it. Twenty canons were in residence; all but four were priests. We ordered the prior to be more zealous than he had been about hearing the confessions of the canons. Brother Robert had conceived rancor amounting to hatred against Brother Walter of Thémericourt, nor has he conversed with him openly; we enjoined Robert to become reconciled with the said Walter without delay, and to conduct himself charitably towards him in the future. They owed about two hundred pounds; about three hundred pounds was owed to them, and they had many provisions. Furthermore, the prior, with apostolic authority, kept a certain cleric, learned in the law, to assist in such cases as were brought before him, but since, as a result, the community did not receive the emoluments of the seal and of the cases, it complained of this practice. We spoke about this to the prior in the presence of the community, and he said that the notary and the said clerk received about ten pounds of the emolument for this sort of thing, and that the rest was dedicated to the needs of the church and to pious purposes, to wit, alms, the repair of the choir stalls and windows, and such things. Item, the community besought us to require the preparation of a written statement of the total expenses and receipts for the entire year, and we ordered this done. Since the said Brother Robert was not very obedient to the prior and had not been, we enjoined him to make his peace with him and to cease from complaining about him any further; otherwise, he should know that he would be punished by the said prior, on our advice and at our mandate.

This day we spent the night at Déville, where the prior gave us procuration. Total for procuration: nine pounds.

MAY 27. With God's aid we visited the monastery of St-Amand-de-Rouen. Forty-five nuns were in residence; of these, four were novices. They had five maidservants. We ordered the abbess frequently to collect the keys of the coffers and boxes of the nuns and to inspect them lest they be in possession of any property. Item, we ordered the abbess to visit the nuns at Saâne more frequently than had been her custom. Item, as we had done before,[1] we forbade them to make alms-bags, frill-collars, needle cases, and such things; nor should they do any work in silk except to make things pertaining to the Divine Service. Item, we ordered them to increase the amount they dispensed for alms. They owed four hundred pounds; they had a supply of provisions sufficient to last out the year.

This day we exchanged with Master John of Soissons the fruits of the prebend which had belonged to Master William of Salmonville for the fruits of the prebend which the said John had in the church of Rouen.

This day we spent the night at Déville, at our own expense.

MAY 28. We visited the abbey of St-Ouen-de-Rouen after we had with God's grace preached His Word there. Fifty-seven monks were in residence, of whom two, to wit, Thomas and Roger, were scholars at Paris. All but twenty were priests. The monks who were living in the priories ate meat freely; we forbade any monk to eat with secular guests, though they might eat with religious. We were not able to obtain a full account of the state of the house; however, we found that they owed eighteen hundred pounds, at interest. A general audit is made at the feast of St. Peter, and it was for this reason that, at the time of our visitation, they could not give an exact statement.

This day we spent the night at Déville.

MAY 29. At Pinterville. MAY 30-31. At the same, the king staying at Vaudreuil. JUNE 1. At Pont-de-l'Arche, where the king was staying also.

[1] See entry for visit of December 12, 1258.

JUNE 2. To wit, Ascension Day. With God's grace we celebrated a High Mass and preached in the royal chapel at Pont-de-l'Arche before the king. We spent the night at this same town. JUNE 3. At the same. JUNE 4. At St-Matthieu, the king residing at Rouen. JUNE 5. God assisting us, we dedicated the Dominican church at Rouen. JUNE 6. At Pont-de-l'Arche. JUNE 7. At Frênes. JUNE 8-19. At Vernon. JUNE 10. At Meulan. JUNE 11. We celebrated the service of the vigil of Pentecost, with God's grace, at royal chapel in Maubisson before the king, and spent the night at St-Martin-de-Pontoise. JUNE 12. To wit, on Pentecost. With God's grace we celebrated the service proper to this day, dined with the king, and slept at St-Martin[-de-Pontoise]. JUNE 13. At Genainville.

JUNE 14. We visited the priory at Villarceaux, where there were nineteen nuns and three lay sisters. They did not have sufficient books, and the ones they did have were in bad condition. We forbade the prioress to allow the nuns to have coffers with keys. They had four maidservants. They owed sixty pounds. They had no provisions. They possessed ten horses, twenty head of cattle, counting both cows and calves, one hundred twenty sheep, and fifteen swine.

This day we spent the night at Genainville.

JUNE 15. At Sausseuse, at our own expense. JUNE 16-18. At Frênes. JUNE 19. With God's grace we conferred Holy Orders at Notre-Dame at Les Andelys.

This day the cleric who was also the former rector of Les Authieux[2] resigned his church into the hands of Brother Harduin, our chaplain, who had our authority to receive it. Present were: John of Morgneval, our clerk; Miles, chaplain at Les Andelys; and Master Bartholomew, rector of the church at Droitecourt.

On the same day we spent the night at Frênes.

JUNE 20. At Mont-Ste-Catherine, Rouen. This day Master Robert of Monceaux resigned the church at Angierville. JUNE 21. God helping us, we celebrated the sacred synod of Rouen. JUNE 22. We held the synod of deans and spent the night at Ste-Catherine. JUNE 23. To wit, on the vigil of St. John the Baptist, at Frênes.

Be it known that when Master John, rector of the church at Suzay, resigned his church not long ago, we, taking compassion upon his pitiful simplicity,

---

[2] This is probably the cleric notorious for drunkenness. See entry for January 15, 1248/49.

granted him a delay until the Pentecostal synod to make an exchange with some
other priest from another diocese. On the morning of the appointed day he
appeared before us at Ste-Catherine and asked us to grant him an extension of
time, but this we were not willing to do. Wherefore he made a verbal appeal
to the Apostolic See, stating that he was appealing rather against the harm
done to his patron than against the harm done to us. In the evening of the
same day he came to us at Frênes and verbally renewed his appeal, as follows:
"My Lord Archbishop, since you have allowed enquiries to be made concerning
a certain cleric, presented for my church at Suzay, I appeal to the Apostolic See,
that you may not admit this cleric or any other to the said church; and I place
myself, my church, and my goods under the protection of the Apostolic See
and I request *apostoli*, the which, if you refuse to grant, I enter another
appeal." Present were: Master J[ohn] of Porte, archdeacon of the Norman
Vexin; Brothers Harduin and Walter of the Franciscans; Master Richard of
Salmonville, canon of Rouen; and many others.

JUNE 24. At Parnes, at our own expense. JUNE 25. At St-Martin, near
Pontoise, at our own expense. JUNE 26-29. At Paris, to attend the Parlement. JUNE 30. At Paris, for the Parlement.

This day Master . . . *[lacuna in MS]*, came before us and read and proposed the following :

Reverend Father, archbishop of Rouen, when Master John of Porte, archdeacon of the church of Rouen in the Norman Vexin, at the time of making
his visitation asserted that ill-fame had arisen about my character — although
the said archdeacon only became aware of this ill-fame through my enemies
and malevolent persons, and those who had accused me of this ill fame did so
rather through malice than zeal for justice — he ordered me peremptorily
to seal a letter of resignation, stating that I should try my best to exchange
my church for another within a stated time, or otherwise regard it as resigned.
Although I am not, according to law, bound to do this, yet, because I could
very easily do so, I was prepared to make this change within the time set,
especially since certain other persons were prepared to exchange with me. You
have refused to accept this; indeed, without observing the order of law, you
have taken steps to withdraw my benefice under cover of the above letter, nor
is it my fault that I have not made the exchange. I offer to prove all these
things before you. Item, you and your archdeacon have proceeded against me
to the extent of withdrawing my benefice on the testimony of laymen and
envious persons; item, although after I had entered an appeal, according to
law, that nothing should be attempted to my prejudice, you have admitted a
certain cleric presented by the patron for my church, to the extent of permitting

an investigation as to his fitness; item, although you, Reverend Father Archbishop, by reason of the charges you lay against me, have proceeded against me to the extent of withdrawing my benefice and although I am ready to purge myself of all ill fame, accusations, crimes or violations of the canons made by me, as well before you as before your archdeacon and to satisfy the law in competent fashion, you refuse to allow me to do these things. Therefore I appeal in writing to the Apostolic See, and I place myself, my church, and all my possessions, under the protection of the Apostolic See, and I request *apostoli* at once. Should you refuse to grant me this, I appeal again in writing to the Apostolic See.

JULY 1. At Paris. On this same day the bishop of Auxerre, the count of Nevers, and the prior of Pré convened with us at our Parisian manor. There was disagreement among them concerning the seizure of some men and other things. They unanimously agreed to submit completely to the decision of our venerable brother Ralph, by God's grace bishop of Evreux, and of ourself. Also, the bishop of Auxerre offered, as surety, for a penalty of one thousand silver marks, the count of Bar, the precentor of Sens, the precentor of Auxerre, and Master Andrew of Verdeuil; the count of Nevers for the same penalty offered as pledges the said count of Bar; Sir Ralph Frechart, knight; and the lord of Tyengnes; the prior of Pré, in respect of a penalty of one hundred marks, gave as his pledge Geoffrey, the provost of Pré.

JULY 2-5. At Paris, attending the Parlement. JULY 6. With God's grace we began our pilgrimage to Chartres on foot. The bishop of Auxerre accompanied us, and we spent the night at Bourg-la-Reine. JULY 7. At Palaiseau. JULY 8. At Château-Gommez. JULY 9. At Rochefort. JULY 10. At Ablis. JULY 11. At Monceaux-sur-Eure, at the grange belonging to St-Jean-du-Val-de-Chartres. JULY 12. At Chartres, at the bishop's palace, at his expense. JULY 13. At Nogent-le-Roi, at the royal castle. JULY 14. At Motelle-sous-Muzy, at Amaury's manor.[3] JULY 15. At Mantes. JULY 16. At St-Côme, near Meulan. JULY 17. At l'Ile-Adam. JULY 18-19. At Beaumont-sur-Oise. JULY 20-21. At Pontoise.

JULY 22. To wit, on the feast of St. Mary Magdalene. We and our venerable brother the bishop of Evreux, in the presence of the king and queen, translated, in procession, two of the eleven thousand virgins from the royal château to the abbey of Notre-Dame at Royaumont. With God's aid we celebrated Mass in the royal chapel, and spent the night at St-Martin.

---

[3] Amaury de Muzy, a nephew of Eudes.

JULY 23. At Mantes. JULY 24. At Vernon. JULY 25-28. At Pinterville. JULY 29-30. At Vernon. JULY 31. At Vernon, with the king. AUGUST 1. At Vernon. This is the feast of St. Peter in Chains. AUGUST 2-3. At the same. AUGUST 4. At Les Andelys.

AUGUST 5. With God's grace we dedicated St. Leonard's church, in the presence of the king and the bishop of Evreux, and we spent the night at Les Andelys, where the prior of St-Leonard gave us procuration, by reason of the said dedication.

AUGUST 6-8. At Frênes. AUGUST 9. At Vesly, at our own expense. AUGUST 10. At Vesly. With God's grace we celebrated Mass in the parish church, preached, and administered Confirmation. AUGUST 11. At Gisors, on the matter concerning the count of Dammartin and the lord of St-Clair-sur-Epte. We spent the night at Frênes. AUGUST 12. At Pont-de-l'Arche. AUGUST 13. At Rouen. AUGUST 14. To wit, on the vigil of the Assumption of the Blessed Mary, at the same. AUGUST 15. At Rouen, where by God's grace we celebrated the feast of the Assumption. AUGUST 16-20. At Déville. AUGUST 21. At Monville, at the manor of the chamberlain of Tancarville, but at our own expense. AUGUST 22. At Longueville, at our own expense. AUGUST 23-24. At Aliermont.

AUGUST 25. At the same. This day Eudes, rector of the church at Imoville, and the former clerk of the late Master Girard of Corio, came before us and [Eudes] promised and swore that he would submit to our orders and will, for that he had fraudulently or incompletely written out the will of the said Master G[irard], and that at his suggestion Luke of St-Nicholas and Enguerrand of St-Amand-de-Rouen, priests, had affixed their seals to a certain document which they said was his will. Item, he swore to assign to Willard, prior of Salle-aux-Puelles, who would act for us, all of the goods belonging to the said Master G. which he had and knew to be in our diocese, and would have these goods assigned to Willard as best he could. The said priests swore and promised to submit to our commands because of the transgression of the law and wrongdoing perpetrated by them in this matter. They offered as pledges for this their churches and all of their moveable and immovable goods. Present were: G., the treasurer; P[eter], the archdeacon of Caux; Master J. of Flainville, and Master J. of Soissons, canons of Rouen; Brother Adam Rigaud; Brother Harduin; Brother Walter of Minières; and Brother John of Morgneval.

AUGUST 26. At Aliermont. This day we cited Master Robert of Houssaye, rector at Conteville, before the above written witnesses, that he might resign his church as he is obliged to do because of his oath. AUGUST 27-29. At Aliermont. AUGUST 30. We received procuration at Nogent near Neufchâtel from Reginald of Aliermont, who was at that time the lessee of the place. Total for procuration: nine pounds.

AUGUST 31. We visited the hospital at Neufchâtel. Present were four canons, three lay brothers and three lay sisters. We enjoined Hugh, called Dominus, that he should confess more frequently, for he had been negligent in this regard. The house in which the sick were lying threatens to collapse. They thought they had a sufficiency of wheat and other provisions, with the exception of oats, to last them until the year was out. With God's grace their condition was good.

This day we visited the two monks from Préaux who are living at Ste-Radegonde, near Neufchâtel. They have a small income.

We spent the night at Beaubec, at the expense of the monastery.

SEPTEMBER 1. We lunched at the manor of Sir John of Robert, knight, and spent the night at Beaussault, where we received procuration that day. Total for procuration: seven pounds, eleven shillings.

SEPTEMBER 2. We visited Beaussault priory, where were two monks from Bec-Hellouin. We ordered them to try to celebrate Mass more often than had been their practice. Alms are given thrice a week to all comers. They had no copy of the Rule; we ordered them to try to get one, and to have a copy written out. They frequently ate meat when there was no need, but they had a good conscience in this matter, because their abbot was fully aware of their practice. They owed one hundred seventeen pounds of Paris and thirty-four pounds of Tours to their abbot; they owed little elsewhere. Everything else was in good condition.

This day we visited the abbey at Bival, where there were thirty-three nuns, of whom one was a novice. They should confess and receive Communion seven times a year. They had three maidservants for their common service. They owed forty pounds; they had few provisions. With God's grace we found everything else to be in a satisfactory state, except that we were displeased at the provision they had made for a priest whom we had taken away from them;[4] we learned that they had assigned to him an annual pension of thirty pounds, and that he was living in the diocese of Amiens.

[4] See entry for January 15, 1256/57.

On the same day we spent the night at Foucarmont, at the expense of the monastery.

This day we received a letter from the cardinals concerning the business of the Tartars,[5] on which the proctors had gone to the Roman Curia. The letter was brought by Master John of Neuilly-en-Thelle and his colleague who had just returned from the Curia.

SEPTEMBER 3. At Eu, at our expense.

SEPTEMBER 4. We visited the abbey there. Thirty-two canons were in residence; of these, four were novices. At our other visitation[6] we had ordered them to have a copy made of the Legend so that the community might use it in the refectory; we again and expressly commanded this to be done, and that they should repair and rebind their Passional. Item, they had neither good vestments nor good ornaments; we ordered them to correct these things. They replied that the sacristan was held to make provision for these things, both to furnish new ones and to have the old repaired. Item, we ordered them to confess more diligently than they had been in the habit of doing. Item, the cloister was visited by lay folk too often, although we had frequently given orders that the cloister be guarded more carefully, both on the monastery side and on the side leading from the kitchen. Once more we ordered them to keep the door next to the kitchen closed, or so guarded that access would be denied to lay folk and they would be unable to enter the cloister as had been their custom. Item, they rarely drew up a statement of receipts, payments, or particular expenses; we ordered them to attend to this more diligently. They owed nine hundred pounds, and eight hundred thirty-three pounds was owed to them. They had enough provisions, with the exception of oats. They had spent a good deal in repairing the granges. Brother William of Arques talked irreverently, volubly, and without restraint in chapter, a thing which much displeased us. We ordered the canons who dined with guests at the house to leave them in time to be present at Compline, and to enter the dormitory with the others. We received procuration there this day. Total for procuration: nine pounds, eight shillings, three pence.

[5] The matter of the Crusade. See entry for the holding of the provincial council of Mantes held April 6, 1260/61. This letter must have been obtained from the College of Cardinals while the Apostolic See was *sede vacante*. Urban (1261-64) was not elected until August 29, 1261, and was consecrated on September 1 of the same year. As the text indicates, Eudes received this letter on September 2.

[6] See entry for March 9, 1259/60.

SEPTEMBER 5. We visited the abbey at Le Tréport, where there were twenty-three monks; one was a novice. We ordered the precentor to have the old books repaired, and especially to have them gathered and bound as he should do. One does not accuse another [in chapter], although we had on several occasions ordered this to be done and corrected;[7] but they said that this was not according to their Usages. Thrice a week alms are given to all laymen who come to them, and once a week to clerics. We ordered the abbot to visit frequently the monks who were living in the outside priories, to restrain them from eating meat, and to inflict the required punishment upon transgressors. They owed three hundred pounds, and about as much was owed to them, although the debts were not very good ones. With God's grace we found everything else to be in good condition. We received procuration there this day. Total for procuration: nine pounds, four shillings.

SEPTEMBER 6. We received procuration at Envermeu. Total for procuration: eight pounds, fourteen shillings.

SEPTEMBER 7. We visited there, where there were thirteen monks; all but one were priests. One did not accuse another [in chapter], because that was the Usage there. However, the prior, subprior, and the other officers accused the delinquents, and then the delinquent was publicly disciplined. Alms are given and bestowed three times a week to all comers. We gave orders that guests should be hospitably received. Item, we ordered them to observe the fasts of the Rule. Sometimes they ate meat when there was no need. It should be known that at the abbot's order an audit ought to be made four times a year. They owed two hundred pounds to the abbot, and a little elsewhere. With the exception of wine, they had sufficient provisions for the year.

This day we spent the night at Aliermont, at our own expense.

SEPTEMBER 8. To wit, on the feast of the Nativity of the Blessed Virgin Mary. We celebrated Mass, and preached at St. Nicholas' church at Aliermont.

This day, we bestowed upon Master John of Gamaches, a priest, a prebend of the Rouen church which had belonged to Master John of Soissons, and in the name of the said priest [John of Gamaches] we invested John of Morgneval, our clerk, by our ring, with this prebend. Present were: Brothers Adam Rigaud, Harduin, and Nicholas of Montebourg.

SEPTEMBER 9. At Dieppe. SEPTEMBER 10. We received procuration at

[7] See entry for January 15, 1259/60.

Longueil, from the lessee of a certain house which the abbot of Bec-Hellouin has there. Total for procuration: ten pouns, three shillings, four pense. SEPTEMBER 11-12. At the same, but at our own expense. SEPTEMBER 13. We received procuration at Bacqueville. Total for procuration: eight pounds, five shillings.

SEPTEMBER 14. We visited there, where there were four monks from Tiron; all were priests, and all four had recently arrived there. Some of them were sleeping on feather beds; we forbade them to use feather beds unless necessity required. We ordered the prior to compel frequent confession and not to permit them to have coffers with keys. The Rule of their order was never read, nor did they observe silence except after Compline. Item, in the presence of a visitor of their own order, we ordered them to observe the fasts according to the Rule of their order and to abstain from eating meat, which they were in the habit of eating freely and without scruples of conscience, except insofar as their Rule permitted them to do so. The visitor stated that this was a matter for his abbot to settle, and that the latter had granted them a dispensation in this matter. We ordered the prior to prepare a written statement of particular expenses, in detail and in total. They owed one hundred twenty pounds. They believed that, with the exception of oats, they had sufficient provisions to last out the year. They said that the prior had found the place in a very run-down condition. Item, we ordered the prior to strive to celebrate Mass more often than was his practice; he explained that he had omitted the celebration of Mass because of his temporal duties.

We came this day to the church at Sauqueville, where there were four canons; there should be six. The treasurer never resides there, although he is bound to do so. The precentor was ill. Walter, called Gross, is unwilling to keep residence; however, those who are in residence do not care about this, for his absence is more advantageous to them than his presence, because of the contentions which he causes in the community; he is illiterate. One of them was deaf, so that he was not able to get up for Matins, and, indeed, he did little at the other Hours. We forbade this deaf canon to allow Stephen, called Briand, and his wife to foregather at his house, by reason of the scandal which might arise therefrom. We must take action against Ferris, the treasurer, for that he has already been defamed many times over of Albereda of Caney. We warned him to keep away from her.

This day, we spent the night at Longueville, at our own expense.

SEPTEMBER 15. We visited the abbey of St-Victor. Eighteen monks were there, and two of them had been sent outside for reasons; one of them was at Bec, the other at Jumièges. All but three were priests. We ordered the abbot and prior to inspect frequently the coffers of the monks, either together or singly, lest they be in the possession of property. Item, we forbade the abbot to receive back any monk who should happen to go out without permission, except in the manner in which a fugitive monk is received back.[8] Item, because quarrels had occasionally arisen amongst them over procuring provisions of better wines and foods, we expressly forbade them to grumble about this in the future. What is more, we urged them to live in charity with one another so far as they could do so. They owed eighty pounds, and about as much was owed to them. Item, we ordered the abbot to issue a complete statement as to the state of their house twice a year in full chapter; to wit, how much they owed, how much was owed to them, and, indeed, upon what the money had been expended. Item, we ordered him to see that the quality of the beer was improved. They were aggrieved because of certain pittances which they received on certain anniversaries, but which the abbot had withdrawn from them; the abbot promised that he would more liberally distribute such pittances on the requisite days. Item, we ordered the abbot to give to those who had been bled, wine and such other things as they were accustomed to receive. Item, that he should see to it that the infirmary was better provided for than had been the case. Item, that he should restore to them what they were in the habit of receiving for increasing the evening meal, to wit, sixty shillings, as some of them said. Alms were not given on definite days, but should be given to all comers on Thursdays and Sundays. We received procuration there this day. Total for procuration: eight pounds.

SEPTEMBER 16. We went in person to St-Thomas, where abbot William[9] was, because we had heard some unpleasant rumors about him from many people, and especially from the visitor of his order, to wit, that he was living incontinently and was conducting himself in worse fashion than he had ever done. We spoke with him in his room. After many rebukes we warned him to abstain completely from the society of women. In the presence of the new abbot, we ordered him to keep two monks with him, and to have one of these with him always and in all places. We ordered the new abbot that if

[8] *Rule of St. Benedict,* Ch. 29.
[9] Abbot William had abdicated. See entry for December 17, 1255.

the pension assigned to the said former abbot was insufficient to maintain him and the monks attached to him, he should at least contribute to the maintenance of the two attached monks.

We spent the night at Déville.

SEPTEMBER 17. We absolved Sir Anselem, knight, bailiff of Gisors, from the excommunication imposed upon him by our vicar of Pontoise, in the matter of a certain twice-married cleric whom the said bailiff had held a prisoner on a charge of homicide and had then returned to us. We had, in turn, returned him to the said bailiff to keep him in custody until such time as we should request him. The said bailiff swore to submit to the mandate of the Church and to our decision in this matter of his excommunication. We spent the night there this day.

SEPTEMBER 18. With God's grace we dedicated the Franciscan church at Rouen, and spent the night at Déville. SEPTEMBER 19. At Déville.

SEPTEMBER 20. We visited the priory at Bondeville, where there were thirty-one nuns, seven lay sisters, and three lay brothers. As we had done before,[10] we expressly forbade any nuns ever to talk with any secular man or woman save in the parlor, that is to say, in some public place. They should confess and receive Communion once a month, but we found that some of them were negligent in these things. The lay brothers confess and receive Communion seven times a year. There is a certain parish there with only nine parishioners. We ought to commit the care of these to a priest whom the prioress should control. Several secular little girls were sent to the priory at their own expense. Item, since we discovered that some of them [the nuns] neglected to receive Communion, we decreed that whosoever did not receive Communion two or three times consecutively with the rest, should abstain for three days from wine and soup. Item, we ordered the prioress to appoint some one over the treasury to receive the money and to supervise expenses, and to be informed and cognizant of expenses. Item, we dismissed Melchior, priest, who for some little time had managed the affairs of the house, because the community did not have complete confidence in him and he had become hateful to them. They owed about two hundred fifty pounds; they had few provisions. Item, we ordered the prioress to be present with the community at least by day, that is to say, she should attend chapter, the refectory, and the choir better than she had been wont to do. We forbade her

10 See entry for November 6, 1259.

to continue her practice of standing out in the churchyard or out of doors after Compline, or to carry on conversations there. Item, the prioress offered us her seal, requesting us to release her from her office; we were, in fact, not willing to concede this to her, but enjoined her to be more zealous in the exercise of her duties.

This day we spent the night at Déville.

SEPTEMBER 21. To wit, on the feast of St. Matthew the Apostle and Evangelist. Through God's grace, we preached and administered the Sacrament of Confirmation at the monastery of St-Patrick and spent the night at Déville.

SEPTEMBER 22. We visited the priory of Notre-Dame-de-Pré. Eighteen monks from Bec were there; all were priests with the exception of one novice who had come there from Bec because of his ill health. There should be twenty-four monks there, but the number had been reduced because of the fire which had damaged the place. They did not confess very often, a fact which much displeased us. We ordered them to keep lay folk out of the cloister, and especially the women who were in the habit of passing through the cloister on their way to the monastery church when memorial Masses for their friends were to be celebrated. We suggested that they should make these women stay in the nave of the monastery church. Alms were dispensed three times a week. They ate meat when there was no need, and they knew they were doing wrong; we ordered them to abstain from eating meat, except as the Rule permitted. We ordered the prior to see that better provision is made for the sick than had been the case. They owed fourteen hundred pounds, of which they owed one thousand pounds to the abbot, with the exception of some sixty marks which he had recently received.

This day we spent the night at Déville, at our own expense.

SEPTEMBER 23. We visited the priory of the St-Mary-Magdalene at Rouen. There were seven canons in residence; ten were outside, one of them staying alone at St-Nichole-de-Bellevue. Item, there were twenty-seven sisters there, some of whom the prior had received without our express approval, although we had forbidden him to do this,[11] and this much displeased us. Item, there were also five lay brothers. All of the canons were priests. Item, we ordered the prior to inspect the coffers of the canons and of the sisters more frequently than was his practice to see that they did not

---

[11] See entry for December 11, 1258.

have any property. Item, Brother Peter was negligent in visiting the sick and in hearing their confessions. We enjoined him to correct his conduct in this regard. Item, the prior had committed himself and his house to provide a certain cleric, Robert by name, with the necessities of life as long as he should live, which displeased us. Item, the brothers and sisters confess and receive Communion thirteen times a year. Item, we expressly forbade the prior, as we had indeed done before,[12] to receive anyone, male or female, as canon, lay brother, or sister, without our special permission. We enjoined a penance upon him because in the face of our prohibition he had received some as sisters. Item, Brother Peter was insensate, drunken, and garrulous, and was at times unwilling to celebrate Mass when requested by the prior, however great the emergency might be. He was disobedient and rebellious, and would walk out of the house in an unseemly manner, with head erect and neck outstretched; wherefore we ordered the prior that, if he did not refrain from such conduct, to send the said Peter to us for punishment. Item, a certain chaplain, Peter by name, whom the prior's predecessor had caused to be brought in had been there for many years, and since this priest and the aforesaid Robert [sic], cleric, had behaved badly and were still doing so, we removed them and ordered them to be sent away without fail.

This day Feris,[13] the treasurer of Sauqueville, stood trial before us and confessed that he was publicly defamed of incontinence with Albereda of Cany; however, he denied the truth of this. Wherefore, we thought it proper to institute an enquiry into this charge against him, that is to say, to find out whether he had cohabited with the said woman and was in the habit of cohabiting with her, as rumor, which he knows about, declares and testifies. We handed over a copy of the charges to him.

This day we dined with the Friars Minor, and spent the night at Déville.

SEPTEMBER 24. With God's grace we conferred Holy Orders at the Dominican monastery in Rouen, dined with the Friars Minor, who had gathered at Rouen to elect a minister,[14] and spent the night at our manor at Rouen. SEPTEMBER 25-27. At Frênes. SEPTEMBER 28. We received procuration at St-Laurent-en-Lyons. Total for procuration seven pounds, four shillings.

[12] Idem.

[13] Seen entry for September 14, above.

[14] That is, a superior: this must have been an election of a local superior. No meeting for 1261 to elect a general superior is recounted in Luke Wadding, Annales Minorum, 1256-75, Vol. III (Florence, 1931), nor in R. M. Huber, Documented History of the Franciscan Order, 1182-1517, (Washington, 1944), I, 830-31.

SEPTEMBER 29. With God's aid we preached and administered Confirmation at the parish church in Beauvoir, and spent the night at St-Laurent, at our own expense. It was the feast of St. Michael.

SEPTEMBER 30. We visited the priory of St-Laurent-en-Lyons. Fourteen canons were in residence, and sixteen were in eight places outside; all but two were priests. Two were under suspension: to wit, Brother Richard, for having clandestinely given his daughter in marriage, a daughter whom he had begotten while a priest; the other for another reason. One did not accuse another [in chapter]; we ordered this corrected. Item, the canons freely went out of the cloister and monastery, especially at our coming and when lay guests arrive; they gossiped with the lay folk; we forbade this to be allowed in the future. We gave orders that lay folk be kept out of the cloister and that the cloister gate be more carefully guarded than had been their practice. Item, we ordered them to confess and receive Communion more often. Item, there were six lay brothers and three lay sisters there; they confess and receive Communion twice a year. Alms are given three times a week to all comers. Item, we ordered them to keep a written record of the house's income. Once a month an audit is made of receipts and expenses. They owe two hundred fifty pounds of Tours. A certain lay brother had burdened the house with a heavy debt. You can see this in the attached schedule.[15]

This day we spent this night at Bellosane, at the expense of the abbey.

OCTOBER 1. We visited the priory of St-Aubin, where were fourteen choir nuns and one lay sister. We expressly forbade them, as we had done before,[16] to receive anyone, whether as choir-nun or lay sister, without our special permission. They are obliged to confess and receive Communion seven times a year; however, we found that they were sometimes negligent about it; they said that they had omitted to do it because they did not have any wine left after Communion. After hearing this, we ordered them never to omit receiving Communion for any such reason and, what is more, to prepare themselves for Communion with the greatest diligence. They had coffers with keys, and the prioress had never inspected them. Item, Alice of Rouen conceived and brought forth a child since our last visitation, and it is said that she has had three children on three separate occasions; likewise, Beatrice of Beauvais had a certain child of which she was delivered at Blacourt, and

15 Now missing from the manuscript.
16 See entry for March 5, 1259/60.

it is rumored that she was made pregnant by the dean of St-Quentin, in the diocese of Beauvais. The prioress told us that these two [Alice and Beatrice] were in grave fault for many days and had performed such penance for their offenses as the Rule of their order required. Item, we expressly forbade them individually or otherwise, or any lay person, to eat at their priest's house; item, [we forbade them] to take in any children to be brought up; item, [we forbade] the juniors to go out either for gainful purposes or for any other reason. Item, we ordered the prioress that if, when the time for receiving Communion came around, anyone should neglect it, to place her under grave fault, unless she had been absent for just cause. They had few provisions.

This day we visited the chapter at Gournay. We found there one canon living with the dean. They did not have the corporals sufficiently clean; the treasurer, or whoever exercised his office, was responsible for washing them. We found other things to be in a satisfactorily good state, and we spent the night at Gournay, at our own expense.

OCTOBER 2. We visited the Hôtel-Dieu at Gournay, where were four brothers, one priest, and five sisters, of whom two lived outside and three within the house. The priest was a [professed] brother of the community, and all of them had taken the three vows. The sick poor received little from the goods of the house, and the town provided them with meat twice a week; item, they had admitted and had received as guests healthy travelers, both priests and clerics, and even the sergeants of the king who watched the forest of Lyons. We forbade them to grant hospitality to men of this kind in the future, unless such men were willing to sleep with the sick. They owed sixteen pounds. Item, the brothers who were staying in the granges had their wives with them. The priest had the cure of those living in the house, and for this they had to come to a satisfactory agreement with the priest at St. Mary's [parish].

This day with God's grace we celebrated Mass at St-Hildevert. The chancellor of Rouen preached, and we administered Confirmation there, with God's aid. We spent the night in the town, at our own expense.

OCTOBER 3. We came in person to the priory at Neufmarché, and visited there. We found three monks from St-Evroult in residence. We could not spend the night there because the buildings were neither adequate nor furnished to receive us. Alms are usually given every Sunday to all comers. They had no copy of the Rule; we ordered them to have one written out.

They ate meat freely when there was no need; we ordered them to abstain from eating meat as the Statutes of the Rule require, and to keep their conscience clear in this matter. The parish priest belonged to their table. They owed two hundred pounds, fifty pounds of which they owed to their abbot for rebuilding the houses. They should have a certain house, with its appurtenances, at Gonneville, which [appurtenances] the abbot had appropriated to the use of the abbey, and from all of them the priory at Neufmarché has only received twenty-three pounds a year, although the entire amount should go to the priory. The said parish priest had no clerk, as was requested for his needs; we ordered the prior to give the priest a clerk who would be suitable to help the priest, both by day and by night, in psalmody, in serving at the altar, and in attending him on his parish calls by day or by night.

This day we spent the night at Frênes, at our own expense.

On the day before, we had the leper hospital at Gournay visited by the dean of Bray and by our almoner. They found the place miserably desolate, that is to say, overburdened with debts and with people, and without provisions to last out the year. They found also that their chaplain had recently died.

OCTOBER 4-5. At Frênes. OCTOBER 6. At Pont-de-l'Arche. OCTOBER 7-10. Attending the Exchequer at Rouen, and we slept at the castle with the other masters. OCTOBER 11. At Bec-Hellouin. OCTOBER 12. At Lisieux. OCTOBER 13-17. At Caen, to attend the Exchequer. OCTOBER 18. The feast of St. Luke the Evangelist. At Caen. OCTOBER 19. At Caen. OCTOBER 20. At Lisieux. OCTOBER 21. At Beaumont-le-Roger. OCTOBER 22. We came to Evreux to restore peace between the bishop and the chapter. OCTOBER 23. By God's grace, through our mediation and by the counsel of good men, peace was restored between the said bishop and chapter, and that day we spent this night at Sausseuse, at our own expense. OCTOBER 24. At Chaumont, at our expense.

OCTOBER 25. With God's grace we celebrated the sacred synod of the Vexin, at the priory at [Notre-Dame] l'Aillerie, and we spent the night there.

This day we assigned the day after Advent as the time when Walter, priest at Hérouville, should purge himself with the seventh hand of priests of the incontinence of which he had been many times defamed, as we have [heard] from trustworthy persons. He has not denied this kind of defamation.

OCTOBER 26. At Frênes. OCTOBER 27. At Pinterville. OCTOBER 28. To wit, on the feast of SS. Simon and Jude. With God's aid we bestowed our benediction upon Sister Jeanne, abbess of St-Amand-de-Rouen, and spent the night there. OCTOBER 29. At Rouen. OCTOBER 30. With God's help we preached a general sermon at the cathedral. OCTOBER 31. At Rouen.

NOVEMBER 1. With God's grace we celebrated the feast of All Saints at Rouen. Today we cited before us the chaplains of the cathedral of Rouen and warned them to celebrate Mass more frequently than they had been doing, and we had them warned about this again by the chapter of Rouen. NOVEMBER 2-4. At Martot.

NOVEMBER 5. At Martot. This day Master Reginald of Campagne, presented for the church at Barville by Sir Robert of Etoutteville, knight, appeared before us and said that he was appealing from us lest we should collate any one to the said church in his stead; beyond that he said nothing.

NOVEMBER 6. At Martot. NOVEMBER 7. At Rouen. NOVEMBER 8. We celebrated the sacred synod of Rouen. NOVEMBER 9. We held the synod of deans.

This day we assigned the day before the Christmas ordinations as the time when the priest of Civières, many times defamed of divers vices, should purge himself with the ninth hand of priests[17] of incontinence, adultery, constant fighting, and frequenting taverns.

We spent the night at Ste-Catherine, at our own expense.

NOVEMBER 10. At Pinterville. NOVEMBER 11. To wit, on the feast of St. Martin *Hiemalis*; at the same. NOVEMBER 12. At Vernon. NOVEMBER 13. At Mantes. NOVEMBER 14. At St-Germain-en-Laye. NOVEMBER 15. At Paris. This day we conferred upon Master Anselm of Bucy the canonry which Brother John of Soissons possessed in the Rouen church, together with the prebend which had belonged to Master Richard of Salmonville. NOVEMBER 16-19. At Paris, to attend the Parlement.

NOVEMBER 20. At Paris. This day Master Reginald of Campagne,[18] cleric, appeared before us and entered the following appeal:

Reverend Father, lord archbishop of Rouen, I, Reginald of Campagne, cleric, was presented to you for the vacant church of Notre-Dame at Barville by the noble man, Sir Robert of Etoutteville, knight, the true patron of this church through Jeanne, his wife, and with the consent of the mother of the said Jeanne, through whom the right of advowson is known to pertain to the said

[17] See above, October 16, 1248, n. 70.
[18] See entry for November 5, above.

knight. Since it is said that you do not wish to receive me at the presentation of this knight, the true patron of the said church, I, feeling myself aggrieved thereby, have appealed to the Apostolic See, and I appeal again, renewing my appeal in writing. And, lest you should receive anyone for the said church or collate anyone in it to my prejudice and hurt, I request you give me *apostoli*.

However, we are not obliged to defer to an appeal of this kind, for it was neither true nor just, and especially since there was a dispute concerning the right of advowson to the said church between the presenter of the said Reginald, on the one hand, and William, lord of Nogent, knight, on the other, and the dispute had not been settled definitely within the legal time limit.

NOVEMBEB 21-29. At Paris, to attend the Parlement. NOVEMBER 30. To wit, on the feast of St. Andrew the Apostle. At the same. DECEMBER 1-4. At Paris.[19] DECEMBER 5. At Louvres. DECEMBER 6. At Senlis, to wit, on the feast of St. Nicholas. DECEMBER 7. At Compiègne. DECEMBER 8. At Noyon. DECEMBER 9. At Gournay-sur-Aronde. DECEMBER 10. At Bulles. DECEMBER 11. At Milly. DECEMBER 12. At St-Laurent-en-Lyons, at our own expense.

DECEMBER 13. At the same, and at our own expense. This day we relieved Brother William, then prior, from his office, with God's grace, and confirmed the election of Brother William of Rouville, a canon of the place, after first making a careful examination of the method of holding the election and of the elected person.

DECEMBER 14. At Sigy, where we received procuration from the prior of the place, who owes us full procuration each year, but which is not to exceed ten pounds of Tours, according to a letter copied out in our cartulary, and which contains a more complete statement of this. Total for procuration: eight pounds, ten shillings.

DECEMBER 15. We visited the priory at Sigy, where there were three monks from St-Ouen-de-Rouen. There should be six, but the abbot of his own free will recalled three of them to his monastery and reduced the income of the priory because of this, cutting it down to about one hundred forty pounds; this displeased us greatly, because of the diminishing of the Divine Service. They had an insufficient number of [liturgical] books. Alms are given thrice a week. They ate meat many times when there was no need.

---

[19] Eudes' clerk has thirty-two days in December. This was done by beginning the month with the V Nones rather than IV Nones.

They did well in observing the fasts of the Rule, as they said. They only made an audit of the state of the house before their abbot once a year, on the feast of St-Ouen. The income of the place was not worth two hundred pounds, as they said. We must speak with the abbot about this withdrawal of income, about restoring it to the said priory, and about replacing the three monks.

This day we spent the night at Déville, at our own expense.

DECEMBER 16. At Déville.

DECEMBER 17. With God's grace we conferred Holy Orders at the church of St-Maclou-de-Rouen.

This day the priest at Civières appeared before us, although yesterday was the day assigned to him for purging himself with the seventh [sic] hand of priests of the vice of incontinence and of many other crimes of which he had been gravely defamed.[20] We assigned him the Friday before Christmas for purgation.

DECEMBER 18. With God's grace we preached at the cathedral of Rouen, and we spent the night at Rouen.

DECEMBER 19. Walter, priest at Aronville, appeared before us, for this day had been assigned to him for purging himself with the seventh hand of priests of the vice of incontinence, about which he had confessed to us before and admitted that he had been defamed. He stated that because of the holy days which were upon us, he could not conveniently bring his compurgators with him. We, although convinced of his bad intention, assigned him the day following the coming Septuagesima, when he should appear before us at Rouen, or before our official should we be absent, and purge himself of the said vice in the manner stated. Item, he then confessed that he was defamed. Present were the venerable men: the archdeacon Stephen, Masters John of Neuilly-en-Thelle, Richard of Salmonville, Richard of Sap, and John of Morgneval.

We spent the night at Martot.

DECEMBER 20-22. At Martot. DECEMBER 23. At Rouen, and we made our O.[21] DECEMBER 24. At Rouen. DECEMBER 25. With God's grace we celebrated the feast of the Lord's Nativity.

DECEMBER 26. At Déville. Today, Girard, priest at Martigny, was per-

[20] See entry for November 9, above. The original purgation was with the ninth hand of priests.

[21] See above, December 23, 1250, n. 135.

emptorily and in person cited to appear before us to answer a charge that he
had wounded Peter of Vivier, a man of Sir Thomas of Beaumont, knight.
He appeared before us, but no one appeared against him. However, we were
in no wise willing to allow a thing of this kind to go entirely undiscussed,
and we asked him whether he had wounded or struck the said man, and he
said, "Yes," and that with a sword but in protection of his own body because
the man had rushed upon him. Then, with his consent, we proposed, with
God's grace, to investigate the said affair, the method of wounding, and the
cause and the nature of the wound.

DECEMBER 27-28. At Déville.

DECEMBER 29. We came to the monastery at Jumièges, not with the intention of making a visitation,[22] but because some of the monks of this
monastery, to wit, the seniors of the community, had come to us and revealed
that the abbot, of his own free will and so far as he could, had renounced
his office and had returned his seal, broken, to the community. We spent the
night there, at our own expense.

DECEMBER 30. We entered the chapter, and with the monks gathered
together, and in the presence of the abbots of St-Wandrille, St-Taurin-
d'Evreux, and St-Georges, and the treasurer and the precentor of Rouen, we
preached God's Word, with His aid. This finished, the abbot[23] appeared
before us who were prepared to exercise the duty of visitation in the usual
manner. Throwing himself on the ground, the abbot besought us most
urgently to accept his abdication from office, and we listened to him in this
matter. On the other hand, the community, on bended knees, humbly prayed
us to compel him to exercise his office as he had been accustomed to do. We
did not at all agree with the reasons that the abbot had set forth alleging his
insufficiency, but rather considered them to be empty and frivolous. We
enjoined him, by virtue of his vow of obedience, to exercise his office as he
ought. Then we sought to obtain from him, and he agreed to comply without
exhortation, a statement concerning the state of the house, in the usual
manner employed at visitations. We found that the fasts were not very well
observed in the priories, and that they ate meat when there was no need.
Item, no monks were as yet at Guisenières; we warned the abbot to put some
there. More was owed to them than they owed. With God's grace we found

---

[22] Eudes did not intend to make a formal visitation, but circumstances compelled
him to do otherwise.

[23] William.

other things to be in a satisfactorily good condition. We received procuration there that day. They did not wish to compute.

DECEMBER 31. At St-Georges, at our expense.

JANUARY 1. To wit, on the Circumcision of the Lord. By God's grace we preached His Word in chapter and visited there. Twenty-five monks were in residence; two of them were novices; they have three others in England, and two at St-Nicole. All but three were priests. The community did not have a good Bible to read. No alms are given there except a tenth part of the bread which is baked in the house and three loaves which the almoner receives every day from the community bread in the refectory. Ill provision was made for those who had been bled, although we had ordered them before to correct this.[24] We repeated our orders to attend to this in a better fashion than they had been doing. They had sufficient provisions. They owed about one hundred pounds, and some five hundred pounds or more was owed to them. We received procuration there this day. Total for procuration: nine pounds, fifteen shillings, six pence.

JANUARY 1 [*sic*]. At Déville, at our own expense. JANUARY 2. We received procuration at St-Saëns. Total for procuration: eight pounds, fifteen shillings.

JANUARY 3. We visited the priory at St-Saëns, where were three monks from St-Wandrille with the prior. They ate meat freely and did not observe the fasts of the Rule very well. Alms are given once a week to all comers. More was owed to them than they owed. Other things we found to be satisfactory.

This day we came to the priory of nuns of St-Saëns, and, having preached there, we visited the nuns. Fifteen choir nuns were there, and one novice. Sometimes they ceased altogether to chant the Hours with notation and the accustomed modulation.[25] Occasionally one of them would go out alone, a thing which greatly displeased us, and we forbade this to be permitted in the future. They have not had their own confessor for a long time; we determined to procure the prior of Cressy for them. At our visitation last year[26] we gave orders to have the two nuns who were staying at Ste-Austreberte removed and recalled to the cloister; the prioress had neglected to do this and gave as her excuse that one of the two, Mary of Eu, was obstreperous,

---

[24] See entry for January 4, 1260/61.
[25] See above, July 9, 1249, n. 36.
[26] See entry for December 1, 1260.

and she feared that if [Mary] returned, she would upset the whole community. However, because of the dangers and scandals which might arise, and from what we had heard about the two nuns who were staying there, as well as on account of the meagreness of the income of the said place, we, with God's grace, proposed to have them removed [from Ste-Austreberte], and decreed that, for the future, no nuns should dwell there under any conditions, but that they [the nuns of St-Saëns] should receive some of the income annually of the said place, from whatever priest should be there at the time. Item, they were keeping two young girls at the priory, to wit, the daughter of the chatelain of Bellencombre and the elder daughter of the lord of Manières; we ordered them to send these girls back home. Item, they begged us to give them permission to receive and give the veil to five nuns, so that their number might be twenty, in order to advance the Divine cult; we, however, did not concede this to them. However, we told and ordered them to send to us the women or their friends whom they wished to have become nuns in the community and, if we judged that it was advantageous to them and to the community, we would permit them to receive and give the veil to some; nevertheless, we expressly forbade them to presume to receive anyone without our special permission. Item, we forbade any of them to eat with lay folk in the priory. They had one lay sister and three maidservants. Item, they had sold about three hundred fifty pounds worth of their wood at Equiqueville of which amount they had already received one hundred twenty pounds. They owed two hundred forty pounds; they had neither wheat nor oats.

This day we spent the night and received procuration at Bures. Total for procuration: nine pounds, ten shillings.

JANUARY 4. We visited the priory there, where there were two monks from Pré. They ate meat and used feather beds; they did not observe the fasts of the Rule. The prior of Pré received everything that was left over to the monks from the income of this house, after the maintenance had been paid. They owed nothing and nothing was owed to them, inasmuch as the prior of Pré provided for them and supplied them with their necessities.

We spent this night at Aliermont.

JANUARY 5. At Aliermont. JANUARY 6. With God's grace we celebrated the feast of the Epiphany there. JANUARY 7-8. At Aliermont. JANUARY 9. We received procuration at Aliermont from the lessee at Wanchy. Total for procuration: nine pounds, seven shillings. JANUARY 10. At Aliermont.

JANUARY 11. At the same, at our own expense. This day we received the following letter from the king:

Louis, by God's grace king of the Franks, to his beloved and faithful . . . [*lacuna in MS*] [Eudes], archbishop of Rouen, greeting and affection. We have been notified by a special letter from Master Nicholas of Sens, a canon of Paris, and by the intimation of merchants, that the Lord Pope has ordained and elevated seven cardinals to the Holy Roman Church, and that amongst these, three members of our Council have been so elevated, to wit, the archbishop of Narbonne,[27] the bishop of Evreux,[28] and the treasurer of St-Martin-de-Tours;[29] the four others are Transmontains, to wit, Simon of Padua, formerly elected bishop of Aversa; Gonfroi of Alatri; Giacomo Sabelli of Urbino; and Hubert of Cocani—all modest and reverend men, according to the letter we received.

Since we have some matters to talk over with you, we command you hasten to us without delay. We also understand that the abovementioned treasurer proposes to talk and consult with you anent the foregoing. Given, etc.

JANUARY 12. At Aliermont. JANUARY 13. At St-Saëns, at our own expense. JANUARY 14. At Déville. JANUARY 15. At Frênes. JANUARY 16-18. At Chaumont, at our own expense. JANUARY 19-20. At Beaumont-sur-Oise. JANUARY 21. At Meulan. JANUARY 22. At Vernon. JANUARY 23-26. At Pinterville. Were with us [Ralph], the bishop of Evreux, and [Simon], the treasurer of Tours. JANUARY 27. At Pont-de-l'Arche. JANUARY 28. At Rouen. JANUARY 29. At Frênes. JANUARY 30. At Chaumont. JANUARY 31. At Asnières. FEBRUARY 1. At the same. FEBRUARY 2. We celebrated High Mass before the king at the church in Royaumont, to wit, on the feast of the Purification of the Blessed Virgin Mary. We spent the night at Asnières. FEBRUARY 3-4. At Asnières. FEBRUARY 5. This day, with God's grace, we preached in the chapter at Royaumont before the king, the local community, and many others. FEBRUARY 6. At St-Denis. FEBRUARY 7-28. At Paris, to attend the Parlement. MARCH 1. At Meulan. MARCH 2. At Vernon. MARCH 3. At Frênes. MARCH 4. With God's grace we conferred Holy Orders at St. Mary's church at Les Andelys, and we spent the night at Frênes. MARCH 5. At Rouen. MARCH 6. At Pinterville. MARCH 7. At

---

[27] Guy le Gros, archbishop of Narbonne (1257), cardinal of St-Sabino (1262), and later Pope Clement IV (1265-68).

[28] Ralph de Grosparmi, cardinal of St-Albano.

[29] Simon de Brie, cardinal of Ste-Cecilia, later legate of Clement IV to France, to preach the Crusade.

Vernon. MARCH 8. At Meulan. MARCH 9-21. At Paris. MARCH 22. At the same. This day, to wit, the Wednesday after *Laetare Hierusalem*,[30] all the cardinals left Paris. MARCH 23. At Meulan. MARCH 24. At Vernon. MARCH 25. At the same, to wit, on the Annunciation of the Blessed Virgin Mary. With God's grace we celebrated High Mass at the monastery of the Friars Minor, and we dined with them. MARCH 26. At Gaillon. MARCH 27. At Pinterville. MARCH 28-31. At Martot.

APRIL 1. At Rouen. That day we deprived Walter, former priest of the church at Aronville,[31] of the said church, using the following formula:

In the name of the Father, and of the Son, and of the Holy Ghost, Amen. Since Walter, rector of the church of Aronville, had been gravely defamed of the vice of incontinence, both in his own parish and elsewhere; and since we ordered him to undergo a purgation with the seventh hand[32] on a definitely appointed day, and in graciousness granted him an extension of the time until the Saturday before Palm Sunday; and since, on the appointed day, the aforesaid Walter completely failed in his purgation, we, weighing the advice of good men, have deprived the said Walter of the aforesaid church at Aronville.

Present were the venerable men: Masters J[ohn] and St[ephen], the archdeacons of the Norman and French [Vexins]; John of Neuilly-en-Thelle; Richard of Sap, canon of Rouen; Brother Adam Rigaud; and John of Morgneval, our clerk.

Item, on this same day appeared before us in person John, priest at Civières,[33] a man who had, on the testimony of good and serious men, been many times defamed of incontinence, of frequenting taverns, of scurrility, and of brawling, concerning all of which, with his consent, we had long ago ordered an enquiry to be made, and he asked us to show him a copy of the said investigation. But since we were convinced, upon examination of the said investigation, that he had been justly accused of the said crimes, we were not willing to grant this part of his request, but we ordered him to undergo a purgation with the seventh hand of his Order. For this purpose we appointed for him the Monday before Easter, when he should come before us at Rouen, or before our official, should we be away. In charity we

---

[30] The fourth Sunday in Lent.
[31] See entry for December 19, above.
[32] See above, October 16, 1248, n. 70.
[33] See entries for November 9, above, and December 17, above.

told him that if he desired to suggest anything to us which might demonstrate his innocence, we would be willing to hear what he might have to say on the day before Palm Sunday. He did not appear on that day, nor did he send a proctor. This day we spent the night at our manor at Rouen.

APRIL 2. That is to say, on Palm Sunday. With God's help we celebrated High Mass at the Rouen cathedral and preached a sermon in the atrium at St-Laurent. This day we spent the night at Rouen.

This day we exchanged the fruits of the prebend which the late Master Richard of Chevrèuses possessed in the Rouen church with Master William of Flavacourt, canon of Rouen, for the fruits of the prebend which the said Master William had possessed in the said church.

APRIL 3. We dined with the Dominicans at Rouen and spent the night at Déville. APRIL 4. At Déville. APRIL 5. We dined with the Friars Minor and spent the night at our manor in Rouen.

APRIL 6. With God's grace we preached a sermon at the cathedral immediately after Matins, and then with His aid we followed the usual custom of granting absolutions at the churches of Ste-Catherine, St-Ouen, St-Amand, and St-Lô[-de-Rouen]. Later, when the penitents had been led into the said cathedral at Rouen, we preached another sermon and performed the ceremonies of the holy chrism.

APRIL 7. With God's aid we performed the ceremonies of the Adoration of the Holy Cross.

APRIL 8. With God's grace we preached the Word of God in Latin in the cloister to the canons and clerks choral, and then we performed the ceremonies of the day.

This day a proxy letter was shown to us, to all appearances sealed with the seal of the court of the deanery of Beauvais, which ran as follows:

To all to whom the present letter may come, the dean of Beauvais gives greeting in the Lord. Be it known that the priest, Walter, rector of the church at Aronville,[34] in the diocese of Rouen, came before us and appointed and delegated Simon, cleric, the bearer of the present letter, as his legal and special proctor in the matter of entering an appeal against the legal process held against the said priest, and the sentence imposed upon him which deprived him of his church; and also in the matter of undertaking whatsoever other business may be pertinent to this affair, and do whatsoever he [Walter] might be able to do were he present before the Reverend Father, the lord archbishop of Rouen.

[34] See entries for December 19, above, and April 1, 1261.

He agreed to regard as valid and agreeable whatsoever the said proctor should negotiate for him in these matters. In testimony whereof we have caused the present proxy letter to be sealed with the seal of our court. Done in the year of our Lord 1261, on the Thursday after Palm Sunday.

When this proxy letter had been read out before us, the said Simon, clerical proctor, spoke in our presence as follows:

Reverend Father and Lord, lord archbishop of Rouen, Simon cleric, proctor for Walter, rector of the church at Aronville in the diocese of Rouen and in the French Vexin, proposes to you that in depriving him [Walter] of the aforesaid church you have proceeded against him evilly, unjustly, and incorrectly, because of unwritten and other reasons in law:

First, because when the aforesaid rector was cited before you and your official, he did not have anyone who might defend his case; he did not have, nor was he able to have, any lawyer who could explain his wishes and who, to defend his rights, could propose defenses and exceptions favorable to him; and when, on several occasions, he urgently besought your official to grant him a lawyer from the official's office, the said official denied his request, and utterly and expressly refused to grant him one;

Item, although he requested articles that he might know how you intended to proceed in your investigation against him, he could not procure a copy of these; indeed, they were completely denied to him;

Item, that you have not proceeded against him according to law in instituting this investigation, although the matter of which he is said to be ill famed did not reach your ears through persistent clamor and rumor;

Item, although the knowledge of this ill fame had its origin in certain malevolent and evil-speaking persons, and not in worthy and upright men, you have undertaken this inquisition without observing due process of law;

Item, you have proceeded against him to an incorrect investigation, although few, indeed, none at all, defamed him to you out of zeal for charity, but they were led rather by the tongue of malice, hate and evil;

Item, when the enquiry was started against him, he was never cited to be present at it;

Item, you did not proceed with this investigation with your canon lawyers, but at your own whim;

Item, although he has never in any way been defamed in the town and parish where he has resided and lived for the past twenty years, your investigation launched against him in foreign and distant parts is arbitrary;

Item, although no one accused or charged this priest with any crime, he was prepared to defend himself if any so accused him; as for those charges now proffered against him, nobody came forward or appeared to charge him with any crime, yet you have proceeded to an investigation against him without an accuser or denouncer;

Item, although he was reported, and that falsely, to have been defamed of a certain woman and to have loved her deeply, he offered to prove in your presence that he was prepared and willing to abjure her completely and wholly; yet, contrary to justice you were unwilling to hear him on this matter;

Item, although in your presence he offered to submit and to undergo an enquiry to be made anent this defamation, among, as it was said, his parishioners and all the priests of his deanery, you would not hear him, but, without due process of law, proceeded against him on your own initiative, hearing strange and unknown persons in strange and distant places;

Item, although he asked to be informed of the names of the witnesses, and that the statements and depositions of these witnesses in the enquiry instituted against him be made public so that he might hear them and defend himself or disprove their statements, you refused to do this for him;

Item, although he requested a copy of the investigation which it was said was made against him, you were unwilling to grant this;

Item, although in your presence he stated and offered himself as willing for you to make enquiry through his parishioners and any of his neighbors concerning his life, morals, and way of life, and that he would freely submit to such an enquiry, you were unwilling to listen to him in this matter, but rather arbitrarily proceeded with the enquiry among strangers and men unknown to him;

Item, although he suggested in your presence that, should he be again defamed of the said woman or of any other, even though the charge be untrue, he would be willing to regard his church as resigned, you were unwilling to grant this to him;

Item, although he had never been warned by you about the said defamation, nor by any other in the requisite and legal manner, you have unduly begun this enquiry against him without any warning anent the foregoing inquiry;

Item, although he has taken the Cross and has a rescript, in proper form, from Pope Alexander IV, of good memory, protecting him in person and in goods, nevertheless you, scorning this and ignoring his apostolic letter which he showed to you and presented in person, have proceeded, as is said, to investigate him and to deprive him;

Item, although he has told you several times that because he lives more than twenty leagues distant from Rouen he is unable, by reason of the great expense and other necessary and justifiable causes, to bring to Rouen from his own region the priests who are laboring in those remote parts to attend his purgation as to whether he were unjustly accused in his defamation or no, yet you have compelled him to come to Rouen, a thing impossible for him to do;

Item, beyond the limits of right, you have ordered him to purge himself of the said defamation with seven priests, when five, or even less, would suffice;

Item, although he has many times suggested that if he has in any way been delinquent he was ready to make amends, humbly to undertake and fulfill any penance, and to submit to your command and decree, you have not been willing to listen to him as a good and benign father;

Wherefore, for the foregoing and other reasons to be set forth in the proper time and place, I, the aforesaid proctor, feeling that the said priest has been and will continue to be aggrieved by the process instituted against him, and by the sentence imposed if thereby he is deprived of his church, appeal in writing to the Apostolic See in his name and in his behalf, and I request that *apostoli* be given to me at once. If you refuse to grant me this I again appeal to the same See, placing the said priest, his church, his parish, and all his goods under the protection of the Apostolic See; and lest anything be instigated or any attempt at instigation be made to the prejudice of this appeal or while it is pending, I again appeal to the same See for him and in his name. I urge that no prejudice may arise through this my appeal as regards the rights of the said priest against your process and sentence, if it be groundless or if it have no value before the law, and I request that this appeal may be strengthened by the addition of your seal in testimony thereof, and, should you refuse to seal it for me, I again appeal in writing to the Apostolic See.

Inasmuch as this appeal contained neither just nor true reasons, we were in no way obliged to defer to it.

APRIL 9. With God's grace we celebrated the feast of Easter at Rouen.

APRIL 10. While we were in our hall at Rouen an accusation was placed before us against Thomas, called Humphrey of Vylemerville, to the effect that he had on many occasions carnally known Valentina, the wife of a relative of his, William Trenchant, and had frequently had associations with her, in spite of the fact that he had once abjured her in our presence under pain of forfeiting twenty pounds of Tours. Since he did not confess to this charge, we assigned to him the vigil of the Ascension of the Lord as the day on which he should legally purge himself in this matter before us at Rouen, or, should we happen to be absent, before our official at Rouen.

This day we spent the night at Déville.

APRIL 11-14. At Martot.

APRIL 15. At Martot. This day we ordered Dom Luke, priest at St-Nicholas-de-Rouen, to begin a pilgrimage to St-Giles within a fortnight and, after he had completed this, to continue his pilgrimage to the shrine of St-Michel-in-Peril-of-the-Sea, as penance for having, with Enguerrand, priest at St-Amand-de-Rouen, committed perjury and born false testimony in connection with the will of the late Master Girard of Corio,[1] of good memory. In our presence they both swore to obey our will and sentence. Item, since the said Luke was gravely defamed of his parishioner, Jeanne, the wife of John Pérrièrs, we bade him to exchange his church for another church outside the city of Rouen.

APRIL 16. At Martot. The lord of Catelon delivered to us five hares taken in the forest at Montfort which he is obliged to pay us every Easter, or in lieu thereof a boar which he may take in the said forest. For this payment the said lord's chapel established there is said to be free and immune from the payments collected on the occasion of synods (*synodaticus*), on the distribution of the chrism, and on the visitations of the archdeacon.[2]

---

[1] See entry for August 25, 1261.

[2] Dues to be given the bishop and archdeacon for taking care of churches, and to be presented when synods were held, when the holy chrism was distributed (usually on the later days of Holy Week) and on the archdeacon's visit. In this case, the lord's chapel was free of such dues in lieu of other things: hares or a boar.

APRIL 17-19. At Martot. APRIL 20. At Mont-Deux-Amants, and at our own expense because, as the prior was away, we could not visit there. APRIL 21. We received procuration at Noyen-sur-Andelle. Total for procuration: seven pounds, fifteen shillings.

APRIL 22. We visited the priory there, finding six monks from St-Evroult with their prior. The chapter house had been closed for many days, being used for storing wines and other inappropriate uses; we ordered it opened and employed properly. Item, since the cloister was unbecomingly uneven, we ordered them to level it and make it even. Item, since the nave of the monastery was exposed to gusts of wind which came through the windows, we ordered them to block up these openings with plaster, or glass, or in any way at all. They owed one hundred eighty pounds, and they had enough provisions to last the year. We left the matter of their eating meat to their own conscience.

This day we spent the night at L'Ile-Dieu, at the expense of the abbey.

APRIL 23. With God's grace we preached and administered Confirmation at Pérrièrs, and we received procuration from the lessee of the house belonging to St-Ouen-de-Rouen. Total for procuration: nine pounds, five shillings.

APRIL 24-27. At Rouen, acting as one of the masters of the Exchequer.

APRIL 28. We conferred upon Master Robert of Les Andelys the rights of a canon which Master Richard of Chevrèuses had had in the church of Rouen and the fruits of the prebend which Master William of Flavacourt had possessed, and we invested him [Robert] with these.

Item, this same day we collated Master Peter of St-Germain to the church at Sassetot, which the said Master Robert had held.

Item, this day we collated Master Peter, called "The Philosopher," to the church at Houville, in the deanery of Gamaches, and, in his name, we invested John of Neuilly-en-Thelle with it.

This day we spent the night at Bec-Hellouin, together with the other masters of the Exchequer, and at the expense of the king.

APRIL 29. At Lisieux. APRIL 30. At Troarn. MAY 1. To wit, on the feast of SS. Philip and James. At Caen. MAY 2-4. In the Exchequer at Caen. MAY 5. At Notre-Dame-d'Estrée. MAY 6. At Thiberville, at the manor of the bishop of Lisieux, but at our own expense. MAY 7. With God's grace we administered Confirmation at Brionne, and slept at Bec. [No entry for May 8].

MAY 9. With God's assistance we preached in the chapter of the abbey of Bec, and visited. Eighty monks were there, including both the professed and the novices. They did not, as of custom, accuse each other [in chapter], save for breaking the rule of silence. The Statutes of Pope Gregory are read out in chapter three times a year. We ordered the abbot frequently to receive and audit the accounts of those who administer the expenses and receipts. In the priories they eat meat in violation of the Statutes of the Rule. With God's grace we found other things to be in good condition. We spent the night there, at the expense of the abbey.

This day we, appointed as judge or executor by the Lord Pope, issued to Master Peter, a clerk of . . . [*lacuna in MS*], the count of Brittany,[3] a certain citation whereby the bishop of Quimper, the bishop of Nantes, and one other, all bishops of Brittany, were summoned to appear against the said count before us at Rouen on the day following Assumption Day, or, if we should be absent, before our official.

MAY 10. With God's grace we administered Confirmation at the church at Montfort-sur-Risle, and received procuration this day at Corneville. Total for procuration: eight pounds, ten shillings, but we remitted one hundred shillings to them because of their poverty.

MAY 11. With God's help we preached a sermon in the chapter of the abbey at Corneville, and visited there. There were ten canons in residence, and ten outside; and two of these, by reason of the meagerness of the local resources, were residing alone in two places. Two of those in the monastery were novices. As of custom, one did not accuse another [in chapter]. We ordered the abbot to visit frequently the canons who were dwelling outside. A certain woman from Pont-Audemer, wearing the habit of a religious, had stayed with them for a long time as a sister and had bound herself by a vow of continence. She had later returned to the world and for a long time had resumed the costume of the laity. However, she had suffered a change of

---

[3] Jean Leroux, count of Brittany, like his father, Pierre Mauclerc, had many disagreements with the bishops and clergy of his county, and especially with the bishop of Nantes. In 1256 Jean Leroux was absolved from the sentence of excommunication laid upon him. Later, further disagreements arose between him and Brittany's bishops and Eudes seems to have been delegated by Rome to make peace. His father played a prominent part in the *Statutarii* movement mentioned above on pp. 323-24, n. 25. Pierre called the barons of Brittany together, and all defied excommunication and forbade the collection of tithes. For this he was excommunicated by Gregory IX, but he retaliated by exiling Brittany's bishops. (Potthast, *Regesta*, I. 706 [8196].) Jean continued the fight after the death of his father.

heart, had redonned her religious garb, and had urgently requested to be received at once. The canons and ourself disagreed about her case and status; after some discussion, it seemed to us that they were obliged to take her back. They owed one hundred thirty pounds, or thereabouts; seventy pounds was owed to them. They had enough wheat to last until the harvest, but that is not the case with the oats; they had barely enough of other provisions to last out the year. This day we spent the night there, at our own expense.

MAY 12. We visited the priory at Bourg-Achard after, with God's grace, we had preached. Thirteen canons were in residence; of these four were novices. There were only four priests; the novices were rude, of low mentality, and incorrigible, at which we were mightily grieved. Silence was insufficiently observed. The novices had neither received Communion nor confessed once a month as we had enjoined upon them at our last visitation;[4] we ordered them again to correct this. Only a small quantity of alms was dispensed there. They had enough provisions to last the year, and the prior believed that the house would entirely rid itself of debt before next Michaelmas, and that without selling or infringing upon future income. Since, indeed, the prior had received many useless and intractable [novices], we forbade him to receive any more without our knowledge and special permission. Item, since John, the cellarer, was spiteful and insolent to the canons and was accused of this by them, we ordered him removed from his office, and we advised the prior to put a secular cleric in his place, and a more honest and faithful one if he could. Item, the aforesaid novices had been there almost three years, and had as yet made no profession because of their rudeness and weak mentality; we ordered the prior to have them make profession, and afterwards he could dispose of them as he saw fit, either sending them to other houses of his Order to be formed by the disciplines of the Rule, or keeping them there, as he preferred. Total for procuration: eleven pounds, ten shillings.

This day we spent the night at Pinterville.

MAY 13. At Pinterville. MAY 14. With God's grace we administered Confirmation at St-Aubin, and spent the night at Gaillon. MAY 15. In the morning we received our homage at Gaillon and spent the night at Frênes. MAY 16. We received procuration at Ste-Catherine. Total for procuration: eight pounds, seventeen shillings.

---

[4] See entry for January 23, 1260/61.

MAY 17. We visited the abbey there, although the abbot was absent. Twenty-three monks were there, and there were thirteen at Blythe, in England. Fewer alms than usual were being dispensed there, because the almoner was heavily in debt by reason of last year's high prices. We enjoined the prior to procure a suitable servant for the infirmary. Brother Nicholas, a monk from St-Georges, had been with them for two years, and the community urgently requested that he be sent away, for he was disobedient to the prior and the subprior and insolent to the community, and they were very annoyed at his general behavior. Item, we ordered that a physician be procured for the sick.

This day with God's grace, we preached in the churchyard before the clergy and the people of Rouen who had come there in procession, and we spent the night at Rouen.

MAY 18. To wit, Ascension Day. We celebrated the feast proper for this day at the cathedral at Rouen.

This day William, rector of the church at Banville, resigned the chapel of Neville into the hands of Master John of Neuilly-en-Thelle, who was acting for us.

MAY 19. We received procuration at St-Wandrille. They would not compute.

MAY 20. With God's aid, we visited there, where there were forty-one monks. They had one lay brother, garbed in secular clothing; we ordered the abbot to be solicitous in getting information about his habits, to wit, whether he confessed and received Communion frequently and conducted himself according to the Rule. Item, we ordered the novices to confess and receive Holy Communion frequently. They have twenty monks in outside priories. There were no monks at Quitri; we ordered the abbot to send two monks there, as soon as he could conveniently do so. The monks ate meat in the priories when there was no need, not observing the statutes of the Rule; we ordered the abbot to take up this matter with them and to deal with them as seemed expedient for the welfare of their souls. They owed three hundred pounds; they had a sufficiency of provisions for the year, and they were still to receive about one thousand pounds of this year's income. Item, certain dissatisfied ones had objected that they were not informed of the value of the income from their granges and that the abbot never gave to the community information concerning leased properties or the value of rents; therefore, we enjoined the abbot to associate five or six of the seniors of the community with him whenever he leased out land, drew up the accounts, and estimated the value of the rents, so that these might be aware of his activities.

We spent the night at Le Valasse, a Cistercian house, at the expense of the monastery.

MAY 21. We received procuration at Graville. Total for procuration: ten pounds, eight shillings, seven pence.

MAY 22. After we had, with God's grace, preached a sermon in chapter, we visited the priory there. Thirteen canons were in residence, and eight were dwelling in assignments outside; ten of the resident canons were priests. They did not owe much, for the prior thought that he could entirely rid himself of debts before the coming feast of St. Remy, from the outstanding accounts and arrears of rent which he would receive this year. With God's grace, we found other things to be in good condition.

This day with God's grace, and with His aid, we preached a sermon to the chapter at Montivilliers, and visited there. Sixty nuns were there, and this is the statutory number. As we had done at our other visitation,[5] we ordered them to see to it that they performed the daily Office with such diligence that it would be performed in its entirety in daylight. Item, we ordered the abbess to make frequent inspection of the nuns' coffers for the purpose of removing any possessions. A general dispensing of alms is made three times a week, but every day, by reason of an old custom instituted by Alice, a former abbess, the abbess is obliged to feed thirteen poor people. They said that they had entirely abandoned the farces which they used to act at the feast of the Innocents; item, we ordered them to abstain from all such things entirely. Item, once a year, to wit, on the feast of the Magdalene, a complete statement of all expenses, outlays, and receipts is read out to the community; the abbess audits and receives the individual accounts. They had on deposit or in the treasury, after all their debts have been paid, six hundred pounds, and enough provisions for the year. The abbess rarely mixed with the community, or appeared at chapter or in the refectory. Item, as we had done before in another visitation,[6] we ordered that the ordering of the Hours be arranged by the precentor and the more discreet nuns, that is to say, those who were older, knew the Use better, and were better acquainted with the ceremonies of the Hours. Item, since the abbess kept putting off

---

[5] See entry for January 12, 1260/61.

[6] *Ibid.* This visitation is based on Eudes' ordinances of January 12, 1260/61.

the allotment of new clothes, head covers, cloth, and other needful things for too long a time, we ordered her to try to handle this matter in better and more harmonious fashion, and to be solicitious about this. Item, we ordered her to see that the sick were better cared for than had been the case and to have the infirmary repaired. Item, that she should provide a physician for the community. Item, that she should call in and have with her some of the seniors of the community whenever the accounts were audited and made up. Item, that keys should be confiscated, as we had ordered before, and that the abbess should punish for a grave fault, and as disobedient, all who should be unwilling to hand over their keys at her request; indeed, we understood that when the abbess asked them to give her their keys, some of them did not care to do so for two or three days, until they had removed their things and had hidden what they did not wish the abbess to see, and for this reason we ordered such nuns to be punished as disobedient and as possessors of property. We received procuration there this day. Total for procuration: ten pounds, fifteen shillings.

MAY 23. We were at Valmont, at our own expense.

MAY 24. With God's aid we preached a sermon in chapter and, with His grace, we visited the abbey at Valmont. Twenty-six monks were there; of these ten were priests. They did not confess frequently, a fact which greatly displeased us. They had one priory in England, in which one monk was dwelling by himself, although at times there had been three monks there. Alms are given four times a week to all comers in summer, but never in winter, although fragments are given to certain poor people of the neighborhood. Item, some of their servants had been unruly and incontinent, and had been so at the time of our other visitation;[7] at that time we had ordered them to be removed or properly punished. However, they had neither been sent away nor disciplined as yet; indeed, since the granary custodian had not expelled them at the abbot's order, we enjoined him, when he asked us to impose penance upon him for this, to get rid of them entirely before the coming feast of St. John and to get some good and upright ones. Six hundred pounds of Tours more than they owed was owed to them, of which four hundred pounds had to be devoted to certain repairs which they intend to make in the chancel of their church; we enjoined them, by virtue of their oath of obedience, to reserve this money particularly for this work, and we expressly forbade them to convert it to any other purpose, or to lend it, or

[7] See entry for January 14, 1260/61.

any part of it, to anybody. Finally, the abbot publicly protested that he was feeble and broken in body, and he humbly besought us to regard his deficiencies with paternal kindness and to release him from his abbatial duties. And we, after consultation with our own staff, and likewise considering his age, debility, and failing sight, received his resignation in the name of the Lord and caused him to be released from an office which he had exercised in a praiseworthy, faithful, and devoted manner for many years. We gave the community permission to elect another, and we asked them as soon as possible to select, with the Lord's assistance, some good man who they thought would be suitable for them and their monastery. We left behind our beloved son in Christ, P.[eter], the archdeacon of Caux, enjoining him to break the seal of the former abbot in the chapter and in the presence of the community. We received procuration there this day. Total for procuration: eleven pounds, twelve shillings, eight pence.

This was the day assigned to Thomas Humphrey of Vylemerville,[8] cleric, to purge himself, according to law, of the charge that he had relapsed with the wife of a relative of his, and whom, in our presence, he had abjured on pain of forfeiting twenty pounds of Tours. Archdeacon Peter of Osny, whom we had delegated to act for us in this matter, afraid lest the said Thomas would become enraged when he appeared before him with his compurgators, and being unwilling to pardon him for his offenses, ordered him to leave his district for the space of two years and to spend his time studying at Paris or at some other distant place.

MAY 25. We came to the priory at Etoutteville. There we found two monks from Lewes, priests, and a lay servant acting as manager of the said house for Master Gilbert of Caux, who has a life interest in the place. The roof of the house was in sad need of repair. Three monks should be there.

This day with God's grace, we preached at Ouville priory, and made a visitation. Ten canons were in residence, there were two at Auteny. They had received a certain cleric who had served them for two years, and whom, God assisting, they intended to accept into their order within a short time. Although we had already issued the same orders on many previous occasions, we ordered one to accuse another [in chapter]. Item, we ordered them to place their relics either on St. Michael's altar, or outside of the choir, so that lay folk could not pass through their choir. They had two lay brothers and one lay sister. They thought that they had enough wheat to last until the

---

[8] See entry for April 10, above.

next harvest, but they did not have enough wine to last until the new vintage. They owed about fifty pounds, and about forty pounds was owed to them. Furthermore, Brother Nicolas, not as yet a professed canon, led on by levity of the spirit, left the house carrying with him his monk's clothes, but with God's grace he returned immediately; because of this action, we enjoined the prior to have him in grave fault, so that he and the others might be impressed. Item, we expressly ordered the prior to give the community ten pounds a year which their benefactors had left to them for pittances. For many years the prior had stopped making this payment. This mightily displeased us, because the community possessed a letter drawn up by the prior which dealt with such money as should be converted into pittances at the desire of the community. We received procuration there this day. Total for procuration: ten pounds, three pence.

MAY 26. At Aliermont. MAY 27. At Dieppe. MAY 27. At Dieppe. MAY 28. To wit, on Pentecost. We celebrated High Mass at the parish church at Dieppe and, with God's grace, preached there. We spent the night at our manor. MAY 29. At Aliermont.

MAY 30. We celebrated Mass at the parish church at Douvrend, and with God's grace we preached there. When this had been done, we received our homage from the men of this town and of certain adjacent hamlets.

This day we spent this night at Aliermont.

MAY 31. At Longueville[-Giffard], at the expense of the priory.

JUNE 1. We visited the priory at Auffay, where there were six monks from St-Evroult; all but one were priests. We forbade the prior to permit the monks to have coffers with keys. Sometimes they ate meat when there was no need. A general distribution of alms is made to all comers once a week, to wit, on Mondays. They owed forty pounds. They had enough wine and wheat to last until the new harvest, but they were out of oats. We received procuration there this day. Total for procuration: ten pounds, nineteen shillings.

JUNE 2. At St-Georges-de-Boscherville, at our own expense. JUNE 3. At the same. With God's grace we conferred Holy Orders there, and we spent the night at our own expense.

JUNE 4. To wit, on the feast of the Holy Trinity. We read and inspected the report of an investigation which we had caused to be carried out by Peter, archdeacon of Caux, at the monastery of Eu, in accordance with the tenor of a certain letter in which the prior and community of the place had given us the power to provide them as we pleased with a shepherd from their own community. After giving much thought to the matter, about the advantage of the monastery, amongst other things, we were led to give them Thomas of Nangi, and we ordered the prior and the chamberlain, who were present, and their fellow canons to obey the said Thomas as their abbot.

This day, with God's help, we gave our benediction to the said Thomas at our chapel at Déville. We spent the night at Déville.

On this same day Michael, the former rector of the church at St-Germain-des-Fontaines, came before us and voluntarily resigned his church into our hands.

JUNE 5. At Déville. Robert, rector at Blosville and proctor of the prior of St-Lô-de-Rouen came before us and, acting for the said absent prior, gave security to the amount of ten pounds of Tours in consideration of the case which was being contested between him and the archdeacon of Rouen. He offered Master William Bienvenu as his surety. We gave the letter of agreement which was made between them and us, and which was still uncanceled and in force, to the said prior, that he might make a copy of it.

This was the day which had been designated as the day when the priests of Civières,[9] Benouville, and Binville, should appear before us to treat with us on certain matters concerned with their actions. Although they did appear, to wit, the said priests of Benouville and Binville, we postponed their business until the morrow, when they were to appear before us at Rouen and in the same manner, even after siesta time.

JUNE 6. With God's aid we celebrated the sacred synod at Rouen. This day we ordered the priests at Benouville and Binville to undergo canonical purgation on the vigil of St. Mary Magdalene at Rouen, because they were gravely defamed of incontinence; and to do this before either us or our official.

We deprived Master Adam, rector of the church at Yvecrique, of his church in the manner written below and in the presence of those venerable men the archdeacons of the French and Norman Vexins and of Grand-Caux, Master John of Neuilly-en-Thelle, canon of Rouen; Dom Roger, chaplain to the archdeacon of Petit-Caux; and John of Morgneval, our clerk:

In the name of the Father, and of the Son, and of the Holy Ghost, Amen. Although Master Adam, rector of the church at Yvecrique, had been cited

9 See entry for April 1, 1261/62.

to appear before us at Rouen on the Monday following the Trinity, in the year of our Lord 1262, to answer to criminal charges laid against him, to wit, charges of incontinence and drunkenness, and to a further charge that, although suspended and struck with various sentences of excommunication, he had frequently presumed to celebrate the Divine service; and although he had been gravely defamed of all these things for a long time and is still so defamed, he completely failed to appear upon the said day, either in person or by any proctor, to stand trial and hear our decision in respect of a promise which he made to us and confirmed by oath, namely, that he would resign his church at our request, a promise which is fully contained in a letter of his; furthermore, inasmuch as he did not appear before us at all on the Wednesday after the feast of St. Mark the Evangelist in the aforesaid year, although he had been cited to do so, we have suspended him; item, since he did not appear before us on the vigil of Ascension, just past, although likewise cited to appear and for the same reasons, we have excommunicated him for his contumacy: wherefore, as a result of the aforesaid acts of contumacy and contempt, we have adjudged the said Adam as convicted and as bound by his promise to regard his church as resigned, and we, by definitive sentence, deprive him of his church at Yvecrique.

JUNE 7. We held a synod of deans and spent the night at Pont-de-l'Arche. JUNE 8. At Pacy. JUNE 9. At Nogent-le-Roi. JUNE 10. At Berchère-l'Evêque, at the manor of the bishop of Chartres, and at his expense. JUNE 11. At Artenay. JUNE 12. At La Ferté-Senneterre. JUNE 13. At Chapelle-d'Angillon, at the manor of Sir Henry Sully. JUNE 14-15. At Bourges, where we found the king and queen. JUNE 16. At Dun-le-Roi. JUNE 17-18. At Sancoins.

JUNE 19. At St-Pierre-le-Moûtier. This day we set out with the Reverend Fathers the bishops of Beauvais and Auxerre, and the noble men Sir Simon of Nigelle, Sir Peter, the chamberlain, and Sir Egide, called Brune, the constable, all representing the king of France, to meet the king of Aragon, who was due to arrive at Clermont in Auvergne, on the day of the Nativity of St. John, to confer with the king of the French.[10]

JUNE 20. At Moulins. JUNE 21. At St-Pourçain. JUNE 22. At Aigueperse. JUNE 23. At Clermont. JUNE 24. At Issoire, to wit, on the Nativity of St. John the Baptist. JUNE 25. At Brioude. This day the king of Aragon

[10] The royal party went to meet the king of Aragon, who was on his way to Clermont-Ferrand to be present at the marriage of his daughter Isabella to Louis IX's son, Philippe le Hardi. Eudes performed this marriage on July 6.

arrived there. JUNE 26. At the same. JUNE 27. At Issoire. JUNE 28. At Clermont. JUNE 29. To wit ,on the feast of SS. Peter and Paul. At the same. JUNE 30–JULY 1. At Clermont. JULY 2. At the same. This day the king of the French arrived. JULY 3. At the same.

JULY 4. At the same. The report of the election of Brother Vincent,[11] monk at Valmont, was presented to us by the prior of Valmont, and by Brother Peter, the former abbot of Valmont. We examined carefully, as we are held to do, both the manner of the election and the worthiness of the elected one. As the law demanded, we quashed this election, not because of any defect in the individual, but because of a flaw in the manner of holding the election. However, acting on the depositions of the said brothers, who had been sent to us about this matter, we agreed that the merits of the said Brother Vincent sufficed for the needs and direction of the said monastery. Seeing that the votes of the monks were almost all in his favor, and the authority of providing for the said monastery thereby devolving upon us, we decided to provide them and their monastery with the said Brother Vincent. We commanded them by our letters patent to regard him as their shepherd and render him canonical obedience.

JULY 5. At Clermont.

JULY 6. With God's aid, and in the presence of the king of the French, the kings of Aragon and Navarre, and of many prelates and barons of France, we married Sir Philip, the eldest son of the king of the French, to Damoiselle Isabella, daughter of the king of Aragon, in the cathedral of Clermont.

JULY 7. At Clermont. JULY 8. At Aigueperse. JULY 9. At St-Pourçain. JULY 10. At Moulins. JULY 11. At St-Pierre-le-Moûtier. JULY 12-13. At Nevers. JULY 14. At La Charité-sur-Loire. JULY 15. At Chassy, at the manor of the bishop of Auxerre, and at his expense. JULY 16. At Lorris. JULY 17. At Montargis. JULY 18. At Nemours. JULY 19. At Corbeil. JULY 20-21. At Paris. JULY 22. To wit, on the feast of St. Mary Magdalene. At the same. JULY 23-30. At Paris. JULY 31. We accompanied the king of the French on his way to meet the king of England,[12] and we spent

---

[11] See entry for May 24, above.

[12] Henry III was at the moment very much occupied with his struggle against Simon de Montfort and the English baronage. Henry left England and went to Paris to discuss the implementation of the Treaty of Paris (1259) and the demands of Simon de Montfort, who actually was a French rather than an English baron. Henry III had made a compromise with his rebellious baronage in 1261 and was

the night at St-Cloud. AUGUST 1. We returned to Paris with the king of the French, to wit, on the feast of St. Peter in Chains, and we spent the night there. AUGUST 2. We arrived and spent the night at Poissy. AUGUST 3. We arrived and spent the night at Juziers, where we received procuration this day. Total for procuration: seven pounds, eight shillings of Paris.

AUGUST 4. On the morrow, to wit, August 4, we visited there, where there were six monks, all of whom were priests. They slept on feather beds. Whenever they were sick they wore pelisses, trimmed with rabbit fur, as they say. Some of them did not celebrate Mass even once a week, but after they had been reproved by us for this they said that they would correct the situation of their own free will. There was a woman there who receives her maintenance in the house and washes their clothes. They did not observe the fasts of the Rule. They ate meat three times a week, but they said that they did this with their abbot's permission; indeed, they said that their abbot knowingly permitted them not to observe the fasts of the Rule. They do not compute in chapter, but the prior and the cellarer, being acquainted with the state of the house, compute with the abbot. They owe one hundred twenty pounds; one hundred pounds is owed to them. This same day we spent this night there, but at our own expense.

This day the venerable father Guy, by God's grace bishop of Auxerre, came to us, and spent the night with us at our expense.

AUGUST 5. We came to Vernon, accompanied by the lord bishop of Auxerre. AUGUST 6-8. At Frênes, and the bishop of Auxerre was with us. AUGUST 9-10. At Pinterville, and the bishop of Auxerre was with us. AUGUST 11. At Martot. AUGUST 12. At Déville.

AUGUST 13. At the same. This day was the Sunday before the Assumption of the Blessed Mary. After we had celebrated Mass in our chapel at Déville, we went to Rouen and preached in the square at St-Gervais. The lord bishop of Auxerre, who was then visiting us, remained at Déville and, acting in our stead, instituted and blessed Vincent as abbot of St. Mary of Valmont.

AUGUST 14. At Rouen, and we celebrated Mass at Notre-Dame, that is to say, at the cathedral. AUGUST 15. This day was the feast of the Assumption of the Blessed Mary, and we celebrated Mass, in pontificals, at the Friars

---

probably hoping that Louis IX would bring his good offices to bear on this and thus keep the peace. (F. M. Powicke, *King Henry III and the Lord Edward* [Oxford, 1947], II, 428-29.)

Minor. Indeed, the lord bishop of Auxerre celebrated High Mass at Notre-Dame. AUGUST 16. We spent the night at Déville.

This same day Humphrey, rector of the chapel at Benouville, and Walter, rector at Binville,[13] promised that they would resign their benefices whenever we should so desire, and they gave us the following letter about this:

To all who may see these presents Humphrey, rector of the chapel at Benouville, [gives] greeting in the Lord. Let all know that when I was found gravely defamed before good and serious men, and especially the Reverend Father E., by God's grace archbishop of Rouen, of the vice of incontinence, particularly with Emmaline, called Plantin, I preferred rather to submit to the will of the said Father than to await the sentence of the law. I, touching the Holy Gospel, promised the said Father that I would resign the aforesaid chapel without the publicity of a trial or of making any difficulty whatsoever, and would regard it as resigned whensoever it should so please the said Father. I likewise promised in good faith that I would never in the future contest the said resignation. Present were: the wise and discreet men Master Richard of Salmonville and Master Robert, called of Dieppe, canons of Rouen; the men in religion the prior of St-Laurent-en-Lyons and Brother Walter of Minières of the Order of Minors, the companion of the said Father; and the wise and discreet men the prior of Salle-aux-Puelles and Master Eudes, the said Father's clerk. Since I did not have the seal which I was accustomed to use, I asked the said Master Richard of Salmonville and the prior of Salle-aux-Puelles to be pleased to seal this letter with their seals. Given at Déville, in the year of our Lord 1262, on the day after the Assumption of the Blessed Mary.

To all who may see these presents Walter, priest and rector of the church at Binville [gives] greeting in the Lord. Let all know that when I was found gravely defamed before good and serious men, and especially the Reverend Father E., by God's grace archbishop of Rouen, of the vice of incontinence, particularly with Heudeline of St-Saëns, I preferred rather to submit to the will of the said Father than to await the sentence of the law, and, with my hands on the Holy Gospel, I promised the said Father that I would resign my church, without the publicity of a trial or any difficulty whatever, and that I would regard it as resigned whensoever it should so please the said Father. Present were: the wise and discreet men Master Richard of Salmonville, Master Robert, called of Dieppe, canons of Rouen; the prior of Salle-aux-Puelles; the men in religion the prior of St-Laurent-en-Lyons and Brother Walter of Minières of the Minorite Order, the companion of the said Father; and Master Eudes, clerk

[13] See entry for June 5, above.

of the said Father. And since I did not have with me the seal which I am accustomed to use, I requested the said venerable men Master Richard of Salmonville and the prior of Salle-aux-Puelles to be pleased to seal this letter with their seals. Given at Déville, in the year of our Lord 1262, on the day after the Assumption.

AUGUST 17. At Martot.

AUGUST 18. At Pinterville. This same day Girard, canon of Autun, came to us at Pinterville and read to us the following letter:

The abbot and the prior of St-Denis-en-France, appointed judges by the Lord Pope, to their beloved son in Christ, Girard, canon of Autun, greeting in the Lord. By the authority of the Lord Pope, by which we are operating in this matter, we order and command you on our authority, or rather on that of the Pope, to proceed in person to the venerable archbishop of Rouen, and diligently and attentively warn him, in the name of the abbot of Néauphles-les-Vieux, the conservator of St-Denis' privileges, since it is reported that there has been a revocation of the sentences and restraints which the precentor of Auxerre, delegated by us, made in respect of the collation of the venerable man Sir Guy de Gebennes, canon of Chartres. And, as the said archbishop has procured this [revocation] to be made, let him [Girard] see that the revocation is made by the said abbot [of Néauphles-les-Vieux], especially since it is not at all our wish or intention to attempt anything against the favors of his [Eudes] privileges. You will cite the said archbishop to appear before us at St-Denis on the day following the Decollation of St. John the Baptist, to show what privileges he has, if any, and to show cause why we should not proceed against him according to the tenor of the apostolic mandate sent to us in this matter of the collation of the said Guy. You will faithfully report to us whatsoever you shall do in this matter. Given in the year of our Lord 1262, on the Saturday after the feast of St. Lawrence.

When we had read the letter through, the aforesaid Girard warned us a second and a third time, immediately and without pause, saying, "I warn you once, twice, and thrice, and once for all, that you have a care diligently to fulfill what is required in the aforesaid letter." Present were: the venerable father in Christ G[uy], bishop of Auxerre; the venerable and discreet men Master Richard of Salmonville, canon of Rouen; our companion Stephen; the companion of the said Father and a canon of Auxerre; the religious Brothers Adam Rigaud and Walter of Minières of the Minorite Order; and Master Peter, our physician, and Henry, our clerk.

AUGUST 19. At Pinterville. This day the venerable Father the bishop of Auxerre, left us. AUGUST 20-23. At Pinterville. AUGUST 24. This was the feast of St. Bartholomew the Apostle. At the same. AUGUST 25. At Gaillon.

AUGUST 26. At Gasny, where we visited. There were two monks there, the prior and his companion; they dwelt in their priory across the river and a large part of his [the prior's] household was in the grange on this side. They did not sing their Office every day with modulation, and they sang the Masses only on feast days. They did not observe the fasts of the Rule; they ate meat, but rarely, as they said. We forbade the prior to invite women to dine in the priory or to eat with them in the village. Since they had but lately come there, they did not know the state of the house. We received procuration there. Total for procuration: seven pounds, sixteen shillings, ten pence of Paris.

AUGUST 27. At St-Laurent-en-Cornecervine, and we visited there. Five monks were there, and this was because of the poverty of the abbey, as they said, for there should be three there normally.[14] They did not hold chapter, nor did they observe the Rule on silence. They used feather beds. We ordered the prior to inspect the coffers of the monks occasionally. They did not observe the fasts, but they said that they had a rescript permitting those who lived outside their chapter to eat meat three times a week, and they asserted that in this way they observed the fasts very well. There was a building there in a state of decay which the prior said he would repair as soon as he could. We received procuration there. Total for procuration: nine pounds, four shillings of Paris.

AUGUST 28. At St-Germain-en-Laye, and the lord bishop of Lysias[15] was with us. AUGUST 29. At Paris. This day was the feast of the Decollation of St. John the Baptist.

AUGUST 30. This day is Wednesday, the day after the Decollation of St. John the Baptist; at Paris, and we celebrated the Mass of the Holy Spirit at our chapel, and then we went to the sacred council, called by the venerable father the bishop of Agen, the Pope's legate. The father began by preaching a sermon in which he brought out the need which the Church of Rome had for financial assistance, not only for repairing the damages which have already been suffered, that is, in recovering the land belonging to Constan-

---

[14] See entry for October 6, 1259. Evidently the mother abbey, Notre-Dame-de-Josaphat-de-Chartres, was in financial difficulties.
[15] Lysias was in Asia Minor.

tinople, which has already been lost; but also to avoid dangers which threaten, that is, to preserve the land of Acre, which was in peril of being lost; and if this were lost, then Christians, according to this Father, would no longer have access to the Holy Land. These matters being presented and demonstrated, the Father concluded by stating that he had been appointed an Apostolic legate to deal with this matter, and that, having called together and in one place all the prelates of the realm of France, he would beseech them to grant a worthy subsidy for the alleviation or avoidance of the above-mentioned perils. Indeed, he revealed an apostolic letter in which he was given authority to do this and to make such a plea. However, with the consent of the said legate, the answer of the prelates to this was postponed until the morrow.

AUGUST 31. On the morrow, to wit, on August 31, at Paris. We convened in the bishop's hall together with the other prelates to give our response to the legate. After we had taken counsel amongst ourselves, and then with the proctors of the chapters, we gave our reply through the reverend father G. [Vincent], archbishop of Tours. He pointed out that the Church in Gaul had been long oppressed with burdens because of subsidies which it had made in response to papal request for the recovery of the Holy Land, namely, a tenth and a twelfth, which it had paid for a long time. Because of certain other special subsidies which it had paid to the Pope on occasion, together with other subsidies for the land of Constantinople, with the common consent of all, he replied that, at present, we were not able to help that land.

On this same day we caused to be read a letter which had been sent from the Apostolic See to us and to the venerable man Eudes of Lorris, canon of Beauvais, concerning the collection of an hundreth[16] for the relief of the Holy Land.

SEPTEMBER 1. The morrow, to wit, September 1, at Paris.

On that same day, the proctors of the Reverend Fathers, the archbishops and bishops noted below, appeared before us and that venerable man, Eudes of Lorris, canon of Beauvais, and tendered us the following letter:

To all to whom the presents may come, we, the archbishops of Bourges, Rheims, Sens, and Tours, together with G[irard], bishop of Autun, G[ilbert], bishop of Limoges, and J[ohn], bishop of Mâcon [give] greeting in the Lord. Be it known that we, archbishops and our suffragans and the aforesaid bishops, have appointed as our proctors the prudent and discreet men Master P[eter],

16 A tax.

archdeacon of the Gâtinais in the church at Sens, Master Matthew, canon of Rheims, and Master Thomas, canon of Limoges, the bearers of this letter, to appeal from all judges, [judges-] delegate, subdelegates, conservators, or any other, and from all complaints, and to request and receive *apostoli*, as well for us as for our suffragans who support us in this matter. We give these proctors full power and special authority to do all and each of the aforesaid mentioned. We will regard as valid and acceptable whatever shall be accomplished or procured by the said proctors in each and all of the aforementioned matters. In testimony whereof we have caused our seals to be affixed to the present letter. Done at Paris in the year of our Lord 1262, on the Friday after the Decollation of St. John the Baptist.

This having been presented, they further presented a second letter in these words:

We, the proctors of the archbishops of Bourges, Rheims, Sens, and Tours, and of G., the bishop of Autun, G., the bishop of Limoges, and J., bishop of Mâcon, in their behalf and that of their suffragans, subjects, and adherents, [appeal] from you, the lord archbishop of Rouen, and from your colleague, Master Eudes [of Lorris], who consider yourselves officially deputized by the Holy See in the matter of a subsidy levied against them [the prelates], their subjects, and their churches to the extent of an hundredth to be exacted from them and their subjects for the succor of the Holy Land. They have many sound reasons why they should not be compelled to pay this at all, and they are prepared to demonstrate these reasons at the proper time and place: first, because for a long time, or for many years, they have been burdened and oppressed by heavy subsidies for the Holy Land, so much so in fact that because of the aforementioned subsidies they, their subjects, and their churches are still under many obligations of debt: second, by reason of the bad harvest there has been a lack of good crops, and the greatest cost of provisions has resulted: third, real danger does not threaten, nor are preparations set for a general passage overseas, nor has any prince or equally powerful man assumed this task for which a subsidy should be extorted from them: fourth, since truces have for a long time been in effect between the Saracens and the Christians overseas, the subsidy is not necessary, and it may be that when the Pope sent the letter to you, there were no truces, or if there were, perchance he was not aware of them. For these and other reasons, to be presented and demonstrated in their time and place, we beseech and supplicate you not to proceed with the matter of this subsidy so far as they and their subjects are concerned. Lest you should so proceed notwithstanding the aforementioned reasons and the others to be presented and proved in time and place, and without giving us a copy of the apostolic letter which is said to have been sent to you, we appeal in writing to the Apostolic See, requesting you that, referring to such an appeal, you will give us *apostoli* about this; which if you refuse to do, we, aggrieved, appeal in writing to the Apostolic See.

This day we conferred upon Master Thomas of Barou a prebend in the church at Rouen which had been vacant since the death of Master Michael of Bercay.

SEPTEMBER 2-5. At Paris. SEPTEMBER 6. We started our journey from Paris in the morning and spent the night at St-Denis. SEPTEMBER 7. At Meulan. SEPTEMBER 8. We preached and confirmed at . . . [*lacuna in MS*], spent the night at Gaillonet, and received procuration there. Total for procuration: seven pounds, thirteen shillings, three pence of Paris.

SEPTEMBER 9. At St-Martin-la-Garenne, where we visited the priory. Three monks were there; there should be more, but because of the poverty of the place some of them had been sent back to the abbey. They did not observe the fasts of the Rule very well. Sometimes they ate meat when the Statutes of the Rule did not permit, but they said that they did this through a scarcity of other foods. They owed about forty-five pounds, in addition to what they owed their abbot. We received procuration there this day. Total for procuration: eight pounds, two shillings of Paris.

The election of Brother Nicholas of St-Croix, canon of Corneville, as abbot of Corneville, was reported to us at St-Martin-la-Garenne by Brother . . . [*lacuna in MS*], a former abbot of this house, and by Brother William, called Mignot, and Brother Henry, a canon of Corneville, the three of whom had been given power by the prior and community of Corneville to elect an abbot, and to provide their house with a shepherd. They had chosen Nicholas, their fellow canon, as abbot and pastor of their monastery at Corneville, as we saw more fully contained in their dossier drawn up to cover this matter. The said three presented the abbot-elect to us on this same day and at this same place. We, having diligently examined both the manner of the election and the elected person, as is fitting that we should do, and, having taken the advice of good and prudent men, confirmed this election as done according to law, and we decided that the said Nicholas should be provided for the aforementioned monastery, giving him our letter to the prior and community of this house and commanding them to show obedience to the said Nicholas and to give him the reverence due an abbot and shepherd.

SEPTEMBER 10. That is to say, on the next day, we conferred the gift of benediction [on Nicholas] in the said monastery.

This day having celebrated Mass, we examined and confirmed the election made of ... [*lacuna in MS*], a nun of Villarceaux, as the prioress of that house. Then we came to Sausseuse.

SEPTEMBER 10. We received procuration at Sausseuse. Total for procuration: seven pounds, fifteen shillings, two pence of Paris.

SEPTEMBER 11. After preaching a sermon in Latin, we visited the priory at Sausseuse. Eleven canons were dwelling in the house. There were fifteen outside, one being alone at Le Thil. Of those dwelling within, six were priests and four were unprofessed novices. Because of the multitude of poor people who flock thither and because of the insufficiency of their own supplies, alms were given but twice a week. There were two lay brothers and two lay sisters there. They owed about five hundred pounds. We enjoined the prior to take some of the more discreet canons into his confidence, and to seek their advice more than he was wont to do.

On the same day after finishing our visitation, we came to Gaillon, where we ate. We went on to Evreux and spent the night there.

SEPTEMBER 12. We dined at Evreux and came to Pinterville. SEPTEMBER 13. At Pinterville. This day William, surnamed Le Turc, resigned his church at Seneville. SEPTEMBER 14. At Pinterville, to wit, on the feast of the Exaltation of the Cross. SEPTEMBER 15. At the same, to wit, on the octave of the Nativity of the Blessed Mary. SEPTEMBER 16. At the same. SEPTEMBER 17-21. At Frênes.

SEPTEMBER 22. At Frênes. That day Sir Reginald, the bailiff of St-Ouen, was informed on the part of the lord archbishop, and in the name of the abbot and community of St-Ouen, that they were taking out of his [Reginald's] hands the land which they held at Fresnelle as a fief of the said Father.

SEPTEMBER 23. With God's grace we conferred Holy Orders at St-Leonard-sur-Andelle, and we spent this night at Sausseuse, at our own expense.

SEPTEMBER 24. At Mantes, where William of Ecrainville offered William Berout and Michael of Porchenville as surety for three barrels of wine for which the bailiff of Mantes is obligated. We gave him a letter to deliver the said barrels to him [William of Ecrainville] at Louviers.

SEPTEMBER 25. At Poissy. SEPTEMBER 26—OCTOBER 4. At Paris. OCTOBER 5. At Meulan. OCTOBER 6. At Vernon. OCTOBER 7. At Pinterville. OCTOBER

8. At Pont-de-l'Arche. OCTOBER 9. At Rouen, at the Exchequer. OCTOBER 10. At Rouen. This same day we bestowed the gift of benediction, with God's aid, upon the abbot-elect of Mortemer.[17] On this same day the choice made by the monks of Ste-Trinité-près-Rouen was reported to us.

OCTOBER 11. At Rouen. This same day we examined the election of Brother Robert of Plainbosc, who had been selected by the monks of Ste-Trinité-près-Rouen. Having examined the abbot-elect, as was fitting, we confirmed the election as done according to law, and we slept at Déville.

OCTOBER 12. At Martot.

OCTOBER 13. At the same. This day Peter, rector of the church at Vernonnet, appeared before us in person, and we revealed to him a certain investigation undertaken against him by the dean of Baudemont, because he had been defamed of the vice of incontinence a little while ago, and particularly with Florence, his parishioner. We had not discovered that he had in any way been acquitted of this ill-fame as a result of the investigation; although we were in a position to take rather severe steps against him, we pardoned him of this offense, because of the infirmity under which he said he was suffering. But we warned him, in a spirit of clemency, to abstain entirely from forbidden action and to persevere in living properly, otherwise we would punish him severely for any future offense.

OCTOBER 14. At Mont-Deux-Amants, where we received procuration this day. Total for procuration: seven pounds, sixteen shillings.

OCTOBER 15. With God's grace we preached in the chapter there and visited. Thirteen canons were in residence, although one of them was outside because of his illness and was dwelling alone at a certain chapel where ordinarily they do not maintain canons unless for a special reason. One did not accuse another [in chapter] as is required; we ordered them to accuse each other [in chapter] frequently. We ordered Brother Simon to be more willing to hear confessions when that charge was committed to him by the prior. They did not read throughout the entire meal, but only a little at the beginning and again at the end; we ordered them, at least in the morning and especially when they were all together, to read continuously throughout the entire meal. There was a novice there; we warned him to make frequent confession and to receive Communion at least once a month. They bestowed the customary alms. They owed about one hundred sixty pounds; they had

[17] There is some confusion regarding the succession of Mortemer's abbots. This is probably Maurice (1262-83). (*Gallia Christiana*, XI, 310.)

neither sufficient oats nor meat to last out the year. They accused the prior of leaving the house more often than was necessary, [and they charged] that he so favored his relatives that in this way the house suffered, that they could not get the twenty pounds which the prior owed them for pittances[18] without a deal of disturbance, and that he was giving away and alienating the goods of the house, to wit, horses and cups, without the permission of the chapter. We ordered the prior to allow them without more ado to collect the twenty pounds from the grange at Nuitreville, which they were entitled to have as their pittances. All of the other statements were merely matters of dispute, as it patently appeared, alleged by a certain brother, named Babot, and therefore were regarded as being frivolous. This day we spent the night at Frênes, at our own expense.

OCTOBER 16. At Chaumont. OCTOBER 17. At Neuville-en-Hez. OCTOBER 18. At Gournay-sur-Aronde. OCTOBER 19. At Noyon. OCTOBER 20. At Villeneuve-le-Roy. OCTOBER 21. At Bresles, at the manor of the bishop of Beauvais, and at his expense. OCTOBER 22. We received procuration at Chaumont. Total for procuration: seven pounds, eight pence.

OCTOBER 23. To wit, on the feast of St. Romain. With God's grace we preached to the entire parish at Chaumont and then visited there. There were two monks there with the prior. Once a week, to wit, on Sundays, alms are given to all comers. Freely and without need they ate meat and used feather beds; we warned them to consult with their abbot about this, and to act with his counsel and permission so that they may not appear to conduct themselves in violation of the Rule. They owed one hundred ten pounds.

This day we spent the night at St-Ouen-de-Gisors, and, in the name of procuration, we received seven pounds of Tours from its prior. It should be known that the prior is held to pay us this sum annually, whenever we turn aside to his priory once a year and spend the night there; but he owes no more, unless as a matter of kindness.

OCTOBER 24. At Gisors, with the king. OCTOBER 25. We spent the night at Chaumont, at our expense.

OCTOBER 26. At Chaumont, where, with God's grace, we held the sacred synod of the Vexin. We spent the night there, at our own expense.

This day, Odeardis, the lady of Boismont-Jove, did homage to us, and as

---

[18] For a general discussion of rents and the financial problems of communities, see R. A. L. Smith, *Regimen Scacarii in English Monasteries*, *T.R.H.S.*, 4th series, XXIV (1934), 74-94.

surety for her relief she offered Sir John Cordele, Sir Peter of Faiel, and Sir Peter of Bertrichières.

OCTOBER 27. We spent the night at Mortemer, at the expense of the abbey. OCTOBER 28. At Ste-Catherine, at our own expense. OCTOBER 29. To wit, on the Sunday before the feast of All Saints. With God's grace we preached at the Cathedral in Rouen and gave our benediction to the abbot of Ste-Catherine and the abbot of L'Ile-Dieu. OCTOBER 30. We received procuration at St-Lô-de-Rouen. Total: ... [*lacuna in MS*].

OCTOBER 31. We preached a sermon in chapter and then visited this priory. Twenty canons were in residence; four were outside, to wit, at Theméricourt and Cressy. They owed one hundred pounds of Paris, but they had a large supply of provisions and the fruits of this year on hand.

This day we spent this night at our palace at Rouen.

NOVEMBER 1. We celebrated the feast of All Saints at Rouen.

NOVEMBER 2. We arrived at the abbey of Ste-Catharine, accompanied by the treasurer of Rouen, Master John of Neuilly-en-Thelle; Master Richard of Salmonville; Brother Adam Rigaud; Brother Nicholas of Montebourg, the prior of Salle-aux-Puelles; and John of Morgneval, our clerk. There, in the presence of the new abbot; the prior; the subprior; the cellarer; the bailiff; Dom Nicholas, the chaplain of the abbot of Mortemer; Simon, his clerk, as well as that of the aforesaid men, we looked into what had been left by the late abbot, and in what condition the new abbot received the house. It should be known that they had, including debts and cash in hand, six thousand six hundred pounds.

We received procuration this day at Quévreville from the lessee of that place. Total for procuration: nine pounds, five shillings.

NOVEMBER 3-4. At Martot. NOVEMBER 5. At the same. This day the bishop and several of the canons of Coutances dined with us, and they agreed upon certain good men who should act as arbiters in a dispute which had broken out between them.[19] NOVEMBER 6. At Ste-Catherine, at our own expense. NOVEMBER 7. With God's grace we celebrated the sacred synod of Rouen.

NOVEMBER 8. We spoke with our deans in the lower hall. Amongst other things, we decreed that any priest might be permitted to confess to a neighboring priest, provided that he see the penitencer about it within two

---

[19] See entry for May 18, 1256.

weeks. This day we conferred the chancellery of Rouen upon Master Richard of Salmonville.

On that same day we spent the night at Ste-Catherine, at our own expense.

NOVEMBER 9. At Frênes. NOVEMBER 10. We received procuration at Vesly, where are two monks from Marmoutier. Total for procuration: seven pounds, nine shillings.

NOVEMBER 11. That is to say, Martinmas. We preached in the parish church at Parnes, and then with God's grace we visited the priory. Three monks were there with the prior; all were priests. They ate meat when there was no need. Alms are given three times a week. The fasts of the Rule were badly observed there. They owed about thirty pounds; about fifteen pounds was owed to them. With the exception of oats, they had enough provisions to last out the year. With God's grace we found other things to be in good condition. We received procuration there this day. Total for procuration: nine pounds.

NOVEMBER 12. We spent the night at St-Martin-de-Pontoise, at our own expense.

NOVEMBER 13. With God's grace we preached in chapter and then visited this abbey. Twenty-five monks were staying there and in residence; sixteen were outside in priories. They possessed a manor in the diocese of Meaux, where there should be monks, but the bishop of Meaux was holding it for life, and the archdeacon of Meaux likewise was holding another of their manors, also situated in this diocese [Meaux], for life. They broke the rule of silence by speaking in the cloister and the monastery, conduct which displeased us, and so we gave orders that the rule of silence be better observed. Some of the juniors were wearing linen shirts; we ordered them to wear light wool and to put away their linen. They drank too often and according to custom after Compline; we ordered them to abstain from this practice, and that no drink should be given to anyone except as an emergency measure. They ate meat beyond necessity; we ordered the abbot to have them abstain from eating meat, save in so far as the Rule permits, and to visit the priories. A certain leprous monk was there. Item, three lay brothers were there, but they rarely confessed or received Communion; we ordered the prior to compel them to make frequent confession, so that they should confess and receive Communion three or four times a year at least; item, [there were] two lay sisters. They owed sixteen hundred pounds, in addition to the annual pensions. Item, the abbot's relatives had been a burden to the monastery and were still injuring it considerably in the matter of bread, wine, and other things. We received procuration there this day. Total for procuration: seven pounds, six shillings.

NOVEMBER 14. After preaching the Word of God, we visited the chapter of St-Mellon-de-Pontoise. The treasurer and Dom Luke were residing there. There are ten prebends. Item, nine vicars are attached to the chapter; of these, three were absent and had absented themselves for a long while and against the treasurer's will. Item, two chaplains were there, and one of these had the cure of St. Peter's parish; but he was not able to serve either benefice very well, and the treasurer was intensely displeased with this. Item, there were two vicars, one of whom should be a subdeacon and the other a deacon. Item, we forbade John, a chaplain, to celebrate his Mass in a loud voice, as was his custom, because it disturbed those who were singing the Psalms in the choir. Item, we ordered, as we had done before,[20] the cape keeper or sacristan to sing his Mass before the Hour of Prime was sounded. Item, they did not have sufficient reading material, and although an enquiry had been made into the question of obtaining reading material—that is to say, whether the king should provide them, or the treasurer, or the chapter—nothing had been accomplished in this matter. Item, we ordered Dom Luke to have the albs, palls, and amices repaired, and to see to it that this was done properly. Item, since we found one great defect, to wit, that few attended the day Offices, we decreed, with their common consent, that the hebdomadary, the precentor, and the succentor should be present at every Hour, and that otherwise the one who was absent should pay a penny of Tours from his own pocket, and that the moneys collected from delinquencies of this kind should be added together at the end of the year and turned over to the common fund. We also decreed that a like fine should be exacted from anyone who was unwilling to obey any of the three aforesaid, to wit, the hebdomadary, the precentor, or the succentor. Item, we forbade anyone to leave the choir while the Divine Office was being celebrated in the choir, nor should anyone be behind the altar, impeding the service; otherwise, the offending person would incur the aforesaid penalty. We ordered Dom Vincent to exact and collect this fine, and to know how much it amounted to each year. Item, we forbade James, the chaplain of Dom Nicholas, who is the king's

[20] This particular item has not been mentioned in the visitations of St-Mellon so far: February 12, 1250/51; March 17, 1251/52; September 2, 1253; November 23, 1254; October 5, 1259.

chaplain, to absent himself from the Hours and Office at St-Mellon, as had been his custom. Item, Luke, a vicar, was still defamed of incontinence, and he often went to sleep in the choir, although he could chant and sing well if he wanted to. Item, we ordered that the vicars, when walking through the town, should wear seemly clothing, to wit, closed gowns or supertunics.

We visited St. Peter's priory this day. Four monks from Bec-Hellouin were there. There should be six, but they had been burdened with debts, and on this account there were fewer of them. All were priests; they ate meat. They owed about one hundred pounds, and seventy-three pounds of this was owed to their abbot; wherefore they had assigned him the manor of Fontenay, that he might receive the fruits and profits of the said manor until he should recover the said debt. Alms are given thrice a week. Other things, through God's grace, we found to be in good condition.

This day we spent the night at St-Martin, and received one hundred shillings of Paris from the chapter of St-Mellon, in which amount, in addition to cups, dishes, straw, beds, and cooking utensils this chapter is annually held to us whenever we visit the said church.

NOVEMBER 15-19. At Paris.

NOVEMBER 20. At Paris. This day Sir John of St-Martin rendered homage to us for a certain small fief which he holds of us at Douvrend. Present were: Sir Jocelin of St-Ouen and Sir William Martel, knights, and Brother Adam Rigaud.

NOVEMBER 21-22. At Paris. NOVEMBER 23. To wit, on the feast of St. Clement. At the same. NOVEMBER 24. At Paris. NOVEMBER 25. To wit, on the feast of St. Catherine, at the same. This day with God's grace, we preached at the cloister of the Franciscans at Paris, celebrated High Mass, and dined with them at their convent. NOVEMBER 26-30. At Paris. DECEMBER 1. At Paris. DECEMBER 2. At Juziers, at our own expense, to wit, on the feast of St. Andrew the Apostle.[21] DECEMBER 3. At Gaillon. DECEMBER 4. At Rouen.

---

[21] Eudes' chronology for December is unbelievably confused. For some unknown reason, the clerk calendred December 2 as VIII Nones December, whereas it should be the IV Nones. Accordingly, this month has 35 days. The feast of St. Andrew is celebrated on November 30, not on December 2. The Conception of the Blessed Virgin is here dated on December 9-10, whereas the correct date is December 8; the feast of St. Lucy is placed on December 15 instead of on December 13; the feast of St. Thomas is put on December 22 rather than on December 21, and the Nativity falls on December 27 rather than on December 25. There seems to be no explanation

DECEMBER 5. To wit, the first Sunday in Advent. We preached at the cathedral at Rouen, celebrated High Mass, and, with God's aid, bestowed our benediction upon the abbot of Bonport, because at this time the see of Evreux was vacant.[22] DECEMBER 6. By apostolic authority we conferred the church of St-Nicaise-de-Rouen upon Luke, the said clerk of . . . *[lacuna in MS]*, the official of Rouen. We slept at Martot. DECEMBER 7-8. At Martot. DECEMBER 9-10. At Pinterville. The Conception of the Virgin Mary.[23]

DECEMBER 11-14. At the same. This day by the authority of the papal Penitencer, we suspended Roger, called Lalemant, cleric, from executing the functions of deacon and subdeacon, in which orders he had been ordained.

This day Master Geoffrey Polart, our proctor at the Roman Curia, took the oath which members of our household are always accustomed to take, that he would not ask for anything in our name at the Curia.

DECEMBER 15. At Pinterville, to wit, on the feast of St. Lucy. This day the said Geoffrey left us to go to Rome. DECEMBER 16-17. At the same. DECEMBER 18. At Sausseuse, at our own expense. DECEMBER 19-20. At Frênes. DECEMBER 21-22. At Pinterville. DECEMBER 23. To wit, on the feast of St. Thomas, at Pont-de-l'Arche. DECEMBER 24. At Rouen. DECEMBER 25. At Rouen. With God's grace we conferred Holy Orders at our chapel, and this day we made our *O*.[24] DECEMBER 26. At Rouen. DECEMBER 27. At Déville. With God's grace, we celebrated the feast of the Nativity. DECEMBER 26-35 [31]. At Déville. JANUARY 1-5. At Déville. JANUARY 6. At Rouen. JANUARY 7. With God's grace we celebrated the feast of the Epiphany. This day John Savarin paid homage to us for the lands he holds of us at Gaillon.[25] JANUARY 8. At Pont-de-l'Arche. JANUARY 9-11. At Pinterville. JANUARY 12. At Gaillon, where we conferred upon Dom Giles of Eu the prebend which had belonged to Master Robert of Grainville, and upon Dom Robert of Puiseux the prebend which had been that of Dom James of Tremblay. JANUARY 13-14. At Vernon, with the king. JANUARY 15-16. At Pacy, with the king. JANUARY 17. At Pinterville. JANUARY 18.

---

for these discrepancies, beyond faulty clerkship. They demonstrate beyond doubt that a clerk and not Eudes kept the Register.

[22] Ralph de Grosparmi had been transferred to the bishopric of Albano. See entry for January 11, 1261/62. His successor at Evreux, Ralph de Chevry, was not consecrated until August, 1263. Bonport was in the diocese of Evreux.

[23] The feast of the Immaculate Conception falls on one day, December 8.

[24] See above, December 23, 1250, n. 135.

[25] Eudes' chronology is still incorrect. The feast of the Epiphany falls on January 6.

At Frênes. JANUARY 19. We received procuration at Beaulieu. Total for procuration: eight pounds, eight shillings.

JANUARY 20. With God's aid we preached His Word, and then, with His grace, we visited. Ten canons were in residence, and there were eleven outside in obediences. There were three lay brothers and three lay sisters. We ordered the prior to take away the keys of the coffers. Item, we ordered him to have a record of the income written out in a register. They owed five hundred pounds. With the exception of oats, they believed that they had enough provisions to last out the year. Richard, priest at Roquemont-sur-Cailly, was living with them, which displeased us, because he had deserted his church without our permission. However, the prior told us that he had done this with the knowledge and consent of the archdeacon, and that the said priest intended, with God's grace, to enrich the temporalities of the priory and to conduct himself amongst them in a praiseworthy manner. There was another priest there, aged and overburdened with debility, to whom they said they were giving the necessities of life, under God's charity.

We received procuration this day at Sigy. It should be known that the prior of Sigy owes us full procuration every year, it being understood that this procuration shall not exceed ten pounds of Tours, as is more fully set forth in a certain letter drawn up about this, which is in our cartulary.[26] Total for procuration: ten pounds, six shillings, one penny.

JANUARY 21. To wit, Sunday, the feast of St. Agnes. With God's aid we preached in the local parish church and administered Confirmation. Afterwards, with His aid, we visited the monks. There were three monks there, including the prior; there should be six, but the prior told us that their abbot had withdrawn the greater part of their income, appropriating it to himself and his monastery, because of the huge expenses which he contracted in requesting and obtaining the [right to wear a] mitre[27]; it was for this reason that he had diminished the number of the monks at the priory. We must discuss this with the abbot. We forbade the men of the village to bring their wives with them when they dined at the priory. Item, alms are given to all comers thrice a week. They owed about one hundred pounds, but they had not as yet sold any of this year's harvest. They said that they did not

26 And thus not included in Eudes' Register.

27 Sigy was a priory of St-Ouen-de-Rouen. The abbot of St-Ouen-de-Rouen mentioned here is Nicholas of Beauvais (1251-67). According to *Gallia Christiana,* Pope Alexander IV conceded to Abbot Nicholas the use of pontifical insignia in the year 1256. (*Gallia Christiana,* XI, 148; Potthast, *Regesta,* II, 1346, [16417].)

have more than one hundred fifty pounds as income. We received procuration this day at St-Saëns. Total for procuration: nine pounds.

JANUARY 22. We visited the priory of nuns at St-Saëns. Seventeen nuns were there, of whom one was a novice, to wit, the niece of Master William of Denestanville. They frequently gave up chanting their Hours with modulation. The almoner of St-Victor was their confessor; we knew of this and approved it. Three maids servants were there. Item, the prioress permitted one nun to go out alone against our prohibition. Because of this we enjoined upon her a penance which we deemed expedient, and forbade her to do this again. Item, we forbade all of them to work anything in silk unless it be such things as pertain to the church. Alms are given twice a week to all comers. Item, [we ordered] that the income be written down in registers or rolls. They owed one hundred sixty pounds. The roofs of their buildings were in need of repair. They had few provisions. Item, they were owed one hundred sixty pounds for the woodland they sold at Equiqueville. Item, we forbade them, as we had already done before,[28] to receive anyone without our special permission.

This day we visited the monks' priory, where there were three monks and their prior. They ate meat and did not observe the fasts of the Rule very well. The prior rarely celebrated Mass. More was owed to them than they owed.

This day we spent the night at Aliermont.

JANUARY 23. At Aliermont, at our own expense.

JANUARY 24. We arrived at the manor belonging to the abbot of St-Ouen-de-Rouen at Wanchy, but we found that the place was inadequate for our reception, so we spent the night at Aliermont, where we received procuration from the lessee of the aforementioned manor. Total for procuration: eleven pounds, three shillings.

JANUARY 25. To wit, on the feast of the Conversion of St. Paul. With God's grace we preached in the chapter at the priory of Envermeu and visited at that place. There were twelve monks from Bec. Sometimes they ate meat when there was no need; we ordered them to abstain from eating it except as the Rule permits. Alms are given thrice a week. They owed one hundred fifty pounds; sixty pounds was owed to them. They had enough supplies to last out the year, as they believed. With God's grace we found other things to be in good condition. We received procuration this day at

[28] See entry for June 28, 1258.

Aliermont from the prior of Envermeu. Total for procuration: ten pounds, eight shillings.

JANUARY 26. With God's grace we visited the priory at Bures. There was a certain monk from Pré, near Rouen, there, not as prior, but acting as a custodian for the prior of Pré. He holds the administration at the prior's pleasure. There should be at least two monks there. We did find two who had arrived with the said custodian, to convalesce, and with the prior's permission. They used feather beds and ate meat when there was no need, nor did they observe the fasts of the Rule very well. They owed nothing, nor was anything owed to them, since the prior of Pré collected everything and kept what remained after paying for the sustenance of the monks and the household. We received procuration there this day. Total: ... [*lacuna in MS*].

JANUARY 27. We visited the house at Nogent, near Neufchâtel, and spent the night at Neufchâtel, where the lessee of the above-mentioned house gave us procuration. Total for procuration: eleven pounds, nine shillings, five pence.

This day we visited the local Hôtel-Dieu, or hospital, where were two canons with their prior. One of them, to wit, Hugh, called Dominus, was useless and broken down by age, wherefore we were pleased to order him [the prior] to receive into the hospital and give the habit to two suitable men as soon as possible; he [the prior] should receive Communion at least once a month. There were three lay brothers and six lay sisters there. The prior has the cure of all those in residence. They have an income of two hundred pounds and more; they owed fifty pounds; more than one hundred pounds was owed to them. With the exception of wine, they had sufficient provisions to last out the year.

JANUARY 28. To wit, Septuagesima Sunday. With God's grace we celebrated Mass and preached at St. Mary's church at Neufchâtel. We spent the night at Mortemer-sur-Eaulne, where we received procuration from the lessee of the local house or priory. Total for procuration: thirteen pounds, eleven shillings.

JANUARY 29. We visited the said house, where there were two monks from Lewes. They receive twenty shillings of Tours every week for their sustenance from Master Eudes of St-Denis, who holds the said house for life.

This day we spent the night at Aumale, at our own expense.

JANUARY 30. Wit God's grace we visited the abbey of this said place.

Nineteen monks were in residence; three were in England. All but four were priests. One did not accuse another [in chapter]. Four lay brothers were there; we ordered the abbot to urge them to make frequent confession and to see that they confessed and received Communion four to six times a year. Silence was badly observed; we ordered this corrected. Item, we gave orders that lay folk be kept out of the cloister and that some monk be appointed to guard the cloister gate so that women and laymen could not have free access as they had had up to this time. Item, we expressly forbade anyone to remain away from Compline or to drink after Compline. Item, we ordered them to dismiss their present baker and to secure some one else who would be more upright and suitable. Item, we ordered the abbot to inspect and take away all keys of coffers and boxes of the monks before Ash Wednesday, lest they should be in the possession of any property. He had been negligent in this matter. Item, we ordered them to have the income written down in registers. They owed five hundred pounds; they had sufficient provisions for the year, and at present some eighty pounds from last year's wool was still owed to them. We advised them to increase both their alms donations and the number of their monks, if they could do so. The abbot's sister sometimes dined with him at the abbey, a thing which displeased us. We forbade him to invite her in the future. He may invite his brother-in-law without his wife. Item, we expressly forbade him, as well as all the monks of the place, and as we had done before,[29] to allow any secular clerics, priests, or laymen to dine in the refectory as had been the custom. Item, we enjoined the monks to obey their abbot in all legitimate and proper things as they were bound to do, or that otherwise we would severly punish those whom we should find guilty of disobedience. Item, Ralph of St-Valery was suspected of owning property; we ordered the abbot to have a careful investigation made into the truth of this, and then to take such action as seemed fitting under the Rule. Item, we found that Enguerrand, the prior, was defamed and that an evil report had been raised against him; but since we were not at that time able to get any definite evidence concerning the truth of the matter, we ordered the abbot to make an inquiry into the evil report as well as into the truth of the matter, as cautiously and honestly as he could, and then to handle it in a proper manner. Furthermore, we were much displeased that the abbot had promoted the said E[nguerrand], as prior, for he had been behaving badly for many years, and an evil report of

29 See entry for September 21, 1251.

long standing had never been cleared up. We received procuration there this day. Total for procuration: nine pounds, eight shillings.

JANUARY 31. At Foucarmont, at the expense of the abbey. FEBRUARY 1. At Eu, at our own expense.

FEBRUARY 2. To wit, on the feast of the Purification of the Blessed Mary. With God's grace we celebrated High Mass in pontificals at the abbey; we preached to the canons of Eu and to a great multitude of people. We received procuration there. Total for procuration: ten pounds, five shillings.

FEBRUARY 3. With God's aid we visited there. There were thirty-three canons, a custodian of the Blessed Sacrament, and an official who exercised the office of watcher;[30] we ordered them to commit this latter office to one of the canons so that it might be better performed. Item, since the Magdalene Chapel had been badly served for some time and was greatly impoverished both as to spiritualities and temporalities, we ordered the abbot to be diligent in seeing that these defects were remedied. All but six were priests. Item, at our other visitation[31] we had ordered them to repair their Passional and to have a copy of the Lives of the Saints for use in the refectory; they had done nothing at all about this, so we again ordered them to attend to it. They had one lay brother and a lay sister. Alms are given thrice a week to poor clerics and thrice a week to laymen. Silence was not well observed there. Item, we were much displeased that lay folk freely entered the chancel, and we discussed this matter at considerable length in chapter with the canons, that is to say, how the entrance and approach might more easily be made impossible for lay folk. They stated that great harm would be done if they did not open the entrances to the choir and chancel, and especially to the relics. Item, we forbade the chamberlain to receive or spend anything without the knowledge of the abbot. Item, we gave orders that more diligence and consideration than had been the case be used in providing food for the community. Item, concerning the money which they had received from bequests, we ordered that it be used to purchase leases or that it be put in reserve in some common chest until something appropriate was offered for sale. Item, since they were burdened with debt, we advised them to try to sell some of their woodland. Item, we forbade the prior to invite anyone to dine while the abbot was away, or during his absence to have

---

[30] The *Rule of St. Benedict* (Ch. 48) made provision for a watcher whose duty it was to see that everything was in good order and everybody was doing his allotted task.
[31] See entry for September 4, 1261.

various kinds of wine drawn for the guests, as he had been wont to do. They owed thirteen hundred pounds; some bad debts were owed to them. They had enough wheat and other grain to last the year, and they thought that they would be in a position to sell thirty *muids* after providing for their own maintenance. Item, we ordered the new abbot to make suitable provision in some quiet place for the old abbot.

This day we spent the night at Le Tréport, where we received procuration. Total for procuration: eight pounds, three shillings.

FEBRUARY 4. With God's grace we visited the said place, where there were twenty-two monks in residence. All but four were priests. We ordered the abbot to forbid them to hold property. They were not very punctual about turning in their old clothes, especially their pelisses, upon the receipt of new ones; however, we ordered them not to make any disposition of the said pelisses without the permission of the abbot. Item, the abbot neither gave them sufficient clothing nor handed the garments out on time. Item, they complained about the smallness of their daily portions of bread; we ordered this corrected. They owed three hundred pounds, and about as much was owed to them. They had sufficient provisions to last the year.

FEBRUARY 5. To wit, on the feast of St. Agatha, at Aliermont. With God's grace, we preached at St. Agatha's church. FEBRUARY 6-7. At Aliermont. FEBRUARY 8. At Longueville, at our own expense. FEBRUARY 9. At Déville. FEBRUARY 10. At Pont-de-l'Arche. FEBRUARY 11. At Pinterville. FEBRUARY 12. At Vernon. FEBRUARY 13. At Meulan. FEBRUARY 14. To wit, on Ash Wednesday, at Pontoise. FEBRUARY 15. At Pontoise. We gave audience to certain monks who had elected Brother Walter.[32]

We slept at Paris.

FEBRUARY 16-21. At Paris. FEBRUARY 22. To wit, on the feast of St. Peter's Chair [of Antioch], at Paris. FEBRUARY 23–MARCH 5. At Paris. MARCH 6. At Poissy. MARCH 7. At Mantes. MARCH 8. At Gaillon. MARCH 9. At Pont-de-l'Arche. MARCH 10. At Rouen.

MARCH 11. To wit, on the Sunday on which *Laetare Hierusalem* is sung.[33] With God's grace we preached at the cathedral in Rouen, and celebrated High Mass.

MARCH 12. Having examined the process of the election of Brother Walter of Serifontaine which was carried out at the monastery of St-Martin-

[32] See entry for March 12, below.
[33] The Fourth Sunday in Lent.

de-Pontoise, on the advice of prudent men and the claims of justice we confirmed this election.

We slept at Déville.

MARCH 13-14 At Déville.

MARCH 15. With God's aid we preached a sermon in chapter at St. Georges' abbey and, with God's grace, visited there. Twenty-four monks were in residence; of these, four were novices; they had three others in England and two at St-Nicolas. A tenth of the bread of the house is given in alms. They had sufficient provisions to last the year. They owed about one hundred pounds, and about four hundred pounds was owed to them. With God's grace we found other things to be in good condition, except that they did not have a Bible to read in the community. We received procuration there this day. Total for procuration: ... [lacuna in MS].

MARCH 16. At Jumièges. MARCH 17. With God's grace we conferred Holy Orders at Jumièges. MARCH 18. With God's aid we bestowed our benediction upon Brother W[alter], the abbot of [St-Martin-de-]Pontoise, celebrated High Mass, and spent the night there, at our own expense.

MARCH 19. With God's grace we visited there, after having, with His aid, first preached a sermon. Fifty monks were dwelling there, of whom six were novices; twenty were in outside priories. They ate meat in the priories when there was no need. We forbade them to diminish in any way the supply of goods intended for alms. Item, we ordered them to have a complete statement of the income of the monastery written out in a register; the abbot made himself rather difficult about this. Item, we ordered the abbot to get an itemized account of expenditures from the kitchener once every six weeks, and at the end of the year to have a total accounting made of all expenses incurred during the year. More was owed to them than they owed. By God's grace we found other things to be in good condition.

We spent this night at Déville, at our own expense.

MARCH 20. By God's grace we visited the priory at Bondeville, where there were twenty-eight [choir] nuns, seven lay sisters, and three lay brothers. They should confess and receive Communion once a month. We ordered the prioress to make frequent inspection of the nuns' coffers. We forbade her to allow any nuns to go to Rouen without proper and dependable companionship. Those who go should return without delay. There is a parish there having nine parishioners; we must assign the cure of it to some priest. They did not have enough chaplains, and they needed a steward to manage the affairs of the house and provide for them. They owed one hundred twenty pounds.

We spent this night at Déville.

MARCH 21. At Déville, to wit, on the feast of St. Benedict.

MARCH 22. With God's aid we preached in the chapter and made a visitation at the abbey of St-Ouen-de-Rouen. Sixty monks were in residence; two were students in Paris; three were at St-Michel; fourteen of the sixty were novices. All but seven of the professed were priests. The fasts of the Rule were not well observed in the priories, and the article covering the eating of meat was badly observed. To date they owed one thousand pounds at interest and three thousand pounds or so in other debts; some debts were owed to them—indeed, many such, they say—but in bad debts. We took the abbot to task in the matter of the three monks who should be sent back to Sigy;[34] he had removed them on his own initiative and called them back to the cloister. We warned him also to restore certain income which he had withdrawn from that priory. With God's grace we found other things to be in good condition.

We spent this night at Déville, at our own expense.

MARCH 23. With God's grace we preached a sermon at the monastery of St-Amand and visited. Fifteen nuns were in residence, and five were at Saâne. They should confess and receive Communion once a month. Item, since we discovered that amongst the nuns there was general discord and bitterness of heart, we charged the abbess and confessor to compel, by restrictions on wine and pittances, those hereafter found thus at fault to become reconciled and live in charity so far as possible. Item, we forbade them to fashion or work on alms-bags, needle-cases, neck-bands, and such things, but rather to work on such as pertained to the divine cult, as best they knew how. Item, we expressly forbade the nuns to reduce their alms or to allow a reduction of them in any way. The abbess did not have available her accounts, or, rather, a record of her total accounts. Consequently, we were unable to get exact knowledge of the condition of the house. However, they were of the opinion that more was owed to them than they owed. We thereupon ordered the abbess to go over her records and report to us on the state of the house. Three hundred seventy-seven pounds, seven shillings was owed to them; they owed one hundred forty pounds and forty shillings. They had sufficient

[34] See entry for January 21, above.

supplies to last out the year. With God's grace we found all else to be in good condition.

With God's grace we spent this night at Déville, at our own expense.

MARCH 23. At Rouen. MARCH 24. To wit, Palm Sunday. By God's grace we celebrated the ceremonies proper to this day at Rouen. MARCH 25. With God's help we celebrated the feast of the Annunciation of the Blessed Mary, which fell on this Sunday. MARCH 26. We dined with the Dominicans at Rouen. MARCH 27. We dined with the Franciscans at Rouen. MARCH 28. gave absolutions in the accustomed manner and at the usual places, and with God's grace preached at the cathedral of Rouen. MARCH 29. With God's aid we performed the Divine Offices proper to this day. MARCH 30. At Rouen.

MARCH 31. With God's grace we celebrated Holy Easter Day at Rouen. APRIL 1. We dined with the greater archdeacon,[1] and spent the night at Rouen. APRIL 2-12. At Pinterville.

APRIL 13. At Pinterville. On this day his lordship [Eudes] conferred upon Master Eudes of Senne the prebend which had belonged to Master Giles Picard, and upon Master Peter of St-Germain the prebend which had been that of Master Richard of Cottévrard.

APRIL 14. At Pinterville. APRIL 15. At Pont-de-l'Arche.

APRIL 16. We came to the priory of St-Paul near Rouen, and with God's grace we made a visitation there. There were six nuns from Montivilliers; there should be only four; the other two were there at the time because of their ill-health. Matilda, the sister-in-law of Peter of Mesnil, was with them. Because of their small number they do not sing their Hours with modulation.[2] They have only one Mass, namely the parochial Mass. They have two maid-servants. We found out that the king's sergeants, the forest wardens, had been imposing upon them and were still imposing upon them, namely by eating at their house often and by molesting without reason their workmen in the forest, although they hold the right to use the forest. They owed forty pounds; they paid a tithe on one hundred forty pounds of income.

This day we spent the night at Rouen in the royal castle, with the other masters of the Exchequer.

APRIL 17-20. At the same. APRIL 21. At Bec-Hellouin, with the other masters of the Exchequer. APRIL 22. At Lisieux. APRIL 23. At Troarn. APRIL 24-28. At Caen, on Exchequer business, at our own expense. APRIL 29. At Le Plessis-Grimoult, at the expense of the king. APRIL 30. At Château-Vire. We entered the diocese of Avranches. MAY 1. We received procuration at the priory of [Notre-Dame-du-]Rocher-de-Mortain. Total for procuration: ten pounds.

MAY 2. With God's grace we visited there, where there were ten monks

---

[1] Jean Cholet de Nointel, the greater archdeacon of the cathedral of Rouen.

[2] See above, July 9, 1249, n. 36.

from Marmoutier, and although they are exempt, they nevertheless answered every question put to them. They used feather beds and ate meat; they did not observe the fasts of the Rule very well. They had one chalice, which much displeased us, for all of them were priests. They had one monk in England and two manors which were of very little profit to them. The priory building was almost unroofed and in ruins. The prior could not give us information concerning the financial condition of the house, that is to say, whether they owed anything or whether anything was owed to them, nor even as to the extent of their income. Item, since the bishop had and received the right of procuration at the priory at Bailleul, we warned the prior who was then in charge and governing here [Bailleul] to pay us procuration. He told us that the house was inadequate to receive us, and that their income was extremely small. We agreed to this and, for this time, we passed it by.

This day we came, by God's grace, to the chapter of St-Firmin,[3] and after preaching, we visited as the Lord directed. There are sixteen prebends there, but the prebendary canons did not maintain residence at all; however, we found four old men in residence. The prior of Le Rocher-[de-Mortain] holds one of these prebends; four of the canons must find four priest-vicars who are obligated to celebrate Masses. The prebends are not of equal value. Bartholomew, the precentor's vicar, was a drunkard, although we had warned him about this before.[4] Morel was violent and a reviler, as he had been before. Firmin, the prior's vicar, was a trader, and had been one for many years. Roger, a canon, was given to wine and frequently drank immoderately; we forbade him to drink up to the gullet in the future, or to frequent taverns. Jocelin, a canon, had been appointed by the bishop as confessor to the canons and to the clerks-choral, although the dean had the cure of their souls. Item, we warned Bartholomew, the precentor's vicar, to abstain from overmuch drinking and to give up further quarreling with his companions, as he had been wont to do.

We received procuration this day from the chapter, at the priory of Le Rocher[-de-Mortain], although the prior was not at all obliged to do this in their chapter. Total for procuration: nine pounds, two shillings.

MAY 3. To wit, the Finding of the Holy Cross. We received procuration at Les Biards. Total for procuration: seven pounds, nine shillings.

MAY 4. With God's grace, we visited the said priory. Two old and feeble

---

[3] A chapter of secular canons. See entry for May 2, 1256.
[4] *Ibid.*

monks of the Benedictine Order were there; they did not observe the statutes of the Rule in any matter; the prior rarely celebrated Mass and often drank with lay folk in the village, as we were informed by certain persons. Of this he was indeed guilty, and we warned him about this. They had an income of forty pounds; they owed about ten pounds, but they said that they had enough in hand to liquidate this conveniently. However, after investigating and learning of the meager income of the house, we graciously remitted, for this time, and returned to the said prior, four pounds of Tours from the total of procuration owed.

This day we spent the night, with God's grace, at the abbey at Savigny, of the Cistercian Order.

MAY 5. We came to the priory at St-Hilaire, and found this place to be in a miserable condition, that is to say, we found that the monastery and the whole manor belonging to the priory had been totally destroyed and consumed by fire. No monks were there, although there should be three monks from St-Benôit-sur-Loire. The said priory had an income of one hundred sixty pounds. The prior was at St-James-de-Beuvron, where, with God's grace, we spent this night, and received procuration from the said prior, on account of the said priory [St-Hilaire]. Total for procuration: seven pounds, seventeen shillings.

MAY 6. To wit, the Sunday before Ascension. With God's aid we celebrated a parochial Mass at the church at St-James-de-Beuvron, and, with His help, preached a sermon in the churchyard. We received procuration there. Total for procuration: eight pounds, eight shillings.

MAY 7. With God's grace, we visited the said priory. There were four monks from St-Benôit-sur-Loire in residence, as was the aforesaid prior of St-Hilaire, who had received the priory of St-James in farm from his abbot. There should be seven monks, but the prior told us that the abbot, with papal permission, was allowed to appropriate to his table the fruits of some of his priories, and had in consequence diminished the number of monks and had leased out this said priory. The monks who were staying there ate meat and used feather beds and linens, but, as they said, they did this with the knowledge and permission of their abbot. Those who were not priests rarely confessed or received Communion; we ordered the prior to instruct them and to bring pressure to bear upon them to confess and to receive Communion frequently. Item, we forbade them to eat with lay folk in their village, or to permit lay folk, especially women, to eat with them. Their grange was in a ruinous condition and its roof needed repair; we ordered this repaired. Item, we ordered the prior to have the houses at St-Hilaire rebuilt and repaired. They have an income of two hundred sixty pounds.

MAY 8. We received procuration this day at Sacey, where were four monks from Marmoutier. With God's grace we visited there, where, as already stated, there were four monks from Marmoutier. All were priests except one, whom we ordered to confess and to receive Communion frequently. Alms are given twice a week to all comers. The fasts of the Rule were not well observed; they frequently ate meat when there was no need. We found the parish priest to be many times defamed of incontinence. They said that they had no scruples about eating meat because their abbot had given them a dispensation in this matter, under a privilege which he had obtained from the Apostolic See. They had an income of two hundred pounds; they said that about as much was owed to them as they owed.

This day, after first preaching, with God's grace, to the chapter of the abbey of Montmorel, we visited there. Seventeen canons were in residence, and there were six more in three of their priories; one was dwelling by himself in a certain parish in Brittany, and this much displeased us. All but four of those at the abbey were priests; we enjoined those who were not priests to confess and to receive Communion at least once a month. It was the custom to give alms to all comers thrice a week, but we discovered that they had curtailed and reduced their almsgiving, since, at the time of our present visitation, a general distribution of alms was seldom or never made. We ordered the abbot to manage this business in a more diligent, devout, and generous manner, to bestow alms as usual, and to give orders that alms be distributed as they had been in times past. As much was owed to them as they owed, and they had a large supply of provisions. We received procuration there this day. Total for procuration: eight pounds, two shillings.

MAY 9. We came to the chapter at Avranches, and there, with God's grace, we preached and visited the chapter. Twenty-one prebends are there, and six rectors or dignities (*Dignitates*), to wit, a dean, a treasurer, two archdeacons, a precentor, and a chancellor or master of the schools. Item, four priest-vicars who are obliged to celebrate Masses; and two deacons and two subdeacons who were obliged to vest themselves for Masses. Each of these received sixty shillings, as we were told, and it seemed to us that this was a moderate stipend for their services. The canons do not vest themselves, unless they desire to do so, at the major feasts, and each is bound to maintain his vicar in the chapter. With God's grace we found everything else to be satisfactory, except that the canons sold the fruits of their prebends at a rather high price in expectation of the harvest. We received procuration this day from the chapter at the bishop's palace; they did not desire to compute.

MAY 10. To wit, on Ascension Day, at Avranches. With God's grace we marched in procession with the bishop and the canons, and we celebrated High Mass. The bishop gave us procuration this day, and he had the entire chapter with us.

MAY 11. With God's grace we preached in the chapter house at St-Michel-in-Peril-of-the-Sea and visited. Forty monks were there. They had many priories scattered in divers regions, in some of which, because of the smallness of the local incomes, monks were dwelling alone. We ordered the abbot to take counsel on this matter. Item, we ordered them to read the Statutes of Pope Gregory more often than they were accustomed to do, and to do this at least twice a year in chapter, and in the presence of the entire community. All but five of the residents were priests. Item, a general distribution of alms is made to all comers every day. Item, we ordered the abbot to make better provision for the weak and infirm than had been the case. Item, that he should see to it that the articles covering the eating of meat and the fasts should be observed in the priories so far as this was possible. More was owed to them than they owed; they had a large supply of provisions, and with God's grace they were, as they said, opulent. We received procuration there this day. Total for procuration: nine pounds.

MAY 12. We spent the night at the abbey at La Lucerne, which is a member of the Premonstratensian Order.

This day William of Bos, cleric, presented for the church at Grainville by Sir Richard of Grainville, knight, appeared in person before us and besought us to undertake an investigation as to the right of advowson in the said church; also, that we should proceed to his reception or should collate him to the said church, since he believed that a half year had elapsed since the church had become vacant. We did not desire to do either of these things, but we set apart for him and the said Richard the Saturday preceding the next Trinity Sunday, when they should appear at Les Andelys to show cause why Master Guy of Ravenel, cleric, presented for the same church by Hugh and John of Grainville, esquires, ought not to be admitted. Thereupon he produced a letter, sealed with the seal of the said knight [Richard] and of William of Grainville, cleric, drawn up relative to the legal renunciation of the advowson which the above-mentioned persons [Hugh and John] held in the church.

MAY 13. At Le Parc, a manor belonging to the bishop of Avranches, and at his expense. MAY 14. At Torigni. This day the abbey of Bec was ruinously burned. MAY 15-16. At St-Etienne-de-Caen, at our own expense. MAY 17. At Beaumont-le-Roger, at our own expense.

MAY 18. With God's grace we visited the abbey at Corneville. There were ten canons in residence and ten more outside, of whom two were dwelling alone in two places. We ordered the abbot to visit the canons who were dwelling outside more often than he was in the habit of doing. All but three of those at the abbey were priests. Alms are given thrice a week to all comers. Item, they had not yet received a certain woman from Pont-Audemer who was living in the monastery in lay habit; she had formerly dwelt with them, garbed as a regular sister. At our last visitation[5] this matter had been discussed and considered by us, together with our associates, and Abbot Waleran and the canons of Corneville. It had then appeared to us that they were obligated to receive her. We told them once again to receive her, or that otherwise we would enjoin our official of Rouen to see that this woman did not fail to get justice. They owed two hundred pounds. We received procuration there this day. Total for procuration: six pounds, two shillings.

MAY 19. We received procuration at Bourg-Achard. Total for procuration: nine pounds.

MAY 20. To wit, on Pentecost. With God's grace we visited the priory of the said place. Ten canons were in residence; there used to be fourteen; nine of the canons were in priories; of those who were in residence, six were priests. Alms are distributed twice a week to all comers. More was owed to them in collectible debts than they owed. They had enough provisions to last out the year. This day with God's grace, we celebrated High Mass and spent the night there, at our own expense. We dined with the canons in the refectory.

MAY 21. At Bourgtheroulde. MAY 22. At the same. We preached and administered Confirmation there, with God's grace, and spent the night at Pinterville. MAY 23. At Pinterville. MAY 24. At Gaillon. MAY 25. At Frênes. MAY 26. With God's grace we conferred Holy Orders at Notre-

---

[5] See entry for May 10, 1262.

Dame-des-Andelys, and spent the night at Frênes. MAY 27. At Frênes. MAY 28. At Ste-Catherine, at our own expense. MAY 29. God helping us, we celebrated the holy synod at Rouen. MAY 30. We held a synod of deans, and spent the night at Rouen. MAY 31. At Pinterville. JUNE 1. At Vernon, at the king's castle. JUNE 2. At Meulan. JUNE 3-16. At Paris, to attend the Parlement. JUNE 17. At Courquetaine. JUNE 18-22. At Samoiseau, a manor belonging to the abbot of St-Germain-de-Paris. JUNE 23. At Nemours.⁶ JUNE 24. At the same. This was the feast of the Nativity of St. John the Baptist. With God's grace we celebrated the blessing of the nuns there [the abbey of Notre-Dame-de-la-Joye]. JUNE 25. At Jard, at our own expense. JUNE 26-27. At Paris. JUNE 28. At Poissy. JUNE 29. To wit, on the feast of the Apostles Peter and Paul. With God's grace we celebrated High Mass at the Franciscan monastery at Mantes. We dined with them and spent this night in the town. JUNE 30. At Gaillon. JULY 1. We entered our château at Gaillon and slept there for the first time. JULY 2-4. At Pinterville.

JULY 5. At Frênes. This day the following matters were presented to us:

In your presence, Reverend Father, lord archbishop of Rouen, I, John of St-Saveur, cleric and proctor of Jane, daughter of the lady of Bucy, wife of Guy of Meru, submit that when Adam, called Fourre, began a matrimonial case against the aforesaid Jane, he stated that he had contracted actual marriage with her.⁷ The action was tried before your representative at Pontoise. Adam stated and admitted at the trial that he could not prove his own case⁸ except by witnesses who, he said, were bound by excommunication. On account of this [excommunication], so he said, he had obtained from the Apostolic See that there be granted to you, by mandatory letters,⁹ the power of absolving provisionally the aforesaid witnesses until they had given testimony in the said case. Then they would be returned to their original sentence of excommunication.

⁶ An Augustinian priory founded by Louis VII, near Fontainebleu. (Cottineau, II, 2046.)

⁷ *Per verba de praesenti matrimonium contraxisse.* In this instance *de praesenti matrimonium* corresponds to today's *sponsalia de praesenti* (actual marriage) as opposed to *sponsalia de futuro* (betrothal). ("Fiançailles," *Dict. de droit can.*, V, 838.)

⁸ *Confessus fuerit se intentionem suam probare non posse.* Though intention is an integral part of the legality of marriage, *intentionem suam* in this instance means *intentio* in the Roman legal sense, the case which the plaintiff must prove in court.

⁹ *Per litteras in mandatis.* There are many classifications of papal letters, among which are the *mandamenta*, which begin with the words *per apostolica scripta mandamus-* and contain information, confidential or otherwise. ("*Lettres pontificales,*" *Dict. de droit can.*, VI, 409.)

unless they had, in the meanwhiele, made full satisfaction for that for which they wore excommunicated. Jane's previous proctor proposed to you, and I now propose, first, that since they [the letters] were obtained by stealth, you cannot and ought not to proceed on the authority of the above mandatory letters to absolve Malachia whom the said Adam produced as a witness in this matrimonial case, because there is no mention in the letters, obtained by stealth, who the witnesses were and especially that Malachia was a witness. Moreover, the said Malachia belongs to another diocese, namely Beauvais, and to another province, namely Rheims, and she has been bound with the knot of several excommunications. If all this had been told, Adam would never have obtained letters addressed to you, but rather [addressed] to the excommunicators, which is in accordance with legal procedure and the methods of the Roman court. Thererefore they were obtained by stealth, and you cannot proceed on their authority. Second, because the said Malachia was excommunicated *latae sententiae*[10] in that she had laid violent hands on Herman, cleric, of the diocese of Beauvais, you cannot proceed to the absolution of excommunications *latae sententiae* on the authority of letters which speak about absolution in general terms and without reference to particulars, because an excommunication of this nature requires a special mandate, just as is most expressly stated in the law.[11] It is according to law that where ever a special mandate is required, a general mandate does not cover it, all of which is understood and can be understood even from the very content of the above letters. We have never heard of the Lord Pope granting absolution from excommunication *latae sententiae*, in general terms. Although it has been stated that the marriage was contracted in the diocese of Rouen and the matrimonial cause was argued before your representative, as is evident from your own decisions, I argue that you cannot proceed to the absolution of the other sentences of other prelates[12] and of other laws on the basis of this general mandate, because

[10] Excommunication incurred by the very fact that the crime is committed. *Ferendae sententiae* is excommunication when imposed by a judge after a trial. An act whose very performance carries with it automatic excommunication, as in this case, laying violent hands on a cleric. ("Censures," *Dict. de droit can.*, III, 176; also III, 187-189.) Excommunicates for laying violent hands on clerics could be absolved only by the Pope. (*Decretales*, lib. V, tit. XXXIX, cap. V; Mansi, XXIII, 382.) However, Malachia, being a woman, could be absolved by her local ordinary without being compelled to go to Rome. Being a woman, she was not *sui juris*. Corp. jur. can., Greg IX Lib. v. Tit. 39. cap. 6.) We here follow the Ms. *in canonem latae sententiae* rather than Bonnin's text, *in canonis latae sententiae*.

[11] *Ibid.* cap. 7.

[12] Absolution requires jurisdiction which may be *personal* in the case of persons in religion, or *territorial* when it is determined by a definite circumscribed territorial area, as in the case of a diocese or a parish. The question here is whether Eudes could absolve from an excommunication incurred automatically in another diocese. ("Absolution," *Dict. de droit can.*, I, 120-121.)

this is contrary to the intention of the Pope. Third, Jane's previous proctor proposed to you, and I now propose, that Malachia should not be absolved because, even though absolved, she cannot bear witness. And if she did bear witness, it would not be of worth because she was corrupted for a price and received her price to prove a marriage contracted between Adam and Jane. All these things, which are facts, the aforesaid proctor undertook to prove and I now offer to prove. Because you, Reverend Father, have cast aside and do cast aside the aforesaid plaintiff's claims and proofs by your interlocutary sentence, and because you have absolved and do regard as absolved the aforesaid Malachia and are willing to receive and do receive her as a witness, I, by reason of the foregoing, feel the said Jane and me, in her name, to be unjustly harmed by your interlocutary decree and, because of the aforesaid grievances or any one of them, appeal in Jane's name, in writing, to the Apostolic See and demand *apostoli* here and now. And I place the aforesaid Jane, her status, and her conjugal way of life with her husband, under apostolic protection, lest you proceed in any particular against them.

JULY 6. At Frênes. JULY 7-8. At Pinterville. JULY 9. At Gaillon. JULY 10-11. At Vernon, with the king. JULY 12. At Les Andelys. JULY 13. At Frênes. JULY 14. At Pont-de-l'Arche. JULY 15-16. At Déville. JULY 17-20. At Pinterville. JULY 21. At Gaillon. JULY 22. To wit, the feast of St. Mary-Magdalene. At Gaillon. JULY 23. At Pinterville. JULY 24-26. At Martot. JULY 27-28. At Rouen. JULY 29. At Rouen. This day with God's grace, we consecrated as bishops our venerable brothers, R[alph] of Evreux and O. [Eudes] of Bayeux. JULY 30. At Pinterville. JULY 31. At Evreux. This day the aforesaid R[alph], bishop, was solemnly received as was fitting and customary. AUGUST 1. To wit, on the feast of St Peter in Chains. At Gaillon. AUGUST 2. At the same, and the bishop of Beauvais was with us. AUGUST 3-6. At the same. AUGUST 7-8. At Frênes. AUGUST 9. At Pinterville. AUGUST 10. To wit, on the feast of St. Lawrence. At the same. AUGUST 11. At Déville. AUGUST 12. We preached a sermon in the churchyard at St-Gervais and we were present there, to wit, on the Sunday before the Assumption of the Blessed Mary. We spent the night at Pinterville. AUGUST 13. At Déville. AUGUST 14. At Rouen. AUGUST 15. With God's grace we celebrated the feast of the Assumption of the Blessed Mary at Rouen. AUGUST 16-17. At Déville. [*No entry for August 18.*] AUGUST 19. We received procuration at Noyon-sur-Andelle. Total for procuration: seven pounds, fifteen shillings.

AUGUST 20. With God's grace we visited there. Present with the prior were six monks from St-Evroult, as well as one monk who was dwelling at Le Héron. All of them celebrated Mass of their own volition and frequently, except the abbot's secretary; we ordered him to give up his writing occasionally and to celebrate Mass more often than was his practice. Item, we ordered the prior once again, although we had given this order several times in the past, to have the path of the cloister leveled off and repaired; to have the openings in the windows and doors of the nave of the monastery [church] blocked up with plaster, glass, or some other material; and to have the barrels altogether removed from the chapterhouse and the place cleaned and kept clean and becoming.[13] They owed about one hundred pounds; they said that they had enough provisions to last out the year. With God's grace we found other things to be in good condition.

We received procuration this day at Pérrièrs. Total for procuration: six pounds, seven shillings, three pence.

AUGUST 21. With God's grace, we came in person to St-Laurent-en-Lyons, where, by His will, we were so afflicted and tormented with pains in the head and stomach that we were unable to exercise our duty of visitation in person, but were obliged to send our dearest brother, Brother Adam, to the chapter there to act for us. With God's aid he preached there, as was fitting, and then made his visitation, first making inquiries into the spiritual condition of the place and then asking about temporal things. From the report of this Brother Adam we learned that fifteen canons were dwelling there, that all but one were priests, and that fourteen were outside in seven places. With God's grace he found everything to be in a satisfactorily good condition. They owed three hundred pounds; they had enough provisions to last out the year. We received procuration there this day. Total for procuration: seven pounds, thirteen shillings.

AUGUST 22. With God's grace we came in person on pilgrimage to the church of St-Hildevert at Gournay, where we heard Mass and kissed the relics. Afterwards we consulted separately with the dean and a resident canon concerning the condition of the place. We discovered that the clerks [-choral], vicars, and chaplains performed their duties carelessly, and that the Divine Office, both day and night, was carried out with great negligence and irregularity. Item, more Masses were celebrated at the High Altar than ought to be. Item, on some of the feast days, particularly that of St. Nicholas, the clerks [-choral], vicars, and even the chaplains conducted themselves in a

13 See entry for April 22, 1262.

dissolute and scurrilous manner, dancing through the town and singing *virelais*.[14] Item, we learned that Matthew, a canon, at present in ill-health, had, as was widely believed, kept a certain woman from Les Andelys for fourteen years, and it was believed that she was still living in his house. However, he had not kept her openly, but so cautiously and secretly that she could be seen by very few people. Item, Simon, chaplain, was over and over defamed of incontinence, and it was said that he had severely beaten a certain woman, by the name of Haise, because she was unwilling to turn over her daughter to him, and that he finally had taken the girl by force. Item, that this same Simon and Lawrence, a chaplain, frequently played at dice. Item, William Moiniat, vicar, and one of his associates, shamefully pommeled a layman in the very center of the town, from which scandal had arisen. The said William had drawn his knife. Reginald, the sacristan's helper, was in the habit of going out at night.

This day Brother Adam, our brother, visited the nuns' priory of St-Aubin. From his account we learned that there were eleven nuns there at present. The prioress was not present. They said that they owed nothing beyond their debt[15] to the king. With God's grace he found everything else to be in good condition.

This same day Dom Willard, the prior of Salle-aux-Puelles, near Rouen, visited the local leper house in our stead. Their chaplain had recently died. There were as many healthy in residence as there were lepers, namely, eleven. They owed twenty-five pounds of Paris; they thought that they had enough wheat to last out the year.

This same day Brother Adam visited the priory at Neufmarché in our stead. Four monks from St-Evroult were there. The parish priest was, by established custom, attached to their table; but inasmuch as this priest was unable to have a clerk or a servant to carry the hand bell through the village whensoever he went to visit the sick, the said brother enjoined the prior, on our behalf, and, indeed, we also enjoined him as we had done before[16] to provide the said priest with a clerk for this service. They owed about one hundred pounds; however, some debts were owed to them. With God's grace other things concerning the place were in good condition, except that they had a serious complaint against the lord of the village, who, as they said,

---

[14] Short rhyming verses, usually accompanied by dances.
[15] The tithe.
[16] See entry for October 3, 1261.

had, without compensation, killed sixteen of their swine. We received procuration there this day. Total for procuration: six pounds, fifteen shillings.

AUGUST 23-26. At Frênes. AUGUST 27-28. At Gaillon. AUGUST 29. To wit, on the feast of the Decollation of St. John, at Pinterville. AUGUST 30. At the same. With God's grace we married Geoffrey, the son of Sir Julian of Péronne,[17] to Petronilla of Pontoise, in our chapel. AUGUST 31—SEPTEMBER 4. At Pinterville. SEPTEMBER 5. At Gaillon. SEPTEMBER 6. At Ste-Catherine, at our own expense. SEPTEMBER 7. With God's grace we preached at the Franciscan chapter, where with God's assistance the brothers had assembled for a provincial chapter. SEPTEMBER 8. To wit, on the Nativity of the Blessed Mary. We were at Rouen, and by God's grace we celebrated the feast of her Nativity. SEPTEMBER 9-13. At Frênes. SEPTEMBER 14. To wit, on the Exaltation of the Holy Cross. We were at L'Ile-Dieu, a Premonstratensian house, at the expense of the abbey. SEPTEMBER 15. At Beaubec, of the Cistercian Order, at the expense of the abbey.

SEPTEMBER 16. With God's grace we visited the abbey of Bival. Thirty-five nuns and one lay sister were in residence. We expressly forbade them to sell on the outside any bread given to them as their portion. They owed more than sixty pounds; they had but a meager store of provisions, nor did they have any wheat for sowing. At this time we were much displeased at the provision made for a certain chaplain, who had been received into their fraternity, for he had been no small burden to the house; so we ordered the dean of Neufchâtel to confiscate into our hands whatever the said chaplain was to receive by way of pension in our diocese, and to forbid him to celebrate Mass in our diocese.

This day we spent the night at Beaussault.

This day, to wit, September 16, we visited the priory at Beaussault, where there were two monks from Bec-Hellouin. We forbade them to invite any women to dine with them. They had no written copy of the Rule; we ordered them to have one written out. They ate meat, but, as they said, with the abbot's knowledge. They owed one hundred seventeen pounds of Paris to their abbot, and about twenty pounds of Tours elsewhere. We received procuration there this day. Total for procuration: six pounds.

SEPTEMBER 17. At Aliermont.

SEPTEMBER 18. We visited the priory at Auffay, where there were six monks from St-Evroult, to wit, Luke of Sap, who was then prior, Dreux of

[17] Sir Julian de Péronne was then bailiff of Rouen.

Neufmarché, Peter of Sap, Nicholas of Cahanges, John of Sap-André, and Henry of Haqueville. All were priests. A general distribution of alms is made once a week, to wit, on Mondays. They owed about thirty pounds; however, they had a sufficiency of wheat, oats, wine, and other provisions. We enjoined the prior to be more considerate and charitable than he had been and to be more careful in insisting that things necessary for the reception of guests, especially of religious, be on hand. We received procuration there this day. Total for procuration: eight pounds, seventeen pence.

SEPTEMBER 19. With God's grace we visited the abbey of St-Victor-en-Caux, where there were twenty-five monks. All but three were priests. We ordered the prior to have the Statutes of Pope Gregory read aloud in chapter more frequently—at least twice or three times a year. They had complained a good deal about the inadequate provision made for the sick; we ordered the abbot to have this corrected and to treat the weaker ones with more care and kindliness, inviting them to eat with him occasionally and seeing that they were provided with essentials. A general distribution of alms is made thrice [a week]. They owed eighty pounds, and about sixty pounds was owing to them. Item, they were unanimous in complaining, just as they had complained these many years, about their abbot, to wit, about certain pittances which they were entitled to receive on certain anniversaries, and which the abbot had entirely appropriated for himself, although we had often warned him to give these pittances to the monks.[18] Item, since they knew almost nothing about the state of the house, we ordered the abbot to have three copies of a statement written down in certain rolls or records giving a total accounting and itemized information, of which he was to keep one copy and to give the others to two seniors of the community; item, we ordered him again, as we had done before,[19] to issue a statement concerning the condition of the house twice a year in full chapter, and in the presence of the community, and in the presence of certain seniors elected by the community to audit the individual accounts and prepare a statement upon this. Item, that he should have the place repaired and kept in good condition. Item, that he should provide his monks with better bread, beer, comestibles, and other things than he had been doing, as far as the finances of the house would permit. Item, we warned him to see that things required

[18] See entries for May 18, 1251; March 8, 1254/55; September 4, 1258; March 12, 1259/60; September 15, 1261.
[19] See entry for September 15, 1261.

by the sick were provided for in better fashion than had been the case. Item, that he restore the aforesaid pittances to the community. Item, that he should behave in an affable and friendly manner toward [former] Abbot William,[20] encouraging him with kindly admonishment to be solicitous in cultivating those things which are requisite for his salvation. Item, that he should at once restore to the community its legal seal. Item, we enjoined him in particular to remove and depose Brother Robert of Quévremont, prior, Brother Roger of Breuil, subprior, and Brother John of Paris, almoner, from their offices within the next week. Item, that before All Saints he reduce his overlarge staff, and in particular Nicholas, his clerk. Item, we forbade the monks to presume to take any bread away from table or to sell it, as they had been doing. Item, we expressly forbade any of them to leave the house or to eat in the town, on pain of having anyone who should do so treated by the abbot as a runaway monk. Item, it should be noticed that William, the cellarer, took an oath in the presence of the community that he had acquired his office with purity and simplicity of heart, and without any taint of simony. Item, we enjoined the abbot to impose proper penance upon the said cellarer for having bathed in the presence of laymen. Item, we ordered [former] abbot William to confess more often than was his practice—at least once a week. Item, we ordered the abbot to make a diligent inquiry, together with the dean, into the charge of sodomy directed against Robert, an old monk, and to send the results of this investigation to us under seal. This day we received procuration from them. Total for procuration: seven pounds, eight shillings.

SEPTEMBER 20-21. At Déville.

SEPTEMBER 22. With God's grace we conferred Holy Orders at Ste-Catherine and spent the night there at our own expense.

This day the following document was placed before us:

In your presence, Reverend Father, archbishop of Rouen, the abbot and convent of St-Josse-sur-Mer, a Benedictine house in the diocese of Amiens, propose and assert that they possess the right of presentation to the church at Mesnil-David, in your diocese, as patently appears in a letter of your predecessor in which their right is set forth, notwithstanding the denial of Richard of Mesnil-David, the father of the late William of Mesnil-David, esquire, who now unjustly contests [their] claim. And you have, to their prejudice and hurt,

---

[20] Abbot William had resigned his office as abbot of St-Victor-en-Caux on December 17, 1255.

refused without reasonable cause to admit Master Dreux of Montreuil, cleric, to this church, though presented to you by the said abbot, and thereby you have aggrieved them. Item, you have injured them in another matter. In their case presented against the said William concerning this advowson, you delayed them a long time, so that it became manifest that this was being done so that time might slip away and the presentation revert to you. It is also evident that, at the expiration of the statutory period for making presentation, you wrongly referred the said abbot, the convent, and Dreux, cleric, presented by the said abbot, to a secular judge, and to one who had no jurisdiction in such a case. Item, you have injured and stil injure them in yet another matter, in that when your predecessor's letter was presented to you in the presence of the said William, which letter asserted how much of the advowson belonged to the possessor, no objection to the said letter was raised, although a day was set on which the said instrument might be spoken against if there were any legal impediment in it. No objection was offered. You were unwilling to follow the said letter and refused to act in accord with its contents. Item, you have also injured them, for that, although it had been suggested to you that possibly the dispute concerning the advowson should be referred to a secular judge, yet anent the possession of the right of presentation to the said church, concerning which possession it was adjudged by your predecessor that this question should not be referred to a secular judge, you have unjustly refused to admit this decision, by referring nevertheless to a secular judge the question of possession as well as that of ownership. Item, you have further injured them in that when on behalf of the said abbot and convent it was suggested to you that they were, and for a long time had been, in the possession of the right of receiving forty shillings of Tours as an annual pension from the priest at Mesnil-David, by reason of the right of advowson to the said church, and which the said religious offered to prove to you if this were denied by the other side, you nevertheless unjustly and to their prejudice refused to permit them to make such proof.

I, Master Dreux, proctor of the said abbot and convent, in their name and in my own behalf, petition that these grievances be removed and that I be admitted to the said church. The which if you should deny, I appeal in writing to the Apostolic See on their behalf and in their name and for myself, and I request *apostoli*. And if this be refused I appeal again in writing; and if you should attempt anything affecting the said church after the said appeal to the Apostolic See has been canonically presented, I again appeal in writing to the Apostolic See lest you undertake anything, and I place the church of Mesnil-David under the protection of the Apostolic See.

This appeal the proctor of the said abbot and convent presented by letters of proxy, sealed, as seemed, to all appearances with their seal. But to this appeal, since it contained nothing of truth or justice, we are not obliged to defer.

SEPTEMBER 23. At Frênes. SEPTEMBER 24. At Chaumont, at our own expense. SEPTEMBER 25. At Bresles, at the manor of the bishop of Beauvais, and at his expense. SEPTEMBER 26. At Gournay-sur-Aronde. SEPTEMBER 27. At Noyon. SEPTEMBER 28. At Villeneuve-le-Roi. SEPTEMBER 29. At Villeneuve-en-Hez. SEPTEMBER 30. At St-Germer-de-Flay, at our own expense.

OCTOBER 1. Since upon a previous occasion[21] we had turned aside to make a pilgrimage to the church of St-Hildevert-de-Gournay and discovered and found certain things connected with the canons, chaplains and clerks[-choral] of that church which needed correction, we came to this church today to make a visitation, and, with God's aid after preaching a sermon, we proceeded to visit it. We found only one dean there with the chaplains and clerks. Two canons were ill, to wit, Matthew and Reginald; because of Matthew's infirmity we were not able to discipline him or punish him for that he had been much defamed of a certain woman from Les Andelys, whom, it is rumored, he had kept for fourteen years and was still keeping. Furthermore, we expressly warned Simon, a chaplain who was gravely defamed of incontinence, particularly with a certain daughter of Haisie, whom he confessed to us to have known carnally, to abstain from things of this kind and to take care not to fall into sin again with this said daughter of Haisie or with any other, else he should know that we would punish him severely. Item, that he should refrain from playing dice and from his practice of making ill-considered accusations against his companions. We enjoined upon him what we considered to be a suitable penance for his delinquencies. We also warned Lawrence, a chaplain, to stop playing dice, and we forbade Reginald, the sacristan's aide, from going about the town at night in the future. Item, we issued a general prohibition against dancing on the feasts of St. Nicholas, St. Catherine, St. Hildevert, or any other, or from conducting themselves in any dissolute manner from which scandal might arise, as had happened in the past. Item, we ordered them to put the tabernacle, which had been made to hold the Blessed Sacrament, in a seemly and decent place near the parish altar. Item, we ordered the dean to punish some laymen of Gournay who were reported to have eaten meat on the Wednesdays of the Ember Days, and we gave him our authority to do this.

[21] See entry for August 22, above.

This day we came to the priory of St-Aubin. Eleven nuns were in residence; two had gone to France in search of alms, and two others, to wit, Alice of Rouen and Beatrice of Beauvais, led away by frivolity of soul, had departed at the devil's instigation; we gave orders that these not be readmitted without our special permission. We also forbade the prioress to receive any new members or to bestow the veil upon any without our special permission. They owed about twenty pounds, in addition to a debt to the king for a certain lease which is a serious burden to them. They had few supplies.

This same day with God's grace, we spent the night at St-Germer-de-Flay, at our own expense.

OCTOBER 2-8. At Frênes. OCTOBER 9. At Frênes, to wit, on the feast of St. Denis. OCTOBER 10-11. At Frênes. OCTOBER 12-13. At Gaillon. OCTOBER 14. At Pinterville. OCTOBER 15. At Martot. OCTOBER 16-17. At Déville. OCTOBER 18. To wit, on the feast of St. Luke the Evangelist, at St-Wandrille, at our own expense. OCTOBER 19. With God's grace we visited the said abbey. There were forty monks in residence and twenty outside in priories; all were priests, with the exception of six and three novices. One does not accuse another [in chapter]. We ordered the abbot to make frequent inspection of the coffers of the monks and that [the monks] turn in their old clothes upon the receipt of new ones. They ate meat freely in the priories and when there was no need. Alms are given daily to all comers, but not, however, at stated hours. We ordered them to make more sufficient provisions for the weak and infirm. More is owed to them than they owe, and in good debts, and they have a large store of provisions; and with God's grace things were well with them. Item, however, we publicly exhorted the abbot to conduct himself charitably toward those who grew fatigued by reason of their labor, to be more sympathetic than he had been, and to provide such recreation for his monks as should seem fitting; item, that he be more affable with them. We received procuration there this day and dined in the refectory with the community.

OCTOBER 20. We spent the night at Le Valasse, at the expense of the abbey. OCTOBER 21. We received procuration at Graville. Total for procuration: seven pounds.

OCTOBER 22. With God's grace we visited the priory of the said place, where there were thirteen canons in residence. We ordered the prior to inspect the canons' coffers to remove any property. We were much displeased that lay folk, both men and women, had free access and entry through the choir to the relics upon the high altar; wherefore we advised and asked them to close off, so far as was possible, such a way and entry for lay folk, and to bring out and display the relics upon some altar outside the chancel in the nave of the monastery. They owed nothing beyond one hundred pounds for which they were beholden to a certain priest, and they had a large stock of provisions.

This day we spent this night at Montivilliers, at our own expense.

OCTOBER 23. With God's grace we visited there. Forty nuns were in residence, and that is the certain and statutory number. They should confess and receive Communion at least once a month. As we had done before at our other visitation, we gave orders that the day and night Offices be celebrated with sufficient diligence that the entire service might be completed in daylight.[22] Item, we ordered the abbess to remove the keys and to make frequent inspection of the coffers lest they have any property. Item, that the nuns should hand in their old garments upon the receipt of new ones. Item, that all the healthy ones should eat together. We expressly forbade them to reduce their alms donations, that is to say, that nothing be held back which should be given as alms. Item, that they should not have many and various dishes in the kitchen. A general distribution of alms should be made three times a week, but they had abandoned making any gifts of this kind since September and would not make any until they had collected their rents. Nevertheless, the abbess was obligated to maintain thirteen poor people every day, by reason of an ancient custom established by Alice, a former abbess. They owed nothing, and they had, either in the chest or treasury or in good and receivable accounts, five hundred pounds. The abbess rarely attended community activities, that is to say, the refectory, chapter, dormitory, and choir. Some of them complained about the austerity of the abbess. We ordered her to appoint one or two to take care of the little needs of the nuns, such as ginger, or some such thing, and with whom the others might talk a little more freely and familiarly. Item, that the quality of the wine drunk by the community be improved. Item, we, as was fitting, being desirous of eradicating all matter for scandal and of preserving them from all perils, expressly forbade the abbess, the prioress, and the subprioress to permit any more processions to be held in the church, as had been done, and to see that the community refrained completely from such processions; however, we

[22] See entry for January 12, 1260/61.

were quite willing and do desire that the prayers, antiphons, and responses which were sung at these processions be sung in the choir. We received procuration there this day. Total for procuration: nine pounds, nine shillings.

OCTOBER 24. William, priest at Mannevillette, who had been cited by the archdeacon, appeared before us, for it was stated that he was bellicose and a brawler and that he had come to blows with his parishioners. In the presence of P[eter], the archdeacon, Brother Adam Rigaud, and John of Morgneval, we expressly admonished him to abstain from such conduct.

This same day we warned Ralph, priest at Valliquerville, to resign his church as he had promised, for we knew that he had relapsed.

This day we spent the night at Valmont, at our expense.

OCTOBER 25. With God's grace we visited the abbey there, where there were twenty-six monks in residence. All but one were priests; one was alone outside, and we ordered that a companion be sent to him; four were [officially] in England, but two of them were at present staying with Sir Robert of Etoutteville and his wife. We ordered those living in the abbey to confess more frequently. One does not, as of custom, accuse another [in chapter]. Alms are given daily to all comers in summer, but in winter three times a week. They had a little carter who was drunken and overly given to wine and whom we ordered discharged. We ordered the abbot to see that the Rule covering the eating of meat was observed both within the abbey and outside. Item, we ordered that the prior and one of the seniors of the community attend the abbot when the individual accounts were drawn up. Their finances were in good condition; they had a certain sum of money for the care of the fabric of the church. Sir Robert, the lord of the village, owed them fifty pounds, and his lady owed them forty pounds; up to the present some eighty pounds in arrears of rents was owed to them. We received procuration there this day. Total for procuration: six pounds.

This same day the priest at Lintot, whose letter we have, came before us admitting his obligation to resign his church whenever we desire. And since we found him to be defamed of incontinence, as had occurred before, we permitted him to exchange this church for another somewhere else before Easter, and we urged him to bring about such an exchange, otherwise he must thenceforth regard the former church as resigned.

OCTOBER 26. We came to the priory at Etoutteville, which we found to be miserably administered in both spiritual and temporal concerns. Two monks from Lewes were there, and a certain English servant provided the monks with necessities on behalf of Master Gilbert of Caux, who holds the place and has it for life. We enjoined Robert, the said servant, to have the place repaired and improved. Nevertheless, we caused the goods of this priory to be seized into our hands and to be held by the dean of Canville until the place should be suitably repaired, together with fifty pounds of Tours, which we likewise had seized for the same reason at our last visitation.[23] Item, we ordered the treasurer and the priest of the parish to have suitable ornaments for their church, for we found it defective therein.

This day we spent the night at Ouville, where we received procuration from the aforesaid servant. Total for procuration: nine pounds, ten shillings.

OCTOBER 27. With God's grace we visited the priory at Ouville. Twelve canons were in residence; all but one were priests; two were at Attigny. They had two lay brothers and one lay sister. We ordered that silence be observed better in accordance with the Rule than had been the case there; the canons should not leave the cloister without the prior's permission. Item, since the prior had been unwilling, although we had several times ordered him to do so,[24] to restore or return to the canons the ten pounds a year which certain faithful deceased had willed to them as pittances, we expressly enjoined him to assign them this ten pounds from definite sources of income. This should be done with the consent of the prior and community. Then we ordered that they, or some one of them deputed for this, should receive seven and one half pounds which was owed to them on a certain house at Rouen, and fifty shillings annually at Corianville, for the above pittances. As much was owed to them in good debts as they owed. Other things, with God's grace we found to be in a satisfactory state. We received procuration there this day. Total for procuration: seven pounds.

OCTOBER 28. To wit, on the feast of SS. Simon and Jude, at Déville.

OCTOBER 29. At the same.

OCTOBER 30. We came to the church of Notre-Dame-la-Ronde at Rouen, and there, with God's grace, we preached and made a visitation. We found a dean residing there with a single canon and some vicars. Indeed, we found that Master Walter of Pérrièrs, a canon who owed residence, did not maintain it and wandered about more than he should. There was some defect in procuring lights, for they had lost almost all the revenue devoted to lighting since the withdrawal of the market. Item, they had no serving

---

[23] See entry for May 25, 1262.
[24] See entry for May 25, 1262.

clerk, nor any distributor of the commons.[25] Item, they had no general chapter. With God's grace we proposed to draw up some ordinances about these things. We spent this night at Déville.

OCTOBER 31. At Rouen. NOVEMBER 1. With God's grace we celebrated the feast of All Saints at Rouen. NOVEMBER 2-5. At Déville, because of our rheumatism. NOVEMBER 6. This was the day of the synod, which we could not hold because of our rheumatism.

NOVEMBER 7. At Déville, where, still being afflicted with rheumatism, we could not speak with the deans whom we had convoked there, as we would have liked to do. However, we sent Peter, the archdeacon of Grand-Caux, Master John of Neuilly-en-Thelle, and the archdeacon of Rouen to them in our stead. These warned them, on our behalf, to be more diligent than they had been in making inquiries and not to allow the priests to ride abroad in short cloaks; item, to order the priests of their deaneries to visit their parishioners in person in times of sickness or need.

This day was opened the inquiry concerning the wounding of Geoffrey of Roncherolles, which was imputed to the priest at Roquette, who was present, and for whom, at his request, we had a copy of the inquiry prepared. We assigned him the day after [the first Sunday in] Advent when the inquiry would be continued and sentence imposed.

This same day we warned and required Baldwin, rector of a certain part of the church of St-Remy-les-Champs, and Ralph, priest at Valliquèrville, to resign their benefices as by their oaths and letters patent they are held to do at our volition; but they were not willing to do this.

NOVEMBER 8. We likewise warned and required Master Robert of Houssay, rector of the church at Conteville, to resign his church as he had promised, on oath, to do. This he did not wish to do.

This day was presented to us the report of the election of [Abbess] Margaret of Cristot to the monastery of Bival; we examined it carefully and rejected it because of faulty procedure. However, with God's aid, having considered and weighed the merits of the person elected and the general utility to the said monastery, we caused her in God's name to be provided to the said monastery. This day we spent the night at Déville.

NOVEMBER 9. In God's charity we conferred upon Master Adam Rigaud, our nephew, the prebend which Master Richard of Salmonville had formerly held in the church at Rouen, and in the hall of our palace at Rouen we

[25] The share of food and revenues to which all canons were entitled.

invested John of Morgneval, our clerk, with this prebend and with our ring, in the name of the said Master Adam. Present were: the venerable men, Master G., the treasurer; Master P[eter], archdeacon of Grand-Caux in the church of Rouen; Master William of Flavacourt, the official; Master John of Neuilly-en-Thelle, canon of Rouen; Brother Adam Rigaud; and John of Morgneval, our clerk.

This day we spent the night at Pont-de-l'Arche.

NOVEMBER 10. At Pinterville. NOVEMBER 11. At the same, to wit, on the feast of St. Martin. NOVEMBER 12. At Gaillon. NOVEMBER 13. At Vernon. NOVEMBER 14. We received procuration at Juziers.

NOVEMBER 15. With God's grace we visited the priory there, where there were five monks. There should be six with a prior; all were priests. They wore rabbit-fur cloaks and used feather beds. Alms are given daily to all comers. They did not observe the fasts of the Rule, and they occasionally ate meat when there was no need; however, their abbot, who was present at this visitation, had excused them and offered a sufficiently reasonable explanation of why they acted so. Here follow the names of the monks who were present at this time: Philip, the sacristan; Geoffrey of Carnot; Bartholomew of Aulnay; and John of Limay. This day we spent the night at St-Germain-en-Laye.

NOVEMBER 16-22. At Paris. NOVEMBER 23. At the same, to wit, on the feast of St. Clement. NOVEMBER 24-29. At Paris. NOVEMBER 30. To wit, on the feast of St. Andrew the Apostle. This day Master Peter of St-Germain died. DECEMBER 1. At the same. This day with God's aid, we married Peter Rigaud to Nazarea, the daughter of the road supervisor of Auxerre, at Ville-juif, near Paris. DECEMBER 2-5. At Paris. DECEMBER 6. To wit, on the feast of St-Nicholas. DECEMBER 7-8. At Paris. DECEMBER 9. At St-Martin-de-Pontoise, at our own expense. This day we conferred the chancellery [26] upon Master Richard of Sap.

DECEMBER 10. With God's grace we visited the said abbey, where there were twenty-four monks. One monk was alone at Tavergny; we ordered a companion for him. We ordered the Statutes of Pope Gregory to be read more often than had been done in the past. Alms are given thrice a week to all comers. They had two lay brothers and four lay sisters. We ordered the abbot to see that they confessed and received Communion more frequently. The monks resident in the priories ate meat; we enjoined the abbot to

[26] The *chancelerie* was the repository of all officially signed documents.

discipline and punish them for this, and to see that they abstained from meat and observed the Rule in this matter. They owed nineteen hundred pounds of Paris, of which eight hundred was at interest; however, they had many annual pensions, and the bishop and the archdeacon of Meaux held two manors of them for life. We received procuration there this day. Total for procuration: nine pounds, six shillings, eight pence.

DECEMBER 11. With God's grace we visited the chapter of St-Mellon. There are ten prebends. Dom Luke was the only resident canon. There were nine vicars and a sacristan in charge of capes, and two chaplains; of the vicars there, one should be a subdeacon, the other a deacon. They need surplices and altar cloths; we ordered Dom Luke, who said that he had cloth for making them at the house, to provide the church with these things. Item, since during the celebration of the Divine Office certain ones murmur in the choir to the detriment of the Divine Services, we expressly forbade them to continue this whispering, but to apply themselves with the greatest and most devout diligence to the Office. Item, we found Luke, a vicar, to be gravely defamed of the vice of incontinence, as we had done before,[27] and especially with a certain lame woman whom he admitted knowing carnally within the past year. Since, indeed, we found him to be incorrigible, obstinate, and disobedient, inasmuch as he had been very frequently warned by us, and careless of his salvation and indifferent to his reputation, we enjoined him to resign his benefice or otherwise we would undertake judicial proceedings against him; this he did not do, but with tears besought some favor in this matter. We, giving ear to his supplications and to certain ones who interceded for him, gave him permission to exchange his church [for another] elsewhere before the feast of the Purification of the Blessed Virgin Mary. He swore and promised of his own free will, and on the Holy Gospels, that he would resign his benefice before the stated day, or that otherwise we might then deprive him of the said benefice without any appeal on his part and without the publicity of a trial. He even swore that from now on he would urge no claim nor contest a deprivation of this kind. Item, we found Luke, a deacon, likewise gravely defamed of incontinence, and he voluntarily confessed that he had had an affair with Emelotte, a neighbor of Dom Luke, his uncle, and that she had had a child by him. In response to his desire to accept penance, we enjoined him to say the Psalter five times before the feast of the Purification, to make a pilgrimage to St-Michael-in-Danger-of-

[27] See entry for November 14, 1262.

the-Sea before Easter. We forbade him to read the Gospel[28] in his church before the feast of the Purification. He swore upon the Holy Gospel and promised that should he be found culpable of this vice again, or even so defamed that he could not purge himself canonically, he would regard his benefice as resigned from that time on. Item, we warned Dom Thomas, who was defamed of incontinence, to abstain from this vice. Item, we warned Dom Walter, likewise defamed of incontinence, to abstain, and we expressly forbade him to continue to maintain his daughter and her mother in his own home, which he had long done with scandal. Item, we warned Michael, defamed of a certain maidservant living at the house of one of the burgesses, to abstain. Item, we warned Robert of Minières to conduct himself more obediently in the community than had been his practice, for we learned that he was rebellious and negligent. Therefore we enjoined him to repeat three times the seven [penitential] psalms[29] and the Litany[30] before next Christmas. Item, we warned them all to refrain from whispering or causing disturbance, especially in the choir. Item, we seized and stopped the income from the prebend of Nicholas of Montlieu, canon of St-Mellon, reported to be deceased, from going to Dom Luke, who has collected it for many years. Item, we ordered them to recover from the dean of St-Aignan the twenty shillings he had received for a certain psalter. Item, we forbade the chaplains to celebrate Masses, Vespers, or any other Office, in the town. Since we found mismanagement in the procuring and rebinding of the books, the roofing of the monastery, as well as in the matter of certain monies left by Master Ptolemy to provide lighting; also that few ever came to the general chapter, that little provision was made for books or reading material, and that they did not have a common proctor, we peremptorily cited the chapter to appear before us suitably represented, at Rouen or in the vicinity, on the day preceding the coming conferring of Holy Orders. Item, we forbade them to strew any more straw in the choir. Present at this visitation were: Peter, the archdeacon of Caux; Master John of Neuilly-en-Thelle; Eudes Bigot, canon of Rouen; Brother Adam Rigaud; John of Morgneval; and the vicars and chaplains of the chapter of St-Mellon. And it should be known that the said Luke, the deacon, gave us a letter concerning the matter mentioned above,

[28] As a deacon, one of his functions at High Mass was the reading of the Gospel to the public.

[29] The seven penitential psalms are Psalms 6, 31, 37, 50, 101, 129, 142.

[30] The solemn Litany which is said on Good Friday and on Rogation Days. ("Litanies," Dict. d'arch. chrét. et de lit., IX², 1540-1570.)

under the seal of the said archdeacon and Master John, the tenor of which is recorded above[31] along with the obligations of the priests.

This day we spent this night at St-Martin, and from Dom Luke, canon of St-Mellon, we received for procuration one hundred shillings of Paris on behalf of the chapter, in which amount the chapter is annually bound to us at our visitation, in addition to housing, straw, wood, cups, dishes, and other utensils.

DECEMBER 12. With God's grace we visited the Hôtel-Dieu at Pontoise, where there were four good men garbed in regular or religious habit, two of whom were priests. They had as their master or rector a certain secular priest, to wit, John of Fenins, given to them by the king. The original four had no definite rule, nor did they follow the observances of any order, nor did they make any profession. Item, thirteen sisters were there, of whom one was the prioress. These lived, as they said, according to a rule,[32] and some of them had made profession of the three vows, to wit, of obedience, chastity, and the renunciation of property. They had an annual income of six hundred pounds; they owed nothing; they had some provisions, wine enough for a year, but not that amount of wheat, and few animals. They had five maidservants.

This day we visited St. Peter's priory, where there were five monks from Bec-Hellouin, to wit, Ralph of L'Honblonnière, prior; and John of Cambremer, William of Ninville, Peter of Olibec, and Ralph of Beaumont, monks. They ate meat when there was no need, which much displeased us. In the prior's presence, the parish priest of St. Peter's complained to us of an incompetent and unworthy clerk whom the prior had sent to him, for the prior is bound to provide him with an efficient clerk; we ordered the prior to correct this. They owed thirty-two pounds to the abbot and a little elsewhere; they believed that they had enough supplies to last out the year.

This same day with God's grace we spent the night at St-Martin[-la-Garenne], at our own expense.

DECEMBER 13. We received procuration at St-Martin-la-Garenne. Total for procuration: seven pounds. We visited the local priory, where were three monks from Bec-Hellouin, to wit, Ralph of Brotonne, prior; William of Olibec; and Henry of Evreux. There should be more, but because of the deficiency of goods and of the barrenness of the vines from which they

---

[31] *Bonnin,* pp. 667-68.
[32] This may be the Rule of St. Augustine.

suffered these many years, the others were recalled to the cloister. They did not observe the fasts of the Rule very well, but they said this was because of their guests. They used meat when there was no need, and then used feather beds. They owed about thirty-two pounds in addition to what they owed to their abbot; they had enough wheat to last out the year. One of the buildings in the courtyard near the stable was in a ruinous state; we ordered the prior to have it repaired.

DECEMBER 14. We visited the priory at Gasny, where there were three monks from St-Ouen-de-Rouen, to wit, Roger of St-Aignan, Geoffrey of Ninville, and William of Magdalene. They dwelt in the manor called St-Nicaise across the river and performed no Divine Services in the other manor. There they had supplies for the animals and a large staff which always stayed at St-Nicaise. They were almost ignorant concerning the state of the house, since they were but lately come there and since they sent to the abbey everything except what was essential for their own maintenance and that of their staff. We received procuration there this day. Total for procuration: seven pounds, six shillings.

DECEMBER 15. At Vernon, with the king.

DECEMBER 16-17. At Pinterville.

DECEMBER 18. At Pont-de-l'Arche.

DECEMBER 19. At Rouen.

DECEMBER 20. At the same, and this day with God's grace we preached the king at St. Matthew's, and the [Dominican] sisters were installed there.

DECEMBER 21. To wit, on the feast of St. Thomas the Apostle, at Déville.

DECEMBER 22. With God's grace we conferred Holy Orders in our chapel at Déville.

This day, Ralph, rector of the church at Valliquerville, voluntarily resigned his church.

DECEMBER 23. We made our O [33] at Rouen.

DECEMBER 24. At the same. This day Baldwin, rector of a part of the church of St-Remy-les-Champs, voluntarily resigned his portion. This day we pronounced the following sentence:

Inasmuch as Robert of Houssaye, rector of the church at Conteville, for legitimate reasons had sworn on the Holy Gospel to resign the aforesaid church without publicity of trial whensoever he should be requested to do so by us, and inasmuch as we have warned and requested him to resign the said church and he

[33] See above, December 23, 1250, n. 135.

has not cared to attend to our admonition, we by sentence deprive him, as perjured, of the said church.

DECEMBER 25. With God's grace we celebrated the feast of the Nativity at Rouen.

DECEMBER 26-29. At Déville.

DECEMBER 30. At Pont-de-l'Arche.

DECEMBER 31. At Gaillon, to wit, the feast of the Circumcision of the Lord.[34]

JANUARY 1-3. At the same.

JANUARY 4-5. At Frênes.

JANUARY 6. To wit, on the feast of the Epiphany, at Frênes.

JANUARY 7. At Frênes.

JANUARY 8. We received procuration at Sigy. Total for procuration:... [lacuna in MS]. It should be known that the procuration to be collected here by us should not exceed ten pounds of Tours, as is more fully set forth in a letter of agreement, copied out in our cartulary.[35] JANUARY 9. With God's grace we visited the priory at Sigy, where there were three monks from St-Ouen-de-Rouen, to wit, Brother Peter of Ruppe, prior; Brother John of Genestoies; and Matthew of Commune. There should be six, but the abbot, because of certain damages suffered by his monastery, has recalled three to the cloister and has appropriated to himself certain incomes which should belong to the priory, which indeed displeased us not a little. However, the said John told us that the abbot had planned to replace the accustomed number of monks before the coming feast of St. Peter[36] and to restore to the priory the income which had been deducted. They ate meat freely and sometimes broke the fasts of the Rule because of their guests. We forbade them to eat meat in the town or to allow women to dine with them. They owed one hundred forty pounds and said that they had enough provisions to last out the year. We spent this night at Aliermont.

JANUARY 10-16. At Aliermont.

JANUARY 17. At the same. This day we inspected a certain letter, sealed with the seal of P.[37] of good memory, by God's grace our predecessor, which

[34] This may be the clerk's error, since December 31 is the vigil and not the feast of the Circumcision. On the other hand, some of the opus Dei for the feast was recited on the vigil, hence the entry may stress the Service rather than the calendar.

[35] See above, November 11, 1254, n. 18; May 18, 1255, n. 6.

[36] Probably the feast of St. Peter's Chair of Antioch, February 22.

[37] Pierre de Colmieu, archbishop of Rouen from 1236 to 1244.

was drawn up anent an agreement made about certain tithes of orchards, woodlands, and the like, and which the present rector was seeking to collect from the prior of the leper house at Arques. After diligently inspecting its intent, we desired and ordered that the agreement be observed, as it had been made according to law.

JANUARY 18-19. At Aliermont. JANUARY 20. We received procuration at Longueville. JANUARY 21. We received procuration at St-Saëns. Total for procuration: nine pounds.

JANUARY 22. With God's grace we visited the priory of monks, where there were four, including the prior, to wit, Dom Philip of St-Riquier, who was then ill, Peter of Aumale, and Ralph of Mouteville. They ate meat frequently when there was no need and did not observe the fasts of the Rule very well. The prior rarely celebrated Mass. More was owed to them than they owed, and they had many supplies. Alms are distributed thrice a week.

We spent the night at Déville.

JANUARY 23. At Pont-de-l'Arche. JANUARY 24. At Pinterville. JANUARY 25. To wit, on the feast of the Conversion of St. Paul, at Pinterville. JANUARY 26. At Gaillon. JANUARY 27-28. At Vernon.

JANUARY 29. At Vernon, where, with God's grace, we celebrated a provincial council at the Franciscan monastery, assisted by our venerable brothers our suffragan bishops, to wit, O.[Eudes], of Bayeux; R[alph], of Evreux; F[ulk], of Lisieux; R[ichard], of Avranches; Th[omas], of Séez, and J[ohn], of Coutances. First we celebrated the Mass of the Holy Ghost in pontificals with the deacon and the subdeacon formally vested, to wit, Master J[ohn], the archdeacon of Petit-Caux in the church of Rouen, acting as deacon; and Master William of Flavicourt, then the official of Rouen, as subdeacon. At the celebration of the Mass our suffragans stood clothed in albs with choral copes. When this had been celebrated, although we and our suffragans, dressed in pontificals, should have ascended the dais erected according to custom near the doors of the church, we agreed to remain before the altar, they being in albs and copes as before. It should be mentioned that the bishops of Bayeux, Evreux, and Lisieux sat on our right upon the dais, and in that order, while on our left were seated in order the bishops of Avranches, Séez, and Coutances. The Gospel was read at once, to wit, the passage beginning, "Jesus appointed seventy-two,"[38] by the deacon who had been vested at the Mass. When this had been read, we began aloud the

[38] Luke 10 : 1-5.

Veni Creator Spiritus, after which two, vested in surplices, sang the Litany, and after the Lord's Prayer in a low voice, we offered the prayer *Assumus.* This ended, with God's grace we preached a sermon, and, the sermon being finished, the letter of convocation and the rescript and the letters of proxy of the cathedral chapters were read; then followed a reading of the statute *Sicut olim,* enacted in general council, concerning the holding of annual councils by archbishops and their suffragans which is contained in the title, *On Accusations:*[39] also the statute, concerning intoxication and drunkenness, etc., was read.

The proctors were as follows: of the Rouen chapter, Master William of Saâne, the treasurer of Rouen; of Bayeux, Master John of Clermont, the archdeacon of that church; of Evreux, Dom Thomas of St-Verane and Nicolas Hurtaud, canons of Evreux; of Lisieux, Master Nicolas, the archdeacon of Pont-Audemer in the church of Lisieux; of Avranches, John of Fontenay, canon of Avranches; of Séez, Michael Estancion, canon of Séez; of Coutances, Master William, called Porte. Then were read all of the following statutes:

It is the pleasure of the holy council that those things which follow below be firmly observed, in such a way that the Reverend Father Eudes, by God's grace archbishop of Rouen, his suffragans, and their subjects, should not be bound to their observance as though they were newly enacted, that is, as regards those things which are expressly to be found in [canon] law, in the Statutes of Pope Gregory IX, or in the episcopal synods.

We will that the decree of the Council of Lyons, in the matter of procurations to be received by the archbishop and bishops by reason of visitation, and in the matter of burdens inflicted by their officials under pretext of performing their duties, be observed.

We will that the statute of the general council concerning those who form leagues, and the statute published concerning the liberties of the Church, be frequently and solemnly promulgated in synods and in parish churches, and that transgressors be canonically punished.

We decree that such secular authorities as shall seize clerics with more violence than the disobedience of the defendant requires, or who shall detain them against or beyond the pleas of the ecclesiastical judge, shall be pronounced excommunicate by a general sentence and by a specific sentence after the fact is proved.

We strictly forbid that in cases pertaining to the Church a secular judge be

[39] See above, January 29, 1259/60, n. 31; January 26, 1260/61, n. 24.

consulted by ecclesiastical persons, particularly regarding personal actions.

We decree that abbots and priors, and other ecclesiastical persons who receive the major tithes of parish churches, shall be obligated to repair the fabric, books, and ornaments in the same proportion as they receive such tithes.

We desire that the synodal statutes, to wit, that ecclesiastical persons who receive the mandates of various judges, delegates, conservators, or executors shall diligently inspect and observe the authenticity of the names of the judges, dioceses, and places to which they cite, be firmly observed.

We forbid any Christian, man or woman, to serve Jews in hospices or presume to dwell with them, and we decree that Jews be obliged to wear distinctive signs whereby they may be distinguished from Catholics.

We strictly forbid any vigils or dances to be held in churchyards and sacred places, and we decree that transgressors be canonically punished.

Let all clerics and especially the unmarried ones be warned in the churches to wear a suitable tonsure, and let all who have taken the Cross be obliged to wear a cross openly.

We will that the statute of the general council in the matter of gilded saddles, bridles, spurs, and cinches, and other superfluities, the use of which is forbidden to the clergy, and especially in the matter of wearing closed gowns by priests, be observed.

We forbid any clerics who are beneficed or ordained in Holy Orders to be carried away by or become addicted to hunting and fowling.

We decree that in those abbeys and priories whose revenues are not curtailed, the requisite number of religious be reestablished, execept perchance, temporarily, by express permission of the superior and for reasonable cause.

We will and decree that what is decreed by law, to wit, that no monk shall dwell anywhere alone, be observed.

Let the monks dwelling in nonconventual priories be warned, under threat of suspension and excommunication or as may seem expedient, that they must strive to observe the Statutes of Pope Gregory pertaining to the eating of meat, confession, and the fasts.

We decree that regulars shall not live with seculars save by the special permission of their own diocesan.

The statute covering the contracting of loans by religious beyond a certain amount, except by permission of their abbot, shall be strictly observed.

We order that rural deans who have such jurisdiction shall neither excommunicate nor suspend, save in writing.

We decree that priests shall not refrain from pronouncing excommunication, even though the parties may have become reconciled, until they are legally absolved from excommunication.

We desire that absolution be made with due solemnity.

We forbid priests to presume to pronounce general sentence of excommunication save in cases of theft or vandalism and after due warning has been given.

We decree that chaplains to whom churches are temporarily entrusted shall be diligently examined as to their learning, way of life, and ordination.

We decree that canons regular to whom a care of souls has to be committed shall be more carefully examined than has been the practice as to their learning, way of life, morals and general conduct, and matrimonial status.

Item, we decree that a special Mass shall be sung in every cathedral, conventual, collegiate, and parish church of the province for any archbishop or bishop of the province who shall die.

These things being completed, and the council harmoniously ended, we sang *Te Deum laudamus* before the altar, and when the canticle was over we offered suitable prayers.

This day we spent the night at Vernon.

JANUARY 30. This day we spent the night at Pinterville, and our venerable brothers the bishops of Avranches and Coutances dined with us. JANUARY 31–FEBRUARY 1. At Pinterville. FEBRUARY 2. To wit, on the feast of the Purification of the Blessed Mary, at the same. FEBRUARY 3-14. At Pinterville. FEBRUARY 15. At Pont-de-l'Arche. FEBRUARY 16. At Rouen. FEBRUARY 17. At the same, and with God's grace we preached in the cathedral. FEBRUARY 18. We received procuration at Quévreville from the abbot of St-Ouen-de-Rouen, who then held this said house in his possession. We did not compute because of the presence of the abbot, who was with us.

FEBRUARY 19. With God's grace we visited the priory of Mont-Deux-Amants, where twelve canons were in residence; two were novices. We ordered these to confess at least once a month. They were not careful about surrendering their old clothing upon the receipt of new; we ordered this corrected. At mealtimes they did not read continually or throughout the meal, but a little at the beginning and again at the end. As a general practice, alms are dispensed every day. They thought they had a sufficiency of wheat, oats, and wine to last out the year, and they had many animals. They owed two hundred pounds, including the debt owed to the priest at Tourville, and about sixty pounds in good debts was owed to them. The sick were not well attended; we ordered this corrected. Many complaints were made against the prior concerning certain pittances, but we judged these to be frivolous. Item, at times the prior engaged personally in outside business which could be done by an ordinary canon. Item, we decreed that one canon be especially appointed to collect twenty pounds from the grange at Muitreville for pittances. We received procuration there this day. Total for procuration: seven pounds, twelve shillings, eight pence.

FEBRUARY 20-21. At Frênes, at our own pence. FEBRUARY 22. To wit, on the feast of St. Peter's Chair, at Mortemer-en-Lyons, at the expense of the abbey.

FEBRUARY 23. At Gisors, at the priory of St-Ouen, where we are entitled once a year to receive, when we turn aside to spend the night there, seven pounds of Tours for procuration, and nothing more unless it be through liberality and grace. Two exempt monks from Marmoutier are there.

FEBRUARY 24. We received procuration at Vesly, to wit, on the feast of St. Matthew the Apostle. Two exempt monks from Marmoutier are there. Total for procuration: seven pounds, six shillings. FEBRUARY 25. We received procuration at Sausseuse. Total for procuration: eight pounds, sixteen shillings.

FEBRUARY 26. With God's help we preached a sermon, and with His grace we visited this priory. Thirteen canons were in residence, of whom three were novices; with the exception of these and two others, all were priests. Some were in parish churches outside, and to these the cure of souls had not yet been committed; we ordered this corrected. Item, we gave orders that the novices confess frequently. Alms are given there twice a week. They owed only one hundred pounds of Tours, and more was owed to them, as they said. They have plenty of provisions, except wheat, to last out the year, and they have much animal fodder. Item, we expressly forbade the prior to allow the canons dwelling outside to run about the neighboring towns in the future, or to go to markets and trade as they had sometimes done. With God's grace we found other things to be in a sufficiently good state.

Note: Concerning the canon at Bacqueville, who had held the church at Ouville in fee.

This day we spent the night at Gaillon.

FEBRUARY 27-28. At Gaillon. FEBRUARY 29—MARCH 2. At Pinterville. MARCH 3. At Pont-de-l'Arche. MARCH 4. At Déville. MARCH 5. To wit, on Ash Wednesday, and with God's grace we performed this day's service in the cathedral at Rouen and preached there. MARCH 6-8. At Déville. MARCH 9. With God's grace we preached at the cathedral at Rouen, and we spent the night there.

MARCH 10. Sir John of Neville, knight, rendered homage to us for the service for which he is held to the archbishop of Rouen, on the day of the reception of the said archbishop, and the said knight should have a cup worth three marks with which he served him on that day.[49]

MARCH 10 [*sic*]. In the middle chamber of our manor at Rouen and in the presence of the venerable men G., the treasurer; J[ohn], the precentor; P[eter] of Ons, archdeacon; J[ohn] of Neuilly-en-Thelle, archdeacon; Master P[eter] of Aumale, canon of Rouen; Master Ralph of St-Gildard, canon of Bayeux; Isembard; and John of Morgneval, Richer [called] the Lombard, the advocate of Haut-Pas,[41] appeared before us. We had undertaken proceedings against him officially for the crime of fraud. The aforementioned P[eter], the archdeacon; Isembard; and likewise Dom Robert of Porte, who had been present when the said Richer, in the presence of the official of Rouen, had confessed to some of the charges laid against him, swore that they would truly tell what they had heard in this matter. The said archdeacon testified under oath that on a certain day, the date of which he could not remember, he was present at our court in Rouen, in the chamber where the official holds his hearings, when the said Richer confessed and admitted, in the presence of the said official, that he believed he had added a clause to the content of an official letter, in a summary which he had used throughout our diocese, to the effect that priests and clerics who should diligently conduct the business of Haut-Pas would be absolved by apostolic authority from all omissions and neglects of duty in their Divine Offices; and the archdeacon heard this, as he recollected.

Master Isembard, when sworn and asked about this, replied in the same manner as the said archdeacon.

Dom Robert, when sworn and asked about the same matter, said likewise that he was present on a certain day, the date of which he could not remember, in the said chamber when the said R[icher], in the presence of the official, admitted that he believed that he had added two clauses of his own to the two clauses of the summary beyond those which were contained in the

---

[40] I.e., the vassal serves his lord at a banquet and receives a silver cup in recompense.

[41] The Order of St-Jacques-de-Haut-Pas of Luca had a house in Paris. ("Hospitaliers," *Dict. de théol. cath.*, VII[1], 192.) As Bonnin points out, the order's objective was to aid pilgrims to cross rivers by using boats and bridges which they themselves had made. Their name came from their original house built on the banks of the river Arno, in Italy, in the twelfth century. (Bonnin, p. 485, n. 2.)

letter from the Curia, to wit, that priests and clerics who attended diligently to the business of Haut-Pas would be absolved from such omissions as they made through negligence in the Divine Office: item, that to all the faithful of Christ who should further the work, whatever the offense committed by them in amassing evil gains, forgiveness [for that offense] would be granted to them on apostolic authority. The said R[obert] heard this, as he remembered.

This day we spent the night at Déville, where we received procuration from the prior of St-Lô-de-Rouen, for the priory was then inadequate and insufficient for our reception.

MARCH 11. With God's grace we came to the priory of St-Lô[-de-Rouen], and there with His aid we preached and made a visitation. There were seventeen canons in residence and five outside, to wit, at Cressy and Théméricourt. Alms are given twice a week to all comers. They owed two hundred pounds because they had been burdened by the heavy expenses entailed in providing food for the chapter. They had sufficient supplies to last out the year.

This day we spent the night at Déville, at our own expense.

MARCH 12. At Déville.

MARCH 13. With God's grace we came to the abbey of St-Amand-de-Rouen, and with His aid we preached and made a visitation. Forty-five nuns were in residence, and there were five at Saâne. Three girls had been received in secular garb, who were to take the veil. A daughter of Lady Alice of Senots was there, and we ordered her to be sent home; we expressly forbade them to receive or give the veil to any one without our special permission. Item, we forbade anyone to leave the cloister without the permission of the abbess, and we ordered the gate of the cloister to be more carefully guarded. Item, we ordered them to observe silence better than had been customary. Item, we ordered them all to go to bed in the dormitory at the same hour. We ordered that the juniors no longer remain in the choir on the Feast of the Innocents, as they had done before, chanting the Office and the Sequences suited to that day, when the seniors had retired and the juniors remained behind. Item, we forbade them to presume to diminish their quota of alms by carrying off anything which ought to be given to alms. Item, we forbade the abbess to be lenient in giving permission to any person or persons to go out, requiring her to give good, sure, and faithful company to those to whom she should grant a favor of this kind. Item, we forbade them to make any laces, needle-cases, or alms-bags. They owed about one hundred pounds, and some debts were owed to them. Item, we ordered the nuns to be equally distributed in the choir, so that there would not be a larger proportion of juniors on one side than on the other.

This day we spent the night at Déville, at our own expense.

MARCH 14-15. At Déville. MARCH 16. To wit, the second Sunday in Lent. We dined with the Dominicans at Rouen, and spent the night at Déville. MARCH 17. At Déville. MARCH 18. At Pont-de-l'Arche. MARCH 19-24. At Pinterville. MARCH 25. To wit, on the Annunciation of the Blessed Virgin Mary, at the same. MARCH 26-27. At the same. MARCH 28. At Pont-de-l'Arche. MARCH 29. At Ste-Catherine, at our expense. MARCH 30. With God's grace we preached at the cathedral at Rouen and spent the night at our manor there.

MARCH 31. We conferred the church of St-Maclou-de-Rouen upon Master Thierry. This day Richer, called the Lombard, against whom we had an action for fraud,[42] appeared before us and swore and promised on the Gospels that because of the matter of which he had been accused he would injure no one. Item, that he would leave the province of Rouen within the coming octave of St. John the Baptist. Item, that he would not re-enter it unless he merited being recalled by us. Present were the venerable men Masters John, archdeacon of Petit-Caux; William of Flavacourt, the official; Ralph of Cottévrard; Nicholas of Savigny, a canon of Rouen; Thierry, the dean of La Chrétienté; the prior of La Salle-aux-Puelles; John of Bully, a priest; and John of Morgneval, our clerk.

This day we spent the night at Déville.

APRIL 1-7. At Déville.

APRIL 8. With God's grace we preached at the priory at Bondeville, and we visited there. There were twenty-eight nuns, two girls received but not yet in religious garb, four lay sisters, and three lay brothers. One of the parishes there is very unsuitably served, which much displeased us. They had few [books of] sermons. They should confess and receive Communion once a month. There were complaints that the food distributions were not fairly made; we ordered the prioress to make these as uniform as possible. The lay brothers and lay sisters should confess seven times a year. They owed one hundred forty pounds, and seventy pounds was owed to them. They believed that with the exception of oats they had sufficient food to

---

[42] See entry for March 10, above.

last them the year. They did not have as many priests as they need. We ordered them to take better care of the sick than they had done, at least so far as they could, and especially during convalescence. With God's grace we found other things to be in good condition.

This day we spent the night at Déville.

APRIL 9. At Déville. APRIL 10. At Déville, and this day with God's grace we visited the Rouen chapter. APRIL 11. At the same. APRIL 12. At Rouen. APRIL 13. This being Palm Sunday, with God's grace we celebrated the proper service at Rouen.

APRIL 14. Richard, priest at Tôtes, appeared before us in the loge of our manor at Rouen, between our chamber and the church, and took oath and promised, on the Gospels and with hand on breast, that he would with no reservations regard his church as resigned from the present octave of the Nativity of the Blessed Mary, and that he would never again reclaim it, whether we should live or die, and that he would submit to our command. Present were: P[eter], archdeacon of Grand-Caux; J[ohn], archdeacon of Petit-Caux; G. [Walter], the treasurer; G. [Walter], the official; Master Ralph of Cottévrard, the prior of Salle-aux-Puelles; Nicholas of Bretteville, knight, brother of the said priest; John, knight and lord of Tôtes; and John of Morgneval, our clerk.

This day we spent the night at Déville.

APRIL 15. At the same. APRIL 16-19. At Rouen, and with God's grace we did what ought to be done on these days, both in the cathedral and outside.

1264

APRIL 20. To wit, Easter Sunday, and with God's grace we celebrated this day's feast at Rouen. APRIL 21. At Rouen. APRIL 22-27. At Pinterville. APRIL 28-29. At Gaillon. APRIL 30. At Frênes. MAY 1-4. At Frênes. MAY 7-11. At Pinterville. MAY 12. At Déville. MAY 13-16. At Rouen, to attend the Exchequer, and we stayed at our manor. MAY 17. At Pinterville. MAY 18. At the same. This day the lord of Bayeux and the other masters of the Exchequer were with us. MAY 19. At Vernon. MAY 20. At Mantes. MAY 21. At St-Germain-en-Laye. MAY 22-24. At Paris. MAY 25. To wit, on the feast of the Translation of St. Francis, and with God's grave we celebrated High Mass in the Franciscan monastery at Paris and dined with them. MAY 26. At Paris. MAY 27. At Poissy.

MAY 28. With God's grace we visited the priory of Notre-Dame-de-l'Aillerie [-de-Chaumont], to wit, on the vigil of the Ascension. Two monks were there with the prior, who had been ill for rather a long time and who was still very feeble from this sickness. Alms were given once a week, to wit, on Sundays. They ate meat and used feather beds when there was no need. They thought they owed two hundred pounds of Tours. Total for procuration: seven pounds, ten shillings of Paris.

MAY 29. To wit, Ascension Day. With God's grace we celebrated High Mass at the nuns' monastery at Gomerfontaine, and with His aid we gave our benediction to Sister Agnes, their abbess.

This day, with God's aid, we visited the priory of St-Martin-d'Es, where there were two monks from St-Magloire-de-Paris, to wit, Brother Nicolas Grimout and Brother Simon of St-Arnoult. The said Brother Nicolas, who was then acting as prior, spoke to us with less respect and reverence than he should have done, and was very wordy. They did not chant the night Matins because, as they said, of the thieves. Item, they did not sleep together, but separately; we enjoined them to sleep together in the same room as becomingly and properly as they could. They owed thirteen pounds; they thought that they had enough provisions to last out the year. They did not observe the fasts of the Rule. They ate meat.

This same day with God's grace, we spent the night at Liancourt, where we received from the prior four pounds of Paris, in which amount he is held to us for procuration, together with lodging and domestic utensils, once a year, when we come to this place and visit it.

MAY 30. With God's aid we visited the said priory. Three monks from St-Père-de-Chartres were there, to wit, Brother Peter of Cerisy, prior; William, called Bird, and Anselm, the prior's nephew. They ate meat three times a weak, but, as they said, with the abbot's permission; they did not observe the fasts of the Rule very well. They owed one hundred forty pounds; with the exception of oats, they had enough provisions to last out the year. With God's grace we found other things to be in a sufficiently good condition.

This day, with God's help, we came to the priory at Sérans [-le-Bouteiller], and with His aid we visited it. There were two monks from St-Germer-de-Flay in residence besides the prior, who was then absent, to wit, Brother Eschelin of Beaumont and Adam of Donne-Médard. They ate meat freely and without any scruples. They did not observe the fasts of the Rule. Eschelin told us that, as he thought, the prior owed one hundred twenty pounds of Paris. We spent the night there and received seventy shillings of Paris, in which amount they are held annually for procuration when we visit them, in addition to wood, charcoal for our common use, such fodder as may be procured in the village, dishes, and domestic utensils. Alms are given thrice a week to all comers.

In the year of our Lord 1264, on the Saturday after the Ascension of the Lord, John of Fagicourt, esquire, appeared before us at Sérans [-le-Bouteiller] and made amends for the violence he had committed in the said priory. He swore that he would submit to our commands in this matter and in the case where he had audaciously raised the hand of violence against a certain monk there. Item, he swore that he would pay sixty shillings and would go to the Holy Land, as a certain Franciscan who had [freed] him from the excommunication incurred by this violence had enjoined him to do. As his guarantor [stood] the lord archdeacon of Petit-Caux and ... [*lacuna in MS*].

MAY 31. With God's grace we visited the priory at Villarceaux, where there were nineteen nuns. We expressly forbade the prioress, and indeed all of them, to receive anyone as a nun or bestow the veil upon anyone without our special permission. They had three lay sisters and three maidservants in common. They owed one hundred pounds of Paris. They had, as they thought, enough provisions to last out the year, that is to say, wheat, oats, and wine, but their buildings needed roofing. They had two horses, six mules, three colts, six cows, and three heifers. With God's grace we found everything else to be in good condition.

We spent this night at Wy, where we received one *muid* of oats from the priest at Gadancourt, for which the priest is held to us annually whenever we happen to stay the night at Wy.

JUNE 1. With God's grace we preached at the parish church at Gasny and visited the priory there. Three monks were there with the prior, to wit, Brother William of Mesnil-David, prior; Henry of Haqueville; Gervaise of Séez; and Peter of Neufmarché. All but one were priests. We ordered him who was not a priest to confess and receive Communion at least once a month. They ate meat when there was no need; we ordered them to observe the Rule covering this so far as they could. They owed forty pounds of Paris; they said that they had sufficient supplies to last out the year. With God's grace we found other things in good condition. We received procuration there this day. Total for procuration: eight pounds, ten shillings.

JUNE 2. At Frênes. JUNE 3. At Beaulieu, at our own expense.

JUNE 4. With God's grace we visited the priory of nuns at St-Saëns. Seventeen nuns were in residence, and two were at Ste-Austreberte. They had one lay brother, Brother Albert. Sometimes they say the Divine Office without modulation.[1] We forbade the prioress to be lenient in giving permission to the nuns to go out, ordering her to give such a one as should receive such permission good company, and also to set a definite time for their return. They had three maidservants in common. Item, we found Petronilla of Dreux gravely defamed of incontinence, especially with Ralph, the priory harvester; she had been defamed before with Ralph of Le Thil, a married man, about which we had warned her in secret before the prioress and some of our suite. We ordered the prioress to remove Ralph at once from his duty as harvester and no longer to permit him to frequent the priory, and so far as possible remove all opportunities for misdeed and for scandal. Item, the prioress was defamed of the priest at L'Hortier, and it was rumored that she frequently went to the manor of Equiqueville and elsewhere, where she had many rendezvous with him and mingled with unworthy company. We emphatically enjoined her to refrain from this sort

[1] See above, July 9, 1249, n. 36.

of conduct and to reform her state and reputation by living as she should. Item, rumor was rife about Nicolette of Rouen, the cantress, and it was commonly stated in the town that she had undergone an abortion within the month, and that she, together with her sister from Rouen, had dined at the house of Master Simon, rector of a church at St-Saëns. However, we were not able during our visitation to find anything really provable about these things, and the nuns said that the last offense was falsely and untruthfully imputed to her. They owed eighty pounds; forty pounds was owed to them for some woodland sold at Equiqueville. Item, almost fifty-five pounds was owed to them from the sale of timber felled from their woods. They believed that they had sufficient wheat and oats to last out the year. Item, we forbade the prioress to receive or give the veil to anyone without our special permission.

This day we spent the night at the monks' priory, at our own expense.

JUNE 5. With God's grace we visited the priory at Bures, where there were two monks from Pré, of whom one was the steward of the place, not as a prior, but holding the administration of the place at the pleasure of the prior of Pré. There should be at least two monks there. They used feather beds, ate meat, and did not observe the fasts of the Rule. They owed nothing, and likewise nothing was owed to them, since they must remit to the prior of Pré all that they can beyond what is necessary to reserve for their own maintenance and that of the staff, or whatever is left after such maintenance. We told them to try to live as becomingly as they could and to celebrate Mass more often than they had been doing. We received procuration there this day. Total for procuration: seven pounds, nineteen shillings, six pence.

JUNE 6. With God's grace we visited the priory at Envermeu, where there were thirteen monks from Bec; all but three were priests. The almoner had two hundred loaves of bread to distribute to the poor every week. The prior said that they owed one hundred thirty-six pounds, and that forty pounds was owed to them; the community, however, asserted that the prior owed forty pounds or thereabouts. Item, they also said that because of the prior's inefficiency and laziness, the properties of the house were badly managed. They claimed that he was weak, useless, and one who saw little either with the eyes of the body or, frequently, with those of the mind. Item, that he rarely if ever celebrated Mass and that even on Easter he did not celebrate Mass because of his eye trouble; that he rarely confessed or received Communion; that he did not compute as he should; that he was unable to ride and had, in consequence, sold his palfrey to the abbot. We must speak with the abbot about all of these things.

We received procuration this day from the said prior at our manor at Aliermont, where we spent the night. Total for procuration: seven pounds, ten shillings one penny.

JUNE 7. To wit, on the vigil of Pentecost, at Dieppe.

JUNE 8. With God's grace we celebrated the feast of Pentecost at Dieppe, that is to say, we celebrated a High Mass at the parish church and preached in the churchyard.

JUNE 9. We received procuration at Longueuil, at the manor which the abbot of Bec holds there of ... [lacuna in MS], a burgess of Dieppe, who was then the lessee of the place. Total for procuration: eight pounds, eight shillings, eleven pence.

JUNE 10. With God's grace we preached and administered Confirmation at the parish church at Longueuil, and immediately afterwards on this day we went to the priory at Bacqueville, where, with His aid, we made a visitation. Three monks from Tiron were there, and, as they told us, one other monk ought to come there within the next week. We ordered the prior to tell his abbot for us to put two monks at Ribeuf,[2] for there is only one there now, which displeased us. They owed one hundred sixty pounds. They believed that they had sufficient wheat to last out the year, but no wine or oats at all. Total for procuration: seven pounds, seven shillings, four pence.

JUNE 11-12. At Aliermont, at our own expense. JUNE 13. We received procuration at Neufchâtel from Boullo, the lessee of Wanchy. Total for procuration: eight pounds, six shillings. JUNE 14. With God's grace we conferred Holy Orders at Notre-Dame-de-Neufchâtel, and spent the night at Beaubec, at the expense of the abbey. JUNE 15-16. At Déville. JUNE 17. With God's grace we celebrated the holy synod at Rouen, and also the feast of the Translation of St. Romain.

JUNE 18. At Rouen, and we held a synod of deans in our middle chamber. The priest at Lintot[3] had been cited to appear before us this day to resign his church and to hear our sentence, as he had promised to do on his own oath according to a letter which he gave to us at little while ago. However, because of the absence of Archdeacon Peter, we assigned him the vigil of the Assumption of the Blessed Mary as the time to determine this matter.

---

[2] St-Laurent, near Dieppe, in the deanery of Brachy. (Cottineau, II, 2459.)

[3] See entry for October 25, 1263.

On that day we came to Pinterville and spent the night there.

JUNE 19. At Vernon. JUNE 20. At Meulan. JUNE 21-23. At Paris. JUNE 24. To wit, on the feast of St. John the Baptist. JUNE 25–JULY 15. At Paris, to attend the Parlement. JULY 16. At Luzarches. JULY 17. At Verberie. JULY 18. At Compiègne. JULY 19. At Noyon. JULY 20. At Compiègne. JULY 21. At Senlis, with the king. JULY 22. To wit, on the feast of St. Mary Magdalene, we celebrated, with God's grace, a High Mass at St. Vincent's monastery, and spent the night there. JULY 23. At Senlis. JULY 24. At Chambly. JULY 25. At Ressons, a Premonstratensian house, at the expense of the abbey. JULY 26. At Marcheroux, a Premonstratensian house, at the expense of the abbey. JULY 27. At Vesly, at our own expense. JULY 28-31. At Gaillon. AUGUST 1. To wit, on the feast of St. Peter in Chains, at Gaillon. AUGUST 2-4. At Pinterville. AUGUST 5. At the same. This day we personally cited Jordan, the rector of the church at Crasmesnil, to appear in person before us at Rouen on the vigil of the Assumption of the Blessed Mary, to answer charges.

AUGUST 6. The abbot of Le Tréport presented Master Geoffrey Polard to us for St. Mary's church at Benouville, and we admitted him to it, investing with our ring John of Morgneval, our clerk, to this place in the place and in the name of the said G[eoffrey]. Present were Master Ralph of Cottévrard, the said abbot; one of his monks; Brother Adam Rigaud; Brother Peter Breton; and the aforesaid John [of Morgneval]. It was the feast of the Transfiguration of the Lord. We spent this night at Pinterville.

AUGUST 7. At Pinterville. AUGUST 8. We received procuration at Ste-Catherine. Total for procuration: nine pounds.

AUGUST 9. With God's grace we preached in the chapter and made a visitation. Thirty-two monks were in residence, three of whom were novices; fourteen were at Blyth, in England. As of custom, they drew up a general statement of all expenses and receipts and the value of the income of the house once a year, to wit, at Michaelmas; on the other hand, individual accounts were rendered once a month and in the presence of the seniors of the community. We ordered the abbot to ride about less than he had been in the habit of doing at his first coming. We found that the treasurer of Rouen had kept in his possession, and had done so ever since the installation of the abbot, the key or keys of the little room in which had been deposited the properties which Abbot John[4] had left; it was our pleasure

---

[4] John de Folleville, the abbot, had died in 1262 and was succeeded by Robert de

that the abbot should again have this key. Their old debts were still owed, and they could not collect them. We found that at the time of the abbot's installation they possessed, in cash and credits, over sixty-six hundred pounds, of which they had not as yet spent anything. With God's grace we found other things to be in good condition.

This day we spent this night at Déville at our own expense.

AUGUST 10. With God's grace we preached in the churchyard of St-Gervaise-de-Rouen, to wit, on the Sunday before the Assumption of the Blessed Mary. We spent the night at Déville.

AUGUST 11. With the Lord's consent we came to the monastery of St-Ouen-de-Rouen, and there, with His grace, we first preached and then made a visitation. Sixty monks were in residence, and many were outside in priories and in many places. Inasmuch as that year we had found many things amiss at the priory at Gasny,[5] concerning the books and other things needful to the monks dwelling there, we ordered the abbot to provide effective remedies. All but fourteen of the resident monks were priests; we ordered them to confess frequently. The Statute covering the eating of meat is badly observed in the priories. With God's grace we found them to be in a good spiritual state, but the same was not true of their temporal affairs, because the abbot's sister and her husband, Master William, did grievous injury to the house in the matter of wine, wheat, food, oats, and other things; item, and also because the abbot had removed the monks from the house at Sigy and had, in consequence, reduced the income of that priory, appropriating it for himself without reasonable cause.[6] And so we went away feeling frustrated because we could not find out what was the material condition of the monks or that of the monastery, as would be necessary and helpful for us.

We spent this night at Déville.

AUGUST 12-13. At Déville. AUGUST 14. With God's grace we preached in Latin at the cathedral at Rouen, to wit, in the vigil of the Assumption, and there were present: ... [lacuna in MS], the bishop of Noyon,[7] and the canons, chaplains, and clerks-choral of the cathedral. AUGUST 15. With God's grace we celebrated the feast of the Assumption of the Blessed Mary at Rouen. The said bishop celebrated High Mass at the cathedral, while

---

Plain-Bose (1262-71). (*Gallia Christiana*, XI, 128-29.)

[5] See entry for December 14, 1263.

[6] See entry for December 15, 1261.

[7] Vermond.

we celebrated Mass at the Franciscan monastery. AUGUST 16. At Déville, and the said bishop was with us. AUGUST 17. At Pinterville, along with the said bishop. AUGUST 18. At Gaillon. AUGUST 19. At Vernon, where with God's grace we treated with our venerable brother, the bishop of Evreux, about certain matters of dispute which had arisen between us. AUGUST 20. At Gassicourt, near Mantes. AUGUST 21. At St-Germain-en-Laye. AUGUST 22-23. At Paris.

AUGUST 24. Along with the other prelates of France we attended upon the Reverend Father, Simon [de Brie], by God's grace, cardinal-priest of Santa Cecilia, then legate of the Apostolic See, at the palace of the bishop of Paris. Here the legate put forth and discussed many aspects of a plan for a three years' tithe to assist the Roman church in furthering the business of . . . [lacuna in MS], the count of Anjou.[8]

AUGUST 25-28. At Paris. AUGUST 29. At Poissy. AUGUST 30. At Gassicourt. AUGUST 31. At Gaillon. SEPTEMBER 1. At Bonport. SEPTEMBER 2-3. At Déville. SEPTEMBER 4. At St-Saëns, at our own expense.

SEPTEMBER 5. We came to the leper hospital at Bellencombre, where with God's grace we preached and made a visitation. Four canons were there with the prior, to wit, Thomas, William, Nicholas, and a certain old man. Item, there were eight lepers, three healthy lay brothers, and four lay sisters. We enjoined the prior to do his best to encourage and exhort the lepers to bear their sufferings. After Compline, the canons grumbled in the dormitory against the orders of the prior and broke the rule of silence in talking to each other; we ordered them to stop this and to obey the prior in this as in other matters. Item, Brother William had received one hundred pounds out of one hundred twenty pounds of Tours which the king had given to them for the improvement of their buildings. They said that the bailiff of Caux owed them the other twenty pounds; we ordered the said Brother William, in the presence of his prior, the canons, and the lepers, to render due account of the one hundred pounds which he had received. Item, we ordered the prior to have the buildings in which the lepers lived suitably repaired and reroofed and to be more solicitous and considerate than he had been in providing them with the necessities of life. Item, we ordered the prior that they should confess to him more often than had been their practice.

[8] Charles of Anjou, brother of Louis IX, to whom Pope Innocent IV had offered the kingdom of Sicily. The Sicilian affair was largely financed by the papacy.

This day, with God's grace, we blessed the churchyard of the church at Les Bosquet, and we spent the night at Aliermont.

SEPTEMBER 6. We received procuration at LeTréport. Total for procuration: eight pounds and eight pence. SEPTEMBER 7. With God's grace we preached in chapter at Le Tréport, and visited. Twenty-one monks were in residence, eleven were in outside priories, and one, to wit, Ralph of Muis, was at Lyre on other business. One does not accuse another [in chapter], and this they have as a custom, so they say. All but three of the residents were priests. Those who are not priests, as of custom, confessed and received Communion once a week, to wit, on Sunday. We had ordered them before to hand in their old pelisses upon the receipt of new ones[9]; we now found that they were still retaining them, and so we forbade them to sell, give, or otherwise dispose of anything without the approval and knowledge of the abbot. Alms are given daily to all comers, and more frequently and abundantly to clerics. They owed three hundred pounds, and about as much was owed to them. They had an abundance of supplies, particularly of wine, and enough of everything to last until next Easter. We ordered the abbot to get a scribe who would write out and prepare a Passional, of which they were in great need.

We received procuration this day at Eu. Total for procuration: ten pounds.

SEPTEMBER 8. To wit, on the feast of the Nativity of the Blessed Virgin Mary. We celebrated High Mass for the community and preached to the canons, clerics, and people who were present. We were here at our own expense.

SEPTEMBER 9. With God's grace we preached in the chapter at Eu, and visited. Twenty-seven canons were in residence, and many more were in the outside priories. The infirmary was insufficiently equipped; we ordered this corrected. There were many things said about the character of the abbot which we regarded as inane and frivolous. They owed eight hundred eighty pounds of Tours, and more than eleven hundred [pounds] was owed to them, partly from the sale of woodlands and partly from other sources. They believed that with the exception of wine, they had sufficient provisions to last out the year. With God's grace we found other things to be in a sufficiently good condition. However, we ordered the Passional to be diligently corrected and improved by four or six canons. We spent this night at Aliermont.

9 See entry for February 4, 1262/63.

SEPTEMBER 10-13. At Aliermont. SEPTEMBER 14. To wit, on the Exaltation of the Holy Cross.

SEPTEMBER 15. We came to the house or priory at Mortemer-sur-Eaulne, which Master Eudes of St-Denis holds for life. We found this place to be entirely marred in things both spiritual and temporal, for there was but one monk there. Most of the buildings were in a ruinous state, a fact to be greatly regretted. We received procuration at the royal castle from the local lessee. Total for procuration: twelve pounds, fourteen shillings.

SEPTEMBER 16. We received procuration at Aumale. Total for procuration: ten pounds, six shillings.

SEPTEMBER 17. With God's grace we preached in the chapter and visited. Twenty monks were in residence, and there were three in England. We had forbidden them before to allow layfolk to eat in the refectory,[10] but this had never been corrected, and so we expressly repeated our prohibition. As we had done before, we expressly forbade the abbot to permit his sister or Lady Agnes of Pré or anyone else to dine within the confines of the abbey, and to see to it that women were excluded from the choir and cloister.[11] Item, the refectory often was without monks, and the reading was sometimes omitted, which much displeased us. We expressly forbade the abbot to permit this state of things to continue, or to allow the monks to eat meat, save in cases of necessity and as the Rule permits. They owed five hundred eighty pounds, of which they thought that they had some eighty marks in England for some time past; some debts were owed to them. Item, we expressly forbade the mothers of the novices to be allowed to eat in any of the abbey rooms in the future, or indeed, anywhere save in the great common hall, for sometimes they had eaten in the abbot's room or in the rooms of the infirmary. Item, we ordered that better provision be made for the sick, and that the abbot show no preferences, but rather deal with each according to his need and the state of his infirmity. Item, we enjoined the monks to obey their abbot in every way possible.

SEPTEMBER 17. With God's grace we spent the night at Foucarmont, at the expense of the abbey. SEPTEMBER 18. We received procuration at St-Saëns from Ralph of Aulages, the lessee of the house or priory at Nogent, near Neufchâtel. Total for procuration: eleven pounds, six shillings. SEPTEMBER 19. We spent the night at Déville, at our own expense. SEPTEM-

[10] See entry for September 21, 1251.
[11] See entry for January 17, 1256/57.

BER 20. With God's grace we conferred Holy Orders at the Franciscan monastery at Rouen.

SEPTEMBER 21. To wit, on the feast of St. Matthew the Apostle and Evangelist, at Déville, where we assigned to the priest at Civières[12] the day following the coming synod as the time for purging himself with the seventh hand of priests[13] of the vice of incontinence, of which he had been many times defamed. Item, this day we investigated there the election of Brother Richard of Bolleville by the monks of Jumièges, and, as justice requires, we approved of the character of the elected one and the mode of election, and conferred our benediction this very day upon the said Richard.[14]

SEPTEMBER 22. At the same. SEPTEMBER 23. At St-Germain-sous-Cailly, at our own expense. SEPTEMBER 24. With God's grace we dedicated St. Martin's church at Critot, and spent the night at St-Germain at the expense of the parishioners of the said church. SEPTEMBER 25. At Banns-le-Comte, at our own expense. SEPTEMBER 26. With God's aid we dedicated the church of Notre-Dame-des-Champs and spent the night there at the expense of the parishioners' rector. SEPTEMBER 27. At Déville. SEPTEMBER 28. At Bonport. SEPTEMBER 29-30. At Pinterville. OCTOBER 1. At Gaillon.

OCTOBER 2. We were at our assizes at Les Andelys, and there we conferred upon Master John of Etoutteville the Rouen prebend, which had belonged to Nicholas of Cubry, but which was then vacant because, as it was said, he had married. We spent the night at Frênes.

OCTOBER 3. At Frênes. OCTOBER 4. To wit, on the feast of St. Francis, at Gaillon, where we entertained the masters going to attend the Exchequer at Rouen. OCTOBER 5. At Gaillon. OCTOBER 6. At Bonport. OCTOBER 7-9. At Rouen, and on this day we conferred upon Master Thomas of Bray the prebend which had belonged to Master Anselm of Buchy. OCTOBER 11. At Rouen. OCTOBER 12. At Déville. OCTOBER 13. We received procuration at Beaulieu. Total for procuration: nine pounds, five pence.

OCTOBER 14. With God's grace we visited there, where there were ten resident canons; ten others were in obedience outside. We enjoined the prior to inspect the coffers of the canons more often than he had been doing, at least twice a year, and to take any property away from them. Two lay brothers and two lay sisters were there. Item, we expressly enjoined the

[12] See entry for June 5, 1262.
[13] See above, October 16, 1248, n. 70.
[14] Richard de Boleville (1264-72). (*Gallia Christiana*, XI, 197.)

prior, as we had done before,[15] to have the general and individual audits recorded in registers; the prior, however, had been negligent in this. They owed four hundred twenty-four pounds of Tours. They thought that they had enough wheat to last out the year, but not enough of other things. With God's grace we found other things to be in a sufficiently good condition.

This day with God's grace, we spent the night at Frênes.

OCTOBER 15. At Chaumont, at our own expense.

OCTOBER 16. With God's grace we celebrated the synod of the French Vexin at the church of Notre-Dame-de-l'Aillerie. This day we assigned to the priest at Le Caable the day following the holding of the synod at Rouen as the time to appear before us to answer charges. We spent the night there, at our own expense.

OCTOBER 17. We received procuration at Neufmarché. Total for procuration: six pounds, ten shillings.

OCTOBER 18. With God's grace we visited the said priory, where were three monks from St-Evroult, to wit, Jocelin, the prior; and Brothers Geoffrey Girourat and William Moter. There should be several there, but because of the war[16] they had not received their English income for several years, and there were fewer [monks] in consequence. The parish church had been insufficiently served for many days because of the priest's absence, for he had set out for the Holy Land; we ordered this corrected. They frequently ate meat when there was no need, and they did this, as they said, with their abbot's knowledge. They owed two hundred pounds, the greater part of which was to their abbot. They did not have enough provisions to last out the year.

This day with God's grace we visited the chapter of the church of St-Hildevert at Gournay. There we found only the dean and Matthew of Montfort in residence. With God's grace we found the church in a sufficiently good condition. We enjoined the dean to act for us in warning Dom John, the priest at Notre-Dame, to keep a chaplain to celebrate Mass at least three times a week in his church, because of the chantry of Sir Bartholomew, knight, of which the said priest receives and has received the income; or that otherwise we would withdraw the income from him.

In this same chapter of St-Hildevert, and in the presence of the dean and

[15] See entry for March 17, 1259/60.
[16] This is a reference to the Barons' War led by Simon of Montfort in England.

Matthew of Montfort, we called before us two brothers from the Hôtel-Dieu, from whom we had made inquiries concerning the state of their house. We discovered that there were three lay brothers and five lay sisters there; that one of the lay brothers, along with his wife, was managing a grange, another a second grange, while a third managed the hospital. The sick and the poor were ill provided for. The said lay brothers and lay sisters had spent almost everything and the chapel of the Hôtel-Dieu was insufficiently served.

This same day we talked with the masters and proctors of the local leper houses, who told us that there were twelve lepers there, six men and six women; that the place also had seven healthy people, including both lay brothers and lay sisters, not counting a small staff. They had no chaplain, but they were getting one before next Easter, for a certain cleric upon whom we had already conferred this chapel had been ordained as a subdeacon for this position, being anxious to be promoted as rapidly as possible to the various degrees of the Higher Orders. They have few provisions to last out the year.

OCTOBER 18. With God's grace we visited the nuns' priory at St-Aubin, where twelve nuns were in residence. Beatrice of Beauvais was a rover, and it was said that she had had several children. The houses badly needed repair, especially the roof of the main monastery where they could hardly stay when the weather was rainy. They did not chant their Hours, especially Matins, because many of them had been sick for a long time. Because of the absence of the prioress, who was then lying ill in bed, we could not obtain complete information concerning the state of the house.

OCTOBER 19. This day with God's grace, we spent this day at Bellosane, a Premonstratensian house, at their expense.

With God's grace we visited the priory at St-Laurent-en-Lyons. Seventeen canons were in residence, and there were fifteen in various obediences. Three lay brothers and two lay sisters were in residence; we gave orders that these should confess and receive Communion at least three times a year. They do not accuse one another [in chapter] as often as they should. Alms are given to all comers thrice a week. They owed three hundred pounds. We received procuration there this day. Total for procuration: seven pounds, fifteen shillings.

OCTOBER 20. We received procuration at Noyon-sur-Andelle. Total for procuration: eight pounds, six shillings, six pence.

OCTOBER 21. With God's grace we visited the priory there, where there were five monks from St-Evroult, to wit, Masters Thomas Surde; William of Orgières, the cellarer; Dreux of Neufmarché; Peter Duval; and Thomas of Silly. The prior was attending the vintage near Meulan, and because of his absence we were not able to learn about the state of the house.

This day we spent the night at Pérrièrs, where we received procuration from the local lessee. Total for procuration: six pounds, sixteen shillings.

OCTOBER 22. To wit, on the vigil of St-Romain, at Rouen. OCTOBER 23. With God's grace we celebrated the feast of St. Romain.

OCTOBER 24. With God's help we visited the Hôtel-Dieu at Rouen, where ten canons were in residence with the prior; six were staying outside in obediences; all were priests. There were twenty sisters. They should confess and receive Communion at least thirteen times a year. We ordered the prior to inspect frequently, at least two or three times a year, the coffers of the canons and of the sisters to see that they had no possessions. Twelve maid-servants were there. One thing much displeased us, to wit, that certain stalls were placed along the chapel wall and at the entrance to the hospital, where hoods and such things were sold in an unseemly fashion, and because of this the chapel was put to improper uses. Item, we enjoined the canons to visit the sick more diligently than had been their practice. They owed four hundred pounds or thereabouts, and almost as much was owed to them.

This day we spent the night at Déville.

OCTOBER 25. At Déville. OCTOBER 26. With God's aid we preached at the cathedral of Rouen. OCTOBER 27. At Déville. OCTOBER 28. At St-Vauberg, at the expense of the Templars. OCTOBER 29. With God's aid we dedicated the chapel there, and we spent the night at Déville, at our own expense. OCTOBER 30. At Déville. OCTOBER 31. At Jumièges, at our own expense.

NOVEMBER 1. To wit, on All Saints. With God's grace we preached in the chapter there and visited the abbey. Forty-eight professed monks and seven novices were in residence; eighteen were dwelling in outside priories; thirty of the residents were priests. We ordered them to confess more diligently and in better fashion than they had been doing; item, that the Statutes of Pope Gregory be read in chapter at least two or three times a year. Alms are given daily to all comers. Item, we gave explicit orders, as we had done before,[17] that the cook and those who made daily and special expenditures

[17] See entry for March 19, 1262/63.

should compute more frequently than was their practice, to wit, every month, or more often if possible. From Richard, the new abbot, and indeed from the entire community, we learned that Abbot Robert had left over to his aforesaid successor[18] some two thousand pounds of Tours in cash and credits amounting to nineteen hundred pounds, although some of this last, according to Abbot Richard, was not readily collectible. With God's grace we found other things to be in sufficiently good condition. Then, with His grace, we celebrated a High Mass in pontificals and dined with the community in the refectory.

NOVEMBER 2. To wit, on Sunday, when no one is permitted to work. At Duclair we came across a certain cart laden with wood and drawn by three horses belonging to Eudes of Duclair. We imposed a fine of ten shillings and instructed the dean of St-Georges, who was with us, to levy and collect this fine, half of which he should give to the local lepers and the other half to the hospital. John of Quesnay stood surety for this fine. We received procuration at St-Georges today. Total for procuration: twelve pounds, sixteen pence.

NOVEMBER 3. With God's grace we visited the abbey of the said place [St-Georges], where twenty-two monks were in residence; all but four were priests. Four were in England, and two at St-Nicolas. The abbot rarely attended the choir or arose for Matins; his reason, as he put it, being that he did not understand the Lessons. Item, he did not eat very often in the refectory, saying that he was more useful and of better service elsewhere, since he mercifully invited to dine with him in his room some of the weak and those whom he believed to be in need of food and recreation. Item, he rarely attended chapter; we ordered him to try and be present more often and to administer discipline in the proper manner. The total alms bestowed is a tenth part of the loaves of bread. They owed about one hundred pounds; and more was owed to them. For a long time they had received nothing from England. The community highly commended the goodness and solicitude of the abbot.

We spent this day at Déville, at our own expense.

NOVEMBER 4. With God's grace we celebrated the sacred synod at Rouen.

NOVEMBER 5. We held the synod of deans there, and, without trial,

---

[18] Robert d'Ettelant was abbot from 1251 to 1264, in which year he was deposed in favor of Richard, who resigned in 1272. In that year Robert was reinstated and ruled until 1288. (*Gallia Christiana* XI, 196-97.)

Reginald of Lintot[19] resigned the church of the said place [Lintot]. Present were: Peter, the archdeacon; Dom William of St-Laurent, priest; Master William of Flavacourt, a canon of Rouen; John of Morgneval; and many others.

This same day, at our palace and in the presence of the said archdeacon and a great many others, we deprived, as justice required, the chaplain of the leper house at Val-Osmond of his chapel because of his continued non-residence.

This day John, priest at Civières,[20] appeared before us, accompanied by seven priests, prepared to purge himself of the many offenses which had been attributed to him and of which he had been many times defamed. But we, fearing that he would be rejected along with these priests and remembering that he had given us a letter[21] about these offenses some time ago, were convinced that such a purgation should be waived. We assigned to him the Tuesday before Christmas as the day upon which he should fulfill what he had said in this letter, and as he had promised on his own oath.

We warned the priest of St. Peter's at Franquevillette to abstain from frequenting taverns, from immoderate wine-bibbing, and from running about and from associating with improper women; of these vices he had been many times defamed. Present were; Peter, the archdeacon; the dean at Pérrièrs; Master William of Flavacourt; and Master Peter of Aumale.

This day we spent this night at Rouen.

NOVEMBER 6. At Pinterville. NOVEMBER 7. At Gaillon. NOVEMBER 8. At Mantes. NOVEMBER 9. At St-Germain-en-Laye. NOVEMBER 10. At Paris. NOVEMBER 11. To wit, on Martinmas, at Paris. NOVEMBER 12-22. At Paris, to attend the Parlement. NOVEMBER 23. To wit, on the feast of St. Clement, at Paris. NOVEMBER 24-29. At Paris. NOVEMBER 30. To wit, on the feast of St. Andrew, at Paris. DECEMBER 1-5. At Paris, because of the Parlement.[22] DECEMBER 6. At Paris. DECEMBER 7. At Paris. On the Feast of St. Nicholas. DECEMBER 8. At Paris. DECEMBER 9. At Paris. On the Feast of the Conception of the Virgin Mary. DECEMBER 10. At Conflans, at our expense. DECEMBER 11. At the same. With God's aid we came to to the church of St-Mellon-de-Pontoise, and with His favor we preached

---

[19] See entry for June 18, 1264.
[20] See entry for September 21, 1264.
[21] Printed in the *Diffamationes*, Bonnin, p. 666.
[22] For some unknown reason, Eudes, clerk has 33 days in December.

in a certain hall near the church which they use as a chapter house. Then we visited. Of the canons, we found only the treasurer and Dom Luke in residence. There are nine prebends. These are the names of the canons: Dom Luke, John of Mont-Lucille, Dom Roger of Corbeil, Master Nicholas of Montherlan, Peter of Bosc-Commines, Vincent, called Pica, Master John of Limoges, Humbert, and Master Robert Picard. Several vicars-perpetual and some chaplains are there. As upon other occasions,[23] we found great defects as to altar cloths and rochets, as to the repair of books, and as to the roofing of the monastery, especially the bell tower. We thereupon ordered Master Simon, our vicar, to sequestrate so much of the canons' property as would be sufficient to supply the church adequately with altar-cloths, rochets, and such things, and to have the hall properly repaired and reroofed, since it was badly and improperly roofed. Item, [we ordered] that our procuration be paid from the same source. We ordered the treasurer to have the monastery, and particularly the bell tower, properly reroofed. Item, we ordered the vicars to break the seal which they had had made and by all means to deface it so that it would be useless. Item, Dom John of Pont, priest at St-Pierre, possessed a certain chapel in the said church for which he is obligated to be present for Matins, Masses, and Vespers at St-Mellon on the feast days of Nine Lessons.[24] He had not attended as he should, because of the duties and occupations of his cure. We ordered him to be more solicitious about this, and he told us that he had intended to give up this chapel and to resign it very soon. Item, Dom Thomas, a chaplain, was in the habit of to celebrating Mass every day at the monastery of nuns at Maudune, but rarely or never at the church of St-Mellon; he said that this was due to his lack of a missal. We ordered him to procure some missal or manual[25] as quickly as possible so that he might be able to celebrate Mass at St-Mellon at least four times a week, as his chaplaincy requires. Item, Dom William celebrated Mass at Val-Roi, which much displeased us; we forbade him to celebrate there in the future, but rather to be sedulous and regular in attending St-Mellon. Item, Fromond, a vicar, was in the habit of going about the town at night in an unseemly and, as it were, fatuous manner; we ordered him to stop this. Item, we ordered Dom

---

[23] See entries for November 23, 1254; October 5, 1259; December 11, 1263.

[24] I.e., on solemn feast days.

[25] According to the Council of Rouen (1235), it was decreed (canon 28) that every parish priest have "a book which is called a manual." (Mansi, XXIII, 377.)

Luke to ask the dean of St-Aignan to pay the twenty-five shillings he owed for a certain psalter. Item, since we discovered that there was, and is, considerable abuse in the church in the cases of those who are guilty of misdemeanors, to wit, those who were not willing to chant the Responses and Alleluias in choir, we ordered Dom Richard Triguel to exact a penny fine for each offense from those who had committed such offenses, to obtain that money from the distributor, and to keep all such moneys as he should collect for a year. Some of the new vicars complained that they were badly paid from the distributions, that they had never received anything from them; wherefore we ordered Master Simon, our vicar, to audit these accounts and when this had been done to act for us as would be just and equitable. Item, Denis, a vicar, was contentious and abusive; we ordered him to be as mild as possible in his conduct in the community.

This day with God's grace, we visited St. Peter's priory. Five monks from Bec were there: Brother Ralph of L'Honblonnière, the prior; Geoffrey of Angeville; William of Noinville; Peter of Albec; and Ralph of Beaumont. They ate meat when there was no need they said that because of the guests they did not observe the fasts of the Rule. We ordered the prior to inspect the monks' coffers more frequently than was his practice. They owed about forty pounds to their abbot and others. We must talk with the abbot [of Bec] about the tithe which he exacted from this priory. They believed that they had sufficient provisions to last out the year.

This same day. We spent the night at St-Martin, where we received from the chapter of St-Mellon, for procuration, seven pounds of Tours, in which amount the said chapter is annually held to us, in addition to cups, dishes, wood, and other utensils.

DECEMBER 12. With God's grace we visited St. Martin's abbey at Pontoise, where there were twenty-four monks. They had two lay brothers and four lay sisters; we ordered the prior to have the lay brothers and lay sisters confess and receive Communion more frequently than they had done—at least three times a year. One monk was dwelling alone at Belle-Eglise, but, as the abbot told us, with the permission of the bishop of Beauvais; however, he said that he planned to send another monk there before the next harvest. The monks who were in the priories ate meat when there was no need. Altogether they owed two thousand pounds of Paris, but nothing at interest. They had eighty *muids* of grain on hand, which was left over from the last year, as well as forty barrels of old wine. They were much burdened with annual pensions and also because the bishop and the archdeacon of Meaux held two of their manors for life.

We received their procuration this day at Juziers. Total for procuration: seven pounds, fourteen shillings.

DECEMBER 13. We received procuration at Juziers. Total for procuration: nine pounds, four pence.

DECEMBER 14. We visited the said priory, finding six monks from St-Père-Chartres, to wit, John, the prior; Geoffrey of Chartres; Lawrence of Chartres; Bartholomew of Aulnay, the sacristan; Giles the Younger; and Arnoul Carrel. They ate meat when there was no need, but, as they said, they did this with their abbot's permission. Some were wearing pelisses of rabbit skins; they did not observe the fasts of the Rule, and this, they said, was because of the guests. They owed about one hundred pounds. They had little wine this year.

This day we spent the night and received procuration at St-Martin-la-Garenne, to wit, on the feast of St. Lucy the Virgin. Total for procuration at St-Martin: seven pounds, nine shillings.

DECEMBER 15. With God's grave, we visited the priory at St-Martin-la-Garenne, where there were four monks from Bec-Hellouin, to wit; Ralph of Brotonne, the prior; Henry of Evreux; Eustace of Caux; and John of Formunville. At of custom, they did not chant all of their Hours with modulation;[26] we ordered them to accustom themselves in the future to doing this, and to chant their Hours together. They ate meat when there was no need; they did not observe the fasts of the Rule very well. We ordered the prior to celebrate Mass more often than he had been doing, and to confess to his companions. Item, we also ordered the monks to confess to their prior and to obey and reverence him as much as possible. They owed thirty pounds over and above their obligations to the abbey; about fifteen pounds was owed to them. Item, we ordered the prior to be more diligent and prompt than he had been in providing his monks and servants with shoes, and to act with courtesy toward the parish priest.

This day we received procuration at Gasny. No computation was made.

DECEMBER 16. With God's grace we visited the priory at Gasny, where there were three monks from St-Ouen-de-Rouen, to wit: John of Fontes-en-Bray, the prior; Geoffrey of Noinville; and John of Beauvais; they dwelt over the river at St-Nicaise. In another manor, to wit, the one in which we

[26] See above, July 9, 1249, n. 36.

were received, they had food for the stock and a considerable staff, but they did not perform any Divine Office there. We ordered them to build a gateway so that a shorter and more private passage might be obtained to the the parish church, as there is in some of their other houses, to wit, at Qué-vreville, Wanchy, Pérrièrs, and elsewhere. They did not chant their Hours with modulation.[27] They did not observe the fasts of the Rule. They owed nothing, for they send and remit to the abbey everything except that which they and their staff use in the said manor.

This day we spent the night at Gaillon.

DECEMBER 17-18. At Vernon. DECEMBER 19. At Gaillon, and the king spent the night there at our castle. DECEMBER 20. At Rouen. DECEMBER 21. With God's grace we conferred Holy Orders at the Dominican convent at Rouen, and we ate with them.

DECEMBER 22. To wit, on the Sunday before Christmas. We were present while the archbishop of Tyre preached the Crusade in the vestibule of the cathedral at Rouen. He spent this night, to wit, the feast of St. Thomas, with us at our manor at Rouen.

DECEMBER 23. Hearing that the king was ill at Pont-de-l'Arche, we visited him and spent the night at Bonport. OECEMBER 24. At Rouen, and we made our O.[28] Today we assigned to Master William, rector of the church at Fontenay, the day after Epiphany as the time when he should show why he had not resided in the said church as he should have done. DECEMBER 25. To wit, the vigil of the Nativity, at Rouen. DECEMBER 26. With God's grace we celebrated the feast of the Nativity. The king was in the city. DECEMBER 27. At Bonport. DECEMBER 28-31. At Pinterville. DECEMBER 32. At Croix-St-Leufroy. DECEMBER 33. To wit, at the same, on the Feast of the Circumcision. With the legate at Evreux. JANUARY 1. At the same. JANUARY 2. At Pinterville, and we had the legate and the bishop of Evreux with us. JANUARY 3. At Pont-de-l'Arche. JANUARY 4-5. At Rouen. JANUARY 6. To wit, on Epiphany, at Rouen. The legate was with us, and he celebrated a High Mass in the cathedral. We entertained him and our entire chapter at our manor, at our expense.

JANUARY 7. At Rouen, and the legate was with us. Today Peter Jouin of Foucarmont was presented by the abbot of Le Tréport for the church at St-Pierre-en-Val.

[27] *Ibid.*
[28] See above, December 23, 1250, n. 135.

This day Master William, rector of the church at Fontenay, voluntarily resigned his church into our hands. Present were the venerable men the treasurer, the precentor, and Master William of Flavacourt, a canon of Rouen.

JANUARY 8. At Rouen, and the legate was with us. JANUARY 9-12. At Pinterville. JANUARY 13-14. At Gaillon, and the legate was with us. JANUARY 15. At Bonport. JANUARY 16. At Déville. JANUARY 17. At St-Saëns, at our own expense. JANUARY 18. Aliermont. JANUARY 19. At Eu, at our own expense. JANUARY 20. At the same, to see about the church of St-Martin-le-Gaillard, and at our own expense. JANUARY 21. At Aliermont.

JANUARY 22. At the same. This day Sir Geoffrey of Cuverville, knight, many times defamed of adultery and found guilty of the same, personally appeared before us and promised on oath and in the presence of Master John of Flainville, precentor; Master William of Flavacourt, a canon of Rouen; Brother Adam Rigaud; the dean of Envermeu; and John of Morgneval, our clerk that under forfeiture of twenty pounds of Tours he would not relapse with the woman of whom he had been defamed and that he would visit the shrine of St-Giles before the coming feast of the Assumption of the Blessed Mary, under penalty of the same fine. Walter of Gamaches, a vassal of the said knight and a parishioner of Glicourt, stood as surety.

JANUARY 23-24. At Dieppe. JANUARY 25. At Aliermont.

JANUARY 26. At the same. Today we submitted the following judgment,[29] in the litigation which had been long standing between William of Sauqueville and Thomas, a miller, both citizens of Dieppe, anent the death of William's brother, for both had chosen us as arbitrator in every respect:

In the name of the Father, and of the Son, and of the Hole Ghost, Amen. As a dispute has arisen between William of Sauqueville and Thomas the Miller and their parties on the occasion of the death of Gilbert of Sauqueville, brother of the aforementioned William, and as Aubin de la Fossé has subsequently appeared against Thomas the Miller and Robert le Feures against Michael the Miller, the father of Thomas, to charge them with responsibility for that death — the one directly, the other circumstantially — be it known that our court is holding them. The contenders agreed to accept our decision in the entire affair, both as to the central point at issue and as to all its ramifications, and subjected themselves and all their properties and possessions to whatsoever

---

[29] The judgement was given and entered in French.

judgment we should pass in the case in any way, and pledges of this were given on both sides. Following up now on the announcement we made, summoning the disputants for our decision on the Tuesday before Candlemas in our house in the forest of Aliermont, we hereby proclaim our determinations in this case as follows. To satisfy the accusers and to appease their hearts, the aforementioned Thomas shall, on a solemn occasion and in the house of William of Sauqueville in Dieppe, if he permits it, or otherwise in the church of St. James in that town, present sixty worthy men—twenty priests, twenty knights, and twenty in holy orders, to swear with him that he did not, out of malice or intrigue or hatred for the dead man, do that which led to his death, and that what had happened was not and had never been any burden on his conscience; and we personally are of the opinion that they can fittingly and properly take this oath. The said Thomas shall then go to the shrine of St. James in Spain and to the shrine of St. Giles in Provence, and he shall be on his way on these pilgrimages before next All Saints Day, unless for some reason he shall have been given permission by us not to do so; in that case he shall send two others on these same pilgrimages, unless we direct otherwise. Further, he shall see to it that two thousand Masses shall be said for the soul of the deceased man, arranging that, beginning with the next Pentecost synod, five shall be said regularly each year for the next five years, and he shall see to it that the remainder of those Masses are said in some other fashion. In addition, for the soul of the departed he shall send overseas four select footsoldiers, to go with the next battalion, which is to be mobilized within a year from St. John's Day. And since it is our opinion that Robert le Feures haled the elder Michael into court without sufficient reason, we wish and order by this decree that he release him from the court, and by way of reconciliation we command that they give each other the kiss of peace and forgive each other all ill feelings, and conduct themselves hereafter in friendly and amiable fashion, for if—which God forbid!—any malevolence should ensue as a consequence of what has been said and done between them, we will see to it that their guarantors answer to us for it. And if there be anything in the decision which is obscure or dubious so that quarreling is continued or flares up again between these parties, we reserve the right to make any further determinations required. The guarantors for Thomas are: the seniors named Michael Miller, the Michaels who are his brothers, and Martin Miffant; the guarantors for the other party are: William of Sauqueville, William Caletot, and John Angis.

As we have said, we carried out the foregoing in the upper hall of our manor at Aliermont on the Tuesday preceding the feast of the Purification of the Virgin Mary, in the year of our Lord 1264. Present were: the said parties, and the venerable men Master G. the treasurer; Master J[ohn] of Flainville, precentor; [William] of Flavacourt; Robert of les Andelys, a canon of Rouen; Brother Adam Rigaud; John of Morgneval, our clerk; Reginald of Tremblay; and many others. This day we spent the night there.

JANUARY 27. With God's grace we visited the priory at Auffay, where there were six monks, to wit, the prior, Luke of Sap; John of Sap-André; John of Bellière; Henry of Jumièges; Robert of Blève; and Simon of Crouttes. We enjoined the prior to inspect the coffers of the monks frequently lest they should have any property. They ate meat in common; they did not observe the fasts of the Rule well, neither did they preserve silence. Item, since we learned that the prior was less devout and sincere concerning the Divine Office than he ought to be, was too severe, and was, as it were, unmerciful and ferocious, we expressly enjoined him to confess and celebrate Mass more frequently and more zealously than had been his practice, to be present at Matins and at the day and night Offices, to speak more gently with his monks, to correct them more discreetly and mercifully than he had done, and to conduct himself more affably and paternally toward them. Item, to be more moderate in his drinking. Item, since the nave of the church was in a bad state of repair, it was much exposed to the weather and the faithful could not stand in it to hear the Divine Office. Since the church had too long been in an unseemly and disordered state, although the parishioners were wealthy and influential, we summoned the treasurers of the church before us, in the presence of the dean of Longueville and the local prior. After we had diligently inquired of them what actually should pertain to the treasury of the church, we ordered the dean to obtain a statement from the treasurers and to find out from them what they received for they church treasury. With our authority, [we ordered them] to force the parishioners to contribute to the rebuilding or repair of the said church and pay a levy of one hundred twenty pounds which had been imposed that year for work on the church and which had not yet been paid nor received. Then indeed, at the petition of several of the parishioners of the said village and with the consent and advice of the present or former treasurers and of the dean, we appointed Richard of Les Andelys, a parishioner of this village, to receive all that should pertain, or had pertained, to the said church, as well as the said impost, and also the balance that remained to the treasurers from the treasury. This day we spent the night there and received procuration. Total for procuration: ten pounds, fifteen shillings.

JANUARY 28. With God's grace we visited the abbey of St-Victor [-en-Caux], where nineteen monks were in residence; usually more were there. All but three were priests. Three were at St-Thomas, although usually only two were there. Alms, that is to say, the leftovers or fragments of the monks' food, were given twice a week. With God's grace we found everything else to be in a sufficiently good condition, except that the abbot and community were still quarreling, as they had been doing for many years, about certain pittances. However, with God's grace we pacified them and agreed that the abbot should remit and acquit himself of all pittances of this kind to the community. We ordered, with the common consent of the abbot and the community, that two of them, to wit, the prior and Brother John of Paris, should collect and receive all incomes devoted or pertaining to the said pittances, and should pay, when proper, the pittances to the community from this money, on the right days and occasion, without any consultation with the abbot. We ordered and enjoined the abbot to restore to the said community whatever revenues he had received and whatever purchases he had made with the money bequeathed and left by certain of the faithful to the community for pittances and on no account to interfer with such things in the future. Abbot William was sickly and close to death, and with God's will afflicted with age and general debility, so that he had almost lost [the use of] all bodily sensations. They owed one hundred pounds; they had sufficient supplies to last out the year, as they believed, with the exception of wine. We received procuration there today. Total for procuration: nine pounds.

JANUARY 29-30. At Déville. JANUARY 31. To wit, on Septuagesima Sunday. With God's aid we preached a sermon at the cathedral at Rouen. FEBRUARY 2. To wit, on the feast of the Purification of the Blessed Mary, we celebrated this day's feast at the cathedral, and we had the entire chapter with us. FEBRUARY 3-4. At Pinterville. FEBRUARY 5. At Vernon. FEBRUARY 6. At Juziers, at our own expense. FEBRUARY 7-17. At Paris, to attend the Parlement. FEBRUARY 18. To wit, on Ash Wednesday. FEBRUARY 19-21. At Paris. FEBRUARY 22. The feast of St. Peter's Chair. FEBRUARY 23. At Paris. FEBRUARY 24. To wit, on the feast of St. Matthew the Apostle. FEBRUARY 25-28. At Paris, to attend the Parlement. MARCH 1. At Paris, to attend the Parlement. MARCH 2. At Conflans.

MARCH 3. With God's grace we came to the Hôtel-Dieu at Pontoise; with His aid we preached and visited it. We found five persons there, including both priests and clerics, one of whom, to wit, Dom John of Fenins, dressed in lay garb, had been appointed rector of the place by the king. We had entrusted other duties to him, and we now committed or gave to him the cure of the residents of the said house, both well and sick, both brothers and sisters. A certain other priest, John, was there, who had been chaplain at Maudun and who was either unwilling or unable to visit the sick. He was impetuous, and we therefore gave orders that he be entirely removed from office, especially since the prioress said that two priests with the said master [Dom John] were quite sufficient. The brothers neither had nor observed any Rule. The sisters were held to observe and conduct themselves according to the Rule of St. Augustine, but, [a copy of] this, however, they did not have. The prioress told us that she was having it written out, and she thought that she would have it ready quite soon. They took the three vows, to wit, of obedience, chastity, and poverty. We forbade them to confess to anyone without the permission of the master and [ordered them] to give him the name of the confessor whom they desired to be given to them. They had no churchyard, and they complained about this. They owed little, and but little was owed to them. They thought that, with the exception of wine, they had enough supplies to last out the year. The greater part of the building looking toward the river was on the verge of ruin.

This day we cited and had before us the priests of the archdeaconry of Pontoise. We ordered them to obey our vicar as though he were ourself, to abide by the synodal decrees, and to govern and conduct themselves accordingly. Item, we ordered the vicar to act for us in visiting every church at least once a year.

This same day we spent this night at St. Martin's, at our own expense.

MARCH 4. We received procuration at Gaillonet, a Premonstratensian house. We did not compute. MARCH 5. We received procuration at St-Laurent-en-Cornecervine. Total for procuration: seven pounds, eleven shillings.

MARCH 6. With God's grace we visited the said priory, where there were four monks from St-Père-de-Chartres, to wit, Brother Philip of Sérans, the prior; Thomas of Guitrancourt; John Bat-la-Bourre; and Simon Scotus. They performed the sacraments of the church for the men residing at Monceux, a practice which has always displeased us, and still does. They used feather beds, they did not observe the fasts of the Rule, and they freely ate meat three times a week, when there was no need. The prior who preceded the said Philip had told us at our last visitation[30] that their abbot, together with certain other abbots of the province of Sens, had obtained this indulgence, to wit, that the monks dwelling in priories outside the monastery might legally eat meat thrice a week. The aforesaid Philip knew nothing about this, so we ordered him to consult with his abbot in this matter. They owed about sixty pounds. With God's grace we found other things to be in a sufficiently good condition.

MARCH 7. We received procuration at Sausseuse. Total for procuration: ... [lacuna in MS].

MARCH 8. With God's grace we visited the aforesaid priory. Fourteen canons, of whom six were novices, were dwelling there; all but these six were priest. They owed one hundred pounds of Paris. They believed that, with the exception of wine, they had sufficient supplies to last out the year. With God's grace we found everything else to be in good condition.

We spent this night at Frênes.

MARCH 9. With God's help we preached and administered Confirmation at Ecouis, and spent the night at Frênes.

MARCH 10. With His aid we came to St. Mary's church at Les Andelys, and, having called before us in the upper hall of our manor the dean, the canons, the chaplains, the vicars, and the clerks [-choral] of this church who were then in residence, we made inquiry concerning their condition. We found that there were six prebends there: the dean was present, and two canons were in residence, to wit, Dom John of Muids and Master Ralph of Salmonville; a third, Master Peter of Fenertine, was in Rome; two, the fourth and fifth, Henry of Mouflaines and John of Morgneval, our clerks, were riding with us; while the sixth, Master John of Yspanne, was a scholar at Paris. Item, there were four vicars present, of whom one should serve continually in the church at La Culture, and these four are held to support the burdens of the parish; two other vicars were there, one a deacon and the other a subdeacon, who are obligated to vest themselves every day for High Mass. The dean has the cure of all the canons and clerics of the church, and of the parishioners, not excepting those of certain adjacent villages. The sacristan is a priest who must sleep in the sacristy and conduct the song school. In our presence it was enacted that those who held benefices in the church should pay whatever procurations the papal legates were, or should be, entitled to receive; that is to say, that each one should contribute

[30] See entries for October 6, 1259; February 8, 1260/61.

in proportion his income. They should hold a general chapter twice a year, on the day following *Quasimodo*[31] and on the morrow of the Nativity of the Blessed Mary, and those who were absent at the time should pay a fine of twenty shillings. Furthermore, we discovered that Master Ralph of Salmonville and Dom Richard, a vicar, had quarreled unbecomingly in the church, and that, not without scandal, they had brawled frequently; we ordered the dean to bring about a reconciliation between them without delay. Item, we ordered that the Graduals be re-bound. With God's grace we found other things in good condition.

This day we spent the night at Frênes, at our own expense.

MARCH 11. We visited the Hôtel-Dieu at Les Andelys. A certain priest was proctor and rector of the house. It had an income of one hundred twenty pounds; it owed little, and, with the exception of those things required by the seriously ill, it had sufficient provisions for the year. We found the house to be in sufficiently good condition with respect to both temporal and spiritual concerns.

This day we spent the night at Gaillon.

MARCH 12. At Gaillon. MARCH 13. At Pinterville. MARCH 14. At Bonport. MARCH 15. At Rouen. MARCH 16. To wit, on the Sunday on which *Letare Iherusalem*[32] is sung. With God's assistance we preached in the cathedral at Rouen, and spent the night at our manor. MARCH 17. At Bonport. MARCH 18-19. At Gaillon. MARCH 20. At Bonport. MARCH 21. At Déville. MARCH 22. With God's grace we conferred Holy Orders at the parish church in Déville. MARCH 23-24. At Déville. MARCH 25. To wit, on the Annunciation of the Blessed Mary. We celebrated this day's feast at Rouen. MARCH 26. At Rouen.

MARCH 27. We came to the nuns' monastery of St-Amand-de-Rouen, and, with God's grace, having preached in the chapter, we visited. In residence were forty-five veiled nuns and four young noble girls already received but dressed in secular garb. One of these, to wit, Margaret of Hodeng, had been received in violation of our prohibition; wherefore we punished the abbess as we had [determined] in council and knew to be proper. We enjoined her to return the said Margaret to her relatives without delay, and that not later than two weeks after the coming Easter, inasmuch as we did not regard her as a received novice. Once more we

[31] Low Sunday, or the First Sunday after Easter.
[32] The Fourth Sunday in Lent.

forbade her ever to receive or veil any other or others without our permission or special mandate,[33] else she should know that she would be punished more severely. Item, four nuns were at Saâne. Item, we forbade the abbess to be as lenient as she had been in giving the nuns permission to go out; we ordered her to inspect their coffers more often, and to make her first inspection before the coming two weeks after Easter. Item, as we had done before,[34] we expressly forbade each nun to diminish her contribution to alms, that is to say, that everything of food, drink, or bits of bread remaining on the table in the refectory should be left there, as is fitting, for we found that little or nothing remained from this source for alms, and so they had cheated the alms supply. Item, we ordered them, when they received new pelisses, shirts, other clothing, and shoes, to give their old ones to the almoness. They murmured a bit about this, which displeased us, and we forbade the abbess to give them new clothes of this kind unless, as has been said, they surrendered their old ones. Item, we forbade them to make lace, needle-cases, or other such things, unless they were suited to the use of the church. Item, we ordered the abbess to compute more frequently than had been her practice. They owed five hundred pounds of Tours; they said that some money was owed to them in bad debts. We ordered the abbess to get rid of the superfluous maidservants. With God's grace we found other things to be in good condition.

We spent this night at Déville.

MARCH 28. With God's grace we visited Bondeville priory. Thirty nuns, four lay sisters, and two lay brothers were there. They should confess and receive Communion once a month. They complained that doves flew through the choir and chancel and created a tumult there which, as they said, disturbed the Divine Office; wherefore we ordered them to block up or plaster most of the windows, for several of them were superfluous. They owed one hundred twenty pounds. With God's grace we found other things to be in good condition. In truth, recognizing the feebleness of Comtesse who had long been prioress there, and wishing to make provision for her comfort, we felt that we should remove her from office, although she was worthily acquitting herself of this position and had done so for many years. We gave the community permission to elect another.

This day we spent this night at Déville.

[33] See entry for March 13, 1263/64.
[34] *Ibid.*

MARCH 29. At Rouen. MARCH 30. To wit, on Palm Sunday. With God's grace we performed the service suitable for this day, and preached in the vestibule of St-Laurent. MARCH 31. At Déville.

APRIL 1. With God's grace we visited the priory of Mont-aux-Malades. Ten priest-canons were in residence, and six were in Burgundy; also there were five healthy lay brothers, sixteen healthy lay sisters, twelve male lepers, and seventeen female lepers, so that five groups were there. One of the canons was contentious, given to wine, and given to swearing. We ordered the prior to take this matter under suitable advisement. Two secular priests were there; one governed the parish, the other celebrated Mass at the chapel at Pigache. They owed about ... [*lacuna in MS*]; they had enough supplies for the year. With God's grace we found other things to be in sufficiently good condition.

APRIL 2. At Rouen. APRIL 3. We bestowed absolutions, preached, and, with God's grace, consecrated the holy chrism, as is customarily done on this day. APRIL 4. To wit, Good Friday. APRIL 5. To wit, the Holy Easter Sabbath. At Rouen, and with God's grace we celebrated the service proper for these days.

APRIL 6. To wit, Easter Sunday, and with God's grace we celebrated this feast at Rouen. APRIL 7. We received procuration at Quévreville from the lessee of the place.

APRIL 8. With God's aid we visited the priory at Mont-Deux-Amants, where eleven canons, including the prior, were in residence. There was a certain lay sister there who had not been in residence a year as yet; we ordered the prior to train her according to the discipline of the Rule and to teach her how to lead a good life and confess frequently. They did not observe the rule of silence very well; as we had often done before,[1] we now expressly ordered them to keep it in a better and more scrupulous manner than had been their custom, and especially so in the cloister, where they were garrulous and overmuch given to gossiping. Item, we discovered that the subprior and several of the canons, in the prior's absence and without his knowledge, had purchased from two brothers who are laymen an annual rental worth ten shillings of Tours to be received from a certain orchard, and this with money fraudently obtained from the late Anselm the Englishman, former doorkeeper there. In this negotiation they had drawn up a contract badly phrased and almost ridiculous, and had signed it with a certain seal in the name of the subprior, although the subprior had no business having his own seal. When we heard of this wrongdoing, we enjoined the prior to remove Guiard of Louvetot, the subprior, from office at once, and not to appoint him to any other position without our mandate or permission. We also ordered him to seize the seal which was used in making out the contract and which was still in his possession. We forbade in perpetuity any subprior ever to use a seal of his own. Item, we gave orders that Brother Eustace of Lambertville be removed from his duties as pittancer and that he not be given any other office without our mandate. Item, since the said ten shillings [annual rental] had been purchased with the aforementioned Anselm's money which should have gone to the prior, we ordered the latter to appropriate the ten shillings for the house. Item, we ordered the prior

---

[1] See entries for July 31, 1259; October 15, 1262.

to punish as seemed proper those who had been involved in this contract. Item, we ordered the prior to furnish Brothers William Babot and Gilbert, the former subprior, who are feeble and infirm, with a worthy servant who would see to their needs. They owed eighty pounds over and above what they owed to the priest at Tourville. With the exception of wine, they had sufficient supplies to last out the year. We received procuration there this day. Total for procuration: eight pounds, nine shillings.

APRIL 9-10. At Frênes. AFRIL 11. At Mortemer-en-Lyons, at the expense of the abbey. APRIL 12. At l'Ile-Dieu, at the expense of the abbey. APRIL 13. At Bonport. APRIL 14-16. At Pinterville. APRIL 17. At Bourg-Achard, at our own expense.

APRIL 18. With God's grace we visited the aforesaid priory, where nine canons were in residence; nine were in outside parishes. A certain canon had been in a certain parish in the deanery of Bourgtheroulde for some little time, although we had never bestowed the cure of the parish upon him. This displeased us, and we ordered it corrected. A young canon from Corneville was there; we ordered him to confess and receive Communion more often than he had been doing. Item, we ordered the prior to receive some more canons, since there were too few of them. More was owed to them than they owed; they had provisions to last out the year. The buildings were badly roofed and uninhabitable in many places, especially the farmhouse behind the garden in which the guests are received; we ordered this corrected. We received procuration there this day. Total for procuration: . . . [lacuna in MS].

We caused all of the priests of the deanery of Pont-Audemer to be called before us at Rougemontiers. We found that Nicholas, vicar at Bliquetuit, did not celebrate Mass in the church of this place as he ought to do; we ordered him to celebrate Mass in a better fashion and more often. Item, because he had been defamed of incontinence, especially with a certain woman named Dinote; of having annoyed several people with apostolic letters which he had unjustly procured; and of engaging in trade, particularly in the purchase and sale of woodlands, he gave us a letter, under his own seal, and swore that if he should again be defamed of the foregoing, or any one of them, so that he could not canonically purge himself, he would regard his vicarate as resigned. Item, Gervaise, priest of Ste-Croix, was defamed of Julianne, his parishioner; we warned him to keep away from her and not to allow her or his own daughter whom he had in the town to enter his house. Item, we ordered the parson at Bliquetuit to find a chaplain. Item, because the chaplain of St. Edmund's in the parish of Ste-Opportune does not keep residence, we ordered his goods to be seized. Item, we forbade all priests to levy contributions on several Sundays or feast days, but on one day only;[2] item, that they shall receive nothing for collecting these contributions; item, that they diligently beware that nothing is contained in the schedules of the collectors of contributions beyond what is to be found in our letters. Item, we ordered the priest at Trouville to procure a cape.

This day, having ended the sermon which, with God's grace, we preached to these priests, and having completed our visitation, we came to the abbey at Corneville and spent the night there, at our own expense.

APRIL 20. With God's grace we preached and administered Confirmation here, and spent the night, at our own expense.

APRIL 21. With God's grace we visited this abbey. Ten canons were in residence, and there were nine outside. Abbot Peter was staying alone at Beaumont, which displeased us. We ordered the prior to compel those who were not priests to confess and receive Communion at least once a month. Item, since we found that one had not accused another [in chapter], we expressly ordered the prior to compel the canons to be assiduous in such accusations. Item, that he should see that silence was better observed than had been the case. They owed two hundred pounds, most of it to a priest at Routot. They believed that they had sufficient provisions to last out the year. With God's grace we found other things to be in good condition. We received procuration there this day. Total for procuration: seven pounds, ten shillings.

APRIL 22. At Bourg-Achard, at our own expense.

APRIL 23. We convoked all the priests of the deanery of Bourgtheroulde before us at Thuit-Herbert. We found that the chaplain of the leper house at Orival seldom resides in his chapel; he had performed a clandestine marriage,[3] was excommunicate, and was also defamed of incontinence. Item, Henry Cornet, chaplain at Vivier, rarely keeps residence; because of his negligence the lord at Harcourt has seized some of his income; we ordered him to maintain residence. Item, the priest at Malleville was contentious

---

[2] Collections authorized by the bishop for defraying the expenses of the diocese.
[3] Clandestine marriage is a marriage performed outside the canonical forms, e.g., in the absence of the parish priest or his delegate, or without witnesses. ("Marriage," Dict. de droit canon., VI, 740; Corp. jur. can., Decretal. Grag. IX Lib. IV. Tit. 3, cap. 1-3.)

and of bad life. Item, Master Ralph of St-Denis-des-Monts, an Englishman, was defamed of one of his nieces, an English girl; we warned him to keep away from her, and by all means to put her out of his house; item, we ordered him [Ralph] to find a chaplain. Item, the priest at Bosrobert was defamed of the wife of a certain cleric named Bigre, and also of a certain English girl; we enjoined him to send away without fail this Bigre and his wife. Item, the priest at St-Philbert was defamed of a certain Emmaline, a married woman.

This day we spent the night at Yville.

APRIL 24. With God's grace we dedicated St. Leger's church at Yville, and spent the night there, at the priest's expense. APRIL 25. At Déville, to wit, on the feast of St. Mark. APRIL 26. At St-Georges, at our own expense. APRIL 27. With God's grace we preached and administered Confirmation at Duclair, and we spent the night at Jumièges, at our own expense. [No entry for April 28].

APRIL 29. With God's grace we visited the abbey at St-Wandrille after we had, with His aid, first preached a sermon in chapter. Forty monks were in residence; there were twenty-two outside in the priories. All but six of the residents were priests. We ordered the abbot to inspect the coffers of the monks more frequently than he was wont to do, for he had been negligent about this. Item, we issued orders, as we had done several times before,[4] that old clothes be returned upon the receipt of new ones. Item, we ordered the abbot to visit those monks who were dwelling outside [in priories], and to restrain them so far as he could from bad conduct. Item, since the income allocated to the infirmary was insufficient to provide necessities for the sick, we decreed, with the consent of all, that the kitchener should receive the said income and should provide the infirmary and the sick as best he could with everything that was needful. They owed six hundred pounds; some debts were owed to them, but the debts were not very collectible. Item, since by the decree and enactment of the visitors of their Order Brother William of Modec was ordered to remain alone in a certain room, entirely shut off and separated from all association with the community and the monks, for that he had inadvisedly and evilly spoken words in open chapter which had scandalized and disturbed the community, we did not care to make any change in such an ordinance. We received procuration there this day. Total for procuration: . . . [lacuna in MS].

[4] See entry for October 19, 1263.

APRIL 30. At Déville. MAY 1-3. At Rouen, because of the Exchequer.

MAY 3. To wit, on the Invention of the Holy Cross, John, priest and rector of the church at Civières,[5] appeared before us in our clerks' room and admitted that upon several occasions he had been grievously defamed by good and serious men of incontinence, of frequent fighting, and of other offenses, concerning which he had recently given us a letter stating that he would resign his church at our request. He had relapsed, and for this reason we had cited him before us. Seeing that we could proceed most harshly against him, he besought our mercy and swore, with hands upon the Holy Gospels, that he would resign his church before the coming octave of St. Mary-Magdalene, and that henceforth he would never make any claim to the said church. He was willing that its patron should be free to make his presentation to it after the said octave. Present were the venerable men Peter of Ons; Stephen, archdeacon of the French Vexin; Richard of Sap, chancellor; William of Flavacourt, the official; John of Jumièges, canon of Evreux; and John of Morgneval.

This day we were at Déville.

MAY 4. At Déville. MAY 5. At St-Wandrille, at our own expense. MAY 6. At Le Valasse, of the Cistercian order, at the expense of the abbey. MAY 7. At Graville, at our own expense.

MAY 8. With God's grace we visited the priory at Graville, where twelve canons were in residence. One did not accuse another [in chapter]; we ordered this corrected. A certain cleric, called Hugh, had been received in perpetuity there, clad in secular garb. He behaved in a depraved and faithless manner towards them; in a furtive and secret manner he had sold part of a certain woodland which had been entrusted to his keeping. In full chapter we announced that unless he reformed and acted more honestly, we would remove him without fail. They owed two hundred forty pounds of Tours; they believed that, with the exception of wine, they had enough provisions to last the year. Then, as we were leaving, we warned this cleric to be more zealous in refraining from illicit acts. With God's grace we found other things to be in good condition. We received procuration there this day. Total for procuration: . . . [lacuna in MS]

MAY 9. With God's grace we visited the abbey at Montivilliers after we had with His grace, first preached in the chapter there. Fifty-eight nuns were in residence; there should be sixty, according to the certain number,

---

[5] See entry for September 21, 1264.

but one had recently died, and Dame Margaret of Cergines was taking her place. They should confess and receive Communion at least once a month. We ordered the abbess, as we had often done before,[6] to make frequent inspection of the nuns' coffers, lest they have any property. We ordered them to return their old clothes upon the receipt of new ones. Item, we ordered them to refrain altogether from games on the feast of the Innocents. Alms are given thrice a week to all comers. The abbess, as a result of an old custom of Alice, a former abbess, is held to provide for thirteen poor people every day. They had five hundred pounds of Tours, both in safekeeping in the treasury and in good debts. They have several silver dishes which they had recently bought; they have supplies enough for the year. A certain glossed psalter, left to them by Sir Arnoul of Jocres of good memory, had been loaned without the knowledge of the community; we ordered the abbess to have this psalter replaced without delay. She said that she could do this quite easily, since Master William of Beaumont had it. Item, before leaving we called the abbess, the prioress, and the subprioress before us in the major chapel of the abbess next to the hall and ordered the abbess to take better care and more suitable charge of the pelisses than she had done. Item, we forbade her to allow any nun to lift any child or children again from the sacred font after baptism, or to stand godmother for any person or persons.[7] Item, we ordered a complete removal of birds. Item we expressly forbade anyone to put ornaments or decorations made of peach-colored cloth or such things on the ends of their pelisses, that is to say, on collars or on cuffs. Item, we forbade them to wear metaled belts or to use unusual knives, made valuable with carved and silvered handles. Item, we ordered them to be more prompt in rising in the morning than had been their custom. Item, we forbade the abbess to cause Philippa of Monchy any trouble, or to be angry with her for some words which the said Philippa had spoken in chapter. Item, we forbade them to make any more needle-cases or lacework. Item, we ordered those who waited upon the sick nuns to eat together in one place and not in scattered groups. Item, that the food from

[6] See entries for January 12, 1260/61; October 23, 1263.

[7] Godparents as an institution in baptism can be traced back to the early days of the Church. Probably, at the beginning, parents were also the godparents. In cases of orphans and slaves, strangers acted as sponsors. In all probability, the institution of godparents other than the real parents dates back to the days of the catechumens, as does the introduction of well-known persons to sponsor those who were about to be baptized.

the refectory and the infirmary intended for alms be better collected and taken care of than it had been. We were there this day at the expense of the abbey. Total for procuration: . . . *[lacuna in MS]*.

Note: Anent new clothes, the infirmary and napkins, and those in charge of the sick.

MAY 10. With God's grace we blessed the nuns there.

MAY 11. When we learned that William, priest at Mannevillette, had been defamed of theft and of frequent brawling, he, of his own free will, admitted in our presence that such a rumor had circulated, although he denied the facts themselves. We ordered him to purge himself with the seventh hand of his neighboring priests,[8] and for this purpose we assigned him the day following the Pentecostal synod.

This day we were at Lillebonne, at our own expense.

MAY 12. With God's aid we conferred Confirmation there and spent the night. MAY 13. At Valmont, at our own expense. MAY 14. To wit, Ascension Day, at the same, and at our own expense. God aiding us, we celebrated the high conventual Mass and preached.

MAY 15. With God's grace we visited the aforesaid abbey. Twenty-six monks were in residence, two of whom were novices; three were in England; all but three of the residents were priests. The Statutes of Pope Gregory were rarely if ever read. We gave orders that the rule covering the fasts be better observed than it had been. A general distribution of alms is made there three times a week; however, on other days the lepers receive it. Item, as we had done before,[9] we issued orders that the prior and some senior from the community be present when the abbot computed. They owed fifty pounds; some bad debts were owed to them. We received procuration there this day. Total for procuration: . . . *[lacuna in MS]*.

Note: concerning the monk who is living with the lord.

MAY 16. We were at Fauville, at our own expense. MAY 17. With God's grace we preached and administered Confirmation there, and spent the night there, at our own expense.

MAY 18. With God's grace we came to the house or priory at Etoutteville. We were extremely grieved to find almost everything about the place in a miserable state of disrepair. This day we received procuration and spent this night at Ouville.

[8] See October 16, 1248, n. 70.
[9] See entry for October 25, 1263.

MAY 19. With God's grace we visited this priory, where eleven canons were in residence. A twelfth canon had, with the prior's permission, gone on pilgrimage to St.-Romuald's,[10] because of a serious illness with which he was afflicted. All were priests; two were at Autigny. The canons need some ordinal for community use; we ordered the prior to obtain one at the coming synod. They owed sixty pounds; some monies were owed to them from past times. They did not have enough wine or oats to last out the year. We ordered the prior to have a general and itemized statement of the priory income put into rolls or registers, and that the community or some seniors from the community who should represent them all should have one copy, the subprior another, and the prior a third; we also ordered that the same statement of revenue be written out in a cartulary. Item, we expressly ordered the prior, as we had done before,[11] to assign the community the ten pounds of Tours which it is entitled to have as pittances, and in particular the income from the house it has at Rouen and the fifty shillings from property at Corbianville; item when leaving, we expressly forbade the prior to claim any of the said ten pounds under any circumstances, nor any of the monies given in alms to the community for the purpose of purchasing rents. We received procuration this day from the lessee of the house at Etoutteville. Total for procuration: eight pounds, fifteen shillings.

MAY 20. We received procuration at Longueville-Geoffroi. Total for procuration: ... [lacuna in MS].

This same day we called before us Brother Ralph, one of the two monks residing at the aforementioned house at Etoutteville, and Robert the Englishman, the caretaker of this house. We warned the said Robert to behave more becomingly than he had been doing, and to eschew the company of disreputable women, and especially not to bring them to the priory in the future; item, that he should do nothing with, or make any disposition of the goods belonging to the said house beyond the value of five shillings of Tours without the knowledge of the dean of Canville. We appointed the said dean as an assistant to the said Robert in making up an inventory of the said goods.

MAY 21-23. At Aliermont. MAY 24. To wit, Pentecost. This day, with God's grace, we celebrated High Mass as St-Nicolas and preached there.

---

[10] St. Romauld was the founder of the Camoldoli in the first years of the eleventh century, in the diocese of Arezzo, Italy. He was a friend of Pope Sylvester II (Gerbert of Aurillac) and of Emperor Otto III.

[11] See entry for October 27, 1263.

MAY 25. At Bellencombre, at our own expense. MAY 26-27. At Déville. MAY 28. At Bonport. MAY 29. At Gaillon. MAY 30. At Mantes. MAY 31. At St-Germain-en-Laye on Trinity Sunday. JUNE 1. To wit, on the Translation of St.-Francis. With God's grace we preached at the monastery of our sisters near St-Cloud, and celebrated High Mass there. We went to Paris.

JUNE 2. At Paris. This day the sacred synod was held at Rouen, but we were absent through necessity. However, by letter patent we appointed the venerable men Master P[eter] of Ons and Master J[ohn] of Neuilly-en-Thelle, the archdeacons of Greater and Lesser Caux in the diocese of Rouen respectively, to act in our stead in certain cases and affairs which some priests and clerics had with us for the day of the Rouen synod and the day following. Dom Thomas, rector of the church at Malleville, a severe and unreasonable man, defamed of serving his church inadequately and ofttimes excommunicated and suspended, promised the said archdeacons on oath that he would carry out completely whatever decisions we should make concerning himself or his church, excepting, however, the resignation of this church. This we learned on the faithful testimony of John of Morgneval, our clerck. Item, the said archdeacons ordered Sylvester, priest at Varangeville, who had taken the Cross, and had already received the pack and staff,[12] to remain in his church until our arrival, that is to say, until he had talked with us.

Item, they assigned the vigil of St.-Mary Magdalene as the day when the priest at Hébécourt should appear before us at Rouen to stand trial for those matters which, on his own oath, he had promised us in a letter.

Item, they assigned the same day to Stephen, priest of Raffetot, to answer for the vice of incontinence of which he was defamed.

Item, they imposed purgation upon Enguerrand, priest at Puchay, for having relapsed into incontinence after he had given a letter to Archdeacon John of Porte and had admitted the rumor, though he denied the fact. For this purgation he was assigned the same vigil of St.-Magdalene when he should appear before us at Rouen.

Item, Thomas Humphrey, cleric from the parish of Vylermerville, appeared before the said archdeacons the day following the Rouen synod, and the said vigil was assigned to him for the purpose of purging himself with the seventh hand of good and trustworthy men[13] of the charge that he had

---

[12] The pack and staff, together with the wearing of the cross on an outer garment, were a sign that the individual had taken an oath to go on Crusade.

[13] See above, October 16, 1248, n. 70.

relapsed with the wife of William Trenchant, his relative, and whom, in our presence, he had abjured under the penalty of twenty pounds of Tours. Although the said Thomas did not have any legitimate compurgators, nevertheless the said archdeacons, dealing kindly with him, assigned him the said vigil of the Magdalene at Rouen, enjoining him to bring thither some of his neighbors of good repute and worthy of being believed when he came to make his purgation.

JUNE 3-23. At Paris, attending the Parlement. JUNE 24. To wit, the Nativity of St. John the Baptist. JUNE 25. At St-Denis. JUNE 26. At Senlis. JUNE 27. At Compiègne. JUNE 28. At Noyon. JUNE 29. At Herthie, at the manor of the Bishop of Noyon, and at his expense; to wit the Nativity of SS. Peter and Paul JUNE 30. At Montdidier. JULY 1. At Conty. JULY 2. At Aumale, at our own expense. JULY 3. At Blangy. JULY 4. To wit, on the Translation of St. Martin, at the same. JULY 5. With God's grace we spent [two] nights and administered Confirmation there for two days. JULY 6-9. At Aliermont. JULY 10. We received procuration at Aliermont from the lessee at Wanchy. Total for procuration: nine pounds, twenty-three pence. JULY 11-13. At Aliermont, and we had Dom Jean of Acre with us. JULY 14. At Aliermont. JULY 15. We received procuration at Bures. Total for procuration: ten pounds, sixteen shillings.

JULY 16. With God's grace we visited the aforesaid priory. Two monks from Pré were there, one of whom had the cure of the house. He administered it in the name of and at the will of the said prior [of Pré]; two monks at least should be there. They used feather beds and ate meat, and in these matters as well as the fasts, they did not observe the statutes of the Rule. Alms are given thrice a week to all comers. They owed nothing, and likewise nothing was owed to them. They are held to remit to the prior of Pré whatever remains to them after providing for their own maintenance and that of their staff. The prior of Pré was personally present at our visitation.

This day we came to St-Saëns and, with God's grace, visited the priory of nuns there. We found the nuns living in disorder and not according to the Rule, particularly the prioress and Marie of Eu. Frequently they recited the day and night Offices without modulation,[14] even on Sundays. They did not confess frequently, nor did they eat together, but in separate groups. We ordered Marie of Eu to return the chalice to the chapel of Ste-Austreberte as soon as possible and to return to the prioress a certain charter or letter

---

[14] See above, July 9, 1249, n. 36.

which she had from the community concerning the manor of Ste-Austre-berte. Item, we ordered the prioress to provide the said chapel with some one would serve it suitably. Item, to inspect the coffers of the nuns more frequently than she had been doing. They owed one hundred pounds; forty pounds was owed to them; they had neither enough wheat nor enough oats to last until the harvest. Since we saw them to be in bad state, especially in the matter of certain observances of the Rule, we earnestly and eagerly sought for ways by which their state might be decently and wholesomely improved, and that they might be better attuned to God and to their own Rule. However, we did not do anything about this at this time. But on the following morning we went to them again, and all, gathered together in chapter before us, submitted themselves entirely to our will and ordinance and promised in good faith that they would more zealously observe whatever, with God's aid, we should be led to ordain for them. They must prepare a letter covering this and sealed with the seals of the prioress and Master J[ohn] of Neuilly-en-Thelle, archdeacon of Petit-Caux, who was then with us.

We received procuration this day at the monks' priory at St-Saëns. Total for procuration: seven pounds, six shillings.

JULY 17. With God's grace we visited this priory, where there were four monks of St-Wandrille, counting the prior, and Brothers Ralph of Mante-ville, Ralph of Butille and William of St-Paterne. They did not observe the fasts of the Rule; they used feather beds and ate meat when there was no need. The prior rarely celebrated Mass. More was owed to them than they owed.

This day with God's grace we visited the priory at Beaussault, where there were two monks of Bec-Hellouin. They did not have a satisfactory Missal. They ate meat and used feather beds and they did not observe the fasts of the Rule. They owed twenty-four pounds; thirty pounds was owed to them. We received procuration there this day. Total for procuration: eight pounds, four shillings, eight pence.

JULY 19. With God's grace we visited the abbey at Bival, where there were thirty-three nuns, one lay sister, and one sister in lay garb. We ordered the abbess to inspect the nuns' coffers more frequently than she had, lest they have any property. Item, we expressly ordered them to be as zealous as possible about eating together in the refectory and in having the same food and drink in common. They owed sixty pounds; they did not have enough wheat to last until the new harvest. We ordered the recall of a certain priest, because we intended to assist the house in the matter of an annual pension which he was receiving from it. He was a brother [professed] in his own [religious] house, who had been sent away from his abbey for cause, some time ago. But many of them murmured about this and were very heavy of heart. They said and asserted that he was worse now than ever he had been and that in consequence they were in no little fear at the prospect of his return and of his way of life. A little later, indeed, at the request of the abbess and by reason of her supplication, we withdrew [our order of] revocation and willed that he be kept away from the house, as heretofore, lest worse ensue.

This day we were at Beaubec, at the expense of the abbey.

JULY 20. With God's grace we preached and confirmed at Sigy, and received procuration there. Total for procuration: ten pounds, five shillings, one penny.

We visited the said priory, where Brothers Nicholas of Talvée, then prior; Gonfroy of Louvièrs; Simon of Pont-Audemer; Luke of St-Aignan; Martin of Frênes; and Clement of Jumièges. Alms are given twice a week to all comers. They ate meat and used feather, and they did not observe the fasts of the Rule well. They owed seventy pounds. It must be known that our procuration may not exceed the sum of ten pounds of Tours, and if we spend any more we must pay for it, as is set forth in a certain letter drawn up concerning this agreement.

This day we were at Déville, at our own expense.

JULY 21. In the morning Girard, priest at Martigny, appeared before us in the hall of our manor at Rouen. He had been summoned and cited by his archdeacon for that he had been again defamed of incontinence. He denied this on oath, and later on we assigned him the day following the Assumption of the Blessed Mary when [the results of] the inquiry, made in the meantime by the archdeacon Robert as to whether he stood defamed or not, would be revealed, and whether proceedings should be taken against him, etc.

Item, Thomas Humphrey, cleric of the parish of Vylermerville, who had been accused and defamed a little while ago of [incontinence with] the wife of William Trenchant, his own relative, and abjured her under the penalty of twenty pounds of Tours, was, however, as it is reported, once again accused and defamed of this and of lapsing. We imposed purgation upon him and assigned him a definite day on which he should bring his compurgators.[15] However, we remitted this purgation. Then of his own volition and on oath he foreswore the village of Vylermerville for an entire year, that is to say, a year from the octave of the coming Nativity of the Blessed Mary, under penalty of ten pounds of Tours, to be exacted from him should he enter the said village within the said year. Peter Muitel, Peter's brother; John Muitel; and Robert Herenc stood guarantors for this fine.

Item, Ralph, priest at Hébécourt, who had been frequently punished by us in the past for wasting the goods of his church, for leaving his church too long unserved, and for other matters, concerning which he had given us a letter [in which he promised] to resign his church at our pleasure, now, on the vigil of the Blessed Mary Magdalene [promised] that he would not claim anything in the said church for any reason whatsoever, but that he would regard it as resigned from now on. He admitted and granted that we could deprive him, present or absent, of this church for any reason whatsoever. This day we were at Bonport.

JULY 22. At Evreux, to wit, on the feast of St-Mary Magdalene. JULY 23-25. At the same, with the king and the legate. JULY 26. At Frênes, where we had the legate with us. JULY 27-29. At Pinterville. JULY 30-31. At Gaillon. AUGUST 1. To wit, on the feast of St. Peter in Chains, at the same. AUGUST 2-3. At Gaillon. AUGUST 4-5. At Frênes. AUGUST 6. At Bonport. AUGUST 7. At Déville. AUGUST 8. At the same, where John, former rector of the church at Civieres,[16] now voluntarily resigned this church into our hands in the presence of Robert, the archdeacon of this place, and of Masters G., the treasurer of Rouen; John of Jumièges, canon of Evreux; Dom Reginald of Muchegros, the chaplain of the said treasurer; and John of Morgneval, our clerk.

AUGUST 9. At Déville. AUGUST 10. To wit, on the feast of St. Lawrence, at the same.

AUGUST 11. With God's aid we came to the priory of St-Lô-de-Rouen, and there with His aid we preached and visited. Seventeen canons were in residence, and four were outside, to wit, at Cressy and Thémericourt. We ordered the prior to have the cloister gate near the entrance to the refectory better guarded than it had been and to keep the lay folk from the refectory. Alms are given twice a week to all comers. They owed two hundred forty pounds; they had sufficient supplies to last out the year; one hundred fifty

---

[15] See above, October 16, 1248, n. 70.
[16] See entry for May 3, 1265.

pounds was owed to them. This day we received procuration from them at Déville. Total for procuration: . . . [*lacuna in MS*].

AUGUST 12. With God's grace we visited the priory of Pré, near Rouen, after we had with His aid preached in the chapter. Eighteen monks of Bec-Hellouin were there; all but four were priests. At one time there had been in residence twenty-four of twenty-five monks, that is to say, before the house had been burned. They make a general distribution of alms thrice a week. They owed six hundred pounds of Tours to the abbey, and another six hundred pounds of Tours elsewhere; they had sufficient provisions to last out the year. With God's grace we found other things in good condition.

This day with God's grace we dined at the Franciscan convent with the minister-general and the minister-provincial.

We spent the night at Déville.

AUGUST 13. With God's help we came to the monastery of St-Ouen-de-Roucn, and with His grace we preached in the chapter and made a visitation. Fifty-eight monks were in residence, and many were outside in priories and in other places. Alms are given every day to all comers; to wit, thrice a week to clerics, and thrice to laymen. The articles of the Rule covering the eating of meat and the observance of the fasts are badly kept in the priories. The spiritual state [of the monastery] with God's grace was good. They owed forty-three hundred pounds; twenty-seven hundred pounds in bad debts was owed to them. We were unable to find out how much income they had received from the first year of vacant churches.[17] However, from the report we received from Master John of Neuilly-en-Thelle, the archdeacon of Petit-Caux, whom we had sent to them on this matter once before, we understand that from such returns, both within the diocese of Rouen and outside, they had received four hundred forty-one pounds of Tours up to the Nativity of the Blessed Virgin Mary, in the year 1264; but they said that they did not know how much [they had received] since then, or after the aforesaid Nativity.

We spent the night at Déville.

[17] The collators of churches ordinarily received, in whole or in part, for one year or more, the revenues of such churches when conferred on the new titularies. This was called the *Jus deporti,* or *jus deportationum.* The collators kept the revenues either for themselves or for the upkeep of the fabric of the church, or other uses. ("Annates," *Dict. de droit canon.,* I, 533.) John's report is not included in Eudes' Register. However, see entry for March 30, 1259/60 and reference to parish churches therein.

AUGUST 14. At Rouen. AUGUST 15. At the same, and with God's grace we celebrated the feast of the Assumption of the Blessed Mary. AUGUST 16. In our great hall Ralph,[18] former rector of the church at Hébécourt, resigned his church into our hands.

We spent the night at Déville.

AUGUST 17. At Déville. This day we made the following announcement:

Since the rector of the chapel at Val-Osmond, who had been absent six months and more from the said chapel without having asked or obtained our permission, and who later had been warned and cited according to law on our authority to return to the said chapel within six months to keep due residence there and to perform [his] required functions, as he is bound by his oath to do, has not seen fit to fulfill these duties nor in any manner to return to this [chapel]: since the said chaplain, legally cited to appear before us on the Monday following the Assumption of the Blessed Virgin Mary to stand trial in these matters failed to appear before us, he was therefore considered by us to be contumacious. We, in consequence, deemed the said rector to have been absent through contumacy. Having taken counsel with men learned in the law, we by this sentence deprive him of the said shapel.

AUGUST 18. At Déville. This day in our smaller hall at Rouen we ordered Girard,[19] priest at Martigny, to undergo purgation before the official of Rouen, with the seventh hand of the priests of his order,[20] on the octave of the Nativity of the Blessed Mary, for that he had been defamed of incontinence after he had given us a letter that he would not relapse.

AUGUST 19-21. At Frênes. AUGUST 22. At l'Ile-Dieu, at the expense of the abbey. AUGUST 23. With God's grace we dedicated the church there, and spent the night at Noyon-sur-Andelle, at our own expense. AUGUST 24. At Noyon [-sur-Andelle], at our own expense. AUGUST 25-27. At Déville, at our own expense. AUGUST 28. At St-Wandrille, at our own expense. AUGUST 29. At the same, and at our own expense. This day, to wit, the Decollation of St. John, with God's grace we preached and confirmed in the local parish church. AUGUST 30. With God's grace we dedicated the church at Louvetot, and spent the night at St-Wandrille, at the expense of the rector of the said church. AUGUST 31. At Jumièges, at our own expense. SEPTEMBER 1-2. At Pont-Audemer.

[18] See entry for July 21, above.
[19] See entry for July 21, above.
[20] See entry for October 16, 1248, n. 70.

SEPTEMBER 3. At the same. With God's grace we celebrated the provincial council[21] in St. Ouen's church at Pont-Audemer, and with us were our venerable brothers O. [Eudes de Lorry], of Bayeux; R[alph] de Chevry, of Evreux; Fulk d'Astin, of Lisieux; Richard of Avranches, of Avranches; Thomas d'Aulnon, of Séez; John, of Coutances; all, with God's grace, being bishops.

SEPTEMBER 4. At the same

SEPTEMBER 5. We came in person to the church at Illeville because of a dispute between the rector of that church and the prior of St-Ymer. The said parties appeared before us and our council after we had with God's grace celebrated Mass. However, we were not able to end the dispute at this time, and we assigned the parties the day following the Rouen synod to appear before us to hear judgment. In the interim, the parties should present their arguments to us before Michaelmas.

This day we were at St-Philbert, at the manor of our venerable brother Richard, by God's grace bishop of Avranches, and at his expense.

SEPTEMBER 6. At Pinterville, and we had the said bishop with us.

SEPTEMBER 7. At Gaillon. This day Archdeacon Peter, on our behalf, presented the following to the official of Evreux:

I, Peter, archdeacon of Grand-Caux in the diocese of Rouen and proctor of the Reverend Father Eudes, by God's grace archbishop of Rouen, revoke in his name and in that of his diocese of Rouen whatsoever John, called Roussel, a sergeant of this Father, has promised concerning the disposition of a certain cleric apprehended at Louviers. And in particular John's promise to provide two men to escort the said cleric to Evreux, at the mandate of the official of Evreux. Furthermore, I, the said Peter, appeal in writing to the Apostolic See in the name of the said Father [Eudes], and of his aforesaid diocese, and of his present or future sergeants, my lord official, lest you should compel them, or any one of them, to escort to Evreux any cleric who had been taken for any crime committed in the territory or district of Louviers, since this competency does not belong to you, either by custom or by right. I also appeal lest you attempt anything similar that would be prejudicial to the said Father and to his diocese, and I request *apostoli* at once. Done in the curia of the official of Evreux, in the presence of this official, sitting in tribunal, and in the year of our Lord 1265, on the vigil of the Nativity of the Blessed Virgin Mary.

Present were the advocates Masters Nicholas Cornouiller; Master William

21 The acts of this council have not been published.

of Laigle, the amice-bearer; and Master Jordan of Tanville; John, called Ruffo, of Louviers; Ralph of Cottévrard, canon of Rouen; and several others.

SEPTEMBER 8. To wit, on the Nativity of the Blessed Mary. With His grace we celebrated Migh Mass and preached at St. Anthony's in Gaillon. After we had breakfasted at our château, we went on to Vernon, and spent the night there.

SEPTEMBER 9. At St-Côme, near Rouen. SEPTEMBER 10-11. At St-Martin, near Pontoise, at our own expense. The king was there. SEPTEMBER 12-13. At Paris. SEPTEMBER 14. At Paris. To wit, on the Exaltation of the Holy Cross. SEPTEMBER 15-16. At Paris. SEPTEMBER 17. At St-Germain-en-Laye. SEPTEMBER 18. At St-Côme, near Meulan. SEPTEMBER 19. With God's grace we conferred Holy Orders at Juziers, and spent the night at St-Côme. SEPTEMBER 20. With God's help we gave our blessing to the abbot of Ressons in St. Mary's church at Meulan, and spent the night at Mantes. SEPTEMBER 21. To wit, on the feast of St. Matthew the Apostle and Evangelist. At Gaillon. SEPTEMBER 22. At Bonport. SEPTEMBER 23. At Déville. SEPTEMBER 24. At St-Victor-en-Caux. This day Ascius, former abbot of this place, ceased to be abbot and resigned his office into our hands. SEPTEMBER 25. At Aliermont. SEPTEMBER 29. To wit, on the feast of St. Michael the Archangel. At the same. SEPTEMBER 30. At Frênes. OCTOBER 1. At St-Victor-en-Caux, at our own expense.

OCTOBER 2. At Déville. This day William, rector of the church at Benouville, accused and likewise defamed of incontinence, as we have learned from the archdeacon of Petit-Caux, appeared before us. The said G. [William] denied both the ill-fame and the fact, and we then assigned him the day following the coming synod to purge himself with the seventh hand of priests.[22]

OCTOBER 3. At Rouen. This day Richard, rector of the church at Grainville, appeared before us. We had assigned him the Saturday following the octave of St. Denis at Rouen as the time when he should appear before us in the matter of the inquiry directed against him by the archdeacon of Petit-Caux.

OCTOBER 4. With God's grace we celebrated the feast of St. Francis at the Rouen cathedral. This day the office of the said Saint with the proper Lessons was celebrated in this church. OCTOBER 5. At Vesly, at our own expense. OCTOBER 6. At Clermont[-en-Beauvais]. OCTOBER 7. At Crépy.

[22] See entry for October 16, 1248, n. 70.

OCTOBER 8. At Soissons. OCTOBER 9. To wit, on the feast of St. Denis. At Laon. OCTOBER 10. At Bouconville, near Vauclair,[23] where we found Lord Othelin.[24] OCTOBER 11. At Jauzy. OCTOBER 12. At Clermont[-en-Beauvais].

OCTOBER 13. At the priory of St-Ouen at Gisors, where there are two monks of Marmoutier. Here we now received, in the name of procuration, seven pounds of Tours, to which we are entitled once every year, when we turn aside to this place and spend the night there. The monks are not held to do anything more for us, unless it be through graciousness alone, as is further set forth in a letter of agreement drawn up in this matter.[25]

OCTOBER 14-16. At Rouen, on Exchequer business.

OCTOBER 17. At Rouen. This day in our great hall at Rouen, and in the presence of Sir Matthew of Triel, the count of Dommartin; Master William of Flavacourt; Master Ralph of Cottévrard, canons of Rouen; the lady of Oirneval, and many others, the lord of Gueiry appeared before us and stated that Sir John de Muchegros, knight, held the fief of Muchegros from him. On the other hand, John said that he held this fief of us. He desired and agreed that we should make an inquiry into the truth of this matter, and stated that he would obey forever whatever decision should follow our findings.

OCTOBER 18-19. At Rouen, because of the Exchequer. OCTOBER 20-21. At Déville. OCTOBER 22. At Rouen. OCTOBER 23. We celebrated the feast of St. Romain at Rouen. OCTOBER 24. At Frênes. OCTOBER 25. At Chaumont. We received procuration there this day. Total for procuration: ... [*lacuna in MS*]. OCTOBER 26. We held a synod of the priests of the French Vexin at the priory [Notre-Dame] at L'Aillerie.

OCTOBER 27. With God's grace we visited the said priory, where there were two monks of St-Germer-de-Flay, to wit, Brother William, and Brother John, who was the treasurer of the aforesaid monastery, and to whom the priory had been entrusted. He never stayed there long because, as they said, the priory was burdened with many debts. The said two monks did not

---

[23] A Cistercian abbey, a daughter house of Clairvaux, founded near Laon, 1134. (Cottineau, II, 3302.)

[24] Eudes, count of Burgundy. At this meeting, at Bouconville near Laon, Eudes negotiated the marriage settlement between Louis IX's fourth son, Jean Tristan, count of Valois (born at Damietta) and Yolande, eldest daughter and heiress of her father, Eudes, count of Burgundy. Yolande's mother was Mathilda de Bourbon, countess of Nevers. Bouconville was her property. The marriage was performed on January 14, 1266/67.

[25] This letter is not contained in the Register.

observe the fasts of the Rule, nor did they observe the Rule so far as it pertains to the eating of meat and the use of feather beds. Because of the poverty of the house no guests were received there. They owed two hundred eighty pounds of Paris. The bell tower was so badly in need of reroofing that it seriously threatened to damage the fabric and vaulting. We pesonally ordered the archdeacon to compel under appropriate censure those who were responsible for having this bell tower properly roofed to attend to this business, and to do this on our authority.

This day we came to the priory at Liancourt, which we found to be in a miserable spiritual and temporal condition. The prior, to wit, Peter of Cerisy, was then absent. Two monks of St.-Pere-de-Chartres were there, to wit, Anselm, the prior's nephew, and Lawrence Petit-Noire. They had for a long time given up performing the Divine Offices, by reason of the many excommunications by which they had been bound, such as the tithe, the hundredth, and other things. Neither alms nor hospitality was offered there. They did not observe the statutes of the Rule in anything. Finally, seeing the desolate state of the house, and fearing that things would become even worse, we sequestrated all the wheat that was on the grange, both that which had been threshed, and that which was to be threshed. We had the threshers removed from the grange by the local dean and by Nicholas, priest of St. Mary's at Liancourt. We ordered them to take charge of the grange until such time as we could make other disposition anent the state of the monks and of the house. The aforesaid Anselm told us that the prior owed one hundred pounds of Paris in addition to the tithe and the hundreth.

This same day we spent the night at Sérans-le-Bouteiller, and we received for procuration the seventy shillings of Paris which they owe us once a year whenever we turn aside to come to them, in addition to wood, coals for general use, and such fodder as may be found in the town, as well as dishes and domestic utensils.

OCTOBER 28. With God's grace we visited the said priory, to wit, on the feast of SS. Simon and Jude. Three monks of St-Germer-de-Flay were there, to wit, Brother Warner of Vaux, prior, and Brothers William of Reilly and Adam of Breteuil. The cloister and the ambulatory near the hall were inadequately roofed. The prior rarely celebrated Mass. They ate meat and did not observe the fasts of the Rule. They owed one hundred forty pounds of Paris.

We received procuration this day at Parnes. Total for procuration: seven pounds, fourteen shillings.

OCTOBER 29. With God's grace, we visited this priory, where there were four monks of St-Evroult, to wit, Brither Nicholas of Villers, prior, Dom John of St-Celerin, and Brothers William of Gratesmesnil and John of Prêtreville. They observed the fasts quite well; occasionally they ate meat when there was no need. They owed fifty pounds of Paris in addition to the tithe and the hundredth. Both the bell tower and the chancel needed re-roofing; we ordered this done.

This day we came by chance to St. Stephen's priory near Hacqueville, where we found three monks of Conches, to wit, Brother Adam of Dieppe, prior, and Brothers William of Hacqueville and Bartholmew. We called them before us in a certain room of the priory and proceeded to make a visitation. They replied to all of our questions. All were priests. Alms are given thrice a week. They ate meat, used feather beds, and did not observe the fast of the Rule. They owed ten pounds. When the visitation had been finished, we asked them for the procuration due to us by reason of this visitation. They absolutely refused, saying that they were not obliged to pay this, and that we had no right to visit them, since no archbishop of Rouen had ever visited this priory.

This day we spent the night at Frênes, at our own expense.

OCTABER 30. We received procuration at Ste-Catherine-sur-Rouen. Total for procuration: ten pounds, fourteen shillings.

OCTOBER 31. With God's grace we visited this abbey after we had preached in the chapter with His aid. Twenty-eight monks were in residence there; two were scholars at Paris, fourteen were at Blyth in England, two were at Hermondsworth, and a few were in priories elsewhere. All but nine were priests. Once a year, to wit, at Michaelmas, they were accustomed to prepare a general audit of all expenses, receipts, and of the value of the rents of the house. Individual audits were drawn up every month in the presence of the seniors of the community. They had a good deal [of money], both in cash and in debts since the time of Abbot John,[26] to wit, sixty-six hundred pounds and over. They had not spent any of this yet, though they had been unable to collect any of the debts.

This day we were at Rouen.

[26] Abbot John had died in 1262. See entries for November 2, 1262, and August 9, 1264.

NOVEMBER 1. To wit, on the feast of All Saints. At Rouen. NOVEMBER 2. At Déville. NOVEMBER 3. With God's grace we celebrated the sacred synod of Rouen. NOVEMBER 4. We held the synod of deans in our middle chamber, and spent the night at Déville. NOVEMBER 5. At Ste-Catherine, at our own expense. NOVEMBER 6-7. At Pinterville. NOVEMBER 8. At Gaillon. NOVEMBER 9. At Mantes. NOVEMBER 10. At St-Germain-en-Laye. NOVEMBER 11. To wit, on the feast of St. Martin, at Paris. NOVEMBER 12-15. At Paris.

NOVEMBER 16. At Paris. This day we exchanged with Master Adam fruits of the prebend which the said A. held at Necy. Present were Master John of Neuilly-en-Thelle, the archdeacon; William of Flavacourt; and John of Morgneval.

NOVEMBER 17-18. At Paris. NOVEMBER 19. At Paris. This day we conferred the said prebend at Necy upon Master John of Jumièges with the canonical rights which the defunct had as a prebendary. NOVEMBER 20-22. At Paris, because of the Parlement. NOVEMBER 23. To wit, on the feast of St. Clement. NOVEMBER 24-29. At Paris, because of the Parlement. NOVEMBER 30. To wit, on the feast of St. Andrew, at the same. DECEMBER 1-2. At Juziers, where we received procuration this day. Total for procuration: ... [lacuna in MS].

DECEMBER 4. We visited the priory at Juziers, where there were seven monks, to wit, John, prior; Geoffrey of Chartres; Bartholomew of Arnet; Giles the younger; William Bird; Stephen Lambert; and Matthew of Alone. They did not observe the fasts of the Rule; they ate meat when there was no need; they wore pelisses of rabbit fur. All but one were priests. We ordered him to confess and receive Communion more often than had been his practice. They owed about sixty pounds; they said that they had enough supplies to last out the year.

This day we spent the night at Vernon.

DECEMBER 5. At Gaillon. This morning with God's grace we bestowed our benediction upon the abbot of Marcheroux in the Franciscan monastery.

This day, to wit, on the feast of St. Nicholas, in the presence of Brother Adam Rigaud and John of Morgneval, we exchanged with Adam of Verneuil, our nephew, the fruits of the prebend of Master Reginald of Bully, deceased, for that which he held. We exchanged this, or rather the fruits of it, with Master John of Jumièges for the fruits which he held, and which likewise we exchanged with Master Ralph of Cottévrard.

DECEMBER 6-11. At Gaillon. DECEMBER 12. To wit, on the feast of St. Lucy, at Pinterville.

DECEMBER 13. At Gaillon, where the election of Brother John of Guine-ville[27] by the monks of Bec was presented to us. As justice required, we quashed this election.[28] However, considering the advantage and quiet of the house, as well as weighing the merits of the said John, since the authority to provide this abbey with an abbot had now devolved upon us,[29] we were led to provide the said monastery with the said John. At Déville.

DECEMBER 17. At Déville, whence we issued the following:

Since Oliver, priest and rector of the church at Tocqueville in the diocese of Rouen, had promised on oath that he would resign his church into the hands of the venerable Peter, archdeacon of Grand-Caux in the diocese of Rouen, before the feast of St. Remy just passed, unless he could exchange this church for another somewhere else, because of the adultery which he was said to have committed with Avicia, his parishioner;

And since he had done neither one thing nor the other although several times requested by us, and has been unwilling to resign the said church, although he has admitted taking such an oath;

Therefore, be it known that the said Oliver has broken his pledge. We, deeming him a violator of the said pledge, deprived him by definitive sentence of the said church, when he appeared before us to stand trial on this, the Friday before Christmas.

DECEMBER 18. With God's grace we conferred Holy Orders at the Franciscan monastery in Rouen, and dined with them in the refectory.

We spent the night at our house in Rouen.

DECEMBER 19. With God's grace we preached in the cathedral at Rouen, and slept at our house. DECEMBER 20. At Déville. DECEMBER 21. To wit, on the feast of St. Thomas the Apostle, at Déville. DECEMBER 22. At Rouen. We made our O.[30] DECEMBER 23. At Rouen. DECEMBER 24-25. With God's

---

[27] John de Guineville (1265-72). (*Gallia Christiana*, XI, 232.)

[28] Eudes gives no canonical reason for his action.

[29] Under certain conditions the electors were deprived of their right to elect, and the right of nomination to office passed to him who had the right to provide; in this case, Eudes. Such conditions would be a too hasty election, non-convocation of the majority of the community to vote. ("Election," *Dict. de droit canon.*, V, 238-47, especially 246-47.)

[30] December 23, 1250, n. 135.

grace we celebrated the feast of the Nativity of the Lord at Rouen. DECEM-BER 26. To wit, on the feast of St. Stephen. With God's grace we celebrated High Mass at the Dominican monastery at Rouen, and dined with them. DECEMBER 27. With God's grace we bestowed our benediction upon Brother John,[31] the abbot of Bec, in our chapel at Déville. DECEMBER 28. At Bonport. DECEMBER 29-30. At Pinterville. DECEMBER 31. At Gaillon. JANUARY 1. To wit, on the Circumcision of the Lord, at the same. JANUARY 2-4. At Pinterville. JANUARY 5. At Brosville, in the manor of the bishop of Evreux, at his expense. JANUARY 6. To wit, on Epiphany, at the same. JANUARY 7. At Pinterville, and we had the said lord bishop with us. JANUARY 8. At Vernon. JANUARY 9. We received procuration at the priory of St-Martin-la-Garenne. Total for procuration: nine pounds.

JANUARY 10. With God's grace we visited this priory, where there were three monks of Bec-Hellouin, to wit, Brother Ralph, prior, and Brothers John of Pont-Authou and Nicholas of Bourg-Achard. There should be four. They did not observe the fasts of the Rule very well; they ate meat when there was no need. It was the custom to bestow alms upon all comers thrice a week. They owed thirty pounds in addition to the three hundred twenty pounds which they owed to the abbot, as was recorderd in the records of Abbot Robert.[32] With God's grace we found other things to be in good condition.

This day we spent the night at Mantes.

JANUARY 11. At Juziers, at our own expense. JANUARY 12-13. At St-Germain-en-Laye. JANUARY 14. At the same, and we attended the blessing of the nuptials of Lord John, the son of our lord king, and the daughter of the countess of Nevers.[33]

We spent this night at Juziers, at our own expense.

JANUARY 15. We came to the priory at Villarceaux, where with God's grace we preached in chapter and made a visitation. Twenty choir nuns were in residence, of whom one had been but very recently received; there were three lay sisters. They confessed six times a year. There were four general servant girls. We forbade the prioress to receive any person or persons without our permission, or to permit any needle-cases, lace, or alms-bags to be made as presents for lay folk. With God's grace we found their spiritual

---

[31] See entry for December 13, above.
[32] Robert de Clairbec (1247-65), abbot of Bec. (*Gallia Christiana*, XI, 232.)
[33] See entry for October 10, above.

condition to be good. They believed that they owed one hundred pounds and more. They had enough wheat, oats, and wine to last out the year, if they are prudent. They had nineteen cows, thirty-eight swine, six horses, five roosters and sixty sheep. The roofs of the buildings needed repair. Because we found six of the choir nuns absent, we forbade the prioress to be lenient in granting them permission to go out. We ordered her to give them reliable companions when they did go out.

Note: Concerning the choral cape and the book of homilies pledged with the prior of Sausseuse. Item, the gilded cup and chalice to John, the priest at Omerville.

This day, we spent the night and received procuration at Gasny. Total for procuration: eight pounds, eighteen shillings, eight pence.

JANUARY 16. With God's grace we visited the priory at Gasny, where there were three monks of St-Ouen-de-Rouen, to wit Brother John of Fontaine-en-Bray, prior, Brother Geoffrey of Noinville, and Brother John of Beauvais. They dwelt across the river [Epte] at St-Nicaise.[34] They kept the food for their animals in another manor, to wit, in that in which they were accustomed to receive or to give us procuration, and where they also kept a large number of their staff, but where they performed none of the Divine Offices. They did not say their Hours with modulation.[35] They did not observe the fasts of the Rule, and they freely ate meat without need. They owed nothing, and nothing was owed to them, inasmuch as they remitted and sent to the abbey everything which they were able to save over and above their own needs and those of their staff.

We received procuration this day at Vesly. Total for procuration: eight pounds, three shillings.

JANUARY 17-19. At Frênes. JANUARY 20. At Vernon. JANUARY 21. At Meulan. JANUARY 22-23. At Paris. JANUARY 24. At Conflans.

JANUARY 25. To wit, on the Conversation of St. Paul. With God's grace we came to the church of St-Mellon-de-Pontoise, and there with His aid we celebrated Mass and preached a sermon to the assembled canons, vicars and clerks[-choral] of the said church, a large gathering of knights, who were awaiting a tournament which was schedulel to be held the following morning near the city of Pontoise, and to many of the people of the said city. Afterwards with God's help we went to the hall which the local canons

---

[34] Not mentioned in Cottineau.
[35] See entry for July, 9, 1249, n. 36.

were accustomed to use as a chapter house, and there we assembled the resident canons, vicars, chaplains, and clerks[-choral] before us. We proceeded to make a visitation. We found three resident canons there, to wit, the treasurer, Dom Luke, and Dom Peter of Bosc-Commin. Nine prebends are there, also perpetual vicars and some chaplains. They chanted too rapidly and precipitately in choir, which we ordered corrected. Item, we ordered Dom William the Norman to impose fines for minor faults and to collect from those who incurred them, to wit, a penny for every minor fault. With the consent of all we ordered that the amount which he might collect from penances of this kind be devoted to the common use and distributed equally amongst those who were present at the Divine Offices. He should know the annual value of the fines collected for such minor faults. Item, we willed that the canons who were present at the Divine Office should be sharers in the monies levied for such faults. Item, we ordered Master Simon, our vicar, to act for us in telling Dom Vincent, chaplain, who had recently been collated to the chapel at St-Lazare with the cure of the brothers, sisters, and lepers of that house, to resign the vicarate which he had in St. Mellon's church and which he could not hold together with the said chapel. Item, we ordered the canons, vicars, and chaplains to remain at the Masses of the Faithful in the church until the *Agnes Dei,* or that otherwise they should go without the distribution made at the Obits.[36] Item, since we found a great lack of church ornaments, we ordered Master Simon to seize enough of the canons' goods that from this source they might have suitable albs, altar cloths, and other things which the canons are held to provide. Item, we ordered the treasurer to have bound together the sections of the Bible which they possessed. Item, we ordered them to have repaired and rebuilt a certain ruinous house adjacent to the chapter hall. Item, we warned Dom John of Mont-Lucille, who was said to be overfond of wine, to temper the wine to himself, and himself to the wine. Item, we ordered Dom John of Pont,

---

[36] The word *obit* has many meanings. It may mean a cleric who is provided with a benefice which has become vacant through the death of its holder; it may mean not only the death of a person but the Office celebrated at his or her death; also, the calendars of religious communities in which were entered not only the departed dead of the community, but the friends and relatives of the community who were to be prayed for. This last is the sense mentioned in this passage. The calendars bore the date of death in order to assure that Masses and prayers would be said on the anniversary of death. Distributions of extra food or money were made on that day, depending on the terms of the will of the deceased. ("Obits," *Dict. de droit canon.,* VI, 1054-55.)

rector of the church in St. Peter's parish, to attend St. Mellon's on the feasts of the Nine Lessons,[37] because of the chapel which he held therein. Item, we found that Fromond, a vicar, was grievously defamed of drunkenness, incontinence, playing dice, frequenting taverns, unreasonable litigiousness, and whispering in choir. Wherefore, he promised on oath that he would resign his vicarate at our pleasure, and a letter was drawn up covering this matter which we have under the seal of Master William of Flavacourt. Item, Dom Denis, a vicar, was not present at the visitation. We found that he had absented himself knowlingly and maliciously, and we could not get hold of him. However, we found that he was incontinent and defamed thereof, especially with a certain girl named Frances, and with another called Alice, whom he had shamefully beaten. Indeed, we learned that a certain loose woman whom he had in his chamber had seized his supertunic and had thrown it out of the window into the street to another of her ribald friends. He was defamed of dicing, of frequenting taverns, and of not confessing to the confessor we had selected for him. Item, Luke was likewise defamed of dicing, frequenting taverns, and incontinence. We discovered that the mayor of the town had held him in prison on the accusation of a certain woman whom he is said to have wanted to attack. The dean of St-Aignan still owed twenty-five shillings for a certain psalter. Thomas, a chaplain, was without a missal and a chalice.

This day we were at St. Martin's, where for procuration we should receive from the chapter of St-Mellon one hundred shillings of Paris, being the amount in which they are held each year when we visit them, in addition to furnished quarters, beds, cups, dishes, drink, and the usual cooking utensils.

JANUARY 26. With God's grace we visited St. Martin's abbey after we had preached in chapter. There were . . . [lacuna in MS] monks in residence; many were two by two in the outside priories. They had two lay brothers and two lay sisters; we ordered the prior to make both [lay brothers and lay sisters] confess and receive Communion more frequently. As we had done before,[38], we ordered them to give up drinking after Compline altogether. We enjoined the refectorian or custodian of the refectory to close and shut the refectory immediately after Collation,[39] and under no circumstances to open it up again until morning, unless given special permission by

---

[37] The major feasts: Christmas, Easter, Ascension, Pentecost, etc.
[38] See entries for February 11, 1250: September 1, 1253.
[39] The reading during the evening meal.

the abbot. Should he fail to do this, he should fast the next day on bread and water. We forbade the further serving of wine in the rooms by special arrangement, as we understood had been done on many occasions. The monks and the priors ate meat freely when there was no need, and did not observe the fasts of the Rule. They owed twenty-one hundred pounds of Paris to the abbey of Ste-Catherine and elsewhere, and one hundred pounds of this was owed at Paris at interest. They were heavily burdened with annual pensions for which they spent annually in wheat, wine, and coin, one hundred forty pounds. They said that they had enough wheat, oats, and wine to last out the year. We received procuration there this day.

JANUARY 27. With God's grace we visited St. Peter's priory, where five monks from Bec-Hellouin were in residence. Ralph of L'Honblonnière, the prior, was not present; William of Noinville was also absent, for they had gone out on business of the house, as the three whom we found there informed us. Their names are: Peter of Calleville, Richard of Jumièges, and Ralph of Beaumont. All were priests. We were much displeased that the prior was absent at this time, for we believed that we had forewarned him of our coming. They ate meat when there was no need. The great hall, to wit, that in which we were accustomed to visit them, was not very clean or properly cared for; there were no windows there. The prior ranted at the many letters of the legate,[40] which displeased us, and we told the monks to tell the prior for us to refrain and desist from such conduct. Because of the prior's absence we could not procure complete information concerning the state of the house; however, they said that they thought they owed little or nothing.

This day with God's grace we visited the Hôtel-Dieu, where with His help we preached. Afterwards we inquired into the state of the house and found that there were thirteen veiled sisters and two who were to be veiled. These last the king had sent there for perpetual residence. A priest dressed in secular garb was also there. He was a canon of Péronne whom the king had temporarily appointed as rector and custodian of this house. His name was Dom John of Fenins, and to him we committed the cure of all the residents of the house, both the healthy and the infirm. Four others were there with him, two priests and two subdeacons, who should, God willing, be advanced

---

[40] Probably the papal legate, Cardinal Simon de Brie. This is undoubtedly a reference to the papal taxes levied for the Crusade of Louis IX and for the "Sicilian Affair" of Charles of Anjou, whose burden fell on the priests who had to pay.

at the proper times successively to the diaconate and the priesthood. But one of these two priests was neither willing nor able to visit the sick as was essential and fitting, and he was, in fact, hot-headed, being indisposed to obey anyone in anything. Wherefore we gave orders that he be sent away. We ordered the said rector and prioress not to keep him there later than the coming Easter. The said brothers had no Rule, but the sisters were bound to live and conduct themselves according to the Rule of St. Augustine, and they took or made the three vows, to wit, of obedience, chastity, and property [i.e., poverty]. We forbade them to confess to anyone without the master's permission. Theen said that they owed more than sixty pounds, and that they did not have enough wheat or wine to last out the year.

We were at St-Martin's this day, at our own expense.

JANUARY 28. At Magny, at the local priory, and at our ouw expense.

JANUARY 29. With God's grace we visited this priory, where there were four canons from the house at Ambazac: a member of the Order of St. Augustine in the diocese of Limoges, to wit, Brother Gerard, prior; and Brothers Heduin, Peter Gilbert, and Gerard of Beaulieu. They have and keep the Rule of St. Augustine. A secular priest who had the cure of the parish was a member of their table. The house was in the habit of making a general distribution of alms three times a week. Each canon was, by custom, to receive only forty shillings a year from the prior for clothing. They owed forty pounds of Paris to the prior of St-Leonard at Les Andelys; they had enough provisions to last out the year. With God's grace we found everything else to be in good condition.

This day we preached with God's grace in the chapter house of the nuns at Le Trésor, and spent the night at Sausseuse, at our own expense.

JANUARY 30-31. At Frênes. FEBRUARY 1. At the same.

FEBRUARY 2. To wit, on the feast of Purification of the Blessed Mary. With God's grace we celebrated High Mass and preached in the church of Our Lady at Les Andelys, dined at our manor near the said church, and spent the night at Frênes.

FEBRUARY 3. We received procuration at Noyon-sur-Andelle. Total for procuration: eight pounds, six shillings, four pence.

FEBRUARY 4. With God's grace we visited the said priory, where there were six monks of St-Evroult, to wit, Brother Robert of Epines, prior; and Masters Thomas Sourd, Dreux of Neufmarché, Hugh of Breteuil, Thomas of Silly, and Nicholas of Cahagnes. A general distribution of alms is made there thrice a week. They ate meat when there are no need. They owed over two hundred pounds. However, they said that they had enough supplies to last out the year. We found everything else to be in good condition, except that the cellarer was a drunken and disturbing element, and because of this amongst other things, he should be removed. We received procuration this day at Pérrièrs from the lessee there. Total for procuration: seven pounds, six shillings.

FEBRUARY 5. We received procuration at Beaulieu. Total for procuration: six pounds, eighteen shillings.

FEBRUARY 6. With God's grace we visited the priory there after we had preached. Thirteen canons were in residence and eleven were in outside obediences; all but three were priests; [there were] two lay brothers and two lay sisters. We discovered that the prior was negligent in that he had not inspected the canons' coffers as we had ordered;[41] we again ordered him to correct this, and we enjoined penance upon him. A general distribution of alms is made thrice a week. They owed four hundred pounds, thirteen of it at interest. They said that they believed that they would be obliged to buy two hundred *mines* of wheat before the next harvest time for use at the house. However, they thought that for the year they had enough oats, though not of wine. They had twelve hundred sheep, one hundred swine, sixteen cows, and several horses and oxen for ploughing.

This day we spent the night at Déville.

FEBRUARY 7-9. At Déville. FEBRUARY 10. To wit, Ash Wednesday, at Rouen, where with God's grace we preached and celebrated the Office for the day.

FEBRUARY 11. With God's grace we came to Salle-aux-Puelles, near Rouen, preached, and made a visitation. Dom Willard, the proctor and custodian of the place, was there, as was a certain priest, to wit, Robert, who had been admitted. There were also six leprous lay sisters; however, one of them, to wit, Isabelle of Avenes, whom we found guilty of fornication and of having had a child by Peter of Couronne, priest, said that she was in good health. And she said that she desired to leave the place, inasmuch as she was of sound health, and especially since, by the tenor of a certain privilege and custom of the place, none but leprous sisters should be there. When we had heard this, we ordered her to be sent home to her father and by all means to be sent away. We ordered the said W[illard] to inflict

___

[41] See entry for October 14, 1264.

punishment and impose penance upon the said sisters for having concealed the shame and offense of the said Isabelle. The sisters were accustomed to attend Matins, which they always said with modulation,[42] they were also accustomed to repeating the seven [penitential] psalms after Prime and keeping silence after Compline. The sisters have definite allotments of food and drink; thrice a week they have meat, and thrice eggs, or fish or herrings, or something else which suffices. The remnants or fragments are given to a certain leprous woman at Moulineaux. They had three maid servants in common. A general distribution of alms is made there three times a week. They had in the wood cows and oxen, mares and colts. The said W[illard] told us that he had about two hundred pound in silver cups, monies, and other things, and that he owed nothing.

We spent this night at Déville.

FEBRUARY 12. At Déville. FEBRUARY 13. At Rouen. FEBRUARY 14. With God's grace we preached a sermon in the vestibule of the cathedral at Rouen, celebrated Mass there, and spent the night at Bonport. FEBRUARY 15. At Vernon. FEBRUARY 16. At Meulan. FEBRUARY 17-28. At Paris, to attend the Parlement. MARCH 1. At Paris. MARCH 2. At Paris. This day we conferred the archdeanery of Rouen upon Master Nicholas of Chécy. MARCH 3-5. At Paris. MARCH 6. At St-Denis-de-Chausée. MARCH 7. At Conflans. MARCH 8. At Wy, where we received from the priest at Gadancourt a *muid* of oats, in which amount the said priest at Gadancourt in annually held to us when we spend one night a year at Wy. MARCH 9. We received procuration at Sausseuse. Total for procuration: nine pounds, eight shillings.

MARCH 10. With God's grace we visited this priory, where there were fourteen resident canons, two lay brothers, and two lay sisters. Two were at Ecos; four of the resident canons were novices. They owed one hundred forty pounds; three hundred pounds was owed to them. With the exception of wine, they had enough provisions to last out the year. With God's grace we found other things to be in sufficiently good condition.

MARCH 11-12. At Gaillon. MARCH 13. At Frênes. MARCH 14. With God's grace we conferred Holy Orders at Notre-Dame-des-Andelys, and returned afterwards to Frênes. MARCH 15. At Frênes. MARCH 16-17. At Gaillon. MARCH 18. At Pinterville. MARCH 19-20. At Bonport. MARCH 21. At Rouen. MARCH 22. To wit, on Palm Sunday. We celebrated the Office of the day at Rouen, and with God's grace we preached in the churchyard at

---

[42] See July 9, 1249, n. 36.

St-Laurent-de-Rouen, as a customary. MARCH 23. We dined with the Dominicans and spent the night at Déville. MARCH 24. At Déville. MARCH 25. We dined with the Friars Minor and spent the night at our manor in Rouen. MARCH 26. To wit, on Holy Thursday. With God's help we granted absolutions at the customary place, and when we had led the penitents inside we preached at the cathedral and blessed the holy chrism. MARCH 27. To wit, on Good Friday. We celebrated the feast of this day at Rouen. MARCH 28. To wit, on Holy Saturday, at the same.

MARCH 29. To wit, holy Easter Day, at Rouen. MARCH 30. At Bonport. MARCH 31. At Pinterville. APRIL 1-2. At the same. APRIL 2-3. At Gaillon. APRIL 4. At Vernon.

APRIL 5. At the same, where was then the legate to France.[1] We together with our venerable brothers the suffragans of the church of Rouen, also the abbots, priors, and proctors of our churches of the province and diocese, discussed with him matters concerning the kingdom of Sicily.[2]

APRIL 6. At Pinterville, where with God's grace we had O. [Eudes], the bishop of Bayeux, with us. APRIL 7-8. At the same. APRIL 9. At Bonport.

APRIL 10. With God's help we visited the priory at Mont-Deux-Amants after we had with His aid preached a sermon. Eleven canons were in residence; nine were outside in four different places, except that the ninth was staying alone at Authieux. A certain lay sister was there, the sister of John of Pérrièrs. All but two of the resident canons were priests. One did not accuse another [in chapter]; we ordered this corrected. They owed sixty pounds in one debt and one hundred pounds to the priest at Tourville; they had sufficient supplies to last out the year. However, on the following day, before we left, we consulted with our companions about the pittances of the community, and of certain monies willed and given to the community for pittances by certain of the faithful, about which a quarrel had broken out between the prior and the community.[3] After diligent deliberation, we ordered and willed, in the presence and with the consent of the prior, the subprior, and the bailiff, that the prior should make suitable satisfaction to the community, giving for pittances to one of their canons chosen for this purpose the annual rent of twenty pounds, which for a long time the community had received and was still receiving from the grange at Muitreville. We also ordered that of the annual rental of four pounds, ten shillings of Tours which he had purchased with the monies given to them by the faithful,

---

[1] Simon de Brie, cardinal-priest of St-Cecilia and later Pope Martin IV, 1281-1285. In 1264, he was instrumental in concluding the treaty which gave the crown of Italy to Charles of Anjou, brother of Louis IX. See entry for May 30, 1254, n. 1.

[2] The records of this provincial council have been lost.

[3] See entry for October 15, 1262.

the prior should have sixty shillings and the community thirty shillings for pittances. And similarly, in the future, [we ordered] that of all rents which might be purchased from such monies, the prior should have two thirds and the community one third as a pittance. With God's grace we found other things to be in a sufficiently good condition. We received procuration there this day. Total for procuration: eight pounds, three pence.

APRIL 11. With God's grace we preached and confirmed at the church at Champ-d'Oisel, and received procuration at Quévreville from the lessee of the said place. Total for procuration: eight pounds, sixteen shillings. APRIL 12-16. At Déville. APRIL 17. At the same. This day we came to Rouen, and we issued our ordinance affecting the nuns at Caen; we provided these nuns with Sister Jeanne, a nun from St-Sauveur-d'Evreux.[4]

APRIL 18. With God's grace we preached near the Mare-du-Parc, where the clergy and people of Rouen had collected after marching thither in a procession. Here we adjudged and condemned as an apostate and heretic one who had been converted from Judaism to the Catholic faith. He had again reverted from the Catholic faith to Judiac depravity, and, once again baptized, had once more reverted to Judaism, being unwilling afterwards to be restored to the Catholic faith, although several times admonished to do so. He was then burned by the bailiff.

We spent this night at Déville.

APRIL 19-20. At Déville; however, we went to Rouen each day to attend the Exchequer. APRIL 21-24. At Déville. APRIL 25. To wit, on the feast of St. Mark the Evangelist, at the same. APRIL 26. At Déville. APRIL 27. We received procuration at Auffay. Total for procuration: eight pounds, eleven shillings, three pence.

APRIL 28. With God's grace we administered Confirmation in the parish church at this place, and then with His help we visited the priory. Six monks of St-Evroult were there, to wit, Brother Luke of Sap, prior; and Brothers Henry of Mont-de-Piété, William of Barr, Alexander of Pontchardon, John

---

[4] Beatrice had been elected abbess by the community in 1262, but her election was not accepted by the ordinary, the Bishop of Bayeux, who nominated in her stead Lucia de Crèvecoeur. Beatrice appealed to Eudes as archbishop of Rouen, who declared both elections null and nominated Jeanne-du-Châtel of St-Saveur-d'Evreux. Though provided for by Eudes, Jeanne did not accept the office. Beatrice, Lucia, and the community at Caen appealed to Rome. Beatrice was abbess in 1270 and died in 1289 and was thus, probably, the choice of Rome as well as of her own community. (*Gallia Christiana*, XI, 433-34.)

of Bellière, and Robert of Blève. All but one were priests, and him we ordered to confess and receive Communion frequently. As we had done before,[5] we ordered the prior to inspect the monks' coffers more frequently than had been his practice. They ate meat when there was no need. They observed neither silence nor the fasts of the Rule very well. They owed sixty pounds; they did not have enough wheat or wine to last out the year. We received procuration this day at Bacqueville. Total for procuration: eight pounds, twelve shillings, eight pence.

APRIL 29. With God's grace we visited the priory, where were three monks of Tiron. There should be four, but the prior told us that the fourth one would be there directly. These are the names of those who were there: Clement de Beaumont; Robert, called Four-Sides; and William of Pérrièrs. With them was also a monk from Crasville. One monk was alone at Ribeuf. We ordered the prior to inform the abbot for us that he should not delay to give a companion to this solitary monk. Occasionally women and their husbands dined at the priory. We forbade the prior to permit this in the future. They did not observe the fasts of the Rule very well, and they frequently ate meat when there was no need. They owed one hundred pounds; they thought they had enough wheat to last out the year. With God's grace we found other things to be in good condition. We received procuration this day at Longueil from a certain burgher of Dieppe who was then holding the house there in farm. Total for procuration: nine pounds.

APRIL 30. At Dieppe. MAY 1. To wit, on the feast of SS. Philip and James, at the same. This day with God's grace we administered Confirmation in the local church. MAY 2. With God's grace we celebrated a parish Mass at Arques, administered Confirmation there, and spent the night at Aliermont. MAY 3. We came to the abbey at Eu and received procuration there. Total for procuration: nine pounds, three shillings.

MAY 4. With God's grace we visited this abbey, after we had with His aid preached in the local chapter. Twenty-eight resident canons were there. As we had done before,[6] we ordered the Passional repaired. Several complaints were made against the abbot, to which we listened with diligent attention and deliberation. We discovered and recognized that they obviously sprang from rancor and hatred, and were born of malevolence; we therefore adjudged them trifling. However, on the following morning we returned to them

---

[5] See entry for January 27, 1264/65.
[6] See entry for September 9, 1264.

from Le Tréport. We then ordered and expressly enjoined the abbot and the bailiff to have three copies of the general income and the individual rents written out in registers, of which the abbot should have one, the prior another, and the bailiff the third. Item, we ordered a record made of the individual accounts, of which the prior should have one transcript for himself and the community, the abbot another, and the bailiff a third. Item, since each individual held three offices, and so was less suitably prepared to perform and carry them out at the same time, we ordered them to appoint one canon as almoner. Item, since many goods with which rents had been purchased had been donated and willed to the church by the faithful, we decreed that on double and triple feasts, and on the days of the anniversaries of princes and prelates, the community should be better treated, to wit, that some generosity be shown to the community in the matter of food and drink.[7] Item, we ordered that from the rents which might be purchased with the monies given or left to the church, one half should go to the abbey's treasury and one third to the community for pittances. Item, we ordered that when they had completed the manor house which they had just begun to build, they should stop selling their woodland. We forbade them to sell any more without the consent of the community. They owed eight hundred pounds; seven hundred was owed to them, but four hundred pounds was in bad debts. And so, after many wranglings over the charges which had been made against the abbot, we departed.

MAY 4 (*sic*). We received procuration at Le Tréport. Total for procuration: eight pounds, sixteen shillings.

MAY 5. With God's grace we visited the monastery there, where twenty-two monks were in residence; one monk from Pontoise was there. One did not accuse another [in chapter]. They say that it is their custom not to do so. We ordered the prior to take better care than he had done of a certain old and feeble monk. They ate meat in the outside priories. As we had done before,[8] we ordered the prior to procure some scribe who would prepare and copy out a Passional and other spiritual reading of which they were in great need. They owed two hundred pounds or thereabouts, and only about the same amount was owing to them in both good and bad debts. With God's grace we found other things to be in good condition.

This day we spent the night at Aliermont, at our own expense.

[7] In the form of pittances of extra food and drink.
[8] See entry for September 7, 1264.

MAY 6. To wit, on the feast of the Ascension. With God's grace we celebrated High Mass at St-Nicolas and preached there.

MAY 7. We came to the priory at Envermeu, where with God's help we
preached and made a visitation. We found only six monks of Bec there.
There should be thirteen, but six had been returned to the priory at Pré and
the monastery at Bec because the prior, when he had first arrived, had undertaken very sumptuous operations about the cloister and other buildings. A
general distribution of alms is made there thrice a week, and the almoner had
two hundred loaves every week. They owed three hundred pounds; sixty
pounds was owed to them. Indeed, they thought that they would be able to
sell some sixty pounds worth of wheat. With the exception of wine, they
had enough supplies to last out the year.

We were at Aliermont this day, and we received procuration there from
the prior of Envermeu. Total for procuration: nine pounds, eleven shillings.

MAY 8. At Aliermont, at our own expense. MAY 9. We received procuration at Neufchâtel from Ralph of Aulages, the lessee of the house at
Nogent. Total for procuration: twelve pounds, twelve shillings.

MAY 10. We sent our companion, Master John of Jumièges, canon of
Rouen; Brother Adam Rigaud; and Dom Willard, prior of Salle-aux-Puelles
near Rouen, to the Hôtel-Dieu at Neufchâtel, to visit it in our stead. From
their trustworthy account we learned with God's grace that the said hospital
was in a spiritually good condition. Three canons were there with the prior;
one of them, called Dominus, was deaf and almost useless by reason of his
age, and debility. They owed about one hundred pounds, and about forty
pounds in good debts was owed to them. With the exception of wine, they
had enough supplies for the year. We received procuration this day at St-
Laurent-en-Lyons. Total for procuration: nine pounds.

MAY 11. With God's grace we visited this priory, after we had preached
in chapter, with His aid. Fifteen canons were staying there; all were priests
but two novices. We gave orders that the said novices should confess and
receive Communion at least once a month. One did not accuse another [in
chapter] as we had enjoined upon them at a previous visitation.[9] We therefore expressly enjoined the prior to be diligent about this and to labor to see
that the accusations were made for the good of their souls. Six lay brothers
and two lay sisters were there. They owed about four hundred pounds; with

[9] See entry for October 19, 1264.

the exception of wine and oats, they had enough provisions for the year. We received procuration this day at Neufmarché. Total for procuration: seven pounds.

MAY 12. With God's help we visited this priory, where there were three canons of St-Evroult, to wit, Brother Victor, prior; Brother William of Falaise; and Brother Clement of Mondreville. At one time there had been more, but they had been reduced to fewer numbers because of their rents especially those which they held in England and which had been reduced. Sometimes they ate meat when there was no need, as frequently as three times a week. We left this matter to their consciences. They kept the fasts of the Rule well.[10] They owed two hundred pounds; they had enough provisions for the year, as they said. Other things [temporal], with God's grace, we found in good condition. Since, indeed, the chapter house and cloister were somewhat dirty, disgraceful, and badly kept, we ordered the prior to keep them cleaner than he had, and to remove the casks and timber, and all of the other things with which they were cluttered.

This day we were at Marcheroux, where we spent the night at the Premonstratensian monastery, at the monastery's expense. They did not care to compute.

This day William of Daubeuf, esquire, appeared before us, and we had read out to him a certain letter which he himself had had prepared about his own business, and which he had handed to us under his own seal and that of Sir Walter, the chamberlain of France, and which ran as follows:

Let all know that when I, William of Daubeuf, esquire, had contracted a clandestine marriage with Mary of Fresnell, against the definite orders of that venerable man the official of Rouen, acting for the Reverend Father [Eudes], by God's grace archbishop of Rouen, I, induced by the counsel of my friends, promised, obligated, and submitted myself to undergo and sustain any corporal punishment for this offense, should I be so instructed or enjoined so to do by the said Father or his said official. However, if I fail or should fail in any way to carry out and fulfill whatever, as has been stated, shall be enjoined or requested of me, I, acting under the authority and consent and express wish of my mediator, that noble man Sir Walter, the chamberlain of France, my immediate and present lord, obligate myself and submit to the aforesaid Father and to his mandate, to collect, raise, and procure one hundred pounds of Tours

---

[10] In view of the previous sentence, this is difficult to explain, as is the whole entry. Eudes may be referring to the Great Fast, from September 14 to Easter Sunday, or perhaps the scribe forgot to include *non* before *servabant*.

as a fine, in which amount I am held because of the forgoing. And I shall pay this within the five years next ensuing, that is to say, in each of the said five years, twenty pounds, ten on the feast of St. Remy and the same at Christmas and I pledge my fief by hauberk[11] which I have and hold from the said chamberlain at Daubeuf. And this shall be paid without any oppostion or obstruction on my part, or that of my heirs, to the said Father or at his order. And, in order that all these things may remain valid and stable, and unbroken throughout the whole of the said period, I, the said William, give to the said Father and at his request the present letter, sealed with my seal. And I, the said chamberlain, approving and confirming this agreement, do ratify it by appending my seal to this letter next to his. Done in the year of our Lord 1266, on the Friday after *Jubilate*[12] and in the month of April.

After considering the affair concerning the said William and consulting and deliberating with our [men], we decided that the following penance should be imposed. We enjoined him to set out before the feast of St. Mary Magdalene next ensuing, on sucessive pilgrimages to the shrines of SS. Peter and Paul and to that of St. Nicholas of Bari, as well as to the Roman Curia and the Apostolic See; that he too should return by way of St-Giles in Provence; that he should bring us letters testifying that all these things had been properly done, under the penalty defined in the above-mentioned letter and to be exacted from him if he should not do what was said. Present in the garden near the chapter house of this monastery were Master John of Jumièges; Brother Adam Rigaud; Dom Willard, prior of Salle-aux-Puelles; and John of Morgneval, our clerk.

MAY 13. At Beaumont-sur-Oise. MAY 14. At Paris. MAY 15. At the same. This day with God's grace we preached in the chapter house of the Minorites at Paris, after we had sung the hymn *Veni Creator spiritus*. The brothers of the Order, to wit, the [minister-]general and the ministers-provincial had convened there from divers parts of the world to celebrate a general chapter. We dined with them in community and celebrated the Office of the day there.

MAY 16. To wit, on the feast of Pentecost. We celebrated High Mass in the monastery of the said brothers, and dined with them. MAY 17-18. At Paris. MAY 19. At Meulan. MAY 20. At Gaillon. MAY 21. At Frênes.

[11] Hauberk knights were those who wore the heavy coats of chain mail. Knights invested with hauberk lands were to be ever ready to fight for their lord. In many respects, they were the predecessers of the mercenary Knights of the later Middle Ages.
[12] The third Sunday after Easter.

MAY 22. With God's grace we conferred Holy Orders at Notre-Dame-des-Andelys. MAY 23. With God's grace we married the daughter of Sir Theobald of Chantemelle to . . . [*lacuna in MS*]. MAY 24. At Ste-Catherine-sur-Mont, above Rouen, at our own expense. MAY 25. With God's grace we held the holy Rouen synod, and spent the night at Rouen.

MAY 26. We held the synod of deans at Rouen. This day we had Peter, the chaplain of the leper house at Quesne-Canu, cited before us, since we had learned that he was laboring under the sin of incontinence, especially with a certain damoiselle formerly living in the house at Salle-aux-Puelles, by whom he was said to have had a child. However, under oath taken about this matter he denied the ill-fame, though he admitted the rumor. We enjoined him to purge himself with the sixth hand of priests.[13] For this purgation we assigned him a day within the octave of St. John the Baptist, or the day following the said octave, should those days be ferial. At that time he should appear before us at Rouen, or before our official should we happen to be away from Rouen or its immediate neighborhood.

This day we were at Bonport.

MAY 27. At Vernon. MAY 28. At St-Côme, near Meulan. MAY 29-JUNE 9. At Paris, to attend the Parlement. JUNE 10. To wit, on the feast of St. Barnabas. At the same. JUNE 11-17. At Paris. JUNE 18. At St-Martin, near Pontoise. JUNE 19. At Gaillonet, where there were four Premonstratensian canons from Dommartin in Ponthieu from whom we received procuration this day. Total for procuration: seven pounds, nine shillings, three pence.

JUNE 20. With God's grace we preached and administered Confirmation in the church at Hardricourt. This day, God helping us, we visited the priory of St-Laurent-en-Cornecervine, where were four monks of Josaphat-de-Chartres, to wit, Brother Philip of Sérans, prior, and Brothers John of Chartres, John of Tymer, and Noah of Châteaux. The prior had never inspected the monks' coffers, although we had ordered him to do this before.[14] Accordingly we ordered him again and forbade the monks to go alone to the wood beyond the priory close, as they were in the habit of doing. We also forbade the prior to permit women, and especially seculars, to eat at the priory. We ordered him to strive so far as he could to keep them away from the priory. They did not observe the fasts of the Rule, and they ate meat. They said that

[13] See entry for October 16, 1248, n. 70.
[14] See entry for August 27, 1262.

they did this with the knowledge and will of their abbot. They owed one hundred pounds of Paris and more. They did not have enough wine, wheat, or oats to last until the new harvest. Total for procuration: seven pounds, ten shillings.

JUNE 21. At Gaillon. JUNE 22. At Pinterville. JUNE 23. At Bonport. JUNE 24. To wit, on the feast of St. John the Baptist. With God's grace we celebrated High Mass in the cathedral at Rouen, and we spent the night there. JUNE 25. At Déville.

JUNE 26. With God's grace we visited St. George's abbey, after we had preached in the chapter house. Twenty-five monks were in residence: of these, three were novices; all but three were priests; four were in England; two were at St-Nicolas. Alms were bestowed of a tenth part of all the loaves baked in the abbey. We found that Brother Samson had been negligent in confessing. More was owed to them than they owed, and with God's grace things were well with them. We ordered the abbot to admonish frequently the said Brother Samson, and any others there who might be similarly negligent, to confess more frequently than they had. We received procuration there this day. Total for procuration: eleven pounds, two pence.

JUNE 27. With God's grace we visited the monastery at Jumièges, where there were forty-nine monks in residence, of whom thirty-five were priests; twenty-one were outside, and one was with the abbot of St-Victor[-en-Caux]. We discovered that they had the Rule read out hardly once a year. We disciplined the prior for neglect of this kind, and we enjoined upon him such penance as we deemed expedient. We ordered the abbot that, so far as possible, he should see that the Rule covering the eating of meat and the fasts be observed by the monks dwelling in the priories outside. Item, as we had done before,[15] we expressly ordered that each house official draw up his individual accounts more often than had been the practice, at least once every six weeks. The abbot had spent the sum of money which Abbot Robert had left them; the latter had left them two thousand pounds in ready cash and in debts of which about eight hundred pounds was still owed to them. We received procuration there this day.

JUNE 28. With God's grace we visited the priory at Bourg-Achard. Ten canons were in residence, of whom four were novices. The prior had loaned the glossed *Epistles* of St. Paul and the *Summa* of Master William of

[15] See entries for November 5. 1254: December 9, 1256: December 6, 1257: November 1, 1264.

Auxerre[16] to Master Nicholas of Bois-Guillaume. We ordered the prior to get them back and to apply them to the use of the community. More was owed to them than they owed; with the exception of wine, they had enough provisions to last the year. Finally, because we had heard that the prior's reputation had been somewhat damaged and that evil rumors were still to some extent being bruited about, we ordered and admonished him to abstain from evil conduct and to be zealous in reforming his past life by future worthiness. Item, [we ordered] him to give to Geoffrey Boîte, the imprisoned canon, some breviary or other book, so that the latter could say his Hours and pray. We ordered the prior to make him confess and receive Communion every week.

JUNE 29. To wit, on the feast of SS. Peter and Paul. With God's grace we celebrated Mass in pontificals in the church at Illeville. We preached and confirmed there, God helping, and received procuration at Corneville. Total for procuration: eight pounds, ten shillings.

JUNE 30. With God's grace we visited the abbey at Corneville, where there were nine canons. One did not accuse another [in chapter]. In this respect we found them to have been most negligent, and once again we expressly ordered them to correct this.[17] Item, we expressly ordered the prior to make those who were not priests confess and receive Communion at least on the first Sunday of every month. Item, we found Brother Adam Picard guilty of having possessions. He had been in an outside obedience, where he had illegally held back the offerings, gifts, and such things, up to thirty shillings, contrary to the orders of his superiors. As he confessed before us, he had given these to one of his sisters-in-law. Wherefore, we deemed him guilty of possessing property, and we ordered the abbot to discipline and punish him for this in accordance with the Statutes of the Rule.[18] We enjoined the said canon to see to it that the said money was

---

[16] William of Auxerre was one among the many famous theologians at the University of Paris in the thirteenth century. His name is to be found in many documents relating to the university. He was archdeacon of Beauvais and a *magister* of the University of Paris, and in 1231 he was appointed, with others, by Pope Gregory IX to prepare an edition of Aristotle's works. A prior edition was condemned in 1210 for inaccuracies in translation. William was the author of the *Summa aurea* which was modeled in form and content on the *Sententiae* of Peter Lombard. William's *Summa aurea* contained much of the correct version of Aristotle and was widely read. ("Foi," *Dict. de théol. cath.* VI[1], 245-46.)

[17] See entry for April 21, 1265.

[18] Possession of property was forbidden by the Rule of St. Benedict, Ch. 33.

restored to his abbot and to undergo penance for his actions, after he had first received absolution from his abbot. Item, since the same canon had said many abusive things to the abbot, we ordered the latter to punish him well. They owed four hundred pounds, the greater part of it to the priest at Routot; with the exception of wine, they had enough supplies to last out the year.

This day we were at Bec, at the expense of the monastery.

JULY 1. With God's grace we visited this abbey, after we had with His aid preached in the chapter. Forty monks were there. With God's grace we discovered they had been and were in excellent condition so far as all the observances of their Rule and their temporal state were concerned. Much money was owed to them, and they owed nothing. They had enough, although they had been heavily burdened because of a disastrous fire. We were there this day, at the expense of the abbey.

JULY 2. At Pinterville. JULY 3. At Gaillon. JULY 4. At the same. This day with God's grace we preached in St. George's church at Aubevoye. JULY 5-6. At Frênes. JULY 7. At Pinterville. JULY 8. At Bonport. JULY 9-14. At Déville. JULY 15. At St-Victor-en-Caux, at our own expense. JULY 16. We received procuration at Longuevile. They did not care to compute. JULY 17-18. At Aliermont. JULY 19. At the same. This day with God's grace we dedicated the church at Martagny.

JULY 20. We received procuration at Mortemer-sur-Eaulne, where there were four Cluniac monks. The house was a dependent of the priory at Lewes. The monks had but recently arrived and as yet had received none of the priory's goods, since Master Eudes of St-Denis had held the place for over fourteen years. They were in litigation over it. Total for procuration: . . . [lacuna in MS].

JULY 21. With God's grace we visited the abbey of St-Martin-d'Aumale. Nineteen monks were in residence, and three were in England. One did not accuse another [in chapter]; we ordered this corrected. All but four of the resident monks were priests. A general distribution of alms is made thrice a week to all comers, an on other days to poor clerics and to the sick. They owed seven hundred pounds of Paris; they had enough wheat, oats, and wine to last until the new harvest. With God's grace we found other things to be in a sufficiently good state. We received procuration there this day. Total for procuration: eight pounds, ten shillings.

JULY 22. To wit, on the feast of St. Mary Magdalene, at Conty. JULY 23.

At Montdidier. JULY 24. At Noyon. JULY 25. At Maucourt, at the château of the lord bishop of Noyon, and at his expense. JULY 26. At St-Martin-aux-Bois. JULY 27. At Bresles, in the manor of the lord bishop of Beauvais, and at his expense. JULY 28. At Ressons, a Premonstratensian house, at the expense of the abbey. JULY 29. At Gournay, at our own expense.

JULY 30. With God's grace we visited the chapter of St-Hildevert-de Gournay. Here we found only the dean, the treasurer, and Master John Savenne, a canon, in residence. They did not have a deacon and a subdeacon at their Masses. We asked the dean, the treasurer, and Master John to discuss and talk over in the general chapter the question of having a deacon and a subdeacon, and to come to some definite arrangement about this. We warned them about it. Item, we enjoined upon them that in the same chapter they should decide upon and appoint one of their canons as proctor for the Hôtel-Dieu and leper house, who, in the company of a canon and of some burgher elected and deputed for this purpose, should visit these houses during the year. A proctor from their community should be appointed for this task every year. Item, we warned them about disciplining offenses already committed or to be committed by them in the town. We found Dom Lawrence, who had the cure of a church, grievously defamed of dicing, of playing ball, and of drinking in the taverns. When he was brought before us, he admitted the facts. Item, he was defamed of incontinence with a certain woman whom he is said to have made pregnant; he admitted the rumor of this but denied the fact. We must have Master John of Jumièges make an investigation of this. The said Lawrence gave us a letter about all this. We ordered Bertrand to have himself advanced through successive Orders. Item, we expressly forbade them to mutter or act tumultuously in future in the choir, since they greatly impeded the Divine Office thereby. We ordered them to pass some statutes about this in their chapter. We ordered the said Dom Lawrence to celebrate his parish Mass earlier in the morning than he had been doing, so that the daily Hours might be said in choir more quietly and with greater freedom.

This day we visited the priory at St-Aubin, where there were thirteen nuns. With the exception of Advent and Lent (Quadragesima) they rarely if ever chant their Hours with modulation on ferial days. As we have done before,[19] we expressly forbade the prioress to receive anyone without our special permission. If they did so we would not regard the one received as a nun.

[19] See entry for March 5, 1259/60.

Two maidservants in common were there; one of them was incontinent and ill famed; we ordered her expelled and definitely sent away. Item, we forbade Richilde, the cellaress, to have the servants of the house eat in the kitchen in the future, as she had allowed in the past. Item, because a certain miller who frequented the priory was reported to be a man of depraved conduct, we gave orders that he be kept away from the house. Item, because several of them had their own hens and chickens, they were often quarrelling. We ordered them to feed all the hens and chickens together and to possess them in common. We ordered that such eggs as might be produced be served equally to the nuns and that occasionally, when it seemed best, some of the chickens be served to the sick. Item, the master of the school at Beauvoir did not show prudence in visiting the said house or priory on various occasions, whence evil report arose. Accordingly, we ordered the dean of Bray to warn him.

This same day Master John of Jumièges and Brother Adam acted for us and visited the leper house and hospital in our stead. A certain lay brother and the chaplain of the leper house were wasting the goods of the place, drinking in the town and buying unnecessary things. They were ordered to refrain from such conduct. They owed twenty-four pounds and had no supplies.

The Hôtel-Dieu was not well administered, for the chaplain there was incontinent. Brother Robert of Fry, a lay brother, spent money needlessly and evilly, and we warned him about this. They owed twenty-four pounds.

This day we were at Bellosane, at the expense of the abbey.

These are the churches in the patronage of the chapter at Gournay: Bos-Yon, Bos-Guilbert, Hodanget, Avênes, Forges, and St-Claire.

JULY 31. At Beaubec, at the expense of the abbey. AUGUST 1. With God's grace we dedicated a certain chapel which is in front of the court of the aforesaid monastery. We were there this day, at the expense of this monastery.

AUGUST 2. With God's grace we visited the abbey at Bival, where there were thirty-two nuns and one lay sister. As we had done before,[20] we forbade the abbess to receive any one without our special permission; and [we ordered] that no one should go out without the permission of the abbess.[21] They owed sixty pounds. With God's grace we found them to be in a sufficiently

[20] See entry for February 27, 1254/55.
[21] See entries for November 23, 1255: January 15, 1256/57: July 17, 1259.

good state, except that they felt themselves burdened with a pension for a priest. We, at their request, proposing to lessen this pension, ordered the sequestration into our hands of an annual income of forty shillings of Tours, which the said priest was receiving at Eu and as much at Rouen. Nothing more had been assigned to him in our diocese.[22]

We received procuration this day at Beaussault. Total for procuration: seven pounds, eight shillings.

AUGUST 3. We visited this priory, where there were two monks of Bec-Hellouin, to wit, Brother Herbert . . . [*lacuna in MS*] and Brother Hugh. They ate meat freely and did not observe the fasts of the Rule. They owed sixteen pounds. We found other things to be in good condition. We received procuration this day at Sigy. Total for procuration: eight pounds, eleven shillings.

AUGUST 4. We visited this priory, where there were six monks of St-Ouen-de-Rouen, to wit, Brothers Nicholas of Talvée, Gilbert of Pîtres, Gonfred of Louviers, Simon of Pont-Audemer, Matthew of Commune, and Anquetil of Hermanville. They owed two hundred pounds; however, they had a sufficiency of provisions. We ordered the prior that he, together with his monks, eat in some room other than the hall and so dine together more becomingly and better than they had been doing. They had been in the habit of eating in the hall in the presence of all of the servants, which we, not without reason, thought to be unseemly and unbecoming.

This day we were at Mortemer-en-Lyons, at the expense of the monastery.

AUGUST 5. At Frênes. AUGUST 6. At L'Ile-Dieu, at the expense of the monastery. AUGUST 7. At Déville. AUGUST 8. At the same. This day with God's grace we preached in the churchyard of St-Gervaise.

AUGUST 9. With God's grace we visited the monastery of St-Ouen-de-Rouen. Fifty-eight monks were there; all but six were priests. One monk was dwelling alone at St-Remy. The abbot said this was because of the meager resources of the place. However, we ordered a companion to be given to him. The almoner had a small income for dispensing alms; we asked the abbot to augment this so far as he could. The itemized accounts of the kitchen, that is to say, of those things which pertain to the kitchen, are prepared every three weeks; once a year, to wit, on the feast of St. Peter, a general audit of all expenses and receipts is made. We willed and ordered that three of four seniors of the community be present at an audit of this

[22] See entry for September 16, 1263.

kind, and that they be specifically called in for this purpose by those officials or administrators who were to make the audit. We learned that they, including several seniors of the community, believed that the house was seriously harmed by the abbot. They said he rode abroad more often than the needs of the house required, and with too large and sumptuous a retinue; he was also too extravagant in food and wines. Item, against the wishes of the community many things had been given to his sister by the administrators in order to gain the good will of the abbot. Item, he had some nephews who they thought were living at the expense of the monastery. I warned him about these things.[23] We also discovered that the house was burdened by reason of the fact that all the foodstuffs, as well as those intended for the guests as for the abbot, were prepared in the community kitchen, and that, in consequence, the kitchener was obliged to seek additional provisions, inasmuch it was necessary to provide more than would otherwise be required. We also found that the Divine Service of the community was greatly disturbed because of the parish which was in their monastery. They agreed that another church, reserved for the parish, should be built near the abbey. They owed fifty-two hundred seventy-eight pounds, sixteen shillings, seven pence; twenty-eight hundred pounds in bad debts was owed to them. We, seeing that the house was in bad state as to temporals, although with God's grace it was well with them in spirituals, thought about ways in which the house might be more conveniently and suitably relieved. With the consent of the abbot and of the entire community, we decreed that upon some specific day we would convene with ten monks from that monastery whom they should nominate, to wit, the prior of the community; the subprior, N.; John, prior of Beaumont-en-Auge; Robert Pésant, the treasurer; Gilbert of Pîtres; Robert of Jumièges; John, the sacristan; Busquet; Roger of les Andelys; Peter of Ruppe; and Thomas of Bruyères. We would discuss the matter of reforming their condition, and with their counsel we would issue orders, especially in the matter of the abbot of St-Victor[-en-Caux], concerning the transfer and separation of the parish church, of the kitchens, and indeed, concerning the whole state of the house, concerning the carelessness or negligence of the abbot, for he seemed to take little heed for the interests of the house.

We were at Déville this day, at our own expense.

AUGUST 10-13. At Déville. AUGUST 14. To wit, on the vigil of the

---

[23] This is the first time the archbishop has used the first person singular in the Register, and is entered as a marginal note in the MS.

Assumption of the Blessed Mary, at Rouen. In the chapter house of the cathedral we preached in Latin to the assembled canons and clerks-choral. AUGUST 15. With God's grace we celebrated the feast of the Assumption of the Blessed Mary, and we had with us B.,[24] by God's grace the bishop of Amiens. AUGUST 16. At Déville, and the said bishop was with us. AUGUST 17-18. At Pinterville. AUGUST 19. At Gaillon. AUGUST 20. At the same, and hither came to us, on his return from Apulia, our dearest Reverend Father,[25] by God's grace bishop of Auxerre. AUGUST 21. At the same, and the said bishop was with us. AUGUST 22-23. At Pinterville. On these days we had the said bishop and the bishop of Evreux with us. AUGUST 24. At Brosville, in the manor of the bishop of Evreux. Here were we and the said bishop of Auxerre, along with the lord bishop of Evreux, and at the expense of the latter. AUGUST 25. We had breakfast at Calleville, in the manor of Sir John of Harcourt, knight. Here we left the said bishop of Auxerre, who was ill, and we spent the night at Bec-Hellouin. AUGUST 26. At Lisieux. AUGUST 27. At Troarn, at our own expense. AUGUST 28. At Fontenay, at our own expense. AUGUST 29. At Condé-sur-Noireau. Here we entered the diocese of Coutances. AUGUST 30. We received procuration at St-Sever. Total for procuration: eight pounds, six shillings.

AUGUST 31. With God's grace we visited the abbey at St-Sever. Fifteen monks were in residence; three were in England; all but three were priests. Abbot Peter was at La Haye-Pesnel and had one monk with him. We ordered the Statutes of Pope Gregory covering the eating of meat to be observed. A tenth part of all the loaves which are made in the abbey is given to the almoner in addition to a definite amount from income which is set aside and designated for alms. Twice a week alms are given to all comers. They owed four hundred pounds, not counting what they owed abbot Peter for his maintenance.

This day with God's grace we received procuration at the Hôtel-Dieu at Saultchevreuil, in the house of the Hospitalers. Ordinarily we did not visit there. Total for procuration: eight pounds, six shillings.

SEPTEMBER 1. By God's grace we visited the abbey at Hambye, where there were twenty-one monks. Alms are given thrice a week to all comers. With God's grace we found the place in good condition as regards both temporals and spirituals. They owed about three hundred pounds. We

[24] Bernard d'Abbeville.
[25] Gui de Mello.

ordered the abbot to have the accounts cast in the presence of the seniors of the community and some members chosen by it, and to have all sources of income for the house listed in registers. We received procuration there this day. Total for procuration: ... [*lacuna in MS*].

SEPTEMBER 2. By God's grace we visited the priory at St-Pair-sur-Mer. Two monks from St-Michel-in-Peril-of-the-Sea were there; they had, they said, come there only recently. We ordered the prior to make frequent distribution of the alms which had been customary there in former times. Item, we forbade him to permit women to eat in the priory in the future, and we enjoined him to have the fasts of the Rule and the article concerning the eating of meat observed. They were obliged to turn over to the abbey whatever remained to them over and above what was necessary for their own upkeep and that of those staying at the house. However, they expected that in the future they would have a definite amount allotted for that purpose by the abbot's revised tax schedule. The abbey, it may be noted, had been well able to collect without any difficulty a thousand pounds and more each year from this house. They did not desire to compute our procuration.

SEPTEMBER 3. We received procuration at Coutances from ... [*lacuna in MS*] [John], the bishop.

SEPTEMBER 4. With God's grace we preached in the chapter house at Coutances, and visited the chapter. We found that in choir they were in the habit of speaking from stall to stall and even from third stall to third stall. There is no dean; the precentor governs the chapter so far as singing is concerned, and the master of the schools does likewise for the reading. The canons told us that the bishop did not have the cure of their souls. However, with the bishop's permission they had confessors whom they had obtained by petitioning him. The chapter attended to the disciplining of the clerks-choral and of the chaplains, but did not know who had the cure of their souls, but they desired that the bishop have it. However, the bishop refused this, on the grounds that he had no jurisdiction over them. We received procuration this day from the chapter, in the bishop's manor. We did not compute. Item, we warned the bishop to be diligent in finding out and knowing to whom the chaplains and clerks-choral should confess. Item, there had been a dispute between the precentor and the chapter as to who should discipline the offenses of the clerks-choral and vicars. We found that this quarrel had been put to rest as the result of an agreement made by them a little while before. Accordingly, Master Harvey, the master of the schools, had corrected where correction was needed. Item, we warned Julian Romain, a canon, to abstain from the vice of incontinence of which we found him defamed.

SEPTEMBER 5. With God's grace we came to Pérrièrs. On this day we celebrated the parish Mass and preached to the entire local parish. We received procuration from the proctor of the abbot and convent of St-Taurin of Evreux, who receive the great tithes of the entire parish along with many other things; wherefore the said religious owe us full procuration. We spent the night at the house of Colin of Grosparmi.²⁶ Total for procuration . . . *[lacuna in MS]*.

SEPTEMBER 6. With God's grace we visited the abbey at Lessay, where there were thirty-one monks in residence; all but five were priests. They wore linen shirts for lack of woolen goods, which, they said, they had not been able to procure for a long time because of the English barons'²⁷ war. Alms are distributed four times a week to all comers. They said they were heavily burdened with the many pensions which they paid out annually to various persons. The abbot,²⁸ who was there at that time, had been installed about last All Saints, and we were not able to obtain full information about the state of the house, that is to say, to find out how much they owed. However, we did discover that at the time of the abbot's installation they owed nine hundred pounds, according to an audit which they had then made and which was put in writing under the seals of the aforesaid abbot and community. Also that there was owed to them three hundred twenty pounds in bad debts, dating from the time of Abbot Humphrey. A certain secular cleric, Master Geoffrey, had for many years received the entire income of the abbey rents and profits, had managed the business of the abbey, and had paid its bills. This much displeased us. With the consent of the abbot and community, we ordered that a monk should be attached to him who should learn and be instructed by this cleric in what manner the temporal affairs of the abbey were run, to know how much they owed and to whom, and, indeed, to become acquainted with the entire state of the house as to temporals, since not for sixteen years had any monk or any other even taken any part in these things. We received procuration there this day. Total for procuration: . . . *[lacuna in MS]*.

---

²⁶ Colin may have been a relative of Ralph de Grosparmi, who had been canon of Bayeux and bishop of Evreux, and was now cardinal-bishop of Albano.

²⁷ The war between Henry III and Simon de Montfort.

²⁸ This is probably Pierre de Creances. (*Gallia Christiana*, XI, 920.)

SEPTEMBER 7. With God's grace we came in person to the priory of St-Germain-sur-Ay,[29] where there are two monks of Mont-Saint-Michel, although they had absolutely refused hospitality to our servants whom we had sent on ahead the day before and had shut the gates against them. We, in the presence of one of their sergeants, and of Bartholomew Fergant, viscount, Master William of Flavacourt, Master John of Jumièges, and of many others who were standing about their door, warned them, whose absence was a fraud and who were withdrawing [from our jurisdiction], that they should receive us for visitation and procuration.

This day we spent the night in the town, and on the following day we went again to the door of the aforesaid priory and warned the monks, although we did not see them, that they must make good our expenses of the preceding day. The total of our expenses for that day was ... [lacuna in MS].

SEPTEMBER 8. To wit, on the Nativity of the Blessed Mary. We celebrated High Mass in the abbey at Blanchelande, a Premonstratensian house, and we were there this day at the expense of the monastery.

SEPTEMBER 9. With God's grace we visited the abbey of St-Sauveur. Twenty-four monks were in residence; all but one were priests. They had been without an abbot for several days. However, they told us that they had elected one of their own number, who was then absent and had gone to the bishop to be confirmed by him. With God's grace we found them in good condition as to spirituals. They owed five hundred twenty pounds; four hundred pounds was owed to them in debts both good and bad. We received procuration there this day.

SEPTEMBER 10. We were at Héauville in a certain priory dependent upon Marmoutier. Four monks were there. They are exempt, and in consequence we cannot visit them fully. However, we warned them to live as uprightly as they could, since in the event of crime we can deal with them.

SEPTEMBER 11. With God's grace we came to the tomb of St. Thomas [Elie] of Biville, by whose merits many and various miracles were there made manifest by the omnipotent Lord Jesus Christ.

Then we went thence to the priory at Vauville, where with God's aid we made a visitation. Three monks of Cerisy were there; there should be four, but the fourth had been sent to England. In the chapel we found some

[29] See entries for May 20 and June 1, 1256.

books in folios and quartos which we ordered bound. They had no copy of
the Rule; we ordered the prior to have one written out and frequently pondered and read. They ate meat freely and, as they said, had no scruples
about this, because of a certain grace or indulgence made to the abbots of
their Order in this regard. They did not observe the fasts of the Rule. They
owed fifty pounds and had few or almost no provisions. Today we received
procuration from the prior of this place at the abbey at Cherbourg. Total
for procuration: seven pounds, fifteen shillings.

SEPTEMBER 12. With God's grace we visited the abbey at Cherbourg,
where twenty-five canons were in residence; twenty were outside in priories
and parishes. They had many and good books for studying. We ordered
them to be carefully kept, diligently and decently placed in one and the
same place, and at least once a year brought out before the community in
chapter and inspected. With God's grace we found them in good condition
as to spirituals. We gave orders that the audits be made in the presence of
the seniors of the community. They owed one hundred pounds; much was
owed to them, and they had many provisions, animals, and many oxen.
We received procuration there. Total for procuration: . . . [lacuna in MS].

SEPTEMBER 13. We were at Valognes, at the manor of the bishop of
Coutances, and at his expense.

SEPTEMBER 14. With God's grace we visited the abbey at Montebourg,
where thirty-six monks were in residence; all were priests with the exception
of certain novices who were there at this time. They said that in accordance
with the custom of this monastery, they remain four years in the novitiate.[30]
We gave orders that the Statutes of Pope Gregory be read out in chapter
twice a year. Alms should be given thrice a week to all comers. With God's
grace they were in good state both as to temporals and spirituals. As much
was owed to them as they owed, and their supplies were plentiful. Item, we
gave orders that the accounts be cast more often than had been the practice,
and done in the presence of the abbot and of some [of the brethren] elected
by the community. We received procuration there this day. Total for
procuration: . . . [lacuna in MS].

SEPTEMBER 15. We came to the house or priory at St.-Côme-du-Mont.
This house had been given to Sir Leonard the Lombard, to have and to hold
for life. We found it to be insufficiently and improvidendly managed. The

---

[30] This was most unusual, since the Rule of St. Benedict, Ch. 58, demanded a
novitiate of one year's duration.

said Lombard had been there only once. The vicar of the priory was living in a great stone house. The garden was almost a waste.

This day we spent the night at Pont-Unvie at the house of Master Nicholas, cleric, where we received procuration from Thomas Hogue, Thomas Aelor, and Ralph of St-Côme, then lessees of the said Lombard. Total for procuration: eight pounds, thirteen shillings, eight pence.

SEPTEMBER 16. At Bohon, a certain priory belonging to Marmoutier, where there were six monks in residence. There should be eight but the prior told us that a certain lay brother had been sent there by the abbot in lieu of one monk, and that, similarly, Brother Amelin, the abbot's chaplain, was sent there to recover his health, for he was ill. They were exempt. However, we warned them to live so far as possible without scandal. We requested the prior to arrange and see to it that the Blessed Sacrament was placed in a vase, pyx, or other such vessel and set in a noticeable and prominent place above the altar or vicinity. This had never as yet been done, which amazed us. We received procuration there this day. They did not wish to compute.

SEPTEMBER 17. We came to the priory of St-Pierre-de-Saintény, and with God's grace we visited this place. There we found two monks from St-Nicolas-d'Angers. We enjoined them to celebrate Mass more frequently than was their practice and to observe the fasts of the Rule just as that Rule prescribes. They ate meat freely, and they had no scruples about it, as they said, because it was done with their abbot's knowledge. Alms are distributed three times[31] to all comers from the beginning of Lent to the feast of St. John the Baptist. As much was owed to them as they owed; they had many provisions. However, they considered themselves somewhat burdened by reason of the construction of a certain stone house, which they had just recently had built near the old hall.

Immediately after these things had been done and heard, on this same day, we went on to the priory at Marchézieux, where with God's help we made a visitation. There we found three monks from St-Paul-de-Cormery. They had no [copy of the] Rule; we ordered them to have one made and written out. From Christmas until the feast of St. Claire they were accustomed to give and distribute alms to all comers. With God's grace we found other things to be in good condition. More was owed to them than they owed.

[31] Probably weekly.

It is to be known that although we had, and can have, full procuration at any of the aforesaid priories, and we have in our own times [32] twice exacted and received it, nevertheless, since we had been summoned by the king of France, we strove to hasten the exercise of our visitation, and for this once we collected these two procurations as one, so that we received procuration at Marchézieux at one and the same time from the local prior [of Marchézieux] and from the priory of Saintény. For the above reason we remitted it to them this day. Total for procuration: . . . [*lacuna in MS*].

This day at Marchézieux Master Geoffrey, former rector of the church at Belleville, resigned this church into our hands.

SEPTEMBER 18. We visited the abbey at St-Lô, where there were twenty-four monks.[33] We gave orders that lay folk be kept away from the cloister. Many of them had keys to their coffers; we enjoined the abbot to remove and by all means take these away lest the canons have property. Alms are given thrice a week to all comers. However, they told us that the number of the poor was increasing and that they came there in streams, so that they were very often compelled to withdraw their hand, since the supplies devoted to charity were not sufficient. With God's grace we found other things to be in good condition. They owed forty pounds to the lord bishop of Coutances, which sum he had loaned them to pay off their tithe.[34] We received procuration there this day. Total for procuration: . . . [*lacuna in MS*].

SEPTEMBER 19. With God's grace we visited the priory at St-Fromond, after we had preached in the cloister to the monks and the parishioners of the parish whom we had had called to the sermon because it was Sunday. Thirteen monks of Cerisy were there; all were priests. Sometimes the refectory remained vacant, at which times the monks ate in the prior's chamber for recreation, as they said; this much displeased us. They wore linen shirts through want of woolen goods.[35] They owed sixty pounds. With God's grace we found other things to be in good condition. We expressly ordered

[32] See entries for September 1, 1250, and May 30, 1256.

[33] This is a scribe's or clerk's mistake, because St-Lô was an abbey of canons of St. Augustine.

[34] Probably the tenth levied by Pope Innocent IV in 1245 for the Crusade of Louis IX.

[35] Another probable reference to the Barons' War in England. Because of the internal conflicts, England had ceased to export wool to the continent. See entry for September 6, above.

the prior to collect the monks' keys and inspect their coffers frequently, and not to permit them to have any private possessions. We received procuration there this day. Total for procuration: ... [*lacuna in MS*].

We sent the following letter to our venerable brother J[ohn], by God's grace bishop of Coutances, regarding the case or affair of the priory of St-Germain-sur-Ay.[36]

Brother Eudes, by God's will the unworthy bishop of the church of Rouen, to his venerable brother and close friend J., by His grace bishop of Coutances, sends eternal greeting in the Lord Jesus Christ.

When by God's grace, in accord with the duty of our office, we were visiting the diocese of Coutances, we sent orders by letter and messengers to the prior of St-Germain in that diocese to prepare to receive us for our required exercise of visitation there upon a definite date. When we in person with God's help, arrived at that place on the vigil of the Nativity of the Blessed Virgin Mary last, the prior was nowhere to be found. We warned those whom he had left there to open the doors for us and receive us for visitation and procuration, since, as we stated before many witnesses, we were ready with God's help to do our duty. As we stood there, locked out and knocking for admission, they absolutely refused to do this and denied us admission. Hence we were compelled to go into the town and spend the night there at our own expense. On the morning of the following day we again went in person to that priory and, as the prior was still absent and the doors still locked, we requested once more of those who were within, representing the aforementioned prior, that the doors be opened and that we be received. We proclaimed formally in the presence of many that we were ready to fulfull our duty of visitation. We warned them in addition that they should, as part of and in the name of procuration, make up for the expenses incurred by us and our staff on that occasion.

We are unwilling to close our eyes to such impertinence and contemptuousness deliberately shown towards us and the church of Rouen; moreover, it is our duty not to do so. This is particularly true since the prior of that same place on another occasion,[37] in the presence of the abbot of the monastery of St-Michel, of which this priory is known to be a dependency, made amends to us for having once before refused to admit us for visitation, and also made satisfaction in the matter of our procuration, as is well known by many. Hence we order you, either personally or through a representative, to inform the aforementioned prior that he must appear before us before next Michaelmas to make amends

[36] See entry for September 7, above.
[37] See entries for May 20 and June 1, 1256.

for the foregoing and pay us for the expenses we incurred on that occasion at St-Germain-sur-Ay. If, after having been properly notified, he fails to do this, we hereby in writing declare him suspended as of that date, and you shall denounce him as suspended and you shall make public proclamation of that denunciation.

You shall, by your letter patent, inform us of whatever steps you take in this matter. Issued at Pont-Unvie, in the year of our Lord 1266, within the octave of the Nativity of the Blessed Virgin Mary.

SEPTEMBER 20. In the early hours of the morning, just as we were about to leave the priory of St-Fromond, brother Ralph, called Brasart, prior of the above mentioned St-Germain-sur-Ay, arrived in our presence and gave us a letter sealed with the seal of the abbot and convent of St-Michel. It read as follows:

To the Reverend Father in Christ and beloved Lord Eudes, by God's grace archbishop of Rouen, brother Nicholas, by Divine dispensation the unworthy abbot of Mont-St-Michel-in Peril-of-the-Sea together with the whole community of that same place, [send] greetings and respects in all reverence and honor.

Whereas, as we have been informed, your venerable Paternity desires to press for and exact, as part of visitation, procuration from the custodian of our manor at St-Germain-sur-Ay, we, respectfully beseeching your Paternity, humbly ask you to withdraw, out of fairness, this demand, since neither you nor your predecessors have ever in times past collected anything at that manor under such a pretext, and we are not aware that you have any right to receive anything for such a reason. The holdings and incomes of that manor were long ago designated by the donors for the common support of our community, as can be clearly shown by our documents and charters.

We, however, have the highest respect for your magnanimity and your unimpeachable and saintly virtue, the fame whereof has spread to the Orient and to the furthest climes of the world. We have neither the desire nor the right to grieve your generous soul in any way or to provoke you to anger in any degree whatsoever. We unanimously wish and have agreed upon this that you have an inquiry made by trustworthy men—men who, as contemplators of the Godhead, are illumined by the light of the truth—to determine whether or not you possess the right to receive such procuration in that manor. For be it known to your venerable Paternity that we hold and ever will hold as approved and acceptable whatsoever you and brother Ralph, called Brasart, the custodian of that manor and our appointed representative in this affair, determine as proper. We promise to accept your decision in all good faith and leave the entire matter up to your generosity and good judgment. To you and to all interested parties we attest this by this letter sealed with the seal of our communiy. May your venerable Paternity flourish long and happily. Issued on the Saturday after the feast of the Exaltation of the Holy Cross, in the year of our Lord 1266, in the month of September.

The said Ralph Brasart agreed and freely consented that we should make the determination for both of us as to what might and ought be done. As proctor and prior of the place involved, he gave his word in good faith that he would regard as approved and acceptable, and would strictly hold to, whatever action or determination we decided upon in this matter. Present were Master William of Flavacourt, the archdeacon of Petit-Caux in the church of Rouen; John of Jumièges; Brother Gervaise of Neaufles of the Minorite Order; Robert of Agy and Roger of St-Quentin, monks of Cérisy who were then staying at the priory of St-Fromond; and Robert of Senlis and John Morgneval, clerks of the said Father [Eudes]. When these things had been completed, we left there early in the morning, to wit, on the nineteenth day of September,[38] and were that day at Douvres, in the manor of the lord bishop of Bayeux, and at his expense.

La Bloutière is a priory of St-Augustine located near Deauville; we did not go there, because of the meagerness of the priory's income.

St-Nicolas-de-Bois-Roger is a priory of Cormery located near Coutances; we did not go there either, because of its poverty.

Savigny is a priory of Ste-Barbe located near Coutances; likewise we did not visit it or receive procuration there, because of its poverty.

SEPTEMBER 21. At Carbon.[39] SEPTEMBER 22. At Bernay, at the abbey, and at our expense. SEPTEMBER 23. At Pinterville. SEPTEMBER 24. At Vernon. SEPTEMBER 25. At St-Côme, near Meulan. SEPTEMBER 26-27. At Pontoise, with the king. SEPTEMBER 28. At St-Germain-en-Laye. SEPTEMBER 29. At Mantes. SEPTEMBER 30. At Gaillon, to wit, on the feast of St. Michael. OCTOBER 1. At Pinterville. OCTOBER 2. At Bonport. OCTOBER 3. At Rouen. OCTOBER 4. At Rouen. Here we celebrated the feast of St. Francis, and we had the chapter [of the cathedral] with us.

OCTOBER 5. At Ste-Catherine-sur-Mont, at our own expense. This day Ralph Mauconduit, rector of the church at Blosville, who for almost a year

[38] The clerk made the entry on the next day, September 20.

[39] O. Darlington, (*The Travels of Odo Rigaud* [Philadelphia, 1940]), in his map for Eudes' travels in 1266, identifies *Pontes Corbonios* as Cabourg on the Channel. On the other hand, Carbon on the Vie, between Troarn and Cambrèmer, is a more likely translation and is on a much shorter route from Douvres to Bernay.

and more had been excommunicated by us for many acts of contumacy, who had not presented himself for Holy Orders, and who had broken into a grange in which his goods were stored and had seized them with violence, [goods] which we had had sequestrated for the above reasons, appeared in person before us. Concerning all of the above he submitted himself to our will, in the presence of those venerable men Master William of Flavacourt, the archdeacon of Petit-Caux; Master John of Jumièges, the bailiff of Ste-Catherine; Master William, called Perfect; John of Morgneval; and many others.

OCTOBER 6. We absolved the said Ralph from the above-mentioned excommunications. We enjoined him to have his church properly serviced and to satisfy us with twenty pounds, to wit, ten pounds before the feast of Saint Andrew, and the remaining ten pounds at the following Purification. This day we were at Frênes.

OCTOBER 7-8. At Frênes. OCTOBER 9. At the château in Gisors, at our own expense.

OCTOBER 10. We reconciled the churchyard at Bouconvillers,[40] celebrated Mass and preached there, with God's aid.

We spent the night at Ivry[-le-Temple] at the Templar's place, and at their expense because of the procuration which we should receive for dedicating their chapel.

OCTOBER 11. With God's grace we dedicated the said chapel, and we spent the night at the manor of Count Dommartin at Frênes-l'Aiquillon, at our own expense. OCTOBER 12. With God's grace we celebrated the synod of the French Vexin at Chaumont, in the priory at [Notre-Dame-] l'Aillerie, where we were then at our own expense.

OCTOBER 13. With God's grace we dedicated the church of the nuns at Gomerfontaine. We spent the night at Gisors at the king's castle, where the prior of St-Ouen-de-Gisors paid us seven pounds of Tours, the amount in which he is annually held to us for procuration, when, once a year, it happens

---

[40] A cemetery or churchyard is a sacred place blessed either by the bishop or his delegate. It is violated or polluted by a homicide which can be imputed to its perpetrator (a person bereft of his or her senses would not be imputable); the shedding of blood unjustly and in an appreciable quantity; sordid misuse, e.g., carrying out capital punishment; or burial of an infidel or an excommunicate. ("Cimitière," *Dict. de droit canon.*, III, 738-39.) The cemetery had to be re-blessed or reconciled before being used again for Christian burial. For the prayers used at reconciliation, see M. Andrieu, *Le Pontifical romain au moyen âge*, III, 604.

that we come to his place. The said prior is held to give us no more than the said seven pounds of Tours.

OCTOBER 14. At Frênes. OCTOBER 15-16. At Déville. OCTOBER 17. On the feast of St. Luke the Evangelist, at Déville. OCTOBER 18-20. At Déville. OCTOBER 21-22. At Bonport. OCTOBER 23. To wit, on the feast of St-Romain, at Pinterville. OCTOBER 24-25. At Pinterville. OCTOBER 26. At Gaillon. OCTOBER 27. At Vernon, with the king. OCTOBER 28. To wit, on the feast of SS. Simon and Jude, at the same. OCTOBER 29. At Vernon. OCTOBER 30. At Bonport. OCTOBER 31. At Rouen. NOVEMBER 1. To wit, on All Saints. With God's grace we celebrated the feast at Rouen. NOVEMBER 2. To wit, on All Souls. With God's grace we celebrated Mass at St. Matthew's at the monastery of the [Dominican] sisters, and spent the night at Déville. NOVEMBER 3-4. At Déville.

NOVEMBER 5. With God's grace we came to the cathedral at Rouen to exercise visitation. In the chapter house we preached in Latin to the canons, chaplains, and clerks-choral, and especially to the holders of benefices in the said church, whom we had collected there by means of a letter which we we had sent to the hebdomadary about this. When we had finished, we proceeded to make a visitation. We found that the canons and clerks-choral talk and gossip from stall to stall, and even from three stalls away, during the Divine Office. The psalms are raced through too hurriedly. We found some things connected with the treasurer's office which needed correction. The chaplains do not celebrate Mass often enough. Item, the chaplains and the clerks-choral quite frequently leave the choir before the completion of the Hour which has been begun. In the matter of personnel, we found many were defamed of incontinence, to wit, Burnet of Aubin, scandalously so; Visus Lupi, with several women; Dom Geoffrey of Soteville; Peter Pilate; Peter of Aulages; and Ralph the Englishman, chaplains all; and a certain clerk-choral named George. Item, Dom Robert, called Fish, of trading. Item, we found that two boys from Basse-Forme, to wit, Picard and Rage-en-Tête, frequented taverns and played dice. Item, the clerks-choral of St-Albano did not sleep together in their house, as they should. Item, we found Dom Gilbert, called Barrabas, priest and rector of St. Stephen's parish, many times defamed. It is said that he had kept his own niece for many years, that he is still keeping her, and that he has had children by her. He did not have his letter of ordination; he could not tell by whom of through whom he had been instituted in his cure; he was also defamed of trading; and he did not celebrate Mass often enough. He was too solitary, that is to say, familiar with few in the parish. We enjoined the rectors and the canons who were at the visitation to discipline the foregoing derelictions before the coming octave of Epiphany, or that otherwise we would stretch forth our hands in these matters, as we can do. We then besought our procuration from the chapter, by reason of the said visitation.

Note: Concerning the man charged with the cure of St-Etienne.

This day we spent the night at Déville.

NOVEMBER 6-8. At Déville. NOVEMBER 9. With God's grace we celebrated the holy synod at Rouen, and spent the night there. NOVEMBER 10. We held the synod of deans, and we had them with us in our upper chamber. NOVEMBER 11. To wit, on Martinmas. At Martot. NOVEMBER 12. At Pinterville. NOVEMBER 13. At Gaillon. NOVEMBER 14. At Mantes. NOVEMBER 15. At Poissy. NOVEMBER 16. At Paris. NOVEMBER 17. At Paris, because of the Parlement. NOVEMBER 18. At the same. Today we collated Master Nicholas of Pérrièrs to the church at Corny, and invested John of Morgneval with it, in the name and place of the said N[icholas]. NOVEMBER 19-22. At Paris, because of the Parlement. NOVEMBER 23. To wit, on the feast of St. Clement. At Paris. NOVEMBER 24. At Paris. NOVEMBER 25. On the feast of St. Catherine. With God's grace we celebrated Mass at the chapel of the Hospitalers for the benefit of the scholars of the Gallic Nation.[41] NOVEMBER 26-29. At Paris, because of the Parlement. NOVEMBER 30. On the feast of St. Andrew the Apostle. At Paris. DECEMBER 1-5. At Paris, because of the Parlement. DECEMBER 6. On the feast of St. Nicolas. At Paris, because of the Parlement. DECEMBER 7. At Paris. DECEMBER 8. On the Conception of the Blessed Mary. We celebrated Mass at St-Severin, on the feast day of the Norman Nation.[42] On Conception Day we conferred a prebend worth fifteen marks upon Master John, called de Gallande. DECEMBER 9. At Paris. DECEMBER 10. At Poissy. DECEMBER 11. We received procuration at Juziers. Total for procuration:. . . [lacuna in MS].

---

[41] The university was composed at that time of four "nations" (France, Picardy, Normandy, and England), each of which had its own special feast days. The scholars of France celebrated the Feast of St. Catherine in the chapel of the Hospitalers of St-Jacques-de-Haut-Pas.

[42] The Feast of the Immaculate Conception of the Virgin, often called the Feast of the Normans. See Robert Wace, L'Etablissement de la fête de la Conception Notre-Dame, dite la fête aux Normands (Caen, 1842); E. Vacandard, "Les Origines de la fête de la Conception dans le diocèse de Rouen et en Angleterre," Revue des questions

DECEMBER 12. With God's grace we visited this priory, where there were seven monks from St-Père-de-Chartres, to wit, John, prior; Geoffrey of Chartres; Bartholomew of Aulnay; Giles the Younger; William Bird; Stephen Lambert; and Lawrence of Chartres; all but Giles the Younger were priests. They did not observe the fasts of the Rule, and they sometimes ate meat when there was no need. Alms are given thrice a week to all comers. They owed about sixty pounds.

This day, to wit, on the feast of St. Lucy, we spent the night at Vernon.

DECEMBER 13. At Gaillon. DECEMBER 14. At Pinterville. [*No entry for December 15*]. DECEMBER 16. At Martot. DECEMBER 17. At Déville. DECEMBER 18. With God's Grace we conferred Holy Orders at the monastery of the Preachers at Rouen, dined with them this day, and spent the night at our manor in Rouen. DECEMBER 19. With God's grace we preached in Rouen cathedral and spent the night at Rouen.

DECEMBER 20. We dined with the Friars Minor at Rouen. This day Master Ph[ilip] of Val-Badone appeared before us and made amends for failing to present himself for Holy Orders. Master William of Porpicie stood as surety for his fine. We spent this night at Déville.

DECEMBER 21. To wit, on the feast of St. Thomas the Apostle. At Déville. DECEMBER 22. At the same. DECEMBER 23. With God's help we made our O[43] at the cathedral in Rouen.

DECEMBER 24. To wit, on the vigil of the Nativity of the Lord. With God's grace we visited the Hôtel-Dieu at Rouen, where eight canons, including the prior, were in residence; eight were in outside obediences; [there were] twenty-two sisters, three lay brothers, and eleven maidservants. We ordered the prior and the prioress to make frequent inspection of the coffers of the canons and of the sisters. The sisters should confess and receive Communion thirteen times a year. Item, we ordered the prior to have sermons preached to the infirm more frequently than had been the custom. They owed about fifty pounds; more was owed to them. We found Brother John, called Magnus, a canon, gravely defamed of incontinence; we also learned that he had behaved badly at Foville and at Hotot, living in incontinence and, contrary to the Rule, carrying things away from the house. We ordered him to

---

historiques, LXI, (1897), 166. Each year, on December 8, the Norman students attended Mass at St-Severin in honor of their patroness.

[43] See above, December 23, 1250, n. 135.

undergo canonical purgation for this before the coming Purification of the Blessed Mary, and we ordered the prior to send him to Mont-aux-Malades, to stay there until the said Purification, and to purge himself in the meantime.

DECEMBER 25. With God's grace we celebrated the feast of the Nativity at Rouen. This day we conferred upon Master Enguerrand of Etrépagny the prebend in the Rouen church which had previously been held by William, the penitencer.

DECEMBER 26-27. At Déville.

DECEMBER 28. On the feast of the Innocents, at Déville. At this time we exchanged with Master Ralph of Cottévrard the prebend[44] which had belonged to Master Adam Rigaud, for the fruits of the prebend which the said R[alph] held at Vicy, and which we likewise exchanged with Master Robert Malet for the fruits of the prebend which he held.

DECEMBER 29. At St-Wandrille, at our own expense.

DECEMBER 30. With God's grace we preached in the chapter house and then visited the abbey. Forty monks were in residence; twenty-three were in outside priories, and two at the Roman Curia; all but six of those in residence were priests. At a preceding visitation we had ordered,[45] with the common consent of the abbot and community, that the kitchener should receive the rents set aside and appropriated to the infirmary and should provide the sick with all the necessities; however, this ordinance has not yet been observed. They owed about five hundred pounds; they believed that they had sufficient provisions to last out the year. With God's grace we found other things to be in good condition. Finally, we requested the abbot to behave more courteously towards the monks, inviting the less healthy and weaker ones to him, as well as those whom he thought needed recreation. Item, that he be more solicitious about advancing the work of his monastery than he had been by giving more liberally than he had done. We received procuration there this day. Total for procuration: ... [lacuna in MS].

DECEMBER 31. At Le Valasse, a Cistercian house, at the expense of the abbey. JANUARY 1. To wit, on the Circumcision of the Lord. We preached at St-Denis at Lillebonne. JANUARY 2. We received procuration at Graville. Total for procuration: eight pounds, sixteen shillings.

JANUARY 3. With God's grace we visited this priory, where eleven canons

---

[44] See entry for November 16, 1265.
[45] See entry for October 19, 1263.

were in residence; eight [were] outside; we ordered the prior to increase the number of resident canons. One does not accuse another [in chapter]; we ordered them to correct this, as we have done on several occasions.[46] Item, that the prior inspect the canons' coffers more often than was his practice. They owed two hundred fifty pounds of Tours and had sufficient supplies to last the year.

This day we conferred the church at St-Machaut upon Master John of Aumerville. We were at Montivilliers today, at our own expense.

JANUARY 4. With God's grace we visited this abbey, after we had with His aid preached a sermon in the chapter house. Sixty-one nuns were in residence; sixty should be the certain number, but the legate had established one there, to wit, the daughter of Thibaut Maurice, a sergeant of the king. They should confess and receive Communion at least once a month. As we had done before,[47] we forbade them to let their hair or tresses grow or to wear palisses of squirrel or of vair, or metaled belts too intricately wrought. Item, we ordered the abbess and the prioress to inspect the nuns' coffers more often than was the practice. Item, we issued orders that the fragments left over from the refectory or infirmary be collected and preserved more carefully and better than had been the case. Alms are given thrice a week to all comers. However, the abbess is held to maintain thirteen poor people every day, because of the old custom of Alice, a [former] abbess. Item, since we discovered that when some of the nuns happen to be admitted to the infirmary for recreation or for slight infirmities, they were accustomed to eat separately and in little gatherings, we forbade this practice for the future, and ordered them to eat together. More was owed to them than they owe. Item, we ordered the abbess to have the pelisses and garments of the nuns carefully repaired and to equip them with more suitable ones. We ordered them to get more workmen than were there, for we found them deficient in this respect. We received procuration there this day.

JANUARY 5. We received procuration at Valmont. Total for procuration: ... [lacune in MS].

JANUARY 6. To wit, on Epiphany. With God's grace we celebrated High Mass, preached, and visited the aforesaid abbey. In residence were twenty-five monks and two simple[-minded] ones; two were in England; two were outside at a certain obedience in Normandy; and one was with the lord of

---

[46] See entries for January 11, 1260/61; May 8, 1265.
[47] See entry for May 9, 1265.

Etoutteville. One did not accuse another [in chapter]; we ordered this corrected. Item, as we had done before,[48] we issued express orders that the Statutes of Pope Gregory be read out in chapter more often than had been the case. Item, we ordered the abbot, when he made his audits, to have the prior or some other person from the community with him. Two hundred pounds was owed to them, and they owed one hundred pounds; they had sufficient supplies to last out the year. We were there this day at our own expense.

JANUARY 7. With God's grace we reconciled the church at Carville, [Ricarville?] in the deanery of Fauville, which had been violated by the shedding of blood.

This day with God's aid we came to the priory or house at Etoutteville, and we found the place in very bad condition as to both temporals and spirituals. Two monks from Lewes were there. They had only twenty shillings a week for their maintenance. We received procuration this same day at the priory at Ouville from Nicholas, priest at Etoutteville, Robert le Nosdier, and William Pencier, who were then the lessees of the said house. Total for procuration: ten pounds, nine pence.

JANUARY 8. Established by God's grace in the priory at Ouville, because we had found the priory at Etoutteville in a ruinous condition and almost destitute of any provender, we enjoined the said lessees, by the oath which they took in our presence, not to pay Master Gilbert of Vauville, who held the said house for life, the one hundred eighty pounds in which they were held to him each year by reason of the said lease. Nor were they to give anything to anyone from now on, except that which the two monks who are living there should have. In addition there should be given the ten pounds, nine pence for our procuration, plus, in accord with existing agreements, whatever should be put aside for the repair of the said manor.

This day with God's grace we visited the priory at Ouville, where there were ten canons in residence. One did not accuse another [in chapter]. At a precious visitation[49] we ordered the prior to provide the community with an ordinal which they needed badly. He has failed to do this, and we ordered him again [to do so]. Item, we ordered him to remove the keys [from the coffers of the canons]. Item, we ordered Brother John of Avremesnil to inscribe the house income in two books, of which the prior should have one and some one elected by the community the other. They owed one hundred

---

[48] See entry for May 15, 1265.
[49] See entry for May 19, 1265.

twenty pounds; with the exception of beverages, to wit, wine and beer, they had sufficient supplies to last out the year. We received procuration there this day. Total for procuration: ten pounds, five shillings.

JANUARY 9-13. At Aliermont. JANUARY 14. At the same. This day there appeared before us the excommunicate, John of Etrans, esquire, who, in the hardness of his heart, had remained for a long time in a state of excommunication. He had hindered and disturbed the church at Etrans, the advowson to which is known to pertain to us, and to which we collate as we wish, so that any one instituted by us may reside there in person. At long last, however, with change of heart he besought the benefit of absolution for himself. We enjoined him to make a [penitential] appearance in the cathedral at Rouen and another in the church at Etrans, on two Sundays or feast days, with naked feet, clad only in a shirt and trunk hose, carrying rods of punishment in his hands, and publicly confessing his offense [while] asking to be disciplined. Nevertheless, we gave him the cross, which he requested with humility and devoutness.

JANUARY 15-19. At Aliermont.

JANUARY 20. On the feast of SS. Fabian and Sebastian. This day with God's grace we visited the house at Wanchy, administered Confirmation at the local parish church, and spent the night at Aliermont, where we received procuration from Richard Boullon, the lessee of Wanchy. Total: ten pounds, six shillings, three pence.

JANUARY 21. We received procuration at Bures. Total for procuration: eight pounds, six shillings.

JANUARY 22. With God's grace we visited this priory, where there were two monks from Pré. One of them managed the house as prior and held this office from the prior of Pré and at the will of the said prior. There should always be two monks there. They ate meat and used feather beds; they did not observe the statutes of the Rule in these matters nor in the matter of the fasts. Alms are given thrice a week to all comers. They owed nothing, and similarly nothing was owed to them, since they are held to remit to the prior of Pré whatever remains to them beyond their own sustenance and that of their familiars.

This same day with God's grace we came to the priory of nuns at St-Saëns, where we first of all preached and then made a visitation. Eighteen nuns were in residence. There was one very young novice. Petronilla of Dreux, the cellaress, was many times defamed of Ralph, a laborer who had worked for them at harvest time. They owed about one hundred pounds. With God's grace we found other things to be in good condition. This day we were at the monks' priory, at our own expense.

JANUARY 23. With God's grace we preached and administered Confirmation in the local parish church. Total for procuration: nine pounds, ten shillings.

JANUARY 24. With God's grace we visited the said priory, where there were four monks of St-Wandrille, to wit, Brother Herbert, prior, and Brothers Ralph of Manteville, William of Parc-d'Anxtot, and Roger of Lympeville. They used feather beds and ate meat when there was no need, and, as they said, with their abbot's knowledge. The prior rarely celebrated Mass. More was owed to them than they owed.

We were at Déville this day, at our own expense.

JANUARY 25. To wit, on the Conversion of Saint Paul. At Déville. JANUARY 26-28. At Martot. JANUARY 29-31. At Pinterville. FEBRUARY 1. At Gaillon. FEBRUARY 2. To wit, on the Purification of the Blessed Mary. With God's grace we celebrated Mass, preached in the church of the canons at Caillon, and were at our château[50] this day. FEBRUARY 3. We received procuration at Gasny. Total for procuration: eight pounds.

FEBRUARY 4. With God's grace, and in the presence of the abbot of St-Ouen-de-Rouen, we visited the priory at Gasny. Here in the manor adjoining the local parish church, where we were accustomed to receive procuration, were three monks of St-Ouen-de-Rouen, to wit, Brother John of Fontaine-en-Bray, prior, Brother Geoffrey of Noinville, and Brother John of Beauvais; they resided across the river in the priory of St-Nicaise. They quite often said their Hours without modulation.[51] They did not observe the fasts of the Rule; they ate meat when there was no need. We ordered the prior to be mindful to celebrate Mass more often than was his practice. Item, we ordered him to ask for and receive the old clothes of the monks when he provided them with new ones. Item, we expressly ordered him to have some suitable repository made wherein the Blessed Sacrament might be reverently and honorably placed above the altar, or nearby, and that the wafer be renewed every Sunday. They did not perform any part of the Divine Office in the manor where we were accustomed to be received, but kept a large staff there and food for the animals. They had provisions in plenty; they owed

[50] At Gaillon.
[51] See above, July 9, 1249, n. 36.

nothing, and nothing was owed to them, since they were held to remit to the abbey whatever surplus remained over and above their own sustenance and that of their staff. We received procuration this day at Vesly. Total for procuration: seven pounds, sixteen shillings.

FEBRUARY 5. We received procuration at Chaumont-en-l'Aillerie. Total for procuration: eight pounds, five shillings.

FEBRUARY 6. With God's grace we visited the said priory, where there were three monks from St-Germer-de-Flay, to wit, Brother Peter of Osmont, the abbot's nephew and the new prior, Brother John of Chaumont, and Brother William of St-Germer. They did not observe the fasts of the Rule; giving their guests as a reason, they ate meat when there was no need. Ever-since the days of Prior Peter the house had been heavily burdened and oppressed with many debts. A general distribution of alms is made twice a week, that is to say, to all comers at a stated hour. They owed two hundred twenty pounds; they had sufficient supplies to last the year. The roof of the bell tower for many years had been so out of shape and so badly in need of repair that, through leaks, the timbers and vaults of the building were in danger. No counsel had as yet been taken about this, although we had several times issued orders[52] through the archdeacon that repairs be made. We should have the archdeacon compel the parishioners to contribute according to each one's obligation.

This day with God's grace we celebrated a parish Mass at Sérans, and we confirmed there. We were there at our own expense, except that we received from the prior seventy shillings of Paris, which in addition to wood and other things we are entitled to receive once a year, whensoever we turn aside to this place, as is contained in the charter.[53]

FEBRUARY 7. With God's grace we visited the said priory. We found it miserably out of order. Two monks of St-Germer-de-Flay were there: Brother Adam of Omericourt, prior, and Brother Adam of Breteuil. They did not observe the fasts of the Rule; they ate meat when there was no need. The prior rarely or never celebrated Mass; we ordered him to be mindful to celebrate Mass more often than was his practice. They owed two hundred eighty pounds and fifteen *muids* of wheat and oats; they had few provisions.

This same day with God's grace we visited the priory at Parnes, where

[52] See entry for October 27, 1265.
[53] The charter is contained in Bonnin, p. 776, dated the Friday after the Nativity of St. John the Baptist, 1227.

there were four monks of St-Evroult, to wit, Brother William of Neuf-marché, prior, Nicholas, called "The Orphan," John of Prêtreville, and John of Duclair. They observed the fasts of the Rule fairly well, except that they ate meat occasionally during the period of the Great Fast.[54] They owed sixty-four pounds. With God's grace we found other things to be in good condition. We received procuration there this day. Total for procuration: eight pounds, twelve shillings.

FEBRUARY 8. At Frênes, at our own expense.

FEBRUARY 9. With God's grace we reconciled the churchyard at Notre-Dame-des-Andelys, which had been violated by the shedding of blood. Immediately afterwards, with His aid, we preached in the upper chamber of our manor which adjoins this church, to the canons, chaplains, and clerks-choral of the said church, who were standing there before us. Six canons are there, of whom four keep residence, to wit, Dom John Muids, who was at this time seriously ill, Master Ralph of Salmonville, and Master John, called of Spain [Yspanne]. The fourth one, Master Peter Ferentino, was at Rome; the fifth was Master Simon, the official of Pontoise, and Henry, our almoner, was the sixth. There were four priests-vicars, one of whom must serve continually in the church at La Culture, and these four are obliged to bear the burdens of the parish. Two other vicars were there, one a deacon, the other a subdeacon, and these are bound to vest themselves for High Mass every day. The dean has the cure of the canons, chaplains, and clerks-choral of the community, as well as of all the men of the town and some of the adjacent villages. The sacristan must always sleep in the vestry and is obliged to keep the song schools. They did not have enough books. We learned that some of them had disturbed the Divine Office by scoffing and murmurs in choir, from which we enjoined all of them at large to abstain. Item, [we ordered] that they should show more reverence to the dean than they had done, and that they should obey him as they ought to do. John Glazer, a deacon, was not in the habit of confessing to the dean, nor had he ever asked his permission to confess to anyone else; we warned him to correct this. Item, we ordered Dom Peter Robillart to get rid of a certain unworthy Breton cleric, who was serving him in the church at La Culture, and to put another and more circumspect one there. Item, we gave them permission to have a cemetery in the fields where they might bury the bodies of those who lived in the parish or at the Hôtel-Dieu. Item, it was enacted with their common

[54] From September 14 to Easter.

consent that the community wine and wheat might be sold as soon as it has been gathered in, so that the proctor of the community might be able to pay each one his daily stipend, as should be done. Item, it was [also] enacted that the canons should not pay anything in the dean's court for the use of the seal for their own business or for business pertaining to the community. We forbade them to permit women to dine with them.

This day we spent the night at Frênes, at our own expense.

FEBRUARY 10. We received procuration at Ste-Catherine, above Rouen. Total for procuration: nine pounds, twelve shillings.

FEBRUARY 11. With God's grace we visited the said abbey, after we had, with His aid, first preached in the chapter house. Thirty monks were in residence; two were scholars at Paris; fourteen were at Blyth priory in England, and some were at other places in Normandy; two were at Hermansworth, in England;[55] all but two of the residents were priests. Individual accounts were made up ordinarily once a month in the presence of seniors, elected by the community. More was owed to them then they owed. With God's grace we found other things to be in good condition.

We received procuration this day at St-Lô[-de-Rouen].

FEBRUARY 12. With God's grace we visited this priory after we had, with His aid, preached in the chapter house. Eighteen canons, including the prior, were in residence; three of these were novices. One blind canon was in the infirmary, two were at Cressy, and two at Thémericourt. They owed four hundred pounds; they had supplies and many provisions for the year. With God's grace we found other things to be in good condition. Total for procuration: nine pounds, sixteen shillings.

We were at our manor in Rouen, at our own expense.

FEBRUARY 13. To wit, on Septuagesima. We preached in Rouen cathedral and were, this day, at our [manor] in Rouen, and at our own expense.

FEBRUARY 14-17. At Martot. FEBRUARY 18. We received procuration at Noyon-sur-Andelle. Total for procuration: ... [lacuna in MS].

FEBRUARY 19. With God's grace we visited this priory, where there were six monks of St-Evroult, to wit, Brother Jordan, prior, and Brothers Thomas of Silly, Master Thomas Surde, John of Bos-Yon, Robert of Manly, and Hugh of Breteuil. They sometimes ate meat when there was no need. They owed about two hundred pounds, and to their abbot sixty pounds, saving ten marks sterling which he had received out of this. They had sufficient sup-

---

[55] In Middlesex.

plies to last out the year. With God's grace we found other things to be in good condition. The prior had lately arrived there. We received procuration this day at Pérrièrs from the lessee there. Total for procuration: ... [*lacuna in Ms.*].

FEBRUARY 20. We preached and administered Confirmation in the church at Grainville, and spent the night at Magny. FEBRUARY 21. At Magny. FEBRUARY 22. At Pontoise, to wit, on the feast of St. Peter's Chair [of Antioch], at our own expense.

FEBRUARY 23. With God's grace we visited St. Peter's priory, where there were six monks of Bec-Hellouin, to wit, Brother William of St-Cloud-en-Alvia, prior, and Brothers Philip of Chambly, William of Noinville, Richard of Hurel, who was a paralytic, Geoffrey of Angeville, and Peter of Mesnil; all were priests. With God's grace we found the house to be in good condition, as to both spirituals and temporals. However, they owed about ten pounds.

This day with God's grace we visited the Hôtel-Dieu at Pontoise, after we had preached a sermon there. Here we found a certain secular priest, appointed by the king as rector and master of the house, to wit, Dom John of Fenins,[56] a canon of St-Mellon, who is bound to take counsel with the prioress concerning the administration of the goods of the said house. Fourteen sisters were there, two priests, dressed as regulars, and one other priest who celebrated Mass in the chapel at the château. The said two priests had not yet made profession of a Rule, nor did they know what Rule to follow. With their consent and that of the prioress, we instructed them to wear a white tunic or a white costume under their surplices, and a black cape over them; we must talk with the king about the Rule under which they should live. The sisters should conduct themselves according to the Rule of St. Augustine, and they have taken the three vows. The said Master had the cure of all the souls inhabiting the said house, as well those of the healthy as those of the infirm. They owed one hundred pounds of Paris to Sir Geoffrey of Chapelle, knight, because of a certain purchase, and another fifty pounds in the town.

We spent this night at St. Martin's, at our own expense.

FEBRUARY 24. To wit, on the feast of St. Matthew the Apostle. We celebrated High Mass at St-Mellon and preached to the canons, chaplains, and vicars then resident in the said community. This done, we came to a certain

---

[56] See entry for January 27, 1265/66.

house near the church in which the canons, as of custom, held their chapter. We proceeded to visit the said canons, chaplains, and vicars gathered there in front of us. We found one resident canon there, to wit, Dom John of Fennins, the rector of the local Hôtel-Dieu; the dean was absent. We discovered a great lack of altar cloths, albs, and rochets; wherefore, we ordered Master Simon, our vicar who was then present, to seize so much of the canons' goods as would provide the community with these things. Item, the roof and the glass above the altar of St. John were in need of repair, and we ordered repairs for these. Item, the vicars and chaplains complained to us that the priests at St-Maclou and St-André did not come to St-Mellon to sing, as is customary, the Collects on the saint's feast day as they were held to do, or to sing the Third Response;[57] we ordered our vicar[58] to find out just what this was about. The deans and the canons were in litigation with the vicars about the house which is called the chapter house. A great contention has arisen amongst them about this before the official of Soissons, referred there through a letter of the lord legate. On the authority of this letter the dean and the canons had dragged the vicars thither into a lawsuit. This displeased us greatly. We ordered the deans and the canons to desist from a nuisance of this kind and to have the case tried before our vicar.

This day we were at St. Martin's, where we received one hundred shillings of Paris from the chapter of St-Mellon, in which amount they are annually held to us for procuration when we visit their church; in addition they are held to supply us with furnished quarters, beds, cups, dishes, pots, and the usual cooking utensils.

FEBRUARY 25. With God's grace we came to the priory at Liancourt, where we should receive each year for procuration four pounds of Paris, together with quarters and domestic utensils. We spent the night there.

FEBRUARY 26. With God's grace we visited the said priory, which we found to be miserably marred in both temporals and spirituals. Three monks of St-Père-de-Chartres were there, to wit, Brother Philip of Fontenay, prior, Brother Geoffrey of St-Martin, and Brother Matthew of Alone. The prior had been excommunicated for failure to pay the tithes,[59] and the other two

---

[57] That is, they were not present at the third nocturn of the office, at Matins.

[58] Pontoise, until an agreement was reached between Eudes and Louis IX, was a royal benefice. Eudes appointed an archdeacon to administer the newly acquired archdeaconry and gave him powers to act in his own stead, or as "our vicar." (Andrieu-Guitrancourt, *Archevêque Eudes Rigaud*, pp. 350-64.)

[59] The tithes levied to defray the expenses of the Crusade of Louis IX.

aforesaid had conducted and were still conducting themselves in everything quite unbecomingly and in a manner not in accord with their vocation as religious. We wrote to the abbot about recalling them to the cloister and about sending some others who should be more mature and of better lives than these. They did nothing so far as the Divine Office was concerned. They owed two hundred pounds; they had few provisions. This day we spent the night at Etrépagny, at the manor of the lord of Dangu, and at our expense.

FEBRUARY 27-28. At Frênes. MARCH 1. At Ste-Catherine, at our own expense. MARCH 2. To wit, on Ash Wednesday. With God's grace we celebrated the Office of the day at the cathedral in Rouen, and spent the night at our manor. MARCH 3-4. At Déville. MARCH 5. At Rouen. MARCH 6. To wit, the First Sunday in Lent. With God's grace we preached at the cathedral in Rouen, and spent the night at our manor. MARCH 7. At Déville. MARCH 8. With God's grace we visited the priory of nuns at Bondeville, after we had first preached, with His aid, in the chapter house. Here were thirty choir nuns, four lay sisters, and three lay brothers. In their custody, as it were, there were some young girls, daughters of burghers of Rouen, which displeased us; two priest in the garb of religious were there, and four secular maidservants. Item, we were displeased that some of the nuns often foregathered in the bakery. They owed about one hundred thirty pounds; sixty pounds was owed to them. They had supplies to last out the year, as they said. The prioress accepted her punishment for having, against our orders to the contrary, allowed [them] to eat and assemble in the bakery,[60] and we enjoined penance upon her for this, as well as for the fact that she had, without our special permission, received a certain girl, to wit, Jeannette, sister of Adolf of Gueures, esquire, although she had not as yet received the veil; we forbade her to be veiled without our special permission. Also, as we had done before,[61] we forbade them to receive anyone without our knowledge and consent. We ordered them to send away that woman of Rouen, to wit, Laurentia, called "Four Men."

This day we spent the night at Déville, at our own expense.

MARCH 9. We received procuration at Beaulieu. Total for procuration: eight shillings, two pence.

MARCH 10. With God's grace we visited this priory, where thirteen canons

---

[60] See entry for June 12, 1255.
[61] This probably refers to the entry for September 20, 1261.

were in residence; all were priests; ten were outside in obediences. We forbade lay folk to talk with the canons in the cloister. There were two lay brothers, one of whom was overly given to wine and drunkenness; there was one lay sister. A general distribution of alms is made thrice a week to all comers. They owed four hundred fifty pounds, fourteen of this at interest. They had almost enough wheat and oats to last out the year. One canon was with the lord of Pré.

This day, with God's grace we were at Martot.

MARCH 11. At Martot. MARCH 12. With God's aid we conferred Holy Orders at the royal chapel at Pont-de-l'Arche, and we spent the night at Martot. To wit, on the feast of St. Gregory. MARCH 13. With God's grace we preached and administered Confirmation at Alizay, and spent the night at Martot. MARCH 14. At Pinterville. MARCH 15. At Gaillon. MARCH 16. We received procuration at Sausseuse. Total for procuration: seven pounds, nine shillings.

MARCH 17. With God's grace we visited the said priory, after we had first preached in the chapter house. Fifteen canons were in residence; of these five were novices, and all of the residents, with the exception of these five, were priests. One thing, however, displeased us, namely, that the canons remained there many years before they made profession. We ordered the prior to oblige every canon to make such profession after a year had elapsed, provided that he desired to remain there and his conduct was suitable. One lay brother and four lay sisters were there; fifteen canons were outside in obediences. Item, we ordered the prior to have all the books of the priory brought out once a year and displayed to the entire community in chapter. We ordered that they should try to get back the ones that had been loaned long enough to be conveyed to and viewed in chapter, and that each book be listed invididually in registers. A general distribution of alms is made there twice a week. They owed one hundred forty pounds; about three hundred pounds in good debts was owed to them. They have sufficient provisions to last out the year.

We received procuration this day at St-Martin-la-Garenne. Total for procuration: eight pounds, three shillings.

MARCH 18. With God's grace we visited the said priory, where there were four monks of Bec-Hellouin, to wit, Brother Ralph of Bretonne, prior, and Brothers Andrew of Rouen, Bartholomew of Meulan, and Geoffrey of Angeville; there ought to be at least five; all were priests. They did not observe the fasts of the Rule very well, and they sometimes ate meat when there was no need. A general distribution of alms is made there thrice a week. They owed sixty-five pounds, twenty-five of this to the abbot, the amount which the abbot had loaned the prior last year to improve the vineyard. In addition they still owed a large debt of long standing which they had owed to Abbot Robert, to wit, three hundred forty pounds. They had, as the prior thought, enough supplies to last the year.

This day with God's grace we came to the priory at Villarceaux, and there, after we had with His aid preached in the chapter house, we made a visitation. Twenty nuns were in residence, [and this was] below the certain and statutory number. However, one was there awaiting her turn, to wit, Perrote of Bosc-Asse, whom they had received with the permission and at the request of their abbess. Four lay sisters were there, and four general maidservants. There were also several secular girls under the custody, so to say, of certain nuns and this displeased us exceedingly. They owed one hundred pounds, and twenty pounds of this was owed at interest to the Jews and Cahorsins [*Catturcensibus*] of Mantes. If they are economical they have enough wheat and oats to last out the year, but they did not have enough wine. After a brief interval, we commanded and enjoined the prioress by letter to have each and every one of the secular girls sent away without fail before the octave of this coming Easter. We forbade her to admit or to permit the admission of any nun or nuns, any lay sister or lay sisters, in the future without our special permission, despite whatever mandate she may receive from the abbess of St-Cyr.[62] Item, we ordered her to have the bell rung twice each day, because by their Rule they are allowed to eat twice a day, that is to say, breakfeast and supper. In this way they are to assemble in the refectory at each ringing in a more suitable manner than they had been doing, for they often ate apart in chambers.

This day we spent the night at Wy, where we received from the priest at Gadancourt the *muid* of oats in which he is annually held to us, when we turn aside and spend the night at Wy.

MARCH 19. At Poissy. MARCH 20-24. At Paris.

MARCH 25. To wit, on the feast of the Annuncation of our Lady, at the same. This day the king of France and three of his children, to wit, my lords Philip, John, and Peter, together with many nobles of the realm of France, counts, barons, and also the countess of Flanders, took the Cross.

[62] Villarceaux was a dependent priory of St-Cyr. See Cottineau, II, 2646, 3381.

MARH 26-29. At Paris. MARCH 30. At St-Denis-la-Chausée. MARCH 31. At Conflans.

APRIL 1. At Clergy. APRIL 2. At Neufmarché, at our own expense. APRIL 3. At Beaubec. APRIL 4. At Grandcourt.

APRIL 5. At Eu. We came thither upon the complaint of many concerning the violent quarrel which had broken out between the abbot and community there. This day we were in the chapter, and we listened to a great many things which the community, or the greater part of it, said against the abbot.

APRIL 6. After we had considered those things which we had heard yesterday about the abbot, we ordained and decreed that the audits should be made in the presence of the prior and the subprior, and of two of the more mature and prudent brothers elected in common by the abbot and community. Item, that wine should be apportioned in suitable manner to the community. Item, that the cellarer shoud serve and minister to the community in a more polite and becoming fashion than he had been doing. Item, that a certain old lay brother be removed from the monks' infirmary. Item, that they should have the advice of physicians. Item, that the chamberlain be permitted to sell woodland only [to the value of] one hundred pounds of Paris. Item, that the two canons who had been sent to us at Paris by the community to treat of the foregoing not be molested. We also enjoined the abbot, and warned him secretly, to attend the community better than he had been doing and to behave with greater clemency towards the canons.

We were at Aliermont today.

APRIL 7. At Bellencombre, at our own expense. APRIL 8. At Déville. APRIL 9. At Rouen. APRIL 10. To wit, on Palm Sunday. With God's grace we took part in the processional at St-Gildard; we preached in the vestibule before the doors of the Rouen cathedral to a multitude of clerics and to a great body of the people gathered there, although by custom the sermon should have been delivered in the vestibule at St-Laurent. But we had returned to the cathedral because, by reason of the multitude of those present and of a badly erected platform, we could not have been easily heard at St-Laurent.

We dined with the Preachers [Dominicans] at Rouen and in their refectory. We spent this night at Déville.

APRIL 12. At Déville.

APRIL 13. We dined with the Friars Minor of Rouen, and spent the night at our manor in Rouen.

APRIL 14. To wit, Holy Thursday. With God's grace we performed the absolutions to be given on this day, and we celebrated the ceremonies of [the blessing of] the chrism at the cathedral. APRIL 15. To wit, on the day of the Passion and Death of the Lord. We celebrated this day's ceremonies in the cathedral. APRIL 16. We celebrated likewise this day's ceremonies there.

1267

APRIL 17. With God's grace we celebrated the holy feast of Easter at Rouen. APRIL 18-20. At Martot. APRIL 21. At Bec-Hellouin, at our own expense. APRIL 22. At Cormeilles, at our own expense. Here we entered the diocese of Bayeux. APRIL 23. At Val-Richer, a Cistercian house in the diocese of Bayeux, at the expense of the abbey.

APRIL 24. To wit, on the octave of Easter. With God's grace we preached in the chapter house of the abbey at Troarn, and visited. We found forty monks in residence; all but two were priests; one lay brother was there. In the outside priories they observed neither the fasts of the Rule nor the article concerning the eating of meat; we ordered these things corrected. A general distribution of alms is made every day to all comers from Holy Thursday to the feast of St. Clair, near the feast St. Mary Magdalene. They owed fifteen houndred pounds. We received procuration there this day. Total for procuration: nine pounds, sixteen shillings.

APRIL 25. To wit, on the feast of St. Mark. With God's grace we came to the abbey of St-Etienne at Caen, and after we had preached in chapter we made a visitation. We found seventy monks in residence; all were priests. Alms are given to all comers during the months of June and July. They owed four thousand pounds, three hundred of this at interest. We ordered them to confess more readily and frequently than was their practice. We received procuration from them this day.

APRIL 26. With God's grace we came to the church of St-Sépulcre, and after we had preached in the choir of this church we adjourned to a certain place below the church which is used for a chapter house. There with His aid we made a visitation. We found sixteen canons in residence, as well as a dean who has the cure of the canons and of all of chaplains and clerks-choral attending the church; no certain number of canons is there. This day we received procuration at the dean's house from the distributor of the chapter. Total for procuration: eleven pounds, six shillings.

APRIL 27. With God's grace we came to the monastery of nuns of the Holy Trinity [at Caen], where with His aid we preached in the chapter house, and proceeded to make a visitation. However, we were able to accomplish but little here, because there was no abbess. A great quarrel had divided them,[1] and there was litigation about this at Rome. We found that there were seventy-five nuns in residence and five outside. They performed the Hours in a confused and unworthy fashion, for one group was in the choir, and another group outside. They owed seventeen hundred pounds.

APRIL 28. With God's grace we came to the Hôtel-Dieu at Caen, and after we had preached we proceeded to make a visitation. There we found five canons, three of whom maintained continuous residence; the other two were serving outside in two churches. Ten weak and aged sisters were there, who, although they did not all wear the usual garb of religious, were held to live according to a Rule under obedience to the local prior, chastely and without property. However, since we found that they did not eat together in one place, but apart and in chambers, we ordered the prior to bring them to a common life so far as he could, to require them to eat and sleep together, and to give them a sufficient supply of things needful to them so that they should not have to buy or sell anything at all in the town. As they said, they had occasionally sold bonnets or firewood and such things in order to procure certain articles which they needed. The prior did not compute well enough, for rarely if ever did he draw up his statements of receipts and expenses in the presence of his canons, or of any one of them, nor of any burgher or burghers of the town, so that no one could know the state of the house, a thing which much displeased us. They had an income of two thousand pounds; they owed three hundred pounds, at which we were greatly amazed, for they had a large income and there were fewer persons there than usual. We ordered the prior to celebrate Mass more often than he had been doing and to cast his accounts in the presence of one or more of the canons of his house and in the presence of some of the burghers of the town.

We received procuration this day at the abbey of Ardenne, a Premonstratensian house near Caen, and at the expense of the abbey.

APRIL 29. We received procuration from the bishop of Bayeux at his manor at Bayeux.

APRIL 30. With God's grace we preached a sermon in Latin in the chapter house of the church at Bayeux to the canons in residence, the chaplains, and the clerks-choral who were gathered there. This ended, we made such visitation as we could, with His aid. We asked who had the cure of their souls;

---

[1] This refers to the disputed election of Beatrice. See entry for April 17, 1266.

some replied that it was the bishop, others said that it was the dean, so we could not be certain about it. The dean was with the legate[2] in England. The church has twelve dignitaries [officials], and forty-nine prebendaries. We found fault with the care of the clothing and with the ringing of the bells. Some complained that occasionally their choral capes were handed out to them in a dirty condition. They did not come to chapter often enough. There was a contention between some of them and the bishop concerning certain uses or usages (*usibus seu usagiis*) of the woodland at Neuilly. We received procuration from the chapter this day at the bishop's house. There was no computation.

MAY 1. To wit, on the feast of SS. Philip and James. With God's grace we came to the priory at Longues, near Bayeux. With God's aid we preached in chapter, and then we proceeded to make a visitation. We found ten monks staying there with the prior; two others were scholars, one at Avignon, the other at Orleans; each year these scholars receive as much as would sustain three monks in the said priory. We, realizing that the prior was burdened because of this, ordered the prior to get the abbot of St-Benigne-de-Dijon, to whom the said priory is subject, either to recall the said two monks from the schools and send them back to the priory, or else to make some other provision for their maintenance. Item, we ordered the prior to have observed that article [of the Statutes of Pope Gregory] concerning the eating of meat and the fasts. Because of the meagerness of the income, two monks were by themselves in two places, to wit, one at La Chapelle-de-Mesnil-Hameau, and the other at Lanfreville. We ordered the priests to celebrate Mass more frequently. We ordered those who were not priests to apply themselves more diligently to the Divine Office, and to confess and receive Communion more often. They had bed coverlets of squirrel fur, which displeased us. Item, we ordered the prior to make frequent inspection of the monks' coffers lest they have any property. Item, we ordered that when he gave out new clothes, he have the old ones turned in to him. He never computes with his community, but only once a year with the abbot at Dijon. They have an income of six hundred fifty pounds; they owed twelve hundred pounds. We received procuration there this day. Total for procuration: . . . [*lacuna in MS*].

MAY 2. We visited the abbey at Longues, where twenty monks were in residence; two were outside. There was a certain place called Carronges, in

---

[2] Cardinal Ottobuono Fieschi, who was in England as peacemaker, 1265-68. He later became Pope Hadrian V (1276).

the diocese of Séez, where there should be monks, but we found that the bishop had seized its income because there were no monks there. All but five of the monks who resided in the abbey were priests, and we ordered them to celebrate Mass more frequently and readily than had been their custom. Alms are distributed daily to all comers. They had, as they said, an income of five hundred pounds; they owed two hundred pounds. Item, we ordered the abbot to see to it that the sick were better taken care of than they had been. We received procuration from them this day. Total for procuration: ... [*lacuna in MS*].

MAY 3. With God's grace we came to the abbey at Cerisy, to wit, on the Finding of the Holy Cross, and with His aid we preached in chapter and proceeded to make a visitation. Thirty-two monks were in residence, and there were several in outside priories; all but seven of the residents were priests. We ordered the abbot to see that necessities were provided for the sick in better fashion than had been the case. More was owed to them than they owed. They had sufficient supplies to last the year. With God's grace we found the house in good condition. We received procuration there this day. Total for procuration: ... [*lacuna in MS*].

MAY 4. We were at Aunay, near Mont-Incote, at an abbey belonging to the Cistercian Order, at the expense of the abbey.

MAY 5. With God's grace we visited the priory at Le Désert, where there were six monks of Troarn, to wit, Brother Robert of Sagy, Hugh, called Larramée, John of Loncelles, John Pagan, Hugh of Alençon, and Richard Acarny; all were priests. They did not have any written [copy of the] Rule; we ordered them to have one written out. They and the parish priest had but one chalice; we ordered them to procure another for themselves. We forbade women to eat with them as they had previously done. We ordered them to observe the Rule in the eating of meat and in the matter of fasts. They owed forty pounds. We received procuration there this day. Total for procuration: eight pounds, eight shillings, eight pence.

MAY 6. To wit, on the feast of St. John before the Latin Gate. We were at Belle-Etoile, an abbey belonging to the Premonstratensian Order, and where, did we so desire, we could be at the expense of the monastery; but we desired to spare them this time, considering their devotion and the work which they were doing for the divine cult and for the betterment of the monastery. We received procuration there this day from the prior of La Lande-Patry.

On the said day with God's grace we came to the said priory at La Lande-Patry, where we found three monks of St-Vincent-du-Mans, to wit, Brother John of Celles, prior, Peter of Brièsche, and John of Vassy. They ate meat freely when there was no need; they did not observe the fasts of the Rule; we ordered this corrected. The prior did not sleep with the other monks, but in a certain lower hall, and this displeased us. The monastery or church was filled with wood and beams and boxes; we ordered them to get rid of material of this kind and to have the monastery kept more becomingly and cleanly than it had been. They had, as they said, an income of one hundred forty-nine pounds; they owed fifty-four pounds. They had provisions for the year. We did not spend the night there because the houses were not adequate to receive us and our staff conveniently, and so, at the prior's request, we returned to Belle-Etoile, where, as has been stated, the prior paid us our procuration. He admitted that he was held to us for full procuration. Total for procuration: seven pounds, fifteen shillings.

MAY 7. With God's grace we came to the priory at Le Plessis-Grimoult, and after we had with His grace preached in chapter, we made a visitation. Fourteen canons were there; there should be twenty, but six had died during the year. We ordered the prior to inspect the canons' coffers more often than was his practice. With God's grace we found the priory in good condition as to both temporals and spirituals. They had an income of fifteen hundred pounds; more than three hundred pounds was owed to them; they owed nothing and they had a large store of provisions. It was well with them, although they had expended a great deal on buildings. We received procuration there this day. Total for procuration: nine pounds, three shillings, nine pence.

MAY 8. With God's grace we visited the abbey at Le Val-Sainte-Marie, where twelve canons were in residence; one was a novice, several were in outside priories, and four were in England. We ordered the abbot to visit the overseas priories more often and in better fashion than he had done. Item, we gave orders to the abbot that at least once a week the entire Rule should be read out to the community. Item, we ordered the abbot to have each and every book belonging to the community recorded in some list or catalogue. Alms are given thrice a week to all comers. Item, we ordered that the novice should confess and receive Communion at least once a month. They owed four hundred pounds; they had an income of four hundred pounds. A certain canon was being kept there in prison. Sometimes he was

given to vociferation and unbridled vituperation and thus disturbed and
molested the community. We then ordered the abbot to put distance between
this simpleton and the community, and to have his prison constructed somewhere else. We received procuration there this day. Total for procuration:
seven pounds, sixteen shillings.

MAY 9. We were at the abbey at Barbery, a Cistercian house, at the expense
of the monastery, and we dined in the refectory with the community.

MAY 10. With God's grace we preached in the chapter house of the monastery at Fontenay, and then, as was fitting, we visited the community. Nineteen monks were in residence; one was in England. We gave orders that a
certain gate between the cloister and the courtyard be kept closed and better
watched, and that lay folk be kept away from the cloister. Item, we forbade
merchants to be admitted there in the future, as they had been in the past.
The monks in the priories ate meat; we ordered the abbot to visit them about
this. They owed four hundred pounds; they had an income of about twelve
hundred pounds. We received procuration from them this day. Total for
procuration: seven pounds, eight shillings.

MAY 11. At Beaumont-en-Auge, at our own expense. MAY 12. At Pont-
Audemer.

MAY 13. With God's grace we visited the abbey at Corneville, although a
year had not as yet elapsed since we had made a visitation there. We came
there at the abbot's request, because of a contention between him and Brother
Osbert, who was accusing the abbot of many crimes. We found that one did
not accuse another [in chapter]; we ordered the abbot to give his diligent
attention to this, and to punish him whom he knew was unwilling to accuse
a deliquent. Item, we ordered them to have all the books catologued in some
list or register, and to try to get back those which they had loaned. Master
William Bienvenu had a certain book of Decretals. We ordered the abbot
to appoint confessors for the canons, reserving certain cases for himself. The
Order's visitors[3] ordered that non-priest canons confess and receive Communion at least every two weeks. Brother Adam Picard had never confessed
to the abbot, nor had he asked his permission to confess to any other; we
ordered him to reform himself in this matter. Brother Henry Surde had conceived a hatred, and for a long time had maintained it, of one of the novices
and of Brother Robert, a fellow-canon who was a priest. This displeased us

---

[3] Corneville was a house of Augustinian canons and, as such, was visited by the
Order's officials.

much, and although at this visitation we caused them to be reconciled in full chapter, nevertheless we expressly ordered the said Henry to watch himself very carefully about this. Item, we ordered the abbot to see that better provision was made for the sick than had been the case. Item, we forbade him to allow lay folk to gossip in future in the cloister or to talk with the canons, as the former had been in the habit of doing. Item, we ordered that, inasmuch as he did not wish to have a bailiff, at all events he himself should strive to have his audits well and suitably drawn up in the presence of some of the seniors of the community. They owed two hundred pounds, of which the greater part was owed to the priest at Routot. Moreover, it should be known that Brother Osbert of Porte had mentioned certain things to us, or rather had repeated what he had stated to our official of Rouen, as is contained in a *libellus*[4] drawn up in the presence of the said official, namely, that they knew of certain crimes committed by the said abbot, Brother Nicholas of La Croix. Both the abbot and Brother Osbert willingly agreed in full chapter that we, in person or by some other one or more, should make a full investigation into the aforesaid crimes, calling upon anyone whom we desired, whether from the community or from outside, either religious or secular, and this without the publicity of a trial. If, in accordance with our judgment, we should find the said abbot culpable of the above-mentioned crimes or of any one of them, we would punish him as seemed expedient to us. Similarly, should we find, in our judgment, that the said Brother Osbert had charged the said abbot with any crime or crimes of which in our judgment we did not find him culpable, we would punish the said Brother O[sbert] as we should deem proper.[5] Present were Master G. [William], the archdeacon of Petit-Caux; Master John of Jumièges, a canon of Rouen; the priors of Bourg-Achard and of the hospital of St-Jean-de-Pont-Audemer; and Brothers Adam Rigaud, Nicholas of Hauteville, Master William Bienvenu, and Herbert, Robert and John, our clerks.

We received procuration this day, and on the following day we went away, with God's grace, leaving Master John of Jumièges there to make the aforesaid inquiries in our stead.

---

[4] The *libellus* was the first step in Roman and canonical court procedure. It is a written document wherein the demandant makes a brief of his demand and then presents it to the authorities.

[5] This is in accordance with the legal principle, *onus probandi incumbit ei qui dicit*: the burden of proof is on the plaintiff. See also Giry, ed., *Les Etablissements de Rouen*, II, Ch. 36. p. 43, for a like punishment in the secular court.

MAY 14. At Martot. MAY 15-20. At Déville, to attend the Rouen Exchequer. MAY 21. At Pinterville, where we had with us our venerable brothers O. [Eudes], by God's grace bishop of Bayeux; R[alph], by His grace bishop of Evreux; and Master Gerald of Poitou. MAY 22. At Vernon, where the king then was.

MAY 23. At the same. This day, on the authority of the lord legate, whose letter about this we had received, we absolved Sir Robert of Frênes, the viscount of Rouen, from the excommunication which he had incurred for detaining and laying hands upon Gilbert, a cleric. We enjoined a suitable penance upon him, to wit, that he should visit the shrine of St-Michel [in-Peril-of-the-sea] before the coming feast of St. Remy, that he should repeat the Lord's Prayer fifty times and as many Ave Marias; that he should bestow five shillings upon the poor; and that he should fast for three days, that is to say, for three Fridays.

MAY 24-25. At Gaillon. MAY 26. To wit, on Ascension Day, at the same.

MAY 27. At the same. This day Gauguin Duret, esquire, the son-in-law of Sir Guy of Mal-Lion, knight, paid homage to us for a certain fief which this knight gave to the wife of the said esquire as a marriage gift. The said knight had held Aubevoie of us. When this had been done, the said knight and Robert Baldwin stood as sureties for the said esquire's relief if we are entitled to one.

MAY 28. At Gaillon. MAY 29. At Vernon. MAY 30. At Mantes. MAY 31. At St-Germain-en-Laye. JUNE 1. At Paris.

JUNE 2. At the same. This day we absolved, or rather had absolved by Brother Adam, our brother, Peter of St-Remy, esquire, from the excommunication by which he had been bound by our official of Rouen because of fifty pounds of Tours in which the said P[eter] was held to the said official by way of a fine. The form of the absolution was as follows: that he shall at once be returned to his former state [of excommunication] if he shall not pay the said official the said quantity of money before the coming feast of St. Remy. Master John of Flainville, precentor of Rouen, offered himself as the chief surety and responsible party for the said fifty pounds, on behalf of the said P[eter], should he not make satisfaction for this within the stated time. Present in our hall at Paris and before Brother Adam, our representative, were: Master J[ohn] of Flainville, precentor; G. [William] of Flavacourt, the archdeacon of Petit-Caux; and Sir Herbert of Villières and Sir Enguerrand Guengenne, knights.

JUNE 3-4. At Paris.

JUNE 5. To wit, on Pentecost, at the same. On this day by God's grace Sir Ph[ilip], the eldest son of the king of France, together with many nobles of the kingdom of France, were girded with the sword of knighthood. We, the king of Navarre, the count of Dreux, the lord of Harcourt, and many other nobles took the Cross, with God's aid, from the lord legate on the island of Notre-Dame, where we preached before the king, the said legate, many prelates and barons of France, a multitude of the clergy, and a great gathering of the people.

JUNE 6. At Paris. JUNE 7. At St-Denis. JUNE 8. At St-Martin, near Pontoise. JUNE 9. At Bray-sous-Baudemont. JUNE 10. At Frênes.

JUNE 11. To wit, on the feast of St. Barnabas the Apostle. With God's grace we conferred Holy Orders at Les Andelys. This day Master John, surnamed Faber, the rector of the church at Chambourgy, was ordained to the priesthood. On oath, he promised to abide by our decision in that he had not taken steps to present himself for orders nor, contrary to his prior oath which he took at the time of his collation, had he resided in the said church nor sought permission from us for not so residing, thereby acting in a rash manner.

We spent this night at Frênes.

JUNE 12. To wit, on Trinity Sunday. We received procuration at Quévreville. Total for procuration: seven pounds, ten shillings. JUNE 13. At Déville. JUNE 14. With God's grace we celebrated the holy synod at Rouen.

JUNE 15. We held the synod of deans in our upper chamber at Rouen. Amongst other things which we accomplished in their presence, we ordained or decreed that every priest who did not attend the Rouen synods should be held to pay forty shillings of Tours for each absence from a synod, unless prevented by some legitimate reason. The monies collected may be distributed in whatever way we should desire.

This day the priest at Chartier appeared before us, by appointment, to purge himself with the seventh hand of priests[6] of the vice of incontinence of which he had been, and was, grievously defamed, especially with Germaine of Asnières. However, since he had brought with him some priests who were not quite suitable, that is to say, such ones as could not possess complete knowledge of his life and manners, we assigned him the day after Assumption to purge himself according to law of the foregoing, as it is stated, with

[6] See above, October 16, 1248, n. 70.

the aid of six well-known priests, neighbors, and of good repute.

We spent this night at Ste-Catherine, at our own expense.

JUNE 16. At Martot. JUNE 17-19. At Pinterville. JUNE 20. At Martot. JUNE 21. With God's grace we married Henry Louvel to Petronilla of Val-Richer, and we bestowed the marriage blessing at Notre-Dame-la-Ronde in Rouen.

This day we spent the night at Déville.

JUNE 22. At Martot. JUNE 23. At Gaillon. JUNE 24. To wit, on the feast of St. John the Baptist. At Gaillon. JUNE 25-26. At Gaillon. JUNE 27. At Vernon. JUNE 28. At Mantes. JUNE 29. To wit, on the feast of SS. Peter and Paul. JUNE 30. At Paris. JULY 1. At Paris. JULY 2. At Paris. On this day with God's help, after seeking and obtaining the permission of the lord bishop of Paris,[7] and after we had examined the process of election and the person of the elect by seeking the advice of prudent and good men in the hall of our Paris manor, we decided, as justice demands, to confirm the election held in the church of Lisieux of Dom Gui de Merle.

JULY 3-9. At Paris. JULY 10. At St-Denis-en-France. JULY 11. At Lu-zarches. JULY 12. At Senlis. JULY 13. At Compiègne. JULY 14. At Noyon. JULY 15. At Gournay-sur-Aronde. JULY 16. At Bresles, at the manor of the bishop of Beauvais, the see [of Beauvais] being vacant, and at our own expense.

JULY 17. With God's grace we visited the priory at Neufmarché, where were three monks of St-Evroult, to wit, Brother Victor, prior, and Brothers William of Falaise, Peter of Noyon, and Hugh of Breteuil. They ate meat thrice a week, and they said that this was with the permission of the abbot. Their service books were in poor condition, especially the Graduals. As we had done at our other visitations,[8] we ordered the prior to keep the cloister clean or at least to close off completely that part adjacent to the cloister. They owed one hundred pounds to their abbot and ten pounds elsewhere. We received procuration there this day. Total for procuration: nine pounds.

JULY 18. With God's grace we visited the priory of St-Laurent-en-Lyons, where sixteen canons were in residence, two of whom were novices. One does not accuse another [in chapter]. Four lay brothers were in the priory;

---

[7] Since Eudes was not in either his own diocese or his own archdiocese, permission from the ordinary in whose diocese or archdiocese he was residing had to be obtained before he could proceed to official acts affecting his own diocese or archdiocese.

[8] See entries for September 17, 1258; October 3, 1261; August 22, 1263.

two were outside. There were two lay sisters. We forbade Brother Richard
... [*lacuna in MS*] to talk any further with his own daughter, for their chats
had scandalized many. We also forbade the prior to permit her to visit or
enter the house, and [we ordered him] to punish the said Richard severely
should he disobey, either by withholding some of his food and wine or by
some other method, as the prior should deem expedient. They owed three
hundred twenty pounds, of which one hundred forty pounds was owed to a
former priest at Buchy. With God's grace we found other things to be in
good condition. We received procuration there this day. Total for procuration: eight pounds.

JULY 19. We received procuration from the lessee of the house or priory
of Nogent, near Neufchâtel. Total for procuration: eleven pounds, ten
shillings.

This day we visited the hospital or Hôtel-Dieu at Neufchâtel, where there
were two canons, with a priest who was also prior, three lay brothers, six lay
sisters, and two secular maidservants to attend the sick. We gave orders that
the lay brothers and the lay sisters should confess and receive Communion at
least five or four times a year. Item, that the canons confess to their prior
more often than they had been doing. They owed one hundred pounds; sixty
was owed to them.

JULY 20. At Aliermont. JULY 21. At Dieppe. JULY 22. To wit, on the
feast of St. Mary Magdalene, at Dieppe. With God's grace we preached in
the local churchyard. JULY 23. At Aliermont. JULY 24. With God's grace
we dedicated St. Agatha's church at Aliermont. JULY 25. To wit, on the
feast of St. James. We celebrated Mass at St-Jacques-de-Tristeville.

JULY 26. With God's aid we visited the priory at Envermeu, where there
were nine monks of Bec. There should be thirteen, but because of the very
many burdens of the house the number had been diminished. We ordered
the prior to inspect the monks' coffers frequently. A general distribution of
alms is made thrice a week to all comers. They owed six hundred pounds.
This day we received procuration from the prior at our manor at Aliermont.
Total for procuration: seven pounds, three shillings.

JULY 27. With God's aid we came to St. Mary's church at Sauqueville,
and we visited as best we could. Out of the entire chapter we found only
Master Ralph, who is charged with the local cure, the precentor, and a deaf
man. We also found the church destitute of persons and defrauded of its
due services. The Divine Office was celebrated with little devotion or so-

lemnity. Inasmuch as we discovered that the absentees had carried off certain of the revenues which had been allocated to the resident canons for at least a very long time, we ordered both the aforementioned Master Ralph and the precentor to warn Ferris, the treasurer, and Walter, called Gross, who had deserted the said church without permission and in violation of the ancient and approved statute of the church, to return thither, and faithfully to keep and maintain due residence as they were held to do. They [Master Ralph and the precentor] should withhold from them entirely the revenues which were due to a resident, and should distribute the revenues to those who were in residence. Item, they should select some suitable and faithful person from the chapter to receive the revenues belonging to the community and distribute them as should be done. Item, they should enact amongst themselves that a general chapter be held at least once a year, and on some fixed day, at which the state of the church might be dealt with. Also in this same chapter, whatever should be done by those who were present should have the stamp of authority. For a long time they have received nothing from England. The church has six prebends.

This day with God's grace we received procuration at Longueil from the lessee there. Total for procuration: eleven pounds, ten shillings.

JULY 28. With God's grace we visited the priory at Bacqueville-le-Martel, where there were four monks from Tiron, to wit, Clement, prior, Ralph of Paris, John of Corbeville, and Walter of Crassville. They ate meat, as they said, thrice a week; they did not observe the fasts of the Rule. They owed fifty-six pounds; they had few supplies. We received procuration there this day. Total for procuration: eight pounds.

JULY 29. We received procuration at Longueville. They did not compute. This same day we exchanged with Master John of Jumièges the fruits of the prebend which he held for the fruits of the prebend which had belonged to Dom Senebald, and we immediately exchanged the fruits of that prebend with the archdeacon John of Neuilly-en-Thelle, for the fruits of the prebend which he held.

JULY 30. With God's grace we visited the priory at Auffay, where there were six monks of St-Evroult, to wit, Brother Nicholas Mahiart, prior, and Brothers Dreux of Neufmarché, Alexander of Pontchardon, Henry of Mont-de-Piété, Robert of Blève, and Ralph of Us. All were priests, with the exception of Brother Ralph of Us, whom we ordered to confess frequently and to receive Communion at least once a month. They occasionally ate meat when there was no need. The prior was new. They owed two hundred fifty pounds, in addition to the king's fine.[9] They had, as they said, a sufficiency of supplies. We received procuration there this day. Total for procuration: eight pounds.

JULY 31. With God's grace we visited the abbey of St-Victor-en-Caux. Ten monks were in residence; because of the poverty of the abbey eight had been dispatched and sent outside to various places. All the residents were priests but one, whom we ordered to confess more often than he had been doing and to receive Communion at least four or five times a year. Item, we ordered the abbot to have the Statutes of Pope Gregory frequently read out in chapter. Item, he should draw up and report his accounts in the presence of some person or persons from the community. They owed about four hundred pounds. With God's grace we found other things to be in a sufficiently good condition, except that Brother Thomas had made himself obnoxious or hateful to all by reason of the shameful words, accusations, and insults which he frequently and unreasonably directed towards many of them; even before us in chapter we found him to be litigious and grumbling. We received procuration there this day. They did not wish to compute.

AUGUST 1. To wit, on the feast of St. Peter in Chains, at Déville. AUGUST 2-3. At the same. AUGUST 4. With God's grace we visited St-Georges-de-Bocherville, where twenty-five monks were in residence, of whom two were novices. All but [these] two were priests. More was owed to them than they owed. With God's grace things were very well with them, for we found them to be in excellent condition as to both temporals and spirituals. We received procuration there this day. Total for procuration: eight pounds.

AUGUST 5. With God's grace we visited the abbey at Jumièges, where forty-five monks were in residence; all but twelve were priests. There were twenty-one outside; one was with the abbot of St-Victor[-en-Caux]. They owed about one thousand pounds; about four thousand was owed to them, but some of this was in bad debts. With God's grace we found them to be in good condition. Nevertheless, since some had held and were holding bad opinions about the conduct and action of the abbot, we privately admonished him the next day, in the chamber where we were in the habit of sleeping and in the presence of Masters J[ohn] of Jumièges; Brothers Adam Rigaud and Henry of Houssaye of the Franciscans; and John Morgneval, our clerk, about the following matters: that with greater willingness than formerly he should

---

[9] The levy for the Crusade of Louis IX.

consult with the prior, the seniors, and the more mature members of the community concerning any future undertakings, in order that he might act more advisedly and surely. Item, that he should not undertake to construct any sumptuous buildings without their advice and consent. Item, that he should try to recover that sum of money which Abbot Robert had left to them [and which was now] scattered about. Item, that he should not gossip and joke with the guests to such a late hour as he had been doing, for, as we understood, he had been in the habit of sitting up late at night with certain guests, telling jokes and drinking, so that his attendant monks felt they were extremely burdened thereby. Item, that he should try to travel in a more seemly and simple fashion, and in all things act and conduct himself more maturely. We not only forbade him to visit the priory at Villarceaux in the future but actually to keep away from it altogether.

This day we were at Caudebec, at our own expense.

AUGUST 6. With God's grace we dedicated the church at Caudebec, and from the priest of this village we received procuration at St-Wandrille, by reason of the aforesaid dedication.

AUGUST 7. With God's grace, we visited the priory at Bourg-Achard, where twelve canons were in residence. One of these, to wit, Geoffrey, called Box, was being held in prison there; nine were in obediences outside. We ordered the prior to visit the outside canons more often than he had been doing, particularly those who are staying at Hernem. We enjoined a penance upon the prior because he had not as we had ordered him to do at our previous visitations[10] fetched back the *Summa* of Master William of Auxerre from Master Nicholas, the rector of the church at Bois-Guillaume, which the prior had loaned him some time before. They owed two hundred sixty pounds; one hundred sixty pounds in good was owed to them from past payments; they had a large supply of provisions. We received procuration there this day. Total for procuration: eight pounds.

AUGUST 8. At Pinterville. AUGUST 9. To wit, on the feast of St. Lawrence, at the same. AUGUST 10-11. At Martot. AUGUST 12. At Ste-Catherine, at our own expense. AUGUST 13. At Rouen. AUGUST 14. To wit, on the Sunday next before the Assumption of the Blessed Mary. We went in procession to St-Gervaise and preached in the atrium there. AUGUST 15. To wit, on Assumption Day. With Gods grace we celebrated this day's feast at Rouen. AUGUST 16-18. At Déville.

[10] See entry for June 28, 1266.

AUGUST 19. With God's grace we visited the monastery of St-Ouen-de-Rouen, where there were fifty-eight monks; all but eight were priests. With God's grace we found them to be in good state as to spirituals. However, the Divine Office was much disturbed because of the parish. They owed four thousand eight hundred twelve pounds, five shillings of Tours; there was owed to them in bad debts, as they said, twenty-six hundred pounds of Tours; five hundred pounds of Tours of the said debt which they owed was at interest.

We were at Déville this day, at our own expense.

AUGUST 20. At Rouen. AUGUST 21. With God's aid we consecrated as bishop our venerable brother G[ui] de Merle[11] in the cathedral of Rouen, our venerable brothers the suffragans of the church of Rouen assisting us. AUGUST 22-23. At Martot. AUGUST 24. To wit, on the feast of St. Bartholomew the Apostle, at the same. AUGUST 25. At Martot. AUGUST 26. At Bourg-Achard, at our own expense. AUGUST 27. At Cormeilles, at our own expense. AUGUST 28. To wit, on the feast of St. Augustine, a Sunday. We were present at the reception of our venerable brother G[ui] de Merle, by God's grace bishop of Lisieux.

We spent the night at Lisieux.

AUGUST 29. At Pont-Audemer, to wit, on the feast of the Decollation of St. John.

AUGUST 30. At the same. This day with God's grace we celebrated a provincial council at the church of St-Ouen. Present were our venerable brothers the suffragans of the church of Rouen: O. [Eudes] of Bayeux, R[ichard] of Avranches, G[ui] of Lisieux, Th[omas] of Séez and J[ohn] of Coutances, all by God's grace bishops. R[alph] of Evreux was absent, and he had offered a legitimate excuse by letter patent. Then with God's aid we acted and ordered as we should in accordance with the demands of business and affairs, amongst which we read and recited publicly those statutes which are herein contained in a schedule herewith inserted.[12]

AUGUST 31. We were at St-Philbert, at the manor of the bishop of Avranches, and at his expense. SEPTEMBER 1-2. At Pinterville. SEPTEMBER 3-4. At Gaillon. SEPTEMBER 5-6. At Frênes. SEPTEMBER 7. At Gournay.

---

[11] Gui de Merle was consecrated bishop of Lisieux. See entry for July 2, 1267.

[12] Apparently the complete record of this council has been lost, but Mansi (XXIII, 1165-68) prints some statutes of the council which are a reproduction of the statutes as printed in Philip Labbé and Gabriel Cossart, *Sacrosancta concilia* (Venice, 1731), XIV, 357-60.

SEPTEMBER 8. To wit, on the Nativity of the Blessed Mary. We celebrated High Mass in St. Mary's church in Gournay and preached in the churchyard there. This day with God's grace we visited the leper house, where there were one chaplain, five lay brothers, two lay sisters, and two lepers. The chaplain received only as much as a lay brother. We forbade them to eat in the village in the future, as they had been in the habit of doing. They owed about twenty pounds, and they had almost enough supplies to last out the year. We spent this night in the said town, at our own expense.

SEPTEMBER 9. With God's grace we visited the chapter of Gournay. In residence we found the dean, the treasurer, and Matthew of Montfort, a canon. Reginald, the sacristan's helper, John of Etrépagny, and the younger brother of the treasurer were defamed, as it was said, of despoiling the Jews, of assaulting the townsmen at night, and of fishing in the king's fish pond. We ordered the chapter to discipline and punish them for the above and to correct all these matters before the coming feast of St. Remy. Furthermore, since the aforesaid Matthew had been defamed for many years of a certain woman of Les Andelys, whom, indeed, he had kept for a long time in his own house, we expressly warned him not to allow her to frequent his house in the future, nor to live in the same house with her, and to abstain from the vice of incontinence. Item, since the treasurer had worn and was still wearing robes and supertunics which were too short, we enjoined him to wear more seemly clothing and to behave and conduct himself in a more becoming fashion than he had been doing.

This day with God's aid we visited the local Hôtel-Dieu, where there were three brothers and six sisters. They owed sixty shillings. With God's grace the house was in good condition.

This same day with God's grace we visited the nuns at St-Aubin. Thirteen nuns were in residence; of these, three were in the vineyards. As we had done before,[13] we expressly forbade them to receive anyone without our special permission. Since Anastasia had by her own choice resigned her duties as subprioress, we rebuked and corrected her for this, enjoined on her a penance which seemed proper to us and forced her to resume the aforesaid office. Item, we ordered Richilde dismissed from her office as cellaress, for she had conducted herself in a manner unsuitable for an office of this kind. Thomas, rector of the church at Forges-les-Eaux, frequented the house to the

[13] See entries for September 17, 1258; March 5, 1259/60; July 30, 1266.

point of scandal, and John of Menerval, a cleric, did likewise; we gave orders that they be completely kept away from the house, so far as possible. Nothing had been done about the orders we gave at our other visitation concerning the roosters and hens.[14] Item, as we had done before,[15] we expressly ordered that a certain miller, named Frongnet, be completely banished from the house. They owed about thirty pounds.

This day we spent the night, to wit, September 10, at Bellosane.

SEPTEMBER 10. We were at La Ferté-en-Bray, at the expense of the village. Total for procuration ... [lacuna in MS].

SEPTEMBER 11. With God's grace we dedicated the church there, and spent this night at Sigy, where we received procuration from the local prior. It should be known that our procuration may not exceed the sum of ten pounds of Tours, as is contained in a letter drawn up to set forth the agreement entered into by the prior and us.[16]

SEPTEMBER 12. With God's grace we visited this priory, where there were six monks of St-Ouen-de-Rouen, to wit, Brothers Nicholas of La Luée, Humphrey of Louviers, John of Génèste, Richard of Goderville, William of Beaumont, and William of Pré. Once a week alms are given to all comers. They owed about two hundred pounds.

This day we spent the night at Déville.

SEPTEMBER 13. At Déville. SEPTEMBER 14. To wit, on the Exaltation of the Holy Cross, at the same. SEPTEMBER 15-16. At the same. SEPTEMBER 17. At Valliquèrville, at our own expense. SEPTEMBER 18. With God's grace we dedicated the church of the said place, and spent the night at the expense of the village. SEPTEMBER 19. At Déville. SEPTEMBER 20. With God's grace we visited the abbey of St-Amand-de-Rouen, where there were seven veiled nuns and seven little girls in secular garb, who had already been received for the purpose of taking the veil. We gave orders that all the maidservants be paid from the common fund and retrained at a definite wage. We forbade that anyone be received without our special permission. Item, [we ordered] that all unnecessary maidservants be sent away. They had one lay brother; we ordered the abbess to show careful and proper attention to the said lay brother, to wit, [to see] that he should confess frequently and receive Communion at the proper times, and [to see that] this lay bro-

---

[14] See entry for July 30, 1266.
[15] See entry for July 30, 1266.
[16] See entries for December 14, 1261; January 8, 1263/64; July 20, 1265.

ther was in charge of the bakery of the house. Item, we ordered the abbess to call in the prioress or the subprioress, or some other senior member of the community, when auditing and drawing up her accounts. Item, that she should try to augment the alms allowance. Item, that she should have the cloister gate most diligently guarded. We also forbade any work in silk to be done there, unless it was exclusively intended for the divine cult. They owed five hundred pounds. At their petition we granted them two confessors, a treasurer, and a penitencer. We spent this night at Déville, at our own expense.

SEPTEMBER 21. To wit, on the feast of St. Matthew. We celebrated Mass at St. Matthew's church near the Rouen bridge, and, God permitting, we preached there. SEPTEMBER 22-23. At Déville. SEPTEMBER 24. At the same. With God's grace we conferred Holy Orders at Déville. SEPTEMBER 25. We spent the night with Sir Richard of Montiarde, knight, at his expense and that of the parishioners of Notre-Dame at Aunay. SEPTEMBER 26. With God's help we dedicated this church, and we spent the night at the house of the priest at Osebosc, at our own expense. SEPTEMBER 27. We dedicated the local church with God's aid, and we spent the day there at the expense of the rector and of the village. SEPTEMBER 28. At the abbey at Le Valasse, at our own expense.

SEPTEMBER 29. To wit on the feast of St. Michael, in Monte Gargano, at Tancarville. We celebrated Mass in the parish church and with God's help preached a sermon. This day we were at the chamberlain's castle, and at his expense.

SEPTEMBER 30. With God's aid we dedicated St. Mary's chapel, which is in this castle, and we were here this day, at the chamberlain's expense. OCTOBER 1. At St-Wandrille, at our own expense. OCTOBER 2. At Déville. OCTOBER 3. At Rouen. OCTOBER 4. To wit, on the feast of St. Francis. At Rouen. OCTOBER 5-8. At Déville, because of the Exchequer at Rouen, which we attended daily, God helping us. OCTOBER 9. To wit, on the feast of St. Denis. OCTOBER 10-12. At Déville, for the Exchequer at Rouen, which with God's aid we attended daily. OCTOBER 13. At Ste-Catherine, at our own expense. OCTOBER 14. At Gaillon. OCTOBER 15. At Frênes. This day we had with us the lord legate[17] to France. OCTOBER 16. At Rouen. OCTOBER 17. At Rouen. The said legate celebrated a council about collecting the

[17] Simon de Brie.

tithe.[18] OCTOBER 18. At Frênes. OCTOBER 19. At St-Germer-de-Flay, at our own expense. OCTOBER 20. At Neuville-en-Hez. OCTOBER 21. At Compiègne. OCTOBER 22. At Soissons. OCTOBER 23. To wit, on the feast of St. Romain. At Jonchery. OCTOBER 24-27. At Rheims, with the king, on the business connected with the count of Bar.[19] OCTOBER 28. To wit, on the feast of SS. Simon and Jude. At Rheims. OCTOBER 29. At Rheims. OCTOBER 30. At Fismes. OCTOBER 31. At Soissons. NOVEMBER 1. To wit, on All Saints. With God's grace we celebrated High Mass at the Franciscan monastery at Soissons, and breakfasted with the lord legate to France at the house of the bishop of Rheims. NOVEMBER 2. At Compiègne. NOVEMBER 3. At Clermont. NOVEMBER 4. At St-Quentin-Beauvais.

NOVEMBER 5. At Gisors, at the priory of St-Ouen, where we received seven pounds of Tours, in which amount only is the said house annually held to us for procuration when we come to them once a year, nor can we nor should we demand anything more for procuration.

NOVEMBER 6. At Frênes. NOVEMBER 7. At Ste-Catherine, at our own expense. NOVEMBER 8. With God's grace we celebrated the sacred synod at Rouen.

NOVEMBER 9. We celebrated the synod of deans. This day had been assigned to Andrew, priest at the chapel of St-Ouen, who had been defamed of Mathilda, his parishioner, and had confessed to this ill fame. It was also assigned to Peter, priest at Busc, in like manner defamed of Agnes; he had confessed to the ill fame. They were assigned this day for the purpose of purging themselves according to law of these charges. Both failed to do so. As they stood before us, we appointed for them the Friday following the coming feast of St. Lucy as the day when they should stand trial on the foregoing, either at Rouen or in the vicinity.

We spent this night at Martot.

NOVEMBER 10. At Vernon. NOVEMBER 11. To wit, on the feast of St. Martin [*Hiemalis*]. At Meulan. NOVEMBER 12-21. At Paris, to attend the Parlement. NOVEMBER 22. On the feast of St. Cecilia. At Paris. NOVEMBER 23-24. At Paris, to attend the Parlement. NOVEMBER 25. On the feast of St. Catherine. At Paris. NOVEMBER 26-29. At Paris, to attend the Parlement. NOVEMBER 30. On the feast of St. Andrew. At Paris. DECEMBER 1-5. At

[18] No record of this council seems to have survived. The tithe refers to the Crusades.

[19] Probably to settle the dispute between Thibaud, count of Bar, and Henry of Luxemburg.

Paris, to attend the Parlement. DECEMBER 6. On the feast of St. Nicholas. At Paris. DECEMBER 7. At Paris, to attend the Parlement. DECEMBER 8. On the Conception of the Blessed Mary. At Asnières. DECEMBER 9. At Asnières. DECEMBER 10. At Verberie. DECEMBER 11. At Noyon. DECEMBER 12. At Ham. DECEMBER 13. At St-Quentin, on the feast of St. Lucy. DECEMBER 14. At Gouy. DECEMBER 15-17. At Cambrai, to attend the council of the five dioceses, to wit, Cambrai, Liège, Toul, Metz, and Verdun.[20] DECEMBER 18. At Bapaume. DECEMBER 19. At Corbie. DECEMBER 20. At Poix. DECEMBER 21. At Foucarmont, at the expense of the abbey. DECEMBER 22. At St-Saëns. DECEMBER 23. At Rouen, and we made our O.[21] DECEMBER 24. At Rouen. This day Gerard, the rector at Vernonnet, resigned this church into our hands. DECEMBER 25. With God's grace we celebrated the feast of the Nativity of the Lord at Rouen. DECEMBER 26. At Déville. DECEMBER 27. At Jumièges, at our own expense. DECEMBER 28. At Pont-Audemer. Here begins the visitation of the diocese of Lisieux. DECEMBER 29. With God's grace we came to the monastery of St-Pierre-des-Préaux, in the diocese of Lisieux, and after we had preached with God's help in the chapter house, we made a visitation. Thirty-two monks were in residence; two were novices; with the exception of these novices, all were priests. In the priories they do not observe the statutes of the Rule pertaining to the eating of meat and to the fasts; we ordered the abbot to have this corrected so far as could be done. More was owed to them than they owed; they had a sufficiency of wheat, oats, and wine to last out the year, and with God's grace things were well with them. We received procuration there this day. Total for procuration: eight pounds, two shillings, two pence.

DECEMBER 30. With God's grace we visited the abbey of the nuns of St-Léger, after we had first preached in chapter. Forty-five nuns were in residence, which is in accord with the certain and statutory number. One of them was staying alone with her mother at Argoulles, which displeased us. We then forbade the abbess to give further permission to any nun to go out, except with good company. Three general maidservants were there, and several private ones, of whose excessive number we disapproved. We ordered her to inspect the nuns' coffers, for the purpose of removing any property,

---

[20] There does not seem to be a record of this particular council. Most probably, Eudes' presence was connected with the Crusade. Eudes had taken the cross at Pentecost, June 5 of this year.

[21] See above, December 23, 1250, n. 135.

more often than she had been in the habit of doing. Item, we forbade them to take any but the three vows taken at their profession, that is to say, of obedience, chastity, and poverty. They owed but little, as they said, and with the exception of wine they had enough provisions to last out the year. We received procuration there this day. Total for procuration: eight pounds, five shillings.

On the same day, to wit, December 30, and at the monastery of St-Léger-des-Préaux, there appeared before us in person Sister Lucy of Crèvecœur, a nun attached to the monastery of the Holy Trinity at Caen, who for a long time had been excommunicate through our authority as metropolitan, seeking absolution from this sentence.[22] After taking counsel with prudent men, we were convinced that we ought to bestow the benefit of absolution upon her. On taking an oath on the Eucharist, she promised that she was prepared [to obey] our commands. Whereupon we enjoined her to accept three disciplines in the chapter of her monastery, to repeat three psalters,[23] to fast for two Fridays on bread and water, and to fast every Friday for a year on common food, as well as to restore and give back to the monastery all the goods which she had taken or which she had been able to take.

DECEMBER 31. With God's grace we came to the monastery at Grestain, where we made a visitation after we had with His assistance preached a sermon. Twenty-six monks were in residence; they had two [monks] in England, two at Ste-Scholasse, in the diocese of Lisieux, and two in the county of Poitou, in the diocese of Angers. We ordered the abbot to visit the outside priories more often than he had been doing. All but one of the resident monks were priests. Item, we ordered the prior to inspect the monks' coffers lest they have any property. Item, we ordered them to make out their individual accounts each month in the presence of some of the seniors of the community. They owed one hundred pounds; they had sufficient supplies to last out the year. With God's grace we found other things to be in good condition. We received procuration there this day. Total for procuration: eight pounds, twelve shillings.

JANUARY 1. On the feast of the Circumcision. We were there [at Grestain], at our own expense.

[22] This refers to the disputed election at Holy Trinity at Caen between Beatrice and Lucia de Crèvecoeur. See entry for April 17, 1266.

[23] The most probable meaning in this instance is the imposition of a penance which consisted of reciting privately the Opus Dei three times in addition to reciting it with the others in choir.

JANUARY 2. With God's grace we visited the abbey at Cormeilles, where there were thirty monks; eight were in England. All but five were priests. Alms are given to all comers every day. They owed nine hundred pounds of Tours; three hundred ten pounds was owed to them; as yet they had not used up any of this year's fruits. With God's grace we found other things to be in good condition. We received procuration there this day. Total for procuration: eight pounds, four shillings.

JANUARY 3. We visited the abbey of nuns at Lisieux, where there were thirty-six nuns; there was no certain or statutory number. They should confess and receive Communion seven times a year. Two general maidservants are there. They owed forty pounds, and they had enough wheat, oats, and beer to last out the year. With God's grace we found other things to be in good condition. The abbess was sick and was not present at the visitation. We received procuration this day from the bishop, and spent the night at his manor.

JANUARY 4. With God's grace we entered the vestry of the mother church of Lisieux, and there we preached in Latin to the assembled canons, chaplains, and clerks-choral of this church. Afterwards, when the aforesaid chaplains and clerks-choral had left and the canons had remained with us, together with our venerable brother G[ui], by God's grace the bishop there, we, with our companions and clerks, proceeded with His aid to make a visitation, as was fitting. Having inquired into the state of the church, we discovered that by God's grace it was in good condition as to both temporals and spirituals, and that at this time there was nothing which needed correction. We received procuration this day at the bishop's palace, from the chapter.

JANUARY 5. With God's grace we came to the priory at St-Hymer, where we preached a sermon and with God's aid made a visitation. Ten monks of Bec-Hellouin were there; all but one were priests. They owed one hundred pounds and had sufficient supplies to last out the year. All other things, including both spirituals and temporals, we found to be in good condition. We received procuration there this day. Total for procuration: seven pounds, two shillings.

JANUARY 6. We received procuration at St-Hymer from its prior, in the name of the priory at Blangy, to wit, on the Epiphany of the Lord. Total for procuration: seven pounds, five shillings.

JANUARY 7. With God's grace we visited the priory at Beaumont-en-Auge.

Twelve monks of St-Ouen-de-Rouen were in residence; all were priests. We issued orders that all the books of the church be catalogued in some roll or principal record at the mother church [St-Ouen-de-Rouen]. Item, that the Statutes of Pope Gregory be copied out and frequently read in chapter. They celebrated Mass but little, and confessed as rarely; we ordered the prior to have this corrected. Item, that he see to it that lay folk were kept away from the cloister. Item, that he inspect the monks' coffers more frequently than he had been doing, for the purpose of removing any property from them. The refectory sometimes remained vacant and empty, which displeased us. They owed one hundred sixty pounds. We found other things to be in good state. We received procuration there this day. Total for procuration: six pounds, sixteen shillings.

JANUARY 8. We received procuration at Ste-Barbe. Total for procuration: eight pounds, three shillings.

JANUARY 9. With God's grace we visited the priory at Ste-Barbe, where thirty-five canons were in residence; all but four were priests; about thirty-six were outside in obediences. We ordered the prior to make frequent inspection of the monks' coffers, and to visit them for the purpose of taking away any property. They owed one thousand pounds, four hundred pounds of which they owed to the abbot of Cormeilles for certain rents. They had enough provisions to last out the year. Other things with God's grace we found in good condition.

We received procuration this day at Crouttes. Total for procuration: seven pounds.

JANUARY 10. We visited the aforesaid priory at Crouttes, where there were two monks of Jumièges, to wit, Brother Roger of Pont-Audemer, prior, and Brother Nicholas; both were priests. Mass should be sung every day in their chapel by one of them. They do not observe the fasts of the Rule, nor do they observe the Rule in the matter of eating meat. The buildings were badly in need of reroofing. They owed four hundred pounds of Tours, which was the debt of William Durescu, the former prior, who had burdened the house inordinately both with this debt and others. However, they thought that they had enough supplies to last out the year.

We received procuration this day at Ticherville. Total for procuration: eight pounds.

This same day with God's grace we visited this priory with our venerable brother in Christ G[ui], by God's [grace] the bishop of Lisieux, who had breakfast with us this day. Three monks of St-Wandrille were there, to wit, Brothers Gerard of Beuseville, William of Muis, and Geoffrey Blondel. We forbade them to [permit] women to dine with them in the future. They did not observe the fasts of the Rule; they ate meat when there was no need. The monks and the parish priest had but one chalice, and the church was very bare and uncleanly kept; neither were there sufficient ornaments there, which displeased us. They had sufficient supplies for the year; they owed two hundred pounds.

JANUARY 11. With God's grace we visited the abbey at St-Evroult, where thirty-seven monks were in residence; all but twelve were priests. We ordered the prior to make frequent inspection of the monks' coffers to remove any property. It was not the custom to accuse another [in chapter], except for violation of the rule of silence. More was owed to them than they owed. We received procuration there this day. Total for procuration: eight pounds, ten shillings.

JANUARY 12. To wit, on the octave of Epiphany. With God's aid we visited the abbey at Bernay. Twenty-six monks were in residence; all but four were priests. They confess and receive Communion once a month. They owed nothing; five hundred pounds was owed to them. They had sufficient supplies to last the year, and with God's grace things were well with them. We received procuration there this day. Total for procuration: seven pounds, eight shillings.

This day we breakfasted at the manor of Sir Henry of Pérrièrs, at Pérrièrs.

JANUARY 13. At Beaumont-le-Roger, at our own expense. JANUARY 14. At Evreux, at the expense of the bishop. JANUARY 15. At Sausseuse, at our own expense. JANUARY 16. At Chaumont, at our own expense. JANUARY 17. At Chambly. JANUARY 18. At Viarmes. JANUARY 19. At Paris. JANUARY 20. At Essones. JANUARY 21. At Milly-en-Gatenais. JANUARY 22. To wit, on the feast of St. Vincent. With God's grace we celebrated Mass and preached in the parish church of Milly. We spent the night at La Chapelle-la-Reine. JANUARY 23. At Chatenay. JANUARY 24. At Montargis. JANUARY 25. To wit, on the Conversion of St. Paul. At Gien. JANUARY 26. At Aubigny. JANUARY 27. At La Chapelle-d'Angillon. JANUARY 28. At St-Palais, at the manor of the lord archbishop of Bourges, and at his expense. JANUARY 29-31. At Bourges, to attend the council. FEBRUARY 1. At Sancerre. FEBRUARY 2. To wit, on the Purification of the Blessed Mary. At the same. Here by God's will we were crushed with rheumatism, and could neither celebrate Mass nor preach, nor do anything fitting for a prelate. With us were the lords and reverend fathers, J[ohn], by God's grace archbishop of Bourges, and G[ui], bishop of Auxerre.[24]

FEBRUARY 3. At Ville-Catule, at the manor of the lord bishop of Auxerre, and at his expense. FEBRUARY 4. At the priory of Espaillac, at the expense of the lord bishop of Auxerre. FEBRUARY 5. At Varzy. At his expense. FEBRUARY 6. At Clamecy. At his expense. FEBRUARY 7. At Vézelay. At his expense. FEBRUARY 8. At Basarnes. At his expense. FEBRUARY 9-10. At Reigny, at the manor of the bishop of Auxerre. FEBRUARY 11. At La Ferté-Louptière. FEBRUARY 12. In the priory at Courtenay, near Chantecoq. FEBRUARY 13. At Nemours. FEBRUARY 14. At Verneuil. FEBRUARY 15. At Courquetaine. FEBRUARY 16. At the same, and we had breakfast at the house of Sir Peter of Cervole. FEBRUARY 17. At St-Maur. FEBRUARY 18. At Royaumont. FEBRUARY 19. We had breakfast at St-Denis, and we spent the night at Paris. FEBRUARY 20-21. At Paris. FEBRUARY 22. To wit, on Ash Wednesday, and, to wit, on [the feast of] St. Peter's Chair [of Antioch]. At Paris. FEBRUARY 23. At Paris. FEBRUARY 24. To wit, on the feast of St. Matthew. At Paris. FEBRUARY 25-27. At Paris. FEBRUARY 28. At Conflans. MARCH 1. At Genainville. MARCH 2. At Frênes. MARCH 3. With God's grace we conferred Holy Orders at Les Andelys, and we spent the night at Frênes. MARCH 4-5. At Frênes. MARCH 6. We received procuration at Gasny. Total for procuration: ten pounds.

MARCH 7. With God's grace we visited the said priory, that is to say, the monks dwelling there. There we found Brother John of Fontaines, prior, and Brothers Geoffry of Renville and Simon of Pont-Audemer. We ordered the prior to have a good missal made for the chapel of St-Nicaise across the river, and to celebrate Mass more often than he was in the habit of doing. They owed nothing, since they remit to the abbey everything that is left over after providing for their own maintenance and that of their staff. They lived in the manor across the river, where they should not receive us but rather here on this side, where we were in the habit of being received and of getting procuration. Across the river they had a large staff and food for the animals. We received procuration this day at Vesly. Total for procuration: eight pounds, ten shillings.

[24] John de Sully (1261-71) and Gui de Mello (1247-70). Gams, *Series episcoporum*, pp. 502, 523.)

MARCH 8. We were at Mortemer-en-Lyons, at the expense of the abbey, and we celebrated a high conventual Mass in pontificals this day, to wit, the feast day of the dedication of the abbey church.

MARCH 9. We were at L'Ile-Dieu, a Premonstratensian house, at the expense of the abbey. This day Master Henry of Bailleul, rector of the church at Touffreville, resigned into our hands his portion of the said church, if we wished to accept such a resignation.

MARCH 10. We received procuration at Pérrièrs from the lessee there. Total for procuration: seven pounds, four shillings.

MARCH 11. With God's grace we preached and administered Confirmation at Pérrièrs, spent the night at Noyon-sur-Andelle, and received procuration there. Total for procuration: nine pounds.

MARCH 12. To wit, on the feast of St. Gregory. With God's grace we visited the said priory, where there were seven monks of St-Evroult, to wit, Brother Jordan of La Chapelle, the prior, who was deaf; Dreux of Neufmarché; John of Duclair; Clement, the cellarer; Robert of Blève; and Thomas of Silly. They have received nothing from England for a long time. They owed four hundred pounds of Tours, sixty pounds of it to the abbot; they had sufficient provisions to last the year. With God's grace we found other things to be in good state.

This same day by God's grace we came to and visited the priory of Mont-Deux-Amants. Twelve canons were in residence, and ten were outside. We ordered the precentor to have each and every one of their books produced at least once a year and publicly displayed to the community, that they might be seen; we also ordered him to get back some which had been loaned, and we forbade him to lend any more to any person or persons without a good acknowledgment or definite letter, and to lend them with the knowledge and consent of the community. Item, we ordered that each and every item of the priory income be recorded in some register or roll. They owed about one hundred pounds; with the exception of oats, they had enough supplies to last the year. We received procuration there this day. Total for procuration: eight pounds, three shillings.

MARCH 13. With God's grace we visited the priory at Beaulieu. Twelve canons were in residence, and ten were outside. We expressly forbade the prior to allow the lay folk to talk or gossip with the canons in the cloister, but rather to keep them away from it as far as he was able to do so. They owed six hundred pounds, and they did not have enough wheat and oats to last the year. Total for procuration: eight pounds.

MARCH 14-16. At Déville. MARCH 17. At Rouen.

MARCH 18. To wit, Mid-Lent Sunday. With God's grace we preached the Crusade at the Halls of the Old Tower,[25] and thence we translated, with great veneration and in procession, relics of St. Mary Magdalene, which the king had, through us, sent to the prior and convent of the Hôtel-Dieu at Rouen. We celebrated High Mass in the cathedral.

MARCH 19. At Déville. MARCH 20. At St-Saëns, at the monks' priory, where we received procuration this day. Total for procuration: six pounds, ten shillings.

MARCH 21. With God's grace we visited the said priory, where there were five monks of St-Wandrille, to wit, Brother Herbert, prior, and Brothers Ralph of Manteville, William of Anxtot, John Godebout, a physician, and John, surnamed Erne, who was not a priest. We ordered this last to confess and receive Communion at least once a year. At their mill they had a certain miller, incontinent and defamed thereof; therefore we ordered him removed. The prior rarely celebrated Mass and was in poor health. Very often they ate meat when there was no need. [The priory] had some debts; however, it had sufficient supplies to last the year, as [the prior] said.

This same day with God's grace we came to the priory of nuns there, and, having preached a sermon, we made a visitation. There were eighteen nuns, three maidservants, and two lay brothers. Jeanne of Morcent, the prioress, was defamed of Reginald, the priest at l'Hortier. Petronilla of Dreux, the cellaress, was over and over defamed, as before,[26] of Ralph of Maintru. We found Agnes of Equetot and Jeanne of Morainville to be liars and perjurers when we asked some questions of them under oath. Wherefore we went away, as it were, sad and out of patience. They owed one hundred forty pounds; with the exception of oats, they had supplies to last the year. They will receive a large amount of money from the sale of woodlands.

We received procuration this day at Bures. Total for procuration: nine pounds, twelve shillings.

MARCH 22. We visited the said priory, where two monks of Pré were staying, to wit, . . . [*lacuna in MS*], who was the companion of the prior,

---

[25] The Old Tower was a former castle of the dukes of Normandy and was destroyed by Philip-Augustus in 1204. In its place the commune of Rouen built the "Halls." (Giry, ed., *Les Etablissements de Rouen*, II, p. 51.)

[26] See entry for January 22, 1266/67.

who was then absent. They do not observe the Statutes of the Rule pertaining
to the eating of meat and the fasts. Two monks of Pré, under obedience to
the prior of Pré, should always be there; these two are held to remit annually
to the said priory whatever remains to them after providing for their own
maintenance and that of their staff.

MARCH 23. We came to the priory or house at Wanchy, where there was
a certain lay lessee who had received it in fee from the abbot of St-Ouen-de-
Rouen, and from him we received procuration this day at our home at Aliermont. Total for procuration: ... [lacuna in MS].

MARCH 23[sic]-24. At Aliermont, at our own expense. MARCH 25. To
wit, on the Annunciation of the Blessed Mary. We celebrated Mass and
preached at St. Mary's church in Aliermont. MARCH 26-27. At Aliermont.
MARCH 28. At St-Victor-en-Caux, at our own expense. MARCH 29-30. At
Déville. MARCH 31. At Rouen. APRIL 1. With God's grace we preached on
Palm Sunday in the vestibule of St-Laurent, as is customary, and with His
aid we performed the Office of this day. APRIL 2-3. At Déville. APRIL 4.
We dined with the Franciscans, and spent the night at our manor in Rouen.
APRIL 5. To wit, on Holy Thursday. We granted the absolutions which are
accustomed to be made at Rouen this day, and we celebrated the Office of
the chrism, with God's help, at the cathedral. APRIL 6. We celebrated this
day's Office at the cathedral. APRIL 7. To wit, on Holy Saturday. At Rouen.
[No entry for April 8.][27]

---

[27] Eudes' clerk's chronology was incorrect; VI Ides April (April 8) was Easter
Sunday. The clerk made no entry for the VI Ides April and incorrectly placed Easter
Sunday on the V Ides April (April 9). Actually, Easter fell on April 8 in 1267/68.

1268

APRIL 9. We celebrated the holy Easter Day at Rouen.

APRIL 10. We came to the monastery of St-Georges-de-Boscherville, where we gave ecclesiastical burial to the body of G[uilelmus] [William], the chamberlain of Tancarville, of venerable memory, who had died the preceding Friday. On this day we buried his heart in the chancel of the Franciscan monastery at Rouen, and we spent the night at Ste-Catherine, at our own expense.

APRIL 11-14. At Pinterville. APRIL 15. At Martot. APRIL 16. At Bec-Hellouin. APRIL 17. To wit, the dedication day of this church. With God's grace we preached in chapter, and celebrated High Mass there. APRIL 18. At Jumièges, at our own expense.

APRIL 19. With God's grace we came to the monastery at St-Wandrille, where we first preached in chapter and [then] made a visitation. Thirty-eight monks were there; all were priests. A stone railing inappropriate and unseemly was placed in the lobby of the entrance to the cloister; we ordered it taken away. One monk was alone at Roeny; we ordered the abbot not to delay in giving him a companion. Outside, in England and elsewhere, there were thirty-three monks. Alms should be given daily to all comers. They owed two thousand pounds, of which two hundred was at interest. We received procuration there this day. They did not wish to compute.

APRIL 20. At Le Valasse, at the expense of the abbey.

APRIL 21. We visited the priory at Graville. The prior was sick at this time and could not be present at the visitation. However, after we had preached, as was fitting, we gathered before us the canons of the place and proceeded in his absence to make a visitation. We learned that there were ten canons in residence, counting the prior. There was no one with the cure of souls at Bellevue; we ordered them to see to it that one was placed there. They owed nothing. A little, as the prior had told us,[1] was owed to them. We also heard the same thing from the community. With God's grace we

---

[1] This probably refers to the sixty pounds owed to them. See entry for January 5, 1259/60.

found other things to be in good condition. We received procuration there this day. Total for procuration: six pounds, two shillings.

APRIL 22. With God's grace we dedicated St. Nicholas' church at L'Eure and spent the night at Graville, at the expense of the rector and parishioners of that place [L'Eure].

APRIL 23. With God's grace we visited the abbey at Montivilliers, where there were sixty-one nuns, although, according to the certain and statutory number, there should be but sixty. However, the legate, on his own wish and authority, had had the daughter of Thibaud, called Cambellanus, placed there. All of them should confess and receive Communion at least once a month. They had four general maidservants. We ordered the abbess and the prioress to see to it that the loaves and fragments from the refectory were more carefully and better looked after than they had been. It was customary for alms to be given thrice a week, and alms were distributed there to all comers and, in accord with the ancient practice of abbess Alice, the abbess must maintain thirteen poor folk every day. More was owed to them than they owed. With God's grace we found other things to be in good condition. We received procuration there this day. They did not care to compute.

APRIL 24. We were at Valmont, at our own expense.

APRIL 25. To wit, on the feast of St. Mark. With God's grace we visited the abbey, where there were twenty-four monks; all but three were priests; two were at St-James. We ordered those who were not priests to confess and receive Communion at least once a month. We ordered the prior to have the Rule and the Statutes of Pope Gregory frequently read aloud in chapter. One did not accuse another [in chapter]; we ordered this corrected. Item, we ordered the kitchener, the pittancer, the sacristan, the infirmarian, and the other officials of the house to draw up their accounts in the presence of the abbot, the prior, and some of the seniors of the community. Item, since we discovered that there were too many boys about the place, as well as boys from the town, and that both frequented the abbey too much, to its expense and loss, we expressly ordered the abbot to try to find some remedy for this, that is to say, that he should permit only necessary servants to stay there and that particularly he should keep them from the cloister, refectory, infirmary, kitchen, and entrance or lobby which is just in front of the kitchen. Also, we ordered him to enjoin the doorkeeper, under pain of dismissal, to watch the gate better than he had been doing. We also forbade the monks to presume to have their own private messengers, as they had. Item, we ordered the abbot to be considerate of Abbot Peter,[2] to study how to act toward him, to visit him frequently in charity and mercy, and to supervise the accounts of his expenditures. We removed the nephew of Abbot Peter from his society, since the former had made himself somewhat of a nuisance to the latter; we ordered the abbot to provide him with another who would be more suitable. Furthermore, since we learned that William Pothon, a monk, to the damage or loss of the abbey, had pledged a certain English manor without the consent of the abbot and community, and that he had lived perversely beyond the seas; since in our presence, when the community had been gathered in chapter before us, he had spoken against his own abbot with irreverence of mind and unbridled contumely, we caused him to be seized and taken to our manor at Rouen to be detained there. Moreover, he had brought from England certain articles, to wit, a coverlet of vair, an ivory horn, a silver cup, and certain other things which he was never willing to confess that he had carried off. Furthermore, we privately warned the abbot to try to conduct himself in such a way that he might be able to restore his reputation, which had been somewhat impaired by the vice of incontinence. Item, we warned Abbot Peter's nephew to mend his ways, for we had learned that he had occasionally and scandalously left the house at night. They owed nothing, and much was owed to them; they had, both in cash on hand and in good debts, up to about four hundred pounds of Tours. We received procuration there this day. Total for procuration: six pounds, eight shillings, two pence.

APRIL 26. We came to the house or priory at Etoutteville, which we found to be miserably deformed as to both spirituals and temporals. Two monks from Lewes were there. They had twenty shillings a week for their support. We received procuration this day at Ouville from the lessee of Etoutteville. Total for procuration: ten pounds, seventeen shillings.

APRIL 27. With God's grace we visited the priory at Ouville, where there were eleven canons. We gave orders that all books should be more frequently brought into the chapter and displayed to the community. We ordered that lay folk be kept out of the cloister. Item, we expressly forbade the canons to drink in the garden in the future. Since we found the prior weak and feeble, we thought that, as he requested, he should be relieved of his office. They owed one hundred twenty pounds. We received procuration

---

[2] On May 24, 1262, Eudes had accepted Abbot Peter's resignation because of old age.

there this day. Total for procuration: seven pounds, twelve shillings.

APRIL 28-30. At Déville. MAY 1. To wit, on the feast of SS. Philip and James. At Déville. We went to Rouen daily to attend the Exchequer. MAY 2. At Déville. MAY 3. At the same. This day we invested John of Morgneval with a portion of the church at Normanville, in the stead and name of Master Robert John, on whom, in our paternal goodness, we had conferred it. MAY 4-5. At Déville. MAY 6. At Martot, on the feast of St. John before the Latin Gate. MAY 7. At Pinterville. MAY 8. At Gaillon. MAY 9. On the Translation of St. Nicholas. At Vernon, with the king. MAY 10. At Vernon. with the king. MAY 11. At Vernon, with the king. This day, as the law requires, we confirmed the election of Brother Robert of Limanville as prior of Ouville.

This same day we conferred on Dom John of St-Benoît the church at Neuville-Royale and invested John of Morgneval with it.

MAY 12-14. At Vernon.

MAY 15. With God's grace we visited the priory at St-Martin-la-Garenne, where there were three monks of Bec-Hellouin. There should be five, but the abbot had recalled two of them to the cloister, partly because of the needs of the priory which was burdened with debts and partly to increase the number of those forming the community of the abbey. These are the names of the monks: Brother John of Bec, prior, and Brothers Geoffrey of Hérouville and Andrew of Rouen. They ate meat and used feather beds when there was no need, and badly observed the fasts of the Rule. They owed one hundred thirty pounds in addition to a large old debt, to wit, of three hundred twenty pounds, which they owed to Abbot Robert. We received procuration there this day. Total for procuration: six pounds, six shillings.

MAY 16. With God's grace we came to the priory at Villarceaux, where there were nineteen nuns. According to the certain and statutory number there should be twenty nuns, four lay sisters, and four general maidservants. Item, as we had done before,[3] we ordered them to remove without fail all damoiselles or secular maidens, if there were any, and not to permit any person or persons to remain except that person or persons intended to take the veil. Item, we ordered the prioress to cast her accounts more frequently than she had been doing in the presence of seniors elected by the community. Eustasia, a former prioress, had a certain bird which she kept to the annoyance and displeasure of some of the older nuns, wherefore we ordered it

[3] See entries for January 15, 1265/66; March 18, 1266/67.

removed. She, because of this, spoke somewhat indiscreetly and irreverently to us, which much displeased us. They did not have wheat and oats to last until the new harvest. They owed seventy pounds.

This day we received procuration at St-Laurent-en-Lyons.[4] Total for procuration: ... [lacuna in MS].

MAY 17. To wit on the feast of the Ascension of the Lord. In the morning with God's grace we visited the aforesaid priory, where there were four monks of Josaphat-sous-Chartres, to wit, Brother Philip of Sérans, prior, and Brothers John Rigaud, Giles of Morete, and Adam of Brie. We ordered them to observe silence after Compline. The prior had never inspected the monks' coffers, although on our former visitations[5] we had several times enjoined him to do this; wherefore we had impossed a penance upon him, to with, that he should repeat the seven [penitential] psalms and the Litany. Once again we ordered him to do the same penance. They ate meat every day but Fridays and Saturdays, which much displeased us. We forbade the prior to permit the monks to go out to the wood alone in the future, or indeed to pass beyond the gate, as they were in the habit of doing. Crispin, the prior's servant, was a person of ill-repute and unsuitable; that is to say, he was a dice player and a haunter of taverns. We were under the impression that the abbot had ordered the prior to remove him and to expel him before the coming feast of St. John the Baptist. The prior, as we discovered, had scarcely celebrated Mass for five months, at which his fellow monks were greatly astounded. We, likewise, were not inexcusably surprised at this. It was believed that this was because of an unpaid tithe; but he told us, when we inquired into the reason, that he had never omitted to celebrate Mass because of any default in the payment of the tithe, and that he intended to give a somewhat secret explanation to his abbot right away. They had neither wheat nor oats; they owed one hundred pounds.

This same day with God's grace we came to the priory at Juziers, where we took part in a procession, celebrated Mass in pontificals, as was fitting, and with God's aid preached a sermon. We received procuration there this day, to wit, Ascension Day.

MAY 18. With God's grace we visited the said priory, where there were

---

[4] Actually St-Laurent-en-Cornecervine. St-Laurent-en-Lyons was a house of Augustinian canons, whereas St-Laurent-en-Cornecervine was a Benedictine priory. The mistake is Bonnin's, since the MS has the correct notation in the margin.

[5] See entries for August 27, 1262; June 20, 1266.

seven monks of St-Père-de-Chartres, to wit, John, prior, William Bird, John of Liancourt, Philip of Fontenay, Anselm of Stampe, Baillet, and Geoffrey of Chartres. They did not have enough chalices. We gave orders that they read the schedule or calendar of the saints every day. They owed forty pounds. They did not observe the fasts of the Rule very well; they ate meat and used feather beds when there was no need.

This same day we came in person with God's permission to the priory at Gaillonet, and immediately we went on to the house of St-Côme, near Meulans, which belongs to Bec-Hellouin. There we received procuration from the prior of Gaillonet.

MAY 19. With God's grace we came to the Hôtel-Dieu at Pontoise, where with His aid we preached to the brothers and sisters of the said house, who were gathered there before us in a certain lobby near the chapel. Then we made a visitation. In residence were Dom John of Fenins, a canon of St-Mellon-de-Pontoise, appointed by the king as custodian and rector of the house, and also two canons dressed in the garb of canons-regular, who celebrated the day and night Offices there and heard the confessions of the sick. The said John, the rector, had the cure of souls of all of the inhabitants of the said house, both sick and well. Also there were fourteen veiled sisters in residence, and one who had already been received for the purpose of taking the veil; there were also four lay brothers. We ordered the prioress that in the future she and the said J[ohn], when making up their accounts, should call in the two aforesaid priests and two of the older and more mature sisters who had been chosen by the others. They owed but little; with the exception of wheat they had sufficient provisions to last the year. We made this visitation with God's aid after *Dormitio*, or, as is said, when the evening reading was over.[6]

We spent the night at our own expense at our manor in the town, where our vicar resides.

MAY 20. With God's grace we celebrated a parish Mass and preached and confirmed at St. Mary's church in Pontoise, to wit, on the Sunday after Ascension.

We spent the night, at our own expense, at our aforementioned manor.

MAY 21. With God's grace we came to St-Mellon and preached in a certain building near the church which the canons use for a chapter house. With His aid we performed the duty of a visitation. Here we found a dean and

[6] I.e., just before Compline.

two resident canons, to wit, Dom John of Fenins, a priest, and Master Robert of Attrabate, a physician. There are nine prebends, and there are perpetual vicars, to wit, Dom Richard, vicar-warden for the treasurer; Robert of Brie, the vicar of Master Robert of Attrabate; Baldwin of Meaux, the vicar of Master Adam of Picardy; William of Longuesse, the vicar of Imbert the almoner; John Small, the vicar of John of Mont-Lucile; Robert of Vernon, the vicar of Dom John of Fenins; William the Norman, the vicar of Dom Robert of Corbeil; Simon, the vicar of Vincent la Pie; Fromond, the dean's vicar; and Peter of Limoges, the vicar of Grosparmi. There were some chaplains there whose number and names we did not record; there were two clerics, one a deacon, and the other a subdeacon, who must vest themselves daily for High Mass. We forbade them to talk in choir in the future, as they were wont to do. Dom Simon and Dom William of Longuesse, above-mentioned vicars, were defamed of the vice of incontinence, and we found that the said Simon, by reason of this vice, had scandalized the entire community, for he had had two children by a certain loose woman whom he was keeping. We enjoined our vicar to act for us in proceeding against them in these matters, and we gave him a letter patent commissioning him to act for us. Fromond, the dean's vicar, and Luke, a deacon, had not performed their duties as canons of the church for a long time, having absented themselves at their own whim and without anyone's permission. Since they are held to maintain continual and personal residence, we had them notified according to law through our vicar to see to it that they returned to the church to take up permanent residence there within six months and to devote themselves to the service due to God, or otherwise we would proceed against them as the law demands. Item, we ordered the dean and the canons to have repaired at once a certain leak which threatened danger and collapse to the wall adjacent to St. John's altar. To speed up this repair work we advanced them the needed cash, through our vicar [of Pontoise], until the next harvest.

Immediately after the said visitation we came this day to St. Peter's priory, and with God's aid we visited as we are entitled to do and as is fitting. Here we found four monks of Bec-Hellouin, to wit, John of St-Cloud, Roger of Estivente, Peter of Mesnil, and John of St-Aubin; all were priests. There should be more, but the abbot had recalled some to the cloister. They owed about sixteen pounds. With God's grace we found them in good condition.

The same day, having made this visitation, with God's aid, we confirmed many children in St. Peter's church, and we spent the night at our manor in the town, where, by reason of the visitation at St-Mellon, we received one hundred shillings of Paris, in which amount the chapter of St-Mellon is held for procuration once each year when we visit this church. The said chapter has to provide us with salvers, dishes, cups, beds, and general cooking utensils, and to find quarters for us should we wish it.

MAY 22. At Asnières. MAY 23. At the same. This day we breakfasted with the legate,[7] at Royaumont. MAY 24. At Bellencourt, at the manor of Anselm of l'Ile, and at his expense. MAY 25. We were at Ressons, at the expense of the abbey. MAY 26. At St-Quentin, near Beauvais, at our own expense. Here with God's aid we celebrated the Office of the day with the community. MAY 27. To wit, on Pentecost. At the same, and on this feast we celebrated High Mass. Afterwards we were present at the reception of the lord bishop of Beauvais, and we ate with him. MAY 28. At St-Germer-de-Flay. MAY 29-31. At Frênes. JUNE 1. At Déville. JUNE 2. At the same. Overcome by the infirmity of our own body, we could not confer Holy Orders. Of his graciousness John, by His grace bishop of Lübeck, a suffragan of the archbishop of Bremen, who was then staying at Grandmont near Rouen, conferred them in our stead.

JUNE 3-4. At Déville. JUNE 5. This day, because of this infirmity, we could not hold the synod. JUNE 6-8. At Déville. JUNE 9-10. At Martot. JUNE 11. To wit, on the feast of St. Barnabas the Apostle. At Martot. JUNE 12-17. At Pinterville. JUNE 18-19. At Gaillon. JUNE 20-23. At Pinterville. JUNE 24. To wit, on the Nativity of St. John. At the same. JUNE 25-26. At Pinterville.

JUNE 27. At the same. This day we conferred upon Robert of Harcourt the prebend which Master Peter of Aumale had previously held in the church of Rouen, and we invested Master John of Jumièges with this, in the stead and name of the said Robert. This was done in our companion's chamber and in the presence of Brothers Adam Rigaud; Nicholas of Hauteville; Henry of Houssaye; Willard, the prior of Salle-aux-Puelles; and John of Morgneval.

JUNE 28. At Pinterville. JUNE 29. To wit, on the feast of SS. Peter and Paul. At the same. JUNE 30. At Pinterville. JULY 1. At Pinterville. JULY 2-3. At Martot. JULY 4. To wit, on the Translation of St. Martin. At Déville. JULY 5-7. At Déville. JULY 8. At St-Victor, at our own expense. JULY 9-10. At Aliermont.

---

[7] Simon de Brie.

JULY 11. To wit, on the Translation of St. Benedict. At the same. This day the men of St-Aubin, at the command of the count of Dreux, their lord, appeared in person before us and made amends for having taken away from one of our clerics, a warden of Aliermont, a stag which he had chased and had captured at St-Aubin. In token of an amend of this kind they brought with them a bull calf which they offered us and which we kept in the name and stead of the said stag. Here are the names of these men: William Esperon, Gilbert Galcet, John Fouchier, Robert Tassel, Walter the Englishman, Ralph of Perrin, Robert Willart, Henry Solles, Nicholas of Boncourt, Peter le Braceor, Peter of Porte, and Ralph Savoulet. The bailiff of the said town [St-Aubin] and his son made the same amend to us on the following day.

We spent this night at Dieppe.

JULY 12. At Dieppe. JULY 13-15. At Aliermont. JULY 16. At St-Victor, at our own expense. JULY 17-21. At Déville. JULY 22. To wit, on the feast of St. Mary Magdalene. At the same. JULY 23. At Martot. JULY 24-28. At Pinterville. JULY 29-31. At Gaillon. AUGUST 1. To wit, on the feast of St. Peter in Chains. At Gaillon. AUGUST 2. At Martot. AUGUST 3. At Jumièges, at our own expense.

AUGUST 4. With God's grace we visited the monastery at Jumièges, after with His aid we had first preached in chapter. Forty-three monks were in residence; twenty-one were outside; all but eleven of the residents were priests. With God's grace we found the community to be in good state concerning the Divine Office and in the matter of the observance of the Rule. Yet they had been exceedingly disturbed about certain things which at the time, both inside and outside the abbey, were being said about the abbot. There was a sinister report about him. There in full chapter, Brother Peter of Neubourg, a monk of this monastery, stood up and uttered many unsuitable and shameful things against the abbot in our presence by way of denunciation,[8] but without binding himself to prove them. However, he did present one formal accusation against his abbot, reading publicly from a certain document all of which follows:

I, Brother Peter of Neubourg, a monk of Jumièges, in my own name and in that of the said monastery, and for the best interest of the same, present before

---

[8] Charges made to an ecclesiastical superior, either orally or in writing. Canon law demanded that proof be furnished with the denunciation. For the canonical procedure of denunciation, see Corp. jur. can., Decretal., Lib. v, Tit. 1. cap. 1-27.

you, Reverend Father [Eudes], by God's grace archbishop of Rouen, accusation
against Richard, the abbot of Jumièges; by way of that he is a forger in that he
falsely wrote, or had written, a certain letter in the name of our community,
for which letter he falsely took the names and implied the consent of our
brothers, though absent and ignorant of the whole, and secretly and at night
he signed or caused to be signed this letter with the community seal. This
letter concerned the revocation of a certain agreement or ordinance in the case
of a dispute moved between you, on the one hand, and ourselves and our
monastery on the other, and which had been drawn up by persons known and
worthy of credit. When this came to the attention of our brothers, they held
it to be invalid, and this I offer to prove in legal form against him.

Wherefore, for the reason aforesaid, I, the said Brother Peter, in my own
name, request that the said abbot be canonically punished by you, and I beg
you to take legal steps in this matter when you shall have received sufficient
evidence of the aforesaid crime. And I subject myself to retaliation should I
fail to prove the said crime.[9]

To further this accusation I request that you appoint me a certain day and a
secure place, and that the said abbot be called to appear against me and hear
your verdict on the said day and at the said time.

Having heard this, we assigned the parties to appear before us, or before
our official of Rouen, on the Monday following the feast of St. Giles, at
Rouen, if the said day be not a feast day; but should it be, then on the Tuesday following. Since, indeed, we quite early realized that the whole monastery was scandalized and upset because of the abbot, and we had heard many
evil things about his actions and his activities, we called him before us the
next day in the chamber where we were accustomed to stay and in the
presence of the abbots of St-Wandrille and of St-Georges, and of the venerable men Masters J[ohn] of Neuilly-en-Thelle, the archdeacon of Grand-
Caux; G. [William] of Flavacourt, the archdeacon of Petit-Caux; J[ohn] of
Jumièges, a canon of Rouen; W[illard,]the prior of Salle-aux-Puelles;
Brother Adam Rigaud; Robert of Senlis; and John of Morgneval. We specifically warned him as follows, to wit, that he should not keep dogs and
birds for the purpose of hunting. Item, that he should keep entertainers
away from his quarters. Item, that he should abstain from superfluous
spending and building. Item, that he should neither dine nor stay up late in

---

[9] If the plaintiff could not prove the guilt of the defendant, the former was
subject to the punishment which would have been that of the latter. This was the
lex talionis.

his room, as was his practice. Item, that he entirely avoid associating with any women whatsoever. Item, that he procure a decent staff of servants (*familiam honestam*). Item, that he farm out his manors better and to greater profit. Item, that he should not burden his monks unduly. Item, that he attend the meeting of the community in better manner and more frequently than he had been doing, and that he try to conduct himself with more understanding and suitability in all things. He promised in the presence of all, taking an oath on the Blessed Sacrament in the presence of the Blessed Sacrament that did he not comply with our admonition in the things aforesaid, he would obligate himself to do whatsoever we should order or tell him to do, and in these matters he expressly submitted himself to our mandate. Two of the abbot's servants, to wit, John of Picardy and John of Gisors, were not of good character. We ordered them removed. They owed five hundred pounds; twenty-five hundred pounds was owed to them, the larger part of it in bad debts. We received procuration there this day. We did not compute.

AUGUST 5. At Martot. AUGUST 6-7. At Frênes. AUGUST 8. At Vernon. AUGUST 9. At Mantes. AUGUST 10. To wit, on the feast of St. Lawrence. At Mantes. AUGUST 11. At St.-Germain-en-Laye. AUGUST 12-13. At Paris. AUGUST 14. To wit, on the vigil of the Assumption. At St-Maur. AUGUST 15. On the said feast. At the same. AUGUST 16-20. At Paris. AUGUST 21. At St-Denis. AUGUST 22. At Luzarches. AUGUST 23. At Creil, where we were bled. AUGUST 24. To wit, on the feast of St. Bartholomew. At Creil. AUGUST 25. At Creil. AUGUST 26. At Compiègne AUGUST 27. At Noyon. AUGUST 28. At Gournay-sur-Aronde. AUGUST 29. At Breteuil. To wit, on [the feast of] the Decollation of St. John. AUGUST 30. At Poix. AUGUST 31. At Aumale, at our own expense.

SEPTEMBER 1. To wit, on the feast of St. Giles. With God's grace, we visited the abbey, after a sermon had been preached in chapter by Master R[obert] of Darnestal, the archdeacon of Eu, who had never preached there as archdeacon, but who now, on our authority and at our request, as our companion, propounded the Word of God. There were . . . [*lacuna in MS*] monks in residence; one was a novice; one, to wit, Dom Eustace, was in England, and he had lately sent back a certain monk whom the abbot had sent to him as a companion, so that he had remained there alone, which much displeased both the abbot and ourself. They did not confess frequently; we ordered this corrected. A general distribution of alms is made there thrice a week. They did not keep the cloister well. Sometimes they went out through the meadows and other places without permission; we ordered this corrected. We forbade them to leave the refectory empty in the future, for they occasionally ate together elsewhere for recreation. We ordered those who were not priests to confess and receive Communion more often than they had been doing. They owed seven hundred pounds; of old wheat they had over three hundred *mines,* and of oats twenty *mines.* Item, we expressly forbade them to allow the Divine Services to be celebrated by anyone in St. Mary's chapel beyond the town, except in the customary manner, that is to say, Vespers on Saturday and Mass on Sunday, or unless it was necessary to perform them at other times for some of the nobles who might perchance wish to have Mass celebrated or hear Vespers there. We also ordered them to appoint some monk to receive the guests and make suitable provision for them, and to take better care of the sick than had been the case. Dom Matthew was defamed of incontinence and was said to have made pregnant Maelota, who lived near the abbey. We received procuration there this day. Total for procuration: eight pounds, three shillings, two pence.

SEPTEMBER 2. We received procuration at the priory of Mortemer-sur-Eaulne, where there were three monks of the Order of Cluny. Total for procuration: eight pounds, six shillings, four pence.

SEPTEMBER 3. At Eu, at our own expense.

SEPTEMBER 4. With God's grace we visited this abbey, after we had first preached in chapter. Twenty-eight canons were in residence, and eight were outside. We gave orders that all the books of the entire monastery be catalogued, frequently inspected, and surveyed, and that they should not be so generous in giving or lending them as they had been. Alms are given to clerics thrice a week, and thrice to poor lay folk. They owed four hundred seventy-four pounds of Tours; they had enough wine to last until the new yield.

However, on the following day, we entered the chapter once more because of the discord and rancors which existed between the community, the chamberlain, and the abbot. There, after we had first taken counsel with our associates concerning those things which were subject to dispute, and after due deliberation, we made the following decision. We ordered Brother Obert, the chamberlain, removed and relieved of his office and another person put in his place. Item, that by the appointed chamberlain, whose office would be temporary, separate accounts be drawn up containing all the expenses both in whole and in particular, and that the community should have one of these copies; that accounts be cast in the presence of some elected by the community more often than had been the case. Item, that the cloister be better guarded than it had been, and that lay folk be kept away from it. Item, that a suitable companion be given to Abbot William. Item, that the abbot be paid the monies due him annually. Item, that the sacristan account for the money which he received to administer his office. We received procuration there this day. Total for procuration: seven pounds, fifteen shillings, ten pence.

SEPTEMBER 5. With God's grace we received procuration at Le Tréport. Total for procuration: . . . [lacuna in MS].

SEPTEMBER 6. With God's aid we visited the abbey at Le Tréport, where there were nineteen monks; eight were outside in priories. We ordered the abbot to see to it that the Passional and the Lessons which he had just begun to have written out be completed as quickly as possible. All but three of the resident monks were priests. Item, we ordered the abbot to provide the community with more confessors. Item, that he should see that the sick were better taken care of than they had been and that a suitable servant be given to the sick, for they had long had a certain servant who was too young; and that they [the sick] should hear or say the Divine Office, and that they should have appropriate service books. Item, we gave orders that one monk should be in charge of the monks' clothing. Brother Richard, a former prior, was considered suspect of leprosy. We ordered him to undergo an examination in the presence of some monks sent with him. Item, we ordered that the accounts be made up every six weeks. Item, we ordered an increase in the pittance, which had customarily been of fifteen eggs. Item, we forbade the cellarer to eat meat with lay folk in the future without the abbot's permission, and we ordered him to eat in the refectory more often than was his practice. They owed five hundred forty pounds; three hundred pounds was owed to them. We found them to be very contentious and quarrelsome, at which we were aggrieved.

This day we spent the night at Envermeu.

SEPTEMBER 6. We received procuration at Envermeu. Total for procuration: nine pounds, nineteen pence.

SEPTEMBER 7. With God's aid we visited this priory, where there were eight monks of Bec-Hellouin. There should be twelve or thirteen, but on account of the multiple burdens of the house the number of monks had been diminished. They owed about three hundred pounds. With God's grace we found them to be in good condition. We were this day at Aliermont, at our own expense.

SEPTEMBER 8. To wit, on the Nativity of the Blessed Mary. At the same.

SEPTEMBER 9. We received procuration at Longueil, at a certain manor belonging to the abbot of Bec-Hellouin. The abbot was then keeping it in his own hands. Total for procuration: nine pounds, sixteen shillings, ten pence.

SEPTEMBER 10. With God's grace we visited the priory at Bacqueville, where there were four monks of Tiron, to wit, Clement of Beaumont, prior, Walter of Crasville, William Morant, and Giles of Illois. In such things as the fasts and the eating of meat they did not observe the Rule very well. We ordered them to celebrate Mass and to confess more frequently than had been their practice. They owed sixty pounds in addition to another ten pound which they owed to the rector of the church for the tithe belonging to him. We received procuration there this day. Total for procuration: . . . [lacuna in MS].

SEPTEMBER 11. At Longueville-Geoffroi, at the expense of the priory.

SEPTEMBER 12. We received procuration at Nogent near Neufchâtel. Total for procuration: . . . [lacuna in MS].

SEPTEMBER 13. With God's grace we visited the abbey at Bival, where there were thirty-two nuns and one lay sister. We forbade the abbess to receive in the future a share of the nuns' pittances. We also ordered her to draw up her accounts in the presence of some of the seniors elected by the community. Item, that she should pay the old abbess[10] the monies due to her annually. Item, that she remove a certain child whom she was having brought up at a house at Pierrement. Item, we warned her to make an effort to conduct herself towards the nuns in all things in a more clement and solicitous manner than she had done. They owed fifty-five pounds. We received procuration this day at Beaussault. Total for procuration: . . . [lacuna in MS].

SEPTEMBER 14. We visited the Beaussault priory, where there were two monks of Bec-Hellouin, to wit, Brother Herbert of St-Etienne, the prior, and Geoffrey of Angeville. With God's grace they were conducting themselves well. They were heavily burdened because of the new building.

Here we assigned to Matthew, the rector of a portion of [the church of] St-Remy-les-Champs, the day following the winter synod as the time when

---

[10] See entry for August 7, 1248.

he should purge himself with the seventh hand of priests[11] of being defamed of incontinence.

This same day we were at Beaubec, at the expense of the monastery. We did not compute.

SEPTEMBER 15. With God's grace we visited the priory at Sigy, where there were four monks of St-Ouen-de-Rouen, to wit, Brother William of Cahanges, prior, John of Jumièges, John of Calleville, and Anquetil of Hermenville. There should be six, but two had been recalled to the cloister for necessary reasons; but, as they said, the abbot was going to send two [more] there in a short while. They owed one hundred thirty-seven pounds, five shillings. We found other thins to be in good condition. We received procuration there this day. Total for procuration: seven pounds, fifteen shillings, ten pence.

SEPTEMBER 16-17. At Déville.

SEPTEMBER 18. With God's grace we came to the priory of St-Lô-de-Rouen, where seventeen canons, including the prior, were in residence. All but three were priests; two were at Cressy, and two at Theméricourt. One did not accuse another [in chapter]; we ordered this corrected. We ordered the subprior to behave in a more friendly manner towards the community than he had been doing. More was owed to them than they owed; they had received their entire yearly quit rents, and they had many supplies. This day we received procuration from the prior, but at Déville. Total for procuration: ... [lacuna in MS].

SEPTEMBER 19. With God's grace we visited the abbey of St-Ouen-de-Rouen, after with His aid we had first preached in Latin in chapter. Fifty monks were in residence; all but three were priests. We ordered the abbot never to permit any monk to dwell alone. We gave orders that the accounts, and in particular the itemized accounts of the kitchen, be drawn up more often than had been the practice, and in the presence of some of the seniors of the community. They owed five thousand one hundred four pounds, ten shillings, three pence of Tours, of which eleven hundred seventy pounds was at interest; fifteen hundred pounds in bad debts was owed to them. In other things concerning their spiritual state, with God's grace, we found them to be in good condition.

We received procuration this day at Ste-Catherine. Total for procuration: ... [lacuna in MS].

[11] See above, October 16, 1248, n. 70.

SEPTEMBER 20. With God's grace we visited the abbey of Ste-Catherine-sur-Rouen, where there were ... [*lacuna in MS*] monks in residence. All but one were priests; fourteen were at Blyth, and two at Hermansworth in England. We ordered the abbot to inspect the monks' coffers more frequently than was his custom. When this portion of the visitation had been completed, the community departed. The abbot, the bailiff, the prior, and the almoner remained behind with us in the chapter house. We questioned them together, and individually in secret, about the condition of the house. We found, indeed, that much was owed to them from the loans made by Abbot John; the Lady of Dangu and Sir Walter Crispin owed them six hundred pounds of Paris; the widow of the chamberlain of Tancarville, two hundred pounds of Tours; the Lady of Anneval, one hundred fifty pounds of Tours; Aelis Michael, three hundred pounds of Tours; the abbot and community of St-Martin-de-Pontoise, that large debt which many had known and [still] knew about.

We received procuration this day at Quévreville, from the lessee there. Total for procuration: eight pounds, fifteen shillings.

SEPTEMBER 21. To wit, on the feast of St. Matthew. At Martot, and we had the bishop of Evreux with us. SEPTEMBER 22. With God's grace the said bishop conferred Holy Orders on our and his own ordinands in the royal chapel at Pont-de-l'Arche, and spent the night with us at Martot. SEPTEMBER 23. At Pinterville. SEPTEMBER 24. At Gaillon, and we had the lord bishop of Evreux there with us. SEPTEMBER 25. At Pinterville.

This day the damoiselle Isabelle, daughter of the late Sir William of Gisors, a deceased knight, came in person to us at our hall at Pinterville, and in the presence of her mother; Master William of Flavacourt, the archdeacon of Petit-Caux, and Master John of Jumièges, both canons of Rouen; Sir Peter, Sir Guy Malvoisin, Sir Walter of Courcelles, and Sir John of Mont-Chevreuil, knights; Anselm of l'Ille and Guy of Roeny, esquires; and many others, swore, touching the Holy Gospels, that she would in no way hinder the executors of the will of the said deceased from freely carrying out his will, and that if it were necessary she would contribute from her own share so that the terms of the said will might be fulfilled. For this she offered as sureties the aforesaid Sir Peter, Sir Guy, and Sir John, knights, and the said Guy of Roeny.

SEPTEMBER 26-28. At Pinterville. SEPTEMBER 29. To wit, on the feast of St. Michael. At the same. SEPTEMBER 30. At Pinterville. OCTOBER 1-2.

At Martot. OCTOBER 3. At Rouen. OCTOBER 4. To wit, on the feast of St. Francis. At Rouen. With God's grace, although weak and infirm, we celebrated High Mass in pontificals at the Rouen cathedral and had the entire chapter at our manor for the feast day. OCTOBER 5. At Déville. OCTOBER 6. At Frênes. OCTOBER 7. With God's grace we came to the priory at Sausseuse, and with His help we visited. In residence were fourteen canons, of whom four were novices; all but six were priests; fifteen were outside in obediences. At our last visitation,[12] we had ordered the prior to have each and every one of the priory books brought out at least once a year and displayed before the community in chapter, and if by chance any had been loaned or given away they should be reclaimed. He had not done this, and therefore we imposed such penance upon him as seemed expedient to us; we repeated this order to him and also to the subprior. They owed two hundred forty pounds; about the same amount was owed to them in both good and bad debts. We received procuration there this day. Total for procuration: six pounds, seven shillings.

OCTOBER 8. At Sérans-le-Bouteiller. This day we received from the prior seventy shillings of Paris, the amount in which he is held to us each year when we turn aside to this place; also, in addition to the said sum, he is held to provide us with household vessels and common utensils, forage for the horses, and other things, as is more fully contained in a letter drawn up about this.[13]

OCTOBER 9. To wit, on the feast of St. Denis. With God's grace we visited this priory, where there ware two monks of St-Germer-de-Flay: Brother Adam of Omericourt, prior, and Brother ... [lacuna in MS]. They ate meat when there was no need, and they did not observe the fasts of the Rule. We ordered the prior to be careful to celebrate Mass more often than was his practice. They were in debt for two hundred pounds and for six muids of wheat.

This day with God's grace we visited the priory at Parnes, where there were four monks of St-Evroult, to wit, Brother William of Neufmarché, John of Ste-Celerine, Thomas Mansel, and Henry of Jumièges. With God's grace we found them to be in good condition. They owed sixty pounds. We received procuration there this same day. Total for procuration: six pounds, three shillings, five pence.

12 See entry for March 17, 1266/67.
13 See entry for February 6. 1266/67, n. 53

OCTOBER 10. We received procuration at Chaumont-en-l'Aillerie. Total for procuration: seven pounds, three shillings, four pence. OCTOBER 11. With God's grace we held the synod of the French Vexin in the church at Chaumont, and we were there this day at our own expense.

OCTOBER 12. With God's grace we visited the said priory of Chaumont-l'Aillerie, where there were three monks of St-Germer-de-Flay, to wit, Brother Henry of Reilly, prior, William of St-Germer, and John of Chaumont. With God's grace they carried themselves well. The bell tower was unroofed and had been badly maintained for a long while. They owed two hundred pounds.

We received procuration this day at Gisors, together with our expenses, at the royal castle.

OCTOBER 13. At Frênes. OCTOBER 14-17. At Déville. OCTOBER 18. To wit, on the feast of St. Luke the Evangelist. At the same. OCTOBER 19-20. At Déville, because of the Exchequer at Rouen. OCTOBER 21. The same. This day we had the lord bishop of Bayeux with us. OCTOBER 22. At Frênes, and the said bishop with us. OCTOBER 23. To wit, on the feast of St-Romain. At Gisors, with the king; the said bishop, being ill, remained this day at Frênes. OCTOBER 24-25. At Gisors. OCTOBER 26-27. At Frênes. OCTOBER 28. To wit, on the feast of SS. Simon and Jude. At Frênes. OCTOBER 29. At Gaillon. OCTOBER 30-31. At Martot. NOVEMBER 1. To wit, on All Saints. At Martot. NOVEMBER 2. At Martot. NOVEMBER 3-5. At Déville. NOVEMBER 6. At Rouen, where with God's aid we held the holy synod.

NOVEMBER 7. At Rouen. This day there appeared in person before us Ralph of Neubourg, rector of the church at Sommery, to whom we had assigned this day to hear our will and verdict, for that he had promised us, when he had appeared according to law before us in our council, that he would resign his church whenever we should so desire, and since he had been defamed of incontinence and had confessed both to the ill-fame and the fact itself. We then enjoined him to exchange his church with some other in another diocese before the coming Lent, and that furthermore, he should not claim anything more from the said church [Sommery] from that time on.

To Walter, priest at Bival, we assigned the day next before the day for ordinations to purge himself with the seventh hand of priests[14] of the vice

---

[14] See above, October 16, 1248, n. 70.

of incontinence, of which he had been and was still grievously defamed ever since he had returned from Rome.

Item, we assigned the same day to Stephen, priest at Denestanville, to pay the fine of twenty pounds of Tours, which we had already imposed upon him and which he had promised to pay, because he had been and was defamed of the daughter of Robert Pesant of Longueville, or else to purge himself of this ill report with the seventh hand of priests.[15]

Item, this day John, the former rector of the church at Neuville-en-Bosc, resigned this church into our hands; however, as a concession, we permitted him to exchange this church for some other in another diocese before the coming octave of the Nativity.

Item, this day Matthew, rector of a portion of the church of St-Remy-les-Champs, failed his purgation.

NOVEMBER 8. At Déville. NOVEMBER 9. At Martot. NOVEMBER 10. At Pinterville. NOVEMBER 11. To wit, on the feast of St. Martin. At the same. NOVEMBER 12. At Gaillon. NOVEMBER 13-16. At Pinterville. NOVEMBER 17-18. At Gaillon. NOVEMBER 19. At Mantes. NOVEMBER 20. At Pontoise. NOVEMBER 21-22. At Paris, to attend the Parlement. NOVEMBER 23. To wit, on the feast of St. Clement. NOVEMBER 24-29. At Paris, attending the Parlement. NOVEMBER 30. To wit, on the feast of St. Andrew. At St-Germain-en-Laye. DECEMBER 1. At Pontoise. DECEMBER 2. To wit, on the first Sunday in Advent. At Mantes. DECEMBER 3. At Caillon. DECEMBER 4-5. At Pinterville. DECEMBER 6. To wit, on the feast of St. Nicholas. At the same. DECEMBER 7. At the same. DECEMBER 8. To wit, on the Conception of the Blessed Mary. At the same. DECEMBER 9. At Vernon. DECEMBER 10. At Mantes. DECEMBER 11-12. At Pontoise. DECEMBER 13. To wit, on the feast of St. Lucy. At Mantes. DECEMBER 14. At Gaillon. DECEMBER 15. At Pinterville. DECEMBER 16. At Martot. DECEMBER 17. At Déville.

DECEMBER 18. With God's grace we came to the priory at Bondeville, and with His aid we exercised our duty of visitation this day. After we had preached, we found that there were thirty nuns, of whom one was a novice; there were also four lay brothers, six lay sisters, and two maidservants. We ordered them to send away Basiria, the daughter of Emmeline of Aulnay, who had been there for a month. We forbade the prioress to keep any female or females there, unless she or they had already been received, and

[15] *Ibid.*

we ordered that they should not receive anyone without our special permission. Some of the nuns had incomes: we ordered that they could be obtained and kept only with the knowledge of the prioress. Item, we ordered Brother Oger, the priest, to obey the prioress better than he had been doing. The building in which guests were received was too near the cloister and the community; we ordered the prioress to try and find some suitable remedy for this. They owed one hundred forty pounds; eighty pounds was owed to them. They had enought wheat to last the year, as they thought; however, they had no oats.

This day we spent the night at Déville, at our own expense.

DECEMBER 19. At Déville.

DECEMBER 20. With God's grace we came to the church of Notre-Dame-la-Ronde-de-Rouen, where with His aid we preached a sermon in Latin in the choir, and then made a visitation. We found the dean staying there with a single canon and certain vicars. With God's grace their state was good. This day, we spent the night at Déville, at our own expense.

This day with God's grace, we visited the clerics of St-Albano. We found that they were living in sufficient harmony, and that their affairs and the state of their house were in good condition, through God's providence.

DECEMBER 21. To wit, on the feast of St-Thomas the Apostle. At Déville.

DECEMBER 22. Our venerable brother R[alph], by God's grace the bishop of Evreux, conferred Holy Orders for us at the Franciscan monastery at Vernon.

This same day, while we remained at Déville, we assigned to Walter,[16] the priest at Bival, [who was] many times defamed of incontinence, and who had already come before us, the Tuesday before the Purification of the Blessed Mary, at Rouen or vicinity, or before our official of Rouen whom we appointed as our agent in this matter, to purge himself of this vice with the seventh hand of priests.[17]

This same day we had before us the priest at Appegart who, as we learned from his own mouth, had not celebrated Mass, nor received Communion, that is, the Eucharist, within four ... [lacuna in MS], and who was serving his church badly. For these matters we assigned him the Tuesday before the Purification to appear before us or our official, at Rouen or vicinity etcetera.

This day we dined at the house of the Friars Minor of Rouen, and spent the night at our manor at Rouen.

[16] See entry for November 7, above.
[17] See above, October 16, 1248, n. 70.

DECEMBER 23. At Rouen, and, as was fitting, we made our *O*,[18] God helping us. DECEMBER 24. To wit, on the vigil of the Nativity of the Lord. At Rouen. DECEMBER 25. With God's grace we celebrated the feast of the Nativity of the Lord at Rouen. DECEMBER 26. At Frênes. DECEMBER 27. At Genainville, at our own expense. DECEMBER 28. To wit, on the feast of the Holy Innocents. At Conflans. DECEMBER 29-31. At Paris. JANUARY 1. To wit, on the Circumcision. At Paris. JANUARY 2-5. At Paris. JANUARY 6. To wit, on Epiphany. At Paris. JANUARY 7-8. At Paris. JANUARY 9. At St-Maur. This day lord Simon, [De Brie] the cardinal, left Paris. JANUARY 10. At Paris. JANUARY 11. At Pontoise. JANUARY 12. At Bray-sur-Baudemont. JANUARY 12-14. At Gaillon. JANUARY 15-16. At Pinterville. JANUARY 17. At Martot. JANUARY 18-19. At Déville. JANUARY 20. To wit, on Septuagesima Sunday. With God's grace we preached in the cathedral at Rouen. JANUARY 21-24. At Déville. JANUARY 25. To wit, on the Conversion of St. Paul. At the same.

JANUARY 26. At St-Victor-en-Caux, at our own expense. On the said Septuagesima and at the entrance to the choir of the cathedral of Rouen, we conferred the archdeanery of Grand-Caux upon Master Stephen of Sens, the former archdeacon of the French Vexin, and the archdeanery of the [French] Vexin we conferred upon Master Th[omas] of Barre. Also we conferred upon John of Morgneval, our clerk, the prebend which Master Nicholas of Checy, former archdeacon of Rouen, had held.

JANUARY 27. To wit, on Sexagesima Sunday. In between the cloister and chapter house at St-Victor-en-Caux, we preached to the local monks and to a large portion of the parishioners of the village who had gathered there. When, with God's grace, we had finished our talk, we remained in chapter with the community, and with His aid we exercised our duty of visitation, as was fitting. We found seventeen monks in residence; two were at St-Thomas, two in England. We ordered the abbot to have the Rule read out frequently in chapter, and also explained in French. Since, indeed, the abbot had omitted to have the Statutes of the Pope read out in chapter, as we had ordered him to do at our other visitation,[19] we imposed upon him such a penance as seemed expedient to us. We again ordered him to do this, that is to say, to have the Statutes of Pope Gregory frequently read out in chapter. Item, we ordered him to inspect the monks' coffers more often

[18] See above, December 23, 1250, n. 135.
[19] See entry for July 31, 1267.

than was his practice, lest they had any property. They owed two hundred pounds; with the exception of wine, they had enough supplies to last the year. A general distribution of alms is made there thrice a week. John, called of Paris, had cast off and put aside his habit and had returned it to the abbot in full chapter, stating that he had entered the order through the crime of simony. We received procuration there this day. Total for procuration: seven pounds.

JANUARY 28. With God's grace we visited the priory at Auffay, where there were six monks of St-Evroult, to wit, Brothers Geoffrey Gravart, John of Vernuces, Alexander of Pontchardon, Henry of Mont-de-Piété, Robert of Manle, and William of Falaise. They owed three hundred pounds. With God's grace we found them in good condition as to spirituals. We received procuration there this day. Total for procuration: seven pounds.

JANUARY 29-31. At Aliermont. FEBRUARY 1. At the same. FEBRUARY 2. To wit, on the feast of the Purification. At the same. With God's grace we celebrated Mass in pontificals, and preached at St. Nicholas' church there. FEBRUARY 3. At St-Victor-en-Caux, at our own expense. FEBRUARY 4-5. At Déville. FEBRUARY 6. To wit, on Ash Wednesday. At Rouen, where with God's grace we performed the Office of this day. FEBRUARY 7. At Déville.

FEBRUARY 8. At the same. This day Walter,[20] a priest and rector of the church at Bival, appeared before us, having been assigned this day for purging himself before us with the seventh hand of priests[21] of the vice of incontinence of which he was repeatedly defamed in particular with the wife of John Taillart, his parishioner. His purgation fell short of being satisfactory. We then assigned him the Saturday next before Palm Sunday to appear before us at Rouen, or wherever we might happen to be in that vicinity, to hear his sentence for the foregoing.

FEBRUARY 9. At Ouville. FEBRUARY 10. To wit, on the Sunday when the *Invocavit me*[22] is sung. We preached in the cathedral at Rouen, and spent the night at our manor, God helping us. FEBRUARY 11. At Ste-Catherine, at our own expense. FEBRUARY 12-13. At Frênes.

FEBRUARY 14. With God's grace we came to St. Mary's church at Les Andelys, and there, having preached with His aid, we proceeded to make

[20] See entries for November 7 and December 22, above.
[21] See above, October 16, 1248, n. 70.
[22] The first Sunday in Lent.

a visitation. We found a dean and four canons in residence, to wit, Masters John Cadot, Ralph of Salmonville, L'Homme-Dieu, and John of Spain; two were absent, to wit, the official of Pontoise and a certain Romain. There are six prebends. There are four priest-vicars, of whom one should serve at La Culture, and the other three must attend the church to support the burdens of the parish. Two other vicars are there, of whom one is a deacon, the other a subdeacon, and who are held to vest themselves every day for High Mass. The dean has the cure of souls of the canons, the chaplains, and the clerks-choral, and, indeed, of the whole village and the adjacent hamlets. The sacristan is held to sleep always in the sacristy and to hold the song school. We ordered them to improve or correct the lighting of the church. Item, we ordered the canons and vicars to revere and obey the dean in better fashion than they had been doing. Item, it was agreeably determined that the sacristan should be held to celebrate the Mass of the Faithful, and for this he should have the purchase, that is to say, the four acres of ground, made from the estate of Master Robert, of good memory, a former canon of this church, now deceased. The dean and canons ought to take this under consideration, to wit, the method of celebrating Mass and how many times a week the said sacristan might conveniently celebrate a Mass of this kind [of the Faithful]. Item, they ought to discuss sometime about who will receive the gross income of their prebends when they die. Item, concerning the acquisition of an area near La Culture to make a cemetery.

This day we spent the night at Frênes.

FEBRUARY 15. At Mortemer-en-Lyons, at the expense of the abbey. FEBRUARY 16. We received procuration at St-Laurent-en-Lyons. Total for procuration: ... [lacuna in MS].

FEBRUARY 17. With God's grace we visited the said priory, after we had first with His aid preached in the chapter house. Sixteen canons were in residence; one was with Dom Peter, the priest at Vibeuf, and we gave orders that he be recalled immediately after Easter. Item, we gave orders that all the books of the house be catalogued and checked over in chapter at least once every year. All but two of the residents were priests. There were six lay brothers, of whom three were in the priory, two were at St-Crepin, and one was at Moulin; there were three lay sisters. They owed three hundred pounds; with the exception of oats, they had enough supplies to last the year.

This day we spent the night at Bellosane, and at the expense of the abbey.

FEBRUARY 18. With God's grace we visited the priory of nuns at St-Aubin, where there were ... [*lacuna in MS*] nuns. We punished Anastasia, a former subprioress, for having given up her office of subprioress on her own authority, and against the wish of the prioress. We also deemed Eustachia and Margaret disobedient for that, to wit, they had been unwilling to receive or undertake the said office at the command of the prioress, and therefore we punished them as seemed expedient to us. They owed eight pounds, ten shillings, and they had few or no supplies.

This day with God's aid we reconciled St-Hildevert's church at Gournay, which had been violated by the spilling of blood.

We were, at our own expense, at Gournay this day.

FEBRUARY 19. With God's grace we visited the chapter of St-Hildevert-de-Gournay, where we found the dean, the treasurer, Matthew of Montfort, and Master Guy of Laudun as resident canons. We issued orders that Stephen, a chaplain of the church, who was and had been staying with the penitentiary at Rouen, be recalled to the chapter at once and be compelled to take up personal residence there, or else to resign his benefice. Item, it was ordained that in their first general chapter they would deal with these things, and should see to what the treasurer is held, and to do this after careful deliberation. Item, that they should strive to have a conventual Mass every day with deacon and subdeacon vested. Item, that they should have a conference among themselves concerning the parochial rights which the priest of St. Mary's claims to have over the Hôtel-Dieu.

This same day we visited the Hôtel-Dieu, where there were two lay brothers and three lay sisters. Peter, the provost of Gournay, was managing the house with the assistance of a lay brother. There was a quarrel between them and the priest of St. Mary's, although there was an ordinance or agreement drawn up by the official of Rouen about this disagreement which had been sealed with the seal of the Rouen Curia, that is to say, concerning the parish rights which the said priest claimed to have over the said house; and the said brothers did not wish to observe this ordinance. They owed one hundred shillings; with the exception of oats, they had enough supplies to last the year. We gave orders, too, that Dom Ralph of St-Julien should hear the confessions of the brothers and those of all the inhabitants of the Hôtel-Dieu until the chapter should pass some regulation about this.

The same day we made inquiries concerning the state of the local leper house from the dean, the canons, and Peter, the provost manager of the place. We found that there was one leper there. They owed six pounds. [The house] was, with God's grace in sufficiently good condition. We received procuration this day at Neufmarché.

FEBRUARY 20. With God's grace we visited the priory at Neufmarché, where there were four monks of St-Evroult, to wit, Brother Victor of Nogent prior, and Brothers William of Orqueil, John of Prêtreville, and Peter of Nogent. William of Orqueil was slothful and negligent about the Divine Office. The prior rarely celebrated Mass. They owed twenty pounds. We ordered the prior to keep the cloister in a cleaner and better condition than had been his practice. Item, that he should have the choir of his priory repaired and so arranged that lay folk should not be able to reach them or see them, as they had been doing, and that the monks and clerics there might be able to serve God more circumspectly than they had been doing. Total for procuration: of this place: . . . . [lacuna in MS].

This day we spent night at Gisors, at the priory of St-Ouen, where, in the name of procuration, we ought to receive seven pounds of Tours annually, whensoever we turn aside once a year to this place. [We ought to receive] nothing else except by the graciousness and will of the prior.

FEBRUARY 21. At Marcheroux, at the expense of the abbey. FEBRUARY 22. To wit, on St. Peter's Chair [of Antioch]. At Beaumont-sur-Oise. FEBRUARY 23. At Paris. FEBRUARY 24. To wit, on the feast of St. Matthew the Apostle. At the same. FEBRUARY 25-28. At Paris. MARCH 1-3. At Paris. MARCH 4. At St-Germain-en-Laye. MARCH 5. At Juziers, at our own expence. MARCH 6. At Vernon. MARCH 7. At Pinterville. MARCH 8. At Martot, and we had Lord R[ichard], the bishop of Evreux, with us. MARCH 9. At Martot. This day the said bishop conferred Holy Orders for us at the royal chapel at Pont-de-l'Arche, and spent the night with us at Martot. MARCH 10-11. At Martot. MARCH 12. To wit, on the feast of St. Gregory. At Martot. MARCH 13-15. At Déville.

MARCH 16. At Rouen. On this day, which had been assigned to him to hear his sentence, there appeared before us Walter,[23] the priest at Bival, who had failed to purge himself one day some time ago of the vice of incontinence of which he had been repeatedly defamed. We, sparing him and giving him fuller grace in this matter, thought we should assign to him the Tuesday next after the Sunday on which . . . [lacuna in MS] is sung, when he should appear before us at Rouen, or wherever we might be in that

[23] See entry for February 8, above.

vicinity, to purge himself of the said vice of incontinence with the seventh hand of known and neighboring priests, men of good opinion and repute.[24]

This same day we warned Dom Stephen, priest at Denestanville, to put himself within forty days into such a position that he would be able to serve his church, or that otherwise we would proceed against him as the law requires.

MARCH 17. To wit, Palm Sunday. With God's grace we preached in the cathedral at Rouen, and spent the night at our manor in Rouen. MARCH 18. We dined with the [Dominican] Preachers of Rouen, and spent the night at Déville. MARCH 19. At Déville. MARCH 20. We dined at the house of the Friars Minor of Rouen, and spent the night at our manor in Rouen. MARCH 21. To wit, on Holy Thursday. With God's grace we bestowed absolutions, as is customarily done at Rouen this day, and we performed the Office of the day at the cathedral in Rouen. MARCH 22. To wit, on the Adoration of the Cross. We performed the office suitable for this day at the cathedral in Rouen. MARCH 23. To wit, on Holy Saturday. At Rouen.

[24] See above, October 16, 1248, n. 70.

MARCH 24. To wit, on holy Easter. At the same. MARCH 25. To wit, on the Annunciation of the Blessed Mary. At Déville.

MARCH 26. With God's grace we visited Saint George's abbey at Boscherville, after with His grace we had first preached in the chapter house. Twenty-four monks were in residence there; all but four were priests; six were outside, to wit, two at St-Nicholas and four in England. One does not, as of custom, accuse another [in chapter]. More was owed to them than they owed. We received procuration there this day. Total for procuration: nine pounds, seven shillings, twenty-three pence.

MARCH 27. At St-Wandrille, at our own expense. MARCH 28. At Fauville, at our own expense. MARCH 29. With God's grace we reconciled the church at Hattenville, which had been violated by the shedding of blood.

We spent the night at St-Wandrille, at our own expense.

MARCH 30. At Jumièges, at our own expense. This day we assigned to Master P[hilip] of Val-Badone, rector of the church at ... [Obertiville] [*lacuna in MS*], in our diocese. He appeared before us in person in the new hall near the abbot's chapel, and we assigned him the Wednesday next after Trinity [Sunday], when he should appear before us at Rouen or wherever we might be in the vicinity, or before our official should we happen to be absent, to answer to a charge of perjury which he had incurred, in that he had omitted to present himself for Holy Orders and had never desired to reside personally in his said church, as he is held to do by his own oath which he took at his collation to it. He is also to receive from us whatever justice will demand.

MARCH 31. To wit, on the octave of Easter. At Corneville, where we received procuration this day. Total for procuration: seven pounds.

APRIL 1. With God's grace we visited the said abbey of Corneville, where there were eight canons in residence; eleven were outside in obediences. There was none with cure of souls in the parishes of Corneville or Ameriville, nor had there been any for many days, due to the carelessness and negligence of the prior. This much displeased us. We then ordered the abbot to see to it that these places had in them priests charged with care of souls within forty days, or that otherwise we would place secular priests in them. Item, we ordered him to have each and every book of the house recorded in registers and checked over every year in chapter, and that he should recall the ones that had been loaned. Master William Bienvenu had certain collections of canon law. We also ordered the abbot that before Pentecost he should recall to the cloister Brother Henry from his association with the priest at Routot, with whom he had now for a long time been staying without our knowledge and permission. They had no prior; we ordered the abbot not to delay in promoting someone as prior, and to receive some good youths or lettered clerics and to gown them as speedily as he could decently do so, in order to augment the number of canons and bring it up to at least twelve, and thus embellish the divine cult. Item, that he should make better provision for the sick than had been made, especially to procure some serving lad who should attend them. They owed two hundred forty pounds; with the exception of oats, they had sufficient supplies to last the year We received procuration this day at Bourg-Achard. Total for procuration: ... [*lacuna in MS*].

APRIL 2. This day we celebrated [the octave of] the Divine Office of the Annunciation of the Blessed Mary. With God's grace we celebrated High Mass in pontificals at the said priory, and later, when we had preached in the middle of the church to the canons of the place and to the local parishioners who were standing by, we visited the community in chapter. We found twelve canons in residence; all but two were priests. More was owed to them than they owed. We enjoined a penance on the prior because he had not yet asked Master William of Bosc-Guillaume for the *Summa* of Master William of Auxerre, as we had ordered him to do at our other visitation.[1] With God's grace, we found other things to be in good condition. We were there this day, at our own expense.

APRIL 3. With God's grace we came to the abbey of Bec-Hellouin, and after, with His aid, we had preached in chapter, we proceeded to make a visitation. We found sixty-four monks and [learned] that three were at St-Nicolas; twenty of the said sixty-four were novices. All were priests with the exception of the novices. We gave orders that all abbey books be viewed before Pentecost and carefully checked over before the entire community in chapter. Item, we ordered the abbot and prior to inspect the boxes and

---

[1] See entry for August 7, 1267.

coffers of the monks, lest they have any property. Item, that the Statutes of Pope Gregory be frequently read in chapter. A single monk was at St-Lambert; we ordered another sent to him. Item, we expressly enjoined the abbot to be diligent about getting accounts of everything which they spent and received from those who had administrative offices, especially from the kitchener, the officer in charge of the grain, and others, and to compel them to make computations. Item, since the community suspected Brother Nicholas of Lendy of leprosy, and abhorred and abominated him because of this, we advised the abbot privately, in the chamber where we, as of custom, slept, to send the said Brother N[icholas] away. The abbot told us that he would send him to St-Lambert, where there is no great concourse of men and where he might receive the benefit of the air and considerable mitigation of his ailment. Item, we requested the abbot to take care to entrust offices or administrative positions to persons whom he thought to be suitable, provident, and honest. Item, we ordered him to discharge from his service his marshal, whom we found to be seriously defamed of incontinence, although he had a wife at Rouen with whom he had never cared to cohabit. We received procuration there this day. They did not compute our expenses.

APRIL 4-10. At Pinterville. APRIL 11-12. At Martot. APRIL 13-21. At Déville, because of the Exchequer. APRIL 22. At Pinterville, and we had with us the lord bishop of Bayeux and the dean of St-Aignan [-d'Orléans]. Here begins the visitation of the diocese of Evreux.

APRIL 23. With God's grace we came to the abbey at Croix-St-Leufroy, in the diocese of Evreux, and after we had preached in the chapter house, we visited. We found sixteen monks in residence, of whom three were novices; all were priests, with the exception of these three novices. We ordered the abbot to visit the outside priories and to have the fasts and other observances of the Rule maintained in them. Item, that he should inspect the monks' coffers more often than had been his practice. They owed eleven hundred pounds. We received procuration there this day. Total for procuration: nine pounds, six shillings.

APRIL 24. We visited the chapter of St. Mary's church at Vernon, after with His aid we had preached the Word of God in the choir of that same church to the chaplains, the vicars, and some of the lay folk who were present. There are nine prebends; none of the canons resided there. There were nine vicars, of whom five were priests; two were deacons, and two were subdeacons. There were four clerics who regularly attended the church in a satisfactory manner, considering the small stipends. The vicars referred to above did not have permanency of tenure to the extent that the canons could remove them at will if the canons so desired. We received procuration this day from the proctor of the chapter, in a house belong to Bec. Total for procuration: eleven pounds, thirteen shillings, eleven pence.

APRIL 25. We received procuration at the priory of Jouy. Total for procuration: nine pounds, five shillings, seven pence.

APRIL 26. With God's grace we visited this priory, where there were two [monks] of Jumièges. They had an income of five hundred pounds, and of this they were required to remit to the abbey whatever they were able to save over and above their own maintenance and that of their staff. Sometimes they ate meat when there was no need.

This day we were at the house of the lord bishop of Evreux, at his expense.

APRIL 27. With God's grace we entered the chapter at Evreux, where, after, with His aid, we had preached before R[alph], by God's grace bishop of that place, and the canons, clerks-choral and chaplains of the church of Evreux who were present, we investigated as fully as we could the state of the house. We found with God's grace that it was in good condition, except for the fact that the dean, though obligated to do so, hardly kept residence at all. We ordered them to give this matter careful and attentive consideration. We received procuration this day from the chapter, in the house of the bishop. Total for procuration: eighteen pounds, nineteen shillings, eight pence.

APRIL 28. With God's grace we visited the abbey at St-Taurin, where there were twenty-three monks; all but six [were] priests. We ordered the abbot to inspect the monks' coffers more frequently than was his practice and to see that they did not have any private property. They owed one thousand pounds; two hundred pounds was owed to them. With God's grace we found other things to be in good condition. We received procuration there this day. Total for procuration: six pounds, eighteen shillings. No inventory of their wine could be had.

APRIL 29. With God's grace we came to the abbey at St-Sauveur, and when with His aid we had preached a sermon, we proceeded to make a visitation. There we found sixty-one veiled nuns, and two who were to receive the veil. Although these had already been accepted into the community, yet they were still awaiting their formal place in the community. We gave orders that the leftovers of each nun's bread be given away as alms. Item, we forbade the nuns to dine with their relatives in the house or in the abbey; we also forbade them to have dogs, birds, and squirrels. Item, that they should not work needle-cases of silk, or make alms-bags or such things, but only such as were destined for the worship of God. Item, that they should not have any metaled belts. Further, we forbade the abbess to give any nun permission to go out, unless with good companionship. The community had three maidservants in common, and there were several private maids at the expense of the house. We gave orders that, for the future, there should be no more private maidservants, but that the number of general ones might be increased if necessary, we ordered the abbess to make better provision for the sick than had been the case. They owed four hundred pounds; they paid a tithe on eleven hundred fifty pounds.

We received procuration from them this day at St-Taurin. Total for procuration: ten pounds, twenty-three pence.

APRIL 30. We received procuration at Ivry. Total for procuration: nine pounds, three shillings, three pence.

MAY 1. To wit, on the feast of SS. Philip and James, and on the vigil of the Ascension. We visited the said abbey at Ivry, where fifteen monks were in residence; all but one were priests. We ordered the abbot, who was a new one, to visit the outside priories at least once a year to see that the monks did not have any [private] property. We ordered the abbot to cast his accounts more frequently than he had been doing, and in the presence of the community or some of the seniors elected and provided by the community. They owed ... [*lacuna in MS*].

This day we were at the abbey at Breuil [-Benoît], a Cistercian house, at the expense of the abbey. We did not compute.

MAY 2. To wit, Ascension Day. We spent the night at Motelle, at the house of Amaury of Muzy, our nephew's squire, since the said squire had been very insistent in inviting us. The prior of Muzy, who was held to receive us and to give us procuration, had buildings which were unsuitable for our reception. Although, indeed, we can, according to law, receive full procuration from the said prior, yet, since he was poor and burdened with debts, we took only one hundred shillings from him in the name of procuration, though, in fact, the prior of this place is held in full procuration to us whensoever we exercise the office of visitation in this diocese.

MAY 3. With God's grace we visited the priory at Muzy, where there were four monks of Coulombs. All were priests. They ate meat when there was no need, and they observed the fasts of the Rule rather unsuitably. The buildings of the place were in bad condition. They owed one hundred twenty pounds; they had few supplies.

This day with God's grace we visited the priory at Heudreville, where three monks of Tiron were staying; they observed no Rule. We found three casks of wine in the church; we forbade them to put anything in the house of God in the future, but to keep it as clean as they were able to do. Item, we ordered them to confess and receive Communion, and even to celebrate Mass more often than was their custom. Item, we ordered them to find maidservants who were older and less subject to suspicion than the ones they had been having. They owed about one hundred pounds; with the exception of oats, they had enough supplies to last the year; they paid a tithe on two hundred pounds. We received procuration there this day. Total for procuration: six pounds, six shillings, six pence.

MAY 4. We visited the house at Coudres, where there were two monks of Bourgueil. The prior did not sleep [in the same room] with his companion; we ordered them to sleep in a single chamber. They did not observe the Statutes of the Rule in any respect. The prior, as he told us, remitted to his abbot two hundred fifty pounds each year, and managed the house with the residue. We received procuration there this day. He did not care to compute.

MAY 5. We came to the house at Tillières, which belongs to the abbey of Bec-Hellouin. We found the buildings in need of reroofing and the whole manor miserably out of condition so far as the buildings were concerned.

We spent the night at Breteuil at the royal castle, where we received procuration from the custodian of the aforesaid manor. Total for procuration: ten pounds, sixteen shillings, eleven pence.

MAY 6. With God's grace we visited the priory of St-Sulpice, near L'Aigle, where there were eight monks of St-Laumer-de-Blois. They did not have enough altars. They did not observe the statutes of the Rule as to the eating of meat, the fasts, and other things. They rarely confessed. With the exception of wine they had sufficient supplies to last the year. They owed little; they had an income of about three hundred pounds. Total for procuration: seven pounds, nine shillings, eight pence.

MAY 7. We visited the priory at Rai, near L'Aigle, where there were two monks of St-Laumer-de-Blois. They observed no Rule; they ate meat occasionally and without scruples. We forbade them [to permit] women with their husbands to dine with them, as they had been in the habit of doing. Sometimes they ate meat, but, as the prior said, they did this with their abbot's permission. The prior's companion was absent at this time. They had an income of ninety pounds, and they paid a tithe based on this amount. We received procuration there this day. Total for procuration: six pounds, seventeen shillings, two pence. We caused sixty shillings of Tours to be returned and given back to them, because [the house] was burdened with debts. Indeed, it owed one hundred pounds.

MAY 8. With God's grace we came to the abbey at Lyre, and after with His aid we had preached in chapter, we proceeded to make a visitation. There we found thirty-seven monks in residence; all but seven were priests; there were fifteen monks in England. We found them at fault in the frequency of their confession, and we expressly ordered them to confess more often than had been their practice. Item, we gave orders that the cloister be better guarded than it had been and that a careful watch be placed at the entrance to the cloister. Alms are distributed there every day. They owed eighteen hundred pounds, of which eight hundred sixty-six was at interest. They have suffered very heavy losses in England, as they said. We received procuration there this day. We did not compute.

MAY 9. We received procuration at the abbey of Conches.

MAY 10. With God's grace we visited the said abbey, where there were twenty-five monks, two of whom were novices. There used to be more, and the abbot told us that he would increase the number. We forbade lay folk to talk with the monks in the cloister. We ordered the abbot to have the Rule as it affected the eating of meat observed in the priories as well as he could. They owed little, and some debts were owed to them; they had enough supplies to last the year. With God's grace things were well with them.

This day we were at the abbey at La Noë, a Cistercian house, at the expense of the abbey. We did not compute.

MAY 11. We received procuration at the priory at Beaumont-le-Roger, which belongs to the abbey of Bec-Hellouin. Total for procuration: nine pounds, twelve shillings, four pence.

MAY 12. To wit, on Pentecost. With God's grace we celebrated Mass in pontificals in the upper chapel of the aforesaid priory, and then we preached near the old royal castle. We were this day at the said priory, but at our own expense. This same day we visited the said priory, where we found six monks of Bec-Hellouin. There used to be more, but the number had been reduced because of the extensive buildings they were constructing. The abbot had sold [property to the value of] forty marks sterling, which should belong to the priory; we must speak with the abbot [of Bec] about this. They owed four hundred pounds; two hundred pounds was owed to them; with the exception of oats, they had enough supplies to last the year.

MAY 13. To wit, the day following Pentecost. We came to the priory or house at Daubeuf, which belongs to the monastery of St-Ouen-de-Rouen, where we found a certain lessee, to wit, Peter of Bicauf, who remitted annually to St. Ouen's monastery eighty *muids* of both wheat and oats, and one hundred forty pounds of Tours. He did not give us procuration this day, but on a following day, as will be explained below.[2]

This same day we visited the priory at Montaure, where there were two monks of St-Ouen [-de-Rouen]; there ought to be three. They had but one chalice for the manor chapel and the parish church; we ordered them to get one for the chapel. We forbade them to allow women to dine with them at their house in the future, as they had been doing. They had an income of two hundred fifty pounds; they owed eighty pounds. With the exception of wine and oats, they had enough supplies to last the year. We received procuration there this day. Total for procuration: ... [*lacuna in MS*].

MAY 14. With God's grace we came to the priory at Bailleul, which belongs to the monastery of St-Ouen-de-Rouen. There we found ... [*lacuna in MS*], the lessee, who paid and remitted annually to the said monastery eighty *muids* each of wheat, rye, and oats, and one hundred pounds of Tours.

This day he gave us procuration at our castle at Gaillon, for the houses at Bailleul were not sufficiently suitable or adaptable to receive us. Total for procuration: eight pounds, fifteen shillings, five pence of Paris.

MAY 15. We were at Bonport at the expense of the abbey. We did not compute. MAY 16. We received procuration at Martot, from the lessee of the aforesaid house at Daubeuf. Total for procuration: nine pounds, fifteen shillings. MAY 17. At Déville. MAY 18. With God's grace we conferred Holy Orders at the parish church at Déville and spent the night at our manor there. MAY 19-20. At Déville. MAY 21. With God's grace we cele-

---

[2] See entry for May 16, below.

brated the holy synod at the cathedral in Rouen and spent the night at our manor there. MAY 22. We held the synod of deans in our upper chamber and spent the night at Déville.

MAY 23. At the same. This day we assigned the priest at Berville the day following the Assumption of the Blessed Mary as the day when he should appear before us at Rouen or vicinity, to hear our order concerning the tenor of a letter which we have from him.[3]

MAY 24. At Martot. MAY 25. To wit, on the feasts of St. Urban and the Translation of St. Francis. At Pinterville. MAY 26. At Pinterville. MAY 27-28. At Gaillon. MAY 29. With God's grace we came to the priory at Gasny and received procuration. Total for procuration: ... [lacuna in MS].

MAY 30. With God's grace we visited this priory, where there were three monks of St-Ouen-de-Rouen, to wit, Brother John of Beauvais, prior, and Brothers Robert of Frênes and Geoffrey of Reuville. We ordered them to procure a good missal and a good copy of Legends, both of which they needed badly. They ate meat occasionally and without scruples and when there was no need, nor did they observe the fasts of the Rule. They owed nothing, since they were held to remit to the abbey everything which remained to them beyond their own sustenance and that of their staff. They had quite a large staff in the manor on this side of the river, where as of custom they received us and gave us procuration. They said that they were not obliged to receive us in the manor of St-Nicaise, on the other side of the river.

This day we spent night at La Roche Guyon, where we received forty shillings of Paris from the monks of Fécamp who were there, the amount in which the resident monks are annually held to us for procuration when, once a year, we happen to turn aside to them, nor ought they to provide us with anything more, unless it be through hospitality.

MAY 31. We were at the priory at Gaillonet, of the Premonstratensian Order, at the expense of the canons who were staying there. Total for procuration: ... [lacuna in MS].

JUNE 1. At St-Germain-en-Laye. JUNE 2-10. At Paris. JUNE 11. To wit, on the feast of St. Barnabas. At St-Denis-la-Chausée. JUNE 12. At Luzarches. JUNE 13. At Verberie. JUNE 14. At Noyon. JUNE 15. At Compiègne. JUNE 16. At Clermont. JUNE 17. At Ressons, of the Premonstratensian Order, in the diocese of Rouen, at the expense of the monastery.

[3] Probably this refers to the entry for March 22, 1259/60, or November 20, 1261.

JUNE 18. At Vesly, where there were two monks of Marmoutier. Here we received full procuration. The prior of Pierrefonds had the house in his possession and had it supervised by a certain monk. Total for procuration: ... [*lacuna in MS*]. JUNE 19. At Frênes. JUNE 20-21. At Gaillon. JUNE 22. At the same. There we had with us the Reverend Father R[alph], by God's grace the bishop of Albano and legate of the Apostolic See.[4] JUNE 23. At Pinterville. JUNE 24. To wit, on the Nativity of St. John the Baptist. At the same. JUNE 25-26. At the same. JUNE 27. At the same. This day we had the said legate with us. JUNE 28. At Martot. This day Ph[ilip] of Val-Badone,[5] former rector of the church at Obertiville, voluntarily resigned his church into our hands. JUNE 29. To wit, on the feast of SS. Peter and Paul. At Déville. JUNE 30. With God's aid we preached the Crusade, in the presence of the legate, to the people who had gathered after a procession at the atrium of St-Gervaise. We had the legate at our manor in Rouen, at our expense. JULY 1. We dined at our manor in Rouen with the said legate, receiving procuration from the Rouen chapter, and we spent the night at Déville. JULY 2-3. At Déville. JULY 4. At the same. This day we had the legate with us, at our expense. JULY 5-8. At the same. JULY 9. At St-Victor-en-Caux. At our own expense. JULY 10-11. At Aliermont. JULY 12. At Dieppe. JULY 13. At Ouville. We received procuration there this day. Total for procuration: ... [*lacuna in MS*].

JULY 14. We visited the said priory, where eleven canons were in residence; two were at Autigny. We ordered the prior to inspect the monks' coffers more frequently than was his wont, lest they have any property. Item, that all of the books of the house be carefully protected and frequently inspected. They owed one hundred forty pounds. With God's grace, we founds other things to be in good condition.

This same day with God's aid we came to the priory at Etoutteville. We found this place miserably deformed as to both temporals and spirituals. Master Gilbert of Vaudeville [-en-Caux], cleric, held the said place for life. There were two monks of Lewes staying there, who had from the said Master G[ilbert] twenty shillings of Tours every week for their sustenance. We received procuration this day from William, called ... [Pencier]

---

[4] Ralph de Grosparmi, former bishop of Evreux and then cardinal-bishop of Albano, replaced, as legate of the Holy See in France, Simon de Brie, cardinal of St. Cecilia, who left France in January, 1268. (Potthast, II 1628 [20221].)

[5] See entry for March 30, above.

[*lacuna in MS*], the then lessee of the place. Total for procuration: eleven pounds.

JULY 15. At Valmont, at our own expense.

JULY 16. With God's grace we visited this abbey, where twenty-two monks were in residence; there was one lay brother of Hambye, to whom the abbot had entrusted the office of almoner, although he did not know his worthiness; two were at St-Jacques. There were four novices at the abbey. All the residents except the novices were priests. We gave orders that the said lay brother of Hambye be removed from his office of almoner. Item, that the abbot should promote someone as prior, for there had been no prior there for many days. The infirmary was badly attended; wherefore we enjoined a penance upon the abbot, punishing him as seemed expedient to us, because we had already given orders that the serving boys and the healthy [monks] be kept away from it. Item, we ordered that better provision be made for the sick than had been done and forbade anyone to eat with the sick in the infirmary without permission of the abbot. Item, we ordered the cellarer to be more careful and proper in administering wine to those who had been bled than he had been in the past. Item, that the excessive number of serving boys be removed from the kitchen. More was owed to them than they owed. We received procuration there this day. Total for procuration: ... [*lacuna in MS*].

JULY 17. With God's grace we dedicated the church at Rouville and stayed at the priest's house, at the expense of the parishioners. JULY 18. With His aid we dedicated the church at Sassetot and stayed this day at the rector's house, and at his expense. JULY 19. God assisting, we dedicated the church at Cany and spent the night at Ouainville, at the house of Dom Matthew of Mailloz, who was rector of the churches at Cany and Ouainville and held both of these by apostolic authority. JULY 20. At Le Valasse, a Cistercian house, at the expense of the abbey. JULY 21. We received procuration at Montivilliers. They did not compute.

JULY 22. With God's grace we visited the said abbey, where we found sixty-one nuns, although under the certain and statutory number there should only be sixty. However, the legate, Simon, at the time of his legateship, had added one on his own authority and power. More was owed to them than they owed; they had many provisions. With God's grace things were well with them.

This same day, to wit, on the feast of the St. Mary Magdalene, we went on to the priory at Graville, where with God's aid, and after *Dormitio*, we gave a talk in the chapter, with the community gathered before us. Eleven canons were in residence; all but one were priests. Brother Ralph, who was said to have hidden and absconded with certain writings after the death of the priest at Fontaines, besought a penalty from us because he had offended and could have offended in the matter of this document; we postponed enjoining any penalty upon him until we could learn more about the matter. They owed sixty pounds; they had many supplies. With God's grace we found other things to be in good condition. We received procuration there this day. Total for procuration: ... [*lacuna in MS*].

JULY 23. At Lillebonne, at our own expense. JULY 24. At Jumièges, at our own expense. JULY 25-26. At Déville.

JULY 27. At the same. There we assigned the prior of St-Lô-de-Rouen the day after the Assumption as the time when he should appear before us at Rouen to set forth all his reasons against those things which were demanded of him by the archdeacon of Rouen. This assignment was made with the agreement of both parties.

JULY 28-29. At Déville, the king staying at Rouen. JULY 30-31. At Martot. AUGUST 1. To wit, on the feast of St. Peter in Chains. AUGUST 2. At Martot. AUGUST 3. At Martot. On this day Brother Adam died.[6] AUGUST 4. At Rouen. With God's aid we buried the body of the said brother at the house of the Friars Minor, and we spent the night at our manor. AUGUST 5. At Frênes. AUGUST 6. At Frênes. We had there with us our venerable brother R[alph], by God's grace bishop of Evreux. AUGUST 7. At Pinterville. The said bishop was with us. AUGUST 8. At Pont-de-l'Arche. AUGUST 9-11. At Déville. AUGUST 12-13. At the same, and the lord bishop of Auxerre was with us. AUGUST 15. To wit, on the Assumption of the Blessed Virgin Mary. The lord archbishop of Lund and the bishop of Auxerre were with us. AUGUST 16. At Ste-Catherine, at our own expense. The said fathers were with us. AUGUST 17. At Pinterville, the said fathers with us. AUGUST 18. At Gaillon, the said fathers with us. AUGUST 19. At Mantes, the lord of Auxerre with us. AUGUST 20. At St-Germain-en-Laye. AUGUST 21-23. At Paris. AUGUST 24. To wit, on the feast of St. Bartholomew. At the same. AUGUST 25-27. At Paris. AUGUST 28. At Poissy.

AUGUST 29. To wit, on the Decollation of St. John. With God's grace

---

[6] This was the archbishop's nephew, who had been attached to the archiepiscopal retinue since 1248.

we visited the priory at Juziers, where there were six[7] monks of St-Père-de-Chartres, to wit, John, prior, Brother William Bird, John of Liancourt, Philip of Fontenay, Anselm of Stampe, Baillet, and Geoffrey of Chartres. They did not observe the fasts of the Rule sufficiently well. The alms quota had been reduced, that is to say, alms were not given there as they used to be and should be; a general distribution of alms is made thrice a week; we ordered this corrected. Sometimes the monks drank in the town; we rebuked the prior for this. A certain Norman cleric in the house was defamed of incontinence; we ordered the prior to find some effective and timely remedy for this. They owed sixty pounds. The prior was at this time excommunicate at the instance of Archdeacon Stephen. We received procuration there this day. Total for procuration: seven pounds, fourteen shillings, six pence.

AUGUST 30–SEPTEMBER 1. At Gaillon. SEPTEMBER 2. At Frênes. SEPTEMBER 3. At Pérrièrs-sur-Andelle, where we received procuration from the local lessee; it is a house belonging to St-Ouen-de-Rouen. SEPTEMBER 4. At L'Ile-Dieu, a Premonstratensian house, at the expense of the abbey.

SEPTEMBER 5. With God's grace we visited the priory at Beaulieu. Twelve canons were in residence; ten were outside; [there were] two lay brothers, one of whom was fatuous and incorrigible; all but one of the residents were priests. They did not have enough chalices; we ordered the prior to provide the priory with one before the feast of the Purification. Item, that he should have all the books of the priory catalogued and checked over, and frequently displayed in chapter; that he should recall those which they had loaned. We expressly ordered the prior to draw up a statement of all receipts and expenses more often than had been his practice. They owed four hundred pounds. We received procuration: seven pounds, sixteen shillings.

SEPTEMBER 6. At St-Victor-en-Caux, at our own expense. SEPTEMBER 7. At Longueville-Geoffroi, at the expense of the priory. SEPTEMBER 8. To wit, on the Nativity of the Blessed Virgin Mary. At the same, at our own expense. SEPTEMBER 9-10. At Aliermont. SEPTEMBER 11. We received procuration at Eu. Total for procuration: nine pounds, ten shillings, six pence.

SEPTEMBER 12. With God's grace we visited the said abbey, where there were twenty-eight canons and one lay brother. We gave orders that all the books of the abbey be inspected and displayed in chapter before the community, and this before the coming feast of All Saints. Item, we expressly

[7] Actually, seven are named.

ordered the prior and Brother Obert, the chamberlain, as we had done before,[8] not to put off paying Abbot William his pension of twenty pounds of Tours, and we enjoined a penance upon the said chamberlain, because he had not wished to pay the said pension. Item, we ordered him to restore and repay to the kitchen the two hundred twenty *mines* of wheat which he had withdrawn from the [supplies] which pertain to the kitchen. Item, we gave orders that individual accounts of all expenses and receipts be drawn up every six weeks before some [of the brothers] elected by the community, and that two copies of these be made, of which one must remain with the community. Item, since the prior was in charge of the cure of the parish, we gave orders that another be deputed to administer the parish. Item, we ordered that one canon be specifically deputed to watch over the Blessed Sacrament. Item, that two canons be located at [the chapel of the] Magdalene, if they can allow the place sufficient supplies for their upkeep. Item, that each and every official should account for the money pertinent to his office. They owed hundred pounds; six hundred pounds was owed to them from lands and woods already negotiated for. We were pleased that they were selling as much of their woodland as seemed expedient to them, but with the understanding that this be done with the common consent of the entire community. We received procuration this day at Le Tréport abbey. Total for procuration: eight pounds, fifteen shillings.

SEPTEMBER 13. With God's grace we visited Le Tréport abbey, where twenty-one monks were in residence; four of these were novices. We ordered the abbot to have completed all the copying which was being done on a Passional. All but seven of the residents were priests. Alms are given thrice a week to all comers. We gave orders that the sick be provided with necessities. Both the abbot and the bailiff owed five hundred pounds.

We received procuration this day at Envermeu.[9] Total for procuration: ... [*lacuna in MS*].

SEPTEMBER 14. With God's grace we visited the said priory at Envermeu, where there were twelve monks of Bec; two of these were novices. Alms are given there thrice a week. They owed three hundred pounds. With God's grace we found other things concerning temporals and spirituals in good condition.

---

[8] See entry for September 4, 1268. At that time Brother Obert had been ordered removed from office.

[9] An inadvertent repetition by the clerk.

This day we came to the house at Wanchy, and we saw the place most desolate and run down. It is dependent on the abbey of St-Ouen-de-Rouen, and we received procuration this day from the local lessee, but at Aliermont. Total for procuration: nine pounds, seventeen shillings, five pence.

SEPTEMBER 15. We visited the priory at Bures, where two monks of Pré were in residence; one of these administered the house. They do not observe the fasts of the Rule concerning the eating of meat and the fasts in general. There must be two monks from Pré there under orders from the prior of Pré, and these two monks are held to remit and restore annually to the priory of Pré whatever remains to them beyond their own maintenance and that of their staff. We received procuration there this day. Total for procuration: ... [lacuna in MS].

SEPTEMBER 16. We visited the house at Nogent, near Neufchâtel, which is dependent on the abbey of Ste-Catherine-de-Rouen. We spent the night at Neufchâtel, where we received procuration from the lessee of the said place [Nogent]. Total for procuration: ... [lacuna in MS].

SEPTEMBER 17. We visited the nuns of St-Saëns. Seventeen nuns were there. Some secular girls were there, and we ordered them removed and sent back to their relatives before the coming feast of All Saints. They owed about one hundred pounds; eighty pounds was owed to them in one debt and one hundred pounds for woodland. We found other things in good condition.

This same day we visited the monks' priory there, where there were three monks of St-Wandrille; there had been five at other times. They did not observe the Rule in the matter of the fasts or that of eating meat. The prior rarely celebrated Mass. More was owed to them than they owed. We received procuration from them this day. Total for procuration: eight pounds, eighteen shillings, ten pence.

SEPTEMBER 18-20. At Déville. SEPTEMBER 21. To wit, on the feast of St. Matthew the Evangelist. We conferred Holy Orders at Déville. SEPTEMBER 22. At the same. SEPTEMBER 23. At Bourg-Achard, at our own expence. SEPTEMBER 24. At Pont-Audemer.

SEPTEMBER 25. At the same, where for the purpose of celebrating the sacred council we had convened with our venerable brothers the bishops R[alph] of Evreux, O. [Eudes] of Bayeux, G[ui] of Lisieux, and Th[omas] of Séez; we dealt with certain matters this day.[10] The see of Avranches was

---

[10] Bishop John of Coutances was absent.

then vacant through the death of that man of venerable memory R[ichard], by God's grace the bishop of that place.

SEPTEMBER 26. With God's grace we and the said bishops celebrated the sacred council in the church of St-Aignan. SEPTEMBER 27. At Bec-Hellouin, at the expense of the monastery, and not by reason of a visitation. SEPTEMBER 28. At Pinterville. SEPTEMBER 29. To wit, on the feast of St. Michael. At the same. SEPTEMBER 30. At the same. OCTOBER 1. At the same. OCTOBER 2. We received procuration at Quévreville from the lessee there. This place is dependent upon the monastery of St-Ouen-de-Rouen. Total for procuration: ... [lacuna in MS]. OCTOBER 3. At Rouen. OCTOBER 4. To wit, on the feast of St. Francis. With God's grace we celebrated High Mass in the cathedral in Rouen, and we had the whole chapter with us at our manor this day. OCTOBER 5. At Frênes. OCTOBER 6. At Genainville. OCTOBER 7. At our manor in Pontoise, at our own expense.

OCTOBER 8. At St-Denis, in France, and at the abbey, and, through generosity and graciousness, at the expense of the monastery. The king of France, the legate, and many of the prelates of France were staying there at this time.

OCTOBER 9. To wit, on the feast of St. Denis. At the same. During these days we were by God's will so overburdened with the infirmity of our own body that we were obliged to take to our bed, and we were not able to attend the Office in the church.

OCTOBER 10-15. At Paris. OCTOBER 16. At St-Martin, near Pontoise, at our own expense. OCTOBER 17. With God's grace we celebrated the synod of the French Vexin at the monastery of St-Martin-de Pontoise, and we spent this night there, at our own expense. OCTOBER 18. To wit, on the feast of St. Luke the Evangelist. We received procuration at the priory at Parnes. Total for procuration: ... [lacuna in MS].

OCTOBER 19. With God's aid we visited this priory, where we found two monks, the prior being absent, for he had gone to the monastery of St-Evroult, on which the said priory depends, because of the death of his abbot who had just died. However, we found there Brother Gervaise of Sigy and William of Barre. There usually were more in residence, but some had died. With God's grace they had been and were in good condition as to spirituals, as we learned. They owed one hundred forty pounds, as the monks staying there believed.

We spent this night at Sérans-le-Bouteiller, where by reason and in the name of procuration we received from the prior of the place seventy shillings of Paris, in which amount the prior there is annually held to the archbishop of Rouen, whenever it happens that once a year he turns aside to this place. However, in addition to the said sum of money, he is held to supply the archbishop with household dishes and common utensils, forage and straw for the horses, and wood and fuel, as is more fully contained in a letter drawn up about this.[11]

OCTOBER 20. With God's grace we visited the said priory, where there were two monks of St-Germer-de-Flay, to wit, Brother Adam of Omercourt, prior, and Brother Reginald of Villières. They did not observe the Rule as to the eating of meat and the fasts very well; we ordered this corrected by their abbot. We ordered the prior to celebrate Mass more often than was his practice. They owed one hundred forty pounds.

We spent this night at Chaumont, at the priory of Notre-Dame-de-l'Aillerie, where we received procuration this day. Total for procuration: six pounds, nine shillings, nine pence.

OCTOBER 21. With God's grace we visited the said priory, where there were three monks of St-Germer-de-Flay, to wit, Brother Henry of Reilly, prior, and Brothers William of St-Germer and John of Chaumont. With God's grace they were in good condition as to spirituals. We ordered the prior to celebrate Mass more often than was his practice. They owed sixty pounds.

This day we were at St-Germer-de-Flay, at our own expense.

OCTOBER 22. We received procuration at Sigy, at the priory dependent upon the monastery of St-Ouen-de-Rouen. It should be noted that they are held to us for procuration, provided that this sum does not exceed ten pounds of Tours. Total for procuration: six pounds, thirteen shillings, nine pence.

OCTOBER 23. To wit, on the feast of St-Romain. With God's grace we visited the said priory [Sigy], where we found three monks of St-Ouen-de-Rouen, to wit, Brother William of Cahagnes, prior, John of Calleville, and William of Bos. There should be more, at least six, but the abbot had recalled some to the cloister because of certain hardships which the priory had temporarily suffered. Sometimes they ate meat when there was no need, and they did not observe the fasts of the Rule. They owed one hundred forty pounds. With God's grace we found other things to be in good condition.

[11] See entry for October 8, 1268.

This day we were at the abbey of Beaubec, a Cistercian house, at the expense of the abbey.

OCTOBER 24. With God's grace we came to the priory at Beaussault, a dependency of the monastery of Bec-Hellouin. We found two monks there, to wit, Brother Herbert of St-Etienne and Geoffrey of Angeville. We ordered the prior to acquire a [copy of the] Rule. They ate meat when there was no need, and this, as they said, was with their abbot's knowledge. They were very heavily burdened by reason of their buildings. They owed thirty pounds.

This day with God's aid we visited the abbey of nuns at Bival, where there were twenty-nine nuns, one lay sister, and three maidservants in common. As we had done before,[12] we forbade them [to eat] with their relatives in the abbey, and [we ordered] punished, as seemed expedient, those who were delinquent in this. We gave orders that the pension of sixty shillings due to the former abbess be paid, and we enjoined a penance upon the present abbess because she had failed to do this. She had not obeyed or complied with the orders which we had given about this at our other visitation.[13] She had not removed a certain boy whom she was having reared at the grange at Pierrement,[14] and whom we once again ordered to be sent away by all means. Item, we ordered the abbess that before the coming feast of All Saints she redeem a certain chalice which the former abbess had pawned. They owed one hundred twenty pounds.

We received procuration this day at Neufchâtel, from the prior at Beaussault. Total for procuration: . . . [lacuna in MS].

OCTOBER 25-26. At Aliermont. OCTOBER 27. At Dieppe. OCTOBER 28. To wit, on the feast of SS. Simon and Jude. We received procuration at Longueil, in a certain house belonging to Bec-Hellouin and from the lessee there. Total for procuration: . . . [lacuna in MS]. OCTOBER 29. We received procuration at Bacqueville. Total for procuration: . . . [lacuna in MS].

OCTOBER 30. With God's grace we visited the said priory, where there were five monks of Tiron. The prior was absent. Here are the names of those who were present: Walter of Crasville, John Rufus, Yvo, John Strabo, and Hugh of St-Prisce. They ate meat, as they said, with their abbot's per-

---

[12] See entry for February 27, 1254/55.
[13] See entry for September 13, 1268.
[14] *Ibid*.

mission. As we understood from the monks then staying there, they owed about one hundred pounds.

We received procuration this day at St-Wandrille. They did not wish to compute.

OCTOBER 31. With God's grace we visited the said abbey, where forty monks were in residence; eight of these were novices. With the exception of the novices, all were priests. We ordered the abbot to visit the outside priories more often than was his practice. Item, that he should have the Blessed Sacrament decently placed upon the altar in some precious repository. A general distribution of alms is made there daily. Item, we gave orders that better provision be made for the sick than had been the practice. They owed about one hundred pounds. We received procuration this day at Jumièges. Total for procuration: ... [lacuna in MS].

NOVEMBER 1. To wit, on the feast of All Saints. We visited the said abbey, where forty-eight monks were in residence, of whom three were novices; twenty-two were outside. With God's grace we found them in good condition as to spirituals. The cellarer owed two hundred pounds, and the abbot owed four hundred pounds; twenty-five hundred pounds in bad debts was owed to them. We were there this day at our own expense.

NOVEMBER 2. At St-Georges-de-Boscherville, at our own expense.

NOVEMBER 3. At Déville, where, with God's aid, having examined both the canonical processes of the election carried out in the church of Avranches, and the person of Master Ralph of Thiéville, the elect, we felt we should confirm this election.

NOVEMBER 4. At Déville. NOVEMBER 5. With God's grace we celebrated the sacred synod at Rouen. NOVEMBER 6. At Rouen, where in our upper chamber we held the synod of deans; and we spent the night at Déville. NOVEMBER 7. We attended the chapter at Rouen and spent the night at Déville. NOVEMBER 8-10. At Déville. NOVEMBER 11. To wit, on the feast of St. Martin. We were at Bondeville, not to make a visitation, but to receive our permission.[15] With God's grace they were in good condition. We spent the night at Déville.

NOVEMBER 12. With God's grace we came to the monastery of St-Ouen-de-Rouen and exercised our office of visitation. Fifty monks were there;

---

[15] It was customary for those departing on the Crusade to journey in the neighborhood and receive a blessing from those who stayed behind. Clerics received the permission and blessings of their superiors and subjects. Eudes was no exception.

all but four were priests. We found the abbey in good condition as to
spirituals. They owed five thousand pounds of Tours, fifteen hundred
pounds of this at interest; three thousand in bad debts was owed to them.
We spent this night at Déville.

NOVEMBER 13. We visited the monastery at St-Amand, where we found
fifty-nine nuns, nine of whom were to be veiled. One lay brother was there;
we gave orders that this lay brother should confess and receive Communion
more often than was his practice, and that he should be punished if he did
not obey well. Item, we ordered the abbess to strive as hard as she could
to have the nuns live in peace and concord. Item, we ordered her to try
to restore to the alms allotment the manor of Calcy, the income of which
had been withdrawn from the almoness. They owed eleven hundred pounds.
This day spent the night at Déville, at our own expense.

NOVEMBER 14. With God's aid we came in person to Mont-aux-Malades
and to the hospital of St. Mary Magdalene, and we received the permission
of these places. Thence we returned to Déville.

NOVEMBER 15. This day we were at the Daughters of God, the Beguines,[16]
at Pré; at Salle-aux-Puelles; at the Sisters of St. Matthew; and at the Fratres
Barrati, to wit, the Carmelite Brethren. We dined this day with the Friars
Preachers of Rouen.

With God's aid we visited the above-mentioned places, and, inquiring
from them about their condition, we found that Mont-aux-Malades, the hospital, and the Salle-aux-Puelles were in good condition. Pré owed two
thousand pounds and they had lost the year's harvest at Bures through bad
weather.

We spent this night at Déville.

NOVEMBER 16. We were at St-Lô[-de-Rouen]; we dined with the Friars
Minor at Rouen, and we spent the night at our manor in Rouen. NOVEMBER
17. We preached in the cathedral at Rouen and received "permission" from
the clergy and the people. This day we had the whole chapter with us.

NOVEMBER 18. We received procuration at Ste-Catherine. They did not
wish to compute.

NOVEMBER 19. With God's grace we visited the said abbey, where thirty

---

[16] Lay women who lived in a community and performed works of mercy. They did
not take the vow of poverty and could leave the community at will. They are said
to have been founded in 1180 by Lambert le Bègue, but their origins are much
controverted.

monks were in residence; several were in England or elsewhere in various places. All of the residents were priests. We gave orders that they should cast their individual accounts of expense and receipts once a month. They owed nothing, and something was owed to them. We received procuration this day at Mont-Deux-Amants. Total for procuration: seven pounds, seven shillings.

NOVEMBER 20. With God's grace we visited the said priory, where eleven canons were in residence; ten were outside in obediences. We ordered them to get back all loaned books and forbade them to lend any more without a good record of the loan. With the exception of two novices, all the resident canons were priests. They owed one hundred pounds.

We received procuration this day at Noyon-sur-Andelle. Total for procuration: nins pounds, eight shillings, five pence.

NOVEMBER 21. With God's grace we visited the priory at Noyon-sur-Andelle, where there were six monks of St-Evroult, to wit, Brother Jordan, prior, and Brothers Peter of Noyon, Dreux of Neufmarché, John of Sap, Robert of Blève, and Thomas of Silly. With God's grace they were well and in good condition.

We spent this night at Frênes.

NOVEMBER 22. At Frênes. NOVEMBER 23. To wit, on the feast of St-Clement. At the same. NOVEMBER 24. At Pont-de-l'Arche. NOVEMBER 25-29. At Pinterville. NOVEMBER 30. To wit, on the feast of St. Andrew the Apostle. At Gaillon. DECEMBER 1. At Gaillon. DECEMBER 2. At Sausseuse, at our own expense.

DECEMBER 3. With God's grace we visited the said priory, where fourteen canons were in residence; fifteen were outside in obediences. There had been no one with the cure of souls in one of the churches for a long time; wherefore we punished the prior and enjoined on him a penance which we deemed expedient. Lay sisters were there. The priory owed three hundred pounds, and bad debts were owed to it. We received procuration there this day. They did not wish to compute.

DECEMBER 4. At Mantes. DECEMBER 5. At St-Martin, near Pontoise, at our own expense.

DECEMBER 6. On the feast of St. Nicholas. With God's grace we visited the said abbey, where fourteen monks were in residence. We ordered the abbot to have individual statements made up every two weeks. We expressly forbade them to assign any more pensions to any persons, as they had done in the past. They owed eleven hundred pounds. With God's grace we found other things to be in good condition.

DECEMBER 7. With God's grace we visited the chapter at St-Mellon. We gave orders that the floor or staging under the belfry be repaired and that the silver cruets be fixed. Item, that Luke, the deacon, should arise for Matins in better fashion than was his practice. Item, we ordered Dom John, the vicar of John of Mont-Lucile, to put out of his house a certain woman who was living there. William of Longuesse and Fromond, vicars, had absented themselves from the church without permission and had not served it for many days. We ordered them cited by our vicar [of Pontoise.] We received procuration there this day. Total for procuration: ten pounds, eight pence.

DECEMBER 8. We visited St. Peter's priory, where there were five monks of Bec-Hellouin, to wit, John of St-Cloud, Roger of Extivent, Robert of Pont-l'Evêque, Peter of Mesnil, and John of St-Aubin. They owed twenty pounds, and as much was owed to them. Other things we found to be in good condition.

We also found that the Hôtel-Dieu, by God's grace, was in good condition as to spirituals and temporals.

We were at Conflans this day, at our own expense.

DECEMBER 9-12. At Paris. DECEMBER 13. To wit, on the feast of St. Lucy. At the same. DECEMBER 14-15. At St-Maur-des-Fosses. DECEMBER 16-17. At Paris.

APPENDIX

The Statutes of Pope Gregory IX
on the Reformation of the Monks
of the order of St. Benedict

IN THE FIRST PLACE, we ordain that all monks constituted in a monastery according to the Rule of St. Benedict, shall, as soon as they have heard the signal hasten to the church with proper dispatch, putting aside whatsoever they were doing, since nothing ought to be preferred to the divine office, and they shall perform the offices in church with both awe and reverence of God and, as the Rule requires, shall participate in the beginning, middle, and end of the Hours. And in purity of conscience and with devotion of spirit they shall offer to the Lord the sacrifice of praise and the harvest of their lips.

Confession shall be made by every brother in the monasteries once a month, and each and every brother shall attend to this without any excuse. The abbot shall see to it that they receive the Body and Blood of our Lord, Jesus Christ, on the first Sunday of the month. If for any reason anyone should think that he ought to abstain, he shall not delay to explain the reason therefor either to the prior or to the penitencers appointed by the abbot, so that he either may abstain through their judgment or go to the Communion. Rigorous discipline is to be maintained in the chapter; silence is to be observed in the church, in the cloister, in the refectory, and in the dormitory, and penalties must be imposed upon transgressors according to the statutory regulations.

Moreover, to all those wishing to become monks, frequent and particular explanation shall be given of these three things: obedience, continence, and poverty. The requirements of the Rule regarding the acceptance and release of novices shall be observed.

Three times yearly the Rule shall be read and expounded to those seeking admission as novices as well as to those already admitted, regarding the harshness and roughness of the means through which God is approached. At the end of the period of probation set down by St. Benedict, a reliable teacher shall be appointed for the novices, and until they have made their profession no administrative post of any kind shall be given them. Therefore, when the year of probation has been completed, the novices shall make their profession and receive the benediction at once; let those who do not wish to make profession withdraw without delay. Moreover, no one shall be admitted who has not reached his eighteenth year, nor shall any promise about receiving such [minors] be given.

The office of prior, dean, provost, and all other administrative positions shall be conferred only upon monks who are discreet and of good reputation, and freely without any venality of collusion. Conventual priories shall be conferred only upon priests or upon those who are to take orders within a year; if they shall not have been ordained within a year let them forfeit their priories.

Moreover, if any monk shall have been found to have given or to have promised anything for any such office let him be regarded as simoniacal and be removed from the office so obtained, and let him never receive any dignity or administrative position in this Order.

But the abbot who shall have sold [an office] shall likewise be punished as simoniacal. Moreover, if, through the mediation of layfolk, anyone should request that an obedience or a priory be conferred upon him, he shall never receive it, nor any other [office] within a year.

Also, the priors of conventual priories shall not be removed without reasonable cause.

No prior shall have any confirmatory letter to the effect that he should not be removed from his priory or obedience; if such a one has been obtained it shall be *ipso jure* of no effect.

Furthermore, we strictly forbid any monk to hold more than one abbey or priory, or an abbey and a priory, or be a monk in more than one monastery. He who holds an office outside the abbey shall have no other office unless, perchance, that office is connected with the administration of his abbey.

Nor shall any monk reside alone in any priory; to him who is thus alone shall be given a companion, or several companions, if the facilities of the place permit; otherwise he shall be recalled to the cloister, provided however, that the church be not deprived of the services of a priest or of its proper offices.

If the abbot shall not have desired to bestow the office of bailiff, or provost, or the supervision of rents on any brother he shall not make any contract with him nor require any security from him. The abbot shall earnestly admonish those who shall be entrusted with administration not to harrass or prosecute anyone unjustly; not to oppress them with injuries or with undue taxation; not to sell more dearly at the fixed day, nor to make any improper agreements.

We decree that those priors, obediencers, and monks holding temporal administration, who have permitted their bailly or stewardship to get into an unhealthy condition shall resign and hand over to the abbot their various offices and all the perquisites thereunto belonging, and this without delay after judgment has been determined and a confession made.

Concerning the quality of the food and raiment, we require all monks to have their clothing from a single wardrobe, and to be refreshed in one refectory with meals prepared in one kitchen. On no account shall the custom be established of serving meals in the cells. Meals shall consist regularly of one dish and one cup, not including the pittances which, on definite warrant, are usually granted at the greater feasts. Exceptions may occur when, perchance, the monks shall eat in the infirmary or privately with the abbot.

From the Ides of September to the beginning of Lent the monks shall eat as the Rule of the Blessed Benedict provides, to wit, at Nones and at other times according to the same Rule. And let them be content with that food which the Rule prescribes, and with the prescribed pittances whensoever they may be given. Nor shall anyone cause anything more delicate in food and drink to be prepared for him or to be served to him beyond the usual fare; nor shall he receive anything which has been sent to him, except whatever has been sent to him by the one who is in charge of the community. The latter shall make such use of it [extra food sent in by the superior], or of other pittances, so that it and they will bring comfort to those who are by nature weak and delicate and cannot fitly partake of the ordinary diet.

Cups of silver or gold, or even those with a gold or silver base or band, shall not be used in the infirmary or refectory; nor shall anyone be permitted to wear or possess any belt or knife embellished with gold or silver.

Moreover, no one shall eat meat in the infirmary except the monk or lay brother who shall have been ill or has been sent to the infirmary because of his weakness of body.

No monk shall eat meat in any place whatsoever, except as is specified in the Rule, whether within the house of his Order or elsewhere.

We absolutely forbid any dishes of meat which in certain monasteries, at stated times, have heretofore been customarily served to the healthy brethren. And as we prohibit the use of meat so also we forbid sophistry concerning certain flesh-foods.

Should anyone presume to eat meat in violation of the aforesaid orders, let him be subjected to the regular discipline once or even twice. If he offend a third time, let him fast the following Wednesday and Friday on bread and water; if his offense become habitual let him receive grave censure. If the abbot shall have offended in this, let him be content with bread and water on Monday, Wednesday, and Friday: should he, however, persist in this and be unwilling to amend his conduct after a warning from the local bishop or the visitors, let him be deprived of his office.

Moreover, we prescribe that the monks who are sick shall be provided with such foods, beds, helpers, and other necessities as their illness requires and the Rule assigns. If, in any of these matters, the infirmirian shall have been found remiss, let him be properly punished by his own abbot or prior. If the faults rests with the abbot or prior let him be properly punished by the visitors when they come to the place.

We also require this rule to be observed: that both monks and lay brothers be furnished, at a suitable time, with the regulation clothing and footwear, and we strictly forbid that monies be given to anyone for this purpose. Monks shall clothe themselves as modestly, in the regular garb prescribed by the Rule, when they go abroad as when they remain in the cloister. They shall not travel without their choirrobe and their regular habit, nor shall they possess a colored mantle. Nor shall anyone presume to ride on a special saddle, or on a costly one superfluously decorated with ornamental nails. They shall not wear gilded or silvered spurs. Decorated metalwork shall be completely removed from the reins, nor shall anyone wear decorated moleskin gloves or boots.

No one, in any place whatsoever, shall wear tunics or coverings of burnet or any other dyed cloth, or the skins of wild beasts, or linen shirts, nor shall they use linen cloth. Monks shall sleep gowned and cinctured as the Rule states, nor shall they have any of their clothes divided in front or behind.

No claustral prior or any other monk shall appropriate for his own use any room, horse, servant, or equipment, or contend for the use of these; but if through necessity or expediency he be obliged to go abroad, he shall receive what is needful from the person in charge.

In addition, we order all abbots and priors, whenever any loan is to be arranged or renewed, to proceed with the counsel of all of the brethren under their control, or with the greater and wiser part of them, and to arrange it in such a manner that everyone may understand for how large is a sum, to what creditors, on what conditions, for what length of time, and for what purposes the loan is to be contracted.

In order that the [financial] condition of the houses may be known with greater accuracy, the officials shall, once every three months, present to the abbot, or to the prior if the abbot is not there, and to the senior members a report from their departments faithfully listing all expenses and receipts.

Twice a year, on October 1, after the yearly harvest has been garnered, and on April 1, abbots and priors shall issue a complete statement covering the condition of their houses either to the Chapter or to its senior members, and also to the Visitors whenever they shall arrive. Moreover, the abbot, prior, or provost, who shall have fraudulently suppressed any serious debts in the said accounts shall be for a certainty removed from the office which he has obtained.

If, indeed, an abbot or prior shall have contracted a loan without the consent of his convent, he shall not keep his monastery unless the extent to which the money borrowed was spent in the interests of the monastery can be proved.

Again, no abbot or prior shall presume to bestow any priory, grange, pension, or monachal prebend upon laymen. He shall not sell, compound for, or alienate any pension except in cases admitted by law; nor shall he grant any. Rather let him know that alienation is absolutely forbidden him.

Monks who are in possession of property shall be excommunicated by their abbots. If any one, after his death, shall be found to have possessed anything, his body shall be interred without the burial service.

No one, unless he absolutely needs it in the administration of his office, shall have a chest provided with a lock except with the abbot's permission. And as often as the abbot shall request it, he shall hand over the key; and if he has anything beyond that required for his office, he shall be deemed a possessor of property to that extent.

Once a year, to wit, on Palm Sunday, the abbot in chapter shall solemnly pronounce sentence of excommunication against proprietary monks. And if, later on, anyone shall have been found to have any property of his own, let him lose his bailly, if he have one, nor let any other be bestowed upon him within a year, and not even then unless he seek it after he has made restitution of the property and has performed penance. The abbot who, knowingly, shall have given property to a monk or shall have scorned to punish a proprietary monk, shall be temporarily suspended.

Moreover, we construe the word "property" in the sense used in St. Benedict's Rule; but no monk or lay brother whatever shall receive in his name, or even in that of the monastery, any loan, lease, or bailment without the special permission of the abbot or convent. However, we do not wish any loan to be assigned by the abbot and chapter beyond a reasonable amount.

Moreover, the abbot himself shall give to each according to his individual need without favoritism and with due consideration of imfirmities.

And we rigidly forbid any abbot to confer any immovable property belonging to his monastery upon a relative in need, or even to give him any movables unless some little thing be bestowed in the name of alms. Whoever shall presume to ignore this order concerning immovables shall be removed from his church. Priors and officials shall be completely removed from their administration if it be proved that they have offended in this respect, and they shall suffer such other severe punishment as the serious nature of their offense demands.

The custody of the cloister, refectory, dormitory, and choir shall be entrusted to certain individuals during the singing of the Office. No woman shall be permitted to enter the aforesaid places or the choir during the service there, unless perchance, on such occasions as the consecrations and indulgences of churches and on the chief festival of the church, or the Office of the Dead when it happens that some women walk through the cloister or choir. An exception may be made of noblewomen who are patronesses of the monastery, or others of noble rank to whom entry may not be refused without serious scandal. To these, admission may be granted for certain hours and periods by the abbot and prior, saving indulgences in this matter granted, or to be granted, to certain persons by the Apostolic See.

If this regulation be presumptuously disobeyed, the official through whose door the woman shall have entered, or the abbot or prior who may have ordered it done, shall fast one day on bread and water for such an offense.

Abbots and priors riding abroad, and accompanied by secular servants, whether their own or belonging to the community, may have only such as are of mature years, of good repute, and not wanton in their costume.

Further, we will and ordain that in any and every monastery or priory the abbot or prior, or, in default of these, the visitors who may be there temporarily, shall require that alms be given in proportion to the ability of the houses; that a suitable hospice be set apart to receive the poor and other guests, and that a suitable servant be deputed to wait upon them. If hospitality shall be denied to any monk, he who shall have been deputed to the hospice shall fast for three days on bread and water.

Under threat of eternal damnation, we forbid that any goods or revenues assigned to or collected for alms, hospitality, or the infirmary be diverted from such uses. If this regulation be presumptuously violated, the revenues shall not be kept, but the funds shall be recalled to the aforesaid purposes. If abbots shall presume to disobey they shall be suspended from office by the visitors. Offending monks shall be suspended by their abbots. Offenders shall remain suspended for such time as shall seem proportionate to the seriousness of the offense.

And since the alms for the poor must not be fraudently administered, no one shall defraud the almonry of the food which is served at table, or of the old clothes and footwear when he receives new ones. All of these things shall be given to the almoner who shall, in turn, give them to the poor. Nor shall new equipment be given to anyone who will not return the old.

And we strictly forbid that permission to wander abroad be freely given to the monks, nor shall a license to visit lay folk be given to residents of monasteries except, perhaps, on very rare occasions for suitable cause, and for a short period, and with a mature companion deputed to watch over them. They shall recite their Hours on the journey and from the book provided for them. Permission shall be refused any monk to speak with a woman except in the presence of two or three reputable witnesses.

The monk who, after sojourning in an abbey or priory, shall have presumed to depart from the cloisters without the permission of the superior, shall be subject to the penalty set forth in the Rule.

We also strictly decree that monks residing in the outside priories shall attend the divine services in proper costume and, in the matter of abstaining from food, shall conform to the custom of their abbeys. They shall sleep clothed and cinctured just as the monks in the abbey dormitory. Also, we order this practice to be observed by all who shall sleep outside the dormitory.

Women shall not be admitted in person to any place for the service of monks.

And finally, since abbots and priors should not wander or roam about, we desire that they should sit with the brothers in the cloister; that they should attend the divine services, especially the Vigils, the Chapter, and Conferences, and other divine offices unless they be prevented by some necessary or useful or worthy cause.

No abbot or monk shall dine or spend the night in a layman's house within a league of his monastery or a cell of his monastery.

Since in many monasteries the Rule, when read aloud, is understood by but a few, we decree that the reading of the Rule, when it is read in Chapter for the benefit of the junior brethren, shall be expounded in the vernacular by him who is holding chapter, or by another upon whom he shall have decided that this duty should be enjoined.

We wish this proper moderation to be observed with respect to the mounted escort of abbots, to wit, that no abbot may have more than ten riders for his permanent household, and of these no monk may carry any banner.

However, let the lesser abbots be content with a smaller number of mounted escorts, as warranted by the facilities of their houses.

Also, all the revenues of the abbey, as well as those belonging to the head as to the members, shall be set down in writing; and items not certainly known shall be honestly estimated. The abbot shall have one copy in his own possession, the prior and convent shall have another, and both copies shall be kept in a secret place in their possession.

We decree also that if the poverty of the place, or the serious violation of the Rule, or punishment for an offense should require it, some monks may be sent away from their own monasteries. The abbots to whom they shall be sent shall not refuse to receive such monks as long as it shall seem expedient to the Visitors, unless they be of such a character that their presence could not be endured without grave scandal. But if they shall not be willing to receive them, though they are able to do so, they may be compelled by the Visitors.

Moreover, we have thought it best to insert here, as a measure of precaution, the manner in which one should proceed against the aforesaid persons, as it is contained in the document covering this matter issued by us and of which the tenor is as follows: that monks having opportunity to wander about may not incur damage to their own salvation and that their blood may not be required at the hands of their superiors, we decree that the presiding officers of chapters, whether abbots or priors, acting according to the statute of the General Council, shall once a year inquire earnestly about the monks who have run away from, or have been ejected from, their Order. If the Rule permits them to be received back into their own monasteries, the local abbots or priors shall be compelled under threat of the aforesaid ecclesiastical censure, to take them back, saving the discipline of the Order. If the Order does not permit this, acting under our authority, they shall see to it that such offenders be provided with the necessities of life in suitable places within their own monasteries, wherever it may be done without serious scandal, or in other religious houses of the same Order, so that they may work out their penance there. But if they find such fugitives and expelled monks to be disobedient, they shall excommunicate them and, at the same time, have them publicly pronounced excommunicate by the superiors of monasteries until such time as they shall humbly heed these commands.

We desire that all abbots, and all priors who have not their own abbot in their monasteries, shall have all the aforesaid regulations inviolably enforced throughout their monasteries, cells, obediences, and all other places under their control. Otherwise, the Visitors shall have the aforesaid observed and shall punish transgressors in accordance with the Rule. Nevertheless, in all the above matters the Rule of St. Benedict, which, as they are aware, particularly looks to the great amending and reforming of the Order, must be preserved and maintained.

Also, we decree that the abbot by virtue of obedience, or the prior if the abbot should be absent, shall cause all of the above to be read and carefully explained in chapter three times a year; to wit, during the Octaves of the feasts of the Nativity, of Easter, and of the Assumption of the Blessed Virgin. The abbot, indeed, shall diligently observe all these things, and have them observed by others. Otherwise, should he prove negligent in these matters, he shall be so punished in proportion to the nature of his transgression or negligence that his punishment shall be an example to others. And if, perchance, it should happen that his offenses make it necessary that he should be removed from the administration of his abbey, no promise of other revenues shall be made to him; but rather let his soul be looked after in his [lost] abbey, that he may work out a salutory penance for the offenses he committed.

Furthermore, we decree, under threat of the Divine Judgment, that abbots who shall temporarily attend the provincial chapter, shall, in that very provincial chapter, appoint as Visitors prudent, cautious, and God-fearing men who shall, within the year, visit all the abbeys and the priories not having their own abbots which are within the same province, and shall proceed to correct and reform them according to this our ordinance. And those things which they order amended they shall [record in writing and] send under their seals to each monastery; and they shall present a report of these actions to the chapter of the following year, which must be handed over to the relieving Visitors so that thus the state of obedience, or lapse, of each monastery may be clearly known. Also, the Visitors of every province shall write to us every five years, detailing what abuses they shall have corrected, and what orders they shall have required to be observed.

EUDES' CALENDAR

January	Medieval dating	Feast
1	I Kalends, January	Circumcision
2	IV Nones, January	
3	III Nones, January	
4	II Nones, January	
5	Nones, January	
6	VIII Ides, January	Epiphany
7	VII Ides, January	
8	VI Ides, January	
9	V Ides, January	
10	IV Ides, January	
11	III Ides, January	
12	II Ides, January	
13	Ides, January	
14	XIX Kalends, February	
15	XVIII Kalends, February	
16	XVII Kalends, February	
17	XVI Kalends, February	
18	XV Kalends, February	St. Peter's Chair, Rome
19	XIV Kalends, February	
20	XIII Kalends, February	SS. Fabian and Sebastian
21	XII Kalends, February	
22	XI Kalends, February	St. Vincent
23	X Kalends, February	
24	IX Kalends, February	
25	VIII Kalends, February	
26	VII Kalends, February	
27	VI Kalends, February	
28	V Kalends, February	Conversion of St. Paul
29	IV Kalends, February	
30	III Kalends, February	
31	II Kalends, February	

February	Medieval dating	Feast
1	I Kalends, February	
2	IV Nones, February	Purification of Virgin Mary
3	III Nones, February	
4	II Nones, February	
5	Nones, February	
6	VIII Ides, February	
7	VII Ides, February	
8	VI Ides, February	
9	V Ides, February	St. Scholastica
10	IV Ides, February	
11	III Ides, February	
12	II Ides, February	
13	Ides, February	
14	XVI Kalends, March	
15	XV Kalends, March	
16	XIV Kalends, March	
17	XIII Kalends, March	
18	XII Kalends, March	
19	XI Kalends, March	
20	X Kalends, March	
21	IX Kalends, March	
22	VIII Kalends, March	St. Peter's Chair, Antioch
23	VII Kalends, March	
24	VI Kalends, March	
25	V Kalends, March	
26	IV Kalends, March	
27	III Kalends, March	
28	II Kalends, March	

March	Medieval dating	Feast
1	I Kalends, March	
2	VI Nones, March	
3	V Nones, March	
4	IV Nones, March	
5	III Nones, March	

6	II Nones, March	
7	Nones, March	
8	VIII Ides, March	
9	VII Ides, March	
10	VI Ides, March	
11	V Ides, March	
12	IV Ides, March	St. Gregory, Pope
13	III Ides, March	
14	II Ides, March	
15	Ides, March	
16	XVII Kalends, April	
17	XVI Kalends, April	
18	XV Kalends, April	
19	XIV Kalends, April	
20	XIII Kalends, April	
21	XII Kalends, April	St. Benedict
22	XI Kalends, April	
23	X Kalends, April	
24	IX Kalends, April	
25	VIII Kalends, April	Annunciation of Virgin Mary
26	VII Kalends, April	
27	VI Kalends, April	
28	V Kalends, April	
29	IV Kalends, April	
30	III Kalends, April	
31	II Kalends, April	

April	Medieval dating	Feast
1	I Kalends, April	
2	IV Nones, April	
3	III Nones, April	
4	II Nones, April	
5	Nones, April	
6	VIII Ides, April	
7	VII Ides, April	
8	VI Ides, April	

9	V Ides, April	
10	IV Ides, April	
11	III Ides, April	
12	II Ides, April	
13	Ides, April	
14	XVIII Kalends, May	
15	XVII Kalends, May	
16	XVI Kalends, May	
17	XV Kalends, May	
18	XIV Kalends, May	
19	XIII Kalends, May	
20	XII Kalends, May	
21	XI Kalends, May	
22	X Kalends, May	
23	IX Kalends, May	St. George
24	VIII Kalends, May	
25	VII Kalends, May	St. Mark, Apostle
26	VI Kalends, May	
27	V Kalends, May	
28	IV Kalends, May	
29	III Kalends, May	
30	II Kalends, May	

May	Medieval dating	Feast
1	I Kalends, May	SS. Philip and James
2	VI Nones, May	
3	V Nones, May	
4	IV Nones, May	
5	III Nones, May	
6	II Nones, May	St. John Before the Latin Gate
7	Nones, May	
8	VIII Ides, May	St. Michael
9	VII Ides, May	Translation of St. Nicholas
10	VI Ides, May	
11	V Ides, May	
12	IV Ides, May	

13	III Ides, May
14	II Ides, May
15	Ides, May
16	XVII Kalends, June
17	XVI Kalends, June
18	XV Kalends, June
19	XIV Kalends, June
20	XIII Kalends, June
21	XII Kalends, June
22	XI Kalends, June
23	X Kalends, June
24	IX Kalends, June
25	VIII Kalends, June	St. Urban Translation of St. Francis
26	VII Kalends, June
27	VI Kalends, June
28	V Kalends, June
29	IV Kalends, June
30	III Kalends, June
31	II Kalends, June

June	*Medieval dating*	*Feast*
1	I Kalends, June
2	IV Nones, June
3	III Nones, June
4	II Nones, June
5	Nones, June
6	VIII Ides, June
7	VII Ides, June
8	VI Ides, June
9	V Ides, June
10	IV Ides, June
11	III Ides, June	St. Barnabas
12	II Ides, June
13	Ides, June
14	XVIII Kalends, July

15	XVII Kalends, July	
16	XVI Kalends, July	
17	XV Kalends, July	
18	XIV Kalends, July	
19	XIII Kalends, July	
20	XII Kalends, July	
21	XI Kalends, July	
22	X Kalends, July	
23	IX Kalends, July	
24	VIII Kalends, July	St. John the Baptist
25	VII Kalends, July	
26	VI Kalends, July	
27	V Kalends, July	
28	IV Kalends, July	
29	III Kalends, July	SS. Peter and Paul
30	II Kalends, July	

July	*Medieval dating*	*Feast*
1	I Kalends, July	
2	VI Nones, July	
3	V Nones, July	
4	IV Nones, July	St. Martin
5	III Nones, July	
6	II Nones, July	
7	Nones, July	
8	VIII Ides, July	
9	VII Ides, July	
10	VI Ides, July	
11	V Ides, July	Translation of St. Benedict
12	IV Ides, July	
13	III Ides, July	
14	II Ides, July	
15	Ides, July	
16	XVII Kalends, August	
17	XVI Kalends, August	
18	XV Kalends, August	St. Clare

19	XIV Kalends, August	
20	XIII Kalends, August	St. Margaret
21	XII Kalends, August	
22	XI Kalends, August	St. Mary Magdalene
23	X Kalends, August	
24	IX Kalends, August	
25	VIII Kalends, August	SS. James and Christopher
26	VII Kalends, August	
27	VI Kalends, August	
28	V Kalends, August	
29	IV Kalends, August	
30	III Kalends, August	
31	II Kalends, August	

August	Medieval dating	Feast
1	I Kalends, August	St. Peter in Chains
2	IV Nones, August	
3	III Nones, August	
4	II Nones, August	
5	Nones, August	
6	VIII Ides, August	
7	VII Ides, August	
8	VI Ides, August	
9	V Ides, August	
10	IV Ides, August	St. Lawrence
11	III Ides, August	
12	II Ides, August	
13	Ides, August	
14	XIX Kalends, September	Assumption of Virgin Mary
15	XVIII Kalends, September	
16	XVII Kalends, September	
17	XVI Kalends, September	
18	XV Kalends, September	
19	XIV Kalends, September	
20	XIII Kalends, September	
21	XII Kalends, September	

22	XI Kalends, September	
23	X Kalends, September	
24	IX Kalends, September	St. Bartholomew, Apostle
25	VIII Kalends, September	
26	VII Kalends, September	
27	VI Kalends, September	
28	V Kalends, September	
29	IV Kalends, September	Beheading of St. John
30	III Kalends, September	
31	II Kalends, September	

September	Medieval dating	Feast
1	I Kalends, September	
2	IV Nones, September	
3	III Nones, September	
4	II Nones, September	
5	Nones, September	
6	VIII Ides, September	
7	VII Ides, September	
8	VI Ides, September	Nativity of Virgin Mary
9	V Ides, September	
10	IV Ides, September	
11	III Ides, September	
12	II Ides, September	
13	Ides, September	
14	XVIII Kalends, October	Exaltation of The Holy Cross
15	XVII Kalends, October	
16	XVI Kalends, October	
17	XV Kalends, October	
18	XIV Kalends, October	
19	XIII Kalends, October	
20	XII Kalends, October	
21	XI Kalends, October	St. Matthew, Apostle
22	X Kalends, October	
23	IX Kalends, October	
24	VIII Kalends, October	

25	VII Kalends, October	
26	VI Kalends, October	
27	V Kalends, October	
28	IV Kalends, October	
29	III Kalends, October	St. Michael Archangel
30	II Kalends, October	

October	Medieval dating	Feast
1	I Kalends, October	St. Rémy
2	VI Nones, October	
3	V Nones, October	
4	IV Nones, October	St. Francis of Assisi
5	III Nones, October	
6	II Nones, October	
7	Nones, October	
8	VIII Ides, October	
9	VII Ides, October	St. Denis
10	VI Ides, October	
11	V Ides, October	
12	IV Ides, October	
13	III Ides, October	
14	II Ides, October	
15	Ides, October	
16	XVII Kalends, November	
17	XVI Kalends, November	
18	XV Kalends, November	St. Luke, Apostle
19	XIV Kalends, November	
20	XIII Kalends, November	
21	XII Kalends, November	
22	XI Kalends, November	
23	X Kalends, November	St. Romanus
24	IX Kalends, November	St. Maclou
25	VIII Kalends, November	
26	VII Kalends, November	
27	VI Kalends, November	
28	V Kalends, November	SS. Simon and Jude

29	IV Kalends, November
30	III Kalends, November
31	II Kalends, November

November	*Medieval dating*	*Feast*
1	I Kalends, November	All Saints
2	IV Nones, November	All Souls
3	III Nones, November	
4	II Nones, November	
5	Nones, November	
6	VIII Ides, November	
7	VII Ides, November	
8	VI Ides, November	
9	V Ides, November	
10	IV Ides, November	
11	III Ides, November	St. Martin
12	II Ides, November	
13	Ides, November	
14	XVIII Kalends, December	
15	XVII Kalends, December	
16	XVI Kalends, December	
17	XV Kalends, December	
18	XIV Kalends, December	
19	XIII Kalends, December	
20	XII Kalends, December	
21	XI Kalends, December	
22	X Kalends, December	
23	IX Kalends, December	St. Clement
24	VIII Kalends, December	
25	VII Kalends, December	
26	VI Kalends, December	
27	V Kalends, December	
28	IV Kalends, December	
29	III Kalends, December	
30	II Kalends, December	St. Andrew, Apostle

December	Medieval dating	Feast
1	I Kalends, December	
2	IV Nones, December	
3	III Nones, December	
4	II Nones, December	
5	Nones, December	
6	VIII Ides, December	St. Nicholas
7	VII Ides, December	
8	VI Ides, December	Immaculate Conception of Virgin Mary
9	V Ides, December	
10	IV Ides, December	
11	III Ides, December	
12	II Ides, December	
13	Ides, December	St. Lucy
14	XIX Kalends, January	
15	XVIII Kalends, January	
16	XVII Kalends, January	
17	XVI Kalends, January	
18	XV Kalends, January	Expectation of Virgin Mary
19	XIV Kalends, January	
20	XIII Kalends, January	
21	XII Kalends, January	St. Thomas, Apostle
22	XI Kalends, January	
23	X Kalends, January	
24	IX Kalends, January	
25	VIII Kalends, January	Nativity
26	VII Kalends, January	
27	VI Kalends, January	St. John, Apostle
29	V Kalends, January	Holy Innocents
29	IV Kalends, January	
30	III Kalends, January	
31	II Kalends, January	

MOVABLE FEASTS

Septuagesima (Circumdederunt Me)	Third Sunday before Ash Wednesday
Sexagesima (Exurge)	Second Sunday before Ash Wednesday
Quinquagesima (Esto Mihi)	Sunday before Ash Wednesday
Feria Quarta Cinerum	Ash Wednesday (Lent)
Quadragesima (Invocabit Me)	First Sunday in Lent
(Reminiscere)	Second Sunday in Lent
(Oculi Mei)	Third Sunday in Lent
(Laetare, Jerusalem)	Fourth Sunday in Lent
(Judica Me, Deus)	Passion Sunday
(Domine, Ne longe)	Palm Sunday
Cena Domini	Holy Thursday
Parasceve	Good Friday
(Resurrexi)	Easter Sunday
Dominica in Albis (Quasimodo)	First Sunday after Easter
(Misericordia Domini)	Second Sunday after Easter
(Jubilate Deo)	Third Sunday after Easter
(Cantate Domino)	Fourth Sunday after Easter
(Vocem Jucunditatis)	Fifth Sunday after Easter
(Viri Galilei)	Ascencion Thursday
(Spiritus Domini)	Pentecost

BIBLIOGRAPHY

MANUSCRIPT SOURCES

Ms 1245, *du fonds latin,* Bibliothèque nationale. Paris.

GENERAL BIBLIOGRAPHY

Andrieu, Michel. *Le pontifical romain au moyen âge.* 4 vols. Rome, 1938-41.

Andrieu-Guitrancourt, P. *Archêveque Eudes Rigaud, et la vie de l'église au XIIIe siècle.* Paris, 1938.

Aubert, M. *Architecture cictercienne en France.* Paris, 1947.

Auvry, D. C. *Histoire de la congrégation de Savigny.* 3 vols. Paris and Rouen, 1896.

Bateson, M. "Origin and Early History of Double Monasteries," *Transactions of the Royal Historical Society,* N.S., XII (London, 1899), 137-98.

Berger, E. *Blanche de Castille, reine de France.* Paris, 1895.

Berliere, U. "Archidiaconés ou exemptions privilegées de monastères," *Revue Bénédictine,* XL (Maredsous, 1928), 116-22.

—— *L'ascèse bénédictine, des origines a la fin du XIIe siècle,* Paris, 1927.

—— "L'exercise du ministère paroissial par les moines," *Revue Bénédictine,* XIL (Maredsous, 1927), 227-50, 340-64.

—— *La familia dans les monastères bénédictines du moyen âge.* Brussels, 1931.

—— "Les Monastères doubles aux XIIe-XIIIe siècles" in *Memoires publiées par l'Académie royale de Belgique.* 2d Ser., Vol. XVIII (Brussels, 1924).

—— *L'orde monastique des origines au XIIe siècle,* 2d edition. Paris, 1921.

—— *Le recruitement dans les monastères bénédictines au XIIIe-XIVe siècles.* Brussels, 1924.

Besse, J. M. *Abbayes et prieurés de l'ancienne France.* 8 vols. Paris, 1906-14.

Bishop, E. "Methods and Degrees of Fasting and Abstinence of the Black Monks in England before the Reformation." *Downside Review,* XLVI (1925), 184-237.

Bongert, Yvonne. *Recherches sur les cours laiques du Xe au XIIIe siècle.* Paris, 1949.

Brown, S. "Eudes Rigaud" *Moyen âge,* 3d Ser., V. II (Paris, 1931), 167-94.

Le Cacheux, P. *L'exemption de Montivilliers.* Caen, 1929.

Cartulaire de l'abbaye de St-Bertin, ed. B. Guérard. Paris, 1841.

Cartulaire de l'église Notre-Dame-de-Paris, ed. B. Guérard. 4 vols. Paris, 1850.

Cheney, C. R. *English Bishops' Chanceries.* Manchester, 1950.

—— *Episcopal Visitation of Monasteries in the 13th Century.* Manchester, 1931.

The Constitutions of Lanfranc, ed. and trans. David Knowles. Oxford, 1951.

Coquelin, F. B. *Histoire de l'abbaye du Tréport*. 2 vols. Rouen, 1879-88.

Corpus Juris canonici, ed. E. Friedberg. 2 vols. Leipzig, 1879-81.

Cottineau, L. H. *Répertoire topo-bibliographique des abbayes et prieurés*, 2 vols. Macon, 1939.

Crossley, F. H. *The English Abbey, Its Life and Work in the Middle Ages*. London, 1903.

Darlington, O. *The Travels of Odo Rigaud*. Philadelphia, 1940.

Delisle, L. "Le clergé normand au XIIIᵉ siècle," *Bibliothèque de l'école des chartes*. 2d Ser., V. III (Paris, 1846), 479-99.

Dictionnaire d'archéologie chrétienne et de liturgie, ed. F. Cabrol and H. Leclercq. 15 vols. Paris, 1902-53.

Dictionnaire de droit canonique, ed. R. Naz. 6 vols. Paris, 1935-.

Dictionnaire d'histoire et de géographie ecclésiastique, eds. A. Boudriallart *et al.* 14 vols. Paris, 1909 ff.

Dictionnaire de théologie catholique, eds. A. Vacant and E. Mangenot. 15 vols. Paris, 1900-50.

Dimier, A. *St. Louis et Cîteaux*, Paris, 1954.

Dugdale, William. *Monasticon Anglicanum*, ed. J. Caley. 6 vols in 8. London, 1846.

Du Cange, Charles Du Fresne. *Glossarium mediae et infimae Latinitatis*. 7 vols. Paris, 1845-50.

Du Plessis, Michel. *Description historique de la haute Normandie*, 2 vols. Paris, 1740.

Dutilleux, A., and A. Depoin. *L'abbaye de Maubisson*. Pontoise, 1882.

Fallue, L. *Histoire de la ville et de l'abbaye de Fécamp*. Rouen, 1841.

Fournier, Paul. *Les officialités au moyen âge*. Paris, 1880.

Franz, D. *Die Kirchlichen Benediktionen im Mittelalter*. 2 vols. Freiburg, 1909.

Gabrilovic, M. *Etude sur le traité de Paris de 1259*. Paris, 1899.

Gallia Christiana. 13 vols. Paris, 1870-74.

Gams, P. *Series episcoporum*. Ratisbon, 1873.

Gasquet, F. A. *English Monastic Life*, 3d edition. London, 1905.

Genestal, R. *Le role des monastères comme établissements de credit, etudié en Normandie du XIᵉ-XIIIᵉ siècles*. Paris, 1901.

Giry, A. *Les Etablissements de Rouen*. 2 vols. Paris, 1883-85.

Glanville, L. *Histoire du prieuré de St-Lo-de-Rouen*. 2 vols. Rouen, 1890-91.

Guignard, Philippe. *Les monuments primitifs de la règle cistercienne*. Dijon, 1878.

Hefele, C. J., and H. Leclercq. *Histoire des conciles*. 10 vols in 20. Paris, 1907-38.

Huber, R. M. *A Documented History of the Franciscan Order*. Milwaukee and Washington, D.C., 1944.

Imbart de la Tour, P. *Les élections episcopales dans l'église de France du IXᵉ-XIIᵉ siècles*. Paris, 1891.

Jacob, E. F. *Studies in the Period of Baronial Reform, 1258-1267*. Oxford, 1925.

Jungman, Joseph A. *Missarum solemnia*, trans. F. A. Brunner as the *Mass of the Roman Rite*. 2 vols. New York, 1950.

Langlois, C. V. *La Vie en France au moyen âge*. 3 vols. Paris, 1927.

Langlois, P. *Histoire du prieuré du Mont-aux-Malades-de-Rouen*. Paris, 1851.

Leduc, Dom, and Dom Baudot. *The Liturgy of the Roman Missal*. New York, n.d.

Le Grand, Leon. *Status d'hôtels-Dieu et de léproseries*. Paris, 1901.

Little, A. G. *The Grey Friars in Oxford*. Oxford, 1892.

Loth, F., and R. Fawtier. *Histoire des institutions françaises au moyen âge*. 3 vols. Paris, 1957-62.

Loth, Julien. *Histoire de l'abbaye de St-Pierre-de-Jumièges*. 3 vols. Rouen, 1885.

Mc Neill, John T., and Helene M. Gamer. *Mediaeval Handbooks of Penance*. New York, 1938.

Mansi, J. D. *Sacrorum conciliorum nova et amplissima collectio*. 53 vols. Florence and Paris, 1901-27.

Martène, C. *De antiquis monachorum ritibus*. Lyons, 1690.

Martène, E. *Histoire de l'abbaye de Marmoutier*, ed. C. Chevalier. 2 vols. Tours, 1874.

Merlet, M. L. *Cartulaire de l'abbaye de Sainte-Trinité-de-Tiron*. Chartres, 1883.

Moorman, J. R. H. *The Grey Friars in Cambridge*. Cambridge, England, 1952.

Histoire de l'abbaye royale de St-Ouen-de-Rouen, par un religieux bénédictin de la congrégation de St-Maur. Rouen, 1662.

Painter, S. *The Scourge of the Clergy*. Baltimore, 1937.

Patrologiae latinae completus cursus, ed. J. P. Migne, 218 vols. Paris, 1844-64.

Porée, A. *Histoire de l'abbaye de Bec*. 2 vols. Evreux, 1901.

Potthast, A. *Regesta Pontificum Romanorum*. 2 vols. Berlin, 1874-75.

Powicke, F. M. *King Henry III and the Lord Edward*. 2 vols. Oxford, 1947.

Pugin, A. W. *Glossary of Ecclesiastical Ornaments*. London, 1846.

Recueil des historiens des Gaules et de la France. 24 vols. Paris, 1868-1904.

Regularis Concordia, ed. and trans. Thomas Symons. Oxford, 1953.

Rule of St. Benedict, ed. and trans. Justin Mc Cann. London, 1952.

Runciman, Sir Steven. *A History of the Crusades*. 3 vols. Cambridge, 1954. (Particularly Vol. III for the Crusades of Louis IX.)

Sauvage, R. N. *L'abbaye de St-Martin-de-Troarn*, in *Mémoires de la Société des antiquaires de Normandie*. 4th Ser., Vol. IV. Caen, 1911.

Schmitz, Philbert. *Histoire de l'ordre de St. Benoît*. 6 vols. Maredsous, 1948-49.

Senn, F. *L'institution des avoueries ecclésiastiques en France*. Paris, 1903.

Saint Leon, Étienne St-Martin. *Histoire des corporation des métiers*. Paris, 1879.

Snape, R. H. *English Monastic Finances in the later Middle Ages*. Cambridge, 1926.

Strayer, J. R. *The Administration of Normandy under St. Louis*. Cambridge, 1932.

—— *The Royal Domain in the Bailliage of Rouen*. Princeton, 1936.

The Theodosian Code, trans. Clyde Pharr. Princeton, 1952.

Thomas, Paul. *Le droit de propriété des laiques sur les églises au moyen âge.* Paris, 1906.

Thomassin, Louis. *Ancienne et nouvelle discipline de l'église,* ed. M. Andre. 7 vols. Paris, 1864-67.

Thompson, A. H. *The English Clergy and Their Organization in the later Middle Ages.* Oxford, 1947.

Viard, Pierre-Paul. *Histoire de la dîme ecclésiastique, principalement en France, XIIe-XIIe siècles.* Paris, 1912.

Wadding, L. *Annales Minorum.* 28 vols. Quaracchi, 1931-41.

Wallon, H. *St. Louis et son temps.* 2 vols. Paris, 1876.

Wolff, Philippe. *Commerce et marchands de Toulouse.* Paris, 1954.

Young, Karl. *The Drama of the Mediaeval Church.* Oxford, 1933.

GENERAL INDEX

INDEX OF VISITATIONS